# Anticipative Criminal Investigation

Marianne F.H. Hirsch Ballin

# Anticipative Criminal Investigation

## Theory and Counterterrorism Practice in the Netherlands and the United States

T·M·C·Asser Press

Springer

Dr. Marianne F.H. Hirsch Ballin
Pels Rijcken & Droogleever Fortuijn N.V.
PO Box 11756
2502 AT The Hague
Zuid-Holland
The Netherlands

ISBN 978-90-6704-842-2 e-ISBN 978-90-6704-843-9
DOI 10.1007/978-90-6704-843-9

Library of Congress Control Number: 2011946091



Published by T.M.C. ASSER PRESS, The Hague, The Netherlands www.asserpress.nl
Produced and distributed for T.M.C. ASSER PRESS by Springer-Verlag Berlin Heidelberg



*Cover design:* eStudio Calamar, Berlin/Figueres

Printed on acid-free paper

Springer is part of Springer Science+Business Media (www.springer.com)

*To my parents*

# Foreword

Law performs three national security functions. It provides substantive authority to act. It provides essential process. And, it conveys essential societal and security values. In United States practice each of these foundational functions is found in Constitutional law, statutory law, and Executive directive.[1]

9/11 put uncommon strain on each of these law functions. In truth, the stress was already evident as the law evolved from the certitude of Cold War substance, structure, and values, to a less certain orientation toward rogue states and trans-national threats, including non-state actors intent on obtaining and, in the case of at least al-Qaeda, using weapons of mass destruction (WMD). There were advents of the future to come; including the 1993 attack on the World Trade Center and the 1995 attack on the Murrah Federal Building in Oklahoma City.

However, legal and especially legislative change was incremental, if it occurred at all. In the mid-1990s, spending was increased on WMD preparedness; the military was authorized to assist in the event of a WMD incident; however, efforts to expand the government's surveillance authorities in the area of roving wiretap and "lone wolf"[2] authority were rebuffed in the Congress. The Executive's identification of the WMD and al-Qaeda threat was more robust as were subsequent overt efforts to target Osama Bin Laden. Less evident were the covert efforts to do the same until referenced in the 9/11 Commission Report. In the 1990s then, the United States had moved, or was moving, from a reactive or law

---

[1] In simplest manifestation, for example, the Constitution provides for a structure of separate and shared powers, which at one time describes the enumerated substantive authority of each branch, describes the process by which the branches coexist and reflects the legal value that power in a democracy should be dispersed rather than concentrated in a single branch or person.

[2] Authority under the Foreign Intelligence Surveillance Act directed toward the would-be terrorist acting alone who by definition would not meet the traditional predicate as an "agent of a foreign power," which definition includes international terrorist organizations.

enforcement paradigm to an intelligence driven preventive paradigm in combating terrorism. However, a collective sense of urgency did not emerge or bind the political branches of government.

9/11 changed all that in the United States as well as in the Netherlands as this thoughtful and important work of scholarship describes. In Europe, the Madrid train attack of 11 March 2004 and London transit attack of 7 July 2005 confirmed this change. To some, it seemed, western democracies faced a zero-sum choice between security and liberty as well as between a criminal and a military paradigm of response. As *Anticipative Criminal Investigation* (*ACI*) reports, the debate was framed among other ways as one between the function of the prosecutorial sword – the tools used by the government to fact-find – and the shield – the safeguards that provide a fair system of justice and that protect individual rights.[3] In the U.S., the paradigmatic debate focused on three subjects: extraordinary rendition, interrogation tactics, and surveillance techniques. ("Targeted killing" would join the debate at a later date.) While the Netherlands did not cross the threshold of targeted killing in the 1990s as the U.S. did, in some respects it has exceeded U.S. law in its anticipative reach in the area of criminal investigation.

In both countries the focus was on the immediate, the next attack. As Justice Jackson noted of government decision-making in the context of the 1952 Steel Seizure Case, "the tendency is strong to emphasize transient results upon policies." *Youngstown Sheet & Tube Co. v. Sawyer*, 343 U.S. 579 (1952) (Jackson, J. concurring). Those who have served in the national security field know this focus well. The pressure is greatest on lawyers when lives are at stake. But those trained in law will also know the rest of the Jackson admonition: "… and lose sight of enduring consequences upon the balanced power of our Republic." That is why a focus on legal process and values, and not just substance, is imperative in time of crisis. That is also why studies such as *Anticipative Criminal Investigation (ACI)* are essential to our understanding of law and its relation to national security.

*ACI* analyzes the transition from a reactive to an anticipatory criminal law framework for preventing terrorism in the Netherlands and in the United States. The focus is on one aspect of the legal debate, what the Dutch refer to as Special Investigative Techniques (SIT) and what U.S. readers will recognize as the intelligence and law enforcement tools of electronic surveillance, physical surveillance, clandestine search, infiltration, mail cover, and more. A number of core questions are asked and analyzed: Who may engage in such activities? Based on what factual predicate, if any? What use may be made of the information obtained? And, what forms of accountability apply?

In U.S. practice, such techniques date to the advent of the Republic, as the rubric "eavesdropping" suggests. As envoy to France, Ben Franklin was an accomplished, albeit amateur intelligence operative. President Lincoln was an avid intelligence consumer, known to read Confederate communications obtained by

[3] P. 14 below.

agents tapping into telegraph wires.[4] Formal legal permit came later in both criminal and intelligence context in the form of Supreme Court case law (*Katz v. United States*, 389 U.S. 347 (1967); *United States v. United States District Court* (*Keith*), 407 U.S. 297 (1972)) and express statutory authorization (Title III of the Omnibus Safe Streets Act of 1968; Foreign Intelligence Surveillance Act of 1978).

There the law more or less settled until 9/11 and the external discovery of an internal "Wall" between criminal and intelligence investigative methods within the Department of Justice and FBI. So too, old proposals for roving authority and "lone wolf" authority were quickly renewed. The "Wall," as it turned out, was based on concerns that the threshold for intelligence surveillance (reason to believe the target is an agent of foreign power or international terrorist organization) would be used to circumvent the probable cause predicate for criminal surveillance (reason to believe a crime had been, was being, or would be committed). However, as the Foreign Intelligence Surveillance Court of Review noted, espionage and terrorism necessarily and simultaneously raise both security and criminal law implications and thus the predicate for "the Wall" was tenuous from a legal and policy point of view.

There followed the serial PATRIOT Act debates over whether to authorize roving intelligence wiretaps, access to business records, and the free exchange of information obtained through intelligence and criminal investigative methods. In each case, prevention ultimately prevailed. The principle of protection was preserved in process, but not by prohibition. And, of course, there was the debate that did not occur: Could the President authorize warrantless electronic surveillance pursuant to his implied constitutional authority as Chief Executive and Commander in Chief?

As *ACI* recounts, the Dutch legal framework applicable to intelligence led investigative activities followed a different path to a comparable end. Dutch law includes a concept of "legality" – "the requirement of a foundation in law for every governmental action that interferes with the rights or freedoms of citizens."[5] In the most intrusive circumstances an explicit basis in law is required.[6] Through application of the European Convention on Human Rights, Dutch law also implies a requirement of "foreseeability" – sufficient transparency in the law that those subject to its force are on general notice of its reach.[7]

The key Dutch authorities are found in criminal context in parliamentary acts dating to the 1926 Dutch Code of Criminal Procedure (CCP), the 1999 Act on Special Investigative Techniques, the 2004 Act on Terrorist Crimes, and the 2006 Act to Broaden the Possibilities to Investigate Terrorist Crimes. The 2004 Act, for

---

[4] Lincoln also served as his own case officer, running a spy named Lloyd from within the White House. We know this, because Lloyd's estate eventually sued to recoup promised payments in the case of *Totten v. United States*, 92 U.S. 105 (1875).

[5] P. 43.

[6] P. 78.

[7] Pp. 50 and 114-116.

example, increased penalties for certain crimes with terrorist motive. It also criminalized conduct preparatory to acts of terrorism, thus shifting both traditional and intelligence investigative resources to an inherently anticipative context. In 2005, the Parliament also created the position of National Coordinator for Counterterrorism to serve as "the spider in the web."[8] In addition, the 2006 Act changed the predicate for SIT from one of "reasonable suspicion" to one of "indications of terrorism," clearly a reduced standard, but one without parliamentary or judicial definition. The 2006 Act also authorized the extraordinary search of objects, vehicles, and people for up to twelve hours and with respect to a specifically indicated area upon determination by the Public Prosecutor that terrorist indications present an immediate threat. Permanent search authorization is also granted within designated security zones, like airports and train stations, pursuant to an administrative decree that the zone is under permanent threat of attack.

The intelligence keystones in Dutch law are more amorphous, for as *ACI* notes,

> "the powers available to the AIVD are regulated by requiring, for the use of the most intrusive powers, the permission of the relevant Minister and, otherwise, on behalf of the Minister, the permission of the head of the AIVD... Because the AIVD's task is to protect the national security and not to collect evidence for criminal prosecution, the AIVD's use of these special powers is not further restrained by some threshold, such as having a reasonable suspicion under criminal procedural law, nor subjected to judicial review."[9]

However, 9/11 brought greater emphasis on the express identification of authority as well as on anticipatory investigation to prevent terrorism. Significantly, it was after 9/11 that the functions of the national Dutch intelligence service, the General Intelligence and Security Service (AIVD), were expressly defined in enabling legislation called the Intelligence and Security Services Act of 2002. In addition, the 2006 Act and corresponding changes to the criminal procedural law, as well as the Shielded Witnesses Act, were intended to trigger the sharing of information between the intelligence service (AIVD) and the public prosecutor at an earlier moment and stimulate such sharing in general.

Most significantly, perhaps, from an enabling perspective, the 2006 Act on Shielded Witnesses permits AIVD witnesses to provide intelligence testimony, including testimony based on liaison sourcing, in the presence of the investigating magistrate alone. While the defendant can participate by telecommunication or through the submission of questions, *ACI* dryly notes, "in the end the interest of national security trumps the criminal procedural interest of equality of arms and adversarial proceedings." "Although the trial judge still has the final say on what sources of evidence a conviction will be based, he cannot further examine the conclusion of the examining magistrate as to the veracity of the AIVD-information."[10]

---

[8] P. 200.

[9] Pp. 88-9.

[10] Pp. 192-193.

In U.S. law, such a limitation would implicate the $6^{th}$ Amendment right of a criminal defendant to cross-examine his accusers. To the extent there is a comparable U.S. law, the Classified Information Procedures Act (CIPA) places the burden on the Government to place the defendant in as good a position as they would have been had they been able to access and use relevant and material classified information, or face judicial dismissal of the charges. In civil context, of course, the State Secrets Doctrine is more comparable to the Dutch Witness Protection Act.

Aside from providing an outstanding review of the law in both countries, *ACI*'s comparative perspective is important and commendable. First, there are the evident bonds between the two legal traditions rooted in a parallel commitment to what the U.S. calls the rule of law and what the Dutch call "*Rechtsstaat*," "the state's subjection to limits on its power as provided by law."[11] There is also the manifest pressure each system faces to prevent catastrophic acts of terrorism. The United States is not alone in its legal values or in facing a catastrophic violence. It is also worth remembering that in a global system of transport, commerce, and communication, the safety of passengers and cargo alike is only as strong as the weakest link – whether that link is found at Schiphol Airport or New York harbor.

Second, understanding the bonds between the Dutch and U.S. legal experience one might also better derive lessons-learned from that experience. In this regard, one is reminded how eerily similar are the 9/11 Commission report and the Canadian report on the 1985 terrorist bombing of Air India Flight 182. Applying a comparative approach, one might avoid mistakes already made as well as benefit from successful example. One might ask, are there measures of accountability in Dutch practice that might better effectuate the substance, process, and legal values in U.S. practice, or conversely?

Some greater perspective is surely useful in both directions. A number of examples illustrate. In Dutch practice, for example, accountability is almost exclusively dependent on a hierarchical process of SIT approval, rather than the judicial approval found in U.S. FISA and Title III practice. The Public Prosecutor is the central actor, and in certain cases, the investigating magistrate. In short, the Dutch system appears to rely on the integrity of decision-makers, rather than on external checks and balances. However, Dutch law also includes an express "duty to draw up records;" a written record of the investigator's activities and findings. And, because the system is premised on criminal prosecution as the ultimate means of prevention, there is ex post judicial review of SIT at trial with the possibility of evidentiary exclusion.

On a privacy continuum, the U.S. debate on governmental access to business records, including library computer and loan records, is given new perspective when considered in light of the Dutch concept of "administrative disturbance," the obtrusive observation of a person for whom cause does not exist to arrest. Administrative disturbance is intended to disrupt the person's daily life in a

---

[11] P. 8.

manner that will alert the suspect that they are under suspicion and that will disturb preparation of criminal conduct.[12] (One is reminded here of the former U.S. State Department and the obtrusive manner in which he was followed by U.S. authorities while under investigation for espionage in 1989.)

Similarly, debates about profiling might be informed by the Dutch experience in applying special security zones or imminent threat searches. Likewise, one might consider the distinctions between a Dutch system based on "legality" – "the requirement of a foundation in law for every governmental action that interferes with the rights or freedoms of citizens"[13] – and a U.S. system in which substantial authority is vested in the President through implied authority derived from Article II. How, for example, do the comparative advantages in flexibility that Article II provides weigh against the reduction in accountability and the risk that critical actors will take fewer risks when the law is not clearly stated or clearly invoked, either because it is invoked in vague constitutional manner, or done so in secret?

As a final illustration, the Dutch principles of proportionality and subsidiarity warrant identification and comment. Subsidiarity equates to necessity; in other words, a determination that the specific method is necessary to achieve an investigative need. This concept corresponds in U.S. law with the concept of last resort, whereas the most intrusive methods will only be used when other methods are unavailing. Proportionality is defined variously within *ACI* as: the principle that "the interference corresponds to a pressing social need and, in particular, that it is proportionate to the legitimate aim pursued;" and the "require[ment] that the 'harm' inflicted' by using investigative powers may not exceed the harm which will result from refraining from the investigative action."[14] As *ACI* notes, this formulation seems to lead ineluctably to the application of "less strict standards for the investigation of serious crimes." Proportionality, while found in the law of armed conflict, has no immediate investigative corollary in U.S. practice. The exigent circumstances doctrine and minimization perhaps come closest. One has to wonder just how slippery the proportionality slope is, especially where catastrophic terrorism is at issue. On the other hand, the concept may also reflect a realistic and honest assessment of the compulsion state actors feel to flexibly use the law when confronted by dangerous facts, in which case proportionality might also be viewed as a refreshing form of decisional transparency.

Third, it is noteworthy that the Netherlands has expressly chosen a law enforcement paradigm for addressing terrorism. ("Because terrorism is considered to be criminal behavior, the Dutch government considered the criminal justice system as the primary area for dealing with terrorists.")[15] As debate in the United States continues as to whether to apply a criminal, military, or mixed paradigm to terrorist interrogation, adjudication, and detention, it is interesting to consider the

---

[12] P. 202.

[13] P. 43.

[14] Pp. 557-558.

[15] P. 168.

strengths and weaknesses of a Dutch system that is committed at the outset to an anticipative criminal paradigm. So too one might consider whether the relative volume and scale make any comparison apt.

However one compares and contrasts the U.S. and Dutch experiences, *ACI* makes clear that in both contexts, 9/11 irrevocably changed the backdrop in which choices about investigative methods are made – the risk and realization of catastrophic terrorism, including the prospective use of WMD. That threat has not disappeared with the demise of Osama Bin Laden, or for that matter Kim Jong-il. However, this is a good opportunity to take a moment to reflect on what has occurred and what might yet occur. That is one reason why this book is important. The book is inherently timely coming as it does soon after the tenth anniversary of 9/11. But it is not a retrospective. It looks to the future through the prism of the past. What started as a WMD problem will continue as a WMD problem, and thus persist long past the death of Bin Laden. The imperative of anticipation and prevention remains.

That means Justice Jackson's admonition is as relevant today as it was in 1952, on 9/10 and on 9/12. This is a book about finding our long-term equilibrium, the enduring consequences of anticipative criminal investigation and law. In my view, it succeeds in doing so for four reasons.

First, *ACI* eschews the false dichotomous choices of security versus liberty, and shield versus sword. It does not treat these concepts as zero-sum exercises in balance. "The 'balancing' approach fails to acknowledge that the protection of certain interests is non-negotiable."[16]

Second, *ACI* avoids the trap of aggregate symbols, like "security" or "liberty," and breaks each down into finite and tangible values like the presumption of innocence, due process, fair trial, *and* the right to a private life free from the violent interference of others. Symbols like "Guantanamo" or "military paradigm" in reality are aggregates of complex and distinct choices about how to prevent terrorism by identifying, capturing, interrogating, and detaining persons while at the same time adjudicating their status and their conduct.

Third, *ACI* returns time and again to all three purposes of law – substance, process, and values. Thus, the book describes with equal care the essential procedural requirements associated with each positive authority. It also places that process in context recognizing that process is neither inherently good nor bad. It is not done to make lawyers happy. Good process exists to ensure that the law effectively serves as both sword and shield. If process is effective, it will prevent the state from overreaching and thereby also cause the state to focus its finite investigative assets on more important targets.

Likewise, one can attempt to "legislate" the creation of an "Information Sharing Environment," as the U.S. Congress has done, but information sharing ultimately depends on process and values. Hence, *ACI* describes and compares the

---

16 P. 606.

Dutch Counterterrorism Information Box, located at AIVD Headquarters, with the U.S. National Counterterrorism Center and Joint Terrorism Task Force structure.

Finally, and most importantly, *ACI* returns us to our roots, the core values law is intended to reflect and protect. As has been said of the common law is also true of national security law. If one is not attentive, the law can move in incremental tacks away from the shore of constitutional intent, until the shore falls out of sight. The author is committed to liberty *and* security, the sword *and* the shield, and the recognition that all are rooted in our fundamental legal values. Those values include a concept of human dignity that imposes on the state "the positive duty to protect any individual present in its territory against violations of his/her fundamental rights by others" and "the negative duty to refrain, as much as possible, from interfering with the personal freedom of individuals."[17] In U.S. law, comparable duties are found in Article II and the Bill of Rights to the Constitution, the preamble to which declares at the outset that the Constitution is established to "provide for the common defense" and "secure the blessings of liberty." The art of national security policy and law is to utilize all the tools of national power and do so in a manner consistent with democratic process and our legal values. *ACI* is a book that goes a long way in the area of SIT to telling us when and how to do just that.

James E. Baker
*Chief Judge, United States Court of Appeals for the Armed Forces and Adjunct Professor of Law, Georgetown University Law Center*

[17] P. 12.

# Acknowledgments

The past decade may be typified by the difficulties Western States had in finding a rule of law-based answer to terrorism. Implementing adequate preventive measures within the criminal justice system turned out to be a complex task. States have usually justified terrorism laws by considering security an interest that overrides traditional protective rules. In this book a rule of law approach is taken in which the term rule of law is understood as requiring attention both for liberty and security. From this perspective this book goes back to the roots of rule of law based legal systems in order to draw borders on the state's powers in terrorism prevention. Albeit focusing on the manner in which the Netherlands and the United States have implemented legislation facilitating anticipative criminal investigations, the rule of law approach of this book surpasses differences between legal systems. With this approach I hope to be able to deliver a contribution for reflection, both on measures taken to confront terrorism and on a changed society trying to control ostensibly not fully controllable threats.

The basis for this book is my PhD-research at the Willem Pompe Institute of Utrecht University between 2007 and 2011. It is to Professor John Vervaele and Professor Stijn Franken at Utrecht University, that I owe the most gratitude: for their always harmonious guidance, the continuing inspiration they give me and their support in finding my own way through the extensive subject-matter of anticipative investigations in the Netherlands and the United States. The manuscript was closed on November 5th, 2011. Any changes in the law that have since occurred could not be included.

I would also like to express my gratitude to the Fulbright Association, from which I received a scholarship. Spending time among the inspiring and energetic staff of the International Human Rights Law Institute of DePaul University in Chicago has been an unforgettable and meaningful experience. Furthermore, I would like to express my gratitude to Judge James E. Baker, who taught me 'national security law' at Georgetown University Law Center in 2007. From that moment, he has been extremely supportive with regard to my research plans into a subject matter which has our shared interest and, in particular, concerning the comparative approach of my research. It is an honor to be able to include his foreword in this book.

To my Thomas I reserve the most gratitude. As the person closest to me, his unconditional love, support and patience have been the most meaningful encouragement while writing this book. My parents are my biggest example. Their devotion in contributing to a just society inspired me to choose law as a study. To my parents, whose love, faith and encouragement has always given me strength, I dedicate this book.

December 2011 Marianne F.H. Hirsch Ballin

# Contents

# List of Abbreviations

| | |
|---|---|
| ACHR | American Convention on Human Rights |
| ACLU | American Civil Liberties Union |
| AG | Attorney General |
| AIVD | General Intelligence and Security Service [*Algemene Inlichtingen- en Veiligheidsdienst*] |
| AUMF | Authorization for Use of Military Force |
| BVD | National Security Service, predecessor of the AIVD [*Binnenlandse Veiligheidsdienst*] |
| CCP | (Dutch) Code of Criminal Procedure |
| CIA | Central Intelligence Agency |
| CIE | Criminal Intelligence Unit [*Criminele Inlichtingen Eenheid*] |
| CIPA | Validity and Construction of Classified Information Procedures Act |
| CT-Infobox | Counterterrorism Information box [*Contraterrorisme Infobox*] |
| CTC | Central Assessment Committee [*Centrale Toetsingscommissie*] |
| DCI | Director of Central Intelligence |
| DIOG | Domestic Investigations and Operations Guide |
| DNI | Director of National Intelligence |
| DoJ | Department of Justice |
| ECHR | European Convention for the Protection of Human Rights and Fundamental Freedoms |
| ECrtHR | European Court of Human Rights |
| EU | European Union |
| FAA | FISA Amendments Act of 2008 |
| FISA | Foreign Intelligence Surveillance Act of 1978 |
| FBI | Federal Bureau of Investigation |
| FOIA | Freedom of Information Act |
| HR | Dutch Supreme Court [*Hoge Raad der Nederlanden*] |

| | |
|---|---|
| IACHR | Inter-American Court of Human Rights |
| ICCPR | International Covenant on Civil and Political Rights |
| JTTF | Joint Terrorism Task Force |
| KLPD | National Police Services Agency [*Korps landelijke politiediensten*] |
| KMar | Royal Netherlands Marechaussee [*Koninklijke Marechaussee*] |
| MIVD | Military Intelligence and Security Service [*Militaire Inlichtingen- en Veiligheidsdienst* |
| NCTb | National Coordinator for Counterterrorism [*Nationaal Coördinator Terrorismebestrijding*] |
| NSA | National Security Agency |
| NSC | National Security Council |
| NSI | National Security Investigations |
| NSL | National Security Letter |
| PPS | Public Prosecution Service |
| RID | Regional Intelligence Service [*Regionale Inlichtingendienst*] |
| SIT | Special Investigative Techniques |
| UN | United Nations |
| US | United States of America |
| WED | Economic Offenses Act [*Wet op de economische delicten*] |
| WIV 2002 | Intelligence and Security Services Act of 2002 [*Wet op de inlichtingen- en veiligheidsdiensten 2002*] |
| WVW 1994 | Road Traffic Act [*Wegenverkeerswet 1994*] |
| WWM | Weapons and Ammunition Act [*Wet wapens en munitie*] |

# Chapter 1
# Introduction

## 1.1 Terrorism, Prevention and the Criminal Justice System

Imagine the following situation: an anonymous tip is received that a certain extremist group is planning to carry out an attack against a central station in a metropolitan city during the rush hour within the coming week. Many innocent citizens may fall victim, which puts the agencies responsible for dealing with threats and violence under great pressure to ensure that an attack is prevented. At the same time there is uncertainty as to the reliability of the tip: the information comes from an unknown source and cannot be substantiated by other information. How do states deal with such dilemmas?

The state has several means at its disposal to respond to a security threat such as this: intelligence powers to obtain more information and knowledge on the extremist group; criminal investigative powers such as electronic surveillance to discover whether a crime is being prepared or committed; and criminal coercive powers such as the power of arrest to make sure that these persons are unable to act as potential perpetrators of a terrorist attack.

At the same time the state, which has subjected itself to several restraints and checks to protect individual liberties, may face several obstacles. For instance, relying on the criminal justice system may be excluded because the applicable threshold for using criminal procedural powers, such as probable cause or reasonable suspicion, cannot be met. Nevertheless, the state needs to use the powers that are capable of most effectively ruling out the possibility that an attack will be carried out in order to protect innocent lives. Moreover, the state wants to rule out the threat not only for the coming week, but also in the long term. For this reason, preferably before turning to the power of arrest, evidence will be gathered regarding plans to commit a terrorist attack in order to be able to prosecute and punish the terrorists.

Faced with this (hypothetical) dilemma, states have sought to adapt their powers to act for the purpose of prevention by enabling a system that starts to operate in anticipation of future harm, already before concrete criminal behavior

M.F.H. Hirsch Ballin, *Anticipative Criminal Investigation*,
DOI: 10.1007/978-90-6704-843-9_1,

can be identified. For this purpose, states have sought to answer this security threat through a combination of their intelligence and criminal justice responses. This investigative approach can be defined as anticipative criminal investigation.

Ten years after the confrontation with the devastating terrorist attacks in the United States, it seems that in particular the government's responsibility to act so as to prevent security threats—for which purpose investigative powers are used in anticipation of future threats—has changed the character and function of the criminal justice system in the longer term. Whereas other measures, such as the introduction of enhanced methods to interrogate terrorist suspects in the United States, have been reversed, the role of the state in anticipating future threats in order to prevent terrorist attacks remains a current one. The criminal investigation has obtained a permanent role in order to anticipate future terrorist threats through the investigation of potential dangerous behavior or activities, which may imply criminal investigative activities before concrete criminal behavior can be identified. The purpose of these criminal investigative activities is both the prevention of terrorist crimes *and* the prosecution and punishment of the 'terrorists'; bringing to justice those responsible for criminal acts, such as the criminal preparation of a terrorist crime, conspiracy to commit a terrorist crime or membership of a terrorist organization. In this book I will examine whether and, if so, how this preventive function of investigative activities can be embedded in the criminal justice system when seeking to pursue such a preventive function while still observing the rule of law.

The chapter will begin to conceptualize the subject-matter of the book by defining 'anticipative criminal investigation' (Sect. 1.2.1) and limiting the assessment of the subject of 'anticipative criminal investigation' to the way in which it has been adopted and implemented in the Netherlands and the United States (1.2.2). Subsequently, Sect. 1.2 draws the theoretical background which is relevant to assess changes to the criminal justice system. For that purpose, the rule of law will be defined as the notion that should regulate all state action and the observance of which legitimizes and restricts state action, because its observance is based on the regulation of state power in observing respect for the human dignity of every individual (Sect. 1.2.3). From the definition adopted, I continue by interpreting the function of criminal law and criminal procedural law. This results in the formulation of the objectives of criminal procedural law (Sect. 1.2.4), which also apply—as will be explained—to investigative activities with the purpose of evidence gathering for criminal prosecution (Sects. 1.2.5 and 1.2.6).

Subsequently, the subject-matter will be contextualized: several developments that transcend the level of states clarify that the phenomenon of criminal investigation for preventive purposes is not limited to the states of examination, but fits within the larger international picture of counterterrorism measures and a call on the state's responsibility to protect its citizens against serious violence and threats (Sect. 1.3)

The chapter will then turn to summarizing the subject-matter on the basis of the manner in which the subject has been framed in Sects. 1.2 and 1.3 (Sect. 1.4). On that basis, the chapter will formulate the main research question which this book will seek to answer (Sect. 1.5) and provide for the approach and methods which have been chosen to answer this research question (Sect.1.6).

## 1.2 Conceptualizing the Subject

### *1.2.1 Defining Anticipative Criminal Investigation*

This book focuses on the phenomenon where the government uses its investigative capacities to obtain a strong information position in order to be able to anticipate future dangers and to prevent future harm in the context of the criminal justice system. This intelligence-led and proactive form of investigation is a phenomenon where the traditional functions of criminal investigation and intelligence investigation have been blended. An increased call on states to provide security as a precondition for citizens to be able to enjoy their liberty, along with an increased responsibility of states to anticipate risks in order to prevent their realization, have resulted in state measures inspired by the 'preventive paradigm' as the general focus of policy with regard to safety and criminality.[1] The 'threat of terrorism' has significantly contributed to the increased call on states to guarantee security and, in particular, to realize the prevention of terrorist crimes. Since the first confrontation with the potential destructive nature of international terrorist attacks on September 11, 2001 in New York and near Washington D.C., states have sought to adjust their traditional means to confront the threat posed by terrorism. Terrorism concerns a danger which is different from ordinary crime, especially because of the arbitrary selection of innocent targets, for which reason prevention is the central notion in counterterrorism policy.[2] Consequently, also the understanding of the role of the criminal justice system has shifted, from not exclusively the *ultimum remedium* to investigate, prosecute and punish criminal offenders for purposes of retribution and general and special prevention, to also being an instrument to control safety risks and preventing harm.[3]

For that reason, the traditional criminal investigation has been adjusted when it comes to the investigation of serious crimes that threaten essential aspects of our democratic society, especially terrorist crimes, so that the primary goal is now to prevent these crimes rather than searching for evidence to enable prosecution. At the same time the barrier between the investigative activities of the intelligence agencies and the investigative activities of law enforcement agencies has been reduced or even been dissipated. The German term of '*Vorfeldermittlung*' very

---

[1] Cole and Lobel 2007, 2-6.

[2] Luban 2002, 12 and McCormack 2008, 258. Compare also the US Attorney General Alberto Gonzales: "[p]revention is the goal of all goals when it comes to terrorism because we simply cannot and will not wait for these particular crimes to occur before taking action." Alberto Gonzales, U.S. Attorney General, Remarks at the World Affairs Council of Pittsburgh on 'Stopping Terrorists Before They Strike: The Justice Department's Power of Prevention' (August 16 2006), available at http://http://www.justice.gov/archive/ag/speeches/2006/ag_speech_060816.html (accessed 30 August 2011).

[3] Compare: Albrecht 2010, 4, Van der Woude 2010, 108-109, Parry 2007 and Dripps 2003 17-19, Cole and Lobel 2007, 12, 30-31.

well characterizes the new phenomenon of the investigative activity of the government, which is by definition proactive, is aimed at the prevention of serious crimes that threaten the safety of many citizens, in particular terrorism, and for which reason the traditional criminal investigative functions (evidence gathering) and intelligence investigative functions (the gathering of information about threats to national security for the purpose of prevention) have been merged. To distinguish this new area of investigation from its traditional forms, these investigative activities will be referred to in this project as *anticipative investigation*. Anticipative investigation thus covers any form of proactive investigation on behalf of the government for the prevention of serious crimes or threats and can typically be characterized by its intelligence-led approach.

Arguably, the term 'proactive investigation' could also be chosen to describe the investigative activities researched. However, to distinguish this investigative area, where intelligence and law enforcement functions have come together, from a traditional criminal investigation, this new term of 'anticipative' investigation has been chosen. 'Proactive' has a clear connotation with a traditional criminal investigation both in the Netherlands and the United States: in the Netherlands 'proactive' has always been understood as the investigative activities before the establishment of a reasonable suspicion that a committed has been crime, whereas in the US 'proactive' is usually understood as a police-invoked as opposed to a citizen-invoked form of investigation. Hence, when choosing the term proactive the focus is on the triggering moment of the investigative action (before instead of after the crime). To emphasize that the distinguishing character of the form of the investigative activity that this book seeks to discuss concerns the *purpose of the prevention* of serious (terrorist) crimes, by taking an intelligence-led approach in anticipation of threats, 'anticipative investigation' has been chosen.

The second defining aspect is the relation of this form of investigation to the criminal justice system. An anticipative investigation includes investigative activities of the government resulting in the gathering of information—information which may, immediately or subsequently, become part of criminal proceedings. Especially this character of anticipative investigation is crucial for the examination in this book. Hence, the form of investigation will be referred to in this book as 'anticipative *criminal* investigation', in order to emphasize the connection with potential future criminal prosecution and to limit the scope of the project to anticipative investigation that has implications for the criminal justice system. Criminal investigation under this definition may therefore include investigative activities of law enforcement agencies and of intelligence agencies, where it appears that intelligence investigation is used to collect information to be used in the criminal process. For example, the activities of the Dutch or US intelligence entities may gather intelligence not only for the purpose of protecting national security, but also for the purpose of using it as criminal evidence. For this reason, also the activities of intelligence entities, with a commensurate purpose of gathering evidence for criminal prosecution, is covered by the concept of anticipative criminal investigation.

The basic assumption and *leitmotiv* of anticipative criminal investigation is the prevention of, in particular, terrorist crimes. Prevention, as it will be used in this project, applies to government action for the purpose of preventing crime through anticipative investigation. Hence, prevention in this respect does not refer to the traditional goal of criminal procedural law: general or special prevention as a consequence of deterrence through the prosecution and punishment of criminal behavior. Nor does the concept of anticipative investigation refer to the criminalization of acts of preparation, expanding the concept of conspiracy, criminalized membership of a criminal or terrorist organization, criminalizing the aiding or abetting of terrorism, criminalizing the financing of terrorism or criminalizing participation in training for terrorism, which are all also aimed at the prevention of 'bigger' crimes. The criminalization of acts that cover the planning and preparation of 'bigger' crimes, such as terrorist attacks, may result in the conviction of terrorists and, by 'placing them behind bars,' this may prevent future terrorist attacks. Nonetheless, the criminalization of these acts does not mean that the investigation in the procedural sense is geared towards prevention; the government has been given investigative powers *especially* for the purpose of guaranteeing the safety of citizens through anticipating future potential harm.

Anticipation and prevention are used in this book in the procedural context: the anticipative use of investigative tools, particularly aimed at the interception of the planning of crimes in order to be able to prevent their commission. Of course, this procedural aspect of anticipation and prevention cannot be assessed completely separately from the developments in substantive criminal law. The expansion in the preventive sphere of substantive criminal law must be taken into account as a factor that significantly reinforces procedural measures aimed at enabling anticipative criminal investigation as well as enabling investigation for the purpose of prevention without such measures. The book will not, however, assess the legitimacy of the criminalization of activities in these early phases, which may raise serious concerns with respect to locating the border between criminalizing thoughts and speech and actual criminal deeds.[4] Because the book focuses on the scope, position and function that a criminal investigation may have under the rule of law, which are all procedural issues, the substantive aspect of anticipative criminal investigation only plays a role as a factor influencing the scope of criminal investigative powers and the effectiveness of criminal investigation under applicable restraints.

Although the preventive paradigm has, as the frame of reference for developing a wide variety of state policy,[5] also influenced other aspects of the criminal justice system, such as preventive detention, rendition and enhanced interrogation methods, this book deals with intelligence-led investigative activities that typically occur before an arrest. Other forms where the state applies criminal procedural tools as instruments for the purpose of preventing serious (typically terrorist) crimes are excluded from the assessment made in this book. Instead, the book

---

[4] See on this subject e.g. for the Netherlands: Lintz 2007.

[5] In the words of Vervaele: "a perception of reality (…) for the definition of social constructs as crime, danger, risk and insecurity." Vervaele 2012 (*forthcoming*).

deals in particular with the use of covert special investigative techniques, which may seriously interfere with the fundamental rights of citizens, such as wire-tapping, physical surveillance and infiltration, as these are the tools that the government will apply during the phase of anticipative criminal investigation.

The concept of anticipative criminal investigation as just defined concerns the subject of assessment in this book. It reflects the development of a new perception concerning the role of the government with regard to security and criminal justice. States have, in answer to an increased call on their responsibility to provide a secure society, adjusted their policies to the prevention of harm, which has also changed ideas concerning the role of the criminal justice system. This development has accelerated since the terrorist attacks of September 11, 2001, for which reason the prevention, rather than the repression, of crimes can now be identified as an independent goal of criminal investigation. Moreover, the approach of this form of anticipative criminal investigation is exclusively proactive, whereas reactive criminal investigation was the rule before the developments in the wake of September 11, 2001.

### 1.2.2 Selection of Countries

The systems of law to be examined encompass the Netherlands and the United States. Both countries face similar problems and have experienced similar developments as to the rise of anticipative investigation. The most dramatic reforms influencing the nature of investigative activities have in both countries been caused by the urge to minimize the possibility of a terrorist attack. Under the 'preventive paradigm' both the Netherlands and the United States have taken many measures, varying from preventive military action to preventive detention and preventive investigation, in order to optimize the state's capability to prevent future terrorist attacks.

Although many other Western countries have undergone similar developments during the last decade, the Netherlands and the United States have been selected for further examination because each of them represents a specific approach of embedding the anticipative criminal investigation into their respective procedural and institutional systems. Moreover, the United States has generally been engaged in pioneering work when it comes to the adoption of counterterrorism measures. The Member States of the European Union, as well as other states, have followed suit by implementing similar counterterrorism measures in their own legal systems and cooperating structures. This may be illustrated by the fact that the main legislative measures facilitating anticipative criminal investigation date from 2001 in the United States and from 2006 in the Netherlands. The Netherlands and the United States thus offer interesting material for comparison as to the regulation of anticipative criminal investigation. The limitation to examining only these two countries follows from conceivable practical considerations.

Despite the similarities as to the rationale behind enabling anticipative criminal investigation, the path chosen by the Netherlands and the United States differs with regard to certain fundamental elements. This study seeks to compare these two approaches as to their compatibility with a legitimate criminal justice system. This comparison is based upon the perception that the goals that the criminal justice systems of both countries aim to realize are equal. For that reason, the viability and acceptability of the concept of anticipative criminal investigation can be assessed on the basis of the objectives that the system as a whole must pursue.[6] The synthesis between these objectives will for both systems function as the touchstone. I will deduce these objectives from the rule of law.

Because of the comparability of the approaches chosen in the Netherlands and the United States—two legal systems based on rule of law values—differences between these legal systems following from the different legal traditions in which these countries are rooted—generally typified as an inquisitorial or adversarial tradition, respectively[7]—will be surpassed. Nevertheless, the specific legal system of a state continues to be the determining factor for specific choices in states' regulation of criminal investigation in general, and of anticipative criminal investigation in particular, and, therefore, for the manner in which shared values are guaranteed.

### *1.2.3 The Rule of Law*

'*Rechtsstaat*' and the 'rule of law' are both concepts that are used all over the world as the notion that should—ideally—govern all state action. In the

[6] Brants et al., 42.

[7] Adversarial and inquisitorial are the terms traditionally used to make a general distinction between two types of criminal justice systems. Adversarial systems are based upon the idea of the trial "as a contest between two equal parties, seeking to resolve a dispute before a passive and impartial judge, with a jury ('the people') pronouncing one version of events to be the truth." Inquisitorial systems have attributed to the state the responsibility to investigate a criminal offense and possible perpetrators "with a view to establishing the truth." The impartial and independent judge has an active role in the truth-finding process in the inquisitorial system. Brants et al. 1995, 42. The primary distinguishing aspects are the mode of "a contest or a dispute" in the adversarial system and the mode of investigation on behalf of the state in the inquisitorial system. The equality of the two adversaries is the basic assumption for the first, whereas the latter is primarily the responsibility of state actors. Damaška 1986, 3. Today, a sharp distinction between adversarial and inquisitorial systems can no longer be upheld. Inquisitorial systems have moved towards the adversarial system, as a consequence of the "ideological domination of adversarial methodology" and, in Europe, to an important extent as a consequence of the jurisprudence of the European Court of Human Rights especially with regard to Article 6 providing for the right to a fair trial, which have caused an increased focus on due process and on "common standards of fairness". Vogler 2008, 11 and Brants and Rignalda 2010/2011, 9. Vice versa, especially the investigative phase in countries such as the US, which are traditionally shaped in accordance with the adversarial system, has largely obtained an inquisitorial nature.

Netherlands adherence to the *'Rechtsstaat'* covers the state's subjection to limits on its power as provided by law. In the United States the 'rule of law' constitutes the originally English notion that aims to protect citizens against the absolute power of the state.[8] Both *Rechtsstaat* and the rule of law reflect the idea of restricting state power by subjecting it to the law and providing for a normative organization of the state that has its origins in the Enlightenment. Although *Rechtsstaat* and the rule of law are concepts that have a different background and also a different and often rather elusive meaning, in this book I adopt a broad rule of law concept that covers also the normative elements aiming to restrict state power that can be attributed to the concept of the *Rechtsstaat*.

This section will continue to provide such a broad definition of the rule of law. It will not set out the differences between the concepts of *Rechtsstaat* and the rule of law, nor attempt to merge them into one concept, although today—arguably—the content of both may extensively overlap. Rather, this section will formulate the basic rule of law principles applying to all states that adhere to a state organization based on respect for human dignity, for the purpose of defining the role of and legitimizing criminal procedural law. For this purpose, I will also go back to the first ideas of restrictions on governmental power as inherited from the Enlightenment and the development of the idea of the *'Rechtsstaat'* in continental Europe, which underlie the adopted (in this book) modern and broad notion of the 'rule of law'. As will be elaborated in the next section, the design of the criminal justice system should follow from this definition of the rule of law.

Before turning to this notion of the rule of law, attention should be given to the notion of respect for human dignity, underpinning the rule of law. The recognition of the human dignity of every human being is closely related to the idea of individual autonomy. Luban considers the concept of human dignity as more than only recognizing everyone's right of "willing and choosing." "Honoring someone's human dignity means honoring their being, not merely their willing."[9] The state which recognizes human dignity shall provide the conditions for enjoying individual autonomy, which it can do by refraining from intermingling with individual liberty. Individual autonomy requires the freedom to pursue the personal objects of (reasoned) choice.[10] According to Rawls the first principle of justice is the "equal right to a fully adequate scheme of basic liberties which is compatible with a similar scheme of liberties for all."[11] This does not mean that the state shall never interfere with individual liberties. Respect for human dignity also requires from the state that the individual autonomy of others is protected or promoted.[12] In addition to the state's responsibility to recognize individual

[8] Blaau 1990, 88-89.

[9] Luban 2007, 76.

[10] Sen 2010, 301.

[11] Rawls 1993, 291.

[12] Ashworth 2009, 25.

autonomy, human dignity as a concept honoring a person's 'being' in general requires the "non-humiliation" of individuals.[13]

The concepts of the rule of law and *Rechtsstaat* are basically understood as either a formal version or a substantive version (also referred to as a 'thin' or 'thick' version), the substantive version which then also adopts the requirements of the formal version.[14] A formal notion of the rule of law requires the regulation of state conduct in the law: rule by the law. It requires rules set out in advance in general and clear terms, which are applied equally to all.[15] When human dignity is considered as the basic assumption for the polity of the state, it is required to give the rule of law, as will be used in this project, a more substantive content. It then includes democracy and individual rights together with formal legality, separation of powers and an independent judiciary. The rule of law as a notion based on respect for human dignity requires that state power is only exercised in recognition of individual liberty. This means that state power is exercised within the borders of the law, that protection against abuse of state power is provided through a state organization based on democracy, separation of powers and an independent judiciary, and, lastly, with respect for fundamental rights both vertically and horizontally.[16] In the thickest variant, the rule of law or *Rechtsstaat* will also include social rights.[17]

A notion of the rule of law without such a substantive content ignores the fact that respect for each individual's right to human dignity gives the fundamental rights that follow from that right an inalienable character. The inalienable character of the right to respect for human dignity and the fundamental rights that can again be derived from that right also make it a basic and inherent element of the rule of law as the notion that regulates state conduct. This observation can be made regardless of whether one considers human dignity as a grant by God and/or as an inherent part of our status as human beings. For that reason, the right to human dignity goes even beyond the democratic legislature and beyond constitutional amendment. Hence, I propose a definition of the rule of law that includes the observance of individual and social rights (collectively referred to as fundamental rights). As will appear later, the substantive content of the rule of law, which, in the first place, restricts state conduct in relation to its citizens as well as obliging the state to protect a society in which every citizen may enjoy his/her individual liberty, concerns the most important normative aspect of the rule of law in order to address the subject of anticipative criminal investigation.

The central position of respect for human dignity can already be recognized in the views of Locke and Kant, and can in general be considered as an important inheritance of the Enlightenment. For Kant individual autonomy was the principal

---

13 Luban 2007, 88.

14 Tamanaha 2004, 91.

15 Tamanaha 2004, 91-101 and Boettke and Oprea 2004, 507-508.

16 Compare Tamanaha 2004, 102-112 and Cole and Lobel 2007, 33.

17 Tamanaha 2004, 112-113.

right, which he interpreted as requiring freedom ("of every member of society as a human being"), equality and the right to property. In Kant's view, the *Rechtsstaat* required compliance with the rule of law, equality before the law and granting citizens the rights attached to their right to individual autonomy.[18] Before Kant, Locke considered natural rights as belonging to the individual, rights which the individual possesses prior to and freestanding from the social contract and civil society. Based on Locke's view, this recognition of inalienable rights imposes on the government the negative duty to refrain from interfering with its citizens' enjoyment of these rights.[19]

Currently, also the positive duty to deter or punish private infringements of fellow-citizens' inalienable rights is considered as an inherent part of the right to respect for human dignity.[20] For this reason, the modern state has a duty to provide for security and act against any violation of the inalienable rights of its citizens by fellow-citizens, whereas at the same time it should provide protection against unlimited state power to interfere with individual rights. This reflects the notion of the modern democratic state governed by the rule of law. Additionally, one should add the positive duty of the state to provide for the circumstances in which its citizens' social rights are guaranteed. This aspect renders the state a 'social welfare state.'

Today, also Dworkin defends the view that law is not only a set of rules, but includes immanent moral principles, which are present, also when not explicitly stated in rules. Rules are just an effort to capture moral rights.[21] Law is more than mere rules, because the right to human dignity transcends the elaboration of this right in human rights, legal principles, constitutional rights and all other legal rules. The modern state governed by the rule of law shall be designed according to this idea, by enshrining fundamental rights and principles as transcending ordinary laws, elaborating human dignity in substantive fundamental rights by adopting fundamental rights in constitutions and human rights documents, and institutionalizing legality, which includes equality to the law, consistency, predictability and the realization of substantive goals. Democracy should then be considered as the ideal form of state authority. Inherent in the right to human dignity, including individual liberty, is the idea of self-government. Rules acquire their legitimization because they are the result of a democratic process (provided that they are also underpinned by fundamental rights and principles).

The universality of embracing the idea of human dignity as the guiding principle in the state governed by the rule of law follows eminently from the Universal Declaration of Human Rights. The preamble to the Declaration starts with:

---

18 See Immanuel Kant's 'Theory and Practice' (1793), published in: Reis 1970, 74–79.

19 Locke 1980 (original edition 1690), 65–68.

20 Rosenfeld rephrased Locke's view with regard to inalienable rights in this sense: Rosenfeld 2001, 1324-1325 and 1333. See furthermore: Rodley 2010, 209-210, Mégret 2010, 130-131 and Sect. 1.3.2.

21 Dworkin 1979, 269.

"[w]hereas recognition of the inherent dignity and of the equal and inalienable rights of all members of the human family is the foundation of freedom, justice and peace in the world". Article 1 of the Universal Declaration of Human Rights then explicitly determines that "all human beings are born free and equal in dignity and rights. They are endowed with reason and conscience and should act towards one another in a spirit of brotherhood."[22] Respect for human dignity as the guiding principle of all state action emphasizes the substantive elements of the rule of law. It goes beyond the formal aspects of the rule of law and is in that way the touchstone of all law and all state action.

It can be concluded that the broad, substantive notion of the rule of law is very important to permanently guarantee—regardless of the organization of the state and even regardless of the democratic legitimate choices made in the state—respect for human dignity. All legal rules and all state action in accordance with the formal aspect of the rule of law shall, in addition, be subjected to an examination on conformity with the substantive counterpart of the rule of law. The rights attached to human dignity shall always be part of the rule of law, regardless of whether or not they are laid down in constitutions or human rights documents or treaties.[23]

This substantive aspect of the rule of law, of respect for human dignity as the guiding principle for the regulation of state power, will be the basic assumption which underpins the role and position of the criminal justice system, as the procedural mechanism reflecting the synthesis found between promoting security (of those who are the victims of criminal offenses and of society in general) and protecting liberty (of those becoming subjected to criminal procedural law, as a suspect or otherwise, and of society in general), and, subsequently, also of the assessment of anticipative criminal investigation.

### 1.2.4 Criminal Procedural Law

Based on the above interpretation of the concept of the rule of law, this section will seek to formulate the function and objectives of criminal procedural law. The rule

---

[22] The Universal Declaration of Human Rights, General Assembly Resolution 217 A (III), 10 December 1948, Preamble and Article 1. See also the Preamble to the ICCPR, General Assembly Resolution 2200 A (XXI), 16 December 1966 and Article 1 of the Charter of the Fundamental Rights of the European Union. Proof that respect for human dignity has also become the basic assumption in states that have traditionally adhered to the notion of 'Rechtsstaat' may also be found in the German Constitution adopted in 1949, taking into consideration that the idea of Rechtsstaat has its origins in Germany. Article 1 of the *Grundgesetz* states that "human dignity shall be inviolable." "To respect and protect it shall be the duty of all state authority."

[23] The fact that fundamental rights have been adopted in constitutions and binding human rights treaties such as the ECHR gives a stronger guarantee that these rights will be taken seriously in practice. Governments are directly bound by a clear set of rules. However, once a democratic legislature touches upon these rights, it should still not violate the rule of law.

of law will be of importance to the design of the criminal justice system for two reasons. First, observing the rule of law imposes on the state the positive duty to protect individuals' fundamental rights by providing for a system that can offer protection to any individual present in its territory against violations of his/her fundamental rights by others. The establishment of a criminal justice system as such is based upon this idea. Second, observing the rule of law imposes limitations on the state's exercise of its positive duty. For that reason, the state shall under the rule of law, as a minimum, exercise its criminal procedural powers in a restrictive way, as people must be protected against this state power to coerce persons. Respect for the rule of law thus also imposes on the state the negative duty to refrain, as much as possible, from interfering with the personal freedom of individuals.

Dworkin formulates "two dimensions of human dignity."[24] Firstly, each human life has objective intrinsic value and, secondly, everyone has a personal responsibility to realize the potential value of one's own life.[25] On the basis of this second dimension of human dignity, everyone is entitled to certain personal decisions on how to live their lives (such as on decisions relating to religion, marriage and political choice), whilst on other issues people have agreed that the state decides how to make decisions.[26] The principal example of issues falling in the latter category concerns criminal law.

Criminal law constitutes a set of norms to which the people have agreed—through democratic decision-making—to adhere. Substantive criminal law encompasses the specific set of rules following from collective decisions with regard to violations of moral principles or rules of order, adopted in order to realize crime control and maintain order in society. The violation of these moral principles and rules of order has been elaborated—by the democratically legitimated legislature—in provisions of substantive criminal law. These criminal offenses shall meet the requirements of formal legality and be formulated in general and clear terms in order to be foreseeable to the people.

Because human dignity includes the responsibility to realize the potential value of one's own life, people have given the state the power to enforce these commonly decided rules of criminal law.[27] This is to a large extent based on the desire to live in a society that is safe; a society that gives its citizens the potential to develop a life that is in accordance with their values. The use of state power is legitimate because citizens have commonly agreed to impose these limitations on

[24] Dworkin 2006, 9.

[25] *Ibid.*, 9-10.

[26] *Ibid.*, 19-21. Dworkin distinguishes these two categories as ethics and morality: "[t]he principle of personal responsibility allows the state to force us to live in accordance with collective decisions of moral principle, but it forbids the state to dictate ethical convictions in that way." *Ibid.* 21.

[27] Compare: *Ibid.* 2006, 20-21.

their personal freedom.[28] Criminal procedural law gives the government these powers to act against those that are suspected of having committed criminal offenses; and, in that way, the powers to contribute to a safe society.

Giving the state this power to interfere with the personal freedom of the individual, however, gives rise to the interrelated need to provide for protection against this power of the state.[29] As argued, both aspects follow from the adopted notion of the rule of law. In the period of the Enlightenment, it was Beccaria who added the function of providing for legal principles and the protection of fundamental rights to the instrumental function of criminal procedural law, on the basis of the idea of the social contract.[30] The Dutch and US criminal justice systems are still designed according to this 'classical approach' towards criminal law. This additional protective function of criminal procedural law makes the criminal process a regulated and restricted form of state power.[31] The classical approach strongly adheres to the idea of respect for the individual within the legal order, which goes hand in hand with a restrictive, regulated design of the criminal process.

The criminal process must focus on the employment of criminal law that enables both an adequate enforcement of the norms elaborated in substantive law, as well as respect for human dignity, including equality to the law and respect for fundamental rights. The employment of criminal procedural law that respects human dignity means that the state must be restrained when using criminal procedural powers. However, respecting human dignity also means that the state will do all in its capacity to convict those who have been found guilty of committing a criminal offense, because through the commission of a criminal offense other individuals' fundamental rights have been violated. Equality to the law forbids the state from using its criminal procedural powers arbitrarily. Respect for fundamental rights prescribes the state to use the criminal process in a manner that the individual liberty of each individual is respected. The criminal process may only be used for the purpose of convicting those who are guilty and the state must be restrained when using its powers by being subjected to principles of proportionality and subsidiarity, also against those who are suspected of a crime. Furthermore, respect for fundamental rights requires the state to provide a fair system and

---

28 Pompe 2008, 15. See also Habermas: "the modern legal order can draw its legitimacy only from the idea of self-determination: citizens should always be able to understand themselves also as authors of the law to which they are subject as addressees." Habermas 1996, 449. Compare also Bassiouni on the functioning of national criminal justice systems in Bassiouni 2008, 238-239: "the criminalization of transgressions against (...) types of protected interests is based on society's assessment of the intrinsic value of the social interest, which in turn reflects the individual and social harm sought to be averted." The legitimacy of the criminalization of such commonly-shared social values depends on the "legitimacy of the protected social interest and/or [the absence of] a claim of higher legitimacy in transgressing the social interest."

29 Van Zuijlen 2008, 2.

30 Beccaria 1971, 305-311. See also Foqué and 't Hart 1990, 84-91.

31 Foqué and 't Hart 1990, 15.

to restrict interference with fundamental rights to that which is necessary for the functioning of the system.

Two main objectives of criminal procedural law can now be formulated. In general the criminal process must be aimed at the establishment of the truth in order to convict the guilty. This goal implies two things: on the one hand, it must be able—by having sufficient tools for this purpose—to adequately ascertain the truth during the process; on the other hand, criminal law must be employed so that it can fulfill the duty to provide for a safe society by investigating, prosecuting and convicting the perpetrators of crimes. The first objective of criminal procedural law is thus to provide the instruments for truth-finding. Furthermore, criminal procedural law must provide for protection against state interference with the rights of individuals. Employing criminal procedural powers should result as little as possible in the subjection of innocent people to criminal procedural powers and may not lead to the disproportionate subjection of suspects to criminal procedural powers. Criminal procedural law should therefore provide for sufficient protection in order to avoid the use of criminal procedural powers arbitrarily or unnecessarily and to guarantee the observance of fundamental rights and due process. Establishing substantive truth includes the exclusion of the arbitrary and unnecessary use of criminal procedural powers. The second objective of criminal procedural law is therefore a protective objective: providing for a fair system that excludes arbitrariness and respects the fundamental rights of citizens.

Both objectives are equally important and both are derived from the rule of law, which underpins the regulation of all state action in recognition of respect for individual human dignity. Considering that criminal law provides the government with powers to control crime and maintain order in society, it can only be justified that the government has been given these powers if the fundamental rights of citizens are respected and the powers are only used for the purpose of convicting the guilty. Each objective puts limits on the other: "they are interrelated in the sense that they may clash and yet at the same time depend on each other for legitimacy."[32] Only the pursuance of both objectives makes the use of criminal procedural powers legitimate and in accordance with the rule of law.

The design of the criminal justice system must be based on its potential to realize these two objectives. The criminal justice system shall include the instruments (the sword) in order to enable adequate truth-finding, as well as the safeguards to guarantee a fair system that observes individual rights (the shield).[33] The shield function of criminal procedural law consists of different protective rules that can be reduced to general principles of criminal law and to specific fundamental rights.

The constitutionalization of criminal procedural law in the United States can be considered as the elaboration of the shield aspect of criminal procedural law, because the Constitutional restraints on the exercise of criminal procedural law

---

[32] Brants et al. 1995, 43.

[33] The terms "sword" and "shield" are derived from: Vogler 2008, 20.

aim to guarantee respect for fundamental Constitutional rights[34] and to protect the innocent from criminal procedural coercion.[35] Constitutional due process and the First, Fourth, Fifth and Sixth Amendments provide for limitations on the use of criminal procedural powers against citizens. Especially the Fourth and First Amendments place restraints on the government's power in order to protect individual liberty. The development of Constitutional doctrines by the courts has resulted from considerations based on the balancing of the interest of prompt and efficient law enforcement against the Constitutional protection of fundamental individual rights from interference by law enforcement activities. Constitutional due process is a constitutional principle that has been derived directly from the rule of law as a principle regulating criminal procedure.[36]

In the Netherlands, different principles of criminal procedural law reflect the shield aspect, such as the principle of legality, the presumption of innocence, and the principle of proportionality.[37] The principle of legality applies to all uses of criminal procedural powers and has a restrictive function on the use of state power in the field of criminal law; the government is bound to use only those powers that have a basis in law. Consequently, the main source of protective rules is the Code of Criminal Procedure. Furthermore, the Dutch Constitution and the European Convention on Human Rights (ECHR) guarantee respect for fundamental rights, including in the exercise of criminal procedural powers. These concern in particular the right to private life—as criminal procedural powers seriously touch upon one's personal freedom—and the right to a fair trial.

To conclude: the exercise of criminal procedural law is based upon and is limited by the contents of the rule of law. The use of criminal procedural powers by the state is legitimized because the rule of law requires that the state strives for a safe society in which citizens are entitled to live. In addition, the state's exercise of criminal powers is restrained by the substantive elements of the rule of law as it provides the state with the power to interfere with its citizens' fundamental liberty in the most far-reaching way, namely through imposing punishment. Hence, criminal law is *ultimum remedium* to be used in order to punish the guilty, which requires the adoption of safeguards to avoid unnecessarily affecting the innocent, such as rules of due process and limitations on the use of coercive and investigative powers. These safeguards have been elaborated in principles of criminal procedural law and follow from fundamental rights protected in human rights documents and constitutions. The protective objective places boundaries on the objective of instrumentality, and, vice versa, instrumentality imposes boundaries

[34] E.g. the Fourth Amendment protecting the "right of the people to be secure in their persons, houses, papers, and effects" by imposing limitations on governmental infringements against these rights, including such infringements in the context of the exercise of criminal procedural powers.

[35] Amar 1997, X.

[36] Nowak and Rotunda 2004, 432.

[37] Foqué and 't Hart 1990, 16.

on one's claim to legal protection.[38] Hence, the synthesis between the two objectives renders a particular system of regulation legitimate.

### *1.2.5 The Relation Between Criminal Investigation and Criminal Procedural Law*

In the introductory section of this chapter a criminal investigation has been defined as a term covering all governmental investigative activities that collect information for the purpose of using it in criminal proceedings. Because of this collocation with criminal proceedings, the manner in which these investigative activities are regulated and conducted need to correspond with the objectives of criminal procedural law as formulated in the previous section. Hence, criminal investigation is only legitimate if it is exercised in a manner that does not undermine the protective objective of criminal procedural law and should be subjected to constraints to ensure that also this objective of criminal procedural law will ultimately be achieved. Otherwise, the criminal justice system loses its legitimacy as such, considering that the realization of each of the formulated objectives underpins the legitimacy of the system as a system based on the realization of respect for human dignity for everyone. For that reason, the sword and shield objectives of criminal procedural law shall be echoed when criminally investigating: providing sufficient means for pursuing the substantive goals of the criminal justice systems and avoiding the use of investigative powers against innocent persons, limiting interference with fundamental rights to that which is necessary and investigating in anticipation of a fair procedure. Hence, a synthesis between sword and shield shall be achieved in the regulation of criminal investigation.

### *1.2.6 The Relation Between Criminal Investigation and Intelligence Investigation*

Criminal investigation and intelligence investigation have traditionally been considered, both in the Netherlands and the United States, as clearly separated matters, because of the institutional and functional separation of the intelligence community and the law enforcement community. The intelligence community, the criminal justice system and the military concern three separate responses to threats and violence, each allocated with a different purpose and, for that reason, also provided with different powers and subjected to different restraints.[39] The military, traditionally aimed at "subdue and control", currently also at "prevention" and

[38] Compare: Groenhuijsen and Knigge 2001, 18, Kelk 1995, 4 and Brants et al. 1995, 43.

[39] McCormack 2007, 35-36.

regulated through the law of armed conflict, will not be dealt with, because the rise of anticipative criminal investigation involves an institutional shift of the intelligence and law enforcement community, due to a merging of their traditional functions without also involving the preventive military response.[40]

The intelligence community has been given responsibility for prevention, whereas the role of enforcement through investigation, prosecution and punishment is attributed to the law enforcement community. The criminal justice system deals with the prosecution and punishment of individuals, which concerns a state power as an *ultimum remedium* to be used when norms determined by a democratic decision-making process have been violated and implies a commensurate set of safeguards to avoid criminal procedural powers from being used arbitrarily or unnecessarily or in a manner which impairs the fairness of the procedure. Also the use of criminal investigative powers shall, therefore, be subjected to safeguards to offer the protection required so as to render the criminal justice system legitimate. As has been explained, criminal investigation has traditionally focused on the investigation of past criminal acts and is, therefore, retrospective. To be able to guarantee the fairness of criminal proceedings, transparency, also of investigative activities, is an important assumption. On the contrary, intelligence investigation is aimed at prevention through gaining competitive advantage by means of intelligence collection.[41] The intelligence investigative activities are, therefore, clearly directed towards the future, making threat analyses and analyzing data, covered by the realm of secrecy, in order to prevent harm.

The rise of anticipative criminal investigation blends this traditional institutional and functional separation between the intelligence and law enforcement community. The phenomenon of anticipative criminal investigation has adopted both intelligence and law enforcement functions. As will follow in the subsequent chapters, this may be realized by attributing a new preventive function to traditional criminal investigation and/or by attributing the function of evidence gathering to the employment of intelligence investigative tools. To put it succinctly: intelligence investigation and criminal investigation have traditionally been separated as different responses to threats and violence and, for that reason, have been subjected to different restraints on the government's powers in either field. However, due to the rise of the phenomenon of anticipative criminal investigation, this clear separation has been blended and the areas have started to overlap. For that reason, this book also involves the activities of intelligence agencies insofar as they influence the 'anticipative' capacity of the criminal investigation.

Because the specific purposes of the investigative activities are decisive for defining these activities as anticipative criminal investigation or as intelligence/national security investigation, it is important that the investigative purposes are clearly defined. The anticipative criminal investigative purpose is two-fold: it

---

[40] McCormack 2007, 35 and 49.

[41] According to Jennifer Sims, cited in the report of the US Director of National Intelligence 'Vision 2015'. McConell 2008, 8.

pursues the purpose of preventing terrorist crimes and, in parallel, it pursues the purpose of gathering information that can be used in criminal proceedings (e.g. in order to meet the threshold for using coercive methods or to charge someone with a criminal offense, with a view to prosecuting and punishing those guilty of having committed a (terrorist) crime). Because of this latter purpose, the investigation concerns a *criminal* investigation with the commensurate regulatory consequences (see Sects. 1.2.4 and 1.2.5). The intelligence and national security investigative purpose concerns exclusively the gathering of information in order to prevent harm, thereby protecting society against threats. However, this does not exclude the possibility of using information gathered for that specific intelligence/national security purpose in criminal proceedings. Decisive is the specific purpose of the *gathering* and not the eventual destination of the information.

## 1.3 Contextualizing States' Preventive Measures

Reforms to criminal investigative activities cannot—apart from modernization measures—be seen separately from the call on states to confront terrorism effectively. This call points to the presence of, and may also even be based upon, the duty of the state to protect its citizens against threats such as, recently most imminently, terrorism. In the past similar developments can be signaled with regard to other 'threats' involving criminal activity, such as drug trafficking and organized crime, that have called for an emphasis on the instrumental aspect of criminal procedural law. States experiencing difficulties in protecting their citizens against these more complex and threatening forms of crime take measures that increase the state's powers to confront these crimes, measures which have also affected criminal investigation.

This call on states to take measures can be derived from different contexts. In the first place, societal and political developments have resulted in an increased call on the states' responsibility to take measures to control risks and guarantee citizens a safe society. Secondly, since 9/11 international institutions such as the United Nations, the European Union and the Council of Europe have put pressure on states to take measures to prevent future terrorist attacks. In the third place, human rights obligations, in particular Article 2 of the ECHR, have been interpreted as also including a duty on the part of states to protect the lives of their citizens, which may require that they take measures which are necessary to prevent terrorist attacks that may threaten the lives of many innocent victims.[42]

Even in the presence of such a duty to prevent terrorism (or other serious threats), this does not necessarily mean that criminal investigation should also be especially geared towards the prevention of terrorism, as also many other measures, such as immigration policies, pure intelligence activities, military activities

[42] Compare Goldschmidt 2005, 14.

as well as education and the prevention of radicalization may very well be capable of reducing the possibility of future terrorist attacks. However, the influence of international institutions in this field and a call on states to take responsibility in protecting their citizens against terrorism have reinforced or sometimes even resulted in a focus on prevention in states' investigative efforts. Considering the pioneering role of the US in the field of counterterrorism in the wake of September 11, 2001, it cannot be said that the US has acted under the influence of international developments. Nevertheless, the developments in the US also fit within the larger international legal picture. In addition, a changed perception of the role of the state in providing safety caused by sociological and political factors applies equally to the United States. Especially these sociological and political factors, derived from theories on the risk society, the culture of control and the precautionary principle, have resulted in the mobilization of particularly the criminal justice system for prevention purposes.

Firstly, this section will address both the increased pressure on states to provide protection against acts of terrorism as a consequence of the influence of regulatory actions and policies by international institutions and the existence of a duty to protect under international human rights law obligations.[43] Subsequently, the sociological and political context which influences the state to take preventive measures will be addressed.

### *1.3.1 The Influence of International Institutions*

The influence from international institutions such as the United Nations (UN) and also the European Union (EU) and—to a more limited extent—the Council of Europe with regard to the Netherlands contextualize the reforms of states' criminal justice systems for the purpose of combating complex forms of crime and, most recently, to effectively confront terrorism. For some states this influence may even be considered as the driving force—at least in part—behind counterterrorism policies, such as the freezing of assets belonging to entities listed as terrorist organizations, the rearrangement of the capacities of intelligence services, anticipative investigative policies with relaxed legal requirements and intensified transnational cooperation between law enforcement services and intelligence services.[44]

At the level of the United Nations the 13 anti-terrorism conventions since 1963 have urged the Member States to act against different manifestations of

[43] See on the 'duty to protect' as a consequence of international legal and human rights law obligations also Hirsch Ballin 2012 (*forthcoming*).

[44] Compare: Luban et al. 2010, 704.

terrorism.[45] Shortly after 9/11 the UN Security Council adopted Resolution 1373, in which it expresses its intention to prevent all acts of terrorism and affirms the need to combat, by all means, "threats to international peace and security caused by terrorist acts." The Security Council recognized the need for all states to take additional measures in order to prevent and suppress, by lawful means, the preparation of terrorist attacks. For that purpose the Security Council has, among other things, decided that States should "take the necessary steps to prevent the commission of terrorist acts, (…) ensure that any person who participates in the financing, planning, preparation or perpetration of terrorist acts or in supporting terrorist acts is brought to justice and ensure that, in addition (…) such terrorist acts are established as serious criminal offences in domestic laws and regulations."[46] The United Nations Security Council Counter-Terrorism Committee, established in 2001, monitors the Member States' implementation of Resolution 1373, for which purpose Member States are required to report their actions in that regard.[47] Several subsequent resolutions of the Security Council have urged Member States to implement and comply with all measures, have urged Member States to combat the financing of terrorism and have established bodies for the monitoring of State efforts in combating international terrorism.[48] In 2006 the General Assembly of the UN adopted a resolution that entails the United Nations Global Counter-terrorism Strategy, which in general includes measures to prevent and combat terrorism in all Member States, encourages cooperation in that regard and strengthens the role of the UN in combating and preventing terrorism.[49] This includes measures for the purpose of "capacity-building in all States" to "prevent and combat terrorism", which includes an "effective and rule of law-based national criminal justice system that can ensure (…) that any person who participates in the financing, planning, preparation or perpetration of terrorist acts or in support of terrorist acts is brought to justice (…)."[50]

Furthermore, the policy of the European Union has had a significant influence on its Member States' (including the Netherlands) efforts to effectively combat

---

[45] For an overview of the 13 major legal instruments and additional amendments by the UN (the'13 Terrorism Conventions'): http://www.un.org/terrorism/instruments.shtml (accessed 6 July 2009). The first Convention in 1963 dealt with offenses and certain other acts committed on board aircraft. The last convention was adopted in 2005 and it deals with nuclear terrorism.

[46] Resolution 1373 (2001), adopted by the Security Council at its 4385th meeting, on 28 September 2001, *S/RES/1373* (2001).

[47] *Ibid.*, para 6. See on this: Van Ginkel 2010, 248–249 and Rosand 2004.

[48] See e.g. Resolution 1455 (2003), *S/RES/1455* (2003), Resolution 1526 (2004), *S/RES/1526* (2004), Resolution 1617 (2005), *S/RES/1617* (2005) and Resolution 1735 (2006), *S/RES/1735* (2006).

[49] General Assembly Resolution 60/288, The United Nations Global Counter-Terrorism Strategy, *A/RES/60/288*. The 'Counter-Terrorism Implementation Task Force' (established by the Secretary General in 2005) coordinates the implementation of the Strategy. See: Van Ginkel 2010, 204-206.

[50] General Assembly Resolution 60/288, The United Nations Global Counter-Terrorism Strategy, *A/RES/60/288,* para III and IV (4).

terrorism. The Council of the EU adopted the Framework Decision on Combating Terrorism on 13 June 2002.[51] This Framework decision starts with the statement that terrorism constitutes one of the most serious violations of the principles of human dignity, liberty, equality and solidarity, respect for human rights and fundamental freedoms as well as the principles of democracy and the rule of law, which are common to the Member States.[52] The Framework Decision has obliged the Member States to penalize the terrorist offenses specified in the Decision and to establish jurisdiction over these offenses.[53] The EU has since 2001 been very active in urging the Member States to contribute to effectively confronting terrorism and to enhance cooperation between the Member States for that purpose. By way of an example, in 2005 the Council of the EU adopted a decision on the exchange of information and cooperation concerning terrorist offenses[54] and by the Council decision of 23 June 2008 (on the stepping up of cross-border cooperation, particularly in combating terrorism and cross-border crime), essential parts of the Prüm Treaty (an intergovernmental treaty between some Member States of the EU) that improve the exchange of information for the purpose of criminal investigations or criminal intelligence operations have become applicable to all Member States.[55] Member States have repeatedly been urged to take the necessary measures for the prevention of terrorist crimes.[56]

Moreover, the Council of Europe has made efforts to canalize the pressure on its Member States, including the Netherlands, to take action in the field of terrorism prevention. The Council of Europe has adopted a Convention on the Prevention of Terrorism, which has imposed a 'duty to investigate' on the Member States "upon receiving information that a person who has committed or who is alleged to have

---

[51] Council of the European Union, 'Framework Decision of 13 June 2002 on Combating Terrorism,' *2002/475/JHA*.

[52] Framework Decision of 13 June 2002 on Combating Terrorism, sec. (1) and (2).

[53] In 2008 another Framework Decision on Combating Terrorism was adopted, which further expanded the mandatory criminalization of certain terrorist offenses. Council of the European Union, 'Framework Decision of 28 November 2008, amending Framework Decision 2002/475/JHA on combating terrorism', 2008/919/JHA.

[54] Council Decision 2005/671/JHA of 20 September 2005 on the exchange of information and cooperation concerning terrorist offenses.

[55] Council Decision 2008/615/JHA of 23 June 2008 on the stepping up of cross-border cooperation, particularly in combating terrorism and cross-border crime.

[56] See e.g.: *Presidency Conclusions—Brussels 4/5 November 2004, The Hague Programme, Strengthening Freedom, Security and Justice in the European Union*, at 28, 14292/1/04 Rev 1 Annex I, and *Communication from the Commission to the Council and the European Parliament, The Hague Programme, ten priorities for the next five years*, at 6, 8, COM (2005) 184 final (May 10, 2005): The fight against terrorism, working toward a global response. And see also: *The European Union counter-terrorism strategy* (adopted in December 2005 by the Council of the European Union), *14469/4/05 REV 4, DG H2,* in which four pillars of the strategy were adopted: prevent, protect, pursue and respond. 'Pursue' includes that "At a national level the competent authorities need to have the necessary tools to collect and analyse intelligence and to pursue and investigate terrorists, requiring Member States to update their policy response and legislative provisions here necessary." (12, under 24).

committed an offence set forth in this Convention may be present in its territory."[57]

The measures at the UN and European level, as described above, entail measures that aim to enhance the capacity—the instruments—of states to effectively combat and prevent terrorism. These measures have been accompanied by an increasing call to combat terrorism in accordance with human rights and international legal obligations. For example, the Convention on the Prevention of Terrorism of the Council of Europe affirmed that "all measures taken to prevent or suppress terrorist offences have to respect the rule of law and democratic values, human rights and fundamental freedoms as well as other provisions of international law, including, were applicable, international humanitarian law." Moreover, the Committee of Ministers of the Council of Europe adopted Guidelines on human rights and the fight against terrorism.[58] In addition, counterterrorism measures in the European Union should be taken in respect of the fundamental rights as guaranteed by the European Convention on Human Rights and Fundamental Freedoms (ECHR) as to Article 6(3) of the Treaty on European Union and in respect of the "the rights, freedoms and principles set out in the Charter of the Fundamental Rights of the European Union" as to Article 6(1) of the Treaty on European Union.[59] Also the General Assembly adopted resolutions regarding the protection of human rights and fundamental freedoms while countering terrorism and appointed a special rapporteur on the promotion and protection of human rights and fundamental freedoms while countering terrorism.[60]

### *1.3.2 A Duty to Prevent Terrorism Under International Human Rights Law Obligations*

Article 9 of the International Covenant on Civil and Political Rights (ICCPR), Article 6 of the Charter of the Fundamental Rights of the European Union and Article 7 of the American Convention on Human Rights (ACHR) explicitly

[57] Article 15 of the Council of Europe Convention on the Prevention of Terrorism, *CETS 196, 16.V.2005 (Trb.* 2006, 34*)*: "(…) the Party concerned shall take such measures as may be necessary under its domestic law to investigate the facts contained in the information."

[58] Guidelines on human rights and the fight against terrorism, adopted by the Committee of Ministers on 11 July 2002 at the 804th meeting of the Ministers' Deputies.

[59] Treaty of Lisbon amending the Treaty on European Union and the Treaty establishing the European Community, 2007/C 306/01. See also: Council of the European Union, 'Framework Decision of 13 June 2002 on Combating Terrorism,' *2002/475/JHA*, sec. (10).

[60] Human Rights Resolution 2005/80, Protection of human rights and fundamental freedoms while countering terrorism. See for more information on the Special Rapporteur as well as his reports: http://www.ohchr.org/EN/Issues/Terrorism/Pages/SRTerrorismIndex.aspx. See also General Assembly Resolution 60/288, The United Nations Global Counter-Terrorism Strategy, *A/RES/60/288,* para IV ("Measures to ensure respect for human rights for all and the rule of law as the fundamental basis of the fight against terrorism").

provide that everyone has the right to liberty and security of person. Article 2 of the European Convention on Human Rights (ECHR) provides for the right to life. This right to life has been interpreted as having a close relation with the positive duty of the state to provide a secure society.[61]

The European Court of Human Rights (ECrtHR) held in *Osman v. The United Kingdom* that Section 1 of Article 2 "enjoins" the state "to take appropriate steps to safeguard the lives of those within its jurisdiction." This duty to protect involves a "primary duty to secure the right to life by putting in place effective criminal-law provisions to deter the commission of the offenses against the person backed up by a law-enforcement machinery for the prevention, suppression and punishment of breaches of such provisions." Here, the Court includes the use of criminal procedural law for the prevention of crime in the state's duty to protect. Moreover, the Court has stated that the duty to protect also extends "in certain well-defined circumstances" to "a positive obligation on the authorities to take preventive operational measures to protect an individual whose life is at risk from the criminal acts of another individual."[62] Furthermore, the Court emphasized that the police need to "exercise their powers to control and prevent crime in a manner which fully respects the due process and other guarantees which legitimately place restraints on the scope of their action to investigate crime and bring offenders to justice, including the guarantees contained in Articles 5 and 8 of the Convention."[63] The protections offered by the state to meet the requirements of the positive duty implied in Article 2 must be "practical and effective" in order to not leave the guarantees of the ECHR as a dead letter.[64] An important factor to consider in assessing whether the state has, in the circumstances of a particular case, violated the right to life is whether "the authorities knew or ought to have known at the time of the existence of a real and immediate risk to the life of an identified individual or individuals from the criminal acts of a third party."[65]

On that basis, the conclusion can be drawn that Article 2 ECHR has been interpreted so as to impose a positive duty on the state to use its criminal procedural powers to establish the truth when a fellow-citizen has violated a citizen's right to life. This includes at least the duty to investigate thoroughly any taking of

---

[61] Some have argued that the duty to protect also implies a fundamental right to security. See on that issue: Van Zuijlen 2008, 184-185 (concluding in the negative). Moreover, also other Articles of the ECHR have been interpreted so as to include positive duties on the state to realize the protection of the interests protected by these articles. For example, Articles 3, 4, 8 and 9 ECHR have been interpreted by the Court to impose on states also the obligation to criminalize acts that violate the rights protected by these Articles. See also: Vellinga-Schootstra and Vellinga 2008, 11–16.

[62] ECHR 28 October 1998, App. no. 23452/94 (*Osman v. The United Kingdom*), para 115. See also ECHR 10 October 2000, App. nos 22947/93 and 22948/93 (*Akkoç v. Turkey*), para 77 and ECHR 3 April 2001, App. no. 27229/95 (*Keenan v. The United Kingdom*), para 89.

[63] ECHR 28 October 1998, App. no. 23452/94 (*Osman v. The United Kingdom*), para 116.

[64] ECHR 24 April 2003, App. no. 24351/94 (*Aktaş v. Turkey*), para 289.

[65] ECHR 28 October 1998, App. no. 23452/94 (*Osman v. The United Kingdom*), para 116.

life (e.g. murder) and any attempt to take a life by a fellow-citizen.[66] From the language used in *Osman* it follows that the duty of the state includes the prevention of violations of the right to life; however, this is limited to "well-defined" circumstances and applies—in the cases the Court has dealt with—to the situation of a concrete threat concerning a specific person. The Court has not (yet) dealt with the question whether the operational measures that must be taken also include the investigation of information regarding a *threat* of terrorism. For this reason, it cannot be said that the duty to protect under Article 2 ECHR includes, according to the ECrtHR, the duty to take general operational measures for the purpose of preventing terrorism. In any event, when a state decides to adopt such general operational measures in criminal procedural law, these measures should observe other protections in the ECHR, which for the use of criminal investigative powers in particular concerns Article 8 ECHR.[67]

In comparison to Strasbourg's interpretation of the duty to protect under Article 2, the "Guidelines on human rights and the fight against terrorism," as adopted in 2002 by the Council of Europe, are somewhat more specific. The guidelines provide explicitly that the right to life implies also a duty to protect everyone against terrorism. Article I of these guidelines provides that "states are under the obligation to take the measures needed to protect the fundamental rights of everyone within their jurisdiction against terrorist acts, especially the right to life. This positive obligation fully justifies States' fight against terrorism in accordance with the present guidelines."[68] Also in the preamble to these Guidelines it is stated that states have "the imperative duty to protect their population against possible terrorist acts."[69] Moreover, the Council of Europe adopted a Convention on the Prevention of Terrorism imposing a 'duty to investigate' on Member States "upon receiving information that a person who has committed or who is alleged to have committed an offence set forth in this Convention may be present in its territory."[70]

It seems that the Council of Europe intends to encourage states to extend their responsibility to protect to the prevention of acts of terrorism, which concerns a threat to the collective instead of a threat to identified persons (as required under the duty to protect following from Article 2 ECHR).

Lastly, also the Inter-American Court of Human Rights (IACHR) has read a duty to protect into Article 7 of the ACHR (the right to personal liberty and security) in conjunction with Article 1(1) of the ACHR (the obligation for State Parties to respect

---

[66] Van Kempen 2008, 45-46. For an overview of operational measures that the state should take under its positive obligation as has been dealt with in ECHR case law, see: Van Kempen 2008, 40-43. See also: Vellinga-Schootstra and Vellinga 2008, 7-10.

[67] Van Kempen 2008, 49.

[68] Guidelines on human rights and the fight against terrorism, adopted by the Committee of Ministers on 11 July 2002 at the 804th meeting of the Ministers' Deputies, Article I.

[69] *Ibid.*, preamble.

[70] Article 15 of the Council of Europe Convention on the Prevention of Terrorism, *CETS 196, 16.V.2005 (Trb.* 2006, 34*)*: "(…) the Party concerned shall take such measures as may be necessary under its domestic law to investigate the facts contained in the information."

the rights and freedoms protected in the Convention) in the case of *Velásquez Rodríguez v. Honduras* concerning forced disappearance.[71] The Court concluded that "[a]n illegal act which violates human rights and which is initially not directly imputable to a State (...) can lead to international responsibility of the State, not because of the act itself, but because of the lack of due diligence to prevent the violation or to respond to it as required by the Convention."[72] This duty to protect includes, according to the IACHR, a duty for the state to investigate situations where rights protected by the Convention have been violated.[73]

### 1.3.3 The Influence of Theories on the Risk Society, the Culture of Control and the Precautionary Principle on Mobilizing Criminal Law for the Purpose of Prevention

Increasingly, citizens have started to expect their governments to guarantee a safe society and to take the measures which are necessary to control danger and guarantee security. A changed sociological and political climate has resulted in different expectations with regard to the government's responsibility in providing a secure society, which includes an expectation that the government takes the measures which are necessary to prevent future terrorist attacks. This development has been identified on the basis of theories such as the risk society, the culture of control and the precautionary principle. Not only as a consequence of the influence of international institutions and a duty to prevent under human rights law obligations, but also the influence of these theories constitute the background to changes in the criminal law, in particular with regard to the use of the criminal justice system as a means to prevent harm.

The risk society is a concept which was introduced by Ulrich Beck, on which basis the changed perception of the role of criminal law in modern society is explained as a consequence of the technological developments in the social welfare state. These technological developments have resulted in uncontrollable risks and citizens have become increasingly aware of these risks, also as a consequence of the mass communication and media coverage of catastrophes including terrorist attacks. For this reason, states have become orientated on controlling and managing risks.[74] David Garland's concept of the culture of control explains that criminal law has become a means to control security risks by eliminating risky elements as part of an overall culture of control, which has arisen due to different sociological, criminological and political factors.[75] The precautionary principle

[71] IACHR 29 July 1988, Series C No. 4 (*Velásquez Rodríguez v. Honduras*).

[72] *Ibid.*, para 172.

[73] *Ibid.*, para 176. See in more detail Mégret 2010, 131-132.

[74] Beck 2005.

[75] Garland 2002.

has been developed by Sunstein as a normative notion obliging the state to take precautionary measures in the presence of a threat of a wide-ranging disaster (for which reason it can also be understood as an anti-catastrophe principle).[76]

All three theories have in common that they identify a change in society focusing on the control and management of risks in order to provide safety.[77] In line with this focus on controlling and managing risks a 'security paradigm' can be identified, which has been the driving force behind changes in states' policies affecting the criminal justice system, the intelligence apparatus, immigration policies, as well as various other state instruments that are considered useful for improving security. Also the criminal justice system has thus, as a consequence of a changed perception in society with regard to risk and safety and the role of the state in controlling risks and providing security, increasingly become one of the state's instruments to fulfill this role. Consequently, criminal law has obtained a character supplementing its traditional character, namely a risk-controlling character with a focus on realizing security through prevention and eliminating risky elements from society. To gear the criminal justice system towards that function, the criminal justice system has been expanded, has become more complex and harsher and has approached the field of work of the intelligence apparatus.[78]

## 1.4 Framing the Subject

After the confrontation with the devastating terrorist crimes on September 11, 2001 (in the United States), and on March 11, 2004 (Madrid) and July 7, 2005 (London) within the EU, states have taken a wide range of measures to minimize the possibility of new terrorist attacks. As described in Sect. 1.3, these measures go hand-in-hand with developments on the international plane. Moreover, human rights law obligations may be invoked as requiring states to take measures to prevent terrorist attacks in order to protect the right to life of their citizens. In addition, states have acted on their own initiatives as a result of domestic societal and political pressure calling for a focus on security, which has in particular resulted in the mobilization of criminal law for the purpose of prevention. These developments forming the background of counterterrorism measures may point to a duty for states to protect citizens against serious security threats and harm.

During the past decade states have become increasingly aware of the importance of setting out a counterterrorism strategy that is in accordance with the fundamental values of a state governed by the rule of law. The legitimacy of counterterrorism measures will ultimately depend on the ability of the state to take these measures while not trading in on the principles that are inherent in the rule of

[76] Sunstein 2005. See also: Borgers and Van Sliedregt 2009, 183-187.

[77] Safety is a broader concept, including security as well as other risks, such as health risks or the risks of natural disasters.

[78] Groenhuijsen and Kooijmans 2010, 452.

law. The report of a worldwide survey by the International Commission of Jurists has demonstrated that "the events of 11 September 2001 have changed the legal landscape in countries around the world." States have "allowed themselves to be rushed into hasty responses, introducing an array of measures which undermine cherished values as well as the international legal framework carefully developed since the Second World War."[79] Many measures affecting criminal law have resulted in a trade-in of criminal procedural principles and standards of due process and in some cases even violating fundamental values such as the prohibition of torture. When we consider these standards and values as being inherent to contemporary citizens, deviating therefrom in the name of security also undermines the legitimacy of counterterrorism measures as it supports the goals of terrorists when there is a failure to uphold the fundamental values of contemporary civilized society.[80] A commitment to the rule of law can be demonstrated by upholding its inherent values also during times of crisis. As the Supreme Court of the United States emphasized in *Hamdi v. Rumsfeld*: "we must preserve our commitment at home to the principles for which we fight abroad."[81]

Many counterterrorism measures were taken outside the scope of criminal justice. Many others have also affected the traditional principles that apply to the criminal justice systems of states, including those enabling anticipative criminal investigations. When the state is called upon to suppress terrorism and applies criminal law for that goal,[82] this inevitably results in tension between the truth-finding objective (the sword dimension) and the protective objective (the shield dimension). The protective function of criminal law towards society, towards the (potential) victims of these serious forms of crime, results in a shift to the instrumental character of criminal law. Many "sword measures" have been taken to confront these crimes, but often, however, without compensating them with additional "shield measures".[83]

Today, the threat of terrorism has resulted in an increase in the practical means of the state to use also criminal procedural powers for the *prevention* of terrorism. This has been realized by watering down procedural restraints that have traditionally governed criminal procedural law and by a merger between intelligence and law enforcement functions, which are traditionally two institutionally separated fields but have obtained a joint primarily goal of prevention through

---

[79] International Commission of Jurists 2009.

[80] Bassiouni 2005, 20 and 25-26.

[81] *Hamdi v. Rumsfeld*, 542 U.S. 507, 124 S.Ct. 2633, 2648 (2004), 531 (sec. III, C, 3).

[82] As explained in Sect. 1.3.2, it must be noted that on the basis of the case law of the ECrtHR an identifiable 'duty to protect' does not oblige states acting under this duty to employ also criminal procedural law for the prevention of future terrorist attacks (as opposed to a concrete danger). Rather, at first sight, it may be more natural to attribute the intelligence community with an enhanced responsibility for the prevention of terrorism.

[83] See Vogler 2008, 20, Groenhuijsen and Simmelink 2008, 379 and Foqué and 't Hart 1990, 16; the Modern Approach to criminal law focuses on the control of crime, which implies a more instrumental character.

intensified cooperation.[84] Traditionally, criminal procedural law has a reactive nature, because the sword function of criminal procedural law is based on the assumption of deterrence and repression through prosecution and punishment. However, today also preventing *ex ante* the fundamental rights of individuals from being violated by other individuals is a task of the state for which criminal law is increasingly employed. Whether or not it is actually required under the duty to prevent terrorism, the preventive use of criminal procedural powers has accelerated due to an increased call on states to give effect to this duty since 9/11.

In order to employ criminal law effectively for that purpose with regard to more threatening forms of crime that may affect a large part of society, the focus has increasingly been placed on crime control, which has developed towards crime prevention. Whilst an increased focus on crime control results in a shift of focus in the synthesis between the instrumental and protective aspect of criminal procedural law, a shift to anticipative investigation goes somewhat further. An independent objective of investigation is now the prevention of crime, which goes further than increasing the focus on crime control at the expense of protection and restraints, for example, by allowing proactive investigation in order to effectively prosecute organized crime. Prevention has become an independent and new sword goal of criminal investigative activities, in addition to the traditional goal of gathering evidence to prosecute crimes with the final objective of repression and prevention through deterrence.

The preventive function of criminal law is, however, at the same time limited by respect for fundamental rights and the principles which are applicable in the relation between the state and individuals. When we consider every human being's right to human dignity as being part of the rule of law and the rule of law as the notion that should govern all state action, then expanding the sword function of criminal procedural law may never occur, in a way impairing the realization of the protective objective in criminal procedural law, due to a trading in on the protection of fundamental rights and principles by deviating from traditional criminal procedural principles during the investigative phase. Nevertheless, respect for the rule of law imposes on the state also the duty to protect its citizens against (terrorist) crimes. In this regard it must be noted that although the taking of preventive measures as such is justified considering the background of an increased call on the duty of states to take such measures, introducing new and/or adjusted frameworks for this purpose needs to conform to the requirements following from the rule of law. Hence, the developments described in Sect. 1.3 cannot as such *legitimize* the adoption of specific measures for the purpose of terrorism prevention under the rule of law. The legitimacy of gearing criminal investigation towards the prevention of terrorist crimes, to be considered against the background of a call on states to prevent future terrorist attacks, depends on the question whether prevention is a goal that can be pursued by criminal investigation without unacceptably trading in on the protective function of criminal procedural law.

[84] Bassiouni 2002, 94. See also: McCormack 2007, 37-38 and 191.

## 1.5 Research Question

The rule of law, as the notion that guarantees the inalienable rights of each citizen attached to his/her individual right to human dignity, imposes on states the duty to guarantee fundamental rights providing equality, liberty and security for each citizen. That duty is two-fold: (1) it entitles citizens to protection against the state interfering with their fundamental rights, attached to their right to human dignity; and (2) it imposes a duty on the state to offer protection to its citizens against any violation of their fundamental rights by fellow-citizens. The first concerns a negative duty on the state to refrain from meddling with the liberty of its citizens, whereas the latter imposes a positive duty on the state to offer protection against (potential) violations against individual liberty by others; to offer security. Both duties are interrelated as security is ultimately realized through the pursuit of liberty and liberty can ultimately only be enjoyed subject to the condition of security.[85] This two-fold duty is also the legitimization for the establishment of a criminal justice system, for which reason the regulation of criminal procedural law shall conform to a synthesis between instruments for confronting crime and restraints and safeguards in order to adequately protect citizens against the state interfering with their fundamental rights.

Since September 11, 2001 states have focused, against the backdrop of the larger context described in Sect. 1.3, on adopting a variety of measures under the umbrella of the preventive paradigm, which has included measures affecting the criminal justice system. Under the preventive paradigm, prevention has also become an independent goal of criminal investigation. This shift to prevention does not concern a revolutionary development only caused by the events of 9/11. Rather, the system had already evolved prior to the events of 9/11 from a primary reactive system to a system that increasingly pursues proactive goals, an evolvement which has accelerated towards an independent goal of preventing crimes in the post-9/11 era.

As a consequence of the emergence of the anticipative criminal investigation, the sword objective of criminal investigation has changed from, exclusively, the enforcement of substantive norms by gathering evidence of criminal acts for the purpose of prosecution, to include also the prevention of crimes by focusing on dangerous behavior that may point to the initial planning of crimes. The synthesis between the sword and shield objective of criminal procedural law has traditionally been found by adhering to principles that make the criminal investigation primarily a reactive enterprise aimed at the repression and deterrence of crime by the prosecution and punishment of criminal offenders. This synthesis has now been affected as a consequence of an increased focus on the prevention of crime by starting to intercept potentially dangerous activities before crimes have actually been committed.

---

[85] Lazarus and Goold 2007, 2.

This brings us to the formulation of the central research question which this book seeks to answer:

*Can a preventive function of criminal investigation be part of a criminal justice system under the rule of law and, if so, under what conditions, and what does this mean for the current regulation of anticipative criminal investigations adopted in the Netherlands and the United States?*

This research question is two-fold: it seeks to answer the question whether the concept of anticipative criminal investigation is *as such* compatible with a criminal justice system under the rule of law, and it seeks to provide for a normative judgment as to the compatibility with the rule of law of the current adopted regulation for anticipative criminal investigation in the Netherlands and the United States.

Before it will be possible to answer the central research question, the parts of the book dealing with the particular situation of the Netherlands and the United States will seek to answer the following sub-questions:

- To which limitations has criminal investigation in the Netherlands and the United States traditionally been subjected in order to realize both the sword and shield objective of criminal procedural law?
- By means of which changes has anticipative criminal investigation in the Netherlands and the United States been realized?
- What are the implications of enabling anticipative criminal investigation for the shield objective of criminal procedural law, the relation between the sword and shield objectives and for the role and position of criminal investigation?

## 1.6 Approach and Methodology

The approach taken in this book differs from the traditional approach of dealing with adjustments to the criminal justice system, where the obligation of crime control is balanced against the duty to offer sufficient protection to citizens.[86] In this book the position is taken that such a balancing approach is unsatisfactory for determining whether a particular regulation reflects the required synthesis between the sword and the shield under the rule of law. Considering protective elements and security interests as factors that can be weighed against each other denies the common ground of protection and instruments under a rule of law notion that is underpinned by the right to respect for human dignity.

This subject, as well as the recommended approach in examining a particular system of regulating anticipative criminal investigation, will be extensively broached in Chap. 8. In Chap. 8 a framework for examination will be adopted by identifying the fundamental rights and principles, attached to the right to respect

---

[86] Groenhuijsen and Knigge 2001, 21.

for human dignity, which provide for the 'common ground' of any system of regulation for criminal investigation. In addition, the assessment will go a step further by reflecting on the mobilization of criminal investigation for the purpose of prevention. For that purpose, it will be addressed whether a focus on prevention can be harmonized with the protective objective of criminal procedural law. This raises new questions as to the relation between anticipative criminal investigation and the traditional character of criminal procedural law as a primarily reactive enterprise aimed at repression and as an *ultimum remedium*. Furthermore, it raises questions as to the relation between the newly obtained function and position of criminal investigation and the function and position of the intelligence community. Only when anticipative criminal investigation can be realized without undermining the protective objective of criminal procedural law is gearing criminal investigation towards prevention, when it comes to terrorism, a legitimate and suitable[87] tool for realizing the state's duty to protect citizens against terrorist attacks.

Before Chap. 8 will continue with the theoretical assessment of the phenomenon of the anticipative criminal investigation, which may be applied to any state governed by the rule of law, the situation in the Netherlands and the United States will be assessed in detail (parts I and II). These two countries will function as examples of, firstly, how anticipative criminal investigation may be embedded into their respective legal systems and, secondly, the implications for the synthesis of shield and sword in their respective regulatory frameworks for criminal investigation. Subsequently, the conclusions drawn for both countries as to the implications for the synthesis considering their traditional framework of regulating criminal investigation will be examined on the basis of the framework for examination formulated in Chap. 8.

On the basis of the foregoing, three levels of analysis can be identified in order to answer the central research question.

In the *first* place, changes made to the framework of the criminal investigation to enable a preventive approach will be examined on the basis of the existing normative framework adopted as the synthesis between the sword and shield objective of criminal procedural law. This legal examination will result in a conclusion as to the implications for the interests that traditional regulatory rules of the criminal investigation seek to protect and the seriousness of the deviation from protective elements as caused by the shift to prevention in the criminal investigation. It will define the position of anticipative criminal investigation in relation to the traditional criminal investigation and in relation to intelligence investigation. The examination will be conducted for the Netherlands (Chap. 4) and the United States (Chap. 7) separately on the basis of an analysis of the traditional design of the criminal justice system of each country (Chaps. 2 and 5 respectively) and an analysis of the measures that have contributed to a shift towards prevention (Chaps. 3 and 6 respectively).

---

[87] Presuming that such anticipative criminal investigation may also be an effective tool to intercept the planning of future terrorist attacks.

The existing normative framework, compounded by traditional criminal procedural restraints based on the idea that the criminal justice system is primarily a reactive enterprise, will not, however, be the eventual frame of examination. The underlying objectives of the criminal justice system constitute the ultimate frame of reference, upon which any adopted regulation of criminal investigation shall be based. Hence, the *second* level of analysis will constitute a theoretical evaluation of the normative frameworks for criminal investigation on the basis of its underlying assumptions regarding the role and function that criminal procedural law should have under the rule of law and the relation of these assumptions to the circumstances of modern society. Arguments will be discussed and assessed, which may currently provide a reason for a different approach towards the role and function of criminal procedural law and which may advocate for or against any deviation from traditional protective criminal procedural notions. On that basis a regulatory architecture for anticipative criminal investigation will be developed, detached from the specific context of the Netherlands and the United States and, hence, applicable to any legal system which is subject to the rule of law. The theoretical analysis will result in the answer to the first part of the research question (Chap. 8), namely whether criminal investigation may at all be employed for the purpose of preventing crimes and, if so, general conditions for the regulation of anticipative criminal investigation will be deduced from the theoretical analysis.

The *third* level of analysis will apply the outcome of the second level to the outcome of the first level of analysis and draw conclusions as to the acceptability of the approaches taken in the Netherlands and the United States to enable anticipative criminal investigation. On the basis of the formulated general conditions, conclusions will be drawn with regard to the acceptability of the determined position of anticipative criminal investigation in both countries and the acceptability of the identified implications for the shield objective of criminal procedural law (Chap. 9). Where appropriate, recommendations will be made, which may bring the adopted regulation for anticipative criminal investigation within rule of law borders. Hence, the comparison between the Netherlands and the United States does not concern an evaluation of the differences and similarities in their regulation of anticipative criminal investigations, but an evaluation of the functionality of the regulation of anticipative criminal investigation to realize a system that does not undermine the legitimacy of the criminal justice system.

The first level of analysis will be conducted on the basis of an assessment of the positive law, using sources of legislation (domestic law and, if applicable, (human rights) treaty law), case law (domestic case law and, if applicable, the case law of the ECrtHR) and legal doctrine.

The second level of analysis will seek the content underpinning the positive law by means of a theoretical reflection based on the concept of the rule of law adopted in this chapter. Hence, sources of legal philosophy and legal theory will be used, whilst seeking confirmation of the fundamental character of rights and principles in the recognition of these rights and principles in human rights documents and constitutional doctrine. Furthermore, the second level of analysis will use not only legal sources but also sources of a criminological or political nature, in order to give effect to normative argumentation in the flexible area of the law where it needs to adapt to the specific circumstances of current society and the specific issues which criminal justice in this current society needs to deal with.

The third level of analysis combines the findings of the foregoing levels in order to subject the positive law to an examination as to its compatibility with fundamental underlying values. This shall result in recommendations as to the further development of the procedural and institutional embedding of the state's role in achieving preventive goals and the desire to employ the criminal investigation for that purpose.

# Part I
# The Netherlands

# Chapter 2
# The System of Criminal Investigation in the Netherlands

## 2.1 Introduction

### 2.1.1 Goals of the Chapter

The assessment of the manner in which anticipative criminal investigation has been embedded in the Dutch system of criminal procedural law and, possibly, cognate legal systems, will require a precise understanding of the system of criminal investigation in the Netherlands. The goal of the underlying chapter is to provide for this precise understanding by drawing the relevant legal background of the system of criminal investigation and to identify the basic assumptions underpinning the regulation of criminal investigation in the Netherlands. Changes to the system that have been adopted in order to make the criminal investigation also suitable for the prevention of terrorism, thereby enabling anticipative criminal investigation, will not yet be dealt with. These changes will be addressed in Chap. 3. The description of the system of criminal investigation in the current chapter will be provided in a serving manner: in anticipation of the changes adopted for terrorism prevention and the implications of these changes for the system of criminal procedural law as the synthesis of the sword and shield elements. Therefore, some aspects which are relevant for understanding the consequences of changes to the system in response to the terrorist attack of September 11th 2001 and the attacks on European soil in Madrid and London in March 2004 and July 2005 will be dealt with in more detail. Other aspects will be addressed more generally and only to provide a correct understanding of the system as a whole. Specific attention will also be attributed to the basic principles and assumptions underpinning the regulation of the Dutch system of criminal investigations, notwithstanding the fact that some of these principles have a regulatory influence on the system as a whole. Addressing these principles is in particular important in order to be able to draw conclusions as to the

M.F.H. Hirsch Ballin, *Anticipative Criminal Investigation*,
DOI: 10.1007/978-90-6704-843-9_2,

implications of the changes (as described in Chap. 3) to the sword and shield objectives of criminal procedural law, which will be done in Chap. 4.

The rights and principles underpinning the Dutch system of criminal investigation follow in the first place from the European Convention on Human Rights, which is directly applicable in the Netherlands. Because the Netherlands does not have a Constitutional Court, the decisions of the European Court of Human Rights have a significant regulatory influence.[1] In addition, Constitutional rights and fundamental principles of criminal procedural law constitute the foundation of the framework for regulating criminal investigation. After providing for some basic characteristics of the Dutch criminal justice system, this introductory section will elaborate on these fundamental principles and rights that are relevant for the regulation of criminal investigations in the Netherlands. Furthermore, the contents of this chapter will largely follow from the manner in which the criminal investigation has found its regulation in the Dutch Code of Criminal Procedure (henceforth: CCP), originally adopted in 1926, which provides for the basic choices for giving effect to the sword objective and shield objective in criminal investigation. On the basis of the provisions of the CCP the specific role and functions attributed to the different actors in the criminal investigation and the adopted restrictive elements on the use of criminal investigative powers can be identified. In order to provide for a correct understanding of these provisions, their interpretation in case law, in so far as is applicable, will be taken into account.

The chapter is divided into two main parts, reflecting the synthesis that the regulation as a whole shall provide between the sword and shield objectives. Section 2.2 will deal with the manner in which the system of criminal investigation is able to give effect to the sword objective of criminal procedural law. The actors responsible for carrying out the sword function of criminal investigation and the criminal investigative powers attributed to these actors will be described. Attention will also be given to the relevance of the activities of the intelligence and security service for the criminal investigation. Subsequently, Sect. 2.3 will address the shield responsibilities of the actors having a role in the criminal investigation and describe the restraints on the powers of criminal investigation in order to give effect to the principles and rights underpinning the shield objective of criminal investigation.

Hence, this chapter will seek an answer to the following two questions:

1. How is the sword objective in the Dutch system of criminal investigation realized? This will firstly require an analysis of the actors that have a truth-finding responsibility and, secondly, an analysis of the investigative powers available to these truth-finding actors.
2. How is the shield objective in the Dutch system of criminal investigation realized? Answering this question will, firstly, require an analysis of the responsibility of the actors during the criminal investigation to contribute to the fairness of the investigation. Furthermore, different elements have been adopted in order to provide for legal protection against arbitrary interferences with the fundamental right to respect for private life and in order to realize a fair criminal process.

[1] See in more detail the introduction to Sect. 2.1.3.

### 2.1.2 The Dutch Criminal Justice System

Contiguous to the objectives of criminal procedural law, as formulated in Chap. 1, the Dutch CCP as established in 1926 clearly formulates that the main goal of criminal procedural law is to establish the truth in order to convict the guilty and to prevent the conviction of those who are innocent.[2] Considering this goal of criminal procedural law, the criminal process must be designed in a manner that is orientated towards truth-finding, while the possibility that the innocent will be convicted is minimized. More specifically, the criminal process must provide for enough safeguards to prevent criminal procedural powers having an adverse impact on the innocent (the shield function of criminal procedural law) and, at the other hand, provide for enough practical means to enable truth-finding by the police and the Public Prosecution Service (henceforth: PPS), the judiciary (pre-trial: the examining magistrate, and, subsequently, the trial judge) and the defense (the sword function of criminal procedural law). The combination of both functions shall result in a system that can, with sufficient certainty, produce the substantive truth.[3] In addition, criminal procedural law shall be attributed a broader and independent shield function: not only guaranteeing the just application of the criminal law, but also generally providing the safeguards against the arbitrary and unnecessary use of criminal procedural powers.[4]

Currently the role of criminal procedural law and, thus, of the CCP, is understood as pursuing the interests of *all* involved—victims as well as suspects—and providing space for a criminal justice system in which fundamental rights and the interests of the accused, witnesses and victims are recognized.[5] The desire to pursue both of these objectives of criminal law and to design a system of criminal justice, accordingly, has resulted in specific choices that have become basic assumptions for criminal procedural law in the Netherlands. These basic assumptions are directly related to the legal tradition of the Netherlands. Hence, this section will start by describing the legal tradition of the Netherlands, followed

---

[2] This view was also adopted by the research into Criminal Procedure in 2001 (an extensive research project into the fundaments of criminal procedural law as a proposal for a possible new Code of Criminal Procedure): Groenhuijsen and Knigge 2001.

[3] Groenhuijsen and Knigge 2001, 17-18.

[4] Brants et al. 2003, 2-6. The authors consider the Criminal Procedure 2001 researchers' view on the objectives of criminal procedural law to be too restrictive: the shield function of criminal procedural law has been reduced to *a* function, instead of *the* (main) function of criminal procedural law. In this book the approach has been taken that criminal procedural law has two main objectives: a shield and a sword objective (see Chap. 1, Sect. 1.2.4). The shield objective will, however, be described more broadly than only making sure that the innocent are not convicted. It has a general protective function against the arbitrary and unnecessary use of criminal procedural powers, which is connected to the *ultimum remedium* character of criminal procedural law.

[5] Groenhuijsen and Simmelink 2008, 379.

by an explanation of the basic assumptions in the system of Dutch criminal investigation that follow from the Dutch legal tradition.

Dutch criminal procedural law is strongly influenced by the French system. The French *Code d'Instruction Criminelle* that entered into force in 1811 also applied, by order of Napoleon, in the Netherlands. This Code strongly followed an inquisitorial model, especially in the pre-trial phase. The Netherlands first adopted its own Code of Criminal Procedure in 1838, which was however basically a copy of the French *Code d'Instruction Criminelle,* although trial by jury had been abolished. In 1926 the current Code of Criminal Procedure replaced the old version. The CCP importantly changed the character of the criminal investigation by regulating the powers of the police and the Public Prosecution Service, providing citizens with legal protection against state power and allowing procedural rights for the suspect (pre-trial) and the accused (after the decision to prosecute has been taken). The reforms aimed to turn the inquisitorial character of the criminal justice system into a more accusatorial process. The explanatory memorandum to the Dutch CCP characterizes the criminal justice system as being moderately accusatorial. In fact, it is neither typically inquisitorial nor accusatorial, but has features of both. The design of the criminal justice system has been based on the compromise between, on the one hand, the need to give the state the powers to repress crime and to protect the victim, and, on the other hand, to provide the defense with all rights that do not obstruct the purpose of the system; the establishment of the substantive truth.[6] The Dutch criminal justice system has evolved from being inquisitorial, with the focus on crime control, towards a system in which also the protective elements of the rule of law are recognized by including safeguards that aim to protect fundamental rights. Moreover, under the influence of the ECHR, the position of the defense during trial has gained in importance.[7]

The Dutch criminal process can be divided into three main stages: the pre-trial stage [*voorbereidend onderzoek*] in which the criminal investigation [*opsporingsonderzoek*] is carried out, the trial stage [*eindonderzoek*],[8] and the execution stage. The trial stage constitutes a debate amongst the actors (the judge, prosecutor and defense) with an active role for the judge, which shall result in the establishment of the substantive truth by the judge.

At the moment of the adoption of the CCP of 1926, the legislature aimed to create a system with emphasis on the truth-finding process within the trial phase, subject to the applicability of the principle of immediacy. However, due to a Supreme Court decision of 1926, where the Supreme Court accepted hearsay

---

[6] Lindenberg 2002, 424 (MvT 17).

[7] Reijntjes 2006, 11.

[8] Currently, two types of investigative phases can be initiated pre-trial: the criminal investigation and the preliminary judicial investigation. Because the Act on Strengthening the Position of the Examining Magistrate, by which the preliminary judicial investigation will be abolished, has been adopted by the Second Chamber of Parliament on June 30, 2011 and, because it can be expected that also the First Chamber of Parliament will adopt the Act in due time, in this book the law is described according to the changes following from this Act. See on this in more detail Sects. 2.2.1.3 and 2.3.1.3.

testimony (*testimonium de auditu*) as evidence, both written and oral, the pre-trial phase has become the most crucial within the truth-finding process.[9] Since this Supreme Court decision the principle of immediacy is no longer interpreted as requiring that all evidence is directly produced in court. Rather, the hearing of witnesses at trial has become rather an exception. Instead, the dossier contains the written testimonials of witnesses heard by the police or examining magistrate and during the trial investigation these testimonials are discussed and verified. As a consequence, the pre-trial phase has obtained increasing importance and the events during the pre-trial phase have become crucial for the final judgment.[10]

Over the past decades the principle of immediacy has again retrieved more attention under the influence of the case law of the ECrtHR. According to Article 6 ECHR the investigation at trial must have an adversarial nature.[11] Consequently, the accused has the right to be present, the proceedings are held in public and the principle of immediacy applies. Because of the principle of immediacy, the judge may only use the materials discussed at trial as evidence. The judge decides what material is discussed. The defense has the right to challenge these materials.

Lastly, it must be noted that many cases, especially regarding misdemeanors, will never make it to the trial stage. A large share of all criminal cases is dealt with by out of court settlements such as fines imposed by the police or the public prosecutor or financial transactions (settlement penalties) offered by the public prosecutor to the suspect.[12]

Whereas the trial phase should have an adversarial character in observance of Article 6 ECHR, in the Dutch system the more determining pre-trial phase shall be typified as being mainly inquisitorial. Pre-trial, the suspect is merely the subject of investigation, especially during the pre-arrest stage. The police and the PPS will collect the evidence in the dossier, which will subsequently constitute the basis for any trial. The police and the PPS act on behalf of the state in the public interest, which implies that they shall investigate impartially. For that reason the PPS is formally part of the judiciary and public prosecutors are referred to as magistrates,

---

[9] HR 20 December 1926, *NJ* 1927, 85.

[10] Pompe 1959, 141-151.

[11] ECHR 28 August 1991, App. no. 11170/84; 12876/87; 13468/87 (*Brandstetter v. Austria*), para 66-67. This does not imply that only Anglo-American adversarial systems should be considered as fair considering their adversarial character. The Court emphasizes that various systems of domestic law can be used to comply with this requirement. Every system, however, should ensure that each party has equal access to filed observations and an equal opportunity to comment on the evidence (para 67). See also: ECHR 23 June 1993, Application no. 12952/87 (*Ruiz-Mateos v. Spain*), para 63.

[12] Corstens 2008, 11-12. The Dutch criminal justice system provides for the possibility to settle criminal cases by way of a transaction which takes the form of a settlement penalty. A transaction involves the voluntary payment of a sum of money to the Treasury in order to avoid further criminal prosecution and a public trial. Entering into such a settlement does not require the offender to admit his or her guilt. The offender even has a right not to be prosecuted if the crime is only punishable by a fine and if he or she pays the maximum fine that can be imposed. Articles 74 and 74A CCP.

a position which reflects the PPS's impartial responsibility, obliged to investigate incriminating and exculpatory circumstances.[13] However, the ECrtHR has recently described the PPS as follows: "although bound by requirements of basic integrity", "in terms of procedure" as a "party", which cannot be attributed the 'judiciary' characteristics of objectivity and impartiality.[14] The PPS has been attributed the discretion to decide whether or not to prosecute (*opportuniteitsbeginsel*). Under this principle of opportunity the public prosecutor will, before resorting to prosecution, determine whether prosecuting criminal behavior also serves the public interest. The latter will be determined positively when, considering the nature of the crime, it will be obvious that a prosecution serves the public interest or when policy guidelines and/or general directions prescribe that prosecuting a particular type of offense is indicated.

It is the task of the defense to control whether during the investigation all procedural rules have been observed. The dossier constitutes the basis for controlling the pre-trial investigation. All investigative actions shall be reported and filed within the dossier. The public prosecutor is mainly responsible for the contents of the dossier with an additional role for the examining magistrate when more interests are at stake. Although during the pre-trial investigation, especially during the pre-arrest stage, the suspect is merely the subject of the investigation, pre-trial the defense is able to play an indirect role in the truth-finding process by requesting the examining magistrate to investigate certain aspects, which the suspect can do from the moment of the first police interrogation.[15]

### *2.1.3 Meaning of Some Principles and Fundamental Rights Relevant to the Criminal Investigation in Dutch Criminal Procedural Law*

According to Article 93 Constitution, the provisions of the ECHR and ICCPR are directly applicable within the Dutch legal order. The Netherlands does not have a constitutional court,[16] but the Constitution obliges the courts to examine the compatibility of national legislation with directly applicable provisions of

---

[13] See on the role of the public prosecutor as a 'magistrate': Verrest 2011, 221-244.

[14] ECHR 14 September 2010, App. no. 38224/03 (*Sanoma Uitgevers B.V. v. The Netherlands*), para 93.

[15] As, upon the soon to be expected entry into force of the Act on Strengthening the Position of the Examining Magistrate (*Kamerstukken I* 2010/11, 32177, no. A), provided in Article 182 CCP (currently: Articles 36a-e CCP).

[16] A proposal to amend the Constitution in order to introduce the authority for the courts to examine statutes on the basis of Constitutional provisions is currently pending as the required second round in order to amend the Constitution is still to take place (private member's bill by Halsema). See *Kamerstukken II* 2001/02, 28 331, nos. 2 and 3, *Kamerstukken I* 2008/09, 28331, *Stb*. 2009, 120 and *Kamerstukken II* 2009/10, 32334, nos. 1-3.

international treaties. The ICCPR will not be dealt with any further, considering that the interpretation of the similar rights protected in the ECHR following from the judgments of the European Court of Human Rights (ECrtHR) provides for considerably more precise and elaborative conditions than the ICCPR monitoring Human Rights Committee.

When national legislation conflicts with treaty provisions, the national legislation is not applicable (Article 94 Constitution). The ECrtHR may not, however, undo national legislation that provides for rights to citizens which are supplementary to the rights guaranteed in the Convention as to Article 60 ECHR. An individual who is of the opinion that state authorities have violated his or her rights as protected by the ECHR may, when domestic remedies have been exhausted, appeal to the European Court of Human Rights (ECrtHR) by filing a complaint. Because almost all provisions of the ECHR are directly applicable in the Dutch legal order and the Supreme Court has understood the interpretation of these provisions by the ECrtHR as being incorporated within the concerned provisions of the ECHR, the judgments of the ECrtHR have an important regulatory effect on Dutch criminal procedural law.[17] Therefore, in this section, next to the fundamental rights protected in the Dutch Constitution, especially some provisions of the ECHR will be dealt with as they have proven to have an important regulatory influence on the procedural framework of the criminal investigation.

#### 2.1.3.1 The Principle of Legality

Article 1 of the CCP can be regarded as the codification of the principle of legality for criminal procedural law. It provides that criminal procedure can only be carried out in the manner provided by law. Also Article 7 of the ECHR recognizes the principle of legality as a fundamental guarantee. However, Article 7 ECHR exclusively applies to substantive criminal law.[18] Hence, the scope and interpretation of this Article are irrelevant for the procedural legality requirements concerning the criminal investigation.

The principle of legality as guaranteed in Article 1 CCP is traditionally understood as expressing the requirement of a foundation in law for every governmental action that interferes with the rights or freedoms of citizens. Hence, the

---

[17] See on this subject: Coomans and Kamminga 2007, 492-493, Besselink and Wessel 2009 and Lawson 1999, 1-132.

[18] Article 7 ECHR embodies the observance of the principles "*nullum crimen, nulla poena sine lege*", a prohibition on construing the criminal law "extensively (...) to an accused's detriment, for instance by anology", the requirement that "an offence must be clearly defined in the law" and the prohibition of "retrospective application of the criminal law to an accused's disadvantage." ECHR 25 May 1993, App. no. 14307/88 (*Kokkinakis v. Greece*), para 52. See also: Bleichrodt 2006, 651-652. The Court has formulated the goal of Article 7 as offering "essential safeguards against arbitrary prosecution, conviction and punishment." ECHR 22 November 1995, App. nos. 20166/92 and 20190/92 (*S.W. and C.R. v. The United Kingdom*), para 34 and 33.

principle of legality is closely related to the protection of the right to respect for private life. Restrictions to the right to respect for private life are, according to Article 8 ECHR, only permissible "in accordance with the law."[19] Law is then understood in the sense of the ECHR as referring to written as well as unwritten law, implying requirements as to the quality of the law,[20] while law in the sense of Article 1 CCP refers to statutory law established by Act of Parliament. The purpose of establishing this requirement of a basis in law is to guarantee legal certainty, equality for the law and to establish democratic legitimacy for governmental action that interferes with the personal freedom of citizens. Democratic legitimacy is guaranteed through requiring an Act of Parliament for every governmental power interfering with rights or freedoms. Legal certainty and equality for the law are guaranteed by codifying the specific power, which makes it—in principle—known to everyone and aims to preclude inequality in exercising the powers and in that way it protects citizens against arbitrary action by the government.

The principle of legality places obligations or responsibilities on the various actors in the criminal justice system. In the first place, responsibilities for the legislature can be derived from Article 1 CCP. The legislature is responsible for establishing law by Act of Parliament for every power that is deemed necessary for the purpose of establishing the truth about criminal offenses and which power interferes with fundamental rights and liberties. Establishing the rules for the truth-seeking process binds the government to the use of the powers subject to the conditions as laid down in law, which will further the integrity of the process. Secondly, the judiciary is responsible for respecting and guaranteeing the law when administering justice, without interpreting the law by analogy. Furthermore, the investigative officers (and any other person exercising criminal procedural powers) are responsible for carrying out their powers in accordance with the law. They shall not use powers that do not have a basis in law, they shall not use their powers for unattributed purposes and they shall use these powers by observing the legal requirements. Lastly, citizens can derive from Article 1 CCP the expectation that the government uses its powers only as provided in the law and in accordance with the law.

The principle of legality is a fundamental principle of the Dutch legal system and of a civil law system in general. It is laid down in the Constitution (Article 107) by providing that the law regulates civil law, criminal law and the civil and criminal procedural law in general codes, except for the authority to regulate certain subjects in special statutes. This provision must actually be considered as a codification principle, which is, of course, closely linked to the principle of legality. The principle of legality is, considering the legal system of the Netherlands, in fact an obligation to regulate in a code all government powers that

---

[19] See on this in more detail Sect. 2.1.3.2.1.

[20] Compare: ECHR 22 November 1995, App. nos. 20166/92 and 20190/92 (*S.W. and C.R. v. The United Kingdom*), para 35 and 33.

interfere with the fundamental rights of citizens. As a consequence, the CCP is also the most important source of regulation with regard to the criminal investigation.

The scope of the principle of legality is unspecified and is subject to different interpretations in the literature and the case law. In practice, the principle of legality is understood as not requiring for every governmental action a basis in law, although the legislature shall further such a basis at any time. When a basis is lacking, the courts can extend the interpretation of the powers regulated in law in accordance with fundamental principles of law.[21] However, this is only possible when the lack of a basis in a statute is not contrary to the goal of Article 1 or in violation of Article 8(2) ECHR or Article 10 of the Dutch Constitution, which means that it can only apply to powers of the government that do not, or only to a minor extent, interfere with rights and liberties. Otherwise, the legislature is obliged to provide a basis in the law before the government may use these powers.

An important factor for determining the scope of Article 1 CCP is the meaning of 'criminal procedure' itself, because Article 1 only takes effect when an action can be considered as a criminal procedural action. Criminal procedure is generally understood as the entity of regulations and fundamental principles with regard to the criminal investigation, prosecution and execution.[22] However, when strictly taking into account the purpose of the principle of legality—giving expression to the rule of law by requiring that every action of the government that interferes with the rights and liberties of citizens must have a foundation in law—it seems that only governmental powers which interfere with rights and liberties are covered by the term criminal procedure in the context of Article 1 CCP.[23] Limiting the term to governmental action that interferes with rights and liberties means that defense rights and procedural activities within the criminal investigation, prosecution or execution that do not interfere with rights or liberties are excluded from the principle of legality. However, because it is desirable that legal protection and the integrity of the process as a whole are guaranteed, also these rights and activities, being elements of the criminal process, have a basis in law. Article 1 of the CCP includes these activities and, for that reason, a basis in law must be established for all aspects during all phases of the criminal process. Thus Article 1 is in fact broader than the scope of the principle of legality itself when taking into account the goal that the principle is meant to serve. As soon as specific action can be considered as criminal procedure, Article 1 takes effect and a basis in law must be established for this action.

The principle of legality or, more precisely, Article 1 CCP is not subject to one unchangeable interpretation regarding its scope. It has generally been accepted that the protections given to the rule of law do not bar the interpretation of the law in

[21] See in this regard also the Opinion of Advocate General Van Dorst para 2 at HR 19 December 1995, *NJ* 1996, 249.

[22] See also: Knigge and Kwakman 2001, 244.

[23] Ibid., 244-245.

accordance with the requirements and necessities of modern society.[24] It is in fact the task of the courts and legal academics to interpret the meaning of Article 1 and of criminal procedure according to the recent state of societal developments.[25] The use of governmental powers must occur according to the provisions determined by law, but these provisions often leave room for a broader interpretation.

To conclude: the principle of legality furthers legal protection, equality for the law and legal certainty by requiring a basis in law for governmental action that interferes with rights or freedoms during the criminal investigation. The principle of legality underpins the regulation of investigative powers by requiring a sufficiently precise regulation, from which citizens can derive legal certainty and protection against arbitrariness. This regulation shall make sufficiently clear under which circumstances citizens can expect that state authorities may use investigative powers against them. Furthermore, it democratically legitimizes the use of governmental power in the criminal investigation as the provisions for using criminal investigative powers have been established through the process of democratic decision-making. Hence, the principle of legality can be understood as a sword and shield with regard to the use of criminal procedural powers. With regard to its shield function the principle is closely related to the protection of the right to private life, considering that the required level of precision of the basis in law is related to the level at which the power intrudes into someone's private life.

#### 2.1.3.2 The Right to Respect for Private Life

Activities that are conducted within the criminal investigation, more specifically the use of investigative powers, almost always affect the private life of the persons under investigation. The mere registration of information about a person already entails an interference with the private life of that person, especially when this is done on behalf of the state authorities. The underlying assumption in creating and adopting fundamental rights and liberties—such as the right to respect for private life—is to protect against unlimited and arbitrary governmental power to invade citizens' personal freedom. The government's obligation under the rule of law to obey the fundamental rights and liberties of its citizens is at the same time also a legitimization for using governmental power according to established conditions under which citizens are willing to give up some of these rights and liberties to serve other interests.[26] Hence, not all these activities are an actual violation of private life as protected in Article 10 of the Dutch Constitution and Article 8 ECHR (and Article 17 ICCPR and Article 7 (and 8) of the Charter for Fundamental

[24] See also ECHR 26 April 1979, App. no. 6538/74 (*Sunday Times v. The United Kingdom*), para. 49: "the law must be able to keep pace with changing circumstances." See also: Berkhout-van Poelgeest 2001, 25-27.

[25] Rozemond 1998, 202.

[26] 't Hart 1994, 210-212.

Rights of the European Union). Whether the right to respect for private life has been violated depends on the scope of the right to private life in the specific circumstances of a case. When there is an actual violation of the private life of a person as protected by these articles, this violation might still be justifiable if it is in accordance with the conditions of the restrictive clauses of these articles adopted to regulate the governmental interest to conduct investigative activities in observance of the right to respect for private life. Especially the interpretation of Article 8 ECHR has an important influence on the regulation of the Dutch criminal investigation.[27] Article 10 of the Constitution provides for additional requirements. The meaning of both Articles and their consequences for Dutch criminal procedural law will be dealt with below.

##### 2.1.3.2.1 Article 8 ECHR

Article 8 ECHR reads as follows:

1. Everyone has the right to respect for his private and family life, his home and his correspondence.
2. There shall be no interference by a public authority with the exercise of this right except such as is in accordance with the law and is necessary in a democratic society in the interests of national security, public safety or the economic well-being of the country, for the prevention of disorder or crime, for the protection of health or morals, or for the protection of the rights and freedoms of others.

The "essential object" of Article 8 is "to protect the individual against arbitrary action by the government."[28] Article 8 does not prohibit all interferences with private life, by providing for a restrictive clause in the second paragraph.[29] The wording of the restrictive clause of Article 8 involves an obligation to regulate to a certain extent the use of its criminal procedural powers when this use possibly interferes with the private life of individuals. The precise scope of Article 8 ECHR and, thus, what activities of state authorities must meet the standards of the restrictive clause, is rather vague. In addition, the Court provides the states with "a certain margin of appreciation" for striking a balance between "the competing interests of the individual and of the community as a whole."[30]

---

[27] The provisions of the ECHR are directly binding on all subjects in the Member States. According to the Dutch Constitution the provisions of international treaties with such a character become an integral part of the Dutch legal order, without it being necessary to implement them in national law. They only need to be properly announced (Article 93 Constitution). The provisions of the ECHR prevail over conflicting national provisions (Article 94 Constitution).

[28] ECHR 27 October 1994, App. no. 18535/91 (*Kroon and Others v. The Netherlands*), para 31.

[29] ECHR 24 June 2004, App. no. 59320/00 (*Von Hannover v. Germany*), para 57.

[30] *Ibid.*, para 31.

To determine whether the use of an investigative power constitutes, in the specific circumstances of a case, a violation of the right to respect for private life, it must, in the first place, be assessed whether the use of the power constitutes an interference with private life as meant in Article 8(1) ECHR. The scope of the right to respect for private and family life is not static, but depends on "present day conditions and developments in social and political attitudes."[31]

In its judgments the Court has decided that the concept of private life includes someone's physical and psychological integrity, aspects relating to someone's personal identity, activities in someone's private as well as professional life and that it entails a "zone of interaction" with other people which can extend to a public context.[32] This flexible interpretation of the right to private life has in the specific circumstances of the case been determined by the Court on the basis of the 'reasonable expectation of privacy test' to determine whether a person with certain activities in the public domain "knowingly or intentionally" involves himself in a situation in which these activities may be reported or recorded.[33] This does not mean that all observations or recordings done in a public setting do not constitute interference with someone's private life. Neither does it mean that all activities "knowingly or intentionally" disposed to the public fall outside the scope of the right to respect for private life: "a person's reasonable expectations as to privacy may be a significant, although not necessarily conclusive, factor."[34] For instance, in the case of *Halford* the Court also considered other factors to determine that someone could have "a reasonable expectation of privacy" in that telecommunications were not intercepted when using internal telecommunications on business premises, such as the "sole use of her office where there were two telephones, one of which was specifically designated for her private use."[35] Moreover, once observations in the public scene, "even without the use of covert surveillance methods", obtain a systematic character and result in the "storing of data (...) on particular individuals," which was the case in *Uzun v. Germany* through the use of GPS surveillance, the Court has concluded that there is interference with private life.[36] On the contrary, the Court has ruled that someone becoming involved in the drugs trade "must have been aware from then on that he was engaged in a criminal act (...) and that consequently he was running the risk of

---

[31] Loof 2005, 204.

[32] See e.g.: ECHR 24 June 2004, App. no. 59320/00 (*Von Hannover v. Germany*) para 50 and ECHR 25 September 2001, App. no. 44787/98 (*P.G. and J.H. v. The United Kingdom*), para 56, ECHR 25 October 2007, App. no. 38258/03 (*Van Vondel v. The Netherlands*), para 48, and ECHR 2 September 2010, App. no. 35623/05 (*Uzun v. Germany*), para 43.

[33] ECHR 25 September 2001, App. no. 44787/98 (*P.G. and J.H. v. The United Kingdom*), para 57 and ECHR 2 September 2010, App. no. 35623/05 (*Uzun v. Germany*), para 44.

[34] ECHR 2 September 2010, App. no. 35623/05 (*Uzun v. Germany*), para 44.

[35] ECHR 25 June 1997, App. no. 73/1996/692/884 (*Halford v. The United Kingdom*), para 45. See also ECHR 24 June 2004, App. no. 59320/00 (*Von Hannover v. Germany*), para 51.

[36] ECHR 2 September 2010, App. no. 35623/05 (*Uzun v. Germany*), para 44-46 and 52.

encountering an undercover police officer whose task would in fact be to expose him."[37] However, this presumes that the government should be convinced beforehand of someone's involvement in a criminal act, whereas the investigation aims to establish the truth about that criminal offense. Hence, someone's involvement in a criminal act has never been repeated by the ECrtHR as a factor to determine the reasonableness of someone's expectation of privacy.[38]

To summarize: the concept of private life is rather broad and interference by public authorities with one's private life is generally not difficult to prove. More important is the question whether such interference constitutes a violation of Article 8 ECHR.

If the activities of public authorities do result in interference with the right to respect for private life as protected in Article 8(1), the restrictive clause of Article 8(2) prescribes that a legitimization for such activities is required under the law. ECHR Article 8 allows limitations if they are "in accordance with the law" and if "necessary in a democratic society in the interests of national security, public safety or the economic well-being of the country, for the prevention of disorder or crime, for the protection of health or morals, or for the protection of the rights and liberties of others."[39]

It is not important what kind of law is sufficient for a restriction that is in accordance with the law. This, in the first place, is an issue for the domestic courts to consider. The Court has at least stated in its judgments that it is irrelevant whether the basis in law concerns case law or an Act of Parliament.[40] The Court "understood the term law in its substantive sense," which includes lower-rank acts and unwritten law.[41] It is the primary task of the domestic courts to determine whether this basis in law can in their legal system count as being 'in accordance with the law'. The requirement of 'in accordance with the law' is meant to refer to a basis in national law that provides for the restriction as well as to the quality of that law. The Court refers to the rule of law, in relation to this condition of being 'in accordance with the law', by stating that the quality of the law means that it should be compatible with the rule of law in the sense that it protects against arbitrary interferences by public authorities.[42] The presence of a basis in domestic law is, thus, insufficient for meeting the requirement of being 'in accordance with

---

[37] ECHR 15 June 1992, App. no. 12433/86 (*Lüdi v. Switzerland*), para 40.

[38] Corstens 2008, 278.

[39] Article 8(2) ECHR.

[40] In the Netherlands, the Constitution requires that the 'basis in law' has been established by Act of Parliament. See on this the next section (2.1.3.2.2).

[41] ECHR 24 April 1990, App. no. 11801/85 and App. no. 11105/84 (*Kruslin v. France and Huvig v. France*), para 29/28; ECHR 2 August 1984, App. no. 8691/79 (*Malone v. The United Kingdom*), para 66.

[42] ECHR 2 August 1984, App. no. 8691/79 (*Malone v. The United Kingdom*), para 67 and ECHR 25 March 1983, App. no. 5947/72; 6205/73; 7052/75; 7061/75; 7107/75; 7113/75; 7136/75 (*Silver and Others v. The United Kingdom*), para 90.

the law'. In addition, this basis in law must meet certain requirements regarding its quality.

The Court defines 'quality of the law' more precisely by formulating the requirements of the foreseeability and accessibility of the basis in the law. The Court has interpreted "prescribed by law" (which wording is understood as having the same meaning as 'in accordance with the law') as referring to "the quality of the law in question, requiring that it should be accessible to the person concerned, who must moreover be able to foresee its consequences for him, and compatible with the rule of law."[43] The ECHR further explained the terms foreseeable and accessible in *Sunday Times* (1979) by ruling that the law providing for the limitation on the right to freedom of expression (Article 10) must be sufficiently adequately accessible and should be sufficiently precisely formulated.[44] The requirement of foreseeability is subsequently mitigated by stating that a person must be able to foresee the consequences of his or her conduct to "a degree that is reasonable."[45] This interpretation of prescribed by law has been adopted *mutatis mutandis* for the interpretation of 'in accordance with the law' as the requirement for legitimate interference with the right to private life in Article 8(2) ECHR.[46] Both requirements have been further developed in the case law of the ECrtHR.

Furthermore, the restriction shall be adopted for a legitimate aim—one of the aims enumerated in Article 8(2)—and be necessary in a democratic society, which means that "the interference corresponds to a pressing social need and, in particular, that it is proportionate to the legitimate aim pursued."[47]

The more precise elaboration of the different requirements of Article 8(2) ECHR will be dealt with in Sect. 2.3.2.1 in order to determine the protective conditions that follow from Article 8 ECHR concerning the regulation of criminal investigative powers.

[43] ECHR 25 March 1998, App. no. 13/1997/797/1000 (*Kopp v. Switzerland*), para 55; ECHR 16 February 2000, App. no. 27798/95 (*Amann v. Switzerland*), para 50 (and 56); ECHR 26 April 1979, App. no. 6538/74 (*Sunday Times v. The United Kingdom*), para 49; ECHR 24 April 1990, App. no. 11801/85 and App. no. 11105/84 (*Kruslin v. France and Huvig v. France*), para 30/29.

[44] ECHR 26 April 1979, App. no. 6538/74 (*Sunday Times v. The United Kingdom*), para 49. The principle applies *mutatis mutandis* to Article 8: ECHR 25 March 1983, App. no. 5947/72; 6205/73; 7052/75; 7061/75; 7107/75; 7113/75; 7136/75 (*Silver and Others v. The United Kingdom*), para 85.

[45] ECHR 26 April 1979, App. no. 6538/74 (*Sunday Times v. The United Kingdom*), para 49.

[46] ECHR 2 August 1984, App. no. 8691/79 (*Malone v. The United Kingdom*), para 66 and ECHR 24 April 1990, App. no. 11801/85 and App. no. 11105/84 (*Kruslin v. France and Huvig v. France*), para 30/29.

[47] ECHR 26 March 1987, App. no. 9248/81, para 58 (*Leander v. Sweden*). See also ECHR 25 March 1983, App. no. 5947/72; 6205/73; 7052/75; 7061/75; 7107/75; 7113/75; 7136/75 (*Silver and Others v. The United Kingdom*), para 97.

#### 2.1.3.2.2 Article 10 Constitution

Besides the requirements for legitimate interferences by public authorities with the private lives of individuals as extensively elaborated by the European Court, also the Dutch Constitution has a regulating influence on the exercise of criminal investigative powers. According to Article 10 of the Constitution everyone has the right to respect for private life, except for limitations on this right provided by the law.[48]

The scope of the right to private life as adopted in the Constitution is rather vague. The legislature intended that the courts would develop the lines for a more precise interpretation of the scope of these rights. Elaborations of the right to private life can be found in the more specific rights formulated in Article 11-13 of the Constitution, providing for the right to respect for the integrity of the body, homes and the confidentiality of mail. The legislature explained the right to private life as the right to live one's life with as little interference from outside as possible. The Dutch Supreme Court has in some cases interpreted the scope of the right to private life as being similar to the reasonable expectation of privacy test, as also applied by the ECrtHR. However—and also similar to the approach of the ECrtHR—this test is not decisive for the Supreme Court to assess whether a particular situation contributes to a violation of the right to private life. In each case the Supreme Court separately balances the concrete circumstances and interests that are relevant for the scope of the right to private life. Important factors to be considered are the assessment of a particular situation by police officers as well as the actual entitlement of a person in a particular situation to privacy.[49]

Restrictions on the right to privacy are, according to Article 10 of the Dutch Constitution, allowed if 'provided by the law', which means according to the letter of the Constitution that an Act established by Act of Parliament shall provide for the restriction. For this reason, Article 10 Constitution is complementary to Article 8 ECHR, considering that requiring law established by Act of Parliament further narrows down the ECHR requirement 'in accordance to the law', which also allows for law of a different nature, such as case law[50] (see the previous section). In fact, this is the most important regulatory consequence of Article 10 in addition to those following from Article 8 ECHR.

---

48 Article 10(1) Constitution of the Kingdom of the Netherlands [*Grondwet voor het Koninkrijk der Nederlanden*].

49 See, for instance, HR 19 March 1996, *NJ* 1997, 85, para 6.2 and the annotation by Knigge, para 2 and 3.

50 In common law countries the principle of legality may be served by referring to a legal basis in case law, which is thus also a permitted interpretation of Article 8(2) ECHR.

#### 2.1.3.3 The Right to a Fair Trial

The right to a fair trial has not been included in the Dutch Constitution,[51] for which reason resort will be had to the ECHR to determine the relevance of the right for Dutch criminal investigation. The right to a fair trial is elaborated in Article 6 ECHR and, as a result, specific fair trial requirements as well as the notion of fair trial, as such, are relevant to Dutch criminal procedural law. Article 6 ECHR provides for the right to a fair trial as a fundamental aspect of the rule of law.[52] Article 6 provides that: "in the determination of his civil rights and obligations or of any criminal charge against him, everyone is entitled to a fair and public hearing within a reasonable time by an independent and impartial tribunal established by law." Furthermore, the "judgment shall be pronounced publicly", save for some exceptions. The presumption of innocence is contained in the second section of Article 6. The third section of Article 6 attributes some specific minimum rights for "everyone charged with a criminal offence".

Article 6 aims to protect against arbitrary state action in criminal law, which has resulted in the formulation of some specific minimum rights that should be guaranteed in criminal proceedings. Most of these rights concern the position of the accused, such as the right to a fair and public hearing within a reasonable time (Article 6(1)), the right to be presumed innocent (Article 6(2)), the right to be informed of the accusation against him (Article 6(3)a) and the right to examine or have examined witnesses against him and to obtain the attendance and examination of witnesses on his behalf under the same conditions as witnesses against him (Article 6(3)d)). This section will, firstly, elaborate on the presumption of innocence and, secondly, address the basic fairness requirements for the criminal proceedings as a whole, following from Article 6 ECHR.

##### 2.1.3.3.1 The Presumption of Innocence

The presumption of innocence, as one of the requirements of the right to a fair trial provided in Article 6(2) (and also recognized in Article 14(2) ICCPR), has only limited consequences for the criminal investigation. As will appear later, the presumption of innocence as a fundamental principle of law does have

[51] The aspects covered by the right to a fair trial were considered as an inherent part of the requirement of an independent judiciary, a fundamental principle of the 'Rechtsstaat' and, hence, implied in the Constitutional provisions requiring an independent judge to decide on legal conflicts (as guaranteed in the Constitution, Articles 112 and 113(1)). Corstens 2008, 53. Currently the inclusion of the right to a fair trial in the Constitution is being considered. The 'State Commission on the Constitution' (*Staatscommissie Grondwet)* concluded in its report of November 2010 in favor of including the right to a fair trial in the Constitution. Rapport Staatscommissie Grondwet 2010. See also: Mevis 2009A.

[52] See also the Preamble to the European Convention on Human Rights.

considerable consequences for criminal proceedings, *including* the criminal investigation.[53]

According to Article 6(2) ECHR "[e]veryone charged with a criminal offense shall be presumed innocent until proved guilty according to the law." Article 6(2) "governs criminal proceedings in their entirety, irrespective of the outcome of the prosecution,"[54] which corresponds with the general interpretation of Article 6 that the fairness of the trial depends on the proceedings as a whole. The applicable principle for determining whether there has been a violation of the presumption of innocence reads as follows:

> "the presumption of innocence will be violated if, without the accused's having previously been proved guilty according to the law and, notably without having had the opportunity of exercising his rights of defence, a judicial decision concerning him reflects an opinion that he is guilty. This may even be so in absence of any formal finding; it suffices that there is some reasoning suggesting that the court regards the accused as guilty."[55]

In the context of the ECHR the presumption of innocence concerns primarily a "rule of evidence and decision."[56] As an element of the fundamental right to a fair trial, the presumption of innocence "constitutes a measure of protection against error in the process and a counterweight to the immense power and resources of the State compared to the position of the defendant."[57]

Article 6(2) ECHR has been applied by the Court so as to cover issues such as the division of the burden of proof (the reversal of the burden of proof is, in principle, forbidden)[58] and a prohibition on any statements made by public officials about the guilt of a person when his guilt has eventually not or not yet been proven according to the law (e.g. in the media).[59]

However, the ECrtHR clearly distinguishes the state of a reasonable suspicion from statements about the guilt or innocence of someone.[60] The state of a reasonable suspicion, in fact constituting some proof concerning someone's guilt, may justify a less strict application of the presumption of innocence. This means, for instance, that in the case of a *prima facie* case the refusal to testify (the right to

---

[53] See on this Chap. 8, Sects. 8.3.1.1 and 2.3.2.3.3.

[54] ECHR 25 March 1983, App. no. 8660/79 (*Minelli v. Switzerland*), para 30, ECHR 6 February 2007, App. no. 14348/02 (*Garycki v. Poland*), para 68.

[55] ECHR 25 March 1983, App. no. 8660/79 (*Minelli v. Switzerland*), para 37. See also: ECHR 28 October 2003 App. no. 44320/98 (*Baars v. The Netherlands*), para 26.

[56] Van Sliedregt 2009, 22 and 27.

[57] Ashcroft 2009, 72.

[58] ECHR 5 July 2001, App. no. 41087/98 (*Philips v. The United Kingdom*), para 32.

[59] ECHR 25 March 1983, App. no. 8660/79 (*Minelli v. Switzerland*), para 37. See also: ECHR 28 October 2003 App. no. 44320/98 (*Baars v. The Netherlands*), para 26, ECHR 28 October 2004, Requêtes nos 48173/99 et 48319/99 (*Y.B. et autres c. Turquie*), para 43 and ECHR 6 February 2007, App. no. 14348/02 (*Garycki v. Poland*), para 66.

[60] ECHR 28 October 2004, Requêtes nos. 48173/99 et 48319/99 (*Y.B. et autres c. Turquie*), para 47, ECHR 28 October 2003 App. no. 44320/98 (*Baars v. The Netherlands*), para 28, ECHR 6 February 2007, App. no. 14348/02 (*Garycki v. Poland*), para 67.

a 'fair hearing' also implies the privilege against self-incrimination and the right to remain silent) may justify drawing adverse interferences, if such adverse interferences do not result in a reversal of the burden of proof.[61] Hence, the presumption of innocence shall also not be understood as a prohibition on investigating crimes, imposing pre-trial detention and initiating criminal proceedings. Instead, in the pre-trial phase, the presumption of innocence shall *in abstracto* be considered as a normative notion that controls, rather than hinders, the criminal procedure.[62] Also the goal of Dutch criminal procedural law has been formulated around the presumption of innocence with more general protective implications: the criminal process must be aimed at establishing the substantive truth; guaranteeing that the Penal Code is applied to the guilty, while minimizing the possibility that the innocent are affected by criminal procedural law.[63]

This more abstract and broader regulatory influence of the presumption of innocence on the criminal proceedings as a whole does not directly follow from the interpretation given to the presumption as provided in Article 6(2) ECHR, focusing on its meaning for the fairness of the criminal proceedings, as a rule of evidence and decision. Instead, it concerns a fundamental notion for the criminal justice system under the rule of law, because it recognizes the inviolability of human dignity and its reflection on the government's use of its powers. From that perspective, the presumption of innocence shall be understood as imposing restrictions on the use of criminal investigative powers, considering that the criminal procedure is aimed at establishing the truth by being continuously orientated towards the possibility that the suspect is innocent until the contrary—his guilt—has been proven in a court of law,[64] and, consequently, limiting the use of criminal investigative powers to that which is necessary and for the purpose of establishing the substantive truth (and not for punitive purposes).[65] This particular regulatory effect of the presumption of innocence will not be dealt with further at this point, as it does not directly impose specific regulatory consequences on the Dutch criminal justice system. Rather, the principle shall be considered as (one of) the rationales behind rights and principles that prohibit arbitrary and unnecessary interferences with privacy rights, the principles of proportionality and subsidiarity,[66] the principle of *détournement de pouvoir*[67] and the idea of the criminal justice system as the *ultimum remedium*.

---

61 ECHR 8 February 1996, Case no. 41/1994/488/560 (*John Murray v. The United Kingdom*), para 51-54.

62 Stuckenberg 1997, 74.

63 Lindenberg 2002, 420 (MvT 3) and Groenhuijsen and Knigge 2001, 17-18.

64 Krauß 1971, 156 and 176.

65 More on the presumption of innocence as a fundamental principle under the rule of law regulating the criminal process, including the use of criminal investigative powers, in Chap. 8, Sect. 8.3.1.1.

66 See Sect. 2.1.3.4.1.

67 See Sect. 2.1.3.4.2.

#### 2.1.3.3.2 Implications of Article 6 ECHR for Pre-Trial Proceedings

The right to a fair trial is connected with the originally common-law notion of due process. Due process or fair trial aims to guarantee the effective realization of other substantive rights and liberties in the course of fair judicial proceedings.[68] The ECHR has interpreted the fairness of proceedings to entail the proceedings 'as a whole': the Court will "ascertain whether the proceedings in their entirety, including in the way in which evidence was taken, were fair."[69] For that reason, Article 6 ECHR also has consequences for the manner in which the criminal investigation is organized and conducted.

When the Court considers the course of the pre-trial phase in relation to the trial phase, it will not assess the rules on the admissibility of evidence that apply under national law (this is a matter of regulation by national law), but will only determine whether the proceedings as a whole were fair.[70] The fairness of the procedure as a whole is a requirement that is read into Article 6(1) ECHR. The ECHR has set three basic conditions in order to determine whether the proceedings as a whole have been fair. Firstly, the trial must have an adversarial character. An adversarial trial implies that both prosecution and defense must have knowledge of and be able to challenge all evidence produced. Secondly, the principle of equality of arms must be observed. Equality of arms gives the accused the right to have the same means as the prosecutor to challenge the evidence and to present his or her own evidence.[71] Thirdly, the principle of immediacy shall be observed, which gives the accused the right to be present at trial and to have the evidence presented during trial.[72] However, the principle of immediacy does not preclude using statements obtained in the pre-trial stage, as often occurs in the Netherlands as a consequence of the acceptance of *de auditu* testimony.[73] The Court accepts this practice provided that the rights of the defense are sufficiently respected in the

---

[68] Ölçer 2008, 71.

[69] See e.g.: ECHR 16 December 1992, App. no. 13071/87 (*Edwards v. The United Kingdom*), para 34 and ECHR 9 June 1998, case 44/1997/828/1034 (*Teixeira de Castro v. Portugal*), para 34.

[70] E.g.: ECHR 12 July 1988, App. no. 10862/84 (*Schenk v. Switzerland*), para 46, ECHR 18 March 1997, Reports 1997-III (*Van Mechelen v. The Netherlands*), para 50, ECHR 9 June 1998, case 44/1997/828/1034 (*Teixeira de Castro v. Portugal*), para 34, and ECHR 12 May 2000, App. no. 35394/97 (*Khan v. The United Kingdom*), para 34.

[71] ECHR 22 July 2003, App. no. 39647/98 and 40461/98 (*Edwards and Lewis v. The United Kingdom*), para 52: "(i)t is in any event a fundamental aspect of the right to a fair trial that criminal proceedings, including the elements of such proceedings which relate to procedure, should be adversarial and that there should be equality of arms between the prosecution and defence. The right to an adversarial trial means, in a criminal case, that both prosecution and defence must be given the opportunity to have knowledge of and comment on the observations filed and the evidence adduced by the other party."

[72] ECHR 20 November 1989, App. no. 11454/85 (*Kostovski v. The Netherlands*), para 41 and ECHR 10 November 2005, App. no. 54789/00 (*Bocos-Cuesta v. The Netherlands*), para 67-68.

[73] See Sect. 2.1.2.

sense that the defense has been given an adequate opportunity to test the evidence introduced, including having been given the opportunity to examine or have examined the witnesses against him or her. All three conditions mentioned have been established in order to guarantee that the defense is not restricted in the exertion of its rights, and to guarantee that the manner in which evidence is obtained and used is fair. In *Teixeira de Castro v. Portugal* the Court stressed that "the general requirements of fairness embodied in Article 6 apply to proceedings concerning all types of criminal offence, from the most straightforward to the most complex."[74]

Considering that it may still be possible to compensate in the trial phase for illegitimate aspects which occurred in the pre-trial phase, only upon the determination that it will be *impossible* to effectuate the right to a fair trial during trial can the conclusion be drawn that illegitimate aspects during the pre-trial phase will constitute a violation of the right to a fair trial. Hence, the rights of Article 6 may also be relevant for the pre-trial phase "in so far as the fairness of the trial is likely to be seriously prejudiced by an initial failure to comply with them."[75] During the criminal investigation the truth-finding actors shall already anticipate the observance of the requirement of adversarial proceedings and the requirement of equality of arms. The accused must be able to challenge the evidence collected during the criminal investigation. This requires a certain level of transparency concerning the investigation: the accused must have sufficient insight into the manner of obtaining the evidence and the source of the evidence.

Directly related thereto is the obligation for the prosecutor "to disclose to the defence all material evidence for or against the accused."[76] However, this is not an absolute right as competing interests such as "national security", the "need to protect witnesses", the need to "keep secret police methods of criminal investigation" or in order to "preserve the fundamental rights of another individual or to safeguard an important public interest" may outweigh certain requirements of a fair trial.[77] In general, as a result of the assessment by the Court of the procedure as a whole, there is a possibility to rectify shortcomings with regard to the position of the defense. For example, in *Doorson v. The Netherlands* "the interests of the defence are balanced against those of witnesses or victims called upon to testify", as the Member States in their criminal proceedings should also protect the life, liberty and security of victims and witnesses.[78] The Court shall ascertain whether the limitations on the defense rights were strictly necessary and permissible under Article 6(1), requiring a decision-making procedure that observes the requirements

---

[74] ECHR 9 June 1998, case 44/1997/828/1034 (*Teixeira de Castro v. Portugal*), para 36.

[75] ECHR 24 November 1993, App. no. 13972/88 (*Imbriosca v. Switzerland*), para 36.

[76] ECHR 16 December 1992, App. no. 13071/87 (*Edwards v. The United Kingdom*), para 36.

[77] ECHR 25 September 2001, App. no. 44787/98 (*P.G. and J.H. v. The United Kingdom*), para 68.

[78] ECHR 26 March 1996, Reports 1996-II (*Doorson v. The Netherlands*), para 70. See also: ECHR 18 March 1997, Reports 1997-III (*Van Mechelen v. The Netherlands*), para 52-53.

of adversarial proceedings and equality of arms, and has incorporated sufficient safeguards to protect the interests of the accused.[79] Decisive for the Court to determine whether in a specific case limitations on the defense rights constitute a violation of the right to a fair trial is the question whether the handicaps for the defense have been sufficiently counterbalanced.

In several cases the Court has assessed events during the pre-trial stage in relation to the fairness of the procedure as a whole. For example, in *Teixeira de Castro* the Court stated that "the use of undercover agents must be restricted and safeguards put in place even in cases concerning the fight against drug trafficking. While the rise in organized crime undoubtedly requires that appropriate measures be taken (…) [t]he public interest cannot justify the use of evidence obtained as a result of police incitement." The applicant was deprived of his right to a fair trial because undercover agents had "instigated the offence and there is nothing to suggest that without their intervention it would have been committed." The Court took into account that the conviction was mainly based on the statements of the undercover agents.[80] Furthermore, in cases concerning the use of anonymous witnesses in the Netherlands, the Court has considered that reliance on anonymous sources is not precluded at the investigation stage, but the "subsequent use of their statements by the trial court to found a conviction is however capable of raising issues under the Convention."[81] The use of undercover agents during the criminal investigation, who then produce evidence as anonymous witnesses at trial, is considered to be permitted if the handicaps of the defense are sufficiently counterbalanced by the procedure followed by the judicial authorities and if the conviction is not solely, or to a decisive extent, based upon the testimony of these witnesses.[82]

Another example concerning the procedure during the criminal investigation is the situation in which evidence has been obtained during the criminal investigation in violation of another right protected by the ECHR. It turns out that the use of evidence gathered in violation of Article 8 ECHR does not automatically result in a violation of the right to a fair trial. For determining whether the trial as a whole is fair in such a situation, the Court assesses whether the rights of the defense were not disregarded taking into account the possibility to counterbalance and whether the

---

[79] ECHR 25 September 2001, App. no. 44787/98 (*P.G. and J.H. v. The United Kingdom*), para 68.

[80] ECHR 9 June 1998, case 44/1997/828/1034 (*Teixeira de Castro v. Portugal*), para 36 and 39.

[81] ECHR 20 November 1989, App. no. 11454/85 (*Kostovski v. The Netherlands*), para 44, ECHR 26 March 1996, Reports 1996-II (*Doorson v. The Netherlands*), para 69.

[82] This assessment has led to the conclusion in ECHR 20 November 1989, App. no. 11454/85 (*Kostovski v. The Netherlands*), para 43-45 and ECHR 18 March 1997, Reports 1997-III (*Van Mechelen v. The Netherlands*), para 59-65, that the right to a fair trial had been violated. In ECHR 26 March 1996, Reports 1996-II (*Doorson v. The Netherlands*), para 74-76, the use of anonymous witnesses endured the test of the ECHR.

illegally obtained evidence is not the only basis for the conviction. Consequently, when evidence obtained in violation of a right protected in the ECHR—e.g. Article 8—is used as evidence in a domestic criminal trial, this does not necessarily mean that also Article 6 ECHR has been violated.[83] Nevertheless, the Court considers questions as to the admissibility of evidence and the question whether or not illegally obtained evidence requires procedural sanctions to be primarily a matter for domestic law.[84]

It would be going beyond the scope of this book to deal with all implications of respecting the right to a fair trial and violations thereof. The previous examples may illustrate the manner in which the Court deals with events during the pre-trial phase in relation to the right to a fair trial. Obviously, it is necessary to anticipate, already during the pre-trial investigation, whether, during the trial phase, the judge will assess the fairness of the procedure as a whole. This influences the manner in which the pre-trial investigation should be organized. The most important consequence seems to be the required transparency of the pre-trial proceedings, in order to enable control and to prevent the defense from being hindered in exercising its rights. A 'secret investigation', without revealing all applied methods and sources before or during trial, seems to clash with the right to an adversarial trial and equality of arms. However, under some circumstances the Court has accepted limitations on defense rights, for instance, if this is in the interest of national security or in order to protect the rights of victims or witnesses. These limitations are only justified if they are sufficiently counterbalanced and if the conviction is not only, or to a decisive extent, based on the evidence regarding which defense rights have been limited.

#### 2.1.3.4 The Principles of the Due Administration of Justice

Principles of the due administration of justice [*beginselen van behoorlijke procesorde*] are unwritten principles that aim to guarantee, supplementary to the statutory conditions, the legitimacy of the criminal process where the law affords discretion, including the criminal investigation. The principles of the due administration of justice can in that regard be understood as guiding the investigative officer or the public prosecutor in the manner in which a criminal investigative power is applied or where the investigative officer has the discretion to choose between different investigative methods.[85] The judge is held to control the exertion of an investigative power and the choice between different investigative possibilities also on the basis of these principles of the due administration of justice.

---

[83] ECHR 12 July 1988, App. no. 10862/84 (*Schenk v. Switzerland*), para 46-48 and ECHR 12 May 2000, App. no. 35394/97 (*Khan v. The United Kingdom*), para 36-40.

[84] See on the relevant domestic law Sect. 2.3.1.4 and Franken 2004A, 14-16.

[85] Corstens 2008, 62-63.

The Supreme Court has acknowledged the regulatory effect of the principles of the due administration of justice in a case where the investigative officer had entered a home, where illegal radio broadcasting activities took place, by breaking a window. The Supreme Court formulated in this case that investigative activities in accordance with the statutory requirements are not per se legitimate. In addition, the judge shall examine the activities on the basis of the principles of the due administration of justice.[86] These principles of the due administration of justice concern principles that have been developed in administrative law: the principle of legitimate expectations, the principle of equality before the law, the principles of proportionality and subsidiarity and the prohibition on *détournement de pouvoir* (or: abuse of power). For the criminal investigation the principles of proportionality and subsidiarity and the prohibition on *détournement de pouvoir* are in particular relevant and will therefore be dealt with in more detail.

#### 2.1.3.4.1 Proportionality and Subsidiarity

The principles of proportionality and subsidiarity have an important regulatory meaning in the Dutch system of criminal procedural law by requiring a reasonable assessment of all the interests involved. The regulatory influence of the principles of proportionality and subsidiarity is present on the abstract level of the adoption of criminal investigative policy as well as on the concrete level in the sense that any use of criminal investigative powers must be in compliance with the principles of proportionality and subsidiarity.

The principles of proportionality and subsidiarity require that the adoption of specific statutory provisions for criminal procedural powers is the product of the assessment of the interest of criminal law enforcement and the interest of protection against arbitrary interferences with the rights and liberties of citizens. This means, for the adoption of statutory law, providing the legal basis for a criminal investigative method so that the scope and nature of the method correspond with the need for a specific investigative power (proportionality) and that the specific method is also necessary for achieving the investigative need (subsidiarity).[87] Providing the government with broader or more investigative powers than necessary in order to pursue the purpose of criminal investigation (truth-finding regarding criminal offenses in order to prosecute and convict the guilty) would be in violation of the principles of proportionality and subsidiarity.

On the concrete level the principles of proportionality and subsidiarity have a regulatory influence in addition to the legal requirements (which are thus themselves a product of an assessment of proportionality and subsidiarity) for the use of criminal investigative powers, as acknowledged by the Supreme Court for the first time in 1978.[88] In this case the breaking of the window to enter the house was

---

[86] HR 12 December 1978, *NJ* 1979, 142 ann. GEM.

[87] Corstens 2008, 71.

[88] HR 12 December 1978, *NJ* 1979, 142 ann. GEM.

considered to violate the principle of subsidiarity.[89] The principles of proportionality and subsidiarity should continuously direct the actors applying criminal investigative powers in addition to the requirements of the law. Also the trial judge should examine whether the investigative activities have been in compliance with these principles, for which purpose the trial judge will only conduct a marginal examination to determine whether the police and/or the PPS could reasonably conduct the specific criminal investigative activities.[90] Furthermore, the application of these principles to the criminal investigation follows from the wording of Article 8 ECHR, which requires any restrictions on the right to respect for private life to be 'necessary in a democratic society'. In addition, some bases in law for the use of investigative methods require an assessment of proportionality and subsidiarity, for example, by subjecting the use of the investigative method to the requirement of 'in the interest of the investigation' or 'upon a pressing investigative need'.[91]

The principles of proportionality and subsidiarity require from the actors deciding on the use of criminal investigative powers and responsible for applying the power in question that in each individual case an assessment is made whether the use of the power in the light of the specific circumstances of the cases is also proportionate and concerns the least intrusive method in order to achieve the intended investigative goal. Consequently, the principles are considered to have an important regulatory influence during the entire criminal investigation influencing particular criminal investigative decisions (such as on the use of intrusive special investigative techniques) and the execution of specific criminal investigative powers on behalf of the police.[92] Nevertheless, the principles are also often used as arguments *justifying* a more intrusive application of criminal investigative powers, for which reason the value of the principles as protective principles appears to be primarily theoretical.[93]

---

[89] *Ibid.*

[90] E.g. HR 12 December 1978, *NJ* 1979, 142 ann. GEM (where the violation of the principle of subsidiarity resulted in the exclusion of evidence), see also HR 30 March 2004, *NJ* 2004, 376, ann. YB. See in more detail on the manner in which the trial judge exerts control on the criminal investigation in observance of the principles of the due administration of justice Sects. 2.3.1.4 and 2.3.2.4.2.

[91] Compare: Franken 2009, 83-84.

[92] As also explicitly mentioned in the Guide for the Criminal Investigative Practice [*Handboek voor de opsporingspraktijk*], supplement: *Stcrt.* 10 December 2007, no. 239/p. 11, 1 and 2. This Guide is not an independent source of regulation, but concerns an explanation of the Directive for criminal investigative powers [*Aanwijzing opsporingsbevoegdheden*], *Stcrt.* 24 February 2011, no. 3240, 2. (the directive also refers in some places to the applicability of the principles of proportionality and subsidiarity).

[93] The actual protective meaning of the principles seems to be currently limited in practice. Franken 2009, 83-84. More on this in Chap. 4, Sect. 4.2.3.2.

#### 2.1.3.4.2 Prohibition on Détournement de Pouvoir

The prohibition on *détournement de pouvoir* limits the use of criminal investigative powers to the purpose for which the power has been attributed. Hence, the prohibition on *détournement de pouvoir* can also be understood as a principle of purpose limitation. For criminal investigative powers, this means that the powers can only be used for the purpose of establishing the substantive truth with regard to criminal offenses (or the making of prosecutorial decisions[94]). Usually the purpose limitation is also implied in the specific statutory provision providing for a criminal investigative power. For example, the threshold of a reasonable suspicion, in combination with a requirement that the power shall be used 'in the interest of the investigation', implies that the use of the power is limited to the clarification of the reasonable suspicion for the purpose of making prosecutorial decisions.

The principle of purpose limitation also applies outside the context of criminal procedural law, for example to intelligence investigative activities or to administrative supervisory powers used for the purpose of the administrative enforcement of the law. The principle of purpose limitation also prohibits the use of these powers for purposes other than, respectively, the protection of national security and the administrative enforcement of the law (maintenance of public order). These powers may thus not be used for criminal law enforcement purposes.[95]

## 2.2 The Sword Function of the Dutch Criminal Investigation

### *2.2.1 The Actors Responsible for Truth-Finding*

The actors responsible for the criminal investigation are the police, the public prosecution service (PPS) and the examining magistrate. The suspect and/or defense are not dealt with, as the criminal investigative phase is in this project limited to the covert, pre-arrest phase, conducted beyond the awareness of the suspect, which means that there is, as yet, no role for the suspect and/or the defense to play with regard to contributing to truth-finding.[96] Hence, it is sufficient to mention that the defense does have possibilities from the moment of the first police interrogation to request the examining magistrate to conduct some specific

---

[94] As the purpose of the criminal investigation has been described in Article 132a CCP, which provides for the definition of the criminal investigation.

[95] Corstens 2008, 69-70.

[96] Although during a covert criminal investigation the suspect will not yet be able to contribute to truth-finding, the suspect, once indentified as such, is entitled to certain procedural protection. See on this Sect. 2.3.1.5.

investigative action (Article 182 CCP[97]) already during the pre-trial phase.[98] This division of responsibility for the criminal investigation among the police, the public prosecution service and the examining magistrate provides for three levels of shared responsibilities, partly in a hierarchical structure. The responsibility with regard to the course of events during the criminal investigation in its entirety is a shared individual responsibility of the public prosecutor and the examining magistrate. For the use of specific investigative powers during the criminal investigation, depending on the interests involved, a 'higher' actor will be responsible and will be given the power to employ or authorize investigative powers.

Article 141 of the CCP determines which actors are responsible for the criminal investigation: public prosecutors, law enforcement (police) officers and members of the Royal Netherlands Military Constabulary designated for that purpose by the Minister of Justice and the Minister of Defense are investigative officers. In addition, Article 142 CCP allots investigative powers to 'special investigative officers', a group which includes people designated as such by the Minister of Justice or the Board of Procurators-General[99] and investigative officers in charge of special investigative services (e.g. for environmental crimes or fiscal crimes).[100] All these people who are responsible for the criminal investigation on the basis of Articles 141 and 142 CCP are collectively referred to as investigative officers, as provided in Article 127 CCP.

Article 148 explicitly provides that public prosecutors are responsible for tracing criminal offenses, within the jurisdiction of the District Court for which the prosecutor is working. Articles 141, 142 and 148 CCP together determine who is responsible for the government's task to investigate criminal offenses and to trace criminal offenders. The designation as an investigative officer gives that officer the authority to exercise the criminal investigative task. It does not give the officer in charge specific powers for pursuing this task, although these powers may again be derived from this task attribution for criminal investigation.[101]

The examining magistrate's (sword) role in the criminal investigation primarily concerns a role as a warrant judge, considering that the *ex ante* authorization of the examining magistrate is required for the use of some investigative powers.

---

[97] Article 182 CCP replaces the 'mini-investigation' on the basis of Articles 36a-36d CCP, as a consequence of the soon to be expected entry into force of the Act on Strengthening the Position of the Examining Magistrate (*Kamerstukken I* 2010/11, 32177, no. A and *Kamerstukken II* 2009/10, 32177, no. 3).

[98] Section 2.3.1.5 will provide a brief description of these pre-trial investigative possibilities for the suspect.

[99] The Board of Procurators General [*College van procureurs-generaal*] is in command of the public prosecutor's department and has the authority to give general and more specific directions to the public prosecutor's department. The board consists of five members with one chairman. Corstens 2008, 119-120.

[100] Articles 141 and 142 CCP.

[101] This will be dealt with in Sect. 2.2.2.1.

Also citizens can in some circumstances be allotted with an investigative task. Citizens can assist in the criminal investigation upon the request of the public prosecutor under the CCP provisions regarding special investigative techniques.[102] They can be requested to act as an informant, to take part as a citizen in an infiltration action or to act in pseudo-deals or services.[103]

This section will deal with the three main actors during the criminal investigation with a direct responsibility for truth-finding: the police, the PPS and the examining magistrate.

#### 2.2.1.1 The Police

Not only the police, but also some other (specialized) services carry out the criminal law enforcement task and thus bear in practice the responsibility for the criminal investigation carried out under the supervision of the public prosecutor. The goal of the activities of these law enforcement services concerns the collection of information for criminal prosecution. The following law enforcement services can be identified: the PPS, the police (including the criminal intelligence unit (CIE)), the Royal Netherlands Military Constabulary, customs and special investigative services such as the FIOD-ECD (the Fiscal Information and Investigation Service and the Economic Investigation Service), and the AID (the General Inspectorate for agriculture). In the context of this research, attention will primarily be devoted to the PPS and the police, which for the police particularly concern the KLPD (the National Police Services Agency) and regional police forces, the criminal investigation service and the CIE.

The police in the Netherlands are organized in 25 regions, each having its own regional police force supervised by a chief of police, one national police force (KLPD) and special police officers.[104] The KLPD is particularly concerned with serious crime which is not restricted to one particular area. Especially for the purpose of advanced criminal investigation the KLPD has a criminal investigation service [*nationale recherche*],[105] which is also responsible in particular for the investigation of terrorist activities. Furthermore, the regional police forces as well as the KLPD have a criminal intelligence unit [*Criminele Inlichtingen Eenheid*] (henceforth: CIE), which collects and verifies criminal intelligence, including information from informants, and analyzes this information insofar as the information concerns serious crimes and is relevant for the tasks of the police. Criminal investigative policy choices may be founded on the analyses of the CIE, or the CIE can provide reports to the police, which can be used to initiate a criminal

[102] Title Va (Article 126v-z) of the CCP.

[103] Articles 126v-126z CCP. For terrorism investigations: Articles 126zt-126zu CCP.

[104] Articles 21, 24, 38 and 43 Police Act 1993 [*Politiewet 1993*].

[105] Regeling nationale en bovenregionale recherche, *Stcrt*. 2004, 19.

investigation.[106] (Political) control over the police is entrusted to the Minister of Security and Justice.[107]

Article 2 of the Police Act 1993 attributes to the police the task of the actual enforcement of the law and the maintenance of order and to provide assistance to anyone in need, while being subordinated to the competent authority and in accordance with the law as is in force.[108] All police officers are authorized to pursue this task anywhere in the territory of the Netherlands.[109] Considering this task the police also have a monopoly on using force, as provided in Article 8 of the Police Act 1993.

This police task is twofold: the first task is the maintenance of public order and offering assistance (administrative supervisory authority or administrative enforcement), in which function the police act under the supervision of the mayor.[110] The second, law enforcement task (the enforcement of criminal law) occurs under the supervision of the public prosecutor.[111] The public prosecutor shall exert this supervisory responsibility impartially, which follows from his position as part of the 'judiciary' and, hence, taking into account all the interests—sword and shield—involved.[112] The criminal law enforcement task of the police is understood to be an *ultimum remedium,* which means that the police shall consider alternatives before turning to the use of their powers attributed for the purpose of exerting the law enforcement task.[113]

During the criminal investigation the investigative officers will in practice conduct the investigative activities. The police are subordinated to the supervision of the PPS, which will include the obligation to act upon the instructions of the PPS. Such instructions can also be given on a more general basis by the issuance of guidelines to direct the police in the execution of their task, for example by describing the situations where the police may offer a transaction (a settlement penalty) in order to avoid a criminal prosecution in the case of minor criminal offenses. Nevertheless, in practice the police usually operate with a high level of

---

[106] Regeling criminele inlichtingen eenheden, *Stcrt.* 2000, 198, Articles 2 and 4.

[107] Until 14 October 2010, the Minister of the Interior controlled the Police. See Organisatieregeling Ministerie van Veiligheid en Justitie, *Stcrt* 2011, no. 1003 and 1004.

[108] Article 2 Police Act 1993.

[109] Article 7 Police Act 1993.

[110] Article 12 Police Act 1993. When the task of maintaining public order has a character which exceeds the normal tasks of the municipality the governor of the province [*Commissaris van de Koningin*] can supervise the police in their task of maintaining public order (Article 16(1) Police Act 1993). When the breach of public order has a national character, the Minister of the Interior, at present the Minister of Security and Justice, can instruct the mayor and governor as to the task of the police and can order that certain objects or facilities be guarded or made secure (Article 15a and Article 16(2) Police Act 1993).

[111] Article 13 Police Act 1993.

[112] See in more detail Sects. 2.2.1.2 and 2.3.1.2. In addition, see for the precise understanding of the formal position of the public prosecutor as part of the judiciary Sect. 2.1.2.

[113] Buruma 2007, 525.

autonomy. The police do not need the permission of a public prosecutor when they want to use a criminal procedural power attributed to them to execute their task. Furthermore, the public prosecutor, the chief of police and the mayor enter into regular consultations concerning which policy should be chosen in a certain area, which implies a mutual influence on policy choices.[114] Lastly, the PPS is largely dependent on the information provided by the police for the building of cases. In sum, this means that the police have a rather large autonomy in executing their task and using investigative powers which have been attributed to them, whilst the PPS bears the primary responsibility for the criminal investigation mainly by means of making strategic choices and prosecutorial decisions.[115]

#### 2.2.1.2 The Public Prosecution Service (PPS)

The PPS is a hierarchical organization: the public prosecutor acts under the supervision of the Chief public prosecutor of the district, who again falls under the supervision of the Board of Procurators General [*College van procureurs-generaal*].[116] The PPS as a whole acts under the supervision of the Minister of Security and Justice, who may give general and specific instructions (which occurs only in exceptional circumstances) to the PPS.[117] The Minister of Security and Justice also appoints, by royal decree, the public prosecutors and procurators general. The Board of Procurators General shall provide all information to the Minister which is relevant to exercising his supervisory task.[118] A similar obligation applies to the members of the PPS in relation to the Board of Procurators General.[119] In that way a hierarchical system of control and supervision is realized, although a certain level of distance has also been created between the Minister of Security and Justice and the PPS—in the form of the intermediary Board of Procurators General—in order to guarantee that the PPS operates free from political pressure.[120]

The PPS is further organized into 19 district public prosecutor's offices [*arrondissementsparketten*], related to the 19 district courts (courts of first instance), and one national public prosecutor's office, which is particularly responsible for the investigation and prosecution of serious crimes, such as

---

114 Article 14 Police Act 1993.

115 Buruma 2007, 555. See also: Krommendijk et al. 2009, 15-16. The PPS has a larger influence in more complex criminal investigations, for example by having the power to order the use of special investigative techniques. For the use of some special investigative techniques the authorization of the examining magistrate is also required. Nevertheless, the primary responsibility for the criminal investigation remains with the PPS. See on this subject in more detail Sects. 2.2.1.2 and 2.2.1.3.

116 Articles 125, 130 and 136 Judiciary Organization Act [*Wet op de rechterlijke organisatie*], *Stb*. 1999, 195, as amended (2011). Hereafter referred to as 'RO'. The public prosecutors at the Courts of Appeal are referred to as Advocates General (Article 138 RO).

117 Article 127 RO.

118 Article 129(1) RO.

119 Article 129(2) RO.

120 See e.g. Article 128 RO. In more detail: Corstens 2008, 112-115.

organized crime or crimes of a national or international character including terrorism. Furthermore, there is one specialized public prosecutor's office that focuses on e.g. fraud and environmental crimes. Lastly, there are five public prosecutor's offices [*ressortsparketten*] at the Courts of Appeal.[121]

The PPS is a crucial actor in the criminal investigative phase by bearing responsibility for the criminal investigation, on the basis of Article 124 of the Judiciary (Organization) Act, Article 13 Police Act and Articles 132a and 148 CCP.[122] Article 132a CCP defines the criminal investigation and includes in that definition that the criminal investigation occurs under the supervision of the public prosecutor. Also according to Article 149 CCP, providing for the task of the public prosecutor, the public prosecutor bears the responsibility for the criminal investigation. In Article 13 Police Act it is provided that the police exert their law enforcement task under the supervision of the public prosecutor. In Article 141 the public prosecutor is indicated as a first in line law enforcement (criminal investigative) officer, although in practice only the police will act as law enforcement officers. Giving the public prosecutor this responsibility for the criminal investigation is a logical decision as it is also the public prosecutor who has the discretionary power to decide on whether to prosecute or not [*opportuniteitsbeginsel*]. The realization of an effective prosecution policy will also depend on the choices already made in the course of the criminal investigation.[123]

In line with the supervisory role for the criminal investigation, the public prosecutor has been given the power to order the use of coercive powers and special investigative techniques. Also the police have been attributed the discretion to use investigative powers for the purpose of fulfilling their law enforcement task, but only the public prosecutor is entrusted with the power to apply more intrusive techniques that intrude on the private lives of citizens. What powers are available during the criminal investigation and, in particular, the use of covert special investigative techniques upon the order of the public prosecutor (and for the most intrusive techniques also the authorization of the examining magistrate) will be extensively addressed in Sect. 2.2.2.

The supervisory role of the PPS over the criminal investigation also has significant consequences for the further development of the proceedings, because the public prosecutor decides on the moment when materials are to be disclosed to the defense (Article 30 CCP) and on the compilation of the file that will constitute the basis for the inquiry at trial.[124] Considering this determining influence on the proceedings it is the task of the public prosecutor to seek the truth by investigating all the circumstances of the case, both incriminating and exonerating, equally. In line with the responsibility for the course of events during the criminal investigation that should be borne in an unprejudiced way, the PPS is viewed as part of the

---

[121] Corstens 2008, 119.

[122] A responsibility which can be derived from Article 124 RO and Articles 148 and 132a CCP.

[123] 't Hart 1983, 137-138.

[124] Corstens 2008, 91, 92, 247 and 248.

judicial organization in a wider sense. At the same time, the Minister of Security and Justice is politically accountable for the functioning of the PPS and, under certain conditions, has the power to give instructions to the PPS.[125] This double line of accountability, an orientation towards the judiciary and the supervision of the Minister of Security and Justice, gives the PPS a special position intended to provide public prosecutors with sufficient independence to fulfill their truth-seeking role while at the same time taking into account criminal policy interests.

#### 2.2.1.3 The Examining Magistrate

At the time of the adoption of the CCP the preliminary judicial investigation still occupied a central place in the pre-trial phase next to the criminal investigation. The preliminary judicial investigation shall be opened once a suspicion is present and, consequently, the examining magistrate, as a judge, obtains the supervisory role over the investigative activities in the pre-trial phase.[126] The idea underpinning this intended central role for the examining magistrate was to guarantee the impartiality and independence of the pre-trial investigation.[127] However, in practice this central position of the judicial preliminary investigation has faded away,[128] partly due to a number of legislative changes reducing the role and function of the preliminary judicial investigation and, consequently, also the central role of the examining magistrate in the pre-trial phase.

A number of incidents, including widely publicized wrongful convictions, have resulted in a call to improve the balance within the pre-trial phase by enhancing the equal attention to exonerating and incriminating circumstances, which goes hand in hand with enhanced judicial control over the pre-trial phase by strengthening the position of the examining magistrate. Consequently, the adoption[129] of the Act to Strengthen the Position of the Examining Magistrate has resulted in abolishing the preliminary judicial investigation in order to strengthen the supervising role of the examining magistrate over the criminal investigation in general without connecting it to the rather obsolete structure of the preliminary judicial investigation. In this way the role of the actors in the criminal investigation have actually been repositioned: the public prosecutor directs the criminal investigation, with a supervisory role over the police, and the examining magistrate exerts judicial

---

[125] Simmelink en Baaijens-van Geloven 2001, 395-396. See also *Kamerstukken II* 1996/97, 25 392 no. 3, 3.

[126] Hielkema 2005, 259.

[127] Franken 2006, 267.

[128] Reijntjes already concluded in 2001 that, in fact, at that time the preliminary judicial investigation had already been abolished. However, the abolition is not yet formal. Reijntjes 2001, 297. This last step will only be taken by the entry into force of the Act on Strengthening the Position of the Examining Magistrate, *Kamerstukken I* 2010/11, 32177, no. A.

[129] On June 30, 2011 the Second Chamber of Parliament adopted the bill. On November 29, 2011 also the First Chamber adopted the bill. It can be expected that the act will enter into force shortly after this book has been finalized. See for the Bill: *Kamerstukken I* 2010/11, 32177, no. A.

control over the course of events in the criminal investigation, in particular over the legitimate use of investigative powers, over the progress of the investigation and over the realization of the duty to seek the truth in a balanced and complete manner.[130] Section 2.3.1.3 will deal in more detail with the role of the examining magistrate and his or her relation towards the other actors in the pre-trial phase, considering that the role of the examining magistrate is primarily a shield role. This section will be further confined to briefly setting out the investigative powers for which authorization by the examining magistrate is required and the investigative powers that shall be exerted by the examining magistrate personally.

The current role of the examining magistrate can primarily be described as a warrant judge or judge of freedoms, responsible for *ex ante* judicial control over the criminal investigation and in particular over the use of the most intrusive investigative methods, namely electronic surveillance (Articles 126l, 126m and 126t CCP) and the subpoena of certain stored or still to be processed personal (other than identifying) information (Articles 126nd, 126ne, 126nf, 126ud, 126ue, 126ug CCP).[131] Authorization by the examining magistrate is also required for the search of homes and offices of persons acting under a privilege of non-disclosure such as lawyers and for the seizure of objects and materials (Articles 97, 110 CCP). Searches are in principle conducted by the examining magistrate in person, although in cases of urgency the public prosecutor may conduct the search upon the authorization of the examining magistrate. The examining magistrate also has the power to seize objects and materials (Article 104 CCP).

The examining magistrate may, furthermore, take investigative steps at the request of the public prosecutor or at the request of the defense (Articles 181 and 182 CCP). When the examining magistrate considers additional investigative steps to be necessary for the completeness of the investigation, he or she may also apply investigative powers *ex officio*. The use of investigative powers at the request of the public prosecutor, the defense or *ex officio* may concern, for example, the hearing of witnesses. This hearing of witnesses may also concern the application of special procedures for hearing shielded witnesses (see on this Sect. 3.4.2, considering that this special procedure has been introduced in order to further cooperation between the intelligence and law enforcement communities as part of the Dutch counterterrorism strategy).[132]

---

[130] *Kamerstukken II* 2009/10, 32177, no. 3, 1-2 and 10. See on the recent Act to Strengthen the Position of the Examining Magistrate also Van der Meij 2010B and Mevis 2009B.

[131] In addition, the examining magistrate has, as a judge, an independent general supervisory role over the course of events pre-trial. This 'shield' role will be dealt with in Sect. 2.3.1.3.

[132] In addition, the examining magistrate bears the important responsibility for determining the legitimacy of pre-trial detention (remanding in police custody [*inverzekeringstelling*] on the order of the public prosecutor or deputy public prosecutor for a period not exceeding 3 days, with the possibility of an extension for another 3 days; Articles 57, 58 and 59a CCP) and has the power to order, upon the request of the public prosecutor, a further extension of pre-trial detention for a period of 14 days [*bewaring*] (Article 63 CCP).

Within the scope of the criminal investigation 'pre-arrest', the task of the examining magistrate is primarily one of a warrant judge, where his authorization is required before some investigative powers may be used. The hearing of witnesses at the request of the public prosecutor may in exceptional circumstances already occur before the suspect has been found and/or is aware of the investigation against him or her. In addition, the examining magistrate has an overall controlling function over the criminal investigation with regard to its progress and completeness. This latter function will be addressed in more detail in Sect. 2.3.1.3.

#### 2.2.1.4 The AIVD (General Intelligence and Security Service)

Although the General Intelligence and Security Service [*Algemene Inlichtingen- en Veiligheidsdienst*] (henceforth: AIVD) cannot be considered as an actor in the criminal investigation, it is included in this section as a relevant actor, because its activities do influence the sword ability of the police and PPS as a consequence of the possibility to send official reports to the police or PPS and on which basis the police and PPS may initiate criminal investigative action or change the focus of an ongoing criminal investigation.

The intelligence services include the AIVD and the MIVD [*Militaire Inlichtingen en Veiligheidsdienst; Military Intelligence and Security Service*]. Furthermore, all regional police forces have a regional intelligence service (RID), which operate as the regional continuation of the AIVD.[133] Since 2002 the tasks of the AIVD have explicitly been defined in law by means of the Intelligence and Security Services Act of 2002 [*Wet op de inlichtingen- en veiligheidsdiensten*] (hereinafter: WIV 2002).[134] With the adoption of this Act, the tasks of the intelligence services have been defined in an Act of Parliament for the first time. The WIV of 2002 enumerates five tasks of the AIVD:

> "(a) conducting investigations regarding organizations that, and persons who, because of the objectives they pursue, or through their activities give cause for serious suspicion that they are a danger to the continued existence of the democratic legal system, or to the security or other vital interests of the state; (b) conducting security clearance investigations as referred to in the Security Investigations Act; (c) promoting measures for the protection of the interests referred to under a, including measures for the protection of information that is to remain secret for reasons of national security, and information pertaining to those parts of the public service and business community that in the opinion of the relevant Ministers are of vital importance for the continued existence of the social order; (d) conducting investigations regarding other countries concerning subjects designated by the Prime Minister, Minister of General Affairs, in accordance with the relevant

[133] Muller 2007, 178-179.

[134] *Stb.* 2002, 148.

> Ministers; (e) drawing up threat and risk assessments at the joint request of the Minister of the Interior and Kingdom Relations and the Minister of Justice for the benefit of the protection of [certain in law specified persons]."[135]

The main task of the AIVD concerns the collection of intelligence for the purpose of protecting the democratic legal order and security or other vital interests of the state (in the following collectively summarized as the protection of national security).[136] Through the collection of intelligence and the distribution of information (in the form of reports or notes) to other government agencies or private organizations, measures can be taken in order to avert a threat. Most relevant in the context of this research is the situation where the AIVD has obtained intelligence on a certain threat to national security and sends an official report regarding information on this threat to law enforcement services on which basis the police (in cooperation with the PPS) can subsequently take action by either directly arresting persons in order to avert the threat or by initiating a criminal investigation for the purpose of collecting further information that can be used in a criminal prosecution.[137] This possibility of transferring information to law enforcement services will be further elaborated in Sect. 2.2.2.4.2.

The AIVD resorts under the responsibility of the Minister of the Interior.[138] In this way the intelligence community is also separated with regard to their political accountability from the law enforcement services, which act under the authority of the Minister of Security and Justice. This separation between the intelligence community and the law enforcement community is established because of shield considerations, for which reason this subject will be further elaborated in Sect. 2.3.2.2.3. The position of the RIDs is slightly different as the RIDs have both an 'AIVD task', acting under the authority of the AIVD, and a task with regard to the enforcement of public order under the responsibility of the mayor.[139]

---

[135] Article 6 WIV 2002 (as amended by *Stb.* 2006, 574, adding the task under e to Article 6). Official translation of the WIV 2002 available at: https://www.aivd.nl/english/aivd/the-intelligence-and/ (accessed February 18, 2011). The five tasks of the AIVD are summarized, maybe more clearly, on their website as follows: (1) To investigate people and organizations reasonably suspected of representing a serious danger to the democratic legal order, national security or to other important interests of the Dutch State; (2) To screen candidates for the so-called "positions involving confidentiality" (this task is provided for under separate legislation, the Security Screening Act or Wvo); (3) To support the institutions responsible for maintaining the security of those sections of the national infrastructure, in both the public and the private sectors, which are vital to maintaining the fabric of Dutch society; (4) To investigate other countries in respect of activities jointly designated by the Prime Minister, the Minister of the Interior and the Minister of Defence; (5) As part of the national Safety and Security System, to supply risk and threat analyses concerning property, services and individuals."

[136] Muller 2007, 171.

[137] The transfer of information from the AIVD to law enforcement services is dealt with in detail in Sect. 2.2.2.4.2.

[138] See Article 1 WIV 2002. The Minister of Defense is responsible for the Military Intelligence and Security Service.

[139] Muller 2007, 179-180.

### 2.2.2 *The Powers Available for Truth-Finding in the Criminal Investigation*

In the previous section the actors that have been designated with the task of truth-finding during the criminal investigation have been described. As a consequence of the principle of legality (see Sect. 2.1.3.1), these actors may only conduct investigative activities if the powers used to that end are provided in the law. Hence, this section will deal with the different bases in law from which these actors may derive the power to conduct investigative activities and apply specific far-reaching investigative techniques.

With regard to the specific basis in law required for using investigative powers, the explanatory memorandum of the CCP is rather vague by providing that 'the police and prosecution must be given all those means that they need for investigating crimes and culprits in order to gather the available evidence as soon as possible and take all measures required for bringing the accused as quickly as possible before a judge. The authorities that are attributed the task of investigating and prosecuting must be able to act quickly and decisively, being able to do what is required under the specific circumstances of a case and shall not be hindered by regulations which are too stringent.'[140]

Until 2000 the police and PPS had a wide discretion in using investigative powers, which could be derived from the provision formulating their task as investigative officers. The growing awareness in the 1990s of the importance of protecting citizens against the unfettered investigative power of the state interfering with their personal freedom and the simultaneously growing arsenal of smart investigative techniques resulted in a more specific regulation of investigative powers, as adopted by the Act of 27 May 1999 (entering into force on 1 February 2000).[141] Consequently, the Dutch CCP currently provides not only general task descriptions for investigative officers, but also for codified provisions that designate specific investigative powers. Notwithstanding the fact that this act intended to increase the protection of the right to respect for private life where the police and PPS sought the use of intrusive special investigative techniques, the Act has also broadened the scope of the criminal investigation to include also proactive investigation. Before 2000 the criminal investigation was understood to be limited to the situation where a reasonable suspicion could be established; the government's use of criminal procedural law was considered to be only justified in the situation where a reasonable suspicion of a crime having been committed could be established. Since 2000 the criminal investigation includes also proactive investigative activities, lacking the establishment of a reasonable suspicion of a *committed* crime. Currently, the criminal investigation covers *all* investigative

---

[140] Lindenberg 2002, 424 (MvT 16).

[141] Stb. 1999, 245, Stb. 2000, 32.

activities conducted for the purpose of making prosecutorial decisions under the supervision of the public prosecutor.

This section will continue to describe the investigative powers that can be used to contribute to the goal of the criminal investigation: the collection of information in order to make prosecutorial decisions.[142] For this purpose the different bases in law will be dealt with separately, whilst in describing these bases in the law the historical development will be taken into account, including the interpretation of the term 'criminal investigation' in the Netherlands over the years. There are four different bases from which the power to use investigative powers can be derived for the purpose of collecting information that can be used in criminal proceedings. These bases differ in accordance with the character of the investigative power as a consequence of the regulatory effect of the right to respect for private life and the principle of legality (see in more detail Sects. 2.1.3.1, 2.1.3.2 and 2.3.2.1).

In the first place, Article 2 of the Police Act of 1993[143] will be dealt with, which provides for the general task of the police. The description of the law enforcement task of the police is understood to provide the basis in law to conduct certain investigative activities that to a limited extent interfere with private life (Sect. 2.2.2.1).

Secondly, more specific provisions in the CCP or in special criminal statutes provide for the basis for using investigative powers that seriously interfere with private life, such as the use of coercive methods[144] and investigative methods such as the searching of homes, electronic surveillance and infiltration. In general, as a minimum, the presence of a reasonable suspicion is required before these methods can be applied.[145] The covert investigative methods that are applied pre-arrest, and, hence, the methods which are relevant for this research are collectively referred to as special investigative techniques (or SIT). Section 2.2.2.2 deals with these SIT by addressing the Act that has created the specific legal bases for SIT (the Act on SIT of 27 May 1999) and the phase of the criminal investigation in which these SIT can be used (the full criminal investigation, that can either be reactive or also proactive). Furthermore, investigative officers may derive the power to use specific investigative methods from some special statutes, where the investigation concerns the offenses criminalized in those statutes, such as the Act on Weapons and Ammunition (Article 49-52), the Act on Economic Offenses (Article 17-26) and the Opium Act (Article 9).

In the third place, the CCP provides for investigative powers in the context of a preliminary investigation, which is only allowed in preparation for the more

[142] Compare Article 132a CCP.

[143] Police Act 1993.

[144] Coercive methods are understood to concern freedom-restricting methods, such as arrest and pre-trial detention.

[145] See for example Article 54 CCP for the coercive method of arrest and Article 126g for the special investigative technique of systematic observation. The most significant and general requirement before coercive methods or special investigative techniques can be applied against someone concerns the establishment of a reasonable suspicion as to Article 27(1) CCP.

complex (full) investigation of organized crime (Sect. 2.2.2.3). This preliminary investigation is an investigative phase separated from the full criminal investigation in the CCP, for which reason it is also dealt with as a separate basis for investigative activities, to be distinguished from the several provisions for using SIT in the context of the (full) criminal investigation. During the preliminary investigation, investigative activities can be conducted that aim to gather sufficient information to start a full criminal investigation.[146] These investigative techniques have a less intrusive character in comparison with those available in the full criminal investigation, such as the search of police databases.[147] Of course, the information collected during the preliminary investigation will equally become part of the criminal investigation, for which reason the investigative power of the preliminary investigation adds up to the sword capacity of the criminal investigation.

Lastly, as already mentioned in Sect. 2.2.1.4, information obtained by the AIVD can be shared with the PPS by means of an official report and can, consequently, result in criminal investigative steps and become part of the information produced in the criminal investigative phase and, hence, of the dossier. The information received from the AIVD may be used to serve the goal of the criminal investigation (collecting information to make prosecutorial decisions), for which reason it is dealt with as a separate basis in this section.

#### 2.2.2.1 Article 2 Police Act 1993

As already briefly explained above, the police may conduct investigative activities in order to fulfill their general policing task as provided in Article 2 Police Act 1993. According to Article 2 it is the task of the police to pursue the actual enforcement of law, to maintain order and to provide assistance to anyone in need, while being subordinated to the competent authority and in accordance with the law as is in force. This includes the police's law enforcement task, for which purpose the police shall investigate and prevent criminal offenses.[148] The relevance of Article 2 Police Act 1993 as a legal basis for investigative powers within the complete arsenal of investigative powers which are available in the criminal investigation follows from the interpretation of Article 2 over the years up until the interpretation which has been currently adopted. Important for this interpretation is the divisibility of the general police task into two types: the law enforcement task and the task of administrative enforcement, which concerns the maintenance of legal order, including the prevention of crime. This distinction made within the policing task can also be found in the organization of the supervision of either task—by the public prosecutor or the mayor—as well as in its regulation.[149] The

[146] Article 126gg CCP.

[147] Article 126hh CCP.

[148] Van Zuijlen 2008, 116-117.

[149] Articles 12 and 13 Police Act 1993 (supervision).

law enforcement task is regulated in criminal procedural law, whereas administrative enforcement is regulated in administrative law.[150]

Criminal investigation and the police's task to conduct criminal investigative activities were initially (mainly before the entry into force of the Act on Special Investigative Techniques in 2000[151]) distinguished from the administrative supervisory task of the police on the basis of the presence of a reasonable suspicion: criminal investigation concerns investigation on the basis of a reasonable suspicion, while the controlling task of the police concerns all other forms of investigation and control. This distinction with a 'reasonable suspicion' as the dividing line resulted in a 'limited interpretation of the criminal investigation' regulated by criminal procedural law. However, in practice, criminal investigation and administrative supervision cannot be strictly separated as both activities often overlap.[152] The powers for administrative supervision and for criminal investigation are often delegated to the same officials, for which reason the demarcation line between administrative supervision and criminal investigation is often difficult to recognize. This is especially apparent when the administrative supervisory authorities are delegated with regard to a special Act (such as drugs) and the activities lead to the establishment of a reasonable suspicion of a criminal offense. Using powers for other purposes than attributed constitutes a *détournement de pouvoir* (an abuse of power).[153] However, most investigative officers will be attributed with the power to use investigative methods for both purposes in order to avoid problems as just mentioned.[154]

Also the Supreme Court upheld a limited interpretation of the criminal investigation in the so-called '*Shadow judgments*' (1986)[155] and in the '*Zwolsman*' case (1995)[156] by determining that the criminal investigation only entails the investigation aimed at the clarification of a reasonable suspicion that a crime has been committed or is being committed, from which proactive activities are excluded. The criminal investigation in the limited sense was at that time understood to entail only the activities regulated in criminal procedural law, which concerned activities that could be conducted upon the establishment of a reasonable suspicion that a crime has been committed. Nevertheless, in the *Shadow judgments* and in the *Zwolsman* case it was also argued that the criminal investigation can be preceded by a proactive phase in which law enforcement officers are entitled to use

[150] For the regulation of the administrative task of the police, see: Title 5.2 of the General Administrative Law Act [*Algemene wet bestuursrecht*]. Stb 1992, 315 (as amended in 2011).

[151] February 1, 2000, Stb. 1999, 245 and Stb. 2000, 32. The implications of this Act on Special Investigative Techniques will be extensively dealt with in Sect. 2.2.2.2.1.

[152] Elzinga et al. 1995, 38-42.

[153] See Sect. 2.1.3.4.2.

[154] The distinction between investigation for the purpose of administrative supervision and for the purpose of criminal investigation, and the overlap between these two functions, will be dealt with more extensively in Sect. 2.3.2.2.2.

[155] HR 14 October 1986, *NJ* 1987, 564 and HR 14 October 1986, *NJ* 1988, 511, ann. ThWvV.

[156] HR 19 December 1995, *NJ* 1996, 249, ann. Sch.

investigative powers on the basis of Article 2 (at that time Article 28) of the Police Act 1993. On the basis of Article 2 of the Police Act of 1993, in combination with Article 141 or 142 CCP, which gives police officers the task of investigating criminal offenses and thus determines who may use the criminal investigative powers derived from Article 2 Police Act 1993, police officers can legitimately conduct these proactive investigative activities.[157]

The limited interpretation of the scope of the criminal investigation was already questioned by the Parliamentary Inquiry Commission (the Van Traa Commission), which was established in December 1994 in order to investigate the use of and the control on investigative powers within the Netherlands. In its report the Van Traa Commission endorsed the fact that the criminal investigation in practice includes phases in which a reasonable suspicion cannot be established. As demonstrated by the case of *Zwolsman*, proactive investigative activities were being applied in practice and they lacked any regulation by criminal procedural law.[158] The acceptance of these proactive investigative activities in fact pointed to a gap in the law, considering that regulation in the CCP is desirable because also these proactive investigative activities aim to trace criminal offenses and to interfere with the private lives of those people involved. In order to offer a solution to this undesirable situation, the Van Traa Commission had proposed a definition of criminal investigation, which included those situations in which a reasonable suspicion cannot yet be established.[159]

Both the report of the Parliamentary Inquiry Commission (1996) and the Supreme Court's decision in *Zwolsman* (1995) can be understood as a call for the legislature to create new legislation providing for a basis in the CCP for investigative methods that (seriously) interfere with privacy rights, which can both be applied in reaction to a crime which has been committed or proactively.[160] The Act of 27 May 1999 on special investigative techniques amended the CCP in order to precisely regulate the use of SIT.[161] This Act entered into force on 1 February 2000.[162] For the first time the Act also provided for a definition of criminal investigation in Article 132a CCP. According to this definition, the criminal investigation occurs under the supervision of the public prosecutor and commences when there is a reasonable suspicion that a crime has been committed or when there is a reasonable suspicion that crimes in an organized context are being

---

[157] HR 19 December 1995, *NJ* 1996, 249, ann. Sch., para 6.4.5, see also the annotation by Sch. para 3 and 4. HR 14 October 1986, *NJ* 1988, 511, ann. ThWvW, para 6.2. See also Fokkens and Kirkels-Vrijman 2009, 109.

[158] HR 19 December 1995, *NJ* 1996, 249 (*Zwolsman*), para 6.4.4 and 6.4.5 and HR 14 October 1986, *NJ* 1987, 564 para 7.3 and HR 14 October, *NJ* 1988, 511, ann. ThWvV para 6.2 (*Shadow Judgments*).

[159] Rapport van de Parlementaire Enquêtecommissie Opsporingsmethoden 1996, 455.

[160] Rapport van de Parlementaire Enquêtecommissie Opsporingsmethoden 1996, 432-437 and HR 19 December 1995, *NJ* 1996, 249, para 6.4.4.

[161] *Stb.* 1999, 245.

[162] *Stb.* 2000, 32.

planned or committed while these crimes result in a serious infringement of the legal order.[163] The latter threshold aims to include proactive investigative activities. The purpose of the criminal investigation must, furthermore, be to 'make prosecutorial decisions', which generally means any decision by the public prosecutor in relation to criminal offenses (e.g. the decision as to whether or not to prosecute as well as the decision to arrest a suspect) and, hence, that the purpose of the investigation shall be the collection of information which is relevant for truth-finding regarding criminal offenses. As a consequence of this definition of the criminal investigation, the relevant investigative activities, which were already used in practice and resulted in a serious interference with private life, are by means of the Act of 1999 also brought within the regulatory context of the criminal procedural law.[164]

As a consequence of the Act on SIT of 1999 and, especially, since the Act to Broaden the Possibilities to Investigate Terrorist Crimes of 2006 (henceforth: the Act on the Criminal Investigation of Terrorist Crimes), the limited interpretation of criminal investigation and the commensurate distinction which is made between criminal investigation and administrative supervision on the basis of the presence of a reasonable suspicion is no longer valid. According to the definition of criminal investigation provided in Article 132a CCP, all police activities conducted for the purpose of making prosecutorial decisions under the responsibility of the public prosecutor concern criminal investigative activities.[165] Hence, the activities of the police belonging to their law enforcement task as included in Article 2 Police Act 1993 concern criminal investigative activities in the context of the criminal investigation phase defined in Article 132a CCP. According to this definition, the two distinguishing circumstances that separate the criminal investigation from administrative supervision are, firstly, that the public prosecutor supervises the police activities and, secondly, that investigative activities shall result in making prosecutorial decisions.[166] Therefore, the term criminal investigation refers to all investigative activities that meet this definition, which thus concerns the law enforcement task of the police regardless of the specific legal basis in law for using investigating powers for exerting the police's law enforcement task.

Nevertheless, the previous distinction which was made between investigative activities requiring a specific legal basis and those activities that can be conducted on the basis of Article 2 Police Act 1993 in the *Zwolsman* case of 1995 is still valid as a consequence of the right to respect for private life as guaranteed in Article 8 ECHR and Article 10 Constitution and of the principle of legality as laid down in

---

[163] This definition was in place until 2007. The Act of 2006 to Broaden the Possibilities to Investigate and Prosecute Terrorist Crimes (Act on the Criminal Investigation of Terrorist Crimes) amended Article 132a CCP by eliminating the threshold of a reasonable suspicion or a reasonable suspicion that crimes are being planned or committed in an organized context from the definition. See on the current demarcation of the criminal investigation phase Sect. 2.3.2.2.

[164] *Kamerstukken II* 1997/98, 25 403, no. 7, 17.

[165] As adopted by the Act of 20 November 2006, *Stb.* 2006, 580.

[166] This subject will be dealt with in more detail in Sect. 2.3.2.2.1.

Article 1 CCP. The Act on SIT of 1999 has provided legal bases for the more intrusive investigative techniques (Title IVA and Title V CCP; Articles 126g-126ui CCP) that can be conducted in the context of a criminal investigation.[167] Article 2 of the Police Act 1993 still concerns the legal basis for those investigative activities of law enforcement officers (under Articles 141 or 142 CCP) within the criminal investigation that do not, or only to a limit extent, interfere with fundamental rights and are not otherwise regulated.[168]

Case law has further defined which specific activities may be conducted on the basis of the general task description of Article 2 Police Act 1993. Especially the Supreme Court's decision in *Zwolsman* still functions as the guideline to determine which investigative activities can be based upon Article 2 of the Police Act 1993 and which activities must be based upon a more specific legal basis, or, in the absence of such a provision, are in fact prohibited. In *Zwolsman* it was explicitly determined that Article 2 of the Police Act 1993 is insufficient for functioning as a basis for using investigative powers that interfere with privacy rights, because a more precise legal basis is required to comply with the requirements of Article 8 ECHR, Article 10 of the Constitution and the principle of legality under Article 1 CCP.[169]

Referring to the *Zwolsman* decision it has been decided, for example, that simple observation concerns only a limited interference with privacy rights, and Article 2 of the Police Act 1993 can thus function as the basis for this authority. Recently, the Supreme Court has accepted the use of a heat sensor on the basis of Article 2 Police Act 1993, because the 'heat image' obtained through the sensor only results in a limited interference with privacy rights.[170] However, when the observation has a systematic character, which depends on the frequency, the duration, the intensity, the specific location observed, the manner of observing and the level of the consequential interferences,[171] the basis under Article 2 is unsatisfactory. Also the purpose of the observation and the specific activities observed shall be taken into account as relevant elements for the intrusiveness of the interference with private life.[172] What matters, for example, is whether the observation took place in public or in a place where someone can expect to be able to rely on privacy, such as the observation of someone at his or her home.[173] Intrusive techniques for which, for instance, places that are exclusively protected

167 See the subsequent section for the legal bases of special investigative techniques.

168 Compare: Fokkens and Kirkels-Vrijman 2009, 123.

169 HR 19 December 1995, *NJ* 1996, 249, para 6.4.4 and 6.4.5.

170 HR 20 January 2009, *NJ* 2009, 225, ann. Borgers, see annotation para 7.

171 For example, HR 5 June 2001, *NJ* 2001, 518, para 1.4 and 4.3 and HR 29 March 2005, *LJN* AS27527, para 3.1.

172 HR 25 January 2000, *NJ* 2000, 279, para 3.5 (concerning observations of business premises for the purpose of determining whether the conditions for a particular permit were being observed) and HR 19 December 1995, *NJ* 1996, 249, para 9.7, 9.8 and 9.9.

173 HR 14 October 1986, *NJ* 1988, 511, para 6.3.

(such as private homes[174]) have to be entered or searched, as well as techniques that violate the confidentiality of mail and telephone communications, require an explicit basis in law for using the technique along with clear procedural conditions. Camera surveillance in public places does not infringe someone's privacy rights, because the observation does not concern a situation in which someone can have a reasonable expectation of privacy.[175] On the other hand, it has been prohibited to enter homes for the purpose of observation, for example in order to install a technical device, whilst the observation of a person at his or her home from the outside is not precluded as long as the observations can be made without a technical device such as a camera or are restricted to the activities that take place outside the house, for example, registering who enters and leaves the house.[176] The Court of Appeal of The Hague has also accepted the requesting of a suspect's IP address from a third person on the basis of Article 2 Police Act 1993.[177] Furthermore, the seriousness of the crimes involved can play a role in deciding whether or not Article 2 suffices as the basis for the investigative authority. With the application of the principle of proportionality the interest of investigating a serious offense is balanced against the interest of the person whose privacy is intruded for the purpose of the investigation, resulting in less strict standards for the investigation of serious crimes. The seriousness does not only entail the nature of the crime itself, but also the circumstances under which it is committed and a possible concurrence with other crimes.[178] The seriousness of the crime is then a factor in deciding on the proportionality of the use of the investigative power, which may also be taken into account for determining whether Article 2 Police Act 1993 is, in a particular situation, a sufficient basis for an investigative power.

---

[174] Private homes are considered to be places where people have a pre-eminent right to freedom and respect for their private life. This is also explicitly stated in Article 8 ECHR, Article 17 ICCPR, as well as protected by Article 138 and 370 Penal Code and Article 12 Constitution. The ECHR has extended the interpretation of the terms "private life" and "home" under Article 8 ECHR to include certain professional or business activities or premises. ECHR 16 December 1992, App. no. 13710/88 (*Niemietz v. Germany*), para 29.

[175] HR 20 April 2004, *NJ* 2004, 525, para 3.3.

[176] *Kamerstukken II* 1996/97, 25 403, no. 3, 70-71. And: HR 29 March 2005, *LJN* AS27527, para 3.2.

[177] Gerechtshof 's-Gravenhage 15 November 2002, *NJ* 2003, 23, para 3.

[178] HR 12 February 2002, *NJ* 2002, 301, para 3.4 and HR 29 March 2005, *LJN* AS27527, para 3.1 and 3.3. See in this regard also Sect. 2.3.2.3 concerning the threshold of a reasonable suspicion. In balancing the interests involved for adopting a threshold of application for SIT, the seriousness of the crime is also an important factor which has to be considered.

#### 2.2.2.2 Investigative Techniques with a Specific Basis in the Law

##### 2.2.2.2.1 The Act on Special Investigative Techniques of 1999

The Act of 27 May 1999,[179] which entered into force on 1 February 2000,[180] amended the CCP in order to regulate the use of certain far-reaching investigative powers. This Act has adopted a definition of the criminal investigation that demarcates the criminal investigation as a phase in which exclusively specific far-reaching investigative powers may be used. As explained in the previous section, currently—in particular since the adoption of the Act on the Criminal Investigation of Terrorist Crimes of 2006[181]—the criminal investigation is not limited to the conditions under which also far-reaching investigative techniques can be applied. The criminal investigation is now the phase which covers all investigative activities (including those based on Article 2 Police Act 1993) for the purpose of truth-finding in criminal law. However, the use of far-reaching SIT is still regulated under more precise conditions that were previously also related to the phase of the criminal investigation.

This section will describe the system adopted for the use of SIT within the criminal investigation by the Act of 27 May 1999, by focusing on the basis for using SIT created by this Act. The goal of the adoption of this Act has been to improve the transparency and, on that basis, the internal and external controllability of criminal investigations. Considering this goal, the regulation in the CCP seems primarily to serve a shield role. Nevertheless, the created bases in law to use special investigative techniques also concern the legitimization for using far-reaching investigative techniques in order to enhance the investigative capacity of the police and PPS. Hence, this section will address the nature and scope of the investigative activities that can be conducted with the help of SIT as a consequence of the Act of 27 May 1999. The Act has resulted in a different approach to the investigative possibilities with the help of SIT for ordinary crime (henceforth: classical investigation[182]) and for organized crime (organized crime investigation). This section will address the scope and nature of these two investigative domains separately. The restraints adopted by this Act on SIT and the shield function served by these restraints will, for each category, be extensively dealt with in Sect. 2.3.2.3.2. Since the entry into force (2007) of the Act on the Criminal Investigation of Terrorist Crimes, 'terrorist crimes' constitute a third category of investigation with its own set of regulations. This category will be dealt with in the next chapter, as part of the counterterrorism measures that have enabled anticipative criminal investigations in the Netherlands.

The same techniques are available in the classical investigation and in the organized crime investigation. These techniques concern: systematic observation

[179] *Stb.* 1999, 245.

[180] *Stb.* 2000, 32.

[181] *Stb.* 2006, 580.

[182] Compare Corstens 2008, 257.

(Articles 126g and 126o CCP); infiltration (Articles 126h and 126p CCP); pseudo-dealing or serving (Articles 126i and 126q CCP); the systematic gaining of information by using informants (Articles 126j and 126qa CCP); the entering of a private place other than homes (Articles 126k and 126r CCP); the interception of private communications (in particular: with the help of a technical device, Articles 126l and 126s CCP; wiretapping and the interception of electronic communications, Articles 126la-126nb and 126t-126ub CCP); and the ordering of stored information (stored or recorded identifying information, Articles 126nc and 126uc; stored or recorded other than identifying information, Articles 126nd and 126ud; information received after the order has been issued, Articles 126ne and 126ue; stored or recorded information that concerns information regarding one's religion, race, political views, health, sex life or membership of a labor union, Articles 126nf and 126uf CCP; and, the information meant in the Articles 126nc-126ne and 126uc-126ue requested from an electronic network service provider, Articles 126ng and 126ug CCP). Some of these techniques have a more intrusive character than others, for which reason one of the enumerated techniques is generally available to law enforcement officers,[183] whereas most of the others are only available upon the order of the public prosecutor[184] or even require additional authorization by an examining magistrate.[185] The specific additional conditions for using SIT will be dealt with in Sect. 2.3.2.3.2.5.[186]

##### *2.2.2.2.1.1 Classical Investigation*

The classical investigation starts with the finding of a circumstance which makes it clear that a crime has been committed or may have been committed (either a notification or the discovery of evidence of a (possible) crime). This renders the classical investigation in principle a reactive form of criminal investigation, whereas it is not required that the suspect has already been found. The terms reactive and proactive are here understood in a similar fashion as is traditionally understood in Dutch criminal procedural law by referring to the triggering moment of the criminal investigation. A reactive investigation concerns an investigation for the purpose of clarifying a committed crime where a reasonable suspicion that a crime has been committed[187] is

---

[183] Ordering of identifying information.

[184] Systematic observation, infiltration, pseudo-dealing or serving, systematic gaining of information, and entering private places.

[185] Interception of private communications and ordering (personal) information other than identifying information.

[186] For more information on these specific special investigative techniques, see Buruma 2001 and Corstens 2008, 441-471.

[187] The requirement of 'suspicion' is defined in Article 27(1) CCP. According to Article 27(1) CCP, a person can be considered to be a suspect, before the prosecution has been initiated, when a reasonable suspicion to believe that he or she is guilty of having committed a criminal offense can be derived from the facts or circumstances. The importance and influence of the central position of this definition of a suspect as a threshold for using SIT will be dealt with in more detail in Sect. 2.3.2.3.

present, whereas a proactive investigation refers to criminal investigative activities before there is a reasonable suspicion that a crime has been committed.[188]

Provided that a suspicion as defined in Article 27(1) CCP is required, and thus a suspicion that a crime has been committed, proactive application, in the procedural sense, is not possible within the classical investigative domain. Nevertheless, proactive investigative goals can be pursued also in the classical investigation, because of the possibility to investigate, on the basis of the threshold which is applicable under Title IVa, the suspected fulfillment of the provisions criminalizing acts of preparation (Article 46 Penal Code and Article 10a Drugs Act), conspiracy to commit certain crimes (Articles 80, 96, 103, 114b, 120b, 122, 176b, 282c, 289a, 304b, 415b Penal Code) and participation in a criminal organization (Article 140 Penal Code).[189] These acts are crimes, although they often concern, at the same time, the planning of the 'full' crimes. Hence, investigations upon a reasonable suspicion of these crimes are, according to the law, reactive and not proactive, although in practice these investigations primarily serve a proactive goal. The investigation will in the first place be limited to clarifying a reasonable suspicion of—for instance—criminal preparation, but does not have to stop if other crimes are simultaneously discovered. As a consequence, these reactive investigations provide the possibility to act for proactive or preventive purposes with regard to other—and more serious—crimes. The Supreme Court has affirmed this practice: 'it is not precluded that an authorization, in this case for infiltration, in the classical investigation is used for the discovery of criminal offenses which are committed after the authorization of the order.'[190] This interpretation thus allows that an investigation upon a reasonable suspicion of a specifically indicated crime is not limited to that crime but can be simultaneously extended to other discovered crimes.

#### *2.2.2.2.1.2 Organized Crime Investigation*

Title V of the CCP provides for the SIT which are available in the investigation of organized crime. These concern the same techniques as are available in the classical investigation. However, the Title dealing with the special investigative techniques which are available in the organized crime investigation differs from the Title dealing with SIT in the classical investigation, because the investigation is not limited to a reaction to the presence of a reasonable suspicion of a committed crime. Instead, the main requirement that has to be met before SIT can be used in organized crime investigations concerns: 'a reasonable suspicion that crimes are being planned or committed in an organized context, which crimes result in a serious infringement of the legal order considering their nature or relation with other crimes and for which crimes pre-trial detention can be imposed as to the

---

188 Compare Corstens 2008, 257-258 and 269. Corstens identifies proactive investigation as 'early detection' [*vroegsporing*].

189 See in more detail: Krommendijk et al. 2009, 119-123, Sikkema 2008, para 4.10, and Van Sliedregt 2006, 9.

190 HR 7 October 2003, *NJ* 2004, 118, para 3.3.

law.' This means that contrary to classical investigations, the proactive use of SIT is permitted, considering that the reasonable suspicion is not limited to committed crimes, but covers also future criminality.

The adoption of the Act on SIT of 27 May 1999 was primarily a consequence of the 'crisis in the investigation' as reported by the Van Traa Commission due to a discrepancy between investigative practice and its regulation in the CCP.[191] The traditional reactive form of criminal investigation was unsuitable for the investigation of organized crime, which concerns a form of criminality that has increased in particular in the 1980s. A strategy of going after separate crimes committed by a criminal organization was unable to stop the criminal organization from planning and committing new offenses. As a consequence, in practice SIT were used to obtain information on the structure and members of a criminal organization and the nature of the criminal offenses committed by this organization. The existence of a proactive investigative practice in the absence of explicit regulation in the CCP was also confirmed by the Supreme Court in the *Zwolsman* case (1995)[192] and by the Van Traa Parliamentary Inquiry Commission.[193]

It was generally acknowledged that the investigation of organized crime calls for a different approach than investigating conventional crime, because of the complexity and serious nature of the criminal activities. The criminal activities of such an organization are not limited to one crime and one suspect. A proactive approach targeting the organization as a whole is required. Hence, for effectively confronting organized crime, it was deemed necessary to adopt a standard for the use of SIT that is different from the standard applied to classical investigations.[194] The adopted threshold for organized crime investigations meets this goal by permitting the use of SIT in relation to multiple people and multiple criminal offenses in order to investigate the planning and committing of serious crimes in the context of a criminal organization. According to the explanatory memorandum of the Act on SIT, the investigation of organized crime according to this threshold cannot be strictly understood as pure proactive investigation, because the investigation of a criminal organization will also always include already committed crime. However, the focus of the investigation is broader and includes also future criminality. Consequently, the focus of the investigation will be proactive: to confront the criminal organization as a whole by investigating the organization and its members, before revealing what is on track by prosecuting a single criminal offense committed by the organization.[195] Nevertheless, a proactive criminal investigation with the help of special investigative techniques remains an exception, created especially for the most complex forms of criminality, considering the

[191] *Kamerstukken II* 1995/96, 24 072, nos. 10-11, 413-415 (Rapport van de Parlementaire Enquêtecommissie Opsporingsmethoden 1996). See also Krommendijk et al. 2009, 10.

[192] HR 19 December 1995, *NJ* 1996, 249, ann. Sch., para 6.4.4.

[193] *Kamerstukken II* 1995/96, 24 072, nos. 10-11, 413-414 and 451 (Rapport van de Parlementaire Enquêtecommissie Opsporingsmethoden 1996) and *Kamerstukken II* 1996/97, 25 403, no. 3, 4.

[194] *Kamerstukken II* 1996/97, 25 403, no. 3, 4.

[195] *Kamerstukken II* 1996/97, 25 403, no. 3, 4 and 5.

limitation to the investigation of organized crime where serious crimes are being committed or will be committed.[196] Considering the additional requirement of the involvement of 'crimes that result in a serious infringement of the legal order considering their nature or relation with other crimes and for which crimes pre-trial detention can be imposed under the law', the proactive investigation will concern criminal organizations that engage in serious criminal activities such as human trafficking, the drugs trade or the arms trade.[197]

##### 2.2.2.2.2 Investigative Methods with a Specific Legal Basis in Special Criminal Acts

Criminal offenses are not only provided in the Penal Code, but also in some special criminal Acts. The CCP applies to the investigation of all criminal offenses, including those criminalized in these special criminal Acts. Hence, the criminal investigation also covers the investigation of these offenses. Where special investigative officers[198] have been attributed responsibility for the criminal investigation of offenses criminalized in these special criminal Acts, they likewise operate under the supervision of the public prosecutor.[199]

Besides defining criminal offenses, some of the special criminal Acts provide for a specific legal basis for the use of investigative methods, additional to the criminal investigative methods provided in the CCP. Some of these investigative methods may be used for the *criminal investigation* of offenses criminalized in the special criminal acts. Others are attributed for exerting *control* over the observance of the special criminal act.

For example, the Road Traffic Act [*Wegenverkeerswet 1994, WVW 1994*] gives investigative officers or special investigative officers (under Article 142 CCP, but also others designated under Article 159 WVW 1994) the power to stop vehicles (Article 160(1) WVW 1994) or to order that someone cooperates with a breath test (Article 160(5) WVW 1994). These powers entail administrative supervisory powers concerning the observance of the Road Traffic Act, for which the presence of a reasonable suspicion is not required.

Furthermore, some of the special criminal Acts also provide for specific criminal investigative methods, some of which can be used subject to lower standards than similar methods regulated in the CCP. For example, the Economic Offenses Act [*Wet op de economische delicten, WED*], provides investigative officers with the power to enter places and to search vehicles for the purpose of the

---

[196] Regardless of the fact that the limited availability of proactive investigative means must be put into perspective because of the possibility of a 'reactive' criminal investigation of preparatory acts, which still means that, except for clarifying a reasonable suspicion of that crime having been committed, also proactive goals will be realized.

[197] Krommendijk et al. 2009, 11.

[198] Article 142 CCP.

[199] Article 157 CCP. In addition, also 'regular' law enforcement officers (Article 141 CCP) are authorized to investigate criminal activities criminalized in the special criminal acts.

criminal investigation of offenses covered by the Act (Article 20-23 WED). The Drugs Act [*Opiumwet*] allows investigative officers and special investigative officers (e.g. customs officers) to search vehicles, to enter places, to frisk persons seriously suspected of a drugs crime and to seize goods (Article 9 *Opiumwet*). Lastly, the Weapons and Ammunition Act [*Wet wapens en munitie, WWM*] provides for some far-reaching investigative powers. Investigative officers can search places for the purpose of seizure if they reasonably suspect that weapons are present in that place (Article 49). Furthermore, investigative officers have the power to search things, including luggage, when there is a reasonable reason to do so: a) after a crime has been committed with the help of a weapon; b) in case of an offense as specified in the Act; and c) in the case of 'indications' that a crime as referred to under a and b will be committed.[200] Moreover, the public prosecutor can order the search of things belonging to every person[201] and the mayor can order that in a security zone things belonging to any person present in that area are to be searched.[202] The same powers have been created with regard to vehicles.[203] The Weapons and Ammunition Act provides, furthermore, for the power to seize things (Article 52(1) and for frisking powers under the same conditions as are applicable to search powers (Article 52(2) and (3)). Especially, the Drugs Act and the Weapons and Ammunition Act provide for some far-reaching powers that have been considered necessary taking into account the nature of the offenses criminalized in these statutes, the safety of the investigative officers or the possibility to mislay, for instance drugs, when there is no immediate action.

The bases for investigative methods provided for in the special criminal Acts differ with regard to two important aspects from the investigative powers attributed in the CCP. In the first place, the majority of the investigative methods specifically provided for in the special criminal acts concern administrative supervisory methods, to be used for the purpose of the preventive enforcement of the special criminal Act by controlling the observance of the Acts. Consequently, the use of these administrative supervisory methods fall outside the scope of the criminal investigation and are, thus, not supervised by the public prosecutor[204] and are not

200 Article 50(1) Weapons and Ammunition Act.

201 Article 50(2) Weapons and Ammunition Act.

202 Article 50(3) Weapons and Ammunition Act.

203 Article 51 Weapons and Ammunition Act.

204 This division of responsibility between the public prosecutor and the mayor on the basis of their respective responsibility for the criminal investigation and the maintenance of order (Articles 2, 12 and 13 Police Act 1993) is not always self-evident. The issue of responsibility for investigative officers exerting administrative supervisory powers, such as for example the power to stop a car in order to control observance with the Road Traffic Act (Article 160 WVW 1994), is less clear, considering that sometimes also persons other than police officers may use this controlling power (compare Article 159 WVW 1994) and, more in general, that the use of administrative supervisory powers on behalf of law enforcement officers very often overlaps or concurs with their criminal investigative task. Luchtman argues on the basis of this latter argument for supervision by the PPS also concerning the use of administrative supervisory powers. Luchtman 2007B, 669-672.

subjected to other criminal procedural safeguards. However, as already indicated in Sect. 2.2.2.1, the use of administrative supervisory powers and criminal investigative powers often overlap, considering that the use of an administrative supervisory power can result in a reasonable suspicion of a criminal offense and that the investigative officer is usually authorized to apply both administrative supervisory powers and criminal investigative powers. The Supreme Court has repeatedly addressed the situation where the task of administrative supervision and criminal investigation overlap,[205] which has resulted in the acceptance of the use of administrative supervisory powers also for a criminal investigative purpose as long as the administrative supervisory powers have not been used *exclusively* to pursue criminal investigative purposes.[206]

For example, in 2006 the Supreme Court allowed the use of the administrative supervisory power to stop a vehicle to control, e.g., the license of the driver, whereas it seemed that the police officers in question were particularly concerned with the possibility that one or more of the passengers were suspected of theft.[207] Hence, the availability of these administrative supervisory powers also strengthens the investigative capacity of the criminal investigation by being able to 'build' a criminal case against someone by using (initially) administrative supervisory powers.[208] Nevertheless, when administrative supervisory powers are used against a suspect, the investigative officers must take into account the rights attributed to suspects, such as the right to remain silent.[209]

In the second place, some criminal investigative methods provided in the special criminal acts can be applied subject to lower standards than the investigative methods regulated in the CCP. As follows from the examples mentioned above, under the WED investigative methods can be used if they serve the interest of the investigation. Also the Drugs Act includes similar methods. Furthermore, the Weapons and Ammunition Act allows for a search on the basis of 'indications' that a crime will be committed with the help of a weapon. Also the requirement under the WED and Drugs Act of 'reasonably serve the interest of the investigation' is understood to refer to 'indications' that one or more regulations of the Act have not been observed. Both criteria concern lower thresholds than the

---

[205] Identified as the 'cumulating of spheres' by Luchtman. Luchtman 2007A, 133-142 and 645-651. See also: Luchtman 2007B, 660-661.

[206] HR 26 April 1988, *NJ* 1989, 390, ann. ThWvV (Leidraadarrest) and HR 21 November 2006, *NJ* 2006, 653.

[207] HR 21 November 2006, *NJ* 2006, 653.

[208] A distinction between administrative supervision and criminal investigation was, in the first place, intended to serve a shield goal, considering that in order to protect the rights of citizens the more far-reaching power of the government to act in the context of criminal procedural law is subjected to more restraints and includes more safeguards than the power of the government to act in the context of administrative law. For this reason the demarcation of the criminal investigation from administrative supervision is dealt with in more detail in Sect. 2.3.2.2.2.

[209] Persons subjected to administrative supervisory powers are obliged to cooperate, whereas under criminal procedural law someone has the right to remain silent as part of the right not to cooperate in someone's own conviction. See HR 26 April 1988, *NJ* 1989, 390.

central requirement of a reasonable suspicion for the use of investigative methods under the CCP, which also allow for a proactive criminal investigation. The latter possibility is even stronger considering the possibility of overlapping purposes when administrative supervisory powers are used.

#### 2.2.2.3 The Preliminary Investigation

By the Act of 1999 regulating the use of SIT, also the 'preliminary investigation' has gained a separate place in the CCP (Article 126gg). The preliminary investigation officially 'precedes' the criminal investigation as defined in 132a CCP. It can be initiated in preparation for a full criminal investigation and is aimed at the gathering of information for that purpose. The intention of formulating the purpose of the preliminary investigation in that manner is to separate it from the phase of the criminal investigation, considering that the purpose of the (full) criminal investigation concerns the collection of information for the making of prosecutorial decisions. This separation seems somewhat artificial since the information collected during the preliminary investigation subsequently becomes part of the criminal investigation and in that way equally forms the basis for making prosecutorial decisions. In addition, the preliminary investigation is, according to Article 13 of the Police Act 1993, also conducted under the responsibility of the public prosecutor. For this reason, in this research the term criminal investigation refers also to the preliminary investigation. When the term full criminal investigation is used, this is explicitly intended to separate the preliminary investigative phase from the full criminal investigation. In addition, the preliminary criminal investigation will be considered as a separate basis for conducting investigative activities with the help of the investigative methods that are exclusively reserved for the preliminary investigative phase. This should be compared to the full criminal investigation, which is the phase where special investigative techniques can be used.

The preliminary investigation can be described as an investigation that aims at taking criminal procedural steps and that generates information which is reducible to specific persons.[210] If the information available is insufficient for establishing a reasonable suspicion and, thus, for initiating a (full) criminal investigation, a preliminary investigation can be started if the information available does show indications that among groups of people crimes are being planned or committed. In such a situation an additional investigation will be desirable in order to collect the necessary information for starting a full criminal investigation.[211] For example, a whole sector (such as a harbor, a transport or airport sector) can be investigated in order to determine in which specific part and in what manner criminal activities are taking place.

[210] Buruma 2001, 134.

[211] *Kamerstukken II* 1996/97, 25 403, no. 3, 49.

The investigative activities that can be conducted in the preliminary investigation are not unrestricted: special investigative techniques are precluded; activities that aim to gather information which is reducible to specific persons fall within the scope of the preliminary investigation. The specific activities that can be conducted within the scope of the preliminary investigation are not explicitly mentioned in the provision. The nature of the permitted activities can be derived from the explanatory memorandum, mentioning, for example, the comparison of information stored in police files with information obtainable from open sources. The information gathered from open sources or with voluntary cooperation concerning personal particulars can be temporarily stored in police files.[212] Information already gathered in another criminal investigation, obtained through using one or more regulated SIT, such as observation or the recording of private communications during a full criminal investigation, can be used in a preliminary investigation in order to prepare a new full criminal investigation.[213] According to the second section of Article 126gg CCP, the public prosecutor can order that a law protecting privacy, which determines that information from public files may only be used and spread for the purpose for which they are stored in that specific file, does not apply.[214] This information can then be obtained within the scope of the preliminary investigation and thus be used for criminal investigative purposes.

### 2.2.2.4 The Investigative Powers of the Intelligence Community in Relation to Criminal Justice

#### 2.2.2.4.1 The Investigative Powers of the AIVD

The AIVD has been attributed far-reaching investigative powers for the purpose of fulfilling its task of averting threats and protecting national security and other vital state interests.[215] These powers have for the first time been specifically attributed by law in the WIV 2002. On the basis of Article 17 WIV 2002 the AIVD has the general authority to collect information[216] from other governmental or private organizations or persons without being hindered by legal rules protecting personal privacy. The person from whom the information is requested is, however, not obliged to cooperate.[217] Apart from its common authority to gather intelligence (Article 17 WIV 2002), the service has "special powers" at its disposal for the

[212] See Act on Police Information [*Wet politiegegevens*], *Stb.* 2007, 300.

[213] According to Article 126dd CCP, information obtained through some SIT can be used in a different criminal investigation, which includes the preliminary investigation.

[214] Personal Data Protection Act [*Wet bescherming persoonsgegevens*], Article 9(1).

[215] Article 6 WIV 2002 (see Sect. 2.2.1.4).

[216] The AIVD collects *information*, which is subsequently combined and analyzed by the AIVD resulting in *intelligence*. Muller 2007, 171.

[217] Muller 2007, 173.

purpose of gathering information, which include: observation, the use of undercover agents, electronic surveillance, searching enclosed places or objects, the opening of personal correspondence and demanding information from automated systems with the help of false keys, signals or identities.[218] These powers are comparable to the special investigative techniques available in the criminal investigation, but without subjecting them to the safeguards provided in the regulation of SIT in the CCP, most notably a threshold such as having a 'reasonable suspicion'. This means that in practice criminal activities that at the same time pose a threat to national security may be investigated by the police and the PPS with the help of SIT in order to prepare a criminal prosecution and, simultaneously, by the AIVD in the light of the protection of national security.

The powers available to the AIVD are regulated by requiring, for the use of the most intrusive powers, the permission of the relevant Minister and, otherwise, on behalf of the Minister, the permission of the head of the AIVD. The mandate of the District Court of The Hague is required before the AIVD can use the special power of opening personal correspondence.[219] Furthermore, the principles of proportionality and subsidiarity must be taken into account at all times. This means, firstly, that the powers will immediately be terminated if the objective of the power used has been accomplished. And, secondly, a power cannot be used when a less far-reaching power would suffice.[220] In this manner internal control is meant to be exerted, which is furthered by requiring a written report after the use of any of these powers.[221] External control over the activities of the intelligence services is, contrary to the control of law enforcement activities, not judicial, but political. Parliament controls through the political accountability of the Ministers responsible for the intelligence services. In addition, the Act of 2002 has provided for an independent oversight committee for the information and security services, which is a controlling body for the work of the intelligence services. This oversight committee has been established in order to provide an external independent controlling body in addition to the internal control.[222] The committee is responsible for supervising the legitimacy of the execution of the intelligence services' tasks, and for informing and advising the relevant Ministers on any findings by the committee as well as on the investigation and assessment of complaints.[223] This control is exerted afterwards and, according to the legislature, meets the requirements of Article 13 and Article 8 ECHR. The committee has access to all information (written reports) and can hear all staff belonging to the services. It also has

---

[218] Article 20-30 WIV 2002. For a translated version of the full list of the AIVD's investigative powers see Articles 20-30 of the English version of the WIV 2001, available at: https://www.aivd.nl/english/aivd/the-intelligence-and/ (accessed July 19, 2011).

[219] The power to open personal correspondence is provided with an additional check, because the confidentiality of mail is protected as a Constitutional right in Article 13 Constitution.

[220] Article 32 WIV 2002.

[221] Article 33 WIV 2002.

[222] *Kamerstukken II* 1997/98, 25 877, no. 3, 78-79.

[223] Article 64 WIV 2002.

the authority to hear witnesses and experts and to access places. The reports of the review committee are public.[224] Lastly, the Minister must inform, five years after the use of special powers against a person, whether that person can be notified about the use of the special powers. This duty to investigate whether the person can be notified does not apply when notification will adversely affect some serious interests, such as the interest in retaining shielded sources of the AIVD or of foreign intelligence services.[225] A person may also request whether personal information regarding him/her has been collected by the AIVD.[226]

It can be concluded that far-reaching special powers are available to the AIVD, which have a comparable or even more far-reaching character than the special investigative techniques available to law enforcement agencies. Because the AIVD's task is to protect national security and not to collect evidence for criminal prosecution, the AIVD's use of these special powers is not further restrained by some threshold, such as having a reasonable suspicion under criminal procedural law, nor subjected to judicial review. The use of the special powers must only relate to the exercise of their tasks as mentioned in Article 6 WIV under a and d (see Sect. 2.2.1.4), which means in general that the use of such powers should concern the protection of national security. Because national security is not a clearly defined term, the AIVD has been given wide discretion in using special powers for exerting its tasks.[227] The AIVD is only regulated through requiring authorization by the relevant Minister, by the principles of proportionality and subsidiarity and subject to political external control and an independent *ex post* oversight committee.

##### 2.2.2.4.2 Transfer of Information Obtained by the AIVD to Law Enforcement Services

Any responsibility of the AIVD for the criminal investigation has been explicitly excluded and, hence, the investigative officers of the AIVD do not have criminal investigative powers in the sense of Article 141 or 142 CCP. The intelligence community, on the basis of its tasks, is strictly separated from the law enforcement community. Nevertheless, when the AIVD encounters information which is relevant to a criminal investigation, it is allowed to transfer this information to the national public prosecutor. In that way the AIVD can incite the law enforcement community to start a criminal investigation or, in more urgent situations, directly resort to the use of coercive methods such as arrest and pre-trial detention in order to avert a threat.

A 1992 note by the Minister of Justice addressing the special parliamentary commission on the intelligence and security service regarding the 'evidentiary

[224] Article 74-79 WIV 2002.

[225] Article 34 WIV 2002.

[226] Article 47 WIV 2002.

[227] Compare: Vis 2010A, 421.

value of information obtained by the BVD (the National Security Service which was the predecessor of the AIVD) already provided that although the task of the AIVD is not and will not be to investigate criminal offenses for the purpose of criminal prosecution, the information and material collected by the BVD can provide a cause for initiating a criminal investigation on behalf of the agencies thereby authorized as well as to establish a reasonable suspicion under Article 27 CCP'.[228] The transfer of information from the AIVD to the PPS has been given an explicit basis in the Act of 2002. The AIVD can, on the basis of Article 38, disclose information to the PPS by means of an official report [*ambtsbericht*] when it appears that the information can also be relevant to the investigation or prosecution of offenses. This provision does not entail an obligation to disclosure and the AIVD will only proceed to disclose when this will not harm national security interests. The official report contains information without revealing the source and the methods applied to obtain that information or the agency's actual level of knowledge. The official report will be sent to one of the two national public prosecutors who bear responsibility for countering terrorism and for other criminal cases that also relate to the activities of the AIVD (henceforth: the national public prosecutor for counterterrorism). These national public prosecutors for counterterrorism will subsequently decide whether or not these reports need to be sent to offices of the PPS in order to initiate a criminal investigation.[229] For making this decision, the national public prosecutor for counterterrorism can, on the basis of Article 38(3) WIV 2002, request from the AIVD all information on which the report has been based, in order to be able to assess the reliability of the report and the usefulness of the information for criminal investigative action. Consequently, the national public prosecutor for counterterrorism is likewise bound by secrecy.[230]

The Supreme Court has also affirmed that there is no legal provision that forbids the use of information gathered by an intelligence agency in the criminal process, which also means that this information can establish a reasonable suspicion under Article 27 CCP and can be used as evidence in a trial.[231] In addition, according to the Supreme Court, no legal rule forbids the PPS or other law enforcement service from requesting more specific information from the intelligence community.[232] This request by the PPS is, however, limited to information in addition to the

---

[228] *Kamerstukken II* 1991/92, 22 463, no. 4, 2 and 6. During the discussion of the bill underlying the current WIV 2002, the responsible Ministers concluded that the main lines of the note of 1992 still concerned the correct and practicable description of the manner in which information gathered by the BVD can be used in furtherance of a criminal investigation. *Kamerstukken II,* 1997/98, 25 877, no. 14, 12. See also Hirsch Ballin 2009, 289.

[229] Muller 2007, 180.

[230] Articles 85-86 WIV 2002.

[231] HR 5 September 2006, *NJ* 2007, 336, para 4.5.1. Also the development where courts give more leeway to the possibility of using intelligence information in criminal investigations and further proceedings will be dealt with in Chap. 3.

[232] HR 13 November 2007, *NJ* 2007, 614, para 3.5.2.

official report, information which is thus already available. It cannot request the intelligence service to conduct a further investigation in a specific case. This would entail an abuse of power (*détournement de pouvoir*) resulting in the circumvention of the protective function of criminal procedural law.[233] It is a violation of the law when the law enforcement community intentionally refrains from using SIT in order to make use of the information gathered by the intelligence community or when the intelligence community uses its powers for prosecutorial purposes.[234] When the AIVD sends an official report to the PPS, this does not mean that the intelligence service must end its investigation. A parallel investigation is possible to the extent that the intelligence agency and the law enforcement agency only use their powers with the intention to fulfill their own task.[235]

An exchange in the other direction—from law enforcement to intelligence—constitutes a duty for the law enforcement services when the information available is relevant for protecting national security. Officers of the PPS will "inform a service of the information brought to their notice if they deem this to be in the interest of this service."[236] The same holds true for police officers.[237] For this purpose an automated system has been established, through which the AIVD can search police files on the basis of a hit/no hit system with their own intelligence. When the AIVD finds a 'hit' within the system, the police are obliged to transfer the information directly to the AIVD on the basis of Article 62 WIV 2002.[238] The intelligence services are also entitled to "render technical support to the bodies responsible for the investigation of offenses."[239]

### 2.2.3 Conclusion

In the explanatory memorandum of the CCP the wish was expressed that 'the actors, who have been attributed the task of investigating and prosecuting for the purpose of repressing crime and protecting the victims, shall be attributed the powers required to act quickly and decisively, being able to do what is required under the specific circumstances of a case, and shall not be hindered by regulations which are too stringent.'[240] For this purpose the CCP clearly delineates which actors have the task of conducting criminal investigative activities for the purpose

---

233 *Kamerstukken II* 2003/04, 29 743, no. 7, 23.

234 HR 13 November 2007, *NJ* 2007, 614, para 3.4.2 and HR 5 September 2006, *NJ* 2007, 336, para 4.7.2 and 6.4.2.

235 HR 13 November 2007, *NJ* 2007, 614, para 5.2.2.

236 Article 61 WIV 2002.

237 Article 62 WIV 2002.

238 Vis 2010B, 130.

239 Article 63 WIV 2002.

240 Lindenberg 2002, 424 (MvT 16-17).

of truth-finding and which powers these actors have at their disposal to exercise this task. This does not mean that on the basis of the CCP also the scope of the sword capacities can be precisely demarcated. The requirements for the use of criminal investigative powers provide investigative discretion to the police or PPS. Moreover, the criminal investigation itself covers all investigative activities conducted for the purpose of making prosecutorial decisions by law enforcement officers and under the supervision of the public prosecutor. Although the system was traditionally developed as a reactive system, today the CCP and the special criminal statutes also provide possibilities to act proactively, especially where (serious) organized crime is involved.

On the basis of the system laid down in the CCP, the conclusion can be drawn that the truth-finding actors have been organized in a stratified system, based on a shared system of responsibilities for the criminal investigation with a hierarchical dimension related to the interests at stake when seeking to use a specific investigative method. Only those actors that have been given the task of criminal investigation may use criminal investigative powers for the purpose of truth-finding (or: 'making prosecutorial decisions'). The PPS is the central actor in the criminal investigative phase, bearing the responsibility for the criminal investigation and supervising the investigative activities of the police. Nevertheless, the police will in practice largely conduct the criminal investigative activities. The examining magistrate, as a warrant judge, may provide the required authorization for using some of the most intrusive techniques.

In addition, the AIVD has been addressed as a relevant actor in the criminal investigation, considering that the AIVD may send 'official reports' to the PPS, which may subsequently be used as information to commence a criminal investigation. Through this path of transferring information between the otherwise strictly separated communities of intelligence and law enforcement, the 'sword capacity' of the law enforcement community is strengthened by the provision of information that may be relevant for establishing the truth concerning criminal activities.

Also the bases for using criminal investigative powers, as required under the principle of legality, can be found in the CCP and the special criminal Acts. In accordance with the requirements of Article 8 ECHR, those investigative powers that interfere more than to a limited extent with the right to respect for private life have been given a precise statutory basis. These statutory bases for the more intrusive techniques have only been created by the Act on SIT of 1999, making a distinction between two investigative domains: the classical investigation and the organized crime investigation. Because of the more complex nature of the criminal investigation of terrorism, the possibilities to use SIT proactively are broader for the criminal investigation of organized crime than for the criminal investigation of conventional crime. In addition, the legislature has provided investigative powers to 'prepare' a full criminal investigation by making it possible to combine and analyze certain files, including the possibility to set aside privacy 'protective purpose limitations' and thus to enable the use of files stored for other purposes also for preparing the criminal investigation. Criminal investigative officers (those attributed with that task on the basis of Article 141 or 142 CCP) may use other, not specifically regulated, investigative powers on the basis of their criminal law enforcement task under Article 2 Police Act 1993. On the basis of Article 2 Police Act 1993 only criminal investigative powers may be used that do not, or only to a limited extent, interfere with the right to respect for private life. In addition, special criminal Acts provide for administrative supervisory powers and criminal investigative powers. Also the administrative supervisory powers (used to control the observance of provisions of the special criminal Acts) may be relevant for the criminal investigation, considering that administrative supervision and criminal investigation may overlap and, in that situation, the use of administrative supervisory powers may *also* be used for criminal investigative purposes.

## 2.3 The Shield Function of the Dutch Criminal Investigation

The shield function of the regulation of the criminal investigation in the Netherlands is primarily realized by a hierarchical system of authorization and, consequently, controlling responsibilities and specific legal protective elements in the system of the CCP, such as specific legal provisions for intrusive investigative powers and requirements that aim to realize control. The main purpose of the regulation can be formulated as protecting against arbitrary interferences with the citizen's right to respect for private life, restricting the use of especially intrusive investigative powers to the minimum and anticipating a fair trial process aimed at establishing the substantive truth. Hence the division of responsibilities between the actors and the other protective elements in the system of criminal investigation as adopted—most significantly—in the Dutch CCP are underpinned by the rights and principles described in Sect. 2.1.3. The second part of the current chapter is dedicated to describing this shield function of the regulation, by firstly dealing with the division of responsibilities between the actors involved in the criminal investigation, including the suspect and any other persons subjected to criminal investigative powers, and, secondly, describing the adopted protective elements.

### *2.3.1 The Responsibility of the Actors Towards a Fair Procedure*

The Netherlands has chosen for a hierarchical structure of authority as a method to realize state accountability by attributing powers to the actors in Dutch criminal procedural law by means of a stratified system. The stratified system is adopted in order to "police" the government's own use of criminal procedural powers.[241]

---

[241] Brants et al. 1995, 44. According to Damaška, this system of realizing state accountability is typical for legal systems with a civil law origin. Damaška 1986, 47-50.

This can, for example, be recognized in the organization of the criminal investigation, where the police require an order by the public prosecutor for using some more far-reaching investigative powers, and where the examining magistrate shall authorize the use of one of the most intrusive investigative powers. The responsibility for the criminal investigation in its entirety concerns a *shared* responsibility between the public prosecutor and the examining magistrate: both have been attributed an individual responsibility to control the legitimacy and the fairness of the course of events during the criminal investigation. Afterwards, the trial judge has been given the power to exert control over the legitimacy of the activities conducted during the criminal investigation.[242]

This section will start with the controlling function of the state and the judicial actors that have truth-finding powers, including the trial judge with a truth-finding task during trial. As will follow in the subsequent sections, the overall responsibility for the fairness of the criminal proceedings is an interrelated responsibility between the different actors. Furthermore, the position of the actors that are mainly the subject of investigation—the suspect and other persons investigated—will be dealt with as well as their possibilities to challenge the legitimacy of the investigation against them and the availability of remedies upon the establishment of illegitimate investigative action.

#### 2.3.1.1 The Police

Although the police operate with regard to the law enforcement task under the responsibility of the PPS,[243] the police also have, as government officials, an independent responsibility to observe fundamental rights when carrying out their function and to contribute to a fair criminal procedure in which the fundamental rights of citizens are observed.[244] As explained in Sect. 2.1.3.3, Article 6 ECHR covers the proceedings as a whole and, therefore, also includes the fairness of criminal investigative activities before trial.

The judge who will examine whether the investigative activities were conducted legitimately, possibly resulting in procedural sanctions upon the establishment of illegitimate behavior, also directs investigative officers to observe fundamental rights, to comply with the legal requirements and to ensure the integrity of the criminal investigative activities in general. Nevertheless, this prospect of being held accountable for investigative action will only occur when someone is also actually prosecuted. In many situations, investigative action does not result in the establishment of sufficient evidence for subsequent criminal procedural steps, especially when investigations are conducted proactively. In addition, the

[242] See also HR 11 October 2005, *NJ* 2006, 625, para 3.5.1 and 3.5.2 and HR 21 November 2006, *NJ* 2007/233, ann. Mevis, para 3.4 and annotation para 3.

[243] Compare Article 2 Police Act 1993.

[244] Muller et al. 2007, 559-560.

anticipation of trial proceedings is usually not a direct concern for police officers. The responsibility of the police for the fairness of the proceedings as a whole (as the touchstone under Article 6 ECHR and relevant for imposing sanctions on illegitimate actions which have taken place during the criminal investigation[245]) is subordinate to the responsibility of the public prosecutor, who is, considering his/her continual role as a prosecutor in criminal proceedings, more aware of the procedural consequences of illegitimate actions during the police investigation.

More precisely, the judge will have to examine whether the investigative officers have acted within the boundaries of the law. The principle of legality imposes on each truth-finding actor the duty not to exceed the limits of their powers as attributed by the law. For the police this entails primarily the responsibility to determine whether or not a reasonable suspicion is present, justifying the initiation of a criminal investigation. Furthermore, except for determining whether the investigative activity is in accordance with the law, the investigative officer is responsible for determining in concrete cases whether the use of a specific investigative power is also justified in the light of the circumstances of that particular case. The trial judge, in line with this responsibility, will not only examine whether the investigative activities have occurred within the boundaries of the law, but also whether the investigative officer has not violated (administrative) principles of the due administration of justice.[246] Principles of the due administration of justice concern the principles of legitimate expectations, the principle of equality before the law, the principles of proportionality and subsidiarity and the principle of *détournement de pouvoir*.[247] For the investigative officer, this means that he/she is required to balance the interests involved in a particular case, which primarily entails an assessment of the proportionality and subsidiarity[248] of the intended activity and a limitation to using the criminal investigative power only for the purpose of truth-finding and, thus, a prohibition on general fishing expeditions. In 1978 the Supreme Court held for the first time that the legitimacy of criminal investigative activities shall not only be examined on the basis of the legal requirements, but additionally, on the basis of the principles of the due administration of justice, resulting in that case in the conclusion that the behavior of police officers who had entered a home by breaking a window was not in compliance with the principle of subsidiarity; the police could have chosen a less intrusive method to enter the home.[249] Hence, not only when the statutory conditions require the principles of proportionality and subsidiarity to be observed (as is e.g. implied in

---

[245] See on this in more detail Sect. 2.3.1.4.

[246] See Sect. 2.1.3.4. The applicability of these administrative law principles to a criminal investigation has been acknowledged by the Supreme Court in HR 12 December 1978, *NJ* 1979, 142 ann. GEM. Muller, Dubelaar and Cleiren formulate 15 different principles for police work which are relevant for all the tasks of police officers. Muller et al. 2007, 597. The mentioned principles nevertheless apply in particular to the criminal investigative activities of the police.

[247] See Sect. 2.1.3.4 and Corstens 2008, 62-73.

[248] See on the contents of these principles Sect. 2.1.3.4.1.

[249] HR 12 December 1978, *NJ* 1979, 142, ann. GEM.

the condition 'in the interest of the investigation' included in the provisions for SIT), but also when the police conduct investigative activities on the basis of Article 2 Police Act 1993, are the police bound by the principles of proportionality and subsidiarity.[250]

When the police require an order from the public prosecutor or also an authorization by the examining magistrate, the balancing of the interests involved is largely the responsibility of the 'higher' authority. This hierarchical system, both for determining whether the investigative method sought is in accordance with the law and for determining the proportionality and subsidiarity of the use of the investigative method, has been acknowledged by the Supreme Court. When a 'higher' authority has been responsible for this determination, also the examination of the trial judge may be more marginal.[251] Nevertheless, during the execution of an order the investigative officers need to continually take into account the proportionality and subsidiarity of the manner in which the special investigative technique is being applied. Obliging the police to observe the principles of the due administration of justice, in particular the principles of proportionality and subsidiarity, is intended to guide police officers in their investigative efforts where they are attributed certain discretion.[252]

Lastly, police officers have the obligation under the law to report all their criminal investigative activities and this aims to facilitate defense rights as these reports largely constitute the basis for challenges regarding illegitimate investigative activities. In addition, these reports, to be included in the *dossier*, are also the basis for the controlling function of the trial judge in relation to the fairness of the criminal investigation. The duty to draw up records as provided in Article 152 CCP obliges police officers to report all investigative activities conducted and in that way to facilitate *ex post* transparency with regard to the course of the criminal investigation. The precise scope and function of this duty will be dealt with in Sect. 2.3.2.4.1.

#### 2.3.1.2 The Public Prosecutor

The public prosecutor is the supervisor of the criminal investigation on the basis of Article 148 and Article 132a CCP. It is his task to control the legitimate conduct of the criminal investigation, which he can do by instructing the investigative officers, and keeping an oversight over the course of the investigation as a whole. One of the main concerns of the Van Traa Parliamentary Inquiry Commission was the

---

250 According to Naeyé criminal investigative methods based upon Article 2 Police Act 1993 shall comply with the following fundamental principles for police action: proportionality, subsidiarity, reasonableness and moderateness (J. Naeyé, *De reikwijdte van fundamentele rechten,* Handelingen NJV 1995-I, 272), referred to in: Fokkens and Kirkels-Vrijman 2009, 124.

251 See also HR 11 October 2005, *NJ* 2006, 625, para 3.5.1 and 3.5.2 and HR 21 November 2006, *NJ* 2007, 233, ann. Mevis, para 3.4 and annotation para 3. See also Franken 2009, 84-85.

252 Franken 2009, 82.

lack of control by the PPS over the quality and the legitimacy of the criminal investigation and the investigative powers used. However, the Commission also acknowledged that, considering the central position which the public prosecutor owes to his authority to decide which cases to investigate in the criminal investigation, the public prosecutor should retain the controlling responsibility.[253] This required, however, some organizational changes in order to strengthen the position of the public prosecutor as the supervisor of the criminal investigation.[254] These recommendations have been implemented in the Act of 1999 on special investigative techniques by requiring an order by the public prosecutor for using SIT. Moreover, the supervisory role of the public prosecutor has been included in the definition of the criminal investigation (Article 132a CCP).[255] Hence, the Act of 1999 has importantly enhanced the responsibilities of the public prosecutor with regard to the criminal investigation.[256] The public prosecutor is now more aware of his role as the central actor in the criminal investigation, including his responsibility to exert control.[257]

As the supervisor of the criminal investigation the public prosecutor has an important responsibility with regard to the legitimacy, fairness and overall integrity of the investigative activities. The constitutional position of the PPS as part of the judiciary should give public prosecutors an impartial and independent position, a position which obliges all interests to be taken into account when carrying out the truth-finding task. In the previous section, it has already been indicated that the responsibility of the police for the fairness of the criminal investigation is subordinate to the responsibility of the public prosecutor. Hence, the principle of legality, the right to a fair trial, the right to privacy and the principles of proportionality and subsidiarity more strongly require the public prosecutor to act according to his responsibility for guaranteeing the legitimacy, fairness and overall integrity of the criminal investigation. Especially considering the prospect of the course of events being examined during the criminal investigation at trial, an important aspect of the supervisory role of the public prosecutor will be to direct and control the police to ensure that their investigative activities are within the borders of the law and that they observe the principles of the due administration of justice.

The supervisory role of the public prosecutor is in particular present when special investigative techniques are used in the criminal investigation. An order by the public prosecutor is required before SIT can be applied by the police, for which reason the public prosecutor shall determine whether the legal requirements are met (in particular, the presence of a reasonable suspicion of a crime or a reasonable suspicion that crimes are committed or will be committed in an organized

---

[253] Article 148 CCP and Article 13 Police Act 1993.

[254] Rapport van de Parlementaire Enquêtecommissie Opsporingsmethoden 1996, 439.

[255] This supervisory role for the PPS has been maintained in the new definition adopted by the Act on the Criminal Investigation of Terrorist Crimes of November 2006, *Stb.* 2006, 580.

[256] Mevis 2005B, 454.

[257] Beijer et al. 2004, 160.

context) and whether the use of the investigative method is also in accordance with the principles of proportionality and subsidiarity.

These principles, which have not been explicitly adopted in the CCP, have been attributed an important regulatory effect in the criminal investigation in addition to the requirements formulated in the law. It is the primary responsibility of the public prosecutor as the supervisor of the criminal investigation to make sure that these principles are observed in all circumstances. Proportionality means that the method used is proportionate to its aims. The investigation of serious crimes implies that more intrusive methods are proportionate to the harm that is done to the rights and liberties of the people investigated. The statutory requirement of 'a serious infringement of the legal order' or the limitation to crimes for which pre-trial detention can be imposed (serious crimes) are in fact references to the application of the principle of proportionality. The use of a special investigative technique that has serious implications for the rights and liberties of the persons being investigated is only justified—proportionate—when it is used for investigating serious crime that results in a serious infringement of the legal order. The principle of subsidiarity implies that less intrusive means are not available for the investigation and for achieving the investigative goal intended. If less intrusive methods are available and adequately produce the information needed, then these methods should be applied instead of the methods with a more intrusive character. Both principles should be taken into account at all times and play an important role throughout the whole procedure.

The prosecutor is required to consistently balance the interests involved in each specific phase of the criminal proceedings, where the law offers discretion. The legal provisions which are applicable to the criminal investigation, in particular those regarding the use of SIT as established by the Act of 1999, are, in fact, a consequence of a theoretical, pre-assessment of the interests involved. These provisions of the law are the first layer of regulation to which, most significantly, the public prosecutor is subjected in his/her criminal investigative activities, while the principles of proportionality and subsidiarity shall guide the public prosecutor in addition to these statutory provisions when conducting (or steering) criminal investigative activities.[258]

Nevertheless, the actual regulatory effect of the principles of proportionality and subsidiarity on the responsibility of the public prosecutor towards the fairness of the criminal investigation is in practice difficult to measure. The examination at trial on the basis of these principles is often rather marginal and has not often resulted in a decision that the investigative activity was illegitimate.[259]

Furthermore, also the public prosecutor, like the police, has a duty to report his/her investigative activities, thereby making it possible for the trial judge to exert control over the criminal investigation and providing a possibility to challenge the

---

[258] Baaijens-van Geloven and Simmelink 2002, 562.

[259] Franken has analyzed the case law in the period 2000–2009 to formulate this conclusion. Franken 2009, 87-92.

legitimacy of the criminal investigative activities by the defense. Article 148(3) provides that the public prosecutor shall compile official reports under his oath of office, when the public prosecutor, as the supervisor of the criminal investigation, conducted the investigative activities personally.

In addition, the public prosecutor bears a specific responsibility for dealing with information originating from the intelligence community when it comes to the fairness of the criminal proceedings. When information obtained by the AIVD is transferred to the law enforcement community, the public prosecutor has the responsibility to decide whether the use of that information does not undermine the fairness of the procedure. As has been explained in Sect. 2.2.2.4.2, this task has been attributed to the national public prosecutor for counterterrorism. Official reports by the AIVD which are to be transferred to the law enforcement community will firstly pass through the national public prosecutor for counterterrorism, who shall decide whether or not it is desirable to start a criminal investigation on the basis of that information. According to Article 38 of the WIV 2002 this especially appointed national public prosecutor is entitled to inspect "all the information on which the notification is based and which is necessary in order to assess the correctness of the notification." Similar to other officers of the AIVD, this national public prosecutor is bound by secrecy regarding this knowledge. Consequently, the national public prosecutor has an important controlling function regarding the reliability of the information and the fairness of using it as starting information for a criminal investigation, taking into consideration that the possibilities to examine this information and the underlying documents at trial are rather limited or even excluded.

Because of its responsibility to contribute to a procedure in which the rule of law is observed, the PPS has established an additional internal controlling procedure for the application of some of the more intrusive SIT. With regard to some investigative techniques, such as infiltration, pseudo-dealing or serving and the recording of private communication with a technical device, the Board of Procurators General must decide on such use. The Board will only decide on the basis of the advice of the Central Assessment Committee [*Centrale Toetsingscommissie*] (CTC).[260] The CTC—founded in 1995—is composed of members of the PPS and members of the police and functions as an internal advisory body for the PPS under the authority of the Board of Procurators General.[261] The CTC advises the Board of Procurators General on the use of SIT and this advice will be based upon the statutory rules, case law, proportionality, subsidiarity and the risks of harm regarding e.g. operational aspects, safety aspects, criminal procedural consequences and political and international aspects.[262] The Board of Procurators General rarely decides differently from the CTC.[263]

---

260 Aanwijzing opsporingsbevoegdheden, *Stcrt.* 2004, 227, para 4.1.2.

261 *Ibid.*, para 4.1.1.

262 *Ibid.*, para 4.1.3.

263 Beijer et al. 2004, 163.

The review by the CTC constitutes an additional safeguard as to the legitimate, proportional and subsidiary use of the investigative technique. The review is a mandatory internal procedure, but is neither legally binding nor a final determination regarding the legitimate use of a special investigative technique. The public prosecutor is not obliged to file documents with regard to advice from the CTC in the dossier as these documents are in principle confidential. Only when these documents concern either incriminating or exculpatory evidence is the public prosecutor obliged to file them in the dossier.[264]

It can be concluded that the public prosecutor has an important responsibility regarding control over the legitimate exercise of the criminal investigation, especially as a consequence of his supervisory role in the criminal investigation. The public prosecutor shall in this regard oversee the police as to whether they operate within the law, in respect of the fundamental rights of citizens and in observing the principles of proportionality and subsidiarity. Entrusting the public prosecutor with this supervisory responsibility as to the fairness of the criminal investigation can be considered as a consequence of his position as a 'magistrate' in the Dutch criminal justice system as this controlling responsibility may even require the public prosecutor to act as a magistrate. In the explanatory memorandum of 1926 the Dutch criminal procedure was described as moderately accusatorial, and this moderation must be sought in the position of the PPS. The PPS has traditionally been given a position as part of the judiciary, which also follows from the position attributed to the public prosecutor in criminal proceedings, such as privileges as a party in the trial process (e.g. the authority to refuse to call witnesses requested by the defense) and the authority to offer a defendant a transaction in the case of minor offenses instead of bringing the case to trial. The presumption of independence and impartiality implied in the position as a magistrate is also important for fulfilling the supervisory role of the public prosecutor during the criminal investigative phase. However, this needs to be put into perspective by also observing that the PPS functions under the responsibility of the Minister of Security and Justice, who has the authority to give general (and in exceptional situations specific) policy instructions to the PPS. Furthermore, the PPS is, especially as a consequence of the current political and societal climate with a focus on strict law enforcement, pressured to work efficiently and to bring as many cases as possible to trial, which further affects the public prosecutor's position as a magistrate.[265] Also the ECrtHR has clearly distinguished the procedural position of the public prosecutor from that of a judge, by considering the public prosecutor as a "party" which cannot be attributed the same characteristics of objectivity and impartiality as a judge.[266]

---

[264] HR 20 June 2000, *NJ* 2000, 502, para 3.3 and 3.4.

[265] See also: See e.g. Schalken 2006, 72-73. In recent years the development described in this Article may have been further accelerated under the influence of a societal and political call for safety, which includes the expectation that a tougher prosecution and punishment policy contributes to a safer society. See on this Chap. 4, Sect. 4.2.3.1.

[266] ECHR 14 September 2010, App. no. 38224/03 (*Sanoma Uitgevers B.V. v. The Netherlands*), para 93. See also Sect. 2.1.2.

Notwithstanding the fact that the public prosecutor may in the current circumstances generally be inclined to strike a balance in favor of truth-finding, an additional willingness to operate in accordance with his task to guarantee the fairness of the criminal investigation is given by the need to anticipate the trial investigation in which the trial judge will have to examine the fairness of the proceedings as a whole. The consequences of any irregularities during the pre-trial investigation may, however, be limited, as will be explained in more detail in the section dealing with the responsibility of the trial judge for a fair procedure (Sect. 2.3.1.4) and the framework under which he/she exerts such control (Sect. 2.3.2.4.2).

#### 2.3.1.3 The Examining Magistrate

Next to the public prosecutor as the supervisor of the criminal investigation, the examining magistrate has an individual controlling role with regard to the legitimacy, fairness and overall integrity of the criminal investigation. In the CCP of 1926 the examining magistrate was attributed a central position, capable of taking into account both the sword interest of truth-finding and the shield interest of legal protection. As a judge, the examining magistrate can exert independent control with a sufficient detachment from the actual investigation. This position could make him a better watchdog regarding all the objectives of the investigation, where the public prosecutor may be inclined to focus on truth-finding. Hence, the involvement of the examining magistrate in the pre-trial phase was understood as an important guarantee towards the fairness of the pre-trial proceedings.[267]

The examining magistrate can exert this shield role through *ex ante* judicial control in the course of a criminal investigation when authorizing the use of some of the more intrusive SIT. This means that the shield function of the examining magistrate can only be carried out when the public prosecutor, seeking the use of some of the most intrusive investigative techniques, requests his involvement.[268] The examining magistrate shall determine whether the public prosecutor has made an assessment in his order in accordance with the legal requirements. The function of the examining magistrate as a warrant judge is only required for the most intrusive techniques, because this 'highest' authority in the hierarchical system of authority during the criminal investigation can be expected to have, as a judge, the highest level of independence and objectivity required to assess all the interests involved before authorizing investigative techniques which seriously interfere with the privacy of citizens.[269]

[267] Van der Meij 2010A, 60.

[268] Compare: Van der Meij 2010A, 64-65. Van der Meij concludes that (also) for this reason, the regulation does not provide for a balanced triangular relationship between the examining magistrate, the public prosecutor and the defense. *Ibid.*

[269] *Kamerstukken II* 1997/98, 25 877, no. 3, 99.

The Supreme Court formulated the role of the examining magistrate, in relation to the public prosecutor and the trial judge, as a warrant judge for the use of a wiretap on the basis of Article 126m CCP, as follows: 'Initially, it is the responsibility of the public prosecutor to assess whether or not a reasonable suspicion under Article 126m(1) CCP is present and whether there is an urgent investigative need for the recording of telecommunications. For assessing the latter requirement, the principles of proportionality and subsidiarity should be taken into account. Subsequently, it is the task of the examining magistrate to determine whether the statutory requirements are met. Lastly, the trial judge shall examine the legitimacy of the execution of the order for wire-tapping. In the statutory system, when the examining magistrate has authorized the investigative method, this examination on behalf of the trial judge implies the question whether the examining magistrate could reasonably authorize the wire-tapping. Furthermore, the examination of the trial judge covers the execution of the order by the public prosecutor as to the manner in which the public prosecutor has used his authority to order the interception of communications and whether the authorization was otherwise reasonable [translated MHB].'[270] It follows from this consideration that the additional control by the examining magistrate prior to using a special investigative technique warrants a more marginal examination by the trial judge as compared to special investigative techniques that can be ordered by the public prosecutor. Furthermore, the control exerted by the examining magistrate before authorizing a wire-tap (or other special investigative techniques for which the authorization of the examining magistrate is required), is limited to an assessment as to whether the statutory requirements are met.

As has been explained in Sect. 2.2.1.3, the position of the examining magistrate in the pre-trial phase has been subject to discussion over the past decades. A brief overview will be given of the developments over, roughly, the past 20 years leading up to the recent intended strengthened position of the examining magistrate during the criminal investigation. Before 1999, the examining magistrate had only a function in the preliminary judicial investigation by having the authority to give law enforcement officers investigative instructions and by having the power to hear the suspect and witnesses. Furthermore, permission from the examining magistrate was already required for some investigative powers, such as the searching of homes and wire-tapping, which, before 1999, could not be provided outside the scope of a preliminary judicial investigation. Hence, the pre-trial investigation could then be divided into two phases: the criminal investigation under the responsibility of the public prosecutor and the preliminary judicial investigation under the responsibility of the examining magistrate. Some investigative methods were exclusively reserved for the preliminary judicial investigation. The preliminary judicial investigation was intended to provide for a stronger safeguard as to the fairness of the pre-trial proceedings, because it can be expected

[270] HR 11 October 2005, *NJ* 2006, 625, para 3.5.2. A similar consideration can be found in HR 21 November 2006, *NJ* 2007, 233, ann. Mevis, para 3.4.

that the examining magistrate is impartial and objective to a greater degree than can be expected from the police and the public prosecutor.[271] However, the examining magistrate was usually not informed about the use of investigative powers which were not statutorily regulated when the public prosecutor requested a preliminary judicial investigation. Consequently, the examining magistrate was unable to completely oversee the scope and nature of the pre-trial investigation.

The Parliamentary Inquiry Commission, in its report of 1996, was rather critical of the controlling role of the examining magistrate and called for improvement. The Commission acknowledged that the authorization of an investigative power was a rather isolated decision, considering that the examining magistrate lacked the required insight into the criminal investigation as a whole, thereby complicating a well-considered assessment of the proportionality and subsidiarity of the investigative method sought.[272] Regardless of these criticisms, a significant strengthened position for the examining magistrate was not adopted in the Act on SIT of 1999. After the Act of 1999, the examining magistrate could, outside the scope of the preliminary judicial investigation, fulfill his role as a warrant judge where his authorization was required for the use of the most intrusive SIT. In addition, it was chosen to adopt a strengthened position for the public prosecutor as the supervisor of the criminal investigation.[273] The legislature had thus chosen to only provide the examining magistrate in the criminal investigation with a controlling responsibility for the most intrusive investigative techniques and, apart from that, to keep his controlling role in the criminal investigation, outside the scope of the preliminary judicial investigation, rather limited. This choice was supported by the following three arguments: 1) more frequent involvement of the examining magistrate will harm the strengthened position of the public prosecutor as the supervisor of the criminal investigation; 2) the possibilities for examination are rather limited, because uncovering all information will be against the interest of the investigation and the examination can only occur on the basis of the information provided by the examining magistrate; and, 3) the trial judge already has the possibility to exert control over the legitimate use of investigative powers, which provides the suspect with more legal protection than expanded control on behalf of the examining magistrate.[274] Requiring authorization for the investigation of telecommunications and the recording of private communications with a technical device is nevertheless considered necessary, because these SIT directly interfere with a constitutional right: the right to the confidentiality of mail and private communications as protected in Article 13 of the Dutch Constitution.[275]

---

[271] Corstens 2008, 313.

[272] Rapport van de Parlementaire Enquêtecommissie Opsporingsmethoden 1996, 389.

[273] *Kamerstukken II* 1998/99, 26 269, no. 4-5 (Rapport Commissie Kalsbeek), 175 and Mevis 2005B, 455.

[274] *Kamerstukken II* 1997/98, 25 403, no. 7, 23.

[275] *Kamerstukken II* 1997/98, 25 403, no. 7, 24.

With this approach to the position of the examining magistrate in the pre-trial phase in response to the 'crisis in the criminal investigation' of the 1990s the debate has not ended. In practice, both the central role of the preliminary judicial investigation and the possibility of fulfilling a meaningful role as a warrant judge have diminished. The public prosecutor rarely requests a preliminary judicial investigation, because of efficiency arguments. As to the function of a warrant judge, the examining magistrate has to rely on the public prosecutor's obligation to disclose all information available to decide on an authorization.[276] Control by the examining magistrate is limited to a marginal examination as to whether the statutory requirements have been met;[277] whereas it is not inconceivable that a prosecutor will submit an incomplete dossier to the examining magistrate in order ensure an authorization for the method intended. According to the final evaluation of the implementation of the Act of 1999 in practice, the task of authorizing SIT covers an important part of the work of the examining magistrate as one district deals with approximately 1000 to more than 7000 requests for wire-taps on a yearly basis, whereas each district only has 1–15 examining magistrates.[278] The final evaluation of the Act on SIT also demonstrates that the examining magistrate almost always authorizes the order of the public prosecutor. Due to time constraints as well as a lack of insight into the complete investigation, the actual examination of the documents supporting a request for authorization according to principles such as proportionality and subsidiarity remains rather limited.[279]

Consequently, the Act to Strengthen the Position of the Examining Magistrate has been introduced.[280] Abolishing the preliminary judicial investigation, this Act focuses on the strengthening of the role of the examining magistrate as a supervisor of the criminal investigation by discarding the previous situation where the involvement of the examining magistrate was spread over different procedural stages and statutory frameworks.[281] Upon the entry into force of this Act, the criminal investigation under the supervision of the public prosecutor is the only investigative pre-trial stage for the purpose of truth-finding in preparation for a criminal prosecution. The role of the examining magistrate during the criminal investigation is to oversee the quality of the criminal investigation, in particular to ensure the legitimate use of investigative powers and the progress, balance and completeness of the criminal investigation.[282] For this purpose, the examining magistrate still functions as a warrant judge and the possibilities to conduct

---

[276] Gerechtshof 's-Gravenhage 22 February 2005, *LJN* AU0235.

[277] Compare: HR 11 October 2005, *NJ* 2006, 625, para 3.5.2 and HR 21 November 2006, *NJ* 2007, 233, ann. Mevis, para 3.4.

[278] Beijer et al. 2004, 149-155 and Franken 2006, 267.

[279] Franken 2006, 269.

[280] *Kamerstukken I* 2010/11, 32177, no. A. Considering that the Act has been adopted by the First Chamber of Parliament, it can be expected, at the time of concluding this book, that it will soon enter into force.

[281] Van der Meij 2010A, 549.

[282] *Kamerstukken II* 2009/10, 32177 no. 3, 8-9.

investigative action at the request of the public prosecutor, at the request of the defense or *ex officio* have been broadened.[283] This latter role is exerted in relation to the function of the examining magistrate to oversee the efficient course of the criminal investigation as regulated in Article 180 CCP. The Act of 2011 is thus intended to strengthen the role of the examining magistrate during the criminal investigation in order to provide for a stronger guarantee with regard to the fairness of the criminal investigation. An important prerequisite for the realization of an actual strengthened position of the examining magistrate is the intended improved information position of the examining magistrate. For this purpose, Article 177a CCP requires that the public prosecutor discloses, in good time, all the information which is relevant for the exercise of the function of the examining magistrate. Furthermore, the examining magistrate may also request additional information on the basis of this provision. Lastly, the examining magistrate may summon the public prosecutor and the defense to attend a procedural meeting in order to discuss the state of affairs in the criminal investigation and to inform them which additional investigative steps shall be taken.[284] From the explanatory memorandum, it also follows that this strengthened position of the examining magistrate warrants a more expedient trial phase, where the trial judge may restrict the assessment of the criminal investigative activities to a more marginal examination.[285]

By the Act on Shielded Witnesses of 2006[286] the examining magistrate has obtained an additional important role when it comes to the use of intelligence information in criminal proceedings. Considering the direct relation of this Act with an increase in the use of intelligence in criminal proceedings, especially in terrorism cases, this Act will be dealt with in the next chapter as one of the developments contributing to a shift towards an anticipative criminal investigation.[287]

#### 2.3.1.4 The Trial Judge

The trial judge exercises control *ex post* over the course of events in the criminal investigation. This control is exerted in the context of an assessment of the right to a fair trial as laid down in Article 6 ECHR, covering the proceedings as a whole. The right to a fair trial under Article 6 and the consequences thereof as developed by the ECHR will play an important role in the determination of the trial judge with regard to the fairness of the procedure. The right to a fair trial can be violated due to events during the criminal investigation as has been explained in

283 *Kamerstukken II* 2009/10, 32177 no. 3, 10-11.

284 Article 185 CCP, *Kamerstukken II* 2009/10, 32177 no. 3, 17.

285 *Kamerstukken II* 2009/10, 32177 no. 3, 18.

286 Act of 18 September 2006, *Stb.* 2006, 460.

287 See Chap. 3, Sect. 3.3.2.

Sect. 2.1.3.3. As also explained in Sect. 2.1.3.3 an investigation in violation of statutory law or in violation of another right guaranteed in the ECHR, such as Article 8 ECHR, does not automatically result in a violation of Article 6 ECHR.[288] In order to determine whether the right to a fair trial has been violated, the procedure as a whole is taken into account, which includes the possibility to rectify or compensate illegitimate actions that have occurred during the criminal investigation. The exact implications of an examination with regard to the fairness of the proceedings by the domestic judge are, as repeatedly emphasized by the ECrtHR, a matter of evidentiary law as regulated in domestic law.[289] Hence, the assessment of the trial judge as to whether the right to a fair trial has been violated and the question whether such violation shall result in procedural sanctions will occur within the framework of evidence which has been illegitimately obtained as provided in the Dutch CCP (Article 359a CCP) and as interpreted in the case law. This framework will be dealt with in Sect. 2.3.2.4.2 as an element adopted in the CCP regulating the criminal investigation by providing the remedies against the illegitimate use of criminal investigative powers.

For this section it is sufficient to note that the *ex post* control function of the trial judge with regard to the course of events during the criminal investigation will be exercised within the context of Article 359a CCP with the possibility to offer procedural compensation in the form of one of the remedies enumerated in Article 359a CCP (barring the prosecution, the exclusion of evidence or mitigating the sentence). This decision will be made in light of the right to a fair trial, and is thus dependent on whether or not imposing a procedural sanction can compensate for any unfairness in the criminal investigative phase and whether it will render the procedure as a whole fair.

#### 2.3.1.5 The Position of the Suspect

The suspect is already entitled to certain forms of procedural protection during the pre-trial phase, including during the covert criminal investigation. These forms of protection are embedded in the system of criminal investigation and have a restrictive function on the power of the state to apply investigative methods against its citizens. During the criminal investigation with an inquisitorial character, the suspect is, however, primarily the subject of the investigation. The suspect's rights during the pre-arrest phase are restricted to the right to be informed about any use of investigative powers against him, as enabled by the duty of notification. This right can however be postponed until the interest of the investigation is not obstructed by disclosure. This means that in practice the suspect will not be aware

---

[288] See e.g. ECHR 12 May 2000, App. no. 35394/97 (*Khan v. The United Kingdom*), para 34. See also Sect. 2.1.3.3.

[289] E.g.: ECHR 24 November 1994, App. no. 13972/88 (*Imbrioscia v. Switzerland*), para 34. See also Sect. 2.1.3.3.

of any investigation against him until his arrest or first police interrogation. Consequently, during the criminal investigation it is exclusively the responsibility of the police, the public prosecutor and the examining magistrate also to take the position of the suspect into account at all times. This concerns an independent obligation, as well as the consequence of the prospect of a subsequent criminal trial where the defense can challenge the fairness of the procedure before the trial judge, as has been described in the preceding sub-sections.

As has already been briefly mentioned in the introductory section of this chapter, the defense has a possibility to contribute to truth-finding if there are doubts about the completeness of the investigation conducted on behalf of the PPS (Article 182 CCP).[290] The suspect can, when interrogated with regard to a criminal offense or when already charged, request the examining magistrate to conduct specific investigative activities. These possibilities for the defense to request the involvement of the examining magistrate for specific investigative action have been expanded by the Act on Strengthening the Position of the Examining Magistrate of 2011.[291] According to the explanatory memorandum, a side-effect of the expanded possibilities for the suspect/defense during the pre-trial phase will be that the trial judge may deal with the admissibility of requests for complementary investigative action during trial more restrictively.[292] Nevertheless, considering that the suspect will not normally be aware of any investigation against him until his arrest or, in less serious cases, until the first police interrogation, the involvement of the defense during the criminal investigation on the basis of these provisions is in the context of this project, being limited to covert criminal investigation, of little relevance.

In particular, the right to a fair trial as guaranteed in Article 6 ECHR is important for the position of the suspect in relation to the fairness of the criminal investigation. The suspect can rely on the forms of protection contained in Article 6 ECHR as a guarantee towards the fairness of the criminal proceedings as a whole and may challenge, in the context of a criminal trial, the fairness of the investigative action against him. Nevertheless, as already explained in the previous sub-section and in Sect. 2.1.3.3, the right to a fair trial is not automatically violated when during the domestic procedure evidence has been obtained in a manner that is incompatible with a provision of the ECHR (most probably Article 8). Moreover, the ECrtHR has repeatedly clarified that it is not its task to determine rules for the consequences that should follow when evidence has been unlawfully obtained. Hence, when the suspect challenges the legitimacy of the investigative activities against him, the judge, on the basis of Article 359a CCP, will assess the course of events of the criminal investigation. The most important prerequisite for

---

[290] *Kamerstukken I* 2010/11, 32177, no. A.

[291] Until the entry into force of the Act on Strengthening the Position of the Examining Magistrate, the suspect could under Article 36a-36e CCP request the examining magistrate to investigate in the context of the preliminary judicial investigation some specified aspects.

[292] As suggested in the explanatory memorandum of this Act, *Kamerstukken II* 2009/10, 32177 no. 3, 18.

the defense during the criminal investigation, in order to be able to challenge the fairness of the procedure and the legitimacy of the use of investigative powers, is to have access to all reports concerning the criminal investigation. This is facilitated by the duty to compile records under Article 152 CCP and by disclosure obligations. The defense must be able to rely on the information in the dossier and have the opportunity to challenge the correctness of this information.

The duty to compile records applies to all reports that are relevant. According to the Supreme Court, reports are relevant when they may affect the evidence and shall thus concern all incriminating and exonerating information which is available.[293] This relevance rule corresponds with the approach of the ECrtHR, determining that it is a "requirement of fairness under paragraph 1 of Article 6 (…) that the prosecution authorities disclose to the defence all material evidence for or against the accused."[294] According to Article 126aa CCP the public prosecutor shall disclose the reports on the use of special investigative techniques to the dossier. The fourth section of this Article determines that this reporting applies to all uses of special investigative techniques in a specific criminal investigation, also when the use of SIT has not produced any relevant results.[295]

To take advantage of the duty to compile records, the suspect must be able to take note of the contents of the dossier. The suspect has the right to have all the contents of the dossier disclosed at the latest when the pre-trial investigation has been closed (Article 30-34 CCP). The disclosure to the defense must take place as soon as the interest of the investigation is not impeded by revealing what is detected.[296] The disclosure of relevant reports may be withheld when the exposure of the information to the public may hinder future investigative activities. The judge will need to balance the interest of disclosure against the interest of secrecy.[297] For example, when the disclosure reveals information about an element of a criminal organization and the investigation of the remainder of the criminal organization will continue, the interest of the investigation allows the postponement of the disclosure. Other conceivable examples are a cross-border investigation or any other ongoing investigation which might be obstructed by revealing the information.[298] According to Article 33 CCP, the latest possibility for disclosing information is when the summons is served on the suspect. Because this obligation is sometimes difficult to fulfill due to the pressing interests of an ongoing criminal investigation, in the case law a rather flexible approach has been adopted towards compliance with this last filing possibility.[299] Ultimately, the trial judge has the

---

293 HR 7 May 1996, *NJ* 1996, 687 ann. Sch, para 5.9.

294 ECHR 16 December 1992, App. no. 13071/87 (*Edwards v. The United Kingdom*), para 36.

295 See Corstens 2008, 249.

296 Article 126aa(3) CCP.

297 Corstens 2008, 249.

298 *Kamerstukken II* 1996/97, 25 403, no. 3, 84.

299 Buruma 2001, 28.

authority to order the disclosure of information to the dossier. He can also decide to order disclosure at the request of the defendant.[300]

According to the ECHR, it is decisive for meeting the disclosure obligations whether the dossier (in this particular case there was no dossier, considering that the scope of the disclosure obligation of the prosecutor under English law was at issue) contains "all material evidence for or against the accused".[301] Also, the suspect must eventually have access to the same information as the trial judge.[302] According to the ECHR case of *Fouchier*, it is essential that the suspect at least receives the information regarding the activities of the criminal investigation and the prosecution against him insofar as the information can influence the suspect's position in the procedure.[303]

#### 2.3.1.6 The Position of Other Subjects of Criminal Investigative Activities

Persons can become the subject of the criminal investigation without ever obtaining the status of a suspect or without ever being criminally prosecuted. The use of investigative powers is not limited to a suspect, but is aimed at the clarification of a reasonable suspicion of a crime. Consequently, the application of special investigative techniques may also result in the gathering of information regarding persons that are never prosecuted. Especially in proactive investigations, groups of persons may be investigated, while only some of them will become suspects and will be prosecuted.

According to Article 13 ECHR everyone is entitled to an effective remedy once his or her rights as protected by the ECHR have been violated. In line with this, a duty of notification has been adopted in order to prevent persons remaining unaware of the fact that they have been subjected to an investigation and, consequently, being deprived of a remedy to challenge the legitimacy of the use of special investigative techniques against them. The duty of notification regarding the use of special investigative techniques has been adopted in Article 126bb(1): the public prosecutor provides written notification to any persons involved concerning the use of special investigative techniques as soon as the interest of the investigation is not obstructed by the notification. Section 2 of Article 126bb provides a definition of persons who are 'involved': (a) persons against whom the SIT was used; (b) the user of telecommunications or of technical devices used for telecommunications where wire-tapping has occurred; and (c) the rightful owner of a dwelling used for the application of SIT.[304] The duty of notification in Article 126bb CCP is complementary to the situation where someone is informed, in the

---

[300] Article 315 and 326 CCP.

[301] ECHR 16 December 1992, App. no. 13071/87 (*Edwards v. The United Kingdom*), para 36.

[302] Buruma 2001, 27.

[303] Myjer 1997, 742.

[304] Article 126bb(2) CCP.

context of criminal proceedings, of the duty to disclose under Article 126aa (1) and (4) CCP and has thus been particularly adopted so as to offer persons other than the suspect the possibility to challenge the legitimacy of the use of SIT against them.[305] Sometimes, also persons who are not individualized will be part of the information obtained through the technique. In such a situation the investigative technique is not applied against those persons and the duty of notification does not apply to them.[306] The notification will take place when the interest of the investigation is not prejudiced by the notification. When the person involved is already aware that an investigative technique has been applied, the government is not indemnified from its obligation to notify. An exception to the duty of notification applies when the notification is practically impossible, for example when the address of the person involved in unknown.[307]

Persons who have been involved in criminal investigative activities may have experienced significant interferences with their private life. The duty of notification is an important procedural requirement enabling persons to challenge the legitimacy of such investigative activities and provide them with an effective remedy as guaranteed by Article 13 ECHR. Article 13 ECHR requires that there should be an effective remedy before a national authority in case of an alleged violation of one of the rights protected in the convention. This means that one should have the opportunity to challenge the legitimate use of an investigative power that has interfered with their private life. In *Kruslin/Huvig v. France* the Court determined that the regulation of far-reaching investigative powers such as wire-tapping should include procedural safeguards for the persons involved to have the opportunity to challenge the legitimacy of the wire-tap used against them.[308] In the *Klass* judgment the Court determined that the German provision that "the person concerned must be informed after the termination of the surveillance measures as soon as notification can be made without jeopardizing the purpose of the restriction" is a regulation which is in conformity with Article 13 ECHR.[309] This provision is similar to the Dutch provision of Article 126bb CCP. After notification, persons prosecuted may file a complaint with the National Ombudsman or initiate civil proceedings in order to seek damages for the illegitimate use of criminal investigative powers. However, there are no additional provisions that facilitate an effective remedy after the notification, which might raise doubts about the effectiveness in practice.[310]

---

[305] Article 126bb(3) CCP.

[306] *Kamerstukken II* 1996/97, 25 403, no. 3, 85.

[307] Article 126bb (1) CCP. See in detail on the manner in which the duty of notification shall be exerted, including the possible exceptions: 'Aanwijzing opsporingsbevoegdheden, *Stcrt* 2011, no. 3240, under 5.4.

[308] ECHR 24 April 1990, App. no. 11801/85 and App. no. 11105/84 (*Kruslin v. France and Huvig v. France*).

[309] ECHR 6 September 1978, App. no. 5029/71 (*Klass and others v. Germany*), para 71-72.

[310] See: HR 21 November 2006, *NJ* 2007, 233, ann. Mevis, annotation para 2. See also: Baaijens-van Geloven and Simmelink 2002, 588 and 593.

An evaluation of the use of SIT after the entry into force of the Act of 1999 regulating these techniques demonstrates that, in practice, the duty of notification is usually not observed. It appears that the most important reason for not notifying is that the investigative technique is usually applied against a suspect who will be notified automatically as a result of compliance with the duty to compile records. The second reason for non-observance is that the notification would undermine the interest of the investigation.[311] The interest of the investigation can also concern, similar to refraining from observing the duty to compile records, the interests of other criminal investigations, for example in the case of different investigations into a criminal organization. The Board of Procurators General has now urged all chief public prosecutors in the different district public prosecutor's offices to comply more effectively with the duty of notification, by affirming the importance of this protecting duty within the system of special investigative techniques.[312]

### *2.3.2 The Protective Elements in the System of Criminal Investigation*

The regulation of the criminal investigation in the criminal procedural law of the Netherlands is a consequence of both the fundamental rights and principles addressed in Sect. 2.1.3 and the specific choices made in the regulation of the criminal investigation in the CCP. This section will address the elements in the regulation of the criminal investigation that serve a protective goal. Firstly, the specific consequences of the protection of privacy for the regulation of criminal investigative powers will be described. These consequences follow from the principle of legality and from the interpretation of Article 8 ECHR (Sect. 2.3.2.1). Furthermore, the definition of a criminal investigation and, consequently, the demarcation from other investigative forms serves an important protective function, considering that the principle of legality and criminal procedural guarantees only apply to investigative activities that can be defined as a criminal investigation. This demarcation of the criminal investigative phase will be addressed in Sect. 2.3.2.2. The chapter will then turn to the specific regulation of the use of criminal investigative powers within the criminal investigation. For that purpose three investigative domains can be identified in which a different 'threshold of suspicion' as a triggering mechanism for the use of investigative powers is applied. Section 2.3.2.3 extensively deals with the different applicable triggering mechanisms and the central role of the reasonable suspicion threshold. Also any other levels of suspicion applicable to specific investigative techniques and additional protective restraints will be dealt with. Lastly, additional protective elements

---

[311] Beijer et al. 2004, 145.

[312] *Kamerstukken II* 2006/07, 29 940, no. 4, 1-2 (Letter of the Minister of Justice regarding the evaluation of the Act on SIT).

adopted in the CCP—the duty of reporting and procedural remedies—will be addressed in Sect. 2.3.2.4.

#### 2.3.2.1 Regulation Following the Principle of Legality and the Right to Respect for Private Life

As has been explained in Sects. 2.1.3.1 and 2.1.3.2, the principle of legality and the right to respect for private life require that the use of investigative powers that infringe upon privacy rights is regulated in the manner prescribed by the principle of legality under Article 1 CCP and meeting certain standards following from Article 8 ECHR and Article 10 Constitution. The principle of legality and the right to respect for private life are clearly related when it comes to the regulation of criminal investigative powers that interfere with privacy rights. Already in 1838, when the first Dutch Code of Criminal Procedure was adopted,[313] the underlying principle of the then adopted Code of Criminal Procedure was that for every governmental power interfering with fundamental rights as protected by the Constitution a basis in law must be established.[314] The main purpose of adopting the principle of legality in Article 1 CCP was to relate the provisions in the CCP to the protection of fundamental liberties in the Constitution. In that way the infringements of fundamental liberties by state authorities as provided for in the CCP obtained their justification with respect to the protection elements contained the Constitution through Article 1 CCP.[315] Also the constitutional provision itself (Article 10 Constitution) requires an Act of Parliament for establishing limitations to the right to private life. Article 8 ECHR, providing for the right to respect for one's private life, also only accepts limitations to this right in accordance with the law. In the Netherlands the requirement 'in accordance with the law' obliges the legislature to provide for codified law by an Act of Parliament.

Already in 1838 the Dutch criminal law specialist De Bosch Kemper recognized the importance of respect for private life in exercising powers under criminal law. He considered the protection against any arbitrary use of criminal procedural powers which disrespected individual liberty as one of the basic requirements of the law. According to De Bosch Kemper, the limits to the use of criminal procedural powers that interfere with private life must be provided in the law, while these provisions are only exceptions to the general rule that the government must respect the private life of its citizens.[316] From the wording used in the explanatory memorandum of the CCP of 1913-1914 it can be derived that in designing the CCP the 'paradox situation has been taken into account that in a *Rechtsstaat* it is

[313] Although based to a large extent upon the French Code d'Instruction Criminelle, used in the Netherlands for the preceding 27 years.

[314] As to J. de Bosch Kemper (1838): Simmelink 1987, 39-40.

[315] Simmelink 1987, 40 and 41, Berkhout-van Poelgeest 2001, 30.

[316] J. de Bosch Kemper (1838), cited in Simmelink 1987, 39.

inevitable that the fundamental rights of some are restricted in furtherance of the rights and liberties of others.'[317] Whereas fundamental rights are the core of the *Rechtsstaat,* it is necessary to restrict these rights when certain criminal procedural measures are needed in order to be able to establish the truth in favor of those whose rights have been violated as victims of crime or of crime-affected society in general. Some investigative powers had already been explicitly regulated in the CCP, while subjecting these methods to certain conditions.

Since the entry into force of the Code of Criminal Procedure of 1926 the right to respect for private life has gained in importance, which follows from the relatively recent adoption of this right in the Dutch Constitution (by the amendment of the Constitution in 1983). Moreover, the European Court of Human Rights has promulgated an approach in which the right to private life was given increasing importance over the years. At the same time, many new investigative powers with a more intrusive character have been developed as a consequence of technological developments, whereas the need for such measures was also fed by the increasing complexity of criminality, often in the context of a criminal organization.

This section will first turn to the general rules for the regulation of criminal investigative powers following from the ECrtHR'S interpretation of the restrictive clause of Article 8 ECHR. Section 2.1.3.2.1 has already described the scope of Article 8 ECHR as well as the interpretation of the different elements of the restrictive clause of Article 8 ECHR. These findings will not be repeated here. Instead, the focus will be particularly on the interpretation of the requirements of 'foreseeability' and being 'necessary in a democratic society' as these two elements of the restrictive clause of Article 8 ECHR set specific standards that the regulation of criminal investigative powers in the Netherlands needs to meet. Secondly, Sect. 2.3.2.1.2 will deal with the particular requirements for regulating criminal investigative powers in the Netherlands, where the regulation shall observe not only the requirements of the restrictive clause of Article 8 ECHR but also the particular requirements following from Article 10 Constitution and the principle of legality.

#### 2.3.2.1.1 The Requirements of the Restrictive Clause of Article 8 ECHR

The principle of legality and respect for the right to private life are thus complimentary with regard to the regulation of the criminal investigation. Both protect citizens against arbitrary interference by the state with their private life; they provide them with legal protection; and they guarantee equality for the law. A basis in law should therefore provide for a clear regulation of the circumstances and conditions under which the use of criminal powers by the government is permitted.[318] In addition, the interpretation of Article 8 ECHR has resulted in

---

[317] See: Knigge and Kwakman 2001, 181.

[318] *Ibid.*, 311.

specific requirements with regard to the quality of the law.[319] The law, established by Act of Parliament as a requirement under the Dutch Constitution, shall protect against arbitrary interferences with the right to respect for private life by only allowing restrictions to this right when the basis in law is adequately accessible, to a sufficient extent, and foreseeable to the person concerned.[320] The restriction must also be necessary in a democratic society. The ECrtHR has further developed these requirements in its case law, providing for conditions that domestic legislation on investigative powers that interfere with the right to respect for private life must meet in order to be compatible with Article 8 ECHR.

The requirement of accessibility has been explained as requiring that someone can relatively easily take note of the legal provision providing for a restriction on his or her right to private life. Someone "must be able to have an indication that is adequate in the circumstances of the legal rules applicable to a given case."[321] When the applicable law has been published, the law is considered accessible.[322] Hence, this requirement is generally met in the Dutch legal system, considering that the principle of legality provides that criminal procedure has to be established by an Act of Parliament, which will be published in the 'State's bulletin of acts, orders and decrees'.

With regard to the regulation of criminal investigative powers, especially the requirement of foreseeability imposes specific conditions.[323] The foreseeability of a specific interference must be considered in relation to the government's specific measure which results in such interference. For example, for the interception of telecommunications it cannot be required that a person must be able to foresee when his communications are being intercepted since that gives this person the opportunity to adjust his conduct. Foreseeability in this regard means that a citizen must be aware of in which circumstances and under what conditions the government is authorized to use such (secret) investigative powers.[324] Furthermore, legislation must at least provide for a "minimum degree of legal protection to which citizens are entitled under the rule of law in a democratic society."[325] This

319 See Sect. 2.1.3.2.1.

320 ECHR 26 April 1979, App. no. 6538/74 (*Sunday Times v. The United Kingdom*), para 49; ECHR 25 March 1998, case 13/1997/797/1000 (*Kopp v. Switzerland*), para 55; ECHR 16 February 2000, App. no. 27798/95 (*Amann v. Switzerland*), para 50 (and 56); ECHR 24 April 1990, App. no. 11801/85 and App. no. 11105/84 (*Kruslin v. France and Huvig v. France*), para 30/29). See in more detail Sect. 2.1.3.2.1.

321 ECHR 26 April 1979, App. no. 6538/74 (*Sunday Times v. The United Kingdom*), para 49.

322 ECHR 30 March 1989, App. no. 10461/83 (*Chapell v. The United Kingdom*), para 56.

323 See ECHR 29 June 2006, App. no. 54934/00 (*Weber and Saravia v. Germany*) (admissibility decision), para 93-94 and ECHR 1 July 2008, App. no. 58243/00 (*Liberty and others v. The United Kingdom*), para 62, for a summary of the Court's case law on the interpretation of and the conditions following from the requirement of foreseeability.

324 ECHR 2 August 1984, App. no. 8691/79 (*Malone v. The United Kingdom*), para 67 and ECHR 24 April 1990, App. no. 11801/85 and App. no. 11105/84 (*Kruslin v. France and Huvig v. France*), para 30/29.

325 ECHR 2 August 1984, App. no. 8691/79 (*Malone v. The United Kingdom*), para 79.

means that the basis in law providing for the power to use covert surveillance techniques must provide "adequate protection against arbitrary interference with Article 8 rights" and provide "adequate and effective guarantees against abuse."[326] Nevertheless, the requirement of foreseeability does not mean that the law must be elaborated in detail, because that "might give rise to excessive rigidity, and the law must be able to keep pace with changing circumstances."[327] The foreseeability requirement may be related in that sense to the principle of legality as laid down in Article 7 of the Convention (see on the principle of legality Sect. 2.1.3.1). "[H]owever clearly drafted a legal provision may be, there is an inevitable element of judicial interpretation."[328]

What basis of law is considered to be of sufficient quality to be in accordance with Article 8(2), depends, again, on all the circumstances of the specific case, such as the "nature, scope and duration of the possible measures, the grounds required for ordering them, the authorities competent to permit, carry out and supervise them, and the kind of remedy provided in national law"[329] and, elsewhere, "the content of the instrument in question, the field it is designed to cover and the number and status of those to whom it is addressed."[330] Dependent on the nature of the interference with the right to respect for private life and the consequences of this interference, the ECHR requires either more or less from the substantive precision of a specific basis in domestic law.[331] The Court seems to impose higher standards for covert investigative techniques: "[e]specially where a power vested in the executive is exercised in secret, the risks of arbitrariness are evident."[332] This may be illustrated by cases where the Court has assessed the compatibility of the basis in law for electronic communications.[333] For example, in *Kruslin/Huvig v. France* the Court set strict requirements for tapping phone communications without permission.[334] The tapping of telephone communications

[326] See e.g. ECHR 2 September 2010, App. no. 35623/05 (*Uzun v. Germany*), para 63.

[327] ECHR 23 September 1998, App. no. 72/1997/856/1065 (*McLeod v. The United Kingdom*), para 41, and ECHR 26 April 1979, App. no. 6538/74 (*Sunday Times v. The United Kingdom*), para 49.

[328] ECHR 2 September 2010, App. no. 35623/05 (*Uzun v. Germany*), para 62.

[329] ECHR 2 September 2010, App. no. 35623/05 (*Uzun v. Germany*), para 63.

[330] ECHR 12 January 2010, App. no. 4158/05 (*Gillan and Quinton v. The United Kingdom*), para 77.

[331] ECHR 2 August 1984, App. no. 8691/79 (*Malone v. The United Kingdom*), para 68.

[332] ECHR 2 August 1984, App. no. 8691/79 (*Malone v. The United Kingdom*), para 67 and ECHR 24 April 1990, App. no. 11801/85 and App. no. 11105/84 (*Kruslin v. France and Huvig v. France*), para 30/29.

[333] E.g. ECHR 2 August 1984, App. no. 8691/79 (*Malone v. The United Kingdom*), ECHR 24 April 1990, App. no. 11801/85 and App. no. 11105/84 (*Kruslin v. France and Huvig v. France*), ECHR 29 June 2006, App. no. 54934/00 (*Weber and Saravia v. Germany*) (admissibility decision) and ECHR 1 July 2008, App. no. 58243/00 (*Liberty and others v. The United Kingdom*).

[334] ECHR 24 April 1990, App. no. 11801/85 and App. no. 11105/84 (*Kruslin v. France and Huvig v. France*), para 33/32. ECHR 25 March 1998, case 13/1997/797/1000 (*Kopp v. Switzerland*).

is considered to be such serious interference—although understandably necessary for the interest of the investigation—that using this investigative method is only permitted if it is accompanied by sufficient guarantees for the person(s) involved. According to the Court it is "essential to have clear, detailed rules on interception of telephone conservations, especially as the technology available for use is continually becoming more sophisticated."[335] In *Weber and Saravia* the Court—after summarizing the general considerations in its case law regarding the requirement of foreseeability in the field of electronic surveillance—formulated the specific minimum safeguards that should be included in statutory law for the investigative power of wire-tapping:

> "the nature of the offences which may give rise to an interception order; a definition of the categories of people liable to have their telephones tapped; a limit on the duration of telephone tapping; the procedure to be followed for examining, using and storing the data obtained; the precautions to be taken when communicating the data to other parties; and the circumstances in which recordings may or must be erased or the tapes destroyed."[336]

In contrast, the balancing of less serious interference with privacy against the interests of the investigation in the case of *Murray* gave rise to imposing less strict requirements for the quality of the law. In *Murray* investigative activities such as the recording of personal details, including a photograph having been taken without consent that did not have an explicit basis in the law, were 'in accordance with the law' as they could inexplicitly be derived from the legal basis of the more intrusive powers of arrest and detention. The less intrusive investigative actions were considered necessary for the successful exertion of the powers to arrest and detain.[337] A similar conclusion was reached in *Uzun v. Germany* where the GPS surveillance of movements in public was not considered to interfere with private life to the same extent as the electronic surveillance of telecommunications, for which reason "more general principles on adequate protection against arbitrary interference with Article 8 rights" applies. For this reason the provision that constituted the basis for the GPS surveillance, stating that "other special technical means intended for the purpose of surveillance may be used to investigate the facts of the case or to detect the perpetrator's whereabouts if the investigation concerns a criminal offence of considerable gravity", was sufficiently foreseeable and with this conclusion the Court also took into account additional safeguards against arbitrariness such as the fact that the principle of proportionality had been taken into account and an *ex post* judicial review was in place.[338]

---

[335] ECHR 29 June 2006, App. no. 54934/00 (*Weber and Saravia v. Germany*) (admissibility decision), para 93 and ECHR 1 July 2008, App. no. 58243/00 (*Liberty and others v. The United Kingdom*), para 62.

[336] Internal citations omitted, ECHR 29 June 2006, App. no. 54934/00 (*Weber and Saravia v. Germany*) (admissibility decision), para 95. See also: ECHR 1 July 2008, App. no. 58243/00 (*Liberty and others v. The United Kingdom*), para 62.

[337] ECHR 28 October 1994, App. no. 14310/88 (*Murray v. The United Kingdom*), para 88.

[338] ECHR 2 September 2010, App. no. 35623/05 (*Uzun v. Germany*), para 29 and 68-74.

The second requirement which is relevant for the regulation of criminal investigative powers and that follows from the restrictive clause of Article 8 ECHR concerns the requirement that the interference must be necessary in a democratic society in order to be legitimate. 'Necessary in a democratic society' is a condition which requires a legitimate aim for the interference and, furthermore, that the "interference corresponds to a pressing social need and, in particular, that it is proportionate to the legitimate aim pursued."[339] The possible legitimate aims are enumerated in section 2 of Article 8: the interests of national security, public safety or the economic well-being of the country, the prevention of disorder or crime, the protection of health or morals, or the protection of the rights and liberties of others. For example, in the ECHR case of *Lüdi v. Switzerland* the wire-tapping of the defendant's private communications was permitted because Swiss law establishes a basis for the use of this method in situations where there is a "good reason to believe that criminal offenses are about to be committed." The goal of this law is the prevention of crime, which the Court considers as a necessity in a democratic society. This meets the requirements of Article 8(2) and, with that, justifies the limitation on section 1 of Article 8.[340] The requirement of 'necessary in a democratic society' is a very important requirement that restricts the possibility for states to adopt legislation that provides bases for interfering with Convention rights. Moreover, it reflects the idea that the state model of democracy is the only possible state organization which is compatible with the Convention.[341] However, the Court primarily leaves a margin of appreciation to the states in this regard and exerts only a marginal examination itself. Interfering with the right to privacy is necessary in a democratic society when there is (in addition to one of the enumerated legitimate aims) a pressing social need for the interfering activities, while the interference must be relevant for achieving the intended aim and it must be proportionate to the legitimate aim pursued.[342] Furthermore, the requirement of 'necessity' in fact implies an assessment of the proportionality and subsidiarity of the restriction. The interference shall not be of such a nature that the essence of the right to respect for private life is undermined, and it must be proportionate to the intended aim. An infringement by a public authority will not be legitimate if the intended aim can be achieved by less intrusive means.[343] Also when a state uses its power to exert the positive duty to protect the lives of citizens under Article 2 ECHR—for example, in order to prevent a terrorist attack—and interferes for that purpose with the right to private life as protected by Article 8 ECHR, such

---

[339] ECHR 26 March 1987, App. no. 9248/81 (*Leander v. Sweden*), para 58.

[340] ECHR 15 June 1992, App. no. 12433/86 (*Lüdi v. Switzerland*), para 39. Furthermore, the Court ruled in this case that the use of an undercover agent, who observed the defendant committing a drugs crime, did not violate the privacy of the defendant (Article 8(1)) because the defendant should have been aware of the risk of being observed in that situation. *Ibid.*, para 40.

[341] Loof 2005, 211.

[342] See e.g. ECHR 23 September 1998, App. no. 72/1997/856/1065 (*McLeod v. The United Kingdom*), para 52. See in general: Arai 2006, 340-341.

[343] Loof 2005, 213-214.

interference must meet the requirements for a legitimate restriction of Article 8 ECHR and must therefore be proportionate in order to be necessary in a democratic society.[344]

#### 2.3.2.1.2 The Requirements of the Principle of Legality and the Right to Respect for Private Life in the Regulation of Criminal Investigative Powers

As has been explained in the section dealing with the legal bases providing for truth-finding instruments, different requirements apply with regard to the precision of the legal basis, which depends on the intrusiveness of the investigative powers in question. Until the mid-1990s the Supreme Court accepted that Articles providing for a general setting of tasks, such as Article 2 of the Police Act 1993 and Articles 141/142 CCP, could serve as a sufficient legal basis for investigative powers interfering with privacy rights. One of the main causes of the so-called 'crisis in the criminal investigation' was that investigative powers were widely applied, while a precise regulation in the law was lacking.[345] It was clearly questionable whether these Articles provided, in all circumstances, a sufficient basis in the law within the meaning of Article 8 ECHR.

Around the same time the Supreme Court slightly changed its position by determining in the case of *Zwolsman* that Article 2 of the Police Act 1993 did not sufficiently meet the requirement of being 'in accordance with the law' when the use of the investigative power results in more serious interference with the right to respect for private life.[346] However, when the interference is rather limited Article 2 Police Act 1993 and Article 141/142 CCP can serve as the legitimate basis in law.[347] Decisive for answering the question whether or not a specific basis in law is required for the use of an investigative power is thus the extent to which the power interferes with private life. For example, the Supreme Court considered that sifting through discarded garbage is a measure that does not infringe on privacy, since it does not constitute a situation in which someone can have a reasonable expectation that his private life will be respected.[348] The same view was taken concerning, e.g., observation in a public place.[349]

The ECrtHR (*Malone*) generally requires that (any) legal basis for a criminal investigative power providing for discretion for investigative officers provides for "a measure of legal protection against arbitrary interferences by public authorities

---

344 See also Chap. 1, Sect. 1.3.2.

345 Rapport van de Parlementaire Enquêtecommissie Opsporingsmethoden 1996, 419-420.

346 HR 19 December 1995, *NJ* 1996, 249, para 6.4.4 and 6.4.5. Although, in this case, the Supreme Court made no explicit reference to either Article 8 ECHR or Article 10 of the Constitution, its judgment can clearly be seen in relation to the forms of protection provided in these Articles.

347 HR 19 December 1995, *NJ* 1996, 249, para 6.3.2 and 6.4.5.

348 HR 19 December 1995, *NJ* 1996, 249, para 8.3.

349 HR 2 June 1998, *NJ* 1998, 783, para 6.2, HR 13 June 1995, *NJ* 1995, 684, HR 11 October 1986, *NJ* 1988, 511, para 6.3.

with the rights safeguarded in Article 8(1)."[350] Furthermore: "a law which confers a discretion must indicate the scope of the discretion, although the detailed procedures and conditions to be observed do not necessarily have to be incorporated in rules of substantive law." The Court continued by stating that: "[c]onsequently, the law must indicate the scope of any of such discretion conferred on the competent authorities and the manner of its exercise with sufficient clarity, having regard to the legitimate aim of the measure in question, to give the individual adequate protection against arbitrary interference."[351] A rather wide scope of discretion may be attributed to investigative officers, but not for the use of all investigative powers. As addressed in the previous section, the degree of precision depends on all the circumstances of the case, and in particular on the nature of the investigative power concerned and, consequently, on the nature of the interference caused by using the investigative power. On that basis, the Court decided in the case of *Malone* that the wide discretion afforded to the public authorities in using secret surveillance of communications was not in compliance with the requirement of being 'in accordance with the law' as contained in Article 8 ECHR.[352]

The Act on SIT anticipates these requirements of Article 8 ECHR and the principle of legality by establishing precise regulations for investigative techniques that interfere in most circumstances with the privacy of the persons involved.[353] The adoption of the Act has been a critical turning point in the regulation of a criminal investigation. The basic assumption of this Act was to make the criminal investigation sound and controllable. From now on, SIT that interfere with rights and liberties can only be applied, as the principle of legality and the protection of the right to private life prescribe in criminal procedural law, on the basis of and in accordance with specific conditions provided by law. The government formulated three objectives that the Act was deemed to achieve: (1) regulation by creating a statutory basis in the CCP for SIT; (2) furthering and guaranteeing a legitimate criminal investigation, by establishing hierarchical control primarily by the public prosecutor as well as furthering transparency regarding the use of investigative techniques; and (3) the effective investigation of (organized) crime.[354] The regulation provides for the circumstances in which the use of investigative techniques is permitted and under what conditions this use must occur. The established system thus importantly strengthens the protection against arbitrary governmental interference by including the right to respect for private life, especially in comparison with the situation before 1999. This does not mean that specifically regulated

---

[350] ECHR 2 August 1984, App. no. 8691/79 (*Malone v. The United Kingdom*), para 67. Repeated in: ECHR 24 April 1990, App. no. 11801/85 and App. no. 11105/84 (*Kruslin v. France and Huvig v. France*), para 30/29.

[351] ECHR 2 August 1984, App. no. 8691/79 (*Malone v. The United Kingdom*), para 68.

[352] *Ibid.*, para 79.

[353] *Stb.* 1999, 245.

[354] Beijer et al. 2004, 29. See also the explanatory memorandum in which codification, enhanced hierarchical supervision and controllability were formulated as the main objectives of the new Act. *Kamerstukken II* 1997/98, 25 403, no. 3, 3.

powers leave no room for different interpretations. Without interpreting the law by analogy, it is the task of the judiciary to fill such gaps in the law in accordance with fundamental principles of law (such as proportionality and subsidiarity) and in accordance with the original intent of the legislature in creating that specific regulation.[355]

Also the preliminary investigation has been given a more precise regulation in the CCP. Although the activities conducted in a preliminary investigation cannot entail one of the regulated SIT, they do concern the collection of personal details concerning persons who are not (yet) suspected of a crime. The character of the specific investigative activities conducted during the preliminary investigation cannot be considered as very intrusive for the right to privacy. However, the nature and scope of the investigation, that can be characterized as nosing through the personal details of members of a 'group' or 'branch' of society, nevertheless have serious consequences for the private lives of the people involved. For this reason, the legislature decided to establish a more specific basis in law for these preliminary investigative activities, rather than deriving the power to conduct these activities from Article 2 of the Police Act 1993.[356] To compensate for the seriousness of the implications for the private lives of persons not (yet) suspected of a criminal offense, it has in addition been established by a guideline that the public prosecutor can only order a preliminary investigation after consulting the Board of Procurators General.[357]

Articles 141, 142 CCP and Article 2 Police Act 1993, as well as similar provisions for special law enforcement officers, have been accepted in the case law as sufficient bases for (at least) all investigative powers that do not interfere with privacy rights. These provisions do not provide investigative officers with complete discretion, considering that the use of investigative powers derived from the general police task is restricted by allowing such use only for the purpose of fulfilling that task: investigating criminal offenses.[358] In the guideline it is stated that investigative powers on the basis of Articles 141-142 CCP and Article 2 Police Act 1993 can be used by investigative officers when necessary for the purpose of their law enforcement task if there are 'indications of criminal activities.'[359] Furthermore,

---

[355] See in this regard HR 19 December 1995, *NJ* 1996, 249, ann. Sch, annotation para 29. Before 1999 the Supreme Court often set standards for using specific investigative authorities for which an explicit basis in law was not yet established. For example: the establishment of the so-called *Tallon* criterion for the use of investigative infiltration. The *Tallon* criterion prohibits undercover agents from acting in such a way that the person being investigated commits criminal offenses other than those which were already the object of his criminal intent. HR 4 December 1979, *NJ* 1980, 356. A similar criterion has also been upheld by the ECrtHR: ECHR 9 June 1998, case 44/1997/828/1034 (*Teixeira de Castro v. Portugal*), para 32.

[356] *Kamerstukken II* 199/97, 25 403, no. 3, 49-51.

[357] See 'Aanwijzing opsporingsbevoegdheden, *Stcrt* 2011, no. 3240, 25 and *Kamerstukken II* 1996/97, 25 403, no. 3, 50 (expressing the intention to establish such a guideline).

[358] Knigge and Kwakman 20010, 311-314.

[359] Handboek voor de opsporingspraktijk 2000-2007, aanv. 5 July 2004 AI 1.1-6.

and very important also in the light of the requirement of being 'necessary in a democratic society' under Article 8(2) ECHR, the use of all investigative powers is bound by the principles of the due administration of justice, such as proportionality and subsidiarity. These principles and limiting the use of investigative powers to investigating criminal offenses (purpose limitation) are decisive for the legitimacy of the use of investigative powers that lack a specific regulation in the law (see in more detail Sects. 2.1.3.4.1 and 2.1.3.4.2).[360] The right balance between using provisions which generally set tasks as the basis for investigative powers and requiring a specific regulation must be found. Investigative powers that (seriously) interfere with privacy rights must in any event be given a specific regulation in the law by means of an Act of Parliament, as the protection of the fundamental right to respect for private life and the interests served by the principle of legality explicitly require protection to be provided against arbitrary interferences with the right to private life by investigative actions by the government.

In closing, it must also be noted that the Act on the Intelligence and Security Services of 2002 (WIV 2002) provides a specific legal basis for the special investigative powers of the AIVD that seriously interfere with the protected right to respect for private life as laid down in Article 8 ECHR. With this Act, the legislature aimed to provide for a regulation that meets the requirements of Articles 8 and 13 ECHR, by explicitly regulating the specific powers of the intelligence services and the circumstances under which they can be used, as well as providing for an internal controlling body which is responsible for examining the proportionality and subsidiarity of the powers used in a specific case.[361]

#### 2.3.2.2 The Separation of Criminal Investigation from Other Forms of Investigation

The demarcation of the criminal investigation phase serves an important protective function, considering that it is generally understood to be the starting point of criminal procedural law under Article 1 CCP. Consequently, the regulations of the CCP apply, providing both for the conditions under which criminal investigative powers may be used and for the legal protection of those subjected to the government's powers in the area of criminal procedural law.[362] Nevertheless, as will be seen in this section, the criminal investigation cannot always be clearly separated from other investigative spheres on the basis of the definition provided in Article 132a CCP. Administrative supervision may overlap with criminal investigation and the status of the preliminary investigation as 'preceding' the criminal investigation is not very clear. At the same time, the separation of the criminal investigation from other investigative spheres serves an important restrictive

[360] See e.g. HR 11 October 2005, *NJ* 2006, 625, para 3.5.2.

[361] *Kamerstukken II* 1997/98, 25 877, no. 3, 2-3.

[362] Compare: Borgers 2011, 457.

function, considering that all activities covered by the definition of criminal investigation are also subjected to the protective regulations of the CPP. In that respect, in particular the separation from administrative supervision and from the intelligence community serves an important protective function. In order to address the separation of the criminal investigation from other forms of investigation, this section will firstly analyze the reasons for adopting the definition as provided in Article 132a CCP (Sect. 2.3.2.2.1). Subsequently, the separation from administrative supervisory authority (Sect. 2.3.2.2.2) and from the intelligence investigation (Sect. 2.3.2.2.3) will be dealt with. Lastly, attention will be given to the relation between the preliminary investigation and the criminal investigation (Sect. 2.3.2.2.4).

##### 2.3.2.2.1 The Definition of a Criminal Investigation

The scope of the criminal investigation phase has gradually developed. Until the adoption of a definition (in Article 132a CCP) in 1999 by the Act on SIT, the scope of the criminal investigation was not defined in statutory law. Before 1999, a limited interpretation of the scope of the criminal investigation was generally favored. The criminal investigation was limited, according to this interpretation, to investigative activities on the basis of a reasonable suspicion, whilst proactive investigative activities were tolerated by considering these activities as being part of the administrative supervisory task of police officers on the basis of Article 2 Police Act 1993. However, this situation was unsatisfactory as the nature of proactive investigative activities required more precise regulation and protective guarantees for the subjects of the investigation.

For the first time, by the Act on SIT of 1999 a legal definition of the criminal investigation was adopted in Article 132a CCP. Article 132a CCP defined the criminal investigation on the basis of the responsible authority, the purpose of the investigation and the specific threshold for initiating a criminal investigation. Firstly, also according to the definition under Article 132a, the public prosecutor is the responsible authority for the criminal investigation. The supervisory authority of the public prosecutor shall be seen in relation to Article 148 CCP, giving the public prosecutor the authority to give orders to law enforcement officers. In the second place, the purpose of the criminal investigation must be the making of a prosecutorial decision, which excludes the use of powers in the criminal investigation for the sole purpose of gathering information (and thus general search or fishing expeditions). Using criminal investigative powers for purposes other than evidence gathering will constitute a violation of the prohibition of *détournement de pouvoir*.[363] This limitation to the purpose of gathering information which is relevant for truth-finding regarding criminal offenses imposes an important restriction on the power to conduct criminal investigative activities, which has been a

[363] See also Sect. 2.1.3.4.2.

principal reason for adopting a definition that includes this specific limitation.[364] Thirdly, the definition limited the criminal investigation to activities conducted upon the establishment of a reasonable suspicion of a crime or a reasonable suspicion that crimes are being planned or committed in an organized context. These specific thresholds in the definition of criminal investigation have been adopted in order to limit the criminal investigative phase specifically to the clarification of a reasonable suspicion of a crime or a reasonable suspicion of involvement in the planning or committing of crimes in an organized context and in order to demarcate the criminal investigative phase from other investigative forms.[365]

Initiated by researchers of the Criminal Procedure Research Project of 2001, a broader definition of the criminal investigation is now favored, by which the specific reason for initiating the investigation is no longer included as a defining element. According to the researchers of 2001 Criminal Procedure Project, the purpose of the criminal investigation shall be the central defining factor, instead of the threshold of a reasonable suspicion.[366] The Act of 20 November 2006 to broaden the possibilities to investigate and prosecute terrorist crimes has, in accordance with this approach, amended Article 132a CCP in order to broaden the definition of the criminal investigation by eliminating the threshold of a reasonable suspicion from the definition.[367] The new definition provided in Article 132a defines a criminal investigation on the basis of supervision by the public prosecutor and the purpose of the investigative activities in relation to criminal offenses shall be to 'make prosecutorial decisions.' This implies a limitation on investigative activities for the purpose of gathering information which is relevant for making criminal procedural decisions regarding criminal offenses, such as the decision to charge or a decision to use coercive measures such as the power of arrest.[368] Now, all investigative activities in relation to criminal offenses for the purpose of making prosecutorial decisions are part of the criminal investigation, whether conducted on the basis of Article 2 Police Act 1993, on the basis of a specific legal basis provided in the CCP (in particular the use of SIT), or on the basis of a provision for investigative powers in special criminal law. This means that any order given by the public prosecutor under Article 148 CCP falls within the scope of the criminal investigation (instead of only those related to SIT) and, with that, establishes the supervisory role of the public prosecutor for all criminal investigative activities.[369] Moreover, all investigative activities that contribute to the purpose of gathering evidence for making prosecutorial decisions are subject to the protective provisions of the CCP rather than being regulated by administrative

---

[364] *Kamerstukken II* 1997/98, 25 403, no. 7, 17 and *Handelingen II* 1998/99, no. 24, 1549.

[365] *Kamerstukken II* 1997/98, 25 403, no. 7, 18.

[366] Knigge and Kwakman 2001, 300-347.

[367] *Stb.* 2006, 580.

[368] *Kamerstukken II* 2005-2006, 30 164, no. 3, 17 and Borgers 2009, 40 and 46. See also Sect. 2.1.3.4.2.

[369] See also: *Kamerstukken II* 2005-2006, 30 164, no. 7, 25.

law. For example, the duty to compile records under Article 152 CCP applies to all criminal investigative activities and the remedies provided in Article 359a CCP apply when investigative rules have been violated.[370] For these reasons, the broadening of the definition of criminal investigation could be understood as being favorable to legal protection. Nevertheless, by adopting this definition the central role of the threshold of a reasonable suspicion has been abandoned, which has traditionally served as an important protective restraint against the government acting within the field of criminal procedural law, which opens the door to also using other thresholds for using investigative methods in the criminal investigation and, consequently, expanding the proactive capabilities of the criminal investigation. The protective role of the threshold of a reasonable suspicion will be further discussed in Sect. 2.3.2.2.

The defining elements of the current definition of the criminal investigation are, according to the language of Article 132a CCP, both the purpose of the investigation and the supervision of the public prosecutor. Although the government referred to the proposals of the researchers of the 2001 Criminal Procedure Project when explaining the choice for adopting this definition, the inclusion of supervision by the public prosecutor in the definition was *not* in line with these proposals.[371] Also Borgers argues that it is only the purpose of the investigation that concerns a defining element, whereas supervision by the public prosecutor (as well as other criminal procedural guarantees such as Article 152 CCP and Article 359a CCP) consequently applies as a regulatory element to all activities that have been defined as a 'criminal investigation.'[372] To determine what investigative activities are criminal investigative activities (and thus conducted for the purpose of 'making prosecutorial decisions) two approaches can be taken. Firstly, when the information produced by the investigative activities is possibly relevant to criminal law enforcement, these activities shall be defined as a criminal investigation. Secondly, only those activities conducted by investigative officers who also have criminal investigative authority (under Articles 141-142 CCP) are criminal investigative activities. Borgers chooses the latter approach, because the first is difficult to fit into the system of criminal procedural law (as will be explained in more detail in the next section).[373] However, the disadvantage of this latter

---

[370] Sikkema 2008, para 4.1. The Supreme Court seems to retain the older interpretation of the criminal investigation when addressing the applicability of Article 152 CCP and distinguishes, for that purpose, a criminal investigation under Article 132a CCP and an investigation for the purpose of gathering information in relation to criminal offenses 'preceding' the criminal investigation (although with the same outcome; Article 152 CCP also applies to the investigative activities 'preceding' the criminal investigation when these activities are conducted for the purpose of collecting information for criminal prosecution). See HR 5 October 2010, *LJN* BL5629. Borgers 2011, 462.

[371] *Kamerstukken II* 2005/06, 30 164, no. 7, 26.

[372] Borgers 2009, 53.

[373] *Ibid.*, 57-59. This approach also seems to be the correct one according to the Supreme Court (upholding the reasoning of the Court of Appeal). HR 7 July 2009, *NJ* 2009 528, para 6.2.3 and 8.4 and Gerechtshof 's-Gravenhage 1 March 2007, *LJN* AZ9644, para 5.1.1.

approach is that criminal procedural safeguards, such as Article 359a CCP, will not apply to investigative activities that have been conducted, in violation of the principle of *détournement de pouvoir,* for criminal investigative purposes.

#### 2.3.2.2.2 Separation from Administrative Supervision

The definition of criminal investigation as provided in Article 132a CCP seems to clearly separate criminal investigative activities from administrative supervisory activities. As has already been explained in the previous section and in Sect. 2.2.2.1, criminal investigative activities were previously separated from other investigative activities with the presence of a reasonable suspicion. The disadvantage of such a 'limited' approach towards the criminal investigation was that proactive investigative activities were conducted outside of the criminal investigation, as part of the controlling task of the police and were thus not regulated by the CCP but by administrative law. And also after the adoption of the first definition of criminal investigation by the Act on SIT of 1999 (which included the threshold for the (partly) proactive investigation of organized crime) other proactive investigative activities based on Article 2 Police Act 1993 (instead of the provisions of Title V) aimed at the discovery of criminal activities for the purpose of generating evidence for criminal prosecution would fall outside the scope of criminal investigation and would be regulated by administrative law. On the basis of this more limited definition of a criminal investigation, administrative supervisory authority would cover the investigative activities preceding the phase of criminal investigation.[374]

The definition of criminal investigation adopted by the Act of 2006 now covers all police investigative activities that contribute to their law enforcement task. In that regard, the current definition of the criminal investigation seems to provide for a clearer demarcation of the criminal investigative phase. Currently, the purpose of the investigative activities concerns the dividing factor between criminal investigation and administrative supervision: the criminal investigation is conducted for the purpose of collecting information for making prosecutorial decisions, while administrative supervision is conducted for the purpose of controlling the observance of the (special criminal) law. Less clear is the element of the definition of Article 132a CCP providing that the criminal investigation occurs under the

[374] Nevertheless, the exact scope of the criminal investigation has been, especially before the entry into force of the Act of 2006, rather ambiguous. On the one hand, the scope of Article 132a CCP was explained as separating criminal investigation from administrative supervision on the basis of the threshold of a reasonable suspicion. On the other hand, Article 148 CCP has been interpreted as referring to a broader definition of criminal investigation, namely also covering the investigative powers attributed in special criminal law, which can be applied 'in the interest of criminal investigation' and, hence, in the absence of a reasonable suspicion. Borgers 2011, 460. Because especially this ambiguity has been overcome by the definition adopted in 2006, the previous lack of clarity as to the scope of the criminal investigation will further be left out of consideration.

supervision of the public prosecutor. As described in Sect. 2.2.2.2.2, there are situations where officers other than those enumerated in Articles 141 and 142 CCP have been attributed the power to employ administrative supervisory powers in special criminal Acts, whereas the use of these administrative supervisory powers may also be conducted for the purpose of tracing criminal offenses (also referred to as repressive control). However, these officers do not act under the supervision of the public prosecutor (under Article 148(2) CCP). Hence, when considering the element of supervision by the public prosecutor as a second defining factor, these activities also fall outside the scope of the criminal investigation as provided in Article 132a CCP and concern administrative supervision.[375] Nevertheless, as already addressed in Sect. 2.2.2.2.2, the use of administrative supervisory powers may result in the discovery of information which provides a reason for initiating a criminal investigation; the administrative supervision will then switch to a criminal investigation. Furthermore, sometimes administrative supervision overlaps with criminal investigation, which is also referred to as the cumulation of spheres.[376] This section will continue to address the situation where administrative supervision switches to a criminal investigation and the situation where both spheres overlap, in order to explain the protective function served by the separation between administrative supervision and criminal investigation.

In its judgment of 1935 the Supreme Court addressed the situation where administrative supervision switches to a criminal investigation. In this case the officer in question, who also had criminal investigative authority on the basis of Articles 141 and 142 CCP, used his administrative supervisory authority to check whether the kitchen of a catering establishment was observing the 'Alcohol Act' and encountered a gun during these supervisory activities. According to the Supreme Court, the officer was authorized to seize the gun, as a continuation of using investigative powers, initially for administrative supervision and, subsequently, for a criminal investigation, also when these investigative powers have a basis in a different Act.[377] When evidence of criminal activities is 'in plain view' during the application of administrative supervisory powers and the investigative officer in question is also authorized to employ criminal investigative powers, the administrative supervision may thus switch to a criminal investigation. The switch from administrative supervision to a criminal investigation would be illegitimate when evidence of criminal offenses is not found to be in plain view except by the application of administrative supervisory powers for criminal investigative

[375] One could also argue that these activities concern criminal investigation and, consequently, the officers shall act under the responsibility of the public prosecutor. In that view, the element of supervision by the public prosecutor in Article 132a CCP is a regulatory element instead of also being a defining element for criminal investigation. In this line: Luchtman 2007B, 669-672, see also footnote 204 of this Chap. 3, and: Peçi and Sikkema 2008.

[376] Luchtman 2007A, 133-142 and Borgers 2011, 455.

[377] HR 2 December 1935, *NJ* 1936, 250, ann. WP.

purposes. This would constitute a violation of the principle of *détournement de pouvoir*.[378]

Furthermore, administrative supervisory officers who are not criminal investigative officers under Articles 141 and 142 CCP may not use criminal investigative powers, for which reason the administrative supervision cannot switch to a criminal investigation in such a case.[379] Nevertheless, most investigative officers are authorized to apply both administrative supervisory powers and criminal investigative powers. In addition, concurrent purposes may be pursued when using administrative supervisory powers, as long as it follows that the controlling power has *also* been used for the purpose for which it has been attributed. Hence, police officers may in fact, with the help of administrative supervisory powers, also trace criminal offenses, for example, by using the controlling power to stop vehicles in order to check that the Road Traffic Act is being observed and concurrently—or maybe even primarily—also to discover evidence of a crime.[380]

The situation when administrative supervision switches to a criminal investigation should be distinguished from the situation where administrative supervisory powers are used when information regarding the commission of a criminal offense is already present. The ‘cumulation of spheres’ may take different forms, varying from the abuse of administrative supervisory powers for the purpose of gathering evidence for criminal prosecution to the parallel use of administrative supervisory powers and criminal investigative powers.[381] Whereas the first, as already indicated, constitutes a *détournement de pouvoir*, the latter is permitted provided that when administrative supervisory powers are used against suspects, the suspect is entitled to his procedural rights as a suspect. Hence, instead of being obliged to cooperate (under Article 5:20 General Administrative Law Act), the suspect who is being subjected to controlling power is entitled to use his fundamental right to remain silent under Article 29(2) CCP and Article 6 ECHR.[382]

#### 2.3.2.2.3 Separation from Intelligence Investigation

The investigative activities on behalf of the intelligence agency (AIVD) are explicitly separated from the criminal investigation on the basis of their different investigative purpose. Similar to the separation from administrative supervisory authority, also the separation from the intelligence community is based on

---

[378] Corstens 2008, 273.

[379] According to Borgers those investigative activities conducted for the purpose of making prosecutorial decisions and conducted on behalf of investigative officers under Articles 141 and 142 CCP meet the definition of a criminal investigation under Article 132a CCP. Borgers 2009, 50. *Kamerstukken II* 2005/6, 30 164, no. 7, 57-59.

[380] Borgers 2011, 478.

[381] See on this subject and in particular the use of administrative supervisory powers under the Tax Act (also) for the benefit of gathering evidence for criminal offenses (such as tax fraud): Luchtman 2007A.

[382] Borgers 2011, 481-492 and Van Sliedregt 2006, 18-19.

differing investigative purposes. However, this separation from the intelligence community is, for protective reasons, more restrictive considering that there are no possibilities for fluent switches from intelligence investigation to criminal investigation and that the cumulation of both investigative spheres is prohibited.

While the law enforcement services aim to investigate offenses for the purpose of making prosecutorial decisions, the intelligence services gather information in the interest of protecting national security. The separation that follows from these distinguished purposes has been considered as a very important and critical separation, because the control over the manner in which evidence is gathered is an essential aspect of realizing the fairness of criminal proceedings in order to be able to assess the reliability of the information gathering. Facilitating this control requires transparency, at least in the trial phase, concerning the investigative activities, which clashes with the secrecy of intelligence investigations as a prerequisite for protecting national security interests. Hence, intelligence and law enforcement investigative activities are separated and subjected to different regulation frameworks.

The framework regulating the criminal investigation is underpinned by the desire to realize both the sword and the shield objective of criminal procedural law, in anticipation of fair criminal proceedings for which (internal and, in principle, also external) transparency, to be achieved in the trial phase, is the most important prerequisite. By contrast, the framework regulating the intelligence investigation (WIV 2002) is aimed in the first place at the effective protection of national security, while building in safeguards realizing control and preventing abuse.[383] In line with this rationale, the use of intelligence powers for the purpose of gathering evidence for a criminal prosecution is forbidden, in order to guarantee that criminal procedural safeguards are not circumvented. Furthermore, the separation between criminal investigation and intelligence investigation is the point of departure and the exchange of information between intelligence and law enforcement communities is a delicate matter.

The legislative basis for this separation can be found in the WIV 2002.[384] According to Article 9 the "functionaries of the services have no powers to investigate offenses." And, while investigative officers may be asked to perform activities ordered by the AIVD, they can never use their criminal investigative powers when performing these activities. In Article 14 of the WIV 2002 the processing of information for the AIVD has been strictly separated from the processing of information by the relevant functionaries for other purposes. By means of these provisions, the separation between the intelligence and law enforcement communities has been given a statutory basis.

---

[383] See on this framework Sect. 2.2.2.4.1.

[384] With that, the Act also meets the concerns of the Van Traa Parliamentary Inquiry Commission regarding the possibility of an overlap between intelligence investigation and law enforcement investigations (and consequently an abuse of power) due to a lack of statutory separation between the two communities. Rapport van de Parlementaire Enquêtecommissie Opsporingsmethoden 1996, 358.

The separation can also be found in the statutory basis for using the investigative powers of both services. While the authority of the law enforcement services to tap private communications is founded on Article 126l-m CCP, the AIVD can tap conversations on the basis of Article 25 WIV 2002 and on the basis of the exemption for services pursuing activities under the WIV of 2002 adopted in Article 139c(2)(3) of the Criminal Code, in which Article the tapping of private communications has been prohibited.[385]

#### 2.3.2.2.4 The Relation Between the Preliminary Investigation and the Criminal Investigation

The legal basis for the preliminary investigation can be found in Articles 126gg-126ii CCP. According to Article 126gg(1) CCP the purpose of the preliminary investigation is to prepare the criminal investigation. Strictly speaking, this purpose differs from the purpose of the criminal investigation under Article 132a CCP, for which reason the preliminary investigation could be understood as a separate investigative phase preceding the criminal investigation.

The separate regulation of the preliminary investigation was also part of the Act on SIT of 1999 in order to provide a specific legal basis for certain proactive investigative activities instead of continuing to base these activities on Article 2 Police Act 1993. Practice had demonstrated that there was a need for proactive investigative activities in complex cases regarding organized crime to decide whether and in what way a criminal investigation into organized crime shall be started. Especially in complex cases, the criminal investigation was—before 1999—often preceded by an orientating investigation in order to determine whether there were sufficient grounds to start a criminal investigation. In practice, the border between the investigative activities covered by the criminal investigation and those excluded from that phase (and thus labeled as administrative supervisory authority) was imperceptible.[386] Considering the then applied limited definition of the criminal investigation, the activities in this orientating, preliminary phase were uncontrollable and unlimited, whereas Article 2 Police Act 1993 can in the light of Article 8 ECHR only legitimize simple information gathering, without the application of investigative powers and not the collection of personal details of groups of people not (yet) suspected of a criminal offense. The legislature considered it necessary to maintain the possibility to conduct such a preliminary investigation, but decided to regulate it in the CCP and to limit it to certain activities and to serious crimes. In fact, the adoption of this preliminary investigative phase in the CCP is a solution to the lack of a basis in law for activities in the proactive phase that might interfere with privacy rights.

---

[385] Although Article 139c(2)(3) CCP also excludes tapping for a criminal investigation from this prohibition, the statutory basis for the powers are the provisions in Articles 126l to 126m CCP.

[386] 't Hart 1983, 158.

The legislature decided to adopt the basis for the preliminary investigation as a separate investigative phase in the CCP, preceding the criminal investigation as defined in Article 132a CCP. Considering the definition of the criminal investigation adopted in the Act on SIT of 1999, including the threshold of a reasonable suspicion, this preliminary investigation would indeed fall outside the scope of that definition. Accordingly, the purpose of the preliminary investigation was formulated so as to prepare the criminal investigation. This purpose of the *preparation* of the criminal investigation means that the preliminary investigation is aimed at making a decision as to whether or not it is necessary to initiate a full investigation. It may produce the initial information for a criminal investigation through the possibility of gathering additional information and comparing and combining information, which may increase the level of the information that is available to a level which is sufficient for initiating a full criminal investigation. Furthermore, the preliminary investigation is limited to activities by law enforcement officers and can only be initiated upon the order of the public prosecutor. Authorization by an examining magistrate is required to obtain access to a private databank. Lastly, the preliminary investigation may only be initiated when indications are present, following from facts and circumstances, that within groups of persons serious (Article 67 CCP) crimes are being planned or committed that, considering their nature or their relation to other crimes planned or committed within those groups of people, (will) result in a serious violation of the legal order. The meaning of the 'indications' threshold in relation to the threshold of a reasonable suspicion will be dealt with in Sect. 2.3.2.3.2.3.

As indicated, the legislature intended to separate the preliminary investigation from the criminal investigation by formulating the definition as described and distinguishing the purpose of 'the preparation of the criminal investigation' from the criminal investigation's purpose of 'making prosecutorial decisions.'[387] Nevertheless, when taking into account the just described defining elements for the preliminary investigation according to Article 126gg CCP and comparing those with the current definition of the criminal investigation, the separation, and the reasons for such a separation, from the criminal investigation seem rather artificial. The purpose of preparing the criminal investigation will eventually contribute to the purpose of the criminal investigation, namely making prosecutorial decisions. The information gathered during the preliminary investigation will be used exactly for that purpose. In addition, Article 126gg could rather be seen as the specific legal basis for conducting these proactive criminal investigative activities under the provided conditions. Considering the preliminary criminal investigation to be part of the criminal investigation would also not affect the established public prosecutor's supervision of the investigative activities conducted by law enforcement officers and would avoid doubts as to the applicability of the duty to compile records and other procedural safeguards, such as Article 359a CCP.[388]

[387] *Kamerstukken II* 2004/04, 30 164, no. 3, 17.

[388] Compare Peçi and Sikkema 2008, 361.

Strictly speaking, the duty to compile records currently only applies to the preliminary investigative activities of Articles 126hh and 126ii CCP in the preparation of the full criminal investigation of terrorist crimes and to those preliminary investigative activities that have produced initial information for a criminal investigation as a consequence of Article 126aa CCP. Considering that beforehand it will be uncertain whether it will be required to provide an account of preliminary investigative activities in the context of a criminal trial—because this information has been used as the initial information or has otherwise been introduced in the criminal proceedings—it is difficult to understand why the duty to compile records should not generally also apply to the preliminary investigative activities of Article 126gg CCP.[389] Regardless of these arguments, the legislature has upheld the distinction between the preliminary investigation and the criminal investigation on the basis of the differing investigative purposes when discussing the Act of 2006 to amend Article 132a CCP.[390]

Because of the adopted definition of criminal investigation in this research and the above demonstrated superfluous nature of a distinction under Dutch criminal procedural law from a normative point of view, the term criminal investigation relating to the Dutch situation shall be understood to cover also the preliminary investigation.[391] Therefore, the preliminary investigative phase will further be understood as a proactive investigative power in the criminal investigation on the basis of a threshold (indications) that is different from the threshold which is applicable to SIT.

#### 2.3.2.3 The Suspicion Requirement

The status of a 'suspect' and the requirement of a 'reasonable suspicion' under Article 27 CCP have traditionally obtained, in the Dutch CCP, a central position as the requirement separating criminal investigative activities from other investigative activities and to impose an important restraint on the government's power to investigative for the purpose of gathering evidence for criminal prosecution.

The suspicion of a crime has traditionally functioned as a mandatory requirement for initiating a criminal investigation and in general as the basic assumption legitimizing activities of the government in the field of criminal procedural law.[392] This strict demarcation of the criminal investigative phase on the basis of a reasonable suspicion of a crime can currently no longer be upheld, considering the possibilities for proactive criminal investigation on the basis of the threshold of a reasonable suspicion that crimes are being planned or committed in an organized context and considering the possibility of conducting a preliminary criminal

---

[389] Feuth 2002, 110-112 and Borgers 2009, 50. *Kamerstukken II* 2005/6, 30 164, no. 7, 53.

[390] *Kamerstukken II* 2004/05, 30 164, no. 3, 17.

[391] Compare HR 8 September 2009, *NJ* 2009, 427, Opinion of Advocate General Jörg para 9. The same position has also been taken by Corstens 2008, 260 and Borgers 2009, 50. *Kamerstukken II* 2005/6, 30 164, no. 7, 53.

[392] Sikkema 2008, para 3.1 and Van Sliedregt 2006, 5.

investigation in preparation for a full criminal investigation. In addition, as already explained in the previous section, the suspicion is no longer part of the definition of the criminal investigation: the criminal investigation covers all investigative activities conducted under the responsibility of the public prosecutor for the purpose of making prosecutorial decisions. Nevertheless, the threshold of a reasonable suspicion still fulfills a central role as the triggering mechanism for many criminal procedural powers and, in particular, for the use of special investigative techniques in the context of the criminal investigation.

This section will continue to focus on this shield function of a reasonable suspicion as a triggering mechanism for SIT in the criminal investigation. For this purpose, firstly the definition of a suspect as provided in Article 27(1) CCP will be analyzed (Sect. 2.3.2.3.1). Subsequently, the meaning and variety of different levels of suspicion in different areas of the criminal investigation—mainly, the classical investigation, the organized crime investigation and the preliminary investigation—will be analyzed (Sect. 2.3.2.3.2). Using SIT for the investigation of conventional crime (the classical investigation) can only commence with the establishment of a suspicion of a crime (Sect. 2.3.2.3.2.1). With regard to the use of SIT in criminal investigations of organized crime, a suspicion threshold with a different content applies. Here, the establishment of a reasonable suspicion that crimes (Article 67 CCP crimes) are being planned or committed in an organized context allows the use of investigative powers in the context of the criminal investigation (see Sect. 2.3.2.3.2.2). For initiating a preliminary investigation another threshold must be met: 'indications'. This threshold of 'indications' can be considered as the lowest level of suspicion, which will be addressed, also in its relation to a reasonable suspicion, in Sect. 2.3.2.3.2.3. Furthermore, Sect. 2.3.2.3.2.4 will deal with the indications threshold as is applied to some investigative powers in special criminal law. Lastly, any other forms of suspicion will be dealt with as well as supplementary 'triggering' conditions, such as 'serious concerns', required for e.g. frisking, which is a stronger version of a suspicion, and the requirement of being 'in the interest of the investigation'. The section will conclude by reflecting on the protective function of the suspicion threshold from the perspective of the right to respect for private life, the right to a fair trial and the presumption of innocence (Sect. 2.3.2.3.3).

#### 2.3.2.3.1 The Definition of a Suspect: Article 27 CCP

A definition of the concept of a reasonable suspicion is not provided in the law. However, for the interpretation of the concept, there is a relation with the definition of a suspect as provided in Article 27(1) CCP.[393] According to Article 27(1) CCP a person can, before a prosecution has been initiated, be considered to be a suspect when a reasonable suspicion that he or she is guilty of having committed a

393 The second section of Article 27 CCP provides for the definition of a suspect during the trial phase, which will be left out of consideration.

criminal offense can be derived from the facts or circumstances.[394] The definition of a suspect as provided in Article 27(1) CCP has a legitimizing as well as a protective consequence. Legitimizing, because once someone is labeled as a suspect the government may use—sometimes in combination with other requirements—specific investigative and coercive methods that intrude on the suspect's rights or freedoms (e.g. arrest, pre-trial detention and SIT). The counter-side of this legitimizing consequence is also a restrictive consequence: the government is restricted to only using these specific investigative and coercive methods against suspects. In addition, once someone is a suspect, he or she is attributed some procedural rights, such as the right to remain silent and the right to be informed about the evidence against him or her (during the pre-trial phase only if the interest of the investigation is not obstructed by disclosure).[395] For this reason, a reasonable suspicion is considered to be the equilibrium between, on the one hand, the interest of providing legal protection against arbitrariness in the government's use of its criminal investigative power and, on the other hand, the interest of criminal law enforcement.[396] For the subject-matter of this book, in particular the meaning of a suspicion as the triggering moment for investigative action is relevant.

Considering the definition of a suspect provided in Article 27(1) CCP, the establishment of a reasonable suspicion requires that from an objective point of view one can reasonably be suspected of being guilty of having committed a criminal offense. This objective degree of reasonableness must be based upon facts and circumstances, which concerns objective and concrete information relating to a criminal offense which has been committed.[397] What facts and circumstances are

---

[394] Article 27(1) CCP. The original wording of Article 27(1) CCP is: "*Als verdachte wordt vóórdat de vervolging is aangevangen, aangemerkt degene te wiens aanzien uit feiten of omstandigheden een redelijk vermoeden van schuld aan eenig strafbaar feit voortvloeit.*" The latter part of 'eenig strafbaar feit' (any criminal offense) is translated as having committed a criminal offence, because the relation of this part of the sentence with 'reasonable suspicion of guilt' implies the fulfillment of the provision defining the criminal offence, and, hence, the commission of the criminal offense described in that provision. Compare: Sikkema 2008, para 7.1 and Van Sliedregt 2006, 8.

[395] Article 30 CCP (as amended by the Act on strengthening the position of the examining magistrate, *Kamerstukken I* 2010-2011, 32 177, no. A). Article 31 CCP provides what particular records must be disclosed to the suspect during the pre-trial phase (such as records of his/her interrogation and records of investigative activities that could be attended by the suspect or his/her lawyer). Disclosure may be delayed if it would obstruct the interest of the investigation (Article 30(2) CCP). During the covert criminal investigation disclosure is, obviously, not yet warranted. Suspects in the criminal investigation will normally not be aware of their status as a suspect, until the (*ex post*) notification (Article 126bb(3) CCP) or the disclosure of the evidence gathered against him on the basis of Article 126aa(1) and (4) as soon as the interest of the investigation so allows (which will usually concur with the first interrogation of the suspect).

[396] Compare: Knigge 2005, 353.

[397] The element of 'facts and circumstances' has no further specific legal relevance. It only requires a degree of objectivity, rather than that only certain information can be defined as either a fact or a circumstance or that both a fact or a circumstance are, as a minimum, required. Compare: Sikkema 2008, para 9.

needed to amount to a suspicion that is reasonable is rather vague. The only point of departure provided by the legislature is that the suspicion shall be reasonable not only in the subjective opinion of the law enforcement officer, but for any reasonable person, which requires a degree of objectivity.[398] Hence, the reasonable suspicion should be based on facts and circumstances that are also visible to others.[399] In the case *Murray v. The United Kingdom* (1994), the ECrtHR also provided a definition of reasonable suspicion as the requirement for an arrest, which includes a certain degree of objectivity: "acts or information which would satisfy an objective observer that the person concerned may have committed a criminal offence."[400] 'Reasonableness' attributes a certain margin of appreciation to the investigative officer, the public prosecutor or the examining magistrate assessing the presence of a reasonable suspicion on the basis of the facts and circumstances. Hence, judges exerting *ex post* control will examine whether the officer in question could reasonably reach the conclusion that a suspicion of a crime was present.[401]

Thus, a reasonable suspicion must be supported by facts and circumstances that are open to objectification, such as the observation of criminal behavior, statements of witnesses or clues as to a criminal offense. Case law has provided for clarification with respect to the question of which specific facts and circumstances can establish a reasonable suspicion. An overview will be given.

A judgment of the Court of Appeal of Amsterdam from 1977 (*Hollende kleurling),* concerning the reasonable suspicion under Article 27, held that the fact that a colored person was seen running away from a café which was known to the police as a place where drugs trafficking took place was insufficient for the establishment of a reasonable suspicion that someone was guilty of having committed a criminal offense.[402] Because this decision has been one of the few where the courts have found that the information present was insufficient for the establishment of a reasonable suspicion as required, this decision is still referred to in order to provide guidance as to the nature of the facts and circumstances which are required to meet the threshold of a reasonable suspicion. In another case concerning only a slightly different situation, the facts and circumstances were considered to be sufficient for establishing a reasonable suspicion. In this case, the observation of a car, known to the police to be in the possession of a drugs trader and to be used by persons also known as drugs traders, that drove away from a place which was known as a place where drugs were traded, was sufficient information for establishing a reasonable suspicion.[403]

---

398 See *Kamerstukken II* 1913/14, 286, no. 3, 39.

399 Sikkema 2008, para 8.1.

400 Compare: ECHR 28 October 1994, App. no. 14310/88 (*Murray v. The United Kingdom*), para 51.

401 Van Sliedregt 2006, 7.

402 Gerechtshof Amsterdam 3 June 1977, *NJ* 1978, 601.

403 HR 8 February 2000, *NJ* 2000, 316.

On the basis of these decisions it seems that there should be some sort of factual information that points to the involvement of these specific persons in the suspected crime. In other words: factual information demonstrating a link between the suspected person and the suspected crime. Another example, where such a nexus was lacking and, hence, a reasonable suspicion was unjustly assumed as the basis for requesting a blood test in relation to a suspicion of drunken driving was at issue in a Supreme Court case in 2005. Here, considerably exceeding the speed limit was insufficient information for also establishing a reasonable suspicion of drunken driving.[404] Nevertheless, the Supreme Court has accepted that investigative officers could establish a reasonable suspicion of an offense criminalized in the Drugs Act on the basis of the knowledge of the investigative officers that persons from the west of the Netherlands often transport drugs to the northern part of the Netherlands (Groningen), when observing a car occupied by persons who were from the western part of the Netherlands at a place known for trading in drugs.[405] Here, facts and circumstances linking these persons to the suspected crime seems to be absent and, hence, one may doubt the insufficiency of the facts and circumstances for establishing a reasonable suspicion in the *Hollende kleurling* case in the light of this more recent case law.[406]

More in general, it follows from the case law that the intuition of police officers is insufficient for establishing a reasonable suspicion, while judgments of police officers based on experience may contribute to establishing a reasonable suspicion.[407] Intuition concerns a mere subjective notion, while the experience of police officers concerns knowledge which is open to objectification. Also the knowledge of police officers that the person is a recidivist with regard to bicycle theft has been accepted as contributing to the establishment of a reasonable suspicion.[408]

Furthermore, it has been accepted that anonymous information can trigger a criminal investigation.[409] Also the ECrtHR has accepted anonymous sources as the basis for using criminal procedural powers in the pre-trial phase.[410] Anonymous information, for example provided through the 'Report Crime Anonymously

---

404 HR 6 September 2005, *NJ* 2006, 447.

405 HR 4 April 2000, *NJ* 2000, 735, 3.4 and 3.5.

406 Compare: Van Sliedregt 2006, 16.

407 As also follows from the described cases, the circumstance that the observed behavior occurs at a place 'known as a place where drugs trading takes place', or the knowledge that persons from the western part of the Netherlands transport drugs to the northern provinces, were relevant circumstances for establishing a reasonable suspicion. See, furthermore, HR 14 January 1975, *NJ* 1975, 207, para 4 and HR 20 March 1984, *NJ* 1984, 549, para 2 and Sikkema 2008, para 9.

408 HR 7 November 2006, *NJ* 2007, 108, para 3.2.2 and Opinion Advocate-General para 6.

409 E.g.: HR 18 November 1980, *NJ* 1981, 125, para 6, HR 13 June 2006, *NJ* 2006, 346, para 3.5, HR 22 January 2008, *LJN* BC1375 and HR 11 March 2008, *NJ* 2008, 328, para 3.5. See also: Brinkhof 2008, 1224-1228.

410 ECHR 20 November 1989, *Kostovski v. The Netherlands,* App. no. 11454/85, para 44: "The Convention does not preclude reliance, at the investigation stage of criminal proceedings, on sources such as anonymous informants. However, the subsequent use of anonymous statements as sufficient evidence to found a conviction, as in the present case, is a different matter."

Foundation' [*Stichting Meld Misdaad Anoniem*], can establish a reasonable suspicion without support from other sources if the information is sufficiently concrete and is subjected to an initial check by the police as to its veracity (not of the source but of the factual information provided).[411] Taking into account the case law available where anonymous information is used as the basis for a reasonable suspicion, it seems that such a follow-up check by the police is required before the anonymous information can be used to establish a reasonable suspicion. Nevertheless, it has not been explicitly excluded that also without this verification through further research the anonymous information may still establish a reasonable suspicion.[412] Furthermore, also official reports of the criminal intelligence unit (CIE, see Sect. 2.2.1.1) have been accepted as sufficient for establishing a reasonable suspicion.[413] The police receive these reports from the criminal intelligence unit as anonymous sources.[414] The veracity of the CIE information may, however, be presumed, because, different from anonymous tips received by the police, the information that the CIE communicates to the police has been subjected to procedural guarantees as to the gathering thereof and its transfer, the CIE has already checked the veracity of informants and the identity of the informants is known to the CIE.[415] In addition, a special CIE public prosecutor can randomly control the information collected at the CIE.[416]

It has also been accepted that a suspicion can be based upon information solely originating from the intelligence service AIVD without any supporting information from a police investigation.[417] This has, however, not been accepted when the AIVD has received this information from anonymous sources and other supporting evidence cannot be found, also after a follow-up check by the police.[418] The

[411] HR 13 June 2006, *NJ* 2006, 346, para 3.4 and 3.5, HR 22 January 2008, *LJN* BC1375 and HR 11 March 2008, *NJ* 2008, 328, Opinion of Advocate General Machielse para 3.3 and HR 3.5.

[412] See also: Annotation Borgers, HR 11 March 2008, *NJ* 2008, 329, ann. Borgers, para 4 and Sikkema, 2008, para 11.1.

[413] HR 14 September 1992, *NJ* 1993, 83, para 5.3, HR 25 September 2001, *NJ* 2002, 97, para 3.5, HR 22 December 2009, *LJN* BJ8622, para 2.4 See also HR 12 May 2009, *LJN* BH: 5249, para 9, referring to a guideline of the PPS, where it has been indicated that CIE information can be used, when it is sufficiently concrete, to establish a reasonable suspicion. However, the reports cannot be used as evidence because the information concerns intelligence, which still needs to be checked (e.g. in the context of a criminal investigation aimed at clarifying a reasonable suspicion). Nevertheless, the Head of the regional CIE unit can be heard as a witness regarding information obtained by the CIE from secret informants and his testimony may then be used as evidence. See e.g. HR 5 October 1982, *NJ* 1983, 297 and HR 2 March 1982, *NJ* 1982, 460. See on the use of CIE information as starting information also in detail Brinkhoff 2009, 117-122.

[414] See e.g. HR 14 September 1992, *NJ* 1993, 83, para 5.3.

[415] Sikkema 2008, para 11.2.

[416] The control exerted by the CIE public prosecutor may *de facto* be rather limited, considering that control over specific CIE reports used as starting information for criminal investigations is not exerted. Brinkhoff, 2009, 114-116.

[417] HR 5 September 2006, *NJ* 2007, 336, para 6.2 and para 6.3.2.

[418] HR 11 March 2008, *NJ* 2008, 329, para 3.4.

Supreme Court has ruled that it is acceptable to use AIVD information for establishing a suspicion when, firstly, it does not appear that the information is used with the intention to set aside criminal procedural powers in order to circumvent criminal procedural guarantees and, secondly, when the activities of the intelligence agency have not violated the fundamental rights of the suspect in a way that is contrary to the right to a fair trial.[419] As explained in Sect. 2.2.2.4.2, the AIVD can send an official report to the PPS, which can thus subsequently trigger a criminal investigation. In Chap. 3, the manner in which the courts have dealt with intelligence information, both as triggering information for criminal investigation and in criminal proceedings in general, will be dealt with in more detail, as it concerns one of the implications of an increased focus on prevention during investigative activities and, hence, an aspect of anticipative criminal investigation.[420]

It can be concluded that the interpretation given to a 'reasonable suspicion of a crime' under Article 27(1) CCP is rather broad. 'Soft' information, such as anonymous tips, CIE reports or AIVD information has been considered as sufficient facts and circumstances open to objectification to establish a reasonable suspicion that someone is guilty of having committed a crime.

#### 2.3.2.3.2 Different Degrees of Suspicion

The previous section has provided an analysis of the threshold of the definition of a suspect under Article 27(1) CCP and the facts and circumstances that have been accepted in the case law as being sufficient for establishing a reasonable suspicion. This specific analysis of the definition of a suspect under Article 27(1) CCP has been made because the concept of a suspect has traditionally been the starting point of activities by the government in the field of criminal procedural law and still fulfills a central role as the threshold for using investigative methods that interfere with privacy. Nevertheless, the definition of a suspect and the related threshold of a 'suspicion of a crime', triggering the use of SIT, is currently no longer exclusively the triggering mechanism for the use of criminal procedural powers that interfere more than only to a limited degree with the right to privacy. Within the criminal investigation different domains can be distinguished, in which a different level of suspicion is used to trigger the use of SIT. Most important in this regard is the distinction between the investigative domain of classical investigation (Title IVa) and the investigative domain of organized crime (Title V). For the use of SIT under Title IVa a reasonable suspicion of a crime is required, which is related to the definition of the suspect provided in Article 27(1) CCP. Under Title V a lower version of suspicion, different from the interpretation of reasonable suspicion on the basis of Article 27(1) CCP, is the triggering mechanism for using

[419] HR 5 September 2006, *NJ* 2007, 336, para 4.7.2.

[420] See Chap. 3, Sects. 3.3.1 and 3.3.3.

SIT. In the preliminary investigation (Title Ve) a threshold that requires information amounting to 'indications' instead of a reasonable suspicion is applied. An analysis of the relationship between these levels of suspicion and the threshold of a reasonable suspicion under Article 27(1) CCP will be made. In addition, within the different domains, sometimes either supplementary conditions or less demanding conditions are required for specific techniques, including stronger and milder versions of suspicion, such as 'serious concerns' for frisking and indications of being 'in the interest of the investigation' in some special criminal statutes. Also these and any other applied degrees of suspicion will be dealt with as to their relation to the 'reasonable suspicion' of Article 27(1) CCP.

#### *2.3.2.3.2.1 Title IVA: The Classical Investigation*

Under Title IV special investigative techniques can be used when a reasonable suspicion that a crime has been committed can be established (sometimes supplemented by other conditions). The threshold of suspicion in classical investigations is satisfied when three requirements are met: (i) there is a reasonable suspicion that a criminal offense has been committed; (ii) there is a reasonable suspicion of the guilt of the person involved—whoever that may be—with respect to the committed offense and (iii) the reasonable suspicion should be based on the facts and circumstances.[421] The consequence of the connection between the reasonable suspicion and the crime, rather than between the reasonable suspicion and the suspect (as in the definition of Article 27(1) CCP as well as in the provisions for some investigative powers that can only be applied against the suspect, such as arrest), is that the use of SIT in the classical criminal investigation is not limited to the person of the suspect only but can concern several persons who can be related to that reasonable suspicion of a crime and the use of SIT against these persons is 'in the interest of the investigation'.[422] This view is supported by the explicit determination in the regulations of the specific special investigative techniques that they can be applied against 'a person' (and not against 'the suspect'). In addition, it is only prescribed that a description of the suspect is provided, which does not necessarily include his or her personal details. After all, the use of SIT will usually be aimed at finding the suspect.

The previous section has already dealt with the facts and circumstances that are sufficient for establishing a reasonable suspicion. For initiating a classical investigation under Title IVa it is primarily relevant to note that rather soft information can establish a reasonable suspicion. An anonymous tip, CIE reports or an official report by the AIVD can trigger the use of SIT under Title IVa.

---

[421] Compare Corstens 2008, 88.

[422] See also Supplement to 'Handboek voor de opsporingspraktijk' (2004), *Stcrt* 10 December 2007, no. 239/p. 11, 2.

#### 2.3.2.3.2.2 *Title V: The Organized Crime Investigation*

The complexity of the organizational context and the seriousness of the crimes committed have justified the adoption of a different threshold of application for organized crime investigations and, consequently, a separate investigative domain for organized crime under Title V. Although the use of the wording 'reasonable suspicion' may suggest otherwise, it should not be interpreted as referring to the definition of a suspect provided in Article 27(1) CCP.[423] The difference between the threshold applicable under Title IVa and Title V concerns the object of the reasonable suspicion. Under Title V the reasonable suspicion shall not concern a committed crime, but the planning or commission of serious (Article 67 CCP) crimes in an organized context, which considering their nature or relation with other crimes committed in that organized context result in a serious infringement of the legal order. Hence, also under Title V the required reasonable suspicion shall be open to objectification and the level of information required to establish a 'reasonable suspicion' does not differ,[424] but the object of the suspicion is broader: not a specific committed crime, but a criminal organization committing or planning to commit multiple but not necessarily specifically identified crimes. The object of the reasonable suspicion of Title V includes different elements: an organizational context; serious (Article 67 CCP) crimes that are being planned or committed; and a serious infringement of the legal order. Whilst the formulation of the reasonable suspicion requirement for organized crime investigation is considerably broader than the 'ordinary' suspicion threshold, these elements as well as the requirement of facts and circumstances establishing a 'reasonable suspicion' do have a restrictive function. The different elements of the threshold for applying SIT under Title V will be analyzed separately and, subsequently, the relation between the investigative domain of Title V and that of Title IVa will be addressed.

The Parliamentary Inquiry Commission has for the first time tried to define the concept of organized crime. According to their definition, organized crime exists when groups of people: (a) primarily aim at gaining unlawful profit; (b) systematically commit crimes with serious consequences for society; and (c) have the ability to mask these crimes in a relatively effective manner, particularly by being prepared to use physical violence or by eliminating people through corruption.[425] In practice, this definition of organized crime as formulated by the Parliamentary Inquiry Commission is not used. The Supreme Court considered the existence of an organized context to be sufficiently proven by a concurrence of different factors, such as the commission of several criminal offenses during a certain period, cooperation with and the involvement of other people, criminal activities ordered by other people or close cooperation between several people in, for example, the

---

423 *Kamerstukken II* 1996/1997, 25 403, no. 3, 23.

424 See HR 23 October 2007, *LJN* BB3067 (Opinion of the Advocate General).

425 *Kamerstukken II* 1995/96, 24 072, nos. 10-11, 25 and *Kamerstukken II* 1996/97, 25 403, no. 3, 4. HR 7 November 2000, *LJN* AA8207 and HR 7 October 2003, *NJ* 2004, 118, para 34.

drugs trade.[426] The 'guide for criminal investigative practice' provides that the specific characteristics of an organized context are cooperation between two or more persons, one or more collective objective(s) and a certain level of continuity.[427] The seriousness of the crimes involved and the expectation that several people are involved are in practice factors which are sufficient to assume an organized context for the purpose of deciding on using SIT.[428] This means that the element of an 'organizational context' in the reasonable suspicion threshold of the investigative domain of Title V is considerably less strict than that which is required for demonstrating a reasonable suspicion of the crime of membership of a criminal organization (Article 140 Penal Code). For the latter, facts and circumstances are required concerning some evidence of participation in that criminal organization, concerning the objective of committing crimes and concerning a more structured and endurable form of cooperation.[429] Demonstrating a reasonable suspicion of the organizational context shall therefore not be seen as a very difficult hurdle.[430]

The second element of serious crimes (under Article 67 CCP) that are being planned or committed enables the proactive application of SIT under Title V. This element requires, firstly, a multitude of crimes and, secondly, crimes for which pre-trial detention can be imposed. The possibility of using SIT under Title V for only the investigation of serious crimes implies that the legislature has only considered the proactive use of SIT which are proportionate to the investigation of serious crimes. A similar limitation is imposed on the use of SIT under Title IVa, when the SIT have a more intrusive character, such as infiltration under Article 126h CCP or wire-tapping under Article 126l CCP. When focusing on organized crime, it will also be a rather simple matter to demonstrate a relation with serious and multiple crimes. Furthermore, the element refers, instead of to committed crimes, to crimes that are *being* committed and to the planning of crimes. The standard differs from the Article 27(1) CCP standard employed under Title IVa, because the reasonable suspicion may concern unspecified crimes.[431] Nevertheless, the organized crime investigation under Title V is not *per se* proactive. The investigation will usually be carried out in relation to crimes which have already been committed. Also, requiring a reasonable suspicion that crimes are being committed implies that there must usually be some commencement of committing the crimes. Moreover, the planning of crimes in an organized context will almost always involve a reasonable suspicion that people are participating in a criminal

---

426 HR 7 November 2000, *LJN* AA8207 and HR 7 October 2003, *NJ* 2004, 118, para 34.

427 Supplement to 'Handboek voor de opsporingspraktijk' (2004), *Stcrt* 10 December 2007, no. 239/p. 11, 2.

428 Beijer et al. 2004, 114.

429 'Aanwijzing opsporingsbevoegdheden' 24 February 2011, *Stcrt* 2011, 3240, 2 and Krommendijk et al. 2009, 115.

430 Krommendijk et al. 2009, 115.

431 Corstens 2005, 259-260.

organization and sometimes a reasonable suspicion as to the criminal preparation.[432] However, the investigation is not limited to clarifying a reasonable suspicion of someone's involvement in a criminal organization and will extend to the planning and commission of crimes in that criminal organization.[433] Moreover, the concept of 'planning' is much broader than criminalized acts that concern the planning of (full) crimes, for which reason the scope of the Title V investigation may be much broader than Title IVa investigations into acts of preparation, conspiracy or membership of a criminal organization. The 'planning' in the threshold which is applicable under Title V does not need to concern a criminal act itself and may concern any activity preceding a criminal offense, such as consultation or the making of plans.[434]

Lastly, the element of 'resulting in a serious infringement of the legal order' applies as an additional requirement for the use of SIT under Title V. The requirement of 'resulting in a serious infringement of the legal order' can also be found in the provisions for some of the SIT under Title IVa. Just as under Title V, this additional requirement has been adopted to subject the use of the more intrusive SIT to an additional test as to the proportionality of the use of SIT: the use of a specific SIT is only proportionate for the investigation of crimes that result in a serious infringement of the legal order. The facts and circumstances of a specific case will demonstrate whether the element of a 'serious infringement of the legal order' has been met. The nature of the crime itself may seriously infringe the legal order, such as murder. But also crimes with a violent character, the multitude of crimes committed, the consequences of the crimes for society and the combination of less serious offenses with other offenses are relevant circumstances in order to determine a serious infringement of the legal order.[435] The Supreme Court has considered the requirement of a 'serious infringement of the legal order' in the context of a SIT under Title IVa to have been met, for example, when the suspected theft or misappropriation of a cell phone from a fire engine within a closed fire station had been committed by personnel of the fire department, as a consequence of which, also because of the possible serious consequences of this offense, the material and personnel reliability and the integrity of the fire department were at stake.[436] Furthermore, the selling of stolen ink cartridges concerned a serious infringement of the legal order because of the amount of stolen goods (200,000 cartridges) and the commensurate serious financial consequences for the aggrieved company.[437] In contrast, however, the case where someone had been caught at Schiphol Airport with 2.2 kg of cocaine—a first

[432] Knigge and Kwakman 2001, 131.

[433] Bokhorst et al. 2002, 53.

[434] Krommendijk et al. 2009, 21 and Supplement to 'Handboek voor de opsporingspraktijk' (2004), *Stcrt.* 10 December 2007, no. 239/p. 11, 2.

[435] *Kamerstukken II* 1996/97, 25 403, no. 3, 24-25.

[436] HR 21 November 2006, *NJ* 2007, 233, para 3.5. See also: Blom 2007, 626 ff.

[437] HR 30 March 2010, *NJ* 2010, 201.

offender—did not constitute a serious infringement of the legal order.[438] Hence, it follows that crimes that do not have a serious character in themselves may in the context of other facts and circumstances result in a serious infringement of the legal order.

With regard to the persons who can be subjected to SIT in the context of a criminal investigation into organized crime under Title V the reasonable suspicion must demonstrate the involvement of these persons in committing or planning serious crimes in an organized context. According to the legislature, this 'involvement' requires more than a coincidental involvement in the criminal activities of the group, which may be proven on the basis of facts and circumstances demonstrating more than incidental contacts with the criminal organization or its members. This does not necessarily require that someone is consciously involved in the group.[439]

In practice the standard of application of 'a reasonable suspicion that crimes are being planned or committed in an organized context' is used in situations where an organized context is assumed, but there is insufficient information as to the role of different people involved with regard to which crimes. As soon as more information is available and a reasonable suspicion can be established, there is usually a switch to an investigation under Title IVa.[440] In other situations, it starts with a classical investigation under Title IVa and, when the information collected in this investigation points to the presence of a larger organizational context, there is then a switch to an investigation under Title V with a broader investigative focus.[441] There are also criminal investigations that retain their broad focus under Title V in order to continue to investigate the organization as a whole.[442]

Nevertheless, on the basis of research into the situations where Title IVa or Title V is used, a clear dividing line between the investigative domains cannot be identified. The purpose of the investigation, either being focused on one or more concrete suspects or being focused on getting a better picture of a criminal organization and its activities as a whole, seems to be the main difference between the investigative domains. Also according to the legislature, deciding whether an order to use SIT shall be based upon the provisions under Title IVa or under Title

---

[438] HR 16 November 2004, *NJ* 2005, 171. See, furthermore, HR 22 March 2011, *NJ* 2011, 144, para 2.3.1, 2.3.2 and 2.5 where the Supreme Court considered that serial poaching, in an organized context, amounted to a serious infringement of the legal order. The Court of Appeal of Amsterdam rejected that fact that the offense of social security fraud (without other facts and circumstances) was a serious infringement of the legal order (Gerechtshof Amsterdam 24 June 2004, *NJ* 2004, 531) and, likewise, the District Court did not accept that breaking and entering was a serious infringement of the legal order (Rechtbank 's-Gravenhage 15 January 2004, *NJ* 2004, 276).

[439] *Kamerstukken II* 1996/97, 25 403, no. 3, 23.

[440] Beijer et al. 2004, 111 and Krommendijk et al. 2009, 46-47.

[441] Krommendijk et al. 2009, 41-44.

[442] Krommendijk et al. 2009, 44-46.

V depends on the purpose of the investigation.[443] This was also affirmed by the Court of Appeal of The Hague in the terrorism case of *Piranha*, noting that the investigative domains of Title IVa and Title V do not necessarily differ as to the investigative phase, but do differ on the basis of the purpose of the investigation.[444] Nevertheless, in another case addressing the question whether the reasonable suspicion as applicable under Title V had been met, the facts and circumstances used to establish the reasonable suspicion did not include a specific 'broader' investigative goal and could likewise be used to meet the threshold for using SIT under Title IVa.[445]

It must also be noted that it has followed from empirical research covering the period 2004–2006 that the investigative domain of Title V is rarely used and that the investigation of organized crime usually occurs under Title IVa upon the establishment of a reasonable suspicion of a crime.[446] This is possible because usually a reasonable suspicion of one or more specific crimes can also be established and the then initiated classical investigation allows, simultaneously, for obtaining more information with regard to the organizational context in which the suspects operate. In addition, most public prosecutors consider the use of SIT under Title V to be only warranted when the requirements of Title IVa cannot be met.[447] For this choice also capacity and efficiency reasons may be relevant, because the criminal investigation upon a reasonable suspicion of a crime has a greater possibility of being successful in the short term.[448] It seems that for the decision whether to choose for the classical investigative domain or the investigative domain for organized crime, the presence of a reasonable suspicion of a crime is more determative than the specific investigative purpose.[449]

#### *2.3.2.3.2.3 Title Ve: The Preliminary Investigation*

The preliminary investigation is the (limited) investigation preceding a (full) criminal investigation in order to prepare for a full criminal investigation to be initiated when the threshold of 'indications that among groups of people crimes are being planned or committed which must be of a serious nature (Article 67(1) CCP crimes; crimes for which pre-trial detention can be imposed), and, due to their nature or connection with other crimes, result in a serious infringement of the legal order' has been fulfilled. The indications do not thus refer to a specific crime, but to groups of people, which can be related to the planning or commission of serious

---

443 *Kamerstukken II* 1996/97, 25 403, no. 3, 23-24.

444 Gerechtshof's-Gravenhage 2 October 2008, *LJN* BF3987.

445 See the Opinion of the Advocate General referring to the argumentation of the Court of Appeal of Den Bosch, para 4, HR 23 October 2007, *LJN* BB3067.

446 Krommendijk et al. 2009, 38-39.

447 *Ibid.*, 53.

448 *Ibid.*, 84-86 and 97.

449 *Ibid.*, 71.

crime(s). Therefore, the preliminary investigation will be used to investigate groups of people about whom indications exist that crimes are being planned or committed within that group. Considering that the indications concern the planning or commission of crimes, the investigation can be proactive, similar to organized crime investigations. Moreover, the use of the wording ‘groups of people’ also implies a slightly less restrictive threshold than the term ‘organized context’ in the threshold for using SIT in organized crime investigations.

Facts or circumstances establishing ‘indications’ can, according to the explanatory memorandum of the Act on SIT of 1999, follow from information regarding crimes committed in a certain sector in combination with information on future criminal activities. Examples mentioned are information concerning the commission or planning of crimes within a certain group where legal and illegal activities are interwoven or the laundering of money obtained by the drugs trade in the real-estate sector.[450] Instead of focusing on a specific person (Title IVa) or on persons involved in an organizational context (Title V), the focus of the preliminary investigation will be less defined by investigating a larger and ‘looser’ group of persons.[451] The purpose of the investigation concerns ‘preparing the criminal investigation’ by determining on what aspects the criminal investigation shall focus. This is done by investigating a large collection of persons who are not necessarily suspected or otherwise related to criminal activities through comparing and collecting information from police files and open files, because there are indications that a certain type of criminal activity is more present than average within that ‘collection’ of persons (or a branch or sector of society).[452]

It follows from the case law that crime analyses shall not be considered as a ‘preliminary investigation’. Preliminary investigative activities require a specific legal basis as provided in Article 126gg CCP, because the collecting and analyzing of personal information may concern persons who are not suspected of a crime or ‘involved’ in criminal activities as such. Crime analyses concern a simpler form of analysis without systematically comparing and collecting information. The crime analysis will be conducted to determine whether indications are present by making an inventory of police files.[453] No case law is available in which the threshold of ‘indications’ and the relation of ‘indications’ to a ‘reasonable suspicion’ is further defined. It only follows that, for example, information from previous criminal investigations may be the reason for initiating preliminary investigations into certain groups of people in order to prepare new full criminal investigations.[454] Sometimes also the presence of a reasonable suspicion has been the reason for opening a preliminary investigation.[455] The threshold of ‘indications’ has been

[450] *Kamerstukken II* 1996/97, 24 403, no. 3, 49-50.

[451] *Kamerstukken II* 1996/97, 24 403, no. 3, 23.

[452] *Kamerstukken II* 1996/97, 24 403, no. 3, 23 and 57.

[453] HR 8 September 2009, *NJ* 2009, 427 and HR 8 April 2003, *NJ* 2003, 420.

[454] Gerechtshof ‘s-Gravenhage 31 May 2002, *LJN* AE3708.

[455] Rechtbank ‘s-Gravenhage 21 November 2000, *LJN* AA 8414.

interpreted more precisely in the case law concerning special criminal law, which will be dealt with in the subsequent section.

Nevertheless, taking into account the purpose and the scope of the threshold which is applicable to the preliminary investigative domain, it is clear that this threshold has a significant wider reach. Personal information relating to persons not suspected of committing a crime or of being 'involved' in an organizational context may be collected from police files or open sources and compared. Furthermore, although also indications shall follow from facts and circumstances, it is clear that the legislature intends to establish a 'lower' threshold than a reasonable suspicion. From the explanatory memorandum it follows that these indications shall point to the presence of criminal activities 'more than on average' in a certain sector or branch of society and, considering the applicable threshold, these indications shall point to serious crimes.

#### *2.3.2.3.2.4 The Threshold of Indications in Special Criminal Acts*

In some of the special criminal Acts the threshold of indications suffices for the use of search powers. The Economic Offenses Act (WED) permits investigative officers that have the authority to investigate economic offenses to apply investigative powers—such as seizure, entering any place and investigating objects and vehicles—if these powers are in the interest of the investigation and the use thereof is reasonably required for the fulfillment of their investigative task (Articles 18-23 WED). In the case law 'the interest of the investigation' has been explained as requiring indications that an economic offense (as enumerated in Article 1 and 1a of the Act) has been committed. Furthermore, the Weapons and Ammunition Act (WWM) allows investigative officers to apply investigative powers such as searching vehicles and luggage when there is 'reasonably cause to do so upon indications that a crime will be committed with the help of weapons or upon indications that someone will be in the possession of a weapon of a specific category' (Articles 50-52 WWM). Further guidance can be derived from the case law with regard to the interpretation of the threshold of 'indications' and the relation of this threshold applied for the criminal investigation of offenses criminalized in special criminal law to the reasonable suspicion threshold as applied in classical criminal investigations.

In a case concerning the power to search vehicles under Article 23 WED the Supreme Court upheld the judgment of the Court of Appeal that the criminal investigation of offenses criminalized in the WED cannot remain limited to a concrete suspicion. The interest of the criminal investigation justifies the use of the power to search when there are indications that an economic offense has been committed. According to the Court of Appeal, the language used in Article 23 WED cannot be explained as requiring a reasonable suspicion under Article 27 CCP.[456] The Supreme Court referred in its judgment to the explanatory

[456] HR 9 March 1993, *NJ* 1993, 633, para 7-9.

memorandum of the WED in which it was explicitly explained that the criminal investigation of offenses criminalized in the WED could not be restricted to situations in which a reasonable suspicion can be established. If there are indications that an economic offense has been committed, the interest of the investigation justifies the use of investigative powers to clarify these indications and to investigate whether an economic offence has in fact been committed.[457] Hence, 'indications' seem to provide for a lower standard than a 'reasonable suspicion.'

Furthermore, a case heard by the District Court of Amsterdam in 2007 demonstrated that the single observation of investigative officers that someone had been fishing did not establish indications that an economic offense had been committed. The Court added that the fact that the investigative officers knew that the person in question had violated fishing regulations in the past did not affect this decision.[458]

Although the investigative powers on the basis of the Hunting Act are currently no longer in force—the criminal investigation of the offenses criminalized by this Act (currently by the Flora and Fauna Act) is now covered by the Economic Offenses Act—court decisions assessing an investigation conducted on the basis of this Act may still teach us something about the interpretation of 'indications'. Two cases concerning the investigation under this Act addressed the possible wider scope of the investigation, in the absence of a reasonable suspicion under Article 27(1) CCP. In the first place, the Advocate General concluded with regard to a Supreme Court case from 1997 that searching vehicles under the Hunting Act does not require the establishment of a reasonable suspicion. According to the Supreme Court the vehicle can be searched on the basis of information that it concerns a vehicle in which possibly objects are transported that violate the Act. The Advocate General explained the power to search in the same way as the explanation in the case law concerning Article 23 WED: upon the establishment of indications of a violation of the Act the vehicle can be searched. He continued by stating that acting in the interest of the investigation supposes that there is some cause for the investigation and that 'indications' are the bottom-line for such a cause. Furthermore, the indications do not need to establish a reasonable suspicion. In this specific case, the power to search could otherwise also be based upon Article 51(3) WWM, requiring indications that a criminal offense would be committed with the help of a weapon criminalized by the Weapons and Ammunition Act.[459] Secondly, a case from 1984 illustrates that the power to search vehicles on the basis of the Hunting Act does not require that the owner of the vehicle is a suspect under Article 27 CCP. According to the Supreme Court, the legislature has aimed to create the possibility to search vehicles in which possibly objects have been transported that violate the Hunting Act, without the driver being a suspect. Investigative officers are authorized to use the power to search in order to control the observance of the Hunting Act for the purpose of tracing

457 Bijl. *Handelingen II,* 1968/69, 9608, no. 5, 2 and HR 9 March 1993, *NJ* 1993, 633, para 5.2.

458 Rechtbank Amsterdam 29 June 2007, *LJN* BA9602 en *LJN* BA9586, para 3.1.

459 HR 27 May 1997, *NJ* 1997, 550, Opinion of Advocate General Fokkens, para 11-13.

criminal offenses.[460] The use of criminal investigative powers 'in the interest of the investigation' thus allows the application of criminal investigative powers without information providing for a nexus with a specific criminal offense.[461]

Furthermore, case law concerning search powers under the Weapons and Ammunition Act provides for some further guidance as to the interpretation of the threshold used under that Act. In a case in 2008 on appeal from the Joint Court of Justice of the Netherlands Antilles and Aruba the Advocate General pointed out in his opinion concerning the firearms legislation of the Netherlands Antilles that the power to frisk upon indications that a crime penalized in the Act would be committed under the law of the Netherlands Antilles differed from the powers under the Dutch WWM Article 52. In Dutch law frisking could also be conducted when there are indications, a threshold which is met when there is information that someone is in possession of a firearm.[462] A Supreme Court case in 2010 has further defined the use of indications under the WWM by determining that the threshold of indications for searching a vehicle (Article 51 WWM) is met when there is a specific identifiable reason to assume that the WWM has been violated or will be violated. It is not required that there is also a specific person that can be identified as a suspect.[463] In another case concerning the use of search powers on the basis of firearms and drugs regulations of the Netherlands Antilles, the Advocate General determined in comparison with the Dutch search powers under the WWM that, in his opinion, the difference between a reasonable suspicion and indications regarding the use of search powers is very subtle and that indications would in any case not require that the person being searched is a suspect.[464]

Taking into account this interpretation of 'indications' in the case law regarding investigative powers under special criminal law and comparing that to the interpretation given to the definition of a suspect under Article 27(1) CCP, it can be concluded that 'indications' (or 'in the interest of the investigation') is intended as a 'lower' standard allowing the use of powers that under the CCP can only be applied against a suspect when there is information available which contains indications that a crime, as criminalized under the WED or WWM, has been or will be committed in the future. Any difference as to the level of proof that can be derived from the facts and circumstances establishing indications or a reasonable suspicion is difficult to identify taking into account the information that may establish a reasonable suspicion of a crime (see Sect. 2.3.2.3.1) and the case law analyzed in this section. It seems that the only conclusion warranted is that

---

[460] HR 30 October 1984, *NJ* 1985, 275, para 6.4.

[461] This goal of controlling the observance of a Special Act should not be confused with the 'administrative supervision' as part of policing tasks.

[462] This would be insufficient under the firearms legislation of the Netherlands Antilles, where indications must also be present that the firearm will in fact be used. HR 10 June 2008, *NJ* 2008, 348, Opinion of Advocate General Vellinga, para 10 and see also: *Kamerstukken II*, 1999-2000, 26 865, no. 5, 7-8.

[463] HR 23 March 2010, *NJ* 2010, 197.

[464] HR 17 October 2006, *NJ* 2007, 80, Opinion of Advocate General Wortel, para 19.

searching or frisking powers under the WED and WWM can be applied against persons who are not suspects (but when there are indications that the special criminal act has been violated), whereas searching and frisking as regulated in the CCP are limited to suspects as well as being subjected to other restrictive conditions (e.g. Articles 55a, 55b(2), 56 and 96b CCP).[465] Nevertheless, the reasonable suspicion threshold used under Title IVa allows the use of SIT against persons who are not suspected of a crime.

#### *2.3.2.3.2.5 Other Degrees of Suspicion and Supplementary Conditions*

It follows from the regulation of SIT, other investigative methods and the preliminary investigation that investigative powers that result in a more severe infringement of the right to respect for private life are subjected to more stringent conditions as to their application. As a general rule all SIT are subjected to the requirement that the SIT is used 'in the interest of the investigation'. For some techniques, such as wire-tapping (Articles 126m and 126t CCP) and infiltration (Articles 126h and 126p CCP), there must be a 'pressing' investigative need for using the SIT in the interest of the investigation. This requirement implies an assessment as to whether the use of the SIT is also, in the context of the specific circumstances of the criminal investigation in question, in accordance with the principles of proportionality and subsidiarity.

For the SIT that result in the least serious interference with the right to respect for private life, such as systematic observation (Articles 126g and 126o CCP), meeting the threshold of a reasonable suspicion of either a crime (under Title IVa) or that crimes are being planned or committed in an organized context (under Title V) and using the SIT in the interest of the criminal investigative purpose is sufficient for applying the technique. For some of the more intrusive techniques additional requirements also apply. For example, for entering places under Title IVa, the reasonable suspicion shall concern a serious, Article 67 crime (Article 126k CCP). For the most intrusive SIT, which are wire-tapping and infiltration (Articles 126m CCP and 126h CCP), the suspected crime shall also result in a serious infringement of the legal order, because of its nature or its relation with other crimes. As explained in Sect. 2.3.2.3.2.2, the conditions of serious (article 67 CCP) crimes and a 'serious infringement of the legal order' apply to all SIT regulated under Title V in order to impose an additional restriction on the more intrusive nature of the proactive use of SIT, which is possible under Title Vb considering that the reasonable suspicion may concern the 'planning or commission of crimes'.

Furthermore, outside the context of the use of SIT in the investigative domains of Title IVa and Title V, also some other investigative methods have been specifically regulated in the CCP or in special criminal law. Other investigative and

---

[465] With the exception of searching and frisking powers introduced by the Criminal Investigation of Terrorist Crimes Act (2006). These powers will be dealt with in the next chapter.

coercive methods specifically regulated in the CCP are, for example, arrest (Articles 53 and 54 CCP), frisking and strip searching (Article 56(1) CCP), a body cavity search (Article 56(2) CCP) and pre-trial detention (Articles 57-58, 63-67a CCP). For the methods that seriously intrude onto the rights and liberties of the person involved, a stronger version of a reasonable suspicion is required. For example, the powers to frisk, strip search, to conduct body cavity search and pre-trial detention can only be used upon the establishment of 'serious concerns' [*ernstige bezwaren*].

#### 2.3.2.3.3 The Protective Function of the Suspicion Threshold

The threshold of suspicion, in its different degrees, but primarily as defined in Article 27(1) CCP, has obtained its central position in the regulation of criminal procedural powers to reflect respect for the right to privacy and for the presumption of innocence. The threshold of a reasonable suspicion has been adopted in order to protect against arbitrary interferences with the right to private life and, hence, to prevent unnecessary interferences with private life and to protect the innocent against any interference.

Restrictions to the right to respect for private life under Article 8 ECHR may only be made when they are 'in accordance with the law' and 'necessary in a democratic society'. The specific regulation of the various investigative domains in the CCP providing for the conditions under which SIT may be applied reflects this requirement of providing for restrictions only 'in accordance with the law.' As has been explained in Sect. 2.3.2.1.1, 'in accordance with the law' requires a law of a certain quality in the sense that it is accessible to and foreseeable for the person concerned. Subjecting the use of SIT to a certain threshold reflecting a degree of suspicion is intended to make it foreseeable when the government may use SIT which interferes with the private life of the person concerned. Once there is a case of involvement in criminal activities, one can foresee that the government may start a criminal investigation into these activities, an investigation which may include the use of SIT which interfere with the right to respect for private life. Furthermore, subjecting the use of SIT to a specific threshold reflecting a degree of suspicion in relation to criminal activities limits the use of criminal investigative powers to establishing the truth with regard to those criminal activities. Governmental action in the field of criminal procedural law has been considered necessary in a democratic society. Hence the reasonable suspicion requirement, limiting interference with the right to respect for private life to the purpose of the criminal law enforcement, also meets the requirement of being 'necessary in a democratic society.'

The presumption of innocence, as described in the introductory section (Sect. 2.1.3.3.1), protects against arbitrary interferences by the government in general; it protects the innocent from interferences with their rights and liberties. In the Netherlands this principle is traditionally guaranteed during the criminal investigation by requiring a reasonable suspicion before the use of SIT with far-reaching consequences for the rights and liberties of the persons investigated is permitted. The threshold of a reasonable suspicion as the central threshold for using investigative or coercive methods against someone was already introduced during the drafting process of the current CCP that entered into force in 1926. The explanatory memorandum of 1914 formulated as the goal of the criminal justice system to pursue the conviction of those guilty of having committed a criminal offense and to avoid subjecting the innocent to conviction and prosecution. From the latter, it can be derived that within the administration of criminal justice it must also be avoided that the innocent are subjected to investigative powers unnecessarily.[466] A balance must be struck between the interest of the investigation in the specific circumstances and the risk that innocent persons are subjected to investigative powers. This is deemed to be guaranteed by establishing the threshold of a reasonable suspicion. The explanatory memorandum of 1914 acknowledged that the state of a reasonable suspicion would create awareness among people that also the suspect, who is brought to trial, is only under a suspicion as to his guilt. The explanatory memorandum further explains that using far-reaching investigative powers against someone such as arrest, strip searches, or pre-trial detention is only possible against a person relating to whom such a reasonable suspicion can be established.[467]

The threshold of a suspicion thus fulfills an important restrictive and protective function of the use of criminal procedural powers. The specific degree required for the use of specific investigative techniques is, therefore, explicitly related to the level of intrusion on privacy caused by using the technique and the commensurate level of protection against involving the innocent in the investigation. Also the ECrtHR has related the level of protection to be offered by the regulation to the level of the intrusion. With regard to wire-tapping, the ECrtHR decided in *Kruslin/ Huvig v. France* that the serious intrusion on the right to respect for private life caused by wire-tapping without permission is in principle acceptable considering the interest of the investigation, but must then be surrounded by sufficient safeguards to counterbalance the interference with private life.[468] This would require a legal basis for the investigative method that is "particularly precise", a requirement not met by the French law in question.[469] In the Dutch regulation of investigative methods the relation between the suspicion and the level of intrusion follows, for example, from allowing preliminary investigative activities on the basis of indications, from the requirement that the reasonable suspicion shall concern serious (Article 67 CCP) crimes and from requiring 'serious concerns' for, inter alia, frisking and pre-trial detention.

---

466 Rozemond 1998, 359.

467 Vaststelling van een Wetboek van Strafvordering, Memorie van toelichting [Explanatory Memorandum for Establishing a Code of Criminal Procedure 1912-1913], in: Lindenberg 2002, 436.

468 ECHR 24 April 1990, App. no. 11801/85 and App. no. 11105/84 (*Kruslin v. France and Huvig v. France*), para 33/32.

469 ECHR 24 April 1990, App. no. 11801/85 and App. no. 11105/84 (*Kruslin v. France and Huvig v. France*), para 33/32 and 36/35.

Lastly, as already indicated in Sect. 2.3.2.3.1, the definition of a suspect under Article 27(1) CCP also has important protective consequences for the person meeting this definition. Once labeled as a suspect, all kinds of procedural rights are attributed.[470] However, these procedural rights will not be relevant for the assessment of the criminal investigation in this project, as it focuses on the covert phase of investigation where the suspect will not yet be aware of the investigation against him/her. Moreover, particularly this phase of the investigation will not be directed only against persons meeting the definition of Article 27(1) CCP.

#### 2.3.2.4 Other Protective Elements Adopted in the CCP

##### 2.3.2.4.1 The Duty to Compile Records

The duty to compile records concerns an important protective element in the system of the regulation of the criminal investigation, considering the importance of this duty for providing a transparent criminal justice system and effectuating defense rights in the trial phase. The duty to compile records is in particular important considering the importance of the pre-trial phase for the investigation at trial, as a consequence of the Supreme Court decision regarding *de auditu* testimony.[471] When the trial phase focuses on the verification of the evidence obtained during the pre-trial phase, it is very important that the manner in which evidence has been obtained has been correctly and completely reported. Furthermore, the duty to compile records fulfills an important role with regard to the supervision of the public prosecutor and, when the examining magistrate is involved, also with regard to the controlling function of the examining magistrate. The police reports enable decisions to be made as to the termination of the criminal investigation or initiating specific additional investigative activities and enable the exertion of control over the investigative activities conducted by the police.

The duty to compile records is provided in Article 152 CCP. All officers responsible for the criminal investigation (those investigative officers that are enumerated in Articles 141 and 142 CCP) are obliged to report all their activities and findings during the criminal investigation as soon as possible. If a law enforcement officer deliberately omits to compile records of relevant information, he is contravening his legal duty to compile records and is committing perjury.[472]

---

[470] These procedural rights are mainly relevant for those suspects who are arrested or detained pre-trial. For the suspect (or other person) under investigation, these rights will not yet take effect, considering that the application of investigative powers will be covert. A different threshold than a reasonable suspicion for coercive measures such as arrest is therefore impossible. However, a different view can be defended for the threshold of application concerning investigative powers in the pre-trial investigation, a threshold which should therefore be considered as flexible. See also: Knigge 2005, 360.

[471] See Sect. 2.1.2.

[472] See in this regard: HR 7 February 2006, *NJ* 2007, 396, para 3.3 and 3.4.

This duty to compile records is further defined in Article 153 CCP, requiring that the report is made under oath of office or under solemn affirmation. Article 153 CCP also requires that the investigative officer discovering the information compiles the official report personally. Furthermore, this investigative officer must date and sign the report as well as reflect as much reasons as possible for his knowledge. For public prosecutors the duty to compile records is laid down in Article 148(3) CCP: the public prosecutor must compile official reports, under his oath of office, of all investigative activities conducted personally.

The duty to compile records has since the first version of the CCP of 1926 functioned as a protective procedural safeguard as it was included as a duty for public prosecutors and other investigative officers.[473] The duty to compile records applies, according to Article 152, to the criminal investigation. However, the Supreme Court has decided in the *Zwolsman* judgment that in all circumstances—within or outside the formal scope of the criminal investigation—the duty to compile records must be observed in case the information is required in order to enable the trial judge to make a final judgment, in accordance with the requirements of a fair trial, concerning the legitimacy of the investigation and the reliability of the evidence obtained.[474] Because of the limited interpretation of the criminal investigation before 1999, the duty to compile records did not apply to the proactive phase and, consequently, was one of the reasons for the secretive and uncontrolled use of investigative powers in the proactive phase.[475]

Considering the important role of the reports regarding the criminal investigative activities for the control exerted in the trial phase as to the legitimacy of these investigative activities and the veracity of the information obtained by these activities, the official report must include all findings (incriminating and exonerating) that are relevant for a judgment about the investigation itself and the value of the evidence obtained and must include a description of the investigative powers applied insofar as a determination on its legitimacy is required.[476] Generally speaking, everything which is relevant for future decisions and judgments falls within the scope of the duty to compile records.

Furthermore, any use of investigative powers that result in an infringement of the privacy rights of people—regardless of the gradation—must be included in official reports. This applies in all circumstances to the use of SIT, as explicitly provided in Article 126aa CCP.[477] However, Article 126aa CCP does not apply to the preliminary investigation.[478] In the light of the criterion formulated in the *Zwolsman* case that all information which is relevant for enabling the trial judge to

---

473 Lindenberg 2002, 421.

474 HR 19 December 1995, *NJ* 1996, 249, ann. Sch para 11.2.2. See also: Rozemond 2000.

475 Rapport van de Parlementaire Enquêtecommissie Opsporingsmethoden 1996, 432-433.

476 Aanwijzing opsporingsbevoegdheden, *Stcrt.* 2004, 227.

477 Aanwijzing opsporingsbevoegdheden, *Stcrt.* 2004, 227.

478 Article 126aa CCP applies to the investigative powers under Title IVa-Vc (see Article 126aa(1) CCP).

make a final judgment, including with regard to the legitimacy of the criminal investigation, must be reported, arguably the preliminary investigative activities shall nevertheless be covered by the duty to compile records. Article 126aa CCP requires that the public prosecutor discloses any reports that relate to the use of SIT. According to Article 126aa(4) CCP, when no official report has been disclosed regarding the use of SIT, at least notification of the use of the method must be made in the dossier.[479] The explanatory memorandum further explains that the reporting must take place regardless of the extent to which the use of SIT is relevant for the case and, hence, the use of SIT cannot be kept secret from persons being prosecuted.[480] In this regard, the duty to compile records regarding SIT is stricter than the duty to compile records concerning other findings during the criminal investigation in order to enable *ex post* control over the legitimacy of using special investigative techniques.

The duty to compile records as provided in Article 152 CCP and, specifically for the use of SIT, in Article 126aa CCP serves an important protective role, facilitating control both during the criminal investigation and at trial. The public prosecutor and, sometimes, the examining magistrate use the written reports as the basis for exerting control over the fairness and the legitimacy of the criminal investigation. *Ex post,* at trial, the written reports drawn up under this duty provide the defense with the possibility to challenge the legitimacy of the use of investigative powers and enable the controlling function of the trial judge concerning the events of the criminal investigation. This protective function of the duty to compile records is, however, not always effectuated in the form of procedural remedies, considering that the consequences of failing to compile records may be limited. This subject will be dealt with in more detail in the subsequent section.

#### 2.3.2.4.2 The Remedies of Article 359a CCP

Only since a Supreme Court decision of 1962 involving the testing of blood without the permission of the suspect, can the trial judge attach consequences to any established illegitimate action during the criminal investigation.[481] Previous to this, the trial judge would only assess challenges regarding the veracity of the evidence obtained during the criminal investigation. The Act on Noncompliance with Procedural Requirements [*Vormverzuimen*] of September 14, 1995, established Article 359a CCP, providing a statutory basis for the power of the trial judge to sanction noncompliance with procedural requirements during the pre-trial phase. Noncompliance with procedural requirements covers the violation of

---

479 Article 126aa(4) CCP.

480 *Kamerstukken II* 1996/97, 25 403, no. 3, 16.

481 HR 26 June 1962, *NJ* 1962, 470 ann. WP. The use of evidence obtained by an investigative method that illegitimately—because a statutory basis was lacking—intruded upon someone's physical integrity violated the rights of the defense and, therefore, the results of the blood test had to be excluded as evidence.

statutory requirements which are applicable to the use of investigative methods, for example, the use of investigative methods in the absence of a reasonable suspicion[482] or nonobservance of the duty to report the investigative activities, in particular the use of SIT.[483] In addition, also investigation in violation of the principles of the due administration of justice concerns a violation of procedural requirements.[484] Sometimes, the noncompliance with procedural requirements, e.g. in violation of statutory requirements or a violation of the principles of proportionality and subsidiarity, also amounts to a violation of a right protected in the ECHR, in the context of the criminal investigation most likely Article 8 ECHR.[485] Since the adoption of Article 359a in the CCP, the trial judge exerts his controlling function within the context of this statutory framework. Nevertheless, it shall be taken into account that the trial judge will only actively investigate events during the pre-trial phase when a defense is raised in that regard or *ex officio* in the exceptional situation that the use of the investigative power seems to be clearly illegitimate. Moreover, as already explained in Sect. 2.3.1.3, when the examining magistrate has already been involved in the criminal investigation, in particular for the authorization of an investigative method, the trial judge will only examine

---

[482] See e.g. Gerechtshof Amsterdam 3 June 1977, *NJ* 1978, 601. The evidence was excluded as a consequence of the use of investigative methods in the absence of a reasonable suspicion. See also, HR 24 February 2004, *NJ* 2004, 226, para 3.6, where the Supreme Court did not exclude the evidence, because the evidence had not been obtained through the alleged illegitimate arrest. Because of this conclusion, the Supreme Court did not reach the merits of the question whether the arrest was illegitimate because a reasonable suspicion was lacking. And: HR 6 September 2005, *NJ* 2006, 447, para 3.6: in this case the use of a blood test in the absence of a reasonable suspicion, but with the permission of the person in question, violated statutory law. The Supreme Court upheld the decision to mitigate the sentence, instead of imposing the more 'severe' sanction of excluding the evidence, because the person's physical integrity had not been violated without his permission.

[483] For example HR 19 December 1995, *NJ* 1996, 249, ann. Sch, para 11.3, HR 30 June 1998 *NJ* 1998, 799 ann. Sch, para 9.5, HR 2 November 1999, *NJ* 2000, 162, para 5.3 and 5.4 and HR 30 November 1999 *NJ* 2000, 344 en 345 ann. Mevis, where the court did not impose sanctions because the nonobservance of the duty could be repaired and had not been done intentionally or in order to substantially limit the controlling function of the judge.

[484] See e.g. HR 12 February 2008, *NJ* 2008, 248, para 4.3, an arrest in violation of the principles of the due administration of justice did not have to result in the sanction of barring the prosecution, because this violation did not deprive the defendant of her right to a fair trial. And HR 14 January 2003, *NJ* 2003, 288, where the Supreme Court acknowledged that violations of the principles of the due administration of justice by investigative officers as well as by actions of private persons may be sanctioned; in this case the respective violations of the principles of the due administration of justice (as well as Article 8 ECHR) were not of such a nature that excluding the evidence or barring the prosecution should follow (*Ibid.* para 3.6, 4.3 and 4.4).

[485] See e.g. HR 18 March 2003, *NJ* 2003, 527, para 3.5.1, where the method of collecting evidence (by a private detective) may have violated Article 8 ECHR, but did result in a violation of the principles of the due administration of justice or the rights of the defense in such way that the exclusion of the evidence was warranted.

whether the examining magistrate could reasonably reach such a decision on authorization, whether the public prosecutor has executed the order legitimately and whether the use was also otherwise legitimate.[486] When the special investigative technique challenged has been used solely on the basis of the order of the public prosecutor, the trial judge will examine more in depth whether the public prosecutor could order the use of the investigative technique and whether the use as a whole was legitimate. According to the explanatory memorandum of the Act on Strengthening the Position of the Examining Magistrate, because of the enhanced role of the examining magistrate during pre-trial, the trial judge may exercise more restraint when assessing challenges regarding illegitimate actions during the criminal investigation.[487]

In a decision on March 30, 2004, the Supreme Court formulated general rules as to the scope and applicability of Article 359a CCP. Only when the noncompliance with procedural requirements results in irreparable consequences for the defense may the trial judge impose procedural sanctions, and he or she has rather broad discretion as to whether or not to attach consequences to established illegitimate actions.[488] For example, when reports of the use of investigative methods during the criminal investigation have not been disclosed in the file, the public prosecutor will have the opportunity to rectify this violation of the duty to compile records before considering any possible procedural sanctions.[489] Article 359a provides for the following possible remedies: mitigation of the sentence; exclusion of the evidence obtained through noncompliance with procedural requirements; and the most drastic: barring the prosecution.[490]

According to the Supreme Court the trial judge shall take into account the interests served by the rule that is not observed, the damage resulting from the noncompliance and the seriousness of the noncompliance in order to decide whether a procedural sanction should follow and to choose between the possible sanctions.[491] According to the Supreme Court, a mitigation of the sentence will only be resorted to when: the suspect has actually experienced harm; this harm is the consequence of the noncompliance with the procedural requirements; the harm can be compensated through the sentence being mitigated; and, mitigating the sentence is also justified considering the interest of the rule that is not observed

---

[486] See Sects. 2.3.1.2 and 2.3.1.3 and compare: HR 11 October 2005, *NJ* 2006, 625, para 3.5.2 and HR 21 November 2006, *NJ* 2007, 233, ann. Mevis, para 3.4.

[487] *Kamerstukken II* 2009/10, 32177 no. 3, 18.

[488] Which would thus also imply (without the sanctioning) a violation of Article 6 ECHR. See HR 30 March 2004, *NJ* 2004, 376, para 3.4.3.

[489] Compare: HR 19 December 1995, *NJ* 1996, 249, ann. Sch, para 11.3, HR 30 June 1998, *NJ* 1998, 799 ann. Sch, para 9.5, HR 2 November 1999, *NJ* 2000, 162, para 5.3 and 5.4 and HR 30 November 1999, *NJ* 2000, 344 en 345 ann. Mevis.

[490] Article 359a(1) CCP. See in general on noncompliance with procedural requirements and the procedural sanctions of Article 359a: Franken 2004A.

[491] Article 359a(2) CCP and HR 30 March 2004, *NJ* 2004, 376, para 3.5.

and considering the seriousness of the noncompliance.[492] For example, this means that in the case of an illegitimate search of a house that is not owned by the defendant, no consequences will be attached to this illegitimate search because the violated rule did not protect the interests of the defendant; no actual harm was suffered by the defendant as such.[493] The exclusion of evidence will only occur when the evidence has also been directly obtained through the illegitimate action and the illegitimate gathering of the evidence has considerably violated an important criminal procedural requirement or legal principle.[494] Only in rare situations will the prosecution be barred: when the investigative officers have seriously violated the fundamental principles of legitimate criminal investigation, resulting in a shortcoming in the suspect's enjoyment of his/her right to a fair trial and this shortcoming was either intended or was the consequence of the interests of the suspect having been gravely disregarded.[495] The Supreme Court, furthermore, has explained that a trial judge is only obliged to take a decision under Article 359a CCP when the defense has pleaded noncompliance and this plea must be well grounded on the basis of the relevant facts.[496] Most important for the trial judge confronted with a challenge as to illegitimate investigative actions in the light of Article 359a is to assess whether rights have been impaired and whether procedural sanctions can rectify this impairment in order to render the proceedings as a whole fair.

### 2.3.3 Conclusion

The second part of this chapter has described an interrelated system of shared and hierarchal attributed responsibilities as well as protective and restricting elements, which are jointly intended to function as safeguards against arbitrary and unnecessary interferences with the right to respect for private life and against unfair criminal proceedings.

The truth-finding actors—the police, the PPS and the examining magistrate—operate in a hierarchical structure, with an increasing assumption of being objective and impartial when it comes to the decision on employing a specific investigative method. The decision to employ investigative methods based on Article 2 Police Act 1993 is entrusted to investigative officers, the decision on using SIT is entrusted to the public prosecutor and the use of the most intrusive SIT requires the authorization of the examining magistrate. The responsibility for

---

[492] HR 30 March 2004, *NJ* 2004, 376, para 3.6.3.

[493] HR 30 March 2004, *NJ* 2004, 376, para 4.4.

[494] HR 30 March 2004, *NJ* 2004, 376, para 3.6.4.

[495] HR 30 March 2004, *NJ* 2004, 376. para 3.6.5, firstly adopted in *Zwolsman,* HR 19 December 1995, *NJ* 1996, 249, ann. Sch.

[496] HR 30 March 2004, *NJ* 2004, 376, para 3.7.

overall control over the criminal investigation is shared between the public prosecutor and the examining magistrate. The public prosecutor, as the supervisor of the criminal investigation, has obtained—with the entry into force of the Act on SIT of 1999—the most central role in the criminal investigation. He is required to ensure that the investigative officers operate within the confines of the law, in observance of the principles of proportionality and subsidiarity and in anticipation of the trial phase, where accountability for the course of events during the criminal investigation needs to be achieved. In addition, the examining magistrate has, next to his/her role as a warrant judge, a general role to oversee the efficient course of the criminal investigation. As a consequence of the Act on Strengthening the Position of the Examining Magistrate, the independent controlling responsibility of the examining magistrate, next to the supervisory role of the public prosecutor, has been given more emphasis. Nevertheless, his/her control function remains largely dependent on the information provided by the police and PPS and is affected by a rather high caseload.

The framework in which the actors operate, both with regard to the application and with regard to the manner in which control is exerted, is provided in the CCP. Some specific conditions that the regulation of investigative methods which interfere with the right to privacy must meet follow from Article 8 ECHR. The main implication of these requirements concerns the specific provisions for SIT and the proactive preliminary investigative methods and the possibility to base those investigative methods that do not, or to a limited extent, interfere with privacy on Article 2 Police Act 1993. The reasonable suspicion threshold has traditionally functioned as the crucial restriction to achieve protection against arbitrary and unnecessary interferences with the right to respect for private life. However, as has followed from the description of different varieties of the suspicion threshold in 2.3.2.3 and considering the current definition of criminal investigation, the idea that the definition of Article 27(1) CCP has a central protective function is currently difficult to uphold. In addition, also the protective ability of the reasonable suspicion threshold may be doubted, considering that the threshold can be met by 'soft' information originating from anonymous sources, such as an anonymous tip-off and CIE or AIVD reports. The threshold has been given a flexible interpretation, for which reason the legislature has taken into account factors such as the seriousness of the crimes and the nature of the investigative technique to deviate from the Article 27(1) CCP suspicion threshold, and for which reason the actors seeking to use an investigative technique on the basis of particular 'facts and circumstances' may take into account the contents of the information, whether the police and/or PPS have independently checked the information, the concrete possibilities to verify the information considering a possible need to act with urgency, and the availability of less-intrusive means to achieve the investigative purpose.[497] Hence, in addition to this 'threshold of application', the principles of proportionality and subsidiarity and the principle of

[497] For the latter compare HR 11 March 2008, *NJ* 2008, 329, ann. Borgers, annotation para 6.

purpose limitation are intended to fulfill an important additional restrictive function to protect against abuse in the discretionary area provided to the investigating police and PPS also under the applicability of the suspicion threshold or other varieties of the suspicion threshold.

On the basis of the principle of purpose limitation, the criminal investigation has also been separated from administrative supervisory authority and from intelligence investigations. For the intelligence investigation the purpose limitation principle applies strictly, resulting in a strict separation between the intelligence and law enforcement community, following from a prohibition on using intelligence powers for the purpose of criminal investigation. Administrative supervision and criminal investigation are separated on the basis of a looser application of the purpose limitation rule. Administrative supervisory powers may also be used for criminal investigative purposes as long as these administrative supervisory powers are not used exclusively to pursue criminal investigative purposes. Because of this looser application of the purpose limitation rule, the use of administrative supervisory powers against suspects also triggers the applicability of procedural rights for the suspect, such as the right to remain silent. Nevertheless, the applicability of the purpose limitation does not obstruct the use of information collected either by administrative supervisory powers or in intelligence investigations within the criminal investigation. When the administrative supervision switches to a criminal investigation or when 'spheres cumulate', such a transfer of information occurs automatically, especially considering that usually the same investigative officer will be active in both spheres. In contrast, the transfer of information from the AIVD to the PPS is a decision made solely by the AIVD and occurs through the procedural mechanism provided in the WIV 2002 (AIVD official reports are transferred to the PPS through the intermediary of the national public prosecutor for counterterrorism) in order to uphold the strict separation between the intelligence community and law enforcement community and to exclude the AIVD's secret methods of operating from the transparency requirements of criminal procedures.

Lastly, control over the legitimate and fair course of the criminal investigation has been hierarchically organized. During the criminal investigation the PPS and the examining magistrate bear this controlling responsibility as to whether the criminal investigative powers are used within the confines of the law and, in addition, in observance of the principles of the due administration of justice. Afterwards, the trial judge shall be enabled to exert full control over the course of events during the criminal investigation and the defense can challenge the evidence collected during the criminal investigation, as required under Article 6 ECHR. For this purpose, the trial judge and defense shall, in principle, have sufficient insight into the manner in which the evidence has been obtained and the source of the evidence. For this purpose, the police and PPS have a duty to compile records of all investigative activities relevant for a judgment regarding the legitimacy of the criminal investigative activities and the defense has a right to have these materials disclosed. The level of control that the trial judge is required to exert depends on the level of control that has already been or could have been exerted during the criminal investigation. In other words, the control on the fairness of the criminal proceedings exerted by the judiciary must be kept in balance. Considering the manner in which the Supreme Court has interpreted the framework of Article 359a CCP, the establishing, at the trial stage, of illegitimate actions which have occurred during the criminal investigation do not necessarily result in a procedural remedy for the accused. Only when such a remedy is required in order to render the trial fair and the remedy is suitable for repairing the fairness of the criminal procedure as a whole, will the judge apply one of the procedural sanctions.

# Chapter 3
# Counterterrorism Measures Affecting Criminal Investigation in the Netherlands

## 3.1 Introduction

The Netherlands' first counterterrorism measures were taken in response to the terrorist attacks of September 11, 2001 in the United States. These attacks committed within the United States also confronted Western Europe, including the Netherlands, with the actual threat of international terrorism. Also within Europe these attacks have had a significant influence on society and politics, when a widespread fear emerged that such attacks endangered a free and secure life in the Western world. Immediately after the terrorist attacks of 9/11 the 'General Affairs Council' of the European Union announced the intensifying of its counterterrorism policy in close cooperation with the United States.[1] This resulted in the presentation of a plan of action for the European Union which its Member States adopted in an extraordinary meeting of the Council of the European Union of September 21, 2001, later further elaborated into a Council Common Position.[2] The action plan included counterterrorism measures in order to intensify police and judicial cooperation in particular by the exchange of information between member states and third states (coordinated by Europol and Eurojust), targeting the financing of terrorism, criminalizing acts of terrorism and increasing penalties for terrorist crimes in domestic law and strengthening air security.[3] Furthermore, the United Nations adopted on September 28th, 2001 Resolution 1373 in particular emphasizing the countering of financing of terrorism and the duty for member states to

---

[1] 'Declaration by the European Union', Special Council Meeting, General Affairs, Brussels, September 12, 2001, Pres/01/318.

[2] 'Conclusions and plan of action of the extraordinary European Council Meeting on 21 September 2001', SN 140/01 and Council Common Position of 27 December 2001 on combating terrorism, 2001/930/CFSP, OJ L 344/90.

[3] *Ibid.*

M.F.H. Hirsch Ballin, *Anticipative Criminal Investigation*,
DOI: 10.1007/978-90-6704-843-9_3,

actively confront terrorism.[4] On October 5th, 2001 the Dutch government sent the 'Action Plan for Countering Terrorism and Safety' to Parliament, which provided for a set of counterterrorism measures in order to prevent terrorist attacks within the Netherlands.[5] This action plan, as well as all counterterrorism measures that have since followed, was explicitly set within the context of the policy at the international level, urging member states to take action in order to effectively confront terrorism. Other terrorist incidents and, in particular, the attacks of March 11, 2004 in Madrid, have been the reason to adopt new or to intensify already established counterterrorism measures.[6]

The Dutch government has chosen for a 'broad' counterterrorism strategy that aims to prevent terrorist attacks by acting in time and to combat the phenomenon of terrorism by confronting radicalization. During the first phase of counterterrorism measures the focus was primarily on the adoption of measures in order to intercept the planning of terrorist crimes through repressive measures, and hence upon a criminal law approach, in cooperation with the intelligence services. This occurred in response to the terrorist attacks of 9/11, 2001 within the United States, but primarily after the first attacks on European soil, the train bombings on March 11, 2004 in Madrid. A letter to Parliament on 10 September 2004 set out the counterterrorism strategy in response to the attacks in Madrid, where the government emphasized that the risk and the possible consequences of a terrorist attack require acting in time in order to prevent an attack. In this letter it was stated that in order to respond in a timely manner to terrorist threats it may not be reasonable to wait for concrete suspicions to develop. Instead, action shall be taken against persons when there are signals or indications that justify distrust. The government immediately put this into practice after the terrorist attacks in Madrid by starting to observe people who, at any point in time, have appeared in the investigations of the AIVD or the police as having some involvement in terrorist networks. The government explained that this approach has resulted in an intensified cooperation between the AIVD, the police and the PPS. The exchange of information has been stimulated by establishing a 'counterterrorism information box.'[7] Over the years, the 'broader' approach has been placed at the forefront, with an important role not only for 'hard' measures in the area of law enforcement but also for 'soft' measures focused on the prevention of radicalization and intervention already during the process of radicalization. This has also involved some measures in the administrative law sphere.[8]

---

[4] Resolution 1373 (2001), adopted by the Security Council at its 4385th meeting, on 28 September 2001, *S/RES/1373* (2001).

[5] *Kamerstukken II* 2001/02, 27 9925, no. 10.

[6] The attacks on the London Underground on July 7th 2005 did not trigger a new European or Dutch counterterrorism action plan. Nor did the murder of Theo van Gogh on November 2, 2004 result in new antiterrorism measures. Rapport Evaluatie Antiterrorismemaatregelen 2011, 39.

[7] *Kamerstukken II*, 2003/04, 29 574, no. 1, 10.

[8] See also: Rapport van de Commissie Evaluatie Antiterrorismebeleid 2009, 13-15 and 45.

This research focuses on that part of the Dutch counterterrorism law where the criminal investigative system is affected as a consequence of the desire to intercept the planning of violent terrorist activities. Hence, the part of the Dutch counterterrorism measures that can be typified as a 'soft' approach, focusing on the prevention of radicalization, will not be addressed in detail. The next section (3.1.1) will nevertheless draw a complete picture of the counterterrorism measures taken for the purpose of prevention. Subsequently, the measures that have facilitated a shift towards anticipative criminal investigation will be identified in more detail (3.1.2). The introductory section will conclude by formulating the goals of this chapter.

### *3.1.1 Counterterrorism Measures Under the Preventive Paradigm*

Prevention of crime has, especially in the post-9/11 era, become the primary goal of policy, which is reflected, for example, in the policy plan for the period 2007–2011 with the slogan 'security begins with prevention.'[9] Security, which implies the prevention of crimes, has over the past 10 years become the highest priority of government action in the field of criminal law and the administrative enforcement of the legal order.[10] This trend has so far only increased, resulting, with a new government taking office in October 2010, in the establishment of the Department of 'Security and Justice' and an increased focus on the role of criminal law in achieving security.[11]

Nevertheless, the preventive paradigm (implied by a security paradigm) has underpinned especially all counterterrorism measures, attributing in particular an important preventive function to the criminal justice system.[12] This focus on prevention was immediately clear when the government initially set out the measures of the plan of action for counterterrorism that was sent to Parliament in October 2001. The measures contributing to the prevention of terrorist attacks within the Netherlands that were announced in this plan concerned, in general: the expansion of the capacity of the intelligence and security services; improved cooperation between the intelligence and security services and the police; improved airport and border security; intensified surveillance and protection of possible targeted persons and objects; enhancing the capacity of law enforcement

---

[9] *Kamerstukken II* 2007/08, 28 684, no. 119.

[10] The prioritization of security is, for example, also visible in debates with regard to the protection of privacy. Security interests are often understood as overriding individual privacy claims. See: Muller et al. 2007, 15-18.

[11] See Regeerakkoord 'Vrijheid en verantwoordelijkheid' VVD-CDA and Gedoogakkoord VVD-PVV-CDA, 30 September 2010, available at: http://www.rijksoverheid.nl/documenten-en-publicaties/rapporten/2010/09/30/regeerakkoord-vvd-cda.html (accessed May 2, 2011). See also: De Roos 2010.

[12] Compare: Van der Woude 2010, 292 and Muller et al. 2007, 22-23.

services to investigate and prosecute terrorist activities; the countering of the financing of terrorism; and, the due implementation of European Union and United Nations' decisions and treaties.[13] In a letter to Parliament on June 24, 2003, the Minister of Justice stated that the security of the Netherlands, with its state organization based on democracy and individual liberty, was seriously threatened. Subsequently, the counterterrorism plan, already announced in 2001, was further defined as pursuing three objectives, which reflects the 'broad' counterterrorism effort of the Dutch government. The key objective is the prevention of terrorist attacks. Secondly, society needs to be prepared for the possibility of an attack and the required surveillance and protection measures need to be taken. The third objective concerns research into the causes of Islamic terrorism and the dichotomy in society.[14] In the light of the first objective, measures were announced that further an intelligence-led investigation and a strengthened information position, both on the side of the intelligence services and on the side of the police, for the purpose of timely intervention and, subsequently, realizing criminal prosecution when possible.[15] Subsequently, the attacks in Madrid on March 11, 2004 were the reason for adjusting the counterterrorism strategy in order to be able to more effectively confront this form of 'catastrophic Islamic terrorism' targeting as many civilian casualties as possible.[16] Consequently, the government announced that it would intensify the collection, exchange, combining and analyzing of information relevant for timely intercepting the preparation of terrorist activities and to strengthen the possibilities to act upon this information.[17]

Over the years many specific measures in various areas of law and policy have been taken in order to implement the 'broad' counterterrorism strategy with a general focus on prevention. The criminal justice system concerns one of the most important areas utilized to confront terrorism, based upon the idea that terrorist activities concern criminal activities and, therefore, that terrorists shall be criminally prosecuted and punished. The first set of counterterrorism measures can primarily be typified as safety measures, aimed at enhancing the capacities of law enforcement and intelligence agencies to intercept the planning of terrorist activities in good time. These measures are usually referred to as repressive measures, because of the use of repressive instruments such as criminal investigation and prosecution. Nevertheless, the goal of these 'repressive' measures is prevention, for which reason the term 'repression' seems inapt or at least confusing.[18] Many of the 'repressive' measures were the implementation of European Union and United Nations policy. This 'repressive' approach of the first set of counterterrorism measures was already

---

[13] *Kamerstukken II,* 2001/02, 27 925, no. 10, 8-14.

[14] *Kamerstukken II* 2002/03, 27 925, no. 94, 2.

[15] *Kamerstukken II* 2002/03, 27 925, no. 94, 3-4.

[16] *Kamerstukken II* 2003/04, 27 925, no. 123, 1 and 3.

[17] *Kamerstukken II* 2003/04, 27 925, no. 123, 7-8.

[18] For that reason, Brouwer refers to this type of counterterrorism measures as 'prepressive'. Brouwer 2006.

announced in the plan of action sent to Parliament in October 2001. The measures that were then announced have resulted in several 'counterterrorism' acts, which largely included the implementation of measures taken on the level of the European Union and the United Nations. An overview will be given of the most significant measures underpinned by the preventive paradigm that have been taken in the Netherlands since September 11, 2001.

The first Act adopted, as part of the set of counterterrorism measures, was the Act on Terrorist Crimes of 24 June 2004, which is the implementation of the European Union Framework Decision on Combating Terrorism of 2002[19] in Dutch law. As a consequence of this Act an additional section has been added to some provisions of the Penal Code (e.g. murder), providing for the possibility to impose a harsher sentence when the offense has been committed with a 'terrorist intent'.[20] Furthermore, the Act has criminalized certain activities in the 'preparatory phase'. The criminal preparation of crimes has been expanded and the crimes of conspiracy to commit a serious terrorist crime and recruitment for the violent jihad have been established.[21] As will be explained in Sect. 3.1.2, the criminalization of these activities also has consequences for the preventive potential of the criminal investigation. The criminalization of terrorist activities was complemented in 2009 when participation and cooperation in terrorist training and provocation to commit a terrorist crime were adopted in the Penal Code as criminal offenses. The Act also adopted a higher maximum penalty for some already criminalized offenses when they are committed with a terrorist intent.[22]

As already announced in the October 2001 plan of action, the Dutch government aimed to realize prevention through the intensified sharing of information and cooperation between the intelligence services, the public prosecution service and the police. Increasing the sharing of intelligence between law enforcement and intelligence agencies, as well as between the agencies of different countries and European Union bodies such as Eurojust, was also stimulated within the Hague Programme, setting out the objectives in the area of freedom, security and justice

[19] Council of the European Union, 'Framework Decision of 13 June 2002 on Combating Terrorism,' 2002/475/JHA.

[20] Defined in Article 83a Penal Code. The offenses which amount to 'terrorist crimes' are defined in Article 83 Penal Code by enumerating the offenses that can be committed with a 'terrorist intent'.

[21] Act on Terrorist Crimes 24 June 2004, *Stb.* 2004, 290. Entry into force on 10 August 2004 (*Stb.* 2004, 373).

[22] Act on Training for Terrorism, 12 June 2009, *Stb.* 2009, 245. Entry into force on 1 April 2010 (*Stb.* 2010, 139). The criminalization of these acts is in fact an implementation of Articles 5-7 of the Council of Europe Convention on the Prevention of Terrorism, *CETS 196, 16.V.2005 (Trb.* 2006, 34*)*, obliging member states to criminalize provocation to commit a terrorist crime, recruitment for terrorism and training for terrorism. Subsequently, also a 2008 EU Framework decision on combating terrorism obliged Member States to criminalize these terrorist acts and, additionally, also the aiding or abetting of, inciting and attempting terrorism. Council of the European Union, 'Framework Decision of 28 November 2008, amending Framework Decision 2002/475/JHA on combating terrorism', 2008/919/JHA.

for the period 2005–2010.[23] The first step within the Netherlands to realize a more effective sharing of intelligence was the establishment of the Counterterrorism information box (2004)[24] and, subsequently, the establishment of the coordinating agency of the National Coordinator for Counterterrorism (2005).[25] In 2006, the Shielded Witnesses Act[26] was adopted which sought a solution for the clash between the transparency of criminal proceedings and the secrecy of intelligence investigations, when intelligence information has been introduced to criminal proceedings.[27] Subsequently, the Act to Broaden the Possibilities to Investigate and Prosecute Terrorist Crimes (or: 'the Act on the Criminal Investigation of Terrorist Crimes') was adopted. The goal of this Act was to enhance the preventive capacity of the criminal investigation by expanding the scope of the criminal investigation of terrorist crimes and increasing the coherence between the activities of the intelligence agencies and the law enforcement agencies with a shared goal of preventing terrorist acts.

Furthermore, the Dutch government considered that it needed to be able to act before criminal law enforcement means can be used. For that purpose the possibility has been created that upon the order of the mayor a person who is considered to be a 'terrorist threat', but cannot be suspected of a crime, will be systematically observed in order to make it clear to that person and his/her daily environment that he/she is the subject of investigation. In that way prevention is realized through disturbing that person's activities.[28]

After these Acts and measures with a focus primarily on the use of 'repressive' means for the purpose of prevention, the focus shifted to social-preventive measures,[29] aimed at obtaining knowledge on groups and individuals where radicalization processes are (possibly) taking place and intervention in order to hinder the radicalization process.[30] This anti-radicalization policy is primarily carried out by the intelligence services and by local communities. Also the method of 'personal disturbance' has shifted in focus: now the method is not only applied to interrupt

[23] The Hague Programme, Strengthening Freedom, Security and Justice in the European Union, Brussels 4/5 November 2004. 1492/1/04 REV 1, 27-29. See also: *Kamerstukken II* 2994/05, 29 754, no. 5, 5.

[24] *Kamerstukken II* 2004/05, 29 754 and 27 925, no. 21 (Letter of the Minister of the Interior, and the attached covenant).

[25] Regeling van de Ministers van Justitie en van Binnenlandse Zaken en Koninkrijksrelaties van 29 juni 2005, nr. DDS5357209, houdende instelling van de Nationaal Coördinator Terrorismebestrijding.

[26] *Stb.* 2006, 460.

[27] *Kamerstukken II* 2003/04, 29 732, no. 3.

[28] See Brouwer 2006.

[29] This shift in focus in the Dutch counterterrorism strategy does not apply to the Dutch security policy in general. The focus of the current government is to make society 'safer' by repressive means (both *ex post* and *ex ante*) within the areas of criminal law and administrative enforcement. These repressive means shall be strengthened and applied rigidly in order to give effect to the key task of the government, i.e. guaranteeing security.

[30] Rapport Evaluatie Antiterrorismemaatregelen 2011, 41-45.

the preparation of a terrorist crime but primarily to offer the person in question an alternative through deradicalization. This is done by paying attention to education, housing and sometimes mental health.[31]

### 3.1.2 The Shift to Anticipative Criminal Investigation

Several of the above-mentioned 'repressive' counterterrorism measures have also contributed to a shift to anticipative criminal investigation. An important part of the 'repressive' counterterrorism measures focused on enhancing the capability of the criminal justice system to contribute to the prevention of terrorist crimes and increasing the coherence between the intelligence apparatus, the administrative law enforcement and the criminal justice system in order to realize a more effective preventive system.

The main legislative measure affecting the criminal investigation has been the Act of 20 November 2006 to expand the investigative possibilities in the criminal investigation for the prevention of terrorist crimes. In addition, the Terrorist Crimes Act, criminalizing acts preceding a terrorist attack, has expanded the preventive capacity of the criminal investigation by the possibility to investigate upon a reasonable suspicion of one of these crimes. In this way, it will be possible to investigate and prosecute the persons suspected of committing these 'preparatory' terrorist crimes in order to prevent the 'full' terrorist crimes. From a legal perspective, this does not, however, affect the system of the criminal investigation as such, as it still limits the use of investigative powers to reacting to a reasonable suspicion of the commission of one of these crimes.[32] Therefore, the legislature has considered that also the powers available in the criminal investigation should be geared towards prevention.

In the aftermath of the terrorist attacks in Madrid, the expansion of criminalization in the preparatory phase as a consequence of the Terrorist Crimes Act was considered insufficient in order to confront the threat and nature of the 'new' terrorism. Hence, this gap was filled by expanding the possibilities to use criminal investigative powers where terrorist crimes are being prepared. The legislature did not consider the role of criminal law to be restricted to a reaction to crimes already committed but to have also a role in the prevention of crimes.[33] By the Act of 2006 on broadening the possibilities for investigating and prosecuting terrorist crimes a special investigative domain has been created for the investigation of terrorist activities with a central focus on the prevention of terrorist crimes (Articles 126za-

[31] *Ibid.*, 89.

[32] See on the changes in the substantive law as a consequence of the Act on Terrorist Crimes and the expansion of criminalization in the 'preparatory' phase, raising issues as to the border between criminalizing intentions or acts: Lintz 2007, Van Wifferen 2007, 196-199 and Van der Geest 2008.

[33] *Kamerstukken II* 2003/04, 29 754, no. 1, 1-4 and 12.

126zs CCP). As a consequence of this Act, the exceptional possibility to investigate organized crime proactively under Title V has been expanded to the investigation of terrorist crimes. Moreover, the central position of a reasonable suspicion has been abandoned for the use of SIT, considering that under Title Vb indications suffice when it comes to the prevention of terrorism. This means that under Title Vb SIT can be used at any time when there is relevant information available for the prevention of a terrorist attack.[34] Contrary to the criminalization of acts in the preparatory phase, allowing the use of SIT under the threshold of 'indications' directly influences the preventive capabilities of the criminal investigation, because it enables the preventive use of the investigative capacity in the procedural sense. Lastly, the Act of 2006 has expanded the preliminary investigation for the preparation of terrorism investigations and established new investigative methods available in the criminal investigation especially for terrorism prevention.

Furthermore, the Act on the Criminal Investigation of Terrorist Crimes as well as other measures, such as the Shielded Witnesses Act and some changes on the level of cooperation between different entities, have been taken in order to reorganize and intensify cooperation between law enforcement and intelligence agencies with a focus on the prevention of (terrorist) crimes. In order to realize a coherent counterterrorism strategy underpinned by the preventive paradigm it was considered necessary to make sure that all information relevant to the prevention of terrorism is available to the right entities. The Counterterrorism Information box and the National Coordinator for Counterterrorism have been established in order to coordinate the required cooperation and the exchange of information. The Act on the Criminal Investigation of Terrorist Crimes was also adopted in order to enable intensified cooperation with the intelligence service. When law enforcement agencies are able to act in an earlier phase, this also stimulates the intelligence service to share information in an earlier phase.

Because terrorism is considered to be criminal behavior, the Dutch government considered the criminal justice system as the primary area for dealing with terrorists. Hence, it must be able to 'use' the criminal justice system in an earlier phase and, subsequently, to prosecute terrorists for preparatory acts. In order to avoid that the increased use of intelligence in criminal proceedings would obstruct subsequent criminal trials, the Shielded Witnesses Act has been adopted in order to increase the utility of official reports from the intelligence service either as initial information for a criminal investigation or as evidence. Both the measures that have touched upon the regulation of the criminal investigation as well as the measures affecting relations with the intelligence services have put prevention at the forefront in the criminal investigation of terrorism and, consequently, the criminal investigation has been geared as a tool for anticipating future terrorist attacks.

Lastly, counterterrorism activities in the administrative law sphere may have a repressive nature, although they focus on the prevention of terrorism. The

[34] *Kamerstukken II* 2003/04, 29 754, no. 1, 12-13.

technique of personal disturbance, conducted by the police, will be used when the criminal investigative possibilities fall short in making sure that terrorism is prevented. Also these police activities, regulated under administrative law, concern anticipative investigation. The border between these activities and criminal investigative activities is relevant for determining the exact scope of anticipative *criminal* investigation.

### 3.1.3 Goals of the Chapter

The different measures described in the previous section that have jointly realized a shift to anticipative criminal investigation in the Netherlands will be dealt with in this chapter in three different categories.

The first category (Sect. 3.2) will primarily be concerned with the measures introduced by the Act on the Criminal Investigation of Terrorist Crimes, which directly affect the preventive capacity of the criminal investigation. The preventive capacity of the criminal investigation has not only been enhanced through legislative measures but, additionally, by some organizational changes within the police. Hence, in addition it will be described how the police have evolved into an intelligence-led organization with an important role for the CIE, especially in the field of counterterrorism.

Dealing with the second category, Sect. 3.3 will describe in what manner the use of intelligence in criminal proceedings has been increased in order to be able to use the criminal justice system to confront terrorism before crimes are committed. Attention will be given to the manner in which the courts have taken a position with regard to the use of intelligence in criminal proceedings, to the adoption of the Shielded Witnesses Act in order to stimulate the use of intelligence in criminal proceedings and to organizational changes enhancing cooperation, namely the establishment of the CT Infobox and the National Coordinator for Counter-terrorism. The goal of this section will be to demonstrate that the work of the law enforcement community and intelligence community have approached each other when it comes to terrorism prevention and that the possibility to use the information collected by the AIVD is an essential feature of the anticipative criminal investigation.

The third category (Sect. 3.5) deals with anticipative investigation in the field of administrative law. In Chap. 2 it has been described how the use of administrative supervisory powers in the field of administrative law may be used for the purpose of criminal law enforcement and, hence, this influences the sword capacity of the criminal investigation. The third section will therefore seek to analyze the method of administrative disturbance in order to determine in what manner this influences the capacity of anticipative criminal investigation.

This section will thus seek to describe the anticipative criminal investigation by focusing primarily on its core—the preventive capacity of the criminal investigation itself, bottomed up by the possibilities to gather criminal intelligence—and, in addition, to assess to what extent and in what way the preventive capacity of the

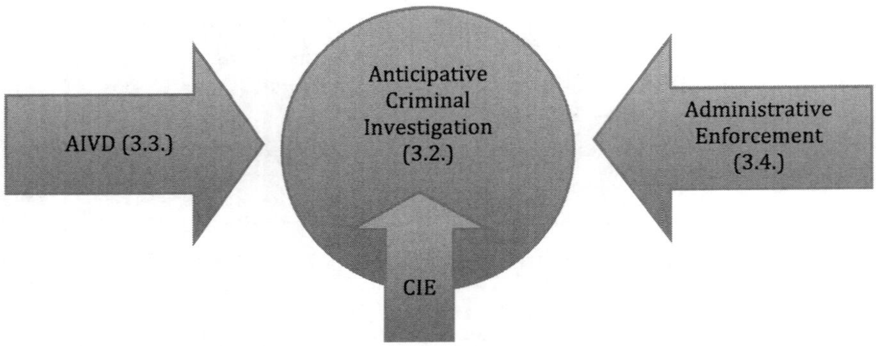


**Fig. 3.1** Hypothetical illustration of the anticipative criminal investigation in the Netherlands

criminal investigation is influenced by cognate legal areas also conducting anticipative investigative activities. Hypothetically, the anticipative criminal investigation can thus be visualized as illustrated below. The goal of this chapter will be to describe the measures in the three categories in order to be able to determine the exact scope and nature of anticipative criminal investigation and whether the interaction between different areas of law conducting anticipative investigative activities indeed reinforces the capacity of the anticipative *criminal* investigation to a greater extent than before the measures of the post-9/11 era. In conclusion, this chapter will assess whether the figure above (Fig. 3.1) correctly reflects the manner in which an anticipative criminal investigation has been enabled in the Netherlands (Sect. 3.5).

## 3.2 Changes Affecting the Criminal Investigation

### *3.2.1 Legislative Measures*

The Act of November 20, 2006 has affected the criminal investigation by adjusting the criminal investigative framework to make it suitable for contributing to the prevention of terrorist crimes. Although most Dutch counterterrorism measures were in fact the implementation of European Policy, most importantly as a result of the adoption of the 2002 Framework Decision on Combating Terrorism,[35] the Act of November 2006 was taken by the Netherlands on its own initiative, considering that no concrete binding obligations in this regard have been established on a European or other international level. The counterterrorism measure was nevertheless in line with European policy, considering that, in general, all

[35] See Chap. 1, Sect. 1.5.

Member States have been urged to take the necessary measures to improve their capability to prevent terrorist attacks.[36]

The Act on the Criminal Investigation of Terrorist Crimes mainly focuses on enhancing the possibilities of the criminal investigation to contribute to the fight against terrorism. In addition, the Act has established adjustments to substantive law, such as to Article 46 Penal Code (criminal preparation) by clarifying the interpretation; by criminalizing the refraining from notifying an intended terrorist crime (in Articles 135 and 136 Penal Code); and providing for a higher maximum penalty on hiding a suspect of a terrorist crime (Article 189 Penal Code). Furthermore, the Telecommunication Act has been adjusted to the application of SIT in terrorism investigations. Finally, the permitted duration of detention before trial has been extended when the suspicion concerns a terrorist crime. The pre-trial detention of a person alleged to have committed a terrorist crime can be extended, after the normal maximum period of 90 days, to a period of not more than two years (Article 66(3) CCP). As a consequence, the non-disclosure of the records of the proceedings to the defense can also be extended during this period. In addition, the stricter suspicion requirement of 'serious concerns' for imposing pre-trial detention is not required for the pre-trial detention of terrorism suspects (Article 67(4) CCP): a suspicion is now sufficient to detain terrorism suspects during pre-trial.[37] The government considered these fundamental changes to be justified because of the continuous threat of terrorist attacks that can result in many innocent victims.[38] Despite the many concerns regarding these fundamental changes, the Second Chamber adopted the bill with only the Green Left Party (*Groenlinks*) voting against. The amendment of the CCP as established by this Act entered into force on 1 February 2007.[39]

This section will only address the measures which have contributed to enabling an anticipative criminal investigation. These are the investigative domain for

---

[36] See e.g.: *Presidency Conclusions—Brussels 4/5 November 2004, The Hague Programme, Strengthening Freedom, Security and Justice in the European Union*, at 28, 14292/1/04 Rev 1 Annex I, and *Communication from the Commission to the Council and the European Parliament, The Hague Programme, ten priorities for the next five years*, at 6, 8, COM (2005) 184 final (May 10, 2005): The fight against terrorism, working toward a global response. And see also: Article 15 of the Council of Europe Convention on the Prevention of Terrorism, *CETS 196, 16.V.2005 (Trb.* 2006, 34*)*, by which the Member States have had a duty to investigate imposed upon them: "upon receiving information that a person who has committed or who is alleged to have committed an offence set forth in this Convention may be present in its territory, the Party concerned shall take such measures as may be necessary under its domestic law to investigate the facts contained in the information". And: *The European Union counter-terrorism strategy* (adopted in December 2005 by the Council of the European Union), *14469/4/05 REV 4, DG H2,* in which four pillars of the strategy were adopted: prevent, protect, pursue and respond. 'Pursue' includes that "at a national level the competent authorities need to have the necessary tools to collect and analyse intelligence and to pursue and investigate terrorists, requiring Member States to update their policy response and legislative provisions here necessary". (12, para 24).

[37] *Stb.* 2006, 580.

[38] *Kamerstukken I* 2006/07, no. D, 21-22.

[39] *Stb.* 2006, 731.

terrorist crimes, the changes affecting the preliminary investigation and the introduction of new criminal investigative methods for the prevention of terrorism. In the first place, a new investigative domain has been adopted where SIT can be used upon 'indications' of a terrorist crime. Secondly, the preliminary investigation has been adjusted to contribute to the prevention of terrorism. Lastly, investigative powers have been established, which are in particular suitable to avert a more urgent threat. These measures will be dealt with in this chapter on the basis of the parliamentary documents regarding the Act to Broaden the Possibilities to Investigate and Prosecute Terrorist Crimes and on the basis of the first experiences in practice with the new investigative domain, the adjusted powers of the preliminary investigation and the new criminal investigative powers. The Act of 2006 has also amended the definition of the criminal investigation as provided in Article 132a CCP, in order to broaden the scope of the criminal investigation to cover these anticipative investigative possibilities. This definition was already introduced as the current definition of a criminal investigation in Chap. 2 in order to avoid confusion about terminology. At this place it should in addition be noted that the direct reason for adopting this new definition by the Act on the Criminal Investigation of Terrorist Crimes was, obviously, the fact that the newly introduced investigative domain for terrorist crimes and the new investigative powers would otherwise fall outside the scope of the criminal investigation.[40]

### 3.2.1.1 The Investigative Domain of Terrorism Investigations: Title Vb

The main consequence of the Act of 20 November 2006 to broaden the possibilities to investigate and prosecute terrorist crimes has been the creation of a new investigative domain within the criminal investigation especially for the investigation of possible terrorist activities. Because the investigation of terrorist activities should be possible whenever there is information available pointing to terrorist activities, a different threshold for using SIT has been adopted, namely 'indications of a terrorist crime'. Upon indications of a terrorist crime it is now possible to apply SIT, such as systematic observation, infiltration, (wire-)tapping and ordering stored information, in the context of a criminal investigation. The amendment also extends to citizens assisting in the investigation which is now also permitted upon indications of a terrorist crime (Article 126zt and 126zu CCP).

In the explanatory memorandum and during the discussion of the bill in Parliament the government tried to explain the interpretation that should be given to the 'indications of a terrorist crime' threshold. The explanatory memorandum even provides for a definition of 'indications of a terrorist crime': 'there are indications if the information available provides for facts and circumstances that point to the

---

40 *Kamerstukken II* 2005/06, 30 164, no. 3, 16-17, *Kamerstukken II* 2005/06, 30 164, no. 7, 25 and see for the objections against eliminating the threshold of application from the definition *Kamerstukken II* 2005/06, 30 164, no. 6, 14. On Article 132a CCP see further Sect. 2.3.2.2.1.

actual commission or future commission of a terrorist crime.' The explanatory memorandum continues by stating that in the criminal investigation into terrorist crimes the most important goal is not only to establish the truth about a reasonable suspicion, but, primarily, the prevention of terrorist attacks.[41]

Notwithstanding this definition provided in the explanatory memorandum, a definition has not been adopted in the law. Members of Parliament repeatedly argued for the adoption of a definition in the law during the discussion of the bill, but the government was unwilling to do so. The government considered it doubtful whether a legal definition would clarify the interpretation of the threshold in practice. Also the reasonable suspicion threshold has not been defined in the law, which does not seem to hinder the operation of the threshold in practice. In addition, a definition would obstruct a sufficiently flexible interpretation of the threshold needed for application in various circumstances. And, adopting a definition in the law would result in confusion with regard to the use of 'indications' at other places in the law, for instance in the Weapons and Ammunition Act and in the Economic Offenses Act.[42] Operating the concept of indications under these Acts without a precise definition does not seem to cause any difficulties. That the indications must follow from facts and circumstances is a logical requirement and would not require explicit adoption in the law.[43] Moreover, according to the government, a definition in the law would not serve legal certainty and would not enforce the controlling role of the trial judge regarding the use of SIT.[44] On the basis of these considerations, Parliament followed the government and rejected the idea of adopting a definition of 'indications' in the law.

The explanatory memorandum of the Act on the Criminal Investigation of Terrorist Crimes provided for several examples in order to clarify the interpretation of 'indications of a terrorist crime.' Facts and circumstances whose accuracy is difficult to verify, or that originate from an unclear source, will be sufficient to justify the use of SIT under Title Vb. Furthermore, rumors that are difficult to verify or threat analyses from the AIVD can serve as the facts or circumstances that establish indications.[45] 'Soft information' will be sufficient, like an anonymous tip-off. As already explained in the previous chapter (Sect. 2.3.2.3.1), an anonymous tip-off can also be sufficient for establishing a reasonable suspicion. The explanatory memorandum explains, however, that in a specific case where the anonymous tip-off is assessed as being insufficient for establishing a reasonable suspicion, it should be possible to use SIT upon 'indications of a terrorist crime.'[46] Another example given in the explanatory memorandum is the situation in which reliable informants report that certain people have a strong interest in the

[41] *Kamerstukken II* 2004/05, 30 164, no. 3, 9.

[42] See Chap. 2, Sect. 2.3.2.3.2.4.

[43] *Kamerstukken II* 2005/06, 30 164, no. 7, 15.

[44] *Ibid.*, 15-16.

[45] *Kamerstukken II* 2004/05, 30 164, no. 3, 8.

[46] *Kamerstukken II* 2004/05, 30 164, no. 3, 10.

constructional aspects of governmental premises and this information can be relevant for the successful commission of a terrorist attack. And: information from a citizen that he has heard from an acquaintance that he intends to cause serious damage to a city center in order to teach the Western world a lesson would be sufficient to trigger the investigative domain for terrorist crime. For establishing 'indications of a terrorist crime' it should not therefore be required that it is clear which specific crime is being planned and the information about the planning does not necessarily have to be verifiable through supporting sources or through the checking of facts.[47]

As a result of questions by Members of Parliament, the Minister of Justice tried to further clarify the level of information needed to establish the threshold of indications. The government emphasized that the indications threshold should not be understood as opening the door to using the criminal justice system to combat certain opinions or thoughts, however adverse they may be, but that the fundamental principle that one can only be criminally prosecuted for his/her acts still has to be observed. As an example: facts and circumstances pointing to the exchange of fundamental religious ideas within a certain group of people would not establish 'indications of a terrorist crime'. Hence, 'terrorist thoughts' cannot trigger criminal investigative activities. However, such information may be used as supporting evidence in combination with a concrete act, together amounting to a terrorist crime. For example, fundamental religious ideas in combination with information that someone has purchased a remarkably large quantity of chemical materials, which cannot reasonably be used for private purposes, will be sufficient for establishing 'indications of a terrorist crime.'[48]

The government also provided some examples regarding the suitability of using specific investigative techniques in the criminal investigation for the prevention of terrorist crimes. The technique of systematic observation could, for instance, be used to obtain a complete picture of someone's involvement in the planning of a terrorist crime. If a sleeping terrorist cell initiates certain activities, it would be useful to observe—upon indications of a terrorist crime—members of the cell and gain information about the committing of preparatory acts regarding a terrorist crime. Pseudo-dealing or serving can be a useful technique to trace alleged terrorists who want to obtain explosives or arms. The technique of the systematic gaining of information (the use of informants) can possibly be applied when it is desirable to intercept communications between members of a terrorist network by, for instance, participating in Internet communities or by participating in a political or religious group.[49] Infiltration (the use of undercover agents) will go one step further: the person infiltrating will actively participate or cooperate in the group or render assistance to the group from the outside.[50]

[47] *Kamerstukken II* 2004/05, 30 164, no. 3, 10.

[48] *Kamerstukken II* 2005/06, 30 164, no. 7, 17-18.

[49] *Kamerstukken II* 2004/05, 30 164, no. 3, 38.

[50] *Ibid.*, 9.

Furthermore, the government stated that the concept of indications has not been newly introduced in criminal procedural law, as it was already used in the Weapons and Ammunition Act (WWM), the Economic Offenses Act (WED) and the Hunting Act for the application of certain investigative or coercive methods.[51] According to the legislature, the interpretation of 'indications' that has been given in the case law with regard to these Acts will also be relevant to the interpretation of 'indications of a terrorist crime' as adopted in the CCP.[52] Although the concept of indications in the special Acts is only linked to specific investigative powers that directly apply to a person or object (search powers), the application of the threshold to these powers has already introduced the concept to the criminal investigation and demonstrates that it can be utilized in practice. Nevertheless, as has followed from Sect. 2.3.2.3.2.4, the interpretation of indications under the special criminal acts has not demonstrated a clear difference in comparison to the level of information required to establish a reasonable suspicion. The main conclusion that can be drawn is that the threshold is intended to cover also situations where a reasonable suspicion is lacking and, thus, not to obstruct the investigation when there is information available that points to the possible (future) commission of specific terrorist crimes.

Also within the investigative domain of the preliminary investigation the concept of indications has since 2000 been used as the threshold for initiating a preliminary investigation on the basis of Article 126gg CCP. The fact that as a consequence of the Act on the Criminal Investigation of Terrorist Crimes both the preliminary investigation and the criminal investigation of terrorist crimes could be initiated upon 'indications' was even considered confusing. This has raised several questions as to the distinction between the two in the advice on the bill and during the discussion of the bill in Parliament. The distinction between the threshold for the preliminary investigations and for the investigative domain of terrorist crimes concerns the object of the indications. For the preliminary investigation the indications concern a group of people, and for the criminal investigation the indications concern a terrorist crime. The preliminary investigation is aimed at determining whether within groups of people terrorist crimes are being planned or committed, which information will result in one or multiple (full) criminal investigations. The focus of the preliminary investigation is on an unspecified group of people, while the criminal investigation of terrorist crimes will be aimed at the clarification of indications of (the preparation of) a specific terrorist crime and the persons who can be associated with that crime.[53]

It is unclear how the examples given by the government actually entail situations in which a reasonable suspicion cannot be established. The adjustment seems to cover the required level of information for starting a criminal investigation. The

---

[51] See Chap. 2, Sect. 2.3.2.3.2.4.

[52] *Kamerstukken II* 2005/06, 30 164, no. 7, 16.

[53] *Kamerstukken II* 2004/05, 30 164, no. 3, 23-24 and *Kamerstukken II* 2005/06, 30 164, no. 7, 13-14.

objective of the 'indications' is the terrorist crime, which means that there must be a connection between the indications and a terrorist crime. However, similar to organized crime investigations it is not required that the terrorist crimes have been committed or that the indications point to a concrete crime. Considering that it is difficult to understand why the required level of information is lower than is required for a reasonable suspicion, the explanation that this lower threshold must result in making it easier for the public prosecutor or examining magistrate to do whatever is needed in the interest of the investigation seems to be more clarificatory in understanding the 'indications of a terrorist crime' threshold. If an investigative technique can be considered to contribute to the prevention of a terrorist crime, it must be possible to use this technique under the threshold of 'indications of a terrorist crime.' The threshold of 'indications of a terrorist crime' shall thus not obstruct the use of a special investigative technique that is assumed to contribute to the prevention of a terrorist crime. Hence, the focus of the use of SIT, as also expressly stated by the government, has now shifted to the interest of the investigation, in anticipation of future crimes, instead of being focused on whether or not a reasonable suspicion can be derived from the information available.[54] When terrorism is involved, it is considered more important than in the case of other crime that the information available will be investigated also when there is a doubt about the accuracy of the information. In fact, the use of SIT will often be aimed at excluding the risk of a terrorist attack by investigating vague information at an early phase.[55] Similar to the proactive organized crime investigations, a concrete terrorist crime does not yet have to have been committed. The central purpose of the investigative domain for terrorist crimes is to intercept the planning of a terrorist crime in time and to prevent the realization of a terrorist crime. The terrorism investigation will, therefore, utilize a proactive approach and put the interest of prevention above the interest of truth-finding in order to make prosecutorial decisions. Moreover, the terrorism investigations have a larger proactive reach than organized crime investigations, because the interest of preventing a terrorist crime will be decisive rather than the question of whether the information available establishes a reasonable suspicion. Considering that the purpose of prevention seems to be the primary purpose within the investigative domain for terrorist crimes, the 'indications of a terrorist crime' threshold will in practice function as a last resort when the information available is insufficient for establishing a reasonable suspicion but using investigative techniques is nevertheless considered to be able to contribute to the prevention of terrorism. With this in mind, also the difference between indications and a reasonable suspicion becomes clearer.[56]

---

[54] *Kamerstukken II* 2004/05, 30 164, no. 3, 11.

[55] See also: De Poot et al. 2008, 43.

[56] Also the legislature pointed to the importance of lowering the threshold for SIT in order to exclude the undesirable situation that the threshold of a reasonable suspicion would hinder effective action for the prevention of terrorist crimes. *Kamerstukken I* 2006/07, 30 164, no. D, 9.

#### 3.2.1.2 Preliminary Investigation for Preparing Terrorism Investigations

The Act of November 2006 to broaden the possibilities to investigate and prosecute terrorist crimes has also enhanced the capability of the preliminary investigation to contribute to the prevention of terrorist crimes. The possibility to 'precede' the criminal investigation by a preliminary investigation was considered a suitable tool to investigate on the basis of indications that a group of people is planning or committing terrorist crimes. The preliminary investigation must then contribute to gaining an understanding of the activities of people within the group and whether these activities may concern the planning or commission of terrorist crimes. A subsequent 'full' criminal investigation can then be conducted on the basis of a more favorable level of information.[57] Two provisions have been added in order to regulate the preliminary investigation of terrorist crimes. On the basis of Article 126hh CCP it is possible to demand information from automated systems. The information can be processed by comparing or combining information from different sources, for example, by combining the information obtained with information already stored in police files. Another newly introduced investigative technique for the preliminary investigation concerns the possibility to obtain the stored identifying information of a person, under Article 126ii CCP. The possibility to obtain such identifying information specifically from telecommunication services has been separately included in the second section of Article 126ii CCP.

These new investigative techniques within the investigative domain of the preliminary investigation were previously only available within the full criminal investigation.[58] Before the entry into force of the Act on the Criminal Investigation of Terrorist Crimes in February 2007, the preliminary investigation was limited to gathering information from police files, from open sources or upon voluntary cooperation. These activities nevertheless interfere with privacy rights considering that the regulation of the preliminary investigation includes an exception to the applicability of the Protection of Personal Data Act and can be applied to persons not yet suspected of a crime or of 'involvement' in organized criminal activities. The preliminary investigation that does not concern terrorist crimes is still restricted to these investigative possibilities. Nevertheless, the legislature considered the possibilities of the preliminary investigation with regard to terrorism to be unsatisfactory. Hence, the investigative possibilities in the preliminary investigation have been

[57] *Kamerstukken II* 2004/05, 30 164, no. 3, 18-19.

[58] See Articles 126na, 126us and 126zi CCP. The investigative techniques concerning the obtaining of information are in fact also quite new to the criminal investigation as they entered into force on 1 January 2006 (*Stb.* 2005, 609). The Act on Powers to Order the Provision of Information (*Stb.* 2005, 390) has added these techniques to the criminal investigation, which actually entailed a measure to keep up with developing technology in the criminal investigation. Some changes have been made by another Act (*Stb.* 2006, 300; Computer Crime II, enacted to keep up with new developments in information technology), which entered into force on 1 September 2007 (*Stb.* 2006, 301).

expanded so as to effectively conduct a preliminary investigation into terrorist activities.[59]

The government explained why the new techniques available in the preliminary investigation are needed in particular for the purpose of preventing terrorism. Through connecting and comparing the information that can be gathered on the basis of Article 126hh CCP (demanding information from automated systems of public and private organizations) it should be possible to find that certain persons repeatedly appear in information originating from different sources. This information can then be analyzed and profiles or patterns can be discovered. Offender profiles, risk profiles or the modus operandi can be found and used as the basis for starting a full criminal investigation. The technique also includes the possibility to demand information from third parties, for example, by ordering the provision of files stored by private companies. In this regard the government pointed to examples where 'indications' are present that within certain companies activities are being employed that might concern the preparation of a terrorist crime or where companies render services to a group of people where indications exist regarding the preparation of a terrorist crime. The government added that the gathering of information from third parties must be restricted to a minimum.[60]

The identifying information that can be gathered on the basis of Article 126ii CCP may concern the name, address, date of birth, gender as well as administrative features, such as the relation of a person to a specific holder of information like a bank account or certain membership. According to the government, the category of information that can be ordered is restricted and, therefore, gathering only interferes, in a limited way, with the right to respect for private life of the people concerned. The government considers the adoption of Article 126ii CCP to be a useful addition, because the information that can be gathered by this specific technique furthers an effective preliminary investigation, which is the more important for the prevention of terrorist crimes.[61]

The preliminary investigation, including the techniques of Articles 126hh and 126ii, can be initiated on the basis of facts and circumstances that establish indications that a group of people is planning or committing serious (Article 67(1) CCP) crimes that result in a serious infringement of the legal order. Hence, the preliminary investigation will be aimed at gaining more specific information from a group of people to possibly identify the nature of the terrorist crime to be planned or committed. Furthermore, the identifying information can contribute to deciding towards whom the criminal investigation should be directed, and what connections between people and between people and situations apply. This should provide a solid starting point for a criminal investigation.[62]

[59] *Kamerstukken II* 2004/05, 30 164, no. 3, 18-19 and *Kamerstukken II* 2005/06, 30 164, nr. 12, 22.

[60] *Kamerstukken II* 2004/05, 30 164, no. 3, 20.

[61] *Kamerstukken II* 2004/05, 30 164, no. 3, 19.

[62] *Kamerstukken II* 2004/05, 30 164, no. 3, 19.

The purpose of the use of the investigative techniques of Articles 126hh and 126ii shall be the preparation of a (full) criminal investigation of terrorist crimes. According to the explanatory memorandum, the preliminary investigation shall still be understood as 'preceding' the criminal investigation and, consequently, the preliminary investigation shall not be covered by the definition of criminal investigation as provided in Article 132a CCP. As already explained in Sect. 2.3.2.2.4, the exclusion of the preliminary investigation from the criminal investigation is actually difficult to uphold (as well as less favorable from a legal protection point of view). Considering that the information collected in the preliminary investigation will be used in the criminal investigation, the preliminary investigation does concern the criminal investigation as defined in this research.

Providing the preliminary investigation with more intrusive investigative powers has also resulted in the adoption of additional protective requirements, which will protect against unreasonable interferences with private life and restrict the use of the information gathered. In the first place, the public prosecutor still maintains responsibility for the preliminary investigation. Furthermore, as an additional safeguard the authorization of the examining magistrate is required for the use of the most far-reaching preliminary investigative technique: the demanding of information from automated systems under the Article 126hh.[63] The examining magistrate will examine, similar to his warrant task in the context of the criminal investigation, whether the public prosecutor has struck a reasonable balance between the interest of the investigation and the privacy implications that follow from ordering the information.[64] Furthermore, the duty to compile records has now been explicitly established for the preliminary investigative techniques that can only be applied to prepare the full terrorism investigation (Articles 126hh(3) and 126ii(3) CCP).[65] According to Article 126hh(3), the public prosecutor shall report what kind of information has been gathered from 'third' parties, in which way the processing of the information has occurred and which facts and circumstances have justified the use of the preliminary investigative technique. When identifying information that has been gathered on the basis of Article 126ii CCP, the public prosecutor shall report what information has been obtained and why this information is in the interest of the investigation.

Furthermore, specific conditions have been adopted in order to restrict the use of the information gathered and to prevent any abuse. It is the task of the public prosecutor to ensure that the information gathered on the basis of Article 126hh CCP will only be further processed if it is relevant for the criminal investigation. Information that can be relevant in order to subsequently control the processing

---

63 Article 126hh(1) CCP.

64 *Kamerstukken II* 2004/05, 30 164, no. 3, 21.

65 Considering the (explicit) applicability of the duty to compile records concerning these preliminary investigative activities, the separation between a preliminary investigation and a criminal investigation (as upheld by the legislature) seems to be even more redundant.

will also be saved.[66] All other information shall be destroyed (Article 126hh(5) CCP). The selected information—after eliminating the information that is not relevant for the interest of the terrorism investigation—can subsequently also be used in the criminal investigation of terrorist crimes (Article 126hh(6) CCP).

The government considered the manner of processing information to be relatively favorable to the right to respect for private life of the persons concerned. The techniques available during the preliminary investigation entail the computerized processing of information, which means that the information will be analyzed and selected without a human being taking note of the contents of the information. A computer will eliminate information that includes personal details which are not relevant for the further investigation. This information can simply be destroyed without the intervention of a human being. Moreover, the computerized processing procedure will include a screening process concerning the relevance of certain information for the prevention of terrorist crimes, which means that persons cannot be 'caught' earlier for other criminal offenses because they become the subject of a preliminary investigation into terrorist crimes on the basis of a certain profile.[67] The government also pointed out that all information will be stored in a temporary police file (in accordance with Article 1(1)(j) Police Files Act) which will be controlled by the Board for the Protection of Personal Data on the basis of Article 27 of the Police Files Act. The Board can randomly control whether personal details relating to citizens have been dealt with sufficiently carefully.[68] This specific procedure for processing the information will limit unnecessary interferences with the private lives of the persons involved.

The Board of Procurators General has also established a guideline by which an internal examining procedure for the preliminary investigation has been adopted. The public prosecutor will have to submit an order for a preliminary investigation to the Chief Prosecutor of the regional district who will subsequently have it examined by the Chief Prosecutor of the national district. The Chief Prosecutor of the national district will examine whether the preliminary investigation meets the requirements laid down in the law and in the guidelines. Moreover, when the preliminary investigation can have certain social implications or has a national or cross-border nature, the permission of the Board of Prosecutors General is additionally required. The government added in the explanatory memorandum that for the preliminary investigation of terrorist crimes, such permission will often be required.[69]

66 *Kamerstukken II* 2004/05, 30 164, no. 3, 21.

67 *Kamerstukken II* 2005/06, 30 164, no. 7, 27-28.

68 *Kamerstukken II* 2005/06, 30 164, no. 12, 20.

69 *Kamerstukken II* 2004/05, 30 164, no. 3, 22 and *Kamerstukken I* 2006/07, 30 164, no. D, 15-16.

#### 3.2.1.3 New Criminal Investigative Powers

Except for creating a specific investigative domain for terrorism investigations and expanding the investigative possibilities within the preliminary investigation to prepare terrorism investigations, the Act on the Criminal Investigation of Terrorist Crimes has also provided for new investigative powers, which can be used within the terrorism investigation. These new powers should contribute to an effective investigation in the situation of an immediate threat. When there is information that at a certain place in the near future a terrorist attack will be committed, these newly introduced powers will contribute to preventing the realization of the attack. The powers include: the search of objects (Article 126zq CCP), the search of vehicles (Article 126zr CCP) and frisking (Article 126zs CCP).

Considering that these investigative powers are available within the investigative domain for terrorist crimes, the threshold for applying the powers is also 'indications of a terrorist crime.' The public prosecutor can order, upon the establishment of 'indications of a terrorist crime', that one or more of the powers will be applied against anyone appropriate considering 'the interest of the investigation.' The public prosecutor can give his/her order orally, which is valid for a period of 12 hours and for a specifically indicated area. It is possible to extend the duration of the order with a period of 12 hours on each occasion. The interest of the investigation will be decisive for determining whether a person or object should be subjected to one of these powers. For example, when there are indications that a terrorist crime will be committed at a governmental building, this would justify the subjection of anyone in the vicinity of that building to the investigative powers. The selection of the specific persons who are eligible to be searched will depend on the interest of the investigation, which concerns an assessment to be made by the investigative officers in charge. For this assessment the investigative officers shall take into account any available additional information, such as the nationality of the persons who are possibly planning to commit the terrorist crime at that specific place.[70] In addition, also the principles of proportionality and subsidiarity shall be taken into account before deciding whether a person or object can be subjected to a search. Internally distributed guidelines have instructed the police to use the new search powers sparingly.[71]

Considering the examples given, the information required to establish such 'indications' is even less concrete than is required for the use of SIT. Again, the interest of the investigation seems to be decisive, which is a criterion that is (even more) easily met when facing the possibility of an imminent terrorist attack. Nevertheless, the indications should follow from facts and circumstances which require a certain level of precision that is open to objectification. The government has therefore rejected the idea that when e.g. an e-mail is received in which it is

[70] Article 126zq(3) CCP, by analogy applicable according to Articles 126zr(3) and 126zs(3) CCP.

[71] De Poot et al. 2008, 32.

stated that 'tomorrow, somewhere in the country, something terrible will happen,' this is a sufficient ground for applying these investigative powers. The information must be more concrete in order to be able to successfully apply these search powers. Continuous rumors among extremists that 'an attack will be committed against a certain sporting event' will be a sufficient ground for initiating a criminal investigation. In such a situation the information is sufficient to decide that, for example, frisking will be employed at the location of the sporting event. From these examples, it follows that the powers can be used when their use will also serve the interest of the investigation from a practical point of view, rather than meeting a certain standard of concreteness and reliability.[72]

Moreover, it is possible to use these new search powers without an order of the public prosecutor in so-called 'security zones.'[73] A certain area can be labeled as a security zone by an administrative decree, which concerns a decision on a semi-permanent basis. If the threat of terrorism with regard to that area has disappeared the decision will again be annulled by an administrative decree. The zones will always concern areas to which a permanent threat of terrorist attacks is applicable, such as governmental premises, airports, large vital industrial areas, nuclear power stations or train or subway stations. By the administrative decree of 21 December 2006 concerning rules for the operation of the regulation of the criminal investigation of terrorist crimes, the specific areas that are security zones have been identified. These zones have not since been changed and concern the following areas: the central train stations of the four major cities, all airports and their direct surroundings, the governmental district in The Hague [*Binnenhof*], the nuclear power station in Borssele and the media district in Hilversum.[74] A security zone will normally concern areas to which a constant threat of terrorist crimes applies, which will for instance follow from threat analyses by the AIVD. For this reason, the legislature has indicated that for the use of search powers in security zones indications of a terrorist need not be present. The investigative officers may search anything or anyone whenever they consider the search to serve the interest of preventing terrorist crimes. In fact, the security zone label replaces the 'indications of a terrorist crime' threshold, as it is assumed that within the security zone indications of a terrorist crime are present on a more permanent basis.[75] Nevertheless, the investigative officers may only use search powers in security zones when the use is 'in the interest of the investigation.' Arguably, in the absence of more concrete 'indications of a terrorist crime' it will be unlikely that the use of a search power will serve the interest of the investigation. Hence, in fact the main difference between using the search powers in security zones and using them

---

72 *Kamerstukken II* 2005/06, 30 164, no. 12, 3-4 and *Kamerstukken II* 2005/06, 30 164, no. 7, 21.

73 Article 126zq(4) CCP.

74 *Stb.* 2006, 730, Article 3(1) and Appendix.

75 *Kamerstukken II* 2004/05, 30 164, no. 3, 44.

outside such zones is that within the security zone the order of the public prosecutor is not required.[76]

Providing the investigative officers with the discretion to select persons to be searched within the security zones, or in the areas that are allocated by an order of the public prosecutor, involves the risk of a selection being made on the basis of discriminatory grounds, for example, by particularly selecting persons on the basis of their Muslim appearance.[77] Also the Council of State touched upon this risk which is involved in the discretionary power of investigative officers when subjecting persons to a search. The Council questioned whether sufficient safeguards have been established to meet the prohibition of discrimination concerning the enjoyment of the right to private life under Article 14 and Article 8 ECHR.[78] It should be prevented that investigative officers make their determination about what is in the interest of the investigation on the basis of incorrect assumptions or maybe even discriminatory ideas. Furthermore, the risk has been addressed that the investigative officers will apply search powers by order of the public prosecutor or in security zones in order to detect other criminal offenses.

In answer to these concerns, the government underlines the presence of different procedural safeguards that should avoid the arbitrary application of search powers. The government emphasized that the investigative officers should realize the exceptional reason to allocate a certain area as an area in which search powers may be used. The government considered that the criterion of 'the interest of the investigation', implying a proportionality assessment, should prevent the selection on the basis of other grounds and shall require an objective and professional judgment by the investigative officers in question. This does not mean that, for example, skin color or specific clothing cannot be used as a selection criterion, because this can be an objective criterion serving the interest of the investigation.[79] Furthermore, according to the government, the protective requirement of the duty to compile records should prevent any abuse of the search powers by facilitating transparency and control.[80] Lastly, the government pointed to the possibility to file a complaint with the chief of police department, the public prosecutor or with the National Ombudsman when someone suspects that he or she has been selected for the wrong reasons.[81]

---

[76] This interpretation is also more close to the exact language of Article 126zq, as the fourth section of Article 126zq only exempts the use of search powers in security zones from the requirement of an order of the public prosecutor and not from the indications threshold. Nevertheless, considering the explanation of the legislature, investigative officers may assume that the indications threshold is met when they seek to apply search methods in security zones. Compare: Corstens and Borgers 2011, 510.

[77] Compare Goldschmidt 2005, 24-26.

[78] *Kamerstukken II* 2005/06, 30 164, no. 7, 21.

[79] *Kamerstukken II* 2005/06, 30 164, no. 7, 23.

[80] Applicable in its strict form, similar to the use of SIT, through Article 126aa CCP.

[81] *Kamerstukken II* 2004/05, 30 164, no. 3, 45 and *Kamerstukken II* 2005/06, 30 164, no. 7, 23 and *Kamerstukken I* 2006/07, 30 164, no. D, 21-22.

The government also pointed to the nature of the newly introduced investigative powers, which differs from SIT. Because these new search methods will not be used covertly but in public, the powers only interfere to a limited extent with the right to respect for private life of the persons concerned. The police and PPS have indicated that they consider these newly created search powers within the criminal investigation to be hardly any different from the search powers they already have within the scope of the Weapons and Ammunition Act, which can also be applied in security zones (although these security zones must be allotted on the basis of Article 151b(1) Municipalities Act, requiring an order of the mayor with the approval of the city council).[82] The police and PPS nevertheless acknowledge the value of the new powers in the potential exceptional situation where they are needed to prevent an imminent terrorist attack. For this reason, the new search powers have been identified not as investigative powers, but as powers that can be used to prevent a terrorist attack in a crisis situation.[83]

### *3.2.2 The Evolvement Towards Intelligence-Led Criminal Law Enforcement*

Intelligence has obtained a central role in countering terrorism, a role which is also still increasing as a consequence of the development of new technological methods to analyze the intelligence collected in combined databases.[84] Also the police have, in the context of the political and societal context where prevention and security are top priorities, undergone an accelerated development towards proactive action, which has triggered a transformation of the methods of operation. This development has accelerated over the past decade, but the process has started since the confrontation with the complexity of investigating organized crime in the 1980s. Consequently, the activities of the police have changed to include the making of risk calculations and have enabled 'intelligence-led policing.'[85] The information-steered operation of the police was also one of the objectives formulated in the report of the working group concerning 'Police in development.'[86] The police operation as an intelligence-led agency is thus a general development, not only suitable for terrorism prevention but also used for detecting (serious) criminal activities in general.

---

[82] Article 50(3), 51(3) and 52(3) Weapons and Ammunition Act.

[83] De Poot et al. 2008, 32-33, 58.

[84] At the same time the focus and further development of measures to strengthen the information position by gathering intelligence also seriously complicates deriving actionable information from the patchwork of information available. See De Hoog 2008, 587 and Muller 2008, 912-913.

[85] See also Vis 2010B, 125-126.

[86] Deelman and Gunther Moor 2010, 373.

Nevertheless, especially for the prevention of terrorism it is required to act in time and, for that purpose, the police not only rely on the information received from the AIVD (e.g. in the context of the CT Infobox[87]), but also independently use their information gathering capacities in order to build a strong information position on which basis the police may initiate criminal investigations of terrorism offences at an early stage. Hence, the national and regional divisions of the CIE have an important role in enabling intelligence-led policing for terrorism prevention considering that the CIE is responsible for collecting 'criminal' intelligence. In order to make sure that criminal investigative capacities are efficiently deployed, the police in practice primarily focus on their investigative gathering capacities in the context of the CIE and with the help of 'regular' police powers on the basis of Article 2 Police Act 1993, instead of using SIT in the context of the criminal investigation.[88] This contributes to avoiding unnecessary use of SIT. In addition, when criminal investigations into terrorism (on the basis of indications or a reasonable suspicion) do not produce results in the sense that the indications or the reasonable suspicion can be substantiated, the police will usually terminate the criminal investigation. To make sure that the remaining 'signals' of terrorist activities do not escape notice, the information is communicated to the RID. Hence, the RIDs—in cooperation with the AIVD—then function as a back-up facility, making it possible to warn the police when the situation has changed and criminal investigative action is required to prevent terrorism.[89]

This policy reflects a focus on a strong information position as the basis for anticipative criminal investigation. It reflects the rationale that a strong information position enables the police and PPS to jump in with criminal investigative activities that include the use of SIT when the information gathered reaches the level of 'indications' or a 'reasonable suspicion' and it will be possible to start gathering additional evidence in order to eventually turn to the prosecution of terrorist suspects.

## 3.3 Changes Affecting the Relation Between the AIVD and the PPS

One of the key elements of the Dutch counterterrorism strategy has been to enhance the coherence between the activities of the AIVD, the PPS and the police by increasing the cooperation and exchange of information between the intelligence community and law enforcement community. Among the measures announced by the government was the linking of the activities of the intelligence agencies and the police and the sharing of information between the intelligence

---

87 See Sect. 3.4.4.

88 Van Gestel et al. 2009, 45-47.

89 *Ibid.*, 47-48.

community and the law enforcement community. For that purpose, AIVD reports shall be sufficient for establishing a reasonable suspicion and it shall be possible to use these reports as evidence in a criminal trial.[90] The adoption of the Act on the Criminal Investigation of Terrorist Crimes was, except for increasing the investigative capacities of the criminal investigation, also intended to increase cooperation and the sharing of information between the intelligence and law enforcement communities, by institutionalizing that the prevention of terrorism has become more of a shared mission of the intelligence and the law enforcement communities.[91] The goal of the possibility to investigate in an 'earlier' phase (as realized by the Act on the Criminal Investigation of Terrorist Crimes, see Sect. 3.2.1) was also to stimulate the transfer of information from the AIVD to the PPS at an earlier point in time in order to combine forces for realizing the prevention of terrorism in the most effective way.[92] Furthermore, also the courts have played an important role in the acceptance of the use of AIVD reports as starting information for a criminal investigation and as evidence in criminal trials as well as a less stringent separation between criminal investigative activities and intelligence activities in general.[93]

Section 3.3.1 will address the acceptance of AIVD reports as starting information for criminal investigations. The Shielded Witnesses Act has been adopted in order to increase the possibilities for using intelligence information in criminal proceedings, either as starting information for criminal investigations or as evidence. The framework for hearing shielded witnesses as an instrument to control the veracity of the intelligence information has especially been created for terrorism cases, but can also be used in other criminal cases with national security implications.[94] The framework will be described in Sect. 3.3.2. Furthermore, as a consequence of the possibility to criminally investigate at an earlier phase and bearing a shared mission of 'prevention', situations where intelligence investigations and criminal investigations are conducted in parallel have increased. Sect. 3.3.3 will deal with parallel investigations and the manner in which the courts have dealt with this situation. Lastly, Sect. 3.3.4 addresses other measures, mainly of an institutional nature, which have been adopted to increase cooperation

---

[90] *Kamerstukken II* 2002/03, 27 925, no. 94, 10.

[91] The acknowledgment that the AIVD and the police have a shared field of action, which means that activities conducted in parallel and with regard to the same subjects/issues are legitimate, was already provided by a commission investigating the activities of the BVD (the predecessor of the AIVD) and the police in 1990. In 1992 the Minister of Justice attached specific legal conclusions to this acknowledgment, such as the use of BVD information as starting information for criminal investigations. Krips 2009, 138 and *Kamerstukken II* 1991/92, 22 453, no. 4, 2.

[92] Rapport Evaluatie Antiterrorismemaatregelen 2011, 15 and 49. See also *Kamerstukken II* 2004/05, 30 164, no. 3, 33, where it was explicitly provided in the explanatory memorandum that as a consequence of the broadening of the criminal investigative domain, an AIVD investigation can in an earlier phase shift to the criminal investigative domain on the basis of an official report by the AIVD under Article 38 WIV 2002.

[93] See also Hirsch Ballin 2009.

[94] Baijer 2006, 959.

and to stimulate the effective sharing of information which is relevant to terrorism prevention

### 3.3.1 AIVD Reports as Starting Information for a Criminal Investigation

The transfer of information from the AIVD to the PPS, through the national public prosecutor for counterterrorism, has been given a specific legal basis in the WIV of 2002.[95] As has been explained in Sect. 2.2.2.4.2, the AIVD will send an official report to the national public prosecutor for counterterrorism who will examine the veracity of the information provided in the report and, on that basis, will decide whether the information should be transferred to the PPS and the police. Because the national public prosecutor has access to the information behind the report, such as the sources and methods of obtaining that information, the national public prosecutor has, similar to employees of the AIVD, a duty of confidentiality (Article 85-86 WIV 2002). Since the establishment of the Counterterrorism Information Box (CT Infobox) such sharing may also occur in the context of the function of this CT Infobox. Sect. 3.3.4 will address the role of the CT Infobox in the exchange of information and the cooperation between the AIVD, the PPS and the police. This section will firstly address the use of AIVD reports as starting information for a criminal investigation, in particular by assessing the manner in which courts have dealt with this issue.

Dutch courts have been, especially in terrorism cases which they have dealt with since 2001, increasingly confronted with the use of AIVD information in criminal proceedings. The fact that the use of AIVD information has especially been at issue in terrorism cases is not surprising considering that the task of the AIVD is to conduct investigations into the activities of persons and organizations, which, considering their objectives, threaten national security.[96] Because the AIVD will usually conduct investigations into terrorist activities already before a criminal investigation may be initiated, it is also not surprising that criminal investigations into terrorist crimes are preceded by the intelligence investigation and are possibly initiated on the basis of information provided by the AIVD on the basis of Article 38 WIV 2002. The intelligence investigation may thus be followed up by a criminal investigation after an official report from the AIVD to that effect. This does not necessarily mean that the AIVD investigation is terminated when a criminal investigation is initiated, as the need for the AIVD to continue investigative activities in order to protect national security may remain. This latter subject of parallel investigations will be dealt with in Sect. 3.3.3.

---

[95] Article 38 WIV 2002, see furthermore Sect. 2.2.2.4.2.

[96] Article 6(2)(a) WIV 2002.

Already in a note from the Minister of Justice dating from 1992, the possibility to use AIVD information in criminal proceedings was explicitly acknowledged. The Minister of Justice concluded in this note that although the task of the BVD (the predecessor of the AIVD) was not to gather evidence regarding criminal offenses, the separation between the intelligence domain and the criminal law enforcement domain did not preclude that the information gathered by the BVD could provide a reason for initiating a criminal investigation and for establishing a reasonable suspicion under Article 27(1) CCP. The possibility to use intelligence as evidence was also acknowledged in this 1992 note, although the final decision as to evidentiary matters is, of course, for the trial judge.[97] Nevertheless, the possibility to use a single AIVD report to trigger a criminal investigation was not yet addressed by the courts. These issues were only addressed when the first 'terrorism case' reached the courts.

The first 'terrorist case' (concerning 'Islamic' terrorism, generally referred to as the '*Eik' case*) was heard by the District Court of Rotterdam in December 2002. The District Court decided that an official report by the BVD could not establish a reasonable suspicion that someone has committed a crime.[98] The acquittal of the suspects in the *Eik* case by the District Court of Rotterdam, as well as the acquittal of other terrorist suspects in June 2003,[99] largely as a consequence of the fact that the AIVD report was not accepted as establishing a reasonable suspicion, triggered political action in order to enable the possibility of using AIVD information in criminal proceedings.[100] This resulted in the adoption of the Shielded Witnesses Act in 2006 which will be addressed in the next section.

Nevertheless, already before the Shielded Witnesses Act had entered into force, the Court of Appeal and, subsequently, the Supreme Court, assessing the *Eik* case on appeal, accepted the AIVD report as establishing a reasonable suspicion. The Court of Appeal argued that the law enforcement services should be able to trust the legitimate operations of the AIVD, considering the framework of the WIV 2002 including an oversight committee under which the AIVD operated. Hence, on the basis of an official report by the AIVD the PPS may initiate a criminal investigation.[101] Since the entry into force of the WIV 2002 an examination of the information provided in the official report is realized by allowing the national

---

97 *Kamerstukken II* 1991/92, 22 463, no. 4, 2 and 6. During the discussion of the bill for the current WIV 2002, the responsible Ministers concluded that the general lines set out in the 1992 note still reflected the current and the correct possibilities for using intelligence in criminal proceedings. *Kamerstukken II* 1997/98, 25 877, no. 14, 12.

98 Rechtbank Rotterdam 18 December 2002, *LJN* AF2141. The suspects in this case were arrested on September 13 2001, as members of an international terrorist network preparing terrorist crimes. Although the court decided that the BVD report could not establish a reasonable suspicion, it also acknowledged that information provided by the intelligence and security services to the PPS could be a reason for initiating a criminal investigation.

99 Rechtbank Rotterdam 5 June 2003, *LJN* AF9546.

100 *Kamerstukken II* 2003/04, 28 463, no. 25.

101 Gerechtshof 's-Gravenhage 21 June 2004, *NJ* 2004, 432 (*Eik*), para 4.3.4 and 4.3.9.

public prosecutor for counterterrorism to examine the background to the official report before passing it through to the law enforcement services. Following the Court of Appeal in its judgment that AIVD reports could (without supporting information) trigger a criminal investigation, the Supreme Court decided that no legal rule obstructs the use of AIVD information (in that particular case BVD information) as starting information for a criminal investigation, and, consequently, the acceptance of a reasonable suspicion against someone (under Article 27(1) CCP) on the basis of that information. The Supreme Court drew this conclusion both on the basis of the legal framework of the WIV 2002 and its predecessor, the WIV 1987, and on the fact that the criminal investigative authorities may in principle presume the correctness of the information provided by the BVD/AIVD.[102]

The Supreme Court thus accepted for the first time in the case *Eik* that also a report by the AIVD could establish a reasonable suspicion of a crime having been/being committed. Subsequently, in the terrorism case of *Piranha,* decided by the Court of Appeal of The Hague in 2008, the initial criminal investigative activities (the criminal investigation 'Paling' conducted under Title V, the criminal investigative domain for organized crime) were based upon official reports by the AIVD, in this case supported by CIE information. Both the District Court that initially decided the case and the Court of Appeal affirmed that the information could establish a reasonable suspicion under Title V and repeated the Supreme Court's acceptance in *Eik* that AIVD information can trigger a criminal investigation.[103] Nevertheless, this does not mean that in all circumstances AIVD information will be allowed to establish a reasonable suspicion. In each case the information available shall be assessed as to whether the facts and circumstances provided can objectively establish a reasonable suspicion (compare Sects. 2.3.2.3.1 and 2.3.2.3.3). In this light the Supreme Court decided in a 2008 case involving a terrorist threat that an anonymously provided tip to the AIVD was insufficient to establish a reasonable suspicion so as to search a home on the basis of Article 49 WWM. Decisive for reaching this conclusion was the fact that the checking of the information as done by the PPS and the police—which was possible considering the time span between the anonymous tip and the mentioned date of the attack—did not establish any additional incriminating information.[104] On the basis of this decision the conclusion can be drawn that it shall be assessed on a case-by-case basis whether the information available provides facts and circumstances that can establish a reasonable suspicion.[105]

AIVD reports, anonymous tip-offs and CIE information are in principle sources upon which a criminal investigation can be initiated. Considering this latter

---

102 HR 5 September 2006, *NJ* 2007, 336, ann. Sch (*Eik*), para 4.6 and 6.3.2.

103 Rechtbank Rotterdam 1 December 2006, *LJN* AZ3589 and Gerechtshof's-Gravenhage 2 October 2008, *LJN* BF3987 (*Piranha*).

104 HR 11 March 2008, *NJ* 2008, 328, para 3.4.

105 Annotation Borgers para 6 at HR 11 March 2008, *NJ* 2008, 329, ann. Borgers.

Supreme Court decision of 2008, the question whether the AIVD report can establish a reasonable suspicion in a particular case also depends on the urgency of the need to act upon the information contained in the AIVD report. If time allows, the police and PPS shall seek to verify the information provided by the AIVD and, on the basis of those findings, decide whether or not the AIVD report can be used as starting information. This reasoning of the Supreme Court, however, also implies that when the AIVD report provides information of an imminent threat, such additional verification may be omitted considering the immediate need to resort to the power of arrest so as to remove that threat.[106] Hence, the question whether or not a reasonable suspicion can be derived from the available facts and circumstances concerns, in fact, a question of balancing the interests involved: between the interest of protection against arbitrary action by the government in the field of criminal procedural law and the interest of criminal law enforcement (including the prevention of a terrorist attack).[107]

The terrorism cases that have been described where the information provided by the AIVD has been used as the starting information for a criminal investigation concerned the question whether this information could establish a reasonable suspicion either as to Article 27(1) CCP or as to the reasonable suspicion threshold applicable to the investigative domain for organized crime. No case has yet been decided where the judge has assessed the facts and circumstances that can establish 'indications of a terrorist crime', as the threshold for using SIT in criminal investigations into terrorist activities. Nevertheless, it is clear that the legislature aimed to establish a 'lower' threshold by adopting the indications threshold and that AIVD reports can therefore also establish 'indications'. Indeed, the legislature even explicitly formulated that the goal of adopting the investigative domain for terrorist crimes was to stimulate that the AIVD would share information at an 'earlier' point with the PPS in order to be able to start criminal investigative activities in an earlier phase.[108] In addition, it follows from the examples mentioned in the explanatory memorandum that information from the AIVD, even including threat analyses, will likely establish indications.[109]

### 3.3.2 The Shielded Witnesses Act

On November 1st 2006 the Shielded Witnesses Act of September 28, 2006 entered into force.[110] This Act has provided for a statutory basis to use AIVD information as evidence by allowing the use of the official report as a full written report, which

[106] Compare: Krips 2009, 148.

[107] Annotation Borgers para 6 at HR 11 March 2008, *NJ* 2008, 329, ann. Borgers.

[108] *Kamerstukken II* 2004/05, 30 164, no. 3, 33.

[109] *Kamerstukken II* 2004/05, 30 164, no. 3, 9.

[110] *Stb.* 2006, 460 and 461.

is one of the accepted evidentiary sources (Article 344(1)(3) CCP) of which its use as evidence is not limited to evidentiary value in relation to other sources of evidence. Not only AIVD information has been accepted as a source of evidence, also information from foreign intelligence services and intelligence collected by international intelligence gathering bodies, such as Europol or Interpol, amount to full written reports.[111]

Furthermore, the Shielded Witnesses Act increases the possibilities to use AIVD information in criminal proceedings by creating a mechanism to examine the veracity of the information provided in the AIVD report. This concerns both the use of AIVD reports as starting information for criminal investigations and as evidence in criminal trials.[112] The duty of confidentiality resting on AIVD employees on the basis of Article 85 WIV 2002 obstructs the hearing of AIVD employees with regard to the information included in the AIVD report in the public setting of the trial and in the presence of the defense, for which reason the use of AIVD information as evidence is usually impossible.[113] Because the legislature has, as part of its counterterrorism strategy, stimulated the use of intelligence information as proactive steering information in criminal proceedings, the legislature has sought a solution to deal with the clash of transparency interests in criminal proceedings and the secrecy of sources and methods in the field of intelligence investigations to protect national security. Hence, the Shielded Witnesses Act is based upon two pillars: firstly, the wish to further the use of intelligence information in criminal proceedings in a way which is compatible with the right to a fair trial and, secondly, the interest of protecting the sources and methods of the AIVD in order to protect national security. In the explanatory memorandum the goal of the Act was formulated as increasing the capabilities for using official reports of the AIVD as starting information for a criminal investigation and as a source of evidence.[114] For this purpose, a mechanism has been provided in the CCP, which can be used in order to hear witnesses as shielded witnesses (Articles 226m-226s CCP).

When the public prosecutor refuses to summon the witness who can testify with regard to the veracity of the AIVD information during trial,[115] the trial judge can refer the case to the examining magistrate to examine the information.[116] The examining magistrate can then hear the AIVD officer as a shielded witness if the protection of national security reasonably demands the hearing of the witness as a shielded witness (Article 226 m(1) CCP). The term national security shall be understood in line with Article 6 WIV 2002, providing for the tasks of the

[111] Article 344(1)(3) CCP, *Kamerstukken II* 2003/04, 29 743, no. 3, 13-14.

[112] *Kamerstukken II* 2003/04, 29 743, no. 3, 1.

[113] As explained in the previous section, the Supreme Court also accepted, prior to the adoption of the Shielded Witnesses Act, the use of AIVD reports as evidence.

[114] *Kamerstukken II* 2003/04, 29743, no. 3, 1.

[115] On the basis of Article 264(2)(b) CCP.

[116] Article 288(2) CCP.

AIVD.[117] It is the task of the AIVD to determine what matters are matters of national security and, hence, the examining magistrate will have to follow any certification of the AIVD employee in that regard.[118] The explanatory memorandum of the Shielded Witnesses Act refers to countering international terrorism, certain serious infringements of the legal order for the purpose of causing political instability and the violent subversion of foreign regimes as matters of national security.[119] The interest of national security may also justify keeping the identity of the witness shielded (Article 226n(1) CCP) and justify hearing the shielded witness in the absence of the defense and public prosecutor (Article 226p CCP). When the shielded witness is examined in the absence of the public prosecutor and the defense, the PPS and the defense are provided with the possibility to participate through telecommunication or, when this method would harm national security interests, through submitting their written questions to the examining magistrate (Article 226p(4)). After the hearing, the examining magistrate shall draw up in writing a report of the examination of the witness. It is the examining magistrate's responsibility to make sure that no information is included that would harm the protection of national security. Nevertheless, the shielded witness has the final say as to whether or not the report of the examination will be disclosed (Articles 226p(3) and 226 s CCP). Hence, in the end the interest of national security trumps the criminal procedural interest of equality of arms and adversarial proceedings.[120]

The main goal of the examination of the shielded witness concerns the conclusion formulated by the examining magistrate as to the veracity of the AIVD information (Article 226q CCP). This conclusion shall be explicitly provided within the written report of the hearing of the shielded witness to be disclosed to the defense, public prosecutor and trial judge. This conclusion may be based upon information which is withheld from disclosure, considering that the examining magistrate may prevent the disclosure of answers given by the shielded witness when these answers may harm the protection of national security (Article 187d(1)(c) CCP). In that light, the examining magistrate shall also consider whether the report is still an adequate reproduction of the hearing of the shielded witness.[121] The examining magistrate can only base his conclusion as to the veracity of the AIVD information on the basis of the hearing of the shielded witness and has thus not had the possibility, like the national public prosecutor for counterterrorism, to examine the underlying documents himself. With this responsibility the examining magistrate has been given a very important role in the truth-finding process. Instead of the trial judge, the examining magistrate shall formulate a conclusion with regard to the veracity of sources of evidence while taking into account both the interest of national security and of a fair trial.

[117] See Chap. 2, Sect 2.2.1.4.

[118] Beijer 2006, 962.

[119] *Kamerstukken II* 2003/04, 29 743, no. 3, 3.

[120] See also *Kamerstukken II* 2003/04, 29 743, no. 3, 1.

[121] See also : Beijer 2006, 971. *Kamerstukken II* 2003/04, 29 743, no. 3, 21-22.

Although the trial judge still has the final say on what sources of evidence a conviction will be based, he cannot further examine the conclusion of the examining magistrate as to the veracity of the AIVD information.[122]

Although adopted in order to enable the usefulness of AIVD information in criminal proceedings in observance of fair trial rights, the use of the framework of the shielded witness impairs the rights of the defense in the light of Article 6 ECHR, in particular as to their right to cross-examine witnesses and to challenge the evidence against them. Although the government considered the framework as a mechanism that, in principle, may sufficiently counterbalance the handicaps for the defense, the government also stated that the framework should only be used when necessary, as required under Article 6 ECHR.[123] So far, it appears that the framework for hearing shielded witnesses has not yet been used in practice.[124]

### *3.3.3 Parallel Investigations*

Another consequence of the possibility to criminally investigate terrorist activities in an earlier phase and for the purpose of preventing 'full' terrorist crimes concerns a possible overlap with the activities of the intelligence and security services, in particular of the AIVD. The investigation of 'indications' of preparatory acts of terrorism likely overlaps with the task of the AIVD to investigate activities that threaten national security (more precisely formulated in Article 6 WIV 2002, see Sect. 2.2.1.4). The possibility of overlapping activities by the AIVD, the PPS and the police already existed prior to the expansion of criminal investigative possibilities in the proactive phase, considering that the proactive criminal investigation of activities that may also constitute a threat to national security may also draw the attention of the AIVD. Nevertheless, especially since the prevention of terrorism has become the shared responsibility of law enforcement and intelligence and since the possibilities of the law enforcement services to investigate in an earlier phase with an eye to prevention have been enhanced as well as stimulated, the phenomenon of parallel investigations has increased.[125]

The separation between the law enforcement services and the intelligence and security services is provided in the law on the basis of their investigative purpose. According to Article 9 WIV 2002 officers of the AIVD do not have criminal investigative powers and may thus not act in the field of criminal law enforcement. Also the processing of information for the benefit of the task of the AIVD needs to be strictly separated from the processing of information by the AIVD for other

---

[122] Beijer 2006, 975.

[123] *Kamerstukken II* 2003/04, 29 743, no. 3, 7 and 9.

[124] Rapport van de Commissie Evaluatie Antiterrorismebeleid 2009, 27 and Van Kempen and Van de Voort 2010, 88.

[125] Krips 2009, 139-140.

purposes.[126] By adopting these provisions the legislature intended to guarantee a strict separation between the intelligence investigation of the AIVD and the criminal investigation on behalf of the PPS and the police.[127] During the discussion of the bill on investigating and prosecuting terrorist crimes, concerns were raised as to the possibility of parallel investigations and the possible intermingling of tasks. The government confirmed the possibility of parallel investigations, which, however, does not alter the fact that the purpose of either investigation is different and, therefore, does not touch upon the separation between the law enforcement and intelligence community.[128]

Nevertheless, the situation of parallel investigations does involve a risk that the criminal investigative authorities cooperate with the AIVD on a level that is inconsistent with the strict separation between the intelligence and law enforcement communities. Firstly, the possibility of parallel investigations may involve a risk that the PPS and the police circumvent the use of criminal investigative powers by relying on the path of sharing AIVD information. Secondly, the AIVD investigation may influence or even steer the course of events during the criminal investigation, whilst this role of the AIVD in the criminal investigation cannot be controlled *ex post*.

These two controversial aspects of parallel investigations have also been addressed by the courts in terrorism cases. Both in the *Eik* and in the *Piranha* cases the defense challenged the practice of parallel investigations. Furthermore, the Supreme Court has addressed parallel investigations in a case concerning an extreme form of animal rights activism. Firstly in the *Eik* case the Supreme Court determined that, whereas no legal rule forbids the use of intelligence in criminal proceedings, the fruits of the intelligence investigation may not be used as evidence: 1) in the exclusive situation where criminal procedural safeguards have intentionally been circumvented by not making use of criminal investigative powers in order to make use of the information gathered by the AIVD; and, 2) where the investigative action of the intelligence agency has violated the fundamental rights of the suspect in a manner which is incompatible with the right to a fair trial under Article 6 ECHR.[129]

Subsequently, the Supreme Court addressed the issue in more detail in the case regarding extremist animal rights activism. Like terrorism, extreme forms of animal rights activism are an issue which has received the shared attention of the AIVD and the criminal investigative authorities. Here, the Supreme Court affirmed that no legal rule forbids the providing of information from the AIVD to the PPS at the request of the PPS or the police, nor the continued requesting of information from the AIVD, except in the situation where there is an intentional circumventing

---

126 Article 14 WIV 2002.

127 See also the explanatory memorandum of the WIV 2002, *Kamerstukken II* 1997/98, 25 877, no. 3, 16.

128 *Kamerstukken II* 2005/06, 30 164, no. 7, 42-43.

129 HR 5 September 2006, *NJ* 2007, 336, para 4.6 and 4.7.2.

of criminal procedural safeguards or in the situation of the use of AIVD investigative powers for criminal investigative purposes (*détournement de pouvoir*).[130] Hence, a parallel investigation is permitted.[131] The Court of Appeal of The Hague reached the same conclusion in the *Piranha* case.[132]

Notwithstanding this general acceptance of parallel investigations and the continued exchange of information, such practice may not result in the circumvention of criminal procedural safeguards by relying on the information of the AIVD, while the law enforcement agencies could use their own criminal investigative powers to obtain this information. This circumvention of criminal procedural safeguards and, thus, *détournement de pouvoir,* concerns the first potential for an abuse of power in the course of parallel investigations. According to the defense in the *Piranha* case the parallel investigation and continued exchange of information did point to the circumvention of criminal procedural guarantees. The District Court concluded, on the basis of the report by the supervisory commission of the AIVD regarding official reports sent in the period January 2004-October 2005 (covering also the official reports sent at the time of the criminal investigation in *Piranha*) and the testimony of the substitute Chief of the AIVD, that the intentional circumvention of criminal procedural safeguards could not be proven.[133] The Court of Appeal followed the District Court in this decision and concluded that it could not be proven that the AIVD, the PPS and the police had cooperated in a far-reaching manner.[134] In the case regarding animal rights extremism, the Supreme Court accepted the rejection of a request by the defense with regard to an alleged abuse of power, when there are insufficient points of departure for further examination.[135]

The manner in which the courts have assessed the challenges regarding abuse in the course of parallel investigations is very marginal. In this regard it is in the first place remarked that Article 359a CCP only applies to irregularities during the criminal investigation and, hence, the investigation conducted by the AIVD falls outside the scope examining the legitimacy of investigative activities in the context of Article 359a CCP.[136] Only in the above-mentioned exceptional situations of either an intentional circumvention of criminal procedural safeguards or a violation of the rights of suspects in a manner which is incompatible with Article 6 ECHR, will the information gathered by the AIVD be excluded from the

[130] HR 13 November 2007, *NJ* 2007, 614, para 3.4.2 and 3.5.2.

[131] HR 13 November 2007, *NJ* 2007, 614, para 3.4.3 and 3.5.2.

[132] Gerechtshof 's-Gravenhage 2 October 2008, *LJN* BF3987. The decision of the Supreme Court is currently still pending.

[133] Rechtbank Rotterdam 1 December 2006, *LJN* AZ 3589.

[134] Gerechtshof's-Gravenhage 2 October 2008, *LJN* BF 3987.

[135] HR 13 November 2007, *NJ* 2007, 614, para 3.6.

[136] HR 5 September 2006, *NJ* 2007, 336, para 4.7.1.

evidence.[137] It appears that in the case of a claim of *détournement de pouvoir* the judge will in the first place trust the legitimacy of the investigative activities of the intelligence agency, unless there are clear indications pointing to one of these 'exceptional situations'. This presumption of trust in the legitimacy of the activities of the AIVD is based upon the presence of controlling mechanisms, namely the oversight commission for the AIVD and parliamentary control.[138] Nevertheless, the Supreme Court in the case *Piranha* did not consider this presumption of trust as decisive to reject the challenge of the defense regarding abuse of power, but the fact that any handicaps for the defense were compensated by the hearing of the national public prosecutor for counterterrorism as a witness with regard to the reliability of the AIVD information.[139] With this approach, the Supreme Court focuses on the evidentiary value of the AIVD information in the light of Article 6 ECHR, considering that the testimony of the national public prosecutor for counterterrorism has not provided for any additional information as to the manner of cooperation between the AIVD and the PPS and, hence, this did not take away any concerns with regard to the legitimacy of the course of events in the parallel investigation.

The second potential for abuse during parallel investigations concerns the possibility that the AIVD influences the criminal investigation in a controlling manner. This potential of abuse was a central issue in the *Piranha* case, where the defense contested that the information provided by the AIVD (concerning tapped telephone conservations) was obtained through entrapment on behalf of the AIVD by instructing the family members of the suspect to have long phone conversations and to ask specific questions.[140] In this regard, the role of the AIVD could have had consequences for the contents of the evidence produced during trial. Moreover, in such a situation the AIVD may have violated the prohibition on entrapment (the *Tallon* criterion).[141] The District Court and the Court of Appeal that assessed the case of *Piranha* rejected this challenge in similar terms as the challenge concerning *détournement de pouvoir*. The courts trusted the legitimate operations of the AIVD, *unless* the activities of the AIVD violated the rights of the suspect to an extent that would take away the fairness of the proceedings as to Article 6 ECHR on its face.[142] Considering that also this challenge concerns the (il)legitimacy of the investigative activities of the AIVD, the trial judge will not

---

137 HR 5 September 2006, *NJ* 2007, 336, para 4.7.2 and HR 13 November 2007, *NJ* 2007, 614, para 3.6.

138 As also explicitly mentioned by the Court of Appeal in *Eik,* Gerechtshof's-Gravenhage 21 June 2004, *NJ* 2004, 432, para 4.3.9. See also Opinion Advocate-General Machielse para 4.2-4.4 HR 5 September 2006, *NJ* 2007, 336.

139 HR 5 September 2006, *NJ* 2007, 336, para 6.3.4.

140 This situation was discussed in the *Piranha* case (Rechtbank Rotterdam 1 December 2006, *LJN* AZ3589 and Gerechtshof's-Gravenhage 2 October 2008, *LJN* BF 3987).

141 See Sect 2.3.2.1.2 footnote 355.

142 Rechtbank Rotterdam 1 December 2006, *LJN* AZ3589 (see also HR 5 September 2006, *NJ* 2007, 336, para 4.7.2).

examine the activities of the AIVD as these actions fall outside the scope of Article 359a CCP (see Chap. 2, Sect. 2.3.2.4.2).[143]

The controlling possibilities of the trial judge concerning the legitimacy of the investigative activities of the AIVD is in that way basically excluded, which is at the same time a logical conclusion considering the strict separation between the intelligence community and the law enforcement community. Because of the institutional separation, also the controlling mechanisms are separated and control by the trial judge over the legitimacy of the investigative activities of the AIVD is excluded. Nevertheless, when the information obtained through illegitimate activities by the AIVD is introduced as evidence this may raise concerns as to the veracity of the information. Currently, an important filtering role is attributed to the national public prosecutor for counterterrorism, who has the task of controlling the information provided in the official reports before sending it to the relevant (regional) PPS on the basis of the underlying file. It can be questioned, however, whether this may substitute for the trial judge's control of the legitimacy of the manner in which evidence has been gathered in the light of Article 6 ECHR.

### *3.3.4 The Counterterrorism Information Box*

The Counterterrorism Information Box (CT Infobox) was established on July 1, 2004 in order to collect, at one point, all information available regarding persons who are involved in terrorist networks or activities or have radicalized viewpoints. The CT Infobox is located in the AIVD headquarters, operates under the responsibility of the AIVD and, hence, under the WIV 2002 and the oversight committee for the intelligence and security services. The CT Infobox was established in response to the terrorist attack in Madrid and the subsequent decision of the government to intensify its counterterrorism strategy, in particular in order to be able to 'keep an eye' on persons who provide reason to believe that they cannot be trusted in relation to terrorist activities or the preparation of such activities. In particular, persons are targeted against whom a concrete suspicion cannot yet be established, but who have emerged in earlier or running investigations by the AIVD or the police.[144] For this purpose, the PPS, the KLPD and the AIVD started to cooperate in order to collect, at a central point, all the information available in their files regarding persons who can be related to terrorism. Later, also the MIVD, KMar, IND (the Immigration and Naturalization Service), FIOD-ECD (the Fiscal Information and Investigation Service and the Economic Investigation Service)

---

[143] Gerechtshof's-Gravenhage 2 October 2008, *LJN* BF3987 and HR 5 September 2006, *NJ* 2007, 336, para 4.7.1 and the Opinion of Advocate General Machielse, para 4.6.

[144] *Kamerstukken II* 2003/04, 29 754, no. 1, 10.

and the FIU-NL (the Financial Intelligence Unit) entered into the cooperation mechanism of the CT Infobox.[145]

The CT Infobox has been established in order to contribute to the countering of terrorism and the radicalization related thereto through collecting and comparing information regarding persons who can be related to (Islamic) terrorism at a central point, within the applicable legal frameworks. Considering the diversity of the cooperating services it is possible to analyze the available information from a multidisciplinary perspective.[146] On the basis of an examination and analysis of the information available, the CT Infobox may provide advice to the cooperating agencies (or other agencies) to share certain information with other agencies or to take action in the field of their task, such as initiating a criminal investigation, taking administrative measures or conducting intelligence investigative activities.[147]

The CT Infobox acts, under the responsibility of the AIVD, in order to make it possible for the AIVD to participate in the cooperation mechanism considering its legal obligations (under the WIV 2002) regarding secrecy and the sharing of information. The cooperation with other services is based upon Article 60 WIV 2002, determining that the other services may conduct activities for the benefit of the AIVD. Nevertheless, the cooperation realized by the establishment of the CT Infobox is considered to function on the basis of equality between the participating services taking due account of the separate specific responsibilities and legal frameworks.[148] Considering the separation between the intelligence community and the law enforcement community, the PPS has been given a special position within the context of the cooperation in the CT Infobox. Hence, the PPS does not have a seat within the CT Infobox, but 'joins' in the cooperation. This means that the National Public Prosecutor for Counterterrorism conducts activities in the context of the CT Infobox.[149] The cooperation is based upon Article 61 WIV 2002, providing that the PPS shall share information with the AIVD when this information is relevant for the task of the AIVD. Vice versa, information available in the CT Infobox which is relevant for the investigation and prosecution of criminal offenses can be sent by means of an official report to the National Public Prosecutor for Counterterrorism on the basis of Article 38 WIV 2002 after advice by the CT Infobox to the AIVD to do so. Contrary to employees of the other cooperating services, the National Public Prosecutor for Counterterrorism does not act under the responsibility of the Minister of the Interior (under Article 60 WIV 2002), but

[145] *Kamerstukken II* 2007/08, 29 754 and 30977, no. 126, 2.

[146] *Kamerstukken II* 2005/06, 29 754, no. 29, 2.

[147] *Kamerstukken II* 2007/08, 29 754 and 30977, no. 126, 2 and 3. See also Rapport van de Commissie van Toezicht op de Inlichtingen- en Veiligheidsdiensten inzake het onderzoek naar de Contra Terrorisme Infobox 2007, 3.

[148] *Kamerstukken II* 2004/05, 29 754 and 27 925, no. 21, 2.

[149] *Kamerstukken II* 2005/06, 29 754, no. 29, 4 and Rapport van de Commissie van Toezicht op de Inlichtingen- en Veiligheidsdiensten inzake het onderzoek naar de Contra Terrorisme Infobox 2007, 7.

acts under the political responsibility of the Minister of Security and Justice.[150] When the CT Infobox sends advice to one of the other partners, this shall be understood as a notification under Article 36 WIV 2002.[151]

Considering the foregoing, the CT Infobox concerns an important mechanism in order to enhance cooperation, in particular with regard to the sharing of information which is relevant to the prevention of terrorism. Because the CT Infobox operates under the responsibility of the AIVD and under the legal regime of the WIV 2002, this cooperation has not touched upon the institutional separation between the PPS and the AIVD. The main purpose of the CT Infobox is to enable the employees of the CT Infobox (and thus of the AIVD) to analyze all relevant information available to the different actors in the field of counterterrorism and, from that position, to coordinate the most effective way to respond to terrorism threats. In that regard the AIVD has obtained a central position in the coordination of counterterrorism policy, although this should be conducted on a presumption of equality between the different cooperating partners. From the perspective of cooperation—for which purpose the cooperating partners enter into consultation on a regular basis[152]—the establishment of the CT Infobox contributes to the proactive sharing of information with the PPS for the purpose of initiating a criminal investigation into terrorist activities.

### *3.3.5 Other Measures Enhancing Cooperation*

In order to improve cooperation between the different actors in the field of counterterrorism (in total about 20), which actors are not always used to cooperation, a coordinating agency has been created.[153] The National Coordinator for Counterterrorism (NCTb) was established on June 29, 2005.[154] The NCTb is responsible for developing policy in the field of counterterrorism, coordinating the cooperation between the different entities responsible for counterterrorism, analyzing intelligence and information for the purpose of an integral analysis and the providing of threat analyses, coordinating protection and security measures and

---

[150] Rapport van de Commissie van Toezicht op de Inlichtingen- en Veiligheidsdiensten inzake het onderzoek naar de Contra Terrorisme Infobox 2007, 8.

[151] *Kamerstukken II* 2004/05, 29 754 and 27 925, no. 21, 2.

[152] For the PPS the Substitute Chief Prosecutor of the National PPS takes part in this consultation. In addition, the National Coordinator for Counterterrorism (see Sect. 3.3.5) attends the consultation. *Kamerstukken II* 2004/05, 29 754 en 27 925, no. 21, 3.

[153] See the website of the NCTb: http://www.nctb.nl/organisatie/wat%5Fdoet%5Fde%5FNCTb/ (accessed 8 May 2011).

[154] Regeling van de Ministers van Justitie en van Binnenlandse Zaken en Koninkrijksrelaties van 29 juni 2005, nr. DDS5357209, houdende instelling van de Nationaal Coördinator Terrorismebestrijding.

directing the providing of information on counterterrorism.[155] The "mission" of the NCTb is formulated on its website, being to "minimise the risk and fear of terrorist attacks in the Netherlands and to take prior measures to limit the potential impact of terrorist acts. The NCTb is responsible for the central coordination of counterterrorism efforts and ensures that cooperation between the parties involved is and remains of a high standard."[156]

The agency of the 'National Coordinator for Counterterrorism' NCTb is relevant for the relationship between the intelligence and law enforcement communities when it concerns their activities regarding counterterrorism. The NCTb is responsible for improving the cooperation between all the different services—intelligence as well as law enforcement services—that are involved in counterterrorism activities. Its goal is to analyze intelligence information and other information regarding terrorism, to develop common policies in countering terrorism and to coordinate all security measures in countering terrorism. The NCTb can be considered as the spider in the web of all organizations working on counterterrorism to improve their coordination and, with that, to increase the effectiveness of combating terrorism. The functions under the responsibility of both the Minister of the Interior and the Minister of Justice, although under the direct supervision of the Minister of Justice.[157]

## 3.4 Changes Affecting the Relation Between Administrative Law and Criminal Procedural Law

Although the government has attributed a central role to the criminal justice system when it comes to terrorism prevention, when the information available in the CT Infobox or shared by the AIVD is insufficient to initiate a criminal investigation or criminal prosecution, the government considered that action in the field of administrative law was warranted. Hence, the government prepared a Bill concerning 'administrative measures for national security', proposing measures that could be used when the information available is insufficient for action in the field of criminal procedural law but nevertheless warrants action.[158] The measures proposed in the Bill would make it possible for the mayor to restrict a person's freedom to move for national security reasons, such as a prohibition on being in a

[155] Regeling van de Ministers van Justitie en van Binnenlandse Zaken en Koninkrijksrelaties van 29 juni 2005, nr. DDS5357209, houdende instelling van de Nationaal Coördinator Terrorismebestrijding, Article 2.

[156] Website of the NCTb http://english.nctb.nl/organisation/about%5Fthe%5FNCTb/mission/ (accessed 8 May 2011).

[157] Regeling van de Ministers van Justitie en van Binnenlandse Zaken en Koninkrijksrelaties van 29 juni 2005, nr. DDS5357209, houdende instelling van de Nationaal Coördinator Terrorismebestrijding.

[158] *Kamerstukken II* 2004/05, 29 754, no. 5, 13 and *Kamerstukken II* 2005/06, 30 566, no. 3, 4.

certain place, within the vicinity of certain persons or in a certain territorial area of the Netherlands or a duty to report to the police.[159] Furthermore, the proposed Act would establish the possibility to deny or repeal permits and subsidies for reasons of terrorism prevention.[160] The Bill has been adopted by the Second Chamber of Parliament and was in consultation in the First Chamber.[161] However, the legislation received much criticism as to the necessity of the proposed administrative powers and the legitimacy of the powers considering the possible punitive character of the measures.[162] In addition, the situations referred to in the explanatory memorandum concerned primarily situations which are now covered by the Act on the Criminal Investigation of Terrorist Crimes, for which the need for additional measures had become doubtful. Also in the evaluation report on the counterterrorism measures of the first decade of the 21st century, it was recommended to withdraw the bill because the proposed legislation seemed to be superfluous and may be in conflict with the ECHR.[163] Consequently, also the government has now decided to withdraw the Bill on Administrative Measures for Counterterrorism.[164]

Nevertheless, this proposed Act has not been the only (proposed) counterterrorism measure in the field of administrative law. The government has also initiated a strategy of 'disturbing' specific persons in order to eliminate them as a risk for committing terrorist crimes. This 'disturbing' of persons was done in the context of the administrative supervisory task of the police to maintain public order under Article 2 Police Act 1993 (see Sect. 2.2.1.1), in combination with Article 12 Police Act 1993 (providing that the police act under the responsibility of the mayor, who can give the police certain directions) and Article 172 Municipalities Act [*Gemeentewet*] (attributing the mayor with responsibility for the maintenance of public order, including the power to give instructions to the police to prevent any disturbance of the public order) and, hence, was not preceded by legislative action adopting a specific legal basis. The goal of the 'disturbance' method is to observe and follow a person in such way that this person and his daily environment realize that he/she is the subject of investigation in order to 'disturb' his/her participation in preparing a terrorist crime.[165] Also this method is applied in order to fill a possible gap between resorting to the criminal justice system and doing nothing: when a criminal investigation and prosecution are not sufficiently effective and the government is nevertheless seeking to reduce the risk of terrorist crimes to the minimum, this method of 'administrative disturbance' can be

---

159 *Kamerstukken II* 2005/06, 30 566, no. 3, 2 and 23-25.

160 *Kamerstukken II* 2005/06, 30 566, no. 3, 31-32.

161 *Handelingen II* 2006/07, no. 50, 2969-2970 and *Kamerstukken I* 2006/07 and 2007/08, 30 566, no. A-D.

162 See e.g. Kuijer 2005, 15-17.

163 Rapport Evaluatie Antiterrorismemaatregelen 2011, 96.

164 *Kamerstukken II* 2010/11, 29 754, no. 199, 2.

165 *Kamerstukken II* 2003/04, 29 754, no. 1.

used.[166] Hence, in order to define the current scope of the criminal investigation, it will be relevant to assess where the possibilities in the scope of the criminal investigation of terrorist crimes falls short and the police in the context of their 'administrative' task under Article 2 Police Act 1993 can 'disturb' the activities of a person through apparent surveillance activities.

### 3.4.1 *Administrative Disturbance*

The administrative disturbance of a specific person's contribution to terrorism-related activities is a form of harassment conducted by means of police surveillance, such as stopping a few times a day in a patrol car in front of the house of the person in question, regularly checking whether that person is at home by calling him/her or ringing his/her doorbell and by accosting any visitors.[167] Considering that under Article 8 ECHR, in combination with Article 10 Constitution, a specific legal basis is required for government activities that interfere more than to a limited extent with the right to respect for private life, it is questionable whether this form of observation can be based upon the general attribution of tasks to the Police under Article 2 Police Act 1993 in combination with the power of the mayor to give instructions to the police regarding the maintenance of public order, including regarding the prevention of possible disturbances to the public legal order (Article 12 Police Act 1993 and Article 172(2) Municipalities Act).[168]

Two court decisions where the plaintiffs sought a temporarily injunction to terminate the police's disturbing activities assessed this issue. In both decisions, the judges considered the interference with the right to respect for private life permissible under Article 8 ECHR, if it is also necessary and executed proportionately.[169] In the first case, the specific information giving rise to the disturbance in relation to the specific disturbing activities conducted was disproportionate and, therefore, illegitimate. Also in the second case the specific reasons for conducting the disturbing activities and the method of disturbance were assessed, this time resulting in the conclusion that the activities were proportionate and thus in accordance with Article 8(2) ECHR. On the basis of these decisions, also in the light of earlier decisions by the Supreme Court assessing the required legal basis

---

[166] Rapport Evaluatie Antiterrorismemaatregelen 2011, 86.

[167] As follows from two temporary injunctions where the plaintiffs sought the termination of the disturbing activities of the police on behalf the city of Amsterdam: Rechtbank Amsterdam 1 December 2005, *LJN* AU 7314 and Rechtbank Amsterdam 9 March 2006, *LJN* AV 4173. See also: Brouwer 2006, 1.

[168] Compare the discussion on for which criminal investigative methods is a specific legal basis required or whether Article 2 Police Act 1993 in combination with Article 141/142 CCP will suffice (Sect. 2.2.2.1).

[169] Rechtbank Amsterdam 1 December 2005, *LJN* AU 7314 and Rechtbank Amsterdam 9 March 2006, *LJN* AV 4173.

for observation in the context of the criminal investigation, it can be concluded that the 'disturbing' activities are conducted at the outer limits of what is legitimate under Article 8 ECHR.[170] Because the government has decided not to provide for a legal basis for the method of administrative disturbance[171] and that the person disturbed may only challenge the practice by means of a (civil) temporary injunction, the method has received a great deal of criticism.[172]

For the purpose of the subject-matter of this book, it is relevant to determine in what situations the government seeks to use the method of administrative disturbance instead of criminal investigative activities. The purpose of the 'disturbance' concerns the prevention of terrorist activities or the prevention of the preparation of terrorist activities. Because terrorist activities are generally also crimes, the purpose of the administrative disturbance is very closely related to the purpose of the criminal investigation of terrorist activities and, therefore, the method of administrative disturbance is used when the criminal investigative possibilities fall short in minimizing the risk of a terrorist crime. Nevertheless, the primary purpose of the activities is to make, by means of harassment, the person and his/her daily environment aware of the fact that he/she is the subject of an investigation and, secondly, to stop the terrorist activities of this person or to obstruct the usefulness of this person within a terrorist network.[173] On the basis of the information available in the CT Infobox the cooperating partners enter into consultation in order to determine which of the available measures are most effective to counter the terrorism threat. These measures may concern the areas of criminal investigation, administrative enforcement or intelligence investigation. The administrative disturbance will only be used when the criminal investigative possibilities fall short in order to eliminate a terrorist threat. This has resulted in the conclusion that the disturbing activities are to be used in the exceptional circumstances that the possibilities to start criminal investigative activities upon the presence of

---

[170] Many simple observational actions do not or to a limited extent interfere with privacy rights, such as non-systematic observations of criminal activity by investigative officers, for which reason Article 2 Police Act 1993 suffices as the legal basis. When the observation activities are 'intensive' and 'frequent' they shall be considered systematic and a specific legal basis for the observation is required. Corstens 2008, 455-456, *Kamerstukken II* 1996/97, 25 403, nr. 3, 26-27 and HR 14 October 1986, *NJ* 1988, 511, ann. ThWvV, HR 25 January 2000, *NJ* 2000, 279, Gerechtshof Arnhem 23 December 2002, *NJ* 2003, 134 (non-systematic observation) and HR 11 November 1994, *NJ* 1995, 400, ann. EAA/HJS (systematic observation).

[171] According to the government such a legal framework is not necessary, considering that the observation in question is not systematic and considering that the method is in practice used sparingly and currently only in a restrictive manner, especially since the broadening of the possibilities to act for the purpose of prevention in the context of a criminal investigation. *Kamerstukken II* 2006/07, 29 754 and 30 977, no. 104.

[172] Brouwer 2006, Muller et al. 2007, 118-119 and Rapport van de Commissie van Toezicht op de Inlichtingen- en Veiligheidsdiensten inzake het onderzoek naar de Contra Terrorisme Infobox 2007, 18-20.

[173] *Kamerstukken II* 2006/07, 29 754, no. 100, 9-10.

indications of the preparation of a terrorist crime fall short and, if used, shall be used in their least intrusive version.[174]

The cases that have been assessed in the context of a temporary injunction concerned the use of administrative disturbance before the Act on the Criminal Investigation of Terrorist Crimes entered into force. Nevertheless, these cases may teach us something about the situations where administrative disturbance is used instead of the criminal investigative track or in addition thereto. The first case in December 2005 concerned an order by the Mayor of Amsterdam to disturb an Islamic woman on the basis of the fact that she had changed her faith from Christian to Islam, changed her manner of dressing, entered into an Islamic marriage, changed to a Mosque where the Muslim faith was more strictly taught, stopped shaking hands with persons of the opposite sex, possessed a tape with a call to Jihad, had contacts with a member of an alleged terrorist organization (the Hofstad Group) and the possible possession of explosives.[175] The judge explicitly rejected using the facts relating to the faith of the woman as constituting a basis for the disturbance. Such facts could only in combination with other facts be used as a ground for conducting administrative disturbing activities.[176] Subsequently, also the other facts were considered insufficient in order to constitute the basis for the disturbing activities as the presence of explosives was dispelled after a search of her house and the other facts could also not be verified or were no longer applicable.[177] Hence, the disturbance was not 'necessary in a democratic society' as required under Article 8(2) ECHR and was thus disproportionate and illegitimate.[178] With regard to the other case which was the subject of a temporary injunction at the District Court of Amsterdam (March 2006), the judge considered the administrative disturbance to be legitimate. This case differed from the case of December 2005 in that the facts concerned verifiable contacts with members of the Hofstad Group and the murderer of the film director Theo van Gogh and of postings on the Internet to recruit for an armed fight against unbelievers. Furthermore, the public prosecutor announced that a criminal prosecution would be initiated regarding a suspicion of recruitment for jihad (Article 205(3) Penal Code).[179] In this light, the judge considered the disturbance 'necessary in the democratic society' under Article 8(2) ECHR. In addition, the specific activities, which were less frequently conducted than in the case of December 2005, were also proportionate.[180]

---

174 *Kamerstukken II* 2006/07, 29754 and 30 977, no. 104, 4-5.

175 Rechtbank Amsterdam 1 December 2005, *LJN* AU 7314, para 1.

176 Rechtbank Amsterdam 1 December 2005, *LJN* AU 7314, para 12.

177 Rechtbank Amsterdam 1 December 2005, *LJN* AU 7314, para 14-16.

178 Rechtbank Amsterdam 1 December 2005, *LJN* AU 7314, para 17.

179 Rechtbank Amsterdam 9 March 2006, *LJN* AV 4173, para 13-14.

180 With respect to the proportionality of the disturbance it is also important that the facts and circumstances justifying the disturbance are regularly reconsidered as to their proportionate relation to the activities conducted. Rechtbank Amsterdam 9 March 2006, *LJN* AV 4173, para 14-16.

In the case decided in March 2006, the administrative disturbance occurred in addition to criminal investigative activities. Here the goal of the disturbance can be described as being to obstruct the development of activities that threaten the public order (terrorist activities) and to reduce the attractiveness and influence of this person within the (terrorist) network.[181] Considering that this goal was pursued parallel to the criminal procedural track, it can be concluded that the disturbance is used in order to more effectively—in the sense of achieving direct results—prevent terrorist activities, whilst apparently the information available is, as yet, insufficient for closing the criminal investigation and initiating a criminal prosecution. The goal of the disturbance in the case decided in December 2005 seemed to be the deradicalization of the woman concerned. The disturbing activities in relation to this goal were considered as unnecessary and disproportionate.

Nevertheless, the government announced in 2007 that the focus of the 'disturbance' of persons would change to a softer approach, focusing on deradicalization by offering the person an alternative to terrorist activities.[182] In the light of the decision of 2005, it is clear that such measures shall not have a 'repressive' character. Rather, changing the focus of the administrative disturbing activities towards 'positive' interference may be considered as a concession to the criticism of this method, based upon Article 2 Police Act 1993 in the context of the police and the mayor's task of maintaining public order.[183]

It can be concluded that the use of administrative disturbance is only of minor significance in the current counterterrorism strategy. Where the government seeks to prevent the commission of terrorist crimes, primarily criminal investigative methods are used. Nevertheless, the 'repressive' nature of the criminal investigative possibilities may also be supplemented by measures in the field of administrative law, including the method of personal disturbance. This method may be used in order to disturb (and in that way to prevent) the preparation of terrorist crimes through harassment, but currently seems to be primarily aimed at the deradicalization of the person giving effect to a 'soft' approach towards counterterrorism.

## 3.5 Conclusion

On the basis of the description provided in this chapter of the measures that have facilitated an anticipative criminal investigation or affected the scope or nature of the anticipative criminal investigation from the sidelines, the figure provided in the introductory section needs to be adjusted and can be expanded as follows:

---

[181] Rechtbank Amsterdam 9 March 2006, *LJN* AV 4173, para 1.

[182] *Kamerstukken II* 2006/07, 29 754, no. 100, 10.

[183] Rapport Evaluatie Antiterrorismemaatregelen 2011, 91-92.

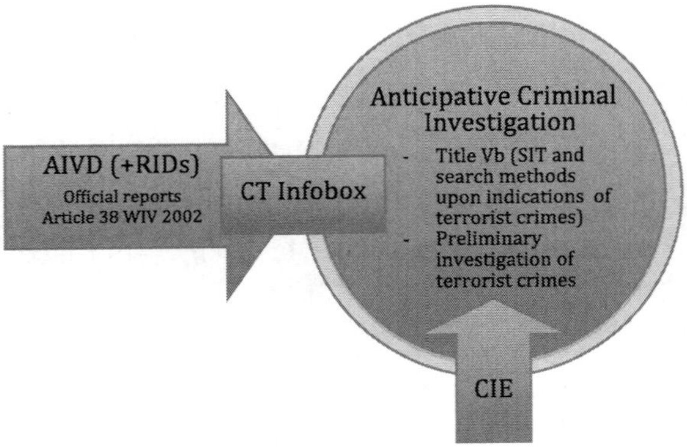


**Fig. 3.2** Conclusive illustration of the anticipative criminal investigation in the Netherlands

This figure requires some further explanation (Fig. 3.2). The large inner-circle concerns the core of the anticipative criminal investigative system. The measures that haven been taken by the Act on the Criminal Investigation of Terrorist Crimes have directly affected the preventive capacity of the criminal investigation: firstly, by allowing the use of SIT upon indications of terrorist crimes (in other words: when the use of SIT can contribute to the prevention of terrorism); secondly, by expanding the investigative possibilities of the preliminary investigation for the purpose of preparing a full terrorist crime investigation; and, thirdly, by introducing search powers to the criminal investigation under Title Vb, which can be used in order to confront an imminent terrorist threat in security zones or in 12-hour zones.

As described in Sect. 3.3 the relation between the AIVD and the law enforcement community has been intensified in the post-9/11 era, aimed at the smooth continuation of the intelligence investigation into an anticipative criminal investigation upon the transfer of an official report under Article 38 WIV 2002 in order to realize the prevention of terrorism *and* the successful prosecution of terrorist suspects. Legislative measures (the Shielded Witnesses Act and, indirectly, also the Act on the Criminal Investigation of Terrorist Crimes), organizational changes (the establishment of the CT Infobox (and in that context consultation between, *inter alia*, the AIVD and PPS) and the coordinating role of the NCtB) as well as the acceptance in case law of intelligence as starting information for criminal investigation and the practice of parallel investigations, have facilitated this intensified relation. Hence, the 'AIVD arrow' and the 'anticipative criminal law circle' have approached each other, operating in close connection although maintaining the institutional separation. The CT Infobox facilitates the sharing of information between the law enforcement community and the AIVD (as well as between other CT entities), although the transfer of information from the AIVD to the PPS/police continues to occur through the procedure on the basis of Article 38 WIV 2002 and through the national public prosecutor for counterterrorism. In fact, the AIVD, with the help of the CT Infobox, provides input to the anticipative criminal investigation on which basis the PPS and the police are strengthened in their capabilities to conduct anticipative criminal investigative activities.

Furthermore, the police, and in particular the CIE, have an intelligence-led focus and use their information collecting entities to obtain a strong information position as the basic assumption for realizing prevention. Likewise, the providing of criminal intelligence to the PPS strengthens the capabilities of using the criminal investigation in anticipation of future harm.

Lastly, Sect. 3.4 has assessed the role of administrative interference. It has been concluded that this administrative preventive counterterrorism method has currently only limited significance and is only used in addition to the preventive capacity of the criminal justice system when such use is considered to contribute to optimizing terrorism prevention. Hence, the outer-circle reflects the field of administrative supervisory authority, used to supplement the preventive capacity of the anticipative criminal investigation, which also means that administrative interference does not further affect the capacity of the anticipative criminal investigation.

The regulation of the anticipative criminal investigation, including the influence of AIVD information and criminal intelligence 'feeding' the anticipative capabilities of the criminal investigation, requires that it is subjected to further scrutiny in order to determine in what manner it affects the synthesis of the objectives of criminal procedural law. Loosening the conditions for a criminal investigation to realize a preventive focus touches upon the previously found balance between the hierarchically operating actors and the protective elements of the CCP in order to protect the innocent against arbitrary and unnecessary interferences with the right to respect for private life. In addition, the broader scope of the anticipative criminal investigation, influenced by the activities of the AIVD and by an increased use of criminal intelligence, requires a reassessment of the demarcation of the criminal investigation, in the light of the definition of criminal investigation under Article 132a CCP and the attached procedural safeguards facilitating control and accountability. These issues will be examined in the next chapter in order to define the implications for the synthesis between the shield and the sword in criminal procedural law.

# Chapter 4
# The Implications of Enabling Anticipative Criminal Investigations to Confront Terrorism for the Objectives of Criminal Procedural Law: The Netherlands

## 4.1 Introduction

As a consequence of the different legislative changes and developments both in case law and in practice, the criminal investigative phase in the Netherlands has obtained a different character, which can be described as anticipative criminal investigation. The previous chapter concluded with defining anticipative criminal investigation as it has been enabled in the Netherlands. This has been done on the basis of the expansion of criminal investigative possibilities so as to prevent crimes, the facilitation of the criminal investigation through the input of criminal intelligence as a consequence of intelligence-led policing (CIE), its input from the AIVD as a consequence of intensified cooperation based on a shared mission to prevent terrorism and, lastly, on the basis of its coherence with other measures, such as administrative disturbance. These features largely correspond with the categories in which the measures and changes have been addressed in the previous chapter. Their effect on the nature and scope of the anticipative criminal investigation is, nevertheless, different. Hence, this chapter will address two separate main issues, which, however, also reinforce each other.

Firstly, in order to assess the implications for the synthesis between the objectives of criminal procedural law, Sect. 4.2 will address in what way the system as described in Chap. 2 has been affected as a consequence of the measures that have touched upon the regulation of the criminal investigation. For this purpose, the scope and nature of the criminal investigation into terrorist activities will be defined (Sect. 4.2.1.1). Subsequently, specific implications for shield elements of the system of criminal investigation will be addressed: the protective value of the indications threshold (Sect. 4.2.1.2) and, partly on that basis, the compatibility of regulating criminal investigations into terrorist activities with the requirements of Article 8 ECHR (Sect. 4.2.1.3). In addition, these implications will be put into the 'broader context' of general trends in criminal procedural law and the manner in which the

M.F.H. Hirsch Ballin, *Anticipative Criminal Investigation*,
DOI: 10.1007/978-90-6704-843-9_4,

new investigative possibilities are used in practice, in order to put the implications into the right perspective (Sect. 4.2.2). Lastly, the implications of these measures that have affected the system of criminal investigation for the division of responsibilities between the actors will be addressed (Sect. 4.2.3).

The second main issue to be addressed concerns the current demarcation of the anticipative criminal investigation. For that purpose, its relation to the intelligence apparatus (Sect. 4.3.1) and to the administrative enforcement of public order (Sect. 4.3.2) will be further defined. On that basis the anticipative criminal investigation as regulated in the Netherlands will be given its final interpretation as to its function and position. Lastly, the following question will be dealt with: whether and, if so, how the anticipative criminal investigation in its broader sense has 'infected' the criminal procedure as to its ability to control investigative activities and accountability for illegitimate behavior, as required under Article 6 ECHR.

## 4.2 Expansion of the Preventive Capacity of the Criminal Investigation

The counterterrorism measures taken by the Dutch government that have affected the criminal justice system were all intended to increase the preventive capacity of the criminal justice system when it comes to terrorist crimes. In particular the criminal investigative phase has been targeted both by expanding the criminalization of preparatory acts and by gearing the criminal investigation towards prevention. Consequently, the sword function of the criminal investigation has been enhanced by making it possible to use SIT upon a 'lower' threshold of application and by expanding the investigative capacities of the preliminary investigation in preparation for a 'full' criminal investigation of terrorist crimes. The possibilities for criminal investigation in anticipation of future harm are reinforced by the measures already taken in substantive criminal law (the Act on Terrorist Crimes and the Act on Training for Terrorism), thereby expanding criminal liability in early phases especially for terrorist offenses. Because the object of the 'indications' threshold concerns a terrorist crime, criminal investigative activities regarding, for example, membership of a terrorist organization or provocation to commit a terrorist crime, may start when the initial acts that can be related to these crimes start to crystallize.[1]

The measures that have affected the criminal investigation concern the investigative domain for terrorist crimes, the enhancing of the investigative possibilities in the investigative domain of the preliminary investigation, especially for the preparation of the full criminal investigation of terrorist crimes and the introduction of new investigative powers for the purpose of preventing a more urgent

[1] Referred to as the 'multiplier effect' in: Rapport van de Commissie Evaluatie Antiterrorismebeleid 2009, 46.

threat of terrorism.[2] Section 4.2.1 will, firstly, draw conclusions as to the sword nature of the criminal investigative possibilities of the three measures following from the Act on the Criminal Investigation of Terrorist Crimes which affect the criminal investigation and, secondly, it will address some specific shield implications of the statutory regulation of the criminal investigation of terrorist crimes. Subsequently, Sect. 4.2.2 will deal with the implications of the legislative changes enabling an anticipative criminal investigation in the broader context of criminal investigative policy. It will be assessed whether also the courts allow the interest of prevention to supersede the interest of legal protection (Sect. 4.2.2.1) and what arguments are decisive in practice for choosing between specific investigative domains (Sect. 4.2.2.2). On that basis the implications of the legislative changes to the criminal investigation for the shield objective of criminal procedural law can be further defined. Section 4.2.3 will address the implications for the distribution of responsibilities on the fairness of the criminal proceedings between the different actors as a consequence of the focus on prevention in terrorism investigations. The section will conclude with some final remarks with respect to the implications of changes that have affected the criminal investigation in order to gear it to terrorism prevention (Sect. 4.2.4).

## *4.2.1 Criminal Investigation for the Purpose of Preventing Terrorism*

### 4.2.1.1 Expansion of the Scope and Nature of the Criminal Investigation of Terrorism

As has been described in Sect. 3.2.1.2, the most important consequence of the Act on the Criminal Investigation of Terrorist Crimes of November 2006 has been the introduction of an additional investigative domain, especially for terrorism, by adopting a new threshold of application for the use of SIT. The emergence of 'indications of a terrorist crime' now suffices for the use of SIT within the investigative domain of Title Vb, especially for the criminal investigation of terrorist crimes. The threshold of indications shall be understood as requiring an assessment as to whether or not, upon the information available, the use of an investigative technique would be in the interest of the investigation. The interest of the investigation will be served when the use of a special investigative technique can contribute to the prevention of terrorist crimes.

The 'indications of a terrorist crime' threshold should be understood as being a lower threshold than a reasonable suspicion. Although the reasonable suspicion threshold has already been interpreted as being satisfied upon the availability of 'soft' information, the 'indications' threshold must nevertheless be considered as

---

2 See Sect. 3.2.1.

'lower', because the decisive assessment for application will be whether the use of a special investigative technique may contribute to the prevention of terrorism. This assessment may justify the use of a special investigative technique also when the verifiability and accuracy of the information available would be insufficient for establishing a reasonable suspicion.

Hence, the investigative domain for terrorist crimes can best be typified as being triggered when the information available requires the police and PPS to take action for the purpose of preventing terrorist crimes. According to Article 132a CCP the purpose of the criminal investigation shall be to make prosecutorial decisions, which in 2010 was still being emphasized by the Supreme Court (repeating the argumentation of the Court of Appeal) so as to fulfill a shield function considering that SIT can only be used for the purpose of making prosecutorial decisions (and when their use is required to further the interest of the investigation).[3] Under Title Vb the purpose of making prosecutorial decisions seems to coincide with the purpose of prevention considering that, ideally, the prevention of a terrorist crime will be realized with the prosecution of the criminalized terrorist activities in the preparatory phase, including membership of a terrorist organization. And, also when the criminal investigation is merely used to exclude risks and does not result in the strengthening of indications, the purpose of making prosecutorial decisions will be met in the sense that insufficient evidence has been found to initiate a prosecution or to use coercive powers. Nevertheless, the interest of preventing terrorism will always supersede the interest of truth-finding for criminal prosecution and will be the decisive consideration for the decision as to whether the threshold of indications of a terrorist crime has been met.[4]

Furthermore, the Act on the Criminal Investigation of Terrorist Crimes has enhanced the investigative capacity of the preliminary investigation especially for preparing the full criminal investigation of terrorist crimes. As a consequence of the expansion of the investigative techniques in the preliminary investigation (the adoption of Articles 126hh and 126iiCCP), the preliminary investigation with regard to terrorist activities has obtained a more intrusive character than the 'regular' preliminary investigation on the basis of Article 126gg CCP. Because it is possible to gather, compare and combine information on a person originating from different sources, the preliminary investigation can become rather intrusive for the persons being investigated. The persons in question will not be aware that their personal information is being investigated, while there is also—of course—no suspicion of a crime. Although the preliminary investigation is surrounded by several safeguards (which will be dealt with in the next section), it is clear that the

---

[3] HR 26 January 2010, *NJ* 2010, 77, para 3.4.

[4] Compare: *Kamerstukken II* 2004/05, 30 164, no. 3, 2: 'It must be possible to conduct criminal investigative activities whenever these activities may contribute to the prevention of terrorism.' And *ibid*., 8: 'terrorism requires a different appraisal. It is undesirable that the government shall have to refrain from criminal investigative activities in the absence of a well-founded suspicion, whilst the criminal investigation can reasonably contribute to the prevention of terrorism.'

nature of the preliminary investigation has considerably changed when it concerns the preparation of the criminal investigation of terrorist crimes: the arsenal of investigative techniques that can be applied has expanded and these techniques have, moreover, a more far-reaching nature. Previously, these techniques were only available in the full criminal investigation. Without a reasonable suspicion people can be investigated in the context of a preliminary investigation simply because they meet a certain profile or show up in certain situations. In addition, third parties, such as companies, can be requested to divulge private information. This new character of the preliminary investigation has raised important concerns as to the risk of 'fishing expeditions' on behalf of the law-enforcement community.[5]

Lastly, the sword capacity of the criminal investigation has been expanded by the introduction of new investigative powers (searching objects and vehicles and frisking) within the investigative domain for terrorist crimes. These search methods are specifically intended to contribute to the prevention of a more urgent threat of terrorism. Police officers have been given wide discretion in selecting people for these investigative powers within a specific area ordered by the public prosecutor on the basis of 'indications of a terrorist crime' or within security zones established by an administrative decree.[6] The scope of the discretion afforded to investigative officers is rather large taking into account that these search powers may be used upon indications of any terrorist crime. Therefore, someone may be searched, not only when there are indications that an attack will be committed (e.g. to check an object for explosives), but also when indications point to membership of a terrorist organization.[7]

Cumulatively, the adoption of the investigative domain for terrorist crimes upon the 'lower' threshold of indications for the purpose of preventing terrorism, the expansion of the investigative possibilities in the preliminary investigation especially for the preparation of the full terrorist crime investigation and the introduction of new investigative powers for the prevention of terrorism, has changed the character of the criminal investigation. In the first place, the interest of preventing crimes has taken the primary place of the criminal investigation, which deviates from the traditionally exceptional nature of proactive criminal investigative activities. In the second place, the central position of the reasonable suspicion threshold has in general been further reduced and has been left as the triggering mechanism for SIT as well as for search methods regulated in the CCP. SIT, the searching of objects and vehicles, and frisking can now be applied also on the basis of 'indications of a terrorist crime', a threshold that is met when the interest of prevention is served by the use of SIT rather than the presence of facts and circumstances linking a person or a group of persons to a specific crime.

[5] See also: Prakken 2004 and Van Kempen 2005b, 8-9 (elaborate version of Van Kempen 2005A).

[6] See Sect. 3.2.1.3.

[7] Van Kempen 2005b, 7 and 11.

Consequently, and in the third place, the scope and nature of the criminal investigation has been affected, both concerning the criminal investigative domain of Title Vb and concerning the preliminary investigation regarding terrorist crimes.[8] A criminal investigation under Title Vb (including the newly introduced search powers) may involve persons who can be related to the 'indications' regarding a specific terrorist crime, or the preparation of a terrorist crime. Because the 'indications' may concern less concrete information, also the group of people being investigated may be larger, which increases the possibility of including persons who cannot be related to terrorist activities.

The preliminary investigation is aimed at the investigation of an unspecified group of people in order to determine whether, within that group, (terrorist) crimes are being planned or committed, rendering the scope of the preliminary investigation even broader. The possibility to apply investigative techniques with a more intrusive character in the preliminary investigation regarding terrorism has changed the nature of the preliminary investigation.

Hence, the criminal investigation in general raises concerns as to compatibility with the right to respect for private life and the principle of legality in the sense that sufficient protection is offered in the current regulation against arbitrary interferences with the right to respect for private life. In addition, the restriction on the right to respect for private life shall be necessary in a democratic society under Article 8 ECHR. To assess compatibility with Article 8 ECHR, it should in the first place be questioned whether the indications threshold, compared to the threshold of a reasonable suspicion, offers sufficient restraints on the use of criminal investigative powers to protect against arbitrariness.

Considering that the enhancement of the sword capacity of the criminal investigation, especially for terrorism, results in various 'shield' concerns, this section will continue to assess the possible shield implications of the current regulation of the criminal investigation as a consequence of the adoption of the Act on Terrorist Crimes. For this purpose Sect. 4.2.1.2 will firstly address the protective function of the indications threshold in comparison to the reasonable suspicion threshold (see Sect. 2.3.2.3), considering that changing the threshold to indications in terrorism investigations has been the key measure in order to realize the criminal investigation for the purpose of preventing terrorism in anticipation of future crimes. Subsequently, Sect. 4.2.1.3 will broaden the scope to the entity of the statutory regulation and address the compatibility of regulating the use of SIT under Title Vb, regulating the preliminary investigation as well as regulating the use of the new search powers under Title Vb with the right to respect for private life and the principle of legality on

[8] As has been explained in Sect. 2.3.2.3.2.3, the preliminary investigation is in this project covered by the term criminal investigation, considering that the (ultimate) purpose of the preliminary investigation coincides with the full criminal investigation when the preliminary investigation is used to prepare the full criminal investigation and the information produced by the preliminary investigative techniques is used as starting information for the full criminal investigation. Nevertheless, the legislature still considers that the preliminary investigation is not covered by Article 132a CCP and precedes the criminal investigative phase.

the basis of the minimum conditions that follow from Article 8 ECHR, Article 10 Constitution and Article 1 CCP (see Sect. 2.3.2.1).

#### 4.2.1.2 The Protective Value of Indications in Comparison to a Reasonable Suspicion

The threshold of a reasonable suspicion has traditionally fulfilled a central protective role in the system of criminal procedural law, reflecting the equilibrium between the protection of individuals against interferences with their rights and liberties on behalf of the state and the interest of criminal law enforcement.[9] From that perspective the suspicion requirement also concerns a crucial restrictive condition for the use of investigative powers that interfere with privacy in order to make a restriction on the right to respect for private life foreseeable to the person concerned and necessary in a democratic society under Article 8 ECHR.[10] In general, the reasonable suspicion threshold shall protect against arbitrary interferences with the right to respect for private life. Article 8 ECHR aims to serve that interest and, in addition, especially in the context of the *ultimum remedium* character of the criminal justice system, the presumption of innocence requires that the government shall use criminal procedural law only when necessary for the purpose of investigating possible criminal activities.[11] This section will compare the protective role fulfilled by the reasonable suspicion threshold with the protective role of the indications threshold in order to draw conclusions regarding the implications for the shield objective of criminal procedural law—in particular with respect to the right to privacy and the presumption of innocence—as a consequence of adopting a lower threshold for using SIT.

In Chap. 2 the conclusion has already been drawn that the criminal investigation is no longer limited to the presence of a reasonable suspicion. Nevertheless, the suspicion threshold, although in different gradations, still has a central role as a triggering mechanism for investigative methods that interfere with privacy. The gradation of the suspicion required for the use of an investigative method depends on the nature of the investigative method as well as on the nature of the crime being investigated. Up until the adoption of the Act on the Criminal Investigation of Terrorist Crimes the reasonable suspicion threshold was the exclusive threshold for using SIT, although also with a different scope for classical investigations and for organized crime investigations.[12]

---

[9] Sikkema 2008, para 8.1, Knigge 2005, 353, and the annotation by Borgers at HR 11 March 2008, *NJ* 2008, 329, ann. Borgers. See also the introduction Sects. 2.3.2.3 and 2.3.2.3.1.

[10] See Sect. 2.3.2.3.3 and for the assessment of the indications threshold in the light of Article 8 ECHR, Sect. 4.2.1.3.

[11] See Sect. 2.3.2.3.3.

[12] See the introduction Sects. 2.3.2.3, 2.3.2.3.2 and 2.3.2.3.3.

The goal of the adoption of the new 'indications of a terrorist crime' threshold for using SIT is clear: avoiding the situation in which a reasonable suspicion cannot be established on the basis of the information available and when a closer investigation is required to make sure that everything is done to prevent a terrorist crime from being committed. The lowered threshold therefore seems to function as a last resort for the rather exceptional situation that a reasonable suspicion cannot be established but the use of a special investigative technique will nevertheless be in the interest of the investigation.

From a practical point of view, choosing the investigative domain for terrorist crimes may be warranted in two potential situations. Firstly, the police or PPS receive vague information (either by an official report of the AIVD or from their own information sources, e.g. the Criminal Intelligence Unit) which may point to the planning of a terrorist crime. Here, the use of SIT could contribute to gathering additional information to initially exclude risks and possibly subsequently to gather evidence for the prosecution of preparatory acts. This concerns a situation where the indications threshold could act as a last resort in order to make sure that risks are excluded where investigation on the basis of a reasonable suspicion would not be possible.

Secondly, the police may receive information pointing to a potential immediate threat. In this situation the information may likely also establish a reasonable suspicion. There will usually not be time for an elaborate criminal investigation in which evidence can be gathered. Rather, the police and PPS will act in a manner so that the threat is immediately removed, most likely by the arrest of the person(s) in question. When the information does not point to specific persons but to a specific place, the search methods within the investigative domain of a terrorist crime can be used at the site of the immediate threat. Furthermore, the technique of systematic observation could be a plausible tool in order to keep an eye on the right person and to intervene at the right moment. Like the first situation, also this situation dealing with an immediate threat clearly reflects the goal of this amendment to the regulation of the criminal investigation: contributing to the prevention of terrorism. For that goal it has been considered necessary at all times that investigative powers can be applied proactively when the information is sufficiently concrete to foresee that the special investigative technique(s) or search method(s) sought to be used can contribute to the prevention of terrorism (and is, therefore, in the interest of the investigation).

In Sect. 2.3.2.3 the case law which has interpreted the threshold of a reasonable suspicion has been examined in order to determine what facts and circumstances are required for meeting the threshold. In the first place, the facts and circumstances shall be open to objectification. Because the indications shall also follow from facts and circumstances, this is not different for the indications threshold.[13] It seems that for the definition of the suspect under Article 27(1) and, hence, for the application of search methods or coercive methods, a nexus between the

[13] *Kamerstukken II* 2005/06, 30 164, no. 7, 15.

suspected person and the suspected crime is required. Furthermore, mere intuition is insufficient, but professional judgments by and the knowledge of investigative officers may contribute to establishing a reasonable suspicion. The investigative domains of Title IVa and Title V apply different versions of the reasonable suspicion threshold: for the classical investigation the 'reasonable suspicion of a crime' and for the organized crime investigation the 'reasonable suspicion that crimes are being planned and committed in an organized context.' These thresholds differ from the definition of a suspect in Article 27(1) in that the reasonable suspicion does not concern a specific person, but a committed crime or 'serious crimes that are planned or committed in an organized context.'

The level of information required to meet the threshold of a reasonable suspicion is, however, similar to the level of information required under Article 27(1) CCP. In Sect. 2.3.2.3.1 it has been concluded that the information required to establish a reasonable suspicion may be 'soft' information. Anonymous information may be used as starting information for a criminal investigation, although it seems that an initial follow-up check by the police as to the veracity of the information is required. Arguably, such verification may be omitted for the criminal investigation triggered by indications, although the anonymously provided information must be sufficiently concrete in order to foresee that the use of a SIT may contribute to the prevention of a terrorist crime. Furthermore, CIE information can establish a reasonable suspicion. It follows from the evaluation reports of the Act on the Criminal Investigation of Terrorist Crimes that CIE information has also functioned as starting information in terrorist crime investigations.[14] As addressed in Sect. 3.3.1, also AIVD reports can trigger a criminal investigation and, hence, establish a reasonable suspicion. Although this development was triggered by the confrontation with intelligence in terrorism prosecutions, the use of AIVD information as starting information does not really break new ground as to the nature of the information establishing the reasonable suspicion, considering that the use of anonymous information and CIE information had already been accepted by the Supreme Court. Similar to anonymous information and CIE information, AIVD information cannot be checked by the public prosecutor who has to decide upon the initiation of criminal investigative activities, for which reason the source of the AIVD report can be compared with these sources (regardless of whether the police shall conduct a follow-up check on the information or whether a check will be made by the national public prosecutor for counterterrorism).[15] Also AIVD information has been used to establish both a reasonable suspicion and indications.[16] Hence, when we take into account the first investigative experiences in practice, it seems that the nature as well as the

[14] Three out of seven of the indications investigations were triggered by CIE information in the period February 2007-February 2009. Van Gestel et al. 2009, 28.

[15] Krips 2009, 146-147.

[16] Although in only one of the seven cases in the period 2007–2009, whereas AIVD information triggered a classical investigation into terrorism on three occasions. Van Gestel et al. 2009, 28.

veracity and accuracy of the starting information for classical investigations or organized crime investigations, in particular in terrorism cases conducted in the context of these investigative domains, does not considerably differ from the veracity and accuracy of the starting information used to establish indications.[17]

The restriction offered by the reasonable suspicion threshold is thus in fact similar to the restriction offered by the indications threshold. Nevertheless, this does not necessarily mean that the indications and reasonable suspicion thresholds do not differ. The adoption of the indications threshold is explicitly done in order to fill the gap where a reasonable suspicion threshold cannot be met and a criminal investigation is nevertheless considered necessary. This gap is largely a misunderstanding because 'soft information' may also establish a reasonable suspicion, enabling preventive action in many conceivable situations. Rather, the adoption of the indications threshold shall be understood against the background of the wish to optimize the prevention of terrorism. Therefore, the establishment of indications legitimizes investigative action whenever this is considered to contribute to the prevention of terrorism. Furthermore, the examination of the case law regarding special criminal law where the indications threshold already applies has warranted the (although modest) conclusion that indications is at least a lower threshold than a reasonable suspicion and, when applied to search methods, does not require that the person searched is also a suspect.[18]

The breadth of the indications threshold thus seems (at least theoretically) to be rather large, with a specific focus on proactive investigation in order to ensure that prevention is realized. Consequently, investigative officers are given a broad discretion with regard to the decision as to what criminal investigative activities may contribute to the prevention of terrorism. Considering that the breadth of the indications threshold has not been compensated with new supplementary conditions and that meeting the threshold may justify the use of far-reaching SIT, it can be concluded that the balance between the interest of providing legal protection against the arbitrary use of SIT and the interest of the criminal investigation (in fact the prevention of terrorism) is struck at a different point. Hence, the (statutory) procedural protection against arbitrary interferences has been traded in with the right to respect for private life in furtherance of the interest of preventing terrorism.[19]

---

[17] Van Gestel et al. 2009, 8 and 27.

[18] See Sect. 2.3.2.3.2.4.

[19] At the same time, these implications must also not be overestimated as it can be concluded that the investigation upon indications will mainly be applied to exclude risks in time. Practical considerations as to the effectiveness of using SIT without knowing sufficiently precisely what to look for reduce the use of SIT on the basis of vague non-verifiable information. In addition, it follows from the evaluations of the use of Title Vb in practice that deploying SIT when there are indications is rarely intended for evidence gathering, but mainly to exclude risks. This implies 'mini-investigations' in which the most far-reaching techniques will not be needed. De Poot et al. 2008, 43. See in more detail on the practical considerations as to choosing between criminal investigative domains Sect. 4.2.2.2.

Nevertheless, adopting a lower gradation of suspicion especially for the criminal investigation of terrorist crimes seems to fit within the already applicable system of the regulation of criminal investigative powers using different gradations of suspicion depending on the nature of the investigative method and the nature of the crimes under investigation. Considering that SIT, and in particular electronic surveillance techniques that intercept communications, are understood to seriously interfere with the right to respect for private life, which in principle requires a rather strict regulation under Article 8 ECHR[20] to protect against arbitrarily targeting persons, the nature of the terrorist crimes has been considered to justify adopting a lower threshold. Because a reasonable suspicion must be understood as the balancing point between the interests involved, this balancing point is flexible considering that different weight must be attached to the interests involved in different circumstances.[21]

In the first place, the legislature has distinguished the use of investigative methods that seriously interfere with the right to respect for private life from methods that only interfere to a limited extent with the private life. This distinction is reflected in the use of different gradations of suspicion as well as in the specific regulation of SIT, whereas less intrusive (or non-intrusive) techniques may be based upon Article 2 Police Act 1993.[22] In the second place, the legislature has established a clear distinction between conventional crime and organized crime, accepting that the seriousness and complexity of organized crime influence the balance to be drawn.

The suspicion threshold has traditionally been considered as the situation in which there is a reason, considering the interests involved and considering the principles of proportionality and subsidiarity, to investigate and use far-reaching investigative powers. Nevertheless, it can also be concluded that the suspicion threshold is not, since it follows from a balancing of interests, inflexible. When there are serious grounds for either additional conditions or allowing a lower central threshold, which can also mean that supplementary conditions compensate a less stringent interpretation of the reasonable suspicion requirement, this will not automatically be in violation of the right to respect for private life or the presumption of innocence. A flexible and broad interpretation seems to correspond

---

[20] See e.g. ECHR 24 April 1990, App. no. 11801/85 and App. no. 11105/84 (*Kruslin v. France and Huvig v. France*), para 33/32.

[21] Compare the annotation of Borgers para 6, HR 11 March 2008, *NJ* 2008. 329. Borgers enumerates the following relevant circumstances for determining the presence of a reasonable suspicion in a particular situation: the contents of the information (in the case addressed in the annotation this information came from an anonymous source); the fact whether the police or PPS have independently checked the information; the concrete possibilities to verify the information, taking into account the need to act with urgency; the possibility to use less intrusive techniques; and the possible alternatives to criminal investigative action.

[22] Compare also HR 18 May 1999, *NJ* 2000, 104, ann. Sch, para 5.3, where the Supreme Court accepted, before the entry into force of the Act on SIT, the use of an intrusive method of investigation (systematic observation) and the continuation of applying such a method on the basis of the level of suspicion present.

with the wording of the Explanatory Memorandum of 1913–1914: 'the authorities responsible for criminal investigation and prosecution must be able to act effectively and decisively, and must be able to pursue those activities that are needed in the circumstances of a specific case and should not be hindered by too stringent and limiting regulations.'[23] In the most recent version of the definition of the criminal investigation under Article 132a CCP, the requirement of a reasonable suspicion is no longer even included. Hence, also this definition leaves more room for differing assessments of the interests involved under varying circumstances.

Any threshold of application shall function as the equilibrium between the necessity to act in order to establish the truth about criminal activities and the need to protect against arbitrary interferences with the right to respect for private life. In the Netherlands this function has traditionally been fulfilled by the threshold of a 'reasonable suspicion'.[24] Nevertheless, different levels of suspicion may apply relating to the intrusiveness of the investigative method or the coercive power involved (compare 'serious concerns' for pre-trial detention' with 'reasonable suspicion' for arrest or the use of SIT) *and* in relation to the crimes involved (compare 'reasonable suspicion of a crime' for the classical criminal investigation with 'reasonable suspicion that crimes are being planned or committed in an organized context' for the criminal investigation of organized crime).[25] According to the government, the serious threat of terrorism has now justified a lower threshold for using SIT in the criminal investigation of terrorist crimes. The only compensating restriction offered to counterbalance the breadth of the indications threshold is the restriction to terrorist crimes. The interest of preventing terrorism has thus been considered so important to strike a balance at a different point at the expense of legal protection.

Nevertheless, balancing the interest involved resulting in different gradations of the suspicion threshold shall not result in a slippery slope of reasoning, where, consequently, the adequate protection of persons against arbitrary and unnecessary interferences with their right to respect for private life can no longer be offered. Whether weakening this safeguard against arbitrary interferences with the right to respect for private life is in conformity, taking into account the entity of the regulation, with the requirements of the restrictive clause of Article 8 ECHR will be addressed in the next section. Furthermore, Sect. 4.2.2.2 will address whether, taking into account the use of the different investigative domains in practice, the adoption of the lower threshold of indications not only theoretically but also *de facto* results in legal protection against arbitrary interferences being traded in with the right to privacy.

---

[23] Lindenberg 2002, 424. This passage has also been cited in the Opinion of the Advocate General (para 34) in the case of *Zwolsman* (HR 19 December 1995, *NJ* 1996, 249, ann. Sch) to support the view that activities falling outside the scope of the criminal investigation (lacking a reasonable suspicion), but which are necessary for investigative officers to carry out their tasks effectively, must be accepted and can therefore be based on Article 2 of the Police Act 1993.

[24] Compare: Knigge 2005, 353.

[25] See in detail Sects. 2.3.2.3.2 and 2.3.2.3.3.

#### 4.2.1.3 The Principle of Legality and the Right to Respect for Private Life

As has been described in Sect. 2.3.2.1, the principle of legality as laid down in Article 1 CCP and the right to respect for private life, as guaranteed in Article 8 ECHR and Article 10 Constitution, complementarily impose conditions upon the regulation of criminal investigative powers. These conditions can generally be summarized as follows: (1) the restriction on the right to respect for private life shall be provided by an Act of Parliament and shall be accessible to the person concerned; (2) the provision in the law must be foreseeable to the person concerned; and, (3) the restriction must be necessary in a democratic society. The first requirement needs no further discussion, as the Act on the Criminal Investigation of Terrorist Crimes provides for the adapted and new criminal investigative powers, which meets the requirements of being 'in accordance with the law' (Article 8 ECHR), being 'accessible' (under Article 8(2) ECHR; the Act is published) and 'established by an Act of Parliament' (Article 10 Constitution and Article 1 CCP). The second requirement requires, more specifically for the intrusive covert technique of wire-tapping that "the domestic law must be sufficiently clear in its terms to give citizens an adequate indication as to the circumstances in which and the conditions on which public authorities are empowered to resort to any such measures."[26] The level of precision required depends on the circumstances of the specific case. In that regard the ECrtHR has enumerated the following factors to be taken into account: "the nature, scope and duration of the possible measures, the grounds required for ordering them, the authorities competent to permit, carry out and supervise them, and the kind of remedy provided in national law"[27] and, elsewhere, "the content of the instrument in question, the field it is designed to cover and the number and status of those to whom it is addressed."[28] Thirdly, the requirement of being 'necessary in a democratic society' requires that the powers introduced by the Act pursue a legitimate aim, that the introduction of the powers meet a "pressing social need" and that they are proportionate to the legitimate aim pursued.[29] This section will seek to examine the regulation of SIT under Title Vb, the preliminary investigation of terrorist crimes and the newly introduced search powers on the basis of these requirements of 'foreseeability' (Sect. 4.2.1.3.1) and being 'necessary in a democratic society' (Sect. 4.2.1.3.2).

---

[26] ECHR 29 June 2006, App. no. 45934/00 (*Weber and Saravia v. Germany*) (admissibility decision).

[27] ECHR 2 September 2010, App. no. 35623/05 (*Uzun v. Germany*), para 63.

[28] ECHR 12 January 2010, App. no. 4158/05 (*Gillan and Quinton v. The United Kingdom*), para 77.

[29] See Sect. 2.3.2.1.

#### 4.2.1.3.1 Foreseeability

##### *4.2.1.3.1.1 Title Vb*

The main aspect on which the regulation of using SIT in the investigative domain for terrorist crimes differs from the classical investigative domain and the investigative domain of organized crime concerns the threshold of application. As has been concluded in the previous section, 'indications of a terrorist crime' is a 'lower' threshold and a vaguer concept, whereas other compensating guarantees have not been adopted in the regulation of SIT. Hence, it shall be determined whether the scope of the regulation is sufficiently defined in order to be foreseeable under Article 8(2) ECHR. Several advisory entities have expressed their concerns as to the compatibility of the regulation of SIT under Title Vb with Article 8 ECHR.[30] The government has unequivocally responded to the concerns of these entities as well as of members of parliament that the regulation of the use of SIT under Title Vb is compatible with the requirements of the restrictive clause of Article 8 ECHR. The Act provides for a precise regulation including different procedural safeguards, such as the order of the public prosecutor, the authorization of the examining magistrate for the more intrusive techniques, the assessment of proportionality and subsidiarity implied in the requirement of 'the interest of the investigation' and the guarantee of reporting and notification. The lower threshold of application is furthermore justified by the significant threat of terrorism, which may victimize many innocent citizens as well as the complex character of the criminal investigation into terrorism.[31]

Nevertheless, the Council of Europe's Commissioner for Human Rights, Hammarberg, has expressed concerns, after visiting the Netherlands, as to the compatibility of the Act on the Criminal Investigation of Terrorist Crimes with Article 8 ECHR, "since the Act lacks the sufficient precision required to regulate conduct."[32] The restrictive function of the threshold of indications in combination with these other procedural guarantees need to be further scrutinized in the light of the case law of the ECHR in order to determine whether the regulation of Title Vb provides the level of precision which is required to provide citizens with an "adequate indication" of the conditions under which the government may apply SIT against them.

As explained in the previous section, the threshold of application is a flexible concept and this flexibility, within the context of the criminal investigation, is related to the nature of the crimes involved. Furthermore, the threshold of application, in combination with supplementary conditions, relates to the nature of the interference caused by using a specific method upon the applicable threshold. Also

---

[30] See *Kamerstukken II* 2004/05, 30 164, no. 3, 3 and 10.

[31] *Kamerstukken II* 2004/05, 30 164, no. 3, 3, 11-12, 16, 28-29 and 31-32, *Kamerstukken II* 2005/06, 30 164, no. 12, 5-6 and *Kamerstukken I* 2006/07, 30 164, no. D, 12-13.

[32] Report by the Commissioner for Human Rights Mr Thomas Hammarberg on his visit to the Netherlands 2009, 38-39 (para 171).

the ECHR in various cases has struck a different balance when a threat of terrorism is involved. For example, the Court acknowledged that the circumstance of a serious threat as terrorism is an argument for accepting a lower standard of evidence required for meeting the threshold of a reasonable suspicion justifying arrest or pre-trial detention. However, there must be "some facts or information that would satisfy an objective observer that the person concerned may have committed the criminal offence (…)."[33] In addition, the preamble to the "Guidelines on human rights and the fight against terrorism" as adopted in 2002 by the Council of Europe declares that states have "the imperative duty to protect their population against possible terrorist acts."[34] Moreover, the Council of Europe has adopted a Convention on the Prevention of Terrorism imposing a 'duty to investigate' on the Member States "upon receiving information that a person who has committed or who is alleged to have committed an offence set forth in this Convention may be present in its territory."[35]

Nevertheless, as has been explained in Sect. 2.3.2.1 the ECrtHR also requires that the use of covert intrusive techniques, such as electronic surveillance, is particularly precisely regulated.[36] This does not necessarily mean that the government may only use electronic surveillance when there is a reasonable suspicion, considering that the Court has also accepted 'broader' forms of electronic surveillance such as 'strategic monitoring' in the absence of a reasonable suspicion.[37] In addition, the ECrtHR has also accepted the use of surveillance in earlier phases for the prevention of crime.[38] The entity of procedural safeguards should "afford

---

[33] ECHR 16 October 2001, App. no. 37555/97 (*O'Hara v. The United Kingdom*), para 34 and ECHR 30 August 1990, App. nos. 12244/86; 12245/86; 12383/86 (*Fox, Campbell and Hartley v. The United Kingdom*), para 32.

[34] *Ibid.*, preamble.

[35] Article 15 of the Council of Europe Convention on the Prevention of Terrorism, *CETS 196, 16.V.2005* (*Trb.* 2006, 34): "(…) the Party concerned shall take such measures as may be necessary under its domestic law to investigate the facts contained in the information."

[36] ECHR 24 April 1990, App. no. 11801/85 and App. no. 11105/84 (*Kruslin v. France and Huvig v. France*), para 33/32.

[37] Nevertheless, these activities are conducted for the purpose of protecting national security (and not in the context of criminal proceedings), which is, however, not a distinction made by the ECrtHR as the Court focuses only on the question whether citizens are afforded sufficient protection against arbitrary interferences with their right to privacy as guaranteed in Article 8 ECHR. ECHR 29 June 2006, App. no. 45934/00 (*Weber and Saravia v. Germany*) and ECHR 1 July 2008, App. no. 58243/00 (*Liberty and Others v. The United Kingdom*). Although not objecting to strategic monitoring as such, in the latter case the Court considered the regulation "not to indicate with sufficient clarity, so as to provide adequate protection against abuse of power, the scope or manner of exercise of the very wide discretion conferred on the State to intercept and examine external communications." *Ibid.* para 69.

[38] ECHR 6 September 1978, App. no. 5029/71 (*Klass and others v. Germany*). The aim of the German G10 legislation assessed in this case was to protect national security and/or to prevent disorder or crime (para 44) and could be used upon 'factual indications' (Tatsächliche Anhaltspunkte) "for suspecting a person of planning, committing or having committed certain serious criminal acts" (para 17 and 51).

adequate safeguards against various possible abuses"[39] and, hence, the absence of a strict threshold of application may be compensated by other procedural safeguards which protect against abusive interferences with the right to respect for private life.[40]

It has been concluded in Sect. 3.2.1.2 that the threshold of 'indications of a terrorist crime' is met when the information available requires action in order to ensure that terrorism is prevented, also when this information would be insufficient to establish a reasonable suspicion. Hence, the protective function should not hinder the preventive action required, basically regardless of the quantum of evidence present. For example, anonymous tip-offs that are difficult to verify may justify the use of SIT against persons which increases the possibility that, for instance, the telephone conversations of persons who cannot be related to terrorist activities are also intercepted.[41] Considering that the threshold of application itself does not impose a clear restriction as to the scope of the criminal investigative power of the government in the investigative domain of Title Vb, it should be assessed whether the other requirements can compensate for the lack of restrictions offered by the indications threshold.

In particular the requirement that the SIT may only be used in 'the interest of the investigation' or, for the most intrusive techniques of infiltration and wiretapping, 'upon a pressing investigative need,' should further narrow down the scope of the legal basis for SIT. This requirement implies an assessment of the proportionality and subsidiarity of the use of a SIT in a specific case.[42] Nevertheless, the assessment of proportionality and subsidiarity must be made on the basis of the information establishing the indications in relation to the interference with the right to respect for private life caused by using the SIT. Hence, when the information is considered to contribute to the prevention of terrorism, it is likely that also the proportionality and subsidiarity of using SIT for this purpose will be accepted.

Furthermore, the specific authority responsible for ordering the SIT concerns an additional safeguard.[43] Like under Title IVa and Title V the public prosecutor orders the use of SIT and, for the most intrusive techniques of electronic surveillance and some of the subpoena powers, additionally, the authorization of the examining magistrate is required (Articles 126zf and 126zm CCP). Hence, also the assessment as to whether the facts and circumstances establish indications and whether the use of the SIT is also 'in the interest of the investigation' or required for a 'pressing investigative need' shall be made by the higher authorities of the public prosecutor and, sometimes, the examining magistrate. This implies an

---

39 ECHR 24 April 1990, App. no. 11801/85 and App. no. 11105/84 (*Kruslin v. France and Huvig v. France*), para 35/34.

40 Compare: Van Kempen and Van de Voort 2010, 69.

41 *Kamerstukken II* 2004/05, 30 164, no. 3, 10.

42 See Sect. 2.3.2.4.2.

43 See also Sect. 2.3.1.

important role for the public prosecutor and the examining magistrate in deciding in concrete cases whether the use of SIT is, in the light of the information available, also proportionate and necessary. However, as indicated in Sect. 2.3.2.4.2, it seems that the regulatory effect of the principles is in practice limited, because judges are inclined to examine investigative practices only marginally on the basis of the principles of proportionality and subsidiarity.[44] It can be expected that the proportionality and subsidiarity of the use of SIT on the basis of information that can be related to terrorist activities will usually be accepted. Moreover, the role of the examining magistrate, who should also particularly assess the proportionality and subsidiarity of the intended method, has become rather limited, due to time constraints as well as a lack of insight into the complete investigation.[45]

The government had also argued that practical considerations will result in further restrictions on the use of SIT: where the information available is very soft, the use of SIT in order to investigate this information will be ineffective and will also be an unreasonable burden on the capacity of the law enforcement community.[46] Nevertheless, such practical considerations do not impose any *legal* restriction on the use of privacy-intrusive investigative powers as required under Article 8 ECHR and, therefore, would not contribute to rendering a restriction on privacy rights foreseeable to the persons concerned.[47]

Lastly, the procedural guarantees of the duty to compile records and to notify also apply to the use of SIT under Title Vb, which enables judicial control *ex post* and may deter any arbitrary use of SIT under Title Vb. Nevertheless, also the control facilitated by these requirements is rather limited and is largely dependent on the subsequent prosecution of the persons investigated.[48] Exactly because the scope of the investigation upon indications is rather broad and may concern anyone who can be related to the 'indications of a terrorist crime', the deterrent function of *ex post* control may in practice be limited, even when there is a possibility for a judicial challenge. As the ECrtHR also noted in *Gillan and Quinton v. The United Kingdom*: "safeguards against abuse (…) provided by the right of an individual to challenge a stop and search by way of judicial review or an action in damages (…)" are rather limited "in the absence of any obligation on the part of the officer to show a reasonable suspicion, [making it] difficult if not impossible to prove that the power was improperly exercised."[49]

---

44 See in detail: Franken 2009, 79-92. See also Sect. 4.2.2.1.

45 Franken 2006, 269 and see Sect. 2.3.1.3. Whether the Act on Strengthening the Position of the Examining Magistrate will change this situation remains to be seen.

46 *Kamerstukken II* 2004/05, 30 164, no. 12, 3.

47 Compare: Van Kempen and Van de Voort 2010, 70.

48 See Sects. 2.3.2.4.1 and 2.3.1.6.

49 ECHR 12 January 2010, App. no. 4158/05 (*Gillan and Quinton v. The United Kingdom*), para 86.

Hence, it seems that the other procedural safeguards in addition to the 'indications' threshold do not impose considerable additional restrictions on the scope of the investigative power. However, when we compare the regulation under Title Vb with the regulation of Title IVa and Title V the only difference concerns the threshold of application.

Especially the vagueness of this newly introduced threshold of application gives reason for concern regarding compatibility with Article 8 ECHR. Because the SIT can in fact be used whenever they can contribute to the prevention of terrorism, the government has been granted a rather wide discretion. In the light of the strict requirements which the ECrtHR has normally imposed on the regulation of electronic surveillance, it may be doubted whether the regulation indicates "the scope of [the] discretion conferred on the competent authorities and the manner of its exercise with sufficient clarity, having regard to the legitimate aim of the measure in question, to give the individual adequate protection against arbitrary interference."[50] In that regard the restriction of using the broad indications threshold only for terrorist crimes, which requires indications of a terrorist intent among those people being investigated, may be important with regard to compliance with Article 8(2) ECHR. However, also the restrictive value of the limitation to terrorist crimes may be questionable, as the term 'terrorist crime' is rather vague. In combination with the threshold of indications, not being precisely defined, the exact scope of the investigative possibilities remains vague.[51] Considering that the sufficiency of the regulation as to its foreseeability largely depends on the manner in which the different procedural safeguards take effect in practice, it will depend on the use of the investigative powers of Title Vb in practice whether this, on a case-by-case basis, may result in a violation of Article 8 ECHR.

This does not mean that adopting a regulation on which basis SIT may be used upon a lower threshold of application in terrorist crime investigations is, on its face value, incompatible with Article 8 ECHR. The Court decided in *Malone* that a regulation which provides for discretion may not mean that the law itself is "somewhat obscure and open to differing interpretation."[52] When we take into account the explanation the government has given as to the applicable procedural safeguards, a conclusion that the regulation for that reason violates Article 8 ECHR is not warranted. Furthermore, the ECrtHR seems to attach weight to the specific circumstances of the threat of terrorism, which may give reason to offer the government more discretion in taking action for the prevention of terrorism. The interpretation of foreseeability leaves a margin of appreciation as the regulation shall be sufficiently precise "to a degree that is reasonable" considering the specific circumstances of the case.[53] In addition, the scope of the right to privacy

---

[50] ECHR 2 August 1984, App. no. 8691/79 (*Malone v. The United Kingdom*), para 68.

[51] Van Sliedregt 2006, 23 and Van Kempen 2005b, 11.

[52] ECHR 2 August 1984, App. no. 8691/79 (*Malone v. The United Kingdom*), para 79.

[53] ECHR 26 April 1979, App. no. 6538/74 (*Sunday Times v. The United Kingdom*), para 49. See Sect. 2.1.3.2.1.

"depends on present day conditions and developments in social and political attitudes,"[54] which concern circumstances that are certainly influenced by the threat of international terrorism in the post-9/11 era. Considering the foregoing, it is unlikely that the ECrtHR will consider the regulation of SIT under Title Vb to be in violation of Article 8 ECHR.

Nevertheless, a risk of abuse because of the lack of restrictions offered by the indications threshold as well as the related limited restrictive potential of the proportionality and subsidiarity assessment mainly lies in the use of the SIT under Title Vb in practice. Section 4.2.2.2 will deal with the practical experiences of Title Vb and, on that basis, the implications for the protection against arbitrary interferences with the right to respect for private life can be further defined.

##### *4.2.1.3.1.2 Preliminary Investigation of Terrorist Crimes*

Within the preliminary investigation the government is granted an even broader discretion considering that the preliminary investigation focuses on a group of people in order to determine whether, within that group, terrorist or other serious crimes are being planned or committed, which result in a serious infringement of the legal order. Because of this wider scope, the use of SIT in the investigative domain of the preliminary investigation is excluded. Hence, notwithstanding its wide scope, the preliminary investigation cannot be compared with strategic monitoring as assessed by the ECrtHR in *Weber and Saravia v. Germany*[55] and *Liberty and others v. The United Kingdom,*[56] because the investigative techniques are limited to demanding stored information in the automated systems of public or private organizations to be made available (Article 126hh CCP) and accessing identifying information (Article 126ii CCP) and cannot involve the interception of private communications.

Nevertheless, concerns regarding the expansion in the preliminary investigation to gather personal information have repeatedly been expressed during the parliamentary discussion of the bill, including by the Board on the Protection of Personal Data, which is a body that controls how the government deals with personal details and its compliance with the Act on the Protection of Personal Data. Because information relating to many people who are not suspected of a criminal offense and, to a minor extent, even information relating to third parties can be processed, the processing of information—data mining—might result in fishing expeditions, and may even pose a risk of racial profiling. The government has also acknowledged that personal details relating to persons who are subsequently cleared of any involvement in terrorist activities will be processed and that also unexpected personal information will be gathered which is irrelevant to the

[54] Loof 2005, 204 and see Sect. 2.1.3.2.1.

[55] ECHR 29 June 2006, App. no. 45934/00 (*Weber and Saravia v. Germany*).

[56] ECHR 1 July 2008, App. no. 58243/00 (*Liberty and Others v. The United Kingdom*).

investigation.[57] This constitutes an interference with the right to respect for private life of persons not (yet) suspected of any crime. The government had attempted to meet these concerns by applying several rules that should guarantee the careful processing of information and adopting procedural safeguards against abuse, thereby limiting the privacy intrusion.[58]

As described in Sect. 3.2.1.2 these safeguards concern the following aspects: the public prosecutor orders the preliminary investigation with the permission of the Board of Prosecutors General; the most intrusive preliminary investigative technique of Article 126hh requires the authorization of an examining magistrate; exceptions to statutory privacy protection are only possible if they are 'necessary' for the investigation; procedural guarantees (by means of an automated system) have been adopted to minimize the privacy implications and to prevent abuse; and the duty to compile records applies.[59] Considering the limited interference with privacy rights, compared to the use of SIT,[60] the entity of the regulation of the preliminary investigative techniques and, especially the applicable procedural safeguards that limit the interference with private life caused by the investigative techniques to a minimum (minimization procedures), it is likely that the procedural safeguards adopted can, from the perspective of the ECHR, compensate for the rather wide initial scope of the preliminary investigation. These safeguards are capable of reducing the scope of the investigation to its legitimate aim.[61] In addition, also here the interest of preventing terrorism may justify the adoption of more intrusive preliminary investigative techniques especially for the preparation of the full criminal investigation of terrorist crimes.

#### *4.2.1.3.1.3 Search Powers for the Prevention of Terrorism*

Under Title Vb and, hence, with the presence of indications, not only SIT but also the searching of vehicles and objects and frisking (collectively referred to as search powers) may be conducted for the purpose of preventing terrorism. The foreseeability of the regulation of these powers under Title Vb differs in a crucial aspect from the regulation of SIT. The selection of persons to be subjected to these search powers is a discretionary authority for the investigative officers, who are

---

[57] *Kamerstukken II* 2004/05, 30 164, no. 3, 21.

[58] Compare: Buruma 2004, 665-675, putting into perspective the intrusion on privacy made by collecting publicly stored information or information stored with third parties. Compare also the approach of the United States, where the collecting of third party information is not considered to be a violation of 'a reasonable expectation of privacy' and, hence, is not covered by the Fourth Amendment (*United States v. Miller*, 425 U.S. 435, 96 S.Ct. 1619 (1976), para 443), see Chap. 5, Sect. 5.1.4.1. Nevertheless, the ECrtHR does consider the method of collecting and analyzing information as conducted in the context of the preliminary investigation to be covered by Article 8 ECHR, see: ECHR 4 May 2000, App. no. 28341/95 (*Rotaru v. Romania*), para 43.

[59] See in detail Sect. 3.2.1.2.

[60] See *supra* footnote 58.

[61] ECHR 2 August 1984, App. no. 8691/79 (*Malone v. The United Kingdom*), para 68. See also the previous Sect. 4.2.1.3.1.3.

entitled to subject anyone in the 12-hour zone (indicated by the order of the public prosecutor in the presence of 'indications of a terrorist crime) or in the security zone (indicated by an administrative decree) to these search powers. The newly introduced powers for the prevention of terrorism resemble the search powers of the UK in the metropolitan area of London, which were recently assessed by the ECrtHR in *Gillan and Quinton v. The United Kingdom* (2010).[62] The Court decided in this case that the search powers are "neither sufficiently circumscribed nor subject to adequate legal safeguards against abuse."[63] The Court reached this conclusion because "the senior police officer (...) is empowered to authorise any constable in uniform to stop and search a pedestrian in any area specified by him within his jurisdiction if he considers it "expedient for the prevention of acts of terrorism"", which gives police officers broad discretion where the selection of persons to be searched is based upon "a "hunch" by or the "professional intuition" of the officer concerned.[64] Furthermore, the Court concluded that there was an absence of any "assessment of the proportionality of the measure" and a "failure of the temporal and geographical restrictions" (considering that an authorization is valid for 28 days and applies to the Metropolitan Police District).[65]

Similar to the regulation of SIT under Title Vb, it shall be determined whether the entity of the regulation affords sufficient precise regulation to compensate for the lack of restrictions offered by the threshold of 'indications of a terrorist crime' or by the status as a security zone.[66] Considering the argumentation of the ECrtHR in *Gillan and Quinton* such additional restrictions may be found in temporal and geographical restrictions. In the Netherlands, the order of the public prosecutor is valid for 12 hours (although extensions are possible) and the area is geographically restricted to where 'indications of a terrorist crime are present.' In addition, it follows from the explanatory memorandum to the Act on the Criminal Investigation of Terrorist Crimes and the discussion of the bill in Parliament that the search powers are used in particular when there is a more urgent threat at a specific location. Here, the investigative officers can contribute to the prevention of terrorism by searching persons at the location and the specific date and time insofar as this follows from the information establishing 'indications of a terrorist crime.'[67] This implies that at least the 12-hour zones are necessarily relatively restricted areas. In addition, also the validity of the order is restrictive, although the

[62] ECHR 12 January 2010, App. no. 4158/05 (*Gillan and Quinton v. The United Kingdom*). See for a detailed comparison of the Dutch search powers for the prevention of terrorism and the *Gillian and Quinton v. The United Kingdom* case Van Kempen and Van de Voort 2010, 73-80.

[63] ECHR 12 January 2010, App. no. 4158/05 (*Gillan and Quinton v. The United Kingdom*), para 87.

[64] ECHR 12 January 2010, App. no. 4158/05 (*Gillan and Quinton v. The United Kingdom*), para 80 and 83.

[65] ECHR 12 January 2010, App. no. 4158/05 (*Gillan and Quinton v. The United Kingdom*), para 80 and 81.

[66] Compare: Van Kempen and Van de Voort 2010, 75.

[67] See Sect. 3.2.1.3.

12-hour period may be extended by 12 hours at a time. The currently established security zones are also comparatively small areas.[68] However, a temporal restriction is absent in the security zones.

Furthermore, the European Court has considered the absence of a proportionality assessment as a reason for insufficient foreseeability. As also emphasized by the government as a procedural guarantee against arbitrary selection, a proportionality assessment is included in the regulation of search powers by requiring that the powers can only be used in the 'interest of the investigation.'[69] However, the proportionality assessment is, unlike the use of SIT, only made on the spot, at the level of the investigative officer and not by the 'higher' authorities of the public prosecutor or examining magistrate.[70] Consequently, the risk of an arbitrary selection will clearly be present. This seems to be comparable with the concerns of the ECrtHR that the selection of persons to be searched will merely be justified on the basis of a "hunch" or "professional intuition."[71]

The proportionality assessment in relation to the lack of temporal restriction in security zones seems to be especially worrisome: these zones are indicated by an administrative decree on a semi-permanent basis and, consequently, the investigative officer can apply the search methods at any time at his/her discretion without involving the public prosecutor. It is assumed that within the security zone indications of a terrorist crime are present on a more permanent basis and, therefore, the use of the powers of Articles 126zq-126zs is a decision which is at the exclusive discretion of the investigative officers.

Furthermore, the applicability of the duty to compile records and the possibility to challenge illegitimate searches have been indicated as additional procedural safeguards which protect against abuse.[72] Nevertheless, as already stated in Sect. 4.2.1.3.1.1 the deterring effect of review and control is limited when the statutory requirement opens the door to broad (and maybe even arbitrary) application.[73]

It can be concluded that compared to the UK's search powers at issue in *Gillan and Quinton v. The United Kingdom*, the Dutch search powers are subjected to more meaningful geographical restrictions. Moreover, the use of search powers in the 12-hour zone is also restricted by time, a restriction which is, however, absent in the security zones. In the 12-hour zone the urgent threat will necessitate a proportionate selection, thereby reducing the risk of abuse. Nevertheless, granting

---

[68] As established by *Stb.* 2006, 730, Article 3(1) and Appendix. Maybe with the exception of the security zone of Schiphol Airport, including its immediate 'environment', which includes highways, bikeways, homes, restaurants and bars, and industrial parks. See Van Kempen and Van de Voort 2010, 76.

[69] See Sect. 3.2.1.3.

[70] See on this issue in more detail Sect. 4.2.3.

[71] ECHR 12 January 2010, App. no. 4158/05 (*Gillan and Quinton v. The United Kingdom*), para 83.

[72] See Sect. 3.2.1.3.

[73] Compare also ECHR 12 January 2010, App. no. 4158/05 (*Gillan and Quinton v. The United Kingdom*), para 86.

investigative officers wide discretion to subject persons to search powers involves a not to be neglected risk of arbitrariness.[74] This risk is especially present in the security zones, where the threat of terrorism is—generally—less urgent. Within the security zones, it will be especially difficult to control whether the investigative officers use these search powers only for the purpose of preventing terrorism. The application of the search methods is a discretionary authority belonging to investigative officers, without the involvement of the public prosecutor. It has not been chosen to require an order by the public prosecutor for using search methods also in the security zones, which would restrict the use of the search methods to situations of a concrete threat and, consequently, reduce the risk of abuse.[75] Considering the foregoing, it is uncertain whether the Dutch regulation can withstand an examination on the basis of Article 8 ECHR.[76]

#### 4.2.1.3.2 Necessary in a Democratic Society

The second requirement of the restrictive clause of Article 8 ECHR on which basis the criminal investigative powers for the prevention of terrorism need to be scrutinized concerns the requirement of being 'necessary in a democratic society'. The adopted measures that interfere with the right to respect for private life shall serve a legitimate aim. Furthermore, the measures must meet a pressing social need and they shall be proportionate to the legitimate aim pursued. States are granted a 'margin of appreciation' in determining what measures are necessary in a democratic society, for which reason the courts only exert a marginal examination with regard to this requirement.[77]

The government has emphasized in the explanatory memorandum that the different measures meet not only the requirement of foreseeability, but are also necessary in a democratic society. In that light the government pointed to the need to take measures to confront the serious threat of terrorism and the proportionality of these measures in relation to that aim.[78] Indeed, the aim of the Act on the Criminal Investigation of Terrorist Crimes is to prevent terrorist crimes, which is also one of the aims enumerated in Article 8(2) ECHR (the prevention of crime and, in relation to specifically preventing terrorist crimes, also the protection of national security).

Furthermore, necessity does not mean "strictly necessary" but the use of the investigative power must be "more than useful or desirable."[79] Arguably, this will require a stricter interpretation of the 'indications' threshold in combination with

[74] Compare also Prakken 2004.

[75] Van Kempen 2005b, 7.

[76] As also concluded in Van Kempen and Van de Voort 2010, 79-80.

[77] See Sect. 2.3.2.1.1.

[78] *Kamerstukken II* 2004/05, 30164, no. 3, 32.

[79] Trechsel 2006, 540.

the requirement of 'in the interest of the investigation' or 'for a pressing investigative need'. The necessity of using investigative powers when very soft information has been obtained or using search methods in security zones in the absence of an urgent threat may be difficult to uphold. Nevertheless, the Court generally accepts the necessity of far-reaching investigative powers, especially where these measures have been adopted for the purpose of protecting national security. However, in order to be also proportionate to the legitimate aim, the Court requires procedural safeguards that protect the individual against abuse.[80] Hence, also in the light of the requirement of being 'necessary in a democratic society' the Court will balance the interest of protecting the individual's privacy against the interest of protecting national security and pay attention in particular to the compensating procedural safeguards protecting against abuse where the government is granted a wide discretion to apply intrusive investigative techniques, for example, as a consequence of an application threshold that does not impose meaningful restrictions.

It is clear that also for the assessment under this Article 8(2) requirement, the involvement of a threat of terrorism will be favorable for reaching a positive conclusion. The conclusion can be drawn that the requirement of being 'necessary in a democratic society' is met, considering the goal of the Act on the Criminal Investigation of Terrorist Crimes and the procedural safeguards adopted in the Act, *in abstracto*. Nevertheless, it shall be assessed on a case-by-case basis whether the information triggering the use of the investigative powers in combination with the applicable procedural guarantees render the use 'necessary in a democratic society.' The use of SIT or search powers in a specific case may not be necessary in a democratic society, exactly because the extent of the discretion granted under Title Vb and the commensurate risk that also the additional procedural guarantees—in particular the proportionality assessment on behalf of the investigative officers as well as on behalf of the public prosecutor or examining magistrate—become rather meaningless.[81]

## *4.2.2 Trends in Criminal Investigative Policy*

### 4.2.2.1 Balancing Prevention Against Legal Protection

The changes described in Chap. 3 that have facilitated the anticipative criminal investigation shall not be considered as isolated developments. On a general level, roughly the last two decades can be characterized by an increasing focus on

---

[80] *Ibid.*, 555.

[81] Compare the remarks in this regard in Sect. 4.2.1.3.1.1. See also Van Kempen and Van de Voort 2010, 80-81.

security, primarily as a consequence of the political and societal climate,[82] which has resulted in a variety of measures in criminal law and administrative law to enhance the powers of the government to combat crime and disturbances to the public order.[83] This societal and political climate, where the prevention of crime and risk reduction are preferred above reacting *ex post*, involving a reasoning that also legal protection may be sacrificed for the purpose of achieving more security, has influenced, in the first place, the legislature and, although to a more limited extent, also the judiciary.[84]

In Chap. 3 the different legislative measures have been described, which are all underpinned by the preventive paradigm. Nevertheless, this does not only apply to anti-terrorism legislation, but to all legislative measures that have been adopted in order to increase security. Moreover, although using the criminal justice system for prevention was already pursued before the attacks of 9/11, the threat of international terrorism has accelerated this development where prevention is the central notion in order to achieve security.[85] Outside the context of anti-terrorism legislation, *inter alia*, the Act on Measures to Confront Football Hooliganism and Serious Public Nuisance has been adopted, and all these measures have a clear preventive focus.[86] On the basis of this Act the mayor can impose bans for certain areas or bans on gathering in the context of the enforcement of public order. If there are serious concerns that a person is intending to commit criminal offences and because of the nature of the offenses or the 'person' of the suspect, the public prosecutor can forbid that person from entering or going a certain place or require that person to report to a police station at certain times. The purpose of this power of the public prosecutor is not to punish criminal offenses, but to prevent them.[87] This Act fits within the development where criminal procedural powers are used as instruments for the prevention of crimes, instead of primarily as an *ultimum remedium* to react to criminal offenses. In addition, it touches upon the relation between administrative enforcement and criminal enforcement, considering the

---

[82] See on this Chap. 1, Sect. 1.3.3.

[83] See for an overview of the catalysts of the main changes in the area of the criminal justice system towards a 'hardening' and expansion of the criminal justice system: Groenhuijsen and Kooijmans 2010. Concerns about this development, in particular since the government of the liberals (VVD) and Christian-democrats (CDA), with the support of Geert Wilders' far-right party (PVV), took office pursuing a harsh, strict and repressive security policy, has come from different angles, see e.g. Van Westerloo 2006 and De Roos 2010.

[84] See on the influence of an increased emphasis on security, and the role of the threat of terrorism as the catalyst for this emphasis on security, on the adoption of legislation in the field of criminal law in the Netherlands: Van der Woude 2010, in particular 2-15, 108-109 and 292. See also Borgers 2007.

[85] Compare: Van der Woude 2010, in particular 7 and 8.

[86] *Stb.* 2010, 325. This Act was one of the measures in the context of the policy program 'Security begins with prevention.' *Kamerstukken II* 2007/08, 28 684, no. 119. See also Sect. 3.1.1.

[87] *Kamerstukken* 2007/08. 31 467, no. 3, 1-2 and 18.

overlap in the purposes of the prevention of crime and the prevention of disturbances to the public order. This latter subject will be assessed in Sect. 4.3.2.

Acts such as this, as well as the range of counterterrorism Acts, have been adopted over the past decade under the denominator of the necessity to act against the serious threat of terrorism, which has justified measures that broaden the government's powers in the field of criminal law and administrative law, sometimes without clear evidence of any necessity, by the rationale of being 'better safe than sorry.'[88] This may also be exemplified by the argumentation of the government in the explanatory memorandum of the Act on the Criminal Investigation of Terrorist Crimes: the measures proposed in the Act are compatible with Article 8 ECHR, because the significant threat of terrorism justifies the use of criminal investigative powers that interfere with the right to respect for private life upon a lower statutory standard.[89]

The political and societal climate resulting in various measures in the field of criminal law in order to use the criminal law for preventive purposes seems to have also influenced the judiciary. Of course, it is also the task of judges to take into account the societal impact of criminal behavior. Likewise, judges have the task of ensuring that defendants are granted the necessary legal protection and that the use of criminal investigative powers has to observe fundamental rights and principles. The courts' sensitivity to social anxiety concerning insecurity and criminality and, in that respect, the importance of establishing the truth with regard to committed crimes, have in particular influenced (and can still influence) the manner in which criminal investigative illegitimate actions have been sanctioned.[90] Consequently, investigative officers have been granted more discretion in their criminal investigative activities, whereas the principles of proportionality and subsidiarity are used, instead of supplementary protective principles, to justify more investigative discretion.[91] Also the courts balance all the interests involved in order to determine whether or not illegitimate interferences with the right to privacy will be sanctioned. When judges follow the societal and political climate where the interest of an expedient criminal justice system and the interest of prevention have obtained the most weight, it is clear that this will result in a less strict application of Article 359a CCP. The decision of the Supreme Court setting out the general rules for the scope and applicability of Article 359a CCP has provided judges with broad discretion, where the interests of an expedient criminal investigation and the prevention of terrorism may be taken into account in order to decide whether or not to attach consequences to illegitimate actions.[92]

---

88 Compare: Van der Woude 2010, in particular 249 and 292.

89 *Kamerstukken II* 2004/05, 30 164, no. 3, 3.

90 Corstens 2008, 706-707 and Franken 2004a, 22-23.

91 Franken 2009. See also: Muller et al. 2007, 36-38.

92 HR 30 March 2004, *NJ* 2004, 376 and Franken 2004a, 24-25. See Sect. 2.3.2.4.3.

#### 4.2.2.2 Choosing Between the Criminal Investigative Domains

The experiences in practice since the entry into force of the Act on the Criminal Investigation of Terrorist Crimes, which have been analyzed in three evaluation reports covering the period 2007–2010, demonstrate that the newly introduced investigative possibilities have been used only reluctantly, also in criminal investigations concerning terrorist activities.[93] Furthermore, none of the criminal investigations based upon indications has resulted in a criminal prosecution.[94] The most important conclusion of the evaluation report two years after the entry into force of the Act on the Criminal Investigation of Terrorist Crimes was that a difference between the nature or source of the information that has triggered a terrorism investigation under Title Vb or that has triggered a terrorism investigation under Title IVa/V could not be demonstrated. Moreover, only 3 of the 15 criminal investigations of terrorist activities that involved the use of SIT were conducted under Title Vb. Hence, it was concluded that the choice for either using Title Vb or Titles IVa or V does not seem to depend on the level of information available, but more on the preferences and specific knowledge of the specific employee of the PPS.[95] The third evaluation report, covering the period 2009–2010, has not warranted a different conclusion.[96] In this period only 3 of the 25 criminal investigations that concerned terrorism were conducted on the basis of 'indications of a terrorist crime.'

On the basis of these practical experiences a few conclusions can be drawn. Firstly, considering that none of the criminal investigations based upon indications has been followed up by a criminal prosecution, it appears that the interest of prevention indeed supersedes the interest of gathering evidence for criminal prosecution. Most of the criminal investigations initiated (under Title Vb but also terrorism investigations under the other Titles) were used to exclude risks and were therefore typically minor and short.[97] Secondly, the investigative possibilities under Title Vb have not resulted in the use of starting information that is vaguer, whereas the use of starting information from the AIVD or CIE is also not typically restricted to the investigative domain for terrorist crimes. Hence, on that basis a clear difference between indications and a reasonable suspicion cannot be demonstrated.[98] Nevertheless, it follows from the last evaluation report that a particular public prosecutor has chosen for the investigative domain of terrorist crimes, because the information available was 'extremely light' and could not establish a reasonable suspicion.[99] Considering this explanation, it seems that

---

93 Van Gestel et al. 2009, 8.

94 *Ibid.*, 9.

95 *Ibid.*, 46.

96 Van Gestel et al. 2010, 13.

97 *Ibid.*, 9.

98 Van Gestel 2009, 27-28.

99 Van Gestel 2010, 9.

although such situations may rarely arise, the indications threshold may indeed be used as a last resort when the information available is insufficient for establishing a reasonable suspicion. In the third place, the PPS and the police seem to prefer to apply SIT within the classical investigative domain rather than using the newly created possibilities especially to act in earlier phases.

To start with this last conclusion, the preference for investigating under the most restrictive threshold of application, namely a reasonable suspicion of a crime having been committed, is not particular to terrorism investigations. In Sect. 2.3.2.3.2.2 it was already indicated that Title V is rarely used and also organized crime investigations are often conducted within the classical investigative domain. Title V was—in the field—already understood as a last resort to be used when the threshold of the classical investigative domain cannot be met, a conclusion which was drawn after the entry into force of the Act on the Criminal Investigation of Terrorist Crimes.[100] The adoption of the Act on the Criminal Investigation of Terrorist Crimes has not changed this trend. When the PPS and the police are confronted with information concerning terrorist activities, a choice can now be made between three investigative domains. The investigative domain of terrorist crimes can in that light be typified as a 'last resort bonus' to be used in the very exceptional situation that an investigation cannot be conducted upon the establishment of a reasonable suspicion. Nevertheless, this does not undermine the preventive purpose of the Act, the reason for which the indications threshold has been adopted. It must be possible to initiate a criminal investigation and use SIT at anytime that information is available and requires to be investigated in order to optimize the realization of preventing terrorism.

The purpose of the investigative activities shall, however, determine the choice for the investigative domain. Also the difference between Title V and Title IVa should concern the purpose of the investigation and, consequently, the phase of the criminal investigation. When the criminal investigative domain of organized crime is used, the reason for choosing this domain has usually—although not exclusively—been the focus of obtaining a better picture of the criminal organization as a whole instead of focusing on one or more concrete suspects. Nevertheless, a clear dividing line between the investigative domains cannot be identified, which is in particular lacking with regard to the investigative phase. The Court of Appeal of The Hague has considered that Title IVa and Title V do not necessarily differ on the basis of the investigative phase, but that the purpose of the investigation concerns the distinguishing element.[101] Nevertheless, the purpose of the investigation has in practice not been decisive for choosing between investigative domains. But when a reasonable suspicion can be established according to the opinion of the PPS and the police, the classical investigative domain is usually chosen.

[100] Krommendijk et al. 2009, 135-137.

[101] Gerechtshof's-Gravenhage 2 October 2008, *LJN* BF3987 (*Piranha*).

An adverse consequence of the emphasis on the classical investigative domain is that the reasonable suspicion threshold is being stretched in order to enable criminal investigations with a wider scope and for proactive or preventive purposes. This may clarify why the indications threshold does not really differ from the reasonable suspicion threshold as to the level of information required.[102] In fact, for determining whether the reasonable suspicion threshold is met the interest of the investigation seems to be decisive, whether this interest concerns truth-finding with regard to a committed crime or the prevention of a terrorist crime. Hence, in fact the classical investigative domain is used to pursue three different purposes, depending on the nature of the crimes to be investigated, whereas the investigative domains of Title V and Title Vb are limited to organized crime, for the purpose of obtaining a picture of the complete organization, and terrorist crimes, for the purpose of prevention.

This does not mean that the value of the investigative domain for terrorist crimes has not been discerned in the field. It has been indicated that the indications threshold in comparison with a reasonable suspicion can be valuable in order to assess observed behavior in the right context, to exclude risks and to assess and evaluate information. The investigative domain has been used for these purposes on several occasions.[103] Furthermore, the indications threshold has been used at least once when the information available was insufficient to establish a reasonable suspicion, but an investigation was nevertheless considered necessary in order to exclude risks.[104] Nevertheless, the fact that the majority of terrorism investigations are conducted upon the establishment of a reasonable suspicion, which does not seem to hinder criminal investigative action for the purpose of prevention, raises doubts as to the necessity of enabling the investigative domain for terrorist crimes.

Considering these findings, the practice in choosing between the different investigative domains does not correspond with some of the expectations of the introduction of the investigative domain for terrorist crimes. A significant goal of the Act on the Criminal Investigation of Terrorist Crimes was to have the situation where (typically) the AIVD or CIE would transfer information to the PPS and the police at an earlier point in time in order to be able to initiate a criminal investigation based upon indications and to gather evidence with regard to preparatory activities concerning terrorist crimes, on which basis a prosecution can subsequently be initiated.[105] Whereas more cooperation between the PPS and AIVD has been established, this development cannot be attributed to the entry into force of the Act on the Criminal Investigation of Terrorist Crimes but rather to newly established cooperation forms (see Sect. 3.3.5) and an increased focus on terrorist

---

[102] See Sects. 2.3.2.3.1 and 4.2.1.2.

[103] De Poot et al. 2008, 43.

[104] Van Gestel 2010, 9.

[105] Rapport Evaluatie Antiterrorismemaatregelen 2011, 15 and 49 and *Kamerstukken II* 2004/05, 30 164, no. 3, 33. That this specific goal of the Act was (initially) also assumed in the field, follows from the interviews conducted for the first evaluation of the Act: De Poot et al. 2008, 47.

activities in the post-9/11 era.[106] Although the adoption of the Act on the Criminal Investigation of Terrorist Crimes was (also) considered to establish a change as to the manner in which the AIVD, the PPS and the police shall jointly work on the prevention of terrorism, this change could also be achieved under the criminal investigative framework as was in force before February 2007.[107] The lack of clear evidence as to necessity also touches upon the legitimacy of the measures that, at least on paper, trade off legal protection.[108]

However, instead of rejecting the adopted legislation because one of the main legitimating reasons for amending the law has lost its validity, it is preferable to retrieve the legitimacy by realizing more attention for the rationale behind choices between the investigative domains on the basis of the purpose of the investigation. This would serve the interest of legal protection as well as the interest of effective criminal investigation and corresponds with the original intention of the legislature. Founding the choice for a specific investigative domain on the purpose of the investigation could stop the development where the reasonable suspicion threshold is further watered down, while broader proactive and preventive investigative possibilities are allowed for organized crime and terrorist crimes. At the same time these broader investigative possibilities are then also restricted to the more complex investigation of organized crime and for pursuing the preventive interest when terrorist crimes are involved. In addition, a stricter distinction on the basis of the investigative purpose would clarify the different investigative possibilities of the investigative domains for those who need to apply them in practice.[109]

Lastly, attention should be paid to the choice between the investigative domain for terrorist crimes and the preliminary investigation. It seems that both in the examples mentioned in the explanatory memorandum and in practice the investigative domain for terrorist crimes is used for 'preliminary investigative purposes.' The preliminary investigation will normally be used to investigate 'certain sectors of industry', such as the harbor sector. It is, however, questionable whether the investigation of a certain sector will be useful for preparing terrorism investigations, considering that it is unlikely that there is a certain branch in which 'terrorism' is rooted. The limited value of the preliminary investigation is supported by the fact that in the period 2007–2010 the preliminary investigative domain has never been used in terrorism cases. The use of SIT within a criminal investigation based upon indications is considered more suitable for investigating multiple companies and groups of persons related to terrorist activities. Hence, 'preliminary investigative purposes' (preparing 'full' criminal investigations within the classical investigative domain) have also been pursued under Title Vb,

---

106 De Poot et al. 2008, 52 and 57-58 and Rapport Evaluatie Antiterrorismemaatregelen 2011, 49 and Van Gestel et al. 2009, 19.

107 See Rapport Evaluatie Antiterrorismemaatregelen 2011, 49.

108 Compare Van Kempen 2005b, 7 and Rapport van de Commissie Evaluatie Antiterrorismebeleid 2009, 62-63.

109 This recommendation will be further elaborated in Chap. 9, Sects. 9.3.1.1 and 9.3.1.2.

for example by checking on persons who are acquainted with a terrorist suspect in order to check whether information can be found that one or more of these persons are also involved in the preparation and planning of terrorist crimes.[110] Hence, in addition the necessity of the expanded preliminary investigative domain can be questioned. However, similar to a more precise distinction between criminal investigative domains on the basis of the investigative purpose, choosing between the preliminary investigation and the full criminal investigation under Title Vb on the basis of a more precise distinction between the purposes of the investigation will further legal protection. Criminal investigations into the circle of acquaintances of a terrorist suspect in order to search for information that can connect one or more of these persons within this circle to terrorist activities concerns, typically, a preliminary investigative purpose, for which purpose the use of SIT has been excluded. When information is found that can indeed link these persons to terrorism investigations, the criminal investigative domain for terrorist crimes can be resorted to.[111]

### *4.2.3 Shifting Responsibilities Among the Various Actors*

The Dutch criminal justice system is operated by actors having a shared responsibility for the legitimacy and fairness of the investigative activities with a hierarchical dimension in order to realize accountability for using criminal procedural powers (see Sect. 2.3.1). The public prosecutor and the examining magistrate both have responsibility with respect to the overall legitimacy and fairness of the criminal investigation. The use of particular investigative methods concerns a hierarchically structured system of responsibility between the actors. The measures that have realized anticipative criminal investigations have touched upon the division of responsibilities between these actors in this hierarchical structure (in particular the police, the PPS and the examining magistrate), primarily by attributing more discretion to the police to enable a preventive focus without compensating for the increased discretion with strengthened supervision.

Different developments in the post-9/11 era can be indicated that have resulted in a shift in the actors' responsibilities. In the first place, the focus on gathering as much information as possible in order to prevent terrorism is not only a responsibility of the AIVD and RIDs, but also of the CIE at the national and at the regional police levels (Sect. 3.2.2). This has resulted in a central role for the police in the prevention of terrorism and increased police action on the basis of information that is difficult to control. Secondly, the Act on the Criminal Investigation of Terrorist Crimes has increased the powers of the PPS and the police, without compensating for more discretion to act for prevention by an expanded check by

---

[110] Van Gestel et al. 2010, 9. See also De Poot et al. 2008, 19.

[111] See further Chap. 9, Sects. 9.3.1.1 and 9.3.1.2.4.

the examining magistrate through additional warrant requirements for the use of SIT based upon indications for preventive purposes. Considering the extent of the indications threshold (as dealt with in Sect. 4.2.1.2), the chances of unjust investigative action based upon information that requires criminal investigative action in order to make sure that everything is done for the prevention of terrorism have increased. Furthermore, in particular the newly introduced search powers have extended the discretion of the police considering that they may use the search powers without further authorization in the 12-hour zones and in the security zones. The hierarchical system of authorization for investigative powers that more than to a limited extent interfere with the right to privacy has been completely left aside with regard to the use of search methods in security zones, considering that the decision to label a particular zone as a security zone is done by means of an administrative decree instead of, like for the 12-hour zone, an order by the public prosecutor.

The legislature has not chosen to compensate for terrorism prevention with increased responsibility, which goes hand in hand with increased investigative discretion, especially for the police and PPS, with strengthened judicial oversight. An exception concerns the increased investigative powers in the preliminary investigation. Here, the legislature has chosen the position that the use of the preliminary investigative technique of Article 126hh CCP (ordering that information from third party automated information files be made available) requires the prior authorization of an examining magistrate to compensate for the more privacy intrusive nature of the technique that can be used against persons who cannot (yet) be connected with criminal activities. Nevertheless, not only the hierarchical structure of authorization enables the shield function of the actors in the criminal investigation. In addition, the principles of proportionality and subsidiarity and the control exerted by the trial judge through the application of Article 359a CCP function as safeguards against illegitimate and unnecessary investigative action.

As has been explained in Sect. 2.3.1 the protective function of the principles of proportionality and subsidiarity, applicable in addition to the legal requirements for using investigative powers, should direct the actors responsible for using criminal investigative powers during the investigation and compliance with these principles is subject to control by the trial judge. The hierarchical organization of attributing powers during the criminal investigation aims to guarantee that higher authorities assess both whether the legal requirements have been met and that the principles of proportionality and subsidiarity have been complied with when the interests involved are more pressing. The above-mentioned developments touching upon the division of responsibilities between the criminal investigative actors affect the protective function of the hierarchically structured decision-making and the possibilities to exert control *ex post*. Hence, it should be assessed whether the complete system of hierarchical control from the police to the trial judge is still in a state of balance. This will be done in this section by addressing three different implications. Firstly, the decision not to change the hierarchical system of authorization for SIT to compensate for the more intrusive nature of using SIT in the investigative domain of terrorist crimes and the manner in which the authorization of search powers is regulated will be subjected to further scrutiny (Sect. 4.2.3.1). Secondly, the ability of the principles of proportionality and subsidiarity and the 'threat' of *ex post* control on the legitimate use of investigative powers to safeguard also the shield responsibility of the police and PPS will be addressed (Sect. 4.2.3.2). Lastly, Sect. 4.2.3.3 will draw some conclusions as to the shifted responsibilities of the actors that have a role in the criminal investigation.

#### 4.2.3.1 Authorization of Investigative Methods

Similar to the use of SIT in the classical criminal investigation and in the organized crime investigation, the public prosecutor is entrusted with a controlling role with regard to the legitimacy (as to the statutory requirements, including an assessment of proportionality and subsidiarity) of the use of SIT upon 'indications of a terrorist crime' in a particular case. The government explained that, although much will depend on the professional judgments of the investigative officers as to whether or not indications of a terrorist crime are present and the use of a special investigative technique is in the interest of the investigation, the public prosecutor should still fulfill a full controlling role with respect to the question whether or not indications can be established in a particular case. The public prosecutor should assess the facts and circumstances on which the indications are based. However, he can include the professional judgments of the investigative officers as to how to interpret and assess the information available. According to the government, factors such as the verifiability and reliability of the information should play an important role when assessing whether a technique can contribute to the prevention of a terrorist crime. The manner of assessing the information shall be similar to the situation in which a reasonable suspicion is required; however, the facts and circumstances in question will be less concrete and verifiable.[112] Only after an independent determination concerning the presence of indications of a terrorist crime will the public prosecutor order the use of a special investigative technique. The same consideration applies with regard to the required authorization of the examining magistrate for some SIT.[113] Emphasizing the similarities with the system of authorization in the classical investigative domain and the investigative domain for organized crime, the legislature considered it unnecessary to adapt the hierarchical system of authorization by expanding the role of the examining magistrate as a warrant judge in the investigative domain for terrorist crimes.[114]

However, the argumentation of the government ignores the fact that the balance in the hierarchical system, where more intrusive powers are compensated by

---

[112] *Kamerstukken II* 2004/05, 30 164, no. 3, 11.

[113] *Kamerstukken II* 2005/06, 30 164, no. 7, 18.

[114] With the exception of the preliminary investigative technique of Article 126hh CCP. This concerns a newly introduced technique with a more intrusive character than the other preliminary investigative techniques, for which reason the legislature considered the additional authorization of the examining magistrate for this technique to be required.

higher hierarchical authorization, has been affected by attributing the PPS and/or the police with more powers to investigate upon a rather vague criterion, allowing investigative activities on the basis of soft information from uncontrollable sources (CIE or AIVD) and involving persons who cannot be suspected of a crime. In this light a member of parliament for the Socialist Party has proposed an amendment to the bill in order to realize judicial control in the form of an authorization by the examining magistrate to compensate for the lower application threshold of SIT by referring to the value attached by the ECrtHR to judicial control over broad investigative discretion.[115] The legislature has, however, not adopted this proposed amendment to the bill, arguing that the nature of the specific special investigative techniques with regard to the seriousness of the interference with privacy rights is the only relevant factor for deciding whether or not an *ex ante* judicial check is required.[116] However, the nature of the specific interference with the right to respect for private life caused by the use of a SIT cannot be determined completely separately from the fact that under the 'indications' threshold the possibilities of subjecting persons who cannot be connected to terrorist activities to SIT have increased.

This means that control over the legitimacy of using a specific investigative power remains primarily with the public prosecutor. The Act on Strengthening the Position of the Examining Magistrate intends to realize his/her strengthened position in the criminal investigation, not by expanding his/her role as a warrant judge but by strengthening his/her position for the purpose of exerting control over the quality of the criminal investigation in general at the request of the public prosecutor or defense or *ex officio*.[117] However, his/her concrete controlling authority with regard to the legitimacy of SIT remains limited, as a consequence of the marginal examination exerted as to whether the statutory requirements are met (which includes an assessment of proportionality and subsidiarity on the basis of the statutory requirement 'in the interest of the investigation' or 'upon a pressing investigative need') and as a consequence of the heavy caseload and the limited insight into the underlying file.[118] Hence, it does not appear that the Act on Strengthening the Position of the Examining Magistrate will also improve the controlling capabilities of the examining magistrate as a warrant judge. In addition, it may be doubted whether the examining magistrate may fulfill an important additional check as a warrant judge for the use of SIT on the basis of indications of a terrorist crime. Because of the breadth of the indications threshold and the dominance of the interest of preventing terrorism when making a proportionality and subsidiarity assessment, it generally seems that points of departure will be absent for refusing a request to authorize a SIT.[119] In this light, the prior

[115] *Kamerstukken II* 2005/06, 30 164, no. 11.

[116] *Kamerstukken II* 2005/06, 30 164, no. 7, 11.

[117] See Sect. 2.3.1.3.

[118] Franken 2006, 269.

[119] Compare: Van Kempen 2005b, 10.

authorization of the examining magistrate may have a more theoretical than a concrete additional protective value.

A special situation concerns the possibility to use search powers on the basis of indications in the 12-hour and security zones. Under the Economic Offenses Act and the Weapons and Ammunition Act the police could already apply search methods when there are indications relating the person (or his/her objects) to an offense criminalized in the Acts without the prior authorization of the public prosecutor. But using search methods against anyone in a particular area requires the authorization of the public prosecutor. For the use of search powers in order to prevent terrorism, the order of the public prosecutor is first required in order to determine the area where and the period during which the search powers can be used because of the presence of 'indications of a terrorist crime' with regard to that area. Subsequently, within that area the police are given the discretion to apply search methods 'in the interest of the investigation', which means that the selection of persons to be searched is made on the basis of an assessment of the proportionality and subsidiarity of the search, in the light of the indications of a terrorist crime. Hence, the search methods in the 12-hour zones are comparable to the use of search methods under the special criminal statutes where such search methods can be used upon an order by the public prosecutor against anyone. However, the broad discretion afforded to the police to apply search methods in security zones without the involvement of a public prosecutor or an examining magistrate seems to break with the hierarchical system of authorities in the criminal investigation. Also the Weapons and Ammunition Act (Articles 50-52 WWM) provides for the possibility to use search powers in security zones, but only upon the order of the public prosecutor and for a period of 12-hours. The investigative officers are thus attributed wide discretion to use search powers in security zones without the involvement of any higher authority in the criminal investigation system. It seems that an administrative decree is intended to replace the indications of a terrorist crime threshold, which, however, may not be expected to replace the assessment of, in particular, the proportionality and subsidiarity of using search powers in that particular area for the purpose of preventing terrorism.[120]

#### 4.2.3.2 Protective Function of the Principles of Proportionality and Subsidiarity and Ex Post Judicial Control

The expanded investigative discretion for the PPS and the police has not been compensated by broadening the control function of the examining magistrate as a warrant judge. Hence, as regulatory elements the principles of proportionality and

[120] Van Kempen advocates additional control by means of an order by the public prosecutor in security zones and an authorization by the examining magistrate before indicting 12-h zones. Compare: Van Kempen 2005b, 6-7.

subsidiarity as well as the *ex post* judicial control of the trial judge should function as sufficient safeguards to prevent an abuse of power by the PPS and the police.

As has been addressed before, police officers will generally be inclined to assume proportionality and subsidiarity when confronted with information requiring action to prevent terrorism. In fact, the principles will generally be used to afford the PPS and the police with more investigative discretion to act upon information concerning a terrorism threat. This may also be recognized in the manner in which the threshold of a reasonable suspicion has been interpreted.[121] At the same time, it follows from the evaluation reports on the Act on the Criminal Investigation of Terrorist Crimes that prosecutors are aware of their responsibility to make a careful assessment of the interests involved by indicating that from a legal protection point of view SIT, based upon indications, should preferably only be used to assess a particular situation and to exclude risks. When SIT are used for the purpose of evidence gathering against someone, it would be important to firstly label this person as a suspect.[122]

The Supreme Court has considered that a more marginal examination of the use of criminal investigative powers is warranted when a higher authority has been involved in the authorization of the investigative powers. Considering the increased investigative discretion of the PPS and the police, this should require a more precise examination by the trial judge under Article 359a CCP.[123] However, this control (which also applies to the control exerted by the examining magistrate when his/her warrant is required for the use of SIT[124]) is impeded as a consequence of the nature of the information generally used as starting information for the criminal investigation of terrorist activities. A substantive check on the reasonableness of basing indications or a reasonable suspicion on information from unknown sources is impeded where the background of the information cannot be checked and an assessment of the proportionality and subsidiarity of the use of a SIT in the light of this information cannot easily be made.

The impeded controlling possibilities of the trial judge may be compensated by procedures for hearing witnesses who can testify with regard to the veracity of the starting information. With regard to the exertion of control over the CIE information, there is the possibility to hear a 'lawfulness witness', who, as an officer of the CIE, is able to testify about the veracity of the information.[125] When AIVD information is used as starting information the procedure as adopted by the Act on Shielded Witnesses can be followed.[126] It will be explained in more detail in Sect. 4.3.3 why these procedures are not capable of fully compensating for the lack of

---

[121] See Sect. 2.3.2.3.

[122] De Poot et al. 2008, 50.

[123] HR 11 October 2005, *NJ* 2006, 625, para 3.5.1 and 3.5.2 and HR 21 November 2006, *NJ* 2007, 233 ann. Mevis, para 3.4 and annotation para 3. See also Sects. 2.3.1.1 and 2.3.2.4.3.

[124] See: Van der Meij 2010a, 554-560.

[125] Brinkhoff 2009, 123-128.

[126] Section 3.3.2.

control over the use of criminal investigative powers on the basis of CIE or AIVD information. This subject will be dealt with there, because the impediments on control are most significantly a consequence of the increased use of intelligence in criminal proceedings and the intelligence-led focus of the PPS and the police.

Furthermore, the control exerted by the trial judge on the basis of the principles of proportionality and subsidiarity cannot be considered to compel the PPS and the police to use more restraint in the course of the criminal investigation. Also the trial judge will be inclined to attach more weight to the threat of terrorism when determining whether the PPS and the police could reasonably decide to use a specific criminal investigative power. In addition, on the basis of an examination of the manner in which courts have used the principles of proportionality and subsidiarity to provide protection in addition to the statutory requirements, Franken has drawn the conclusion that in recent case law proportionality and subsidiarity are primarily used as arguments for not sanctioning illegitimate actions in the course of the criminal investigation.[127] And the legislature has also emphasized that the central role of the principles of proportionality and subsidiarity with regard to the fairness of the use of a technique in a particular situation may also lead to the conclusion that such an examination would result in the balance normally struck for conventional crime now being different as a result of the nature of terrorist crimes.[128]

In this regard it can be questioned to what extent *ex post* judicial control may compensate for a lack of *ex ante* control over the use of investigative powers. This conclusion is here drawn on the basis of an assessment of the legislative developments that have touched upon the division of responsibilities between the actors. It may even be strengthened when taking into account the manner in which prevention is balanced against legal protection in the post-9/11 era (Sect. 4.2.2.1) which also influences the 'judge who is responsive to societal and political developments.'[129]

The ECrtHR has emphasized the importance of effective judicial control over investigative powers that interfere with Article 8(1) ECHR: "The rule of law implies, inter alia, that an interference by the executive authorities with an individual's rights should normally be assured by the judiciary, at least in the last resort, judicial control offering the best guarantees of independence, impartiality and a proper procedure."[130] In *Sanoma Uitgevers B.V. v. The Netherlands*, the European Court emphasized in this regard the value it attaches in particular to *ex ante* judicial control in order to *prevent* serious intrusions of rights protected in the Convention, in this particular case Article 10 ECHR with regard to the protection

---

[127] Franken 2009, 8.

[128] *Kamerstukken I,* 2006/07, 30 164, no. D, 3-4.

[129] Franken 2004a, 22-24.

[130] ECHR 6 September 1978, App. no. 5029/71 (*Klass and Others v. Germany*), para 55.

of journalistic sources.[131] Especially where state authorities seek to use intrusive investigative techniques, *ex ante* control by a judge is preferred and in some situations, such as in *Sanoma* where the criminal investigative interest clashed with the privilege of confidentiality with regard to journalistic sources, is even necessary to provide an adequate procedural safeguard.

Furthermore, a challenge regarding a violation of Article 8 ECHR, although it may be recognized in court, may not be remedied through the application of Article 359a CCP, considering that the judge will determine, in the light of Article 6 ECHR, whether the defendant can no longer, without imposing a sanction, receive a fair trial, which may result in the decision not to attach consequences also to investigative activities in violation of Article 8 ECHR. Arguably, the defendant is then denied an effective remedy as to Article 13 ECHR.[132] Nevertheless, an effective remedy may also be provided outside the context of the criminal proceedings, for example, through civil proceedings or a complaint addressed to the National Ombudsman.

#### 4.2.3.3 Conclusion

An increased focus on affording the investigative actors, the PPS and the police, with sufficient discretion in order to act for the purpose of preventing terrorism has not resulted in measures which rebalance the division of responsibilities in the criminal investigation. In addition, partly as a consequence of the nature of the information used as starting information for criminal investigations for the prevention of terrorism and partly as a consequence of the manner in which the courts have approached the controlling role of the judiciary on the legitimacy of criminal investigative activities, the core of the shield responsibility is vested with the public prosecutor. At the same time, the PPS will be confronted with information requiring investigative action to exclude risks. Although it follows from the evaluation reports that public prosecutors take the balancing of all interests involved seriously before choosing specific criminal investigative activities, considering their reluctance to use SIT on the basis of indications and the preference for 'mini-investigations' to exclude risks, the possibility that persons will be subjected to criminal investigative powers without a sufficient reason has increased. After all, acting upon vague information to ensure that terrorism is prevented involves a considerable risk that it will subsequently become apparent that the information was inaccurate.[133] This may be illustrated by some of the terrorism arrests and searches that have been in the media in the last couple of years. For example, on December 25, 2010 twelve Somali men were arrested on

---

[131] ECHR 14 September 2010, App. no. 38224/03 (*Sanoma Uitgevers B.V. v. The Netherlands*), para 88. 90, 92 and 98-100.

[132] See on this: Franken 2004b, 219, Franken 2004a, 18 and Berkhout-van Poelgeest 2001, 31.

[133] Rapport van de Commissie Evaluatie Antiterrorismebeleid 2009, 46-47.

the basis of a suspicion that they were planning an imminent terrorist attack. Several houses were searched, thereby focusing on ensuring prevention. Subsequently, no evidence was found that could substantiate the suspicions based on an official report by the AIVD.[134] Control over the use of SIT in similar cases will not at all be realized in the context of criminal trials, considering that the persons involved will never be prosecuted. Considering that this is primarily a consequence of the new relation between the intelligence community and the law enforcement community to enable anticipative criminal investigation, the implications signaled for a balanced system of control on legitimate criminal investigations in this section will even be reinforced and, therefore, the issue of control over using criminal investigative powers will be further discussed in Sect. 4.3.4.

### 4.2.4 Final Remarks

The legislative measures and, additionally, intelligence-led policing, have put the prevention of terrorist crimes at the forefront of the criminal investigation. The conclusion can be drawn that this development has, however, not been limited to the investigative domain for terrorist crimes, which is primarily a consequence of the fact that the different criminal investigative domains are not applied exclusively for the purpose for which they have been attributed. Consequently, implications for the shield objective of criminal procedural law affect the system as a whole, although most significantly when the criminal investigation is actually used for the prevention of terrorism. This has affected the balance between the different actors with regard to their responsibility concerning the fairness of the criminal process. Investigative officers have been granted wide discretion to do what is necessary to prevent terrorism, whereas the controlling roles of the examining magistrate and the trial judge have been watered down, both as a consequence of the difficulty in exerting control on the basis of criteria which afford wide discretion and as a consequence of the developments where security interests outweigh the interests of legal protection.

In addition, the statutory framework regulating the criminal investigative powers for the purpose of preventing terrorism may raise doubts with regard to their compatibility with Article 8 ECHR, considering that the extent of the applicable criteria may be insufficiently foreseeable. Nevertheless, considering the restrictive use of the newly attributed and broadened investigative powers, it seems that in practice the additional implications of the legislative measures under Article 8 ECHR are rather limited. At the same time, this conclusion, combined with the finding that the additional value of the legislative measures seems to be

---

[134] See also Vermaas 2011, 25 and 'Schadevergoeding voor opgepakte Somaliërs', *Volkskrant* 14 January 2011.

rather limited in comparison to the criminal investigative possibilities that already existed, may cast doubts as to the necessity of the changes adopted by the Act on the Criminal Investigation of Terrorist Crimes.[135] Unnecessary legislation that provides for government powers that interfere with privacy rights is also incompatible with Article 8 ECHR and the principles of proportionality and subsidiarity.

Nevertheless, instead of rejecting the measures adopted by the Act on the Criminal Investigation of Terrorist Crimes it may be favorable for legal protection in the criminal investigation in general, as well as in order to make sure that the government has the necessary criminal investigative tools to prevent terrorism, to relate the use of criminal investigative powers more strictly to the specific investigative purpose. This would make the choices between different investigative domains, on the basis of the level of the information available and the nature of the crimes involved, more transparent and could facilitate a more meaningful control over the use of criminal investigative powers.[136]

## 4.3 Demarcating the Anticipative Criminal Investigation

### *4.3.1 The Relation Between Anticipative Criminal Investigation and Intelligence Investigation*

The realization of anticipative criminal investigation in the Netherlands has touched upon the relation between an anticipative criminal investigation and an intelligence investigation. This concerns different aspects of the system. In the first place, because the purpose of the anticipative criminal investigation concerns the prevention of terrorist crimes (combined with truth-finding), the anticipative criminal investigative activities may overlap with the activities of the AIVD in the light of their task as to Article 6 WIV 2002. This section will first address this possible overlap. It will do so by taking into account the manner in which the AIVD cooperates with the PPS. In what situation does the AIVD investigate and where do the criminal investigative authorities start to play a role? In how far does this practice differ for the investigative domain concerning terrorist crimes as compared to the classical investigative domain and the investigative domain for organized crime? Secondly, because of the possibility of overlapping investigative purposes, the practice of parallel investigative activities has increased. The implications of 'parallel investigations' for the relation between the criminal investigation and the intelligence investigation will be identified.

---

[135] See e.g. also Van Kempen 2005b and Rapport van de Commissie Evaluatie Antiterrorismebeleid 2009.

[136] This suggested recommendation will be further elaborated in Chap. 9, Sects. 9.3.1.1 and 9.3.1.2.

Cooperation between the AIVD and the PPS is realized and intensified by legislative measures as well as by changes of an organizational nature. The stimulation of information sharing between the AIVD and the PPS in order to be able to initiate criminal investigative activities at an earlier moment has been the indirect objective of adopting the Act on the Criminal Investigation of Terrorist Crimes.[137] Furthermore, the function of the CT Infobox is to analyze information made available by the different participating agencies, which enables the AIVD to send out notifications or official reports to the agencies that can best act upon the information in order to optimize the prevention of terrorist attacks.[138] This also includes the sending of official reports on the basis of Article 38 WIV 2002 to the national public prosecutor for counterterrorism in order to trigger a criminal investigation, possibly on the basis of 'indications of a terrorist crime.' In addition, the adoption of the Shielded Witnesses Act[139] was intended to stimulate an intensified sharing of information between the AIVD and the PPS by providing a solution to the clash of the interest of secrecy in the AIVD investigation and the interest of transparency in criminal proceedings.

Enabling the PPS and the police to investigative at an earlier phase by leaving the central threshold of a reasonable suspicion for the application of special investigative techniques was intended to go hand in hand with an earlier transfer of information from the AIVD to the PPS. The adoption of the Shielded Witnesses Act should further reinforce the transfer of information. The advantage of having the criminal investigative authorities take over the investigation of terrorist activities or to start a criminal investigation parallel to an intelligence investigation is that it will be more likely that also the law enforcement agencies can gather information regarding preparatory activities. This would increase the chances of successfully prosecuting alleged terrorists. In order to successfully use the new criminal investigative possibilities in an 'earlier' phase, it will however be beneficial if the AIVD would decide to send out an official report somewhat earlier than before in order to enable the PPS and the police to initiate a criminal investigation and gather evidence for the purpose of a criminal prosecution. Normally, the AIVD will only send an official report to the PPS when there is an urgent threat, in order to not give away its information position when this is not yet necessary. After such an official report the PPS will immediately use its power of arrest to remove this threat without having the time to initiate a criminal investigation and gather evidence. Furthermore, the AIVD will generally send an official report when it encounters, more or less coincidentally, information regarding criminal offenses in the context of an investigation regarding a threat to national security.[140] In order to allow the law enforcement services to initiate a criminal investigation into terrorist activities earlier than before, it will, however, be essential that the

---

137 *Kamerstukken II* 2004/05, 30 164, no. 3, 33.

138 See Sect. 3.3.4.

139 See Sect. 3.3.2.

140 De Poot et al. 2008, 52.

AIVD will change its practice as to sending official reports. In most situations the AIVD (or the CT Infobox) will possess information that can trigger a criminal investigation based upon indications. Whether or not the AIVD will provide the PPS with such an official report is an independent decision to be taken by the AIVD and will primarily depend on the interest of the AIVD investigation and not so much on the fact that a criminal investigation may be initiated upon the information.[141]

On the basis of the experiences in practice, the conclusion can be drawn that the criminal investigative domain for terrorist crimes is only used exceptionally and the purpose of the criminal investigation seems to be primarily to remove a threat at an early phase and to gather information regarding the group of persons associated with a terrorist suspect. Furthermore, the nature and source of the information do not generally seem to differ for investigations commenced upon indications or commenced upon a reasonable suspicion. The source of the starting information in terrorism cases usually concerns either AIVD reports or CIE information. However, considering that AIVD reports have more often resulted in the initiation of a classical criminal investigation, the conclusion that the AIVD has changed its policy as to sending AIVD reports does not seem, on that basis, to be warranted.[142] The AIVD has also indicated that it prefers not to share information at an earlier point, considering the commensurate risk of losing its information position.[143] Also from the cases dealt with in the courts concerning the interpretation of the reasonable suspicion threshold and from the examples mentioned in the explanatory memorandum, the exact difference between establishing a reasonable suspicion on the basis of the AIVD reports and establishing indications upon the AIVD reports remains unclear.[144]

Considering the results of the evaluations of the implementation of the Act on the Criminal Investigation of Terrorist Crimes, it does not appear that the legislative action has affected the relation between the AIVD and the PPS in the sense that information is shared earlier than before. Nevertheless, in the latest evaluation of the counterterrorism measures taken in the last decade, the conclusion was drawn that although it has taken some time, at this moment the right form of cooperation has been found between the AIVD, the PPS and the police, where the prevention of terrorist crimes is the shared and central mission instead of the role

[141] As is repeatedly stated in the context of cooperation between the AIVD and the PPS/police, the interest of national security prevails above the interest of criminal proceedings. See e.g. explanatory memorandum to the Shielded Witnesses Act *Kamerstukken II* 2004/04, 29743, no. 3, 1. See also the 2007 Amendment to the WIV 2002, amending Article 38 WIV 2002 in order to provide the AIVD with more discretion as to the situations where it shall send an official report to the PPS: the interest of national security prevails above the interest of prosecuting criminal offenses, for which reason the AIVD is no longer obliged to inform the PPS when criminal offenses are discovered during its investigations. *Kamerstukken II* 2006/07, 30 553, no. 8, 2.

[142] De Poot et al. 2008, 43, Van Gestel et al. 2009, 46 and Van Gestel et al. 2010, 9.

[143] De Poot et al. 2008, 53 and 63.

[144] See Sects. 3.2.1.1, 4.2.1.2 and 4.2.2.2.

or position of the separate services.[145] This was primarily the consequence of the established regular consultations between the AIVD, the PPS and the police in the context of Article 61(2) WIV 2002 in order to harmonize the responses to counterterrorism, in combination with the coordinating function of the NCTb and the centralizing of the responsibility for counterterrorism policy at the Department of Security and Justice, rather than the possibilities for the PPS and the police to initiate criminal investigations at an earlier point in time. In addition, also the CT Infobox may continue to play an important role, especially where there is still time to develop covert criminal investigative activities, considering that the information gathered within the CT Infobox concerns information in the context of the regular investigative phase and not information regarding urgent threats.

The observation that countering terrorism, with a primary focus on the prevention of terrorist crimes, has become a shared mission of the AIVD, the PPS and the police has possibly not really affected the relation between the AIVD, the PPS and the police as to the moment when investigative activities are initiated. Nevertheless, the fact that clear.

Examples are absent *in practice*, as a consequence of the limited use of the investigative domain for terrorist crimes and because investigations initiated, based upon indications, have never resulted in a criminal prosecution, does not mean that *theoretically* the PPS and the police cannot resort to SIT in the criminal investigative domain of terrorist crime at an earlier phase.[146]

Furthermore, considering that the 'prevention of terrorism' has become the shared mission of the AIVD, the PPS and the police and that the services cooperate so as to realize the prevention of terrorism in the most effective manner, this results in concerns as to an overlap between the activities of the AIVD and the PPS thereby affecting the institutional separation between the intelligence community and the law enforcement community. The prevention of terrorism has traditionally been the exclusive task of the AIVD.[147] When the criminal investigative authorities start to investigate for preventive purposes, their work becomes similar to that of the intelligence services. That might involve a risk that the cooperation becomes too intense and that the AIVD will start to investigate for criminal investigative purposes and vice versa. Such practice would depart from the traditional separation between the two communities based upon the purposes served—for the intelligence community: conducting investigations to protect against dangers to the democratic legal system or to the security or other vital interests of the state; and, for the law enforcement community: making prosecutorial decisions. Section 3.3.3

---

[145] Rapport Evaluatie Antiterrorismemaatregelen 2011, 102.

[146] See Sect. 4.2.2.2. This difference between the current experiences in practice and the possible theoretical implications may be supported by the fact that it has followed from the interviews conducted for the evaluation reports that the investigative possibilities under Title Vb are understood to be 'broader'. However, the use of Title Vb seems currently to be more dependent on the preferences and knowledge of the persons in charge than the actual nature and concreteness of the information available. See Van Gestel 2009, 46.

[147] Rapport Evaluatie Antiterrorismemaatregelen 2011, 49.

has addressed the manner in which the courts have dealt with parallel investigations. This raises, in particular, concerns as to the controllability of the abuse of investigative powers in the course of parallel investigations. These implications will be addressed in Sect. 4.3.4. In the context of the current section the conclusion can be drawn that the relation between the AIVD, the PPS and the police is affected because the primary purpose of the criminal investigative domain for terrorist crimes is similar to the purpose of the AIVD investigation, for which reason also cooperation between the AIVD, the PPS and the police has been increased and intensified. Although this does not necessarily result in criminal investigations on the basis of 'softer' information than would have been possible in the classical investigative domain or in the investigative domain for organized crime, the different communities do endorse the interest of consultation and of handing over information to the service where the best results can be expected concerning the prevention of terrorism.

The possibilities for overlapping purposes of the AIVD investigation and the criminal investigation may even be more apparent when taking into account the purpose of the preliminary investigation. The Act on the Criminal Investigation of Terrorist Crimes has also expanded the investigative capacity of the preliminary investigation (see Sect. 3.2.1.2) especially for the purpose of preparing a criminal investigation of terrorist crimes. The preliminary investigative function may become rudimentary when Title Vb is typically triggered by AIVD information and this information offers sufficient points of departure to initiate a criminal investigation under Title Vb. Especially considering that the need for preliminary investigative activities can then be removed by requesting the intelligence service to provide more information about the already communicated official report.[148] However, when such additional information cannot be provided or if information is received from the CIE, it is still conceivable that preliminary investigative activities are employed (although in such a situation usually mini-investigations will be conducted under Title Vb in order to exclude risks). Nevertheless, the necessity of the expanded possibilities to gather information for the preparation of a full criminal investigation into terrorism seems to be rather limited, considering that the tools have so far not been used at all.

Vice versa, the law enforcement services may also enter the working field of the AIVD when parallel investigations are conducted regarding the preparation of a terrorist crime, especially because the police have moved towards operating on an intelligence-led basis with an important role for the CIE. When the law enforcement services initiate a criminal investigation, for instance upon information collected by the CIE, the use of SIT will often be used to strengthen the information position of the police and the PPS about groups of people (in particular in organized crime investigations or terrorism investigations), which will enable a more effective criminal investigation of specific persons and a more effective

[148] HR 13 November 2007, *NJ* 2007, 614, para 3.5.2.

gathering of evidence against these persons.[149] This building up of information regarding groups of people is closely related to the work of the AIVD (investigating groups of people for threat assessments). Still, the goal of the criminal investigation shall not be the mere strengthening of the information position, but the gathering of information in order to investigate criminal offenses.[150]

In order to prevent that the investigation of the law enforcement services and that of the intelligence services have adverse influences on each other, the services need to cooperate and harmonize their investigative activities. Consultation between the two communities has a legal basis in Article 61(2) of the WIV 2002 and is, furthermore, facilitated by the creation of the CT Infobox.[151] This seems to be also the current approach of the AIVD and the law enforcement community to give effect to their shared mission of preventing terrorism.

In conclusion: the AIVD, the PPS and the police have overlapping purposes when it comes to the prevention of terrorism. This has been the reason for intensifying cooperation, although based on their separate setting of tasks (and thus the eventual investigative purpose). The intensified cooperation does affect the anticipative criminal investigation. Rather, an anticipative criminal investigation is in fact enabled by this intensified cooperation, where information analyzed in the CT Infobox constitutes the proactive starting information for a criminal investigation into terrorism.[152]

### *4.3.2 Relation Between Anticipative Criminal Investigation and Administrative Supervisory Authority*

Because administrative measures have also obtained an important function in the Dutch counterterrorism policy, underpinned by the same politico-legal considerations as the measures in the field of criminal law,[153] the action in the field of administrative law and in the field of criminal investigative law have in many situations become alternatives in the sense that the measures in both areas of the

[149] In fact, the use of SIT in the context of a criminal investigation based upon indications in order to strengthen the information position in order to prepare a more effective criminal investigation (most likely upon a reasonable suspicion) with regard to the gathering of evidence against persons for the purpose of prosecution is similar to the goal for which the preliminary investigation has been created.

[150] De Poot et al. 2008, 46-47.

[151] See Sect. 3.4.4 and also: De Poot et al. 2008, 17 and 35-36.

[152] Although the practical implementation of the policy pursued may face obstacles considering that the risk that the AIVD loses its information position as a consequence of sharing information with the PPS and the police will remain and, consequently, also the 'reversed' criminal investigation (first an arrest to remove a threat and then collecting the evidence). See also De Poot et al. 2008, 52-53 and Vermaas 2011.

[153] See Sect. 3.1.1.

law may be suitable for action in early phases for the purpose of preventing terrorism. The purpose of the use of the measures in both areas concerns the prevention of terrorism, although the administrative powers are to be conducted in the context of the enforcement of public order and the criminal investigative powers in the context of criminal law enforcement. This distinction is still explicitly made for all measures in either area, as has followed from the description in Chap. 3. Nevertheless, the border between activities in the field of administrative enforcement and in the field of criminal investigation is even less clear, because the activities in early stages when persons cannot yet be suspected of a crime have been expanded as a consequence of the adoption of the indications threshold and the preventive focus in anticipation of future harm of criminal investigative activities.[154] Previously, activities during these phases were not considered to be matters of criminal law enforcement, but as the prevention of disturbances to the public order.

The border between administrative supervision and criminal investigation has always been the subject of discussion, as a consequence of the possibility that the administrative supervision may switch upon the discovery of evidence of a criminal offense to a criminal investigation or that the purposes of administrative supervision and criminal investigation overlap (cumulating spheres).[155] Although the purposes of administrative enforcement and criminal investigation in the context of counterterrorism largely overlap, the legislature has clearly defined, for each measure, to what area of the law the measures belong and, hence, which legal framework is applicable. For that reason, the measures themselves do not affect the way in which this shifting between spheres and the cumulating of spheres, as briefly touched upon in Sect. 2.3.2.2.2, is dealt with. Nevertheless, a new situation of cumulating spheres may have arisen in the context of administrative disturbance.[156] This administrative disturbance may occur parallel to criminal investigative activities, as has followed from one of the two cases that have dealt with the method of administrative disturbance, in order to optimize the risk reduction of the actual commission of a terrorist crime. Nevertheless, currently the use of the method of administrative disturbance seems to focus on the (exceptional) phase preceding the criminal investigative domain of terrorist crimes for the purpose of deradicalization.[157] Whereas the purpose of the 'repressive' use of the administrative disturbance overlaps with the purpose of criminal investigative activities into terrorism, the current 'softer' application of the method seems to fit more clearly in the context of the task of maintaining public order. In fact, the current

154 As also concluded by Luchtman 2007, 678.

155 See Sect. 2.3.2.2.2.

156 The discussion as to whether administrative disturbance can actually be considered as criminal law enforcement, considering the repressive nature and the purpose of preventing terrorist crimes, for which reason the public prosecutor instead of the mayor shall have the authority to order this method of disturbance, falls outside the scope of the subject of this research. See on this subject: Brouwer 2006, 12 and Muller et al. 2007b, 118-119.

157 See Sect. 3.4.1.

use of the method can be better described by the term interference than by the more repressive term of disturbance. The method of administrative interference supplements criminal investigative activities in order to maximize risk reduction. Hence, because of a clearer demarcation of the purposes, the method does not (any longer) affect the relation between the criminal law enforcement task and the task of maintaining public order which belong to the police.

In addition, the clearer demarcation of the purposes of the criminal investigative domain of terrorist crimes and of administrative disturbances has improved the transparency of the rationale for choosing a specific method from the broad arsenal of available measures, for example, on the basis of the information in the CT Infobox, and will improve the refining of the counterterrorism strategy in the context of the consultation between the different partners responsible for counterterrorism and the coordinating role of the NCtB.[158]

Another aspect concerns the introduction of search powers that can be used for the prevention of terrorism and which are comparable to the search powers that were already provided in special criminal statutes (the WED and the WWM).[159] In general, the regulation of the search powers in the CCP makes clear that these methods shall be used only for the criminal investigative purpose and under the applicability of other CCP provisions, which in the light of the issues implicated by cumulating spheres is favorable for legal protection and will avoid misunderstanding as to the purposes of their use.

The only remarkable aspect, where the legislature has refrained from making a clear distinction between the supervisory authority over the criminal investigation and over the administrative enforcement of public order, concerns the fact that the police may use the search powers in security zones without an order by the public prosecutor. In the context of the Weapons and Ammunition Act, the police may conduct preventive frisking and may search objects and vehicles in security zones, indicated as such by the mayor and approved by the city council, upon the order of the public prosecutor (Articles 50-52 WWM).[160] By establishing the supervision of the public prosecutor, the use of search methods under the Weapons and Ammunition Act is more clearly defined as concerning the criminal investigative sphere.[161] Nevertheless, considering the regulation in the CCP, it is clear that the

---

158 Rapport van de Commissie Evaluatie Antiterrorismebeleid 2009, 47-50.

159 See Sect. 2.2.2.2.2.

160 See on these search powers in security zones from the point of view of the ECrtHR decision in *Gillan and Quinton v. The United Kingdom* (ECHR 12 January 2010, App. no. 4158/05): Ölçer 2010, 21-30.

161 On April 6, 2011 the Minister of Security and Justice announced that the possibilities for preventive frisking and searches in security zones will be expanded by allowing the mayor to assign security zones without the intervention of the municipal council. Nevertheless, for the use of search powers on the basis of Articles 50-52 WWM the order of the public prosecutor is still required according to the first version of the bill (available at: http://www.rijksoverheid.nl/documenten-en-publicaties/regelingen/2011/04/07/wetsvoorstel-preventief-fouilleren-voor-consultatie.html (accessed May 18, 2011)), although the public prosecutor may be replaced by an assistant public prosecutor in the case of urgency.

criminal procedural law framework applies to the use of search methods for the prevention of terrorism also in security zones.

### 4.3.3 *Defining and Positioning the Anticipative Criminal Investigation*

Considering the conclusions of the preceding two sections, the realization of anticipative criminal investigation has not affected the demarcation of the criminal investigation from the intelligence investigation and from administrative supervisory authority. The distinction between the three areas on the basis of the investigative purpose has remained in place. Although the purposes of the AIVD and the PPS/police have moved towards each other by adopting a shared mission of preventing terrorism, this does not mean that distinguishing tasks on the basis of investigative purposes can no longer be made. Especially the CT Infobox has been attributed an important role in coordinating the use of counterterrorism measures in the different areas, by taking into account the specific legal context of the measure and the responsible agency.[162] The specific investigative purpose has, for that reason, a significant regulatory impact. This seems to correspond with the preferable interpretation given to the definition of the criminal investigation under Article 132a CCP. The purpose of the criminal investigation—'making prosecutorial decisions'[163]—concerns the only defining element, whereas the supervision of the public prosecutor and the applicability of other criminal procedural guarantees, in particular the duty to compile records, are regulatory elements which are applicable as a consequence of defining investigative activities as criminal investigative activities under Article 132a CCP.[164]

Nevertheless, the criminal investigation has also adopted another purpose, namely the prevention of terrorism, which was a purpose previously exclusively carried out by the intelligence service. Consequently, the AIVD, the police and the PPS have moved towards each other, which means that they may have a shared interest in the objects of investigation and that cooperation has increased. This involves a risk that cooperation will increase to a level where it amounts to an abuse of investigative powers. However, this has not been the objective of the regulation enabling anticipative criminal investigation, but concerns a risk implicated by the shared mission of preventing terrorism.

[162] Rapport van de Commissie Evaluatie Antiterrorismebeleid 2009, 52, 67-69 and 58.

[163] More precisely: 'making prosecutorial decisions' implies a limitation to the collection of information that is relevant for the making of criminal procedural decisions with regard to criminal offenses, such as the decision whether or not to charge or a decision to arrest a suspect. Borgers 2009, 40 and 46. See also Sect. 2.3.2.2.1.

[164] Borgers 2009, 52-53 and Knigge and Kwakman 2001, 305.

Defining the criminal investigation on the basis of the investigative purpose, which seems to be, regardless of the fact that also the supervision of the public prosecutor has been included in the definition,[165] the only defining element for the criminal investigation, has significantly widened the possible scope of the criminal investigation. Any investigative activity, whether proactive or reactive, for the purpose of making prosecutorial decisions (or: gathering information which is relevant for the purpose of truth-finding regarding criminal offenses) and conducted by criminal investigative officers under Article 141 or 142 CCP[166] concerns a criminal investigation.[167] According to the government, the threshold for applying SIT has not been detached from the definition of a criminal investigation in order to achieve a general broadening of the requirements for applying SIT. Nevertheless, the detachment of the reasonable suspicion threshold has made it possible to expand criminal investigative powers in the proactive phase and to include also search methods, which were previously typically regulated outside the context of the CCP.[168] Still, also this development is comparably favorable from a legal protection point of view, considering that on the basis of the current definition of the criminal investigation it is clear that these activities occur under the supervision of the public prosecutor, that the duty to compile records under Article 152 CCP applies and that the trial judge may exert control under the applicability of Article 359a CCP.

Although the criminal investigative phase itself may currently be more precisely defined on the basis of its investigative purpose, the broader definition

---

[165] This does not correspond with the approach of the Criminal procedure 2001 researchers, who firstly opted to define the criminal investigation on the basis of the investigative purpose, whereas the supervision of the public prosecutor is consequently an applicable regulatory element (as well as the applicability of other procedural guarantees). According to Borgers, the choice of the legislature to retain the element of the supervision of the public prosecutor in the definition is erroneous. Borgers 2009, 53.

[166] According to Borgers the criterion that the criminal investigative activities are conducted by the investigative officers under Articles 141 and 142 CCP should be favored above a material criterion that the information collected has potential relevance for the criminal investigation. The latter criterion would make it impossible to establish the supervision of the public prosecutor over all criminal investigative activities, because of the factual situation that many administrative supervisory powers may result in the discovery of information which is relevant for criminal investigations. Also the duty to compile records under Article 152 only applies to investigative officers and the application of Article 359a CCP to investigative activities beyond the responsibility of the public prosecutor would be troublesome. In other words: a material criterion to determine what activities are conducted for the purpose of criminal investigation will, although arguably being more accurate, diverge from the current system of the CCP. Borgers 2009, 57-58. This interpretation can now also be recognized in the case law interpreting Article 132a CCP. See HR 7 July 2009, *NJ* 2009, 528, ann. Buruma, para 6.2.3, citing the argumentation of the Court of Appeal, Gerechtshof's-Gravenhage 1 March 2007, *LJN* AZ9644, para 5.1.1.

[167] Compare also the Supreme Court, repeating the argumentation of the Court of Appeal: including the regulation of SIT in the CCP is intended to guarantee that these SIT are only used for the purpose of criminal investigation under Article 132a CCP, when the interest of the investigation requires the use of SIT for that purpose. HR 26 January 2010, *NJ* 2010, 77, para 3.4.

[168] *Kamerstukken II* 2005/6, 30 164, no. 7, 24-25. See also Borgers 2009, 49-50.

has also opened the door to a further transformation of the criminal investigation than follows on the basis of the legislative measures of the Act on the Criminal Investigation of Terrorist Crimes. As a consequence of the intelligence-led policing, through the assistance of the CIE, and of the increased cooperation between the AIVD, the PPS and the police, the criminal investigation has obtained a preventive focus. In fact, the concept of anticipative criminal investigation as introduced in the first chapter covers also these 'preparatory information-gathering activities' producing the starting information for the criminal investigative domain of terrorist crimes, including the possibility to use SIT. In the context of the Dutch legal system the purposes of these investigative activities would not be defined as 'the making of prosecutorial decisions'. However, the transfer of information from the AIVD to the police, in particular in the context of the CT Infobox and the intelligence-led policing, in which the CIE has the most important role, are exactly the aspects that give the criminal investigation its anticipative character. The decision on initiating a criminal investigation based upon indications or a reasonable suspicion is typically made on the basis of the information available in the CT Infobox or at the CIE, which is a procedure geared towards the anticipation of future harm with the objective being to prevent such future harm.

The implications of this broader concept of anticipative criminal investigation become typically visible in the criminal trials of terrorist suspects. The defense and the trial judge are confronted with starting information from shielded sources and, possibly, also with evidence originating from the AIVD or CIE. Because these 'preparatory information-gathering activities' are not covered by the concept of criminal investigation in Article 132a CCP, the use of the information gathered by these activities results in impediments to controlling the legitimacy of using SIT, considering the lack of transparency regarding the origin and the veracity of the starting information used. This should not be considered as an attempt to formulate arguments in favor of further broadening the definition of the criminal investigation in order to extend the applicability of criminal procedural safeguards. Such a development would be contrary to the criminal procedural system of the CCP,[169] would impair the work of the AIVD and would only have adverse consequences for legal protection, considering that it would require a loosening or even the setting aside of the purpose-limitation requirement. As a consequence thereof, the gathering of evidence for a criminal prosecution could be left to the AIVD without the 'hindrance' of criminal procedural requirements, which would currently constitute a flagrant violation of the prohibition of *détournement de pouvoir*. However, assessing the implications for criminal procedural law of a preventive focus by criminal investigative activities requires the broader concept of anticipative criminal investigation to be taken into account. These implications cannot be separated from the broader context of the facilitating activities *before* SIT can be used for the purpose of prevention and, hence, are broader than one would suggest only on the basis of the Act on the Criminal Investigation of Terrorist Crimes. This

[169] See the argumentation provided in footnote 166 of this chapter.

conclusion will be further substantiated in the subsequent section, where the implications of the anticipative criminal investigation for the fairness of the criminal process will be assessed.

This section will conclude by characterizing the concept of anticipative criminal investigation as it has taken shape in the Netherlands also on the basis of the findings of Sect. 4.2. The central aspect of the anticipative criminal investigation concerns the possibility to use special investigative techniques and search methods when such use is considered to serve the interest of preventing terrorism on the basis of the information available. In order to enable such a preventive focus the relation between the AIVD, the PPS and the police have been intensified in order to make sure that the AIVD can share information with the PPS whenever the initiation of (also) a criminal investigation is considered to contribute to the prevention of terrorism.[170] In addition, the police have obtained an intelligence-led focus in order to be able to inform the PPS whenever a criminal investigation needs to be initiated to prevent terrorism. This concerted action between the AIVD, the police and the PPS aims to enable an anticipative criminal investigation. This 'anticipative criminal investigation' has several implications for the shield responsibilities of the actors and the shield elements of the statutory system of criminal procedural law. These implications have been addressed in the previous sections where they concern the element of the anticipative criminal investigative phase that can be defined as a criminal investigation under Article 132a CCP. The subsequent section will, lastly, deal with the implications as a consequence of the broader concept of anticipative criminal investigation, which touch upon the fairness of the criminal process.

### *4.3.4 Using Intelligence in Criminal Proceedings: An Infected Criminal Process?*

Article 6 ECHR imposes three basic requirements on fair criminal proceedings: an adversarial nature, equality of arms and the principle of immediacy.[171] The purpose of these requirements is to guarantee that the defense is not restricted in exercising its rights and that the manner in which evidence has been obtained, and

---

[170] This does not mean that the AIVD has obtained a different task. The task of the AIVD is still exclusively to protect national security (in the sense of the precise task description in Article 6 WIV 2002). It only means that also the AIVD is aware of the shared mission of preventing terrorism, for which reason the agencies cooperate (in the context of the CT Infobox by entering into regular consultations and under the auspices of the NCTb) and the AIVD shares information with the PPS whenever they consider a criminal investigation to be required in order to realize prevention. When the AIVD considers that sharing information is harmful to its own information position and that the protection of this information is more important for the purpose of realizing prevention, the AIVD will refrain from sharing information with the PPS.

[171] See Sect. 2.1.3.4.

is used, is fair. A prerequisite for giving effect to these three requirements for fairness is that the criminal investigative activities achieve a sufficient level of transparency at trial. Furthermore, to enable the defense to exercise its rights, the prosecutor is obliged "to disclose to the defense all material evidence for or against the accused."[172] These basic principles of the right to a fair trial seem to be at stake in the context of an anticipative criminal investigation, where the starting information for criminal investigative activities typically concerns AIVD or CIE information. The requirements of transparency and the disclosure of all evidentiary material to the case in order for the criminal proceedings to be fair tend to clash with the interest of the AIVD and the CIE in keeping their sources secret and, also for the AIVD, in shielding their methods in order to exercise their tasks effectively.

Although this clash of secrecy and transparency interests is not new to criminal proceedings, the use of AIVD and CIE information in Dutch criminal proceedings has increased and has the potential to further increase as a consequence of the enabling and further exploration of the investigative possibilities of anticipative criminal investigation in practice. The possibility to send official AIVD reports at an earlier moment in time to the PPS has been stimulated by different counter-terrorism measures and policy. In particular the creation of the CT Infobox, the Act on the Criminal Investigation of Terrorist Crimes and the Act on Shielded Witnesses intended to stimulate the cooperation, by means of sharing relevant information and in that way bundling forces to optimally realize the prevention of terrorist crimes, between the AIVD, the PPS and the police. As has been concluded in Sect. 4.3.1, this has not necessarily resulted in the AIVD also actually sending official reports at an earlier moment in time. Nevertheless, the increased cooperation between the AIVD and the PPS as an aspect of realizing anticipative criminal investigation has also resulted in an increase in the use of AIVD information in criminal proceedings. Furthermore, as a consequence of the intelligence-led operation of the police, also the CIE has an important role in facilitating anticipative criminal investigation when their reports are used to trigger criminal investigation activities.

Section 3.3 has dealt with three different situations where the use of intelligence originating from the AIVD affects the criminal proceedings: 1) the use of AIVD information (accepted in case law) as starting information for criminal investigations; 2) the circumvention of criminal procedural safeguards, as a consequence of parallel investigative activities, by relying on the investigative activities of the AIVD, in other words *détournement de pouvoir* by using investigative powers for other purposes than attributed; and 3) the controlling influence of the AIVD during parallel investigative activities through the sharing of information on the basis of Article 38 WIV 2002. The use of CIE information as typical starting information in anticipative criminal investigations can be added to the first category, considering that this information cannot, similar to AIVD information, be checked as to

[172] ECHR 16 December 1992, App no. 13071/87 (*Edwards v. The United Kingdom*), para 36.

its underlying sources by the persons responsible for deciding on the use of SIT or other criminal procedural powers.[173]

As described in Sects. 3.3.1 and 3.3.3, the courts have addressed these issues in the light of Article 359a CCP and Article 6 ECHR. The central problem faced by the controlling trial judge and the defense seeking to exerts its rights in the light of the principle of equality of arms and under the applicability of the immediacy principle concerns the limited possibility, or maybe even the impossibility, to obtain access to the underlying documents containing the information as well as the sources and the methods by which this information has been gathered. The implications for the realization of control over the pre-trial proceedings will be dealt with separately for defense challenges regarding the use of AIVD or CIE information as starting information for criminal investigations and for defense challenges regarding illegitimate actions following from the situation of parallel investigations.

#### 4.3.4.1 Control over the Use of AIVD or CIE Reports as Starting Information

The Supreme Court has generally accepted the use of AIVD reports and CIE reports as starting information for a criminal investigation.[174] Also the ECrtHR allows, in principle, information from secret sources to be used for establishing a reasonable suspicion, as long as the essence of the safeguard of a reasonable suspicion is not undermined, which means that it depends on all the circumstances of the case and that there must be some information available that can satisfy an objective person that there was a reasonable suspicion concerning the person in question.[175] The Court has accepted that it is not required to make all the information public in order to establish a reasonable suspicion taking into account all the circumstances, such as the involvement of terrorism, which can understandably require that sources of information are shielded.[176]

When the judge controls whether the starting information triggering the criminal investigation was sufficient for establishing a reasonable suspicion (or

[173] See Sect. 4.2.1.2.

[174] *Inter alia*, HR 5 September 2006, *NJ* 2007, 336, ann. Sch (*Eik*) and HR 25 September 2001, *NJ* 2002, 97.

[175] ECHR 30 August 1990, App. nos. 12244/86; 12245/86; 12383/86 (*Fox, Campbell and Hartley v. The United Kingdom*), para 32 and 34. In this case the Court assessed the reasonableness of the suspicion required for an arrest under Article 5 ECHR. The Court considered the information available to be insufficient for justifying the arrest as there were no facts or information that could satisfy the Court that the arrested person was reasonably suspected of having committed a criminal offense, because this information could not be disclosed.

[176] ECHR 30 August 1990, App. nos. 12244/86; 12245/86; 12383/86 (*Fox, Campbell and Hartley v. The United Kingdom*), para 34 and ECHR 16 October 2001, App. no. 37555/97 (*O'Hara v. The United Kingdom*), para 35.

indications), the *ex post* interpretation of the information is irrelevant. Rather, the judge will check whether, on the basis of the information available, the police, the PPS or the examining magistrate (depending on what particular authorization is required for the use of a specific criminal investigative power) could reasonably establish a reasonable suspicion. When a higher authority has authorized the criminal investigative technique, the trial judge will more marginally (re-)examine the legitimacy of the use of criminal investigative powers on the basis of the information available.[177]

As has been explained in Sect. 4.2.1.2 the reasonable suspicion threshold is a flexible threshold, leaving room for the authorizing actors to take certain interests into account, such as the urgency of the need for criminal investigative action following from the information, the seriousness of the crimes involved and the concrete possibilities for the information to be independently verified.[178] These factors have resulted in the decision of the Supreme Court that an anonymous tip-off received by the AIVD is insufficient for establishing a reasonable suspicion, because the verification activities have not substantiated the information,[179] and that a single AIVD report can be accepted for establishing a reasonable suspicion in, inter alia, the cases *Eik* and *Piranha*.[180] In *Fox, Campbell and Hartley v. The United Kingdom* the ECrtHR stated that when anonymous sources are used to establish a reasonable suspicion (in that case for the arrest of a terrorist suspect) it must be ascertained that "the essence of the [reasonable suspicion] safeguard has been secured."[181] Although the authorizing actors generally lack concrete points of departure when assessing the veracity of AIVD reports or CIE information, trial judges have generally accepted that anonymous sources can establish a reasonable suspicion without entering into a substantive examination of the veracity of the information. Decisive for this decision have been factors such as the presence of internal controlling mechanisms on the operating of the AIVD (warranting a relation based on the principle of trust, according to the Court of Appeal in the case of *Eik*), the fact that the national public prosecutor for counterterrorism has examined the information as to its veracity and its value for criminal investigative activities before further transferring it to the correct (national or regional) public prosecution office and, similarly, the internal controlling mechanisms of the CIE and the random check of the public prosecutor for the CIE.[182] The internal controlling mechanisms applicable to the AIVD (the supervisory commission and

---

177 HR 11 October 2005, *NJ* 2006, 625, para 3.5.1 and 3.5.2 and HR 21 November 2006, *NJ* 2007, 233, ann. Mevis, para 3.4 and annotation para 3.

178 Compare the annotation by Borgers para 6, HR 11 March 2008, *NJ* 2008, 329.

179 HR 11 March 2008, *NJ* 2008, 329, ann. Borgers.

180 HR 5 September 2006, *NJ* 2007, 336 and Gerechtshof's-Gravenhage 2 October 2008. For the acceptance of CIE information as starting information see e.g. HR 14 September 1992, *NJ* 1993, 83 (see in more detail Sect. 2.3.2.3.1 and footnote 413 of Chap. 2).

181 ECHR 30 August 1990, App. nos. 12244/86; 12245/86; 12383/86 (*Fox, Campbell and Hartley v. The United Kingdom*), para 34.

182 See Sects. 3.3.1 and 2.3.2.3.1 and see Brinkhoff 2009 10, 127-128, 136 and 138-139.

parliamentary control) in fact replace the need for an in-depth examination by judges, both *ex ante* and *ex post*.[183] Therefore, also the Supreme Court could conclude that there is no legal rule forbidding the use of intelligence information as starting information for a criminal investigation.[184] This being the basic presumption for using intelligence as starting information, the Supreme Court nevertheless also acknowledged that the trial judge will need to examine whether the proceedings as a whole were fair. However, this examination can subsequently easily be set aside, because the intelligence information has not been introduced as evidence.[185]

#### 4.3.4.2 Control over Parallel Investigations

When confronted with challenges regarding an abuse of the intelligence investigative power to circumvent criminal procedural safeguards or regarding an impermissible influence by the AIVD on the course of events during the criminal investigation by means of sharing information (see Sect. 3.3.3), the courts have strongly relied on the fact that the AIVD is controlled by other mechanisms outside the context of criminal proceedings. In the first place it is emphasized that Article 359a CCP does not apply when illegitimate activities have occurred outside the scope of the criminal investigation, which means that the trial judge will only examine the legitimacy of the activities of the AIVD, to a very limited extent, when there are strong indications that *evidence* has been gathered by seriously violating fundamental rights.[186] This means that when AIVD information is not used as evidence, the court may refrain from any examination. When AIVD information is also used as evidence the courts will only conduct a marginal examination. Only where it appears that criminal procedural safeguards have intentionally been circumvented or where the rights of the suspects have been violated in a manner that, on face value, is incompatible with Article 6 ECHR, will the evidence obtained through AIVD investigations be excluded.[187] Defense requests concerning an examination of the veracity of CIE information and the legitimacy of obtaining this information have been rejected with similar

---

[183] HR 5 September 2006, *NJ* 2007, 336, ann. Sch, annotation para 2.

[184] HR 5 September 2006, *NJ* 2007, 336, ann. Sch, para 4.6.

[185] According to the annotator, the Supreme Court undermines its own stance with this reasoning.

[186] HR 5 September 2006, *NJ* 2007, 336, para 4.3.9. Compare: ECHR 16 October 2001, App. no. 37555/97 (*O'Hara v. The United Kingdom*), para 35, affirming the importance of shielding confidential sources in the case of a suspicion of a terrorist crime.

[187] HR 5 September 2006, *NJ* 2007, 336 para 4.7.2 and HR 13 November 2007, *NJ* 2007, 614, para 3.6.

arguments: when there are no indications pointing to illegitimate activities, the judge will not resort to an examination.[188]

In the case involving the leaking of state secrets by an employee of the AIVD to a journalist, the Court of Appeal rejected the defense's argument that the AIVD operated as a 'law enforcement agency' with the factual observation that the AIVD does not have a criminal investigative task and no criminal investigative officers have conducted the investigative activities of the AIVD, and considering that AIVD employees are not criminal investigative officers under Articles 141 and 142 CCP. In other words: the investigative activities of the AIVD are not covered by the definition of a criminal investigation as provided in Article 132a CCP. In this way the defense's challenge was parried by interpreting it in its literal meaning, without addressing the essence of the defense, namely an alleged *abuse* of power and without giving the defense the required insight into the activities of the AIVD to substantiate such a defense as a consequence of the secrecy of the information.[189]

#### 4.3.4.3 An Infected Criminal Process?

The approach of the courts towards controlling the legitimacy of the way in which evidence has been gathered seems to contradict the requirements of Article 6 ECHR, in particular the right to challenge the reliability and method of obtaining evidence against the defendant where the AIVD or the CIE have been involved. Where the ECrtHR seems to attach significant weight to the presence of a form of judicial control on the criminal investigative activities, also where shielded information is involved, this control seems to be exerted in only a marginal fashion in the Netherlands. The interest of protecting national security prevails over criminal procedural interests as repeatedly emphasized by the government, for example in the explanatory memorandum to the Shielded Witnesses Act.[190] Taking into account this classification of interests, judges have not considered it a necessity to exclude the results of intelligence investigations from criminal proceedings, but rather to avoid an in-depth examination of the activities of the intelligence agencies.

---

188 See e.g. Gerechtshof Amsterdam 9 June 1994, *NJ* 1994, 709. See in more detail Brinkhoff 2009.

189 The Supreme Court did not address this particular issue once again, but upheld the argumentation of the Court of Appeal (Gerechtshof's-Gravenhage 1 March 2007, *LJN* AZ9644, r.o, 5.1.1), HR 7 July 2009, *NJ* 2009, 528, ann. Buruma para 6.2.3 and 8.4. See also the Opinion of the Advocate General at para 5.8. agreeing with the argumentation of the Court of Appeal. See also the annotation by Buruma at para 3, warning that relying on secrecy should not result in a "secret of convenience" when the AIVD fears that a particular plea could adversely affect the service.

190 *Kamerstukken II* 2003/04, 29 743, no. 3, 1.

The ECrtHR has accepted limitations on defense rights in its case law, subject to the condition that these limitations are sufficiently compensated.[191] The ECrtHR has accepted that when national security is at stake due to the threat of terrorism the police are required to act upon the information available also if this information originates from secret sources. Especially in the situation of a suspicion of a terrorist crime, the Court has acknowledged the importance shielding confidential sources.[192] However, relying on the interest of national security may not result in the exclusion of judicial control.[193] As the Court stated in *Klass and Others v. Germany*: "an interference by the executive authorities with an individual's rights should be subject to an effective control which would normally be assured by the judiciary (…), judicial control offering the best guarantees of independence, impartiality and a proper procedure."[194]

Considering the preceding two sections, it can be concluded that the defense is considerably impaired in its fair trial rights when confronted with the implications of an anticipative criminal investigation, namely the reliance on AIVD or CIE sources as the basis for initiating the criminal investigation and the practice of parallel investigations when both are acting in the field of preventing terrorism. The Dutch courts have so far relied on a rather marginal examination regarding the origin and veracity of information from shielded sources and/or having been obtained through shielded methods, especially where the use of this information has only played a role in the pre-trial phase and has not been introduced as evidence. Indeed, there is, in principle, no concrete reason to automatically suspect the AIVD of illegitimate investigative activities, considering the existence of the controlling mechanisms on the activities of the AIVD, the results of the examination by the oversight committee regarding the veracity of AIVD reports transferred to the PPS on the basis of Article 38 WIV 2002,[195] the fact that it would be contrary to the AIVD's own interest to pursue criminal investigative interests, and the possibilities for the national public prosecutor for counterterrorism to first check the veracity of the information and the value of the information for pursuing

---

[191] See for more detail on this issue: Alink 2004.

[192] ECHR 16 October 2001, App. no. 37555/97 (*O'Hara v. The United Kingdom*), para 35.

[193] See e.g.: ECHR 30 August 1990, App. nos. 12244/86; 12245/86; 12383/86 (*Fox, Campbell and Hartley v. The United Kingdom*), para 34 and ECHR 15 November 1996, *NJ* 1997, 301 (*Chahal v. The United Kingdom*), para 131. See in this regard also: Vervaele 2005, 20-23 and Aksu 2007, 98-100.

[194] ECHR 6 September 1978, App. no. 5029/71 (*Klass and Others v. Germany*), para 55.

[195] The main conclusion of the report of the supervisory commission on the intelligence and security services, investigating the issuance of official reports by the AIVD in the period January 2004-October 2005, was the following: the contents of all examined official reports were supported by the content of the underlying files. In addition, the precision of the process for determining that the information underpinning the official reports is reliable is sufficiently guaranteed. Rapport van de Commissie van Toezicht betreffende de Inlichtingen- en Veiligheidsdiensten inzake het onderzoek naar de door de AIVD uitgebrachte ambtsberichten in de periode van januari 2004 tot oktober 2005, 2006, 7-8.

the task of the law enforcement community.[196] The same can be said for the CIE, which also has internal controlling mechanisms as to the veracity of the information provided to the PPS (the CIE report includes a label reflecting its opinion as to the veracity of the information).[197] In addition, the controlling issues following from the use of CIE information are narrower, because CIE information that is only used as starting information for criminal investigations is in principle not used as evidence and the CIE powers for information gathering are very limited for which reason the complications with regard to parallel AIVD investigations do not apply.

Also the ECrtHR seems to consider this presumption of trust to be legitimate. When judicial control is impossible, the Court has considered that this may still be acceptable in the absence of evidence that the executive authorities have violated the law and if there are other independent authorities that can effectively and continuously control the surveillance activities. As was formulated in the *Klass* judgment, where the Court assessed the German 'G10' regulation for electronic surveillance to protect national security:

> "The rule of law implies, inter alia, that an interference by the executive authorities with an individual's rights should be subject to an effective control which would normally be assured by the judiciary, at least in the last resort, judicial control offering the best guaranteed of independence, impartiality and a proper procedure. [...] Nevertheless, having regard to the nature of the supervisory and other safeguards provided for by the G10, the Court concludes that the exclusion of judicial control does not exceed the limits of what may be deemed necessary in a democratic society. The parliamentary board and the G10 Commission are independent of the authorities carrying out the surveillance, and are vested with sufficient powers and competence to exercise an effective and continuous control. [...] While the possibility of improper action by a dishonest, negligent or over-zealous official can never be completely ruled out whatever system, the considerations that matter for the purposes of the Court's present review are the likelihood of such action and the safeguards provided to protect against it. [...] In the absence of any evidence or indication that the actual practice followed is otherwise, the Court must assume that in the democratic society of the Federal Republic of Germany, the relevant authorities are properly applying the legislation in issue."[198]

Nevertheless, this does not change the fact that the defense, seeking to challenge the legitimacy of certain activities in the pre-trial phase, is facing a wall of secrecy and unwillingness on the part of the courts (and the AIVD) to seek possibilities to break through this secrecy.[199] To provide for concrete information

---

[196] See also Krips 2009, 161. The supervisory commission for the AIVD has argued that the AIVD shall include in its reports, similar to the CIE, a judgment with regard to the veracity of the information provided as a matter of general practice. Rapport van de Commissie van Toezicht betreffende de Inlichtingen- en Veiligheidsdiensten inzake het onderzoek naar de door de AIVD uitgebrachte ambtsberichten in de periode van januari 2004 tot oktober 2005, 2006, 7-8.

[197] Critical: Brinkhoff 2009.

[198] EHRM 6 September 1978, App. no. 5029/71 (*Klass and others v. Germany*), para 55, 56 en 59.

[199] A similar conclusion was drawn by Advocate General Machielse in the *Piranha* case: HR 15 March 2011, *LJN* BP7544 (CPG 08/04418), para 5.20 and 5.21. The decision of the Supreme Court in this case is still pending.

pointing to illegitimate investigative activities that would open the door to a more substantive examination by the trial judge, the defense will first need to have access to all information available on the investigative activities. In addition, it seems that a plea regarding an abuse of power can easily be countered with reference to the definition of the criminal investigation and, on that basis, concluding that the AIVD cannot exert criminal investigative activities.[200] Lastly, it will generally be rather simple to prove that the AIVD has conducted the investigative activities *also* for its own investigative purpose, in particular in the context of parallel anticipative criminal investigations. This approach in fact resembles the 'looser' version of the purpose-limitation principles applied to the separation between criminal investigation and administrative supervisory authority, with the essential difference being that administrative supervision is not covered by a veil of secrecy and is usually conducted by investigative officers, who also act in the field of criminal investigation.[201] Hence, the manner in which courts address defense challenges that involve the CIE or the AIVD seems to concern a circular reasoning in order to avoid the need to exert control in conflict with the national security interest to keep certain information shielded. Moreover, as already concluded in Sect. 4.2.3, also *ex ante* control seems to be rather limited, which is thus subsequently not compensated by the control at the trial phase.

The ECrtHR generally takes the approach that such handicaps for the defense must be sufficiently compensated in order to render the trial fair. The Shielded Witnesses Act has been adopted in order to provide such a compensating procedure as a mechanism enabling the veracity of AIVD information to be controlled (see Sect. 3.3.2). However, the procedure where an AIVD employee can testify before the examining magistrate as to the veracity of the AIVD information cannot be used in order to exert control over the legitimacy of the investigative activities of the AIVD. After all, Article 359a CCP does not provide possibilities to exert control over investigative activities falling outside the scope of the criminal investigation under Article 132a CCP. Only when the results of the AIVD investigation are used as evidence is it necessary for the trial judge to examine the AIVD information and—although marginally—its method of obtaining such information. In this regard the Council of Europe's Commissioner for Human Rights, Thomas Hammarberg, has reported:

> "(…) the commissioner noted with concern that, in the interest of national security, the defence cannot always attend the examination of the witness. He finds that the position of the defence is weakened, considering that the witness remains anonymous in most cases and has a decisive say in the decision as to whether the official report of the investigating judge will become part of the case file and accepted as evidence. The commissioner questions how the principle of equality of arms, an essential guarantee of the right to fair

[200] Gerechtshof's-Gravenhage 1 March 2007, *LJN* AZ9644, para 5.1.1 and HR 7 July 2009, *NJ* 2009, 528, para 6.2.3 and 8.4.

[201] Compare the approach that the courts have taken to assess issues following from the 'cumulating spheres' of administrative law and criminal law. See Sect. 2.3.2.2.2.

trial, is safeguarded by the Act and recalls the right of the individual to know the full case against him or her."[202]

More in general, the Shielded Witnesses Act has been subject to extensive criticism as to its compatibility with fair trial rights, in particular the principle of immediacy and the right to cross-examine. After all, the witness can be heard as a shielded witness, which may occur *ex parte*[203] and *in camera;* the witness may at any time rely on his/her duty to keep information secret, which will result in a judgment of the examining magistrate being provided to the trial judge as to the veracity of the information, whereas neither the examining magistrate nor the trial judge has been able to examine the underlying documents or the methods used for obtaining the information.[204] It is clear that the defense is limited in its right to cross-examine and that the system contradicts the principle that the trial judge will need to exert control over all evidence used to prove a case.

Nevertheless, it must also be noted that, to date, the procedure has not been used. Quite the contrary, a District Court considering the possibility of using the construction for controlling AIVD information expressed that in the absence of a request by the PPS or the defense to use the shielded witnesses construction, it should demonstrate a reluctance to use this procedure and, hence, it concluded that there were no other ways to examine the veracity of AIVD reports.[205] It would be going beyond the scope of this research to subject the framework provided in the Shielded Witnesses Act to a precise examination as to its compatibility with Article 6 ECHR, considering that this primarily applies to the use of AIVD information as evidence and not to the manner in which intelligence information affects the criminal investigation.[206] At this place it suffices to conclude that although the procedure may be useful for examining whether the veracity of the AIVD reports is sufficient for establishing a reasonable suspicion (the value of such *ex post* examination is, however, rather limited, considering that it should be determined whether at the time the police, the PPS or the examining magistrate could reasonably establish a reasonable suspicion from the information, a decision which may also involve other factors such as the required urgency for action) or when introduced as evidence (with the necessary remarks as provided above), any

---

[202] Report by the Commissioner for Human Rights, Mr. Thomas Hammarberg, on his visit to the Netherlands 2009, 37-38.

[203] Although there is the possibility to follow the examination through telecommunication facilities or to submit written questions to the examining magistrate.

[204] Compare: annotation Schalken para HR 5 September 2006, *NJ* 2007, 336. In the end it will be the trial judge who needs to decide whether he/she considers the information from uncontrollable sources to be sufficiently reliable to use as evidence. The ECrtHR has decided, as a safeguard, that a conviction may not exclusively or to a decisive extent be based upon anonymous sources. ECHR 17 November 2005, App. no. 73047/01 (*Monika Haas v. Germany*).

[205] Rechtbank Rotterdam 1 December 2006, *LJN* AZ3589.

[206] See on this e.g. Vervaele 2005, 16-27, Coster van Voorhout 2006, 123-130 and 137-143, Beijer 2006 and Krips 2009, 167-188.

control over the course of events in the situation of parallel investigations seems to be excluded.

In fact the adherence to the strict separation between the PPS and the police, on the one hand, and the AIVD, on the other, in combination with the inescapability of using intelligence especially in criminal investigations into terrorism and the desire to successful prosecute terrorist suspects, results in a very reserved attitude by the courts towards exerting control over the activities of the AIVD. Only when the results of the AIVD investigation are also used as evidence will the trial judge conduct a marginal examination in the light of Article 6 ECHR. Hence, it can be concluded that, whilst seeking to uphold a separation on the basis of the purpose of the investigation between intelligence investigation and anticipative criminal investigation, the criminal process is indeed infected, in the sense that controlling possibilities on the method of obtaining evidence and on the legitimacy of the criminal investigation in general have been impaired, as a consequence of the increased use of intelligence in the anticipative criminal investigation. This reduces the controlling abilities of the trial judge on the complete course of pre-trial events and deprives the defendant of a remedy for possible illegitimate investigative activities when they have been conducted outside the scope of the criminal investigation under Article 359a CCP.

## 4.4 Conclusion

In conclusion, this section will, on the basis of the analysis provided in the preceding sections, characterize the anticipative criminal investigation as it has taken shape in the Netherlands. Subsequently, an overview will be given of the implications for the shield objective of criminal procedural law, as identified in this chapter. This characterization and the identified implications will constitute the legal substantive basis for the further analysis provided in Chaps. 8 and 9.

### *4.4.1 Characterizing the Anticipative Criminal Investigation*

An anticipative criminal investigation has been defined in Sect. 4.3.3 as covering the criminal investigation under the definition of Article 132a CCP, a definition which defines criminal investigation on the basis of its purposes: 'making prosecutorial decisions.' This purpose of the criminal investigation, which can be understood to concern a limitation to only collecting information which is relevant for the purpose of making criminal procedural decisions such as the decision whether or not to charge someone with a criminal offense or to arrest someone, separates the anticipative criminal investigation from other investigative activities conducted by state authorities, such as the intelligence investigation and the administrative supervisory authority. However, the anticipative criminal investigation shall be distinguished from other forms of criminal investigation, because it is typically enabled through starting information from 'preparatory information-gathering activities' conducted by the AIVD or the CIE. Hence, without stretching the definition of the criminal investigation on the basis of the purpose provided in Article 132a CCP, these preparatory information-gathering activities provide the criminal investigation with its anticipatory character and has implications for further criminal proceedings.

Furthermore, the anticipative criminal investigation as allowed in the Netherlands is characterized by the possibility to use SIT upon a lower threshold in order to investigate for preventive purposes. In order to prepare this anticipative criminal investigation of terrorist crimes, new and more intrusive preliminary investigative techniques have been adopted. Furthermore, search methods have been made available in the criminal investigation of terrorist crimes in order to avert more urgent threats. Consequently, the scope and character of the anticipative criminal investigation differs concerning two main aspects from other criminal investigative activities. Firstly, the interest of the prevention of terrorist crimes is first and foremost the objective of the criminal investigation, whilst for the criminal investigation of other crimes proactive action is still the exception. Secondly, the lowered threshold of indications instead of a reasonable suspicion legitimizes the use of SIT and search methods, which makes it possible to investigate persons who constitute a potential danger, because they can be associated with indications of terrorist activities.[207]

Lastly, the anticipative criminal investigation is typically intelligence-led. Prevention is aimed to be realized through a strong information position. For this reason, the preparatory investigative activities of the AIVD or CIE typically precede the anticipative criminal investigation, providing for the proactive steering information for the subsequent criminal investigation.

### *4.4.2 Implications for the Shield Objective of Criminal Procedural Law*

The implications of the above characterized 'anticipative criminal investigation' in the Netherlands for the shield objective of criminal procedural law touch upon two different aspects. Firstly, the allowing of an anticipative criminal investigation has weakened the protection against arbitrary interferences with the right to respect for private life and has reduced the regulatory value of the presumption of innocence. Secondly, as a consequence of anticipative criminal proceedings, the criminal proceedings following on from an anticipative criminal investigation are infected. Both implications will be briefly explained on the basis of the findings of this chapter.

---

[207] See Sect. 4.2.1.1.

#### 4.4.2.1 Weakened Protection of the Right to Respect for Private Life and the Presumption of Innocence

The weakened protection of the right to respect for private life and the presumption of innocence is an implication that follows from the lowered threshold of application, the lack of a clear connection between a criminal investigative purpose and the threshold of application, the current classification of interests in the criminal investigation and the shifted responsibilities among the actors resulting in growing investigative discretion and watered-down control. It will be briefly recapitulated why and how these four aspects have contributed to this first shield implication.

As a consequence of the *lowered threshold of application* for SIT and search methods, the scope of the terrorist crime investigation may be rather broad. Because of the vaguer information upon which a criminal investigation is initiated, it may be more difficult to relate specific persons to the indications present. This involves an increased risk that persons who cannot be related to (indications of) terrorist crimes, who do not constitute a 'danger', will be subjected to investigative techniques that interfere with their right to respect for private life. As concluded in Sects. 4.2.1.3.1.1 and 4.2.1.3.2, the compatibility with Article 8 ECHR largely depends on the manner in which the threshold is construed in practice; whether the application of the indications threshold broadens the scope of the investigation to an unforeseeable scope, thereby unnecessarily investigating certain persons. Such a scope for the investigation would also be contrary to the fundamental presumption of innocence, requiring a general restraint in using investigative powers. 'Suspicion' concerns a flexible threshold, reflecting the equilibrium between investigative interest and protection against interferences with the right to respect for private life and, from that point of view, also the indications threshold may be a justifiable legitimization for investigative activities. However, the equilibrium between sword and shield interests is currently struck at a different point, with adverse implications for the safeguards afforded against arbitrary interferences with the right to respect for the private life and for the presumption of innocence.[208] This implication for the shield objective has been identified because of the *theoretical* breadth of the indication threshold as well as the absence of meaningful other restrictive procedural safeguards. Nevertheless, *in practice* the new investigative possibilities have been explored only exceptionally and with restraint (see Sect. 4.2.2.2).

Secondly, it has been observed that in the criminal investigative practice insufficient attention is attributed to the *relation between the specific threshold of application for an investigative domain and the purpose of the legislation*. Consequently, the threshold of a reasonable suspicion has been stretched in order to pursue also proactive investigative purposes in order to confront organized crime and to pursue preventive purposes when dealing with terrorism. Because the courts

[208] See Sect. 4.2.1.2.

accept the use of the reasonable suspicion threshold for these purposes and, consequently, Title V and Title Vb are rarely used in practice, the adopted legislation loses its legitimacy in the absence of necessity. It has been suggested that instead of rejecting the legislation for this reason, it is preferable to retrieve legitimacy by devoting more attention to the rationale underlying the adopted investigative domains, including the preliminary investigation. The realization of more attention for the relation between the threshold of application and the specific investigative purpose could not only render the legislation enabling anticipative criminal investigation necessary but would also be favorable to legal protection considering the commensurate restriction to terrorist crimes and, likewise, to organized crime and to preliminary investigative activities.[209]

In the third place, Sect. 4.2.2.1 has identified a trend where the *interest of prevention generally supersedes the interest of legal protection against arbitrary interferences with the right to private life*. This is recognizable in antiterrorism legislation, where the interest in acting to prevent terrorism or to protect national security is understood to supersede the legal protection interest of criminal procedural law and, hence, is used both to justify new legislation and as a point of departure in applying the newly introduced methods. Furthermore, this trend is recognizable in the manner in which the courts have dealt with the principles of proportionality and subsidiarity. Instead of applying them as restrictive principles, the courts have used these principles as an argument to grant more investigative discretion.

Lastly, it has been observed that, as a consequence of the increased investigative discretion, *control over the legitimate and fair use of investigative powers has been traded in* by the 'higher' authorities. This has been caused by the willingness to attribute investigative officers with sufficient investigative discretion to act whenever needed for the prevention of terrorism and by vesting the core shield responsibility in the public prosecutor, who will also be inclined to give decisive weight to preventing terrorism. Judicial control, both *ex ante* and *ex post*, is thereby weakened rather than strengthened. Whereas the position of the examining magistrate as to his/her overall controlling responsibility has been strengthened, his/her role as a warrant judge has not been expanded. In addition, the judges' controlling role is complicated because of the criteria that offer a wide discretion and because of the classification of interests where security interests outweigh legal protection interests.[210]

Cumulatively, these developments result in weakened legal protection against arbitrary interferences with the right to respect for private life on behalf of state authorities. This is primarily a consequence of the breadth of the 'indications threshold', which is not compensated by a clear demarcation of investigative domains or strengthened control through the judiciary. The risk involved in the theoretically granted breadth of the investigative domain for terrorist crimes is

[209] See Sect. 4.2.2.2. This idea will be further discussed in Chap. 9.

[210] Section 4.2.3.

even larger considering the current classification of interests where prevention supersedes legal protection.

#### 4.4.2.2 An Infected Criminal Process

The second main implication for the shield objective of criminal procedural law concerns the infected criminal process as a consequence of the nature of the information used as proactive steering information in the anticipative criminal investigation. The information collected during the investigative activities of the AIVD and CIE is used as starting information or is otherwise introduced in the criminal proceedings (e.g. in the course of 'parallel investigations'). These 'preparatory investigative activities' also influence the legitimacy and fairness of the criminal investigation, which becomes typically visible in the criminal trials of terrorist suspects.

Control over the legitimacy of initiating criminal investigative activities on the basis of AIVD or CIE reports and control over the practice of parallel investigations are impeded because of the limited possibility to have access to the underlying documents and the sources and methods by which information has been gathered. Internal mechanisms of control over the activities of the AIVD and the CIE replace the need for an in-depth examination by judges, both *ex ante* and *ex post.* When AIVD information is not used as evidence, trial judges refrain from exerting any control because of the strict applicability of Article 359a CCP to the criminal investigation as defined in Article 132a CCP. Only a marginal examination is exerted where the AIVD reports are used as evidence. Consequently, the defense faces a wall of secrecy when seeking to challenge the legitimacy of anticipative criminal investigative activities. Also the Shielded Witnesses Act seems to be unsuitable for offering recourse when it comes to control over the course of events during parallel investigations.

On this basis it has been concluded that the courts have demonstrated a very reserved attitude with regard to exerting control over the preparatory investigative activities of the anticipative criminal investigation. Consequently, the defense is impaired in its rights where seeking to challenge the legitimacy of initiating a criminal investigation on the basis of AIVD or CIE information and, in particular, when seeking to challenge the illegitimate aspects of parallel investigations (*détournement de pouvoir* or an impermissible steering influence by the AIVD). Hence, the criminal process has been infected as a consequence of the preparatory investigative activities which are typical of the anticipative criminal investigation and as a consequence of the increased cooperation between the AIVD, the police and the PPS because of the shared mission to prevent terrorism.[211]

[211] See in detail Sect. 4.3.4.

# Part II
# The United States

# Chapter 5
# The System of Criminal Investigation in the United States

## 5.1 Introduction

### *5.1.1 Goals of the Chapter*

In order to obtain a correct understanding of all developments in the United States that have facilitated a shift in emphasis to criminal investigation for the purpose of preventing crimes, this chapter will provide for the relevant background: the legal framework and its development which is necessary to understand the impact of changes in the law and policy in order to enable an adequate system of anticipative criminal investigation.[1] The contents and scope of this chapter are thus based on the relevance for the required understanding of the implications of changes in criminal procedural law, in particular those that have been adopted since September 11, 2001 in order to adequately prevent terrorist attacks (as discussed in the sixth chapter). Hence, this chapter will provide a baseline for the post-9/11 sword and shield developments, evaluated in Chap. 7, in criminal procedural law as described in Chap. 6.

An important part of this chapter will be dedicated to Fourth Amendment law: regulating the governmental powers of search and seizure. Physical search and seizure are techniques that are typically not covered by the subject-matter of this book, focusing on the use of covert investigative techniques during the pre-arrest investigation.[2] However, as will hereafter be explained, surveillance techniques have also been included in the concept of 'search' as covered by the Fourth Amendment. Hence, also special investigative techniques such as wire-tapping, the electronic interception

---

[1] Defined in Chap. 1, Sect. 1.2.1 as: any form of proactive investigation on behalf of the government aimed at the prevention of serious crimes or threats, typically characterized by its intelligence-led approach, and resulting in the gathering of information, which information may, immediately or subsequently, come to play a role in criminal proceedings.

[2] Except for exceptions created for covert sneak-and-peak searches.

M.F.H. Hirsch Ballin, *Anticipative Criminal Investigation*,
DOI: 10.1007/978-90-6704-843-9_5,

of communications and the use of undercover agents are limited by the requirements of the Fourth Amendment. Moreover, the Fourth Amendment also applies to the work of the intelligence entities within the United States. These intelligence entities conduct 'national security investigations,' which concern investigations—to be distinguished from law enforcement investigations—"to acquire information about foreign threats to the national security," such as "international terrorism or espionage."[3] These national security investigations are usually conducted within the United States by the Federal Bureau of Investigation (FBI)[4] and have found specific regulation in legislation in observance of the protection that the Fourth Amendment offers against governmental interferences with privacy through the use of their search and seizure authority. Not only the Fourth Amendment, but also due process, as a notion implicated in the due process clauses of the Fifth and Fourteenth Amendment has some, although significantly more limited, normative consequences for criminal investigation. The concept of due process does have some implications for the actors—the police and the prosecutor—in their task to trace criminal evidence and confront criminal behavior and, primarily, sets fairness requirements for trial. Hence, the due process clause has in particular normative consequences for the use of the results of the investigative activities of the government as evidence.

The remainder of this introductory section will give a basic explanation of the US criminal justice system and of the Constitutional principles that regulate the investigative phase. Thereafter, the chapter will be divided in two main parts. The first part (5.2) will deal with the sword function as it has been given effect in the pre-trial phase, with regard to both the conventional criminal law enforcement context and the national security (or intelligence) context. The second part (5.3) will deal with the restraints on the use of investigative powers pre-arrest, following from procedural due process, the Fourth Amendment, additional statutory legislation and guidelines.

Hence, this chapter will seek an answer to the following two questions:

1. How is the sword objective in the US system of criminal investigation realized? This will firstly require an analysis of the actors that bear responsibility to investigate criminal activities (either past or future), and, secondly, an analysis of the investigative powers available to these investigating actors.
2. How is the shield objective in the US system of criminal investigation realized? Answering this question will, firstly, require an analysis of the responsibilities of the actors in play during the criminal investigation to contribute to the fairness of the investigation. Furthermore, the requirements that follow from the Fourth Amendment imposing restraints on the power to search and the statutory regulation of law enforcement and national security surveillance will be analyzed, in order to illustrate the manner in which the system of criminal investigation is organized to reflect the realization of the protection offered by the Fourth Amendment. The limitations of the Fourth Amendment and the

[3] Kris and Wilson 2007, vii.

[4] *Ibid.*

concept of due process together give effect to the protective aspect of criminal procedural law under the rule of law.

### *5.1.2 Framing the Subject*

The United States' criminal process is primarily regulated by the restraints following from the US Constitution. There is no direct influence of international human rights law documents, such as the ICCPR or the ACHR, on US criminal procedural law. The US has not ratified the optional protocol to the ICCPR in order to allow individuals to file human rights complaints with the United Nation's Human Rights Committee. Furthermore, although it signed the ACHR in 1977, the United States has not proceeded with its ratification. Treaties to which the United States are party are part of the Supreme Law of the Land (Article VI US Constitution). Non-self-executing treaties are distinguished from self-executing treaties, in the sense that non-self-executing treaties first need to be implemented in order to become supreme law of the land (notwithstanding the international law obligations that, also without implementation, follow from the ratification of a treaty).[5] Nevertheless, under this 'Supremacy Clause' the US Constitution always takes precedence over federal legislation and treaties. For this reason, the US courts are generally reluctant to use international sources for Constitutional interpretation.[6] However, this approach is also subject to debate and on some occasions the Supreme Court has started citing international sources when it is confronted with new Constitutional questions.[7]

Considering the limited influence of international (human rights) law on US law and, in particular, on the US criminal justice system, the US Constitution (henceforth 'the Constitution') and its interpretation by the Supreme Court and lower courts are the most important source for drawing the legal framework which regulates the criminal investigation.[8] In addition, Congress has enacted legislation for certain areas of criminal investigation, which constitutes an additional source of regulation also for the criminal investigation.

The US consists of multiple jurisdictions that can be roughly divided into a federal jurisdiction, 50 state jurisdictions and the exceptional status of the

---

[5] The Supreme Court recently decided on this distinction between self-executing treaties and non-self-executing treaties in *Medellin v. Texas,* 552 U.S. 491, 128 S.Ct. 1346 (2008). See on this subject: Nokes 2011, 829-855.

[6] *Ibid.*, 853-854.

[7] Glashausser 2008.

[8] This does not mean that international law could not be useful, for example, for transnational issues involved in national security policy. Using international law principles as the baseline for "good process" in national security activities with a transnational aspect may further such good process (providing good legal policy and good national security policy) as well as efficient cooperation in national security matters. See on this: Baker 2007, 644-658.

jurisdiction of the District of Columbia. In addition to these jurisdictions, there is the Article III military jurisdiction and the special jurisdiction of the Military Commissions. Of all criminal prosecutions, only a very small amount (approximately 1%) of all prosecutions occur before a federal court and approximately 97% of all criminal cases are resolved by plea bargaining.[9] The federal jurisdiction does not cover the prosecution of all crimes, but only those to which the Constitution grants legislative authority to Congress. This legislative authority is granted to Congress in Article I of the Constitution, section 8, containing different clauses that provide for the powers of Congress. Most significant for the power to enact federal criminal legislation are the 'commerce clause' and the 'necessary and proper clause.'[10] Federal crimes are particularly those crimes that are criminalized in order to protect the interests of the federal government, such as espionage or the bribery of federal officials, the robbery of facilities in which the federal government has a financial interest and crimes related to Congress' authority over interstate commerce (including sex offenses, financial crimes, crimes committed by criminal organizations and terrorist crimes).[11]

Article I(8)(3) provides for the federal commerce clause, which grants Congress the power "[t]o regulate Commerce with foreign Nations, and among the several States, and with the Indian Tribes." The commerce clause is today interpreted as granting broad power to enact federal legislation. It covers basically anything that has a possible economic impact or is related to an activity of commerce among the states.[12] Furthermore, according to Article I(8)(18) of the Constitution, Congress may enact federal legislation when such legislation is "necessary and proper" to give effect to its powers granted in the preceding clauses of Article I(8). This 'necessary and proper clause' has been interpreted as giving Congress the authority to enact federal legislation if such legislation relates to the carrying out of an express granted power and is not otherwise limited by the Bill of Rights or other restrictions following from the Constitution, which means that Congress may enact federal legislation when it reasonably finds that the legislation relates to one of the federal powers (thus including the federal commerce power) as granted in the Constitution.[13] In fact, the necessary and proper clause has become a catch-all

---

9 Allen et al. 2005, 9-21.

10 Nowak and Rotunda 2004, 139.

11 Israel et al. 2006, 1-2 (ftnt. 1). The adoption of health-care legislation by the federal government is a currently debated and litigated example of whether such health-care legislation exceeds Congress' power to regulate interstate commerce.

12 Nowak and Rotunda 2004, 181. The Supreme Court in *United States v. Lopez*, 514 U.S. 549, 115 S.Ct. 1624 (1995), 558-559, indicated three broad categories of activities where Congress may enact legislation under its federal commerce power: 1) "the use of the channels for interstate commerce"; 2) "to regulate and protect the instrumentalities of interstate commerce, or persons or things in interstate commerce, even though the threat may come only from intrastate activities"; and, 3) "to regulate those activities having a substantial relation to interstate commerce."

13 Nowak and Rotunda 2004, 145. The Supreme Court has interpreted the necessary and proper clause in *McCulloch v. Maryland,* 17 U.S. (4 Wheat.) 316 (1819).

phrase, which can be extended to any area in which the federal government seeks to exert power. The investigation and prosecution of terrorist activities is such area in which the federal government has claimed authority, because such power is considered necessary to protect national security and public safety.

Because the investigation of acts of terrorism is the main subject of this research project, the legal background provided in this chapter focuses on the federal system. As will be seen in Chap. 6, anticipative criminal investigation is conducted principally through the interaction between the intelligence community and law enforcement community on the federal level. Notwithstanding this limitation to the federal system, all jurisdictions in the United States are sufficiently similar concerning the basic structure of the criminal process, as a result of the common heritage of English common law[14] as well as the regulatory influence of the Constitution on all US jurisdictions. This regulatory influence has been a consequence of the Supreme Court's interpretation of the Fourteenth Amendment resulting in the incorporation of parts of the Bill of Rights within the States. The guarantees of the Bill of Rights that relate to the investigative phase have been equally applied to the states under the incorporation doctrine of the Fourteenth Amendment.[15] Consequently, a rather high level of similarity is achieved between the various US jurisdictions considering that the Constitutional restraints on the use of criminal investigative powers apply equally to the States. Therefore, most of the findings in this chapter will also be relevant to the States' jurisdictions.[16] Moreover, most states have adopted similar legislation as enacted on the federal level with regard to the surveillance and investigation of terrorism. The federal regulation of investigative power is often used as a 'model code' for similar legislation on the state level. Nevertheless, because the complete Bill of Rights does not apply to the states, considerable differences between federal criminal procedural law in general (covered by all Bill of Rights' provisions) and state criminal procedural law (covered only by those Bill of Rights' provisions made applicable by the Fourteenth Amendment) as well as among the 50 states' jurisdictions remain in existence.

This chapter will seek to describe the federal system of the criminal investigation of criminal behavior with its powers and protections in order to understand and assess the reforms that have aimed to facilitate a system that can also *prevent* crimes, in particular crimes of terrorism.

---

[14] With the exception of the state of Louisiana, where the legal system is partly based on the French and Spanish (civil) law.

[15] *Duncan v. Louisiana,* 391 U.S. 145, 88 S.Ct. (1968). See also: Allen et al. 2005, 93-100. The incorporation of the Bill of Rights under the Fourteenth Amendment will be dealt with in more detail in Sect. 5.1.4.2.

[16] Allen et al. 2005, 6.

### 5.1.3 The US Criminal Justice System

The goals of the US criminal procedural system,[17] as they are traditionally formulated, correspond with the two main objectives of criminal procedural law in general as formulated in Chap. 1. The Supreme Court has stated that the establishment of the substantive truth is a "fundamental goal of our legal system"[18] and that "the central purpose of a criminal trial is to decide the factual question of the defendant's guilt or innocence."[19] According to the Supreme Court, "[t]he dual aim of our criminal justice system is that guilt shall not escape or innocent suffer. To this end we have placed our confidence in the adversary system, entrusting to it the primary responsibility for developing relevant facts on which a determination on guilt or innocence can be made."[20]

According to Israel, for example, each system of criminal procedural law shall aim at implementing the enforcement of substantive law. This goal then implies that the process shall be structured in a manner that firstly "achieves the best enforcement of substantive law" (the sword as well as the shield objective) and, secondly, "achieves "fairness" in the process" (the shield objective).[21] Others consider the criminal process as being designed either according to the 'due process model,' limiting the use of criminal procedural powers to protect individual dignity and autonomy, or according to the 'crime control' model, which focuses on efficient and expeditious law enforcement.[22] However, as explained in the first chapter it is preferable to view both models not as alternatives, but as two objectives that need to be reconciled with each other within the model underlying the criminal justice system of a particular state. This seems to be in conformity

---

[17] This refers to the federal criminal justice system. As explained in the previous section, there are in fact many US criminal justice systems, considering the differences between federal and local systems, between all local systems and considering differences in resources and crimes concerning which the different 'systems' have jurisdiction. The elements analyzed in this chapter will generally also apply to the other systems.

[18] *United States v. Havens,* 466 U.S. 620, 100 S.Ct. 1912 (1980), 626.

[19] *Delaware v. Arsdall,* 475 U.S. 673, 106 S.Ct. 1431 (1986), 681.

[20] *United States v. Noble*, 422 U.S. 225, 95 S.Ct. 2160 (1975), 230.

[21] Israel 1993, 6. Israel states on this fairness objective: "While this amorphous concept of "fairness" may have a somewhat different connotation in different societies, its fundamental elements are fairly uniform in democratic society." "Fairness imposed both substantive and procedural norms that restrain state power in criminal law enforcement. Substantive norms recognize such interests as human dignity and personal autonomy, while procedural norms reflect values such as community participation, a prescribed procedure, regularity, integrity, and promptness in application, and equality of treatment of like cases. Because the precise content of these independent values is derived in large part from political ideology, tradition, and culture, restraints imposed on the criminal justice process in service of such values will vary from one country to the next. Yet general agreement exists that some "fairness" restraints are needed, even when they reduce the efficient enforcement of substantive criminal law through the criminal justice process."

[22] Packer 1966, 238-239.

with what Griffiths called the family model: a model based on the assumption that the interest of the individual accused is competing with the interest of the state, for which reason the criminal justice system should be designed in accordance with a model based on a reconciliation or battle between these interests.[23] Also Damaška explained Packer's due process model and crime control model as actually contending a single model based on the clashing tendencies of crime control and due process.[24]

Israel formulates nine cornerstones of the US criminal process as the choices that have been made in the US design of criminal procedure to give effect to both the crime control objective and the protective objective. These cornerstones are: "(1) the discovery of the "truth"; (2) utilizing an adversarial process of adjudication; (3) utilizing an accusatorial system of proof; (4) minimizing erroneous convictions; (5) minimizing the burdens of accusation and litigation; (6) providing for lay participation; (7) respecting the dignity of the individual; (8) maintaining the appearance of fairness; and (9) achieving equality in administration."[25]

The adversarial process of adjudication, an accusatorial system of proof and lay participation, is typical for the US following the English common law tradition. A neutral decision-maker is responsible for deciding on guilt or innocence on the basis of the evidence presented by the parties (the trier of fact). A defendant has the right to be adjudicated by a jury, usually composed of 12 persons, as the neutral decision-maker, but may also waive his right to a jury trial and choose for a decision on the facts by the trial judge. The American adversarial procedure can be characterized as a "modified" adversary system, as the judge is not totally inactive and parties are not always strictly opposed but may in some situations be under a duty to assist the other party in evidence gathering (disclosure obligations). The Supreme Court has, on the basis of the presumption of innocence, imposed the burden of proof on the government.[26] On the basis of the evidence presented the prosecution establishes the guilt of the defendant beyond a reasonable doubt to obtain a conviction. Also the presumption of innocence which applies to the defendant follows from the government attorney's burden of the proof.

These being the basic characteristics of the US criminal process, the total process from the beginning of a criminal investigation to the conviction or acquittal at trial requires different procedural steps, which will now be briefly described.

Usually, the commission of a crime triggers the criminal process. The reporting of a committed crime or criminal behavior that comes to the attention of the police in a different manner may result in the initiation of a pre-arrest investigation, usually soon followed by the arrest of the suspect. After the arrest, a decision to charge will have to be made. The police and, subsequently, the prosecutor have

---

[23] Griffiths 1970.

[24] Damaška 1973, 576.

[25] Israel 1993, 6.

[26] *Coffin v. United States,* 156 U.S. 432, 15 S.Ct. 394 (1895).

to decide whether or not the available evidence should lead to a decision to charge. There is a system of prosecutorial discretion, where the prosecutor should consider whether prosecution is also in the interest of justice before making its decision to charge, which includes considerations as to the nature of the crime, the expected attitude of the victim during the criminal process, the criminal record of the suspect, and the aptness of an out-of-court settlement that avoids initiating criminal procedures.[27] When the prosecutor has decided to charge, the subsequent step in the procedure constitutes the preliminary hearing or grand jury review. On a federal level this review is, as a matter of Constitutional law, carried out by the grand jury, which is a jury composed of private citizens.[28] In some states a magistrate judge fulfills the task of the grand jury during a preliminary hearing.[29] The review is aimed at a determination as to whether there is sufficient evidence to support the charge. This sufficiency should meet a standard of probable cause. Only the prosecutor presents the evidence under secrecy to the grand jury, whereas the preliminary hearing is held in an adversarial mode.[30] When the majority of the members of the grand jury are satisfied as to the probable cause against the suspect, the suspect is indicted. The indicted suspect will be informed before the trial court of the charge or charges against him/her (arraignment) and he/she then the opportunity to plead guilty, not guilty or *nolo contendere*. When the defendant pleads not guilty, the case will be set for trial. The actual fact-finding process will then take place in the (rather exceptional) trial phase. The nature of the trial process is adversarial, which means that there is a division within the system between the decision-maker and the parties, who are together responsible for developing the legal and factual issues of the case. The neutral decision-maker (the jury and/or judge) will decide in the light of the materials presented by the two parties, being the defense and the prosecution. The jury shall make a decision with respect to the facts and the judge with respect to questions of law.

It is the responsibility of the parties—and not of the judge—to investigate the facts of the case, including interviewing witnesses and consulting possible experts. Each party decides what and what not to present and gives its view of how the law should be interpreted.[31] Both parties should pursue this in a way which is most favorable to their position. Besides, each party may provide counter-arguments with respect to the presentation of the other party and cross-examine any witnesses or experts. After the parties have completed their presentations and cross-examinations, it is for the judge and the jury to decide impartially about the questions of law and fact at issue.

---

[27] LaFave et al. 2004, 10.

[28] U.S. Constitution, Amendment V.

[29] This part of the Fifth Amendment (the grand jury indictment) has not been incorporated to the states through the Fourteenth Amendment. See on the incorporation clause of the Fourteenth Amendment, Sect. 5.1.4.2.

[30] LaFave et al. 2004, 12.

[31] Before the jury start with their deliberations, the judge will give them the final instruction about the law which is applicable to the case.

At the pre-arrest stage, there is not yet a role for the defense to play and, hence, the pre-arrest criminal investigation is solely conducted on behalf of the government. The United States has always heavily relied upon a reactive criminal justice system, with deterrence being the most effective way of controlling crime. Hence, the criminal process is normally triggered when a crime has been committed. Only in limited situations do the police act proactively. These proactive investigations usually aim to intercept those criminal activities that are consensual, such as the activities of members of a criminal organization, who willingly participate in criminal activities such as the illicit trade in drugs.

### *5.1.4 Constitutional Principles*

The US' criminal process is significantly regulated by the Constitution, in particular by the First, Fourth, Fifth and Sixth Amendments to the Constitution. The provisions of the Constitution that aim to protect individual liberties are usually referred to as the 'Bill of Rights', which basically refers to the first eight amendments to the Constitution. The Amendments were added to the Constitution in 1791 to protect individual liberty against any misuse of power by the national government. Most of these Amendments specifically deal with the protection of individual rights within the criminal process. Although some criminal procedural areas have also been regulated through legislation, the statutory schemes largely follow the restraints that follow from the Constitution as developed by the Supreme Court. The 'constitutionalization' of the criminal process is in fact the result of judgments by the Supreme Court on the interpretation of the Constitutional provisions. The Supreme Court has interpreted the Bill of Rights guarantees expansively and has also extended the application of many of these guarantees to the states by their decisions on the Fourteenth Amendment.[32] The constitutionalization of criminal procedure primarily occurred during the 1960s when Justice Earl Warren was the Chief Justice of the Supreme Court. However, after this era of focusing on the protection of Constitutional values in criminal procedural law, many of the Constitutional requirements set have since been interpreted flexibly and a wide range of exceptions have been created in order to give more leeway to law enforcement officers' efforts to confront more effectively the rising crime rates and the emergence of complex criminality. This happened in particular when Chief Justice Warren Burger presided over the Supreme Court from the 1970s until the mid-1980s. During this period the Court focused on crime control to promote 'truth' and deviated from the rights and due-process orientation of the Warren Court. Nevertheless, the Constitution remains the source of regulation for criminal procedural law. Its interpretation, however, largely depends on a willingness to focus either on the protective aspect of criminal procedural law or on effective and

[32] LaFave et al. 2004, 82.

expeditious law enforcement. According to Amar, the correct normative role of the Constitution in criminal procedural law should be found in Constitutional interpretation that is able to offer protection to the innocent, albeit without needlessly providing an advantage to the guilty.[33]

This section will start by setting out the Constitutional principles that influence the criminal investigation and the general interpretation given to these Constitutional principles insofar as they concern criminal investigation. Thereafter, the chapter will elaborate on the precise restraints on criminal investigative activities that aim to protect against arbitrary and unreasonable invasions of Constitutional rights and principles through the investigative activities of the government.

The specific provisions of the Constitution that are relevant to the regulation of the investigative phase are, first and foremost, the Fourth Amendment, providing for numerous restraints on the use of investigative powers that constitute search or seizure, and, secondly, the due process clauses of the Fifth Amendment and the Fourteenth Amendment.

This section will start with a description of the contents of the Fourth Amendment and, secondly, with the meaning of due process for the criminal investigation. The specific regulatory consequences of the Fourth Amendment and of due process for the investigative phase will be dealt with in Sects. 5.2 and 5.3.

#### 5.1.4.1 Unreasonable Searches and Seizures and the Right to Private Life: Fourth Amendment

The Fourth Amendment of the Constitution of the United States limits the government's power to carry out searches and seizures against US citizens and anyone present in US territory. It poses a limitation on the power of the police to investigate crime while using investigative techniques that constitute searches and seizures. The Fourth Amendment, protecting against "unreasonable searches and seizures," reads as follows:

> "The right of the people to be secure in their persons, houses, papers, and effects, against unreasonable searches and seizures, shall not be violated, and no Warrants shall issue, but upon probable cause, supported by Oath or affirmation, and particularly describing the place to be searched, and the persons or things to be seized."[34]

The Fourth Amendment of the US Constitution contains two clauses that are relevant to searches and seizures within the context of the criminal process. It protects people against unreasonable searches and seizures and establishes that no warrant shall be issued except when there is probable cause. Two different approaches are developed to interpret these clauses of the Fourth Amendment. The first approach is the 'reasonableness Fourth Amendment approach,' where the Supreme Court has interpreted the Fourth Amendment as containing two

---

[33] Amar 1997, 154-155.

[34] U.S. Constitution, Amendment IV.

independent clauses. This means that in some exceptional situations searches and seizures can be reasonable despite the absence of probable cause or a warrant. The relevant test is whether or not the search or seizure as a whole is reasonable.[35] This first approach currently seems to be a correct understanding of the Fourth Amendment, considering the Court's allowance of a variety of exceptions to the probable cause and warrant requirement.[36] However, the Supreme Court has also often—especially during the Warren Court—ruled in favor of the second approach, interpreting the clauses of the Fourth Amendment in a way that a search or seizure is unreasonable if it is not based upon probable cause, in order to ensure that no less stringent requirements apply to warrantless searches and seizures than to searches and seizures explicitly authorized by a warrant.[37] No detailed explanation of the seizure will be given, because the focus of this research will be on special investigative techniques as covered by the term 'search'.

The two clauses of the Fourth Amendment can be divided into several independent issues that must be taken into account in order to define the regulatory law which is applicable to searches and seizures. In the first place, the interpretation of the specific areas and interests that are protected by the Fourth Amendment requires attention. Furthermore, there are specific requirements for the procedure that—save for the exceptions—should be followed before a 'reasonable' search can be conducted: the search or seizure must be preceded by the issuance of a warrant; there must be 'probable cause'; the warrant must be supported by oath or affirmation; and the place to be searched and the things to be seized shall be described. The exclusionary rule—a product of the decisions of the Supreme Court dealing with violations of the Fourth Amendment—comes into play when the police or prosecutor has violated one of the requirements of the Fourth Amendment. This section will elaborate on what areas and interests are protected by the Fourth Amendment. The specific requirements that searches must meet in order to comply with the Fourth Amendment will be the subject of Sect. 5.3.2.1. This section intends to describe the importance and scope of the Fourth Amendment for the criminal investigation and, hence, only covers the interpretation of the Fourth Amendment with regard to its scope: the areas and interests that are protected.

To determine the scope of the Fourth Amendment it is important to note, in the first place, that the Fourth Amendment addresses the 'people'. The Supreme Court interpreted the word 'people' in the Fourth Amendment as covering only members of the "national community," which includes every US citizen, illegal residents or tourists in the US, and corporations, but excludes aliens living outside the US.[38]

---

[35] Harr and Hess 2002, 174.

[36] Amar 1997, 2 and 31. This will be affirmed through the findings of the subsequent Chaps. 6 and 7.

[37] *Wong Sun v. United States*, 371 U.S. 471, 83 S.Ct. 407 (1963), 475 and LaFave et al. 2004, 141.

[38] *United States v. Verdugo-Urquidez,* 494 U.S. 259, 110 S.Ct. 1056 (1990) and see: Israel and LaFave 2006, 50-51 and Nowak and Rotunda 2005, 213.

Subsequently, it must be determined whether the specific investigative activities of the police actually contribute to a search or seizure. The answer to this question depends upon the reasonable expectation of privacy that the person in question exhibits and, thus, upon the interests that the Fourth Amendment aims to protect. If the person or his/her property is searched in a situation where he or she could not have a reasonable expectation of privacy, no Fourth Amendment rights are infringed and there are no limitations on the power of the police. The Supreme Court adopted this 'reasonable expectation of privacy test' in *Katz v. United States* (1967).[39] In *Katz v. United States* the Supreme Court emphasized that the Constitution protects people and not places and for that reason a privacy intrusion does not depend on the place searched but on the person's expectation of privacy in that specific place.[40] *Katz* dealt with the electronic interception and recording of the telephone communications of the defendant while using a public telephone booth. The Court held that this means of electronic interception by the FBI constituted a search and seizure within the meaning of the Fourth Amendment on the basis of the fact that the defendant could have a reasonable expectation of privacy within the walls of the booth, regardless of the manner in which the conversations had been intercepted, and that the requirements of the Fourth Amendment should thus have been followed. For the first time, the Court refused in *Katz* to follow the approach that a search occurs only in those situations in which a "physical invasion" has been made into the area in which the defendant was present, from which perspective wire-tapping from outside is not a search considering that no physical invasion has occurred. Justice Stewart, delivering the opinion of the Court, emphasized that the Constitution "protects people, not places. What a person knowingly exposes to the public, even in his own home or office, is not a subject of Fourth Amendment protections. But what he seeks to preserve as private, even in an area accessible to the public may be constitutionally protected." The fact that the defendant was visible to the public when making calls from the telephone booth was considered irrelevant. A person in a telephone booth, who shuts the door and places a call, is "surely entitled to assume that the words he utters into the mouthpiece will not be broadcast to the world."[41] Justice Douglas explained in his concurring opinion that the rule should be understood as "a twofold requirement, first that a person [has] exhibited an actual (subjective) expectation of privacy and, second, that the expectation be one that society is prepared to recognize as 'reasonable.'" Since *Katz,* the scope of the Fourth Amendment has been interpreted in accordance with this 'reasonable expectation of privacy test' with a subjective element (the actual expectation of privacy) and an objective element (one that society is prepared to recognize as reasonable). As a consequence, not only physical searches fall under the protection of the Fourth Amendment, but also, for instance, the electronic interception of communications or personal information.

39 *Katz v. Unites States,* 389 U.S. 347, 88 S.Ct. 507 (1967).

40 *Ibid.*, 351.

41 *Ibid.*

After *Katz* the Court has taken narrower view to determine whether a particular privacy expectation is justified. In that regard the Court allowed a police examination of abandoned property such as a garbage can without following the conditions of the Fourth Amendment (*California v. Greenwood*[42]). Also a search of abandoned property such as vehicles or even private houses does not violate one's reasonable expectation of privacy. Furthermore, federal agents are allowed to observe people in public as well as in their private property as long as they can be observed from a public location, such as from a public road in front of a house. Decisive is whether the observations, also within private areas, are made from a point that is publicly accessible or concerns a private area to which police officers (or others) have been invited. In *California v. Ciraolo* and *Florida v. Riley*, the Court held that warrantless aerial observation of a fenced yard with the naked eye did not violate the Fourth Amendment.[43] In both cases observation by a police officer with the naked eye at an altitude of 1000ft from a plane, and 400ft from a helicopter, respectively, served as evidence for obtaining a warrant to search the premises. The Court recognized in *California v. Ciraolo* that a fence shielded a yard from observation from the street and the defendant, for that reason, may have had a subjective expectation of privacy with regard to observations from the street. However, the expectation was not reasonable in a sense that society is prepared to honor, because it was unreasonable to extend it to observations from "public navigable airspace" in a "physically non-intrusive manner."[44] The Court reached the same result in both cases by recognizing that the Fourth Amendment does not protect all areas attached to a dwelling from police observation. This includes police aerial observations from the public airspace in order to observe what is visible to the naked eye. Another example of an area where one may not have a reasonable expectation of privacy is a prison cell (*Hudson v. Palmer*[45]) and parolees may also be searched without suspicion (*Samson v. California*[46]).

Furthermore, the use of pen registers has been accepted as a technique that does not violate one's reasonable expectation of privacy, because one cannot have such a reasonable expectation of privacy with regard to information that can be obtained through these techniques (phone numbers).[47] Similar reasoning has resulted in decisions to the effect that the use of investigative tools known as track and trace devices does not constitute a search.[48] Another important restriction on the

---

[42] *California v. Greenwood*, 486 U.S. 35, 108 S.Ct. 1625 (1988).

[43] *California v. Ciraolo,* 467 U.S. 207, 106 S.Ct. 1809 (1968) and *Florida v. Riley*, 488 U.S. 445, 109 S.Ct. 693 (1989).

[44] *California v. Ciraolo,* 467 U.S. 207, 106 S.Ct. 1809 (1968), 212-214.

[45] *Hudson v. Palmer,* 468 U.S. 517, 104 S.Ct. 3194 (1984), 525-526.

[46] *Samson v. California,* 547 U.S. 843, 126 S.Ct. 2193 (2006), 848-857.

[47] *Smith v. Maryland,* 442 U.S. 735, 99 S.Ct. 2577 (1979), 742-746.

[48] *United States v. Knotts,* 460 U.S. 276, 103 S.Ct. 1081 (1983), 278 *United States v. Karo,* 468 U.S. 705, 104 S.Ct. 3296 (1984), 712-713. In the latter case, the Court declined to extend the use of tracking devices as a tool that does not violate one's reasonable expectation of privacy to one's home.

applicability of the Fourth Amendment concerns the decision of the Supreme Court in *United States v. Miller* (1976), where the Court explicitly excluded personal information entrusted to others, such as records kept by banks, from being covered by the Fourth Amendment. "[T]he Fourth Amendment does not prohibit the obtaining of information revealed to a third party and conveyed by him to Government authorities, even if the information is revealed on the assumption that it will be used only for a limited purpose and the confidence placed in the third party will not be betrayed."[49] As a consequence, the Fourth Amendment does not cover the issuing of subpoenas by the government to obtain personal records or documents possessed by third parties.

It follows from the Court's rulings on questions whether the Fourth Amendment protects a certain area that premises in general always receive protection under the Fourth Amendment. Within premises people can in general reasonably expect to be entitled to privacy. The expectation of privacy with regard to personal effects such a luggage has in most cases been judged as reasonable, whereas vehicles have generally received the least Fourth Amendment protection.[50]

The scope of the protection under the Fourth Amendment thus depends on the outcome of the reasonable expectation of privacy test. All circumstances of the particular case shall be taken into account when applying the test. Hence, the Fourth Amendment protects invasions by the government into the private lives the citizens. The Fourth Amendment must not, however, be seen as constituting a general right to private life. Protection under the Fourth Amendment goes further than only the protection of private life as it imposes specific requirements to be observed by police officers conducting searches and seizures. At the same time, the Fourth Amendment covers only these specific governmental intrusions into private life—those by a search and seizure—whereas other Amendments protect against other governmental conduct that may interfere with private life (e.g. the First Amendment).[51]

#### 5.1.4.2 Due Process of Law: Fifth and Fourteenth Amendments

The Bill of Rights was adopted to impose limits on the federal government. Since the adoption of the Fourteenth Amendment in 1868 some have argued that this Amendment made all the guarantees of the first ten Amendments applicable to the states by interpreting the "privileges and immunities clause"[52] and the "due

---

[49] *United States v. Miller,* 425 U.S. 435, 96 S.Ct. 1619 (1976), 443. Compare also *Katz v. United States* (1967) at 351: "[w]hat a person knowingly exposes to the public (…) is not a subject of Fourth Amendment protection."

[50] Israel et al. 2006, 188.

[51] Compare: *Katz v. United States,* 389 U.S. 347, 88 S.Ct. 507 (1967).

[52] The Supreme Court has interpreted the Fourteenth Amendment Privileges and Immunities clause (Section 1) as only protecting citizens as citizens of the federal government. Hence, this privileges and immunities clause typically guarantees equal claims to federal rights, such as the right to petition in Congress, the right to vote in federal elections, the right to interstate travel or commerce, or the right of *habeas corpus.*

process clause" of the Fourteenth Amendment according to the theory of "total incorporation."[53] Since the mid-1960s, however, the Supreme Court has adopted a theory of "selective incorporation" applying only those guarantees to the states which it considers "of the very essence of the scheme ordered liberty."[54] The Supreme Court determines whether a specific right that has been found in the Bill of Rights is deemed to be fundamental, looking not only at the meaning of that right in the specific circumstances of the case, but also at the totality of that right as guaranteed by the particular Amendment.[55] In *Duncan v. Louisiana* (1968) the Court considered trial by jury to be a fundamental procedural right, because it is "fundamental to the American scheme of justice" and "necessarily fundamental to fairness (…) in the context of the criminal processes maintained by the American States."[56] Since then, a right determined by the Supreme Court as a fundamental procedural right obtains the same meaning for the states as it has for the federal government.[57]

This section will not further elaborate upon the specific consequences of the Fourteenth Amendment interpretation as a result of which Bill of Rights guarantees are made applicable to the states and specific guarantees have so far been 'selectively incorporated,' because the analysis of criminal procedural law within the confines of this book concerns the system on a federal level. Instead, this section will continue to elaborate on the specific meaning of 'due process.' The due process clauses of the Fourteenth[58] and Fifth Amendments[59] have been interpreted as having an additional meaning; additional to the rights provided in the Bill of Rights. The due process clauses have in that regard a meaning that overlaps partly with specific guarantees of the Bill of Rights and may also impose additional restrictions on governmental power that are required to provide for "fundamental fairness." This section will analyze the

53 Nowak and Rotunda 2005, 210.

54 Israel et al. 2006, 33.

55 *Ibid.*, 43.

56 *Duncan v. Louisiana*, 391 U.S. 145, 88 S.Ct. 1444 (1968), 149 and 150.

57 See: *Malloy v. Hogan*, 378 U.S. 1, 84 S.Ct. 1489 (1964), 10.

58 U.S. Constitution, Amendment XIV, Section 1: *"All persons born or naturalized in the United States, and subject to the jurisdiction thereof, are citizens of the United States and of the State wherein they reside. No State shall make or enforce any law which shall abridge the privileges or immunities of citizens of the United States; nor shall any State deprive any person of life, liberty, or property, without due process of law; nor deny to any person within its jurisdiction the equal protection of the laws."*

59 U.S. Constitution, Amendment V: *"No person shall be held to answer for a capital, or otherwise infamous crime, unless on a presentment or indictment of a Grand Jury, except in cases arising in the land or naval forces, or in the Militia, when in actual service in time of War or public danger; nor shall any person be subject for the same offence to be twice put in jeopardy of life or limb; nor shall be compelled in any criminal case to be a witness against himself, nor be deprived of life, liberty, or property, without due process of law; nor shall private property be taken for public use, without just compensation."*

contents of this 'independent' or 'free-standing' due process, which has both a substantive and a procedural counterpart.

The existence of substantive due process was first recognized in *Mugler v. Kansas* (1887).[60] Substantive due process gives the judiciary the power to examine the substance of the law in order to control whether the legislature has not surpassed its authority. If the law does not have a "reasonable relation to a legitimate end," the judiciary may render the law void.[61] Moreover, because of substantive due process the Supreme Court may determine certain rights other than those included in the Bill of Rights or other Constitutional provisions as fundamental. For example, the Supreme Court has adopted the right to private life as a fundamental right.[62] Any legislation passed by Congress that limits such a fundamental right must "satisfy strict scrutiny, that is, the restriction must be narrowly tailored to serve a compelling government interest."[63] Substantive due process thus constitutes a judicial check on the legislature's power to pass legislation which shall have a reasonable relation to a legitimate end and must not unnecessarily or arbitrarily limit fundamental rights. One of the consequences of the Supreme Court's ruling based on the substantive content of due process has been the incorporation of many of the provisions of the Bill of Rights in the States.

The procedural counterpart of due process guarantees a process with certain fairness requirements when someone is deprived of life, liberty or property. The difference between procedural and substantive due process is that procedural due process protects against "arbitrary takings" by the government, whereas substantive due process protects against "governmental power arbitrarily and oppressively exercised."[64] This means that procedural due process covers the execution of the law, including, primarily, the judicial proceedings, whereas substantive due process imposes qualitative standards on the law in order to exclude arbitrariness and oppressive power in respect of fundamental rights. When a state action contributes to a taking of life, liberty or property, the person affected has a subsequent right to a procedure in which the basis and legitimacy of such an action is determined.[65] The taking of life, liberty or property (the wording of the due process clauses of the Fifth and Fourteenth Amendments) should be understood as a taking on behalf of the government, as a consequence of which an individual suffers some burden, or as a governmental decision impairing the life, liberty or property of an individual.[66] Any action by a public officer relating to his/her office concerns an action on behalf of the government, which thus includes

---

[60] *Mugler v. State of Kansas,* 123 U.S. 623, 8 S.Ct. 273 (1887).

[61] Nowak and Rotunda 2004, 439 and 442.

[62] *Griswold v. Connecticut,* 381 U.S. 479, 85 S.Ct. 1678 (1965).

[63] E.g. recently applied in *Pleasant Grove City, Utah v. Summum*, 555 U.S. 460, 129 S.Ct. 1125 (2009), 1132.

[64] *Sacramento v. Lewis,* 523 U.S. 833, 118 S.Ct. 1708 (1998), 846.

[65] Nowak and Rotunda 2004, 593 and see US Constitution Amendments V and XIV.

[66] Nowak and Rotunda 2004, 403.

the actions of police officers.[67] In *Goldberg v. Kelly* (1970) the Supreme Court determined some "rudimentary" procedural requirements demanded by due process. These requirements include the "fundamental requisite" of the "opportunity to be heard" and "a hearing (..) at a meaningful time and in a meaningful manner." The Court elaborated on these requirements by demanding: "timely and adequate notice" for a taking; an "effective opportunity to defend by confronting any adverse witnesses and by presenting his own arguments and evidence orally"; "to appear personally with or without counsel (...) to present evidence (..) orally"; "an opportunity to confront and cross-examine adverse witnesses"; and the disclosure of "evidence used to prove the Government's case" to the individual who has been damaged by the governmental action.[68] A due procedure should comply with all the safeguards of the Bill of Rights and constitute a fair adjudication procedure observing the requirements just set out.[69] Many of the specific rights elaborated in the case law that follow from procedural due process have been included in the Federal Rules of Criminal Procedure.[70]

In *Dowling v. United States* (1990), however, the Supreme Court held that "beyond the specific guarantees enumerated in the Bill of Rights, the Due Process Clause has limited operation." Therefore, the Supreme Court has "defined the category of infractions that violate "fundamental fairness" very narrowly."[71] A few years later the Court added that "[t]he Bill of Rights speaks in explicit terms to many aspects of criminal procedure, and the expansion of those constitutional guarantees under the open-ended rubric of the Due Process Clause invites undue interference with both considered legislative judgments and the careful balance that the Constitution strikes between liberty and order."[72] Nevertheless, also after these judgments the Court has regularly based the constitutional regulation of criminal procedure on the independent content of due process. In such judgments the Court has applied a totality-of-circumstances test to determine whether the procedure has been "due." Moreover, these judgments on the procedural aspect of due process turn on the realization of fairness in the process to be followed to establish the truth and in that sense protect against the conviction of the innocent. This means, in principle, that procedural due process affects every stage of the process, including the investigative stage.

Procedural due process only covers the situation where life, liberty or property is at stake and, hence, only in such a situation is the person in question entitled to a fair process in which the protections of the Bill of Rights are guaranteed and fair

---

[67] *Ibid.*, 571.

[68] *Goldberg v. Kelly,* 397 U.S. 254, 90 S.Ct. 1011 (1970), 267-270. The Supreme Court applied the requirements of procedural due process to a case concerning the termination of welfare benefits. See also: Orth 2003, 88.

[69] Nowak and Rotunda 2004, 593.

[70] Another procedural due process requirement for fundamental fairness is that guilt must be established by proof 'beyond a reasonable doubt.'

[71] *Dowling v. United States*, 493 U.S. 343, 110 S.Ct. 668 (1990), 352.

[72] *Medina v. California*, 505 U.S. 437, 112 S.Ct. 2572 (1992), 443.

adjudication is provided.[73] The concept of procedural due process is a concept which is primarily underpinned by the desire to guarantee accuracy and to avoid arbitrariness in the government's decision-making process, but its fundamental basis may be extended—according to critics of the limited interpretation of the Supreme Court narrowing its assessment to the accuracy of the decision-making process—to include other procedural values, such as respect for individual dignity, the right to notification and participation and equality under the law.[74] Notwithstanding the uncertainty with regard to the precise values underpinning the concept of due process, the Supreme Court in *Matthews v. Eldridge* (1976)[75] provided for a test that courts can use to determine whether in a specific case procedural due process has been violated. Any adverse impact on the rights of an individual during a criminal procedure should be balanced by the courts on the basis of the following three factors: "The private interest that will be affected by the official action; second, the risk of an erroneous deprivation of such interest through the procedures used, and the probable value, if any, of additional or substitute procedural safeguards; and finally the government's interests."[76] Hence, rulings on the procedural aspect of due process have resulted in important fundamental fairness requirements which are applicable during trial. However, procedural due process has only little meaning for other stages of the procedure additional to the Bill of Rights. Court judgments on procedural due process that covered the investigative phase have only resulted in the establishment of violations of procedural due process in cases of arbitrary police behavior that 'shocks the conscience' or 'violates the decencies of civilized conduct.' This is a rather high standard and seems to cover only deliberate harmful conduct by the police, where harmful is understood as resulting in bodily harm to the suspect.[77] The normative effect of procedural due process for the investigative phase is thus limited to preventing the government from engaging in conduct that 'shocks the conscience.'[78] During the trial phase, procedural due process does cover the fairness

---

[73] Nowak and Rotunda 2005, 318.

[74] Barron and Dienes 2003, 245-246.

[75] *Matthews v. Eldridge,* 424 U.S. 319, 96 S.Ct. 893 (1976).

[76] *Matthews v. Eldridge,* 424 U.S. 319, 96 S.Ct. 893 (1976), 321. This SC case did not concern a criminal procedure, but a termination of disability benefit. Due process covers all aspects of governmental actions and procedures, not only criminal. Therefore, this test may generally reflect the manner in which the courts balance the interests when they assess a claim of due process violation, also in the criminal law context.

[77] Compare *Rochin v. California,* 342 U.S. 165, 72 S.Ct. 205 (1954) (this case concerned the forced pumping of the suspect's stomach to retrieve the evidence) and *Sacramento v. Lewis,* 523 U.S. 833, 118 S.Ct. 1708 (1998) (A "high-speed automobile chase aimed at apprehending a suspected offender" that resulted in the death of the suspect did not violate substantive due process as "in such circumstances only a purpose to cause harm unrelated to the legitimate object of arrest will satisfy the element of arbitrary conduct shocking to the conscience, necessary for a due process violation." *Ibid.,* 836).

[78] LaFave et al. 2004, 71 and *Rochin v. California,* 342 U.S. 165, 72 S.Ct. 205 (1954), 209 and *Sacramento v. Lewis*, 523 U.S. 833, 118 S.Ct. 1708 (1998), 846-847.

of the use as evidence of information gathered through specific investigative techniques and, therefore, has regulatory consequences for the acceptance of the use of specific investigative techniques for the purpose of evidence gathering.[79]

To sum up, independent due process, as derived from the due process clauses of the Fifth and Fourteenth Amendments, may have consequences for the investigative phase both in a substantive and a procedural sense. The substantive counterpart focuses on the propriety of the law passed by Congress: legislation may not unnecessarily or arbitrarily limit fundamental rights. This may, hypothetically, cover laws that allow for wire-tapping under lower standards when terrorism is involved, where terrorism is insufficiently defined, and, consequently, the law's application may become rather arbitrary. Courts have primarily used procedural due process in order to achieve a certain level of fairness for the trial proceedings. Although, in theory, procedural due process covers the fairness of the proceedings as a whole, its direct meaning during the investigative phase has so far been limited to cases in which police conduct has shocked the conscience. However, its regulatory consequences for the trial phase may include questions such as whether the introduction of classified evidence violates the fundamental fairness of the trial.

## 5.2 The Sword Function of the US Criminal Investigation

### *5.2.1 The Actors Responsible for Truth-Finding*

This section will deal with the four different actors that are directly or indirectly concerned with the criminal investigation in the sense of gathering information that can be used in criminal proceedings to establish the truth. In the first place these actors concern those that have been explicitly attributed a role in the truth-finding process. These are the police, responsible for the investigation of crimes either after they have been committed or in some situations proactively; the prosecutors, responsible for initiating federal prosecutions and taking investigative steps in that regard; and the grand jury, attributed with investigative authority in relation to its power to screen the indictment. In addition to these actors, also the intelligence community with investigative power under the executive's national security power is a relevant actor for the information collected for the purpose of truth-finding in criminal proceedings. Although the primary function of investigations under the national security power is not truth-finding, the information that can be collected may concern information on criminal offenses and be used as evidence in criminal proceedings. Hence, also the national security power and the intelligence community acting under this power will be dealt with in this section.

[79] The regulatory effect of procedural due process on the investigative phase will be dealt with in more detail in the Sects. 5.3.1.1 and 5.3.1.2 and in Sects. 5.3.1.2 and 5.3.1.3 as to the trial phase.

The role of this particular actor is even more important considering that in the next chapter it will appear that the role of the intelligence community in the truth-finding process has substantially increased.

#### 5.2.1.1 The Police

The police within the United States are not a uniform body. Police agencies can be found in over 18,000 different, mostly local, governmental agencies among the US, resulting in a decentralized and fragmentized division of police authority. The agencies are qualified as the police, because they are given the task of enforcing criminal statute(s) and at least some of the officers working within the unit have been given special enforcement powers, such as the power to arrest.

According to the Constitution's Tenth Amendment "[t]he powers not delegated to the United States by the Constitution, nor prohibited by it to the States, are reserved to the States respectively, or to the people."[80] This so-called 'police power' attributes responsibility for public safety and the welfare of citizens to the states, which constitutes the Constitutional basis of the decentralized organization of the police.[81] The underlying rationale for the far-reaching decentralization of the police is, similar to the reason behind the creation of a federal state, spreading power in order to safeguard against the subversion of democracy.[82] Additionally, decentralization enables local communities to maintain control over the administration of criminal law and to set their own priorities, which reflect the interests and needs of that specific community. However, as a consequence of the discretion given to the police in administering criminal law, inequality has developed between the policies of police communities, which concerns a clear disadvantage of decentralization. Moreover, it can often occur that different police agencies concurrently have the power to enforce the law within a particular area, which may result in conflicts.[83]

The organization of the police within the federal jurisdiction is less fragmented in comparison to the organization on the state level. For the subject-matter of this book, the Federal Bureau of Investigation (hereafter FBI), being the primary general police agency on the federal level with also some intelligence elements, will be the most relevant actor. The FBI was founded in 1908 as the investigative service on the federal level functioning under the Department of Justice in order to investigate federal crimes. Today, the FBI has become a powerful and, although still a division of the Department of Justice, largely autonomous agency comprised of both law enforcement and intelligence divisions. The mission of the FBI is currently formulated to "[p]rotect and defend the United States against terrorist

---

[80] U.S. Constitution, Amendment X.

[81] Baker 2007A, 261.

[82] White 2004, 17.

[83] Israel et al. 2006, 16-18.

and foreign intelligence threats; uphold and enforce the criminal laws of the United States; and provide leadership and criminal justice services to federal, state, municipal, and international agencies and partners."[84]

In general, the police constitute autonomous organizations independent of the prosecutor and independent from political branches within the community in which they operate. Also, every police officer has an independent position within his department, which gives him a margin of discretion as to its law enforcement task.[85] The police authorities are not specifically delegated in the law, which means that police officers have a discretionary power to develop activities that are part of their general duties to "enforce the law and keep the peace."[86] The courts have increasingly created constraints on this discretion, especially during the 'criminal procedural revolution' of the 'Warren Court'[87] during the 1960s. The limits placed on police discretion by the Supreme Court have also resulted in more political interference through advice and sometimes legislation and in the issuance of internal guidelines by police units. Since the Warren Court era the Supreme Court activity in regulating police conduct has decreased, which can be partly attributed to the degree of self-regulation established as a consequence of the decisions of the Warren Court. In addition, at this moment the Supreme Court seems to be more deferential, again giving more leeway to the police in fulfilling their law enforcement task in a period of increased focus on crime control since 9/11.[88]

Police officers are usually referred to as law enforcement officers. However, this does not imply that law enforcement—the enforcement of the criminal law—is the only task of the police. Police officers have many other tasks, including providing assistance to those in need and maintaining security and order.[89]

---

[84] According to the website of the FBI: http://www.fbi.gov/libref/historic/history/text.htm. Accessed 25 August 2009.

[85] Israel et al. 2006, 19.

[86] Amsterdam 1974, 386.

[87] Justice Earl Warren was the Chief Justice of the Supreme Court between 1953 and 1969.

[88] Stuntz 2002, 2138, 2140-2141 and (Anonymous) Note 2009, 1717-1718.

[89] Israel et al. 2006, 18. On the police see additionally: Manning 1977. In the American Bar Association Standards on Urban Police Function (1979), the following "Major current responsibilities of police" are listed: "a) indentify criminal offenders and criminal activity and, where appropriate, to apprehend offenders and participate in subsequent proceedings; b) reduce the opportunities for the commission of some crimes through preventive patrol and other measures; c) aid individuals who are in danger of physical harm; d) protect constitutional guarantees; e) facilitate the movement of people and vehicles; f) assist those who cannot care for themselves; g) resolve conflict; h) identify problems that are potentially serious law enforcement or governmental problems; i) create and maintain a feeling of security in the community; j) promote and preserve civil order; and k) provide other services on an emergency basis." Standards available at: http://www.abanet.org/crimjust/standards/urbanpolice.html (accessed 4 October 2010).

#### 5.2.1.2 The Prosecutors

The prosecution service within the United States is established in an office of public prosecution. The authority of the public prosecutor is divided between state officials, responsible for criminal prosecutions under state law, and federal officials (United States Attorneys), who are responsible for the criminal investigation and prosecution under federal law. The federal system is divided into districts. Each district has a US attorney (or federal prosecutor), who is granted full authority with regard to all federal criminal matters in the district. The federal prosecutor has a duty to prosecute all federal offenses and is vested with the broadest discretion to exercise his authority and to fulfill this duty.[90] This duty to prosecute does not imply a form of mandatory prosecution: rather, the provision exclusively[91] authorizes US attorneys to prosecute federal offenses, for which responsibility they are afforded the widest discretion. The US Attorney "possesses an absolute and unreviewable discretion as to what crimes to prosecute."[92] All federal prosecutors are appointed by the President, subject to confirmation by the Senate, and act under the supervision of the Attorney General as the chief of the office of federal prosecution.[93] The Attorney General is appointed by the President "by and with the consent of the Senate as the head of the Department of Justice."[94] Federal prosecutors are thus part of the executive branch, operating under the control of "administrative mechanisms" and "hierarchical governmental supervision."[95] Therefore, under the separation of powers doctrine "the courts are not to interfere with the exercise of discretionary powers of Attorneys of United States and their control over criminal prosecutions."[96] This does not mean that the prosecutors shall operate only in the interest of the executive, without taking into account the interest of justice in general. As 'officers of the court' and 'servants of the law' prosecutors are bound by integrity requirements in order to seek justice.[97] The police (or law enforcement agencies) are largely an independent organ, acting on behalf of the executive branch and having the power to investigate and refer cases to the prosecutor for prosecution. The prosecutor is dependent on the police for its information in order to prosecute and the two often cooperate during the investigation.[98] On the basis of the information provided by the police, the prosecutor shall determine its decision whether or not to institute a prosecution "upon matters of

---

[90] 28 U.S.C. § 547 (2010).

[91] Others, such as citizens, are consequently not authorized to institute federal prosecutions. See *Martinez v. Ensor,* 958 F. Supp. 515, (D.Colo. 1997), 518 and *People of State of New York v. Muka,* 440 F. Supp. 33 (N.D.N.Y. 1977), 36.

[92] *People of State of New York v. Muka,* 440 F. Supp. 33 (N.D.N.Y. 1977), 36.

[93] Contrary to state prosecutors, who are elected by the local community and operate rather autonomously. Walther 2000, 285.

[94] 28 U.S.C. § 503 (2010).

[95] Walther 2000, 286.

[96] *United States v. Cox,* 342 F.2d 167 (5th Cir. 1965), 171.

[97] See on this in more detail Sect. 5.3.1.2.

[98] Walther 2000, 287.

policy wholly apart from any question of probable cause."[99] This means that the prosecutor not only takes into account evidentiary aspects but primarily policy arguments for deciding on whether or not to prosecute a particular case. Considering their dependence on police information, the offices of public prosecutors usually cooperate with the police agencies, regardless of the fact that they are separate organizations. The public prosecutor cannot order the police to conduct certain investigative activities, but the police are usually inclined to follow the legal advice of the public prosecutor, as their interaction is essential for a successful law enforcement policy.

On the federal level the FBI and US attorneys are subject to the supervision of the Attorney General. This supervision extends to all "litigation to which the United States or any agency thereof is a party" and includes the possibility to direct US attorneys with regard to the exertion of their duties.[100] Hence, the hierarchical structure provides the possibility to enable close cooperation and uniformity in law enforcement policy. Nevertheless, the individual US attorney maintains responsibility and authority for the decision to prosecute.[101] This situation with hierarchical supervision on behalf of the Attorney General is different from the organization on the state level, where local police and local public prosecutor offices are autonomous organizations that are not subject to any higher supervising authority. Similar to the reasons behind the fragmented organization of the police, the rationale of the decentralization of the public prosecutor offices is that it gives the operating public prosecutor local democratically legitimized support, requiring him to act in the interest of and in accordance with the values of the local community, which is usually reflected by the prosecutor's selection of cases. The commensurate disadvantage of such an organization is inequality and legal uncertainty as to the administration of criminal law through the country, with possible diverging prosecuting policies between two relatively close districts.[102]

The police initiate most criminal investigations. When the police encounter multiple crimes, usually within the context of a criminal organization, the prosecutor is often asked to take over the primary responsibility for the investigation. The prosecutor will then direct the use of investigative powers by the police or will use its own investigative powers.[103] The role of the prosecutor is important in these cases as a prosecutor has the possibility to apply more invasive investigative techniques than the police have, such as the authority to apply for a search warrant[104] and the possibility to request a grand jury to use its subpoena power

---

[99] *United States v. Cox*, 342 F.2d 167 (5th Cir. 1965), 171.

[100] US Attorney's Manual, para 3-2.140. Available at: http://www.justice.gov/usao/eousa/foia_reading_room/usam/index.html (accessed 4 September 2011).

[101] *Ibid.*

[102] Israel et al. 2006, 21.

[103] Subin et al. 1993, 162.

[104] Although the police will in most situations carry out these investigative methods, access to the court is generally reserved for the prosecutor only.

(see Sect. 5.2.1.3). When the prosecutor wants to acquire testimony from a witness or specified physical evidence in the possession of the witness, the grand jury subpoena will be the appropriate investigative method.[105]

### 5.2.1.3 The Grand Jury

The grand jury is a jury comprising up to 23 private citizens and has both a screening and investigative function. Because of these screening and investigative functions the grand jury has been referred to as the "shield and sword" of the criminal justice process.[106] Regardless of this dual function, the grand jury will only be dealt with in this section, because its implications for the subject-matter of this project are limited to its investigative (sword) power. The shield role of the grand jury concerns the screening of evidence that supports the indictment. A prosecutor can only bring charges after this grand jury screening of the indictment. With that function, the grand jury acts as a shield between the government and citizens, protecting citizens from unwarranted prosecutions.[107]

The investigative power of the grand jury includes the power to subpoena witnesses in order to have them testify with regard to the crimes under investigation. The grand jury can issue a court order to subpoena a person in order to testify or, upon a subpoena *ducus tecum,* to produce physical evidence.[108] For the production of physical evidence, the police would normally need a search warrant issued upon probable cause, whereas the grand jury can obtain such evidence without a showing of probable cause and without particularly describing the place from which such evidence should be obtained.[109] The use of the grand jury's subpoena power aims to "inquire all information that might possibly bear on its investigation until it has identified an offense or satisfied itself that none has occurred."[110] The subpoena authority is very powerful as refusing to cooperate with the grand jury may result in severe sanctions including imprisonment. Moreover, the grand jury acts in secrecy as it is prohibited to disclose any matter occurring before the grand jury (with some exceptions), in the absence of defense attorneys and without the involvement of a judge.[111] This setting enables the prosecutor to largely direct the grand jury, serving as a legal adviser and directing

---

105 LaFave et al. 2004, 0-11.

106 Israel and LaFave 2006, 446.

107 Allen et al. 2005, 988.

108 Perrine 2005 (providing for a description of the grand jury subpoena power to compel the production of records and things).

109 Although subpoenas requesting the production of documents from third parties (knowingly provided to the third party by the person to whom the records pertain) are not subjected to protection by the Fourth Amendment. See *United States v. Miller,* 425 U.S. 435, 96 S.Ct. 1619 (1976), 443 and Sect. 5.1.4.1.

110 *United States v. R. Enterprises Inc.,* 498 U.S. 292, 111 S.Ct. 722 (1991), 297.

111 See Rule 6(d) and (e) of the Federal Rules of Criminal Procedure (2009).

the investigative steps in order to determine "whether a crime has been committed and whether criminal proceedings should be instituted against any person."[112] To pursue this function, the scope of the grand jury's subpoena power is rather broad. Nevertheless, it is not completely unlimited. The Supreme Court has decided that the subpoena power "may not itself violate a valid privilege, whether established by the Constitution, statutes, or the common law." Furthermore, "a grand jury's subpoena ducus tecum will be disallowed if it is 'far too sweeping in its terms to be regarded as reasonable' under the Fourth Amendment."[113]

Allowing the grand jury to apply such powerful tools is based upon the reasoning that "the people" themselves apply the tools, for which reason there is no need to apply the usual Fourth Amendment restriction intended to protect citizens against an abuse of governmental power.[114] Furthermore, the grand jury does not decide on matters of guilt or innocence, for which reason the evidentiary restrictions that normally apply to criminal trials do not apply in grand jury proceedings.[115]

Federal grand juries play an especially important role in complex criminal cases through the use of these subpoena powers when conventional law enforcement techniques fall short. For example, to confront organized crime it can be crucial to hear witnesses under the seal of secrecy of the grand jury. However, despite being effective and powerful, invoking the grand jury may seriously slow down the investigative proceedings.[116] For this latter reason, the investigative role of the grand jury in 'regular' criminal cases has diminished over the years. Because of efficiency arguments, the responsibility for these investigations is now primarily born by the police.

Hence, grand jury investigations primarily deal with revealing complex criminal structures or obtaining information from witnesses who are unwilling to cooperate. The grand jury may grant immunity to witnesses and hear witnesses under the applicability of secrecy requirements, which may prohibit the disclosure of any information produced before the grand jury without a court order.[117]

#### 5.2.1.4 National Security Power and the Intelligence Community

The principal goal of the intelligence community is to protect national security. The concept of national security, although widely used in the different acts of government documents, is ambiguously defined and sometimes not even defined at all. The US government usually refers to national security in terms that relate to

112 *United States v. Calandra,* 414 U.S. 338, 94 S.Ct. 613 (1974), 343-344.

113 *United States v. Calandra,* 414 U.S. 338, 94 S.Ct. 613 (1974), 344 and 346.

114 Allen et al. 2005, 998.

115 *United States v. R. Enterprises Inc.,* 498 U.S. 292, 111 S.Ct. 722 (1991), 298.

116 Allen et al. 2005, 988 and Israel and LaFave 2006, 446.

117 LaFave et al. 2004, 420-421.

'defense' and 'foreign affairs', as the two central functions of the executive under the US Constitution.[118] From the perspective of the executive, the ambiguity of the national security concept provides the necessary flexibility in order to cover new and unpredictable situations. Nevertheless, general themes can be identified in the definition of national security. According to Baker these themes concern "an element of physical security, or freedom from coercion, both for the individual and the state."[119] This may cover a wide variety of topics, including e.g. AIDS, climate change and transnational organized crime, but focuses particularly on threats such as terrorism and other more immediate threats with a potential catastrophic character.[120]

The national security investigation can be defined, according to the 'Guidelines for FBI National Security Investigations and Foreign Intelligence Collection,' issued by the Attorney General Ashcroft on October 31, 2003, as "counterintelligence investigation (…) conducted to obtain information concerning or to protect against a threat to the national security."[121] The scope of the investigative activities is not limited to the investigation as normally understood in the context of law enforcement—investigations in reaction to crimes committed and the gathering of evidence for use in criminal prosecutions—but these activities may also be aimed at the gathering of "critical information needed for broader analytic and intelligence purposes authorized by Executive Order 12333 and these Guidelines to protect the national security."[122]

---

[118] Baker 2007A, 16. For example, in Executive Order 12333 the goals of the US intelligence community are described as follows: "The United States Intelligence effort shall provide the President, the National Security Council, and the Homeland Security Council with the necessary information on which to base decisions concerning the development and conduct of foreign, defense, and economic policies, and the protection of United States national interests from foreign security threats." Executive Order 12333: United States Intelligence Activities, as amended by Executive Order Nos. 13284 (2003), 13355 (2004), and 13470 (2008), 73 Fed. Reg. 45325 (July 30, 2008), section 1.1.

[119] Baker 2007A, 19.

[120] AIDS and climate change are national security threats referred to in the National Security Strategies of President Clinton and President Bush (Baker 2007A, 19), as well as in the National Security Strategy of President Obama (2010), available at: http://www.whitehouse.gov/sites/default/files/rss_viewer/national_security_strategy.pdf (accessed 15 March 2011). On 'transnational organized crime' as a national security threat (including trafficking networks and cybercrime and possibly extending to terrorist activities) see particularly: the "Strategy to Combat Transnational Organized Crimes. Addressing Converging Threats to National Security," issued by Obama in July 2011, available at http://www.whitehouse.gov/sites/default/files/Strategy_to_Combat_Transnational_Organized_Crime_July_2011.pdf (accessed 4 September 2011).

[121] The Attorney General's Guidelines for FBI National Security Investigations and Foreign Intelligence Collection, issued by John Ashcroft, October 31, 2003 (declassified by Attorney General Gonzales on August 2, 2007), part VIII(Q), 36. These Guidelines have now been replaced by the Mukasey Guidelines on FBI Operations (2008), which have also abolished the distinction between FBI national security investigations and criminal investigations. See on this Chap. 6, Sect. 6.4.2.3.

[122] AG Ashcroft Guidelines on NSI (2003), part II, 11.

This broader power to gather intelligence by investigating behavior that may also constitute criminal behavior and which information may be used as evidence in trial is vested primarily within the executive and is subject to less legal restraints than investigative authority in the conventional law enforcement context. This section will continue to deal with the attribution of powers in the national security context and the organization of the intelligence community.

National Security is shared between the three branches of government (Executive, Congress and the Judiciary), according to Articles I, II and III of the Constitution. According to the Constitution, the President is granted power as the Chief Executive and the Commander-in-Chief. He also has the authority to deal with foreign affairs and to ensure that laws are faithfully executed. His national security responsibilities are derived from these powers, because intelligence is an element of his Commander-in-Chief power and his power to conduct foreign affairs.[123] The legislative power is vested in Congress, most importantly through the 'necessary and proper clause,' which enables Congress to do whatever is "necessary and proper to carrying into execution" its constitutionally enumerated powers. Furthermore, Congress has the authority to raise revenue, which gives it the power to direct how state funds are spent, including those funds allocated for national security purposes.[124] The judicial power is vested in the Supreme Court (Article III of the Constitution). The Judiciary can exercise control over the President's exercise of his Commander-in-Chief power, through their power to interpret the Constitution, which also provides for the President's Commander-in-Chief power. However, the "abstention doctrines", such as the political question doctrine, impose restrictions on the judiciary's power to control the executive. Consequently, issues such as the (political) decision on resorting to war and unreviewable standards, such as a claim of using force required to protect national security, are excluded from judicial review. Hence, access to the courts is very restricted and courts have generally been reluctant to interfere in executive, and Congressional, national security powers.[125]

The National Security Act of 1947[126] has constituted the basis of the organization of the intelligence community. Although the different national security agencies introduced by that Act have now been succeeded by new versions, the

[123] Baker 2007A, 35 and 72. Congress follows this interpretation by its texts in different statutes, such as the National Security Act of 1947, by stating that the President has authority next to the Director of National Intelligence to perform functions and duties related to intelligence and sharing the responsibility to keep the intelligence committees informed. Besides, different presidents have actually used their national security power by establishing national security agencies for different purposes. This corresponds with the view of the Supreme Court in *Totten, Administrator v. United States,* 92 U.S. 105, 1875 WL 17758 (1876). and more recently in *Tenet* et al. *v. Doe et Ux*, 544 U.S. 1, 125 S.Ct. 1230 (2005). Baker 2007A, 72-73.

[124] US Constitution, Article I, section 8(1) and (18).

[125] See in more detail Baker 2007A, 46-50.

[126] National Security Act of 1947, Act of July 26, 1947 (2007) (50 U.S.C. 401 and further). Source: Kris and Wilson 2007, Appendix A.

organizational structure has been retained. In combination with Executive Order 12333,[127] the National Security Act of 1947 makes up much of the organization of the intelligence community. According to these documents the intelligence agencies are the Department of Defense, the Department of State, the Department of Homeland Security, the Department of Justice, which includes the FBI, the Central Intelligence Agency (CIA) and numerous smaller agencies that are again part of the just mentioned departments and agencies.[128] Now, in total 16 separate intelligence entities can be identified. Only some of them are relevant for the purpose of this research as they have the authority to conduct national security investigations. The agencies that can conduct national security investigations are attributed powers for that purpose in the Foreign Intelligence Surveillance Act of 1978 (henceforth: FISA).

The intelligence elements of the FBI contribute most significantly to national security investigations. Furthermore, the National Security Agency (NSA) has the power to gather intelligence within the US and the CIA has a limited role in national security investigations as it is primarily a foreign intelligence agency. The FBI, in addition to being an intelligence agency, is also, and primarily, a law enforcement agency. However, its activities in the intelligence field have increased during its history of existence. The FBI now has, next to its division that investigates federal crimes, a Counterintelligence Division, a separate Counterterrorism division, and a Directorate of Intelligence (with the mission to protect the US against foreign intelligence operations and espionage).[129] Furthermore, there are several 'Field Intelligence Groups' operating outside the headquarters of the FBI at the Department of Justice. The FBI, although officially a division of the Department of Justice, operates highly independently.[130]

The National Security Council (NSC) is the coordinating entity for all agencies and is chaired by the President. The function of the NSC is to advise the President about all intelligence-related issues. The main function of the NSC (under 50 U.S.C. § 402(a)) is to advise the President on policies with regard to

---

[127] Executive Order 12333: United States Intelligence Activities, as amended by Executive Order Nos. 13284 (2003), 13355 (2004), and 13470 (2008), 73 Fed. Reg. 45325 (July 30, 2008).

[128] National Security Act of 1947, Section 3(4) and Executive Order 12333 (as amended) sections 1.7-1.13 and 3.5(h).

[129] Kris and Wilson 2007, 1-30. The mission of the FBI Counterterrorism Division is described as follows: "(…) to help our nation prevent acts of terrorism against the U.S. and U.S. targets. The priorities of the Division are to: Detect, disrupt, and dismantle terrorist sleeper cells in the United States before they act; [i]dentify and prevent acts of terrorism by individuals with a terrorist agenda acting alone; [d]etect, disrupt, and dismantle terrorist support networks, including financial support networks; [e]nhance our capability to quickly ascertain the reliability, implications and details of terrorist threats and to improve our capacity to disseminate threat-related information to local, state, and federal agencies, and to the private sector as needed; [e]nhance our overall contribution to the U.S. intelligence community and to senior policy makers in the government by providing timely and accurate in-depth analysis of the terrorist threat and other information of value on an ongoing basis."

[130] Kris and Wilson 2007, 1-29.

national security. In exerting this function, the NSC has proven to be a flexible institution, adapting to the preferences and political color of the different presidents.[131] Furthermore, the National Security Act of 1947 has established the Director of Central Intelligence (DCI), who is the head of the CIA as well as the manager of the intelligence community as a whole. The DCI has the task of coordinating the intelligence community, has substantive control over the intelligence community's budget and generally has access to all intelligence information in the possession of any agency.[132] However, also the DCI's activities are subject to the directions of the President and to the NSC.[133]

In 2004 the agency of 'Director of National Intelligence' was created, which has more coordinating power than the DCI. The DNI has been created to enable a more effective coordination of the intelligence community for the purpose of confronting terrorism. The need for better coordination followed from the results of the 9-11 Commission Report[134] leading several months later to the enactment of the Intelligence Reform and Terrorism Prevention Act, by which the DNI was established. The DNI is not a head of any individual intelligence agency, but has been placed above all individual intelligence agencies in order to have stronger authority to coordinate the intelligence community and, therefore, now presides over the intelligence community.[135] However, in practice the DNI, as head of the intelligence community, faces implementation problems, because the separate agencies refuse to hand over authority for their agency to the DNI and, consequently, also within the agencies a preference remains to give account to their own head of the agency.

### *5.2.2 The Powers Available for Truth-Finding in the Criminal Investigation*

The power to use special investigative techniques is basically dependent on the Fourth Amendment law on searches and seizures. Surveillance has been interpreted as constituting a search, as has been explained in Sect. 5.1.4.1. Other investigative activities do not always amount to a search as meant in the Fourth Amendment, and are, therefore, not as strictly regulated. The scope of a search under the Fourth Amendment is not limited to the physical entry of places; also the investigative technique of observation and forms of electronic surveillance are

[131] Kris and Wilson 2007, 1-5.

[132] *Ibid.*, 1-13.

[133] *Ibid.*, 1-11.

[134] Report of the National Commission on Terrorist Attacks upon the United States 2004.

[135] National Security Act of 1947, 50 U.S.C., Chapter 15 National Security, § 401-442a (2007), Executive Order 12333: United States Intelligence Activities (as amended by Executive Orders 13284 and 13355), December 4, 1981 and Kris and Wilson 2007, 1-3 to 1-30.

considered to be a 'search' once they constitute a violation of a reasonable expectation of privacy. Physical search and surveillance therefore follow the same Fourth Amendment law.

Surveillance will be dealt with in this chapter as a separate category, because the law covering the application of surveillance has experienced its own development in the case law and is also strictly regulated by legislation. Surveillance includes any interception of communications through means such as (wire-)tapping. Pen registers and trap and trace devices are aimed at the interception of identifying information relating to the person under investigation. The use of undercover agents (for the purpose of infiltration) and informants is not constitutionally restricted at all, because it will always involve the consent of the interlocutor who reveals the contents of the communications, and observations, made in situations in which one cannot have a reasonable expectation of privacy, are not protected.

The investigative powers that are applied secretly are primarily relevant within the context of this research project. Hence, surveillance in criminal investigations and national security investigations will acquire most attention. However, the regulation of these areas depends to a large extent on the Fourth Amendment law regarding search in general, as the Fourth Amendment aims to protect the interests that are also at stake when applying surveillance techniques or conducting domestic national security investigations. As a consequence, also this section, elaborating merely the powers available and not the regulatory scheme, will start by elaborating the power to conduct physical searches (5.2.2.1.1) before turning to surveillance and other techniques (5.2.2.1.2). Section 5.2.2.2 will address the law enforcement's capabilities to investigate proactively. The power to conduct national security investigations will be dealt with separately (5.2.2.3).

### 5.2.2.1 Conventional Criminal Investigation

The Fourth Amendment protects the right to private life by prohibiting unreasonable searches on behalf of the government. Section 5.3.2.1 will deal with the restraints that follow from the specific Fourth Amendment requirements and the goals served by these Constitutional limitations. This section will elaborate on the scope of the powers granted to the government to investigate at the pre-arrest stage.

The Constitution imposes negative duties on the state to refrain from certain actions in the criminal law context to protect civil liberties.[136] As a consequence, the police in the US are free to conduct any investigative activity that they consider necessary, except for those activities that violate the Fourth Amendment. Some use of investigative powers is allowed subject to the conditions of the regulatory scheme of the Fourth Amendment. To determine whether or not specific investigative activities are regulated and restricted by the Fourth Amendment, it should

[136] Van Kempen 2008, 56.

firstly be assessed whether the fundamental right protected by the Fourth Amendment is at stake by conducting the investigative activity. As already extensively described in Sect. 5.1.4.1, this depends on the outcome of a two-prong test to determine whether a reasonable expectation of privacy has been violated. The first sub-section will, first, briefly recapitulate which powers the Fourth Amendment law covers, and, second, this section will explain which types of search are not limited under the Fourth Amendment. The second sub-section will continue to elaborate on the search powers that can be applied secretly: a variety of surveillance techniques and infiltration.

#### 5.2.2.1.1 Search Powers

The investigative powers of the police that constitute a search or seizure find their regulation under the Fourth Amendment and, in addition, under Rule 41 of the Federal Rules of Criminal Procedure.[137] A search includes the regular meaning of a search of any place as well as surveillance: the interception—regardless of in which form the interception takes place—of communications.

The scope of the Fourth Amendment, and with that the powers governed by Fourth Amendment law, is determined by the area that it aims to protect, for which reason the Supreme Court adopted the 'reasonable expectation of privacy test' in *Katz v. United States* (1967).[138] In *Katz v. United States* the Supreme Court emphasized that the Constitution protects people and not places and for that reason a privacy intrusion does not depend on the place searched but on the person's expectation of privacy in that specific place.[139] The first step for requiring Fourth Amendment protection for wire-tapping activities was already set in *Silverman v. United States* (1961).[140] Before this, the Court had decided that wire-tapping did not constitute a search in the sense of the Fourth Amendment, because a physical entry of private property was lacking, and the eavesdropping of conversations did not amount to the seizure of "things" in the sense of physical objects.[141] However, in *Silverman v. United States* the Court reasoned that the electronic eavesdropping and seizure of the conversations in question constituted an "illegal search and seizure," for which conclusion the Court did not take into account that a physical trespass was lacking. That a physical trespass was no longer a necessary requirement for being covered by the Fourth Amendment followed, subsequently, more clearly from the Court's reasoning in *Clinton v. Virginia* (1964)[142]

137 Rule 41 of the Federal Rules of Criminal Procedure has codified the federal practice regarding search and seizure. The rule has obtained statutory authority through 18 U.S.C. § 3103.

138 *Katz v. United States,* 389 U.S. 347, 88 S.Ct. 507 (1967).

139 *Katz v. Unites States,* 389 U.S. 347, 88 S.Ct. 507 (1967), 351. See in detail Sect. 5.1.4.1.

140 *Silverman v. United States,* 365 U.S. 505, 81 S.Ct. 679 (1961).

141 *Olmstead v. United States,* 277 U.S. 438, 48 S.Ct. 564 (1928).

142 *Clinton v. Virginia*, 377 U.S. 158, 84 S.Ct. 1186 (1964).

determining that it was irrelevant whether the eavesdropping device was "driven into the wall" or "stuck in it." With the adoption of the reasonable expectation of privacy test in *Katz* the trespass doctrine was set aside, bringing all electronic surveillance activities under the scope of the Fourth Amendment, except those involving the consent of one of the parties (see below).[143]

Although the interpretation of the Supreme Court in *Katz* has significantly broadened the application of the Fourth Amendment, in judgments after *Katz* the courts have, for other areas, taken a "narrower view" in determining which situations concern "justified" expectations of privacy.[144] For example, the Supreme Court rejected the idea of someone having a reasonable expectation of privacy with regard to his/her garbage[145]; it has accepted the aerial surveillance of people within the confines of their garden[146]; and it has allowed the use of electronic tracking devices[147] on the ground that one could not have a reasonable expectation of privacy with regard to the observations or interceptions made when taking into account the manner in which it has been observed or intercepted.

Except for the scope of the concept of search under the Fourth Amendment based on the reasonable expectation of privacy analysis, other circumstances of a particular case have warranted an exemption from the usual Fourth Amendment requirements. Warrantless searches are permissible under emergency circumstances such as a danger to police officers or the destruction of evidence.[148] Exceptionally, courts have also authorized so-called 'sneak-and-peek searches,'[149] when it is important to the investigation that the owners are not aware that they are under suspicion. Sneak-and-peak searches are primarily used in terrorism and narcotic cases to search places without revealing to the suspects that they are under investigation in order to seize intangible evidence (to observe or photograph the presence of evidence on the premises) or to install bugging devices. The appellate courts that have examined the issue have upheld sneak-and-peak searches, under narrowly defined conditions.[150]

Moreover, the police always have the possibility to search without a warrant when they receive the consent of the person involved. Asking for permission can

---

[143] LaFave et al. 2004, 262-264.

[144] Israel et al. 2006, 86.

[145] *California v. Greenwood,* 486 U.S. 35, 108 S.Ct. 1625 (1988).

[146] *California v. Ciraolo*, 476 U.S. 207, 106 S.Ct. 1809 (1989) and *Florida v. Riley*, 488 U.S. 445, 109 S.Ct. 693 (1989).

[147] *United States v. Karo*, 468 U.S. 705, 104 S.Ct. 3296 (1984).

[148] LaFave et al. 2004, 195-198.

[149] Search with a delayed notice of the search.

[150] See in more detail on the notification requirements, the exceptions to notification and the reasoning of the appellate courts dealing with sneak-and-peak searches, Sect. 5.3.2.1.3. The possibilities for conducting sneak-and-peek searches have been broadened by the USA PATRIOT Act. See for this subject Chap. 6. Furthermore, in the national security context physical searches with delayed notice or even no notice at all have been permitted under the Foreign Intelligence Surveillance Act. This subject will be dealt with in 5.2.2.3.1.

be a solution in situations where probable cause is lacking, or when there is not enough time to obtain a warrant. Of course, the consent must be given voluntarily and cannot be the unconscious waiving of a constitutional right, which would not be the case if there were any police coercion.[151]

Once the police intend to use an investigative technique that constitutes a search under the Fourth Amendment, Rule 41 of the Federal Rules of Criminal Procedure applies, which prescribes the specific requirements for conducting the search and/or seizure. According to Rule 41 only magistrate judges may issue a warrant upon "the request of a federal law enforcement officer or an attorney for the government."[152] The warrant may only be issued for the purpose of the seizure of evidence or contraband, for the search of "property designed for use, or intended for use, or used in committing a crime" or for the purpose of arrest or to obtain access to property where a person is unlawfully restrained.[153] The procedure to be followed from the issuance until the execution of a search warrant is, furthermore, specified in Rule 41.

##### 5.2.2.1.2 The Search Powers of Surveillance and the Use of Undercover Agents and Informants

As has been explained, in 1961 the Supreme Court decided in *Silverman v. United States* (affirmed six years later, even more emphatically, in *Katz v. United States*), for the first time, that the electronic seizure of conversations without a trespass affects the constitutional protections of the Fourth Amendment. The electronic interception of conversations constitutes a seizure within the meaning of the Fourth Amendment.[154] With *Katz*, surveillance became a form of search and seizure governed by the protections of the Fourth Amendment, broadening the Fourth Amendment doctrine beyond that of only physical intrusion.[155]

Surveillance includes investigative techniques that intercept any "wire, electronic or oral communication through the use of any electronic, mechanical or other device."[156] Police use tools such as electronic surveillance, pen registers, trap and trace devices, consensual monitoring, physical searches, human surveillance and informants to intercept communications.[157] The character of surveillance activities can generally be considered as more powerful than physical

---

[151] LaFave et al. 2004, 250 and Israel et al. 2006, 260.

[152] Rule 41 (b), Federal Rules of Criminal Procedure (2009).

[153] Rule 41 (c), Federal Rules of Criminal Procedure (2009).

[154] LaFave et al. 2004, 264.

[155] *Katz v. United States*, 389 U.S. 347, 88 S.Ct. 507 (1967), 357-359. Before this, the so-called *Olmstead* trespass doctrine applied until 1967, prescribing that Fourth Amendment limitations are only effective when there is a governmental exercise of power concerning a physical invasion, particularly with respect to private homes. Baker 2007A, 246.

[156] Title 18 Crimes and Criminal Procedure, 18 U.S.C. § 2510(4).

[157] Baker 2007A, 75.

searches, as a warrant can legitimize a search for up to 30 days with possible extensions upon a single showing of probable cause.[158] Moreover, surveillance occurs beyond the knowledge of the person in question. Surveillance is primarily regulated by the so-called 'Title III' of The United States Code on Crime and Criminal Procedure (Title 18),[159] which was enacted shortly after the Supreme Court's judgment of *Katz* and its decision in *Berger v. New York* (1967),[160] holding a state's eavesdropping statute to be in violation of the Fourth Amendment. Title III prohibits the interception, disclosure and the use of wire, oral or electronic conversations as evidence, except in situations specifically provided for in Title III.[161] Title III can be considered as the recognition by Congress that surveillance is an important technique which is necessary for confronting especially organized crime. Surveillance techniques are necessary to "develop adequate strategic intelligence concerning organized crime, to set up specific investigations, to develop witnesses to corroborate their testimony, and to serve as substitutes for them—each a necessary step in the evidence gathering process in organized crime investigations and prosecutions."[162]

The Attorney General, the Deputy Attorney General, the Associate Attorney General, or any (acting) Assistant Attorney General or (acting) Deputy Assistant Attorney General, as well as a state or county prosecutor if authorized by state law, may request that a federal judge authorizes the interception of wire or oral communications by the FBI or other federal agency having responsibility for the investigation.[163] The interception of oral and wire communications is limited to the investigation of crimes enumerated in § 2516(1). These federal crimes typically have a serious nature. The interception of electronic communications—which, as a consequence of technological developments, is a possibility that was added to Title III in 1986 (§ 2516(3))—is permitted for investigations of "any federal felony." The interception of electronic communications has thus been accepted for a wider category of crimes than the interception of other types of communications.

The federal judge may only issue an order (in accordance with § 2518) for surveillance if he determines that there is probable cause to believe that the individual is committing, has committed, or is about to commit a specific enumerated offense. Surveillance is thus, just like search and seizure, only permitted upon a warrant and the establishment of probable cause, because of the Fourth

---

[158] 18 U.S.C. § 2518(5).

[159] Title III, as a part of the 'Omnibus Crime Control and Safe Streets Act of 1968', adopted in 18 U.S.C. Part I, Chapter 119, §§ 2510-2522 and, added in 1986, §§ 2701-2710.

[160] *Berger v. New York*, 388 U.S. 41, 87 S.Ct. 1873 (1967).

[161] 18 U.S.C. § 2511-§ 2515.

[162] According to the 'Crime Commission' appointed by President Johnson (Report by the President's Commission on Law Enforcement and Administration of Justice, the Challenge of Crime in a Free Society 201 (1967)). Cited in: *United Sates v. United States District Court for the Eastern District of Michigan,* 407 U.S. 297, 92 S.Ct. 2125 (1972), 311 (ftnt. 9).

[163] 18 U.S.C. § 2516(1).

Amendment protection of an individual's reasonable expectation of privacy in most non-public settings. Moreover, for surveillance a showing of probable cause is required with regard to the belief that communications will be intercepted that are connected to the offense under investigation and probable cause that the communications can be intercepted from a particular place or facility. To the latter an exception has been created for 'roving taps' (18 U.S.C. § 2518(11)). A specification of the facility or place from which the communications shall be intercepted is not required, if such specification is not practical. Through a roving tap it is possible to intercept a suspect's communication, regardless of the communication device he is using. Through the 'roving bug' it is even possible to eavesdrop on conversations when no communication device is used at all. The 'roving bug' concerns a technique that makes it possible to switch on the microphone of a mobile phone also when the phone is not used or even switched off. The police can then also intercept the conversations of a suspect when that suspect is aware of the possibility of being eavesdropped by the police and meets instead with other people in person.[164]

The specific regulation of surveillance techniques as provided by Title III will be dealt with in Sect. 5.3.2.2. That section will elaborate on the application procedure, the procedure for the approval of an order for surveillance and will deal with the restraints imposed on the execution of a surveillance order, as the statutory requirements are intended to offer protection against unfettered use of these intrusive covert surveillance techniques. This section will continue to describe the scope of surveillance techniques by dealing with the exceptions to the regular restraints following from the statutory scheme of Title III in order to determine the scope and nature of the sword power of surveillance in conventional criminal law.

Similar to searches, consent for the interception of communications substitutes the requirements of Title III. A court order for the interception is no longer needed when one of the parties to the conversation gives permission for interception. This exception is also included within Title III for persons "acting under the color of law" and any other person, if one of the parties to the communication "has given prior consent to such interception."[165] Because surveillance typically occurs secretly and before the persons whose communications are intercepted are aware of the fact that they are part of a criminal investigation, consent for the interception is unlikely. Involving an undercover agent or informant, however, does offer the police the possibility to intercept communications without observing the regular conditions of Title III. Any information intercepted by undercover agents or informants is obtained with the consent of one of the parties—the consent of the

---

[164] See e.g. *United States v. Tomero*, 462 F.Supp.2d 565 (S.D.N.Y. 2006), where the roving bug was installed on an attorney's phone during an organized crime investigation where the suspects chose to communicate via their attorney so as to avoid interception through government surveillance. The Court held that the roving bug did not violate the Fourth Amendment's particularity requirement and that a roving bug could be authorized through electronic surveillance warrants for roving surveillance.

[165] 18 U.S.C. § 2511(2)(c) and § 2511(2)(d).

undercover agent or informant—to a conversation or has been observed by the undercover agent or informant in circumstances where someone did not intend to keep his activities shielded from that agent or other person (consensual monitoring). The undercover agent can carry a tape recorder or radio transmitter or the police can wire-tap his/her phone conversations.

The Supreme Court assessed in *United States v. White* (1971) whether the interception of conversations by an undercover agent—a communication in a restaurant between the defendant and the undercover agent with a concealed radio transmitter—constituted a search. The Court held in White that its consideration in *Hoffa v. United States* (1966)[166] "was left undisturbed by Katz," namely that "however strongly a defendant may trust an apparent colleague, his expectations in this respect are not protected by the Fourth Amendment when it turns out that the colleague is a government agent regularly communicating with the authorities." The Court continued by stating that "[i]f the law gives no protection to the wrongdoer whose trusted accomplice is or becomes a police agent, neither should it protect him when that same agent has recorded or transmitted the conversations which are later offered in evidence to prove the State's case."[167] The rationale of these decisions of the Supreme Court is that a criminal who decides to share his criminal activities with someone else accepts the risk that this person is a government agent or that this person will share this information with the police. Hence, there is no constitutional barrier to the interception of communications by one of the participants to that conversation and thus to the use of undercover agents and informants in general.[168]

The use of undercover agents is therefore an investigative technique whose application is not restricted by the Fourth Amendment protections. Observations and interceptions of communications by undercover agents concern situations in which the persons under investigation cannot have a reasonable expectation of privacy. A general limitation to the unlimited use of the method of investigation concerns the defense of entrapment, which the person investigated, once charged, may raise. The defendant can use entrapment as a defense when the police have induced him or her to commit a crime as a result of the investigative techniques applied, in general with respect to informants or undercover agents. The defense attorney can raise the entrapment defense against investigations by a law enforcement officer if the officer induced the defendant to commit a criminal offence, by knowingly stating that the behavior is not criminal or by inducing the defendant to do something that he would otherwise have refrained from doing.[169] Entrapment must be distinguished from encouragement: the latter is still a lawful investigative technique, unless the undercover agent is responsible for making the unwary innocent (rather than the unwary criminal) commit the crime or if the

---

166 *Hoffa v. United States,* 385 U.S. 293, 87 S.Ct. 408 (1966).

167 *United States v. White*, 401 U.S. 745, 91 S.Ct. 1122 (1971), 749 and 752.

168 LaFave et al. 2004, 272.

169 Mauriello 2007, 18.08.

undercover agent has gone too far with his tactics in inducing the crime, in which case, the defendant can, justifiably, raise the defense of entrapment.[170]

#### 5.2.2.2 The Possibilities for Proactive Criminal Investigations

Although probable cause for a committed crime or a crime being committed is in principle required for a search, this does not necessarily mean that investigative techniques cannot be applied proactively, without evidence of a concrete crime. Investigative techniques such as observation in a public setting and the use of undercover agents—activities that do not infringe upon a reasonable expectation of privacy and for which, consequently, probable cause is not required—are often broadly used in the proactive context.

The power to conduct searches that fall under the scope of the Fourth Amendment is restricted to the presence of probable cause that criminal activity is taking place. Hence, in principle, places cannot be searched when a crime has not yet been committed or is not being committed. This does not mean that Fourth Amendment searches may not be used for proactive purposes, considering that searches on the basis of probable cause regarding, for example, possession of contraband, may lead to the discovery of other (future) criminality, such as drug trafficking. In addition, the probable cause standard that must be met for the authorization of an order under Title III is formulated more broadly and also permits proactive use. The standard under Title III can be met by evidence showing probable cause that a crime is about to be committed, which standard seems to give somewhat more leeway as compared to the definition given for the conventional Fourth Amendment probable cause requirement: "the facts and circumstances within [the officers'] knowledge and of which they had reasonably trustworthy information sufficient in themselves to warrant a man of reasonable caution in the belief that an offense has been or is being committed."[171] In addition, it follows from the legislative history of Title III that one of the reasons for its creation was to combat organized crime more effectively by using electronic eavesdropping for the purpose of strengthening the information position regarding organized crime, which implies a proactive approach.[172]

Furthermore, the crime of conspiracy does provide an important and rather broad possibility for the police to investigate proactively in the context of conventional criminal law, as a consequence of the development of a wide interpretation of the crime of conspiracy in the US criminal justice system. Probable cause with regard to the crime of conspiracy can lead to an extensive application of searches in the proactive field. The concept of conspiracy is somewhat vague. It is a common law

---

170 Israel et al. 2006, 276-277.

171 *Brinegar v. United States,* 338 U.S. 160, 69 S.Ct. 1302 (1949), 175-176.

172 For the acceptability of the broader application of physical search and electronic surveillance, also proactively, especially to confront organized crime, see: Marcus 1998.

concept established in statutes initially in medieval England by Edward I. *Poulter's case* in 1611, interpreting the concept, established a doctrine that is still valid today, providing that "the gist of conspiracy is the agreement, and so the agreement is punishable even if its purpose was not achieved."[173] Over the years, the concept of conspiracy has broadened, leading to the definition of conspiracy as "a combination between two or more persons formed for the purpose of doing either an unlawful act or a lawful act by unlawful means." The crime of conspiracy thus requires both an act (the agreement) and a mental state (the intention to achieve the objective).[174] Additionally, an 'overt act' in furtherance of the conspiracy is often statutorily required, as is formulated in the federal general conspiracy statute. Only an overt act by one of the conspirators is required, which does not need to be criminal or unlawful itself.[175] Furthermore, the supplier of goods and services may be found guilty of conspiracy, provided that he has the requisite criminal intent and not just knowledge of the criminal objective. Criminal intent must be proven in common law to fulfill the requisite *mens rea* with regard to the *actus reus* (the guilty act) in order to establish criminal liability. Mere knowledge of the criminal objective does not establish sufficient *mens rea.*[176] The boundary of sufficiency between intent and knowledge shifts according to the seriousness of the criminal objective.[177] Probable cause for conspiracy to commit a crime can result in a warrant to search a home or other private asset or in an order for Title III surveillance. Moreover, Title III provides for an exception to the warrant requirement in the case of "conspiratorial activities threatening the national security" and in the case of "conspiratorial activities characteristic of organized crime."[178] Considering these options, a proactive enforcement system has been created, especially to confront organized crime or crime constituting a threat to national security.

#### 5.2.2.3 The Powers Available in National Security Investigations in Relation to Criminal Justice

As has been explained in the section dealing with the organization of the intelligence community, primarily the FBI is responsible for conducting national security investigations on the federal level. This section will explain the background of the enactment of FISA in order to regulate national security investigative authority and will describe what powers FISA grants to (primarily) the FBI to conduct national security investigations. As will be explained in Sect. 5.2.2.3.1, the scope of these investigations may be significantly broader than criminal investigations

---

173 LaFave 2003, 465.

174 *Ibid.*, 466.

175 *Ibid.*, 475.

176 Luban et al. 2010, 863.

177 LaFave 2003, 481.

178 18 U.S.C. § 2518(7). See in more detail Sect. 5.3.2.1.2.

where surveillance techniques must be applied under the limitations of Title III. Nevertheless, national security investigations often also focus on criminal behavior and the information gathered in national security investigations may be used in a criminal trial. The transfer of this information to the law enforcement community will be the subject of Sect. 5.2.2.3.2.

#### 5.2.2.3.1 The National Security Investigation: FISA

The 'enabling acts', which grant the FBI the power to conduct national security investigations, are the National Security Act of 1947 and Executive Order 12333 (see Sect. 5.2.1.4). In the context of national security investigations, the FBI may conduct electronic surveillance. Title III, regulating surveillance in the criminal investigative context, explicitly provides that its prohibition on the interception of conversations does not "affect the acquisition by the United States Government of foreign intelligence information from international or foreign communications, or foreign intelligence activities conducted in accordance with otherwise applicable Federal law."[179] Until the enactment of FISA the executive branch faced no legislative restraint on conducting electronic surveillance activities in furtherance of national security.[180]

Before FISA was enacted in 1978, in the case of *United States v. United States District Court for the Eastern District of Michigan* (1972)[181] (henceforth referred to as the '*Keith*' decision) the Supreme Court dealt with the scope of the constitutional power of the President to conduct intelligence surveillance for national security interests. The Supreme Court held in this case that the Fourth Amendment was also applicable to the government's domestic electronic surveillance activities to investigate domestic threats to national security. The Court concluded that prior judicial approval was needed when the government intends to conduct electronic surveillance for domestic security purposes.

---

[179] 18 U.S.C. § 2511(2)(f).

[180] When Title III was enacted in 1968 § 2511(3) provided that nothing in Title III "shall limit the constitutional power of the President to take such measure as he deems necessary to protect the Nation against actual or potential attacks or other hostile acts of a foreign power, to obtain foreign intelligence information deemed essential to the security of the US, or to protect national security information against foreign intelligence activities. Nor shall anything contained be deemed to limit the constitutional power of the President to take such measures as he deems necessary to protect the United States against the overthrow of the Government by force or other unlawful means, or against any other clear and present danger to the structure and existence of the Government." Moreover, it was explicitly provided that any contents intercepted by means of the executive's just mentioned powers "may be received in evidence in any trial, hearing, or other proceeding only where such interception was reasonable (..)."

[181] *United Sates v. United States District Court for the Eastern District of Michigan,* 407 U.S. 297, 92 S.Ct. 2125 (1972). This decision is usually referred to as the '*Keith*' decision, after the U.S. District Court Judge Damon J. Keith who had ruled against warrantless domestic electronic surveillance, a decision later upheld by the Supreme Court.

The Court explicitly included that its decision in *Keith* did not address the Executive's activities against foreign powers or their agents.[182] The Court applied the usual Fourth Amendment test of reasonableness to the surveillance activities conducted for the purpose of protecting national security.[183] The surveillance practices were thus primarily assessed from the regular law enforcement perspective. This resulted in the Court's conclusion that "Fourth Amendment freedoms cannot properly be guaranteed if domestic security surveillance may be conducted solely within the discretion of the Executive Branch." Executive officers cannot be qualified as "neutral and disinterested magistrates" as "[t]heir duty and responsibility are to enforce the laws, to investigate, and to prosecute."[184] The warrant requirement of the Fourth Amendment also applies to electronic surveillance for domestic security purposes. Despite the recognition of the President's constitutional power in domestic security, surveillance for that purpose must be exercised in a way that is compatible with the Fourth Amendment. An appropriate balance is desirable, also in domestic security matters.[185] However, this balance involves a different assessment than in ordinary criminal surveillance cases. Considering that "domestic security surveillances may involve different policy and practical considerations from the surveillance of 'ordinary crime,'"[186] the contents of the probable cause showing required under the Fourth Amendment may be different than required under Title III.

Furthermore, a history of abuses of the national security investigative power preceded the enactment of FISA. The potential for abuse was to an important extent the result of the vagueness of the regulation of surveillance for domestic security purposes. Since World War II, the intelligence community has repeatedly conducted domestic investigations in a manner which violates the constitutional rights of citizens. This problem was also endorsed by Congress, which, after the resignation of President Nixon in 1974, realized that it was not aware of what the Government's intelligence agencies were doing. For this reason, the House of Representatives and the Senate, the two houses of Congress, established special investigative committees. The most important of these was the Church Committee. Their conclusions included the establishment of congressional oversight committees over the intelligence agencies. On behalf of the Senate, the Select Committee on Intelligence was established in 1976, followed, in 1977, by the Permanent Select Committee on Intelligence on behalf of the House of Representatives.[187] The Church Committee also found that national security surveillance

---

182 *Ibid.*, 321-322.

183 *Ibid.*, 309.

184 *Ibid.*, 316-317.

185 *Ibid.*, 317, 320.

186 *United States v. United States District Court*, 407 U.S. 297, 92 S.Ct. 2125 (1972), 322.

187 Snider 2003, 1-4. Snider concludes 25 years after the establishment of the oversight committees that their work has been successful because it has been intensive and intrusive, whereas it does not obstruct security activities. The Committees have provided for a check on otherwise unchecked activities that affect civil liberties. *Ibid.*, 33. See also: Kris and Wilson 2007, 2-3 to 2-13.

without a warrant had been used to spy on several people not engaged in any criminal activity.[188]

Moreover, the Church Committee advised the creation of a legal framework for the intelligence agencies that conduct domestic national security investigations. The Attorney General should be the person responsible for overseeing compliance by the intelligence agencies with this legal framework.[189] Executive order 12333 (1978) was the most important piece of regulation created by the Executive that is still in force. Executive order 12333 is intended to "provide for the effective conduct of United States intelligence activities and the protection of constitutional rights" for the purpose of using "all reasonable and lawful means (...) to ensure that the United States will receive the best intelligence possible."[190] The tasks of the different agencies have been defined within this order. This has resulted in the CIA being prohibited from conducting electronic surveillance activities within the US and only the FBI—save in exceptional circumstances—may engage in physical searches or physical surveillance within the US.[191] Conducting intelligence activities has been regulated by aiming to "achieve the proper balance between the acquisition of essential information and protection of individual interests." The intelligence agencies are only permitted to "collect, retain or disseminate information concerning United States persons" if done "in accordance with the procedures established by the head of the agency concerned and approved by the Attorney General."[192]

As an answer to this history of abusing the national security investigative power as well as to the decision of the Supreme Court that the Fourth Amendment applies to domestic security surveillance, the Foreign Intelligence Surveillance Act of 1978 (FISA) was adopted. FISA built on the Supreme Court's decision in *Keith* by providing a statutory scheme that included judicial authorization for electronic surveillance for the purpose of gathering foreign intelligence information. FISA provided that a court should be created by the Chief Justice "which shall have jurisdiction to hear applications for and grant orders approving electronic surveillance anywhere within the United States under the procedures set forth in this chapter."[193]

The precise regulation as provided by FISA will be dealt with in detail in Sect. 5.3.2.4. This section will continue to elaborate on the scope of national security investigations under the law currently in force. For the purpose of this section, it is sufficient to state that the regulation under FISA provides a wider power to conduct investigative activities and, regardless of the restriction to the

---

188 Howell 2006, 119.

189 Kris and Wilson 2007, 2-14/15.

190 Executive Order 12333 (as amended), preamble.

191 Executive Order 12333 (as amended) § 2.4(a), (b) and (c).

192 Executive Order 12333 (as amended) § 2.3.

193 50 U.S.C. § 1803(a)(1).

gathering of foreign intelligence information, the electronic surveillance activities under FISA may occur within the US and may concern US persons, as long as their activities are not protected by the First Amendment. Warrantless FISA surveillance is only permitted when no US person is involved. The objective of adopting FISA was, primarily, to achieve intelligence goals concerning international terrorist organizations, with targets abroad and possibly fund-raising and other activities within the United States. Foreign intelligence was aimed at including criminal as well as non-criminal activities of agents of foreign powers. With respect to criminal activities, before 9/11 the foreign intelligence information included mainly espionage and not terrorism.[194]

Normally, searches, seizures and surveillance are significantly limited by Fourth Amendment requirements, most importantly by being restricted to a showing of probable cause that a crime is being or will be committed. The reach of national security investigations is broader, as these investigations aim to gather domestic intelligence in order to prevent unlawful activity and in order to enhance knowledge regarding potential security threats.[195] Hence, for national security investigations a statutory scheme with less stringent standards compared to those applicable to Title III was considered justified (taking into account the opinion of the Supreme Court in *Keith*) and necessary for an effective national security policy. Therefore, FISA simplifies the procedures for granting search and surveillance authority when the investigation deals with foreign intelligence information and the suspect is an agent of a foreign power, which includes those affiliated to international terrorism.[196]

Contrary to surveillance, as well as searches, under conventional criminal law (save for some exceptions created in case law) an order of the FISA Court can authorize surveillance as well as physical searches without notice or with delayed notice to the targets and for an extended period of time. FISA has been determined not to violate the Fourth Amendment, because the statutory safeguards of FISA are considered to provide sufficient protection for the rights guaranteed in the Fourth Amendment when the surveillance concerns intelligence activities. In agreement with the *Keith* decision, the rights protected by the Fourth Amendment are considered to be guaranteed by the realization of prior judicial approval in FISA, which no longer leaves foreign intelligence surveillance solely to the discretion of the executive. In addition, domestic security surveillance and the surveillance of foreign powers and agents of foreign powers have been distinguished from the surveillance of ordinary criminal activities, warranting a different assessment under the Fourth Amendment, i.e. as to the standard of probable cause. The decision of the federal court with regard to the constitutionality of FISA has been based, corresponding with the rationale of *Keith,* upon a balancing of the

[194] Musch 2003, 72.

[195] Compare: *United States v. United States District Court*, 407 U.S. 297, 92 S.Ct. 2125 (1972), 322.

[196] Etzioni 2004, 28.

governmental interest in gathering foreign intelligence for national security against the infringements of individual rights and the result is a (substantially) different assessment than in ordinary criminal investigations.[197]

The power of the FBI to conduct national security investigations is granted by the National Security Act of 1947 and Executive Order 12333 and should be exercised in accordance with the legal framework of FISA. Hence, the scope of a national security investigation largely depends on the interpretation of foreign intelligence information. FISA defines foreign intelligence information as "information that relates to, and if concerning a United States person is necessary to, the ability of the United States to protect against (A) actual or potential attack or other grave hostile acts (..); (B) sabotage or international terrorism (..); (C) clandestine intelligence activities," all on behalf of either a foreign power or an agent of a foreign power.[198] The definition of a foreign power and an agent of a foreign power is, in the second place, important for the scope of national security investigations.[199] The term foreign power also covers "groups engaged in international terrorism or activities in preparation therefor" and "a foreign-based

[197] *United States v. Pelton*, 835 F.2d 1067 (4th Cir. 1987), 1075.

[198] 50 U.S.C. § 1801(e) (2011).

[199] See 50 U.S.C. § 1801(a) and (b) (2011) for the definitions of a foreign power and an agent of a foreign power: "(a) "Foreign power" means—(1) a foreign government or any component thereof, whether or not recognized by the United States; (2) a faction of a foreign nation or nations, not substantially composed of United States persons; (3) an entity that is openly acknowledged by a foreign government or governments to be directed and controlled by such foreign government or governments; (4) a group engaged in international terrorism or activities in preparation therefor; (5) a foreign-based political organization, not substantially composed of United States persons; or (6) an entity that is directed and controlled by a foreign government or governments. (b) "Agent of a foreign power" means—(1) any person other than a United States person, who—(A) acts in the United States as an officer or employee of a foreign power, or as a member of a foreign power as defined in subsection (a)(4) of this section; (B) acts for or on behalf of a foreign power which engages in clandestine intelligence activities in the United States contrary to the interests of the United States, when the circumstances of such person's presence in the United States indicate that such person may engage in such activities in the United States, or when such person knowingly aids or abets any person in the conduct of such activities or knowingly conspires with any person to engage in such activities; (C) engages in international terrorism or activities in preparation therefore [sic] [the definition under C was added by the Intelligence Reform and Terrorism Prevention Act, Pubic Law 108-458-Dec. 17, 2004, sec. 6001(a)]; or (2) any person who—(A) knowingly engages in clandestine intelligence gathering activities for or on behalf of a foreign power, which activities involve or may involve a violation of the criminal statutes of the United States; (B) pursuant to the direction of an intelligence service or network of a foreign power, knowingly engages in any other clandestine intelligence activities for or on behalf of such foreign power, which activities involve or are about to involve a violation of the criminal statutes of the United States; (C) knowingly engages in sabotage or international terrorism, or activities that are in preparation therefor, for or on behalf of a foreign power; (D) knowingly enters the United States under a false or fraudulent identity for or on behalf of a foreign power or, while in the United States, knowingly assumes a false or fraudulent identity for or on behalf of a foreign power; or (E) knowingly aids or abets any person in the conduct of activities described in subparagraph (A), (B), or (C) or knowingly conspires with any person to engage in activities described in subparagraph (A), (B), or (C)."

political organization, not substantially composed of United States persons."[200] Agents of foreign powers may either concern non-US persons or "any person".[201] Their activities typically concern "clandestine intelligence activities" and "sabotage or international terrorism." The requirements for meeting the definition of an 'agent of a foreign power', when this agent is a US person—either a US citizen or a permanent resident—are, however, somewhat more stringent by requiring that the "activities for or on behalf of a foreign power" or "pursuant to the direction of an intelligence service or network of a foreign power" involve or may involve a violation of the criminal statutes of the United States.[202] Thus, although the term 'foreign' may imply otherwise, FISA orders authorize national security investigations within the US and may also involve US citizens.

FISA originally only covered electronic surveillance and not physical searches, although a physical entry could be used to effectuate the surveillance.[203] However, physical searches in national security cases have occurred through Presidential authorization under the President's national security power.[204] Moreover, by an Act of October 1994, physical searches (any physical intrusion within the United States into premises or property) for foreign intelligence purposes are permitted upon a court order of the FISA Court. An order can be issued after authorization from the President, certification that the purpose of the search is to obtain foreign intelligence information and the FISA Court finds that probable cause exists to believe that the target of the physical search is a foreign power or an agent of a foreign power.[205]

The use of pen registers and trap and trace devices is, like in conventional criminal law, subject to less stringent requirements. A FISA judge can issue an *ex parte* order for pen registers and trap and trace devices upon approval from the Attorney General or from a designated attorney for the Government and "a certification by the applicant that the information likely to be obtained is relevant to an ongoing foreign intelligence or international terrorism investigation being conducted by the Federal Bureau of Investigation under guidelines approved by the Attorney General" is sufficient. In addition, the application shall include information demonstrating a standard of reason to believe that the telephone line or other instrument or device to which the pen register or trap and trace device is attached has been or is about to be used by an individual "who is engaging or has engaged in international terrorism or clandestine intelligence activities that involve or may involve a violation of the criminal laws of the United States" or by "a foreign power or agent of a foreign power under circumstances giving reason to

[200] 50 U.S.C. § 1801(a)(4) and (5).

[201] 50 U.S.C. § 1801(b).

[202] 50 U.S.C. § 1801(b)(2)(A)(B).

[203] 50 U.S.C. § 1804(a)(8) and § 1805(c)(1)(D).

[204] Baker 2007A, 84.

[205] The part on physical searches has the same structure concerning its conditions as the part on electronic surveillance. 50 U.S.C. § 1821-§ 1829.

believe that the communication concerns or concerned international terrorism or clandestine intelligence activities that involve or may involve a violation of the criminal laws of the United States."[206]

#### 5.2.2.3.2 The Transfer of Information Gathered During a National Security Investigation to the Law Enforcement Community

The authority to share information collected by an intelligence agency with the law enforcement agencies or cooperation between the two communities is not explicitly prohibited, which follows from both the National Security Act of 1947 (implicitly referring to such sharing in Sec. 105B(b)) and from Executive Order 12333, providing that "[n]othing in this Order shall be construed to apply or to interfere with any authorized civil or criminal law enforcement responsibility of any department or agency."[207] Furthermore, Executive Order 12333 permits intelligence agencies to "participate in law enforcement activities to investigate or prevent clandestine intelligence activities by foreign powers, or international terrorist or narcotics activities."[208] Under the National Security Act of 1947 law enforcement agencies may even request an intelligence agency to "collect information outside the United States about individuals who are not United States persons." This information may be collected "notwithstanding that the law enforcement agency intends to use the information collected for purposes of a law enforcement investigation or counterintelligence investigation."[209]

Regardless of the absence of explicit legal barriers, information sharing between the intelligence agencies and law enforcement agencies was before the enactment of the USA PATRIOT Act very limited or did not occur at all. This was importantly due to the 'purpose language' of FISA. The interpretation given to the 'purpose language' used in FISA has over the years created a 'wall' of separation between law enforcement agencies and intelligence agencies. FISA permits, according to several of its provisions, electronic surveillance and physical searches in the presence of a "purpose" to gather "foreign intelligence information."[210] Each FISA application must include a statement concerning the purpose of the search or surveillance. Before the enactment of the USA PATRIOT Act, this requirement was interpreted as requiring that the primary purpose of the investigation must have been to obtain foreign intelligence information.[211] As a

[206] 50 U.S.C. § 1842(c), before amendment by the USA PATRIOT Act.

[207] Executive Order 12333 (as amended), § 2.2.

[208] Executive Order 12333 (as amended), § 2.6.

[209] National Security Act of 1947 (as amended), Section 105A(a).

[210] See e.g. 50 U.S.C. §§ 1802(b) and 1804(7)(B).

[211] 50 U.S.C. § 1804(a)(7)(B): FISA Court approves application of electronic surveillance "[...] of a foreign power or an agent of a foreign power for the purpose of obtaining foreign intelligence information [...]."

consequence, if information was gathered about a person that should lead to criminal prosecution, the primary purpose of the national security investigation was not to gather foreign intelligence information. This interpretation resulted in a "wall" between law enforcement investigations and national security investigations and between the law enforcement community and the intelligence community in general.[212]

Furthermore, the decision of the Fourth Circuit Court in *United States v. Truong* (1980),[213] assessing surveillance activities that occurred also prior to the enactment of FISA, clearly separated investigative activities for national security purposes from investigative activities for law enforcement purposes. *Truong* built on the *Keith* decision in order to further define the scope of national security investigations. In this decision the Fourth Circuit Court made a distinction between investigation for the purpose of gathering foreign intelligence information and investigation for the purpose of gathering evidence for criminal prosecution. The court acknowledged that the Fourth Amendment does not necessarily apply to the executive power's activities against foreign powers or agents of foreign powers and, on that basis, upheld the warrantless surveillance during the first part of the investigation where the *primary* purpose of the investigation was to gather foreign intelligence information.[214] However, this 'foreign intelligence exception' to the Fourth Amendment shall be carefully limited to the situation where the object of the search is "a foreign power, its agent or collaborators." In addition, the exception is limited to the situation where "the surveillance is conducted "primarily" for foreign intelligence reasons." "[O]nce the surveillance becomes primarily a criminal investigation, the courts are entirely competent to make the usual probable cause determination (…)."[215] For that reason, the Fourth Circuit Court excluded all evidence obtained through the surveillance since the investigation's purpose had changed from a primary foreign intelligence purpose to a primary criminal investigative purpose.[216] Hence, by applying the Supreme Court's decision in *Keith* to the case of *Truong,* the Fourth Circuit Court further specified that the level of protection offered by the Fourth Amendment depends on the primary purpose of the investigation and, consequently, the court clearly separated the criminal investigation from the foreign intelligence investigation. This distinction made by the Fourth Circuit Court—decided after the enactment of FISA, but assessing an investigation occurring prior to its enactment—can also be recognized in the 'purpose language' of FISA.

---

212 Kris and Wilson 2007, 10-6 to 10-8.

213 *United States v. Truong Ding Hung*, 629. F.2d 908 (4th Cir. 1980).

214 The court reached this conclusion by referring to the *Keith* decision in order to analogously apply the analytical approach of the Supreme Court in *Keith. United States v. Truong Ding Hung*, 629. F.2d 908 (4th Cir. 1980), 913-914.

215 *United States v. Truong Ding Hung*, 629. F.2d 908 (4th Cir. 1980), at 915.

216 *Ibid.*, 916.

Since the 1980s, guidelines have also been distributed that further limit the use of foreign intelligence surveillance for law enforcement purposes. The Attorney General issued two sets of guidelines: one applicable to the FBI's task in law enforcement ('The Attorney General's Guidelines on General Crimes, Racketeering Enterprise and Domestic Security/Terrorism Investigations'); and the second one applicable to the domestic intelligence activities of the FBI ('The Attorney General's Guidelines for FBI Foreign Intelligence Collection and Foreign Counterintelligence Investigation').[217] The Guidelines governing the FBI's national security investigation concern still largely classified documents and it is therefore not necessary to deal with them in detail.[218]

Since 1995 the Department of Justice, seeking a more effective use of all its FBI resources, has again tried to demolish this wall by distributing guidelines prescribing that information obtained under FISA could be shared with law enforcement officers when such information shows that a crime "has been, is being, or will be committed." This determination had to be made solely by intelligence officials.[219] FISA investigators were permitted to disclose FISA information to prosecutors, but not the other way round. Likewise, the decision in *United States v. Rahman* (1994, affirmed by the Second Circuit in 1999) shows that the court does not need to exclude evidence gathered in conformity with FISA, when the principal purpose of that surveillance was to gather evidence in a criminal case if the person is suspected of conspiracy to conduct war or urban terrorism against the United States. The court concluded that FISA was enacted in anticipation that information, specifically foreign intelligence information, gathered from those defined as agents of a foreign power violating criminal laws, would be used in criminal cases. As long as the executive branch official has certified that the purpose was to gather foreign intelligence information and when, on the basis of the facts provided in the application, it appears that this certification is not clearly erroneous, the FISA Court shall authorize the surveillance and a reviewing court should not "second-guess" this decision.[220]

However, the 'wall' nevertheless resulted in a cultural separation between law enforcement agencies and intelligence agencies, further thwarting cooperation between the two. On the other hand, the creation of this wall did not occur without reason. The intelligence community and the law enforcement (as well as the military) community were established as two institutionally separated areas to respond to threats and violence. Each response comprises a different governmental

---

217 Becker 2003, 597.

218 The Attorney General's Guidelines on criminal investigation that were applicable prior to the issuance of the Ashcroft Guidelines in 2002 will be analyzed in the 'shield' section of this chapter as their main goal was to restrain the FBI's investigative authority by formulating thresholds and protective conditions.

219 U.S. Department of Justice, Office of Legislative Affairs, Office of the Assistant Attorney General, May 13, 2003, 15.

220 *United States v. Rahman*, 861 F.Supp 247 (S.D.N.Y. 1994), affirmed 189 f.3d 88 (2nd Cir. 1999), 251.

reaction to threats and violence. Intelligence is focused on prevention, whereas law enforcement traditionally seeks information about past wrongdoing for the purpose of prosecution and punishment in order to deter future wrongdoing. Each institutional response has been designed in order to effectively fulfill its goal, being subjected to its own restraints and controls, which have been developed over extended periods of time importantly as a consequence of Constitutional interpretation.[221] Hence, law enforcement agencies gather information for the purpose of criminal prosecution within the boundaries set by the courts in interpreting the Fourth Amendment, whereas the intelligence agencies gather information to protect the national security without the need to adhere to the boundaries set for evidence-gathering. This distinction is based on institutional choices as well as on the regulation of governmental power through the Constitution.[222] The wall resulting from this distinction was aimed at preventing FISA warrants from being applied for conventional criminal matters, which are normally protected by more stringent Fourth Amendment protections.[223]

### *5.2.3 Conclusion*

It can be concluded that the FBI is the most relevant actor which is responsible for both the criminal investigation of federal felonies and for national security investigations. Most investigative activities will be conducted by the FBI or by its subdivisions in the federal districts. However, to apply special investigative techniques in conventional criminal investigations, prosecutors or officials of the Department of Justice must a priori apply for a warrant before a magistrate judge.

Fourth Amendment law governs the use of special investigative techniques. Therefore, it has been necessary for describing the powers available during the investigative phase to analyze the concept of search as covered by the Fourth Amendment. Applying the two-prong reasonable expectation of privacy test has resulted in different categories of circumstances in which the use of special investigative techniques find a different level of restraint by the Fourth Amendment and in different categories of techniques finding more or less restrictions due to Fourth Amendment interpretation. The most important consequence of this test has been the extension of Fourth Amendment protections to surveillance. Furthermore, the areas in which people exhibit most Fourth Amendment protections are particularly homes and other non-public premises. Search powers invading a person's privacy with regard to these areas therefore face the most restrictions. Searching vehicles or personal assets such as luggage is subject to somewhat

---

221 McCormack 2007, 35-38.

222 White 2004, 19.

223 The enactment of the USA PATRIOT Act of 2001 as well as other measures of the post-9/11 era have now dismantled this wall. See on this in detail Chap. 6, Sect. 6.4.

loosened Fourth Amendment restrictions. Furthermore, those techniques that do not interfere with privacy expectations that society is prepared to recognize as reasonable do not face any Fourth Amendment restrictions. This has paved the way for the police to make free use of undercover agents and informants as the consent of one of the parties to a conversation deprives the other party of his or her reasonable expectation of privacy. The invasive character of a specific technique has also been a reason to loosen or strengthen the restrictions which are applicable to the use of that technique. Pen registers and trap and trace devices can be used without a showing of probable cause. The use of invasive electronic eavesdropping techniques, however, requires additional restrictions to comply with the Fourth Amendment, which have been adopted in statutory law (Title III).

Investigative techniques are traditionally primarily used to solve cases concerning past wrongdoing, due to the probable cause standard and the traditional reactive nature of US criminal procedural law. However, the adoption of Title III was aimed at enhancing the government's capacity to confront organized crime by providing the means to secretly eavesdrop on members of criminal organizations. The use of Title III surveillance is limited to serious felonies, but allows for proactive secret investigations with regard to these crimes. Furthermore, the concept of conspiracy enables powerful proactive law enforcement, which has consequences, also primarily for the investigation of organized crime.

Except for these investigative powers purely in the law enforcement context, the investigation of criminal behavior within the US may be done in the context of national security investigations. These investigations are conducted on behalf of intelligence agencies, particularly the intelligence elements of the FBI. In the *Keith* decision the Fourth Amendment restrictions were interpreted as also extending to electronic surveillance and physical searches within the context of a national security investigation. However, considering the interest of adequately protecting national security investigations these restrictions are looser than those applicable to electronic surveillance and physical searches in the context of regular law enforcement investigations. FISA has been created to regulate the use of these techniques in compliance with the Fourth Amendment. The investigative powers available during national security investigations are relevant for the subject of research as the information gathered often concerns criminal conduct and may be exported to the law enforcement community. Regardless of the absence of explicit legal barriers, the possibility to transfer information to the law enforcement community was not common practice before 9/11 due to the explanation of the 'purpose language' of FISA resulting in a wall between the intelligence community and the law enforcement communities. Despite several attempts by the Department of Justice to remove this barrier, the intelligence community and the law enforcement community continued—at least until the events of 9/11, 2001—to operate independently of each other without a willingness to share information, which was most importantly due to a cultural separation that has arisen between both communities and is intended not to allow the introduction of information that has not been gathered under the Fourth Amendment restraints as normally applicable in the law enforcement context.

## 5.3 The Shield Function of the US Criminal Investigation

### *5.3.1 The Responsibility of the Actors Towards a Fair Procedure*

#### 5.3.1.1 The Police

The concept of procedural due process, as derived from the Fifth and Fourteenth Amendments' due process clauses, aims to protect suspects and defendants against misconduct by the government during the process, which also covers police action during the investigative phase. Moreover, the exclusionary rule, as a sanction for violations of the Fourth Amendment, aims to deter police misconduct. Both due process and the potential sanction of the exclusion of evidence at trial should induce the police to take into account the fairness of their actions when acting in the context of law enforcement.

Due process protects, in the first place, against arbitrary limitations of fundamental rights, and, secondly, guarantees a fair process once the government deprives an individual of life, liberty, or property.[224] As has been explained in Sect. 5.1.4.2, procedural due process seems primarily to take effect after the taking of life, liberty or property and had been interpreted as including principles to be taken into account during the adjudication process. Moreover, claims of substantive due process have only been accepted in situations not covered by other Constitutional provisions in the situation where the police conduct has shocked the conscience. Hence, both concepts seem to have little or no consequences for police investigative activities during the investigative pre-arrest phase.[225] Rather, the conduct of the police in the investigative phase must primarily be tested according to the reasonableness standard of the Fourth Amendment covering also the execution of search warrants (or warrantless searches). Only if the activities of the police do not constitute a search or seizure under the Fourth Amendment may due process play a role.

Hence, police conduct during the investigative phase seems to be primarily restrained by the Fourth Amendment. Violations of the Fourth Amendment always concern the manner in which the police have conducted the search and/or seizure. Moreover, when "a particular Amendment 'provides an explicit textual source of constitutional protection' against a particular sort of government behavior, that Amendment, not the more generalized notion of 'substantive due process,' must be the guide for analyzing these claims."[226] Hence, primarily the threat of the exclusionary rule of the Fourth Amendment, potentially resulting in an unsuccessful prosecution due to the exclusion of critical evidence, will encourage the

[224] Nowak and Rotunda 2005, 317-318.

[225] A more detailed explanation of the contents and scope of procedural and substantive due process has been provided in Sect. 5.1.4.2.

[226] *Albright v. Oliver,* 510 U.S. 266, 114 S.Ct. 807 (1994), 273.

police—possibly under the direction of the prosecutor—to comply with Fourth Amendment requirements. The function of the Fourth Amendment prohibition of unreasonable searches and seizures is to protect the privacy and security of people against unreasonable arbitrary invasions by the government. The exclusionary rule has been created to actually give effect to these protections, as it aims to deter the police from violating the Fourth Amendment. Its meaning and, with that, its restraining effect has, however, been watered down in recent Supreme Court decisions. In *Herring v. United States* the Supreme Court explained the goal of the exclusionary rule as to "deter deliberate, reckless, or grossly negligent conduct, or in some circumstances recurring or systemic negligence."[227] As will be explained in more detail in Sect. 5.3.2.1.4, over the years the meaning of the exclusionary rule has been watered down to be only applicable if the suppression of the evidence substantially deters the police.[228] Simple negligence by the police that has resulted in a violation of Fourth Amendment requirements is, therefore, not covered.

It can be concluded that the Fourth Amendment concerns the most important restraint on police conduct in their investigative efforts contributing to search and seizure, in particular as a consequence of the remedy of the exclusionary rule. However, because of the Supreme Court's recent explanation of the scope of the exclusionary rule, the police have been given more leeway in their search and seizure activities. Furthermore, although difficult to enforce before the courts, the concept of due process is an important fundamental notion of criminal procedure in the US criminal justice system, which should be resounded also when police officers are engaged in criminal investigative activities. Nevertheless, the courts seem only to recognize a violation of procedural due process when the conduct in question "shocks the conscience." Hence, as a mechanism of enforcement, procedural due process places restraints on police conduct, but only to a limited extent. Most control on police conduct follows from internal manuals and guidelines. Most important for this project are the guidelines issued by the Attorney General governing the criminal investigative activities of the FBI. This latter source of regulation will be extensively dealt with in Sect. 5.3.2.3.

#### 5.3.1.2 The Public Prosecutor

According to the 'standards for criminal justice' of the American Bar Association, it is "the duty of the prosecutor to seek justice, not merely to convict."[229] This duty, which follows from his position as an 'officer of the court', implies that if the prosecutor finds evidence that appears to exclude the guilt of the accused, he must inform the court about this exculpatory evidence. The Supreme Court has ruled in

---

[227] *Herring v. United States,* 555 U.S. 135, 129 S.Ct. 695 (2009), 9.

[228] *Ibid.,* 12.

[229] American Bar Association. Standing Committee on Association Standards for Criminal Justice (1980), p. 3.6: Standard 3-1.1 *The function of the prosecutor.*

*Berger v. United States* (1935) that "[t]he United States Attorney (...) interest (...) in a criminal prosecution is not that it shall win a case, but justice shall be done." The prosecutor is "the servant of the law, the twofold aim of which is that guilt shall not escape or innocence suffer." The Court continued to phrase the duty of the prosecutor as "to refrain from improper methods calculated to produce a wrongful conviction."[230] In the case of *Berger v. United States,* the prosecutor had not refrained from such methods contributing to prosecutorial misconduct in violation of his duty, as he had not corrected the testimony of a witness, which he knew was false.[231] Regardless of such duty, their supervisors, given the social and political pressure, often instruct individual prosecutors to aim at a guilty verdict in order to seek redress for society by a conviction.[232] To fulfill his obligation to seek justice, the prosecutor should comply with the standards of professional conduct and with the requirements to establish a fair trial, in particular the rules with respect to pre-trial disclosure. American criminal procedural law recognizes a right to the pre-trial disclosure of specific evidence to the defense. Simultaneously, the defense is required to disclose specified pre-trial evidence to the prosecution. Both parties have the right to be aware of the evidence that will be introduced by their opposite party. Within the Federal Rules of Criminal Procedure it is laid down which evidence qualifies for pre-trial disclosure. Non-compliance with a disclosure obligation may be challenged before the court by a pre-trial motion.[233] In addition, the American Bar Association Standards for criminal justice with respect to the prosecution function consider it "unprofessional conduct for a prosecutor intentionally to fail to make disclosure to the defense, at the earliest feasible opportunity, of the existence of evidence which tends to negate the guilt of the accused (...) or which would tend to reduce the punishment of the accused."[234] The prosecutor should comply with the discovery procedures in good faith and not avoid looking for and disclosing exculpatory evidence because he thinks it will damage the prosecution's case or support the defendant's case.[235]

The Supreme Court held in *Brady v. Maryland* (1963) that the prosecutorial duty to disclose is a matter of constitutional law: "we now hold that the suppression by the prosecution of evidence favorable to an accused upon request violates due process where the evidence is material either to guilt or to punishment, irrespective of the good faith or bad faith of the prosecution."[236] A failure to disclose violates the Fourteenth Amendment due process clause.[237] The obligation

---

230 *Berger v. United States*, 295 U.S. 78, 55 S.Ct. 629 (1935), 88.

231 *Ibid.,* 84.

232 Senna and Siegel 1998, 265-266.

233 Rule 12 (b) Federal Rules of Criminal Procedure.

234 American Bar Association, Standing Committee on Association Standards for Criminal Justice (1980), 3.61: Standard 3-3.11(a) *Disclosure of evidence by the prosecutor.*

235 *Ibid.*, p. 3.62: Standard 3-3.11(b) and (c).

236 *Brady v. Maryland,* 373 U.S. 83, 83 S.Ct. 1194 (1963), 87.

237 *Ibid.*, 86 and 91.

to disclose extends to all evidence in the possession of the government that has exonerating content, including classified information in the possession of intelligence agencies. Under the United States Attorney's Manual prosecutors are required to ask the intelligence agencies whether they dispose of information which is relevant to a criminal case in the presence of "objective articulable facts" that such agency possesses information that "fall[s] reasonably within the scope of the prosecutor's affirmative discovery obligations to the defendant."[238] If such information is indeed in the possession of an intelligence agency the "Department attorneys" need first to determine whether the information can be declassified before seeking recourse to the procedures of the 'Validity and Construction of Classified Information Procedures Act'[239] (hereafter: 'CIPA') to introduce the evidence in a classified manner.[240]

These obligations of prosecutorial conduct and pre-trial disclosure make the prosecutor aware that all evidence, and not only incriminating evidence, should be taken into account also during the investigative phase when the investigative activities are still being conducted in secret. However, a violation of *Brady v. Maryland* will only be determined if the defendant can establish, after his conviction, that the conviction was erroneous because the government withheld evidence in discovery.

Moreover, the functioning of the Fifth Amendment and Fourteenth Amendment due process clauses provides all US citizens with a criminal procedure in which "fundamental fairness essential to the very concept of justice" is guaranteed. This procedural due process protects the defendant against prosecutorial misconduct, which is considered as an aspect of the right to fundamental fairness.[241] This primarily covers, however, the decision to prosecute and the violation of discovery rules.

When a court holds that the Fourth Amendment has been violated during the investigative phase this violation always concerns a police violation of the Fourth

---

[238] United States Attorney's Manual (available at http://www.usdoj.gov/usai/eousa/foia_reading_room/usam/), para 9-90.210(B)(2).

[239] 18 U.S.C. App. 3 § 1-16 (2009). About this Act see Sect. 5.3.1.3.

[240] Kris and Wilson 2007, 24-7. The procedures of CIPA apply when classified materials are sought to be used in criminal proceedings. In civil litigation, the government can withhold information under the 'state secret privilege' "if there is a reasonable danger that its disclosure would harm national security." The state secret privilege has an absolute character, which cannot be balanced in court against the interest of the private litigant to have access to the information. Congress believed that the state secret privilege could not apply in criminal proceedings, considering the tension with the Constitutional right to disclosure. Congress enacted CIPA to provide the possibility to protect classified information also in criminal cases, without necessarily being forced to drop charges when complete declassification is not possible. Kris and Wilson 2007, 24:8. In addition, Congress enacted CIPA "in an effort to combat the growing problem of graymail, a practice whereby a criminal defendant threatens to reveal classified information during the course of his trial in the hope of forcing the government to drop the charge against him." *United States v. Smith*, 780 F.2d 1102 (4th Cir. 1985), 1105.

[241] Israel et al. 2006, 797-799.

Amendment. The prosecutor's conduct is therefore not directly determined by the Fourth Amendment. When a prosecutor, for example, falsifies a search warrant while the executing police officers are not aware of this falsification, the Fourth Amendment will not be violated as the police act in good faith. Such action will, however, constitute prosecutorial misconduct, in violation of due process obligations.

Nevertheless, in general it is in the interest of prosecutors to make sure that the police act in observance of the Fourth Amendment to avoid that the evidence obtained will be excluded as a consequence of a Fourth Amendment violation. For that purpose, prosecutors often train the police to search and seize in observance of Fourth Amendment requirements.

Furthermore, discovery obligations to disclose any exculpatory evidence in its possession to the defense and standards for prosecutorial conduct may urge the prosecutor to take due account of any exculpatory evidence that appears during the investigation. However, considering the societal and political pressure to confront crime and to succeed in obtaining a criminal conviction, prosecutors, like police officers, are normally inclined to focus on crime control. For that reason, the judgment of an independent magistrate judge is required when the techniques that the prosecutor intends to apply become more invasive.

#### 5.3.1.3 The Defense

The defense can challenge the legitimacy of the use of investigative techniques at trial for the purpose of having evidence obtained through the alleged illegitimate use of investigative techniques excluded. Alleged violations of the Fourth Amendment may invoke the 'exclusionary rule,' which will be dealt with in detail in Sect. 5.3.2.1.4. Furthermore, when someone suspects that unlawful surveillance techniques have been used during an investigation against him, that person has, on the basis of 18 U.S.C. § 3504(a)(1), a claim for the suppression of evidence obtained through such surveillance activities as fruits of an unlawful act. When such a claim has been raised the government shall "affirm or deny the occurrence of the alleged unlawful act," which is normally done by means of sworn testimony or an affidavit.[242]

The applicability of discovery rules and the pre-trial proceedings in which such discovery should be made are decisive for the position of the defense with regard to being able to dispose of all information material to its case, enabling the defense to challenge also the manner in which that information has been obtained. As has already been explained in the preceding section, discovery is a matter of Constitutional law as the Supreme Court in *Brady v. Maryland*[243] determined that the defense has the right to receive material exculpatory information held by the

[242] 18 U.S.C. 3504(a)(1) and LaFave et al. 2004, 295.

[243] *Brady v. Maryland*, 373 U.S. 83, 83 S.Ct. 1194 (1963).

prosecution or by agencies closely aligned with the prosecution. Moreover, the Federal Rules of Criminal Procedure regulate discovery. Rule 16(a)(1) of the Federal Rules of Criminal Procedure provides that "[u]pon a defendant's request, the government must disclose to the defendant" any oral, written or recorded statements made by the defendant, its prior criminal record, documents and objects in the possession of the government that are "material to preparing the defense" or are intended to be used in trial by the government, and a written summary of the testimony of expert witnesses.[244] Lastly, 18 U.S.C. § 3500 of the 'Jencks Act', dealing with the disclosure of witness statements, provides that the government must produce, at the defense's request, any statement by a government witness in its possession relating to the subject-matter to which the witness has testified.

When information has been obtained in the context of a national security investigation, discovery under these rules may be troublesome, because of the classified nature of the information.[245] Normally discovery rules oblige that when information sharing between the intelligence community and law enforcement community results in a criminal investigation and prosecution, this information shall also be disclosed to the defense. Under the prosecutor's discovery obligations it is required to disclose to the defense any exculpatory evidence and the prosecutor should also ask intelligence agencies (if appropriate) to check their files for the presence of such information. However, when the prosecutor introduces information with a classified character and does not intend to declassify the information, CIPA is applicable.[246] CIPA provides extensive statutory regulation regarding the use of classified information[247] in criminal proceedings. It covers both the introduction of classified material by the defense and the use of such material by the government, and is intended to offer protection in both directions by providing mechanisms intended to provide the defense with fair trial rights and to protect classified information. Either party "may move for a pretrial conference

---

[244] Federal Rules of Criminal Procedure, Rule 16(a)(1).

[245] Additional requirements regarding the disclosure of information collected by FISA surveillance or physical searches are provided in FISA. Disclosure to "Federal officers" is allowed under FISA under the applicability of the minimization procedure as provided in FISA (50 U.S.C. § 1801(h), 50 U.S.C. 1821(4) and 50 U.S.C. § 1861(g)) and may only be used for lawful purposes. FISA information may also only be used in criminal proceedings with the permission of the Attorney General. See on the use of information obtained by investigative tools authorized under FISA: Kris and Wilson 2007, Chapter 26.

[246] Also Rule 16 contains a provision on the basis of which an exception may be made to ordinary discovery rules. Rule 16(d)(1) of the Federal Rules of Criminal Procedure allows a court "for good cause" to "deny, restrict, or defer discovery or inspection or grant other appropriate relief." The government may under this rule submit a written statement to the court to be inspected *ex parte*. However, the government has preferred to use CIPA when seeking to keep information shielded from the defense. See: Kris and Wilson 2007, 24-21.

[247] Classified information is defined as "any information or material that has been determined by the United States Government pursuant to an Executive order, statute, or regulation, to require protection against unauthorized disclosure for reasons of national security and any restricted data [regarding atomic energy]." 18 U.S.C. App. 3 § 1.

to consider matters relating to classified information that may arise in connection with the prosecution."[248]

Section 3 of CIPA provides how to deal with information already disclosed by the government that has a classified nature.[249] The government may request the court to "issue an order to protect against the disclosure of any classified information disclosed by the United States to any defendant in any criminal case in a district court in the United States." The defense counsel is usually obliged to obtain security clearance in order to be allowed to review classified documents that are produced in discovery. An order issued under CIPA Section 3 may, however, also be used to prohibit the defense counsel with such security clearance from discussing and sharing any of this classified information with his client. In such a situation the court needs to balance the government's interest to keep this information shielded against the defense interest to be able to review any evidence produced in discovery, which is an important presumption guaranteed in the Fifth and Sixth Amendments and a due process right. In most cases, such balancing will have an outcome which is favorable to the government protecting the national security, in particular in those situations where the defendant's counsel with security clearance has been authorized to review the information and challenge its admissibility.[250]

Whereas section 3 applies to classified information that has already been disclosed to the defense and, therefore, covers the subsequent handling of this information, section 4 of CIPA provides for the procedure in order to prevent the full discovery of classified information to the defense. According to section 4 "[t]he court, upon a sufficient showing may authorize the United States to delete specified items of classified information to be made available to the defendant through discovery under the Federal Rules of Criminal Procedure, to substitute a summary of the information for such classified documents, or to substitute a statement admitting facts that the classified information would tend to prove." Before the Court will assess the request of the government to avoid full disclosure of classified evidence, the Court will first determine whether the information sought by the defense in discovery is also subject to discovery under Rule 16 of the Federal Rules of Criminal Procedure. The Court will do so by applying the regular standard of Rule 16 of being 'material to the case', without taking into account the classified nature of the materials.[251] After having determined that the materials are subject to disclosure under Rule 16 of the Federal rules on Criminal Procedure, the court will hear the request of the government under section 4 CIPA and examine the classified documents *ex parte* and *in camera*. If the government can make a "sufficient showing" to the court that the information should remain classified, this may result in a complete denial of parts of the information to be obtained in discovery by the defense. Such a showing will normally be sufficiently

---

248 18 U.S.C. App 3 § 2.

249 Kris and Wilson 2007, 24-10.

250 *Ibid.*, 24-18.

251 Dycus et al. 2007B, 859.

established if the government can convincingly show that declassification will or may harm national security.[252] The fact that the government may submit such a request *ex parte* excludes the defense from challenging the need to withhold these documents from discovery, whereas in *Brady v. Maryland* discovery has been rendered essential to obtain a fair trial.[253]

Furthermore, issues with regard to the introduction of classified evidence, either on behalf of the defendant or of the government, may appear at trial. CIPA also provides for procedures for the use of classified evidence at trial, without being previously sought or produced in discovery. When a defendant seeks to use classified information in trial or pre-trial procedures, Section 5 of CIPA obliges the defense to make this intention known to the government. The government may then invoke the procedures set forth in Section 6 in order to try to block the introduction of this evidence. The hearing in accordance with section 6 deals with "the use, relevance, or admissibility" of the information as would otherwise be dealt with during the regular proceedings. This section 6 procedure, in combination with the notification obligation on the defense as to section 5, has been the main purpose of adopting CIPA, because it provides the government with the possibility to protect sensitive material from becoming public and damaging national security before such issues would unexpectedly be raised at trial.[254]

All hearings in accordance with section 6 are held *in camera* when "the Attorney General certifies [...] that a public proceeding may result in the disclosure of classified information."[255] When the court authorizes the disclosure the government may move for the court to order that the classified information be disclosed by means of either a "substitution [...] of a statement admitting the relevant facts that the specific classified information tends to prove" or a "substitution [...] of a summary of the specific classified information."[256] When the court determines that the classified information is unsuitable for disclosure or when the Attorney General (*in parte* and *in camera*) files an affidavit permanently blocking the disclosure of the classified information, the court will in general "dismiss the indictment or information." However, if the court determines that such dismissal does not serve the interests of justice it may, for example, also seek redress in lesser sanctions, such as "dismiss[ing] specified counts" or "striking or precluding part of the testimony of the witness."[257]

Section 6 may not be used to put the defense in a worse position than before.[258] Once the court has ordered disclosure because the information is relevant and

---

252 Kris and Wilson 2007, 24-26 and 24-27.

253 18 U.S.C. pp. III § 4 and Kris and Wilson 2007, 24-24 and 24-25.

254 Kris and Wilson 2007, 25-28.

255 18 U.S.C. App 3 § 6(a). The defendant or his counsel has a right to be present at these hearings. Kris and Wilson 2007, 25-14.

256 18 U.S.C. App 3 § 6(c).

257 18 U.S.C. App 3 § 6(e).

258 Kris and Wilson 2007, 25-13. See on this subject also: Becker 2008, 6.

material to the defendant's case (as to Rule 16 of the Federal Rules of Criminal Procedure), any motion by the government seeking to submit a statement or summary of the classified information may only be granted if "the statement or summary will provide the defendant with substantially the same ability to make his defense as would disclosure of the specific classified information."[259] The court may not use the interest to protect national security as an argument to limit the rights of the defense by accepting such a statement or summary.[260] This understanding of the use of CIPA was at issue in *United States v. Zacarias Moussaoui* (2004),[261] a case concerning the accusation of Moussaoui's involvement in the September 11, 2001 attacks. The district court that initially decided this case had rejected the government substitutions as being insufficient to substitute the full witnesses' testimony. However, the Court of Appeals reversed the decision, holding that the substitution of the testimony could contain "sufficient indicia of reliability" as the government would have a "profound interest in obtaining accurate information from the witnesses and in reporting that information accurately to those who can use it to prevent acts of terrorism and to capture Al Qaeda operatives." Hence, the government's substitutions were nevertheless permitted to replace the classified witnesses' testimony.[262]

#### 5.3.1.4 Position of Other Subjects of Criminal Investigative Activities

The Supreme Court has established in *Bivens v. Six Unknown Agents of Federal Bureau of Narcotics* (1971) that someone who has been subjected to a search or seizure in violation of the Fourth Amendment is entitled to a federal cause of action under the Fourth Amendment.[263] In this particular case, the violation concerned a search of plaintiff's apartment and the arrest of plaintiff on narcotic charges without probable cause. To reach this conclusion, the Court cited *Marbury v. Madison* (1803): "the very essence of civil liberties certainly consists in the right of every individual to claim the protection of the laws, whenever he receives injury."[264] Consequently, "everyone is entitled to recover money damages for any injuries he has suffered as a result of the agent's violation of the Amendment."[265] In this way the Supreme Court has established accountability for investigative activities in violation of the Fourth Amendment for persons who are not subsequently

---

[259] 18 U.S.C. App 3 § 6(c).

[260] Kris and Wilson 2007, 25-25.

[261] *United States v. Zacarias Moussaoui,* 382 F.3d 453 (4th Cir. 2004).

[262] See in more detail: Becker 2007, 28-32.

[263] *Bivens v. Six Unknown Agents of Federal Bureau of Narcotics,* 403 U.S. 388, 91 S.Ct. 1999 (1971), 389-394.

[264] *Marbury v. Madison*, 1 Cranch 137, 2 L.Ed. 60 (1803), 163 and *Bivens v. Six Unknown Agents of Federal Bureau of Narcotics,* 403 U.S. 388, 91 S.Ct. 1999 (1971), 397.

[265] *Bivens v. Six Unknown Agents of Federal Bureau of Narcotics,* 403 U.S. 388, 91 S.Ct. 1999 (1971), 397.

prosecuted. Since then, comparable civil claims for damages have been referred to as '*Bivens* claims'. Before *Bivens*, civil liability for violations of Constitutional or other rights was only guaranteed in statutory law (42 U.S.C. § 1983) with regard to state actors. Since *Bivens* such civil liability has been extended to the federal government.[266]

Furthermore, also statutory law provides for bases for action on the basis of illegitimate investigative activities. Under Title III (18 U.S.C. § 2510(11)) any "aggrieved person" may move for the suppression of "other or wire communications" gathered in violation of the requirements of Title III. This statutory exclusionary rule will be dealt with in more detail in Sect. 5.3.2.2.4. Moreover, the Privacy Act of 1974[267] provides a basis for civil actions whenever any agency has gathered information regarding that person and/or maintained the records in violation of the requirements of the Privacy Act, e.g. records that include incorrect information, are kept for an indefinite period or include information regarding the exercise of that person's First Amendment rights.[268]

An example of such civil action under the Privacy Act regarding records maintained by the FBI is *Bassiouni v. FBI* (2006).[269] In the suit it was alleged that the FBI maintained files on the international law professor M. Cherif Bassiouni that were "untimely, inaccurate and contained information with respect to his First Amendment activities," which would violate the Privacy Act. The Court of Appeals decided in favor of the FBI, which was allowed to maintain the file on Bassiouni. The Court came to this conclusion by balancing the interests served by the Privacy Act: offering protection against potential abuse by the Government "allowed to collect political dossiers about American citizens" without risking "overly restrictive limitations on the Government's ability to collect criminal intelligence" as that may "hamper legitimate law enforcement efforts."[270] The Court concurred with the FBI that it has a "legitimate law enforcement purpose for maintaining the file" which is formulated as an exception under the Privacy Act. However, it has always remained secret what this law enforcement purpose entails as the FBI submitted to the court a declaration *in camera* and *ex parte*. Although the FBI admitted that Bassiouni did not have any ties with terrorist groups, the records were needed "to provide context" to evaluate new

266 42 U.S.C. § 1983: "Every person who, under color of any statute, ordinance, regulation, custom, or usage, of any State or Territory or the District of Columbia, subjects, or causes to be subjected, any citizen of the United States or other person within the jurisdiction thereof to the deprivation of any rights, privileges, or immunities secured by the Constitution and laws, shall be liable to the party injured in an action at law, suit in equity, or other proper proceeding for redress, except that in any action brought against a judicial officer for an act or omission taken in such officer's judicial capacity, injunctive relief shall not be granted unless a declaratory decree was violated or declaratory relief was unavailable. For the purposes of this section, any Act of Congress applicable exclusively to the District of Columbia shall be considered to be a statute of the District of Columbia."

267 5 U.S.C. § 552a.

268 5 U.S.C. § 552a and Becker 2005, 63.

269 *Bassiouni v. FBI*, 436 F.3d 712 (7th Cir. 2006) and see Becker 2008, 14-15.

270 *Ibid.*, 718.

information, especially in the light of the, at that time, new top priority of the FBI to investigate terrorism.[271]

Lastly, in order to be able to make use of the possibilities to challenge the legitimacy of investigative activities in civil litigation, the person in question must have been notified that he or she has been subjected to search and seizure as covered by the Fourth Amendment. In *Berger v. New York* (1967) the Supreme Court indicated that such notification requirement shall be included in the warrant in order to render the search reasonable. At least the absence of such notification requirement casts "strong doubts on its constitutional adequacy."[272] Although the postponement of notification is possible ('delayed notice'), notification shall be given within a reasonable time. The subject of notification both for search and surveillance will be dealt with in more detail in Sects. 5.3.2.1.3 and 5.3.2.2.3.

### 5.3.1.5 Magistrate Judge

The magistrate judge can be considered as the actor having primarily the task to guarantee the fairness of an intended physical search or surveillance activity. Also the Supreme Court has repeatedly emphasized the importance of the role of the independent magistrate judge in making a determination on probable cause and, for Title III surveillance, also some additional issues. According to the Supreme Court a magistrate judge must meet two tests to be able to determine whether a search is justified and lawful before issuing a warrant: "[h]e must be neutral and detached, and he must be capable of determining whether probable cause exists for the requested arrest or search. This Court long has insisted that inferences of probable cause be drawn by a neutral and detached magistrate instead of being judged by the officer engaged in the often competitive enterprise of ferreting out crime."[273] For example, in *Coolidge v. New Hampshire* (1971) the Supreme Court confronted the question whether a state attorney general could issue the warrant, whereas the same state attorney general was in charge of the murder investigation and would be in charge as the chief prosecutor at trial. The Supreme Court strongly rejected this course of events by stating that it constituted "a *per se* rule of disqualification rather than a case-by-case evaluation of all the circumstances." The "whole point" of the "basic rule" that a magistrate judge should issue a warrant and make the probable cause determination "is that prosecutors and policemen simply cannot be asked to maintain the requisite neutrality with regard to their own investigations—the 'competitive enterprise' that must rightly engage their single-minded attention."[274]

[271] *Ibid.*, 720 and 724.

[272] *Berger v. New York,* 388 U.S. 41, 87 S.Ct. 1873 (1967), 60.

[273] Internal citation omitted. *Shadwick v. City of Tampa*, 407 U.S. 345, 92 S.Ct. 2119 (1972), 350. See also: *Illinois v. Gates*, 462 U.S. 213, 103 S.Ct. 2317 (1983), 240.

[274] *Coolidge v. New Hampshire,* 403 U.S. 443, 91 S.Ct. 2022 (1971), 450.

Regardless of this repeatedly emphasized importance of the shield function fulfilled by the magistrate judge when issuing a warrant, there are many instances[275] in which a warrantless investigation is permitted and the physical search or surveillance is not preceded by the "neutral and detached" judgment of a magistrate judge on the lawfulness and necessity of the investigative activities. The judgment with regard to the fairness (or reasonableness) of the investigative activities is then left to the police officers in question.

## *5.3.2 The Protective Elements in the System of Criminal Investigation*

### 5.3.2.1 Regulation Following from the Fourth Amendment

To describe the protection offered by the Fourth Amendment, this section will primarily focus on the restraints imposed on searches in general. Where the restraints imposed on surveillance have been given a different interpretation under the Fourth Amendment, this has also been included. The section will start by analyzing the probable cause requirement as the most important restriction on the government's power to conduct searches. Subsequently, the warrant requirement, the general requirement of reasonableness and the remedy of the exclusionary rule will be dealt with.

#### 5.3.2.1.1 Probable Cause

##### *5.3.2.1.1.1 What is Probable Cause?*

According to the Fourth Amendment "no warrants shall issue but upon probable cause." A valid warrant to search can only be issued if the issuing authority (the magistrate judge) is convinced of a showing of probable cause. Considering that there may be many situations in which the police search without first obtaining a warrant,[276] the search must still be "reasonable" to comply with the Fourth Amendment. The Supreme Court held in *Wong Sun v. United States* (1963)[277] that a warrantless arrest and search is unreasonable if not based upon probable cause.

[275] Warrantless searches have been upheld in emergency circumstances, such as exigent circumstances for the police, when there is a risk that evidence will be destroyed, when there is a danger to police officers or others, but also in situations where the privacy intrusion is more limited and for 'any other reasons' for which the police cannot reasonably obtain a warrant before searching. Furthermore, Title III provides some statutory grounds for warrantless surveillance (section 18 U.S.C. 2518(7)). See in more detail about warrantless searches Sect. 5.3.2.1.2.

[276] See the previous footnote and Sect. 5.3.2.1.2.

[277] *Wong Sun v. United States*, 371 U.S. 471, 83 S.Ct. 407 (1963), 479-480.

This implies that the presence of probable cause is the primary and most important requirement for any search to be lawful.[278]

Considering that probable cause is the central threshold restricting governmental powers that fall under the scope of the Fourth Amendment, it is important to understand the contents of probable cause, the manner in which a magistrate judge or, in the case of a warrantless search, a police officer should determine whether the required quantum of evidence is met and the standard of evidence required to establish probable cause. This section will elaborate on the development of the interpretation given to the probable cause requirement and the manner in which a showing of probable cause is generally established until the events of September 11, 2001.

The specific probable cause standard is different in the circumstances under which it is applicable. The reasonableness of a particular search is determined on the basis of a balancing test between the consequences of the search for the privacy of the persons concerned and the specific quantum of information that constitutes probable cause. Whether the standard is met depends on the facts and circumstances of each case. The specific required facts and circumstances differ between the different types of search. For example, the probable cause standard concerning physical searches requires evidence (facts and circumstances) that there is a connection between the items sought and the criminal activity and evidence is needed that those items will be found in the place to be searched.[279] It is not required that the specific suspect is already known.[280] When the intended investigative technique is a surveillance technique, meeting the probable cause standard requires a showing that someone is committing, has committed, or is about to commit one of the enumerated offenses.[281] Like with searches and seizures, this must be shown by the facts and circumstances of the situation, which entails more than bare suspicion.[282]

The Supreme Court formulated in *Brinegar v. United States* that "[i]n dealing with probable cause [...] we deal with probabilities. These are not technical; they are the factual and practical considerations of everyday life on which reasonable and prudent men, not legal technicians, act. The standard of proof is accordingly correlative to what must be proved."[283] The Supreme Court continued to explain the contents of probable cause by repeating previous definitions of the Court such as "reasonable ground for belief of guilt," meaning "less than evidence which would justify condemnation or conviction" and "more than bare suspicion." This comes down to the following definition of probable cause: "the facts and

[278] LaFave et al. 2004, 141.

[279] LaFave et al. 2004, 141. For an arrest, probable cause that a crime has been committed is required and that the person arrested has committed the crime.

[280] LaFave et al. 2004, 141.

[281] 18 U.S.C. § 2518(3)(a).

[282] Baker 2007A, 75.

[283] *Brinegar v. United States*, 338 U.S. 160, 69 S.Ct. 1302 (1949), 175.

circumstances within their (the officers') knowledge and of which they had reasonably trustworthy information (are) sufficient in themselves to warrant a man of reasonable caution in the belief that an offense has been or is being committed."[284]

The Supreme Court has applied different tests for determining whether in a specific case probable cause is present until it finally adopted the 'totality of circumstances test' in *Illinois v. Gates* (1983), which has since been the single method to be applied for making decisions on the presence of probable cause. With the adoption of the totality of circumstances test in *Illinois v. Gates* (1983) the Supreme Court abandoned previous balancing tests and the so-called "Aguilar/ Spinelli test."[285] The totality of circumstances test concerns a "practical," "commonsense" decision of the magistrate judge issuing a warrant on the basis of all the circumstances that are given in the affidavit.[286] The Court considered such a "totality of circumstances approach" to be more consistent with their "prior treatment of probable cause" than "rigid" interpretations of previously used tests.[287] The Supreme Court assessed in *Illinois v. Gates* whether a magistrate can issue a search warrant on the basis of a "partially corroborated anonymous informant's tip."[288] The Court considered the "veracity," "reliability" and the "basis of knowledge as "highly relevant" to determine whether probable cause exists. However, the Court added: "these elements should not be understood as entirely separate and independent requirements to be rigidly exacted in every case." Rather, these elements "should be understood simply as closely intertwined issues that may usefully illuminate the commonsense, practical question whether there is "probable cause" to believe that contraband or evidence is located in a particular place."[289] Probable cause should be a concept that can be used by law enforcement officers in practice, rather than being a theoretically specified concept: "the evidence (…) collected must be seen and weighed not in terms of library analysis by scholars, but as understood by those versed in the field of law enforcement." A totality of circumstances test would, according to the Court, be the most appropriate tool to make determinations of probable cause for law enforcement officers.[290] Critics, however, considered the approach taken in *Illinois v. Gates* to be a watering down of the probable cause standard as, for example, was used in *Aguilar v. Texas* (1964). In *Aguilar* the Court considered a search warrant to be insufficient if it only stated that "reliable information from a credible person" pointed to the presence of narcotics at a certain place. The affidavit should additionally have provided for information about the

284 *Ibid.*, 175-176.

285 According to this test the issuing magistrate should determine, firstly, the reliability of the informant, and, secondly, the reliability of the basis of the knowledge. LaFave et al. 2004, 144.

286 LaFave et al. 2004, 147.

287 *Illinois v. Gates,* 426 U.S. 213, 103 S.Ct. 2317 (1983), 230-231.

288 *Ibid.*, 216.

289 *Ibid.*, 230.

290 *Ibid.*, 232.

informant's basis of knowledge and information from which it could be verified that the informant was credible and reliable. *Illinois v. Gates*, although emphasizing that all of these factors are highly relevant, also allows probable cause determinations when information pointing to one of these factors is lacking, as long as the 'totality of circumstances' justifies the probable cause determination.

The manner in which the presence of probable cause should be determined still does not clarify what information contributes to the presence of probable cause. Justice Scalia, delivering the opinion of the Court in *Virginia v. Moore* (2008), stated that "in a long line of cases" the Court has said "that when an officer has probable cause to believe a person committed even a minor crime in his presence, the balancing of private and public interests is not in doubt."[291] Hence, when a police officer observes what he thinks is the commission of a crime, probable cause will always justifiably be present. When the information comes from a victim or witness of criminal activity the veracity may be assumed and the information may constitute the basis for probable cause for the acting police officers. This is different when the information comes from informants or from a witness who refuses to identify himself to the police. Some additional information pointing to the reliability or basis of knowledge of these victims or witnesses will be needed before probable cause can be established.[292] Also after *Illinois v. Gates,* general statements about the veracity of the informant have been accepted as sufficient, for example, by referring to the past performances of that informant. It seems that also the Supreme Court in *Illinois v. Gates* would not have aimed at accepting this type of information to support the veracity and reliability of the statements of the informant as the Court reaffirmed that "sufficient information must be presented to the magistrate to allow *that official* to determine probable cause; his action cannot be a mere ratification of the bare conclusions of others."[293] Nevertheless, considering that in several post-*Gates* judgments information without direct supporting information of either the reliability or basis of knowledge has been accepted, it is still unclear in how far Fourth Amendment probable cause actually requires additional information as to the reliability or basis of knowledge.[294]

It can be concluded that probable cause has a variable content, which differs according to different circumstances. Basically, to initiate a regular investigation police officers need to believe that reasonable suspicion is present that a crime has been committed.[295] In order to use investigative powers that interfere with rights protected by the Fourth Amendment, probable cause that a crime has been committed or is being or is about to be committed is the applicable threshold for either a physical search under rule 41 of the Federal Rules of Criminal Procedure or

---

291 *Virgina v. Moore*, 553 U.S. 164, 128 S.Ct. 1598 (2008), 1604.

292 LaFave et al. 2004, 152-153.

293 *Illinois v. Gates,* 426 U.S. 213, 103 S.Ct. 2317 (1983), 239.

294 LaFave et al. 2004, 147-149.

295 See also the thresholds for initiating different investigative steps under the AG's guidelines for criminal investigations on behalf of the FBI, as described in Sect. 5.3.2.3.

surveillance under Title III. The information about criminal activity that is required to meet this threshold may originate from police officers' own observations of criminal activity, from victims or witnessess, or from undercover agent informants or corroborating witnesses. When the information originates from the latter the investigation may often be based upon a probable cause standard concerning future criminal activity, allowing e.g. Title III surveillance of the activities of criminal organizations. Also the degree of the intrusion on privacy by using the intended method legitimized by the probable cause showing is arguably relevant to the standard of evidence required for probable cause and shall be taken into account in the totality of circumstances assessment. Support for this observation can be found in the concurring opinion of Justice Stewart in *Berger v. New York* (1967), who argued in favor of including the aspect of intrusiveness in the probable cause determination in his concurring opinion by holding that "the affidavits on which the judicial order issued in this case did not constitute a showing of probable cause adequate to justify the authorizing order. The need for particularity and evidence of reliability in the showing required when judicial authorization is sought for the kind of electronic eavesdropping involved in this case is especially great. The standard of reasonableness embodied in the Fourth Amendment demands that the showing of justification match the degree of intrusion. By its very nature electronic eavesdropping for a 60-day period, even of a specified office, involves a broad invasion of a constitutionally protected area. Only the most precise and rigorous standard of probable cause should justify an intrusion of this sort."[296] Justice Stewart thus concluded that for the more intrusive method of electronic eavesdropping, considering its scope and duration, the quantum of evidence required to meet the probable cause standard is also higher. Arguments based on this reasoning have, however, never reached the courts.[297]

For the use of some investigative techniques the Supreme Court has accepted that a lower standard is used than the regular probable cause standard as required by the Fourth Amendment. Here, a threshold of a lesser evidentiary basis of criminal activity has been accepted as reasonable under the Fourth Amendment. Most important in that regard has been the Supreme Court's judgment in *Terry v. Ohio* (1968) adopting a reasonable suspicion threshold as sufficient to 'stop and frisk' a person. Such use of power by police officers is considered as a lesser intrusion than arrest and search and, therefore, the total quantum of evidence

[296] *Berger v. New York*, 388 U.S. 41, 87 S.Ct. 1873 (1967), 69.

[297] LaFave et al. 2004, 268-269. However, without explicitly relating it to the nature of the investigative method, the Supreme Court has also in many other instances explained that reasonableness is determined by "assessing, on the one hand, the degree to which it intrudes upon an individual's privacy and, on the other, the degree to which it is needed for the promotion of legitimate governmental interests." (See e.g. *Virginia v. Moore*, 553 U.S. 164, 128 S.Ct. 1598 (2008), 1604 and *U.S. v. Knights*, 534 U.S. 112, 122 S.Ct. 587 (2001), 119). In general, the degree of the intrusion is thus a factor to be considered in the reasonableness assessment, which may include all kinds of considerations including the method used and, in particular, the level of the expectation of privacy with regard to the place searched.

required to undertake such activities may also be lower. Although the Court concluded in *Terry v. Ohio* (1968) that stopping a person on the street constitutes a seizure and the frisking activities constitute a search, a lesser quantum of evidence[298] was required for conducting these activities. This consideration was based upon the balancing test as used in *Camara v. Municipal Court,* where for determining the "reasonableness" of a housing inspection the "need to search" was balanced "against the invasion which the search entails."[299] The Court concluded that some Fourth Amendment activities should still be judged by applying a balancing test, which results for stop and frisk in the acceptance of a lesser evidentiary standard. "Reasonable suspicion" of criminal activity was sufficient to stop and frisk a person; however, at that time, only in combination with the presence of an imminent danger for the police officers.[300] More recently, in *United States v. Place* the Court has extended the power to seize on the basis of a reasonable suspicion for the inspection of luggage, although rendering the seizure in that case unreasonable because of the length of the detention of the luggage.[301]

Furthermore, inspections and regulatory searches, which are used to trace violations of administrative regulations such as housing code violations, do not need to follow the conventional Fourth Amendment requirements. A warrant is not necessary; neither does probable cause have to exist. Inspections have been upheld upon a reasonable suspicion or upon some neutral criteria that should prevent the arbitrary selection of places for such inspections. Similar reasoning has also resulted, for example, in upholding an even suspicionless search of a parolee.

---

298 The exact difference as to the quantum of evidence required for probable cause and for a reasonable suspicion has not been precisely defined. In *Terry v. Ohio,* 392 U.S. 1, 88 S.Ct. 1868 (1968), 27, it was only indicated that "the officer need not to be absolutely certain." In another case, building upon the *Terry* decision, the Court went further to define the reasonable suspicion threshold: "The officer, of course, must be able to articulate something more than an inchoate and unparticularized suspicion or 'hunch.' (...) The Fourth Amendment requires some minimal level of objective justification for making the stop. (...) That level of suspicion is considerably less than proof of wrongdoing by a preponderance of the evidence. We have held that probable cause means a fair probability that contraband or evidence of a crime will be found (...) and the level of suspicion required for a *Terry* stop is obviously less demanding than that for probable cause. (...) The concept of reasonable suspicion, like probable cause, is not readily, or even usefully, reduced to a neat set of legal rules. We think the Court of Appeals' effort to refine and elaborate the requirements of "reasonable suspicion" in this case creates unnecessary difficulty in dealing with one of the relatively simple concepts embodied in the Fourth Amendment. In evaluating the validity of a stop such as this, we must consider the totality of the circumstances-the whole picture." [internal citations omitted]. *United States v. Sokolow,* 490 U.S. 1, 109 S.Ct. 1581 (1989), 7-8. "Considering that reasonable suspicion is lower than probable cause and probable cause is understood as a "fair probability", reasonable suspicion could be understood a standard of a "moderate chance" in the sense of the objective level of knowledge of the police officer." Compare: Feld 2011, 898, Taslitz 2010, 148 and *Safford Unified School District No. 1 v. Reddings,* 129 S.Ct. 2633 (2009), 2639.

299 *Camara v. Municipal Court*, 387 U.S. 523, 87 S.Ct. 1727 (1967), 536-537.

300 *Terry v. Ohio*, 392 U.S. 1, 88 S.Ct. 1868(1968), 27.

301 *United States v. Place*, 462 U.S. 696, 103 S.Ct. 2637 (1983), 706 and 709-710.

In these types of cases a deviation from the usual Fourth Amendment requirements was accepted, because of a "special need" that is "distinct from ordinary law enforcement."[302] These exceptions are usually referred to as the "special needs doctrine."[303] Courts applying the special needs doctrine balance the intrusion on the interests protected by the Fourth Amendment against the legitimate governmental interest (the special need), for instance, for alcohol controls on highways or controls on the use of drugs by athletes. Considering the importance of the legitimate 'special need' to be different from ordinary law enforcement, courts may render the search reasonable when a warrant issued upon probable cause is absent.[304] In *Illinois v. Lidster* (2004) the Supreme Court has specified the following factors to consider whether the search (in *Lidster* the brief stopping of motorists to seek information regarding a recent fatal hit-and-run accident) is reasonable when applying the special needs doctrine: a) "the gravity of the public concerns served"; b) "the degree to which" the search advances the public concern (efficacy); and c) "the severity of the interference with individual liberty."[305]

---

302 Israel et al. 2006, 251-252 and LaFave et al. 2004, 229. Exceptions for 'administrative searches' were for the first time labeled as searches for the purpose of a special need, other than a law enforcement purpose in *New Jersey v. T.L.O.,* 469 U.S. 325, 105 S.Ct. 733 (1985) in the concurring opinion of Judge Blackmun (at 351). The special needs doctrine has subsequently been explicitly applied in other cases (see e.g. *Griffin v. Wisconsin*, 483 U.S. 868, 107 S.Ct. 3164 (1987), 873-874, concerning searches for the purpose of enforcing probation system). In *United States v. Knights,* 534 U.S. 112, 122 S.Ct. 587 (2001) the Supreme Court, however, rendered a search of a probationer's home upon a standard of a reasonable suspicion reasonable by an "ordinary Fourth Amendment analysis" where the reasonableness is the final touchstone, without questioning whether the "official purpose" of the search gave reason for a "special needs" exception like in *Griffin v. Wisconsin* (at 122)), *Vernonia School District v. Acton,* 515 U.S. 646, 115 S.Ct. 2386 (1995), 653 (regarding random urine analyses for participants in interscholastic athletics serving the "substantial need of teachers and administrators for freedom to maintain order in schools"), *National Treasury Employees Union v. Von Raab,* 489 U.S. 656, 109 S.Ct. 1348 (1989), 666 (concerning the drug testing of employees of the Customs service for the purpose (special need) of deterring drug use among employees) and *City of Indianapolis v. Edmond,* 531 U.S. 32, 121 S.Ct. 447 (2000), 47-48 (concerning motor vehicle checkpoints for the purpose of preventing illegal drugs from entering the city of Indianapolis. The Supreme Court held the checkpoints violated the Fourth Amendment, because "the primary purpose of the Indianapolis checkpoint program is ultimately indistinguishable from the general interest in crime control." However, the Supreme Court explicitly considered that its holding: "does not affect the validity of border searches or searches at places like airports and government buildings, where the need for such measures to ensure public safety can be particularly acute. Nor does our opinion speak to other intrusions aimed primarily at purposes beyond the general interest in crime control. Our holding also does not impair the ability of police officers to act appropriately upon information that they properly learn during a checkpoint stop justified by a lawful primary purpose.").

303 Recently, courts have also used the 'special needs doctrine' as an argument to permit investigative activities in furtherance of national security without adhering to the usual Fourth Amendment restriction applicable to surveillance in the context of a criminal investigation. See on this Chap. 6, Sect. 6.2.2.

304 See: Fenske 2008, 351-352.

305 *Illinois v. Lidster,* 540 U.S. 419, 124 S.Ct. 885 (2004), 427.

Furthermore, for the use of pen registers and trap and trace devices, which only register tones and data and not the contents of the communications (for example, the numbers dialed from someone's phone (pen register) or the numbers from which incoming calls originate (trap and trace devices), probable cause is not required. Pen registers or trap/trace devices do not meet the definition of "interception"[306] as to Title III, because the "contents"[307] of the communication are not acquired. Therefore, Title III does not apply to pen registers and trap and trace devices.[308] An authorization by a court through an *ex parte* order is sufficient, which will be issued if the Government's attorney can demonstrate that the use of the tool is relevant to an ongoing criminal investigation.[309] This considerably less stringent standard was justified because this information was not considered private, as it does not reveal the individual's identity or the contents of the communication and, therefore, does not need to meet the requirements of the Fourth Amendment.[310]

The explanation given in this section for the quantum of evidence required for meeting the probable cause standard seems to cover primarily criminal offenses which have been committed. However, the proactive use of, in particular, surveillance techniques is very common and is often applied in organized crime investigations. According to the definition of probable cause under section 2518(3)(a) of Title III, surveillance is allowed when someone is committing, has committed, or is about to commit one of the enumerated offenses, which enables a proactive approach once information has been received regarding possible future criminal activity. Furthermore, the possibility to investigate upon a probable cause of conspiracies, as has been explained in Sect. 5.2.2.2, provides important possibilities to investigate proactively.

---

306 18 U.S.C. § 2510(4).

307 Defined in 18 U.S.C. § 2510(8).

308 See: LaFave et al. 2004, 276-277.

309 18 U.S.C. § 3123(a)(2). Currently, using pen registers or trap and trace devices on cell phones will also reveal the location of the user. The constitutionality of the application of the existing law for these purposes is under discussion as the courts do not seem to agree on the acceptance of the extension of the information intercepted by the tools under the current regulation of pen register and trap/trace device authority. See e.g.: *In re Application of United States for an Order for Prospective Cell Site Location Information on a Certain Cellular Telephone*, 460 F.Supp. 2d 448, 2006 WL 3016316 (S.D.N.Y. 2006) and *In the Matter of an Application of the United States of America for an Order Authorizing the Use of a Pen Register with Caller Identification Device Cell Site Location Authority on a Cellular Telephone*, 2009 WL 159187 (S.D.N.Y. 2009).

310 *Smith v. Maryland*, 442 U.S. 735, 99 S.Ct. 2577 (1979), 744, established that "a person has no legitimate expectation of privacy in information he voluntarily turns over to third parties" which is the case when someone uses a phone, resulting in conveying the numerical information to the telephone company.

#### *5.3.2.1.1.2 The Protective Function of Probable Cause*

The protective importance of the 'probable cause' threshold was emphasized by the Supreme Court in *Brinegar v. United States* (1949) when the Court characterized probable cause as the "compromise" between the shield and sword function of criminal procedural law: "these long-prevailing standards seek to safeguard citizens from rash and unreasonable interferences with privacy and from unfounded charges of crime. They also seek to give fair leeway for enforcing the law in the community's protection." The function of probable cause is to provide for a practical tool to "accommodat[e] these often opposing interests."[311] The connection between probable cause and the Fourth Amendment, which seeks to protect people so that they are secure with respect to their persons, homes, papers, and effects, makes clear that the probable cause standard aims to protect persons against unfounded interferences by the government with their private lives. The probable cause standard can be considered as the equilibrium between the sword and shield objective of criminal law, as also clearly follows from the Court's consideration in *Brinegar* as has just been quoted.

#### 5.3.2.1.2 Warrant

The requirement that a warrant must be obtained before a search can be conducted is another important restriction and safeguard concerning the government's power to search places or conduct electronic surveillance activities. On the one hand, a warrant gives the police the necessary legitimization to conduct searches ("to get through the door"), while, on the other, the warrant provides for *ex ante* judicial control of the government's power to intrude into the privacy of citizens through search and seizure.[312] The Fourth Amendment provides for a few requirements that a warrant must meet before it can be issued: probable cause, supported by oath or affirmation and particularly describing the place to be searched, and the persons or things to be seized.

Although a warrant is not required in every situation for a search to be lawful, obtaining a search warrant before conducting a search is preferred because a "neutral and detached magistrate" decides on the question whether the information presented in the affidavit constitutes probable cause. In the previous section it has already been explained that when a magistrate issues a warrant, he/she must determine whether the standard of probable cause is met by taking into consideration "the totality of circumstances," which have been described in the affidavit. This should result in a "common-sense decision" as to whether there is, for physical searches for example, "a fair probability that contraband or evidence of a crime will be found in a particular place."[313] Another requirement is that it must be issued upon oath or affirmation,

---

311 *Brinegar v. United States*, 338 U.S. 160, 69 S.Ct. 1302 (1949), 176.

312 Considering this legitimizing and protective role, the warrant has been identified as "a key and a shield." Pfeiffer 2004, 234-235.

313 Coquillette et al., para 641.10.

which means that the information provided to the magistrate judge, upon which he/she will determine whether a warrant supported by probable cause can be issued, must be sworn evidence. This regards both the written information in the affidavit and any additional information given orally.[314]

The final requirement, which a lawful warrant must meet, is that it must particularly describe the place to be searched and the things to be seized. The warrant should describe the place so that "the officer with a search warrant can with reasonable effort ascertain and identify the place intended" for which there is probable cause.[315] This usually means that a street address must be stated within the warrant, although other descriptive facts concerning the place may be sufficient if a street address cannot be given. For searching vehicles a combination of descriptive factors can be given, such as a license plate or make, to meet the particularity requirement of the Fourth Amendment. Furthermore, the warrant should indicate the things to be seized in order to prevent general searches. The permissible length and intensity of the search depends on the goal of the search: the seizure of the things that are described in the warrant. Also the description of the things to be seized must be given with sufficient clarity in order to identify them with reasonable certainty. *Go-Bart Importing Co. v. United States* (1931) formulated that, except for the prevention of general searches and assuring that the officer can identify the property sought, one of the goals of the particularity requirement of the description of the things to be seized is that "it prevents the issuance of warrants on loose, vague or doubtful bases of fact" and that "[i]t emphasizes the purpose to protect against all general searches."[316] This requirement must also be seen in relation to the probable cause requirement: there must be probable cause that the things to be seized are connected to criminal activity and can be found in the place searched.[317]

In a similar fashion to physical searches, the warrant for surveillance should include, with clarity, what type of communication the government agency seeks to intercept.[318] Because communications are not tangible objects, unlike places, the particularity requirement is met when the surveillance warrant specifically describes the person under surveillance and the facilities from which, or the place where, the communication is to be intercepted. Nevertheless, Title III includes an exception to the requirement that the warrant should specify the communications sought if the specification from which the communications are to be intercepted is "not practical" or where there is "probable cause to believe that the person's actions could have the effect of thwarting interception from a specified facility."[319]

---

[314] LaFave et al. 2004, 161.

[315] *Steele v. United States*, 267 U.S. 498, 45 S.Ct. 414 (1925), 503.

[316] *Go-Bart Importing Co. v. United States,* 282 U.S. 344, 51 S.Ct. 153 (1931), 357.

[317] LaFave et al. 2004, 165.

[318] 18 U.S.C. § 2518(1)(b) and (4)(c) (2007).

[319] In general, when the interception of oral communications is not practical: 18 U.S.C. § 2518(11)(a), and when the person whose communications are to be intercepted thwarts the interception by switching devices in the case of the interception of wired or electronic communications: 18 U.S.C. § 2518(11)(b).

Surveillance aimed at a specific person instead of the type of communication is usually referred to as 'roving' surveillance (see Sect. 5.2.2.1.2) and concerns a powerful surveillance tool for the government, which makes it possible to follow every step of a particular target. Under this 'roving surveillance' provision of Title III it is also possible to authorize roving bugs which can intercept communications even when the target is not using any communication device. Federal courts have considered that roving surveillance, and also the roving bug, does not violate the Fourth Amendment's particularity requirement.[320] Because the Supreme Court has explained that "[t]he manifest purpose of [the] particularity requirement was to prevent general searches", roving surveillance is permissible if it is "carefully tailored to its justifications, and will not take on the character of the wide-ranging exploratory searches the Framers intended to prohibit."[321] The manner in which roving surveillance under Title III is permitted was understood as being carefully tailored, because the potential for abuse is limited considering that the surveillance is limited to devices used by the specified target, minimization procedures apply to conversations that are not relevant to the investigation of the criminal activity and the government must demonstrate to the court the presence of a particular situation that necessitates the roving surveillance, e.g. that it is the "suspect's purpose to thwart interception" by changing facilities.[322] It was concluded that also roving surveillance, in combination with the "many safeguards mandated by statute", constitute "no greater invasion of privacy than necessary" to meet "the legitimate needs of law enforcement."[323]

Although the warrant requirement is an important control on the use of search and seizure techniques by the police, there are important exceptions to the warrant requirement giving the police many instances in which they may conduct warrantless searches. The courts have accepted a warrantless search and seizure for a variety of reasons in the presence of emergency and exceptional circumstances. Warrantless searches (other than warrantless searches with consent) have so far been accepted in five emergency or exceptional circumstances, which can in general terms be identified as: 1) exigent circumstances for the police, including the risk that evidence will be destroyed; 2) a danger to police officers, to others, or to property; 3) to render assistance to a person; 4) situations in which there is a lesser intrusion of Fourth Amendment interests by the search, justifying a warrantless search; or 5) for any other reasons for which the police officers cannot reasonably obtain a warrant before conducting the search activities. Still, when the police search without a warrant there must be probable cause (as has already been explained in Sect. 5.3.2.1.1.1) and the search must, on the whole, be reasonable. The meaning of this latter requirement will be explored in the next section.

320 See e.g. *U.S. v. Petti,* 973 F.2d 1441 (9th Cir. 1992), 1444-1445 and *United States v. Tomero,* 462 F.Supp.2d 565 (S.D.N.Y. 2006).

321 *U.S. v. Petti,* 973 F.2d 1441 (9th Cir. 1992), 1444.

322 *Ibid.*, 1445.

323 *Ibid.*, 1445 and *Katz v. United States,* 389 U.S. 347, 88 S.Ct. 507 (1967), 355-356.

Title III, regulating surveillance, also provides for the possibility of an emergency interception without a warrant and these possibilities are broader than the emergency circumstances established by the courts. Section 2518(7) provides that interception without a warrant is permitted if there are grounds for such an interception and one of the following emergency situations is present: "(i) immediate danger of death or serious physical injury to any person; (ii) conspiratorial activities threatening the national security interests, or (iii) conspiratorial activities characteristic of organized crime, that requires a wire, oral, or electronic communication to be intercepted before an order authorizing such interception can with due diligence be obtained."[324] In fact, this provision gives wide powers to the police to intercept communications without prior judicial approval, especially in the proactive field for the purpose of confronting organized crime and national security threats, as it permits emergency interception in the case of conspiratorial activities. Nevertheless, an order must be obtained within 48 hours after the interception begins.

The Supreme Court has never assessed the constitutionality of this broad exception to the warrant requirement of the Fourth Amendment.[325] Only the lower courts have assessed the presence of an emergency situation when this is used to intercept communications without a warrant. Recently (on July 30, 2009), a District Court in Texas held that it depends on the totality of circumstances whether the Director of the FBI and the Attorney General could determine that an emergency situation as to § 2518(7) existed in order to justify the warrantless interception of communications. "Approached under the "common sense" reading of the affidavits, and a view of the entire circumstances, the information from the informants, together with the corroborating facts garnered from the agents' own investigations, there was probable cause for [subsequently] issuing the order approving the emergency interception."[326] The courts have so far not assessed the use of the second and third exception; it seems that there has virtually been no use of these grounds for an exception to the warrant requirement.

#### 5.3.2.1.3 Reasonableness

Except for the explicit requirements of probable cause and having to obtain a warrant, the Fourth Amendment contains yet another requirement: that of reasonableness, covering the arrest or search and/or seizure as a whole. It seems that the requirement of reasonableness is currently the final and ultimate test for the constitutionality of a particular search and/or seizure, regardless of the other Fourth Amendment requirements, as many exceptions to these other requirements have been created.[327] Nevertheless, also when an exception to other Fourth

---

[324] 18. U.S.C. § 2518(7).

[325] LaFave et al. 2004, 270.

[326] *United States v. Duffey,* 2009 WL 2356156 (N.D.Tex. 2009), 6.

[327] See in this regard: Amar 1997.

Amendment requirements is applicable, the arrest, search and/or seizure must still be reasonable. Compliance with the other Fourth Amendment requirements usually implies, however, that also the arrest, search and/or seizure are reasonable. For example, both the presence of probable cause and a warrant also imply the reasonableness of the arrest or search and/or seizure. The Supreme Court in *Katz* emphasized that "the mandate of the (Fourth) Amendment requires adherence to judicial processes."[328] However, as has been explained, there are many exceptions to the warrant requirement and in some instances also to the probable cause requirement, which have not rendered the arrest or search unreasonable under the Fourth Amendment.

In *Virginia v. Moore* (2008) the Supreme Court dealt with the question whether an arrest and search incident was reasonable when the officers had not followed the applicable state law which provided for an additional regulation to the Fourth Amendment requirements. Justice Scalia, delivering the opinion of the Court, explained that a warrantless arrest is reasonable when it is based upon probable cause, regardless of possibly more stringent regulations for an arrest which are applicable under state law. The Court concluded that: "[w]hen officers have probable cause to believe that a person has committed a crime in their presence, the Fourth Amendment permits them to make an arrest, and to search the suspect in order to safeguard evidence and ensure their own safety."[329] The reasonableness of an arrest or search would thus normally be based on the presence of probable cause. When probable cause is present the arrest will be *per se* reasonable, without requiring compliance with any additional conditions. Although the reasonableness of the search is thus an independent test for the constitutionality of the search and seizure, its determination is, in the first place, strongly intertwined with the other Fourth Amendment requirements of probable cause, having to obtain a warrant and particularity.

Furthermore, the reasonableness requirement governs the execution of the search. In *Maryland v. Garrison* (1987) and *Richard v. Wisconsin* (1997) the Court elaborated on the question of what conditions must be met to render the execution of a valid search warrant reasonable. The reasonableness of a search aims to ensure that people are secure in their homes. Therefore, the execution of a validly issued search warrant must still be reasonable and must not unreasonably violate the right of people to be secure in their own homes. In *Maryland v. Garrison* the Court assessed the question whether the execution of a search warrant indicating the home of Mr. Webb to be on the third floor of a specified apartment building was unreasonable when it transpired that there were two apartments on the third floor and the other apartment not occupied by Mr. Webb had also been searched. The Court repeated its previous statement that "sufficient probability, not certainty, is the touchstone of reasonableness of the Fourth Amendment and on the record before us the officers' mistake was understandable and the [search] a reasonable

[328] *Katz v. United States*, 389 U.S. 347, 88 S.Ct. 507 (1967), 357.

[329] *Virginia v. Moore*, 553 U.S. 164, 128 S.Ct. 1598 (2008), 1608.

response to the situation facing them at the time."[330] The reasonableness of the search of the entire third floor "depends on whether the officers' failure to realize the overbreadth of the warrant was objectively understandable and reasonable."[331] In this case, the Court concluded it was reasonable.

Furthermore, the rule that the police must knock and announce their presence before entering any place may, when not observed, render a search unreasonable. In general, the police are obliged to first knock and announce their presence and the purpose of their visit (the 'knock and announce rule') before entering a home or business. Subsequently, they must provide the owner with a copy of the warrant, which includes the specific authority to search and a specification of what can be seized.[332] These notice requirements are aimed at protecting the privacy of those being searched by preventing so-called 'fishing expeditions.'[333] The requirements limit the scope of the search to the areas and things for which the warrant shows there is probable cause. Moreover, the notification provides the subject of the search with the opportunity to challenge the legitimacy of the search warrant and its execution and to prevent law enforcement officers from making 'good faith' mistakes in the execution of the search warrant.

An announcement was held to be "an element of the reasonableness inquiry under the Fourth Amendment" in *Wilson v. Arkansas* (1995).[334] In general, when the police do not follow these notification requirements, a court will find the search unreasonable and thus in violation of the Fourth Amendment. However, also in its decision in *Wilson v. Arkansas* the Supreme Court held that the requirement of an announcement shall be understood as a flexible requirement, which does not require an "announcement under all circumstances."[335] Courts have allowed exceptions to the knock-and-announce rule and have also permitted searches with a delayed notice (sneak-and-peek searches). *Richard v. Wisconsin* (1997) dealt with the question whether a failure to meet the knock-and-announce requirement makes the execution of a further valid search warrant unreasonable. The Court declined a *per se* exception to the knock-and-announce rule in felony drug investigations, stating that it must be a determination on a case by case basis whether the facts and circumstances justify entry without knocking and announcing the police's presence. However, the Court did establish an exception

---

330 *Maryland v. Garrison,* 480 U.S. 79, 107 S.Ct. 1013 (1987), 87.

331 *Ibid.*, 88.

332 See Rule 41(f) of the Federal Rules of Criminal Procedure.

333 General, wide searches. The following goals of the knock-and-announce rule can be formulated: "(i) it decreases the potential for violence, as an unannounced breaking and entering into a home could quite easily lead an individual to believe that his safety was in peril and cause him to take defensive measures; (ii) it protects privacy by minimizing the chance of entry of the wrong premises and even when there is no mistake, allows those within a brief time to prepare for the police entry; and (iii) it prevents the physical destruction of property by giving the occupant the opportunity to admit the officer." LaFave et al. 2004, 167.

334 *Wilson v. Arkansas,* 514 U.S. 927, 115 S.Ct. 1914 (1995), 929 and 933.

335 *Ibid.*, 934.

to the 'knock-and-announce rule' when the police have a reasonable suspicion that knocking and announcing their presence, under the particular circumstances, would be dangerous or futile, or that it would inhibit the investigation of the crime by, for example, allowing the destruction of evidence.[336] Such a showing strikes a balance between the law enforcement interests and privacy interests at a different point and results in the reasonableness of the execution of a search warrant without complying with the knock-and-announce requirements. *United States v. Ramirez* (1998) added an exception to this where the police have "a reasonable suspicion that knocking and announcing their presence might be dangerous to themselves or to others."[337]

More reluctantly, the courts have also permitted sneak-and-peek searches of property. Such searches are conducted covertly so as to not reveal to the person whose property is being searched that he/she is under investigation. In *Dalia v. United States* (1979) the Supreme Court assessed whether the covert entry of business premises to install a bugging device, necessary for the execution of a valid order under Title III, was reasonable. Here, the Supreme Court held, for the first time explicitly, that "[t]he Fourth Amendment does not prohibit *per se* a covert entry performed for the purpose of installing otherwise legal electronic bugging equipment."[338] Only the federal district courts and appellate courts have dealt with the reasonableness, under the Fourth Amendment, of sneak-and-peek searches. These are covert physical searches of property (sneak) without the seizure of any tangible evidence (peek) and they are not within the context of executing a valid Title III order. In *United States v. Freitas* (1986) the Court of Appeals of the Ninth Circuit assessed the surreptitious entry of a home on the basis of a search warrant. The Court of Appeals referred to *Dalia v. United States* to clarify that not all surreptitious entries are forbidden by the Fourth Amendment, but it considered "the absence of any notice requirement in the warrant" to cast "strong doubt on its constitutional adequacy."[339] This latter requirement was derived from *Berger v. New York* (1967).[340] Such a notice requirement included in the warrant should then prescribe a delayed notice no later than seven days after the entry "except upon a strong showing of necessity."[341] With that, the Court of Appeals made clear that considering the nature of the privacy invasion as a consequence of sneak-and-peek searches, such searches must be "closely circumscribed" in order to be reasonable.[342] The Second Circuit Court of Appeals also concluded that "covert entries without contemporaneous notice may be

336 *Richards v. Wisconsin*, 520 U.S. 385, 117 S.Ct. 1416 (1997), 394.

337 *United States v. Ramirez,* 523 U.S. 65, 118 S.Ct. 992 (1998), 71.

338 *Dalia v. United States*, 441 U.S. 238, 99 S.Ct. 1682 (1979), 248.

339 *United States v. Freitas,* 800 F.2d 1451 (9th Cir. 1968), 1456.

340 *Berger v. New York,* 388 U.S. 41, 87 S.Ct. 1873, 60 (1967). See also Sect. 5.3.2.2 footnote 363.

341 *United States v. Freitas,* 800 F.2d 1451 (9th Cir. 1968), 1456.

342 *Ibid.*, 1456.

authorized." However, "there must be some safeguards to minimize the possibility that the officers will exceed the bounds of propriety without detection." For this purpose it formulated two limitations. Firstly, "the court should not allow the officers to dispense with advance or contemporaneous notice of the search unless they have made a showing of reasonable necessity for the delay", which should be understood as a standard of "good reason for delay." Secondly, when such a showing has been made "the court should nonetheless require the officers to give the appropriate person notice of the search within a reasonable time after the covert entry." What is reasonable depends on the circumstances of the case, but, in agreement with *Freitas*, the court held that "as an initial matter" the court shall not authorize a delayed notice after seven days after the entry. "For good cause, the issuing court may thereafter extend the period of the delay (...), [which requires] a fresh showing of the need for further delay."[343]

On the basis of the aspects that are relevant for a determination regarding the reasonableness of a search on which this section has elaborated, the conclusion can be drawn that the primary indication for the reasonableness of a particular search is the presence of probable cause. Nevertheless, to ultimately determine the reasonableness of a particular search under the Fourth Amendment, an assessment should be made of the search on the basis of "on the one hand, the degree to which it intrudes upon an individual's privacy and, on the other, the degree to which it is needed for the promotion of legitimate governmental interests."[344] This test should be applied whenever a determination has to be made concerning the reasonableness of a search under the Fourth Amendment, regardless of the presence of (e.g. state) law providing for additional requirements for the execution of a search.[345] The particular circumstances of a case may justify striking a balance somewhat differently, which would normally result in additional requirements for e.g. the execution of a valid search warrant. For example, the execution of a valid search warrant would under normal circumstances be unreasonable in the case of a search of someone's home which was not intended by the warrant or when the officers have failed to knock and announce their presence. The reasonableness of the search, however, ultimately depends on the particular circumstances of the case, which requires a balancing of the interests involved. Reasonableness therefore concerns a flexible requirement rendering the regulation of the search flexible and adjustable to law enforcement needs in particular situations, because it allows for exceptions to other Fourth Amendment requirements, which may be reasonable in specific circumstances.

343 *United States v. Villegas,* 899 F.2d 1324 (2nd Cir. 1990), 1337.

344 *Virginia v. Moore*, 553 U.S. 164, 128 S.Ct. 1598 (2008), 1604.

345 *Ibid.*, 1604 and 1605.

#### 5.3.2.1.4 The Exclusionary Rule

Under the applicability of the exclusionary rule, a violation of Fourth Amendment requirements results in the exclusion of evidence obtained through an illegal search (the exclusion of the fruits of an illegal search). The main purpose of this prophylactic 'exclusionary rule' is to deter the police from conducting unreasonable searches and seizures. In addition, it emphasizes the integrity of the judiciary and ensures that the government cannot profit from its unlawful conduct and, consequently, builds upon trust in the government.[346] Hence, the exclusionary rule is an important sanction for violations of the Fourth Amendment that deters the government from not observing Fourth Amendment requirements. In that regard the exclusionary rule aims to function so as to ensure that the restrictions on the governmental power to search and the protection against unreasonable interferences with private life are actually realized in practice.

The Fourth Amendment does not explicitly provide for an exclusionary rule. In 1886 the Supreme Court construed the exclusionary rule for Fourth Amendment violations by relating the Fourth Amendment to the Fifth Amendment: evidence obtained in violation of the Fourth Amendment cannot be allowed at trial as allowing such evidence would not be so different from compelling someone to testify against him/herself.[347] Since then, the Court has, on several occasions, tackled the question whether state courts are also required to exclude evidence obtained in violation of the Fourth Amendment. In *Mapp v. Ohio* (1961), the Court finally reasoned that, considering that the interpretation of the due process clause of the Fourteenth Amendment makes the Fourth Amendment applicable to the states, states' violations of the Fourth Amendment should be confronted with the same sanction of exclusion as violations by the federal government.[348] In *Mapp,* and in several other judgments, the Court emphasized that the main goal of the exclusionary rule is to deter police officers from unreasonable searches and seizures.[349]

The Supreme Court established in *United States v. Leon* (1984) that evidence obtained by officers acting in 'good faith' under a search warrant issued by a magistrate, which is later held not to be supported by probable cause, should not be barred by the exclusionary rule as a result. The Supreme Court wished to establish this exception because the exclusionary rule "cannot be expected, and should not be applied, to deter objectively reasonable law enforcement activity."[350] The exclusionary rule is aimed at deterring the police and not the magistrate judge who

---

[346] LaFave et al. 2004, 107-108.

[347] *Byod v. United States,* 116 U.S. 616, 6 S.Ct. 524, 633 (1886). The Fifth Amendment provides that: "No person (…) shall (…) be compelled in any criminal case to be a witness against himself (…)" US Constitution, Amendment V.

[348] *Mapp v. Ohio,* 367 U.S. 643, 81 S.Ct. 1684 (1961), p. 655.

[349] *Ibid.*, 648.

[350] *United States v. Leon,* 468 U.S. 897, 104 S.Ct. 3405 (1984), 919.

has erroneously issued the warrant. Since the police could justifiably rely on the warrant, it would be ineffective to apply the exclusionary rule to such situations when it is clear that a deterrent effect would be absent. The same reasoning applies in a situation where officers objectively reasonably rely on a statute authorizing a specific search, and the statute is later found to be unconstitutional.[351] Police officers cannot however rely on a warrant issued when "the officer will have no reasonable grounds for believing that the warrant was properly issued."[352] This will likely occur where a warrant is deficient at face value, or is based upon erroneous facts provided in the affidavit of which the police officer was aware, or in the situation of obviously unconstitutional statutory law.

In *Hudson v. Michigan* (2006), the Supreme Court determined that failing to 'knock and announce' could never result in the suppression of evidence, because it would have been "inevitably discovered."[353] With this decision, the Court removed the important remedy of the exclusionary rule for police invasions, without notice, of someone's private life by providing for a cost-benefit analysis by balancing the purpose of the exclusionary rule (considering that that purpose is to deter illegitimate action by the police) against the social cost of acquitting a guilty suspect. In that respect, *Hudson v. Michigan* did not provide for an additional exception to the 'knock-and-announce' rule, but actually undermined the rationale of the exclusionary rule.[354] The burden of proof for the application of an exclusionary rule normally rests upon the defense, except when the police have acted without a warrant: then, the burden of proof lies with the prosecution to prove that there is an exception to the exclusionary rule.[355] Since the Court's creation of the exclusionary rule, its meaning has been gradually watered down by only applying the exclusionary rule when "the deterrent effect of suppression" is "substantial and outweigh[s] any harm to the justice system."[356] Fourth Amendment violations have increasingly been found by the Court without applying the exclusionary rule to the evidence obtained through an unlawful search. *Hudson v. Michigan* set aside the exclusionary rule for any failure to meet the knock-and-announce rule; in *Herring v. United States* (2009) the Court refused to apply the exclusionary rule to the situation where police officers had mistakenly relied upon a search warrant, but only due to isolated negligence. The exclusionary rule will only apply to "reckless, grossly negligent conduct or in some circumstances recurring or systemic negligence."[357] In *Herring* the Court reached the conclusion that the exclusionary rule is "a last resort" to be only applied when "substantial

[351] *Illinois v. Krull*, 480 U.S. 340, 107 S.Ct. 1160 (1987), 350.

[352] *United States v. Leon,* 468 U.S. 897, 104 S.Ct. 3405 (1984), 922-923.

[353] *Hudson v. Michigan*, 547 U.S. 586, 126 S.Ct. 2159 (2006), 594.

[354] Bal 2007.

[355] LaFave et al. 2004, 543.

[356] *Herring v. United States,* 555 U.S. 135,129 S.Ct. 695 (2009), 12.

[357] *Ibid.*, 9. See also Sect. 5.3.1.1.

deterrence" can be realized. This should be determined by an objective "analysis of deterrence and culpability."[358]

In addition to the exclusionary rule, the 'fruit of the poisonous tree' doctrine applies. This theory applies to evidence that follows not directly or primarily from an illegal search, but is the secondary or derivative result of such a search. With respect to this type of evidence, it should be determined whether that evidence is the "fruit of the poisonous tree," which means that the court shall determine whether the derivative evidence was "tainted" by the established Fourth Amendment violation.[359] The exclusion of tainted derivative evidence is not always appropriate considering society's interest in a conviction after a crime has been committed. For that reason, exceptions are established, such as in the case of an inevitable discovery: the "[e]xclusion of physical evidence that would inevitably have been discovered adds nothing to either the integrity or fairness of a criminal trial."[360] Another exception to the 'fruits of the poisonous tree' doctrine that has been adopted by the Court concerns the situation of an independent source pointing to the same evidence as the fruits of the poisonous tree. The exclusion is only warranted if it puts the police in "the same, not a worse, position that they would have been in if no police error or misconduct had occurred.... When the challenged evidence has an independent source, exclusion of such evidence would put the police in a worse position than they would have been, absent any error or violation."[361] In fact, the inevitable discovery exception is an extrapolation of the independent source exception: "[s]ince the tainted evidence would be admissible if in fact discovered through an independent source, it should be admissible if it inevitably would have been discovered."[362]

#### 5.3.2.2 Restrictive Function of the Statutory Regulation of Surveillance Under Title III

Although surveillance is covered by the Fourth Amendment and, therefore, the same Fourth Amendment conditions are applicable to the use of surveillance techniques as to physical searches, Title III provides for an additional regulation of the use of surveillance techniques by the federal government. The contents of the Act were to an important extent based upon the constitutional requirements enumerated by the Supreme Court in *Berger v. New York* (1967) and *Katz v. United States* (1967). Surveillance techniques can be considered as more intrusive than

---

[358] *Ibid.*, 5, 10 and 12.

[359] *Nardone v. United States,* 308 U.S. 338, 60 S.Ct. 266 (1939), 341. See also LaFave et al. 2004, 509.

[360] *Nix v. Williams*, 467 U.S. 431, 104 S.Ct. 2501 (1984), 446.

[361] *Murray v. United States,* 487 U.S. 533, 108 S.Ct. 2529 (1988), 537, citing *Nix v. Williams*, 467 U.S. 431, 104 S.Ct 2501 (1984), 443, in which the independent source exception was applied in a Sixth Amendment context.

[362] *Murray v. United States,* 487 U.S. 533, 108 S.Ct. 2529 (1988), 539.

regular searches as the interception of communications occurs in secret and thus, contrary to physical searches, without prior notification. The success of the interception depends on the secrecy, for which reason advance notice of the interception is not required.[363] Instead, Title III includes a provision prescribing that the judge who has issued a surveillance order shall, "within a reasonable period but not later than 90 days", after the termination of the surveillance notify the persons whose communications have been intercepted.[364] Moreover, the duration of the execution of a warrant is usually much longer than the execution of a regular search warrant. A physical search will entail the entry and subsequent search of the place and the seizure of the things that are being looked after. Surveillance techniques, such as a wire-tap, can be continued for 30 days, which may also be extended.[365]

Surveillance techniques thus have a significantly more intrusive character than conventional, physical searches and, therefore, the use of surveillance techniques is, in addition to the applicable Fourth Amendment conditions, more precisely regulated in statutory law. Especially the application procedure for the authorization of a Title III order is more demanding in order to safeguard the restrictive and justifiable use of surveillance techniques. As was described in *United States v. United States District Court*: "[t]he Act represents a comprehensive attempt by Congress to promote more effective control of crime while protecting the privacy of individual thought and expression."[366] While enabling the use of more effective surveillance techniques to confront complex, mostly organized, crime, Title III provides for requirements which are additional to the Fourth Amendment restraints on physical searches to regulate the more invasive surveillance techniques. Title III limits the use of surveillance in the law enforcement context to the techniques defined in § 2510 and to serious crimes as enumerated in § 2516(1) a to r. Many of the provisions of Title III provide for similar requirements as the Fourth Amendment and the interpretation given to the Fourth Amendment requirements in the case law. Sections 5.3.2.1.1 and 5.3.2.1.2 have already elaborated on the probable cause and warrant requirements that also apply to Title III surveillance. This section will assess the additional restraints imposed by Title III. It will do so

[363] See also *Katz v. United States,* 389 U.S. 347, 88 S.Ct. 507 (1967), 356: "In omitting any requirement of advance notice, the federal court that authorized electronic surveillance in Osborn simply recognized, as has this Court, that officers need not announce their purpose before conducting an otherwise authorized search if such an announcement could provoke the escape of the suspect or the destruction of critical evidence." Also in *Berger v. New York* (1967) the Supreme Court had emphasized that notice prior to eavesdropping cannot reasonably be given as it undermines the whole purpose of the eavesdropping. However, here the Supreme Court suggested that, considering the relevance of a notification requirement for the reasonableness of a conventional search warrant, some showing of exigent circumstances shall be provided to compensate for the absence of a notification requirement in the warrant authorizing eavesdropping. *Berger v. New York,* 388 U.S. 41, 87 S.Ct. 1873 (1967), 60.

[364] 18 U.S.C. § 2518(8)(d) (prior to the amendments by the USA PATRIOT Act of 2001).

[365] 18 U.S.C. § 2518(5).

[366] *United States v. United States District Court*, 407 U.S. 297, 92 S.Ct. 2125 (1972), 302.

by, firstly, dealing with the statutory scheme imposing additional restraints on the application procedure for Title III surveillance. Secondly, the review of the application by the authorizing judge as to Title III will be dealt with. Lastly, the section will assess the restraints on the execution of an order for Title III surveillance and say something about the statutory exclusionary rule of Title III.

##### 5.3.2.2.1 The Application Procedure

An application under Title III must be made by an official higher in hierarchy than the officer who can file an order for the issuance of a conventional search warrant.[367] Since 1986, this official may be any attorney for the government. This statutory requirement "plainly calls" for "the mature judgment of a particular, responsible Department of Justice official (…) as a critical precondition to any judicial order," in order to safeguard a deliberate decision before an application under Title III is made.[368] The applications, similar to an application for a regular search, shall be done "in writing" and "upon oath or affirmation to a judge of competent jurisdiction."[369]

Specific requirements for the information that must be included in the application are given in § 2518(1). This concerns additional specific information regarding the interception. These additional 'particularity' requirements include: "(i) details as to the particular offense that has been, is being, or is about to be committed, (ii) except as provided in subsection (11) [authorizing a roving tap], a particular description of the nature and location of the facilities from which or the place where the communication is to be intercepted, (iii) a particular description of the type of communications sought to be intercepted, (iv) the identity of the person, if known, committing the offense and whose communications are to be intercepted."[370] The language of § 2518(1)(b)(iv) (providing for the particularity requirement as to the identity of the person) has been interpreted by the Court as requiring only the identification of a person in the application if against that person probable cause is present for believing that he/she is actually committing one of the offenses specified.[371] The Court concluded that the judge could justifiably approve an order stating that there was "probable cause to believe that Irving Kahn and 'others yet unknown' were using the two telephones to conduct illegal gambling."[372] Special agents of the FBI could then intercept all communications by

---

[367] LaFave et al. 2004, 280-281. The officials entitled to submit an order for the authorization of surveillance are enumerated in 18 U.S.C. § 2516(1).

[368] *United States v. Giordano*, 416 U.S. 505, 94 S.Ct. 1820 (1974), 515-516.

[369] 18 U.S.C. § 2518(1).

[370] 18 U.S.C. § 2518(1)(b).

[371] *United States v. Kahn,* 415 U.S. 143, 94 S.Ct. 997 (1974), 152 and 155.

[372] *Ibid.*, 146.

Kahn and communications to which Kahn was not a party, from and to the named telephones, as long as these communications related to the offenses specified.[373]

Especially the particularization requirement of the "type of communication sought to be intercepted, and a statement on the particular offense to which it relates" are intended to be important limitations on the discretion of police officers when conducting surveillance.[374] This information in the order will provide the officers with guidance as to where to look for the interception of the communications and when to record the communications based on their relevance with regard to the offense described. However, the lower courts have now generally accepted that the particularization requirement of Title III complies with and meets the Fourth Amendment requirement of particularity when the order only provides for the offense under investigation, by indicating the general nature of the criminal conduct under investigation rather than referring to a particular statutory provision in which that conduct is criminalized.[375]

Furthermore, the application shall include "a statement of the period of time for which the interception is required to be maintained."[376] Normally the authorization for the interception will then end. However, Title III provides for an exception in this regard when "the nature of the investigation is such that the authorization for interception should not automatically terminate when the described type of communication has been first obtained." In such a situation the order should include "a particular description of facts establishing probable cause to believe that additional communications of the same type will occur thereafter."[377]

The last additional statutory requirement for the application procedure of Title III surveillance that must be mentioned is the requirement aiming to prevent 'judge shopping.' Together with the application, any information "known" to the person filing the application with regard to previous applications to any judge must be disclosed.[378]

#### 5.3.2.2.2 A Review of the Application by the Magistrate Judge

Before a magistrate judge may authorize an order for an interception of communications he/she has to determine on the basis of the facts provided in the application whether probable cause can be established that someone is committing, has

[373] *Ibid.*, 158.

[374] 18 U.S.C. § 2518(4).

[375] Lower courts have held that compliance with the statutory requirements (by merely indicating the offense under investigation) of Title III is in compliance with the Fourth Amendment. LaFave et al. 2004, 269 and 282. For the importance of the particularity requirement in surveillance cases, as set out by the Supreme Court before the enactment of Title III, see *Berger v. New York,* 388 U.S. 41, 87 S.Ct. 1873 (1967), 55-56.

[376] 18 U.S.C. § 2518(1)(d).

[377] 18 U.S.C. § 2518(1)(d).

[378] 18 U.S.C. § 2518(1)(e).

committed, or is about to commit one of the offenses enumerated in § 2516(1).[379] This limits the use of surveillance techniques to the investigation of specific serious crimes and to situations in which probable cause is present. In addition, according to § 2518(3)(b), probable cause is also required for the belief that an interception will be the adequate means to obtain communications that are related to that offense. Also the place or facility from which the communications are to be intercepted shall be places or facilities regarding which probable cause can be established of a connection to the commission of the offenses or to the suspects.[380]

Moreover, the authorizing judge should take into account the principle of subsidiarity: the use of Title III techniques is only permitted if normal investigative procedures have either been tried before and have failed, or if normal investigative procedures reasonably appear to be unlikely to succeed or are too dangerous to be followed (§ 2518(3)(c)). The application should include "a full and complete statement" about this issue (§ 2518(1)(c)). This requirement must be considered as an important restraint on the use of electronic surveillance. The Supreme Court emphasized the following in *United States v. Giordano*: "[C]ongress legislated in considerable detail in providing for applications and orders authorizing wiretapping and evinced the clear intent to make doubly sure that the statutory authority be used with restraint and only where the circumstances warrant the surreptitious interception of wire and oral communications. These procedures were not to be routinely employed as the initial step in criminal investigation. Rather, the applicant must state and the court must find that normal investigative procedures have been tried and failed or reasonably appear to be unlikely to succeed if tried or to be too dangerous."[381] However, although intended as an important restraint on electronic eavesdropping in order to secure the spare use of these techniques, in practice the actual assessment of subsidiarity is marginal by only requiring a demonstration of investigatory utility without any showing of the necessity within the application.[382]

---

[379] 18 U.S.C. § 2518(3)(a).

[380] 18 U.S.C. § 2518(3)(d). This does not apply when the exception for the 'roving tap' is applicable under 18 U.S.C. § 2518(11) (the specification of the facilities or place may be omitted upon a particularized showing of need). The examination that the authorizing judge must conduct is described in § 2518(3), providing that the judge must determine "on the basis of the facts submitted by the applicant that: (a) there is probable cause for belief that an individual is committing, has committed, or is about to commit a particular offense enumerated in section 2516 of this chapter; (b) there is probable cause for belief that particular communications concerning that offense will be obtained through such interception; (c) normal investigative procedures have been tried and have failed or reasonably appear to be unlikely to succeed if tried or to be too dangerous; (d) except as provided in subsection (11), there is probable cause for belief that the facilities from which, or the place where, the wire, oral, or electronic communications are to be intercepted are being used, or are about to be used, in connection with the commission of such offense, or are leased to, listed in the name of, or commonly used by such person."

[381] *United States v. Giordano*, 416 U.S. 505, 94 S.Ct. 1820 (1974), 515.

[382] LaFave et al. 2004, 283.

When the authorizing judge has approved the presence of probable cause regarding the several issues mentioned and has assessed the subsidiarity of the use of the interception techniques, he/she may issue an order for the surveillance. This order must specifically provide for the information regarding these determinations on probable cause (the identity of the person, the facilities or places regarding which the authority to intercept has been granted, the type of communications to be intercepted and a statement of the offense to which the interception is related).[383] In addition, the order must specify the period for which interception has been authorized and must include directives regarding the execution of the order. These directives shall include a directive according to which the interception must "be conducted in such a way as to minimize the interception of communications not otherwise subject to interception."[384] This latter minimization requirement will be dealt with in more detail in the next subsection. When an application for interception has been denied by the judge, the government may appeal against this decision.[385] The court may only overturn a denial of an application when this decision was clearly erroneous.[386]

#### 5.3.2.2.3 Execution of an Order Under Title III

Considering the more intrusive nature of the execution of a surveillance order than of the execution of a warrant for a physical search, Title III also includes some additional safeguards for execution. These requirements concern 'recording and sealing', 'minimization,' and 'post-surveillance notice.'

Section 2518(8)(a) requires the recording of any intercepted communication in a such way that editing the recording will be excluded. Subsequently, immediately after the termination of the surveillance the recording shall be made available to the judge who has issued the order so that he/she can 'seal' the recording and prevent the government from having an opportunity to tamper with the contents of the recording. In this way the reliability and integrity of the evidence will be guaranteed.[387] Within Title III the exclusion of evidence obtained in violation of this recording and sealing procedure is guaranteed.[388]

In the second place, the minimization requirement aims to minimize the interception of communications that are not relevant for the investigation.[389] The law enforcement officer executing the order shall make sure that the minimization

---

383 18 U.S.C. § 2518(4).

384 18 U.S.C. § 2518(5).

385 18 U.S.C. § 2518(10)(b).

386 See: LaFave et al. 2004, 285.

387 LaFave et al. 2004, 90.

388 18 U.S.C. § 2518(8)(a).

389 18 U.S.C. § 2518(5): "(…) in such a way as to minimize the interception of communications not otherwise subject to interception under this chapter."

procedures are observed by terminating the electronic surveillance immediately upon the conclusion that the communications intercepted have nothing to do with the offense under investigation or are protected by a specific privilege. If it is not reasonably possible to determine what communications are subject to interception during the execution of the order, the minimization shall take place after the fact. The minimization is understood as a 'good faith' effort of the law enforcement officer in question, for which reason the burden of proof with regard to compliance with the minimization procedures lies on the defendant.[390] When the government is not able to make a *prime facie* showing that the minimization procedures have been observed, the court will determine whether the execution of the order was objectively reasonable. A negative conclusion may render the surveillance unreasonable under the Fourth Amendment. The exact manner of compliance with the minimization requirement depends on the circumstances of a particular case. The Supreme Court made such an assessment in *Scott v. United States* (1978). This case concerned the interception, on behalf of government agents, of "all the phone conversations over a particular phone for a period of one month", whereas "only 40% of them were shown to be narcotics related."[391] The Supreme Court concluded that the minimization requirement had not been violated and the interception was reasonable under the Fourth Amendment. The Court took into account the particular circumstances of the case to reach that conclusion, such as the fact that "many nonpertinent calls may have been very short", "ambiguous in nature" or "one-time conversations" and the fact that the investigation concerned a "widespread conspiracy" justifying "more extensive surveillance."[392]

A third safeguard regarding the execution of a Title III order included in statutory law concerns the requirement of a 'post-surveillance notice.' When the surveillance activities have been terminated, the magistrate judge must give notice to the persons named in the order "and such other parties (…) as the judge may determine in his discretion that is in the interest of justice."[393] The notification must be done 90 days after the termination of the surveillance (or 90 days after an order for interception has been denied). The notification shall include the fact that an order for interception has been issued, the period for which the interception was authorized and whether communications have actually been intercepted.[394] A delayed notice may be permitted: "on an *ex parte* showing of good cause to a judge of competent jurisdiction the serving of the inventory required by this subsection may be postponed."[395]

---

[390] American Bar Association Standards for Criminal Justice (2001), *Electronic Surveillance, Third Edition, Section A: Electronic Surveillance of Private Communications,* 56, 126-139 and 135-144 and Blum et al. 2010, para 412-415.

[391] *Scott v. United States,* 436 U.S. 128, 98 S.Ct. 1717 (1978), 130-131 and 132.

[392] *Ibid.*, 140 and 142.

[393] 18 U.S.C. § 2518(8)(d).

[394] 18 U.S.C. § 2518(d) (1)-(3).

[395] 18 U.S.C. § 2518(8)(d).

#### 5.3.2.2.4 Exclusion of Evidence Obtained in Violation of Title III

When the use of surveillance techniques violates the Fourth Amendment the judicially created exclusionary rule applies, as has been dealt with in Sect. 5.3.2.1.4. In addition, Title III provides in 18 U.S.C. § 2518 for a statutory exclusionary rule covering evidence obtained, directly or indirectly, in violation of Title III. The scope of this statutory exclusionary rule thus appears to be broader than the regular exclusionary rule, considering that it also targets information obtained through surveillance techniques in violation of the restraints imposed by Title III. However, submitting a motion to suppress the evidence obtained in violation of Title III is only possible when: "(i) the communication was unlawfully intercepted; (ii) the order of authorization or approval under which it was intercepted is insufficient on its face; (iii) the interception was not in conformity with the order of authorization or approval."[396]

Also the Supreme Court has somewhat limited the scope of this statutory exclusionary rule. In *United States v. Giordano* the Supreme Court interpreted the unlawful interceptions referred to in § 2518(10)(a) under (1) to "require suppression where there is failure to satisfy any of those statutory requirements that directly and substantially implement the congressional intent to limit the use of intercept procedures to those situations clearly calling for the employment of this extraordinary investigative device."[397] The suppression of evidence obtained in violation of a Title III provision must follow, according to the Court, when the statutory requirement that has been ignored (in this case the provision for pre-application approval by a senior official at the Department of Justice) "was intended to play a central role in the statutory scheme."[398] Also in *United States v. Chavez* (1974) the Court emphasized that in *Giordano* they "did not go so far as to suggest that every failure to comply fully with any requirement provided in Title III would render the interception of wire or oral communications 'unlawful'."[399] Furthermore, in *Giordano* the Supreme Court noted that according to the legislative history the exclusionary provision "should serve to guarantee that the standards of the new chapter will sharply curtail the unlawful interception of wire and oral communications."[400]

Because of this interpretation of the statutory exclusionary rule, in practice the provision is usually not interpreted substantially different from the scope of the Fourth Amendment exclusionary rule. Rather, the interpretation of the Fourth

---

[396] 18 U.S.C. § 2518(10)(a). It is remarkable that the provision only mentions that someone may move for the suppression of the contents of any wire or oral communication intercepted, without referring to electronic communications. When the interception of electronic communications was added to Title III in 1986, no changes were made to the language of this exclusionary rule. LaFave et al. 2004, 291.

[397] *United States v. Giordano*, 416 U.S. 505, 94 S.Ct. 1820 (1974), 527.

[398] *Ibid.*, 528.

[399] *United States v. Chavez*, 416 U.S. 562, 94 S.Ct. 1849 (1974), 574-575.

[400] *United States v. Giordano*, 416 U.S. 505, 94 S.Ct. 1820 (1974), 528.

Amendment exclusionary rule is also used to interpret the scope of the exclusionary rule of Title III. Still, the statutory exclusionary rule has been intended, as has also been affirmed by the Supreme Court, to stimulate adherence to the statutory requirements for surveillance by providing a remedy for violations of these statutory requirements.

#### 5.3.2.3 Regulation of the FBI's Authority to Investigate Through the Issuance of Guidelines by the Attorney General

The Attorney General's guidelines concern the most important source that further defines and regulates the investigative authorities of the FBI. The most important function of these guidelines—and also the reason for their adoption—has been to protect against any abuse of investigative power by the FBI (both its criminal investigative power and its domestic intelligence gathering power), by providing for limitations and principles to be observed in FBI investigations in order to ensure that the FBI's investigative activities occur within Constitutional limits.[401] Taking this initial purpose of the first set of the Attorney General's guidelines (the 'Levi Guidelines') into consideration, the guidelines are dealt with as part of the sources that constitute the shield aspect of criminal investigation, although they are at the same time and also increasingly aimed at improving effective investigation by the FBI by providing guidelines as to how to allocate its resources most effectively in criminal investigations. Arguably, the guidelines have by now, and especially after the events of September 11, 2001, become a sword tool, although initially introduced as a tool of supplementary regulation.

The FBI derives its power to investigate domestically from Executive Order 12333 and from the Attorney General's power to appoint officials for the detection and prosecution of federal crimes.[402] As delegated in the law, the FBI's authority is rather broad, although it is of course subject to the limitations on the use of investigative techniques as follows from the Fourth Amendment, Title III and FISA. Although all guidelines by the Department of Justice concern internal guidelines, which do not become part of the Code of Federal Regulations and thus are not enforceable as legislative standards in the courts, these guidelines are (or were originally) intended to protect citizens' constitutional rights against the unfettered use of investigative powers.[403] In particular in response to the findings of the Church committee (see Sect. 5.2.2.3.1) Attorney General Levi issued the first guidelines in 1976 in order to enhance internal controls and oversight to

[401] Jones 2009, 137 and 141-142.

[402] 28 U.S.C. § 533.

[403] Podgor 2004, 170 and Elliff 1984, 786.

prevent future abuses of investigative powers in domestic matters.[404] The guidelines do not include a detailed regulation of the use of specific investigative techniques; however, they do provide for different types of investigations to be initiated under different conditions and which techniques may be used in these investigations. In addition, the guidelines provide some general principles to be observed in the FBI's investigative activities. This section will continue to analyze the Levi Guidelines and, in more detail, its successor, the Smith Guidelines. The Smith Guidelines 'on General Crimes, Racketeering Enterprise and Domestic Security/Terrorism Investigations largely remained in place[405] until the Ashcroft Guidelines on 'General Crimes, Racketeering Enterprise and Terrorism Enterprise Investigations', which were issued in 2002. The effect of these Guidelines (and its successor) in comparison to the Smith Guidelines will be addressed in Sects. 6.4.2.2 and 6.4.2.3 of the next chapter. In addition to these guidelines dealing with the criminal investigative authority of the FBI, the Attorney General has issued and revised guidelines on the use of confidential informants, on FBI undercover operations, on the consensual monitoring of verbal communications and on National Security Investigations.

#### 5.3.2.3.1 The Levi Guidelines

The 'Domestic Security Investigation Guidelines' by Attorney General Levi (hereafter: the 'Levi Guidelines') became effective on 6 April 1976. Contrary to what might be suggested by its title, the guidelines are understood to deal not only with domestic security investigations, but also with the FBI's general criminal investigations.[406] The Levi Guidelines distinguish three types of domestic security investigations: 1) preliminary investigations; 2) limited investigations; and, 3) full investigations. These three types of investigations differ in scope and in the investigative techniques which may be used.[407] In general, domestic security investigations aim to "ascertain information on the activities of individuals or the activities of groups, which involve or will involve the violation of federal law for

---

[404] See: Special Report of the DoJ's Office of the Inspector General 2005, 34-36. In addition, on December 15, 1976, Attorney General Levi issued guidelines on the "Use of Informants in Domestic Security, Organized Crime, and Other Criminal Investigations," which aimed to minimize the use of informants, to protect individual rights and to adopt policy preventing the government from violating the law when using informants. These guidelines on the use of informants were importantly revised by the Civiletti Guidelines of 1980 and, subsequently, by the Reno Guidelines of 2001. See Special Report of the DoJ's Office of the Inspector General 2005, 37-38, 39-41 and 57-58.

[405] In 1989 Attorney General Dick Thornburgh issued some amendments to the Smith Guidelines, primarily in order to implement some legislative changes. In essence, the Smith Guidelines were untouched and remained into place until the Ashcroft Guidelines of 2002. Jones 2009, 146.

[406] Special Report of the DoJ's Office of the Inspector General 2005, 37 (footnote 55).

[407] Section I, Levi Guidelines, *FBI Statutory Charter*. Hearings Before the Senate Committee on the Judiciary, 95th Cong. Pt. 1, 20-26 (1978) (henceforth: Levi Guidelines), 20.

the purpose of: (1) overthrowing the government of the United States or the government of a State; (2) substantially interfering, in the United States, with the activities of a foreign government or its authorized representatives; (3) substantially impairing for the purpose of influencing U.S. government policies or decisions: (a) the functioning of the government of the United States; (b) the functioning of the government of a State; or (c) interstate commerce; (4) depriving persons of their civil rights under the Constitution, laws, or treaties of the United States" (hereafter collectively referred to as 'purposes threatening domestic security).[408]

A preliminary investigation may be initiated upon "allegations or other information that an individual or a group may be engaged in activities which involve or will involve the use of force or violence and which involve or will involve the violation of federal law for one or more of the "purposes threatening domestic security." The objective of such a preliminary investigation is to determine "whether there is a factual basis for opening a full investigation."[409] The techniques that may be used in preliminary investigations are limited to the examination of FBI indices and files, public records or other public sources, federal, state and local records, as well as an inquiry into existing sources and previously established informants and physical surveillance and to interview other persons for the purpose of identifying the subject of investigation.[410]

The second category of 'limited investigations' allows additional investigative tools when the techniques permitted in the preliminary investigation are inadequate to ascertain whether the initiation of a full investigation is required. As an additional check, authorization in writing by a 'Special Agent in Charge' or by 'FBI Headquarters' is required before the limited investigation may be opened. The techniques available in the limited investigation are those of the preliminary investigation, supplemented by the possibility of "physical surveillance for purposes other than identifying the subject of the investigation" and the "interviewing" of those persons not covered by the investigative tools available in the preliminary investigation "for purposes other than identifying the subject of the investigation." This latter technique may only be used with the authorization of the Special Agent in Charge and "after full consideration of such factors as the seriousness of the allegation, the need for the interview, and the consequences of using the technique." Moreover, if there is doubt as to whether or not this technique shall be used, "the Special Agent in Charge shall seek approval of FBI Headquarters."[411]

Techniques such as the use of informants, mail covers and electronic surveillance are explicitly excluded from use both in the preliminary investigation and the limited investigation.[412] Moreover, the duration of a preliminary and limited

---

408 Section II(A) Levi Guidelines, 20.

409 Section II(C) Levi Guidelines, 20-21.

410 Section II(E) Levi Guidelines, 21.

411 Section II(F) Levi Guidelines, 21-22.

412 Section II(G) Levi Guidelines, 22.

investigation together is limited to 90 days. FBI headquarters may authorize extensions for another 90 days when "facts or information obtained in the original period justify such an extension."[413]

For the third category of 'full investigation' the Levi Guidelines prescribed a threshold of "specific and articulable facts giving reason to believe that an individual or group is or may be engaged in activities which involve the use of force or violence and which involve or will involve the violation of federal law for one or more of the [purposes threatening domestic security]." Moreover, the Guidelines enumerate some factors that should be taken into consideration when determining whether to open a full investigation: "(i) the magnitude of the threatened harm; (2) the likelihood it will occur; (3) the immediacy of the threat; and (4) the danger to privacy and free expression posed by a full investigation."[414] All lawful investigative techniques may be used in a full investigation; however, the guidelines provided some specific conditions that should be observed for the most intrusive techniques, concerning, e.g. the duration of the use of informants, the observance of the privilege against self-discrimination, a prohibition on obtaining privileged information through informants and electronic surveillance, the use of mail covers under the applicable regulations and the use of electronic surveillance under the requirements of Title III.[415]

Furthermore, the Levi Guidelines prescribed internal review procedures for all investigative activities in order to avoid investigations being continued, whereas the threshold for opening such investigations is no longer satisfied. A general review of FBI investigations shall be carried out by the Department of Justice; extensions or long-term investigations and all full investigations shall also be reported to and reviewed by the Department of Justice. The dissemination of "facts or information" to other federal authorities or local and state authorities was permitted if such information falls within the investigative jurisdiction of such other agency, is required for the prevention of use of force or violence, is otherwise prescribed by regulation published in the Federal Register, or is needed to protect the integrity of a law enforcement agency."[416]

The Levi Guidelines were aimed at restraint in the FBI's investigative activities that interfere with privacy rights. FBI agents needed the approval of a Special Agent in Charge of FBI Headquarters even for initiating a limited investigation; the most intrusive techniques, including mail covers, informants and attending demonstrations and meetings, were only available in the full investigation and, before initiating any investigation, the necessity and proportionality thereof in relation to the adverse consequences for Constitutional (First and Fourth Amendment) rights should be taken into account.[417]

---

413 Section II(H) Levi Guidelines, 22.

414 Section II(I) Levi Guidelines, 22.

415 Section II(J) Levi Guidelines, 22-23.

416 Section IV Levi Guidelines, 24-25.

417 Jones 2009, 142.

#### 5.3.2.3.2 The Smith Guidelines

In 1983 Attorney General Smith issued a new set of Guidelines, replacing the Levi Guidelines, in order to "ensure protections of the public from the greater sophistication and changing nature of domestic groups that are prone to violation." The FBI should be able to effectively monitor and prevent violence. However, sufficient protections should be upheld to guarantee respect for behavior protected by the First Amendment.[418] Attorney General Smith furthermore stated that "the time has come [...] to eliminate separate regulations for domestic security/terrorism investigations and treat these matters as an integral part of FBI's general law enforcement responsibilities."[419] Hence, the Smith Guidelines integrated into a single document the guidelines for the FBI in general crime investigations, racketeering enterprise investigations and domestic security and terrorism investigations. The regulation of the FBI's investigative authority with regard to foreign intelligence, foreign counterintelligence and international terrorism matters was maintained in a separate set of guidelines. The Smith Guidelines were explicitly applicable to investigative activities with a nexus to criminal activity.[420] The Guidelines distinguished two types of investigation: (1) General Crimes Investigations, and (2) Criminal Intelligence Investigations (racketeering enterprise investigations and domestic security/terrorism investigations). Each category will be dealt with separately below. The section will conclude with some general consequences of the Smith Guidelines.

##### a. General Crimes Investigations

General crimes investigations could include a "preliminary inquiry" and (full) "investigations." The preliminary investigation addressed under the section 'general crimes investigation' is subject to the same conditions when preceding a criminal intelligence investigation or domestic security investigation.

Preliminary inquiries are intended to cover the situation in which the information available is insufficient to open a full investigation, which means, under the Smith Guidelines, that the information falls short of establishing "reasonable indications." However, the information available is of such a nature that "further scrutiny" is required beyond the "prompt and extremely limited checking out of initial leads." The preliminary inquiry is conducted with "as little intrusion as the needs of the situation permit", is of "short duration" and is done for the purpose of "obtaining the information necessary to make an informed judgment as to whether a full investigation is warranted."[421]

---

[418] Hearing before the Subcommittee on Security and Terrorism on the Committee on the Judiciary United States Senate, 98th Congress, First Session on Attorney General's Guidelines for Domestic Security Investigations (Smith Guidelines), March 25, 1983, Serial No. J-98-25, S. Hrg 98-176 (henceforth: Smith Guidelines 1983), 47 (Appendix).

[419] Smith Guidelines 1983, 48 (Appendix).

[420] See: Smith Guidelines 1983, 53.

[421] Section II(B) Smith Guidelines 1983, 55.

The preliminary inquiry may last for 90 days, with possible extensions for 30-day periods to be granted by FBI Headquarters. Such extensions may only be granted "upon receipt of a written request and statement of reasons why further investigative steps are warranted when there is no "reasonable indication" of criminal activity." Before using an investigative technique in the preliminary inquiry, it should be considered whether "less intrusive means" may also be used to obtain the information in "a timely and effective way." Factors to consider are "adverse consequences to an individual's privacy interests and avoidable damage to his reputation" as well as "the seriousness of the possible crime and the strength of the information indicating the possible existence of the crime."[422] The techniques of mail covers, mail openings and non-consensual electronic surveillance or any other technique covered by Title III are prohibited in the preliminary inquiry. All other lawful investigative techniques are not explicitly prohibited. However, in general the techniques applied should be less intrusive than those applied in full investigations. The techniques previously authorized for preliminary investigations under the Levi Guidelines may now be used in the preliminary inquiry without prior authorization from a supervisory agent. All other lawful techniques must be authorized by a supervisory agent, "except in exigent circumstances." When the technique has a highly intrusive nature, authorization should only be given in "compelling circumstances."[423]

Full general crimes investigations may be initiated when meeting the threshold "facts and circumstances reasonably indicat[ing] that a federal crime has been, is being, or will be committed." The goal of the general crimes investigation is to "prevent, solve and prosecute such criminal activity." It is explained that the threshold of a "reasonable indication" is "substantially lower than probable cause." Factors to consider in order to determine whether the standard is satisfied are those "facts or circumstances a prudent investigator would consider," but must include "facts or circumstances indicating a past, current, or impending violation." An "objective, factual basis" must be present; "a mere hunch is insufficient" for opening a full investigation.[424]

The general crimes investigation can operate proactively in the investigation of criminalized conspiracies and attempts. When the investigation involves future criminal activity, whereas a "current criminal conspiracy or attempt" is not yet involved, the guidelines prescribe "particular care [...] to assure that there exist facts and circumstances amounting to a reasonable indication that a crime will occur."[425]

Furthermore, the guidelines prescribe regular consultations between the Special Agent and the appropriate federal prosecutor. More intensive consultation is warranted when the investigation involves a "sensitive criminal matter."[426]

---

422 Section II(B)(2)–(4) Smith Guidelines 1983, 56.

423 Section II(B)(4)–(6) Smith Guidelines 1983, 56-57.

424 Section II(C)(1) Smith Guidelines 1983, 57.

425 Section II(C)(2) Smith Guidelines 1983, 57.

426 Section II(C)(4) Smith Guidelines 1983, 57-58.

All lawful investigative techniques may be used during the general crimes investigation that is not a preliminary inquiry. The principles of subsidiarity and proportionality apply to the use of investigative techniques as well as statutory regulations and Department regulations and policies.[427]

b. Criminal Intelligence Investigations

The Smith Guidelines included the concept of a 'criminal intelligence investigation.' The criminal intelligence investigation can have a broader scope by investigating enterprises either involved in obtaining "monetary or commercial gains or profits through racketeering activities" or furthering "political or social goals through activities that involve criminal violence."[428] The criminal intelligence investigation is distinguished from the general crimes investigation, because the criminal intelligence investigation is not aimed at investigating who committed a completed criminal act, but at "determining the size and composition of the group involved [in the ongoing criminal enterprise], its geographic dimensions, its past acts and intended criminal goals, and its capacity for harm." The criminal intelligence investigation is, furthermore, not necessarily terminated with the decision as to whether or not to prosecute one or more of the participants. The guidelines refer to the *Keith* decision to indicate that criminal intelligence investigations may, considering their subject of investigation, be "less precise than that directed against more conventional types of crime." The criminal intelligence investigation "requires the fitting together of bits and pieces of information [...] to determine whether a pattern of criminal activity exists." The guidelines also warn that specific care should be taken in these investigations so as to sort out activities protected by the First and Fourth Amendment from those "which may lead to violence or serious disruption of society."[429]

Two types of criminal intelligence investigations are distinguished in the guidelines: racketeering[430] enterprise investigations and domestic security/terrorism investigations.

Racketeering enterprise investigations target criminal organizations that involve "violence, extortion, narcotics, or systematic public corruption." The authority to investigate under this category is limited to racketeering enterprises involved in these activities. However, in exceptional circumstances the Director of the FBI, concurring with the Attorney General, may authorize the investigation of racketeering enterprises not involved in such activities. The threshold for initiating a racketeering enterprise investigation is again a "reasonable indication"; more specifically: "facts or circumstances reasonably indicat[ing] that two or more persons are engaged in a continuing course of conduct for the purpose of obtaining monetary or commercial gains or profits wholly or in part through racketeering

427 Section IV Smith Guidelines 1983, 63.

428 Section III Smith Guidelines 1983, 58.

429 Section III Smith Guidelines 1983, 59.

430 Racketeering activities are those activities that were included in the Racketeer Influenced and Corrupt Organizations Act (18 U.S.C. 1961(1) (1983)).

activity."[431] 'Reasonably indicate' should be understood as requiring "an objective factual basis for initiating the investigation, but […] not […] specific facts or circumstances indicating a past, current, or impending violation."[432] The purpose of the racketeering enterprise investigation is "to obtain information concerning the nature and structure of the enterprise […] with a view to the longer range objective of detection, prevention, and prosecution of the criminal enterprise."[433] The racketeering enterprise investigation may be authorized by the Director of the FBI or the designated Assistant Director (with the concurrence of the Attorney General when no violence, extortion, narcotics, or systematic public corruption is involved) for a period of 180 days, with the possibility of extensions by renewed authorization for additional periods not exceeding 180 days.

The second category of criminal intelligence investigations concerns the "domestic security/terrorism investigations," which should aim to investigate enterprises "whose goals are to achieve political or social change through activities that involve force or violence." This does not include international terrorism, as that was understood as a matter for national security investigations. The standard for full domestic security/terrorism investigations was lowered by replacing the standard of "specific and articulable facts giving reason to believe" by "facts or circumstances [that] reasonably indicate that two or more persons are engaged in an enterprise for the purpose of furthering political or social goals wholly or in part through activities that involve force or violence and a violation of the criminal laws of the United States." All circumstances shall be taken into account to determine whether this threshold is met, "including: (1) the magnitude of the threatened harm; (2) the likelihood it will occur; (3) the immediacy of the threat; and (4) the danger to privacy and free expression posed by an investigation."[434] The guidelines exclude the investigation of mere "speculations that force or violence might occur during the course of an otherwise peaceable demonstration" in order to avoid the investigation of activities protected by the First Amendment.[435] However, a possibility has been created to continue domestic security/terrorism investigations also when the enterprise is temporarily inactive by not engaging in "recent acts of violence" and without concerning an "immediate threat of harm." When the "composition, goals and prior history of the group" nevertheless justifies continued "federal interest," the investigation may be continued through monitoring the "status of the criminal objectives of the enterprise."[436] Furthermore, the purpose, scope and authorization procedures for domestic security/terrorism investigation are similar to those of the racketeering enterprise investigation.[437]

431 Section III(A)(1)–(2) Smith Guidelines 1983, 59.

432 Special Report of the DoJ's Office of the Inspector General 2005, 48.

433 Section III(A)(3) Smith Guidelines 1983.

434 Section III(B)(1)(a) Smith Guidelines 1983.

435 Section III(B)(1)(c) Smith Guidelines 1983.

436 Section III(B)(4)(d) Smith Guidelines 1983.

437 See Section III(B)(2)–(4) Smith Guidelines 1983.

### c. Consequences of the Smith Guidelines

The most important consequence of the Smith Guidelines was the lowering of the evidentiary threshold for initiating a full (either general criminal or criminal intelligence) investigation by replacing the standard of "specific and articulable facts giving reason to believe" by "facts or circumstances [that] reasonably indicate." 'Reasonably indicate' should be understood as requiring "an objective factual basis for initiating the investigation, but [...] not [...] specific facts or circumstances indicating a past, current, or impending violation."[438] From internally circulated instructions by the FBI in 1995 it has followed that the standard of 'reasonably indicate' should be understood as being "substantially lower than probable cause" and that the standard to initiate preliminary inquiries is an even lower standard. Before, 'reasonably indicate' was construed as a standard "requiring evidence of an imminent violation of a federal law." The Oklahoma City bombing in April 1995 caused this reinterpretation of the standard to be be satisfied when there is information showing that the group has an "ability to carry out violent acts that may violate federal law."[439]

The Smith Guidelines provided, in comparison with the Levi Guidelines, for more lenient standards for the FBI's investigative activities. Nevertheless, the main purpose of the Guidelines was still to provide guidance to the FBI in order to make sure that investigative activities are carried out within the confines of the Constitution and the law.[440] The possibilities of preliminary inquiries, the lowering of the evidentiary standard for full investigations, the scope of criminal intelligence investigations, and the possibility of the low-level monitoring of sleeping cells, concern important proactive investigative possibilities for the FBI. However, the use of non-consensual surveillance is still subject to the requirements of Title III, including a showing of probable cause. Also the use of other more intrusive techniques, such as informants and undercover operations, shall be made in accordance with guidelines governing these techniques.[441] Moreover, all investigative activities "shall be based on a "reasonable factual predicate and shall have a valid law enforcement purpose." Hence, the investigations under these guidelines are clearly separated from national security investigations, as they shall always have a nexus with criminal activity and their purpose is to develop evidence for prosecution.[442] However, the prevention of violations of federal criminal law was already included as a valid investigative purpose, without restricting such prevention to the investigation of criminal conspiracy or attempt. Furthermore, the Smith Guidelines included two general restrictions on the FBI's investigative

---

[438] Special Report of the DoJ's Office of the Inspector General 2005, 48.

[439] Special Report of the DoJ's Office of the Inspector General 2005, 56.

[440] Jones 2009, 144-145.

[441] Section IV Smith Guidelines 1983.

[442] Transcript of the press briefing by Attorney General Smith and the Director of the FBI Webster on the new guidelines, Washington, D.C., March 7 1983, published in: Smith Guidelines 1983, 72.

activities by prohibiting initiating an investigation on the basis of someone's exercise of First Amendment rights and by subjecting all investigations to the principle of subsidiarity. These restrictions still apply.[443]

#### 5.3.2.4 The Restrictive Function of the Regulation of National Security Investigations Under FISA

At first sight one would categorize the subject of the regulation of national security investigations under the sword aspect of criminal procedural law, considering that the information obtained in national security investigations may be used as evidence taking into account that, in theory, there are no explicit legal barriers prohibiting the sharing of information obtained through the looser FISA framework with law enforcement agencies. Nevertheless, because FISA has been adopted in order to bring national security surveillance into conformity with the Fourth Amendment, the regulation provided by FISA has a shield function. Moreover, the language of FISA as it was originally adopted in 1978 has been interpreted as to bar the use of FISA for criminal procedural sword purposes.[444] Hence, also from the perspective of criminal procedural law, the FISA of 1978 can be understood to contribute to the shield objective.

##### 5.3.2.4.1 The Regulation of National Security Investigations

As set out before, surveillance is limited by Fourth Amendment protections and by the statutory conditions of Title III if it is carried out against persons within the United States in the context of ordinary law enforcement. Title III, however, does not limit the President's constitutional power, under Article II, to take measures to obtain foreign intelligence information by, for example, warrantless electronic surveillance, if the information sought is essential to the security of the United States.[445] Also the Supreme Court determined in the *Keith* decision that "domestic security surveillance may involve different policy and practical considerations from the surveillance of ordinary crime" and for that reason Congress may enact different standards for domestic security surveillance than already exists for enumerated crimes under Title III (see in detail Sect. 5.2.2.3.1).[446]

To create a statutory scheme of regulation for national security investigations, FISA was enacted in 1978. This Act imposes checks and balances upon the

---

443 See Section I (General Principles) of the Smith Guidelines 1983, 54 and the Special Report of the DoJ's Office of the Inspector General 2005, 49.

444 See Sect. 5.2.2.3.2.

445 LaFave et al. 2004, 265.

446 *United States v. United States District Court*, 407 U.S. 297, 92 S.Ct. 2125 (1972), 322.

President's power to gather foreign intelligence information through surveillance by providing for statutory standards and guidelines and a judicial review of certain investigative activities.[447] The draft FISA was aimed at providing statutory limits and conditions for the use of electronic surveillance for foreign intelligence as opposed to law enforcement purposes. FISA has now been importantly amended by the USA PATRIOT Act of 2001. In addition to this statutory regulation of national security investigations, the guidelines of the Attorney General have regulated, similar to criminal investigations, the FBI's authority in national security investigations. These guidelines also existed prior to the events of 9/11 (and the issuance in 2003 of the Ashcroft Guidelines on "FBI National Security Investigations and Foreign Intelligence Collection").[448] The documents are still largely classified, making a detailed analysis in this section a needless exercise.[449]

The statutory regulation of national security investigations under FISA provided for a "separate track" with respect to electronic surveillance in national security investigations, which loosened the applicable standards for electronic surveillance for the purpose of foreign intelligence gathering as compared with ordinary criminal investigations.[450] Electronic surveillance under this Act has to be approved by a special Foreign Intelligence Surveillance Act Court (the FISA Court). A request for an order of the FISA Court can be made by a federal officer provided that the Attorney General approves.[451] Electronic surveillance is permissible under FISA when there is probable cause to believe that the suspect being investigated is a foreign agent or power, or a US person acting on behalf of a foreign power.

The FISA probable cause standard crucially differs from the probable cause standard in a conventional criminal investigation, considering that the probable cause standard in national security investigations concerns the identity of the person (a foreign agent or power or a US person acting on behalf of a foreign power) and not the criminal activities in which the person engages. Furthermore, the primary purpose of the investigation should be to gather foreign intelligence

---

[447] Howell 2006, 118. The two congressional oversight committees also played an important role in the enactment of FISA.

[448] The Attorney General's Guidelines for FBI National Security Investigations and Foreign Intelligence Collection, issued and classified by John Ashcroft on October 31, 2003 (declassified by AG Gonzales on August 2, 2007), available at: http://www.fas.org/irp/agency/doj/fbi/nsiguidelines.pdf (accessed October 14, 2010). See on these guidelines, Chap. 6, Sect. 6.4.2.2.

[449] The Guidelines preceding the current guidelines on NSI are the Attorney General Reno Guidelines issued on May 25, 1995, available at: http://www.fas.org/irp/agency/doj/fbi/terrorismintel2.pdf (accessed October 14, 2010). The Guidelines intended to govern all "foreign intelligence, foreign counterintelligence, foreign intelligence support activities, and intelligence investigations of international terrorism" on behalf of the FBI as to their task as an intelligence agency in accordance with Executive Order 12333.

[450] Lawson Mack and Kelly 2004, 127.

[451] Title 50 War and National Defense, Chapter 36 Foreign Intelligence Surveillance, 50 U.S.C. § 1804(a).

information.[452] The latter was the key threshold of FISA before the enactment of the PATRIOT Act, and limited the application to foreign intelligence cases only. The language of FISA stated that "the purpose of the surveillance is to obtain foreign intelligence information." This language has been explained by means of a "primary purpose" test, which meant that obtaining foreign intelligence should be the primary purpose but not necessarily the sole purpose of the surveillance.[453] There was no requirement that intelligence gathering was the purpose of the broader investigation; only that it was the goal of the surveillance itself. With that, FISA created an exception to the standards in conventional surveillance, which in general only permitted surveillance if probable cause to believe that a crime has been committed, is being committed or is about to be committed was established and a judge issued a warrant. As first explicitly decided in *Truong* (1980),[454] also several other court decisions, assessing the law prior to the changes of the post-9/11 era, have pointed out that FISA surveillance cannot continue if and when the primary purpose of the case changes from obtaining foreign intelligence into the collection of evidence and, hence, in an ordinary criminal case.[455] The information gathered in FISA surveillance can, however, result in a criminal prosecution.

The application of electronic surveillance under FISA is, furthermore, only permissible when the information sought cannot be obtained through normal investigative techniques.[456] FISA also establishes the so-called "minimization procedures," comparable with the minimization provision of Title III, in order to minimize the invasion of privacy for non-consenting United States' persons subjected to surveillance.[457] These minimization procedures concern an important source of restraints on and conditions for foreign intelligence surveillance and the use of the information obtained by this surveillance. A court order for foreign

[452] 50 U.S.C. § 1804(a)(7)(B): FISA Court approves application of electronic surveillance "[…] of a foreign power or an agent of a foreign power for the purpose of obtaining foreign intelligence information […]."

[453] Musch 2003, 72.

[454] *United States v. Truong Ding Hung*, 629. F.2d 908 (4th Cir. 1980). See in detail Sect. 5.2.2.3.2.

[455] E.g.: *United States v. Sarkissian*, 841 F.2d 959 (9th Cir. 1988), *United States v. Biasucci*, 786 F.2d 504 (2nd Cir. 1986) and *United States v. Johnson*, 952 F.2d 565 (1st Cir. 1991).

[456] 50 U.S.C. § 1804(a)(7)(C) (2007).

[457] *In re Kevork*, 634 F.Supp 1002 (C.D.Cal. 1985), affirmed *In re Kevork,* 788 F2d 566 (9th Cir. 1968), assessed compliance with the minimization procedures: the use of an automatic tape recorder does not violate the minimization procedures, because the minimization of the gathered information can occur in several stages instead of at the moment of the acquisition itself when coded or cryptic language is used, the recording was necessary to avoid the loss of fragile information and Congress has intended that the Government has the opportunity to analyze the information acquired in a counterintelligence and counterterrorism case, particularly when the critical conservations were in a foreign (in this case Armenian) language.

intelligence surveillance can only be issued if the Government meets those minimization requirements as prescribed by the Attorney General.[458]

As already stated above, under FISA, it is not required that a crime "has been, is being, or will be committed," like under Title III. Rather the threshold question is whether the surveillance concerns a foreign power or an agent of a foreign power. This means that for the use of electronic surveillance the government has to establish probable cause that the person under surveillance is an agent of a foreign power. As already indicated in Sect. 5.2.2.3.1, in order to be defined as an agent of a foreign power, different standards apply to foreigners and US persons.[459] Predictably, the threshold requirement is lower for foreigners than for US persons. *Any* person can be deemed an agent of a foreign power, whether a US person or not, if that person:

> "(A) knowingly engages in clandestine intelligence gathering activities for or on behalf of a foreign power, which activities involve or may involve a violation of the criminal statutes of the United States;
> (B) pursuant to the direction of an intelligence service or network of a foreign power, knowingly engages in any other clandestine intelligence activities for or on behalf of such foreign power, which activities involve or are about to involve a violation of the criminal statutes of the United States;
> (C) knowingly engages in sabotage or international terrorism, or activities that are in preparation therefor, for or on behalf of a foreign power;
> (D) knowingly enters the United States under a false or fraudulent identity for or on behalf of a foreign power or, while in the United States, knowingly assumes a false or fraudulent identity for or on behalf of a foreign power; or
> (E) knowingly aids or abets any person in the conduct of activities described in subparagraph (A), (B), or (C) or knowingly conspires with any person to engage in activities described in subparagraph (A), (B), or (C)."[460]

The definition of a "foreign power" also includes "a group engaged in international terrorism or activities in preparation therefor."[461]

The process of obtaining approval for surveillance from a special FISA Court is subject to less judicial control, with a commensurate less stringent application of probable cause.[462] Before issuing a warrant, the judges of the FISA Court have to be satisfied on the basis of the information provided by the federal officer filing the application that there is probable cause to believe that the target of the surveillance is a foreign power or an agent of a foreign power and that there is probable cause to believe that the facilities upon which the electronic surveillance is to be applied are being used or are about to be used by that foreign power or agent of a foreign power.[463] According to § 1805(b), in order to determine whether or not probable

---

[458] 50 U.S.C. § 1805(a)(4).

[459] 50 U.S.C. § 1801(b)(1) determines what is covered by an agent of a foreign power not being a US person and 50 U.S.C. § 1801(b)(2) determines when a US person can be considered as an agent of a foreign power.

[460] 50 U.S.C. § 1801(b)(2).

[461] 50 U.S.C. § 1801(a)(4).

[462] Lobel, 787.

[463] 50 U.S.C. § 1805(a)(3).

cause exists, a judge should consider "past activities of the target, as well as facts and circumstances relating to current or future activities of the target."[464]

According to section 1801(b)(2)(E) electronic surveillance can also be employed against individuals knowingly conspiring with or aiding or abetting persons, who can be subject to electronic surveillance under FISA. The Government would have to prove probable cause that the individual both knows that the person with whom he is conspiring, or who he aids or abets, is engaged in activities which threaten national security, is acting as an agent of a foreign power and knows that he, himself, is furthering or assisting in these activities.[465]

A valid order can approve the electronic surveillance for the "period necessary to achieve its purpose, or for ninety days, whichever is less."[466] Every decision to initiate a surveillance investigation of foreign powers or their agents within the United States is subject to a review not only by the FISA Court and the FISA Court of Review (which heard its first and only case (*In re Sealed*) in 2002), but also to extended Congressional oversight. Congressional oversight functions, as a mechanism for review and accountability, through the provision of both secret and public reports about the surveillance activities. Furthermore, the executive branch itself has some review responsibility by making sure that the primary purpose of the surveillance is to obtain foreign intelligence. In this regard the institution of the 'Inspector General' fulfills an important role. This concerns, however, to a large extent a closed circle of review because it all depends on secrecy.[467]

Federal courts have held the FISA of 1978 to be constitutional. For example, in *United States v. Duggan* (1984) the Second Circuit Court decided in the light of the Supreme Court's decision in *Keith* that "the procedures fashioned in FISA [can be regarded] as a constitutionally adequate balancing of the individual's Fourth Amendment rights against the nation's need to obtain foreign intelligence information." The court in particular assessed the FISA probable cause standard and held that the standard of 'probable cause that the target is a foreign power or an agent of a foreign power' does not violate the Fourth Amendment's probable cause requirement, but rather "make[s] it reasonable to dispense with a requirement that the FISA Judge find probable cause to believe that surveillance will in fact lead to the gathering of foreign intelligence information."[468]

---

464 50 U.S.C. § 1805(b).

465 Musch 2003, 108-109.

466 50 U.S.C. § 1805(e)(1).

467 Baker 2007A, 84.

468 *United States v. Duggan,* 743 F.2d 59 (2nd Cir. 1984), 73-74. See also: *United States v. Falvey*, 540 F.Supp. 1306 (E.D.N.Y. 1982), 1313.

### 5.3.3 Conclusion

Part 5.3 of this chapter has sought to set out the shield aspects of regulating the criminal investigation. These shield aspects can be recognized in the responsibilities of the actors—the one more than the other—during and after the investigative phase, and, more clearly in Fourth Amendment law, statutory regulation and regulative guidelines.

Police and prosecutors are primarily occupied with their task of confronting crime. However, some constitutional protections should also affect the behavior of these actors during the criminal investigation. It turns out that constitutional due process has only limited consequences for police conduct at the pre-arrest stage. Procedural due process which is applicable to the investigative pre-arrest phase has until now only been invoked in cases concerning flagrantly outrageous conduct; conduct that shocks the conscience. Procedural due process has more meaningful consequences for the conduct of prosecutors during the adjudication process, such as the obligation to comply with discovery rules and to take into account the presumption of innocence. The awareness of this obligation during the adjudication process should already be present when conducting investigative activities pre-arrest, in particular when relying on information sources (such as intelligence information) regarding which the defense cannot be granted full access while seeking to exercise defense rights.

The most important source of regulation for the police officers responsible for carrying out the investigative activities concerns the Fourth Amendment. The Fourth Amendment forces police officers to act with restraint when investigating. It is also in the interest of prosecutors to make sure that investigating officers act in compliance with Fourth Amendment requirements to avoid losing cases because of evidence being excluded. The goal of the Fourth Amendment exclusionary rule is to deter the police from investigative activities in violation of the Fourth Amendment. However, in the latest Supreme Court decisions the exclusionary rule has been construed in a way that limits its applicability to the deterrence of police conduct that is "deliberate, reckless or grossly negligent conduct, or in some circumstances recurring or systematic negligence."[469] Hence, the functioning of the exclusionary rule so as to deter law enforcement officers' behavior against the protective interests of criminal procedural law is now limited to deterring the most extreme misconduct.

Furthermore, the defense is in a position to file motions regarding the unlawfulness of the use of special investigative techniques during the investigation in order to have evidence that has been obtained by these techniques excluded. Moreover, discovery rules are very important to the exercise of defense rights so as to challenge the legitimacy of the manner in which evidence has been obtained. Full discovery being the basic assumption, exceptions are created for classified information. For example, when either the prosecutor or the defense seeks to use

[469] *Herring v. United States,* 555 U.S. 135, 129 S.Ct. 695 (2009), 207.

classified intelligence information as evidence, CIPA procedures may apply and the defense may be restricted in the discovery process. Persons subjected to criminal investigative activities who are not prosecuted may rely on civil actions in order to request the agency to delete the files obtained and to seek damages for illegitimate interferences with their private lives. The notification requirement, which is a constitutional requirement, is an important prerequisite to realize a remedy for subjects of criminal investigations other than those prosecuted.

The magistrate judge fulfills the most important protective role, as his function is to examine, before issuing a warrant for a physical search or electronic surveillance, that probable cause is present, particularity requirements are met or whether a warrant may reasonably be issued including exceptions to the regular procedures, such as roving surveillance. The magistrate judge shall, before application, determine whether the use of the investigative technique will be reasonable in the given circumstances. In the context of a national security investigation, the FISA court judge will have this task.

The shield elements of the legal framework covering the criminal investigation can be divided into three categories. The first category concerns the requirements of the Fourth Amendment: probable cause, the issuance of a warrant, reasonableness and, as a remedy, the exclusionary rule. Secondly, Title III provides for additional statutory constraints on the use of the more invasive electronic surveillance techniques. In the third place, the regulation under FISA provides for a different regime for the gathering of foreign intelligence information. In addition to the first and second level, the guidelines issued by the Attorney General have regulatory consequences for the FBI's authority to conduct domestic criminal investigations.

The Fourth Amendment requirement that has the potential of being the most important restraint on the power to search concerns the standard of probable cause, which reflects the compromise between competing interests of privacy protection and law enforcement. The interpretation of the standard for probable cause depends on the outcome of a totality-of-circumstances test, which makes the standard practicable and adaptable to the interests involved. Probable cause concerns an important Fourth Amendment restriction, but a restriction that adapts to the circumstances of a specific case to give also sufficient leeway when the interests of law enforcement should prevail. Nevertheless, the probable cause requirement restricts the use of the governmental power to search to investigations in reaction to the commission of a criminal offense and is, therefore, generally understood as the basic requirement rendering the investigation permissible for the purpose of evidence gathering for a criminal prosecution.

Furthermore, "adherence to the judicial process" as realized by the warrant requirement is an important safeguard protecting against arbitrary use of governmental power and leaving the balancing of interests involved to a "neutral and detached magistrate" rather than to police officers or prosecutors to whom the "competitive enterprise of fettering out crime" prevails. The magistrate judge should independently determine whether the quantum of evidence available meets the probable cause standard and whether the warrant sufficiently and precisely describes the places to be searched and the things to be seized to prevent fishing expeditions. Nevertheless, many exceptions to the warrant requirement have been accepted allowing officers to act immediately in situations such as exigent circumstances, the risk of the destruction of evidence or a danger to police officers. Also Title III includes important exceptions to the requirement that an order for surveillance must be issued by a magistrate judge, which also apply when the nature of the crimes involved is very serious, e.g. threatening national security or conspiratorial activities characteristic of organized crime.

Reasonableness is the ultimate test to be met regardless of the other Fourth Amendment requirements. The reasonableness of a search under the Fourth Amendment depends on the assessments of all interests involved and a balancing of the degree to which private life has been violated against the degree of the necessity of governmental investigative activities in order to confront crime. The particular requirements included in the Fourth Amendment are in principle (save for some exceptions) required to render a search reasonable, such as (especially) the requirement of probable cause and the authorization by a warrant upon oath or affirmation, a particular description of the place to be searched and the things to be seized and a notification requirement.

The exclusionary rule has been created as a remedy for Fourth Amendment violations. This remedy, providing for the exclusion of evidence obtained in violation of the Fourth Amendment, is, however, only applied when it is capable of substantially deterring the police from Fourth Amendment violations.

These being the Fourth Amendment restrictions, the more intrusive electronic surveillance techniques have additionally found specific regulation in 'Title III'. The reason for enacting Title III has been, on the one hand, to enable the use of electronic eavesdropping as an effective means to confront especially organized crime, and, on the other, to guarantee the constitutionality of these intrusive techniques calling for more stringent requirements to comply with the Fourth Amendment. The application procedure for an order authorizing electronic surveillance is, therefore, more demanding by requiring a high-ranking official to file the application and by requesting additional particularity specifications within the application. The issuance of an order can also only proceed when the magistrate has reviewed this application and determined probable cause that someone 'is committing, has committed, or is about to commit' one of the specific enumerated serious offenses. This limits Title III surveillance to probable cause and specific serious offenses. Moreover, the magistrate judge should determine whether probable cause exists that the interception is adequate to obtain communications that relate to the offense and whether there is probable cause that these communications can be intercepted from the place or facility particularized in the application. Furthermore, Title III surveillance is a tool whose use is restricted to the principles of subsidiarity and proportionality; to those situations in which other, less intrusive, techniques will not be effective and the use of Title III techniques has investigative value. Finally, the safeguards of recording and sealing, minimization, and post-surveillance notice aim to guarantee that the order for Title III surveillance is executed in a way that minimizes the consequences of this powerful and intrusive investigative technique of the government. Evidence obtained in violation of the provisions of Title III must be excluded, as provided in the statutory exclusionary rule of Title III. However, the meaning of this statutory exclusionary rule has, similar to the Fourth Amendment exclusionary rule, been watered down as to cover only those provisions "intended to play a central role in the statutory scheme."

It can be concluded that the use of Title III surveillance techniques is intended to provide the means to effectively investigate but only as a 'last resort.' The techniques shall be used with restraint and, according to a strict application, are subject to the authorization and execution procedure. Nevertheless, some exceptions to this protective statutory scheme have been created, particularly when national security is involved or the investigated conspiracy is widespread and serious.

The third level of regulation has been adopted for national security investigations. The techniques involved concern the same techniques as those regulated under Title III. However, because these techniques are used for the purpose of investigating threats to national security, the applicable restrictions may be weaker than in the context of regular law enforcement. As has been explained in Sect. 5.2.2, the scope of national security investigations may be rather wide, involving the criminal behavior of US persons. Moreover, the restraints imposed by the regulatory scheme as provided under FISA are rather loose in comparison with the regulatory scheme under Title III. Nevertheless, FISA has been enacted to put an end to the undesirable situation that warrantless domestic electronic surveillance could be conducted solely on behalf of the executive without oversight and judicial control. With the creation of the FISA court, judicial control has now also been created for electronic surveillance in national security investigations, by requiring a warrant from the FISA court for such surveillance.

The guidelines of the Attorney General concern an additional source of regulation, which direct investigative policy. This does not concern a legally enforceable level of regulation, but rather internal regulation in order to prevent abuses of investigative power by the FBI. Guidelines have been created both for the FBI's criminal investigative authority and for its national security investigative authority. The latter has, however, not been dealt with because the precise meaning and regulatory implications cannot be determined, as a consequence of the largely classified character of these documents. The influence of the guidelines for criminal investigations is, however, especially important for those investigative activities that are not governed by the Fourth Amendment or by Title III, namely those investigative activities which—considering the method used, e.g. undercover operations—do not interfere with a reasonable expectation of privacy. Thresholds have been established in order to regulate also these investigative activities by requiring some factual basis and a nexus to criminal activity. The possibility to initiate investigations in general has under the Smith Guidelines been lowered to a standard allowing effective proactive investigation. Moreover, the guidelines are intended to prohibit investigative activities into someone's exercise of First Amendment rights.

It can be concluded that three different main schemes of regulation are applicable to evidence gathering during the criminal investigation. The first one is the scheme provided by the Fourth Amendment, applicable to all searches. The second permits the use of electronic surveillance techniques to investigate serious crimes under additional statutory requirements, whereas this statutory scheme also aims to render the use of these techniques in compliance with the Fourth Amendment. The third scheme concerns FISA. When the investigative techniques in a national security investigation are used for the primary purpose of gathering foreign intelligence information, but also information relevant for criminal prosecution is discovered, this information can be transferred to the law enforcement community for the purpose of prosecution. This latter scheme permits the use of far-reaching methods without the usual requirements of either the Fourth Amendment or Title III. Still, the regulation under FISA is deemed not to violate the Fourth Amendment, because it is used for the primary purpose of gathering foreign intelligence information, which may not include an intention to also gather evidence for use in a criminal prosecution.

## 5.4 Final Remarks

To facilitate the correct understanding of a shift in emphasis from reactive to preventive in the criminal investigation as has been created since the events of September 11, 2001 to combat terrorism and the implications of such a shift for the system of criminal procedural law, this chapter has framed the system of criminal investigation for the United States. The system has been described by an analysis of the elements that are part of the system in order to give effect to the sword and to the shield objectives of criminal procedural law. A few important observations need to be made before turning to the next chapter, where the measures will be described that have contributed to a general shift to an anticipative criminal investigation of activities related to terrorism.

In the introductory chapter it has been explained that the US Constitution should be understood as placing restraints on the use of criminal procedural powers. The Bill of Rights aims to protect the civil liberties of citizens, for which reason some of the Amendments include specific limits on the government's use of criminal procedural power in order to protect citizens' rights. The Fourth Amendment and the due process clauses of the Fifth and Fourteenth Amendments regulate the criminal investigation. The Fourth Amendment affords direct regulation of the criminal investigation, by subjecting the use of investigative techniques to particular conditions. The due process clauses of the Fifth and Fourteenth Amendments are indirectly able to exert regulatory influence on the criminal investigation when the information collected during investigative activities is introduced during pre-trial procedures or trial procedures. In that regard the Constitution seems to be a powerful source of regulation for criminal investigation. However, as clearly follows from the description given of the interpretation of the individual requirements of the Fourth Amendment and the limited enforcement of due process during the investigative phase, the constitutional interpretation has since the 'due-process revolution' of the Warren Court been used to give law enforcement officers sufficient leeway and discretion to effectively combat crime. The judiciary has chosen a more deferential review in particular when it comes to the police's investigative activities with regard to complex structures of criminal organizations or when the protection of national security is involved.

Furthermore, the most important sources of regulation that have been described cover only the use of intrusive investigative tools; those that violate someone's reasonable expectation of privacy and, consequently, are subject to Fourth Amendment protection. The requirements of probable cause, obtaining a warrant, particularity and reasonableness are only applicable to those investigative techniques that constitute a search. Title III provides regulation for electronic surveillance in criminal investigation and FISA for electronic surveillance and physical search in national security investigations. All these investigative techniques touch upon the interests that the Fourth Amendment aims to protect. Other investigative activities only find internal regulation, for example by rules for police or the prosecution's conduct, or more importantly, by means of the Attorney General Guidelines for the FBI's investigative activities.

The differences in the level of protection are, in the first place, based upon a balancing between the interests protected by the Fourth Amendment and the interests of powerfully investigating certain activities. Hence, the loosened statutory scheme of FISA applies to national security investigations, whereas in regular criminal investigations the Fourth Amendment is more strictly enforced and surveillance shall be conducted in accordance with the more stringent framework of Title III. Although the Fourth Amendment protects against any unreasonable search or seizure on behalf of the government, a distinction has been made between search and seizure for the purpose of evidence gathering and for the purpose of intelligence gathering to protect national security. The latter still requires some Fourth Amendment protection; however, not on the same level as required in the conventional criminal context. This distinction also underlies the institutional separation between law enforcement and intelligence agencies and the 'wall' that has been created between these agencies. This means for the functioning of the FBI that the intelligence counterpart and law enforcement counterpart operate separately and are each directed by a separate set of guidelines.

It can be concluded that the regulation of the criminal investigative phase is to a significant extent a consequence of the interpretation of the scope of the Fourth Amendment and the meaning of its independent requirements, both for conventional criminal investigations and for national security investigations. The Court's decisions that have provided for this Fourth Amendment interpretation have made the regulation of the criminal investigation a complex entity, with many exceptions to protective requirements when particular investigative activities are considered reasonable in the interest of crime control. In addition, the notion of due process should cover the investigative phase. However, the implications of due process are mainly limited to enforcement after the closure of the investigative phase, because procedural due process aims to protect the defense against use of evidence obtained by uncontrollable means.

Nevertheless, from this complex entity of regulation of criminal investigative activities, three important general sources of regulation have been identified: Fourth Amendment interpretation applicable to searches in conventional criminal investigations, the statutory regulation of surveillance in a conventional criminal investigation under Title III, and the statutory regulation of surveillance and physical searches in national security investigations under FISA. Furthermore, the Attorney General's guidelines provide for an additional internal source of regulation for the FBI's investigative actions. The next chapter will, from this basic structure of the organization of criminal investigation, describe the developments that have changed the nature of each of these regulated areas, that have changed the relation between these sources of regulation or that have blended previously distinguished areas. These developments have together resulted in the creation of a system in which prevention is the shared goal of criminal investigative activities in order to protect the national security.

# Chapter 6
# Counterterrorism Measures Affecting Criminal Investigation in the United States

## 6.1 Introduction

In response to the 9/11 attacks on the World Trade Center in New York City and the Pentagon in Arlington, Virginia near Washington D.C., President Bush started what he called the 'war on terror.' A wide variety of measures at home and abroad were taken in order to prevent future terrorist attacks. The leading principle for all these measures has been the 'preventive paradigm,' justifying preventive military actions in Afghanistan and Iraq, the preventive detention of terrorism suspects in Guantanamo Bay, coercive interrogation and preventive investigation.[1] The 9/11 attacks, being the first foreign attack on American soil after Pearl Harbor in 1941, have had a tremendous influence on the American people and raised the question whether the protection of civil liberties should be traded in in return for an effective system of national security. People felt a conflict between their highly esteemed civil liberties and security. Inquiries into people's willingness to give up some liberties in order for the government to confront terrorism, made before and shortly after 9/11, show that people over a short period of time have become much more willing to trade in some of their liberties for that purpose after experiencing the terrorist attacks of 9/11 than they were before.[2]

---

[1] Cole and Lobel 2007, 1. As also emphasized by Attorney General Alberto Gonzales: "[p]revention is the goal of all goals when it comes to terrorism because we simply cannot and will not wait for these particular crimes to occur before taking action." Alberto Gonzales, U.S. Attorney General, Remarks at the World Affairs Council of Pittsburgh on 'Stopping Terrorists Before They Strike: The Justice Department's Power of Prevention' (August 16 2006), available at: http://www.justice.gov/archive/ag/speeches/2006/ag_speech_060816.html (accessed 30 August 2011).

[2] The moments of inquiry were April 1995, May 1995, August 1996, September 2001 and January-March 2002. In September 2001 66% of interviewees were "willing to give up liberties in order to crack down on terrorism," whereas before 9/11 this percentage varied between 52 and 59%. The inquiry between January and March 2002 showed that 78% considered themselves to be "more willing to give up certain freedoms to improve safety and security" than before 9/11. Etzioni 2004, 18.

M.F.H. Hirsch Ballin, *Anticipative Criminal Investigation*,
DOI: 10.1007/978-90-6704-843-9_6, 

This societal and political climate has resulted in the adoption of many measures that significantly expand the government's power to investigate, coerce citizens and engage in covert actions, all aimed at preventing the United States from facing new terrorist attacks. The US government has directly stated that all means at their disposal will be used to confront this threat. At the same time President Bush and Attorney General Ashcroft have claimed that the United States has never permitted and will not permit that American values fall victim to terrorism.[3] However, security and liberty were seen as contradicting concepts, which need to be balanced at the cost of liberty during dangerous times.[4] In response, many referred to the warning of Benjamin Franklin, one of the 'founding fathers' of the United States: "those who would give up essential liberty to purchase a little temporary safety deserve neither liberty nor safety."[5]

In the post-9/11 era, the Bush Administration took many counterterrorism measures that touch upon the individual liberties of American citizens, which were justified by the preventive paradigm. Obama campaigned against certain aspects of the counterterrorism strategy adopted under the Bush Administration.[6] However, so far, his Presidency has been more a continuity than a change with regard to the counterterrorism policy, in particular with regard to the counterterrorism measures addressed in this book.[7]

### *6.1.1 Counterterrorism Measures Under the Preventive Paradigm*

Although the indefinite preventive detention of terrorism suspects without any form of hearing, the use of the material witness statute to detain suspects instead of witnesses, and the enhanced interrogation of persons (arguably constituting 'torture') that has been justified as a method to obtain information vital to the prevention of terrorist attacks may concern the most discussed aspects of 'the war on terror' and are also clearly controversial under the rule of law, this Chapter will not deal with these aspects of the US counterterrorism strategy. This project deals

---

[3] E.g.: Testimony of Attorney General John Ashcroft before the House Committee on the Judiciary, 24 September 2001: "We were attacked for our nation's values. We will not allow our values to become victims. The Justice Department will never waiver in our defense of the Constitution nor relent our defense of civil rights." See also: Dinh 2002, 401.

[4] Compare e.g. Judge Richard Posner. See: Donohue 2008, 4.

[5] O'Harrow Jr 2002, 18.

[6] See e.g.: Position paper Barack Obama 2008.

[7] Nevertheless, in some other aspects the Obama Administration's approach towards countering terrorism did constitute a change: the enhanced interrogation techniques adopted under Bush have been condemned, the Iraq policy substantially changed and, instead of strongly relying on the 'executive power', Obama seeks Congressional approval for his policy. Despite his efforts to seek a solution for the Guantanamo Bay detainees, Obama has not yet succeeded in closing Guantanamo Bay.

with the anticipative criminal investigation,[8] which covers the pre-arrest phase, specifically targeting the covert investigation phase by means of, in particular, surveillance techniques. The definition of anticipative criminal investigation—as provided in Chap. 1—excludes also the arrest and forms of illegal arrest, such as rendition, from the assessment.

At home, the enabling of a system of anticipative investigation has been the most important consequence of the preventive paradigm to enhance protection against terrorism. The government considered it necessary for the prevention of a terrorist attack to be able to keep track of what persons are doing before evidence is present that they are engaging in criminal activity.[9] Many amendments to the law, an enhanced role for the FBI as the leading investigative agency and bureaucratic changes facilitating the sharing of information have resulted in proactive investigative activities with the help of intrusive techniques in order to strengthen the information position of law enforcement agencies to take action when this is needed to prevent a terrorist crime. The facilitation of anticipative investigation for the purpose of prevention has been realized through a wide variety of measures that have affected different agencies and areas.

The 'National Commission on Terrorist Attacks upon the United States' indicated four main reasons for the failure to prevent 9/11: "imagination, policy, capabilities, and management."[10] These identified failures touched upon all aspects of the government's law enforcement and intelligence efforts and have triggered a variety of measures concerning changes to the law, changes of policy and changes to the bureaucratic organization.[11]

At the basis of enabling an anticipative investigation was the widespread belief, already directly after 9/11, that failing to prevent the attacks and to intercept their planning was to be attributed to the intelligence agencies not having access to essential legal tools. At the same time, the Department of Justice lacked sufficient investigative powers to intercept this planning.[12] It was questioned whether the restraints following from the Fourth Amendment contributed to the incapability to intercept the planning of terrorist crimes. This fear has resulted in rhetorical

---

[8] Defined in Chap. 1 as investigative activities that are aimed at the prevention of terrorism by intercepting their planning and resulting in the collection of information that may be used in criminal proceedings. See Chap. 1, Sect. 1.4.

[9] Cole and Lobel 2007, 30 and 31. See also: Dycus et al. 2007A, 83–86 and White 2004, 7 and 14.

[10] Report of the National Commission on Terrorist Attacks upon the United States 2004, 339. For an explanation of these four failures see *Ibid*. 339-360.

[11] Report of the National Commission on Terrorist Attacks upon the United States 2004, 399-428. For an overview of the measures taken to implement the recommendations of the 9/11 Commission Report: Progress Report 2011, 3-6 and 9-10.

[12] Schulhofer 2005, 14-15.

proclamations such as, in the words of Justice Jackson, that "the Constitution is not a suicide-pact."[13]

The 'National Commission on Terrorist Attacks upon the United States' endorsed these issues as aspects of improvement to prevent future terrorist attacks. The Commission urged the FBI to "more fully institutionalize" the "Bureau's shift to a preventive counterterrorism posture."[14] Only in that way could the FBI overcome criticism that is was too "backward-looking" as an agency primarily focused on law enforcement and evidence gathering in reaction to already committed federal crimes.[15] Furthermore, in particular 'the wall' between law enforcement agencies and intelligence agencies, developed after the FISA enactment, was blamed for having obstructed cooperation and essential information exchange.

In the light of these assumptions and the very apparent fear in the nation of this new terrorist threat, a shift to the preventive investigation of terrorist activities has been instigated by enhancing both the capacities of conventional criminal investigation and national security investigations as well as increasing the interaction between both areas and introducing aggressive intelligence investigative tools. The first and most drastic step toward realizing this shift was taken directly after 9/11 by the enactment of the USA PATRIOT Act of October 26, 2001.[16] After the PATRIOT Act, other legislative action and policy measures gave further effect to the strategy of combining forces in order to be able to "prevent acts of terrorism on American soil". In the latest 'National Security Strategy' of May 2010 President Obama again stated that "we must enlist all of our intelligence, law enforcement, and homeland security capabilities."[17]

## 6.1.2 *The Shift to Anticipative Criminal Investigation*

As said, the shift to anticipative investigation has been jointly realized through a variety of measures and developments. As the subject is further demarked to anticipative *criminal* investigation, only those anticipative investigative activities that gather information which may, immediately or subsequently, be used in

---

[13] *Terminiello v. City of Chicago,* 337 U.S. 1, 69 S.Ct. 894 (1949), dissenting opinion of Justice Jackson joined by Justice Burton, 911. Recently Judge Richard Posner breathed new life into this phrase by using it in the context of counterterrorism policy: Posner 2006.

[14] Report of the National Commission on Terrorist Attacks upon the United States 2004, 425.

[15] Cole and Lobel 2007, 12 and Report of the Office of the Inspector General 2003, *The Federal Bureau of Investigation's Efforts to Improve the Sharing of Intelligence and Other Information*, ii.

[16] The full name of this Act is: Uniting and Strengthening America by Providing Appropriate Tools Required to Intercept and Obstruct Terrorism Act of 2001; USA PATRIOT Act, October 26, 2001, *107 Pub. L. No. 56, 115 Stat. 272, (2001) Enacted H.R. 3162; 107 Enacted H.R. 3162.*

[17] National Security Strategy, May 2010. Available at: http://www.whitehouse.gov/sites/default/files/rss_viewer/national_security_strategy.pdf (accessed March 21, 2011), 20.

criminal proceedings are included. The current section will briefly elaborate on the developments underlying the shift to anticipative criminal investigation.

In the first place, the provisions of the USA PATRIOT Act that enhance investigative capacities and promote cooperation and sharing between different agencies will concern an important component of analysis. The drafting of the USA PATRIOT Act started only 8 days after 9/11 and was rushed through Congress. The House of Representatives voted by 357 votes to 66 in favor of the Act, which, subsequently, passed through the Senate by 98 votes to 1.[18] President Bush signed the PATRIOT Act into law on October 26, 2001, only seven weeks after the attacks.[19] Other legislative measures have since followed, including the Reauthorization and Improvement Acts of the 2001 PATRIOT Act.

Attorney General John Ashcroft stated that the USA PATRIOT Act "provides the security that ensures liberty." According to Ashcroft, the Act fills the gaps that had previously hindered the optimal investigation of terrorism by adjusting the law to modern technology and enhancing cooperation between the different participants in the investigative field.[20] His goal was to enable a system to confront terrorism by proactive action for the purpose of prevention. Critics reject many of the provisions of the Act because they believe that it enhances the Government's search and surveillance authorities towards US citizens at the expense of civil liberties and at the expense of checks and balances on the Government's investigative powers.[21]

Under Title II—"Enhanced Surveillance Procedures"—the Act deals with the enhancement of possibilities for law enforcement as well as intelligence officials in the proactive stage, in order to establish a system of terrorism prevention instead of going after the perpetrators after the crimes have been committed.[22] The

18 Vervaele 2005, 207.

19 The USA PATRIOT Act makes amendments to criminal law as well as to the national security law on a federal level. Many states implemented the USA PATRIOT Act on a state level through Fellow Patriot Acts, although some states were reluctant to adopt all the provisions of the federal Act due to concerns about the compatibility with civil rights. Vervaele 2005, 207.

20 Sidel 2004, 10. Citing from: Attorney General Ashcroft, "Attorney General Ashcroft Speaks about the Patriot Act" (prepared remarks, Boise, Idaho, August 25, 2003).

21 E.g. the American Civil Liberties Union (ACLU), see Sidel 2004, 10.

22 USA PATRIOT Act of October 26 2001 and Hitz 2002, 772. Except for the provisions that are dealt with in this Chapter, the USA PATRIOT Act also provides for stricter immigration laws (under Title IV of the Act), such as the refusal of entry into the US for any immigrant who supports terrorism through, for example, speech or writing and the removal of immigrants upon terrorism grounds, while the terms 'terrorism' and 'engaging in terrorist activity' are expanded in the Act. Furthermore, the Act grants authority to the Attorney General to detain aliens charged with a criminal or immigration violation when that individual is involved in terrorist activities or other activities that threaten national security (Lobel 2002). The Act also redefines and expands the term 'domestic terrorism' and some terrorism offences (Title VIII of the Act) and provides for more stringent money-laundering laws (Title III). Lastly, the USA PATRIOT Act provides for compensation regulations for terrorism victims (Title VI). Many of the PATRIOT Act's provisions do not only aim to combat terrorism, but are primarily applied in criminal and administrative cases (Schulhofer 2005, 3-4).

amendments of the USA PATRIOT Act are twofold: some of them amend FISA and deal with foreign intelligence investigations, while others amend U.S.C. Title 18 (Title III) or the Federal Rules of Criminal Procedure and deal with conventional criminal investigations. At the same time, the strict separation of these two separate regimes has decreased or, as will be discussed, may also have been even abandoned. Although the primary goal of the PATRIOT Act was to enable a system that can effectively prevent terrorism, many of the PATRIOT Act's amendments are not limited to investigations into terrorism, but are applicable in any criminal investigation.

The USA PATRIOT Act was the first and most dramatic step, but there are many other developments that have increased the capability of the US government to act for preventive purposes by investigative means, developments which are not limited to legislative action only. The transformation of the FBI has and is being realized to a large extent by changes in internal policy, such as the issuance of new Guidelines by the Attorney General that govern the investigative activities of the FBI. These new guidelines have reformulated the investigative priorities of the FBI and have sought the borders of the investigative discretion attributed to the FBI in order to enable the most aggressive anticipative investigation possible. The implications of more aggressive law enforcement and the introduction of classified materials obtained under FISA in domestic terrorism cases have become visible in the prosecutions that have occurred in the post-9/11 era. A trend allowing for a more preventive focus in the investigative phase may also be derived from the constitutional interpretation of the Fourth Amendment requirements of post-9/11 decisions of the federal courts and the Supreme Court. Furthermore, Congress has passed other acts that have either amended the 2001 PATRIOT Act provisions or further enhanced preventive investigative activities. Relevant amendments include provisions of the Intelligence Reform and Terrorism Prevention Act of 2004, the USA PATRIOT Act Reauthorization and Improvement Acts of 2005 and 2006, the Protect America Act of 2007 and the FISA Amendment Act of 2008.

Lastly, this Chapter needs to deal with investigative activities outside the scope of conventional law enforcement or FISA: the 'Terrorist Surveillance Program', which concerns NSA surveillance in its original form exclusively conducted on the basis of Executive authority,[23] and the warrantless issuance of National Security Letters. The latter does not concern a new investigative power. However, the frequency of using this warrantless investigative tool has exploded since 9/11. The information obtained also through these investigative tools may, due to sharing obligations, become part of criminal proceedings.

To conclude, it must be noted that the shift to anticipative investigation is not a revolutionary change. Rather, expanding law enforcement and intelligence powers and using them for a preventive purpose is an evolution, which has been

[23] Since the FISA Amendments Act of 2008 a FISA Court order is required for the surveillance authorities that were previously authorized without a warrant under the Terrorist Surveillance Program.

accelerated in the post-9/11 era. Prior to the events of 9/11 the government had already repeatedly sought to expand its investigative powers. This resulted in the adoption of various Acts expanding the government's investigative powers, such as the Counterintelligence and Security Enhancements Act of 1994 and the relaxing of the standards for roving surveillance under Title III in order to adjust law enforcement techniques to technological developments.[24] Also many of the provisions of the PATRIOT Act were proposed prior to 9/11. However, only after the devastating confrontation with the threat coming from international terrorism was Congress willing to adopt also these provisions.

### *6.1.3 Goals of the Chapter*

Chapter 5 has identified three different regulatory schemes: 1) the almost purely reactive investigation in conventional criminal law regulated by traditional Fourth Amendment law (upon probable cause that a crime has been, is being or will be committed); 2) Title III investigation in conventional criminal law under Fourth Amendment law and additional statutory regulations, but with the possibility and the inclusion of exceptions to enable the proactive investigation of organized crime; 3) national security investigations regulated through a weaker form of Fourth Amendment protection provided in a significantly different statutory scheme (FISA) and conducted on behalf of the intelligence community for the purpose of the proactive investigation of national security threats. In addition, guidelines issued by the Attorney General provide, on an internal informal level, for the regulation of the FBI's authority to investigate.

This Chapter will aim to frame the shift in the system of criminal investigation from reaction to prevention as it has taken shape in particular since the terrorist attacks of 9/11, 2001. The changes that will be dealt with in this Chapter will demonstrate that: 1) the possibilities to act proactively in conventional criminal law are widened; 2) the investigative means under FISA have been expanded and 3) they may now be used to gather evidence for a criminal prosecution; and 4) far-reaching investigative powers of the intelligence community, (originally) solely on behalf of the executive, have been created, which also affect the 'sword' capacity of a criminal investigation without creating the restraints in observing the Fourth Amendment. Together these developments will demonstrate the shift in the system of US criminal investigation from a primarily reactive system, with some exceptions to enable proactive investigation, to a system in which anticipative investigation has become the tool for the prevention of criminal acts, especially of terrorism.

---

[24] Counterintelligence and Security Enhancements Act (1994), Public Law 103-359 and amending Title III, 18 U.S.C. § 2518(11)(b)(ii) to relax the roving surveillance provision (introduced in 1986): Public Law 105-272, § 604(a)(1).

## 6.2 Changes Affecting Search and Surveillance in the Conventional Law Enforcement Context

This section will be further divided into three different sub-sections in order to categorize the changes that have jointly resulted in a shift to prevention by the use of search and surveillance powers in the conventional law enforcement context. The first category concerns the legislative measures, the relevant provisions of the PATRIOT Act of 2001 and sometimes their later amendments, which have enhanced the surveillance capacities under Title III and, in one case, the physical search capacities as to their regulation under Rule 41 of the Federal Rules of Criminal Procedure. The second category concerns the case law of the post-9/11 era pointing to a watering down of Fourth Amendment requirements in cases where an interest in protecting national security or preventing terrorism was also at stake. The last and third subsection will focus on other developments that have enhanced the proactive investigative activities of law enforcement agencies.

### *6.2.1 Legislative Measures*

The enactment of the USA PATRIOT Act of 2001 (as amended) has contributed to enhancing proactive investigative possibilities in the criminal law enforcement context. Title II—"Enhanced Surveillance Procedures"—of the USA PATRIOT Act of 2001 deals with both measures affecting search and surveillance in the law enforcement context and measures affecting FISA. This section will be limited to those changes that affect powers in the conventional criminal context: Title III. Each relevant amendment will be briefly described in the numerical order of the provisions of the PATRIOT Act.

#### 6.2.1.1 Broadening the Scope of Title III

The first two sections of Title II (sections 201 and 202) add crimes to the crimes enumerated in 18 U.S.C. § 2516(1)(q) for which Title III surveillance is permitted. These newly added crimes under section 201 concern specific terrorist crimes and crimes related to chemical weapons. Section 202 adds felonies relating to mail and computer fraud and abuse to the crimes for which Title III surveillance may be authorized. These amendments have broadened the scope of Title III surveillance to certain other categories of serious crimes, especially in order to cover the applicability of Title III surveillance to all terrorist crimes.

#### 6.2.1.2 Emergency Disclosure

Section 212 of the PATRIOT Act provides for the possibility of emergency disclosure by adding as an exception to the prohibition on the disclosure of communications by service providers (as provided in section 18 U.S.C. § 2702) "if the provider reasonably believes that an emergency involving immediate danger of death or serious physical injury to any person requires disclosure of the information without delay." This exception has been added so as not to prohibit service providers from disclosure when such disclosure may save lives. The USA PATRIOT Improvement and Reauthorization Act of 2005 has added enhanced congressional oversight on such emergency disclosures.[25]

#### 6.2.1.3 Delayed Notice Warrant

Section 213 of the 2001 PATRIOT Act has created a statutory basis to conduct 'sneak-and-peak searches.' This may be considered as the most far-reaching amendment by the USA PATRIOT Act in the context of conventional law enforcement. Notification before the execution of the (physical) search warrant has been the rule, only to be deviated from in exceptional circumstances, such as the risk of the destruction of evidence or an imminent danger to police officers or others. Nevertheless, in conventional criminal practice the issuing of search warrants permitting for delayed notice had already been introduced as an investigative tool, on an exceptional basis, particularly in organized crime investigations.[26] A delayed notice search allows a physical or virtual search (other than surveillance under Title III) of someone's property, including entering their home or business premises, whereas the government need not leave evidence or notification that it has conducted the search.[27] These searches are typically aimed at observing or copying evidence without the seizure of any tangible evidence. Normally, such searches are—save for some exceptions—rendered unreasonable because of the risk of 'fishing expeditions' and the consequences for the privacy of the people involved. The knock-and-announce requirement has been introduced to secure notice before entry and was considered as an important element to render a search reasonable.[28] The PATRIOT Act adds a paragraph to § 3103a of Title 18 concerning additional grounds for the issuing of a warrant for searches and seizures. Before this, there was no general statutory ground for this exception to the Fourth Amendment regular warrant

---

[25] Public Law 109-177, 109th Congress, section 107(a).

[26] See Sect. 5.2.2.1.1. In addition, in the context of a national security investigation 'sneak-and-peek' searches were already broadly authorized under FISA.

[27] Mart 2008, 481.

[28] Notwithstanding the fact that the Supreme Court has rescinded the consequences of violations of the knock-and-announce rule in *Hudson v. Michigan* (2006) (See Chap. 5, Sect. 5.3.2.1.4). See also: Donohue 2008, 235.

requirements as specified in Rule 41 of the Rules of Federal Criminal Procedure.[29] Only in the case law and in rare situations had exceptions been accepted.

Three requirements are formulated that the court shall observe when issuing a warrant that allows for a delayed notice. In the first place, the PATRIOT Act requires that the court issuing the delayed notice warrant establishes the presence of a "reasonable cause to believe that providing immediate notification of the execution of the warrant may have an adverse result." What an 'adverse result' entails is defined in § 2705 (part of the 1986 Electronic Communications Privacy Act).[30] This section already gave a definition of this concept, in the light of the already existing delayed notice exception for the disclosure of the contents of stored wire or electronic communications by a provider or remote computing service. It defines an adverse result as: "(a) endangering the life or physical safety of an individual; (b) flight from prosecution; (c) destruction of or tampering with evidence; (d) intimidation of potential witnesses; or (e) otherwise seriously jeopardizing an investigation or unduly delaying a trial."[31] The latter gives law enforcement officers a rather broad discretion to conduct sneak-and-peak searches and can be considered to undermine the otherwise strictly circumscribed notification requirement.[32] However, since the adoption of the USA PATRIOT Act Improvement and Reauthorization Act of 2005 the ground of "unduly delaying a trial" can no longer constitute the single ground for a delayed notice.[33]

Secondly, the warrant shall include a requirement prohibiting the seizure of "any tangible property, any wire or electronic communication (…), any stored wire or electronic information, except where the court finds reasonable necessity for the seizure."[34] This seems to be an important restriction, which is, however, followed by a broad exception: when the court finds a reasonable necessity for the seizure, the seizure can be allowed. As a result, not only is a delayed notice for a sneak-and-peek search, that is the search and seizure of 'intangible' evidence, e.g. by copying hard disks or photographing the contraband, allowed under this section, but, under some circumstances, a delayed notice for the seizure of tangible evidence is permitted as well.[35]

As a third requirement, the warrant shall provide "for the giving of such notice within a reasonable period of its execution, which period may thereafter be extended by the court for good cause shown."[36] The person owning the property

---

29 Although a delayed notice was already included in the 1986 Electronic Communications Privacy Act and was also accepted under certain conditions by the Courts of the Ninth, Second and Fourth Circuit. See: Donohue 2008, 235 and Duncan Jr 2004, 12-24.

30 USA PATRIOT Act, sec. 213(2)(b)(1).

31 18 U.S.C. § 2705(a)(2) (Electronic Communications Privacy Act of 1986).

32 Cole and Dempsey 2006, 210.

33 Section 114(a), USA PATRIOT Improvement and Reauthorization Act of 2005.

34 USA PATRIOT Act, sec. 203(2)(b)(2).

35 Considering the covert nature of the seizure, this newly created possibility has been defined as 'sneak-and-steal'. See: Shumate 2006.

36 USA PATRIOT Act, sec. 203 (2)(b)(3).

searched must be given the delayed notice within 'a reasonable period' to be determined by the court. To give some guidance as to the length of a reasonable period, the Justice Department had indicated that 90 days could be considered as reasonable.[37]

The USA PATRIOT Improvement and Reauthorization Act of 2005 also included a specific limitation on the length of the delay by requiring the "giving of such notice within a reasonable period not to exceed 30 days after the date of its execution, or on a later certain date if the facts of the case justify a longer period." The court may allow extensions by "good cause shown" and "each additional delay should be limited to 90 days or less, unless the facts of the case justify a longer period of delay."[38] Moreover, the USA PATRIOT Improvement and Reauthorization Act of 2006 included enhanced oversight for delayed notice searches. The judges issuing such warrants shall now report to the Administrative Office of the Court not later than 30 days after issuance whether an application has been made, whether it was granted, modified or denied, the duration of the delay, any applicable extensions and the criminal offense in question. The same information shall be submitted to Congress in order to enable also more substantive Congressional oversight.[39]

It can be concluded that section 213 of the PATRIOT Act provides for a rather broad and vague delayed notice exception to the Fourth Amendment warrant requirement through applying this 'adverse result' requirement, especially by including in the definition "seriously jeopardizing the investigation" or "unduly delaying a trial." Moreover, this section of the PATRIOT Act does not limit its applicability to terrorism investigations, but makes it applicable in any criminal investigation. The USA PATRIOT Improvement and Reauthorization Act of 2005 has narrowed the conditions for the delayed notice provision by placing limitations on the period for which the notice may be delayed. Nonetheless, the grounds upon which a delayed notice can be granted remain rather broad.

#### 6.2.1.4 Pen Registers and Trap and Trace Devices

Section 216 of the PATRIOT Act amends Chapter 206 of Title 18 of the United States Code that regulates the use of pen registers and trap and trace devices. In conventional criminal law, such an authorization already depends on a much less stringent standard than the normal probable cause standard, namely a mere showing of relevance to an ongoing criminal investigation, because the use of these investigative tools does not violate someone's reasonable expectation of

---

[37] Cole and Dempsey 2006, 209. The Justice Department determined this period by relating to other statutes, such as 18 U.S.C. § 2518(8)(d) (providing that the judge who authorizes an order for Title III surveillance shall notify the persons whose communications have been intercepted at the latest 90 days after the termination of the surveillance). Smith, 2003, 437.

[38] Section 114(a), USA PATRIOT Improvement and Reauthorization Act of 2005.

[39] Section 114 USA PATRIOT Improvement and Reauthorization Act of 2006.

privacy as to the contents of communications. The PATRIOT Act broadens the definition of the information that can be intercepted by pen registers and trap and trace devices by including the "routing, addressing, and signaling information" in the definition of pen register.[40] Before the PATRIOT Act amendments, the definition of pen registers limited its use to information relating to telephone numbers,[41] while the information intercepted by trap and trace devices could include "incoming electronic or other impulses which identify the originating number of an instrument or device from which a wire or electronic communication was transmitted."[42] The latter was held to include telephone data as well as analogous information of Internet communications, which made trap and trace devices—thus—already broader in scope than pen registers.[43] Now, the scope of both pen registers and trap and trace devices has been extended to dialing, routing, addressing, and signaling information.[44] The amendments explicitly provide that the information shall not include the contents of any communication. Although the use of pen registers and trap and trace devices remains limited to data and the changes seem, at first sight, a logical adjustment to modern techniques and communication methods, the applicability to different types of information, such as routing information for e-mail including the addressees of the e-mail and the size of the e-mail), web surfing and internet search terms has raised significant privacy concerns, because it can reveal much more about the identity of the user and the subject-matter of the communications.[45]

#### 6.2.1.5 Consensual Monitoring

Section 217 of the PATRIOT Act adds the definitions of a "protected computer" and "computer trespasser" to § 2510 of Title III.[46] This section provides for a statutory solution to a gap in the existing law with respect to tracing computer hackers. Section 217 allows the surveillance of communications by an unauthorized user who accesses a protected computer, because the person in question does not have a reasonable expectation of privacy as a trespasser (consensual monitoring). The unauthorized user shall not have a contractual relationship with the owner of the computer for accessing the computer. Furthermore, the owner of the protected computer shall authorize the interception of the trespasser's

---

40 USA PATRIOT Act, sec. 216(c)(2).

41 18 U.S.C. § 3127(3), which read, before the amendments of the USA PATRIOT Act of October 26, 2001: "(…) records or decodes electronic or other impulses which identify the numbers dialed or otherwise transmitted on the telephone line to which such device is attached."

42 18 U.S.C. § 3127(4), before the USA PATRIOT Act amendments.

43 Schulhofer 2005, 86 and footnote 28, 149.

44 USA PATRIOT Act, sec. 216(c)(3).

45 Schulhofer 2005, 86 and Smith 2003, 440-443.

46 USA PATRIOT Act, sec. 217(1).

communications and the investigator shall have reasonable grounds to believe that the contents of the communications will be relevant to the investigation.[47] No judicial oversight is required for this type of surveillance, because surveillance with the consent of one of the parties to the communications is generally allowed in conventional criminal investigations. The section was enacted for the purpose of preventing terrorism and was supposed to last until December 31, 2005 in the expectation that the terrorist threat at that time would be diminished or would have disappeared. This provision was repealed in the USA PATRIOT Improvement and Reauthorization Act of 2005 making section 217 permanent. It was argued that because the threat is still present and because the section has also turned out to be very useful in ordinary computer hacking cases, this amendment should continue to exist. Nevertheless, the Department of Justice has declared that the authorities of section 217 have also been used on several occasions for the purpose of identifying and dismantling terrorist networks.[48]

#### 6.2.1.6 Nationwide Applicability of Search Warrants

Lastly, the PATRIOT Act of 2001 has created nationwide applicability for search warrants. Section 219 amends Rule 41(b) of the Federal Rules of Criminal Procedure, by adding that a federal magistrate judge in any district has the authority to issue a warrant "in an investigation of domestic terrorism or international terrorism (...) in which activities related to the terrorism may have occurred, for a search of property or for a person within or outside the district."[49] Section 216(b)(1), likewise, provides for the authorization of pen registers and trap and trace devices with nationwide reach and section 220 provides for the nationwide application of search warrants for electronic evidence stored at internet service providers in another district. The nationwide applicability of pen registers, trap and trace devices and search warrants for electronic evidence (section 216(c) and 220) is not limited to investigations into domestic or international terrorism. The necessity for nationwide applicability is much higher for wired and electronic communications due to the easy transmission beyond district borders than for search warrants. Through the PATRIOT Act amendments, it is also possible for federal officers to apply for a pen register or trap and trace device for one suspect anywhere in the United States, irrespective of the communication device used by the suspect, which was not permitted under conventional criminal law and neither under FISA. As a result, it is no longer required to apply for a new order every time the investigation leads to another jurisdiction.

---

47 USA PATRIOT Act, sec. 217(2).

48 As follows from a letter to the House of Representatives from the Assistant Attorney General Jamie E. Brown of May 13, 2003, answering questions of the House of Representatives about the USA PATRIOT Act implementation and related matters. U.S. Department of Justice, Office of Legislative Affairs, Office of the Assistant Attorney General, May 13, 2003, 24.

49 USA PATRIOT Act, sec. 219.

All three sections recognize, as a threshold, that the activities or offenses should have been (partly) committed in the district were the court issues the order. Furthermore, the nationwide applicability of search warrants (section 219) is limited to terrorism investigations. The reason for adopting this amendment has been to enable a system without unnecessary delays in investigating terrorist networks. According to the government, this could be realized by the possibility to obtain a single search warrant in one district, where terrorism activities have occurred, that is applicable in multiple places in different districts at the same time.[50]

### *6.2.2 Developments in Case Law*

Also in the case law of the post-9/11 era a trend can be identified allowing for reasoning in favor of expedient and efficient law enforcement by watering down Fourth Amendment restraints or expanding doctrinal exceptions to Fourth Amendment requirements. The requirement of probable cause has been loosened because of national security arguments, warrantless searches have been considered reasonable in situations involving threats to national security and the special needs doctrine has been expanded so as to be applicable to searches and seizures for the purpose of terrorism prevention.

The Warren Court already made the first step towards diminishing probable cause as a necessary requirement to render a search reasonable when confronted with societal upheaval as a consequence of the racial riots at the end of the 1960s.[51] By deciding *Terry v. Ohio* in 1968 the Court adopted a narrow exception to the probable cause requirement by allowing frisking upon a reasonable suspicion of criminal activity in the presence of an imminent danger.[52] The so-called Terry stop and frisk was reasonable when "the officer's action was justified at its inception, and [when] it was reasonably related in scope to the circumstances which justified the interference in the first place."[53] The Court allowed this Fourth Amendment intrusion of frisking without a warrant or probable cause only "[w]hen an officer is justified in believing that the individual whose suspicious behavior he is investigating at close range is armed and presently dangerous to the officer or to others," which is a reason that goes beyond the governmental interest in investigating crime.[54] Since *Terry v. Ohio*, the rather narrowly defined Terry stop and frisk has been slightly extended to remain a practical investigative tool for law enforcement officers in new exigent situations. Stopping and frisking upon

---

[50] The Department of Justice, 'The USA Patriot Act: Myth vs. Reality', available at: http://www.justice.gov/archive/ll/subs/add_myths.htm (accessed July 29, 2011), sec. 219.

[51] Roth 2009, 2795-2796.

[52] See in more detail about *Terry v. Ohio*, 392 U.S. 1, 88 S.Ct. 1868 (1968), Sect. 5.3.2.1.1.1

[53] *Terry v. Ohio*, 392 U.S. 1, 88 S.Ct. 1868 (1968), 1879.

[54] *Ibid.*, 1881.

reasonable suspicion may now include handcuffing and taking the suspect into custody, which falls short of constituting an arrest, for the purpose of further investigating once a law enforcement officer feels the need to investigate potential suspects in the presence of a reasonable suspicion that criminal activity is afoot.[55] The courts' expansion of Terry authorities has usually been a consequence of an increased focus on effective crime control due to contemporaneous societal concerns, which started with the racial riots of the late 1960s, to the 'war on drugs' of the 1980s and the threat of terrorism since 9/11. The latter has now been used as the decisive consideration for accepting the stopping of a vehicle.

In *United States v. Ramos* (2010)[56] an inspector of the Massachusetts Bay Transit Authority (MBTA) observed a van with passengers having, in her opinion, a 'Middle Eastern' appearance. The van was parked at a place where commuters almost always left their cars, it had a Texas license plate and tinted windows. These circumstances were a sufficient reason for the inspector to call the police, who upon their arrival observed the same circumstances. It was feared that the men intended to commit a terrorist attack with explosives. On the basis of these circumstances, the police opened the door of the van and ordered the passengers to get out. It turned out that the passengers were illegal Brazilians. In court the defendants claimed that their Fourth Amendment rights had been violated as the police did not have a reasonable, articulable suspicion to stop the vehicle. Addressing the case at first instance (2008), District Judge Wolf held that "in the instant case, common sense indicated that the conduct in question was occurring at a public transportation facility which, as the then recent Madrid bombing suggested, might be a particularly attractive target for a terrorist attack."[57] "A series of acts, each of them perhaps innocent if viewed separately" may, "taken together", warrant "further investigation."[58] Furthermore, "the gravity of the potential danger being addressed is one of the totality of the circumstances to be considered" when determining whether the stop was reasonable.[59] Judge Wolf continued by stating that "[a]lthough the courts must be vigilant and rigorous in preventing 9/11 from being casually or carelessly used as an excuse for ignoring the requirements of the Fourth Amendment, common sense compels the conclusion that in certain circumstances, including those involved in the instant case, conduct that arguably might not have been sufficiently threatening to justify a brief investigatory stop in an earlier era may be reasonable in a nation that experienced a terrible terrorist attack only several years before."[60] The First Circuit Court upheld this decision on appeal, although, other than the District Court, it focused

---

[55] Roth 2009, 2800-2802.

[56] *United States v. Ramos,* 629 F.3d 60 (1st Cir. 2010). The First Circuit Court upheld the District Court's Judgment of 2008: *United States v. Ramos,* 591 F.Supp.2d 93 (D.Mass. 2008).

[57] *United States v. Ramos,* 591 F.Supp.2d 93 (D.Mass. 2008), 103.

[58] *Ibid.* and see *Terry v. Ohio,* 392 U.S. 1, 88 S.Ct. 1868 (1968), 22.

[59] *United States v. Ramos,* 591 F.Supp.2d 93 (D.Mass. 2008), 103.

[60] *Ibid.*, 104.

particularly on the question whether the particular circumstances were sufficient to establish a 'reasonable suspicion that criminal activity was afoot.' Nevertheless, the First Circuit Court similarly attached decisive weight to the specific context of a terrorist threat in order to reach the conclusion that a reasonable suspicion was present. Because of the 'Middle Eastern' appearance of the occupants of the car and taking into account the contextual circumstances that "[t]he location involved was a major urban transit system, the threat was highly timely, the risk involved many lives, and the concern about terrorism was intense," the '*Terry* stop' was reasonable under the totality of circumstances test.[61]

The interest of preventing terrorism thus had a decisive weight in establishing a reasonable suspicion required to justify a *Terry* stop, whereas the remaining circumstances would have been insufficient to hold a *Terry* stop reasonable under the Fourth Amendment in the absence of a terrorist threat.

Furthermore, the New York District Court has used the interest of preventing terrorism by expanding the special needs doctrine.[62] *Macwade v. Kelly* (2006)[63] concerned the alleged violation of the Fourth Amendment by New York City's program of random, suspicionless subway baggage searches. The court, applying the special needs doctrine by assessing the factors set out in *Illinois v. Lidster* (2004),[64] decided as follows: "the special needs doctrine may apply where, as here, the subject of a search possesses a full privacy expectation. Further, we hold that preventing a terrorist attack on the subway is a "special need" within the meaning of the doctrine. Finally, we hold that the search program is reasonable because it serves a paramount government interest and, under the circumstances, is narrowly tailored and sufficiently effective." The special needs doctrine is used to create exceptions to regular constitutional restraint. The circumstances of the case constituting such a special need justify search and seizure without a warrant and without probable cause. In *Macwade* the special needs doctrine was expanded to include random searches of bags on the NY subway, as the protection against the possibility that bags contain explosives trumps the regular constitutional restraints. Whereas the special needs doctrine was previously limited to suspicionless searches of cars near the Mexican border to confront illegal immigration, highway alcohol checkpoints, checkpoints to gather information and the drug testing of student athletes, now the 'prevention of terrorism' has been accepted as a valid reason to invoke the special needs doctrine.[65]

---

61 *United States v. Ramos,* 629 F.3d 60 (1st Cir. 2010), 67-68.

62 See Chap. 5, Sect. 5.3.2.1.1.1.

63 *Macwade v. Kelly,* 460 F.3d 260 (2nd Cir. 2006).

64 See Sect. 5.3.2.1.1.1 (*Illinois v. Lidster,* 540 U.S. 419, 124 S.Ct. 885 (2004), 427).

65 Crocker 2008, 248.

Lastly, the U.S. Court of Appeals of the Second Circuit Court has *In re Terrorist Bombings of U.S. Embassies in East Africa* (2008)[66] (also referred to as the *Kenya* case) excluded the Fourth Amendment warrant requirement from searches of US citizens by US agents conducted abroad. According to the court "such searches of U.S. citizens need only satisfy the Fourth Amendment's requirement of reasonableness."[67] The search of the defendant's Nairobi home and the electronic surveillance of the defendant's Kenyan telephone lines were reasonable, because "the searches' intrusion on [defendant's] privacy was outweighed by the Government's manifest need to monitor his activities as an operative of al Qaeda because of the extreme threat al Qaeda presented, and continues to present, to national security."[68] Furthermore, "[b]ecause the surveillance of suspected al Qaeda operatives must be sustained and thorough in order to be effective, we cannot conclude that the scope of the government's electronic surveillance was overbroad. While the intrusion on El-Hage's privacy was great, the need for the government to so intrude was even greater."[69]

More in general, the courts are inclined to focus more on the interest of efficient and expeditious law enforcement in times of increased societal unrest or fear, which has clearly been the case in the post-9/11 era, as a consequence of the confrontation with the devastating crimes of terrorism on US soil. Not only the measures on behalf of the legislature and the executive are influenced by a climate of fear, but also the judicial branch is sensitive to such circumstances. Although it is the task of the judiciary to provide consistency and to slow down too rapid legal changes as the watchdog of constitutional values, the judiciary has never been insensitive to such societal circumstances asking for more power for law enforcement. In addition, it is also the task of the judiciary to explain the law in the light of current circumstances within constitutional parameters. Such a more general trend seems, for example, to follow from two Supreme Court cases in 2006. Although the main issue in these cases was not whether or not probable cause could be established, the Court dealt with situations where probable cause would normally have been required, but explained the standard to be applied in similar terms as reasonable suspicion. In both *Georgia v. Randolph*[70] and *Brigham City v. Stuart*,[71] the Supreme Court allowed, also in cases where the 'special needs

---

66 *In re Terrorist Bombings of U.S. Embassies in East Africa,* 552 F.3d 157 (2nd Cir. 2008). Decision on appeal from the U.S. District Court for the Southern District of New York in *United States v. Bin Laden,* 126 F. Supp. 2d 264 (S.D.N.Y. 2000), which court held that US citizens abroad, who are subjected to search activities on behalf of the US government, can bring Fourth Amendment challenges.

67 *In re Terrorist Bombings of U.S. Embassies in East Africa,* 552 F.3d 157 (2nd Cir. 2008), 167.

68 *Ibid.*, 172-173.

69 *Ibid.*, 176. The Second Circuit also considered that the *ex parte, in camera* evaluation of the evidence submitted by the government in opposition to El-Hage's suppression motion was appropriate in light of national security considerations.

70 *Georgia v. Randolph,* 547 U.S. 103, 126 S.Ct. 1515 (2006).

71 *Brigham City v. Stuart,* 547 U.S. 398, 126 S.Ct. 1943 (2006).

exception' cannot be applied, the standard of a "reason to believe", which is normally used to describe a reasonable suspicion and not probable cause.[72] The Court stated in *Georgia v. Randolph* (a case primarily dealing with the question whether the warrantless search of a home was permissible with the consent of a co-occupant, whereas the occupant in question refused to consent to the search) that the police can enter a house when they have "good reason to believe" that someone needs to be protected against domestic violence.[73] In *Brigham City v. Stuart* this standard of an "objectively reasonable basis for believing" could justify a warrantless entry by officers after they observed through the screen door that someone was being and may continue to be assaulted. This standard could apply regardless of whether the subjective motive of the police was to gather evidence or to render emergency aid, but was objectively justified because of "compelling law enforcement needs."[74] These cases are examples of cases where the Court focuses on the reasonableness of the search rather than on the importance of the presence of probable cause or a valid warrant.[75] As a consequence, not only the warrant requirement but also the central position of the probable cause requirement for the reasonableness of a search or seizure is diminished. Again, the interest of efficient law enforcement to enhance security has been used as an argument to water down and diminish the protective meaning of probable cause.[76]

### 6.2.3 Other Developments Enhancing Proactive Capacities of Law Enforcement Agencies

On a lower level, law enforcement agencies have taken measures in order to enhance the sharing of criminal intelligence and come to an effective 'intelligence-led policing' which is able to 'connect the dots' in time to prevent acts of terrorism. During the 2001 "International Association of Chiefs of Police Criminal Intelligence Sharing Summit" the initiative was taken to form the "Global Justice Information Sharing Initiative Intelligence Working Group" which developed "The National Criminal Intelligence Sharing Plan." Attorney General Ashcroft endorsed this plan in May 2004. One of the key aims of the plan was to "overcome the long-standing and substantial barriers that hinder intelligence sharing," for example, as a consequence of the "hierarchy within the law enforcement and

[72] Kinports 2009, 660.

[73] *Georgia v. Randolph,* 547 U.S. 103, 126 S.Ct. 1515 (2006), 118.

[74] *Brigham City v. Stuart,* 547 U.S. 398, 126 S.Ct. 1943 (2006), 403 and 406.

[75] Antkowiak 2007, 575.

[76] Antkowiak 2007, 569. For the recent diminishment of Fourth Amendment protections by the Supreme Court (with regard to probable cause, individualized suspicion and the exclusionary rule) and socio-politically inspired proposals for alternatives under the Fourth Amendment see: Slobogin 2007. See also: Sydejko 2006 and Winter 2006.

intelligence community." One of the results of the endorsement of the "National Criminal Intelligence Sharing Plan" was the establishment of the "Fusion Center" as "an effective mechanism to exchange information and intelligence" between law enforcement agencies on the local, state and federal level.[77]

Currently 72 recognized fusion centers have been established throughout the country, involving all relevant actors on the "federal, state, local, tribal, territorial" level as well as involving the private sector.[78]

## 6.3 Changes Affecting the Powers in National Security Investigations

Besides changes to conventional criminal investigation, the USA PATRIOT Act of 2001 has significantly contributed to an expansion of powers in the context of a national security investigation by amending the Foreign Intelligence Surveillance Act of 1978. These amendments include extending the scope of surveillance powers under the statutory regime of FISA and creating a virtually new power to obtain "tangible items" (more often referred to as section 215 orders or orders to obtain library and bookstore records) through an order authorized by the FISA Court. Both categories will be dealt with separately below.

### *6.3.1 Increased FISA Surveillance Powers*

One of the most meaningful amendments of the PATRIOT Act of 2001 concerns the introduction of the possibility of 'roving surveillance' to national security investigations. Section 206 aims to enable roving surveillance under FISA, which means that a specific suspect can be followed, irrespective of the communication device that he is using. In addition, the nationwide applicability of FISA orders is now permitted, which means that the target can be followed throughout the US without applying for a new order and regardless of the communication devices that he uses.[79] Roving surveillance was already possible under Title III, when it can be demonstrated that the exceptional circumstance applies that the person's actions are thwarting the interception.[80] A similar wording is now included in FISA to enable roving surveillance also in foreign intelligence investigations. Section 105(c)(2)(B) of the FISA 1978 has been amended by inserting, "or in

---

[77] See: Global Justice Information Sharing Initiative 2003 and Global Justice Information Sharing Initiative 2006.

[78] Progress Report 2011, 3.

[79] Section 206 USA PATRIOT Act of 2001.

[80] 18 U.S.C. § 2518(11)(b)(ii) (2007). See Chap. 5, Sect. 5.3.2.1.2.

circumstances where the Court finds that the actions of the target of the application may have the effect of thwarting the identification of a specified person, such other persons," after "specified person".

The USA PATRIOT Improvement and Reauthorization Act of 2005 has slightly tightened the conditions under which an order for roving surveillance may be issued. Before this, it was sufficient to specify in the application and order the identity of the target and, otherwise, to include a description of the target. Since the 2005 Act such a description must concern the "specific target."[81] However, an order for roving surveillance still does not need to identify the "nature and location of each of the facilities or places at which the electronic surveillance will be directed" if such facilities and places are unknown.[82] The latter requirement concerns the most problematic aspect of roving surveillance as the Fourth Amendment does require that an order must "particularly describe the place to be searched."

The USA PATRIOT Improvement and Reauthorization Act of 2005 includes in section 50 U.S.C. § 1805(c)(3) "special directions" to be included in an order approving roving surveillance, which require "the applicant to provide notice to the court within ten days after the date on which surveillance begins to be directed at any new facility or place, unless the court finds good cause to justify a longer period of up to 60 days [...]" This notification must also include "the facts and circumstances relied upon by the applicant to justify the applicant's belief that each new facility or place at which the electronic surveillance is directed, is or was being used, or is about to be used, by the target of the surveillance."[83] Furthermore, congressional oversight of the use of all foreign intelligence electronic surveillance authority has been enhanced (section 108(c)).

The roving surveillance provision under FISA was originally intended to expire in 2005. This 'sunset' provision was extended by the USA PATRIOT Improvement and Reauthorization Act of 2005 to December 31st 2009. On February 27, 2010 President Obama signed the Act 'To extend expiring provisions of the USA PATRIOT Act Improvement and Reauthorization Act of 2005 and Intelligence Reform and Terrorism Prevention Act of 2004 until February 28, 2011', thereby immediately extending the roving surveillance provision (section 206) as well as other expiring provisions for another year.[84] After another extension for three months, with an eye on reviewing the PATRIOT provisions in question, it has

[81] Section 108 USA PATRIOT Improvement and Reauthorization Act of 2005 and see Yeh and Doyle 2006, 17.

[82] See 50 U.S.C. § 1805(c)(1)(B) (2009).

[83] Section 108(b)(3) USA PATRIOT Improvement and Reauthorization Act of 2005 and 50 U.S.C. § 1805(c)(3).

[84] Public Law 111-141, Feb. 27, 2010, 124 Stat. 37, 111th Congress, An Act 'to extend expiring provisions of the USA PATRIOT Act Improvement and Reauthorization Act of 2005 and Intelligence Reform and Terrorism Prevention Act of 2004 until February 28, 2011.' Except for the provision for roving surveillance, also the seizure of certain business records and the lone wolf provision has been extended.

finally been decided to extend all expiring PATRIOT provisions, including the roving surveillance provision under FISA, until June 2015 without further changes.[85]

In the second place, the period in which an order may be used for FISA surveillance, FISA physical searchers, and FISA pen registers and trap and trace surveillance devices has been extended. Section 207 of the 2001 PATRIOT Act extends the period of surveillance to a maximum of 120 days (formerly 90 days) when the target is an agent of a foreign power *and*—as explicitly added by section 105 of the Reauthorization and Improvement Act of 2005—does not concern a US person.[86]

Similarly, for physical searches the maximum period of a search order against non-US persons is extended to 120 days, whereas the maximum time period in general is also extended from 45 days to 90 days.[87] The maximum surveillance duration permitted now differs for three categories. In principle, an order for surveillance under FISA is permitted for the "period necessary to achieve its purpose" which shall not exceed 90 days. When the electronic surveillance is targeted at a foreign power, the maximum duration may be for the "period specified in the application or for one year." As an exemption to the 90 days maximum, the surveillance against an agent of a foreign power not being a US person may last for 120 days. Similarly, extensions for the first category may be provided under the same conditions as the initial order; extensions for orders targeting foreign powers "may be for a period not to exceed one year if the judge finds probable cause to believe that no communication of any individual United States person will be acquired during that period; and extensions of orders targeting non-US agents of foreign powers can be given for up to one year.[88]

The USA PATRIOT Improvement and Reauthorization Act of 2005 has also extended the permissible period for orders that authorize the use of pen registers and trap and trace devices to obtain foreign intelligence information that does not concern a US person from 90 days to one year.[89]

These amendments to extend the period specifically for the surveillance of agents of foreign powers not concerning US persons do also target the so-called '*lone wolf*.' The Intelligence Reform Act of December 2004 included the 'lone wolf amendment,' which includes in the definition of an agent of a foreign power not only those persons involved with foreign-based groups, but also persons who cannot be linked to a specific group and seem to be acting alone. These 'lone

---

[85] PATRIOT Sunsets Extension Act of 2011, S.990, 112th Congress, 1st Session.

[86] See 50 U.S.C. § 1805(d)(1) and (2). To compare: under Title III the maximum period of surveillance is thirty days, extensions to this period being very limited. 18 U.S.C. § 2518(5).

[87] 50 U.S.C. § 1824(d).

[88] 50 U.S.C. § 1805(d)(2).

[89] Section 105 of the USA PATRIOT Improvement and Reauthorization Act of 2005 amending 50 U.S.C. § 1842(e).

wolves' can only concern "any person other than a United States person, who (...) engages in international terrorism or activities in preparation therefore."[90]

Thirdly, the PATRIOT Act of 2001 and the Reauthorization and Improvement Act of 2005 have amended the existing authorities for the use of pen registers and trap and trace devices in foreign intelligence investigations. The broadening of the definition of pen registers and trap and trace devices by section 216 under conventional criminal law (as dealt with in Sect. 6.2.1) equally applies to national security surveillance.[91] The amendments of section 214 broaden the scope of the information that can be intercepted by pen registers and trap and trace devices. In addition, the language of § 1842(a)(1) and (c)(2) has been changed, which arguably makes the requirement at the same time more stringent than before. It restricts the target of the pen register and trap and trace device to non-US persons in any investigation to obtain foreign intelligence information or to protect against international terrorism or clandestine activities, which may also include US persons if the investigation is not solely based upon "activities protected by the First Amendment." Before, pen registers and trap and trace devices could be used in any investigation to gather foreign intelligence information, irrespective of whether the persons involved were US citizens or not.

Section 128(a) of the USA PATRIOT Improvement and Reauthorization Act of 2005 expands the scope of the pen register or trap and trace device more drastically. Now the FISA Court shall, if requested by the application, direct a service provider to disclose certain information about the customer or subscriber against whom the pen register or trap and trace device is directed, which information may include the name, address, telephone or instrument number, local or long-distance telephone records, the number of any credit card or bank account used to pay the service, and identifying information about the customers or subscribers of incoming or outgoing communication.[92] As the scope of the authority to use pen register and trap and trace devices was previously more restrictive under FISA than under Title III, it was argued that similar authority should exist in national security investigations as is available in conventional criminal investigations. As a consequence of the PATRIOT Act Reauthorization Act of 2005, the information that can be requested from the service provider under a FISA order has now become more extensive than permissible in the law enforcement context (see section 18 U.S.C. § 2709). However, this information is not as extensive as the scope of information under a FISA section 215 "tangible item" order.[93]

Lastly, the threshold upon which a FISA judge can issue an order to use a pen register or trap and trace device has been amended to read: "a certification by the applicant that the information likely to be obtained is foreign intelligence

[90] 50 U.S.C. § 1801(b) heading and under (C).

[91] Schulhofer 2005, 41.

[92] See section 128(a) of the USA PATRIOT ACT Reauthorization and Improvement Act of 2005.

[93] 50 U.S.C. § 1842(d)(2)(C).

information not concerning a United States person or is relevant to an ongoing investigation to protect against international terrorism or clandestine intelligence activities, provided that such investigation of a United States person is not conducted solely upon the basis of activities protected by the first amendment to the Constitution."[94] In addition, and more importantly, the previous additional requirement to be included in the certification of some evidentiary support connecting the information to be intercepted to an individual or a foreign power or agent of a foreign power involved in terrorism or clandestine intelligence activities, which may also involve a violation of criminal law, has been completely eliminated.[95] These amendments make it possible that also information regarding individuals who cannot themselves be related to international terrorism or clandestine intelligence investigations is intercepted through the new pen register or trap and trace authority, which eliminates an important protective restraint.

### *6.3.2 FISA Court Document Production Orders*

Already before the enactment of the PATRIOT Act and PATRIOT Reauthorizations Acts, it was possible under FISA to request the production of transportation-related business records by a FISA Court order, an order which could be issued upon a certification by the applicant that "there are specific articulable facts giving reason to believe that the person to whom the records pertain is a foreign power or an agent of a foreign power."[96] Section 215 of the 2001 USA PATRIOT Act has amended the FISA provisions dealing with the production of business records by broadening its scope, lowering the threshold for such productions and including a permanent and broad non-disclosure requirement. Section 215 has been considered as one of the most controversial sections of the USA PATRIOT Act. It is often referred to as the 'library provision,' because it has the effect of broadening the scope of the order to include library and bookstore records. Since 2001, the section has again been changed substantially by the Reauthorization Acts of 2005 and 2006.

While FISA Court document production orders were originally limited to common carriers, public accommodation facilities, physical storage facilities and vehicle rental facilities, which together included basically all travel-related services, section 215 broadened the scope to "the production of any tangible things (including books, records, papers, documents, and other items)."[97] This makes the

[94] Section 214(2) of the USA PATRIOT Act of 2001, amending 50 U.S.C. § 1842(c)(2).

[95] Section 214(3) of the USA PATRIOT Act of 2001, striking subsection 50 U.S.C. § 1842(c)(3). See for this requirement Sect. 5.2.2.3.1.

[96] As to the unamended language of 50 U.S.C. § 1862(b)(2).

[97] Section 215 of the USA PATRIOT Act of 2001.

order similar to grand jury investigative powers; however, without the protective elements of the grand jury institution.

According to section 215 and the amendment of this section by the Reauthorization Act "the Director of the Federal Bureau of Investigation or a designee of the Director (whose rank shall be no lower than Assistant Special Agent in Charge) may make an application."[98] An application for the production of any tangible things may be made by "the Director of the Federal Bureau of Investigation or a designee of the Director (whose rank shall be no lower than Assistant Special Agent in Charge)." Applications for orders requesting the production of more privacy-sensitive information ("library circulation records, library patron lists, book sales records, book customer lists, firearms sales records, tax return records, educational records, or medial records containing information that would identify a person") may only be made by three high-ranking officials (the Director of the FBI, the Deputy director of the FBI and the Executive Assistant Director for National Security).[99] The requirement of the personal approval of these high-ranking officials has been introduced by the Reauthorization Act of 2005 as a more stringent application procedure for section 215 orders, when the order concerns categories of more privacy-sensitive information.[100]

An application may be made "for an investigation to obtain foreign intelligence information not concerning a United States person or to protect against nternational terrorism or clandestine intelligence activities, provided that such investigation of a United States person is not conducted solely upon the basis of activities protected by the First Amendment to the Constitution." The requirement of some evidentiary support concerning the person to whom the records belong, as was included in the original wording of 50 U.S.C. § 1861, no longer applies. The current threshold which is applicable is "a statement of facts showing that there are reasonable grounds to believe that the tangible things are relevant to an authorized investigation (other than threat assessment)." Such authorized investigation must either be aimed at obtaining foreign intelligence information that does not concern a US person or must be aimed at the protection against international terrorism or clandestine intelligence activities. The section continues by enumerating some circumstances in which document production orders are "presumptively relevant to an authorized investigation." If the tangible things sought "pertain to—(i) a foreign power or an agent of a foreign power; (ii) the activities of a suspected agent of a foreign power who is the subject of such authorized investigation; or (iii) an individual in contact with, or known to, a suspected agent of a foreign power who is the subject of such authorized investigation" the order should be considered presumptively relevant.[101] The new threshold for document production

[98] 50 U.S.C. § 1861(a)(1).

[99] 50 U.S.C. § 1861(a)(3) and section 106(a)(3) Reauthorization Act.

[100] Section 106(a)(2) USA PATRIOT Reauthorization Act of 2005.

[101] 50 U.S.C. § 1861(b)(2).

orders under FISA thus no longer requires any level of suspicion concerning the person to whom the documents pertain.

The FISA Court shall approve the (*ex parte*) order if the statutory requirements for the application are met.[102] The order shall include details, such as a sufficient particular description of the tangible things sought and the date on which the tangible things must be provided.[103] An order cannot be issued if the tangible things sought can also be obtained by the more protective investigative power of the grand jury or any other order of a US court seeking the production of records or tangible things.[104]

Furthermore, section 215 includes a non-disclosure requirement, prohibiting the recipient from disclosing to any other person that the FBI has sought the tangible things described in the order. This permanent non-disclosure requirement has been extensively criticized and is typified as a "permanent and extremely broad gag order," which even forbids section 215 recipients to consult with their lawyer.[105] The recipient of a section 215 order was not allowed to "disclose to any person (other than those persons necessary to produce the tangible things under this section) that the Federal Bureau of Investigation has sought or obtained tangible things under this section."

The constitutionality of this gag order has been challenged in courts with regard to a similar provision applicable to recipients of National Security Letters (NSL, see on NSL Sect. 6.5.2). *Doe v. Ashcroft*[106] (Doe I) and *Doe v. Gonzales*[107] (Doe II) are civil cases challenging the unamended Patriot Act provisions that authorized the issuance of NSL and that permanently barred the disclosure of the fact that a NSL had been received. John Doe is an acronym for an unidentified Internet service provider supported by the American Civil Liberties Union (ACLU). The cases dealt primarily with the non-disclosure gag order, for which reason the outcome of these cases is also relevant to the similar non-disclosure gag order that accompanies section 215 orders. Hence, insofar as these cases deal with this subject they will already be addressed in the current section.

The plaintiffs in Doe I argued that the non-disclosure provision violated the First Amendment to the Constitution as it "burdens speech categorically and perpetually, without any case-by-case judicial consideration of whether that speech burden is justified."[108] The court observed that when limiting freedom of speech the government should observe "strict scrutiny."[109] Although the court acknowledged that the government "should be accorded a due measure of

[102] 50 U.S.C. § 1861(c)(1).

[103] 50 U.S.C. § 1861(c)(2).

[104] 50 U.S.C. § 1861(c)(2)(D).

[105] See e.g. Mart 2008, 438.

[106] *Doe v. Ashcroft,* 334 F.Supp.2d 471 (S.D.N.Y. 2004) (Doe I).

[107] *Doe v. Gonzales,* 386 F.Supp.2d 66 (D.Conn. 2005) (Doe II).

[108] *Doe v. Ashcroft,* 334 F.Supp.2d 471 (S.D.N.Y. 2004), 475.

[109] *Ibid.*, 513.

deference when it asserts that secrecy is necessary for national security purposes," the fact that the recipient of a NSL was confronted with perpetual secrecy without any form of judicial process imposed a "disproportionate burden on free speech."[110] District Court Judge Marrerro, J. granted the motion of the plaintiffs and concluded that "the ban on disclosure contained in § 2709(c) [the provision in 18 U.S.C. authorizing NSL], which the Court is unable to sever from the remainder of the statute, operated as an unconstitutional prior restraint on speech in violation of the First Amendment."[111]

In Doe II a similar conclusion was reached with regard to the non-disclosure requirement accompanying NSL. In that case another district court decided that the non-disclosure requirement failed to satisfy "strict scrutiny," entailing both a violation of the First Amendment with regard to the prohibition on the NSL recipient ever revealing its identity and with regard to the content-based restriction on speech as a consequence of the non-disclosure requirement.[112]

When Doe I and Doe II were being litigated the USA PATRIOT Improvement and Reauthorization Act of 2005 was passed by Congress. This Act also included some changes with regard to the non-disclosure requirement of Section 215 (and regarding NSL). Section 106(e) of the Reauthorization Act has expanded the list of exceptions to the 'gag order,' which included an express permission to disclose to "an attorney to obtain legal advice or assistance," as well as to "other persons as permitted" by the Director of the FBI or his designee." A recipient of a section 215 order shall "at the research of the Director of the FBI or the designee of the Director (...) identify (...) the person to whom such disclosure will be made or to whom such disclosure was made prior to the request, but in no circumstance shall a person be required to inform the Director or such designee that the person intends to consult an attorney to obtain legal advice or legal assistance."[113] Section 4 of the USA PATRIOT Act Additional Reauthorizing Amendments Act of 2006 exempts from the disclosure also the identity of the attorney sought to obtain legal advice, as earlier the "chilling effect" of the non-disclosure requirement on the individual's right to seek legal counsel was criticized.[114]

The Reauthorization Act of 2005 also included in camera judicial review for section 215 orders by judges of the FISA Court. Section 106(f) of the Reauthorization adds a paragraph to 50 U.S.C. § 1861 dealing with the procedures for such a review. A recipient of a section 215 order can challenge the legality of such an order. The FISA court judge has to conduct an initial review of such a petition. When the judge determines that the petition is not "frivolous," he or she will consider the review. When the order does not meet the prescribed requirements or

---

110 *Ibid.*, 524.

111 *Ibid.*, 475 and 526.

112 *Doe v. Gonzales,* 386 F.Supp.2d 66 (D.Conn. 2005) (Doe II), 79-80.

113 Section 106(e) Reauthorization Act of 2005.

114 Yeh and Doyle 2006, 8.

"is otherwise unlawful," the judge may modify or set aside the order.[115] This does not cover general findings that the order as such is, for example, overly broad.[116] When the order is not modified or set aside, the judge "shall immediately affirm the order and order the recipient to comply therewith."[117] In that regard the possibility for judicial review can also result in a judicial order to comply with a section 215 order. The FISA Court of Review and the Supreme Court are granted jurisdiction to consider appeals against the FISA Court judge's decision to affirm, modify, or set aside a section 215 order.

The Additional Reauthorization Act of 2006 has also provided for judicial review with regard to the non-disclosure provision. However, a challenge in that regard can only be filed a year after a section 215 order has been issued. After one year the recipient may file a petition to modify or set aside the non-disclosure requirement, which will be reviewed by the judge if the petition is not frivolous.[118] The judge is not free to decide whether or not to modify or set aside the non-disclosure requirement: the judge may only do so if he finds "no reason to believe that disclosure may endanger the national security of the United States, interfere with a criminal, counterterrorism, or counterintelligence investigation, interfere with diplomatic relations, or endanger the life or physical safety of any person."[119] If the AG, deputy Attorney General, an assistant Attorney General, or the Director of the FBI makes a certification in that regard, the judge must treat that certification as conclusive, unless he or she finds that "the certification was made in bad faith."[120] When the judge decides not to modify or set aside the non-disclosure requirement, the non-disclosure requirement will remain in force for another year. After one year, the recipient may again seek a decision with the FISA Court to modify or set aside the non-disclosure requirement.[121] The recipient or the government may appeal a decision to affirm, modify or set aside the non-disclosure order before the FISA Court of review. Pending such an appeal, the order is stayed.[122]

Because of these amendments of the Reauthorization Act the Court of Appeals of the Second Circuit vacated Doe I and dismissed Doe II, as the amendments of the Reauthorization Act substantially changed the provisions on which the findings in Doe I and II were based. The Court of Appeals remanded Doe I to the district court of New York to assess the amended provisions.[123] This third case about the amended provisions concerning NSL before the New York District Court is known

115 50 U.S.C. § 1861(f)(2)(A).

116 Mart 2008, 440.

117 50 U.S.C. § 1861(f)(2)(A)(ii) and § 1861(f)(2)(B).

118 50 U.S.C. § 1861(f)(2)(A).

119 50 U.S.C. § 1861(f)(2)(C)(i).

120 50 U.S.C. § 1861(f)(2)(C)(ii).

121 50 U.S.C. § 1861(f)(2)(C)(iii).

122 Yeh and Doyle 2006, 9-10.

123 *Doe v. Gonzales,* 449 F.3d 415 (2nd Cir. 2006).

as 'Doe III' (*Doe v. Gonzales* (2007)[124]). District court judge Marrero, J. assessed whether the now amended non-disclosure provision of 18 U.S.C. § 2709(c)) and § 3511(b), concerning the non-disclosure order for NSL and the judicial review of such non-disclosure order were "unconstitutional on their face and as applied under the First Amendment and the principle of separation of powers."[125] The district court held that also the amended non-disclosure provision was unconstitutional on its face as it violated both the First Amendment and the separation of powers. The First Amendment was violated because the non-disclosure provision "functions as a licensing scheme that does not afford adequate procedural safeguards, and because it is not a sufficiently narrowly tailored restriction on protected speech. The separation of powers is violated because the court is, unless in bad faith, bound by the government's certification."[126]

The government appealed the decision of Doe III to enjoin the government from enforcing the provisions covering NSL. The Court of Appeals of the Second Circuit only assessed in *Doe v. Mukasey* (2008)[127] the non-disclosure requirement for NSL. The Court of Appeals took a slightly more moderate view holding that the "John Doe, Inc., has been restrained from publicly expressing a category of information, albeit a narrow one, and that information is relevant to intended criticism of a governmental activity."[128] Whether or not assessed under strict scrutiny, the Court of Appeals contested, two aspects of the non-disclosure requirement remain at issue: "the absence of a requirement that the Government initiate judicial review of the lawfulness of a nondisclosure requirement and the degree of deference a district court is obliged to accord to the certification of senior governmental officials in ordering nondislosure."[129] Considering these issues the court construed the provisions regarding non-disclosure and judicial review in a manner limiting the imposing of a non-disclosure requirement to orders related to "an authorized investigation to protect against international terrorism or clandestine intelligence activities" and placing the burden of proof as to the necessity of the non-disclosure requirement on the government. Furthermore, the court held the provisions unconstitutional "to the extent that they impose a nondisclosure requirement without placing on the Government the burden of initiating judicial review of that requirement." Lastly, the provision directing the court reviewing the non-disclosure requirement to treat the government's "certification that disclosure may endanger the national security of the United States or interfere with diplomatic relations" as conclusive, was held to be unconstitutional.[130] Under the

---

124 *Doe v. Gonzales*, 500 F.Supp.2d 379 (S.D.N.Y. 2007) (Doe III).

125 *Ibid.*, 386.

126 *Ibid.*, 425.

127 *Doe v. Mukasey,* 549 F.3d 861 (2008).

128 *Doe v. Mukasey,* 549 F.3d 861 (2nd Cir. 2008), 878.

129 *Ibid.*, 878.

130 *Ibid.*, 883.

conditions for a judicial review set forth by this Court of Appeals, the provisions at issue would survive constitutional challenge.[131]

The case was again remanded to the US District Court S.D. New York in order to assess whether the "government is justified in continuing to require nondisclosure of a National Security Letter (..) issued to Doe." This issue was assessed in *Doe v. Holder* (2009) under the conditions for judicial review set forth by the Second Circuit. This resulted in the October 2009 order, where the court refused to set aside the non-disclosure requirement for reasons provided by the government *ex parte*, *in camera*, under seal. According to the Court, the government had demonstrated that the continuation of the non-disclosure requirement on the recipient was justified.[132] The plaintiffs moved for a partial reconsideration of the order, resulting in *Doe v. Holder* (2010), where the court only assessed whether the government was justified in continuing to impose the non-disclosure requirement on the attachment to the national security letter received by the plaintiffs. The court directed the government to lift the non-disclosure requirement with regard to the categories of information requested in the attachment, namely "(1) material within the scope of information that the NSL statute identifies as permissible for the FBI to obtain through use of NSLs, and (2) material that the FBI has publicly acknowledged it has previously requested by means of NSLs."[133] With regard to the remainder of the attachment, the court concluded that "the Government has demonstrated that good reason exists to believe that disclosure of the information withheld plausibly could harm an authorized ongoing investigation to protect against international terrorism or clandestine intelligence activities."[134] To support this latter conclusion the court referred to the Supreme Court decision in *CIA v. Sims* (1985), where it "upheld the nondisclosure of intelligence information by the Central Intelligence Agency under analogous circumstances" by "cautioning that "bits and pieces of data *may* aid in piecing together bits of other information even when the individual piece is not of obvious importance in itself."[135]

In May 2010 John Doe filed a notice of appeal against the October 2009 order and the March 2010 decision. However, the plaintiffs and the FBI reached a settlement on July 26, 2010 based on the FBI's statement that "due to a change in circumstances, the FBI no longer believes that non-disclosure of the identity of the recipient of the NSL [was] necessary."[136] It was agreed that the plaintiffs would not reinstate their appeal and that John Doe would be "permitted to identify himself and his company as the recipient of the NSL." John Doe, the acronym for 'Nicholas Merrill', president of the New York-based Internet company 'Calyx',

---

[131] *Ibid*., 884.

[132] *Doe v. Holder,* 665 F.Supp.2d 426 (S.D.N.Y. 2009).

[133] *Doe v. Holder,* 703 F.Supp.2d 313 (S.D.N.Y. 2010), 316.

[134] *Ibid*., 316.

[135] *Ibid*., 317, referring to *CIA v. Sims,* 471 U.S. 159, 105 S.Ct. 1881, 178 (1985).

[136] *Doe v. Holder,* 04 Civ. 2614, 30 July 2010, 2 (Available at: http://www.wired.com/images_blogs/threatlevel/2010/08/Doe-vs-Holder_NSL.pdf, accessed 23 November 2010).

may now publicly discuss the case, albeit without revealing what information was sought through the NSL.[137]

In addition to the changes regarding the procedural requirement for application and order, the non-disclosure requirement and judicial review, the USA PATRIOT Improvement and Reauthorization Act of 2005 contains provisions that are intended to prevent abuses of section 215 authority, such as enhanced Congressional oversight. Section 106(h) of the Authorization Act of 2005 directs the Attorney General to submit to several Congressional committees a report that includes the total number of section 215 orders, the number of section 215 orders that are "either granted, modified, or denied," including the purpose of such orders (either library circulation records, library patron lists, book sales records, or book customer lists; firearms sales records; tax return records; educational records; and medical records containing information that would identify a person). This improves the manner in which Congressional oversight was previously organized considering that previously only the total number and the number granted, modified or denied had to be submitted to Congress, without revealing the nature of the orders.

Litigation regarding section 215 was aimed at retrieving information regarding the frequency in which the government has used its power to obtain section 215 orders. The American Civil Liberties Union has publicly tried to obtain this information under the Freedom of Information Act in two cases, known as ACLU I (2003) and ACLU II (2004).[138] The government had until then only provided some information in that regard to Congress in a classified form. The courts did not compel the government to release the information, deferring to their claim that the information may harm national security.[139] Nevertheless, in 2003 the Attorney General declassified the number of times section 215 orders had been used, from which it followed that an order for the production of business records had until then never been used. ACLU II sought to obtain information as to the number of occasions an application had been made for section 215 orders, which remained classified, however. The amendments of the Reauthorization Act have solved the issue by requiring the government to submit this statistical information unclassified to Congress. From these 'annual reports' it can be derived that in 2005 the FISA Court authorized 155 section 215 orders. Since then, numbers have decreased as a

[137] Nakashima 2010.

[138] See: Mart 2008, 443-444 and *ACLU v. United States Department of Justice (ACLU I),* 265 F. Supp. 2d 20 (D.D.C. 2003) and *ACLU v. United States Department of Justice (ACLU II),* 321 F. Supp. 2d 24 (D.D.C. 2004).

[139] *ACLU v. United States Department of Justice (ACLU I),* 265 F. Supp. 2d 20 (D.D.C. 2003) and *ACLU v. United States Department of Justice (ACLU II),* 321 F. Supp. 2d 24 (D.D.C. 2004). As it was stated in the latter case: the Court considered itself "mindful of the "long-recognized deference to the executive in national security issues."

consequence of the broadening of the definition of pen registers and trap and trace devices.[140] In 2010 the number of authorized section 215 orders was 96.[141]

Furthermore, the Reauthorization Act has made the observance of minimization procedures compulsory. Section 106(g) instructs the Attorney General to "adopt specific minimization procedures governing the retention and dissemination by the Federal Bureau of Investigation of any tangible things." These minimization procedures intend to "minimize the retention, and prohibit the dissemination, of nonpublicly available information concerning unconsenting United States persons, consistent with the need of the United States to obtain, produce, and disseminate foreign intelligence information."[142] Both the application and the order must include the applicable minimization procedures.[143]

Section 215 was originally intended to expire on December 31, 2005. The Act of 2005 included a new 'sunset' provision for section 215, providing that section 215 would expire on December 31, 2009. The 'PATRIOT Act Sunsets Extension Act of 2011' has extended, after a few shorter periods of extension, the sunset provision of Section 215 until June 2015.[144]

## 6.4 Changes Affecting the Interaction Between the Intelligence and Law Enforcement Communities

Many of the provisions of the USA PATRIOT Act were particularly directed at doing away with 'the wall' created as a result of the provisions in FISA and the interpretation of the 'primary purpose' language. The amendments have affected both provisions under Title III and the provisions under FISA and were aimed at the realization of more effective information sharing between the intelligence and law enforcement communities. These amendments and their interpretation will be analyzed in Sect. 6.4.1. Furthermore, internal policy documents, such as the guidelines issued by the Attorney General, have aimed to enhance cooperation between the intelligence and law enforcement communities. These documents will be analyzed in Sect. 6.4.2. Lastly, Sect. 6.4.3 will deal with other legislative amendments in order to increase cooperation and information sharing between the law enforcement and intelligence communities. Most of the changes that will be dealt with and have resulted in increased cooperation between the law enforcement

---

140 See Sects. 6.3.1 and 7.3.2.1.

141 See FISA Annual Reports to Congress, 2005 and 2010, available at: http://www.fas.org/irp/agency/doj/fisa/#rept (accessed August 1, 2011).

142 Section 106(g) Reauthorization Act 2005.

143 Section 106(b) Reauthorization Act 2005.

144 PATRIOT Sunsets Extension Act of 2011, S.990, 112th Congress, 1st Session.

and intelligence communities affect especially the role and functioning of the FBI, which has been transformed into an agency primarily focusing on the prevention of terrorism, for which reason all its relevant counterparts are enhanced and shall intensively and effectively cooperate.

## *6.4.1 Provisions of the USA PATRIOT ACT of 2001*

### 6.4.1.1 Enhancing the Sharing of Information

Section 203(b) of the PATRIOT Act amends Title III (18 U.S.C. § 2517) and the National Security Act of 1947 in order to enhance information sharing. The section authorizes law enforcement officers, who have obtained any knowledge of foreign intelligence, counterintelligence or foreign intelligence information through surveillance means permitted under Title III, to disclose the contents of the communications to any other federal law enforcement, intelligence, protective, immigration, national defense, or national security official.[145] Section 203(c) of the USA PATRIOT Act provides that the Attorney General shall establish procedures for the disclosure of such information when this information concerns a US person according to the definition of a US person in FISA (50 U.S.C. § 1801). A paragraph with the same tenor has been included in the National Security Act of 1947 as amended (50 U.S.C, § 403-5d), which determines that it is lawful to disclose foreign intelligence or counterintelligence or foreign intelligence information obtained as part of a criminal investigation to any other federal agency.[146] For this reason, also a definition of foreign intelligence information has now been

[145] USA PATRIOT Act, sec. 203(b)(1). This section of the Patriot Act amends section 2517 of Title 18 U.S.C. (Title III): "Any investigative or law enforcement officer, or attorney for the Government, who by any means authorized by this chapter, has obtained knowledge of the contents of any wire, oral, or electronic communication, or evidence derived therefrom, may disclose such contents to any other Federal law enforcement, intelligence, protective, immigration, national defense, or national security official to the extent that such contents include foreign intelligence or counterintelligence (as defined in section 3 of the National Security Act of 1947 (50 U.S.C. § 401a) or foreign intelligence information (as defined in subsection (19) of section 2510 of this Title), to assist the official who is to receive that information in the performance of his official duties. Any Federal official who receives information pursuant to this provision may use that information only as necessary in the conduct of that person's official duties subject to any limitations on the unauthorized disclosure of such information."

[146] USA PATRIOT Act, sec. 203(d)(1).

included in both Title III and in the National Security Act of 1947.[147] According to this definition it is irrelevant whether this information concerns a US person or not; decisive is whether the information relates to "the ability of the United States to protect against—(i) actual or potential attack or other grave hostile acts of a foreign power or an agent of a foreign power; (ii) sabotage or international terrorism by a foreign power or an agent of a foreign power; or (iii) clandestine intelligence activities by an intelligence service or network of a foreign power or by an agent of a foreign power;" or when the information concerns a foreign power or foreign territory "related to—(i) the national defense or the security of the United States; or (ii) the conduct of the foreign affairs of the United States."[148] The definition of foreign intelligence and counterintelligence can be found in the National Security Act of 1947, as amended by the PATRIOT Act (50 U.S.C. § 401a). Foreign intelligence means "information relating to the capabilities, intentions or activities of foreign governments or elements thereof, foreign organizations, or foreign persons, or international terrorist activities." Counterintelligence covers the "information gathered, and activities conducted, to protect against espionage, other intelligence activities, sabotage, or assassinations conducted by or on behalf of foreign governments or elements thereof, foreign organizations, or foreign persons, or international terrorist activities."[149]

Moreover, section 203 of the USA PATRIOT Act now allows the disclosure of grand jury information to national security investigators. The Federal Rule of Criminal Procedure 6(e) has been amended to allow for the sharing of grand jury information with national security investigators. Prior to the USA PATRIOT Act amendments of 2001, the disclosure of grand jury information was prohibited as the secrecy of everything occurring before the grand jury is considered as the legitimization of its far-reaching investigative powers (see Chap. 5, Sect. 5.2.1.3). Also this amendment is particularly aimed at dismantling the wall between law enforcement agencies and intelligence agencies and promoting information

---

[147] A definition of foreign intelligence information was already provided in FISA (50 U.S.C. § 1801(e)). This definition has not been changed (see Sect. 5.2.2.3.1). The definition as now adopted in Title III and the National Security Act of 1947 slightly differs from the FISA definition, as the latter distinguishes between US persons and non-US persons, requiring that the information concerning US persons shall be *necessary* for the ability of the United States to protect against the enumerated threats. In the Guidelines concerning FBI operations (covering both the intelligence and law enforcement counterpart) foreign intelligence has been defined as "information relating to the capabilities, intentions, or activities of foreign governments or elements thereof, foreign organizations or foreign persons, or international terrorists" (Mukasey Guidelines for FBI Operations (2008), 8 (para A(3)), which is clearly less tailored than the statutory definitions.

[148] Section 203(b)(2) and 203(d)(2), including this definition respectively in 18 U.S.C. § 2510(19) and 50 U.S.C. § 403-5d.

[149] 50 U.S.C. § 401a(2) and (3), amended by the section 902 of the USA PATRIOT Act of 2001. As a consequence of this amendment the definition of foreign intelligence and counterintelligence was extended to include also international terrorist activities.

sharing and cooperation, which was considered necessary for an effective investigative system for the prevention of terrorism.

Especially the sharing of grand jury information concerns an amendment of a fundamental character, as it gives national security investigators access to the information obtained by the powerful investigative tool of grand jury document production orders or the subpoena power of witnesses.[150] Rule 6(e)(2) of the Federal Rules of Criminal Procedure used to prohibit prosecutors from sharing any "matters occurring before the grand jury".[151] This excluded the sharing of any intelligence information obtained that would be relevant to other agencies. A few limited exceptions already existed before the adoption of the PATRIOT Act, to be applied under the authorization of the court that supervised the grand jury in question. The exceptions to grand jury secrecy (Rule 6(e)(2)) include, since the adoption of the USA PATRIOT Act, the sharing of "any grand-jury matter involving foreign intelligence, counterintelligence (as defined in 50 U.S.C. § 401a), or foreign intelligence information (as defined in Rule 6(e)(3)(D)(iii)) to any federal law enforcement, intelligence, protective, immigration, national defense, or national security official to assist the official receiving the information in the performance of that official's duties."[152] The amendments of the PATRIOT Act allow the sharing of grand jury information when the matters involve foreign intelligence, counterintelligence or foreign intelligence information.[153] As a consequence, all information that can be defined as foreign intelligence information, regardless of its content or nature, may now be disclosed to any federal officer who could use it "for the performance of that official's duties."[154]

Vice versa, national security investigators are encouraged to cooperate with law enforcement officers. Section 504 of the USA PATRIOT Act, addressing 'coordination with law enforcement,' provides that "federal officers who conduct

---

[150] Kris 2006, 523.

[151] Rule 6(e)(2) of the Federal Rules of Criminal Procedure, before the Patriot Act Amendments.

[152] Rule 6(e)(3)(D) of the Federal Rules of Criminal Procedure (2009).

[153] Section 203(a)(V). The definition of intelligence, foreign intelligence and counterintelligence can be found in the National Security Act of 1947: 50 U.S.C. § 401a. "Intelligence includes foreign intelligence and counterintelligence. (…) Foreign intelligence means information relating to the capabilities, intentions or activities of foreign governments or elements thereof, foreign organizations, or foreign persons, or international terrorist activities. (…) Counterintelligence means information gathered, and activities conducted, to protect against espionage, other intelligence activities, sabotage, or assassinations conducted by or on behalf of foreign governments or elements thereof, foreign organizations, or foreign persons, or international terrorist activities."

[154] Kris and Wilson 2007, 21–3.

electronic surveillance to acquire foreign intelligence information under this title [FISA] may consult with federal law enforcement officers." This provision, like the other provisions of Title V of the PATRIOT Act, is dedicated to "removing obstacles to investigating terrorism." The wall between the law enforcement community and the intelligence community was considered one of the obstacles that previously obstructed the investigation of terrorism. PATRIOT Act section 504 amends 50 U.S.C. § 1806 (FISA electronic surveillance) and § 1825 (FISA physical searches) by inserting a paragraph on coordination with law enforcement regarding the use of foreign intelligence information. Federal officers acting under FISA can now consult with federal law enforcement officers to "coordinate efforts to investigate or protect against" national security-related matters, including international terrorism.[155] This, however, shall not preclude the FISA 'purpose threshold.'[156] What such consultation entails was further detailed in the Memorandum of the Attorney General of 6 March 2002. This Memorandum will be addressed below and in Sect. 6.4.3.

#### 6.4.1.2 Changing the Purpose Language

The change that can be considered to have eventually dismantled the wall was the PATRIOT Act amendment that changed the purpose language of FISA. Section 218 changed '*the* purpose' into '*significant* purpose.' This very subtle change and, primarily, the interpretation that has been given thereto by the FISA Court of Review, has had significant consequences for the circumstances under which FISA warrants can be issued and, with that, for dismantling the wall as well. Both in § 1804(a)(7)(B) and § 1823(a)(7)(B)—thus for electronic surveillance as well as for physical searches—a significant purpose of the surveillance or search now has to be to obtain foreign intelligence information. The Bush Administration had proposed to change 'the purpose' into 'a purpose.' After a long debate in Congress 'a significant purpose' was adopted as a compromise, to which Congress added that it had the intention to promote information sharing between the law enforcement community and intelligence community. This means that this amendment aims to remove the incompatibility between gathering foreign intelligence and gathering evidence for a criminal prosecution, which had resulted from the 'primary purpose test.'[157]

---

[155] USA PATRIOT Act, sec. 504(a)(1) and 504(b)(1): Federal Officers may consult with Federal law enforcement officers "to coordinate efforts to investigate or protect against—(A) actual or potential attack or other grave hostile acts of a foreign power or an agent of a foreign power; (B) sabotage or international terrorism by a foreign power or an agent of a foreign power; or (C) clandestine intelligence activities by an intelligence service or network of a foreign power or by an agent of a foreign power." See 50 U.S.C. § 1806(k)(1) and § 1825(k)(1).

[156] USA PATRIOT Act, sec. 504(a)(2) and 504(b)(2) and 50 U.S.C. § 1806(k)(2) and § 1825(k)(2).

[157] Swire 2004, 1330.

The FISA Court of Review decided its first case ever by interpreting the statutory language of 'a significant purpose' in '*In re Sealed*' (2002). It was reviewing a unanimous decision by the FISA Court '*In re All Matters Submitted to Foreign Intelligence Surveillance Court* (2002) in which the FISA Court interpreted minimization procedures in a manner which bolstered the wall between national security investigations under FISA and criminal investigations.[158]

The FISA Court assessed whether the Memorandum 'Department of Justice Intelligence Sharing Procedures' issued by the Attorney General on 6 March 2002,[159] to provide guidance as to how to understand the amended FISA provisions by adopting new minimization procedures, was in accordance with the definition of minimization procedures as provided in the Act (50 U.S.C. § 1801(h) and § 1821(4)). In the memorandum it was stated that the amended FISA provisions should be understood as allowing FISA surveillance and physical searches "primarily for a law enforcement purpose, so long as a significant foreign intelligence purpose remains."[160] The FISA Court decision focused only on the proposed minimization procedures in this Memorandum, which expanded the possibilities for information sharing and cooperation with the Criminal Division of the Department of Justice. In its decision the FISA Court stated that the FBI had repeatedly erroneously informed the FISA Court in its applications, which in "virtually every instance" concerned "information sharing and unauthorized dissemination to criminal investigators and prosecutors" in violation of "wall" procedures.[161] Considering this history, the FISA Court rejected the proposed minimization procedures of the 2002 Memorandum in which "the bright line" was eliminated that "prohibit[ed] direction and control by prosecutors."[162] Moreover, the 2002 Memorandum allows "extensive consultations between the FBI and criminal prosecutors "to coordinate efforts to investigate or protect against" actual or potential attack, sabotage, international terrorism and clandestine intelligence activities by foreign powers and their agents."[163] Such coordination includes full access for criminal prosecutors to the information gathered in counterintelligence investigations, including the information gathered under FISA, and the providing of advice by criminal prosecutors to intelligence officials, which "may include advice about criminal investigation and prosecution as well as the strategy and goals for investigation, the law enforcement and intelligence methods to be used in

---

[158] The FISA court is granted jurisdiction to evaluate proposed minimization procedures: 50 U.S.C. § 1805(a)(4) and § 1824(a)(4).

[159] See Kris and Wilson 2007, Appendix E: 'Department of Justice Intelligence Sharing Procedure (March 6, 2002), Memorandum to the Director of the FBI, Assistant Attorney General, Criminal Division, Counsel for Intelligence Policy and United States Attorneys, from the Attorney General Ashcroft.

[160] *In re All Matters Submitted to the Foreign Intelligence Surveillance Court,* 218 F.Supp.2d 611 (Foreign Int. Surv. Ct. 2002), 615.

[161] *Ibid.*, 621.

[162] *Ibid.*, 622.

[163] *Ibid.*, 622.

investigations, and the interaction between intelligence and law enforcement components of investigations." The Court regarded the permission granted to criminal prosecutors to advise FBI intelligence officials with regard to "the initiation, operation, continuation, or expansion of FISA searches or surveillance" to be most important for its final decision. According to this provision criminal prosecutors can request intelligence officers to seek a FISA Court order for criminal investigative interests, while also the surveillance authorized by the order may now primarily pursue law enforcement purposes.

According to these guidelines the FISA track has become an alternative investigative means for criminal prosecutors in cases involving terrorism. The FISA Court held that these guidelines, which governed the now applicable minimization procedures, did not meet the definition of such procedures, because it now had to "[balance] the government's use of FISA surveillance and searches against the government's need to obtain and use evidence for criminal prosecution, *instead of* determining the "need of the United States to obtain, produce, and disseminate foreign intelligence information" as mandated by § 1801(h) and § 1821(4)."[164] Hence, the Court modified the proposed minimization procedures in a manner which bolstered the wall and prohibited criminal prosecutors from directing FISA investigations and furthering law enforcement objectives through FISA procedures.[165]

Regardless of this decision by the FISA Court explicitly condemning the government's measures dismantling the wall, the FISA Court of Review held that the FISA Court had wrongly interpreted the statutory scheme of FISA as requiring a wall between the law enforcement and intelligence community, without addressing the USA PATRIOT Act amendment changing the purpose language.[166] According to the FISA Court of Review it is "quite puzzling" why FISA has been read, since shortly after its enactment, as to require the government to certify that the purpose of the surveillance is to obtain foreign intelligence information, as the definition of foreign intelligence information as provided in § 1801(e) includes evidence of crimes.[167] The FISA Court of Review held that "FISA as passed by Congress in 1978 clearly did *not* preclude or limit the government's use or proposed use of foreign intelligence information, which included evidence of certain kinds of criminal activity, in a criminal prosecution."[168] Furthermore, the FISA Court of Review considered the reasoning of the FISA Court to be erroneous as it "misinterpreted and misapplied minimization procedures it was entitled to impose;" it exceeded its jurisdiction by adopting the Memorandum guidelines as minimization procedures and modifying its content; and it erroneously refused to consider the PATRIOT Act amendments to FISA.[169]

---

164 *Ibid.*, 624.

165 *Ibid.*, 625.

166 *In re: Sealed Case,* 310 F.3d 717 (FISA Ct. Rev. 2002), 721.

167 *Ibid.*, 723-724.

168 *Ibid.*, 727.

169 *Ibid.*, 732-733.

According to the FISA Court of Review, Congress was "keenly aware that by replacing 'the purpose' for 'a significant purpose' it "relaxed a requirement that the government show that its primary purpose was other than criminal prosecution."[170] However, the PATRIOT Act amendment also unnecessarily emphasized a dichotomy between law enforcement and foreign intelligence purposes of investigation under FISA.[171] These considerations resulted in the most important finding (for the statutory interpretation) by the FISA Court of Review in interpreting the now applicable 'significant purpose' requirement: "as a matter of straightforward logic, if a FISA application can be granted even if "foreign intelligence" is only a significant—not a primary—purpose, another purpose can be primary. One other legitimate purpose that could exist is to prosecute a target for a foreign intelligence crime."[172] Thus: another purpose could be the primary purpose of the surveillance, including a purpose of gathering evidence for the prosecution of a target's criminal activities. The FISA Court of Review contended that this interpretation of the requirements for FISA surveillance and physical search was consistent with the Fourth Amendment.[173]

As a consequence of the changed 'purpose language' and its interpretation by the FISA Court of Review, the government may now obtain orders for covert surveillance and searches under FISA if the primary purpose of the surveillance is to gather evidence of domestic criminal activity, as long as the gathering of foreign intelligence information is also a significant purpose of the surveillance. In practice this gives the government the possibility to circumvent Fourth Amendment probable cause and warrant requirements by asserting before the FISA Court that there is also a desire to gather foreign intelligence information from the person investigated, whilst the actual intention of the investigation is prosecution. The FISA Court has to accept such a showing, unless it is clearly erroneous.

### *6.4.2 The Influence of the Internal Policy of the Department of Justice and the FBI*

The Attorney General can issue guidelines in order to direct the policy of its divisions within the Department of Justice, which it has done since the issuance of the Levi Guidelines in 1976.[174] The issuance of guidelines concerns an important tool to use the discretion that the law provides for developing and steering

---

170 *Ibid.*, 732.

171 *Ibid.*, 735.

172 *Ibid.*, 734.

173 *Ibid.*, 746.

174 Executive Order 13470 (2008), 73 Fed. Reg. 45325 (July 30, 2008), sec. 1.7(g)(1), explicitly prescribes the issuance of such guidelines to regulate the gathering, analyzing, producing and dissemination of foreign intelligence and counterintelligence.

investigative policy and was originally intended to avoid abuses of such discretion by the FBI.[175] However, the Attorney General's Guidelines that have been issued since 9/11 were particularly aimed at directing the manner in which criminal investigations and national security investigations are carried out in order to confront terrorism more effectively. Contrary to the shield goal of the Levi and Smith Guidelines to restrain the investigative activities of the FBI in order to prevent abuse and guarantee that the FBI operated within the borders of the law and the Constitution, the Ashcroft Guidelines and, subsequently, the Mukasey Guidelines have granted the FBI almost unlimited discretion when national security is involved and were intended to guide the FBI in seeking the limits of its authority.[176] This difference in the principal objective of the Guidelines can be related to the fact that the Levi and Smith Guidelines were an answer to the abuse of investigative power as it came to light in, *inter alia*, the Watergate scandals, whereas the Ashcroft and Mukasey Guidelines were a response to the failure to prevent 9/11.

The post-9/11 guidelines have reformulated the investigative priorities of the FBI and have promoted information sharing and cooperation between the divisions responsible for criminal investigations and those responsible for intelligence gathering.[177] Furthermore, two memoranda have been issued: one by the Attorney General; the other by all agencies involved, in order to promote and even to oblige the sharing of information. In addition to the AG Guidelines and the memoranda, the FBI drafts its own manual as a policy guide implementing the AG Guidelines in detailed provisions. This internal policy manual of the FBI has always been a classified document. However, in answer to repeated requests under the Freedom of Information Act (FOIA), the 'Domestic Investigations and Operations Guide' of 16 December 2008, which standardized the investigative policy of the FBI in observance of the 'AG Guidelines for Domestic FBI Operations' (issued September 29, 2008), was almost completely declassified in August 2009. This extensive document provides a detailed insight into the manner in which the powers granted in law, and the general directions provided in the AG Guidelines with regard to the use of these powers, results in concrete investigative policy. This section will chronologically and categorically deal with the policy documents that have been issued since 9/11: with the AG and interagency memoranda; with the AG Guidelines replacing the Smith Guidelines of 1983 that almost unaffectedly remained in place until 2002: and, lastly, with the now declassified FBI Domestic Investigations and Operations Guide, in order to demonstrate a shift in policy aiming at increased interaction between the law enforcement and intelligence counterparts of the FBI and a primary focus on the prevention of terrorism.

---

[175] See Sect. 5.3.2.3.

[176] Jones 2009, 63-165.

[177] The investigative policy of the DoJ has not changed since the Obama Administration took office: to date, Attorney General Holder has not decided to adopt new guidelines.

#### 6.4.2.1 The Memorandum of Attorney General Ashcroft of 6 March 2002 and the Interagency Memorandum of 2003

The Memorandum of 6 March 2002 (as already dealt with in Sect. 6.4.1.2 as the subject of litigation before the FISA Court and the FISA Court of Review) especially set new procedures for the sharing of information and advice between the law enforcement and intelligence officials within the Department of Justice. According to these guidelines, and as later affirmed by the FISA Court of Review, FISA may be used "primarily for a law enforcement purpose, as long as a significant foreign intelligence purpose remains." The authority given in the USA PATRIOT Act (section 504) to consult with federal law enforcement officers has been set out in more detail in the Memorandum so as to include exchanging "a full range of information and advice" concerning efforts "to investigate or protect against foreign threats to national security," which may include "information and advice designed to preserve or enhance the possibility of a criminal prosecution."

Moreover, the Memorandum states that "all relevant Department of Justice components, including the Criminal Division (…) [are] to be fully informed about the nature, scope, and conduct of all full field FI [Foreign Intelligence] and FCI [Foreign Counterintelligence] investigations, whether or not those investigations involve FISA." More in particular, "the Criminal Division and the OIPR [the Office of Intelligence Policy and Review; an expert office of the Department of Justice, now the 'National Security Division'] shall have access to all information developed in full field FI and FCI investigations," except for some restrictions that may apply in particular cases. The Criminal Division and the OIPR should therefore receive all relevant information from the FBI, which includes "both foreign intelligence information and information concerning a crime which has been, is being, or is about to be committed." Information originating from FISA surveillance or a physical search that has been obtained in accordance with these procedures may only be used in criminal proceedings upon the authorization of the Attorney General.

Most far-reaching, and also the aspect that the FISA Court considered to be impermissible as it breaks with previously set safeguards aimed to prevent criminal investigators relying on FISA investigations in order to circumvent Fourth Amendment requirements, is the manner in which advice may be provided by the Criminal Division to the intelligence investigators of the FBI. Consultations between the different components of the DoJ may include advice and recommendations concerning all aspects of the investigations, including "the initiation, operation, continuation, or expansion of FISA searches or surveillance." To sum up, this Memorandum aimed to enable a full information exchange and cooperation between all Department of Justice components that may have an interest in foreign intelligence investigations or counterintelligence investigations, particularly when terrorism is involved. It allows prosecutors to use similar authorities as national security investigators to initiate, operate, continue or expand FISA investigations. All barriers that were established in previous guidelines preventing such a free sharing of information and cooperation have been banned and replaced by guidelines stimulating and directing intense sharing and cooperation. The need to protect national security was considered to be the justification for such "full and free exchange of information and ideas."[178]

The second relevant memorandum that has been issued in the post-9/11 era concerns the "Memorandum of Understanding Between the Intelligence Community, Federal Law Enforcement Agencies, and the Department of Homeland Security Concerning Information Sharing."[179] This Memorandum, issued on March 4, 2003, concerns a binding agreement between these different agencies, which became public in March 2005 after a successful FOIA request. The Memorandum "provides a framework of guidance to govern information sharing, use and handling" between the signing agencies and its subdivisions.[180] The goal of the agreement is to avoid situations in which there is reluctance to share because it may disrupt prosecutorial or investigative purposes, whereas such sharing could serve the "overriding priority of preventing, preempting, and disrupting terrorist threats to our homeland."[181] Hence, the Memorandum provides for policies governing the sharing of information which are based only on the substance of the information.[182] Considering its binding character, the agreement aims to function as an important guarantee that information that is relevant for the prevention of terrorism will indeed be shared between all agencies that can contribute to its actual prevention.

#### 6.4.2.2 The AG Ashcroft Guidelines of 2002 and the AG Ashcroft Guidelines on National Security Investigations of 2003

On May 30, 2002 Attorney General John Ashcroft issued a new set of Guidelines: 'The Attorney General's Guidelines on General Crimes, Racketeering Enterprise and Terrorism Enterprise Investigations.'[183] These Guidelines replaced the 'Smith Guidelines' of 1983 which until then had regulated the investigative authority of the FBI. In 2003 Ashcroft also issued a new set of Guidelines for FBI National Security Investigations and Foreign Intelligence Collection, the contents of which

---

[178] 'Department of Justice Intelligence Sharing Procedures (6 March 2002), Memorandum from the Attorney General Ashcroft (Section I: Introduction and Statement of General Principles).

[179] Memorandum of Understanding Between the Intelligence Community, Federal Law Enforcement Agencies, and the Department of Homeland Security Concerning Information Sharing, 4 March 2003. Available at: (http://fas.org/sgp/othergov/mou-infoshare.pdf) (accessed 27 December 2009). Henceforth: Memorandum of Understanding on Information Sharing (2003).

[180] Memorandum of Understanding on Information Sharing (2003), 1.

[181] *Ibid.*, 4.

[182] *Ibid.*, 5.

[183] *The Attorney General's Guidelines on General Crimes, Racketeering Enterprise ad Terrorism Enterprise Investigations*, Office of the Attorney General, Washington D.C., 2002, 20530. Available at: http://www.fas.org/irp/agency/doj/fbi/generalcrimes2.pdf (accessed 27 December 2009). Henceforth: Ashcroft Guidelines 2002.

are mainly classified. At that time Ashcroft still issued two sets of guidelines with different standards, restraints and conditions for criminal investigations and national security investigations, upholding a separation of policy for both areas. However, an important step towards merging the two areas was already taken in these Guidelines. Moreover, the collective goal of these new guidelines was to enhance the investigative capacities of the FBI in order to be able to effectively confront terrorism in the first place by allowing the FBI to initiate full investigations sooner than was previously the case.[184] The 2002 Guidelines claimed to provide for a "consistent policy" to give effect to the FBI's "highest priority," which is "to protect the security of the nation and the safety of the American people against the depredations of terrorists and foreign aggressors." The Ashcroft Guidelines remained in place until 2008 when Attorney General Mukasey issued new guidelines 'for domestic FBI operations' on September 29, 2008 superseding the Ashcroft Guidelines of 2002 and 2003.

The Ashcroft Guidelines are briefly dealt with in the underlying section—although considering that the separation of criminal and national security investigations by issuing two sets logically belongs to Sects. 6.2 and 6.3—to provide a complete chronological order of events since 9/11 that have influenced the internal policy of the DoJ and FBI resulting in the transformation of the role of the FBI.

The Guidelines on General Crimes, Racketeering Enterprise and Terrorism Enterprise Investigations provide "guidance for general crimes and criminal intelligence investigations by the FBI."[185] The Guidelines provide for three different levels of investigative activity, reorganizing the investigative levels of the previous Smith Guidelines,[186] in order to allow "the FBI the necessary flexibility to act well in advance of the commission of planned terrorist acts or other federal crimes." These levels are: "(1) the prompt and extremely limited checking of initial leads, (2) preliminary inquiries, and (3) full investigations."[187] These levels do not considerably differ from the investigative levels distinguished under the Smith Guidelines. The most important difference is that a full or preliminary investigation may immediately be initiated when "the available information shows at the outset that the threshold standard for a preliminary inquiry or full investigation is satisfied (…) without progressing through more limited investigative stages."[188] Although the classification of investigative activities differs from the investigative levels under the Smith Guidelines and the wording of some of its thresholds has been changed, the investigative possibilities and the thresholds for starting these investigative activities have not been considerably expanded. For this reason and because the Guidelines have been superseded by the Mukasey Guidelines, this Section will not elaborate in detail on the requirements for each

184 Ashcroft Guidelines 2002, 2. And see: Donohue 2008, 249.

185 Ashcroft Guidelines 2002, preamble.

186 See Chap. 5, Sect. 5.3.2.3.2.

187 Ashcroft Guidelines 2002, 1.

188 *Ibid.*, 2.

investigative level. It suffices to note that the Guidelines indicate that when the information relates to the obtaining of material from which weapons or explosives may be developed or to terrorist activities, the threshold for the investigative activity in question is generally met.[189] Moreover, the Guidelines mitigated requirements to initiate full terrorism enterprise investigations, by now allowing any Special Agent in Charge to authorize the investigation with notification to the FBI Headquarters.[190]

More important are the provisions of the Guidelines regarding the methods available to give effect to counterterrorism priorities and the adjustment of the investigative tools to current technological developments such as the advent of the Internet. The guidelines include several provisions to enhance cooperation between the intelligence and law enforcement counterparts of the FBI, including the maintaining of a database of information collected by the investigative activities authorized in the Guidelines for the purpose of information dissemination to counterparts or other agencies.[191] Furthermore, the FBI is required to maintain a special information system "for the purpose of identifying and locating terrorists, excluding or removing from the United States alien terrorists and alien supporters of terrorist activity as authorized by law, assessing and responding to terrorist risks and threats, or otherwise detecting, prosecuting, or preventing terrorist activities."[192] Moreover, FBI officials are authorized to visit "places and events which are open to the public for the purpose of detecting or preventing terrorist activities" and "surfing the internet as any member of the public might do to identify, e.g., public websites, bulletin boards, and chat rooms (...), and observing information open to public view in such forums to detect terrorist activities and other criminal activities."

Lastly, the Ashcroft Guidelines also included 'General Principles,' again similar to the Smith Guidelines, to provide for some principles in order to prevent abuses of investigative power. It is indicated that the choice for investigative methods is subject to the principle of proportionality; however, it was added that the "FBI shall not hesitate to use any lawful techniques consistent with these Guidelines, even if intrusive, where the intrusiveness is warranted in light of the seriousness of a crime or the strength of the information indicating its commission or potential future commission." The latter in particular deals with the "investigation of terrorist crimes and (...) investigation of enterprises that engage in terrorism." All full investigations following from the preliminary investigations "shall be based on a reasonable factual predicate and shall have a valid law enforcement purpose." The full investigation "shall be terminated when all logical leads have been exhausted and no legitimate law enforcement interest justifies

189 *Ibid.*, 2.

190 *Ibid.*, 17.

191 Department of Justice, other Federal agencies and state or local criminal justice agencies, *Ibid.*, 20-21.

192 *Ibid.*, 21-22.

their continuance." The use of investigative methods authorized in the Guidelines in order to "anticipate or prevent crime," whereas criminal activity is not yet taking place, shall "not be based solely on activities protected by the First Amendment or on the lawful exercise of any other rights secured by the Constitution or laws of the United States." However, when such statements "advocate criminal activity or indicate an apparent intent to engage in crime, particularly crimes of violence, an investigation under these guidelines may be warranted unless it is apparent, from the circumstances or the context in which the statements are made, that there is no prospect of harm."

In a separate set of Guidelines, which were issued on October 31, 2003, Attorney General Ashcroft adopted new guidelines "For FBI National Security Investigations and Foreign Intelligence Collection."[193] According to the introductory section, these Guidelines aim to "realize as fully as possible the critical objectives of the Executive Order 12333." Furthermore, the Guidelines are part of the "overall response of the United States to threats to the national security," including enhancing cooperation and information sharing with other agencies.[194]

The Guidelines explicitly stated that the "[d]etecting, solving, and preventing" of crimes "and in many cases, arresting and prosecuting the perpetrators are crucial objectives of national security investigations under these Guidelines." In addition: "threats to the national security, including international terrorism and espionage, almost invariably involve possible violations of criminal statutes." Herewith, an overlap between "counterintelligence and "criminal" investigations" was acknowledged.[195]

Three levels of investigative activity are distinguished for FBI National security investigations: "(1) threat assessment, (2) preliminary investigations, and (3) full investigations."[196] Threat assessments concern the proactive collection of information without any specific investigative predication by means of relatively non-intrusive investigative techniques, which makes it comparable to the checking of initial leads under the Ashcroft Guidelines for criminal investigations.[197] Secondly, a preliminary investigation may be initiated upon "information or an allegation indicating that a threat to the national security may exist." Such investigation (as well as the full investigation) "may relate to individuals, groups, organizations and possible criminal violations."[198] The investigative authorities are again comparable to the preliminary investigations of the 2002 Ashcroft

[193] The Attorney General's Guidelines for FBI National Security Investigations and Foreign Intelligence Collection, Issued and classified by John Ashcroft on October 31, 2003 (declassified by AG Gonzales on August 2, 2007), available at: http://ftp.fas.org/irp/agency/doj/fbi/nsiguidelines.pdf (accessed 17 December 2009).

[194] The Attorney General's Guidelines for FBI National Security Investigations and Foreign Intelligence Collection 2003, 1.

[195] *Ibid.*, 2.

[196] *Ibid.*, 3.

[197] *Ibid.*, 3.

[198] *Ibid.*, 3-4.

Guidelines. The last category of full investigations requires a showing of "specific and articulable facts giving reason to believe that a threat to the national security may exist."[199]

The Guidelines define when a person concerns a US person and when a group should be considered as a US-based group, which provisions have remained, however, largely classified.[200] The interpretation given to these terms is important with regard to the applicability of restrictions on investigative authorities, such as under FISA. Also many other provisions of the Guidelines have remained classified, such as some of the circumstances warranting investigations, some authorized investigative techniques, and extraterritorial authorities.

Furthermore, the Guidelines include some important provisions with regard to information sharing. As a matter of "general principle" it is provided that "information should be shared as consistently and fully as possible."[201] In principle, the Department of Justice's criminal division "shall have full access to all information obtained through activities under these Guidelines." Furthermore, the "FBI shall keep the Criminal Division and the Office of Intelligence Policy and Review apprised of all information obtained through activities under these Guidelines that is necessary to the ability of the United States to investigate or protect against threats to the national security."[202] Consultations between the FBI and the Criminal Division and the Office of Intelligence Policy and Review shall also take place regularly. Likewise, US Attorney's Offices shall "receive information and engage in consultations to the same extent as the Criminal Division."[203]

#### 6.4.2.3 Mukasey Guidelines on FBI Operations (2008)

In the introduction of the Mukasey Guidelines the important role of the FBI is emphasized as the leading agency for investigating violations of federal law and investigating domestic threats to national security. This task includes "investigating international terrorist threats to the United States" and "conducting counterintelligence activities to meet foreign entities' espionage and intelligence efforts directed against the United States." The FBI is also a member agency of the intelligence community[204] and has in addition, therefore, the task of gathering foreign intelligence information. In this document the law enforcement and the intelligence objectives are for the first time combined into one document. The previous wall between the law enforcement and intelligence community was clearly reflected in

[199] *Ibid.*, 4.

[200] *Ibid.*, 9-10.

[201] *Ibid.*, 24.

[202] *Ibid.*, 25.

[203] *Ibid.*, 26.

[204] See Executive Order 12333 and 50 U.S.C. § 401a(4).

the issuance of two separate sets of guidelines: one governing investigations with a nexus to criminal activity and aimed at the gathering of evidence for prosecutions and the other governing the FBI task of gathering foreign intelligence, protecting national security and conducting counterintelligence investigations.[205] The general objective of this new set of guidelines that govern all these topics is, hence, the "full utilization of all authorities and investigative methods [...] to protect the United States and its people from terrorism and other threats to the national security, to protect the United States and its people from victimization by all crimes in violation of federal law, and to further the foreign intelligence objectives of the United States." At the same time the new guidelines were intended, contrary to the Ashcroft Guidelines, to underline that all investigative activities of the FBI shall be conducted "consistent with the Constitution and the Laws of the United States, [...] in a lawful and reasonable manner that respects liberty and privacy and avoids unnecessary intrusions into the lives of law-abiding people." Hence, the guidelines now also include oversight mechanisms "to ensure that all FBI activities are conducted in a manner consistent with law and policy."[206]

The Mukasey Guidelines on FBI Operations state that the law enforcement (federal crimes investigations and investigations of threats to national security) and intelligence investigative objectives of the FBI are overlapping: e.g. the investigation of international terrorism will involve a violation of federal law, a threat to national security as well as the gathering of foreign intelligence information.[207] Therefore, the Mukasey Guidelines do away with the long upheld distinction between criminal investigations, national security investigations and investigations for the purpose of gathering foreign intelligence information, and provide uniform guidelines for all investigative activities, promoting a single investigation in which a "number of the [FBI's] authorities" may be exercised.[208] This approach breaks with previous DoJ investigative policy, although the guidelines are at the same time an acknowledgment of the investigative policy as was developed in the post-9/11 era.

The Guidelines generally authorize the FBI to "conduct investigations to detect, obtain information about, and prevent and protect against federal crimes and threats to the national security and to collect foreign intelligence." If the investigation has one of these authorized purposes, the focus of the activities "may be whatever the circumstances warrant." The concept of investigation under these Guidelines is not interpreted in a "narrow sense" as being limited to "solving particular cases or obtaining evidence for use in particular criminal prosecutions." Investigation may now also include the gathering of "critical information needed for broader analytic and intelligence purposes to facilitate the solution and

---

205 See also: Becker 2005, 63.

206 Introduction (2-3) of The Attorney General's Guidelines for Domestic FBI Operations (2008) (henceforth: Mukasey Guidelines for FBI Operations 2008).

207 Mukasey Guidelines for FBI Operations 2008, 6 (under A).

208 *Ibid.*, 6-7 (para A).

prevention of crime, protect the national security, and further foreign intelligence objectives."[209]

To give effect to this uniform investigative task the FBI is authorized to conduct information-gathering activities on different levels. The first level of investigative activities concerns "assessments" in order to "detect, obtain information about, or prevent or protect against federal crimes or threats to the national security or to collect foreign intelligence."[210] This investigative level of "assessments" replaces the previous 'prompt and limited checking out of initial leads' of the AG's Guidelines on General Crimes, Racketeering Enterprise and Terrorism Enterprise investigations and the "threat assessment" under the AG's Guidelines for FBI National Security Investigations and Foreign Intelligence Collection. The FBI is authorized to conduct these assessments for the aforementioned purpose, without requiring a showing of any factual predicate. The investigative activities are limited to the "checking of investigative leads" by general searches for information, e.g. through: publicly available sources; FBI and DoJ records; requesting such records from other agencies; searches on the internet, interviewing "members of the public and private entities"; observation and surveillance for which a court order is not required; or through "grand jury subpoenas for telephone or electronic mail subscriber information."[211] "Assessments" aim to enhance the position of the FBI acting proactively for the purpose of "detecting and interrupting criminal activities at their early stages, and preventing crimes from occurring in the first place."[212]

The second level of investigation is the "predicated investigation." The purpose of this investigation is similar to assessments; however, it is limited to a showing of "circumstances warranting investigation" and requires supervisory approval. The circumstances warranting a predicated investigation are the following: "(a) an activity constituting a federal crime or a threat to the national security has or may have occurred, is or may be occurring, or will or may occur and the investigation may obtain information relating to the activity or the involvement or role of an individual, group, or organization in such activity; (b) an individual, group, organization, entity, information, property, or activity is or may be a target of attack, victimization acquisition, infiltration, or recruitment in connection with criminal activity in violation of federal law or a threat to the national security and the investigation may obtain information that would help to protect against such activity or threat; (c) the investigation may obtain foreign intelligence that is representative to a foreign intelligence requirement."[213] From the general description of the investigative authority it follows that a classified direction has

[209] *Ibid.*, 16 (para II).

[210] *Ibid.*, 9 (para II(A)).

[211] *Ibid.*, 19-20 (para II(A)(3) and (4)).

[212] *Ibid.*, 7 (para II).

[213] *Ibid.*, 21 (para II(B)(3)).

been issued "providing further specification concerning circumstances supporting certain predicated investigations."[214]

The predicated investigation is subsequently divided, similar to previous guidelines, in either a preliminary investigation or a full investigation. The "information or an allegation indicating" circumstance (a) or (b) warranting a predicate investigation may trigger a preliminary investigation. The duration of a preliminary investigation has been extended to a maximum of 6 months, with possible extensions. All lawful investigative techniques may be used in the preliminary investigation, except for electronic surveillance under Title III or FISA, a physical search under Rule 41 of the Federal Rules of Criminal Procedure or FISA, and the "acquisition of foreign intelligence information" under Title VII of FISA (concerning FISA surveillance of persons located outside the US, as dealt with in Sect. 6.5.1).[215] For full investigations the threshold is somewhat higher by either requiring "an articulable factual basis for the investigation that reasonably indicates" that circumstance (a) or (b), warranting a predicated investigation, exists *or* the circumstance under (c) exists. The FBI is authorized to use any lawful investigative technique during the full investigation.[216] No limits to the duration of full investigations are prescribed in the Guidelines.

Furthermore, the FBI is still authorized to engage in "enterprise investigations." The character of the enterprise is described as a "full investigation" permitting "a general examination of the structure, scope, and nature of certain groups and organizations." The threshold requirement and the requirement of supervisory approval is similar to that of the full investigation; however, the investigation targets "groups or organizations that may be involved in the most serious criminal or national security threats to the public" and aims to broadly investigate the characteristics and activities of the group or organization.[217]

Except for the unification of investigative standards for the FBI authorities as a law enforcement agency and as an intelligence agency, the Mukasey Guidelines include an extensive regulation of "the retention and sharing of information" and enhanced interaction with other intelligence agencies and between its own law enforcement and intelligence counterparts. With regard to the latter, the Guidelines authorize the FBI to "provide investigative assistance (including operational support) to authorized intelligence activities of other Community agencies."[218] Furthermore, the Guidelines provide that the FBI may, in order to exert its intelligence functions, rely on all its lawful sources of information, including sources built by its own investigative activities (which may already have concurrent law enforcement and intelligence purposes).[219]

[214] *Ibid.*, 18 (para II).

[215] *Ibid.*, 21 and 32 (para II(B)(4)(a) and V(A)(11)-(13)).

[216] *Ibid.*, 22 (para II(B)(4)(b)).

[217] *Ibid.*, 18 and 23 (para II and II(C)).

[218] *Ibid.*, 25 (para III(A)).

[219] *Ibid.*, 29 (para IV).

The sharing of information is generally permitted with those other agencies for which the information is relevant for carrying out the responsibilities of that agency.[220] Such sharing is required when so ordered under law or policy documents, such as the AG's Memorandum of 2002 regarding the "Department of Justice Intelligence Sharing Procedures."[221] Prosecutors shall be informed of investigations involving criminal activity. When the information gathered during the investigation is sufficient to warrant prosecution, the relevant information must be communicated to the prosecutor. A prosecutor may also request information.[222]

Sharing is more urgent when the information gathered involves national security information: as a matter of "general principle [...] there is a responsibility to provide information as consistently and fully as possible to agencies with relevant responsibilities to protect the United States and its people from terrorism and other threats to the national security, except as limited by specific restraints on such sharing." The requirements of the "Memorandum of Understanding between the Intelligence Community, Federal Law Enforcement Agencies, and the Department of Homeland Security Concerning Information Sharing (March 4, 2003)" is applicable. Furthermore, "the National Security Division shall have access to all information obtained by the FBI through activities relating to threats to the national security or foreign intelligence." The National Security Division has been given the task of maintaining oversight on all information gathered by the different agencies that relates to threats to the national security. The Guidelines also provide that "relevant United States Attorneys' Offices shall have access to and shall receive information from the FBI relating to the threats to the national security." US Attorneys are even authorized to "engage in consultations" with the FBI about such information in a similar fashion as is permitted for the National Security Division. With regard to counterintelligence investigations (concerning "espionage and other intelligence activities, sabotage, and assassination, conducted by, for, or on behalf of foreign powers, organizations, or persons"[223]), the National Security Division should give permission before the FBI is allowed to consult with US Attorneys.[224] Lastly, the FBI is instructed to disseminate certain "foreign intelligence and information relating to international terrorism and other threats to the national security" to the White House.[225]

It can be concluded that the 2008 Guidelines concern the most far-reaching policy change with regard to the interaction between the law enforcement and intelligence counterparts of the FBI, transforming the role of the FBI and clearly combining the forces of the different FBI divisions in order to jointly confront threats to national security, such as terrorism. This one set of guidelines, aimed at

---

220 *Ibid.*, 35 (para VI(B)(1)).

221 *Ibid.*, 35 (para VI(B)(2)).

222 *Ibid.*, 35 (para VI(C)).

223 *Ibid.*, 45 (para VII(S)(2)).

224 *Ibid.*, 37-38 (para VI(D)(1)).

225 *Ibid.*, 37-38 (para VI(D)(2)).

providing consistent investigative policy for the FBI as a whole and eliminating bureaucratic barriers between law enforcement and intelligence counterparts of the FBI, breaks with the previously upheld distinction between the law enforcement and intelligence investigative activities of the FBI, which was still the case under the Ashcroft Guidelines. Moreover, information sharing and cooperation, also with agencies outside the FBI, are promoted.

#### 6.4.2.4 Domestic Investigations and Operations Guide of the FBI (2008)

The FBI has drafted its own guide with internal rules and procedures on domestic investigations and operations (Domestic Investigations and Operations Guide or DIOG) to implement the Mukasey Guidelines of 2008. This extensive guide of December 16, 2008, counting 258 pages, was released, almost in its entirety, to the public in September 2009 after a FOIA request.[226] Some parts remain classified so as not to give away too much of its investigative strategy to "those who pose a threat to the nation." According to the FBI website, this guide (like the AG's Guidelines) was promulgated "to ensure that the FBI is equipped with all lawful and appropriate tools so that it can transform itself into an intelligence-driven organization that assesses and investigates criminal and national security threats to our nation and its people."[227] The Guide includes the whole range of internal policy for the FBI in its effort to "protect the people of the United States against crime and threats to the national security and to collect foreign intelligence information."[228] Only those aspects of this extensive guide that provide for additional information with regard to the situations that trigger investigative action by the FBI, and that provide information on what level of investigation or nature of techniques is justified in particular situations will be dealt with here.

The Guide begins by setting out its scope of authority, including its leading investigative authority concerning 'federal crimes of terrorism'. A federal crime of terrorism is any "offense that is: (i) calculated to influence or affect the conduct of government by intimidation or coercion or to retaliate against government conduct; and (ii) is a violation of a federal statute relating to" any of the offenses enumerated in a list of 51 criminalized acts that may relate to terrorism.

The Guide provides for a detailed explanation of the scope of Constitutional rights, such as the freedom of speech, freedom of religion and the Equal Protection Clause in order to make the FBI officers aware of the exact limits of their investigative activities. According to the guidelines, FBI employees may, for

[226] 'Domestic Investigations and Operations Guide, Federal Bureau of Investigation (FBI), December 16, 2008 (unclassified) (henceforth: DIOG FBI (2008).' Available at: http://foia.fbi.gov/foiaindex/diog.htm (accessed 9 February 2010).

[227] See: http://foia.fbi.gov/foiaindex/diog.htm (accessed 9 February 2010).

[228] DIOG FBI (2008), preamble, XI.

example, observe, collect and consider any form of the protected speech if done for a valid law enforcement or national security purpose and if not obstructing the person in question from using his right to free speech.[229] Furthermore, religious practitioners or religious facilities may be examined in the context of an "assessment" or "predicated investigation."[230] FBI employees may also "take appropriate cognizance of the role religion may play in the membership or motivation of a criminal or terrorism enterprise" or investigate members of a criminal or terrorist group's possible religious motive. However, group members' mere affiliation with a particular religion may not form the basis of an assessment or investigation, absent any connection of a particular member to the threat under investigation.[231] The Constitutional protection of freedom of association does not preclude, according to court decisions, activities such as "undercover participation in group activities; physical and video surveillance in public areas; properly authorized electronic surveillance; recruitment and operation of sources; collection of information from government, public and private sources (with consent); and the dissemination of information for a valid law enforcement purpose."[232] Furthermore, race and ethnicity "may be a relevant factor to consider" when deciding to initiate investigative activities; however, "it should not be the dominant or primary factor" and never the sole factor.[233]

The choice for the 'least intrusive method' is, as a matter of general principle, prescribed in the Mukasey Guidelines and further specified in the DIOG. The DIOG prescribes a balancing test between the level of intrusion and investigative requirements. The following factors shall be considered in order to determine whether a particular technique is proportionate: "seriousness of the crime or national security threat; strength and significance of the intelligence/information to be gained; amount of information already known about the subject or group under investigation; and requirements of operational security, including protection of sources and methods."[234]

The DIOG further explains the purpose and goal of 'assessments' as to act proactively in "detecting criminal or national security threats" without waiting for leads to come in by using the techniques available for the purpose of early intervention and prevention.[235] Preliminary investigations and full investigations may have a reactive or proactive purpose. Preliminary investigations are in particular aimed at: "determining whether a federal crime has occurred or is occurring, or if planning or preparation for such a crime is taking place;

---

229 *Ibid.*, 26.

230 *Ibid.*, 27.

231 *Ibid.*, 27-28.

232 *Ibid.*, 29-30.

233 *Ibid.*, 31.

234 *Ibid.*, 37.

235 *Ibid.*, 40.

identifying, locating, and apprehending the perpetrators; obtaining evidence needed for prosecution; or identifying threats to the national security."[236]

Full investigations are initiated for the purpose of: "determining whether a federal crime is being planned, prepared for, occurring or occurred; identifying, locating, and apprehending the perpetrators; obtaining evidence for prosecution; identifying threats to the national security; investigating an enterprise (…); or collecting positive foreign intelligence."[237] It is added that the full investigation's objective of gathering "positive foreign intelligence" allows the FBI to conduct information-gathering activities "beyond federal crimes and threats to the national security" and "regarding a broader range of matters relating to foreign powers, organizations, or persons that may be of interest to the conduct of the United States' foreign affairs."[238]

Lastly, enterprise investigations can be initiated and operated on the same grounds and under the same conditions as full investigations and they examine "the structure, scope, and nature of the group or organization including: its relationship, if any, to a foreign power; the identity and relationship of its members, employees, or other persons who may be acting in furtherance of its objectives; its finances and resources; its geographical dimensions; its past and future activities and goals; and its capacity for harm."[239] The threshold for initiating an enterprise investigation as provided in the Mukasey Guidelines is further explained in the DIOG as being met also when the group or organization "may have or may be engaged in, planning or preparation or provision of support" of matters such as international terrorism. Moreover, according to the DIOG the "articulable factual basis" is established with the "identification of a group whose statements made in furtherance of its objectives, or its conduct, demonstrate a purpose of committing crimes or securing the commission of crimes by others. The group's activities and statements of its members may be considered in combination to comprise the "articulable factual basis," even if the statements alone or activities alone would not warrant such a determination."[240]

Furthermore, the DIOG contains a detailed description of all authorized investigative techniques. Especially the instructions for the most intrusive techniques are still partly classified. Also the guidelines with regard to the sharing of information as provided in the Mukasey Guidelines have been implemented in the DIOG.

---

[236] *Ibid.*, 76.

[237] *Ibid.*, 85.

[238] *Ibid.*, 85.

[239] *Ibid.*, 94.

[240] *Ibid.*, 95-96.

### *6.4.3 Other Developments Enhancing Cooperation Between Intelligence and Law Enforcement*

Besides the amendments of the 2001 USA PATRIOT Act and the explanation of the new FISA statutory language by the FISA Court of Review, also some other post-9/11 legislation was adopted in order to increase cooperation between the law enforcement and intelligence community and to promote information sharing. The 'Intelligence Reform and Terrorism Prevention Act of 2004'[241] has created the position of the Director of National Intelligence (DNI), who is to be "appointed by the President, by and with advice and consent of the Senate." The main responsibility of the DNI is to head the intelligence community in order to ensure the effective cooperation of the different intelligence agencies and to "oversee and direct the implementation of the National Intelligence Program."[242] Moreover, the DNI "shall establish requirements and priorities for foreign intelligence information to be collected under [FISA], and provide assistance to the Attorney General to ensure that information derived from electronic surveillance or physical searches under that Act is disseminated so it may be used effectively for national intelligence purposes."[243] The DNI should also promote the sharing of intelligence.

Furthermore, the Intelligence Reform and Terrorism Prevention Act of 2004 creates a National Counterterrorism Center as the "primary organization in the United States Government for analyzing and integrating all intelligence possessed or acquired by the United States Government." This National Counterterrorism Center also has responsibility to "conduct strategic operational planning for counterterrorism integrating all instruments of national power, including [...] law enforcement activities within and among agencies."[244]

The last contribution of this Act to dismantling the wall can be found in the provision governing the "improvement of intelligence capabilities of the Federal Bureau of Investigation," according to which each FBI agent "employed after the date of enactment of this Act shall receive basic training in both criminal justice matters and national intelligence matters" as part of the full institutionalization of the "shift" of the FBI "to a preventive counterterrorism posture."[245]

Furthermore, bureaucratic changes have to a significant extent contributed to the realization of enhanced cooperation between the intelligence community and the law enforcement community. Most notably, in 2002 the FBI established the Joint Terrorism Task Force (JTTF), which concerns a mechanism with a national

---

241 Pubic Law 108-458-Dec. 17, 2004.

242 Intelligence Reform and Terrorism Prevention Act of 2004, sec. 1001(a).

243 *Ibid.*

244 *Ibid.*, sec. 1021.

245 *Ibid.*, sec. 2001 (a) and (c).

and multiple regional offices sharing information relevant to counterterrorism between all relevant federal, state and local entities.[246]

## 6.5 Other Relevant Investigative Powers

Outside the scope of conventional criminal investigations and, as it was firstly introduced, also outside the context of FISA, the executive has introduced a surveillance program authorized by the executive order of the President. Moreover, the government has expanded its use of national security letters in the fight against terrorism. Both the NSA surveillance and the issuance of national security letters did not require a (FISA) court order. Although these tools are primarily intended as intelligence tools, they are now available to the FBI and the information gathered may and will be transferred to the law enforcement community due to current sharing obligations.

Many other measures have been taken for the purpose of preventing terrorism, such as changes in immigration law, border security and combating the financing of terrorism, and also information available to the agencies responsible for these actions may be introduced to criminal proceedings. However, this section will only deal with the 'NSA surveillance program' and with 'National Security Letters.' Only those powers, although also to a limited extent, are relevant to the subject of research as it concerns investigative power that can be conducted by the FBI and concern similar powers available to the FBI in the context of conventional criminal law and national security law, but without the usual restrictions and checks on their use. In addition, the information gathered through these investigative powers may, in conformity with agreements on information sharing policies, be transferred to the law enforcement agencies with regard to the NSA Surveillance Program, especially since its current regulation under the Foreign Intelligence Surveillance Act.

### *6.5.1 The NSA Surveillance Program and its Incorporation in FISA*

NSA surveillance, also referred to as the 'Terrorist Surveillance Program,' concerns a classified surveillance program authorized under the President's authority as Chief Executive. In December 2005 the New York Times published a series of articles revealing the existence of the program.[247] In reaction, Attorney General Gonzales confirmed that the President had authorized the NSA to intercept, without a warrant, phone calls and e-mails that either originate or terminate with a

[246] Baker 2007A, 246-247 and 259 and Progress Report 2011, 12-13.

[247] See in particular: Risen and Lichtblau 2005.

US person, when there "is a reasonable basis to conclude that one party" was linked to Al Qaida. The NSA surveillance program was consciously referred to as the 'Terrorist Surveillance Program' in order to create sympathy for the far-reaching and secretive interception of communications, including the communications of Americans, by suggesting that it is only used to monitor terrorists.[248] Until 2005 the program had already operated completely classified for four years and, although aspects of the Terrorist Surveillance Program had been made public, most of the program remained classified, including authorized activities other than surveillance.[249]

The position of the Bush Administration, defending the legality of the Program, was that the President as Commander-in-Chief and under his foreign affairs power as granted in Article II of the Constitution, in combination with the enactment of the 'Authorization for Use of Military Force' (AUMF), was allowed to authorize these surveillance activities. FISA provides that the interception of electronic communications is prohibited, except as authorized under Statute.[250] Section 2(a) of the AUMF, providing that the President shall "use all necessary and appropriate force against those nations, organizations, or persons he determines planned, authorizes, committed, or aided the terrorist attacks that occurred on September 11, 2001," was considered as such a statute permitting for electronic surveillance outside the scope of FISA.[251] The program remained, however, highly controversial and has received extensive criticism as to its legality. The NSA surveillance seems incompatible with the history of abuses of unchecked government surveillance powers preceding the enactment of FISA, the interpretation that has since been given to the Fourth Amendment requirements applicable to surveillance for domestic security purposes and the explicit requirements of FISA covering all domestic surveillance.[252] Moreover, it follows from the joint unclassified version of the report of all involved Offices of Inspectors General on the 'President's Surveillance Program' that in 2004 the Department of Justice was in conflict with the White House, when the Department of Justice seriously disputed the legality of the program.[253]

The Supreme Court has until now not addressed the question whether the President may also engage in warrantless surveillance under these powers.

---

[248] See also Baker 2007A, 87-89.

[249] Report of the Offices of the Inspectors General on the President's Surveillance Program 2009, 6.

[250] 50 U.S.C. 36 § 1809(a).

[251] See in more detail: Cooper Blum 2009, 285-286.

[252] Bloom and Dunn 2006.

[253] Report of the Offices of the Inspectors General on the President's Surveillance Program 2009, 21-29. This report was drafted as a result of the established oversight by the FISA Amendments Act of 2008, requiring the Inspectors General to review the program. See Foreign Intelligence Surveillance Act of 1978 Amendments Act of 2008, Public Law 110-261-July 10, 2008, 122 Stat. 2472, sec. 301(c).

However, district judge Anna Diggs Taylor held in *American Civil Liberties Union v. National Security Agency* (2006) that the Terrorist Surveillance Program violated the Fourth Amendment as it departed from congressional intention with the enactment of Title III and FISA, for which reason surveillance without a warrant is unconstitutional.

In the meantime the government sought a solution to the remaining concerns regarding the legality of the program, which resulted in the enactment of the Protect America Act of 2007, which amended FISA. The Protect America Act allowed the warrantless surveillance of communications between two foreign parties that were routed through the United States as well as the warrantless surveillance of communications of US citizens with a party located outside the US, whereas it is "reasonably believed" that the target of the surveillance is located outside the US. The statutory phrasing of the surveillance power as previously used in the Terrorist Surveillance Program seems to leave little protection that the surveillance does not in fact target US persons. However, the FISA Court of Review in *In re Directives Pursuant to Section 105B of the Foreign Intelligence Surveillance Act* considered the provisions of the Protect America Act to be lawful as the court could not frustrate the government's "efforts to protect national security" when it "has instituted several layers of serviceable safeguards to protect individuals against unwarranted harms and to minimize incidental intrusions."[254]

The highly controversial Protect America Act of 2007 expired in February 2008 and was succeeded by the FISA Amendments Act of 2008 (FAA). Under the FAA "the Attorney General and Director of National Intelligence may authorize jointly for a period of up to one year [...] the targeting of persons reasonably believed to be located outside the United States to acquire foreign intelligence information."[255] The FAA includes some specific restrictions on the use of this surveillance power, which are intended to prevent abuse by targeting US persons. Hence, the following limitations apply: "an acquisition [...]: (1) may not intentionally target any person known at the time of acquisition to be located in the United States; (2) may not intentionally target a person reasonably believed to be located outside the United States if the purpose of such acquisition is to target a particular, known person reasonably believed to be in the United States; (3) may not intentionally target a United States person reasonably believed to be located outside the United States; (4) may not intentionally acquire any communications as to which the sender and all intended recipients are known at the time of the acquisition to be located in the United States; (5) shall be conducted in a manner consistent with the fourth amendment to the Constitution of the United States."[256] Moreover, an order of the FISA Court is required for the surveillance. This order can be given after a review by the FISA Court of the certification submitted by the AG and DNI including whether

[254] *In re Directives Pursuant to Section 105B of the Foreign Intelligence Surveillance Act*, 551 F.3d 1004 (FISA Ct. Rev. 2008), 1016.

[255] FISA Amendments Act 2008, Sec. 702(a) (50 U.S.C. § 1881(a)).

[256] *Ibid.*, Sec. 702(b) (50 U.S.C. § 1881(a)).

'targeting procedures' are in place to ensure that the surveillance is limited to targeting persons outside the US, minimization procedures are in place, a "significant purpose of the acquisition is to obtain foreign intelligence information" and that the certification is consistent with the Fourth Amendment.[257] As additional mechanisms to prevent abuses of this foreign intelligence surveillance targeting non-US persons outside the US, congressional oversight has been established in order to control whether the communications of innocent US citizens will be acquired and retained. Moreover, the Inspectors General of the relevant departments and agencies are instructed to review the use of these surveillance powers *ex post.*

Although the use of these surveillance powers shall be limited to targeting non-US persons outside the US, the intercepted communications may still include those with US citizens. Because FAA explicitly provides that the minimization procedures of FISA apply to orders for such surveillance, "information that is evidence of a crime which has been, is being, or is about to be committed" may "be retained or disseminated for law enforcement purposes."[258] With the incorporation in FISA, not only the NSA but also the FBI can use these surveillance powers targeting non-US persons outside the US, as is also explicitly provided in the DIOG of the FBI as an available investigative tool in full investigations.[259] Moreover, under discovery obligations the information collected under these authorities is required, in principle, to be disclosed when it is relevant to a prosecution.[260] Also the FBI has acknowledged that the information collected through NSA surveillance included valuable "leads" for the FBI's efforts to prevent future terrorist attacks.[261]

To conclude: NSA surveillance and its current statutory basis in FISA concern an alternative scheme for surveillance with even weaker protection against arbitrary interferences with the private lives of US citizens. Although a FISA order is now required for this surveillance targeting overseas non-US persons, any form of probable cause against the targeted persons is not required and the order by the FISA Court is limited to a review of the certification of the AG and DNI. The main goal of the program is intelligence gathering in order to prevent terrorist attacks against the US that are being planned abroad. However, the information that is intercepted may become relevant for domestic counterterrorism investigations as also information of US persons may be intercepted. Under the FISA minimization procedures such information may even be retained once it is relevant for a future criminal prosecution. The use of information gathered under these procedures, considering that these procedures are still to a large extent classified, may face

---

[257] *Ibid.*, sec. 702(g) and (i) (50 U.S.C. § 1881(a)).

[258] 50 U.S.C. § 1801(h)(3).

[259] DIOG FBI (2008), 115.

[260] See: Report of the Offices of the Inspectors General on the President's Surveillance Program 2009, 18-19.

[261] Report of the Offices of the Inspectors General on the President's Surveillance Program 2009, 32.

difficulties once access is sought in discovery. Although the implications in practice as a consequence of use in criminal procedures will probably remain limited, such use has not been excluded, in particular since explicitly applying the FISA minimization procedures.

### *6.5.2 National Security Letters*

The investigative tool of the 'National Security Letter' (henceforth: 'NSL') concerns a warrantless investigative tool to be used in national security investigations that has been included in different statutes since 1978.[262] However, its scope was significantly expanded by the USA PATRIOT Act of 2001. Moreover, whilst the FBI rarely used the NSL before 2001 (a couple of hundred times in total), the FBI has relied on the tool very frequently since 9/11 (in 2010 the FBI made 24,287 NSL requests, seeking information regarding 14,212 different US persons).[263] The amount of NSLs issued contrasts strongly with the use of section 215 orders, a difference which can reasonably be attributed to the fact that the FBI does not have to obtain a court order for issuing NSL. As a result, authority to issue national security letters has become the subject of litigation and extensive criticism, resulting in changes to its regulation.

The FBI can issue an NSL as a document production under the applicability of a non-disclosure requirement similar to the non-disclosure requirement accompanying section 215 orders (see Sect. 6.3.2). Before the enactment of the 2001 Patriot Act, the use of NSL could only be sought for information pertaining to a foreign power or an agent of a foreign power. Section 505 of the PATRIOT Act lowers the threshold for the issuance of an NSL by requiring that the production concerns information "relevant to an authorized investigation to protect against international terrorist or clandestine intelligence activities, provided that such an investigation of a United States person is not conducted solely on the basis of activities protected by the first amendment to the Constitution of the United States."[264] Before this, the government could only issue NSL upon a showing of

---

[262] The Right to Financial Privacy Act of 1978 (the non-disclosure requirement was included in 1986), the Electronic Communications Privacy Act of 1986, the Fair Credit Reporting Act of 1970, which included NSL authority since 1996, and the National Security Act of 1947, amended in 1994 in order to include NSL authority. See in more detail on NSL authority in these Acts: Report of the Office of the Inspector General 2007, *A Review of the Federal Bureau of Investigation's Use of National Security Letters*, 11-15.

[263] FISA Annual Report to Congress 2010, available at: http://www.fas.org/irp/agency/doj/fisa/#rept (accessed 1 August 2011). For an overview of the amount of FISA Court orders and NSLs for the years 1979-2010, composed on the basis of annual and general reports, see: 'Foreign Intelligence Surveillance Act Court Orders 1979-2010', Electronic Privacy Information Center, available at: http://epic.org/privacy/wiretap/stats/fisa_stats.html (accessed 29 July 2011). See also: Nieland 2007, 1202.

[264] Section 505 USA PATRIOT Act 2001.

"specific articulable facts giving reason to believe that the person or entity to whom the information sought pertains is a foreign power or an agent of a foreign power." This means that currently the NSL can be used in the investigation of international terrorism, whether or not for law enforcement purposes or for foreign intelligence purpose or for multiple purposes. Hence, also in the DIOG of the FBI the use of NSL has been included as an authorized investigative tool in the FBI's preliminary investigations and full investigations.[265] Furthermore, not only senior FBI Headquarters Officials are now authorized to issue NSLs, but any "Special Agent in Charge in a Bureau field office" may also authorize NSLs. The explosive growth of NSLs can be attributed to this latter adjustment.[266] The information that can be sought by issuing a NSL is related to the Acts in which the authority for the tool is provided,[267] which limits the use to information from "communication providers, financial institutions, and consumer credit agencies about persons other than the subjects of national security investigations."[268] The PATRIOT Act extended the latter category by amending the Fair Crediting Reporting Act to extend the scope from information regarding the financial institution and the identity of the consumer, to full consumer credit reports when such reports are relevant to an investigation of international terrorism.[269]

The most important changes to the power of NSL as a consequence of the enactment of the USA PATRIOT Act of 2001 have thus been the allowance of any Special Agent in an FBI Field Office to issue an NSL and the lowering of the threshold to a mere certification of relevance to an authorized investigation relating to international terrorism or clandestine intelligence activities. In addition, the scope of NSL is rather ambiguous and has been able to expand, primarily as a result of technological developments. For example, the category of 'electronic communications service provides' has since the enactment of the Electronic Communications Privacy Act in 1986 grown to include all electronic communications through the Internet. The FBI has interpreted the category to include all businesses and organizations, such as libraries, universities and political organizations, using systems for communication through the Internet. Furthermore, according to this Act the NSL may request 'electronic communications transactional records', which according to the FBI includes the addresses of websites a user has visited, the recipients of e-mails sent by a user and the subject line of e-mails.[270]

---

265 DIOG FBI (2008), 114-115.

266 Section 505(a)(1), (b)(1) and (c)(1)-(3) USA PATRIOT Act 2001.

267 See footnote 262 of this Chapter.

268 Report of the Office of the Inspector General 2007, *A Review of the Federal Bureau of Investigation's Use of National Security Letters*, 8-9.

269 Section 505(c) USA PATRIOT ACT 2001.

270 Nieland 2007, 1214 and Mart 2008, 456-457.

The FBI thus has a large degree of discretion in using its NSL authority, considering that it may choose its target without any judicial overview on relevance for an investigation. The usefulness of the tool has also significantly increased considering that the request may include a wide and not particularly defined range of personal information. Moreover, NSL authority is a very powerful tool because of the applicability of the non-disclosure requirement, which allows the FBI to act in complete secrecy without risking facing a challenge to the lawfulness of using the tool. Altogether, these circumstances have resulted in an explosion in the use of NSL since 9/11.

As a consequence, civil liberties movements have also become more concerned about the government's NSL power. This has resulted in litigation (the *Doe* cases) concerning the constitutionality of the accompanying non-disclosure requirement, which has already been extensively dealt with in Sect. 6.3.2. As a result of district court judgments finding the NSL authority with the non-disclosure requirement unconstitutional and in violation of the separation of powers, the USA PATRIOT Act Amendments Act of 2005 and 2006 have narrowed the non-disclosure requirement by allowing the recipient to consult with his attorney and have provided for a judicial review by a U.S. District Court with regard to the legitimacy of the NSL and the applicable non-disclosure requirement.[271] The contents of the amendments or the similar aspects of these amendments will not be repeated here. Similarly, a judicial review of the scope of a NSL and of the imposed non-disclosure requirement has been introduced, a review which may, however, also result in a court order to comply with the NSL. Likewise, consultation with an attorney has now been exempted from the non-disclosure requirement. However, section 116 of the Amendments Act of 2005 narrowing the non-disclosure requirement for NSL is more far-reaching than the amendments to section 215 orders. The non-disclosure requirement no longer automatically applies and may now only apply to NSL recipients if the FBI official "certifies that otherwise there may result danger to the national security of the United States, interference with a criminal, counterterrorism, or counterintelligence investigation, interference with diplomatic relations, or other danger to the life or physical safety of any person."[272] Nevertheless, the required certification by the government is still unreviewable and, according to guidelines on the use of NSL, such certification is in most situations appropriate.[273] Furthermore, section 5 of the PATRIOT Act

[271] Sections 115 and 116 USA PATRIOT Act Amendments Act of 2005.

[272] Section 116(a) USA PATRIOT Act Amendments Act of 2005.

[273] According to a review in 2006 at least 97% of issued NSLs were still accompanied by the non-disclosure requirement. Report of the Office of the Inspector General (2008), *A Review of the Federal Bureau of Investigation's Use of National Security Letters, Assessment of Corrective Actions and Examination of NSL usage in 2006*, 124.

Amendments Act of 2006 excludes libraries from the entities from which information may be obtained, as they would not fall under the definition of "electronic communication service."[274] Lastly, the Amendment Acts have enhanced congressional oversight on NSL. Nevertheless, the reports produced by the Office of the Inspector General demonstrate that the FBI has repeatedly abused its powers to issue national security letters, for example in media leak cases.[275]

In addition, it needs to be observed that subjects of NSL may never discover that NSLs concerning them have been issued. The Court of Appeals of Illinois has dealt with a case against Robert Mueller, the Director of the FBI, in which someone sought information under FOIA whether he has been the subject of NSLs.[276] The Court agreed with the FBI that it could not disclose the subjects of NSLs as that would "enable terrorist groups to vet their members and circumvent the law by shifting operations to those free of government suspicion."[277] For this reason, exemption 7(E) to FOIA applied and the FBI is not obliged to reveal who have been subjects of NSLs.[278]

## 6.6 Conclusion

This Chapter has analyzed, in four different categories, the legal developments since the events of 9/11, 2001 that have realized a shift of focus in the criminal investigation from reactive to proactive action for the purpose of prevention. On the basis of the measures described in these four categories, an anticipative criminal investigation has been realized, which can be illustrated as in Fig. 6.1.

As illustrated, the anticipative criminal investigation can be conducted under the investigative frameworks of conventional criminal law as well as under FISA, previously exclusively reserved for national security investigations. In addition, because of the realization of full information sharing also the information collected with the use of investigative techniques in pure national security investigations can become part of the anticipative criminal investigation or of criminal proceedings in general.

---

274 Section 5 USA PATRIOT Act Additional Reauthorizing Amendments Act of 2006.

275 This was last concluded in the Report of the Office of Inspector General 2010, A *Review of the Federal Bureau of Investigation's Use of Exigent Letters and Other Informal Requests for Telephone Records*.

276 *Catledge v. Mueller,* 323 Fed.Appx 464, 2009 WL 1025980 (7th Cir. 2009).

277 *Ibid.*, 465 and 467.

278 Compare *Bassiouni v. CIA,* 392 F.3d 244, (7th Cir. 2004) and *Bassiouni v. FBI,* 436 F.3d 712 (7th Cir. 2006), as dealt with in Chap. 5, Sect. 5.3.1.4.

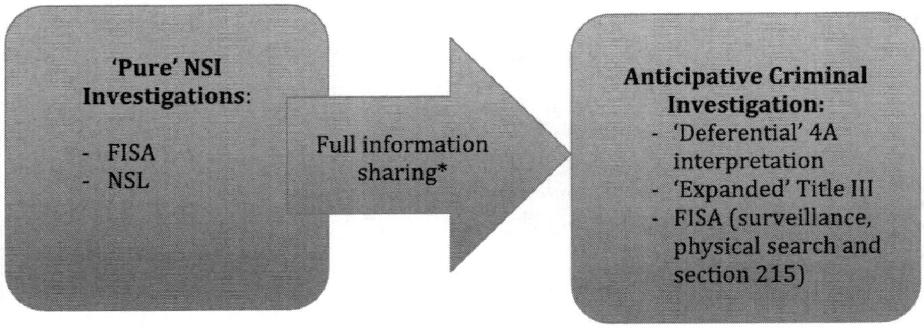


- Full sharing of information is instructed by DoJ Memoranda and enabled through fusion centers.

**Fig. 6.1** Conclusive illustration of the anticipative criminal investigation in the United States

The criminal investigation was traditionally a function to be exercised only through the traditional criminal investigative means as regulated by Fourth Amendment law, Rule 41 of the Federal Rules of Criminal Procedure and Title III. Currently, national security investigations have become an important additional context for criminal investigation when it comes to investigations dealing with 'threats to the national security,' such as international terrorism, aimed both at the collection of foreign intelligence information and at evidence gathering regarding criminal activities. This latter development, realized through changing the 'purpose language' of FISA, may be considered as the most meaningful change towards anticipative criminal investigation, affecting previous institutional choices and accepting investigative standards created especially for the purpose of foreign intelligence gathering, which significantly deviate from traditional standards for criminal investigations. The FBI has, by means of guidelines of the Attorney General, been transformed into an investigative agency combining its intelligence and law enforcement capacities to be able to investigate proactively for the purpose of preventing future terrorist attacks. Intelligence and law enforcement functions are combined within one investigative operation and the investigative powers of conventional law enforcement and FISA can be applied under the statutory requirements which are applicable.

Considering the foregoing, the investigative areas of national security and law enforcement have been merged, for which reason national security investigations have obtained a law enforcement purpose and the collection of evidence occurs as a secondary purpose in investigative operations that are primarily concerned with prevention. On top of that, the investigative powers under FISA have been strengthened in order to be able to act even more effectively for the prevention of future terrorist attacks and to enhance the information position on potential threats to national security. A FISA order may now also authorize roving surveillance, orders targeting 'lone wolves' are valid for 120 days and the FISA Court may issue document production orders for the production of 'any tangible things'. In addition, the possibility of electronic surveillance upon a single showing of relevance to an authorized investigation and targeting non-US persons outside the US is now incorporated in FISA.

As a consequence of the blending of national security and law enforcement functions and the expansion of powers under FISA, the legality of the powers authorized for national security investigations cannot be considered separately from its consequences for criminal procedural law and the protective objective that criminal procedural law must pursue. Hence, renewed questions arise as to the compliance of national security investigative powers with the Fourth Amendment, the relation between the secrecy of national security investigative actions and transparency and due process standards as protective elements of criminal procedural law, as well as the institutional position of the criminal justice system in relation to the intelligence system.

This being the most significant development that has contributed to enabling 'anticipative criminal investigation', in the post-9/11 era also the character of conventional criminal investigations has changed in order to give law enforcement officers acting in the context of conventional criminal law sufficient leeway and effective powers to act proactively and expediently when it comes to the protection of national security or, more in general, to further public safety.

The enactment of the USA PATRIOT Act of 2001 has extended some conventional investigative powers to improve covert investigative capacity. Most importantly, through the expansion of the delayed notice exception the possibilities for sneak and peak searches have been extended. Furthermore, the scope of the information that can be obtained through pen registers and trap and trace devices has been broadened and a single search warrant has nationwide applicability. In combination with an order for roving surveillance under Title III, the latter makes it possible to follow suspects throughout the country without delays due to bureaucratic impediments. Moreover, through an analysis of the case law, a trend has been signaled in post-9/11 court decisions where the interest to protect national security or to prevent terrorism has been used as an argument to deviate from the *Terry v. Ohio* requirements for investigatory stops, to invoke the special needs doctrine, or to outweigh privacy interests rendering the search reasonable. The latter seems to be a general trend in favor of crime control when the interpretation of Fourth Amendment requirements is based upon a balancing of protecting civil liberties against expedient law enforcement needs, which has also resulted in less oversight on police conduct by eroding the remedy of the exclusionary rule.

Lastly, the surveillance of targets outside the US and the issuing of national security letters have been dealt with in a separate category as they neither belong to conventional criminal law nor to national security law due to their origin or to their manner of regulation. However, both are investigative tools available to the FBI and may be used, especially under the current circumstances where sharing obligations apply and the FBI's intelligence and criminal investigative capacities are combined, to investigate also criminal activity and produce information that can be used as evidence. Nevertheless, the surveillance targeting non-US persons outside the US is subject to less regulation than FISA surveillance and the powerful tool of NSL is easily available to any special agent in charge and may, under complete secrecy, lead to the interception of privacy-sensitive information such as the subject line of e-mails. Because of the fact that the information intercepted by these tools may under the current circumstances become part of criminal proceedings, the regulation of these tools raises questions as to their compliance with the Fourth Amendment and as to the relation of the covert nature of these tools to transparency as an important value of criminal procedural law, in particular with regard to the consequences for procedural due process when the information obtained is sought in disclosure or used as evidence.

The description of the developments for each of the categories as given in this Chapter and the signaled rise of 'anticipative criminal investigation' provides a reason for a further analysis of the implications for the shield objective of criminal procedural law. This conclusion has already initially set out the potential implications of the changes since September 11, 2001 with regard to the shield objective of criminal procedural law. The next Chapter will build upon these findings by identifying the precise implications of the measures and developments described in this Chapter and by assessing them in the light of the legal background provided in Chap. 5.

# Chapter 7
# The Implications of Enabling Anticipative Criminal Investigations to Confront Terrorism for the Objectives of Criminal Procedural Law in the United States

## 7.1 Introduction

The previous Chapter has described, in detail, a variety of measures taken by the US government in the post-9/11 era and some general developments in criminal procedural law which have resulted in the realization of the anticipative criminal investigation. These measures and developments have been divided into four categories: 1) measures and developments expanding the preventive capacity of the conventional criminal investigation; 2) measures expanding the powers of national security investigation; 3) cooperation and information sharing between the law enforcement and intelligence communities to enhance preventive capabilities; 4) introducing new or exploiting existing exceptional techniques to enhance capabilities outside the framework of the regulation of conventional criminal law or FISA. Jointly, these measures and developments realize the government's efforts to improve its preventive capabilities through investigative activities. Jointly, as well as individually, the measures and developments also have consequences for criminal procedural law as they alter conventional and sometimes fundamental restraints on the use of criminal investigative powers and they alter the role and purposes of criminal investigation as such.

This Chapter will analyze for each category, or generally where the changes of two categories cannot be separately assessed in relation to each other, the implications for traditional institutional choices as to the role and position of a criminal investigation and the implications for the constitutional protective elements of the system of criminal investigation that have been established to give effect to the protective—shield—objective of criminal procedural law as identified in Chap. 5. The assessment of the implications of the changes described in Chap. 6 will thus be limited to the implications with respect to the shield objective of criminal procedural law and, consequently, the implications for the traditionally established equilibrium between the sword and shield in the criminal investigation following from

M.F.H. Hirsch Ballin, *Anticipative Criminal Investigation*,
DOI: 10.1007/978-90-6704-843-9_7,

constitutional and additional statutory regulation as well as internal policy. Therefore, the changes described in Chap. 6—on which basis a shift to prevention by means of an anticipative criminal investigation has been signaled—will be assessed in the light of the legal background of the criminal investigation provided in Chap. 5.

Section 7.2 will commence by addressing the implications for the conventional criminal investigation and will focus, in particular, on the current state of the protective elements that follow from Fourth Amendment law. The current understanding of the regulatory influence of the Fourth Amendment is important not only for mapping out the implications in conventional criminal law, but also for understanding and assessing the measures in the national security context as a consequence of the intermingling of the two areas. For this reason, the assessment of the implications for conventional criminal law will be comparatively elaborative.

Subsequently, Sect. 7.3 will address the expansion of investigative powers under FISA. Setting out these changes is particularly important in relation to the findings of Sect. 7.4, as the implications of the enabled interaction between the law enforcement and intelligence communities can only be fully understood in the light of the nature of the current 'sword' power available in national security investigations.

Section 7.4 deals with the interaction, or the intermingling, between the law enforcement community and the intelligence community as the principal aspect of the anticipative criminal investigation in the United States. The core of the US approach towards realizing the prevention of future terrorist attacks by anticipating possible threats lies in the combination of gathering as much information as possible in order to be able to anticipate future harm and to make it possible to deal with terrorist suspects through criminal prosecution. Hence, this section will redefine the institutional positions and functions of criminal investigations and national security investigations as well as the law enforcement and intelligence communities (in particular the FBI, composed of both law enforcement and intelligence divisions) and thus, in fact, define the nature, position and purposes of an anticipative criminal investigation. The fusion of investigative purposes through the interaction of law enforcement and intelligence by the two previously separated communities is closely related to Fourth Amendment interpretation, which has shifted under the influence of the preventive paradigm. Hence, the implications signaled in Sect. 7.4 also have a clear relationship with the implications signaled in Sect. 7.2.

Lastly, Sect. 7.5 will deal with the two 'external' influences' of the NSA surveillance program (Terrorist Surveillance Program) adopted in FISA and national security letters. Both concern very powerful and largely unchecked investigative powers, which—especially because of their powerful and secretive nature—further define the nature of the sword power of the anticipative criminal investigation. The implications of these investigative powers with regard to the shield objective of criminal procedural law are, however, no different from the findings of Sects. 7.3 and 7.4. Hence, the goal of this section is to demonstrate that the implications of an anticipative criminal investigation as described in Sects. 7.3 and 7.4 are intensified by the investigative possibilities of the surveillance of non-US persons outside the US and of national security letters.

The final, concluding, Sect. 7.6 will draw a complete picture—in summary—of the implications of enabling anticipative criminal investigations for the sword and shield objective of criminal procedural law as dealt with in the underlying Chapter.

## 7.2 Expansion of the Preventive Capacity of Conventional Criminal Law

### *7.2.1 Expansion of the Scope and Nature of Electronic Surveillance*

#### 7.2.1.1 In General

As a consequence of the amendments of the USA PATRIOT Act, the scope and nature of electronic surveillance in conventional criminal investigations have been expanded. Compared to the situation prior to the events of 9/11, the 'sword' capacity of the government in the context of a conventional criminal investigation has increased, which is a development that also results in implications for the shield objective, in particular constitutional implications.

The measures taken to strengthen the sword aspect of surveillance in conventional criminal investigations have been described in Sect. 6.2.1 and can be summarized as follows. The instances in which Title III surveillance can be used in criminal investigations have grown, because of the inclusion of new terrorist crimes on the list for which Title III surveillance is permitted. Furthermore, the scope of pen registers and trap and trace devices has expanded through changes to the definitions regarding the information that may be intercepted. The USA PATRIOT Act of 2001 has also provided a rather broad statutory basis for search warrants permitting a delayed notice, for which reason the possibilities for a sneak-and-peak search have been increased. In combination with the nationwide applicability of search warrants through the amendment of the Federal Rule of Criminal Procedure 41, the nationwide applicability of orders for pen registers or trap/trace devices and the already existing possibility, under Title III, of roving surveillance and the roving bug, electronic surveillance has become a powerful investigative tool and has been considerably expanded as a tool that can be applied proactively and covertly. Electronic surveillance can take place secretly over a considerable period of time and may follow a target through the country and irrespective of what communication device he is using or, maybe, not using at all.

Changing the scope and nature of electronic surveillance in conventional criminal investigations touches upon the equilibrium between the need for effective investigate tools in criminal investigations and the observance of the Fourth Amendment, protecting people against unreasonable searches and seizures. This equilibrium was earlier found by means of constitutional interpretation, as the source of limitations on the government's power to investigate in order to protect civil liberties. In the landmark Supreme Court decision of *Berger v. New York* (1967),[1] the Court dealt with the manner in which Fourth Amendment requirements apply to surveillance activities. Title III was again the statutory elaboration of the Supreme Court's decision that the Fourth Amendment applies to surveillance. Also the regulation of pen registers and trap/trace authority has been based upon the interpretation of the limited applicability of the Fourth Amendment to pen register and trap/trace authority. The regulation has now been adjusted so as to advance effective criminal investigation at the expense of previous limitations.

In conclusion, the USA PATRIOT Act adjustments to the legal framework of Title III electronic surveillance and pen register and trap and trace authority have enhanced the sword power of Title III. Title III was understood to provide the necessary means for effective criminal investigations, but only as a last resort. The principle of subsidiarity intends to restrict investigative officers' reliance on Title III so that it is only used as a last resort when this is necessary for effective investigation. As a consequence of the PATRIOT Act amendments the possibilities for effective investigation under Title III and the situations in which Title III may be invoked have increased. This also follows from the increase in authorized Title III orders in the post-9/11 era by 168% in the years 2000–2010.[2] Except for the enhanced sword aspect, also some specific constitutional implications have been raised. This section will continue to address these constitutional implications, which concern the use of delayed notice warrants and the more intrusive nature of the current pen register and trap/trace authority.

#### 7.2.1.2 Delayed Notice Warrants

Sneak-and-peek searches have been conducted, primarily in narcotic investigations, since many years before the events of 9/11. Several federal courts have rendered the searches reasonable when sufficiently circumscribed.[3] Although different federal courts have addressed the issue and the relation of delayed notices to the Fourth Amendment and to the Federal Rule of Criminal Procedure 41, it cannot be said that the concerned decisions have developed a uniform standard for sneak-and-peek searches. Moreover, Supreme Court guidance is underdeveloped with regard to the (delayed) notice as a Fourth Amendment requirement.

Section 213 of the USA PATRIOT Act can be understood as action by the legislature to settle the issue.[4] However, it remains questionable whether the

---

[1] *Berger v. New York*, 388 U.S. 41, 87 S.Ct. 1873 (1967).

[2] This concerns a significant increase compared with the increase of 36% over the period 1990–2000. In 2010 judges issued 1207 intercept orders on the federal level, against 479 in 2000. See Wiretap report 2010, 10 and Table 2 and Wiretap report 2000, 13 and Table 2. All statistical information regarding wiretaps is available at: http://www.uscourts.gov/Statistics/WiretapReports.aspx (accessed August 1, 2011).

[3] See Sect. 5.3.2.1.3.

[4] See Sect. 6.2.1.

regulation adopted by the USA PATRIOT Act of 2001 for issuing delayed notice warrants upon rather sweeping grounds will withstand the reasonable test under the Fourth Amendment. The delayed notice provision is not restricted to terrorism investigations, but is applicable to any federal criminal investigation. Federal prosecutors and investigators even describe the new possibilities for delayed notices as a tool that has proven to be most effective in conventional criminal investigations.[5] The power to search with a delayed notice is not accompanied by a 'sunset' provision. The broad and covert nature of the government's authority to search the property of its citizens has raised many concerns among civil rights advocates, which is in sharp contrast to the limited attention which has so far been given to the notice requirement by the Supreme Court. These circumstances render the constitutional assessment of this provision even more urgent.

As has been analyzed in Sect. 5.3.2.1.3, federal appellate courts have held that not all "surreptitious entries" are necessarily unconstitutional.[6] The courts have made clear, however, that sneak-and-peek searches can only be reasonable when there are sufficient safeguards that police officers will not act beyond "the bounds of propriety without detection." Some specific conditions have been formulated upon which there seemed to be agreement among the federal appellate courts. The presence of a "notice requirement in the warrant" is, for example, an indication of "constitutional adequacy."[7] Furthermore, officers applying for a delayed notice warrant must show good cause to the issuing judge for the delayed notice.[8] Lastly, although the reasonableness of the sneak-and-peek search depends on all circumstances of the case, as an initial matter notification shall be given within seven days after the surreptitious entry.[9] More in general, a notice shall be given "within a reasonable, but short, time subsequent to the surreptitious entry. Such time should not exceed seven days except upon a strong showing of necessity."[10]

When seeking to formulate a conclusion as to the constitutionality of the provision for a delayed notice under 18 U.S.C. § 3103a (as created by section 213 of the USA PATRIOT Act of 2001) it shall be determined whether the provision is sufficiently circumscribed to avoid police officers acting beyond the bounds of propriety. For this purpose the current conditions imposed on the issuing of delayed notice warrants can be compared with the conditions previously formulated by the courts. In particular, it shall be determined whether the grounds for a delayed notice can be considered as a demonstration of good cause for the delay to

---

[5] Information based upon conversations with several federal prosecutors and investigators.

[6] *United States v. Freitas,* 800 F.2d 1451 (9th Cir. 1968), 1456 and *United States v. Villegas,* 899 F.2d 1324 (2nd Cir. 1990), 1337 (referring to the Supreme Court decision in *Dalia v. United States*, 441 U.S. 238, 247, 99 S.Ct. 1682, 1688 (1979)).

[7] *United States v. Freitas,* 800 F.2d 1451 (9th Cir. 1986), 1456 (referring to *Berger v. New York* (1967)).

[8] *United States v. Villegas,* 899 F.2d 1324 (2nd Cir. 1990), 1337.

[9] *United States v. Freitas,* 800 F.2d 1451 (9th Cir. 1968), 1456 and *United States v. Villegas,* 899 F.2d 1324 (2nd Cir. 1990), 1337.

[10] *United States v. Freitas,* 800 F.2d 1451 (9th Cir. 1986), 1456.

the issuing judge and whether the 30-day restriction on the period for a delay can still be reasonable, considering the previous indication of 7 days to render the delay reasonable and the relation between the reasonableness of the time delay and the necessity. In addition, the intrusiveness of this type of search in relation to the need for such sneak-and-peek searches for effective criminal investigation is relevant to constitutionality. The Second Circuit Court in *United States v. Villegas* (1990) had noted that sneak and peek should be considered as less intrusive than a conventional search, because a sneak-and-peek search will only result in the seizure of intangible things, which does not deprive the owner of "the use of his property."[11] Moreover, the Second Circuit Court considered sneak and peek to be less intrusive than wire-tapping or video surveillance, because the "physical search is of relatively short duration, focuses the search specifically on the items listed in the warrant, and produces information as of a given moment, whereas the electronic surveillance is ongoing and indiscriminate, gathering in any activities within its mechanical focus."[12] On the other hand, the sneak-and-peek search implies a higher potential for abuse or mistakes, because the owner of the property cannot control the execution of the warrant in accordance with the contents thereof, cannot oppose the legitimacy of the warrant before execution and cannot safeguard law enforcement officers from making 'good faith' mistakes in the execution of a validly issued warrant.[13] The possible implications of a sneak-and-peek search became apparent in the *Mayfield* case, where the FBI had repeatedly conducted sneak-and-peek searches (authorized under FISA) of the Mayfield's family home, but "so incompetently that the FBI left traces of their searches behind, causing the Mayfield family to be frightened and believe that they had been burglarized."[14]

On the basis of these above-mentioned factors established in the case law in order to consider the constitutionality of sneak-and-peak searches, it is possible to assess the delayed notice provision of section 213 as to Fourth Amendment compatibility. In general, the conditions under which a delayed notice of the execution of a search warrant is permitted shall be clearly defined and limited in order to avoid officers acting beyond the bounds of propriety. The provisions of the USA PATRIOT Improvement and Reauthorization Act of 2005 seem to be an improvement in that regard considering its limitations on the period of a delayed notice. However, the grounds upon which a delayed-notice search warrant may be issued remain rather sweeping.

In the first place, a showing of "reasonable cause to believe that providing immediate notification of the execution of the warrant may have an adverse result" shall constitute a "good reason for delay," which has been related by the courts to

[11] *United States v. Villegas,* 899 F.2d 1324 (2nd Cir. 1990), 1337. Section 213(2)(b)(2) of the USA PATRIOT Act, however, also allows the seizure of tangible property during the sneak-and-peek search, when the court finds "reasonable necessity for the seizure."

[12] *United States v. Villegas,* 899 F.2d 1324 (2nd Cir. 1990), 1337.

[13] Smith 2003, 439.

[14] As alleged by the plaintiffs, *Mayfield v. United States,* 504 F.Supp.2d 1023 (D.Or. 2007), 1028.

the presence of necessity.[15] To further circumscribe this ground for a delayed notice, the definition of an 'adverse result' in § 2705 is referred to, which provides rather precisely defined situations (such as fleeing from prosecution, the destruction of evidence and the intimidation of witness), except for the last ground of "otherwise seriously jeopardizing an investigation or unduly delaying a trial." Because the latter may only be used in combination with another ground, it shall be considered whether "otherwise seriously jeopardizing an investigation" is a sufficiently circumscribed ground. It is obvious that by the broad formulation of this last ground a reservoir of grounds has been created and, consequently, not all reasons that may be raised under this ground will also provide a "good reason for delay." Hence, except for examining whether these statutory grounds are met, the issuing judge will need to assess, as an additional and final touchstone, whether the reason is also a "good reason" that reasonably necessitates the delay of notification, which assessment shall be based upon all the circumstances of the case. In the light of previous reasoning regarding the compatibility of a physical search with a delayed notice with the Fourth Amendment, as provided in different federal courts' decisions, all circumstances of the particular case shall be assessed in order to determine the reasonableness of the sneak-and-peek search, which shall be done in addition to examining whether the statutory requirements have been met.

In the second place, also the period for which a delay is granted shall be sufficiently circumscribed. Section 213 prescribed—in accordance with earlier decisions of federal courts—that the warrant must provide for the time within which reasonable notice must be given, without, however, setting a limit for the period after which notification will be *per se* unreasonable. The USA PATRIOT Act Improvement and Reauthorization Act of 2005 has offered an important improvement in that regard, by requiring that notification shall be given within a reasonable period, but not later than 30 days after execution. Extensions may be provided for "good cause shown", but not exceeding 90 days.[16] Here the statutory provision clearly deviates from the time limit of seven days set by the federal appellate courts as an initial indication of what should be considered as reasonable. Since *Freitas* it has been taken as a rule of thumb that notice shall be given no later than seven days after the surreptitious entry, unless good cause is shown.[17] However, courts differ on the question whether the specific conditions regarding the notification provision to be given in the warrant are inherent to the Fourth Amendment (as to the *Freitas* court) or are an interpretation of Rule 41 of the Federal Rules of Criminal Procedure (the position taken by the Second Circuit Court in *Villegas* and, more strongly, in *Pangburn*).[18] In 2000 the Fourth Circuit

---

[15] *United States v. Villegas,* 899 F.2d 1324 (2nd Cir. 1990), 1337 and *United States v. Freitas,* 800 F.2d 1451 (9th Cir. 1968), 1456.

[16] Which was also the time limit set by the Department of Justice, which determined this period through relating it to the notification requirements of Title III. See Sect. 6.2.1.3 (footnote 37).

[17] See e.g.: *States v. Villegas,* 899 F.2d 1324 (2nd Cir. 1990), 1337 and *United States v. Pangburn*, 983 F.2d 449 (2nd Cir. 1993), 453.

[18] See: *United States v. Pangburn*, 983 F.2d 449 (2nd Cir. 1993), 454-455.

Court also dealt with a warrant for surreptitious entry, where notice was given 45 days after executing the warrant. The Fourth Circuit seemed to rely on *Pangburn* to deal with a surreptitious entry upon a validly issued warrant as an issue not covered by the Fourth Amendment. The court therefore found no basis to render the 45-day delay unconstitutional.[19] For that reason, and lacking any Supreme Court guidance regarding a delayed notice, it will be difficult to demonstrate that on the basis of the previous decisions of the lower courts the time limit provided in the USA PATRIOT Act will be unconstitutional. Moreover, because courts have also rendered longer periods of delay reasonable while applying the *Villegas* standard and because courts may apply, by analogy, the 90-day period of Title III to determine what is reasonable, it seems unlikely that courts will hold the 30-day standard, with possible extensions upon good cause being shown, to be unconstitutional at face value. Nevertheless, it can be concluded that the current time limit, with a possibility to extend the notice for an indefinite time, will be insufficiently circumscribed to serve the interest of the people whose property has been searched or, possibly, under the current provision, even seized to challenge the legitimacy of the sneak-and-peek (or in some circumstances sneak-and-steal[20]) warrant that has been issued.

Although there seems to be no doubt that the possibility of delayed notice warrants as such does not violate the Fourth Amendment, it is important that the powers granted to the government are sufficiently circumscribed to avoid executing officers carrying out the covert search without propriety. Additional guidance by the Supreme Court in that regard will be desirable. On the basis of the view taken and the guidance given by the Courts of the Ninth, Second and Fourth Circuit, the delayed notice provision cannot be rendered unconstitutional on its face. However, the courts that have dealt with the issue seem to require that this sneak-and-peek power is sufficiently precisely defined. More in general, the covert nature of the search makes the delayed-notice search a very powerful law enforcement tool, which is a considerably intrusive infringement on the privacy of citizens with a potential for abuse. For that reason, once a choice has been made to statutorily regulate this tool, it is important to clearly define the grounds for a delay, the limits on the execution of the surreptitious entry and the limits on the delay of the notification. The current regulation, in particular the sweeping last ground for delays and the indefinite possibility of extending the delay by periods of 30 days, seems to lack sufficient precision or limitation. As a consequence of a delayed notification, also judicial control over the government's search power is adversely impacted or, in the case of an indefinite extension, even excluded. This deprives citizens of the important check on arbitrary searches and a remedy to challenge the legitimacy of the search in the courts.

---

[19] *United States v. Simons,* 206 F.3d 392 (4th Cir. 2000), 403.

[20] As to: Shumate 2006.

### 7.2.1.3 Pen Registers and Trap/Trace Devices

For the use of pen registers and trap or trace devices an *ex parte* order is sufficient, which can be issued without probable cause upon a showing of relevance to an ongoing criminal investigation. Pen register or trap/trace authority does not violate the Fourth Amendment, because the technique was understood by the Supreme Court as not violating someone's reasonable expectation of privacy as the information that could be obtained was limited to one's phone number (dialing and signaling information), which concerns only identifying information without revealing the contents of the communication.[21] Hence, the use of pen register and trap trace authority is regulated through weaker restraints provided in a separate Chapter in Title 18[22]: a judicial order is required, which will be given upon a certification by the government that the information "likely to be obtained" by the installation of the pen register or trap or trace device is "relevant to an ongoing criminal investigation."[23] Through the amendment of the USA PATRIOT Act, however, the nature of the technique has changed as the information that can be intercepted has been expanded to include more privacy-sensitive information, namely not only dialing information, but also routing, addressing and signaling information, which may include internet search terms, websites visited, the addressees of e-mails and the size of e-mails. The content of communications is explicitly excluded.

Courts have so far only assessed the expansion of the use of pen registers to obtain cell site information. In a 2006 case District Judge Kaplan assessed whether the information obtained through pen registers and trap/trace devices applied to cell phones may extend to location information on the basis of transmission information received by the nearest antenna tower. The district court allowed the extension of the information that can be intercepted on the basis of the provisions of the Chapter, as already amended by the USA PATRIOT Act, that regulate the use of pen registers and trap/devices and in conjunction with section 18 U.S.C. § 2703(d), upon a showing of 'specific and articulable facts' demonstrating the relevance of the information to the ongoing investigation (which is the standard of the latter provision).[24] However, the Court did not resolve the related Fourth Amendment issues that arise because of this extension. It only noted that according to *Smith v. Maryland* (1979)[25] one does not have a reasonable expectation of privacy to one's phone numbers and, according to *United States v. Karo* (1984),[26]

---

[21] *Smith v. Maryland,* 42 U.S. 735, 99 S.Ct. 2577 (1979), 742-746 and *United States v. Karo,* 468 U.S. 705 104 S.Ct. 3296 (1984), 712-713.

[22] Title 18, Chapter 119: 18 U.S.C. § 3121-3127.

[23] 18 U.S.C. § 3123(a)(2).

[24] *In re: Application of the United States for an Order for Prospective Cell Site Information on a Certain Cellular Telephone,* 460 F.Supp.2d 448 (S.D.N.Y. 2006), 460-461.

[25] *Smith v. Maryland,* 42 U.S. 735, 99 S.Ct. 2577 (1979).

[26] *United States v. Karo,* 468 U.S. 705 104 S.Ct. 3296 (1984).

the user of a cell phone has at least some reasonable expectation of privacy with regard to his location if this location concerns a private home.[27] The interpretation of the scope of pen registers provided by Judge Kaplan is still strongly disputed. In previous as well as later court rulings the extension to cell site information upon this 'lower' evidentiary standard—although higher than the standard of 18 U.S.C. § 3123 of relevance to an ongoing criminal investigation—has been rejected, reasoning that the acquiring of this type of information is not intended by the current regulation of pen register and trap/trace device authority and, hence, probable cause, will be required.[28]

The broadening of the information that can be intercepted by pen registers and trap/trace devices, through the amendments of the USA PATRIOT Act, concerns, however, information of a different nature. Nevertheless, similar questions as those dealt with in these cases with regard to cell site information arise under the Fourth Amendment. Like in these cases, it is possible to apply the reasoning of the Supreme Court decisions regarding the use of pen registers or trap/trace devices in order to determine whether one may have a reasonable expectation of privacy with regard to the information that is currently covered by 'dialing, routing, addressing and signaling information.'

In *Smith v. Maryland* (1979) the Supreme Court only assessed the constitutionality of the devices assuming that the information intercepted is limited to phone numbers. In *Karo v. United States* the Supreme Court set as a minimum that someone at least has a reasonable expectation of privacy with regard to one's location when at home. Whether someone has a reasonable expectation of privacy with regard to internet search terms and routing information of e-mails will need to be determined on the basis of the reasonable expectation of privacy test of *Katz v. United States*: does someone justifiably rely on an expectation of privacy that society is prepared to recognize as reasonable with regard to Internet search terms and navigation behavior and the addressees of e-mails sent. Applying the test to these types of information can be compared with the reasoning of *Smith v. Maryland* applying the test to phone numbers. The pen register is still installed on the phone company's property and, hence, someone's property has not been invaded or physically intruded by the police.[29] The fact that the devices do not hear sound and thus do not reveal the contents of any communication and, in addition, that everyone who uses a phone realizes that they "must 'convey' phone numbers to the telephone company", which are for legitimate purposes also

---

[27] *In re: Application of the United States for an Order for Prospective Cell Site Information on a Certain Cellular Telephone,* 460 F.Supp.2d 448 (S.D.N.Y. 2006), 462.

[28] See e.g. *In the Matter of an Application of the United States of America for an Order Authorizing the Use of a Pen Register with Caller Identification Device Cell Site Location Authority on a Cellular Telephone,* 2009 WL 159187 (S.D.N.Y. 2009) and *In re Applications of the United States of America for Orders Pursuant to Title 18, United States Code, Section 2703(d),* 509 F.Supp.2d 76 (D.Mass. 2007). See for a discussion of the Fourth Amendment issues involved in the tracking of cell site information: McLaughlin 2007.

[29] Compare: *Smith v. Maryland,* 442 U.S. 735, 99 S.Ct. 2577 (1979), 741.

recorded by the phone company, has resulted in the conclusion by the Supreme Court that one does not have a reasonable expectation to the information that is intercepted by pen registers.[30] Arguably, intercepting the addressees of e-mails is similar to dialing information of phone numbers, as the contents of e-mails will not be intercepted and the routing information will, for sending purposes, necessarily also be transmitted to the internet service provider. This would also correspond with the decision of the Sixth Circuit Court in *Warshak v. United States* (2010), assessing a court order under 18 U.S.C. § 2703(d) for obtaining from an Internet Service Provider also the contents of e-mail conversations.[31] The Court considered whether the users of an e-mail account, stored on a 'third-party' server, have a reasonable expectation of privacy with regard to the content of their e-mails. The Court concluded that the user does have a reasonable expectation of privacy with regard to the content of the e-mail—"given the fundamental similarities between email and traditional forms of communications",[32]—for which reason probable cause would be required to obtain e-mail content. The fact that the third-party Internet Service Provider has "the mere *ability* (…) to access the contents of the communication cannot be sufficient to extinguish a reasonable expectation of privacy."[33] This judgment particularly focused on the *contents* of e-mail. Previously, in *Warshak I*, the Sixth Circuit Court explicitly distinguished between the "subscriber information and related records" and the contents of e-mail. Applying the 'third-party' doctrine, similar to *Smith v. Maryland*, it concluded that the e-mail user does not have a reasonable expectation of privacy with regard to the former.[34] Considering also this distinction between e-mail content and subscriber information, it can be concluded that the broadening of the information that can be intercepted by pen registers and trap and trace devices to e-mail addressees and e-mail size will not give rise to Fourth Amendment issues.

Internet search terms and websites visited, however, concern more privacy-sensitive information, to which one may at least have a subjective expectation of privacy. Whether this subjective expectation of privacy is also an expectation that society is prepared to recognize as reasonable will again depend on whether someone is aware of the fact that the information will be revealed to a third party, which implies an assumption of an awareness of the risk of disclosure of that third party to the government.[35] The Supreme Court relied on this latter consideration in *Kyllo v. United States* to draw a general line in Fourth Amendment application to new technological developments. The Fourth Amendment can be invoked when new technologically developed information tools are acquired to gain information

[30] *Smith v. Maryland,* 442 U.S. 735, 99 S.Ct. 2577 (1979), 742.

[31] *Warshak v. United States,* 631 F.3d 266 (6th Cir. 2010).

[32] *Warshak v. United States,* 631 F.3d 266 (6th Cir. 2010), 285.

[33] *Warshak v. United States,* 631 F.3d 266 (6th Cir. 2010), 286.

[34] *Warshak v. United States,* 490 F.3d 455 (6th Cir. 2007), 471.

[35] *Smith v. Maryland,* 442 U.S. 735, 99 S.Ct. 2577 (1979), 742.

about the interior of a home, unless such tools are "in general public use."[36] Considering this past Supreme Court reasoning, it will be unlikely that the Supreme Court will hold the current regulation of pen register and trap/trace authority without the requirement of probable cause to be unconstitutional only on the basis of broadening the scope of information that can be intercepted, as realized by the amendment of section 216 of the USA PATRIOT Act of 2001. Nevertheless, it is clear that the government has sought the outer limits of the regulation in order to derive as much information as possible with regard to a person on the basis of dialing, routing and signaling information. It seems that technological advances have surpassed the Supreme Court decisions on pen registers and trap/trace devices based on the very limited scope of information that could be intercepted through these tools.[37] Currently, the distinction between content and non-content information is less clear than at the time of these decisions. Moreover, with current technology the contents of e-mail communications can be intercepted together with non-content information such as the addressees. Subsequently, software such as the FBI's Carnivore system filters, without the intervention of a human being, the content from the non-content information.[38] Such a system is, of course, not free from risks of abuse or mistake, which may result in considerable privacy invasions.

### 7.2.2 A Trend in the Case Law Towards Diminishing the Protective Meaning of the Fourth Amendment for National Security or Terrorism Prevention Interests

The cases dealt with in Sect. 6.2.2 in order to demonstrate a trend in the case law of the courts focusing on crime control and prevention at the expense of usual Fourth Amendment requirements can be divided into two categories: 1) cases that include terrorism prevention or the protection of national security under existing doctrines that exempt particular situations from ordinary criminal investigative searches and, hence, from usual Fourth Amendment requirements; and, 2) cases that use terrorism prevention or the protection of national security as a factor to be considered in the weight to be attached to Fourth Amendment requirements (e.g. when applying the 'totality of circumstances' test) and, therefore, eroding Fourth Amendment protections. Both categories will be dealt with separately.

[36] *Kyllo v. United States,* 533 U.S. 27, 121 S.Ct. 2038 (2001), 34. Justice John Paul Stevens dissented and strongly rejected this limitation on Fourth Amendment application as it can be expected that the exclusion of Fourth Amendment applicability to technical devices also used by the general public may give rise to serious privacy concerns in the future due to the rapid development of technology. See also: Casey 2008, 995-996.

[37] Compare: Casey 2008, 1027-1033.

[38] Smith 2003, 448-449.

#### 7.2.2.1 Applying the Special Needs Doctrine to Searches for the Prevention of Terrorism

New exceptions to Fourth Amendment requirements accepted in the case law shall be compared to exceptions created prior to 9/11, 2001 in order to determine whether the interest of preventing terrorism has, after 9/11, become a ground for deviating from conventional Fourth Amendment protections. The general doctrine for exempting particular situations that need to be distinguished from 'ordinary law enforcement' from the usual Fourth Amendment requirements is the 'special needs doctrine.' Currently 'the protection of the national security' or the 'prevention of terrorism' has been identified as a special need, for which reason an escape from regular Fourth Amendment requirements has been justified. This does not concern an isolated development affecting only the Fourth Amendment. Also under the Fifth Amendment a significant broader 'public safety exception' than would apply in ordinary criminal cases has been considered justified in order to be able to interrogate terrorist suspects concerning terrorist threats before informing them of their *Miranda* rights.[39]

In *Macwade v. Kelly* the New York Court held the random search of bags due to the 'Container Inspection Program' in the New York Subway to be a special need, which allows police officers to search bags without a warrant and without probable cause.[40] The purpose of the Program, introduced shortly after the London Underground bombings, was to curtail the possibility of a terrorist attack on the New York Subway system by randomly searching containers that may contain explosives in order to both screen persons and to deter persons from committing an attack on the Subway system.[41] The Supreme Court has developed the 'special needs doctrine' to allow searches without a warrant and upon less than probable cause or even without any form of individualized suspicion in the situation that the search serves a "special need" of the government "distinct from ordinary law enforcement." When such a special need is present, the ultimate touchstone for compatibility with the Fourth Amendment is 'reasonableness,' without the warrant requirement and probable cause requirement being essential factors for the reasonableness. Under this doctrine courts have allowed searches without a warrant and even without individualized suspicion in different situations where the 'administrative purpose' was the primary purpose of the search rather than law enforcement purposes, such as checkpoints for sobriety regarding alcohol or drugs on highways, controls on drug use by employees or school athletes and airport

---

[39] As instructed by a (classified) FBI Memorandum of October 21, 2001. Savage 2011, 16. See on this subject: Kris 2011, 71-77.

[40] *Macwade v. Kelly,* 460 F.3d 260 (2nd Cir. 2006), see Sect. 6.2.2.

[41] Coveny 2007, 333.

security checks[42] to promote air security.[43] Except for the main purpose of the search, an important factor to consider when applying the 'special needs' doctrine has always been the diminished expectation of privacy of the persons subjected to the search, such as probationers, school children and employees of a particular company. Furthermore, there is also the interest of effectively ensuring that the 'special need' is balanced against the privacy intrusion.[44]

When we consider the wide acceptance by courts (as well as by society) of the appliance of the special-needs doctrine to bag searches at airports to prevent air piracy, it seems comparably likely that in times when attacks on the subway system are an actual threat, similar bag searches in the subway may be considered a special need. This special need then concerns the prevention of an attack on the subway system. To be acceptable under the special needs doctrine, the prevention of an attack must be the purpose of the search, rather than searching for contraband in bags, which concerns clearly a law enforcement purpose. For that reason, to render the random inspection of bags in the New York Subway reasonable by applying the special needs doctrine, it is important that the purpose of preventing terrorist attacks is sufficiently urgent and realistic to avoid situations in which it is more likely that the random search is used to find contraband as evidence for criminal prosecutions. The latter may even be more likely when law enforcement officers conduct the bag inspections, like in *Macwade*. Nevertheless, highway and border inspections by the police were also already accepted under special-needs reasoning.

For that reason, courts considering the reasonableness of this type of search must primarily take into consideration the legitimate interest to undertake these random inspections in subway systems for the prevention of attacks and the effectiveness of such inspections (or the ineffectiveness of requiring a warrant for the realization of the special need), in order to avoid abusing safety inspections for law enforcement purposes. This is even more urgent since the police are responsible for conducting the bag searches, contrary to most special need cases where other people conduct the searches (e.g. teachers or airport security personnel). Requiring some sort of demonstration of the urgency of pursuing this legitimate interest for the purpose of preventing attacks may be compared with the approach taken by Justice Scalia in his dissenting opinion in *National Treasury Employee's Union v. Von Raab* (1989). Justice Scalia was worried about the possibility of

---

42 Airport security checks were permitted under 'special needs reasoning' by courts already prior to the explicit development of the special needs doctrine in *New Jersey v. T.L.O.* (1985), see e.g. *United States v. Skipwith,* 482 F.2d 1272 (5th Cir. 1973) and *United States v. Edwards,* 498 F.2d 496 (2nd Cir. 1974). The Court reasoned that the purpose of the search, namely to prevent persons taking dangerous items on board of an aircraft and, thus, to prevent air piracy, outweighed the commensurate privacy concerns. The Court also noted that the searches would be illegal if used "as a general means of enforcing the criminal law." See also: Power 2010, 656-657 and Coveny 2007, 352.

43 See Sect. 5.3.2.1.1.1 and footnote 302 of Chap. 5.

44 Sydejko 2006, 236-238.

conducting drug testing without a true connection with a problem necessitating such testing, which would be an "immolation of privacy and human dignity in symbolic opposition to drug use." Hence, courts must demonstrate the "social necessity" of the 'special need' served by the search.[45] This may be compared with a more generalized group suspicion regarding the prevention of the threat involved.[46] After demonstrating such a social necessity or urgency for a random inspection, the efficacy of the inspection for curtailing the threat involved also needs to be demonstrated.[47] It is conceivable that bag inspections in the subway of a major US city are sufficiently urgent in the context of the post-9/11 era and shortly after the attacks on the subway systems of Madrid and London, which can be founded e.g. on intelligence reports providing for threat analyses or risk assessments. Moreover, bag inspections at the entrances to the Subway system are presumably efficient for the interception of those bringing in explosives and knowledge about the presence of such inspections may also have a deterring effect.[48] Presumably, because a judgment on the efficacy of the inspection necessarily concerns a (classified) assessment on behalf of the officials, who are themselves responsible for the measures aiming at the prevention of terrorism, which assessment cannot be 'second-guessed' and will always concern the 'future unknown.'[49] Considering the interest of preventing an attack on the subway system, which is not only a governmental interest but, in the first place, the interest of those using the subway and, hence, a public interest, it will be reasonable to consider the expectation of privacy of those commuters who are subjected to random bag inspections to be diminished. Hence, the reasonableness of the search seems, to a large extent, to be based on the urgency of the public concern of preventing a terrorist attack, which is likely to be more urgent in a time of social unrest and fear like in the post-9/11 era and, especially, shortly after the attacks on the London Underground.[50] Nevertheless, special need searches for the purpose of preventing terrorism will need to be based on some factual information regarding

---

45 *National Treasury Employees Union v. Von Raab,* 489 U.S. 656, 109 S.Ct. 1348 (1989), 681.

46 Compare: Slobogin 2007, 613.

47 Compare the factors of *Illinois v. Lidster* (2004) (Sect. 5.3.2.1.1.1), also applied in *Macwade v. Kelly,* 460 F.3d 260 (2nd Cir. 2006), including 'the degree to which the search advances the public concern'. See: Coveny 2007, 370-372.

48 The efficacy of the Container Inspection Program and the level of deterrence have also been criticized, considering the possibility to walk away when encountering such inspection and testimony in the case of *Macwade* has indicated that also deterrence was not likely to be achieved by the Program. See Coveny 2007, 371.

49 See *Macwade v. Kelly*, 460 F.3d 260 (2nd Cir. 2006), 274.

50 The public fear of future terrorist attacks brings about a level of tolerance for far-going governmental measures (including giving up Fourth Amendment protections to allow expedient search powers) taken for the purpose of preventing future terrorist attacks. See Luna 2009, 120-121 (providing a criminological analysis of the relation between fear and the deviation from traditional restraints on employing criminal law and criminal procedural law). Albeit according to this criminological research fear is not the correct basis for deviating from Fourth Amendment requirements designed to protect the civil liberty of privacy.

the threat and, presumably, be efficient in curtailing the threat in order to render the search reasonable for safety purposes.

To sum up, random inspections or searches on the basis of some sort of individualized suspicion[51] may be justified under the special needs doctrine, when the circumstances are defined by some particular conditions. There must be some proof regarding the presence of the special need of 'preventing a terrorist attack' or 'protecting the national security.' The place of the search must reasonably be a place at risk from acts of terrorism, rendering the inspections necessary and to avoid situations where safety inspections are used as a means to pursue law enforcement aims. Only in that situation may the special needs of prevention and protection be considered as a social necessity and, for that reason, a shared interest of society and the government, thereby justifying a diminished expectation of privacy on the part of commuters. As an additional protection to avoid abuse for law enforcement purposes not related to the threat, one could argue for adopting a prohibition—which would also be an exception to the plain view doctrine—on the introduction, as evidence in a criminal prosecution, of any contraband found during such inspections.[52] Such a prohibition should of course not apply if the police have found contraband related to the threat justifying the special need search, such as explosives. Nevertheless, considering the current state of the case law regarding the plain view doctrine and the absence of such a prohibition (although the fact that information is not communicated to the police has been interpreted by the courts as an indication that the search pursued a special need other than ordinary law enforcement purposes) in other special needs cases, such a prohibition will break with the current law and it is unlikely that courts will prohibit the introduction of evidence found in plain view during a legitimately executed search authority. In addition, in *Whren v. United States* (1996) the Supreme Court accepted a search of a car on the basis of a minor traffic violation, whereas the subjective intention of the law enforcement officers was to search for narcotics, but they were unable to establish a founded suspicion regarding the possession of narcotics.[53]

Extending the exempting special needs doctrine to include the special need of 'terrorism prevention' or 'protecting the national security' may also be related to the distinction made in the *Keith* decision between national security surveillance and the surveillance of "ordinary crime." In *Keith* the Supreme Court held that the Fourth Amendment also applied to intelligence surveillance activities conducted for the purpose of investigating domestic threats to national security. The Court then added that the Fourth Amendment standards applied to these intelligence investigative activities may be different from the Fourth Amendment and Title III

[51] This type of search will reasonably be either random or selective. When selective, such selection shall not be conducted solely on the basis of racial characteristics (e.g. selecting persons with a Middle-Eastern appearance only), but on the basis of some sort of individualized suspicion being more than racial characteristics only in order to avoid discrimination.

[52] Simmons 2010, 916-921.

[53] *Whren v. United States,* 517 U.S. 806, 116 S.Ct. 1769 (1996).

standards that apply to law enforcement surveillance as the "domestic security surveillances may involve different policy and practical considerations from the surveillance of 'ordinary crime'."[54] The FISA Court of Review has *In re: Sealed Case* (2002) explicitly related this distinction made by the Court in *Keith* (indeed using similar language as the courts applying the special needs doctrine) to the special needs doctrine.[55] The FISA Court of Review explicitly interpreted the acceptance of a different statutory framework to be the consequence of considering the government interest in collecting foreign intelligence information as an interest (or a special need) distinct from ordinary law enforcement. By referring to the special need cases of *City of Indianapolis v. Edmond* (2000) and *United States v. Martinez-Fuerte* (1976) the FISA Court of Review held that as long as "FISA's general programmatic purpose" concerns the protection of the nation "against terrorist and espionage threats directed by foreign powers" this purpose needs to be distinguished from "ordinary crime control" and, therefore, when balancing the interests involved, including "the most serious threat our country faces", surveillance under the amended FISA is reasonable.[56]

In *Keith* and *In re: Sealed* the statutory regimes of national security investigations and law enforcement investigations have been distinguished in order to assess the constitutionality of the investigative activities under the Fourth Amendment. The purpose of protecting national security is decisive for rendering the activities during national security investigations reasonable, which is comparable to the current extension of the special needs doctrine to law enforcement search activities for the purpose of terrorism prevention. Both for these intelligence investigations and for law enforcement searches like in *Macwade v. Kelly* it will be important to consider in how far the special need search may also be used for law enforcement (evidence-gathering) purposes. In *City of Indianapolis v. Edmonds* the Supreme Court decided that the search was unreasonable because the primary purpose was not to make the street safer but to catch drug users or traffickers.[57] Hence, in the light of this decision it seems that when a search is assessed under the special needs doctrine only plain view evidence gathering is permissible when the primary purpose of the search is a government special need other than law enforcement. Section 7.4.2 will further elaborate on the relation between the purpose of FISA surveillance to be distinguished from Title III surveillance and the special needs doctrine applied to 'administrative interests' of law enforcement, thereby justifying deviations from the regular restraints on law enforcement investigative activities.

---

[54] *United States v. United States District Court (Keith)*, 407 U.S. 297, 92 S.Ct. 2125 (1972), 322. See in more detail Sect. 5.2.2.3.1.

[55] *In re: Sealed Case*, 310 F.3d 717 (FISA Ct. Rev. 2002), 745-746.

[56] *Ibid.*, 746. See also: Power 2010.

[57] Differently: *Michigan Department of State Police v. Sitz*, 496 U.S. 444, 110 S.Ct. 2481 (1990) where the primary purpose was to curtail the grave threat of driving while intoxicated for society, outweighing the privacy interest also when the primary tool was a law enforcement tool conducted by the police.

#### 7.2.2.2 Balancing Liberty Against Security in Fourth Amendment Analysis in Terrorism Cases

The contents of Sect. 6.2.2 have also demonstrated that in the post-9/11 era several courts have used the interest of preventing terrorism or protecting the national security as a reason to diminish the protective meaning of probable cause and a warrant. More in general, courts, ruling under the influence of the societal impact of the recent confrontation with terrorist attacks, have mainly focused on the interest of crime control and expedient law enforcement, which have further watered down Fourth Amendment requirements and the remedy of excluding Fourth Amendment violations. This section will draw some conclusions as to the current protective meaning of the Fourth Amendment requirements due to the recent interpretation of these requirements by courts.

The cases dealt with in Sect. 6.2.2 concern an extension of those situations in which the *Terry v. Ohio* stop and frisk is permitted (*United States v. Ramos* (2010)) and the exclusion of the applicability of Fourth Amendment protections to searches of US citizens outside the United States (*In re Terrorist Bombings of U.S. Embassies in East Africa* (2008)). In both cases the 'threat of terrorism' was used as a ground for granting an exception to Fourth Amendment requirements. Furthermore, considering several other (non-terrorism) cases of the post-9/11 era in which the meaning of Fourth Amendment protections have been watered down, the interest of efficient and expeditious law enforcement has often prevailed over the protective meaning of Fourth Amendment requirements in an era characterized by risk-policing, increased societal unrest and fear.

In some of the cases dealt with in Sect. 6.2.2 the interest of preventing terrorism or protecting national security has explicitly been balanced against the privacy interest of the persons involved. The seriousness of the terrorist threat seems to convince the courts rather easily to rule against meaningful protection through the Fourth Amendment. More in general, the focus on security and for that purpose expedient law enforcement has pushed courts into the direction of focusing on crime control. This development has consequences for the protective meaning of probable cause and a warrant and for the effectiveness of the remedy of the exclusion of evidence and thus to the protective meaning of the Fourth Amendment as such. The protective elements of the Fourth Amendment will be dealt with separately below to draw some conclusions as to their current protective meaning, as a consequence of the focus on the prevention of terrorism in the case law of the post-9/11 era.

##### 7.2.2.2.1 Probable Cause

Probable cause shall be understood as a protective value reflecting the compromise between the sword and shield objective of criminal procedural law in order to "safeguard citizens from rash and unreasonable interferences with privacy and from unfounded charges of crime (…) [and to] give fair leeway for enforcing the law in the community's protection."[58] The 'totality of circumstances' test[59] adopted by the Supreme Court to determine the presence of probable cause in a particular situation reflects this balancing of interests and the commensurate flexibility of the standard. Considering this role of probable cause and the manner of demonstrating its presence, it seems that the standard is designed to fluctuate along with the urgency of investigative activities and, thus, will not obstruct investigative activities aimed at intercepting the planning of a terrorist crime. However, probable cause is also a crucial and arguably the most important threshold for exercising criminal procedural powers, as it is the reason, the legitimization, for criminal procedural action against someone. The watering down of the meaning of probable cause by lowering the substance on which it is based because of giving law enforcement officers sufficient leeway to act for the prevention of terrorism or, more in general, in the interest of crime control or prevention, shall be assessed from this protective background.

In *United States v. Ramos* (2010) the First Circuit Court accepted the stopping of a vehicle on the basis of circumstances (the 'Middle Eastern' appearance of the occupants of the car), which would be insufficient to establish a reasonable, articulable suspicion, the standard adopted for such a stop in *Terry v. Ohio*, in times or at places where a terrorist threat is not present.[60] This conclusion was drawn after a totality of circumstances analysis in which the "lessons of Madrid" and the "highly timely" risk of future attacks "involve[ing] many lives" were decisive for rendering the stop reasonable and, consequently, diminishing the already lowered standard of reasonable suspicion required for the *Terry* stop.[61]

Other court decisions of the post-9/11 era have, as described in Sect. 6.2.2, especially watered down the requirement of probable cause by balancing the interest involved and then finding the search reasonable without the presence of probable cause as a standard with clear substantial protective meaning. As to its 'traditional' definition provided in *Brinegar* (1949): "the facts and circumstances within their (the officers') knowledge and of which they had reasonably trustworthy information (are) sufficient in themselves to warrant a man of reasonable caution in the belief that an offense has been or is being committed."[62] In recent cases the Supreme Court has explained the probable cause standard in less substantial terms, otherwise used to describe the lower standard of reasonable suspicion. Here, also the interest of allowing expedient law enforcement action outweighed a higher protective threshold for the use of search powers. The reasonableness of the search has been, especially when the need to act is more urgent, decisive for the compatibility of the search with the Fourth Amendment, whereas

---

[58] *Brinegar v. United States,* 338 U.S. 160, 69 S.Ct. 1302 (1949), 176, see Sect. 5.3.2.1.1.2.

[59] See Sect. 5.3.2.1.1.1.

[60] *United States v. Ramos,* 629 F.3d 60 (1st Cir. 2010). See Sect. 5.3.2.1.1.1.

[61] *Ibid.*, 67-68.

[62] *Brinegar v. United States,* 338 U.S. 160, 69 S. Ct. 1302 (1949), p. 175-176. See Sect. 5.3.2.1.1.1.

probable cause is then not considered as an essential requirement for reasonableness. When bluntly assessing the reasonableness of a search on the basis of the balancing test provided in *Camara v. Municipal Court* (1967),[63] without including the requirement of probable cause and a warrant as essential elements, any urgent need to search can be justified on the basis of balancing the interests involved.

However, traditionally probable cause has served as the basis for reasonableness in the absence of a warrant.[64] The probable cause requirement has been the requirement that, if met, automatically renders the search reasonable, save for the important exception of the *Terry* stop and frisk. As explicitly stated in *Virginia v. Moore* (2008): "when an officer has probable cause to believe a person committed even a minor crime in his presence, the balancing of private and public interests is not in doubt."[65] Exceptions to the warrant requirement have always been broader (e.g. under exigent circumstances or with regard to subjects covered by a more limited expectation of privacy such as automobiles), which affirms the importance of probable cause as a crucial requirement and as the requirement compensating for the absence of a warrant. Moreover, both from the perspective of the interests that the Fourth Amendment seeks to protect and from the institutional justification for the employment, on behalf of the government, of criminal investigative techniques, the probable cause requirement has a crucial restraining and protective meaning. The Fourth Amendment requirements come into effect once someone's reasonable expectation of privacy has been violated.[66] Only then must the governmental search activities be considered to interfere with privacy rights, for which reason the Fourth Amendment requirements apply in order to protect against unfounded and arbitrary interferences with privacy rights and against an overreaching government.

Considering the described cases in which courts have watered down the meaning of probable cause by examining the search on the basis of its reasonableness and attaching more weight to the interest of preventing a terrorist attack or in general of "compelling law enforcement needs,"[67] the protective value of the probable cause standard has become less meaningful and increasingly flexible. Considering the importance of the protective value traditionally offered by the probable cause requirement, one may doubt whether the reasonableness test alone may offer sufficient comparable protection when this test exclusively concerns the balancing of the interests involved. If we take into account the protective goals, in particular probable cause as the justification for using criminal investigative powers and excluding arbitrary interference with privacy rights, a form of

---

[63] *Camara v. Municipal Court*, 387 U.S. 523, 87 S.Ct. 1727 (1967), 536-537. See Sect. 5.3.2.1.1.1.

[64] Section 5.3.2.1.3.

[65] *Virginia v. Moore*, 553 U.S. 164, 128 S.Ct. 1598 (2008), 1604 (see Sect. 5.3.2.1.1.1).

[66] *Katz v. United States,* 389 U.S. 347, 88 S.Ct. 507 (1967).

[67] *Brigham City v. Stuart,* 547 U.S. 398, 126 S.Ct. 1943 (2006), p. 403 and 406, see Sect. 6.2.2.

suspicion will be an essential restraint on the government's criminal search power and shall be understood as the core of Fourth Amendment protection. Nevertheless, the current interpretation of the clauses of the Fourth Amendment have paved the way for treating probable cause (or even another form of suspicion) as not being a mandatory requirement for reasonableness.[68]

It can be concluded that the current approach of the courts dealing with the Fourth Amendment probable cause requirement has considerable consequences for the protective objective of criminal procedural law and these consequences are fundamental, especially because the value of the probable cause requirement as a safeguard and restraint has now become rather unpredictable without clear guidance to the lower courts on how to apply the requirement. This has resulted in an approach which is solely guided by the reasonableness of the search in which probable cause or a suspicion in general no longer has a central and crucial role.

#### 7.2.2.2.2 Warrant

The Supreme Court held in its landmark judgment in *Katz* concerning electronic surveillance that the warrant requirement is mandatory under the Fourth Amendment: "searches conducted outside the judicial process, without prior approval by judge or magistrate, are per se unreasonable under the Fourth Amendment."[69] *Ex ante* judicial review has thus traditionally been understood as a shield requirement that is essential for legitimizing law enforcement officers to conduct searches that fall under the scope of the Fourth Amendment. Regardless of the protective importance and the assumed fixed nature as a Fourth Amendment requirement, also prior to the events of 9/11, many instances have been considered by the Supreme Court to justify warrantless searches. These instances typically have the character of emergency or exigent circumstances, but they also include situations in which the police cannot reasonably be expected to have obtained a warrant prior to the search. In addition, Title III also includes statutory grounds for an exception from the warrant requirement, which have, similar to the grounds for exceptions developed in Fourth Amendment jurisprudence regarding physical searches, emergency or exigency characteristics.[70]

---

[68] See Sect. 5.1.4.1. Textualists would therefore likely reject such an interpretation of the Fourth Amendment, because the language suggests that the drafters' intention was different (see e.g. Amar 1997, 17-20 and 31-32 and Arcila 2010, 1294). However, when solely looking at the purpose of the protection offered, the restraints that should be imposed on the governmental exertion of criminal procedural powers in relation to the presumption of innocence and in relation to the role of criminal procedural law, some sort of threshold shall apply when the government intends to use search powers that violate one's reasonable expectation to privacy. Therefore, a form of suspicion shall be read as a minimum requirement for the reasonableness of the search.

[69] *Katz v. United States*, 389 U.S. 347, 88 S.Ct. 507, 357.

[70] See Chap. 5, Sect. 5.3.2.1.2.

Since the events of 9/11, the autonomous status of the warrant requirement as a mandatory protective requirement under the Fourth Amendment has been further reduced. In the first place, this has been illustrated in Sect. 6.2.2 by reference to the terrorism case of '*In re Terrorist Bombings of U.S. Embassies in East Africa* (2008)', which particularly dealt with exempting the warrant requirement from the overseas search covered by the Fourth Amendment. According to the Supreme Court in *United States v. Verdigo-Urquidez* (1990) the 'people' protected under the Fourth Amendment concern every US citizen, but excludes aliens living outside the US.[71] The search in the *Kenya* case concerned the surveillance of US citizens abroad and, hence, considering the Supreme Court judgment in *Verdigo-Urquidez*, the Fourth Amendment would apply. Again, the court reiterated that the ultimate touchstone of Fourth Amendment searches is reasonableness. The Second Circuit Court then balanced the intrusion on privacy against the involved threat that Al Qaeda posed to national security and concluded, although the privacy intrusion of "sustained and thorough" electronic surveillance was also great, that prior judicial approval in the form of a warrant was not required to render the surveillance activities reasonable. Here, the court accepted a new and more general exception to the Fourth Amendment warrant requirement, where the government seeks to search US citizens abroad. The Court determined the warrant requirement to be of little legal value in the sense of legitimizing the (sword) activities; however, in that respect denying the protective (shield) value of prior judicial control over the reasonableness of the intrusion on privacy rights, which applies irrespective of whether the search involving US citizens is conducted within or outside the US.[72]

Furthermore, this case also illustrates the development that courts increasingly focus on the overall reasonableness of the search, rather than on the requirements of a warrant and probable cause. Also in the *Kenya* case the court used the reasonableness of the search clearly as the ultimate touchstone when it assessed whether a warrant was required for the surveillance activities. For this purpose, the court, balancing the interests involved, took into account that the search was conducted abroad where a warrant has no legal value, for which reason the governmental interest in ensuring that terrorist attacks are prevented outweighs the interests served by prior judicial authorization. The manner in which the court dealt with the warrant requirement in respect of US citizens' searches abroad is comparable to the manner in which it has dispensed with the requirement of probable cause by relying on reasonableness as the final touchstone of the Fourth Amendment.

Not only in search cases abroad, but also domestically, courts have accepted warrantless searches in situations of 'compelling law enforcement needs'. In Chap. 6, Sect. 6.2.2, the cases of *Georgia v. Randolph*[73] and *Brigham City v.*

---

[71] *United States v. Verdigo-Urquidez,* 494 U.S. 259, 110 S.Ct. 1056 (1990). See Sect. 5.1.4.1.

[72] Forgang 2009, 244.

[73] *Georgia v. Randolph,* 547 U.S. 103, 126 S.Ct. 1515 (2006).

*Stuart*[74] have, by way of an example, been mentioned as cases where the Supreme Court has accepted warrantless searches under the Fourth Amendment by focusing its reasoning on the overall reasonableness of the search, which involves a balancing of all the interests involved without providing autonomous status to specific protective procedural requirements, such as obtaining a warrant.

On the basis of the foregoing it cannot be said that the warrant requirement has been set aside, particularly since 9/11, as a mandatory requirement for the reasonableness of the search. The analysis of the warrant as a shield element in the regulation of criminal investigation, as provided in Chap. 5, has demonstrated that exceptions to the warrant requirement have been rendered permissible under the Fourth Amendment and have obtained a statutory basis in Title III. Hence, considering the broad range of exceptions to the warrant requirement that were already created by the Court, it is difficult to uphold the warrant requirement as a *per se* requirement to render the search reasonable.[75] The developments since 9/11 have, therefore, not changed the status of the warrant requirement in the sense that it has since lost its autonomous position as a Fourth Amendment requirement. Rather, the warrant should be understood as a parameter for determining the reasonableness of the search. When a warrant has not been obtained prior to the (non-consent) search, the judge shall a posteriori assess whether the circumstances involved render the search nevertheless reasonable. The stronger the probable cause present before conducting the search in combination with the presence of exigent circumstances, such as a danger for the officers or other people or the possibility that contraband will be eliminated, the more likely the search shall be considered as reasonable. Reasonableness is indeed the ultimate touchstone, which means that the warrant requirement is advisable to make sure that the search is reasonable and even necessary if a warrant could reasonably be obtained before conducting the search. The approach has thus not really changed through cases like *In re Terrorist Bombings of U.S. Embassies in East Africa*, *Georgia v. Randolph* and *Brigham City v. Stuart*. Rather, these cases have reinforced the development towards reasonableness as the ultimate touchstone of the Fourth Amendment and a warrant only as a parameter that should be taken into account for determining reasonableness.

In addition, it can be concluded that the strength of the warrant as a parameter has weakened as a consequence of developments in the case law, especially when taking into account the general exception created for the searches of US citizens conducted abroad. For searches within the US the absence of a warrant can, generally with the applicability of the principle of proportionality, be compensated by the undoubted correct assumption of probable cause of the law enforcement officers. Furthermore, the warrant is understood as being required in principle, unless exigent circumstances are present that justify the postponement of a judicial

---

[74] *Brigham v. Stuart,* 547 U.S. 398, 126 S.Ct. 1943 (2006).

[75] Amar 1997, 4-10.

review until after the search.[76] Thus, courts continue to consider the judicial review (*ex ante* or *ex post*) of the use of search powers to be necessary, with a clear preference for *ex ante* review by means of a warrant in order to prevent unreasonable searches. However, an *ex ante* review is not considered as an inherently better form of review compared to an *ex post* review. Both forms are considered to be a sufficient check on the government's power to search.

The prioritizing of *ex ante* review seems to have weakened by extending a premise of exigent circumstances to include the interest of preventing terrorism (*In re Terrorist Bombings of U.S. Embassies in East Africa* (2008)). Nevertheless, one of the three statutory grounds for emergency interception without a warrant under Title III also already concerned the presence of a situation of conspiratorial activities threatening the national security interests, which is comparably broad. However, the constitutionality of this particular exception has so far not been assessed by the courts, for which reason it seems that this ground for an exception has virtually not been used. In addition, the exception crafted under *In re Terrorist Bombings of U.S. Embassies in East Africa* (2008) actually seems to fall outside this general scheme, because it is not the interest of preventing terrorism (and thus the presence of 'exigent circumstances'), but the fact that the warrant has no legal value abroad that seems to be the decisive reason for rendering the search reasonable.

To conclude: the case law that has emerged since the terrorist attacks of 9/11 has not clearly changed the understanding of the Fourth Amendment requirement of a warrant. Rather, the case law in which the warrant requirement was at issue corresponds with a general trend of focusing on the overall reasonableness of the search in which the function of (especially) a warrant and probable cause can be better described as parameters than as mandatory requirements.

#### 7.2.2.2.3 Reasonableness

As has already been emphasized in the previous two sub-sections, it can be concluded, especially since the developments in the post-9/11 era, that reasonableness is the ultimate touchstone of the Fourth Amendment.[77] Focusing on reasonableness was a development which was already initiated before the terrorist attacks of 9/11.[78] However, this development accelerated in the post-9/11 era, where especially the interest of protecting national security was the reason for focusing on

---

[76] Compare Slobogin who proposes to apply the proportionality and exigency principle in order to govern the power to search. For non-exigent searches a warrant would be required. Christopher Slobogin 2007, 615 and 617.

[77] In Sect. 5.1.4.1 the Reasonableness Fourth Amendment approach has already been identified as the current mainstream interpretation of the clauses of the Fourth Amendment.

[78] It was already determined in Sect. 5.3.2.1.3 that, considering the multitude of exceptions that had been created to the other Fourth Amendment requirements, reasonableness is the final and ultimate test for the constitutionality of a particular search and/or seizure.

reasonableness by the lower courts. This development clearly breaks with the standards once set in *Katz*[79] and *Keith*,[80] namely that a warrant supported by probable cause is required to protect someone's reasonable expectation of privacy and that the Fourth Amendment protections extend to the national security context. The exceptions created to the framework of strong protections as offered by *Katz*, and extended to the national security context in *Keith*, have been used and extended to allow for expedient law enforcement when the interests of law enforcement are sufficiently urgent, thereby generalizing the reasonableness test as the ultimate Fourth Amendment test upon a balancing inquiry at the expense of the other central Fourth Amendment requirements of a warrant and probable cause.

Considering that this development has evolved gradually, already before the events of 9/11, it cannot be exclusively attributed to the influence of the threat of terrorism.[81] However, as a consequence of the confrontation with the terrorist attacks of 9/11, the exceptions that had already been established have been further exploited to accommodate more expedient law enforcement activities for preventive purposes. The cases described in Sect. 6.2.2 demonstrate the tendency of new deviations from Fourth Amendment requirements when the interest of preventing terrorism (or in general expedient law enforcement in a society confronted with a fear of future terrorist attacks) is involved. Because reasonableness (or in fact proportionality, taking into account all the interests involved) has now become the only mandatory Fourth Amendment requirement, the Court's assessment will concern a balancing of interests, for which reason any urgent governmental interest may be considered to outweigh the protection of privacy rights. In 2008 the Supreme Court judgment in '*Virginia v. Moore*' affirmed this interpretation of applying the Fourth Amendment in a particular case as a matter of proportionality: an assessment should be made of the search on the basis of "on the one hand, the degree to which it intrudes upon an individual's privacy, and, on the other, the degree to which it is needed for the promotion of legitimate governmental interests."[82] Nevertheless, in this case the Supreme Court also indicated that a primary (thus not decisive) indication for the reasonableness of a search is the presence of probable cause.[83]

The current Fourth Amendment test, with reasonableness as the ultimate touchstone, results in a deviation from the other Fourth Amendment requirements, in particular those that are understood to form a threshold for investigative action,[84] in order to allow expedient law enforcement when terrorism is involved. When it is required to act proactively in order to make sure that terrorism is prevented, the

---

79 *Katz v. Unites States,* 389 U.S. 347, 88 S. Ct. 507 (1967).

80 *United States v. United States District Court*, 407 U.S. 297, 92 S.Ct. 2125 (1972), 316-317.

81 See for example Amar, concluding in 1998 that the ultimate touchstone of the Fourth Amendment can only be 'reasonableness,' considering that the multitude of exceptions deprives the other Fourth Amendment requirements of their status as mandatory requirements. Amar 1997, 2 and 31-32.

82 *Virginia v. Moore*, 553 U.S. 164, 128 S.Ct. 1598 (2008), 1604.

83 *Ibid.*, 1608. See Sect. 5.3.2.1.3.

84 Considering that reasonableness also covers the execution phase. See Sect. 5.3.2.1.3.

requirement of probable cause will likely be set aside under the reasonableness test, a conclusion already drawn in Sect. 7.2.2.2.1. The same applies to the warrant requirement (see the previous section). This approach has opened the door to an unlimited balancing test, providing the flexibility to consider the interests of preventing terrorism and protecting national security to outweigh competing protective requirements. Different Fourth Amendment standards will likely apply to cases involving the investigation of crimes having been committed than to cases where similar investigative powers are used proactively because activities are in some way related to terrorism or other threats to national security (compare, for example, the case of *United States v. Ramos* (2010)).[85] Focusing on reasonableness without giving an autonomous status to other Fourth Amendment requirements may result in the protection offered by the Fourth Amendment becoming a slippery slope.

#### 7.2.2.2.4 The Exclusionary Rule

The cases described in Sect. 6.2.2 have not affected the exclusionary rule. However, the expansion of law enforcement powers sought by the legislature in order to give both the FBI and local police officers more discretion to do what is necessary for prevention, which has been added to by the courts granting law enforcement officers a large degree of flexibility to act in anticipation of terrorist or national security threats by focusing on reasonableness, has not been compensated with expanded judicial oversight. Supreme Court cases during the post-9/11 era have eroded judicial oversight on the police even more, rather than reinforcing it.[86] *Hudson v. Michigan* (2006) and *Herring v. United States* (2009) both importantly reduced the meaning of the exclusionary rule as the remedy against Fourth Amendment violations by firstly setting aside the exclusionary rule for failing to comply with the knock-and-announce rule (*Hudson*) and then limiting the applicability of the exclusionary rule to "reckless, grossly negligent" police conduct (*Herring*).[87]

### *7.2.3 The Changed Role of the Relevant Actors*

The changes in conventional criminal law in the post-9/11 era have in particular changed the role of the police as to the relationship between solving committed crimes and acting to prevent crimes (in particular terrorism). Because of the expanded authorities as a consequence of the legislative measures and the trend in the case law to give the police more leeway in their investigative efforts—both assessed

---

[85] Fenske 2008, 345.

[86] (Anonymous) Note 2009, 1717-1718 and Stuntz 2002 (Arguing why Fourth and Fifth Amendment protections should fluctuate with crime).

[87] *Hudson v. Michigan*, 547 U.S. 586, 126 S.Ct. 2159 (2006), 594 and *Herring v. United States*, 555 U.S. 135,129 S.Ct. 695 (2009), 9. See in more detail also Chap. 5, Sect. 5.3.2.1.4.

in Sects. 7.2.1 and 7.2.2—the police have been given more powers to act for the prevention of terrorism, while, at the same time, they have been attributed more leeway to act for the prevention of terrorism. The protective role of the magistrate judge to consider the reasonableness of a search *ex ante* is not a certainty considering the many exceptions that have been accepted to the warrant requirement and especially since the current development towards focusing on reasonableness where the parameters of probable cause and a warrant are considered less urgent when the interests of preventing terrorism or protecting national security are involved.

Moreover, neither has a more powerful judicial check on abuses of law enforcement power *ex post* been created considering the erosion of the exclusionary rule in Supreme Court decisions during the last few years, in the sense that the deterrent function of the exclusionary rule has been limited to apply only when the suppression of evidence can substantially deter the police. In addition, courts have in general exerted a more deferential review of Fourth Amendment requirements in the post-9/11 era. Hence, the additional mechanisms that trigger the shield responsibility of police offers—namely the reasonableness assessment under the Fourth Amendment and substantive due process—also have only a limited steering influence. As we have seen in Sect. 7.2.2.2.3 the interests of preventing terrorism and protecting national security are soon considered as arguments that outweigh protective interests taking into account the totality of circumstances in order to determine the reasonableness of a particular search and/or seizure. In addition, substantive due process only covers police conduct that shocks the conscience (see Sect. 5.3.1.1). Considering that the deterrent meaning of the most significant restraint—the exclusionary rule—on police conduct has been reduced, the potential for abuse has increased, because of the expanded discretion and power to act, especially for the purpose of preventing terrorism. The other mechanisms regulating police conduct are unable to compensate for the reduced deterring effect of the exclusionary rule, whereas also judicial oversight has not been enhanced to compensate for the increased potential for abuses of investigative power.

Furthermore, new internal guidelines which are applicable to the activities of the FBI offer FBI officers more freedom to act for the purpose of preventing terrorism. In Sects. 6.4.2.3 and 6.4.2.4 the Mukasey Guidelines on FBI Operations (2008) and the Domestic Investigations and Operations Guide of the FBI (2008) have been described, from which it can be concluded that all FBI officers, therefore including those previously exclusively concerned with law enforcement investigations, should make the transformation towards an intelligence-driven organization in order to combine forces for the purpose of protecting against terrorism and other threats to national security. Hence, the nature of the task instruction for FBI officers has changed to focus in particular also on gathering as much information as possible in order to make sure that terrorism or other national security threats are prevented.[88] Moreover, also local police officers have been included in the national intelligence-gathering systems in order to contribute to the

[88] More on this in Sect. 7.4.1.

prevention of terrorism. Local police officers make use of databases for the purpose of information sharing and have generally obtained an aggravated responsibility to use the police capacities to make sure that terrorist crimes are prevented.[89] In this way intelligence-led policing has been enabled. As a consequence of changing the task description of the police to focus also on protecting national security through collecting as much information as possible, the police will be encouraged to use their increased discretionary power to investigate for the purpose of preventing terrorism and to share police criminal intelligence especially when they encounter potential security-threatening situations. Police criminal intelligence is included in advanced databases, such as fusion centers (e.g. the JTTF), for the purpose of collection, storage and dissemination.[90] Data aggregation and data mining make it possible to integrate data collected by different agencies and to reveal otherwise undiscoverable patterns and relationships. Consequently, the nature of the police work has become more privacy-sensitive.

The changed function of the police influences the established relation between the actors in the criminal process, and, for that reason, the shield function pursued through the distribution of responsibilities between the different actors. The responsibility of the public prosecutor and the defense with regard to a fair criminal procedure is affected as a consequence of the changed focus of the police towards intelligence-led policing with an eye to protecting the national security. Because of the increased intelligence-led character of the police investigation and the use of databases in which information is included from different sources, including intelligence sources, the use of classified evidence in criminal prosecutions increases. The disclosure procedures that can be applied when classified information is involved (CIPA) have been described in Sects. 5.3.1.2 and 5.3.1.3. The use of classified information in criminal proceedings results in tension between the duty of the prosecutor to disclosure as a matter of constitutional (due process) law (*Brady v. Maryland* (1963)) and the interest of shielding the information for national security reasons. As this tension and the invoking of the classified procedures is primarily a consequence of the dismantling of the wall between law enforcement and intelligence and the commensurate sharing obligations between law enforcement and intelligence agencies, this subject will be specifically broached in Sect. 7.4.3.

Moreover, the role of the judiciary as such has changed with regard to exerting control over investigative activities, as a consequence of the focus on gathering information in the context of national security investigations. The core responsibility for exerting control over anticipative criminal investigative activities is not borne by the judiciary but by alternative mechanisms of control, such as Congressional oversight and the review exerted by the Inspector General of the Department of Justice. This subject will be touched upon in Sect. 7.4.3 as it concerns, likewise, an implication of the dismantling of the wall.

---

[89] White 2004, 14 and 15.

[90] See Sect. 6.2.3.

At this place, it is sufficient to say that the relationship between the actors in criminal investigations has changed, mainly because the police, who have primary responsibility for criminal investigative activities, have become an intelligence-driven organization, with larger investigative discretion and an intensified responsibility to keep an eye on terrorism-related or other national security-threatening activities.

## 7.3 The Expansion of the Preventive Capacity of National Security Investigations

### *7.3.1 Expansion of the Scope and Nature of FISA Surveillance and Physical Searches*

The USA PATRIOT Act has also expanded investigative powers, both in their scope and nature, which can be used in national security investigations (see Sect. 6.3). This section will first draw a more general conclusion as to the expanded surveillance powers in national security investigations (Sect. 7.3.1.1). Secondly, the section will address some particular measures and their relation to the previous regulation of national security investigations. The enabling of roving surveillance and the current regulation of pen register and trap and trace authority under FISA raise some specific renewed questions as to their constitutionality under the Fourth Amendment, for which reason these techniques have been singled out and will be addressed in Sects. 7.3.1.2 and 7.3.1.3. The goal of this section is to draw a conclusion as to the current nature of national security investigations considering the regulation of the available investigative powers. Hence, this section concerns the basis for assessing the full impact of dismantling the wall (as addressed in Sect. 7.4) for the shield objective of criminal procedural law.

#### 7.3.1.1 General Development

The nature of investigative powers in national security investigations has changed due to several amendments to the USA PATRIOT Act of 2001. Roving surveillance is a new possibility within the FISA framework, which already existed under Title III. In addition, FISA orders are now applicable nationwide and orders for FISA surveillance, physical searches or pen register and trap/trace authority can be used over longer periods. Orders for surveillance and pen register or trap/trace authority that target non-US persons who are foreign powers, agents of foreign powers or lone wolves[91] may last for up to one year.[92] Moreover, the information that can be intercepted by pen registers and trap/trace devices under FISA has been expanded to include some personal information concerning the customer or

[91] Non-US persons engaging in international terrorism or activities in preparation therefor without connections to a foreign-based group. 50 U.S.C. § 1801(b) heading and under (C).

[92] See Sect. 6.3.1.

subscriber to be requested from the service provider by changing the definition of pen register and trap/trace devices (similar to the changed definition in the context of a conventional criminal investigation). The scope of surveillance and pen register and trap and trace authority has also been expanded by introducing the possibility to target not only foreign powers or agents of foreign powers that have a connection with a foreign-based group, but also the 'lone wolf.' As a consequence of these expanded powers in combination with the broader scope of FISA as a consequence of the lone wolf amendment, the nature of FISA investigations has become considerably more intrusive. In addition, the amount of FISA court orders has increased since its adoption in 1978 and, in particular, since the years after 9/11. Between 2000 and 2007 the number has even doubled.[93]

The reasoning of the Supreme Court in *Keith* significantly influenced the specific choices made in the statutory scheme of the FISA of 1978. When the nature of FISA surveillance is changed both in nature and in scope, also the choices for adopting a specific regulation framework in order to provide for legal protection need to be reassessed. Many changes that have affected the investigative powers under FISA were supported by the argument that the same techniques should be available under FISA as well as under Title III. Although at first sight this argument may seem plausible, one should take into account that the protective framework of FISA is much weaker than the framework of Title III covering conventional criminal investigations and, hence, also the potential for abuse might be higher.[94] This applies in particular to the level of *ex ante* review exerted to authorize an order for surveillance, the considerable difference between the standards to be reviewed before an order can be authorized and the scope and duration of a FISA Court order.

Under Title III the federal judge may only issue an order (in accordance with 18 U.S.C. § 2518) for surveillance if he determines that there is probable cause to believe that the individual is committing, has committed, or is about to commit a specific enumerated offense. The applicable threshold under FISA contrasts sharply by requiring only probable cause that the target of the surveillance is a foreign power or an agent of a foreign power.[95] Hence, FISA surveillance can be

---

[93] Followed by a decrease in authorized applications in 2009 and 2010. In 2010 1,506 FISA electronic surveillance applications were approved by the FISA Court, in 2005 the number was 2,072 (reaching its highest point in 2007 with 2,370 authorizations) and in 2000 the number of authorized applications was 1,012. Numbers derived from FISA Annual Reports to Congress, available at: http://www.fas.org/irp/agency/doj/fisa/#rept (accessed August 1, 2011). For an overview of the amounts of FISA Court orders and NSLs for the years 1979–2010, composed on the basis of annual and general reports, see: 'Foreign Intelligence Surveillance Act Court Orders 1979–2010', Electronic Privacy Information Center, available at: http://epic.org/privacy/wiretap/stats/fisa_stats.html (accessed July 29, 2011).

[94] Compare the rather strict framework of Title III, intended to provide sufficient protection against unnecessary interference with private life through surveillance, the most intrusive form of search (described in Sect. 5.3.2.2) with the FISA framework (described in Sect. 5.3.2.4).

[95] For the definition of a foreign power or an agent of a foreign power see Sect. 5.2.2.3.1, footnote 199 and Sect. 5.3.2.4.1 (50 U.S.C. § 1801(a) and (b)).

authorized with a showing that concerns the nature of the target rather than an evidentiary showing regarding the nature of the activities in which the target is involved.[96] Considering the broad scope due to the absence of a substantial threshold and, in addition, a weaker *ex ante* judicial review, it is not self-evident that the same investigative techniques shall be available under FISA as under Title III.

The Supreme Court held in the *Keith* decision that also national security investigations are covered by the Fourth Amendment, where the individual's Fourth Amendment rights need to be balanced against the government's need to obtain foreign intelligence information. The FISA of 1978 has been understood as the outcome of this balancing. For example, the government's interest in gathering foreign intelligence information was considered to justify longer periods of surveillance[97] without violating the particularity requirements because the national security investigation is "often long range and involves the interrelation of various sources and types of information."[98] As a consequence of the expansion of the investigative powers under FISA by the USA PATRIOT Act of 2001 at the expense of protective restraints and checks, the nature of FISA surveillance and physical searches has become more intrusive, which touches upon the previous balance between the individual's Fourth Amendment interests and the government's interest in gathering foreign intelligence information achieved in the FISA of 1978. Congress tried to compensate the enhanced sword capacity of FISA investigative powers by strengthening Congressional oversight.[99] However, it is questionable whether Congressional oversight can sufficiently counterbalance the diminished form of judicial control.

For these reasons, the expansion of investigative powers available in national security investigations—as well as the rather intrusive nature of electronic surveillance in general and in particular the comparably long validity of FISA surveillance order—will be assessed in the light of the weaker protection against arbitrary intrusion on privacy rights offered by the statutory framework of FISA.[100] Nevertheless, the overwhelming majority of courts that have assessed the constitutionality of the amended FISA have decided that FISA does not violate the Fourth Amendment. A complete assessment of the constitutionality of the current

---

[96] In addition, it should be taken into account that FISA investigations cover the gathering of foreign intelligence information. Like the definition of a foreign power or agent of a foreign power also the definition of foreign intelligence information is rather broad: "Information that relates to, and if concerning a United States person is necessary to, the ability of the United States to protect against" certain national security threats that can be related to a foreign power or an agent of a foreign power. 50 U.S.C. § 1801(e) (see for the precise definitions Sect. 5.2.2.3.1).

[97] Compare, for example, *Berger v. New York,* 388 U.S. 41, 87 S.Ct. 1873 (1967) where the Court struck down an eavesdropping statute authorizing surveillance over a period of two months with the validity of the FISA court order of 120 days (previously 90; see Sect. 6.3.1).

[98] *United States v. United States District Court*, 407 U.S. 297, 92 S.Ct. 2125 (1972), at 322.

[99] Section 108(c) of the USA PATRIOT Act Reauthorization Act of 2005. See Sect. 6.3.1.

[100] Compare also: Power 2010, 679-681.

FISA cannot be made, however, without also taking into account the development that national security investigations have obtained a quasi-law enforcement function by allowing national security investigations for the primary purpose of gathering evidence. Hence, this assessment overlaps with the second and third category and will be dealt with under the third category.

#### 7.3.1.2 Roving Surveillance

Normally an order for surveillance shall include a specification of the particular place or facility from which the communications will be intercepted. This requirement is included in Title III in order to give effect to the particularity requirement of the Fourth Amendment. An exception to this particularity specification is permitted under Title III when such specification is not practical because the target is evading surveillance by switching communication devices.[101] The regulation of roving surveillance under Title III has been considered by the federal courts as not violating the Fourth Amendment's particularity requirements, because the regulation carefully tailors the power in a way that general searches are prevented. In particular, courts have pointed to the requirement of specifying the person whose communications are to be intercepted, the application of minimization procedures and the showing that must have been made and reviewed by the judge that either specifying the facilities is not practical (in the case of intercepting oral communications; 18 U.S.C. § 2518(11)(a)) or that probable cause can be established that "the person's actions could have the effect of thwarting interception from a specified facility" (in the case of wire or electronic communications; § 2518(11)(b)).[102]

The roving surveillance provision as adopted in FISA does differ, in some aspects, from the regulation in Title III. It should therefore be questioned whether the limitations and protective conditions that currently surround the provision render the roving provision similar to that of Title III. The roving surveillance provision in FISA allows roving surveillance "in circumstances where the Court finds that the actions of the target of the application may have the effect of thwarting the identification of a specified person" and when the facilities and places at which the surveillance will be directed "are unknown."[103] The specific target must be described in the application. In addition, the applicant shall notify the court "within ten days after the date on which surveillance begins to be directed at any new facility or place," although this notification may be extended until 60 days if the court considers a longer period to be justified. Furthermore, the applicant should also demonstrate facts and circumstances that point to the fact that the facility "is or was being used, or is about to be used, by the target of the surveillance" and

---

[101] See Sect. 5.2.2.1.2.

[102] See Sect. 5.3.2.1.2.

[103] See Sect. 6.3.1.

Congressional oversight on electronic surveillance is in place. Lastly, also under FISA, minimization procedures shall be applied to the surveillance.

Considering this regulation of roving surveillance under FISA, the authority cannot be considered to allow—on its face—for general searches. Especially the requirement of describing the particular target in the application seems an important restriction on the surveillance. In addition, considering the circumstances of modern society, it seems logical that the possibility for roving surveillance has also been adopted as an investigative possibility in national security investigations. Nevertheless, it must also be taken into account that the possibility for roving surveillance, including the roving bug, in combination with the nationwide applicability of FISA orders and the wider scope of FISA investigations in general considering its considerably weaker version of probable cause, render the investigative technique of FISA roving surveillance one of the most intrusive. Allowing for this investigative power in national security investigations brings along a greater risk that the communications of individuals who are not the target of the investigation will be intercepted.

#### 7.3.1.3 Pen Register and Trap and Trace Devices

Similar to the PATRIOT Act amendment to pen register and trap and trace authority in conventional criminal law, the PATRIOT Act has also broadened the scope of pen register and trap and trace authority under FISA. As has been explained in Sect. 6.3.1, the changed definition of the pen register and trap and trace devices under FISA broadens the scope of the techniques. The same concerns as addressed in Sect. 7.2.1.3 apply to the amendment to pen register and trap and trace authority under FISA, although it must be taken into account that section 214 also resulted in a new restraint on these techniques. Section 214 has namely restricted the target to non-US persons in national security investigations, which may include US persons if the investigation is not solely based upon activities protected by the First Amendment.

However, remarkably the PATRIOT Improvement and Reauthorization Act of 2005 took another, more dramatic, step to broaden the scope of the pen register and trap and trace device. Pen registers and trap/trace devices may now be used under FISA to obtain from service providers more personal information relating to their customers or subscribers, which makes the category of information that can be intercepted broader than under the pen register and trap and trace authority in a conventional criminal investigation. Albeit the information that can be obtained through pen registers and trap/trace devices is still considerably more limited than that which can be obtained through document production orders—the FISA power created through section 215 of the PATRIOT Act. Hence, privacy concerns due to broadening the scope of the information that can be intercepted by pen registers and trap and trace devices seem to fade away in comparison with the current scope of document production orders, which will be dealt with in the next section.

In addition, Sect. 6.3.1 has described the amendment that has significantly relaxed the threshold for using pen registers and trap and trace devices. The PATRIOT Act has struck out from the requirements to be met in the application that information shall be delivered demonstrating reasons to believe that the telephone lines or other instruments from which information is intercepted are being used or have been used by someone "who is engaging or has engaged in international terrorism or clandestine intelligence activities that involve or may involve a violation of the criminal laws of the United States."[104] This previous requirement was also an important difference with Title III, where a showing of relevance to an ongoing criminal investigation was already sufficient for a judge to issue an *ex parte* order.[105] Although the amendment seems to equalize the threshold, the scope of national security investigations is, by definition, broader than that of criminal investigations and, hence, so is the scope of the pen register and trap and trace authority. Nevertheless, the threshold which is applicable to pen register and trap and trace authority is still comparable to the threshold which is applicable to document production orders and, hence, also when taking this amendment into account, FISA pen register and trap and trace authority cannot exceed the nature or scope of document production orders.

This section will therefore conclude that considering the weaker regulation provided by FISA in general with regard to an individual's Fourth Amendment rights (see the remarks on this respect in the preceding Sect. 7.3.1.1) and considering the scope of information that can now be intercepted by pen register and trap and trace devices, pen register and trap and trace authority under FISA concerns more invasive authority than under the regulation in conventional criminal law.

### 7.3.2 FISA Document Production Orders

Section 215 of the USA PATRIOT Act of 2001 has changed the FISA investigative tool to request the production of transportation-related business records through a FISA Court order into a rather broad and intrusive tool by authorizing the FISA Court to order the production of any tangible things. The amendment touches upon three different aspects: the scope of the order has been broadened to "any tangible things," including library and bookstore records; the threshold has been lowered to a statement of facts of "relevance to an authorized investigation"; and a non-disclosure requirement applies to the recipient of the order.

Previously, a similar powerful authority to subpoena documents containing personal information on US citizens in the investigative stage was only attributed to the grand jury. The grand jury has been described in Sect. 5.2.1.3 as the sword and shield of the criminal justice system. Moreover, the grand jury is underpinned by the idea that "the people" shall be able to control and exercise the use of very

[104] See Sect. 6.3.1 and, in comparison, Sect. 5.2.2.3.1.

[105] See Sect. 5.3.2.1.1.1.

intrusive techniques, including the possibility of issuing document production orders. With the expansion of the scope of document production orders to 'any tangible things' a similar tool has now been given to the government in the context of national security investigations. Hence, this section will further scrutinize the current regulation of the document production order in comparison to other investigative techniques in national security investigations in order to determine the nature and implications of this basically new investigative tool. For this purpose this section will first address the relevant restraints and protective elements of the system in which the document production order is embedded, namely the threshold for issuing a document production order, the prior judicial control exerted by the FISA Court, the applicable minimization procedures, the nature of the information that can be obtained and the importance of the tool for the government in NSI investigations in relation to the protections offered by the First and Fourth Amendments. Secondly, the results of the litigation concerning the non-disclosure requirement will be compared with the manner in which the FISA document production order is currently regulated.

#### 7.3.2.1 The Regulation of Document Production Orders Under FISA

The significant enlargement of the scope of document production orders through Section 215 of the USA PATRIOT Act of 2001 from transportation-related records to a rather sweeping category of all kinds of 'tangible things' permits the FISA Court to order the production of these 'tangible things', including privacy-sensitive categories of information normally subjected to privacy protection.[106] No restriction has been adopted as to the type of records that can be requested by the government. As a consequence, this FISA authority is now analogous to grand jury subpoenas. Considering the categories of privacy-sensitive information that can be obtained, the applicable threshold seems to be rather low. The current threshold of "a statement of facts showing that there are reasonable grounds to believe that the tangible things are relevant to an authorized investigation (other than threat assessment)" is comparable with the threshold that applies to the use of pen registers and trap/trace devices,[107] whereas the information that can be obtained through section 215 orders is considerably more privacy-sensitive than the information that can be obtained through the pen registers and trap and trace devices, also after the scope of these techniques has been broadened (see Sect. 7.3.1.3). Also for document production orders the requirement of any

[106] Although not protected through the Fourth Amendment, considering that the Supreme Court in *United States v. Miller,* 425 U.S. 435, 96 S.Ct. 1619 (1976), 443 (see also Chap. 5, Sect. 5.1.4.1) has considered that someone cannot have a reasonable expectation of privacy relating to personal information already entrusted to others.

[107] "[T]he information likely to be obtained is relevant to an ongoing foreign intelligence or international terrorism investigation being conducted by the Federal Bureau of Investigation under guidelines approved by the Attorney General," See: 50 U.S.C. § 1842(c)(2).

evidentiary support has been eliminated, which makes the threshold less strict than before and applicable to anyone, instead of only to the target of the investigation.

In 2009 the judiciary committees of Congress introduced a bill in order to extend certain expiring provisions of the PATRIOT Act, including section 215, and to implement some protective improvements. One of these improvements concerned the proposition to change the language of section 50 U.S.C. § 1861 regarding the circumstances where the document production order shall be understood to be "presumptively relevant."[108] The proposed change would subject these presumptively relevant circumstances to an evidentiary standard of "reasonable grounds." If this proposed change had been adopted, evidentiary support regarding the persons to whom the records pertain would at least again be required, although still the persons whose documents can be obtained are not necessarily the targets of the investigation.[109] However, the Bill did not obtain enough priority and, instead, in February 2010 Obama signed into law the Act 'to extend expiring provisions of the USA PATRIOT Act Improvement and Reauthorization Act of 2005 and Intelligence Reform and Terrorism Prevention Act of 2004 until February 28, 2011,' straightforwardly extending the provision until February 28, 2010.[110] Subsequently, in May 2011, the provision has once again without amendments been extended until June 2015.[111]

Hence, as follows from Sect. 6.3.2, until now only the rather weak restraints of personal approval by an FBI official (a high-ranking FBI official for categories of more privacy-sensitive information such as library records and medical records) and an application specifying that there are reasonable grounds to believe that the records sought are relevant to an authorized investigation are applicable. What amounts to an authorized investigation follows from the Mukasey Guidelines on FBI Operations of 2008 (see Sect. 6.4.2.3) which state that the investigation must (also) be aimed at either obtaining foreign intelligence information or protecting against international terrorism or clandestine intelligence activities—thus, the order can be used in any authorized national security (FISA) investigation. There are some circumstances in which the records are presumptively relevant, including where the tangible things sought pertain to "an individual in contact with, or known to, a suspected agent of a foreign power who is the subject of such authorized investigation."[112] Actually, the main requirement restraining the government's use of document production orders is the presence of an authorized investigation (according to the Attorney General Guidelines) other than a threat assessment. In addition, US persons receive more protection, because the

[108] See Sect. 6.3.2.

[109] Section 3(a) (2) Bill of 22 September 2009 'to extend the sunset of certain provisions of the USA PATRIOT Act and the authority to issue national security letters, and for other purposes', 111th Congress. 1st Session S.1692.

[110] Public Law 111-141, Feb. 27, 2010, 124 Stat. 37, 111th Congress.

[111] PATRIOT Sunsets Extension Act of 2011, S.990, 112th Congress, 1st Session.

[112] See Sect. 6.3.2.

investigation of US persons may not solely be based upon activities protected by the First Amendment.[113]

Considering the nature of the document production order and the regulation surrounding the technique, it is not surprising that section 215 is generally understood as one of the most controversial PATRIOT Act products, which is also reflected in its nickname: the 'library provision.' The potential for abuse is high and an attempt has been made to compensate for this with the amendments of the Reauthorization Acts of 2005 and 2006 by enhancing judicial review and Congressional oversight. Prior judicial review exerted by the FISA Court is restricted to determining whether the statutory requirements are met, which thus concerns controlling formalities without being able to second-guess the government statements. An important restriction, however, seems to be that the FISA Court may only order production if the things sought cannot be obtained by the more protective investigative power of the grand jury or any other order of a US court seeking the production of records or tangible things (e.g. under rule 17 of the Federal Rules of Criminal Procedure, providing for the power of subpoena in criminal proceedings). Furthermore, it should be taken into consideration that, similar to pen registers and trap and trace devices, the Supreme Court has excluded subpoenas for obtaining personal information entrusted to third parties from Fourth Amendment protection.[114] For this reason, the government is not held to observe the usual Fourth Amendment requirements. Nevertheless, Congress, recognizing the privacy-sensitive nature of personal information, in e.g. medical records, student records and financial records, and taking into account that as a consequence of the Supreme Court's interpretation the person to whom the records pertain is deprived of prior judicial control through the warrant supported by probable cause, has subjected the power of the government to obtain records with personal information to statutory limitations, for example, by demanding a grand jury subpoena and enabling the person concerned to challenge the subpoena before a court.[115] In comparison with these statutory limitations, in particular the requirement of a grand jury subpoena, it is remarkable that under the FISA framework documents, without any distinction as to its nature, a document may be requested without imposing limiting, privacy-protecting conditions. It is questionable whether the subsidiarity requirement—the requirement that section 215 orders may only be issued if the documents cannot be obtained through the power of the grand jury or an order of a US court—may count as a meaningful restriction, when it comes to the privacy protection of exactly those persons who are not suspected of any crime. In addition, it follows from the statistical information

---

[113] Swire 2004, 1331-1332.

[114] See *United States v. Miller,* 425 U.S. 435, 96 S.Ct. 1619 (1976), 443, and Chap. 5, Sect. 5.1.4.1.

[115] Schulhofer 2005, 57-58.

annually provided to Congress that the FISA judges have never denied an application for a document production order.[116]

Because of the large scope of both the information that can be obtained (any tangible things) and the reach of the section 215 order, considering the rather sweeping relevance threshold to an authorized investigation, cumulatively, serious privacy concerns remain. Although also in the context of the criminal investigation the possibilities to obtain a wide range of documents has expanded over the years, these documents may only be obtained in relation to a crime that has been, is being or will be committed, which imposes an important restraint on its scope.[117] The amendments of the USA PATRIOT Act have targeted different aspects of the system of checks and balances that represent the protective objective. Without distinction as to the privacy sensitivity of particular documents, a wide range of information can be obtained if relevant to an authorized FISA investigation.[118] Also the subsidiarity requirement seems not to be an adequate restriction. US persons receive more privacy protection compared to non-US persons by prohibiting the collection of information of activities by the First Amendment. Furthermore, the requirement of observing minimization procedures as introduced by the Reauthorization Act of 2005 includes important additional protection to US persons by requiring the minimization of "the retention and prohibit[ing] the dissemination, of nonpublicly available information concerning unconsenting US persons, consistent with the need of the United States to obtain, produce, and disseminate foreign intelligence information." The 2009 Bill proposed to go one step further by also requiring that the Attorney General directs that the minimization procedures are followed.[119]

Nevertheless, it must also be observed that, as a consequence of the litigation directly concerning FISA document production orders, the Attorney General revealed in 2003 that the order had been issued on zero occasions. In the period 2004–2008 the order to produce documents was issued 236 times. Apparently, however, the order was used on 173 occasions in combination with FISA or trap and trace device orders during the period 2004–2006, which is the period before the definition of the pen register and trap and trace device was broadened by the Reauthorization Act of 2005. Hence, seemingly the majority of document production orders were issued primarily in order to fill the gap in the prior pen register and trap and trace authority, namely also to obtain information about the customer

[116] FISA Annual Reports to Congress 2005–2010, available at: http://www.fas.org/irp/agency/doj/fisa/#rept (accessed August 4, 2011).

[117] Swire 2004, 1332.

[118] *Ibid.*, 1357.

[119] Section 3(a)(3)(B) Bill of 22 September 2009 'to extend the sunset of certain provisions of the USA PATRIOT Act and the authority to issue national security letters, and for other purposes', 111th Congress, 1st Session S.1692.

or subscriber.[120] Moreover, the remainder of the orders were used to obtain transactional information and no recipient has so far challenged the legitimacy of the document production order since the introduction of a judicial remedy by the Reauthorization Act of 2006.[121] Despite this differentiation on the basis of the information revealed by the government regarding the frequency and purpose of the use of the document production order showing that the tool has rarely been used for the purposes most feared (e.g. on a wide scale to obtain library records or medical records of US citizens),[122] the (theoretical) potential for abuse remains high considering the lack of restraints on the FISA document production order.

#### 7.3.2.2 The Non-Disclosure Requirement

Courts have repeatedly held the non-disclosure requirement (in cases dealing with the requirement accompanying NSLs) unconstitutional, including the improved conditions under which the non-disclosure requirement may be imposed as realized in the USA PATRIOT Act Reauthorization Acts of 2005 and 2006. The most recent judicial decisions scrutinizing the non-disclosure requirement have been the decision of the Court of Appeals in *Doe v. Mukasey* (2008) holding the amended non-disclosure requirement constitutional if construed in the manner prescribed by the Court in its decision and the 2009 decisions of *Doe v. Holder* resulting in the lifting of the non-disclosure requirement imposed on 'John Doe'. The decision in *Doe v. Mukasey* of 2008 has been the latest most important decision where the court has conducted a substantive assessment of the constitutionality of the non-disclosure requirement, which was applied in the *Doe v. Holder* (2009) order and decision. In 2008 the Court of Appeals placed the burden on the government instead of on the NSL recipient to prove the necessity of the non-disclosure requirement and to initiate a judicial review of the non-disclosure requirement. In addition, the court held the narrow judicial review of the certification of the government "that disclosure may endanger the national security of the United States or interfere with diplomatic relations" unconstitutional.[123] It was stated that "the fiat of a government official, though senior in rank and doubtless honorable in the execution of official duties, cannot displace the judicial obligation to enforce

---

[120] See Sect. 6.3.1 and 'Statement of David Kris, Assistant Attorney General, Before the Committee on the Judiciary United States Senate, entitled *"Reauthorizing the USA PATRIOT Act: Ensuring Liberty and Security"*, September 23, 2009, 3. See for additional statistical information regarding the use of section 215 in the period 2002–2005 (although largely classified): Report of the Office of the Inspector General 2007, *A Review of the FBI's Use of Section 215 Orders for Business Records*, 15-46 and 77-78.

[121] See Sect. 6.3.1 and the Statement of David Kris, Assistant Attorney General, before the Committee on the Judiciary United States Senate 2009, 3.

[122] See also: Report of the Office of the Inspector General 2007, *A Review of the FBI's Use of Section 215 Orders for Business Records*, 79-80.

[123] See *Doe v. Mukasey*, 549 F.3d 861 (2nd Cir. 2008), 884-884. Section 6.3.2.

constitutional requirements. 'Under no circumstances should the Judiciary become the handmaiden of the Executive.'"[124] The *Doe* cases came to an end through a settlement between the FBI and the plaintiffs at the end of July 2010 (see Sect. 6.3.1). Years of litigation have resulted in the lifting of the non-disclosure requirement as to the identity of the recipient and the possibility to publicly discuss the cases, without revealing the full scope of the data demanded.

The main objection against the non-disclosure requirement—a violation of the requirement is a federal crime—is that it deprives the recipient of a judicial remedy. Outside the national security context the recipient has the possibility to challenge the subpoena before complying. Persons who are subjected to a FISA physical search or surveillance lack that possibility, whereas it must also be admitted that the Fourth Amendment standards applicable to searches (including prior judicial authorization—the warrant) do not apply to subpoenas received by third parties. In addition, one may question the willingness of the third party, for example a bank, to challenge the legitimacy of the order to protect the privacy interests of its clients.[125] Nevertheless, the non-disclosure requirement that accompanies document production orders issued by the FISA Court deprives the recipient of any prior challenge to the legitimacy of the order as well as of any other meaningful form of accountability other than the marginal review of the FISA Court. Except for depriving the recipient of a possibility of prior judicial control, notification after the fact to the persons involved is also impossible and, consequently, the persons involved may never become aware that the government has collected documents containing their personal information. The Reauthorization Acts have made it possible for the recipient to consult an attorney and, after one year, the recipient is allowed to challenge the necessity of continuing the non-disclosure requirement.[126] However, the standard upon which the judge may set aside the non-disclosure requirement is rather high, as the court shall only do so if there is no reason to believe—probably against the certifications of the government to the contrary—that disclosure may endanger national security. The FISA Court judge is generally reluctant to pass over such certifications on behalf of the government, although the decision in *Doe v. Holder* might suggest otherwise. Hence, it can be concluded that there remains a lack of accountability with regard to the majority of document production orders, which involves a high potential for abuse considering the lack of a meaningful judicial check on executive power that intrudes on citizens' privacy rights. Notification, which is not at all provided to those persons to whom the documents actually pertain, is understood as one of the most basic checks against abuse, because it results in publicity being given to governmental activities. Hence, criticism of the FISA document production order has particularly focused on the non-disclosure requirement and also the most notable litigation has concerned the non-disclosure requirement (although of the NSL).

---

[124] *Doe v. Mukasey,* 549 F.3d 861 (2nd Cir. 2008), 882-883.

[125] Compare: Schulhofer 2005, 56, 58-59.

[126] See Sect. 6.3.2.

The manner in which the Court of Appeals in *Doe v. Mukasey* (2008) has interpreted the non-disclosure requirement concerns an important improvement, although still insufficient to restore judicial review and accountability to the usual level. As a consequence of the interpretation of the Court of Appeals the judicial review introduced by the Reauthorization Act of 2005 has become more meaningful, considering that the court has rendered a mere certification by the government that disclosure might endanger national security as insufficient to count as judicial review. Nevertheless, as a consequence of this decision the non-disclosure requirement as such is rendered constitutional and will only be set aside if the recipient is willing to challenge the gag order and if the judge has sufficient reasons to bypass the government's national security claims. Hence, it must be concluded that a solid and general level of accountability cannot be achieved under the current regulation of the non-disclosure requirement accompanying document production orders of the FISA Court.

#### 7.3.2.3 Conclusion

The power to seek the production of 'tangible things' by means of a FISA Court order is one of the most controversial powers introduced by the USA PATRIOT Act of 2001. The section has been revised to include more protective elements in the Reauthorization Acts. However, also parts of the provisions of the latest version of section 215 have been held unconstitutional by the Court of Appeals of the Second Circuit (*Doe v. Mukasey* (2008)), because of the non-disclosure requirement accompanying such orders and the insufficiency of the provided judicial review.

The amendments of section 215 of the USA PATRIOT Act of 2001 have affected different aspects of the totality of restraints and safeguards that are intended to constitute the protective objective of the regulation. The cumulative effect of the substantive broadening of the scope of the order to any tangible things, relaxing the threshold by the removal of the requirement to furnish factual proof and by indicating a wide category where the threshold of relevance to an authorized FISA investigation is presumptively met in combination with depriving recipients of a judicial remedy and reducing accountability to the minimum, renders section 215 a very intrusive and aggressive investigative tool, lacking substantial restraint to protect against arbitrariness and lacking a guaranteed form of accountability or judicial review to prevent abuse. The participation of the FISA Court judge provides some degree of accountability, which is, for example, absent when the government relies on the national security letter. However, as has been concluded in the previous section, the control exerted is only minimal considering that the judge's task is to issue the order (*ex parte* and *in camera*) when the statutory requirements are met.

The Reauthorization Acts have established the possibility for a judicial review of both the order and, one year after its issue, of the non-disclosure requirement. Reviewing the order is rather limited, considering that the FISA Court judge will only consider the review when not frivolous and the review will subsequently only result in a modification to or setting the order aside when the statutory requirements have not been met or the order is "otherwise unlawful." The judicial review with regard to the non-disclosure requirement was held to be constitutional by the *Doe v. Mukasey* (2008) court but only when the government bears the burden to prove the necessity of non-disclosure and only where the court does not treat a certification to that end as conclusive. Compared to the previous situation this has increased judicial review and accountability to a more meaningful level. The recipient may seek to quash the order before the FISA Court and the recipient may seek relief from the non-disclosure requirement one year after the order has been issued. Furthermore, accountability has been improved by the Reauthorization Acts by enhancing Congressional oversight. This oversight is limited to statistical information, which makes it possible to check the government on the frequency of relying on the document production order and on the purposes for which the orders have been issued. Especially the latter aspect has been an important improvement, as it may and has so far demonstrated that the government uses the tool in particular to obtain personal information not belonging to the most intrusive category of information, such as library records and medical records.

Nevertheless, the potential for abuse remains high because of the absence of meaningful restraints on the scope of the order and the lack of a meaningful judicial review and accountability in particular before the fact. Considering that this tool was first introduced by the USA PATRIOT Act of 2001, a test on the basis of substantive due process seems warranted.[127] Any legislation passed by Congress must satisfy the strict scrutiny test: "the restriction must be narrowly tailored to serve a compelling government interest." When comparing the document production order to similar authority in the context of a conventional criminal investigation, it must be observed that the important restraint of a connection to a crime that has been, is being or will be committed; a meaningful possibility for the recipient to challenge, before a court, the legitimacy of the order before complying; the requirement of notification as a check on abuse; and democratic legitimization as realized through grand jury authority, are all lacking. Hence, the document production order is, obviously, not as narrowly tailored as similar authority in conventional criminal law. Furthermore, in order not to violate substantive due process, the legislation must have a 'reasonable relation to a legitimate end' and it shall not 'unnecessarily or arbitrarily limit fundamental rights.'[128] Considering its incorporation in FISA, the reasonable relation of the investigative tool to the government's legitimate need to gather foreign intelligence is obvious. At the same time it must be observed that the need to use the FISA document production order has been reduced as a consequence of expanding the definition of the information that can be obtained through pen register and trap and trace device orders. In addition, one of the consequences of dismantling the wall has been the

[127] See Sect. 5.1.4.2.

[128] See Sect. 5.1.4.2.

availability to intelligence investigators of grand jury information by lifting the prohibition on prosecutors to disclose any matters occurring before the grand jury.[129] Therefore, the necessity of this investigative tool is doubtful.[130] According to David Kris, the Assistant Attorney General for national security, in addition to these other possibilities, the need for similar investigative tools in the context of FISA investigations remains, because of the veil of secrecy that is afforded to FISA authority.[131] It is however questionable whether this limited necessity for the tool outweighs the substantial lack of meaningful protective elements in the regulation of the document production order and the commensurate potential for abuse.

## 7.4 Interaction Between Law Enforcement and Intelligence Communities for the Purpose of Enabling a Preventive Approach

As a consequence of changing the FISA 'purpose language' by amending the USA PATRIOT Act and the interpretation given to this new threshold for FISA surveillance or a physical search by the FISA Court of Review, 'the wall' between the intelligence and the law enforcement communities has been dismantled. In addition, Guidelines issued by the Department of Justice in the post-9/11 era were particularly aimed at increasing cooperation and information sharing between the intelligence and law enforcement communities. Prosecutors are allowed to advise FBI intelligence officials with regard to "the initiation, operation, continuation, or expansion of FISA searches or surveillance." Moreover, FBI national security and criminal investigations are no longer separated areas, but are understood to perform at any time both counterintelligence and law enforcement functions. Lastly, the position of the DNI has been established to coordinate the joint efforts of all federal agencies to protect, in cooperation, the national security. As a result of these amendments and policy changes, previously separated law enforcement and intelligence functions and goals have now been blended. National security investigations have obtained a law enforcement function and have become the investigative context for criminal activities that at the same time pose a threat to national security. The current reliance on the framework for national security investigations when prevention and evidence-gathering are co-existing purposes has enabled the phenomenon defined in the first Chapter as an anticipative criminal investigation.

---

[129] See Sect. 6.4.1.

[130] In 2010 a total of 96 applications for a section 215 order were authorized by the FISA Court, in 2005 the number was 155. See FISA Annual Reports to Congress (2010 and 2005), available at: http://www.fas.org/irp/agency/doj/fisa/#rept (accessed August 1, 2011).

[131] Statement of David Kris, Assistant Attorney General, Before the Committee on the Judiciary United States Senate 2009, 3.

Firstly, this section will briefly redefine, on the basis of the findings of Sect. 6.4.1, the institutional position and the functions of a conventional criminal investigation and of national security investigations. In this new context also the position and role of the FBI will be defined, as the agency composed of both an intelligence and law enforcement division that has undergone a transformation as a consequence of its primary function of conducting anticipative criminal investigations. Secondly, the consequences of the current institutional positions and functions of the different actors responsible for anticipative criminal investigations and the frameworks in which they operate for the protective objective of criminal procedural law will be identified. In particular, attention will be given to the reasons underpinning the previous institutional separation between intelligence and law enforcement and the manner in which the Supreme Court has previously made a distinction between national security investigations and conventional criminal investigations when applying the Fourth Amendment. Thirdly, the manner in which the criminal process is 'infected' due to the dismantling of the wall and sharing obligations will be assessed in particular with regard to guaranteeing procedural due process.

### *7.4.1 Redefining Institutional Positions and Functions*

The issue of a lack of cooperation between law enforcement agencies and intelligence agencies and the impediments to the sharing of information between agencies is repeatedly blamed as one of the main causes of the incapability to prevent 9/11 and, hence, was the subject of many changes in order to create a system capable of preventing future attacks.[132] Especially the FBI was meant to undergo a transformation from an agency that was primarily focused on law enforcement and building cases for prosecution to an agency that is at the forefront in combating terrorism. This resulted in the adoption of the FBI's 'highest priority' of preventing terrorist attacks on the United States and many measures in order to create a well-developed intelligence division, close cooperation between the intelligence and law enforcement divisions of the FBI and adequate information sharing between any appropriate agency.[133]

The increased interaction between the law enforcement community and intelligence community, which is in particular apparent in the transformation of the

---

[132] Although there were no explicit legal barriers prohibiting the sharing of information, 'the wall'—a consequence primarily of a history of abuse and the purpose language—and the cultural separation between law enforcement and intelligence that had followed, prevented any sharing. See Sect. 5.2.2.3.2.

[133] See the Unclassified Report of the Office of the Inspector General: The Federal Bureau of Investigation's Efforts to Improve the Sharing of Intelligence and Other Information' 2003. Most of the recommendations in this report have resulted in the concrete memoranda or guidelines (as dealt with in this section) in order to enhance cooperation and sharing.

functioning of the FBI, has been caused by both changing legal requirements concerning investigation and the dissemination of information as well as by changes governing the investigative policy of the FBI including the removal of bureaucratic impediments to the full sharing of information between different state entities. In the first place, the amendment of the USA PATRIOT Act of 2001, which has changed the threshold for the use of FISA investigative tools from 'the purpose' to 'a significant purpose' and the sweeping interpretation that has been given to this subtle change of language, has been the most significant legislative measure to dismantle the wall and to enable anticipative criminal investigations. In the second place, the guidelines on FBI Operations of 2008 concern an important switch in policy with regard to the investigative activities of the FBI.

According to the FISA Court of Review the new purpose language shall be interpreted as the primary purpose of the national security investigation being the gathering of evidence, as long as there is also a significant purpose for gathering foreign intelligence information.[134] On the basis of the definition of foreign intelligence information provided in FISA—"information that relates to, and if concerning a United States person is necessary to, the ability of the United States to protect against certain national security threats that can be related to a foreign power or an agent of a foreign power"[135]—terrorism investigations with the primary purpose of collecting evidence for prosecution may in any event be conducted under the FISA investigative framework. In addition to changing the purpose language, also other amendments of the USA PATRIOT Act were particularly aimed at doing away with the wall previously separating the national security investigation from the criminal investigation. As described in Sect. 6.4.1, these amendments concern the sharing of information obtained through the criminal investigative framework of Title III with national security investigators, the disclosure of grand jury information—normally shielded by the principle of grand jury secrecy—to national security investigators and the promotion of cooperation and consultation between national security investigators and law enforcement officers.[136] It follows from the definitions of foreign intelligence and counterintelligence provided in the National Security Act of 1947 (as amended) that the information to be shared under these provisions concerns a rather wide range of information related to "capabilities, intentions or activities" of foreign governments, foreign organizations, foreign persons or international terrorist activities or related to the protection against "espionage, other intelligence activities, sabotage, or assassinations" on behalf of these actors.[137] As a consequence of these legislative measures the regulatory framework—mainly either

---

[134] *In re Sealed Case:* 310 F.3d 717 (FISA Ct. Rev. 2002), 734. See also Sect. 6.4.1.

[135] See 50 U.S.C. § 1801(e) (2011).

[136] Sections 203 and 504 of the USA PATRIOT Act 2001. See in detail Sect. 6.4.1.

[137] See 50 U.S.C. § 401a(2) and (3), amended by the USA PATRIOT Act, sec. 902 to include also international terrorist activities as foreign intelligence and counterintelligence information. See Sect. 6.4.1.

Title III or FISA—which is applicable to investigative activities is no longer dependent on the main (primary) purpose of the investigation. Especially when the investigation concerns activities that may threaten national security, anticipating the averting of potential future harm has been considered an interest to supersede law enforcement and prosecutorial interests. Hence, it is now possible to apply investigative techniques in these types of investigation under the more flexible framework of FISA, even when the main purpose of the investigation is to collect evidence for prosecution.

As the second main development resulting in the dismantling of the wall, the changed internal policy of the Department of Justice, in particular of the FBI, has been addressed in Sect. 6.4.2. Internal memoranda were distributed calling for a full exchange of information and cooperation between the different components of the Department of Justice. A binding agreement (the Memorandum of March 4, 2003) was issued making it obligatory to share information when the substance of that information is relevant for other federal agencies and their efforts to protect national security, regardless of the fact that such sharing may adversely affect investigative or prosecutorial interests. In addition, bureaucratic changes have significantly contributed to strengthening close cooperation between the law enforcement community and intelligence community. In that regard the Joint Terrorism Task Force as well as other fusion centers fulfill an important role in the realization of the full sharing of information. Furthermore, the Director of National Intelligence has been established through the Intelligence Reform and Terrorism Prevention Act of 2004 in order to promote the sharing of intelligence between different agencies. Also a National Counterterrorism Center was established in order to be the central repository of all intelligence possessed or acquired by different agencies and to integrate and analyze those data.[138]

In the post-9/11 era two new sets of Guidelines of the Attorney General were issued covering the FBI's investigative activities. It is remarkable that both the 2002 and the 2008 Guidelines were aimed at enhancing the investigative capacities of the FBI in order to give effect to the FBI's 'highest priority' of effectively confronting terrorism. President Bush and, following, Attorney General Ashcroft announced soon after 9/11 2001 the central paradigm of prevention to cover the US government's counterterrorism strategy. As a consequence, also the Department of Justice "added a new paradigm to that of prosecution—a paradigm of prevention." In order to give effect to this new paradigm of prevention "[w]e have broken down some of the artificial barriers separating needlessly our law enforcement and intelligence communities."[139] Whereas the internal Guidelines were distributed in 1976 and 1983 (the Smith Guidelines, preceding the Ashcroft Guidelines) in order to give guidance in the FBI's discretionary field in order to

---

[138] See Sect. 6.4.3.

[139] Prepared Remarks of Attorney General John Ashcroft, Council on Foreign Relations, February 10, 2003. Available at: http://www.justice.gov/archive/ag/speeches/2003/021003 agcouncilonforeignrelation.htm (last visited on December 9, 2010). See also Ashcroft 2006, 131-142 ('New Priorities: From Prosecution to Prevention').

avoid abuse,[140] the Guidelines of 2002 and 2008 (and the DIOG of the FBI, providing even more detailed guidance on the basis of the Mukasey Guidelines) particularly aimed at seeking the limits of the FBI's discretionary field in order to enhance the investigative capacities of the FBI and to combine its forces in combating terrorism. For this purpose the 2002 Ashcroft Guidelines directed the creation of information systems to be accessible by the different counterparts of the FBI and generally allowed for more expedite investigative action when terrorism is involved. Ashcroft indicated in these guidelines that the use of authorized investigative methods to "anticipate or prevent crime" is permitted also when criminal activity has not yet taken place, save for situations where investigative actions target activities entitled to full First Amendment protection or protection following from other constitutional rights or US laws. Moreover, the necessity of establishing an evidentiary standard before initiating investigative activities has been abandoned and, in general, thresholds are understood to be met when the government claims a national security interest.[141] The Mukasey Guidelines of 2008 can be understood as having completed, in a legal sense, the FBI transformation into an agency with primary responsibility for the anticipative criminal investigation of national security crimes/threats, by issuing one set of guidelines covering, without distinction, the FBI's national security investigative activities and criminal investigative activities. Similar to the interpretation of the purpose language, these uniform guidelines have set aside the relation between the regulation and purpose of investigative activities. Rather, the forces of the different FBI divisions have been combined in order to jointly confront threats to national security, such as terrorism.[142] This has also transformed the role of the FBI, which will be further assessed below.

Considering the background of removing the wall between the intelligence community and the law enforcement community, namely offering the most powerful investigative capacities and the least protective regulatory bumps in order to be able to anticipate averting future harm, the form of investigation resulting from the merger between criminal investigations and national security investigations, especially when terrorism is involved, can be defined as an anticipative criminal investigation. With the removal of both legal restraints and policy restraints precluding joint investigations with law enforcement and foreign intelligence purposes, the statutory scheme of FISA can now be qualified as a quasi-law enforcement area. Typically, investigations involving terrorist crimes, or in fact all federal crimes that also constitute a threat to national security and can be linked to a foreign power or an agent of a foreign power—and, hence, also receiving the attention of the intelligence community—will be conducted under the looser statutory framework of FISA.

---

[140] Hence, in Chap. 5 the Guidelines were dealt with as part of the 'shield' of regulating criminal investigations. See Sect. 5.3.2.3.

[141] See Sect. 6.4.2.2.

[142] See Sect. 6.4.2.2.

Under the new FBI Guidelines (the Mukasey Guidelines of 2008) a single investigation will be initiated when, for example, investigating terrorism and all the authorized investigative tools available for the level of investigation may be used. One may assume that the FBI will prefer to choose FISA tools above Title III when conducting full or enterprise investigations. Thus, considering the criminal investigative purposes (collecting evidence) that investigative activities conducted under the FISA framework may currently have (and are likely to have when terrorism is involved), the FISA framework—as a quasi-law enforcement area—can be brought under the definition of a criminal investigation. The most important goal of the FISA investigation will remain, however, preventing the realization of terrorist or other national security crimes, an interest understood to supersede the interest of collecting evidence. *In re Sealed Case* (2002) the FISA Court of Review observed that "the main purpose of ordinary criminal law is twofold: to punish the wrongdoer and to deter other persons in society from embarking on the same course. The government's concern with respect to foreign intelligence crimes, on the other hand, is overwhelmingly to stop or frustrate the immediate criminal activity." These goals have now been intertwined. "[T]he criminal process is often used as part of an integrated effort to counter the malign efforts of a foreign power."[143] Hence, FISA investigations can be defined as anticipative criminal investigations.

In addition, we have seen in Sect. 7.2 that also the conventional criminal investigation has obtained a preventive function and that criminal investigations are conducted in anticipation of future criminality, especially when terrorism is involved. Considering these two developments, it can be concluded that the law enforcement community and intelligence community have moved towards each other; criminal investigations may sometimes pursue a preventive goal superseding the interest of the investigation of a crime and the collection of evidence, whereas the national security investigation may now also pursue law enforcement goals. Anticipating future harm for the purpose of prevention is in both situations the main objective. As the FISA Court of Review put it: "[p]unishment of the terrorist or espionage agent is really a secondary objective; indeed, punishment of a terrorist is often a moot point."[144]

Whereas the intelligence community and law enforcement community were previously strictly separated areas to offer the level of regulation that is in conformity with its investigative purpose, currently the purposes of investigation may overlap and concur both in the context of conventional criminal investigations and in the context of national security investigations.[145] For that reason, the distinction traditionally made between a conventional criminal investigation and a national security investigation can under the current circumstances no longer be upheld. The investigation pursuing both a preventive purpose and law enforcement

[143] *In re: Sealed Case,* 310 F.3d 717 (FISA Ct. Rev. 2002), 744.

[144] *Ibid.*, 744-745.

[145] Compare: Power 2010, 624-625.

purpose shall be defined as an anticipative criminal investigation. As a consequence, the applicable regulation framework is no longer imperatively connected to the purpose of the investigation, but seems largely to be a matter of discretion for the investigative officers.

The FBI can be considered as the organization in which the redefinition of the position and goals of the law enforcement community and intelligence community in their shared task of anticipative criminal investigations has been incarnated. Most significantly as a consequence of the 2008 Mukasey Guidelines and their implementation in the DIOG, especially the FBI, as an agency composed of both an intelligence and a law enforcement division, has been transformed into an agency primarily responsible for the prevention of terrorist crimes through combining both its preventive intelligence function and its evidence-gathering function. The guidelines issued since 2001 (both the Ashcroft Guidelines and the Mukasey Guidelines) particularly aim at directing national security *and* criminal investigative authority to confront terrorism more effectively. Although the Smith Guidelines had already eliminated the separate regulation for domestic security and terrorism investigations by treating them both as an integral part of the FBI's general law enforcement responsibilities, the Smith Guidelines of 1983 were still only applicable to investigative activities with a nexus to criminal activity. Foreign intelligence (FISA) investigations were clearly excluded from the scope of the guidelines and thus from the law enforcement task.[146] As a consequence of the Mukasey Guidelines, the different investigative purposes of the FBI have been merged, which can be pursued by the different investigative phases (assessment, preliminary or full predicated investigation, enterprise investigation). The same standards apply, regardless of the specific (or multiple) purpose pursued by the investigative activities. As we have seen above, in the case of multiple purposes, it is also possible to use surveillance techniques or physical searches under the FISA framework, even when the primary purpose is to gather evidence for a criminal prosecution.

It clearly follows from the Mukasey Guidelines and their implementation in the DIOG that the US government intended to make the FBI the organization with primary responsibility for anticipative criminal investigations. Hence, the 'highest priority' of the FBI and of its investigative activities is to protect against terrorism. The prosecution of the perpetrators of crimes is in second place. In the DIOG it was even explicitly mentioned that the goal of this guide supplementing the Attorney General's guidelines was to realize the transformation of the FBI into an intelligence-

[146] For an overview of the precise differences between the Smith Guidelines of 1983 and the Mukasey Guidelines of 2008, see the two tables (Tables 7.1, 7.2) at the end of this Chapter. Except for the main difference between the two sets of guidelines as to their scope (the Mukasey Guidelines cover the investigative activities for national security (including foreign intelligence) purposes and for law enforcement/criminal justice purposes, whereas the Smith Guidelines only cover investigations for law enforcement and national security (not foreign intelligence) purposes where there is a clear nexus to criminal activity), these tables demonstrate the differences and common features as to the type of investigation, its goal, the threshold and other restraints applicable and the powers available.

driven organization. In that regard the Guidelines, supplemented by the FBI, can be understood as setting out the borders (following from the Constitution and US federal law) of the investigative authority, which enables FBI agents to use all available powers to gather as much information as possible and, on that basis, to become an intelligence-driven organization. Furthermore, considering the training that FBI agents currently receive in both national intelligence and criminal justice matters as a consequence of the Intelligence Reform and Terrorism Prevention Act, not only on the organizational level but also on the individual level, the full institutionalization of the FBI as the agency responsible for anticipative criminal investigations (or: as "preventive counterterrorism posture") has been realized.[147]

### 7.4.2 Consequences of the Institutional Position and Functions of the Anticipative Criminal Investigation

As a consequence of the interpretation given to 'a significant purpose' by the FISA Court of Review, the primary purpose test, which was applied prior to the PATRIOT Act amendment, was rejected. This primary purpose test was established as a threshold to separate surveillance and search warrants in a national security context from conventional law enforcement, with a different assessment of the Fourth Amendment protections. The adoption of FISA and a clear distinction between investigations for law enforcement purposes and investigations to protect national security was the deliberate result of the Supreme Court decisions of *Berger* (1967),[148] *Katz* (1967)[149] (on regulating electronic surveillance for law enforcement purposes) and *Keith* (1972)[150] (on the application of the Fourth Amendment to national security investigations) and the findings of the Church Committee following a history of abuses of executive surveillance power.[151] Already prior to the adoption of the USA PATRIOT Act the purposes of the broader investigation could differ as long as the primary purpose of the FISA surveillance applied within the context of this broader investigation was to gather foreign intelligence. The rationale behind the primary purpose language was clear: to prevent evading Title III to pursue law enforcement objectives through the looser statutory framework of FISA, which would result in a violation of the Fourth Amendment (as affirmed in the *Keith* and *Truong* cases). Now that a 'significant purpose' of FISA investigations shall be the collection of foreign intelligence information, the path has been cleared for a fusion between foreign intelligence and law enforcement purposes under FISA. This raises concerns as to the constitutionality of FISA investigative activities for the purpose of gathering

---

[147] See Sect. 6.4.3.

[148] *Berger v. New York*, 388 U.S. 41, 87 S.Ct. 1873 (1967).

[149] *Katz v. Unites States,* 389 U.S. 347, 88 S.Ct. 507 (1967).

[150] *United States v. United States District Court*, 407 U.S. 297, 92 S.Ct. 2125 (1972).

[151] See Sect. 5.3.2.3.1.

evidence, considering the previous statutory distinction between Title III and FISA and the Supreme Court's decisions in *Berger* (1967) and *Katz* (1967) and especially the Supreme Court's decision in *Keith* (1972) and the Fourth Circuit Court's decision in *United States v. Truong* (1980).[152]

In *Keith* the Supreme Court distinguished electronic surveillance for law enforcement purposes from electronic surveillance for intelligence purposes. As described in Sect. 5.2.2.3, the Court concluded that the Fourth Amendment covered electronic surveillance for either investigative purpose and, therefore, a warrant is required. The Fourth Amendment applies to intelligence purposes concerning "domestic aspects of national security" and not to "foreign powers or their agents." At the same time, the *Keith* Court distinguished between law enforcement purposes and intelligence purposes by emphasizing that "domestic security surveillances may involve different policy and practical considerations from the surveillance of 'ordinary crime.'"[153] Thus, according to the Supreme Court in *Keith*, although a warrant is required and the Fourth Amendment applies in order to protect the privacy interests impinged by electronic surveillance, there can be a differentiation in the applicable regulatory standards in accordance with the investigative purpose. The Supreme Court distinguished three investigative purposes of electronic surveillance and a physical search: criminal law enforcement purposes (covered by the Fourth Amendment and Title III), domestic national security investigations (covered by the Fourth Amendment, requiring a warrant, although looser conditions may apply than provided by Title III), and foreign intelligence investigations with no domestic connection (not necessarily covered by the Fourth Amendment). Taking into account the *Keith* decision, the blending of investigative purposes and, consequently, breaking with the relation between investigative purpose and the applicable regulatory framework in order to safeguard Fourth Amendment interests may be disputable as to compatibility with US constitutional law.

In *United States v. Truong* the Fourth Circuit Court decided a case where the investigation initially had a foreign intelligence purpose but changed into a criminal investigation, which had occurred prior to the enactment of FISA.[154] According to the Fourth Circuit Court, a warrantless electronic surveillance was permissible when the "surveillance is conducted 'primarily' for foreign intelligence reasons," but the evidence obtained after the purpose of the investigation had shifted to a primary criminal investigative purpose was excluded as a consequence of violating the Fourth Amendment.[155] The FISA Court of Review (*In re: Sealed*) actually rejected the *United States v. Truong* decision and even held that the ruling, "whether correctly understood or not," may have contributed "to the FBI missing opportunities to anticipate the September 11, 2001 attacks."[156]

---

152 *United States v. Truong*, 629 F.2d 908 (4th Cir. 1980).

153 *United States v. United States District Court*, 407 U.S. 297, 92 S.Ct. 2125 (1972), 322.

154 See Sect. 5.2.2.3.2.

155 *United States v. Truong*, 629 F.2d 908 (4th Cir. 1980), 915.

156 *In re Sealed Case*, 310 F.3d 717 (FISA Ct. Rev. 2002), 744.

The US District Court of Oregon has been confronted with the issue of the constitutionality of the use of FISA investigative powers under the current statutory scheme for the purpose of gathering evidence against Brandon Mayfield who was allegedly involved in the 2004 terrorist bombings in Madrid. The FISA Court had authorized extensive search and surveillance activities relating to Mayfield, his family and his law firm, on the basis of what seemed more like a random and, in any event, disputable fingerprint match, in combination with speculative circumstances such as Mayfield's Muslim faith. After being arrested and detained, Mayfield was finally released when the Spanish authorities matched the Madrid fingerprint with an Algerian man.[157] The government made a showing that Mayfield was an agent of a foreign power, which the FISA Court could only reject if this was clearly erroneous. The court observed that the primary purpose of the FISA surveillance was in this case the gathering of evidence to prosecute Mayfield for crimes. According to the district court such FISA surveillance with a "programmatic purpose" of generating evidence for law enforcement purposes is unconstitutional, as the activities were conducted while lacking probable cause and a warrant. For that reason, also the PATRIOT Act Amendments to FISA that have changed the purpose language were rendered unconstitutional.[158] The basis for this conclusion is similar to the reasoning of the Fourth Circuit Court in *United States v. Truong* in 1980.[159] Unfortunately, the Court of Appeals of the Ninth Circuit vacated and remanded the judgment without reaching the merits of Mayfield's Fourth Amendment claim, because Mayfield lacked standing for a declaratory judgment.[160] However, several other federal courts have considered the constitutionality of FISA under the Fourth Amendment, all ruling—following the *In re: Sealed* case—that it does not violate the Fourth Amendment.[161] On that basis the conclusion seems warranted that also US courts have discarded, in line with the approaches of the US government by amending FISA and the Department of

[157] See the reports of the Inspector General on this fingerprint misidentification: Report of the Office of the Inspector General 2006, *A Review of the FBI's Handling of the Brandon Mayfield Case* and Report of the Office of the Inspector General 2011, *A Review of the FBI's Progress in Responding to the Recommendations of the Office of the Inspector General Report on the Fingerprint Misidentification in the Brandon Mayfield Case*.

[158] *Mayfield v. United States,* 504 F.Supp.2d 1023 (D.Or. 2007), 1033, 1038-1039 and 1042-1043.

[159] See in detail Sect. 5.3.2.3.1.

[160] *Mayfield v. United States,* 599 F.3d 964 (9th Cir. 2010). 970.

[161] E.g.: *United States v. Ning Wen,* 477 F.3d 896 (7th Cir.2007), *United States v. Mubayyid,* 521 F.Supp.2d 125 (D.Mass. 2007), *United States v. Warsame,* 547 F.Supp.2d 982 (D.Minn. 2008) and *United States v. Abu-Jihaad,* 630 F.3d 102 (2nd Cir. 2010). The Court in *United Stated v. Ning Wen* took a slightly different approach in reasoning why FISA was constitutional under the significant purpose test: as long as the statutory requirements are met (the government could satisfy the requirement of probable cause that the target was an agent of a foreign power and a significant purpose of the surveillance was to gather foreign intelligence) any evidence obtained by the FISA surveillance was legitimate as being discovered in plain view during legitimately authorized surveillance.

Justice by its new internal policy, the imperative relation between the level of Fourth Amendment protection required and the purpose of the investigation.

As has already been touched upon in the section dealing with the special needs doctrine (7.2.2.1), the FISA Court of Review referred in *In re*: *Sealed* to the applicability of the reasoning of the special needs doctrine also to investigations with overlapping intelligence and law enforcement purposes. The surveillance for the purpose of intelligence gathering, also an administrative purpose, could also be treated as a special needs search and, on that basis, could be exempted from the warrant and probable cause requirement. The same result will be realized as under *Keith*: national security investigations are exempted from full Fourth Amendment protection. An important difference, however, is that the administrate searches that are indicated as special needs searches are typically searches that are considered not to seriously interfere with private life, such as airport security searches, border controls or sobriety checkpoints.[162] Nevertheless, in *Macwade v. Kelly* (2006) also the purpose of preventing terrorism has been accepted as a special need justifying the warrantless and random search of bags in New York City's subway.[163] In general, the analogy can certainly be recognized between the exceptional treatment, under the Fourth Amendment, of searches for legitimate government needs beyond ordinary law enforcement needs under the special needs doctrine and the distinction made between national security investigations and law enforcement surveillance as follows from the differences between FISA and Title III.

More surprising is the justification which the FISA Court of Review in *In re*: *Sealed* (2002) has sought in the special needs doctrine, in order to support its argument that the 'significant purpose language' allows for a FISA investigation with a primary law enforcement purpose.[164] The courts that have assessed special needs cases have repeatedly warned that the special needs doctrine may not be used to circumvent Fourth Amendment requirements by the law enforcement officers responsible for conducting the special need search or control and the Supreme Court has decided that a special need search was unreasonable when primarily used for a law enforcement purpose instead of the special need.[165] Nevertheless, the FISA Court of Review did use the doctrine to allow for a merger of purposes in a national security investigation. In 2008 the FISA Court of Review even more strongly applied the special needs doctrine to FISA searches. According to the FISA Court of Review in *In re Directives Pursuant to Section 105B of the Foreign Intelligence Surveillance Act* (2008) the Supreme Court "excluded compliance with the Warrant Clause when the purpose behind the governmental action went beyond routine law enforcement and insisting upon a warrant would

[162] See Sect. 5.3.2.1.1.1.

[163] *Macwade v. Kelly*, 460 F.3d 260 (2nd Cir. 2006).

[164] *In re Sealed Case*, 310 F.3d (FISA Ct. Rev. 2002), 745-746. See also: Donohue 2008, 234.

[165] See Sects. 7.2.2.1 and 5.3.2.1.1.1.

materially interfere with the accomplishment of that purpose."[166] Decisive for whether the special needs doctrine applies by analogy to national security investigations, it depends on the "programmatic purpose of the [FISA] surveillance and whether—as in the special needs cases—that programmatic purpose involves some legitimate objectives beyond ordinary crime control."[167] The approach taken by the FISA Court of Review until now seems to be at odds with the federal courts when assessing the special needs doctrine. Recently in *Macwade v. Kelly* (2006), it was still emphasized that to qualify as a special need search the purpose of the search is "narrowly tailored and sufficiently effective" and shall not be used as a "general means of enforcing the criminal law."[168]

When we combine the findings of the previous and the current section, a development can be identified where the interest of preventing terrorism trumps the interest of protecting privacy rights, which is recognizable in legislative changes, the change of internal policy, and the use of the special needs doctrine to justify the deviation from regular constitutional limitations. This reasoning applies to conventional criminal searches, FISA searches and the general policy of the Department of Justice and the FBI. It also easily fits within today's Fourth Amendment examination, as Fourth Amendment analysis has developed into an ultimate reasonableness assessment of the search as a whole based on the totality of circumstances. Consequently, balancing the interest of preventing terrorism against privacy interests generally results in an outcome in favor of the interest of preventing terrorism.

The current approach of the FISA Court of Review as to the fusion of investigative purposes in FISA investigations can be summarized as follows: as long as the programmatic purpose of the search is to gather foreign intelligence information[169] in order to protect national security also other purposes may be present, whereas full Fourth Amendment protection is not required. The FISA Court of Review reaches this conclusion by relying on *Keith* and observing that *Keith* did not assess the constitutionality of the surveillance of agents of foreign powers but only domestic security. However, these two activities, under the current definitions

---

[166] *In re Directives Pursuant to Section 105B of the Foreign Intelligence Surveillance Act*, 551 F.3d 1004 (FISA Ct. Rev. 2008), 1010.

[167] *Ibid.*, 1011. *In re Directives* dealt in particular with the 'terrorist surveillance program' as regulated in the Protect America Act of 2007 (see Sect. 6.5.1).

[168] *Macwade v. Kelly,* 460 F.3d 260 (2nd Cir. 2006), 263 and 268.

[169] Also in this context it is important to realize the scope of the definition of foreign intelligence, which is not limited to intelligence concerning non-US persons or relating to activities abroad. Domestic activities, whether or not by US persons, which can (ideologically) be related to international terrorism fall within the definition of foreign intelligence. 50 U.S.C. § 401a (2) and (3) and see Sect. 6.4.2.

of agents of foreign powers and foreign intelligence information, can no longer be separated.[170] It is unclear how the difference between the programmatic purpose and the primary purpose is to be understood. Considering the developments in conventional criminal law and the redefining of the primary mission of the Department of Justice, and in particular the FBI, it seems that anticipating future national security threats for the purpose of prevention seems to supersede the conventional law enforcement purposes of gathering sufficient information for prosecution. Hence, the programmatic purpose of the investigation can in all counterterrorism investigations reasonably be defined as the gathering of foreign intelligence information in order to protect national security. Consequently, the collection of evidence during a FISA investigation goes beyond what could be understood as plain-view gathering. The collection of evidence may be the primary purpose of the search; however, the interest of protecting national security by collecting 'foreign intelligence' will nevertheless always surpass—as a 'top priority'—the interest of collecting evidence.[171]

The programmatic purpose appears, at face value, to offer more protection against abuses of FISA power to circumvent Fourth Amendment requirements which are applicable to criminal investigations. Exactly on that basis, also the US District Court of Oregon held that the FISA surveillance and search of Mayfield as well as the PATRIOT Act amendments changing FISA's purpose language were unconstitutional, because the programmatic purpose was to collect information to be used as evidence in a criminal prosecution.[172] Also other federal courts have in line with *In re: Sealed* considered that the FISA Court judge can deny the order when the 'programmatic purpose' is likely to be a law enforcement purpose: "[w]hatever the bounds of the "clearly erroneous" standard, a judicial officer plainly has the ability to deny a request intended solely for domestic law enforcement purposes, or where the foreign intelligence purpose is not significant."[173] Although the review of a FISA application by the FISA Court judge is rather marginal and largely dependent on the certifications of the government, federal courts have considered the marginal review "far from a meaningless

170 In fact, also the FISA of 1978 was based on the *Keith* decision with regard to domestic national security activities, considering that FISA provides for a weaker version of Fourth Amendment requirements such as probable cause and a warrant. Already at that time, foreign intelligence activities were likely to include also domestic national security activities. Compare also: Swire 2004, 1339.

171 Compare the new policy of the DoJ on the basis of the new paradigm of prevention and, in particular, the redefinition of the FBI's highest priority "to protect the security of the nation and the safety of the American people against the depredations of terrorists and foreign aggressors." See Sect. 6.4.2.2.

172 *Mayfield v. United States*, 504 F.Supp.2d 1023 (D.Or. 2007), 1033, 1038-1039 and 1042-1043.

173 *United States v. Mubayyid*, 521 F.Supp. 2d 125 (D.Mass. 2007), 136. The FISA Court judge is held to accept the showing of the government regarding the 'significant purpose' unless this is clearly erroneous.

rubber-stamp."[174] Nevertheless, it must be noted that it follows from the statistical information annually submitted to Congress that the FISA Court has over the past decade rarely denied an application for FISA electronic surveillance.[175]

However, the current prioritizing of interests within the Department of Justice and the definition of foreign intelligence makes it impossible to draw a clear line on the basis of a programmatic purpose test. Promoted by internal policy, FISA investigations are likely to pursue multiple purposes without a precise demarcation of the situations where additional restraints need to apply as required under the Fourth Amendment for the investigation of crime for prosecutorial purposes. As will be dealt with in the next section, the use of information gathered under FISA in criminal proceedings has implications for the exertion of procedural due process rights. Hence, the current approach seems to deviate from the intention of the Supreme Court in *Keith* (and even more specifically as to distinguishing purposes, the Fourth Circuit Court in *Truong*), namely making the required level of Fourth Amendment limitations to the power to search dependent on the purpose of the investigation.[176]

### *7.4.3 An Infected Criminal Process?*

Before turning to the implications of an anticipative criminal investigation for the criminal process, it must be noted that the role of criminal proceedings and judicial review in general with regard to realizing accountability for anticipative criminal investigative activities has decreased. This decreased role of judicial review has two reasons.

In the first place, as already indicated in Sect. 7.2.3, courts have been more deferential where investigative activities have been conducted for the purpose of prevention. However, this does not apply to judicial review in general. In many other areas the judiciary has stepped in in order to halt the executive in broadening its powers, for example, with regard to the detention policy and procedure of terrorist suspects. In addition, civil litigation has played a significant role in reviewing new and amended legislation, such as the review of the NSL authority (as dealt with in Sect. 6.3.2). Nevertheless, in criminal proceedings, courts have demonstrated a more deferential review of investigative standards where the protection of national security is involved.

In the second place, the possibilities for a review of an anticipative criminal investigation in the context of criminal proceedings are comparably limited. Many persons investigated in the context of an anticipative criminal investigation will never

---

[174] *United States v. Mubayyid*, 521 F.Supp. 2d 125 (D. Mass. 2007), 136.

[175] FISA Annual Reports to Congress 2000–2010. Available at: http://www.fas.org/irp/agency/doj/fisa/#rept (accessed August 4, 2011).

[176] Compare: Power 2010, 682-687.

face criminal charges.[177] Moreover, especially national security investigative techniques are not in the first place controlled by the judiciary, but primarily by means of alternative controlling mechanisms. More intrusive techniques have generally not been compensated by an extended judicial review, but by enhanced Congressional oversight.[178] In addition, the internal review exerted by the Inspectors General concerns an important controlling mechanism, which has been capable of bringing an investigative overreach to light, for example, with respect to the issuing of NSLs.[179]

Nevertheless, where persons investigated in the context of an anticipative criminal investigation are subsequently prosecuted, the specific nature of the information used and collected in the anticipative criminal investigation and the secretive nature of the national security investigative techniques affect the criminal proceedings. The US Constitutional system is based on the presumption of an open government and transparency as a prerequisite for accountability.[180] The secrecy required in national security investigations is the exception to this general presumption of transparency. Secrecy in national security investigations is considered to be so crucial for the success of the effective protection of national security because intelligence sources and methods shall not be compromised and the often long-lasting investigation shall

---

[177] Although any person whose rights have been violated is entitled to instigate a civil action for damages under *Bivens v. Six Unknown Agents of Federal Bureau of Narcotics,* 403 U.S. 388, 91 S.Ct. 1999 (1971). See Sect. 5.3.1.4.

[178] See e.g. Sect. 6.2.1 (enhanced Congressional oversight for expanded law enforcement powers, such as on emergency disclosure and delayed notice), Sect. 6.3.1 (enhanced Congressional oversight on FISA surveillance), Sect. 6.3.2 (enhanced Congressional oversight on document production orders, although the Reauthorization Acts have also expanded the previously very limited possibilities for judicial review), Sect. 6.5.1 (enhanced Congressional oversight to compensate for the surveillance of non US-persons outside the US) and Sect. 6.5.2 (enhanced oversight on the use of NSL).

[179] See Report of the Office of Inspector General 2010, *A Review of the Federal Bureau of Investigation's Use of Exigent Letters and Other Informal Requests for Telephone Records.*

[180] Sales 2007, 816. Immediately after taking Office, on January 21st 2009 President Obama issued a Memorandum for the Heads of Executive Departments and Agencies on 'Transparency and Open Government' in order to enhance the government's openness and transparency in order to improve accountability. Memorandum available at: http://www.fas.org/sgp/obama/transparency.pdf (accessed December 12, 2010). In another Memorandum by President Obama issued on the same day regarding the Freedom of Information Act, Obama directed that a presumption of disclosure and thus in favor of transparency shall be guiding when dealing with FOIA requests. Memorandum available at: http://www.sec.gov/foia/president-memo-foia-nov2009.pdf (accessed December 12, 2010). See also the preamble to Executive Order No. 13526 'National Security Information', *75 Fed. Reg. 707* (Dec. 29 2009), stipulating that: "[o]ur democratic principles require that the American people be informed of the activities of their Government. Also, our Nation's progress depends on the free flow of information both within the Government and to the American people. Nevertheless, throughout history, the national defense has required that certain information be maintained in confidence in order to protect our citizens, our democratic institutions, our homeland security, and our interactions with foreign nations. Protecting information critical to our Nation's security and demonstrating our commitment to open Government through accurate and accountable application of classification standards and routine, secure, and effective declassification are equally important priorities."

not be obstructed by revealing to the public information on the goals, methods and targets of the investigation.[181] Transparency, on the other hand, is in particular of the utmost importance to the state's authority in the area of criminal justice. In order to be able to realize a fair criminal justice system based on the principle of adversariality, due process rights shall be effectuated. One of the most important due process rights facilitating a fair adversarial procedure is the right to the disclosure of all information which is material to the criminal case.[182] Moreover, disclosure is essential for realizing accountability, during trial proceedings, of the government's investigative activities to collect information that will be used for the execution of the government's most far-reaching and intrusive power, namely the power to prosecute and punish the perpetrators of crimes.

As a consequence of the obligations to share information between all agencies, information with a secretive nature comes also into the possession of those agencies that operate under the presumption of openness and transparency. The USA PATRIOT Act of 2001 included amendments of the National Security Act of 1947, FISA and Title III to realize the sharing of information obtained in the context of a conventional criminal investigation and in national security investigations between all agencies and divisions that have a role in the common effort to prevent terrorism. Increased cooperation between national security investigators and law enforcement officers is realized through allowing the "federal officer" to consult with federal law enforcement officers and to coordinate efforts to investigate or to protect national security. The Memoranda issued by the Attorney General prescribing the minimization procedures for sharing information included provisions even further realizing intense cooperation and the sharing of information, so as to ensure that all agencies are informed about the information available that may be relevant for the protection of national security and, in particular, providing full access for criminal prosecutors to information gathered in national security investigations. Lastly, the DNI shall promote information sharing and ensure that agencies comply with the sharing directives.[183] Altogether, these measures have resulted in unlimited information sharing and even an obligation to share information that is relevant to protect the US against terrorism.

Not only because of the sharing obligations, but also as a consequence of the likeliness that the FBI, when possible, will prefer to choose the investigative frameworks offering them the most powerful investigative tools, information relevant to criminal proceedings will most probably be obtained through FISA investigations without the regular Fourth Amendment requirements which are applicable to criminal investigations. The persons investigated, who may include US persons, are then not guaranteed the full Fourth Amendment protection as would apply, for example, under Title III. Probable cause that the target is a foreign power or an agent of a foreign power suffices. Any non-US citizen is an

[181] Sales 2007, 817.

[182] See in detail Sects. 5.1.4.2 (on due process) and 5.3.1.2–5.3.1.3 (on disclosure).

[183] See Sects. 7.4.1 and 6.4.

agent of a foreign power, including the lone wolf, as well as US citizens who work for a foreign power or an international organization.[184]

The significant increase in the possibilities to gather evidence through FISA investigations, supported also by a factual increase,[185] and the increase in intelligence information in the possession of law enforcement officers and federal prosecutors as a consequence of sharing obligations will automatically also result in an increase in criminal cases where the government seeks to introduce classified evidence against the accused or where the defense seeks access to classified information in the disclosure process.[186] Several cases have already been dealt with where the court reviewed *in camera* and *ex parte* the FISA Court orders, while the examination is limited to a determination of whether the order was clearly erroneous. CIPA procedures apply upon a mere certification by the Attorney General that disclosure would harm national security. Where the amount of 'FISA evidence' is rather large and also designated as classified, courts face the challenge of carefully balancing defense disclosure rights against national security interests under CIPA.[187] In addition, the prosecutor's duty to actively search for exonerating evidence, including information in the possession of other agencies, is complicated where intelligence agencies are widely involved.[188] The increased impact of classified information on criminal proceedings thus touches upon two different aspects. Firstly, the use of classified materials as evidence and, secondly, the possibility to challenge the legitimacy of evidence gathered under FISA. Both aspects will be subjected to further scrutiny.

When the government seeks to use classified information as evidence, the CIPA procedures can be relied upon. CIPA has been introduced as the solution to deal with classified evidence in a manner in which the adverse impact on defense rights is compensated as much as possible.[189] Section 5.3.1.3 has addressed the case of *United States v. Zacarias Moussaoui* (2004), where the Court of Appeals permitted the government's substitutions replacing classified witnesses' testimony under CIPA.[190] Also within this case the interest of protecting sources of information that may be paramount to the prevention of terrorism outweighed the interest of the defense to disclosure, justifying the sufficiency of disclosing only government substitutions of the witnesses' testimony. In *United States v. Abu Ali* (2008), the court also assessed the constitutionality of the use of redacted versions of classified

---

184 50 U.S.C. § 1801(a) and (b). Although the order which is applicable to US citizens cannot be based upon First Amendment protected activities. 50 U.S.C. § 1842(c)(2).

185 As follows from the FISA Annual Reports to FISA (934 authorized applications in 2001 versus 2,370 in 2007 and 1,506 in 2010), available at: http://www.fas.org/irp/agency/doj/fisa/#rept (accessed 4 August 2011).

186 See on the role that information collected in FISA investigations has played in 'terrorist' trials: Zabel and Benjamin Jr. 2008, 80-81 and 95-96.

187 Zabel and Benjamin Jr. 2008, 96.

188 Zabel and Benjamin Jr. 2008, 98.

189 See on the CIPA procedures Sects. 5.3.1.2 and 5.3.1.3.

190 *United States v. Zacarias Moussaoui,* 382 F.3d 453 (4th Cir. 2004). See Sect. 5.3.1.3.

documents as evidence under CIPA. The court considered the use of the redacted version on the basis of "an ex parte showing that the disclosure would jeopardize national security interests" to be an "appropriately balanced" decision of the district court based upon "a reasonable determination that disclosure of the redacted information was not necessary to a fair trial."[191] However, submitting to the jury not the same version of the evidence, but instead the unredacted classified documents is a violation of the Confrontation Clause under the Sixth Amendment. The Court of Appeals considered that "[i]f classified information is to be relied upon as evidence of guilt, the district court may consider steps to protect some or all of the information from unnecessary public disclosure in the interest of national security and in accordance with CIPA, which specifically contemplates such methods as redactions and substitutions so long as these alternatives do not deprive the defendant of a fair trial. However, the government must at a minimum provide the same version of the evidence to the defendant that is submitted to the jury."[192]

CIPA intends to provide the defense with fair trial rights while protecting classified information. If the judge orders that disclosure is warranted (the information is material to the case), but the government certifies that declassification will harm national security, the judge will order that only a statement or summary of the classified evidence shall be disclosed. Although this may not put the defense in a worse position than before, it deprives the defense of a full possibility to challenge the veracity of the information, while the defense (nor the judge) can examine the reasons for keeping the information classified.[193] Nevertheless, it has been generally acknowledged that under CIPA courts have carefully balanced the defense's interests in disclosure against the government's interests to keep certain information classified considering the experiences with the use of CIPA in courts.[194] For this reason, CIPA may be considered an adequate solution for courts to deal with the clashing interests of transparency and secrecy in evidentiary matters.

However, the possibilities for controlling the legitimacy of the gathering of information under FISA are particularly limited. In several cases in the post-9/11 era courts have held, sometimes with the help of CIPA, upon the required certification of the Attorney General, that disclosure or an adversary hearing would harm national security and have reviewed *in camera* and *ex parte* the affidavits underlying the FISA Court orders.[195] Federal courts shall conduct the same review

---

191 *United States v. Abu Ali,* 528 F.3d 210 (4th Cir. 2008), 253.

192 *Ibid.*, 253. Nevertheless, the establishment of the violation of the Sixth Amendment did not have any procedural consequences, as the court considered it to be a 'harmless error.' *Ibid.*, 257.

193 See Sect. 5.3.1.3.

194 Zabel and Benjamin Jr 2008, 87. See also: Zabel and Benjamin Jr 2009, 25 and 26 and Kris 2011. Others consider the criminal justice system to be unsuitable, because the application of CIPA is considered detrimental to national security interests, for trying terrorists. See on this discussion: Guiora 2008.

195 See: *United States v. Mubayyid,* 521 F.Supp.2d 125 (D.Mass. 2007), *United States v. Abu-Jihaad,* 531 F.Supp.2d 299 (D.Conn. 2008) and *United States v. Warsame,* 547 F.Supp.2d 982 (D.Minn. 2008).

as conducted by the FISA Court itself, which means under the presumed validity of the required certifications given by the government unless they are clearly erroneous.[196] It is clear that the defense is seriously impaired in its rights to challenge the legitimacy of evidence obtained under FISA, whereas it can only speculate as to the correctness of the findings by the government and the *in camera* and *ex parte* review of the materials.

For example, in *United States v. Abu-Jihaad* (2010) the defense sought to suppress the evidence obtained through FISA surveillance because, allegedly, FISA was unconstitutional on its face, the evidence was acquired in violation of the Fourth Amendment, the evidence was obtained in violation of FISA requirements and the FISA orders were based on material misstatements on behalf of the government.[197] The previous section already dealt with the first two arguments supporting the motion to suppress the evidence which was, on similar grounds, rejected. The Court of Appeals emphasized that the ultimate touchstone of the Fourth Amendment is reasonableness and followed the reasoning of the FISA Court of Review in *In re: Sealed* as well as several other similar cases.[198] With regard to the arguments that touch upon the controllability of the legitimacy of the method of investigation and the evidence obtained through the FISA surveillance and search, the Court of Appeals recalled the provision of FISA that when the government claims that disclosure will harm national security, the court shall review *in camera* and *ex parte* the application and order to determine whether the FISA surveillance (or a physical search) was lawfully authorized. Moreover, "disclosure of FISA materials is the exception and *ex parte*, *in camera* determination is the rule."[199] This 'FISA' approach conflicts with the presumption in conventional criminal law, as also adopted in CIPA, that disclosure is the rule and, therefore, only in exceptional situations may alternative procedures be chosen above the full declassification of information which is material to the case. According to the District Court in *United States v. Abu-Jihaad*, the court was, on the basis of the *ex parte* and *in camera* inspection, able to reach a conclusion as to the legitimacy of the FISA investigation, a review which does not "deprive a defendant of due process", because "Congress made a "thoroughly reasonable" effort to balance the competing rights and interests of defendants and the Government."[200] It is remarkable that it was not the actual procedural position of the defense that was the basis for this conclusion, but the legitimacy of the FISA

---

[196] Compare: *United States v. Mubayyid,* 521 F.Supp.2d 125 (D.Mass. 2007), 131.

[197] *United States v. Abu-Jihaad*, 630 F.3d 102 (2nd Cir. 2010), 108. See also the District Court's decision: *United States v. Abu-Jihaad,* 531 F.Supp.2d 299 (D.Conn. 2008).

[198] *United States v. Abu-Jihaad*, 630 F.3d 102 (2nd Cir. 2010), 117-129.

[199] Internal citations omitted, *Ibid.*, 129. See also *United States v. Abu-Jihaad,* 531 F.Supp.2d 299 (D.Conn. 2008), 310 and *United States v. Stewart,* 590 F.3d 93 (2nd Cir. 2009), 129.

[200] *United States v. Abu-Jihaad,* 531 F.Supp.2d 299 (D.Conn. 2008), 310-311. Affirmed in *United States v. Abu-Jihaad*, 630 F.3d 102 (2nd Cir. 2010), 129.

framework.[201] Lastly, the court would only allow the defense to challenge the statement of the government upon which the FISA Court orders were based, if they were able to "make a substantial showing that a false statement knowingly and intentionally, or with reckless disregard for the truth, was included in the application and that the allegedly false statement was necessary to the FISA Judge's approval of the application." The defendant was unable to meet this rather high standard.[202]

In another case, *United States v. Warsame* (2008), the court also assessed whether or not the *ex parte* proceedings violated due process. The court considered the proceedings not to violate due process, because "FISA attempts to protect the rights of individuals not through mandatory disclosure but through "indepth oversight of FISA surveillance by all three branches of government and by a statutory scheme that to a large degree centers on an expanded conception of minimization that differs from that which governs law enforcement surveillance."[203] Again, a reasoning has been decisive that has nothing to do with procedural due process rights, where disclosure is understood as a mandatory requirement for the fundamental fairness of the proceedings, namely the legitimacy of the FISA framework as such.

An increase in classified information relevant to criminal proceedings is the automatic consequence of the fusion of investigative purposes in FISA investigations and of the sharing and cooperation obligations applicable to government agencies and, in particular, between the different divisions of the FBI. As a consequence, the constitutional presumption of disclosure under the due process clause is put under strain.[204] The presumed secrecy of national security investigations clashes with the presumed transparency of criminal proceedings in order to allow the defense to challenge the legitimacy of investigative activities and the veracity of information introduced as evidence. Especially the possibilities to control the lawfulness of FISA investigative activities are rather limited as the judge can only subject the application and order to a marginal review which takes place *in camera* and *ex parte*. Hence, it is unlikely that the defense is able to raise a successful challenge under the exclusionary rule once evidence has been obtained through FISA techniques.

It can be concluded that the increase in the possibilities to collect evidence through FISA investigations as well as the increase in the sharing of intelligence information with law enforcement officers and US attorneys have affected the

[201] Compare also the case of *United States v. Zacarias Moussaoui,* 382 F.3d 453 (4th Cir. 2004): it was not the determination whether or not the defense has been put in a worse position by allowing the introduction of classified information but the nature of the government's national security interests that were decisive for permitting the substitutes under CIPA instead of full disclosure. See Sect. 5.3.1.3.

[202] *United States v. Abu-Jihaad,* 531 F.Supp.2d 299 (D.Conn. 2008), 311. Affirmed in *United States v. Abu-Jihaad*, 630 F.3d 102 (2nd Cir. 2010), 130-131.

[203] *United States v. Warsame,* 547 F.Supp.2d 982 (D.Minn. 2008), 988-989.

[204] *Brady v. Maryland,* 373 U.S, 83, 83 S.Ct. 1194 (1963). See Sects. 5.3.1.2 and 5.3.1.3.

criminal procedure in the sense that the veil of secrecy surrounding this information conflicts with the constitutional obligation of disclosure and transparency as the prerequisite of fairness and accountability in criminal proceedings. In general, courts confronted with this clash between secrecy and transparency cannot second-guess the government's interest in operating under the veil of secrecy in order to protect national security. Consequently, there is trade-in on the interest of disclosure, which is traditionally considered a mandatory requirement of procedural due process in order to guarantee the fundamental fairness of the criminal proceedings.

On more occasions than before the position of the defense will be adversely affected as they will be compelled to exercise their defense rights in trial proceedings under the applicability of CIPA. Although it has been concluded that CIPA, as it has been applied, enables the courts to make a careful assessment between the interest of the defense to disclosure and the interest of courts to keep information shielded when classified materials are introduced as evidence, it deprives the defendant of a full possibility to challenge the veracity of the method of obtaining the evidence against him/her. However, in particular, the exertion of defense rights when seeking to challenge the legitimacy of the manner in which evidence has been obtained under FISA is problematic, considering that the FISA orders are only subjected to the marginal examination common to national security investigations. This latter development may be even more worrisome when taking into account the fact that also the *ex ante* review by the FISA Court judge is rather marginal and cannot be understood to compensate for the lack of accountability and controllability concerning the legitimacy of the method of evidence-gathering during the trial phase. Hence, it must be concluded that the criminal process is indeed 'infected' as a consequence of the dismantling of the wall when it comes to the realization of the fundamental shield aspect of due process.

Moreover, the infection of the criminal process as a consequence of the general acceptance of gathering evidence through FISA investigative techniques and the adverse consequences for realizing procedural due process must be taken into account in order to formulate a final judgment as to the fusion of investigative purpose and the abandoning of the institutional separation between the intelligence and law enforcement communities.

### 7.4.4 Dismantling the Wall: Some Final Remarks

The dismantling of the wall that previously separated the intelligence community from the law enforcement community shall be considered as the most important change of the post-9/11 era that has enabled anticipative criminal investigations. As a consequence of the dismantling of the wall, FISA has become an alternative framework for gathering information relevant for criminal proceedings, especially in investigations relating to terrorist activities. Although the majority of the courts have rendered this development constitutional, some significant implications with regard to the shield objective of criminal procedural law can be observed.

In the first place, there has been a break with the previous fundamental imperative connection between the purpose of the investigation and the specific framework of regulation.

Secondly, no clear choice has yet been made whether to assess the constitutionality of FISA under the special needs doctrine, thereby exempting national security investigations from regular Fourth Amendment restraints (the approach of the FISA Court of Review), or under usual Fourth Amendment interpretation, where reasonableness is the ultimate touchstone. Nevertheless, the acceptance of FISA as a quasi-law enforcement framework, justified by relying on the special needs doctrine, reinforces the development of focusing on Fourth Amendment reasonableness at the expense of other Fourth Amendment requirements, whether as a consequence of accepting a broad national security exception or as a consequence of deviating from Fourth Amendment requirements on a case-by-case basis by applying the 'totality of circumstances' test. The development involves a slippery slope of reasoning based on balancing the interests involved and, consequently, the devaluing of privacy protection afforded by the Fourth Amendment through requirements such as the warrant, probable cause and particularity. As has been concluded in Sect. 7.2, similar developments can be observed in conventional criminal law, also as a consequence of focusing on investigation in anticipation of future harm. For that reason, the step towards accepting FISA as a quasi-law enforcement framework was rather small and vice versa rendering the dismantling of the wall constitutional in line with the tone set in the Fourth Amendment jurisprudence of, roughly, the past ten years.

Thirdly, the dismantling of the wall 'infects' the criminal process in the sense that criminal procedural transparency and national security secrecy clash when the information obtained in FISA investigations is used in criminal proceedings. Accountability and controllability concerning the method of evidence-gathering, which are important due process principles, are principles which are under pressure. In addition, it must be noted that at least the possibility to try to challenge the legitimacy of FISA surveillance or physical searches is provided to those where the information obtained is used as evidence against them, whereas other targets of FISA surveillance or searches may not be notified of the investigation at all. This may involve a risk that FISA surveillance is used to spy on domestic political groups which have ideas related to terrorism groups, which can be compared to the abuses of national security powers before the enactment of FISA.[205] This risk is even more compelling when taking into account that the scope of FISA investigations may be rather broad and, for example, document production orders do not even necessarily concern the target of the investigation.

Schulhofer has strikingly summarized the concerns that have arisen as follows: "[g]ranting prosecutors carte blanche to invoke FISA, rather than ordinary

[205] Lobel 2002, 788.

criminal law processes, poses significant risks in four areas: overly intrusive surveillance, dangerously diluted oversight, weakened remedies, and impairment of the tools to effective defense for individuals ultimately charged with crimes."[206]

## 7.5 FISA Surveillance Targeting Non-US Persons Outside the US and National Security Letters

The third category of regulatory schemes that has been provided to the government to engage in surveillance activities, which is additional to Title III and the 'regular' FISA, concerns the FISA surveillance of non-US persons outside the US and the national security letter. The first concerns a framework for surveillance with even weaker restraints and safeguards than the 'regular' FISA surveillance. The second is comparable to the document production order, although wider in scope and also with weaker restraints and safeguards. In comparison to the assessment of the implications of enabling anticipative criminal investigations for the shield objective of criminal procedural law of Sects. 7.2–7.4, the assessment of the implications of FISA surveillance targeting non-US persons outside the US and national security letters will be rather short. Albeit both tools are highly controversial and raise some serious concerns with regard to the protection of privacy rights, only a few aspects, additional to similar aspects already dealt with in the previous section, are relevant for the assessment of the implications for the shield objective of criminal procedural law. FISA Surveillance targeting non-US persons outside the US and the national security letters will be addressed separately below.

### *7.5.1 FISA Surveillance Targeting Non-US Persons Outside the US*

The NSA surveillance program was originally introduced as a classified and warrantless surveillance program conducted by the NSA, in which phone or e-mail conversations are intercepted when either beginning or terminating with a US person and at least one of the parties could be linked to Al Qaida. Now the program has been incorporated in FISA and limited to the targeting of non-US persons reasonably believed to be located outside the US. The whole procedure, in particular the applicability of targeting procedures and minimization procedures, aims to reduce the scope of this category of FISA surveillance to targets that are located outside the US and are not US persons. However, this does not preclude that the intercepted communications involve US persons. In addition, as a consequence of the incorporation in FISA and under the FBI's DIOG, the FBI may use

[206] Schulhofer 2005, 48.

this type of surveillance in its investigation with overlapping foreign intelligence and law enforcement functions. Moreover, because of the applicability of FISA minimization procedures, information obtained through this type of surveillance, which concerns US citizens who are being criminally prosecuted, may be introduced as evidence against them.[207] For these reasons, also the possibility for the FISA surveillance of non-US persons outside the US shall be taken into account for assessing the full implications of anticipative criminal investigations.

The legal framework of surveillance targeting persons outside the US offers even less protection and restrictions than the 'regular' procedure under FISA. No form of probable cause is required against the targets: the surveillance of foreign targets is permitted when the significant purpose of the surveillance is to gather foreign intelligence. Furthermore, the FISA Court shall issue the order upon a very limited review by the FISA Court. Hence, in comparison with the 'regular' FISA surveillance, the FISA surveillance of non-US persons outside the US is subjected to an even more marginal judicial review. Although in the current regulation a FISA Court order is required, the review to be exerted is limited to the certification to be given by the AG or DNI. In addition to the marginal judicial review, *ex post* Congressional oversight and a review on behalf of the Inspectors General have been established.

The main goal of the surveillance of non-US persons outside the US is to intercept the planning outside the US of terrorist attacks on the US. This is clearly a foreign intelligence goal targeting foreign powers or agents of foreign powers falling outside the scope of the domestic national security investigation and, hence, also outside the scope of the *Keith* decision (as the *Keith* Court emphasized). According to the Supreme Court in *Keith* the Fourth Amendment does not necessarily cover these investigative activities.[208] In line with this decision, also the Fourth Circuit Court in *Truong* upheld the warrantless foreign intelligence surveillance.[209] Hence, the surveillance itself cannot be held to conflict with constitutional interpretation, also prior to the events of 9/11.[210] In some regards the implementation of the NSA surveillance program in FISA through the FISA Amendments Act of 2008 offers even more protection compared to the previous situation, where the surveillance of non-US persons outside the US was understood as being covered neither by the Fourth Amendment nor by FISA and was considered a non-regulated executive power.[211] However, as a consequence of the incorporation into FISA and the applicability of the FISA minimization procedures in combination with the dismantling of the wall, it must be concluded that similar implications arise as addressed in Sect. 7.4.3. The lack of accountability and controllability may even be more compelling when the information obtained under this framework for surveillance is also introduced as evidence.

---

207 See Sect. 6.5.1.

208 *United States v. United States District Court*, 407 U.S. 297, 92 S.Ct. 2125 (1972), 321-322.

209 *United States v. Truong Ding Hung*, 629. F.2d 908 (4th Cir. 1980), 913-914.

210 See also: Forgang 2009, 245-249 and (Anonymous) Note 2008, 2220.

211 Compare: Cooper Blum 2009, 299-300.

### 7.5.2 National Security Letters

National Security Letters concern warrantless document production orders, the use of which has explosively increased since 9/11. The scope of the NSL has been significantly broadened by the USA PATRIOT Act, allowing the order of a rather ambiguous category of private information which has grown along with technological advancements. Any FBI Special Agent can issue an NSL upon a showing of relevance to an authorized investigation relating to international terrorism or clandestine intelligence activities and this showing is not subjected to judicial review before its execution. The recipient of the NSL is subjected to a non-disclosure requirement when the FBI agent certifies that disclosure will result in a danger to national security. Similar to the document production order, as a consequence of the *Doe* cases, consultation with an attorney is now exempted from the non-disclosure requirement and the scope of the NSL is subjected to judicial review. In addition, the non-disclosure requirement accompanying an NSL no longer applies automatically, but only upon the—non-reviewable—certification of the government that national security will otherwise be endangered or will result in interference with ongoing investigations.[212] The NSL concerns a considerably more frequently used tool in comparison to document production orders under section 215 of the USA PATRIOT Act, a difference which can be attributed to the fact that a warrant is not required for the NSL and the NSL can be used at the discretion of any special agent in charge.

This powerful investigative tool may be used during any authorized investigation to protect against international terrorism or clandestine intelligence activities. Fourth Amendment requirements such as probable cause and a warrant do not apply. NSLs can be issued upon a standard of 'relevance to an authorized investigation relating to international terrorism or clandestine intelligence activities.' Taking into account that under the Mukasey Guidelines of 2008 investigations into, in particular, international terrorism will constitute a single investigation for multiple purposes, the authority to issue NSL is available in investigations with also criminal investigative purposes.[213] Moreover, no explicit limitation as to the purpose of the use of the national security letter has been included in the regulation. Hence, the remarks made in Sect. 7.3.2.1 regarding document production orders under FISA equally apply to national security letters. In addition, albeit the scope of the NSL is more limited (only the information related to the Acts in which the

---

[212] See Sect. 6.5.2.

[213] The availability of NSL authority in FBI investigations, both in preliminary investigations and in full investigations, pursuing multiple purposes is explicitly acknowledged in the DIOG of the FBI: DIOG FBI (2008), 114-115. Also the National Security Act provides that NSL are available to conduct i.e. law enforcement investigations: 50 U.S.C. § 436(a)(1). See also Sect. 6.5.2.

authority is provided, instead of 'any tangible things'),[214] the concerns expressed in Sects. 7.3.2.1 and 7.3.2.3 with regard to privacy protection are even more urgent considering that the national security letter may be used without judicial authorization and without any other meaningful limitation.

Furthermore, as also already extensively addressed in Sect. 7.3.2.2, courts have repeatedly held the non-disclosure requirement to be unconstitutional ('*Doe*' cases with, lastly, the lifting of the non-disclosure requirement accompanying an NSL in *Doe v. Holder* (2010)), including the improved conditions under which the non-disclosure requirement may be imposed as realized in the USA PATRIOT Act Reauthorization Acts of 2005 and 2006. Compared to the current regulation of the non-disclosure requirement of document production orders, the statutory improvements of the Reauthorization Act of 2005 regarding the non-disclosure requirement accompanying NSL have been more far-going. The non-disclosure requirement for an NSL cannot be applied automatically, unless the government certifies that a danger to national security may otherwise occur. Nevertheless, such certification is considered appropriate in most situations and, in that form, is still insufficient to be rendered constitutional according to the court in *Doe v. Mukasey* (2008), which required the government to bear the burden of proving the necessity of imposing the non-disclosure requirement and required from the judge not to simply follow the certification of the government.[215] Hence, the remarks in Sect. 7.3.2.2 with regard to the achievable level of accountability apply equally to the regulation of the non-disclosure requirement accompanying NSLs.

Lastly, considering that the FBI may use NSL when relevant to any authorized investigation involving international terrorism and counterintelligence, it is very well possible that the information obtained by NSL will also be introduced as evidence in criminal prosecutions. Again, similar concerns with respect to the realization of procedural due process arise as addressed in Sect. 7.4.3.

## 7.6 Conclusion

In conclusion this section will firstly provide a final characterization of the anticipative criminal investigation in the United States (Sect. 7.6.1) and, secondly, enumerate in three categories the implications identified in this Chapter for the shield objective of criminal procedural law.

---

[214] The Obama Administration proposed, in the spring of 2010, to expand the scope of national security letters to records concerning an individual's Internet activity. See: Nakashima 2010.

[215] See Sects. 6.5.2 and 6.3.2.

### 7.6.1 Characterizing the Anticipative Criminal Investigation

The anticipative criminal investigation has been realized in the United States through a combination of measures and developments in the field of conventional criminal law and in the field of national security law as well as a crucial change in law and policy that has eliminated the separation between criminal investigations and national security investigations.

The most important feature of the anticipative criminal investigation concerns the possibility for the FBI to initiate a single investigation for multiple purposes (protection of national security as well as collecting evidence for a criminal prosecution) when investigating terrorist crimes or other national security crimes. The FBI's highest priority is now to confront terrorism effectively with the adoption of the preventive paradigm. For this purpose, the FBI no longer separates its NSI investigations from criminal investigations, but, when it comes to terrorism, initiates a single investigation (concerning terrorist crimes, or in fact all crimes that also constitute a threat to national security and can be linked to a foreign power or an agent of a foreign power) with a free choice as to the available investigative means: either FISA or Title III surveillance. This is possible as a consequence of the PATRIOT Act changing the FISA purpose language and the interpretation given to this change by the FISA Court of Review, which have detached the choice between the investigative framework and the primary purpose of the investigation. Choosing the way of least resistance, the FISA framework will be the context for gathering evidence in terrorism cases. Therefore, the applicable framework of regulation is no longer imperatively connected to the purpose of the investigation, but seems largely to be a matter of discretion for the investigative (FBI) officers. Moreover, the investigative possibilities under FISA have been expanded.

In addition, as a consequence of the contents of the Mukasey Guidelines and the DIOG, the incorporation of the NSA surveillance program in FISA and the applicability of minimization procedures, FISA surveillance targeting non-US persons outside the US and the NSL are also available in FBI investigations. Because these techniques are primarily used in purely national security investigations, unlike 'regular' FISA techniques, these techniques are used for gathering foreign intelligence information. Nevertheless, the information collected through these techniques may contribute, because of sharing obligations, to the information flow to criminal proceedings.

A parallel development has occurred in conventional criminal law. In the first place, the sword power of the criminal investigation has been enhanced through adjusting the framework of Title III and pen register and trap and trace authority. In addition, a trend in case law has been identified where courts have given the police more leeway under the Fourth Amendment to act for the prevention of terrorism (or the protection of national security). This has been done, firstly, by exempting situations involving terrorism or other national security issues from ordinary criminal investigative searches and, hence, from usual Fourth Amendment requirements; and, secondly, attaching more weight to terrorism/national security interests than to protective requirements such as probable cause and a warrant under the general and ultimate Fourth Amendment assessment. Lastly, internal policy has contributed to focusing on gathering as much information as possible that may be relevant for preventing terrorism, which has realized intelligence-led policing on the level of the FBI as well as on the state and local level.

## *7.6.2 The Implications for the Shield Objective of Criminal Procedural Law*

The above-characterized anticipative criminal investigation as it has been realized in the United States in the post-9/11 era touches upon different shield aspects of the system of regulating criminal investigations. In the first place, several of the evaluated measures have touched upon the protection offered by the Fourth Amendment against arbitrary and unnecessary interference with the right to respect for private life as a consequence of the investigative activities conducted in the anticipative criminal investigation. In the second place, the availability of the FISA framework, previously exclusively reserved for national security investigations, breaks with the separation between law enforcement investigations and national security investigations in order to safeguard that investigative activities conducted for the purpose of gathering evidence for a criminal prosecution are subjected to the highest level of protection. In the third place, implications of the anticipative criminal investigation for the fairness of the trial proceedings have been identified. The measures and developments that have resulted in these implications will be briefly recapitulated below.

### 7.6.2.1 Weakened Fourth Amendment Protection

The realization of the anticipative criminal investigation in the United States has resulted in weakened Fourth Amendment protection against arbitrary and unnecessary investigative activities of state authorities interfering with the privacy rights of individuals. This weakened Fourth Amendment protection touches upon three different aspects: weaker legitimization for anticipative criminal investigative action, reduced control over investigative action in compliance with the Fourth Amendment and the availability of more intrusive techniques. It will be briefly recapitulated for each category which particular measures and developments have contributed to weakened Fourth Amendment protection in the anticipative criminal investigation.

1. Weaker Legitimization
Two key characteristics of the realization of the anticipative criminal investigation have resulted in weaker legitimization for investigative activities that interfere

with the interests protected through the Fourth Amendment: the enabling of FISA as a quasi-law enforcement area and the focus on reasonableness in Fourth Amendment interpretation.

FISA may now be used for the purpose of gathering evidence for criminally prosecuting terrorist crimes or other national security crimes. Consequently, *the FISA probable cause standard may legitimize electronic surveillance and physical search in the anticipative criminal investigation*, which is a considerably lower threshold than the probable cause standard of the Fourth Amendment in conventional criminal law and of Title III, namely probable cause that the target is a foreign power or an agent of a foreign power. This threshold crucially differs from the conventional criminal law standard by focusing on the nature of the identity of the target, instead of on the criminal nature of the activities in which the target is involved (compare: probable cause that a crime has been, is being or will be committed).[216] In addition, the FISA document production order may be used when *'relevant to an authorized investigation'*, which is a standard for which evidentiary support is not needed. It is clear that when using these 'national security investigation' standards in the anticipative criminal investigation, the likelihood has substantially increased that individuals who cannot be related to criminal investigative activities nor constitute a 'danger' will in fact be investigated.

Secondly, also in the context of a conventional criminal investigation the protective value of Fourth Amendment probable cause has been reduced, in particular in cases where national security interests are involved. A development in the case law of *focusing on reasonableness* has been identified (Sect. 7.2.2.2), especially in cases where the government's interest in preventing terrorism or protecting national security is involved. This focus on reasonableness opens the door to an unlimited balancing test, providing the flexibility to consider that the interests of preventing terrorism and protecting national security outweigh competing protective requirements. Consequently, also the protective value of the probable cause standard has become less meaningful and increasingly flexible. One may doubt whether the reasonableness test alone may offer sufficient comparable protection when this test exclusively concerns the balancing of the interests involved without taking into account the importance of a specific legitimization for investigative action. As concluded in Sect. 7.2.2.2.1, in order to exclude arbitrary interference with privacy rights, a form of suspicion is an essential restraint and actually concerns the core of Fourth Amendment protection.

2. Reduced Control

The FBI's powers to act for the prevention of terrorism have been expanded. In addition, internal policy has promoted an intelligence-led approach for FBI officers in order to make sure that the information needed to avert terrorism or national security threats is gathered. The enhanced investigative powers have, however, not

---

[216] See Sect. 7.3.1.1.

been compensated by enhanced control on the compliance of the anticipative criminal investigative activities with the Fourth Amendment. Five different implications of realizing anticipative criminal investigations, resulting in reduced control, have been identified.

In the first place, *ex ante judicial control over investigative activities is weakened when the FISA framework is used* to conduct the anticipative criminal investigation. The FISA Court judge authorizes an order for the use of FISA techniques when the statutory requirements are met, which the FISA Court judge accepts on the basis of the certifications of the government in that regard, unless such certifications are clearly erroneous.[217]

In the second place, in the post-9/11 case law concerning the conventional criminal search power, the *strength of the warrant requirement as a parameter for the reasonableness of the search has been reduced.* The warrant is generally understood as being in principle required, unless exigent circumstances are present that justify the postponement of a judicial review until after the search. Nevertheless, both *ex ante* and *ex post* judicial control are concerned as a sufficient check on the government's power to search. The prioritizing of the *ex ante* review seems to be weakened by extending a premise of exigent circumstances to include the interest of preventing terrorism.

Thirdly, in general the courts in the post-9/11 era have exerted a *more deferential review* in order to grant the investigating authorities sufficient leeway to act for the prevention of terrorism. This has been demonstrated in cases where the courts have focused on the reasonableness of the search as the ultimate touchstone under the Fourth Amendment (Sect. 7.2.2.2). In addition, courts have considered the *interest of protecting national security as a special need*, which justifies exceptions to the Fourth Amendment. Consequently, the shield function of the Fourth Amendment has been reduced especially in terrorism/national security investigations (Sect. 7.2.2.1).

Fourthly, more investigative discretion in the criminal investigation, especially to do whatever is considered necessary to contribute to the prevention of terrorism, has not been compensated with expanded judicial oversight through a strict application of the exclusionary rule. Instead, recent Supreme Court decisions on the exclusionary rule have *reduced the meaning of the exclusionary rule* as the remedy against Fourth Amendment violations.[218]

In the fifth place, the emphasis on controlling mechanisms has *shifted from the judiciary to alternative controlling mechanisms*. In order to compensate for both the expansion of investigative powers and the erosion of judicial control *ex ante* and *ex post*, alternative review mechanisms have been strengthened. Congressional oversight has been enhanced, in particular through the PATRIOT Act Reauthorization Acts, and the importance of minimization procedures has increased. This applies in particular to the investigative techniques regulated under

---

[217] See Sects. 7.4.2 and 7.4.3.

[218] See Sect. 7.2.2.2.4.

FISA. Moreover, the Inspectors General have an important reviewing responsibility. Nevertheless, it remains questionable whether this form of accountability and control can replace judicial control.

3. Expanded Investigative Powers

Both Title III and FISA have been amended in order to enhance the investigative capacities of the government. Consequently, Fourth Amendment protection through statutory regulation has in general been reduced. In addition, some of the newly adopted or amended techniques may be incompatible with the Fourth Amendment.

In the first place, the PATRIOT Act has *enhanced the investigative techniques regulated in Title III* and expanded the situations in which Title III may be invoked. Consequently, the proactive use of techniques regulated in Title III in conventional criminal investigations has increased, whilst Title III was originally intended as a last resort in the criminal investigation subject to the applicability of the principle of subsidiarity.[219]

Furthermore, in particular the regulation of delayed notice warrants and pen registers and trap and trace devices have resulted in constitutional concerns. The rather sweeping ground for a delayed notice and the possibility of extending the delay by periods of 30 days has been identified as being possibly incompatible with the standard of sufficient precision or limitation as developed in the case law under the Fourth Amendment for sneak-and-peek searches (see Sect. 7.2.1.2). With regard to pen registers and trap and trace devices it has been concluded that the risk of abuse or mistakes, with the commensurate privacy invasions, has significantly increased as a consequence of broadening the definition of the information that can be intercepted (Sect. 7.2.1.3).

In the second place, the nature of FISA surveillance and physical searches has become more intrusive, touching upon the previous balance between the individual's Fourth Amendment interests and the government's interest in gathering foreign intelligence information achieved in the FISA of 1978. Especially the enabling of roving surveillance under FISA, the expanding of the scope of pen register and trap and trace authority and the introduction of the document production order may give FISA investigations a more intrusive character.[220] Of these techniques, in particular the FISA document production order concerns a powerful and intrusive tool, considering its broad scope (any tangible things), a threshold of relevance to an authorized investigation and the applicability of the non-disclosure requirement. Because of the weak legitimization for using the tool and the exclusion of a solid and general level of accountability through the non-disclosure requirement, the potential for abuse is rather high. Hence, it has been questioned whether the limited necessity for the tool outweighs the substantial lack of meaningful protective elements in the regulation and the commensurate risk of abuse.[221]

---

219 See Sect. 7.2.1.1.

220 See Sect. 7.3.

221 See Sect. 7.3.2.

#### 7.6.2.2 Abandoning Purpose Limitation

The dismantling of the wall and, hence, the availability of the FISA framework in the anticipative criminal investigation fits within a general trend where the interest of preventing terrorism trumps the interest of protecting privacy rights. This applies to conventional criminal searches, FISA searches and the general policy of the DoJ and the FBI. It also easily fits within today's Fourth Amendment examination, which has developed into an ultimate reasonableness assessment of the search as a whole based on the totality of circumstances. Consequently, purpose limitation, realized through the wall, has been abandoned for which reason the most stringent form of Fourth Amendment protection (as realized in the statutory framework of Title III) is no longer guaranteed for anticipative criminal investigative activities.

Considering the *Keith* and *Truong* decisions, the blending of investigative purposes and, consequently, breaking with the relation between the investigative purpose and the applicable regulatory framework in order to safeguard Fourth Amendment interests may be disputable as to compatibility with the US constitutional law. Not only the government has taken this step (by changing the purpose language through the PATRIOT Act and by adopting new internal DoJ policy), also the US courts have discarded the imperative relation between the level of Fourth Amendment protection required and the purpose of the investigation (primarily: *In re Sealed*). It is questionable whether this approach can be justified by the special needs doctrine (as US courts have done), considering that a broad national security exception is not particularly "narrowly tailored and sufficiently effective" to count as a social necessity.

In Sect. 7.4.2 it was concluded that the programmatic purpose requirement as a method to protect against abuses of FISA investigative powers for law enforcement purposes could not be upheld considering that the interest of anticipating future national security threats for the purpose of prevention will always override the conventional law enforcement purpose of gathering sufficient information for prosecution. Hence, the programmatic purpose of the investigation can reasonably be defined in all counterterrorism investigations as the gathering of foreign intelligence information in order to protect national security. Consequently, the collection of evidence during a FISA investigation goes beyond what could be understood as plain-view gathering. The collection of evidence may be the primary purpose of the search; however, the interest of protecting national security by collecting 'foreign intelligence' will nevertheless always surpass—as a 'top priority'—the interest of collecting evidence. The current prioritizing of interests within the DoJ and the definition of foreign intelligence makes it impossible to draw a clear line on the basis of a programmatic purpose test. Promoted by internal policy, FISA investigations are likely to pursue multiple purposes without a precise demarcation of the situations where additional restraints need to apply as required under the Fourth Amendment for the investigation of crimes for prosecution purposes.

#### 7.6.2.3 Infected Criminal Process

As a consequence of the obligations to share information between all agencies, information with a secretive nature also comes into the possession of those agencies that operate under the presumption of openness and transparency. Measures have resulted in unlimited information sharing and even an obligation to share information that is relevant to protect the US against terrorism. In addition, also as a consequence of the likelihood that the FBI, where possible, will prefer to choose the investigative frameworks offering them the most powerful investigative tools, information relevant to criminal proceedings will be obtained through FISA investigations without the regular Fourth Amendment requirements which are applicable to criminal investigations.

This has implications in particular for the possibilities of the defense to challenge the legitimacy of the gathering of information under the FISA framework. Courts have addressed such challenges from a 'FISA' approach, with *in camera* and *ex parte* inspections of the affidavits underlying the orders. Gathering evidence under FISA automatically deviates from the presumption of CIPA that disclosure is the rule and, therefore, that only in *exceptional* situations may alternative procedures be chosen instead of the full declassification of information which is material to the case. As a consequence of the current 'FISA' approach taken by the courts, it is no longer the actual procedural position of the defense that is taken into account when deciding on mechanisms for the use of classified materials in criminal cases, but the presumed legitimacy of the FISA framework for investigating for the protection of national security. The conclusion has been drawn that the criminal process has been affected, because the veil of secrecy surrounding a FISA investigation conflicts with the constitutional obligation to disclosure and transparency as the prerequisite for fairness and accountability in criminal proceedings.[222]

These concerns with regard to procedural due process are even more compelling when information is obtained by using the framework for surveillance targeting non-US persons outside the US or when information has been obtained through national security letters. The first is subjected to even more marginal *ex ante* judicial review, whereas the latter can be used without prior judicial control.[223]

---

[222] See Sect. 7.4.3.

[223] See Sect. 7.5.

**Table 7.1** Smith Guidelines 1983 (criminal investigations)[224]

| Type | Purposes | Threshold + other restraints | Powers |
|---|---|---|---|
| General crimes investigation: preliminary inquiry | –Preceding the general crime investigation, criminal intelligence investigation or domestic security investigation.<br>–For the purpose of obtaining the information necessary to make an informed judgment as to whether the full investigation is warranted. | –Information available falls short of 'reasonable indications'; however, the information available is of such a nature that 'further scrutiny' is required beyond the 'prompt and extremely limited checking out of initial leads.'<br>–Conducted with "as little intrusion as the needs of the situation permit."<br>–Short duration.<br>–Duration up to 90 days, possible extensions of 30-day periods (upon receipt by FBI headquarters of a written request and statement of reasons why further investigative steps are warranted when there is no "reasonable indication of criminal activity").<br>–Before using technique it shall be considered whether there are less intrusive means available, by taking into account the "adverse consequences to an individual's privacy interests and avoidable damage to his reputation" as well as "the seriousness of the possible crime and the strength of the information indicating the possible existence of the crime." | –All lawful investigative techniques, except for mail covers, mail openings and non-consensual electronic surveillance or any other technique covered by Title III, with the general note that the techniques applied should be less intrusive than those in full investigations.<br>–Techniques other than the examination of FBI indices and files, public records or other public sources, deferral, state and local records, inquiry of existing sources and previously established informants and physical surveillance and interview of other persons for the purpose of identifying the subject of investigations, requires the authorization of a supervisory agent, except in exigent circumstances.<br>–Authorization of techniques with a highly intrusive nature shall only be given in "compelling circumstances." |

(continued)

224 Hearing before the Subcommittee on Security and Terrorism on the Committee on the Judiciary United States Senate, 98th Congress, First Session on Attorney General's Guidelines for Domestic Security Investigations (Smith Guidelines), March 25, 1983, Serial No. J-98-25, S. Hrg 98-176, Appendix

**Table 7.1** (continued)

| Type | Purposes | Threshold + other restraints | Powers |
|---|---|---|---|
| General crimes investigation: (full) investigation | –Prevent, solve and prosecute (such) criminal activity. | –"[f]acts and circumstances reasonably indicat[ing] that a federal crime has been, is being, or will be committed" (Reasonable indication is substantially lower than probable cause; factors to consider are those facts and circumstances a prudent investigator would consider, but must include facts or circumstances indicating a past, current, or impending violation; an objective factual basis must be present, a mere 'hunch' is insufficient).<br>–Proactive operation is possible in the investigation of criminalized conspiracies and attempts. When the investigation involves future criminal activity, whereas a "current criminal conspiracy or attempt" is not yet involved, the guidelines prescribe "particular care [...] to assure that there exist facts and circumstances amounting to a reasonable indication that a crime will occur."<br>–The investigation is terminated with the decision whether or not to prosecute.<br>–Regular consultations between the Special Agent and the appropriate federal prosecutor. | –All lawful investigative techniques (subjected to the principles of subsidiarity and proportionality and to statutory and internal regulations and policies). |

(continued)

**Table 7.1** (continued)

| Type | Purposes | Threshold + other restraints | Powers |
|---|---|---|---|
| Criminal Intelligence Investigation: racketeering enterprise investigation | –"To obtain information concerning the nature and structure of the enterprise (…) with a view to the longer-term objective of the detection, prevention, and prosecution of the criminal enterprise" ("in general the criminal intelligence investigation is aimed at: determining the size and composition of the group involved [in the ongoing criminal enterprise], its geographic dimensions, its past acts and intended criminal goals, and its capacity for harm"). | –"[F]acts or circumstances reasonably indicat[ing] that two or more persons are engaged in a continuing course of conduct for the purpose of obtaining monetary or commercial gains or profits wholly or in part through racketeering activity."<br>–Authority to investigate limited to racketeering enterprises involved in violence, extortion, narcotics, or systematic public corruption upon authorization by the Director of the FBI or designated Assistant Director (except in exceptional circumstances by authorization of the Director of the FBI and the Attorney General).<br>–The investigation is not necessarily terminated with the decision whether or not to prosecute one or more of the participants: considering the subject of investigation the investigation is "less precise than that directed against more conventional types of crime."<br>–Duration: up to 180 days, extensions possible by renewed authorization for additional periods not exceeding 180 days. | –All lawful investigative techniques (subjected to the principles of subsidiarity and proportionality and to statutory and internal regulations and policies). |

(continued)

**Table 7.1** (continued)

| Type | Purposes | Threshold + other restraints | Powers |
|---|---|---|---|
| Criminal Intelligence Investigation: domestic security/terrorism investigation | –investigate enterprises "whose goals are to achieve political or social change through activities that involve force or violence" (not including international terrorism, which is a matter for national security investigations). | –"facts or circumstances [that] reasonably indicate that two or more persons are engaged in an enterprise for the purpose of furthering political or social goals wholly or in part through activities that involve force or violence and a violation of the criminal laws of the United States."<br>–All circumstances shall be taken into account to determine whether this threshold is met, "including: (1) the magnitude of the threatened harm; (2) the likelihood it will occur; (3) the immediacy of the threat; and (4) the danger to privacy and free expression posed by an investigation."<br>–Investigation of mere "speculations that force or violence might occur during the course of an otherwise peaceable demonstration" is excluded. | –all lawful investigative techniques (subject to the principles of subsidiarity and proportionality and to statutory and internal regulations and policies).<br>–Investigation of inactive enterprises may be continued when the "composition, goals and prior history of the group" justifies continued "federal interest," through monitoring the "status of the criminal objectives of the enterprise." |

**Table 7.2** Mukasey Guidelines 2008 + DIOG of the FBI (2008)[225]

| Type | Purposes | Threshold + other restraints | Powers |
|---|---|---|---|
| Assessment | Mukasey Guidelines: Detect, obtain information about, or prevent or protect against federal crimes or threats to the national security or to collect foreign intelligence<br>DIOG: proactively "detecting criminal or national security threats" without waiting for leads to come in by using the techniques available for the purpose of early intervention and prevention. | –No threshold (no showing of any factual predicate required). | –Activities limited to the checking out of investigative leads.<br>–General searches for information, e.g.: searching publicly available sources, FBI and DoJ records, requesting records from other agencies, searching the internet, interviewing "members of the public and private entities", observation and surveillance for which a court order is not required, or through "grand jury subpoenas for telephone or electronic mail subscriber information. |
| Predicated investigation: preliminary investigation | Mukasey Guidelines: Idem.<br>DIOG: "determining whether a federal crime has occurred or is occurring, or if planning or preparation for such a crime is taking place; identifying, locating, and apprehending the perpetrators; obtaining evidence needed for prosecution; or identifying threats to the national security." | –(a) An activity constituting a federal crime or a threat to the national security has or may have occurred, is or may be occurring, or will or may occur and the investigation may obtain information relating to the activity or the involvement or role of an individual, group, or organization in such activity; *or* (b) an individual, group, organization, entity, information, property, or activity is or may be a target of attack, victimization acquisition, infiltration, or recruitment in connection with criminal activity in violation of federal law or a threat to the national security and the investigation may obtain information that would help to protect against such activity or threat.<br>–Duration: maximum of 6 months, extensions possible.<br>–Supervisory approval. | –All lawful investigative techniques, except for electronic surveillance under Title III or FISA, a physical search under Rule 41 of the Federal Rules of Criminal Procedure of FISA, and the acquisition of foreign intelligence information under Title VII of FISA (concerning persons located outside the US). |

(continued)

[225] The Attorney General's Guidelines for Domestic FBI Operations (2008) (Mukasey Guidelines).

**Table 7.2** (continued)

| Type | Purposes | Threshold + other restraints | Powers |
|---|---|---|---|
| Predicated investigation: full investigation | Mukasey Guidelines: Idem.<br>DIOG: "determining whether a federal crime is being planned, prepared for, occurring or occurred; identifying, locating, and apprehending the perpetrators; obtaining evidence for prosecution; identifying threats to the national security; investigating an enterprise (…); or collecting positive foreign intelligence." | –*An articulable factual basis for the investigation that reasonably indicates:* (a) an activity constituting a federal crime or a threat to the national security has or may have occurred, is or may be occurring, or will or may occur and the investigation may obtain information relating to the activity or the involvement or role of an individual, group, or organization in such activity; or (b) an individual, group, organization, entity, information, property, or activity is or may be a target of attack, victimization acquisition, infiltration, or recruitment in connection with criminal activity in violation of federal law or a threat to the national security and the investigation may obtain information that would help to protect against such activity or threat.<br>–*Or*: the investigation may obtain foreign intelligence that is representative to a foreign intelligence requirement.<br>–Supervisory approval | –Any lawful investigative technique.<br>–DIOG: the full investigation's objective of gathering positive foreign intelligence allows the FBI to conduct information-gathering activities "beyond federal crimes and threats to the national security" and "regarding a broader range of matters relating to foreign powers, organizations, or persons that may be of interest to the conduct of the United States' foreign affairs." |

(continued)

**Table 7.2** (continued)

| Type | Purposes | Threshold + other restraints | Powers |
|---|---|---|---|
| Enterprise investigations | Mukasey Guidelines: Idem.<br>DIOG: examine "the structure, scope, and nature of the group or organization including: its relationship, if any, to a foreign power; the identity and relationship of its members, employees, or other persons who may be acting in furtherance of its objectives; its finances and resources; its geographical dimensions; its past and future activities and goals; and its capacity for harm." | Similar to full investigation<br>DIOG:<br>–The threshold is met also when the group or organization "may have or may be engaged in, planning or preparation or provision of support" for matters such as international terrorism.<br>–Articulable factual basis is established with the "identification of a group whose statements made in furtherance of its objectives, or its conduct, demonstrate a purpose of committing crimes or securing the commission of crimes by others. The group's activities and statements of its members may be considered in combination to comprise the "articulable factual basis," even if the statements alone or activities alone would not warrant such a determination." | –Targeting groups or organizations that may be involved in the most serious criminal or national security threats to the public.<br>–All lawful investigative techniques with an aim to broadly investigate the characteristics and activities of the group or organization. |

# Part III
# Theory, Evaluation and Conclusions

# Chapter 8
# Regulating the Anticipative Criminal Investigation Under the Rule of Law

## 8.1 Introduction

In order to give a final normative judgment with regard to the implications for the shield objective of criminal procedural law as identified in Chaps. 4 and 7, this Chapter will identify the conditions for regulating anticipative criminal investigations. On the basis of these conditions the current regulation as adopted in the Netherlands and the United States can be assessed in the next Chapter. These conditions will be formulated through combining two normative, legal interpretive, theoretical concepts, which will result in the development of a three-dimensional approach to the formulation of the conditions regulating criminal investigations. This approach is based on the idea that, on the one hand, certain underpinnings of the system, those that can be derived from the right to respect for human dignity, are perpetual. These underpinnings have a procedural character or an institutional character. On the other hand, a specific system of regulation is subject to change and, hence, within the boundaries of the procedural and institutional principles there is room for adjustments on the basis of policy choices.

The first theoretical concept that will be applied recognizes that certain principles and rights underlying the regulation of a criminal investigation have an intrinsic moral value; certain principles have a fundamental character, to be upheld under all circumstances, because they are the minimum guarantees for state action in respect of the right to human dignity (Sect. 8.3).[1] These principles can be separated into two categories: 'constitutive principles'[2] (Sect. 8.3.1) and parameters (Sect. 8.3.2). Constitutive principles concern rights with a fundamental character that provide for the first dimension of the non-derogable procedural regulation of the criminal investigation. The second dimension is provided by the parameters, which regulate the manner in which state institutions may pursue their

---

1 Dworkin 1979, 269, Brants et al. 2001, 4 and Franken 2008, 10.
2 Term derived from: Finn 1991, particularly 28-35.

M.F.H. Hirsch Ballin, *Anticipative Criminal Investigation*,
DOI: 10.1007/978-90-6704-843-9_8,

substantive goals within the context of the procedure. Hence, the parameters concern fundamental principles of criminal procedural law of an institutional character. Together, the constitutive principles and parameters that will be formulated concern the unchangeable underpinning of any chosen system of regulation for the criminal investigation.

The second theoretical concept to be applied concerns the ability of the law to be open and flexible, when proportionality and/or the circumstances of modern society require an adaptation of the law (8.4). The application of this second theoretical concept provides for the third dimension, which fills up, along the parameters and above the constitutive principles, the area of the law that requires further definition on the basis of a normative assessment (the 'flexible area of the law') of different arguments, which will provide conclusions as to the validity of changing the law in a particular manner and indicate the factors which are relevant for a judgment on the proportionality (as one of the parameters) of newly developed law, such as the anticipative criminal investigation.[3]

In fact this three-dimensional approach, which follows from the application of two normative theoretical concepts concerning the foundation of the law and the rules that built a legal system, can be compared with the building of a house. The constitutive principles provide for the essential foundation of the house, required for the purpose of giving it a solid, inviolable basis. The parameters are the blocks which are required for building the house, which concern irremovable elements of the architecture. Whilst these building blocks will always be needed for a solid architecture, they may be positioned differently. This reflects the flexible area of the law, which provides the possibility to take into account the specific circumstances of a particular time and make it suitable for dealing with specific circumstances. However, without the building blocks, the house will collapse, which limits the flexibility for adjusting the architecture.

Before giving substance to the three dimensions of the regulation of the anticipative criminal investigation, this introductory section will firstly return to the theoretical framework adopted in Chap. 1 and on that basis continue to draw the path to be followed for building the architecture of the criminal investigation. It will do so by explaining why the approach will provide the soundest assessment of *any* system of criminal investigation as well as why the approach will be able to deliver concrete leads in order to formulate a normative judgment as to the regulation of the anticipative criminal investigation in the Netherlands and the United States. Hence, the Chapter will be completed with the formulation of the conditions that can be applied as the touchstones for a normative judgment on the current regulatory imbedding of anticipative criminal investigation in the Netherlands and the United States (Sect. 8.5).

---

[3] Habermas 1996, 218.

### 8.1.1 *The Path Towards Formulating the Framework of Examination*

In Chap. 1 it has been explained that the range of counterterrorism measures taken on the domestic level fit within the larger picture where international policy and human rights law have called on and obliged states to take measures to prevent future terrorist attacks. Moreover, under the influence of concepts such as the risk society, the culture of control and the precautionary principle, citizens have expected governments to guarantee a safe society with measures that aim to control danger and guarantee security. Especially the latter has prompted states to adopt counterterrorism measures, sometimes beyond international and human rights law obligations.

For the Netherlands international policy has to a large extent influenced the counterterrorism policy and some specific Dutch counterterrorism measures concern the implementation of international measures. For the United States it cannot be said that its counterterrorism measures have been triggered by international and/or European policy. Rather, the focus on preventing terrorism has been a parallel development in the United States and on the international plane. International institutions, such as the United Nations, the European Union and the Council of Europe, have urged states to take measures to combat and prevent terrorism.[4] Moreover, the protection of the human right to life (Article 2 ECHR and Article 4 ACHR) or to liberty and the security of the person (Article 9 ICCPR, Article 5 ACHR and Article 6 Charter of Fundamental Rights of the EU) impose on states the positive duty to protect, including a duty to take preventive measures in order to protect citizens against terrorist attacks. The developments in the international legal domain can be considered as the justification for the taking of preventive measures on the national level. The societal and political circumstances on the national level, which are partly also a consequence of the international legal context, have further nourished and shaped the actual preventive measures that have been taken in a particular country.

The establishment of the anticipative criminal investigation, and thus the mobilization of criminal law for the purpose of prevention must be understood against the international public and human rights legal background[5] and the political and societal context, providing for legitimizing grounds, in order to understand these measures and to put them in the right perspective. However, this background cannot be the *justification* for specifically enabling an anticipative

---

[4] Notwithstanding the fact that these institutions have also taken measures of their own volition and that some of the measures taken by the European Union not only urged states to take measures, but also imposed an obligation to implement certain measures. See in detail Chap. 1, Sect. 1.3.1.

[5] In addition, human rights also have, of course, an important restrictive function, subjecting the government's discretion to adopt counterterrorism measures to the human rights standards that aim to protect fundamental rights and liberties.

criminal investigation to give effect to the state's duty to protect against acts of terrorism. The factors that need to be taken into consideration in order to determine whether establishing an anticipative criminal investigation is justified and, if so, whether the regulation of anticipative criminal investigations is also justified under the rule of law—including the protective function of human rights law—will be provided in this Chapter. Hence, this Chapter will provide for the examination framework in order to answer the research question formulated in the first Chapter: can a preventive function of a criminal investigation be part of a criminal justice system under the rule of law and, if so, under what conditions, and what does this mean for the current regulation of the anticipative criminal investigation adopted in the Netherlands and the United States? For this purpose it will first be explained why a balancing approach is inapt for formulating a framework that is capable of examining a regulation for an anticipative criminal investigation under the rule of law (Sect. 8.1.1.1). Secondly, the manner, recommended in this study, of formulating the conditions for examining the current regulation of anticipative criminal investigations in the Netherlands and the United States (and in fact in any state governed by the rule of law) will be provided with a solid ground and further elaborated.

#### 8.1.1.1 The Shortcomings of the Balancing Approach

The rule of law has in the first Chapter been explained as a notion governing state action, including action in the field of criminal law, based on the assumption of respect for human dignity. For this reason, the benchmark for realizing a legitimate and justified regulation of the anticipative criminal investigation is guaranteeing respect for human dignity. It has also been explained in the first Chapter that when we apply an understanding of the rule of law which is based on respect for human dignity to the criminal justice system, the regulation of the use of criminal procedural powers is based on the realization of two fundamental objectives, reflecting the idea that respect for human dignity in governmental action has a legitimizing consequence and a restricting consequence.

The ostensible contradiction between the state's duty to protect its citizens and the protective function of criminal procedural law for those subjected to criminal procedural powers has usually provided a reason to balance the duty of crime control against the duty to offer sufficient protections to citizens. Such balancing easily results in a determination that greater security can only be achieved at the expense of respect for fundamental rights,[6] which has often been used to justify loosened restrictions on governmental power. Indeed, if we take into account the changed political and social climate contributing to an expanded duty to protect that includes the prevention of terrorism, and that criminal law should meet the normative notions of the society to which it applies, one may consider it justified to

[6] Compare: Lazarus Goold 2007, 16-17.

argue that criminal investigative powers should be expanded.[7] When the interest of protecting national security prevails and the urgency for the government to act under its 'duty to protect' increases, one should trade in on civil liberties. In general, the problematic aspect of measures inspired by focusing on managing and controlling risks is that this focus seems to become the arbiter when seeking the justified balance between the sword and the shield. As a consequence, a 'sliding scale' of protection for civil liberties by putting different levels of restraints on the use of investigative powers will be applied. However, an equally important objective of criminal procedural law is to offer legal protection, which has been elaborated in criminal law principles and restraints. This protective objective should also protect against radical changes to the system of criminal procedural law, which expand the government's power to interfere with fundamental rights.[8]

At the other end of the spectrum, the measures to enable anticipative criminal investigations are often rejected on the basis of the mere conclusion that they deviate from the traditional principles regulating criminal investigations.[9] Also this approach is dissatisfactory as it denies that these traditional principles are the product of a search for the synthesis between sword and shield, found under particular circumstances at a particular time, for which reason these principles are not static. In fact, they are not principles as such, but rules based upon principles.

A mere balancing approach clearly has its shortcomings, considering that it is incapable of distinguishing the rules from fundamental principles, resulting in a slippery slope of argumentation either in favor or against enhancing the sword function of criminal investigation at the expense of protective rules.[10] As we have seen, the guarantee of the enjoyment of fundamental rights and the duty to provide security are interrelated and, therefore, are not two components that can be balanced against each other.[11] Relying on balancing involves the danger that interests and principles are, indistinctively, attributed to a "degree of objectivity", which they do not possess, therefore undermining the validity of the balancing operation.[12] Instead, considering the two objectives of criminal procedural law under the rule of law, which are both directly derived from respect for human dignity, one should seek to find the justified *synthesis* between the shield and sword objective for the purpose of regulating the anticipative criminal investigation.

On a more tangible level, this can be illustrated by the comparison Sottiaux has made between argumentation used by the ECrtHR and by the US Supreme Court when assessing interferences with the right to respect for private life. For instance, in order to assess whether electronic surveillance in a particular case constitutes a

---

[7] Rozemond 2006, 164-165.

[8] Franken 2008, 10 and Rozemond 2006, 165-166. For similar reasoning with regard to the interpretation of human rights, see: Van Kempen 2008, 67.

[9] As was also indicated by Van der Woude and Van Sliedregt 2007, 217.

[10] Compare: Tsakyrakis 2008, 30.

[11] Compare: Ashworth 2007, 208.

[12] *Ibid.*, 210.

legitimate interference with one's private life, the ECrtHR typically relies on a mere balancing approach to determine whether or not the right to respect for private life has been violated, thereby balancing the state's obligations to counter terrorism effectively against the protection of the individual's private life. In addition, the Court provides the national state with a margin of appreciation, which is typically wide in the national security context. In the words of Sottiaux: the reliance on a mere balancing approach provides "open-ended" flexibility, which "may result in the under-protection of privacy rights at the benefit of the government's security concerns."[13] As an example to the contrary, the Supreme Court acknowledged in the *Keith* case that certain protective aspects (in this particular case the warrant requirement) cannot simply be "an inconvenience to be somehow "weighed" against the claims of police efficiency."[14] Hence, the Supreme Court imposed limits on balancing by recognizing that some protective elements cannot be compromised.[15]

A slightly different approach was proposed by Borgers and Van Sliedregt: assessing the legitimacy of 'precautionary measures' is a matter of preferences, which can be determined with the help of drawing the complete picture of taking 'precautionary measures' that requires the making of a cost-benefit analysis of the pros and cons of the precautionary measures.[16] However, although a two-sided approach, and with that surpassing the problematic aspect of the mere balancing approach, it still lacks the essential basis, as seeking for a synthesis is not only a matter of preferences to be determined by taking into account the complete picture of measures that aim to realize anticipative criminal investigations, but, primarily, a matter of enlightening the underlying fundamental principles of criminal investigation before setting (new) preferences that reflect changed societal and political circumstances. It is important that when we are seeking to escape from traditional protections in order to be able to prevent threats, that we distinguish protective rules from the fundamental principles and try to assess the traditionally adopted rules in the light of these fundamental principles. In that way we are able to adopt new frameworks or adjust existing frameworks to reflect new preferences

---

[13] Sottiaux 2008, 321.

[14] *United States v. United States District Court*, 407 U.S. 297, 92 S.Ct. 2125 (1972), 315.

[15] Sottiaux 2008, 322. This example, however, would only fit within the approach taken in this book when the warrant requirement also obtains the status of a fundamental principle and not only concerns a 'rule' underpinned by such a fundamental principle. Moreover, as we have seen in Chaps. 6 and 7, the Supreme Court has in the post-9/11 era increasingly relied on 'reasonableness' in order to be able to create (complete) trade-offs of all protective requirements of the Fourth Amendment to provide the government with sufficient leeway to protect national security, an approach comparable to the balancing approach of the ECrtHR. Moreover, the *Keith* decision suggested that a foreign intelligence exception might apply to the warrant requirement of the Fourth Amendment: a gap eagerly filled by the legislator.

[16] Borgers and Van Sliedregt 2009, 189.

inspired by the changed societal and political climate that are also legitimate under the rule of law.[17]

Previous Chapters have demonstrated that the Netherlands and the United States, confronted with an increased call to take action to prevent terrorist attacks, have taken measures to enable anticipative criminal investigations, but with serious consequences for protective values that have governed the system before these measures were taken. The goal of the assessment made in this book is to demonstrate whether or not the current regulation of anticipative criminal investigations in the Netherlands and the United States, in whole or in part, does undermine the legitimacy of the criminal justice system, should it break with or deviate from traditional protective principles in a way that no longer reflects the synthesis required under the rule of law between the sword and shield in criminal procedural law. For this purpose, the above-indicated three-prong analysis will be applied in order to determine the conditions that the regulation of anticipative criminal investigations shall meet under the rule of law. This approach requires some additional explanation and a foundation as to its combination of two different legal interpretive theoretical concepts.

#### 8.1.1.2 Building the Architecture of the Anticipative Criminal Investigation Under the Rule of Law

In Chap. 1, a broad and substantive notion of the rule of law has been adopted, which governs all state action. This broad notion of the rule of law is based on the assumption that the right to respect for human dignity underpins the state organization and all state action. The rule of law then reflects a democratic state organization with separation of powers and an independent judiciary, and a government acting within the borders of the law, established through a democratic process and in accordance with the principle of formal legality, and with due respect to the fundamental rights of its citizens.[18]

The state is thus at any time subjected to the principles that directly follow from the understanding of the rule of law on the basis of respect for human dignity. Dworkin is an important advocate of acknowledging the importance of principles with an intrinsic moral value, derived from the recognition of the human dignity of every human being, as a starting point for establishing rules. Dworkin considers (moral) principles as the underpinning of the whole body of law and as providing the law with its justification.[19] I will distinguish between two types of such fundamental principles, which have a different character and a different regulatory consequence. The fundamental principles to be formulated in this project to underpin the procedural regulation of criminal investigations will be identified as the constitutive

---

[17] Compare: Finn 1991, 7.

[18] See Chap. 1, Sect. 1.3.

[19] See Dworkin in e.g. Dworkin 1979.

principles (Sect. 8.3.1). These constitutive principles are the direct elaboration of principles attached to the right to respect for human dignity. Because of their foundation in rule of law principles, the constitutive principles following from the first prong of analysis cannot be subjected to a balancing exercise.[20] The term 'constitutive principles', borrowed from Finn, reflects that these principles are the fundamental presuppositions on which protective rules are based; they are the solid basis underpinning the measurement of a system of restraints and guarantees to which government action in the field of criminal law is subjected.[21]

The traditional design of the criminal justice system, composed of rules that aim to realize the government's "substantive goals" of "public good" and to restrain the government in its powers to pursue these goals in order to protect individual liberty, comes down to the constitutive principles upon which they are based.[22] Upside down, this means that the rules of legislation and/or jurisprudence should aim to guarantee the constitutive principles and, thus, respect for human dignity. The constitutive principles thus places limits on the development of procedural rules adopted on the basis of a balancing of interests for the purpose of enhancing governmental powers under the influence of societal circumstances.[23]

The procedural rules that follow from the constitutive principles do not limit government action with meticulous detail. Rather, within the boundaries of the procedural regulation the government has discretion. Nevertheless, also institutions are regulated on the basis of fundamental principles that follow from the right to respect for human dignity. These principles, which will be referred to as the parameters, shall thus be distinguished from the constitutive principles, because they cover the conduct of institutions in the context of the criminal justice system instead of the procedure to be followed. The manner in which the procedure will be applied by the institutions responsible needs to be capable of guaranteeing the fundamental principles of criminal procedural law that will be identified as parameters (Sect. 8.3.2). In combination with the constitutive principles, the parameters provide for the non-derogable part of the regulation of criminal investigations; the foundation and building blocks of the house. On the basis of the constitutive principles the procedural framework can be drafted, whilst the parameters require the adoption of rules enabling the subjection of the institutions pursuing their tasks to these fundamental principles.

The second prong of analysis to be provided in this Chapter will assess different arguments that influence the synthesis (Sect. 8.4). This assessment will result in the crystallizing of conditions that are additional to the constitutive principles and the parameters. Moreover, it will result in the identification of the factors

---

20 In fact all rules have a dimension of principles; however, the rules that serve the guarantee of constitutive principles reflect minimum guarantees towards observing rule of law principles. Soeteman 2009, 6. See also: Franken 2008, 11-12 and Dworkin 2006, 27.

21 Finn 1991, 23 and 28.

22 Compare: Finn 1991, 29.

23 Franken 2008, 10 and Peters 1999, 276-277.

influencing specific policy choices made in regulating the anticipative criminal investigation to realize the parameters, 'above' the constitutive principles. The second prong of analysis will thus concern the flexibility of the law in so far as the law needs to be elaborated above the baseline of principled requirements following from the constitutive principles and parameters. It will determine the justified synthesis—taking into account that synthesis reflects the optimization of shield and sword objectives and can thus not be realized by the minimum achievable—between sword and shield in the societal and political philosophical circumstances of today.[24] These arguments will be theoretical arguments of a philosophical, societal, political and criminological nature and will be assessed on the macro-level, detached from the specific situation of the Netherlands or the United States. Their assessment will not go further than required in order to bring the formulation of the conditions that reflect the synthesis between sword and shield in the anticipative criminal investigation to the next level and will thus not be complete as to the scope, contents and potential impact of the separate arguments. This intended next level concerns the validity of the specific choices made that apply to the 'sword aspect' of the anticipative criminal investigation and the proportionality or appropriateness of these choices in relation to protective elements.

Before turning to the elaboration of the three dimensions of the regulation, which should bring us to the synthesis sought between sword and shield on an abstract, theoretical, level, the next section will first conclusively define and position the concept of an anticipative criminal investigation. On the basis of the findings of Chaps. 4 and 7 it will be possible to identify the assumed problematic issues of the current regulation of the anticipative criminal investigation as to the relation with traditional protective requirements (rules) of criminal investigation. Subsequently, the Chapter will turn, firstly, to deducting the constitutive principles and parameters of the anticipative criminal investigation (Sect. 8.3) and then, secondly, to the assessment of the different relevant arguments (Sect. 8.4). Lastly, the findings of Sects. 8.2–8.4 will be integrated, resulting in the substantiation of the concrete conditions, categorized in three pillars of regulatory rules, which can be applied in order to provide for a normative and comparative judgment regarding the current regulation adopted in the Netherlands and the United States in the next and final Chapter.

## 8.2 Conclusive Characterization and Positioning of the Anticipative Criminal Investigation

The anticipative criminal investigation has a long and gradual development, which has accelerated since the events of September 11, 2001. A proactive and intelligence-led investigation was already practiced before 9/11, mainly to confront

[24] Rozemond 2006, 164-165.

organized crime. However, since 9/11 different legislative measures and developments in case law and policy have resulted in the establishment of an investigative framework that differs in crucial aspects from traditional frameworks, for which reason it can now be identified as a separate investigative framework with specific characteristics that gives it its anticipatory character.

Chapter 1 has already taken the initial step to define the concept by emphasizing that this form of investigation is exclusively proactive and is conducted for the purpose of prevention. The goal of prevention is the *leitmotiv* for establishing this form of investigation. Because of this goal of prevention, an anticipative criminal investigation is typically intelligence-led so as to be able to act in anticipation of threats and it is typically covert in order not to divulge the information position (with the exception of search methods that are used to avert an imminent threat). Moreover, and crucially, because prevention is the basic assumption of counterterrorism measures, it has become an independent goal also of the anticipative criminal investigation, even surpassing the goal of evidence-gathering for prosecution. Prevention *ex ante*,[25] a goal previously reserved for the intelligence investigation, has diffused the distinction between intelligence and law enforcement, rendering the anticipative investigation a concept which lies somewhere in between these two areas and pursuing functions of both areas. This touches upon the *ultimum remedium* character of the criminal justice system. Traditionally, the criminal justice system was considered as a last resort to deal with serious wrongful or harmful conduct through prosecution and punishment.[26] Currently the criminal justice system has also become an instrument to contribute to realizing a safe society and to avert harm. The criminal justice system has obtained this additional function, because the realization of the *prevention* of serious wrongful or harmful conduct is considered to require—as an *ultimum remedium*; as a necessary means in addition to other state powers that can be applied to realize prevention (e.g. the intelligence apparatus)—also the employment of the methods and powers attributed to the criminal justice system.

The assessments made in Chaps. 4 and 7 further characterize and position the anticipative criminal investigation by demonstrating for the Netherlands and the United States what aspects the regulation of anticipative criminal investigations breaks with or deviates from previously established protective elements. On the basis of the findings of these Chapters the critical issues for the synthesis sought between sword and shield in criminal procedural law have been identified.

These critical issues will now be briefly recapitulated in order to be able to draw a full picture regarding the character and position of the anticipative criminal investigation. In the first place, the regulation of anticipative criminal investigations raises questions as to the required threshold to legitimize a *criminal* investigation. The adopted threshold in the Netherlands of 'indications of a

[25] As opposed to the realization of prevention after the fact, as a consequence of the deterrent effect of punishment.

[26] Ashworth 2009, 32-33.

terrorist crime' offers the investigating agencies broad discretion to use criminal investigative methods, such as surveillance, for the prevention of terrorism, which deviates, at least theoretically, from the threshold of a reasonable suspicion of a crime having been or being committed or of involvement in a criminal organization. At the same time, also the reasonable suspicion threshold is interpreted as not obstructing criminal investigative activities for the prevention of terrorism. Moreover, the information establishing indications or reasonable suspicion in an anticipative criminal investigation will usually directly and exclusively come from the intelligence and security service or from the criminal intelligence unit and, therefore, from anonymous sources. In the United States, national security investigations have become the primary form for investigating crimes that are at the same time threats to national security. As a consequence, the threshold of probable cause that someone is an agent of a foreign power, rather than probable cause with a nexus to a crime as a requirement included in the Fourth Amendment and in Title III (regulating surveillance in the law enforcement context), must be met, whereas the information intercepted can be used as evidence in a criminal trial. Moreover, under current Fourth Amendment analysis probable cause is no longer a per se requirement in order to render a search reasonable.

The threshold to be met before anticipative criminal investigation activities can be initiated has thus been lowered, resulting in broad discretion to operate in the field of criminal investigation for the prevention of terrorism and expanding the scope of the criminal investigation in general. This development raises questions as to its legitimacy under the rule of law. These questions touch upon the (institutional) relation between criminal (law enforcement) investigation and intelligence investigation and the required legitimization to justify investigative action that interferes with fundamental liberty. The required legitimization for justifying investigative action shall be considered for the separated contexts of criminal investigation and intelligence investigation as well as for a possible 'shared' context where the traditional investigative goals have been combined. Furthermore, this characteristic of an anticipative criminal investigation raises questions which touch upon the role traditionally fulfilled by the presumption of innocence and the right to privacy in relation to the required level of evidence that amounts to a sufficiently good reason for taking criminal investigative steps against someone.

Secondly, the nature of the anticipative criminal investigation, typified as intelligence-led, raises concerns with respect to privacy rights and the protection of the innocent, because of the broadening of the scope and nature of the investigation, the diverse and wide range of the information collected, the stimulation of exchange between different agencies and the limited control over the methods of collecting information by the government agencies. The scope and nature of an anticipative criminal investigation clearly differs from traditional forms of criminal investigation, as explained in Chaps. 4 and 7 for the Netherlands and the United States. This raises questions as to the necessity and proportionality of the adverse consequences for the right to respect for privacy in relation to the effectiveness of this method of investigation.

In the third place, the consequences of the nature of the intercepted information or the context in which the information has been intercepted has implications for the fairness of the proceedings. Both in the Netherlands and the United States, particularly in criminal proceedings that follow an anticipative criminal investigation, parts of the materials that are normally covered by disclosure obligations remain classified. Moreover, the legitimacy of the manner in which the evidence has been obtained cannot be controlled because the method is protected or the information amounting to the required threshold for application is classified. The lack of control over investigative activities increases the risk of abuses of state power. Furthermore, the protection of the right to a fair trial under Article 6 ECHR and the US constitutional guarantee of procedural due process in criminal proceedings are at issue, because the implications of anticipative criminal investigations for subsequent proceedings touch upon due process principles and fair trial rights.

## 8.3 The Common Ground of the Regulation of Criminal Investigations

When assessing the legitimacy of the regulation of the anticipative criminal investigation under the rule of law, we are in fact reconsidering the regulatory choices once made when developing the system of criminal procedural law on the basis of the synthesis found between both objectives in order to realize both optimally. To do so, we need to identify the underlying values of the rule of law that govern the state's authority in criminal procedural law, which must obtain protection through the shield aspect of criminal procedural law. State adherence to the rule of law is intended to protect against an unlimited, absolute state. In the first Chapter (Sect. 1.4) the notion of respect for human dignity has been understood as regulating all state power under the rule of law in a manner which transcends ordinary laws and even Constitutions. It has been explained in what way this notion of respect for human dignity has also determined the function and objectives of criminal procedural law (Sect. 1.5). Under the sword objective of criminal procedural law the state has been attributed the powers to investigate, prosecute and punish those who have committed a crime and in that way to contribute to providing citizens with a secure society. The shield objective of criminal procedural law subjects the system to restraints and checks, based upon the distrust of a too powerful government, in order to protect citizens against an arbitrarily operating and unlimited government. Section 1.6.1 has provided the conclusion that a criminal investigation, because of its connotation with the procedure of prosecution and punishment, should include the safeguards in anticipation of the eventual realization of the shield objective in the criminal process.

The constitutive principles and parameters that will be formulated in this Chapter are the fundamental basis of the shield objective and, hence, the common ground of the regulation of any system of criminal investigation. Criminal investigation powers regulated and used within the borders set by this 'common ground' of fundamental rights and principles guarantee that the state's institutions operate under the rule of law. These fundamental rights and principles govern the state authorities in the exercise of their investigative function and are a guarantee of their integrity with regard to conducting their task in respect of the human dignity of citizens. The legitimization of the use of the power attributed to the state agencies responsible for criminal investigation thus depends on their ability to act within the procedural context of the constitutive principles and directed by the parameters. The restraints and checks on governmental power guarantee the individual liberty of citizens, free from arbitrary authority, in a state that subjects itself to the rule of law.

The adopted 'thick' notion of the rule of law has been understood as subjecting the government to the law (law in the sense of rules meeting the requirements of formal legality) that imposes restraints, as well as obligations, on the government in relation to its citizens for the purpose of guaranteeing respect for human dignity. The constitutive principles and parameters underpinning the regulation of anticipative criminal investigations reflect this restricting and legitimizing aspect of state power under the rule of law. Restraints on governmental power in order to protect human dignity aim to promote equality within the law, to exclude arbitrariness and to guarantee respect for fundamental rights through the protection of the innocent in the criminal justice system and guaranteeing the fairness of the proceedings. Obligations on the state following from the basic assumption of respect for human dignity legitimize the use of power which is necessary to conduct investigative activities for the purpose of providing security—as a prerequisite for the enjoyment of liberty—and punishing those that have violated the norms of the criminal law (as the norms that prohibit violations of the fundamental rights of individuals by other individuals and the violation of norms considered necessary to maintain a free and safe society). The powers provided should be proportionate to their aim. Furthermore, in order to guarantee the integrity and fairness of state activities—that the state uses its powers for legitimate purposes and within the borders of the law—accountability, enabled by a certain level of transparency, is required in order to enable control. Moreover, the legitimacy and integrity of the activities of the criminal investigating institution are guaranteed by regulating discretionary areas through the principles of proportionality and necessity. Lastly, the fairness of the criminal process must be guaranteed in order to make sure that, ultimately, the guilty will be punished and the innocent acquitted; that the truth will be established. The fairness of the procedure is realized by making it possible that also when the procedure resulting in the imposition of punishment is preceded by an anticipative criminal investigation, this procedure is followed while observing fair trial rights and due process principles.

### 8.3.1 Three Constitutive Principles

It is now possible to formulate and further substantiate three constitutive principles for the regulation of an anticipative criminal investigation. Some of these constitutive principles are interrelated and simultaneously promote each other's rule of law values. However, all of them also have an independent constitutive function with regard to the regulation of criminal investigations. Also, the realization of some of the constitutive principles may boil down to the same rules. These rules are then founded on multiple constitutive principles, which give them an even stronger rule of law character. Together the constitutive principles will provide the baseline to regulate anticipative criminal investigations.

The regulation of anticipative criminal investigations may, partly depending on the particular legal tradition, be composed of statutory law, possibly supplemented by internal guidelines, and case law. In other words: the regulation shall be in compliance with the rule of law requirement of formal legality. For the Netherlands, the principle of legality is part of the baseline for regulation, like it is for any law providing a power for the state to interfere with individual liberty. However, in the United States, the principle of legality has obtained a different understanding and does not play a role as a fundamental principle of criminal procedural law as such. Rather, the concept of substantive due process may be compared with the principle of legality as they serve the same goals. Moreover, also the required 'quality of the law' under Article 8(2) ECHR limits the power of the government to interfere with rights and liberties to a well-defined scope and to a legitimate purpose. Because of the different approach in the United States and considering that in the Netherlands the requirements of formal legality are also implied in the conditions following from the protection of the right to respect for private life,[27] legality has not been adopted as a separate constitutive principle as it does not impose specific additional requirements on the substantive body of the regulation of anticipative criminal investigations. Without denying the fundamental status of the principle of legality in the Netherlands, the requirements following from the principle of legality and substantive due process[28] are in this way absorbed in the right to respect for private life.

This section will continue to explore the meaning of the following three constitutive principles: the presumption of innocence, the right to respect for private life and due process/fair trial. These constitutive principles will be identified on the basis of a theoretical reflection based on the rule of law perception underpinned by

[27] Compare the manner in which the right to respect for private life (as guaranteed in Article 8 ECHR and Article 10 of the Dutch Constitution) integrates with the principle of legality (as guaranteed in Article 1 CCP). See on this also Chap. 2, Sect. 2.3.2.1. Article 8 ECHR requires a basis in the law for restrictions on the right to respect for private life that is of sufficient quality to be foreseeable to the person concerned (*lex certa*). In addition, the requirement of being in 'accordance with the law' implied in Article 8(2) ECHR requires a basis (case law or statutory law) for restrictions on the right to respect for private life and requires that the restriction is proportionate to a legitimate aim (implying a purpose limitation).

[28] The powers made available to the government to conduct anticipative criminal investigative activities by means of special investigative techniques shall be provided in the law with sufficient quality (*lex certa*) in order to exclude arbitrariness and promote equality within the law. Furthermore, the powers shall be clearly demarcated so that they are limited to a legitimate aim and shall not *prima facie* concern an unjustified violation of fundamental rights. See also: Van Klink and Lembcke 2007, 10.

the right to respect for human dignity and, hence, the right to individual liberty. In addition, the recognition of certain rights as fundamental human rights in human rights treaties and national constitutions will be taken into account as a strong indication of the validity of attributing these rights the status of constitutive principles in relation to the regulation of anticipative criminal investigations.

#### 8.3.1.1 The Presumption of Innocence

The presumption of innocence is directly connected to the notion of personal autonomy, which requires that the government refrains from intermingling with individual liberty as well as providing the justification for doing so when a person has (of his/her own free will) transgressed substantive norms. Hence, the principle of no punishment without guilt also implies a presumption of innocence and to be free from government interference until guilt has been established.[29]

The fundamental *presumptio innocentiae* is also recognized in various international treaties, most importantly in Article 14(2) ICCPR, Article 6(2) ECHR and Article 8(2) ACHR. This presumption is considered to be an element of the right to a fair trial and can generally be considered as a fundamental principle of law, as it recognizes the inviolability of human dignity and its reflection in the government's use of its power. The presumption of innocence is in this respect the fundamental notion that has its effect on the elaboration of criminal procedural law as a whole in the sense that the entire criminal procedure is aimed at establishing the truth by being continuously orientated towards the possibility that the suspect is innocent until the contrary—his guilt—has been proven in a court of law.[30]

The presumption of innocence is primarily understood as an element of the right to a fair trial, which also follows from its inclusion in the provisions providing for the right to a fair trial in the ICCPR, ECHR and the ACHR. In Chap. 2, Sect. 2.1.3.3.1., the meaning of the presumption of innocence as an element of Article 6 ECHR and its interpretation by the ECrtHR has already been touched upon.[31] It has been explained there that the presumption of innocence primarily obtains its meaning in the context of the trial proceedings and then most significantly for evidentiary purposes, thereby imposing the (legal) burden of proof on the prosecutor and requiring proof 'beyond a reasonable doubt'.[32]

During the investigative stage the presumption implies a right to be treated as being innocent.[33] From that point of view, the presumption of innocence has a

---

[29] Albrecht 2010, 119-120.

[30] Krauß 1971, 156 and 176.

[31] See in more detail on the presumption of innocence and the relation between (anticipative) criminal investigation and the presumption of innocence also Hirsch Ballin 2008.

[32] According to Van Sliedregt the presumption of innocence should be understood "first and foremost [as] a rule of evidence and decision. In addition, it is a limitation on excesses in the preliminary investigation." Van Sliedregt 2009, 15.

[33] *Ibid.*, 11.

normative effect on the regulation of criminal procedural powers.[34] In domestic legal systems, the presumption of innocence is increasingly elaborated in procedural guarantees, which depend on the specific procedural phase and on what level of evidence regarding the guilt of the person involved is present. By way of an example, compare the phase in which wire-tapping techniques are used against an individual, the phase in which pre-trial detention is imposed, and the phase in which a prosecution is initiated. The extent to which the presumption of innocence must be taken into account increases contemporaneously with the severity of the governmental interference in civil rights in each phase of the proceedings, which is demonstrated by the level of proof required for imposing the criminal procedural measures of these phases.[35] The presumption of innocence thus implies that one should be subjected as little as possible to any criminal procedural measures having implications for the (private) life of the person in question. The use of criminal procedural investigative powers against someone will be experienced to a certain extent as being a presumption of guilt. In 1764 Cesare Beccaria, inspired by Pietro Verri,[36] used the *presumptio innocentiae* as an argument for rejecting the use of torture as an investigative method for establishing the truth (a confession), because using torture is a punishment imposed before guilt has been established in a court of law.[37] Also the *Déclaration des Droits de l'Homme et du Citoyen* (1789) formulates, in its Article 9, the regulation of coercive powers in the criminal investigation on the basis of the presumption of innocence.[38]

Although primarily an element of the right to a fair trial that governs the law of evidence, the presumption of innocence, as a principle of criminal procedural law, thus has normative implications for the criminal process as a whole. In this particular meaning the presumption is here identified as a constitutive principle for regulating the anticipative criminal investigation. As a constitutive principle, the presumption of innocence is a normative notion that places restraints on the criminal investigation for the purpose of protecting the innocent without hindering all use of investigative or coercive powers because guilt has not yet been proven in a court of law.[39] It is important to distinguish the meaning of guilt and innocence in the trial phase from the meaning of guilt and innocence in the investigative phase. In the trial phase someone can only be considered guilty once there is sufficient evidence regarding his guilt to convict him/her in a court of law (e.g. upon the establishment of proof beyond a reasonable doubt). All others are innocent. In the investigative phase guilt is understood in the sense of a suspicion:

---

[34] Keijzer 1987, 243.

[35] Krauß 1971, 158.

[36] In his 'Dei delitti e delle Pene' Beccaria largely reproduced an essay by Verri in which he criticized torture and pleaded for the presumption of innocence. This essay, published posthumously in 1804, was used for discussions in the 'Academia dei Pugni,' an academic-philosophic club founded by, inter alia, Verri and Beccaria. See: Verri 1988.

[37] Beccaria 1986, 29-33.

[38] Keijzer 1987.

[39] Stuckenberg 1997, 74 and Keijzer 1987, 243.

some evidence regarding the possible involvement of someone in criminal activities.[40] In contrast, everyone who has nothing to do with criminal activities is innocent. The regulatory impact of the presumption of innocence is therefore directed at the exclusion of involving innocent persons in criminal investigative activities, while it aims to include those persons who, in the procedural sense, are still 'presumed innocent'.

The rules that are based upon the presumption of innocence as a constitutive principle are, therefore, capable of promoting equality within the law, excluding arbitrariness and providing for legitimate interference with the fundamental right to respect for private life during the criminal investigative phase. The presumption of innocence is related to promoting equality within the law and excluding arbitrariness in that the principle reflects that everyone who has not violated criminal law should not become involved in criminal proceedings and, *vice versa*, everyone who transgresses criminal law may expect to become the subject of criminal proceedings and, as a consequence of the notion of individual autonomy and, hence, the "capacity and fair opportunity to do otherwise", lose some of his/her individual liberty.[41] This selection, based on a level of guilt regarding the commission of a criminal offence, aims to exclude any arbitrary use of criminal investigative powers. In addition, the presence of some information pointing to the guilt of someone regarding his/her involvement in a criminal offense is also the necessary legitimization for interfering with the right to respect for private life.

The constitutive principle of the presumption of innocence thus requires the establishment of rules providing a threshold that reflects some involvement in criminal activities (a level of guilt) in order to avoid that the situation where innocent persons are subjected to criminal investigative activities. Furthermore, rules should be adopted that aim to reduce the scope of criminal investigative activities to those against whom a certain level of guilt can be established. Lastly, the presumption of innocence has a regulatory effect prior to trial in that suspects are treated as being innocent, for which reason the government should generally use restraint in the use of investigative powers (see also the parameter of necessity).[42]

---

[40] Guilt during the investigative phase could also be understood as hypothetical innocence within the meaning of the presumption of innocence as an element of the right to a fair trial: (any level of) suspicion requires some evidence of guilt and legitimizes the use of criminal investigative and coercive powers, which can also be understood as a form of pre-trial punishment considering the implications for individual liberty whilst, however, in the criminal procedural sense one is still innocent.

[41] Compare: Ashworth 2009, 24-25, Hart 2008, 28-53 and Albrecht 2010, 119-120.

[42] Compare: Van Sliedregt 2009, 13.

#### 8.3.1.2 Respect for the Fundamental Right to Private Life

The fundamental right to respect for one's private life follows directly from the rule of law requirement that the government shall not enter into the zone of citizens' individual liberty.[43] The fundamental character of the right to a private life is also recognized through its inclusion in all human right treaties (most notably in Article 17 ICCPR, Article 8 ECHR and Article 11 ACHR), the Constitutions of the Netherlands and the United States (Article 10 Dutch Constitution and, although limited to the search and seizure context, the Fourth Amendment of the US Constitution) and Articles 7 and 8 of the EU Charter of Fundamental Rights). This clearly gives the right a fundamental character and its status as a constitutive principle to be observed and guaranteed by any state that considers itself as being subject to the rule of law.[44] Although the right is not an absolute right, it limits the government's activities in the field of criminal procedural law to certain restrictions requiring a specific well-defined justification for interfering with the privacy rights of citizens.

Because the protection of this human right to respect for one's private life underpins the regulation of anticipative criminal investigations, it is required to deduce the interpretation given to this right, as to its scope and permissible restrictions, from the case law of the ECrtHR and the US Supreme Court. On that basis, the precise impact of this constitutive principle will be determined. The right to private life is not an absolute right: restrictions are permitted, for instance in the context of the criminal justice system. As a constitutive principle, this right aims to protect citizens against arbitrary interferences with their private lives, imposing restraints on the power of the government to conduct criminal investigative activities.[45] For the interpretation and scope of the right to respect for one's private life under Article 8 ECHR and the US Constitution's Fourth Amendment, reference can be made to the extensive explanation provided on Article 8 ECHR (Chap. 2, Sects. 2.1.3.2.1 and 2.3.2.1.1) and on the Fourth Amendment (Chap. 5, Sects. 5.1.4.1 and 5.3.2.1).

As a constitutive principle, the right to respect for one's privacy affects different aspects of a regulation of the criminal investigation. Firstly, the rules that follow from this constitutive principle concern the legitimization of investigative activities that interfere with the right to respect for one's private life and the observance of privacy rights during investigative activities (and thus apart from their legitimization). Hence, rules reflecting a threshold on which basis the use of investigative powers is permitted also serve the realization of this constitutive principle. These

[43] Compare: Muller et al. 2007, 19 and 27-30.

[44] The implication of the fundamental right to respect for one's private life for the regulation of criminal investigations has also clearly followed from the analysis of the traditional regulation of the criminal investigation in the Netherlands and the United States. It may even be considered as the constitutive principle having the most significant limiting consequences for the government's criminal investigative authority.

[45] Compare: Sottiaux 2008, 266.

rules should reflect the justification for the governmental agency to interfere with one's private life, relating the information providing the grounds for the interference with the purpose of using the investigative method.[46]

Secondly, the protection of data concerns another aspect of the right to respect for one's private life, which governs the process of the investigation once the investigation has been legitimately initiated.[47] Especially the storage and sharing of information impinges on the right to data protection, which falls beyond the scope of this book focusing on the legitimacy of the gathering process. Hence, without going into the whole range of protective conditions following from the right to informational privacy and which is included in regulations concerning the protection of personal data that are applicable to any government system *storing* personal data, the *gathering* of data in the particular context of criminal proceedings does impose some specific additional requirements. For this reason, the protection of privacy regarding the storage of data on behalf of the government will not be dealt with.[48] Instead, the right to data protection in relation to the legitimacy of the criminal justice system is only relevant as to the realization of the right to *habeas data*, which also concerns an aspect of parameter accountability (see section 8.3.1.4 on parameter accountability).

Lastly and also touching upon the parameter of accountability, any governmental activities that interfere with the right to respect for one's private life shall be subject to supervision. Establishing a system of control and accountability as to the legitimacy of interfering with privacy rights concerns an important check on the integrity and fairness of state actions with regard to the carrying out of its investigative functions.

Hence, the parameter of accountability as to the legitimacy of the interference with the right to privacy in general and the right to *habeas data* are also underpinned by the constitutive principle of the right to privacy. The constitutive principle of the right to privacy itself directly underpins the regulation of the anticipative criminal investigation, by requiring rules that limit interference with the right to privacy to a circumscribed justification.

---

[46] This implies a purpose limitation: interference with the right to respect one's private life is limited to the clarification of the information establishing the grounds that legitimize the interference. Compare: Muller et al. 2007, 76.

[47] As recognized by the ECrtHR as being implied in Article 8 ECHR: ECHR 16 February 2000, App. no. 27798/95 (*Amann v. Switzerland*), para 65 and ECHR 4 May 2000, App. no. 28341/95 (*Rotaru v. Romania*), para 43. Compare also Article 8 of the Charter of Fundamental Rights of the European Union (inspired by the German Constitutional right to '*informationnelle Selbstbestimmung*', based upon Articles 1 and 2 Grundgesetz), explicitly guaranteeing also the right to the protection of one's personal data. The manner in which personal data require protection when voluntarily transferred to 'third parties', such as banks or libraries, is perceived very differently in the United States and in the European Union. See on this: Hirsch Ballin 2012 (*forthcoming*).

[48] On this subject see e.g. De Busser 2009.

### 8.3.1.3 Due Process/Fair Trial[49]

The information collected within the context of an anticipative criminal investigation may be used for the purpose of prosecuting and punishing persons who have violated the criminal law. In order to guarantee that only the guilty are convicted and punished the procedure aims to establish the material truth, which is only permissible through a fair procedure. To serve justice in general, the shield objective of criminal procedural law demands that during the trial proceedings the rights of the defendant are respected based on his/her fundamental right to human dignity, which results in the creation of a procedure of checks and balances for the benefit of the defendant.[50] These procedural checks and balances boil down to principles of due process or fair trial rights.

Due process is a concept with a fundamental character that directly follows from the protection of individual liberty against the power of the state to prosecute and punish individuals. Guaranteeing due process provides fundamental protection for the individual to be precluded from any unlawful and arbitrary deprivation of his/her individual liberty. Hence, the right to a fair trial/due process is a basic human right, guaranteed in Article 14 ICCPR,[51] Article 6 ECHR,[52] Article 8 ACHR and the US Constitution, as a consequence of the Supreme Court decisions regarding the Fifth and Fourteenth Amendments.[53] The general right to a fair trial has been supplemented by a multitude of specific fair trial rights that apply to different aspects of the fairness of the proceedings, such as, most significantly, the right to legal counsel, the right to habeas corpus, the right to equality before the law and the courts, the right to a trial by a competent, independent and impartial tribunal established by law, the right to equality of arms, the presumption of innocence (as a rule of evidence and proof[54]) and the right to call and examine

[49] (Procedural) due process here embraces the right to a fair trial (the former concerns the terminology which is applicable to the US system, the latter to the Dutch system), as both the right to a fair trial and due process aim to guarantee the fairness of trial proceedings which amounts to different fair trial rights/due process principles. When, in the text, reference is made to either due process or fair trial, in both cases this is understood as the fundamental conception of the fairness of the criminal proceedings. Compare the dissenting opinion of Justice Holmes in *Frank v. Mangum*, 237 U.S. 309, 35 S.Ct. 582 (1915), 347: "[w]hatever disagreement there may be as to the scope of the phrase 'due process of law,' there can be no doubt that it embraces the fundamental conception of a fair trial."

[50] Pati 2009, 2-3.

[51] The Commission on Human Rights has even proposed to include the right to the fair trial as a non-derogable right in Article 4(2) of the ICCPR. Pati 2009, 31.

[52] See Chap. 2, section 2.1.2.4.

[53] The Supreme Court has, on the basis of the Fifth and Fourteenth Amendments, developed a concept of constitutional procedural due process, composed of different due process principles which are applicable to trial proceedings. See in more detail Chap. 5, Sect. 5.1.4.2.

[54] See, for the distinction between the presumption of innocence as a constitutive principle and as an element to the right to a fair trial, Sect. 8.3.1.1 and Chap. 2, Sect. 2.1.3.3.1.

witnesses.[55] Not all of these fair trial rights are relevant for the regulation of anticipative criminal investigations within the scope of this project, considering that the majority apply to the trial phase and/or do not relate to information-gathering activities in the trial phase. The implications of the constitutive principle of due process for the regulation of the anticipative criminal investigation are limited to the consequences of introducing information collected within the context of an anticipative criminal investigation to criminal proceedings for the purpose of prosecution. In order to guarantee the fairness of the trial proceedings it is important that the introduction of information that originates from the anticipative criminal investigation (with its—by now—well-known characteristics) does not undermine the adversarial character of the proceedings and the equality of arms. To facilitate adversarial proceedings and equality of arms, as due process guarantees,[56] the defendant has the right to the disclosure of evidence. The influence of due process as a constitutive principle is thus limited to the inclusion of rules that concern the disclosure of evidence in order to facilitate the fairness of the trial proceedings, which is closely related to the concept of internal transparency. The assessment regarding the fairness of prosecution and punishment proceedings in this study will thus not go further than the specific aspect of due process that covers control over the legitimacy of anticipative criminal investigative activities by which evidence has been collected.

The rules to be included in the regulation of anticipative criminal investigations that are based upon the constitutive principle of due process should then concern the formulation of conditions that cover the use of information collected in the

[55] For a complete overview of fair trial rights see Pati 2009, 35-37.

[56] The ECrtHR defines the right to a fair trial by referring to the principle of equality of arms ("each party must be afforded a reasonable opportunity to present his case under conditions that do not place him at a disadvantage *vis-à-vis* his opponent") and the right to adversarial proceedings ("both prosecution and defense must be given the opportunity to have knowledge of and comment on the observations filed and the evidence adduced by the other party"), without clearly distinguishing them. Trechsel 2005, 85, 90 and 96. See e.g.: ECHR 28 August 1991, App. no. 11170/84; 12876/87; 13468/87 (*Brandstetter v. Austria*), para 66 and ECHR 16 February 2000, App. no. 28901/95 (*Rowe and Davis v. The United Kingdom*), para 60. In *Goldberg v. Kelly* (1970) the US Supreme Court interpreted the due process clause of the Fifth and Fourteenth Amendments as containing several specific and "rudimentary" due process rights, including (among others): the "opportunity to be heard"; "a hearing (…) at a meaningful time and in a meaningful manner"; an "effective opportunity to defend by confronting any adverse witnesses and by presenting his own arguments and evidence orally"; "an opportunity to confront and cross-examine adverse witnesses"; and the disclosure of the "evidence used to prove the Government's case" to the individual who has been injured by the governmental action. See *Goldberg v. Kelly*, 397 U.S. 254, 90 S.Ct. 1011 (1970), 267-270. As follows from the content of these rights, they aim to guarantee equality, which underpins the fairness of the adversarial process as the process upon which the US criminal justice system is based. Pati 2009, 213. Hence, in the text a more general formulation derived from the ECrtHR is chosen rather than enlisting specific due process requirements applicable to one particular legal system. The right to disclosure, the specific right which is relevant to the assessment in this project, is in both the ECHR and in US jurisdiction understood as a specific fundamental right derived from the right to a fair trial/due process.

context of an anticipative criminal investigation as evidence. These rules shall reflect the relation between secrecy during the process of collection and the need to eventually achieve, after the covert investigative phase, transparency in the criminal procedure. For this purpose, it should be taken into account that the right to a fair trial/due process is an absolute right, but the specific methods by which to achieve fairness may vary. Hence, the exercise of specific defense rights may be subjected to certain restrictive conditions, but these restrictive conditions cannot be simply the product of balancing the interest of the accused against the interest of the state to keep certain information shielded. Instead, restrictions on defense rights should be strictly necessary and be counterbalanced by procedural mechanisms in order to guarantee the fairness of the proceedings as a whole.[57] Due process/fair trial concerns a flexible concept which can be realized through a structured approach, as long as the essence of due process/fairness is guaranteed.[58] The rules to be adopted in the regulation of anticipative criminal investigations should concern such a structured approach, aiming to facilitate control over the legitimacy of the manner in which the information has been obtained and over the reliability of the information as evidence in order to guarantee the fairness of the process as a whole and reflecting the essence of the due process/fair trial right of disclosure.

### *8.3.2 Three Parameters*

The parameters to be realized in the regulation of criminal investigations, as fundamental principles of criminal procedural law, cover the institutional framework of criminal justice in action, which is based upon the idea that not only the procedure to be followed by the institutions is underpinned by the fundamental right to respect for human dignity, but also the manner in which the government pursuit of its substantive goals within the context of this procedure is underpinned by the right to respect for human dignity. This requires the subjection of the conduct of state institutions within the framework of constitutive principles to parameters that concern the legitimacy of their conduct within the criminal justice

[57] Compare: ECHR 16 February 2000, App. no. 28901/95 (*Rowe and Davis v. The United Kingdom*), para 61. Ashworth 2007, 214-216.

[58] Ashworth 2007, 216-217. Compare also Sottiaux, citing US Justice Frankfurter: "[Due process], unlike some legal rules, is not a technical conception with a fixed content unrelated to time, place and circumstances. Expressing as it does in its ultimate analysis, respect enforced by law for that feeling of just treatment which has been evolved through centuries of Anglo-American constitutional history and civilization, 'due process' cannot be imprisoned within the treacherous limits of any formula. (…) Due process is not a mechanical instrument. It is not a yardstick. It is a process. It is a delicate process of adjustment inescapably involving the exercise of judgment by those whom the Constitution entrusted with the unfolding of the process" (original source: *Joint Anti-Fascist Refugee Committee v. McGrath*, 341 U.S. 123, 71 S.Ct. 624 (1951), concurring opinion of Justice Frankfurter at 162-163). Sottiaux 2008, 331.

system and the integrity of their actions. Because the parameters are also directly derived, as will be explained, from the right to respect for human dignity, the observance and/or realization of the parameters is a permanent, non-derogable, requirement for the legitimate regulation of anticipative criminal investigations. They are to be used in order to guide the institutions in the discretionary area within the boundaries of the constitutive principles and impose limits on the use of arguments in the flexible area of the law (as dealt with in Sect. 8.4).

The parameters can be directly related to the adopted understanding of the role of the state in criminal law, as established in Chap. 1: they address the government in a positive and negative sense in their realization of substantive (positive) goals (including the sword aspect of criminal procedure) and in a restrictive way, protecting citizens against government action (including the shield aspect of criminal procedural law). The three parameters that will be identified below—accountability, proportionality and necessity—concern the standards that the regulation of the anticipative criminal investigation shall meet. Because the parameters cover the acts of state institutions, the principles show similarity with principles of good governance, regulating the conduct of state institutions by aiming, on the one hand, at the realization of their substantive goals, while at the same time taking into account the interests of the individual.[59]

#### 8.3.2.1 Accountability

Accountability is a principle of criminal procedural law[60] requiring that governmental actors account for the manner in which they use their powers and the legitimacy of the choices made when pursuing their substantive goals. Accountability as a principle governing state action is essential for realizing respect for human dignity in a democracy, as it requires the government to provide reasons that justify any interference with individual liberty. Accountability is closely related to the transparency of the criminal justice system, as transparency (both internally and externally) is a condition for accountability, enabling control over the government's activities and enabling citizens to call the government to account.[61]

Accountability is adopted as a parameter, as (an anticipative) criminal investigation concerns a far-reaching power of the government that interferes with fundamental rights, which requires accountability towards the persons affected and towards society in general as to the use of the powers in observance of the constitutive principles and the other parameters. Accountability for criminal

---

[59] Addink 2010, 4-7.

[60] Finn identified 'review' as a constitutive principle. This affirms the rule of law status of the comparable principle of 'accountability'. I consider accountability, however, not as a constitutive principle but as a parameter, because of the distinction between principles touching upon procedure and those touching upon institutions. Finn 1991, 36.

[61] Brants and Van Lent 2001, 75, Brants et al. 2001, 8 and Borgers 2003.

investigative activities shall in the first place be realized within the context of criminal proceedings, under the scrutiny of the judiciary. In addition, political control mechanisms can be established when the context of criminal proceedings is inapt. Control over anticipative criminal investigative activities, also when these activities do not result in a criminal prosecution, is an important guarantee with regard to the integrity of the state agencies involved. The possibility to hold the government to account when it has acted outside the confines of the law concerns an important check on the integrity of the state agency responsible for the anticipative criminal investigation and on the fairness of possible criminal proceedings. For this reason, access to a judge when someone's individual liberties have been violated is considered to be a fundamental right and a basic element of the rule of law.[62] Moreover, the persons affected and the public at large shall have the possibility to assess and challenge the legitimacy and integrity of the government's investigative efforts, which requires transparency regarding the application of rules that legitimize investigative activities interfering with the fundamental right to privacy.[63]

To realize this, accountability rules shall be adopted which are applicable to all aspects of the anticipative criminal process and which establish control and realize accountability, through requiring (internal and external) transparency. However, especially in the context of an anticipative criminal investigation secrecy is often warranted. Hence, accountability will need to be realized while avoiding excessive transparency requirements as they might prevent the government from effectively protecting national security.[64] For this purpose it should be taken into account that the realization of accountability is an absolute requirement, whereas transparency is not. Transparency is an instrument for realizing accountability and is thus not a fundamental principle following from the right to respect for human dignity.[65] Hence different procedural mechanisms, within and outside the context of criminal proceedings, may be adopted, the combination of which realizes control over state agencies conducting sound and fair investigative tasks and a reasonable opportunity for citizens affected by the agencies' investigative activities that have exceeded the boundaries of their authority to have a fair remedy. The required level and form of transparency within these procedural mechanisms is a matter of proportionality, depending on a balance of interests between secrecy and the interests served by transparency. Nevertheless, in their coherence these mechanisms must achieve accountability. Moreover, as will also follow in Sect. 8.5, accountability and the constitutive principle of due process are closely related. In fact, the proportionality of mechanisms for realizing accountability (through establishing control over the basis

[62] As recognized by the US Supreme Court in *Marbury v. Madison*, 1 Cranch 137, 2 L.Ed.60 (1803), as guaranteed by Article 13 ECHR (effective remedy) and by Article 2(2) and (3) (effective, judicial remedy) ICCPR.

[63] Finn 1991, 37.

[64] (Anonymous) Note 2008A, 1556.

[65] *Ibid.*, 1557-1558.

of a certain level of transparency) is framed by the constitutive principle of due process and by the parameter of accountability. The procedural mechanisms adopted must be able to guarantee a fair procedure for the accused and must realize accountability for state activities within the context of the anticipative criminal investigation in the broader sense.

#### 8.3.2.2 Proportionality

Proportionality requires that the 'harm' inflicted by using investigative powers may not exceed the harm which will result from refraining from the investigative action. In general, proportionality has a very important regulatory influence on criminal law as the system, as such, does reflect the realization of the interests of the suspect, society and the victim.[66] As a parameter, proportionality applies to two levels: within the framework of regulating anticipative criminal investigations on a case-by-case basis where the law provides for discretion; and on the level of regulation itself, which guides the determination of regulatory rules in the flexible area of the law *above* the foundation of the regulation following from the constitutive principles.[67]

In its first meaning, the fundamental principle of proportionality gives further mandatory guidance to the criminal investigative activities of state institutions where they have discretionary power within the framework of the constitutive principles. Some level of discretion is necessary in order to provide state institutions with sufficient flexibility in conducting their investigative tasks so as to deal with individual, differing cases. To ensure the integrity of the state's authority where it has discretionary power, it should be subjected to the principle of proportionality, which is then also a factor to be taken into consideration by those who exercise control, most importantly the judge, over the investigative activities of the state.

Secondly, the regulation adopted for anticipative criminal investigations must be proportionate. Hence, the principle of proportionality imposes important limits on the use of arguments in the flexible area of the law used to gear criminal investigative activities towards prevention. It reflects the idea that not all means are permitted to realize prevention and thus imposes limits, additional to the limits following from the constitutive principles, on the legislature and the judge to develop rules for optimizing the prevention of terrorism.

Factors to be taken into account in determining the proportionality of a certain investigative action concern the specific interests involved (e.g. the interest of protecting the privacy of the individual versus the interest of preventing terrorism in a particular case as well as *in abstracto* on the regulatory level). In the context of the restrictions on human rights (e.g. in the structure of the ECHR)

[66] Rozemond 2006, 161.

[67] See also Corstens 2008, 77.

proportionality (or a means/ends) assessment is part of the necessity element. Interferences with the right to respect for one's private life are, for instance, only permitted when 'necessary in a democratic society,' a requirement which is met when the restriction is 'proportionate to a legitimate aim.'[68] Nevertheless, proportionality and necessity are here adopted also as separate parameters, because necessity has, especially in the context of criminal procedural law, an important independent meaning for the criminal justice system considering its character as an *ultimum remedium.* In that sense, necessity applies to the aim, rather than to the means. Furthermore, proportionality is not limited to an assessment as to whether the means are necessary for achieving the aim; the means shall also be in proportion to the aim considering the commensurate interference with privacy and the necessary means shall be applied proportionately. Lastly, proportionality is closely related to the aim of specific investigative activities, which implies that in a certain framework measures may only be proportionate in order to achieve a specific aim, the aim for which the investigative powers have been attributed. In that sense, proportionality may imply a purpose limitation.[69]

#### 8.3.2.3 Necessity

Considering that proportionality implies necessity as to the manner in which investigative powers are used for a specific goal, the meaning of necessity as a parameter is limited to the *abstract* level. The principle reflects the fact that the state should always have legitimization, in the sense of a legitimate substantive goal, to pursue criminal investigative activities. The government shall not use powers beyond those that are necessary for fulfilling its investigative task. The principle of necessity also gives the criminal justice system its character as an *ultimum remedium.* The power to impose punishment is the state power with the most far-reaching consequences for individual liberty and is, therefore, only permitted if necessary in order to fulfill the state's substantive goals of providing the preconditions for the enjoyment of liberty: safety and protection against the violation of fundamental rights by fellow citizens. When less intrusive means are conceivable to achieve the substantive goals of the criminal justice system, these less intrusive means should be chosen, such as civil liability (compare the principle of subsidiarity). The criminal justice system should thus be used as a last resort, in order to deal with "seriously wrongful or harmful conduct."[70] With regard to the regulation of an anticipative criminal investigation, the parameter of necessity requires rules reflecting the urgency to prove the necessity of either pursuing functions of a criminal procedural nature or warning functions regarding threats to national security.

---

68 See Chap. 2, Sect. 2.3.2.1.1. See also De Moor-van Vugt 1994, 242-244.

69 Compare De Moor-van Vugt 1994, 243 and 259.

70 Ashworth 2009, 33.

## 8.4 Seeking Synthesis in the Flexible Area of the Law in the Light of the Circumstances of Modern Society

Societal and political ideas on the role of the state in guaranteeing a safe society have changed under the influence of the conceptualization of society as a risk society, the culture of control and the precautionary principle. The changed role of criminal law, as an instrument to control risks, may be explained in the light of these social theories. Also the regulation of anticipative criminal law is influenced by these societal and political developments. Within the framework of constitutive principles and parameters just discussed, the law is flexible in order to be able to adjust to changing societal and political circumstances. The setting of other 'preferences' because of reasoning derived from the indicated theories may justify adopting an investigative framework that also aims at prevention.

The search for a synthesis between the sword and shield objectives of criminal procedural law should, therefore, also include an assessment of this flexible domain of the law. For this purpose this section will assess two types of arguments.

Section 8.4.1 will first turn to the arguments that can provide legitimization for specific choices made on the sword side of an anticipative criminal investigation. The validity of different relevant arguments will be assessed.[71] Hence, these arguments shall be taken into account as to the *manner* in which the parameters, possibly deviating from traditional systems of regulation, can be realized within the context of an anticipative criminal investigation in the flexible domain 'above' the constitutive principles.[72]

The principle of proportionality (including necessity) has been formulated as a parameter, in the sense that it permanently regulates, on a case-by-case basis, the use of investigative powers under the conditions provided in the law. The meaning of the parameters 'proportionality' and 'necessity' are, in addition to this meaning of proportionality, in particular important in the context of determining the synthesis between shield and sword in the flexible area of the law and, hence, for the

[71] These arguments should be distinguished from the explanation provided in Chap. 1 on the international public law domain and the international human rights domain and the theories on the risk society, the culture of control and the precautionary principle, forming the background of preventive measures in states, which in some situations have even obliged states to take preventive measures in order to protect their citizens against terrorism. These developments on the international legal level and on the societal/political level justify the efforts of states to adjust their law and policy for the purpose of combating and preventing terrorism. The arguments that will be dealt with in Sect. 8.4.1 concern the justification for choosing to enable anticipative criminal investigations through these preventive measures; the validity of arguments that could legitimize the sword objective of an anticipative criminal investigation, namely pursuing both a preventive function by anticipating threats and a criminal procedural function by gathering evidence for prosecution and are therefore part of the examination framework.

[72] Compare: Tsakyrakis 2008. The ECrtHR and continental European States predominantly take the approach that rights and other interests are formally indistinguishable, for which reason proportionality is the solution to *any* clash of rights and other interests. Rivers 2006 and Tsakyrakis 2008, 10-12 and 29.

assessment to be made in the current section. Arguments that may amount to proof of setting preferences in favor of adopting a system of an anticipative criminal investigation shall be considered as indications as to the necessity and proportionality of such a system. At the same time, some of these arguments may provide for counter-indications regarding proportionality and/or necessity. The interests to be taken into account in observing the principles of proportionality and necessity further inspire the formulation of regulatory rules for anticipative criminal investigations as long as absolute rights are not included in the proportionality or necessity assessment.[73]

The manner in which the eventual rules for the regulation of anticipative criminal investigations will be determined in the light of the right to respect for one's private life may illustrate the implications of the parameters in the context of the flexible area of the law and 'above' the rules following from the constitutive principles. The right to respect for one's private life has been formulated as a constitutive principle, but does not concern an absolute right. Interferences with the right to respect for one's private life are permissible under certain circumstances. The meaning of the right to respect for one's private life as a constitutive principle for regulating anticipative criminal investigations comes down to the requirement of a specific standard provided in law justifying the interference and the adoption of rules that guarantee respect for one's private life during investigative activities. In addition, the minimum rules following from the constitutive principle of the right to respect for one's private life can be further substantiated by balancing the interest of the protection of one's private life against the sword interests of an anticipative criminal investigation.[74] Because the restrictions on the right to respect for one's private life involve, to a certain extent, also an assessment (on the regulatory level[75]) of the proportionality and necessity of the restriction in the light of the legitimate aim to be pursued, this section will assess different arguments that may or may not be used in this context.

Secondly, Sect. 8.4.2 will assess, assuming that a validation of the legitimization of the sword approach chosen by the anticipative criminal investigation can

[73] Balancing or applying the principle of proportionality is a legitimate method to develop law or rules, as long as it does not concern absolute rights. Tsakyrakis 2008, 8.

[74] Compare the approach adopted to interpret the scope and applicability of the fundamental rights guaranteed in the ECHR. The balancing approach is recognizable both in the formulation of the rights in the Convention as well as in the way the ECrtHR determines whether a right protected by the Convention has been violated. In general the Court determines whether the interference with the right serves a legitimate aim, whether the interference is necessary in a democratic society and whether it is proportionate to the legitimate aim pursued. The US approach is slightly different: courts assess whether a specific reason of public interest is a proportionate limitation on the exercise of a fundamental right.

[75] Proportionality and necessity shall also further regulate specific investigative action on a case-by-case basis. However, the current section only takes into account the regulatory level. In addition to the regulation the parameter of proportionality (including necessity) shall always further regulate state institutions carrying out their investigative activities within the context of regulatory rules. See Sect. 8.3.2.2.

be provided in Sect. 8.4.1, whether blending criminal investigative functions with intelligence investigative functions is permissible from an institutional perspective. The assessment of this argument is relevant in order to determine whether also the parameter of accountability can be achieved when adopting a proportionate and necessary framework for an anticipative criminal investigation within the boundaries of the constitutive principles. Furthermore, the ultimate validity of some of the arguments assessed in Sect. 8.4.1 will depend on the outcome of the assessment of the fundamental nature and implications of the traditionally provided institutional separation between the law enforcement and intelligence communities. Hence, this section will provide an answer to the first part of the central research question as to whether prevention can be a legitimate goal of a criminal investigation.

Lastly, Sect. 8.4.3 will provide for an integrated conclusion on the findings of the second prong of analysis and, on that basis, it will formulate additional conditions for the regulation of anticipative criminal investigations.

### *8.4.1 Legitimacy of the Anticipative Criminal Investigation with Regard to the 'Sword Side'*

#### 8.4.1.1 The Argument of Necessity or Exigency Justifying 'Emergency Powers' Outside the Traditional Legal Framework

Necessity and exigency are interests that since 9/11 have often been raised in order to justify counterterrorism 'emergency' measures at the expense of the protection of individual liberty.[76] In a situation including a more long-standing state of necessity or exigency, exceptions should be allowed to conventional restrictions on criminal investigative powers. The necessity to prevent future terrorist attacks by using all resources to trace potential terrorists is used as a general exception for new and broader proactive powers to intercept the planning of a terrorist crime as early as possible. In a situation of necessity or exigency exceptional actions are justified, because e.g. the protection of national security invoking the necessity or exigency argument concerns a legitimate goal for actions which are otherwise prohibited.

In its strongest meaning, the necessity argument is used as an unconditional free hand for the government to do whatever it considers necessary in order to avert the threat. According to Carl Schmitt, deciding on the exception is the exclusive authority of the sovereign. In his view, only the sovereign can and is entitled to decide on the question whether there is a situation of necessity or exigency and whether for that reason an exception to the normal legal order applies.[77] Hitler's

[76] E.g.: Ackerman 2006, Posner 2006 and Posner and Vermeule 2007.

[77] Schmitt 2005 (originally published in 1922), 5-15.

Nazi Germany demonstrated the danger of his approach in attributing unlimited power to the so-called sovereign to set aside the normal legal order.

Currently, the 'war on terrorism' or the 'ticking time-bomb scenario' is frequently used to indicate that a state of exception applies, justifying a deviation from the normal legal order.[78] A successful terrorist attack is understood as the failure of the (traditional) system to prevent that attack, which is then the justification for acting outside the (traditional) system in order to prevent new attacks.[79] Also Locke acknowledged that the government may depart from the law in the case of accidents and necessities: "a strict and rigid observation of the laws may do harm, (...) [for which reason the government must be able to act] according to discretion, for the public good, without the prescription of law, and sometimes even against it [...], because also it is impossible to foresee, and so by laws to provide for, all accidents and necessities that may concern the public".[80] In line with this reasoning, the government shall thus have the legitimate power to deviate from existing frameworks in a state of emergency, when there is also the necessity or exigency to do so.

Decisions on a legitimate deviation from the law on the basis of a state of emergency shall only be permitted in certain well-defined situations. Acting outside the traditional system on the basis of necessity or exigency can only be permitted when there is in fact a necessity or exigency to act for the purpose of prevention: the state of emergency must be clear, currently present and incontestable. This also implies that the measures are necessary and urgent (the traditional frameworks are inadequate and adopting new ones through a democratic process is too time-consuming), that the measures may only be used for the purpose of preventing the (urgent) threat and that the measures shall have a temporary character.[81] The state of emergency and the emergency powers outside the traditional framework, which are justified because of the state of emergency, must thus be well delineated in time, scope and purpose. Furthermore, because of that character, the emergency escape must be orientated towards maintaining the traditional legal order including the full guarantee of traditional protective elements.[82] Terrorism, however, has now become a rather steady and continuous threat and the measures to combat terrorism have obtained a permanent character

[78] For a thorough current analysis of the subject of the state of exception, discussing i.a. Carl Schmitt's theories and explaining why using the state of exception involves a danger of transforming democracies in totalitarian states, see Agamben 2005. On that basis, Agamben also rejects the use of the 'state of exception' to justify certain exceptional measures in the fight against terrorism (e.g. introducing the status of enemy combatants, deprived of legal status).

[79] Compare Thomas Hobbes' theory, laid down in *Leviathan* (Hobbes 1998), of the state of nature leading to a war against all, which can be avoided by a social contract establishing a civil society: the traditional framework fails to take away the threat and, hence, the agreed upon order ceases and the state of nature returns and emergency measures are justified.

[80] Locke 1980, 84.

[81] Compare: Finn 1991, 18.

[82] See in detail: Loof 2005, in particular 690-711.

and may sometimes be used also for the prevention of other crimes or threats to national security. As a consequence, the measures that have been taken in order to prevent acts of terrorism cannot be considered as emergency measures, justified by necessity or exigency.

It can be concluded that using necessity or exigency as arguments to justify emergency measures and to escape from the traditional legal order is limited to well-delineated states of emergency, typically in times of immediate danger such as an armed attack. Hence, this argument is invalid as a justification for escaping from traditional protective elements in the context of an anticipative criminal investigation in order to control potential (terrorist) threats. An anticipative criminal investigation cannot be understood as reflecting measures in response to a state of emergency. The regulation of anticipative criminal investigations is intended to function on a more permanent basis[83] as a safety net around terrorist threats; to intercept the planning of terrorist crimes by investigating those who are engaged in such activities, primarily through the gathering of sufficient information about these activities in order to create a position in which the government is able to take action when there is sufficient evidence for prosecution or when immediate action is required to prevent the actual realization of their plans.

If terrorism is indeed a more continuous threat and the traditional frameworks are not able to deal with this threat, one could alternatively choose to add a new framework to the existing frameworks or to adjust the existing frameworks through a democratically legitimized procedure. The phenomenon of anticipative criminal investigation could be understood as such a new framework which is, nevertheless, chiseled into the existing frameworks and is created through the adaptation of existing frameworks. The justification for adapting the existing frameworks in order to create a new framework may be sought in either providing the government with leeway on an *ad hoc* basis within the existing frameworks because of necessity or exigency; in the changed perception of the role of the government with regard to the prevention of crime, in particular terrorism; and in the different nature of the terrorist crime to which the government needs to respond in its investigative activities. The legitimacy of these arguments for the purpose of adopting a new framework, which differs from traditional frameworks because it enhances the sword objective of the criminal investigation while trading in on protective elements, will be dealt with separately in the next sub-sections.

---

[83] Although 'sunset' provisions are still applicable to some of the USA Patriot Act Provisions, the main provisions of the Patriot Act that have realized anticipative criminal investigation have obtained a permanent status. In addition, also the provisions accompanied by a sunset provision have now been in force for approximately 10 years and will continue to be in force until at least 2015, and cannot, therefore, be understood as emergency powers.

#### 8.4.1.2 The Argument of Necessity or Exigency Justifying Exceptions to the Shield Elements within the Traditional Legal Framework

Necessity and exigency (to protect national security) are also used as arguments to seek not a complete escape, but a different balance within the traditional framework between sword and shield: the compelling government interest of dealing with necessity should be balanced against the interest of the protection of fundamental liberties. Necessity or exigent circumstances can then be considered as a categorical justification for departing from (traditional) fundamental values and influencing the proportionate balance between sword and shield.

The validity of using the arguments of necessity and exigency as the basis for finding a different balance between sword and shield can be compared to already existing exceptions to conventional restrictions on the criminal investigation, such as the US 'special needs doctrine' and 'exigent circumstances' as grounds to deviate from conventional Fourth Amendment requirements. The possibilities created in the US Fourth Amendment jurisprudence to depart from Fourth Amendment protective elements are already institutionalized exceptions based on arguments of necessity or exigency. Since the attacks of 9/11 a general development is recognizable where arguments of necessity or exigency are more frequently used in order to deviate from the normally applicable protective requirements. This popularity of the necessity or exigency argument is closely related to the development where the government has obtained greater responsibility to take measures to reduce risks as a consequence of increased feelings of fear, the conception of society as a risk society in which the government has been attributed the responsibility to reduce the risks and is guided by the precautionary principle.[84]

The advantage of the approach of allowing an escape from protective requirements because of necessity or exigency could be that this departure from traditional fundamental protective principles is limited to the specific category in which a deviation is deemed necessary or the *ad hoc* situation of necessity or exigency. However, only the government is in a position to invoke the necessity argument and is thus in the position to create more leeway for itself in its investigative actions in order to avert the threat. This involves the risk that the government will rely on necessity arguments too often in order to escape from protective restraints. The prevention of terrorism or the protection of national security may then become the denominators for categorical exceptions to protective requirements. Moreover, the government will always be granted this leeway as the argument not only has great rhetorical value but will usually also be uncontrollable, based on *ad hoc* risk assessments or on classified information. And, because the argument of necessity then applies in the context of the *prevention* of

[84] See Chap. 1, Sect. 1.3. These developments are distinguished from the arguments of necessity and exigency, because these create *ad hoc* exceptions to the traditional framework, whereas arguments derived from theories on the risk society, the culture of control and the precautionary principle are used as the justification for adopting preventive mechanisms as such.

*future* harm, such as future terrorist attacks, based upon the 'unknown', it is difficult to determine beforehand the actual necessity or exigency for which enhanced investigative powers are sought in order to prevent terrorist crime.[85] Creating an adjusted framework of anticipative criminal investigation in order to give the investigative agencies the necessary sufficient leeway to prevent terrorist crimes would be such a categorical exception to the normally applicable protective requirements. Necessity and exigency can, therefore, also not in themselves serve as arguments within the traditional frameworks, justifying categorical exceptions to protective requirements in order to provide more leeway to respond to terrorism threats.

Nevertheless, on an incidental basis, necessity and exigency may continue to be valid reasons for an *ad hoc* departure from protective principles, such as, for example, in the case of an immediate danger to persons. Furthermore, the argument of necessity or exigency may never be used to escape from the constitutive principles, as that would contravene the goal of subjecting governmental action to such principles, namely providing for restraint in governmental action. Hence, necessity may never trump the restraints that reflect the government's adherence to the rule of law, as that would create a government area with no limits and would thus violate the rule of law.[86]

#### 8.4.1.3 The Argument of the Specific Nature of Terrorist Crimes

Acts of terrorism can be considered as threats to national security as well as criminal offences, for which reason terrorism can be dealt with from both a law enforcement framework and an intelligence framework.[87] At the same time terrorist crimes cannot be dealt with exclusively from either framework. The natural distinction between punishing criminal behavior (law enforcement) and national security (foreign intelligence policy) seems unsuitable for dealing with terrorism, for which reason it is a phenomenon to be dealt with from both frameworks.[88] The development of anticipative criminal investigations, adopting characteristics of both the criminal law framework and the intelligence framework, can, therefore, very well be explained from the specific nature of terrorism. Hence, the suitability of an anticipative criminal investigation for confronting terrorism, which can be

---

[85] See also Loof 2005, 235-236.

[86] Compare: Crocker 2008, 223.

[87] In addition, the military framework may aim, by using "lethal force", to "subdue and control" terrorism. The military framework has been a serious and significant approach as part of the "war on terror", declared by President Bush in reaction to the terrorist attacks of 9/11. In general the military framework—constrained by the law of armed conflict—is applicable because terrorism is considered to be an illegal form of warfare (and the terrorist is considered to be an illegal enemy combatant) or because a state may use the military framework as a form of self-defense against a terrorist attack. See further on the military framework: McCormack 2007, 35 and 44-47.

[88] Martin 2002, 5.

understood as a hybrid framework, may be assessed on the basis of the nature of acts of terrorism. This section will continue to elaborate on the suitability and validity of using the nature of terrorism as an argument for creating anticipative criminal investigations.

To date, there is no universally applicable definition of or any agreement on the definition of terrorism. Nation states have adopted different definitions of terrorism in their penal codes and in the international legal context an internationally agreed upon definition, despite efforts by the UN Security Council, is also lacking. Nevertheless, leading academic studies into terrorism have provided definitions in which some common elements can be identified. According to Bassiouni, terrorism can be defined as "a strategy of violence designed to instill terror in a segment of a population or society in order to achieve a power outcome, propagandize a cause, or inflict harm for a vengeful purpose."[89] Hoffman defines terrorism as "the deliberate creation and exploitation of fear through violence or the threat of violence in the pursuit of political change."[90] And Saul formulates the following identifying elements: "(1) [a]ny serious, violent, criminal act intended to cause death or serious bodily injury, or to endanger life, including by acts against property; (2) where committed outside an armed conflict; (3) for a political ideological, religious, or ethnic purpose; and (4) where intended to create extreme fear in a person, group, or the general public, and: (a) seriously intimidate a population or part of a population, or (b) unduly compel a government or an international organization to do or to abstain from doing any act."[91]

Common elements in all definitions are that an act of terrorism concerns an act of a criminal nature ((a strategy of) violence, threat of violence, violent criminal act) and that this act has a specific motive of an ideological nature. This latter characteristic distinguishes terrorism from other criminal acts. Although the violent act may be similar, the motive for committing the criminal act is different. In the context of organized crime, the criminal act is generally committed in order to obtain material gain. Isolated criminal acts of a similar character usually also have a personal motivation; it may be personal material gain, directed against the victim for other (egocentric) personal motives or be a consequence of psychological or psychiatric circumstances. Terrorists, however, believe they are serving a higher 'good cause' by committing their criminal acts.[92]

Moreover, the organized context in which the modern terrorist group operates differs from criminal organizations. The organizational structure of the terrorist group is generally not very easily recognizable as terrorists tend to operate in "phantom cell networks", "autonomous cells" or as lone wolves. Terrorist groups follow a more nodded structure, organized in a "looser, flatter and linear" fashion than criminal organizations and the lone wolves are affiliated to terrorist

[89] In: Bassiouni 2002, 84 and Bassiouni 2008, 233.

[90] Hoffman 2006, 40.

[91] Saul 2006, 65-66.

[92] Compare Hoffman 2006, 36-40.

organizations simply because their ideological inspiration is drawn from terrorist organizations such as al Qaeda or, as recently seen in Norway, from right-wing xenophobic extremism.[93] Similar to most manifestations of organized crime, terrorist groups often operate transnationally and are not usually located within one country. This characteristic complicates the investigation of the terrorist group. Lastly, terrorism is not only a form of crime, but, considering that the target of a terrorist attack is randomly selected and, therefore, many innocent citizens may fall victim, is also understood as a serious and diffuse threat to national security, and, therefore, a concern for the intelligence community.[94] This is also a characteristic which is not typically shared by 'organized crime' and 'ordinary crime'.

Clearly, there are significant differences between terrorist crimes and ordinary or even organized crime, which also influence the manner of investigation. The criminal investigation is traditionally designed on the basis of the assumption that there is one suspect who has committed one or some criminal offenses and the criminal process should be geared towards apprehending, prosecuting and punishing that individual. Today's law of criminal procedure is still largely, and at its core, based upon this assumption of criminality, although adaptations have been made to gear it more towards modern circumstances. The law is part of a dynamic society and should be able to adapt to differing societal circumstances.[95] It has proved to be able to do so in response to organized crime. Today, society is again confronted with a relatively new type of criminality: terrorism,[96] which makes adjustments in investigative practice necessary. Because of the complex and vague organizational structure of terrorist groups, any investigation often results in new leads about different 'radicalized' people, without proof of any direct nexus with the planning of a particular terrorist crime as the focus of a specific investigation. However, the investigation of these other people may result in new leads. As a consequence, the investigation of terrorism obtains the character of being intelligence-led.

In addition, because of the randomly selected goals of the terrorist crimes against innocent victims, preventing the crime is more important than an adequate reaction after the crime and fulfilling the traditional goals of crime and punishment.[97] The importance of prevention, above prosecution and punishment, has become evident by the increased call on governments to protect their citizens against acts of terrorism.[98] Also for the purpose of prevention, an intelligence-led approach aiming at a strong information position is the most effective way to

---

[93] Hoffman 2006, 38-39.

[94] McCormack 2010, 17.

[95] Groenhuijsen 1991, 44-45 and 47.

[96] Although terrorism is a phenomenon of all ages, the character of contemporary (international) terrorism, as described above, is different and relatively new.

[97] Bassiouni 2002, 94.

[98] See Chap. 1, Sect. 1.3.

realize, in the first place, prevention. At the same time, this character also gives the investigation its secretive nature, as an intelligence-led investigation can only be successful if the sources and methods, as well as the information position obtained, can remain confidential.[99] Moreover, the investigation of terrorism is typically long-lasting, because of its intelligence-led focus resulting in the discovery of new indications regarding terrorism, which places high capacity burdens on law enforcement.[100]

Adjusting the manner of the investigation to the nature of the criminal behavior is not a new phenomenon. For example, compare the possibility of more expedient investigative techniques that can also be applied proactively since the rise of organized crime, such as Title III in the US and the different statutory framework for the use of special investigative techniques in organized crime investigations in the Netherlands. Considering the nature of terrorist crimes, as described above, their investigation needs to be intelligence-led and proactive, aiming at prevention.[101] Taking into account the interest of keeping sources and methods secret, also after the closure of the investigative phase, which contrasts with the notion of internal and external transparency in criminal procedural law, and the capacity limitation of law enforcement to continue long-term investigative activities without being able to initiate a prosecution, the manner of investigating acts of terrorism seems to fit the intelligence community somewhat better. On the other hand, the involvement of the criminal justice system is required in order to be able to use also coercive methods and, eventually, to bring the perpetrators of terrorist crimes to justice. This applies not only to the complete realization of terrorist crimes, but also to the planning of the 'bigger' terrorist crimes, as states have actively criminalized the planning and preparation of attacks over the past ten years.

It can be concluded that not only the possibility to apply both frameworks to investigating terrorism but also the necessity to blend the approaches in order to

---

99 McCormack 2010, 17.

100 *Ibid.*, 17. and Van Gestel et al. 2009, 47.

101 Also the ECrtHR has acknowledged that the state needs to deviate from the traditional investigative approach in order to effectively counter threats such as "highly sophisticated forms of espionage and by terrorism". To do so states "must be able (…) to undertake the secret surveillance of subversive elements operating within its jurisdiction." Hence, the nature of the terrorist threats, according to the ECrtHR, may also be taken into account when assessing the legitimacy of a specific investigative framework; however, "states may not, in the name of the struggle against espionage and terrorism, adopt whatever measures they deem appropriate." (ECHR 6 September 1978, App. no. 5029/71 (*Klass and others v. Germany*), paras 48 and 49. The distinction between terrorism and ordinary crime has also been acknowledged in the *Malone* case, concerning electronic surveillance in the criminal procedural law context (contrary to the intelligence context of *Klass*). Judge Pettiti suggested in his concurring opinion that "there were (…) factors permitting the Court to draw a distinction between the dangers of a crisis situation caused by terrorism (the *Klass* case) and the dangers of ordinary criminality, and hence to consider that two different sets of rules could be adopted (ECHR 2 August 1984, App. no. 8691/79 (*Malone v. The United Kingdom*), concurring opinion Judge Pettiti). Sottiaux 2008, 284-285.

effectively investigate the diffuse nature[102] of terrorism and to answer the changed societal and political circumstances in which the government bears responsibility to prevent terrorism and bring the perpetrators to justice, have been the reason for combining methods and purposes of intelligence and law enforcement. Consequently, the hybrid investigative framework of an anticipative criminal investigation has been adopted. Hence, from the perspective of the nature of terrorism, choosing for a new framework that can be typified as a hybrid investigative framework with intelligence and law enforcement functions is, as the very least, understandable and may concern a valid argument which *justifies* the realization of anticipative criminal investigations. Moreover, the nature of the criminal behavior has traditionally been understood as a factor to be taken into account in order to assess the proportionality of investigative action.[103] Where the criminal behavior is more serious and dangerous, a proportionality assessment is more likely to favor an adequate investigative action rather than the protection of the personal liberty of the persons involved.

However, creating a hybrid framework can only be justified by the argument of the nature of terrorist crimes, when combining two investigative purposes into one framework is also effective compared to the traditional approach (the subject of the next sub-section) and when the creation of a hybrid system, both of purpose and of method, is also legitimate, from an institutional perspective, under the rule of law (the subject of section 8.4.2).

#### 8.4.1.4 The Argument of the Effectiveness of Preventing Harm

An important justification for creating the hybrid framework of an anticipative criminal investigation, which in its relation to the criminal justice system deviates from traditional protective elements, would be the effectiveness of this 'new' approach to prevent harm and to deal with the diffuse nature of terrorist crimes compared to traditional approaches. This effectiveness covers success in prevention by the intelligence-led approach of an anticipative criminal investigation in which the functions of law enforcement and intelligence are blended and the

---

[102] Terrorism constitutes a 'diffuse risk' rather than a 'concrete danger'. Huster and Rudolph 2008, 12. The authors enumerate the following characteristics of terrorism (corresponding with those enumerated in the main text): 1) committed in the context of a network that 'recruits' terrorists and thus not individualized crimes; 2) transnational character; 3) the damage resulting from terrorism is enormous, comparable with mass atrocities; 4) the deterrent effect of prosecution and punishment does not apply to terrorists; 5) the structure of the terrorist threat is not identifiable on the basis of recognizable networks and is not aimed at identifiable persons or groups, but against everyone, rendering the character of the threat diffuse. *Ibid.,* 14-15.

[103] In the Netherlands as a factor to be considered by determining the proportionality of investigative action, including the required level of suspicion (see Chap. 2, primarily Sect. 2.3.2.3). In the United States the nature of the crimes involved may, for instance, justify an exception to the Fourth Amendment warrant requirement. (See Chap. 5, Sect. 5.3.2.1.2).

starting of investigative activities on the basis of 'soft' information. Both aspects of effectiveness will be dealt with separately below.

The intelligence-led approach chosen since 9/11 in order to obtain sufficient information to be able to prevent a terrorist attack has resulted, especially in the US, in the emergence of many agencies responsible for intelligence gathering and the collection of an enormous amount of information by all responsible agencies, which also share the information collected with each other. The Washington Post has conducted an investigation into the US intelligence world, revealing its conclusions in July 2010 that 'top-secret America' has become "so large, so unwieldy and so secretive" that is has grown "beyond control", producing an enormous amount of information, but lacking the necessary focus to efficiently prevent harm.[104] The failure to prevent the 'Fort Hood shooting[105] and the Christmas-Day attempted bombing[106] could not be attributed to the lack of intelligence present at different agencies (such as information on the radicalization of the persons involved, on direct links with Yemen al Qaeda operatives and intended attacks against/or within the US), but had to be ascribed to the inability to 'connect the dots' and getting the crucial information to the right people in time.[107] These incidents may illustrate that the gathering of as much information as possible is not necessarily the most effective way to realize prevention. Also in the Netherlands, the different agencies responsible have faced difficulties in finding the right balance between gathering as much information on possible threats and turning at the right moment to criminal investigative action so that capacities are used efficiently and sufficient evidence is gathered for the prosecution and prevention of terrorist crimes.[108]

The examples mentioned above concern primarily the effectiveness of the work of the intelligence community. However, the intelligence agencies should typically

104 Priest and Arkin 2010.

105 On November 5, 2009 Nidal Malik Hasan, a U.S. Army major and psychiatrist, shot 13 people and wounded 30 others at the large military base 'Fort Hood' in Texas.

106 On December 25th, 2009 a young Nigerian man (Umar Farouk Abdulmutallab) boarded a plane in Amsterdam, heading for Detroit, aiming to commit a suicide bombing by explosives he had carried on board in his underwear. A Dutch fellow passenger was able to overpower the suicide bomber and he prevented a serious explosion immediately before landing in Detroit.

107 See New York Times, Lipton et al. 2010 and The Washington Post, DeYoung and Fletcher 2010.

108 Rapport van de Commissie Bestuurlijke Evaluatie Algemene Inlichtingen- en Veiligheidsdienst 2004, 103-107. Van Gestel et al. 2009, 9, 18 and 47 and Rapport van de Commissie evaluatie antiterrorismebeleid (Rapport Commissie Suyver) 2009, 51-53, 85 and 88. Nevertheless, the latest evaluation report on counterterrorism measures in the Netherlands has drawn a positive conclusion: counterterrorism measures and the expansion of preventive powers have resulted in increased cooperation in order to harmonize the response of different responsible institutions, but not in increased problems as to harmonizing the responses to terrorist threats: Rapport Evaluatie Antiterrorismemaatregelen 2011, 101 and 102. Nevertheless, in a recent publication the two public prosecutors for counterterrorism have indicated that as a consequence of cultural differences optimal cooperation in counterterrorism has not yet been realized: Vermaas 2011.

communicate 'actionable intelligence' to law enforcement agencies to realize the arrest of persons when a terrorist attack is impending. Also the law enforcement approach is currently very much driven, when it comes to criminal activities in the category of threats to national security, by the intelligence-led approach. Moreover, law enforcement agencies are included in sharing strategies and fulfill their functions not only on the basis of internally-gathered intelligence, but also on the basis of this shared information originating from the intelligence agencies. An anticipative criminal investigation includes all these forms of investigative activity on the basis of intelligence or aimed at the gathering of intelligence, where there is also a connection with criminal investigation. In particular, the intelligence-led strategy through cooperation between intelligence and law enforcement agencies is generally aimed at obtaining a strong information position, which should enable the law enforcement agencies to turn to the arrest of persons who are preparing/ have prepared a terrorist attack and the subsequent prosecution of these persons. As may be demonstrated by the mentioned examples within the US, this strategy does not (yet) seem to be functioning properly, because the right information was not available to the right persons at the right moment; it seems difficult to produce 'actionable intelligence' from the enormous amount of intelligence collected. By implementing the intelligence-led approach based on sharing and cooperation between intelligence and law enforcement agencies, the appropriate balance between gathering as much information as possible and producing actionable intelligence needs to be found.[109] Hence, especially the effective functioning of anticipative criminal investigations does not seem to be optimally realized, whereas there is also a general agreement that the set-up of an anticipative criminal investigation should be (as explained in the previous sub-section) the best answer to effectively prevent terrorism *and*—although inferior to prevention—dealing with those planning a terrorist attack within the criminal justice system. Efficiency should be understood as the appropriate manner to realize this purpose of investigative action, which is, for an anticipative criminal investigation, the intelligence-steered investigation, primarily in order to prevent terrorist crimes, and secondly in order to collect evidence for the purpose of prosecution and punishment.[110] Improvement can be achieved by working on a better implementation of the anticipative criminal investigative strategy.[111]

However, the implementation of what is understood as the most effective answer to realize prevention *and* prosecution seems to be obstructed precisely by the blending of investigative purposes. The blending of investigative purposes adversely influences the realization of the independent purposes of the intelligence and law enforcement communities and, because of that, also their shared intelligence.[112]

---

[109] Moore 2007, 847-848.

[110] Jackson and Brown 2007, 121.

[111] Compare: Jackson and Brown 2007, 111.

[112] Bassiouni 2002, 94.

Efficiency with regard to the separate purposes of intelligence and law enforcement applies to the efficiency of realizing the prevention of national security threats for the former and collecting evidence for prosecution and punishment for the latter. Intelligence and law enforcement agencies still operate primarily for the purpose of adequately realizing their own purpose and not their shared purpose in the context of anticipative criminal investigations. It is obvious that the efficiency of intelligence work suffers from the obligation to share information earlier than before with law enforcement agencies, which might result in the exposure of their sources or methods. Furthermore, when prosecutors are able to meddle in the investigative activities of intelligence agencies in order to safeguard their own interests, this is likely to have an adverse impact on the effective realization of intelligence goals. *Vice versa*, it is difficult for law enforcement agencies confronted with a new goal—the prevention of crimes—to find the right balance between taking immediate action to avert threats and to continue investigative activities to collect sufficient information for the purpose of prosecution. Anticipative criminal investigations, where intelligence and law enforcement agencies cooperate, are primarily aimed at prevention and only on a secondary basis at the law enforcement purpose of gathering evidence.

In addition, law enforcement agencies are now sometimes confronted with information that is shared with them by intelligence agencies, which they find difficult to interpret as information on its context, source and how it has been obtained is lacking. It is difficult to determine whether a criminal investigation should be commenced and it is uncertain whether the information received can be used as evidence in a criminal prosecution. Moreover, when law enforcement agencies implement the intelligence-led strategy, they face capacity problems as the investigation aimed at gathering general intelligence on threats, rather than conducting a focused investigation for the purpose of gathering evidence, is likely to continue for a long period, requiring the use of expensive and burdensome special investigative techniques. Law enforcement agencies then face the dilemma whether to continue these long-lasting investigations that require a large share of their capacity or rather trust in the work of the intelligence agencies and focus on the investigation of ordinary and organized crime with more success in efficiently fulfilling, in the short term, their traditional goal of evidence-gathering for prosecution.

To summarize these findings: the anticipative criminal investigation has been created on the basis of the assumption that it is the most appropriate manner to confront terrorism by being primarily focused on the prevention of terrorist crimes, thereby also making it possible that the persons responsible for preparing these terrorist attacks are brought to justice. However, because this requires the blending of traditional separate functions of intelligence and law enforcement and because intelligence and law enforcement agencies are at the same time confronted with this new role and eventually bear primary responsibility for fulfilling their individual traditional purposes, the implementation of the intelligence-led strategy of the anticipative criminal investigation faces opposition when it comes to effectiveness. This new and shared responsibility of also pursuing each other's interests has been attributed to traditionally competing agencies, traditionally operating separately and only for the effective realization of their own purposes, which now need to cooperate in order to effectively conduct anticipative criminal investigations.[113]

Here we may notice a clash of two interests. On the one hand, there is the desire to combine prevention with prosecution and, on the other, effectiveness should be realized. The cultural distinction between intelligence and law enforcement, where different agencies are primarily focused on their own traditional purposes and not on their shared objectives, makes it difficult to implement anticipative criminal investigations in the most effective manner. In order to solve this issue the United States and the Netherlands have both chosen to establish a cooperating structure and/or a coordinating agency (the CT Infobox and in that context consultations between the participating partners as well as the National Coordinator for Counterterrorism and, in the United States, the Joint Terrorism Task Force (JTTF) and the Office of the Director of National Intelligence), but these agencies have not yet proved to be able to completely solve the cultural division and to remove the obstacles regarding sharing and cooperation.[114] In addition, when the function of prevention is combined with evidence-gathering, the shield objective of criminal procedural law automatically also places limitations on the effectiveness of intelligence gathering. It may be clear that the latter category of limitations on effectiveness cannot be overcome when it has been chosen to fulfill both the preventive and evidence-gathering function and the information collected during the anticipative criminal investigation is or can be brought into the criminal justice system. However, to realize the more effective implementation of the intelligence-led strategy through an anticipative criminal investigation, which is a shared responsibility of the intelligence and law enforcement communities, the organizations could improve their effective functioning by a reformulation of their respective purposes. Except for more effectiveness, a reformulation of the purposes could also contribute to more effectively realizing the shield objective of criminal procedural law. Nevertheless, such a reformulation might be understood as a further blending of the institutionally separated areas of intelligence and law enforcement. The implementation of this objective would thus depend on the legitimacy of blending the functions of these traditionally separated institutions, which will be dealt with in the next sub-section.

The other aspect of the effectiveness of anticipative criminal investigations concerns the effectiveness of investigative activities through the use of special investigative techniques, initiated on the basis of 'soft' information. An anticipative criminal investigation is also characterized by the possibility to initiate investigative activity within the law enforcement context on the basis of softer information than the traditionally required level of evidence establishing a

[113] Compare: Bassiouni 2002, 94.

[114] Bekke and De Vries 2007, 45-46 and for the current flaws in the cooperation between AIVD and PPS: Vermaas 2011. See also: Jackson and Brown 2007, 119.

reasonable suspicion or probable cause. The possible adverse consequences with regard to effectiveness may be illustrated by the findings of the evaluation report on the practical implementation of the Dutch legislation allowing for the use of special investigative techniques on the basis of indications instead of a reasonable suspicion, in which several closed criminal investigations regarding terrorist threats have been studied. It appeared that the investigation on the basis of indications (established by rather soft information) lacked focus and, therefore, was ineffective compared to the more focused investigation based on a reasonable suspicion of guilt regarding involvement in criminal activities. Some of the criminal investigations did not lead to the verification of the starting information, and therefore the investigation was terminated. Other criminal investigations initiated on the basis of indications also did not result in more concrete suspicions or in the enervation of the indications. These investigations were also discontinued and left to the discretion of the AIVD (or RID), because of the large capacity burden for the law enforcement agency when these investigations, without producing more concrete information, are continued.[115] It seems that especially investigations that cannot be directed against people regarding whom concrete suspicions are present, but rather focus on groups of people in order to find some information that may be the basis for further actions, may become countereffective as they lack any focus.[116]

The foregoing description of the difficulties in making anticipative criminal investigations as effective as possible demonstrates the tension between the need to take action when certain information regarding a threat is in the possession of the government and the commensurate capacity issues and adverse consequences for the effectiveness of criminal investigations on the basis of vague information and with a primary focus on the prevention of terrorist crimes. The formulation of preconditions that realize a focused investigation, applicable before deciding whether to initiate a law enforcement investigation, seems advisable to improve effectiveness in the law enforcement context.

When it appears that the parameters of proportionality and necessity cannot be achieved as a consequence of the lack of efficiency of (parts of the) framework adopted to regulate anticipative criminal investigations, the regulation will have to be rejected under the rule of law. In that regard it must be acknowledged that the state cannot guarantee a risk-free society. The role of the state stops where its investigative activities lack the required focus to be effective and, therefore, its investigative activities are no longer proportionate and necessary. In addition to the role of the state in preventing terrorism, people have an individual responsibility to contribute to a secure society. This individual responsibility is in particular important where the borders of the state's responsibility have been reached.

---

[115] Van Gestel et al. 2009, 9.

[116] Understood by Kate Martin as a "dragnet approach of collecting all information, relevant or not" versus "focused law enforcement investigation aimed at identifying, surveilling, and arresting those involved in criminal activity." Martin 2002, 7.

Emphasizing this individual responsibility towards a secure society, low-level investigations based on a principle of social solidarity could be strengthened. This 'social solidarity' implies a moral obligation for citizens to cooperate with their government in its efforts to provide a safe society and implies a different perception of the government's responsibility in providing a safe society.[117] The task of the government to ensure safety should then be distinguished from the criminal investigative task. Whereas for the criminal investigative task the protection of innocent citizens against becoming involved in the criminal process is at the forefront, the task of ensuring safety is an interest of society as a whole, involving a moral obligation for citizens to 'warn' in order to contribute to realizing and ensuring the safety of fellow citizens.[118] Rather, low-level investigative activities for the purpose of furthering safety are then an area which is independent of and supplementary to the state functions of gathering intelligence and enforcing criminal law.

Being able to rely also on the individual responsibility of citizens with regard to a secure society, it is possible to initiate focused criminal investigations with the help of intrusive investigative techniques on the basis of more concrete investigative leads, while also optimizing prevention. In combination with the reformulation of investigative purposes for anticipative criminal investigations, the formulation of preconditions for investigation on behalf of the law enforcement agencies would improve the effectiveness of the use of expensive special investigative techniques in criminal investigations.

### *8.4.2 The Fundamental Nature of an Institutional Distinction Between Criminal Investigation and Intelligence Investigation*

In the previous section the possible adverse impact on the effectiveness of blending the functions of intelligence and law enforcement have been addressed. The issues indicated concerned the effectiveness of realizing the sword objective of criminal procedural law. However, concerns also arise as to the possibility of realizing the sword aspect of criminal procedural law, once the functions of intelligence and law enforcement are blended, and the institutional distinction between a criminal and an intelligence investigation becomes blurred. Traditionally, the intelligence and law enforcement communities have been distinguished on an institutional level. This section will assess whether this distinction is of a fundamental nature,

---

[117] An example of strengthening such low-level investigations with the help of the people concerns the "If You See Something, Say Something™ Campaign" launched in the US, intended to create public awareness of indicators of terrorism and crime. See Progress Report 2011, 14-15.

[118] Compare e.g. the obligation to render assistance to someone in distress or the obligation to take out health insurance in order to be medically treated.

prohibiting the blending of intelligence and law enforcement functions, or whether there is a need to reconcile the characteristics of intelligence and law enforcement in order to be able to investigate terrorism.

Traditionally, intelligence and law enforcement have been created as institutionally separated answers to violence and threats. The one aims to protect national security by strengthening the information position of the government regarding threats, making threat assessments and, on that basis, warning the government. Its effective functioning is based upon a competitive enterprise with foreign intelligence agencies to obtain the best information position. The other—law enforcement—aims to collect evidence for the purpose of prosecuting criminal perpetrators in order to repress crime. Because of this relation with the punishment of people, the legitimacy of the use of criminal procedural powers is based on the sufficient protection of the innocent against being subjected to criminal procedural powers and the design of the system based on restraints and protection.[119]

The creation of the framework of anticipative criminal investigations is based on the assumption that a framework that has characteristics of both can best confront terrorism (see Sect. 8.4.1.4). However, such an approach breaks with the clear institutional distinction and separation between law enforcement and intelligence, which has been created in order to guarantee civil liberties while at the same time being able to effectively protect national security and has proven to be an important protection against abuse developed over the years on the basis of fundamental arguments.[120]

The separation between intelligence and law enforcement communities has an institutional nature, because these communities have been established in order to carry out different state functions. Intelligence, law enforcement and the military are three different responses to threats and violence, each having its own specific purpose and, because of that purpose, being subjected to its own framework of limitations and guarantees to protect rights and the integrity of the state. The specific goal attributed to the institutions is thus the reason why intelligence investigations may be initiated when they lack a level of suspicion against identifiable persons, while such standard is traditionally required for initiating criminal investigations. Intelligence investigations may also be wider in scope and be continued for longer periods of time under the veil of secrecy, whereas law enforcement operates within the strict and transparent confines set by the law. The difference between the goals attributed to intelligence and law enforcement is, furthermore, the reason to subject the one only to internal and parliamentary control, whereas the other is subjected to judicial control.[121] Considering that the specific state function attributed to the institution is decisive for the type of regulation, the institutional separation itself is not of a fundamental nature. However, the relation between the state function and a specific set of limitations and

119 See also: McCormack 2007, 35.

120 Compare: Martin 2002, 5 and McCormack 2007, 35.

121 Compare: Sottiaux 2008, 274.

guarantees regarding the protection of fundamental rights and accountability does have a fundamental nature.

An anticipative criminal investigation has adopted the goals of both intelligence and law enforcement by enhancing cooperation and sharing (in the Netherlands and in the US), by also attributing a preventive function to law enforcement agencies (the Netherlands) or also attributing an evidence-gathering function to the intelligence agencies (US). The new challenge for anticipative criminal investigations is thus to realize the prevention of crimes through effective investigation, whereas realizing the shield objective of criminal procedural law is also anticipated. It is important that when the purposes of intelligence and law enforcement are blended, also a regulation is adopted that provides the necessary checks in order to guarantee that the different nature of the investigative action does not influence the fairness of the procedure resulting in prosecution and punishment. This regulation should acknowledge the different nature of the purposes of prevention, prosecution and punishment; they overlap but also maintain separate identities.[122] This may be realized by including a differentiation of the purposes of investigative action in the regulation of anticipative criminal investigations, acknowledging the different character of these purposes. Furthermore, with an eye to guaranteeing the legitimacy of the criminal justice system, the regulation shall provide for rules that aim to exclude the involvement of the innocent in the criminal process, that guarantee the protection of the right to private life during investigative action, and that guarantee the fairness of the criminal process and the integrity of any governmental investigative action.

### *8.4.3 Conclusion*

In this section arguments have been discussed in two different categories: the first category dealt with different arguments that could legitimate anticipative criminal investigations with regard to the 'sword aspect' or, on the contrary, deprive the sword aspect of an anticipative criminal investigation of any legitimacy; the second category dealt with the fundamental nature of the separation of the intelligence and law enforcement communities, coming together in the phenomenon of the anticipative criminal investigation. As has also been indicated within the different subsections, the arguments discussed are often interrelated and can only provide for an integrated conclusion with regard to the regulation of anticipative criminal investigations. The arguments have been addressed in order to draw conclusions as to the validity and implications of the different arguments, which shall then be taken into account when realizing the three formulated parameters

[122] Compare: McCormack 2010, 5. McCormack compares the structure of the different models for confronting violence (intelligence, war, law enforcement) with the structure of the separation of powers: overlapping, but maintaining a separate identity.

through the rules that shall complete the regulation of the anticipative criminal investigation, in addition to the rules that follow from the constitutive principles. The separate conclusions will shortly be summarized and, subsequently, in Sect. 8.5 will be combined in a pattern of regulation for anticipative criminal investigations that can then be recommended.

Necessity and exigency, in the context of measures regarding the investigation of terrorist activities, cannot function as arguments justifying emergency powers, thereby justifying action outside the traditional framework without limitations. The framework of anticipative criminal investigations has not been created in response to an emergency, but functions on a more permanent basis as the instrument to prevent terrorist crimes. These arguments are thus inapt in any assessment of the proportionality or necessity of the regulation of anticipative criminal investigations.

Section 8.4.1.2 has subsequently discussed the use of the arguments of necessity and exigency within the traditional framework justifying the striking of a different balance between the necessity or exigency to act and traditional protective requirements. Also this argument has been qualified as invalid as the 'prevention of terrorism' should not obtain the status of a categorical exception on the basis of an uncontrollable state of necessity/exigency. Necessity and exigency may continue to function as *ad hoc* grounds for deviating from protective elements. Because this deviation then reflects a different balance within the applicable framework, the deviation may never result in the setting aside of constitutive principles. Moreover, these exceptions are only supplementary to available investigative frameworks and do not influence or justify the creation of a framework of anticipative criminal investigations.

In Sect. 8.4.1.3 the conclusion has been drawn that the nature of terrorist crimes differs as regards various aspects from ordinary and organized crime. The specific nature of terrorist crimes may justify changes to investigative practices. A hybrid framework that pursues both law enforcement and intelligence functions seems to be a valid choice on the basis of the nature of the criminal behavior, which the framework needs to deal with. Moreover, the proportionality assessment involving the interests of expedient investigative action of the serious and potentially harmful terrorist crime and the protection of individual liberty is likely to be decided in favor of investigative action.

Lastly, the effectiveness of anticipative criminal investigations has been addressed (8.4.1.4), because proven effectiveness may contribute to the legitimacy of the system. In the first place, this section has provided for the conclusion that, because we are seeking to both prevent terrorist crimes and bring the people responsible for planning terrorist crimes to justice a hybrid framework in which both purposes are pursued seems to be the most effective approach. However, because anticipative criminal investigations are implemented by blending traditional purposes of law enforcement and intelligence agencies, whereas these agencies have traditionally been competing and have now been attributed the task of pursuing shared purposes, the effective implementation of anticipative criminal investigations is being hindered. A reformulation of the purposes of the relevant agencies may contribute to a more effective implementation of anticipative criminal investigations. Secondly, law enforcement agencies are required to initiate investigative actions for the primary purpose of prevention on the basis of soft information. These investigative activities seem to be counterproductive with regard to the realization of their evidence-gathering function. Conditions which are applicable to the decision-making process as to whether or not to initiate criminal investigative activities may be capable of avoiding unfocused and burdensome investigative activities and realize more effective law enforcement investigations. The absence of such a focus contradicts the necessity and proportionality of particular investigative possibilities. By not trading in on the preventive function, low-level investigative actions can be improved, for example, through the implementation of a renewed vision of the government-citizen relationship when it comes to the government's task to provide security, thereby preventing the endangerment of citizens.

Lastly, Sect. 8.4.2 has assessed how the traditional separation between the intelligence and law enforcement communities should be interpreted: is the separation of a fundamental nature or does the combination of purposes not cross a fundamental line? The conclusions of this section are very important in order to attach concrete consequences to the conclusions drawn in the preceding subsections that apply to the regulation of anticipative criminal investigations. It has been explained that the institutional separation itself is not of a fundamental nature, but is a consequence of the different purposes attributed to the different communities, each requiring a different regulation providing for restraints, the protection of rights and procedural checks and balances. The framework of regulation to which the agencies of either category is subjected shall concern the fundamental counterbalance attributed to the state function: protecting national security by warning the government of any risks (prevention) versus the prosecution and punishment of persons who have transgressed the norms adopted as criminal law. The blending of the functions of prevention with prosecution and punishment may not undermine the legitimacy of either state function, which means that the regulation that counterbalances the function of prosecution and punishment is the most ponderous. Hence, the regulation of anticipative criminal investigations should explicitly acknowledge the different nature of the purposes of prevention and evidence-gathering for prosecution and punishment and, because the procedure may result in the latter, is not adversely influenced by the first when it comes to the protection of the innocent, the protection of the right to respect for one's private life and the fairness of the procedure. This requires regulatory provisions regarding the relation between secrecy and transparency in order to realize accountability, which is necessary to guarantee the integrity of the investigative action and to prevent abuse.

An integrated conclusion based on the above findings may now be provided. This integrated conclusion is also the initial answer to the first part of the research question as it was formulated in Chap. 1, namely *if* a preventive function of criminal investigation can be part of a criminal justice system under the rule of law. This section has demonstrated that the criminal investigation can indeed have a preventive function within the criminal justice system under the rule of law. The confrontation with the diffuse nature of terrorist crimes and the desire to effectively realize prevention, as well as evidence-gathering for the purpose of prosecution and punishment, justify the adoption of a hybrid framework that can be defined as an anticipative criminal investigation. The next section will complete the answer to the first part of the research question by formulating the conditions under which a preventive function of criminal investigation can be part of the criminal justice system under the rule of law. On the basis of the findings of this section the following intermediate conclusions may be drawn that should be taken into account when crystallizing these conditions for regulating anticipative criminal investigations in the next section:

1. Achieving the intended synthesis between sword and shield across the constitutive principles shall be realized by applying the parameters of proportionality and necessity, for which purpose the following *factors* shall be taken into account: the nature of the criminal behavior and the effectiveness of investigative action in relation to the interference with fundamental rights.
2. The *regulation* of anticipative criminal investigations shall be based upon a relationship between the substantive goal of investigative activities and the required framework of protective regulation in order to guarantee accountability for investigative activities.

## 8.5 Three Pillars of Regulatory Conditions: Legitimization, Integrity and Fairness

Building on the previous sections—identifying the problematic issues that have emerged in the examination of the relation between the current regulation of anticipative criminal investigations and traditional shield elements of criminal investigation in the Netherlands and the United States (8.2), articulating the constitutive principles (8.3.1) and the parameters (8.3.2), and analyzing the flexible area of the law governing anticipative criminal investigations (8.4)—the current section will connect these findings in order to crystallize the conditions that should apply to the regulation of anticipative criminal investigations.

The analysis of the manner in which the regulation of anticipative criminal investigations deviates from the traditional framework of investigation has demonstrated, both for the Netherlands and the United States, three main aspects of the regulation where there are deviations from or even the avoidance of traditional basic requirements in the criminal investigative context. These aspects concern the grounds upon which the investigation can be initiated, control over the fairness of the investigative activities, in particular as to the relation between investigation and the procedure resulting in prosecution and punishment, and the procedural safeguards that surround the investigative action in order to secure minimum interference with individual liberty. The constitutive principles formulated in Sect. 8.3.1 and the arguments assessed in Sect. 8.4 in relation to the parameters formulated in 8.3.2 can be connected to one or more of these aspects of regulation and provide guidance as to how to assess the identified deviation. On that basis the crucial underpinnings—the architecture—of a regulation for anticipative criminal investigations can be deduced. These underpinnings follow directly from the constitutive principles and the parameters and have been given further substance through using arguments in the flexible area of the law, also along the parameters of proportionality, necessity and accountability. On that basis three pillars of protective conditions can be identified upon which the regulation of anticipative criminal investigations shall rest: the legitimization, integrity and fairness of the criminal proceedings. Because the pillars directly follow from the principles (constitutive principles and parameters) derived from the recognition of the human dignity and personal autonomy of every human being, these pillars concern the rule of law underpinnings of the regulation. With the help of human rights law and the constitutional interpretation of fundamental rights as well as substantiating the parameters on the basis of the arguments addressed, these pillars can be given content, providing for the rules that shall regulate anticipative criminal investigations.

Underpinned by the constitutive principles, corroborated by the parameters and directed by the provided analysis of the arguments in the flexible area of the law, the rules for the regulation for anticipative criminal investigations will be further crystallized within the context of each pillar. In fact the conditions to be formulated, categorized in the three pillars, provide for the building plan of the architecture. Building a regulation for anticipative criminal investigations on the basis of the essential coherence between these three pillars will be legitimate under the rule of law.

### *8.5.1 Legitimization*

The first pillar of regulatory rules is legitimization: the legitimization of the criminal investigative activities and the use of special investigative techniques. Legitimization must be understood as the required justification for conducting criminal investigative activities in general and specifically for the use of special investigative techniques, which, in particular, have an intrusive character for the individual liberties of the persons against whom the techniques are applied. The constitutive principles of the presumption of innocence and the right to respect for one's private life are relevant for the formulation of rules regarding the legitimization.

In the first place, the presumption of innocence prohibits arbitrary criminal investigative action. Rules legitimizing investigative action should, therefore, provide specific grounds that justify criminal investigative actions against someone. The normative influence of the presumption of innocence on investigative activities has been explained in Sect. 8.3.1 as being different from the procedural implications of the presumption. During the criminal investigative phase the presumption of innocence guarantees that the innocent (those who cannot be related to criminal investigative activities) are left alone, free from investigative activities that interfere with their individual liberty, but it does permit the use of investigative powers against persons who can be related to criminal activities, implying a level of guilt. This means that the presumption of innocence does not forbid the investigating, for example, of radicalized persons who can be connected to terrorist organizations which are known to recruit people in order to commit terrorist crimes or radicalized persons who have expressed an intention to commit terrorist crimes.[123] However, the grounds which legitimize criminal investigative activities should not be formulated too broadly. If formulated broadly, the scope of the permitted investigative activities may be too wide and include many persons who cannot be related to (future) criminal activities. For this reason, the formulated grounds upon which a criminal investigation can be initiated must be able to reduce the scope of the investigation so as to provide adequate protection for the innocent, which can be realized by providing for a threshold that can be met upon a showing of evidence regarding involvement in criminal activities. A specific nexus between the persons under investigation and specified criminal offenses is required in order to afford adequate protection for the innocent.

In the second place, the constitutive principle of the fundamental right to respect for one's private life is important in order to determine the justified threshold legitimizing investigative action. The right to respect for one's private life further differentiates the required legitimization of criminal investigative activities, because this constitutive principle only imposes different standards on the legitimization when the investigative activity impinges on the right to respect for one's private life. Thus, whereas the realization of the constitutive principle of the presumption of innocence requires a certain legitimization of any criminal investigative activity, the right to respect for one's private life sets additional standards for the use of intrusive investigative techniques. In the context of anticipative criminal investigations, these techniques typically concern electronic surveillance techniques. As a consequence, there is a direct relation between the nature of the investigative technique with commensurate implications for private life, and the required level and nature of the threshold that legitimizes the use of the investigative technique.

The relation between the right to respect for private life and the required legitimization for using investigative powers that intrude upon privacy also clearly follows from the interpretation given to the protection of the right to respect for one's private life by the ECHR and the US Supreme Court in the criminal investigative context. The ECrtHR requires restrictions on the right to respect for

---

[123] Whereas prosecution on the basis of one's thoughts alone is clearly prohibited by general principles of criminal law and by the fundamental right to freedom of expression, the *presumption of innocence* does not obstruct the investigation of persons who display behavior that may result in the commission of serious crimes.

one's private life so that it is 'in accordance with the law' and that law should have the quality of providing the individual with adequate protection "against arbitrary interferences with the rights safeguarded by paragraph 1 [of Article 8 ECHR]".[124] To be in accordance with the law, the law should meet the test of 'foreseeability', which requires the meeting of certain conditions as to the quality of the law that exclude vagueness and provisions that are open to different interpretations.[125] The foreseeability of the provision is also a requirement to realize the parameter of accountability: transparency is required with regard to the grounds upon which the government is entitled to interfere with citizens' private lives. The requirements of the quality of the law must be more stringent when the interference is more serious.[126] At the same time the Court has acknowledged that the 'foreseeability' of the law should be interpreted more leniently in the context of secret surveillance, as it is necessary for effective surveillance that it is not clear beforehand that the state will engage in surveillance in a given situation.[127] To render a law foreseeable the ECrtHR requires that it provides for the specific grounds upon which electronic surveillance can be authorized. According to the Court, for the law—that provides for the power to use electronic surveillance in the criminal procedural law context—to be of sufficient quality, it must "afford adequate safeguards against various possible abuses" by "for example, [providing for] the categories of people liable to have their telephones tapped by judicial order and the nature of the offences which may give rise to such an order."[128]

In US Constitutional law, the relation between a specific ground for investigation and the protection of private life follows directly from the wording of the Fourth Amendment, (in principle) requiring probable cause before warrants for searches can be issued, which implies both a relation to specific persons and a relation to a crime. The first Supreme Court jurisprudence on electronic surveillance emphasized this relation by determining that "only the most precise and

---

124 See e.g. ECHR 2 August 1984, App. no. 8691/79 (*Malone v. The United Kingdom*), para 67, and ECHR 24 April 1990, App. no. 11801/85 and App. no. 11105/84 (*Kruslin v. France and Huvig v. France*), para 30/29.

125 See in more detail on the interpretation of Article 8 in the context of criminal investigation Chap. 2, Sect. 2.1.3.2.1 and 2.3.2.1.1.

126 ECHR 24 April 1990, App. no. 11801/85 and App. no. 11105/84 (*Kruslin v. France and Huvig v. France*), para 33/32.

127 ECHR 2 August 1984, App. no. 8691/79 (*Malone v. The United Kingdom*), para 67.

128 ECHR 24 April 1990, App. no. 11801/85 and App. no. 11105/84 (*Kruslin v. France and Huvig v. France*), para 35/34. Whereas the Court in the case of *Kruslin/Huvig v. France* suggests that the law should provide, as the threshold for investigative actions, a standard defining the categories of people liable to surveillance and the nature of the offenses which may give rise to surveillance, these specific requirements have become settled in the vast ECHR jurisprudence by the enumeration of specific safeguards to be adopted in the law in ECHR 30 July 1998, App. no. 27671/95 (*Valenzuela Contreras v. Spain*), including the "categories of people liable to have their telephones tapped by judicial order and the nature of the offences which could give rise to such order" (see: 'Case of Valenzuela Contreras v. Spain', *The International Journal of Human Rights, Volume 3, Issue 1 Spring 1999,* 126).

rigorous standard of probable cause should justify an intrusion of this sort,"[129] which has resulted in the adoption of the probable cause standard in the statutory regulation of electronic surveillance in Title III. Title III has further restricted the possibility for using electronic surveillance techniques to the investigation of certain serious offenses to which the probable cause is related.

In this understanding of the relation between a specific ground for investigative action and the protection of the right to respect for one's private life, both in the context of the ECHR and the US Constitution, the recognition of the constitutive principles of the presumption of innocence and the right to respect for private life come together as both recognize individual autonomy. Limiting the use of special investigative techniques to categories of persons liable to be subjected to electronic surveillance (as the primary method of investigation in an anticipative criminal investigation) or to persons against whom probable cause can be established and, in addition, requiring a connection with criminal offenses, implicates a showing of evidence regarding the involvement of persons in criminal activities. In addition, the right to respect for one's private life requires the law to be more stringent once the intrusion into private life increases. Hence, the initial conclusion can be drawn that the threshold legitimizing the use of criminal investigative powers, underpinned by the presumption of innocence and the right to respect for one's private life, shall concern a standard that restricts the use, firstly, to (a group of) persons against whom a level of suspicion can be established and, secondly, to activities that can be related to criminal offenses.

The rules that reflect the required legitimization of anticipative criminal activities shall be further substantiated by subjecting their formulation to the parameter of the principle of necessity. The principle of necessity has specific consequences for the legitimization of *criminal* investigative action in comparison to *intelligence* investigative action. The criminal justice system has the goal of prosecuting and punishing the perpetrators of crimes, which amounts to a criminal justice system in which state institutions have been attributed the most far-reaching powers when it comes to interference with individual liberty. Under the applicability of the principle of necessity, the criminal justice system has, therefore, traditionally obtained the character of an *ultimum remedium.* For this reason, the law enforcement system is traditionally subjected to more rigid restraints than the intelligence community. However, the perception of the *ultimum remedium* character of the criminal justice system has changed, because the criminal justice system, according to the current view, is not only considered to deal exclusively with apprehending, prosecuting and punishing criminals, but has also obtained a function in contributing to security, investigating risks and preventing their realization. This choice may be justified on the basis of the nature of the terrorist crimes and the effectiveness of the need to deal with these crimes by combining prevention with evidence-gathering (Sects. 8.4.1.3 and 8.4.1.4). As has been explained in Sect. 8.4.2, the separation between the law enforcement community

[129] *Berger v. New York*, 388 U.S. 41, 87 S.Ct. 1873 (1967), 69.

and the intelligence community is based on the relation between the function of the agency and the required level of protection provided in the regulatory framework. For this reason, taking into account the now additional function of the criminal justice system to provide security, criminal procedural law is not longer exclusively an *ultimum remedium* for prosecution and punishment, but is also necessary for striving for preventive purposes, considering the nature of the terrorist crimes and considering the necessity to combine prevention with prosecution and punishment.

The formulated conditions on the basis of the constitutive principles of the presumption of innocence and the right to respect for one's private life still concern rather broad, basic conditions. As the last step to further substantiate these conditions, the acknowledgment of the distinction between investigating for the purpose of prevention and for the purpose of prosecuting terrorist (or national security) crimes, in relation to the required level of protection for the individual's right to a private life, shall be taken into account. Hence, in order to complete the above findings so as to find the justified synthesis regarding legitimization, the principle of proportionality shall be applied in order to give further substance to the flexible area of the law, which concerns the area left undefined after having determined the basic procedural conditions that follow from the relevant constitutive principles.

Each of the constitutive principles which is relevant has a clear connotation with the factors that influence the proportionality of the investigative action. With regard to the level of the standard in order to justify the use of special investigative techniques, preferences need to be set that either favor the responsibility of preventing harm by providing a less rigid standard legitimizing investigative activities or favor the protection of the fundamental right to private life. Whether preference may be given to the prevention of harm depends on the necessity of the need to use criminal investigation for that purpose. This necessity can be derived from the assessment of the nature of terrorism and the effectiveness of specific investigative action for the purpose of prevention. Because the criminal justice system is primarily orientated towards prosecution and punishment and also the preventive function of criminal procedural law is connected to this purpose, the criminal investigation should still be distinguished from mere intelligence work, which requires a strict application of the principle of necessity concerning the necessity of using a specific criminal investigative technique for preventive purposes. This section will continue to address these arguments in order to determine the sought after preferences in the flexible area of the law, either in favor of the minimum acceptable legitimizing standard, on the basis of the constitutive principles, or in favor of additional protection for the right to respect for one's private life.

It has been concluded on the basis of the analysis of the nature of terrorist crimes that the investigation shall focus on the preparatory acts of terrorist crimes in order to prevent attacks, that such investigation is complicated by the complex and vague organizational structure of terrorist groups and that, therefore, the investigative approach of gathering information about radicalizing persons most likely provides for leads regarding the actual preparatory acts of terrorist crimes.

Considering that, from the perspective of the nature of the terrorist crime, a preventive investigative focus is preferred, a threshold reflecting a reasonable suspicion of guilt or probable cause regarding a committed crime is unsuitable. It should be possible to initiate the investigative activities already before crimes have been committed in order to be able to deal with the diffuse nature of terrorism. The nature of terrorist crimes is thus an indication that a preference shall be set in favor of a less stringent standard for using investigative powers, allowing for a proactive approach that results in the prevention of attacks.

The analysis provided in the previous section regarding the effectiveness of an intelligence-led investigative approach, combining the goal of prevention with evidence-gathering and initiating criminal investigative activities on the basis of soft information, has compounded the fact that these characteristics may work counterproductively. At the same time, the approach of pursuing both prevention and evidence-gathering is adopted because of the duty to take measures to prevent terrorist attacks and to deal with terrorists by bringing them to justice. An anticipative criminal investigation is adopted as the most effective answer to meet both demands. In order to enhance effectiveness, it has been suggested that the investigative purposes should be reformulated and that the information on the basis of which investigative action is initiated should provide the investigation with sufficient focus. On the basis of the assessment of the argument of effectiveness in relation to the principle of necessity, it can be concluded that the threshold legitimizing criminal investigative action shall limit the scope of the investigative action to specific persons or groups of persons who can be related to preparatory activities of a terrorist crime.

Furthermore, the distinction shall be taken into account between the purpose of the prevention of terrorism, or more in general of protection against threats to national security, and the purpose of gathering evidence for the prosecution of terrorist or national security crimes in relation to the required threshold that can legitimize the investigative activities. It has been provided above that in the criminal investigative context the presumption of innocence and the right to respect for one's private life require at least a threshold reflecting a level of suspicion relating to specific persons with regard to specified criminal offenses. The requirements set for the rigidity of the law providing the grounds for investigation in the context of ordinary crime by means of intrusive special investigative techniques are comparably strict considering the ECrtHR and Fourth Amendment jurisprudence.[130] However, the ECrtHR and the US Courts have considered Article 8/the Fourth Amendment to be interpreted less rigidly in a national security context. With regard to the legitimization of investigative activities the ECrtHR held that the German standard of the "G 10" legislation (regulating electronic surveillance for the protection of national security): "factual indications

[130] See particularly ECHR 24 April 1990, App. no. 11801/85 and App. no. 11105/84 (*Kruslin v. France and Huvig v. France*) and *Berger v. New York* and *Katz*, and the adoption of the standards developed in these cases in the statutory framework of Title III.

(*tatsächliche Anhaltspunkte*) for suspecting a person of planning, committing or having committed criminal acts punishable under the Criminal Code, such as [certain serious crimes against national security]", as a ground for using special investigative techniques in order to protect national security, is sufficiently foreseeable.[131] As has been explained in Chap. 4, the US Foreign Intelligence Surveillance Act, applying a different probable cause standard to national security investigations than the probable cause standards of Title III applicable in the context of criminal investigations, has also been held constitutional under the Fourth Amendment. Whereas the US courts made, prior to the PATRIOT Act amendments, a clear distinction between the goal of preventing national security offenses and the goal of prosecuting any criminal offenses, the ECrtHR seems to distinguish primarily the prevention and prosecution of national security crimes from the (prevention and) prosecution of ordinary crime.[132]

As has been explained in Sect. 8.4.2 there must be a relation between the specific purpose of the investigative activities and the required level of protective safeguards. This implies a distinction between regulatory standards applicable to investigation for the purpose of preventing national security crimes and those which are applicable to investigation for the purpose of prosecuting these crimes. When these purposes are combined in one investigative enterprise, as in the anticipative criminal investigation, the legitimacy of the criminal justice system depends on the presence of procedural safeguards that guarantee the fairness of the criminal process and the integrity of the state agencies responsible for the anticipative criminal investigation and not necessarily on the basis of the applicability of the most rigid standard traditionally reserved for criminal investigations.[133] This approach seems to correspond with the distinction laid down by the ECHR between the investigation (for the purpose of prevention *and* prosecution) of national security crimes and the investigation of ordinary crime. This means for the required legitimization of the anticipative criminal investigation only that it should include a condition limiting the anticipative criminal investigative framework to the investigation of crimes that threaten national security, in particular terrorist crimes.

The preceding findings result in the following conclusion: rules providing for the legitimization of anticipative criminal investigations may concern a considerably lower standard than those traditionally applicable to criminal investigations in order to be able to give effect to the investigative goal of prevention and in order

---

[131] ECHR 6 September 1978, App. no. 5029/71 (*Klass and others v. Germany*), para 17.

[132] Sottiaux draws this conclusion on the basis of an assessment of the applicability of exceptional standards in the fight against terrorism for the use of electronic surveillance and the compatibility of these standards with Article 8 ECHR and the Fourth Amendment. Sottiaux 2008, 294. Nevertheless, the ECHR requires compensation through procedural safeguards (more guarantees as to the integrity of the investigative action) when the foreseeability of the law is weaker. See on this subject in more detail the section dealing with the pillar of integrity (Sect. 8.5.2).

[133] See Sect. 8.4.2.

to be able to confront terrorist crimes. However, in order to realize the constitutive principles of any regulation of criminal investigation, the rules regarding the legitimization of an anticipative criminal investigation must meet, as a minimum, the following three conditions:

1. the use of investigative powers that results in interference with the right to respect for one's private life shall be explicitly legitimized in the law by providing the grounds, in the form of a threshold, upon which the investigative powers may be used;
2. the threshold shall reduce the investigative activities to identifiable (groups of) persons;
3. the threshold shall include a standard that reflects the presence of evidence that provides for a nexus between these (groups of) persons and crimes that threaten national security.

## 8.5.2 Integrity

The second pillar of regulatory rules covers the entire process of the anticipative criminal investigation. The rules categorized under this heading aim to guarantee that the state institutions, responsible for anticipative criminal investigation, do not abuse their powers. It aims to guarantee that the state institutions carry out the substantive goals within the confines of the law, in respect of the presumption of innocence, the right to private life, the principles of necessity and proportionality and in anticipation of the subsequent realization of a fair trial. A system of checks and balances shall apply to the authorities when engaging in anticipative criminal investigations, which covers the interaction between shield and sword objectives.[134] Guaranteeing the integrity of the state institutions that are responsible for an anticipative criminal investigation by means of a system of checks and balances concerns a pillar of regulation rendering the whole system of regulation an integrated body in balance through the coherence between the three pillars. Integrity covers the following aspects of the regulation of anticipative criminal investigations: regulating the discretionary area within the borders of the law, control on abuse of power or on exceeding the limits following from the principles of proportionality and necessity and realizing accountability and redress for abuses of power. Each aspect will be dealt with separately.

---

[134] Adopting a system of checks and balances is identified by Vervaele as the constitutional dimension of the regulation of criminal procedural measures, as a third dimension next to the shield and sword dimension. Here the combination of checks and balances is understood as the measures to realize the integrity of the investigative agency. Vervaele 2009, 83.

#### 8.5.2.1 Minimization Mechanisms

Rules that are intended to guarantee the integrity of the state institutions relate to the legitimization of the investigative action in order to provide checks on the discretionary area following from the adopted threshold for investigation. These checks aim to guarantee that, regardless of the discretion allowed to state institutions, they act in respect of the presumption of innocence and in respect of the right to private life. In the first place, the regulation of anticipative criminal investigations shall include an explicit rule providing that the investigating agency is subjected to the principle of proportionality in all its activities. In addition, it is desirable that guidelines are distributed internally in order to further this proportionality by taking specifically into account the nature of the crimes that are dealt with, the nature of the investigative techniques in a particular context and the effectiveness of investigative action. In the second place, as has been observed in the previous sub-section, a lower threshold for investigative activities is permissible, but shall be backed up by procedural mechanisms as additional safeguards on the state's investigative activities in accordance with the restriction, granted within the law, on the right to private life and in accordance with the principles of necessity and proportionality.

In the ECrtHR case law, the Article 8 requirement that restrictions must have a sufficient 'quality' to be foreseeable has been understood as requiring, except for the grounds justifying a restriction, also the applicability of 'minimization procedures' in order to reduce the interference with private life to the minimum and to protect against abuse.[135] Also in US constitutional law the establishment of procedural safeguards as a means of an integrity back-up has been considered as a constitutional requirement in order to meet the reasonableness test under the Fourth Amendment. In the first place, the Fourth Amendment itself requires the 'particularity' of searches. Warrants must describe what places are to be searched or what conversations are to be intercepted. The requirement of particularity importantly reduces the scope of the search to what is actually necessary for the investigation.[136] Moreover, the US Courts have considered the presence of minimization procedures essential for the reasonableness of the investigation. The adoption of minimization procedures as a procedural safeguard is also a requirement under Title III and FISA. Minimization procedures are a procedural guarantee in order to make sure that only those communications which are relevant to the crime under investigation are intercepted and stored and/or shared (when irrelevant communications have accidentally been intercepted).[137]

---

[135] ECHR 24 April 1990, App. no. 11801/85 and App. no. 11105/84 (*Kruslin v. France and Huvig v. France*), para 35/34.

[136] Also the ECrtHR has read a particularity requirement into Article 8 by requiring that a warrant provides "minimal indications as to the scope of the investigation it authorizes." Sottiaux 2008, 318.

[137] See Chap. 5, Sects. 5.3.2.2.3 and 5.3.2.3.1.

The adoption and applicability of procedures for the purpose of minimizing the intrusion on private life to that which is necessary and avoiding the inclusion of innocent persons in the investigation aim to guarantee the integrity of the state agency, where the agency has been given discretion. These minimization mechanisms provide the investigation focus, by limiting the collection of information to that information which is relevant for the investigation of specific criminal activity. This reduces the adverse impact on the right to respect for one's private life, protects the innocent, limits the criminal investigation to that which is necessary and enhances effectiveness. In the context of an anticipative criminal investigation, where the grounds legitimizing the investigative activities may be comparably weak and, consequently, granting more discretion to the investigating authorities, the applicability of such minimization mechanisms limiting the scope of the investigation is especially important. Even more so when we take into account that the judiciary tends to step back once the government claims it needs to act for the purpose of protecting national security, often under the cloak of secrecy. As we have seen in both the Dutch/ECHR context[138] and the US context,[139] the judiciary prefers not to second-guess the government's claims to national security interests and provides the state with the desired discretion to act in furtherance of national security interests (or in the words of the ECrtHR: granting the states a wide margin of appreciation to decide what measures are necessary for the protection of the national security[140]).[141] The applicability of minimization mechanisms that are adopted to safeguard the government's integrity in their investigative steps are then a necessary requirement in order not to leave protection against arbitrary and unnecessary interference with privacy rights a dead-letter.

#### 8.5.2.2 Controlling Mechanisms

The constitutive principle of accountability requires the adoption of control mechanisms as a check on the integrity of the investigative agencies. These mechanisms shall extend control in order to determine whether the state agency acts within the confines of the law. This control should cover adherence to procedural mechanisms in order to minimize the gathering and storage of 'surplus information',[142] which concerns an important safeguard against

---

[138] See Chap. 4, Sects. 4.2.3.2 and 4.3.4.

[139] See Chap. 6, Sect. 6.2.2.

[140] ECHR 26 March 1987, App. no. 9248/81 (*Leander v. Sweden*), para 58-59 and ECHR 8 February 1996, App. no. 18731/91 (*John Murray v. The United Kingdom*), para 90. See also: Loof 2005, 256-265.

[141] Ramraj 2007, 188-189.

[142] Surplus information concerns all information that does not concern the activities under investigation. Sottiaux 2008, 287.

abuse.[143] Furthermore, control should be established on the whole procedure of surveillance: from the decision to initiate an anticipative criminal investigation until the closure of the investigation. The ECrtHR has considered the establishment of "effective control" as a mandatory requirement in order to review whether the restriction on the right to respect for private life is necessary in a democratic society.[144] This effective control should then concern an assessment of the surveillance procedures as well as realizing a form of accountability when the state agency has acted outside the law or in violation of the principles of necessity and proportionality.

The ECrtHR has given a clear preference to prior judicial control where the interests at stake are particularly pressing, because of the "preventive nature" of such "objective and impartial" control "to make the necessary assessment of the various competing interests."[145] For this reason, in *Sanoma* the Court considered the absence of a prior judicial review, where the government sought to obtain information which would require the breaching of the principle that journalistic sources should be protected, to be an inadequate safeguard to protect against arbitrary interferences with a Convention right (Article 10).[146] In other cases, the Court, similar to its general method of assessment, has taken into account the totality of safeguards applicable to a given situation where the state interferes with the right to respect for one's private life through investigative activities.[147] Whereas in the law enforcement context the *Kruslin/Huvig* judgments seem to suggest, although less clearly than in *Sanoma*, that the measure of effective control should concern a judicial order,[148] in the national security context the Court has not explicitly required effective control to be exerted by a judicial body but has

[143] See e.g. ECHR 6 September 1978, App. no. 5029/71 (*Klass and Others v. Germany*), para 52 and ECHR 29 June 2006, admissibility decision, App. no. 54934/00 (*Weber and Saravia*), para 99-101, where the Court considered the fact that control was exerted on the scope of the information collected by the intelligence agency by someone qualified to hold judicial office, as an important additional safeguard against arbitrary interference with private life, and therefore, as an "adequate indication as to the circumstances in which and the conditions on which the public authorities were empowered to resort to monitoring measures, and the scope and manner of exercise of the authorities' discretion." *Weber and Saravia v. Germany, ibid.*, para 101.

[144] The Court does not focus on the necessity of the restriction on the right to private life, but on the question whether an 'adequate and effective guarantee against abuse' has been established through the realization of effective control. ECHR Judgment 6 September 1978, App. no. 5029/71 (*Klass and Others v. Germany*), para 55 and ECHR 24 August 1998, App. no. 23618/94 (Lambert v. France), para 31.

[145] ECHR 14 September 2010, App. no. 38224/03 (*Sanoma Uitgevers B.V. v. The Netherlands*), para 92-93.

[146] ECHR 14 September 2010, App. no. 38224/03 (*Sanoma Uitgevers B.V. v. The Netherlands*), para 98-100.

[147] Sottiaux 2008, 288-289.

[148] ECHR 24 April 1990, App. no. 11801/85 and App. no. 11105/84 (*Kruslin v. France and Huvig v. France*), para 35/34.

considered the establishment of other supervisory bodies to be sufficient.[149] The Court only requires from these supervisory bodies that they "have sufficient independence to give an objective ruling."[150]

In the US a warrant is clearly preferable, considering that it is also one of the conditions under the Fourth Amendment. In order to nevertheless give effect to secrecy interests, the specialized FISA Court operating *in camera* and *ex parte* is attributed the task of asserting prior judicial control on the use of FISA investigative powers in national security investigations, whereas in the law enforcement context a magistrate is responsible for the authorization of search warrants, including surveillance. Despite this preference for prior judicial authorization, exceptions are widely available, for instance under Title III when the nature of the crimes involved is very serious.

The realization of control over an anticipative criminal investigation concerns both intelligence agencies and law enforcement agencies, as both are attributed the task of anticipative criminal investigation. The manner in which control has been established depends on the specific function fulfilled by the agency that conducts the investigation, similar to the distinction made by the ECrtHR between national security investigations and law enforcement investigations and in the US between warrants issued in regularly constituted courts and FISA court orders. Typically, control over the intelligence agencies is organized internally, through special parliamentary commissions, through internal oversight, and/or through special courts operating *in camera*. By contrast, control over the law enforcement community typically concerns judicial control through prior authorization or a posteriori in the context of trial proceedings, on behalf of the independent and impartial judiciary. When information is shared between the intelligence agency and the law enforcement agency and, as a consequence, the destination of the information changes from intelligence in order to make threat assessments to information that can be used as evidence for prosecution and punishment, this raises new questions as to the nature of the effective control to be exerted on the information-gathering process.

The ECrtHR has also dealt with this possibility in the case of *Weber and Saravia v. Germany*. The Court acknowledged that the sharing of personal information constitutes a "further separate interference" and especially the sharing of information collected "without any specific prior suspicion" with law enforcement agencies "in order to allow the institution of criminal proceedings against those being monitored constitutes a fairly serious interference with the right of these persons to secrecy of telecommunications."[151] Nevertheless, the

---

[149] ECHR Judgment 6 September 1978, App no. 5029/71 (*Klass and Others v. Germany*), para 56: although emphasizing that it is "in principle desirable to entrust supervisory control to a judge[,] (...) the exclusion of judicial control does not exceed the limits of what may be deemed necessary in a democratic society."

[150] *Ibidem.*

[151] ECHR 29 June 2006, admissibility decision, App. no. 54934/00 (*Weber and Saravia*), para 79 and 125.

Court considered that this fairly serious interference with private life did not violate Article 8 ECHR, because the use of the information for other purposes was limited: "merely in order to prevent or prosecute [specific] serious criminal offences." In the view of the Court the applicability of additional procedural safeguards[152] renders the interference with privacy proportionate and necessary in the democratic society.[153] In the US the choice for a particularly regulatory framework (either Title III or FISA) was traditionally determined on the basis of a primary purpose test. Through this approach the choice for a particular framework, including the form of control over the investigative activities, was also directly dependent on the purpose of the information gathering.[154]

An anticipative criminal investigation concerns a shared responsibility between the intelligence and law enforcement communities, where prevention is likely to be understood as overriding prosecution and punishment interests. Considering the foregoing, it is important that when the intelligence agency is responsible for the information gathering and this information is transferred to the law enforcement community for evidentiary purposes, sufficient procedural mechanisms are in place in order to guarantee the integrity of the information-gathering process. This shall not necessarily have consequences for the manner in which control is exerted over the intelligence agencies.

Especially with regard to the effectiveness of the intelligence work, it is important to maintain the current differences in the organization of control (characterized by secrecy versus transparency). Otherwise, the effectiveness of carrying out the primary function of the intelligence community to warn against threats to national security would be incommensurately obstructed by requiring transparency where secrecy is essential for maintaining a strong information position.[155] Hence, as long as a form of control has been established, capable of exerting control independently from the state agency responsible for the investigation, this, in combination with other protective procedural measures, would be a sufficient control over the integrity of the intelligence agency, also in relation to the ultimate fairness of the criminal proceedings.

Nevertheless, it should be avoided that, because of the combination of lower standards upon which investigative action can be initiated with a different, more secretive, system of control, cooperation between law enforcement and

---

[152] Such as: "specific facts—as opposed to mere factual indications—aroused the suspicion that someone had committed one of the offences listed"; "the transmission had to be recorded in minutes"; "the decision to transmit data had to be taken by a staff member of the Federal Intelligence Service qualified to hold judicial office, who was particularly well trained to verify whether the conditions for transmission were met; and, an independent commission ("the G10 commission") is authorized to review to verify "that the statutory conditions for data transmission were complied with." *Ibid.* para 127-128.

[153] *Ibid.*, para 126-130.

[154] Since the changing of the 'purpose language' into a significant purpose, the relation between the investigative goal and the regulatory framework has been clouded. See Chap. 6, Sect. 6.4.1.

[155] Compare section 8.4.1.5. See also: (Anonymous), Note 2008A, 1556.

intelligence results in escaping from more stringent criminal procedural safeguards. Procedural safeguards such as prior judicial authorization and the establishment of a level of suspicion regarding specified crimes may not be circumvented by leaving the investigative activities for the purpose of evidence-gathering to the intelligence agencies. For this reason—and under the parameter of necessity in combination with the assessment of the argument of effectiveness (8.4.1.4) as well as because of the fundamental nature of the institutional separation between law enforcement and intelligence (8.4.2)—always the most protective investigative framework should be chosen, once the investigation is conducted for the specific purpose of evidence-gathering and there is a choice between either the intelligence framework or the criminal procedural law framework in their traditional forms, attributed with their traditional functions. Hence, not only the specific legitimization required for investigative activities, but also the required additional procedural safeguards, such as judicial control, shall be related to the investigative purpose.

This also implies that if the intelligence agencies carry out the anticipative criminal investigative task (information collection both for prevention and evidence-gathering), the intelligence agencies become bound by the specific purposes of this form of investigation. Considering the relation between the purpose of the investigation and the required regulatory framework, the intelligence agencies can carry out the anticipative criminal investigative task under the following two conditions: 1) the intelligence agencies observe the conditions for regulating an anticipative criminal investigation, in particular those under the pillar of legitimization; and, 2) the information produced by the intelligence agencies that becomes part of the criminal process is subjected to judicial scrutiny, who shall guard the fairness of the procedure resulting in prosecution and punishment (see the subsequent pillar).[156] The particular implications for the regulation of anticipative criminal investigations will be further evaluated in Chap. 9.

Considering the foregoing, rules regarding control, other than the already existing mechanisms of control over state agencies, which concern the integrity of the state organ, thus do not need to be established specifically in the regulation of an anticipative criminal investigation. Rather, when regulating anticipative criminal investigations, it is important to precisely define the specific purposes of the relevant investigative activities in order to choose for the right investigative framework. Insofar as the investigative activities of the intelligence agencies are involved and these activities are not specifically conducted for the purpose of evidence-gathering, a more pragmatic approach is preferable, in order not to adversely influence the intelligence agencies' efforts in protecting national security by demanding transparency for controlling mechanisms. The combination of procedural safeguards concerning integrity, the applicable standards legitimizing

[156] Compare section 8.6.2: "It is important that when the goals of intelligence and law enforcement are blended, also a regulation is adopted that provides the checks in order to guarantee that the different nature of investigative action does not influence the procedure resulting in prosecution and punishment."

the investigative activities and the possibility of guaranteeing the fairness of the criminal proceedings shall be sufficient to counterbalance a reduced, less transparent, form of control over the integrity of the intelligence agency. When such a coherence of protective measures provides the safeguards for an institutional culture that is incorruptible, presumed trust in the information-gathering process may guide the transmission of information from intelligence to law enforcement agencies, either for the purpose of starting a criminal investigation or directly for the purpose of prosecution (the latter under the applicability of the conditions formulated under the third pillar).[157]

#### 8.5.2.3 The Availability of a Remedy

Another aspect of the parameter of accountability requires that citizens are provided with the possibility to hold the government accountable for conducting investigative activities by which they are affected. When the agency responsible for the anticipative criminal investigation abuses its powers and acts outside the borders demarcating its powers, accountability shall be realized. Contrary to the realization of control over investigative activities, realizing retrospective accountability does require specific rules in the regulation of anticipative criminal investigations. To guarantee integrity it is important that it is also possible to hold a state agency accountable when it has acted outside the law or has disregarded rights and principles that aim to protect individual liberty.

When someone is prosecuted, accountability is realized in the (traditional) criminal process compensating illegalities or irregularities during the investigation by excluding evidence, reducing the sentence or even prohibiting the prosecutor from continuing a prosecution. Here the accountability for illegitimate actions or irregularities during the investigative phase influences and becomes an aspect of the fairness of the proceedings and, hence, will be dealt with in more detail under the next pillar. Here, it is sufficient to note that the availability of procedural remedies for illegitimate action during the anticipative criminal investigation is not only a fair trial guarantee, but the threat of these remedies also functions as a procedural mechanism forcing the investigative agencies to act within the borders of the law and, thus, as a safeguard for the integrity of actors that have been attributed an evidence-gathering task.

However, also persons who are not subsequently prosecuted may become the subject of an anticipative criminal investigation. This is even more likely than in traditional forms of criminal investigation, because, despite rules that aim to protect the innocent, the wider scope of the investigative activities focusing on the initial activities in preparation of the commission of terrorist crimes is likely to involve persons against whom sufficient evidence can never be produced for the purpose of prosecution. In addition, and even more importantly, accountability

[157] Ramraj 2007, 200.

must be realized when the investigative agencies abuse their power, for example, by targeting innocent persons.[158] These persons should be able to challenge the legitimacy of the interferences with their private lives. Moreover, they shall be provided with the right to *habeas data*, considering that the personal information of both those legitimately investigated and those illegitimately investigated may be collected, stored and shared, which impinges upon the right to informational privacy.

Realizing accountability outside the context of criminal proceedings is only possible if the persons included in the anticipative criminal investigation are notified. As the ECrtHR observed in *Klass*: "[a]s regards review a posteriori, it is necessary to determine whether judicial control, in particular with the individual's participation, should continue to be excluded even after surveillance has ceased. Inextricably linked to this issue is the question of subsequent notification, since there is in principle little scope for recourse to the courts by the individual concerned unless he is advised of the measures taken without his knowledge and thus able retrospectively to challenge their legality."[159] The Court continued to observe, however, that notification can in practice reasonably not always be required as "subsequent notification to each individual affected by a suspended measure might well jeopardize the long-term purpose that originally prompted the surveillance (…), it might serve to reveal the working methods and fields of operation of the intelligence service and even possibly to identify their agents."[160] Although the presence of a statutory notification requirement is a procedural safeguard that the Court takes into account when assessing the proportionality of a specific restriction on privacy rights,[161] the Court considers post hoc notification not to be essential for guaranteeing the integrity of the state agency carrying out its investigative tasks within the borders of the law.

The US Supreme Court has been stricter as the notification requirement has been considered as an essential safeguard for the constitutional adequacy of a search.[162] Nevertheless, also the US Courts have accepted that a notification requirement should not be adopted in the warrant in the presence of exigent circumstances and in certain circumstances the notification may be postponed.

---

[158] Compare the distinction laid down in Sect. 8.3.1.1 on the constitutive principle of the presumption of innocence between guilt and innocence in the prosecutorial sense (where guilt is established upon evidence proving beyond reasonable doubt/according to the law and the conviction of the judge, that someone has committed a criminal offense) and guilt/innocence in the investigative sense (where innocence concerns those who cannot in any sense be connected with criminal activities and guilt reflects information regarding possible involvement in (future) criminal activities).

[159] ECHR Judgment 6 September 1978, App. no. 5029/71 (*Klass and Others v. Germany*), para 57.

[160] *Ibid.*, para 58.

[161] Sottiaux 2008, 319.

[162] *Berger v. New York*, 388 U.S. 41, 87 S.Ct. 1873, 60.

It should be taken into account that it is not transparency that is a fundamental principle, but the realization of accountability. Again, the presence of a coherent system of procedural safeguards and controlling mechanisms should result in the presumption that the government has acted in due regard of individual rights, for which reason the interest of shielding investigative activities prevails above the interest of the individual in notification. In the words of the Court: "[w]hile the possibility of improper action by a dishonest, negligent or over-zealous official can never be completely ruled out whatever the system, the considerations that matter for the purposes of the Court's present review are the likelihood of such action and the safeguards provided to protect against it."[163]

Nevertheless, realizing accountability for all state actions concerns a fundamental principle of the law, which includes providing citizens with a remedy once they have been subjected to an investigation, and it is important that notification is the rule with possible exceptions for the postponement of the notification. Considering that an anticipative criminal investigation will likely involve the subjection of persons to investigative activities, whilst these persons will never face criminal charges, a general level of accountability can only be achieved with the observance of notification requirements. Therefore, the regulation of anticipative criminal investigations should include provisions requiring the notification of those persons whose right to respect for private life has been affected by anticipative criminal investigative activities. Possible exceptions, allowing for a delayed notice, should also be circumscribed in the regulation in order to be foreseeable. Actual accountability may occur through a civil procedure, with the possibility of financial compensation.

#### 8.5.2.4 Conditions Concerning Integrity

The pillar of integrity is crucial in order to uphold the two other pillars of legitimacy and fairness and, hence, it makes the entity of the regulation a coherent set of rules providing for a structured approach in order to give effect to the shield and sword objective of criminal procedural law. In order to guarantee the institutional integrity of the state agency responsible for an anticipative criminal investigation, the regulation of anticipative criminal investigations shall meet the following conditions:

1. All anticipative criminal investigative activities shall be subjected to the principle of proportionality to be explicitly provided in the law and supplemented by guidelines.
2. Minimization procedures shall be adopted that guarantee that the investigative activities are limited to the legitimized scope and purpose.

[163] See ECHR Judgment 6 September 1978, App. no. 5029/71 (*Klass and Others v. Germany*), para 58.

3. When intelligence agencies and law enforcement agencies maintain their traditional functions (regardless of enhanced cooperation through sharing), the primary purpose of the investigation shall be decisive for choosing the regulatory framework.
4. If intelligence agencies explicitly have an active and direct role in gathering information in the context of an anticipative criminal investigation, the substantive goals of intelligence agencies need to be redefined. Because of the relationship between the investigative purpose and regulatory framework, the intelligence agency shall, when carrying out the anticipative criminal investigative task, be subjected to the following conditions (or be rejected): a) the intelligence agencies shall adhere to the grounds that legitimize an anticipative criminal investigation; and, b) the information produced by the intelligence agencies that becomes part of the criminal process shall be subjected to judicial scrutiny, which shall guard over the information-gathering process in furtherance of the fairness of the procedure resulting in prosecution and punishment;
5. A mandatory notification requirement shall be adopted in the regulation of anticipative criminal investigations, including circumscribed exceptions to this notification obligation;
6. Accountability for impropriety in investigative activities requires rules that provide affected persons with a remedy, either in the context of a criminal trial or in the context of civil proceedings.

### *8.5.3 Fairness*

The pillar of 'fairness' does not actually cover the regulation of anticipative criminal investigations. Nevertheless, it has here been adopted as a separate pillar, because the legitimacy of establishing an anticipative criminal investigation ultimately depends on the ability to guarantee the fairness of the entirety of the criminal proceedings. Hence, the legitimacy of the framework of an anticipative criminal investigation rests, besides the regulatory conditions of legitimization and integrity, also on the possibility to realize the fairness of subsequent trial proceedings given the conditions applicable to the investigative phase.[164]

---

[164] Of course, the information collected in the process of an anticipative criminal investigation may also be relevant in pre-trial detention hearings (see on the relation between due process and pre-trial detention: Pati 2009). The right to *habeas corpus* should entail a meaningful possibility to challenge the legitimacy of the detention. Access to evidence on which the pre-trial detention has been ordered is an important requisite for guaranteeing the right to *habeas corpus*. Moreover, in the wake of 9/11 some countries have sought recourse to incommunicado detention and control orders, implying detention based on secret evidence and sometimes suspects being even deprived of the right to *habeas corpus*. This concerns another form of the preventive use of criminal procedural law, falling outside the scope of this research project. For the compatibility of these practices with the fundamental right to *habeas corpus* see: International Commission of Jurists

The rules to be formulated under the pillar of fairness seek to provide conditions under which information collected during the anticipative criminal investigation can be introduced to criminal proceedings without undermining the guarantee of a fair trial/due process. As has followed from the explanation of the constitutive principle of due process/fair trial, these rules will therefore concern the right to the disclosure of materials relevant to truth-finding as that right is the primary step for facilitating adversarial proceedings and equality of arms. The right to disclosure under both Article 6 ECHR and US constitutional law regarding procedural due process has been understood as entailing the right to the disclosure of all material evidence for or against the accused, which imposes an obligation to disclose on the prosecution.[165]

The realization of adversarial proceedings and equality of arms depends on both parties being aware of all the evidence present, including the way in which the evidence has been obtained. Only then is the defense provided with the possibility to challenge the veracity and legitimacy of the evidence against him, which is essential in order to guarantee a fair trial.[166] In addition, the possibility to challenge the legitimacy of the investigative activities and the information collected during the criminal trial is also required in order to realize accountability when the investigative authorities have acted beyond the scope of their powers. Also for this purpose the defense shall have access to the information regarding the investigation procedure in order to be able to challenge the legitimacy of initiating criminal investigative activities and the integrity of the course of the investigation. In order to guarantee the fairness of the proceedings, a challenge resulting in a finding of illegitimate behavior or irregularities during the investigative phase, which affects the fairness of the procedure as a whole shall be compensated procedurally, for instance, by the exclusion of the evidence collected through an illegitimate criminal investigative power.

---

(Footnote 164 continued)
2009, 60 and Vervaele 2009, 106. An in-depth analysis of the right to *habeas corpus* will exceed the limits of this research project. In this project only the right to disclosure will be dealt with as one of the prerequisites for the fairness of the proceedings as a whole. These findings may also apply to the fairness of detention hearings. However, it is likely that further limitations on the right to disclosure are warranted because of the interest of continuing investigations regarding the person detained. For a detailed assessment of the use of secret evidence in terrorist detention hearings see: Barak-Erez and Waxman 2009 and, on the right to individual liberty and habeas corpus in the context of terrorism: Sottiaux 2008, 197-263.

165 ECHR 16 December 1992, App. no. 1307/87 (*Edwards v. The United Kingdom*) and *Brady v. Maryland,* 373 U.S. 83, 83 S.Ct. 1194 (1963).

166 A detailed explanation of the right to a fair trial, procedural due process and in particular the right to disclosure has already been provided in Chap. 2, Sects. 2.1.3.3 and 2.3.1.5 (the Netherlands) and Chap. 5, Sects. 5.1.4.2 and 5.3.1.3 (the United States). This section will therefore not further elaborate, beyond the aspects necessary for the contents of the current section, on the interpretation that has been given to the right to a fair trial/due process and, in particular, disclosure in the Netherlands and the United States.

One of the main characteristics of an anticipative criminal investigation is the classified character of the information underlying starting information for criminal investigations or the sources of methods themselves by which evidence is gathered, because the investigation concerns threats to national security and relies heavily on the work of (criminal) intelligence agencies. Because access to information and evidence is a prerequisite for realizing the fairness of the trial proceedings (adversarial proceedings and equality of arms) and realizing fairness through establishing accountability, the veil of secrecy surrounding parts of the investigative phase seriously complicates the effectuation of fairness. The secrecy of information which is relevant to the trial proceedings may have an adverse impact on the fairness of the proceedings in the sense of reaching the required accuracy for judgment in order to protect the innocent. Furthermore, secrecy deprives the accused of his defense right to be able to participate in the proceedings, which is an inherent aspect of the right to human dignity in protection against the powerful state. Lastly, secrecy may reduce accountability for abuses of power as it isolates the investigative practice from control, challenge and accountability.[167] In order to be able to prosecute terrorist and national security crimes states have sought recourse to restrictions on disclosure obligations. These restrictions may not undermine the realization of the constitutive principles of due process/fair trial and accountability.

Both in the US and in the European context[168] the right to disclosure is not an absolute right. The ECrtHR has taken the approach that the defendant's rights shall be weighed against the interest of protecting national security, the safety of witnesses or to keep investigative methods shielded. Possible restrictions on the right to disclosure shall be strictly necessary and require the adoption of sufficient safeguards that can guarantee a fair decision-making procedure.[169] The Court shall ascertain whether the limitations on defense rights were strictly necessary and permissible under Article 6(1), requiring a decision-making procedure that observes the requirements of adversarial proceedings and equality of arms, and has incorporated sufficient safeguards to protect the interests of the accused. The procedural safeguards must sufficiently counterbalance the handicaps for the defense in order to render the procedure fair as a whole, which, as a minimum, shall include the involvement of a judge to assess the legitimacy of the non-disclosure.[170] The adoption of the CIPA procedures in the US provides for a special procedure in order to admit classified information in criminal trials, pre-

---

[167] Barak-Erez and Waxman 2009, 31-47.

[168] The Dutch Constitution does not provide for a right to a fair trial; hence, for the interpretation of the right to disclosure as an element of the right to a fair trial, the ECrtHR's Article 6 jurisprudence is decisive for the Netherlands.

[169] See for the relevant case law and a more detailed explanation Chap. 2, Sect. 2.1.3.3.2.

[170] ECHR 16 February 2000, App. no. 28901/95 (*Rowe and Davis v. The United Kingdom*), para 63-65.

scribing that the judge shall engage in a similar balancing of interests and shall determine whether to admit the evidence as classified or to require substitutions.[171] Also the Act on shielded witnesses as applicable in the Netherlands is such a special procedure, where the examining magistrate has been attributed the task of determining the veracity of evidence where sources and methods of obtaining it remain undisclosed.

Information originating from anticipative criminal investigative activities and introduced as evidence will most likely originate from the intelligence agencies. The intelligence agencies operate in particular under the veil of secrecy and may have compelling interests to keep their sources or methods of investigation confidential. Nevertheless, also 'police intelligence' may contain information that shall remain classified in order to protect national security or witnesses or other individuals, especially in the case of prosecutions for terrorist or other national security crimes. However, the use of criminal procedural investigative powers on behalf of law enforcement agencies is embedded in a system composed of more procedural safeguards in order to guarantee the integrity of the investigative activities than applies to the intelligence community. Hence, in order to guarantee the fairness of the trial proceedings it is important that the regulation of anticipative criminal investigations includes strong procedural mechanisms regarding the integrity of the investigation. Moreover, a judicial body should be involved for the purpose of determining whether it is necessary to withhold information from the defense and whether such information may be used as evidence.[172] The involvement of a judicial body in this decision is considered an essential safeguard in both the ECHR and the US constitutional context.[173] Lastly, the essence of the defense rights shall be guaranteed by the adoption of procedural mechanisms that are capable of counterbalancing restrictions on the right to disclosure. Backed up by the impartial and independent control by a judge, the realization of effective control over the integrity of the intelligence agencies and the adoption of procedural mechanisms as alternatives to give effect to the essence of fair trial rights can then counterbalance restrictions on disclosure rights. Under these conditions, by providing for a structured approach in order to guarantee the fairness of the proceedings,[174] a reasonable and proportionate balance is achieved between the

---

[171] See in detail Chap. 5, Sect. 5.3.1.3.

[172] Compare: Report by the International Bar Association's Task Force on International Terrorism 2003, 63: "The potential dangers in the blurring of the roles of law enforcement and intelligence service underline the importance of ensuring that the judiciary retains the authority to determine the admissibility of evidence and its effect on due process guarantees."

[173] See also: Sottiaux 2008, 361-369.

[174] The aspects of fairness that touch upon evidentiary matters are not further elaborated, considering that the pillar of fairness is limited to the regulation of the criminal investigation and not the trial phase. Hence, only the aspect of disclosure is dealt with under the pillar of fairness, as the prerequisite for realizing fair trial proceedings. Such other aspects may, for example, concern the requirement of sufficient other evidence when deciding whether the products of an anticipative criminal investigation can contribute to the establishment of guilt.

interest of withholding information and the interest of the defense in having access to all information which is relevant to the case.[175]

Hence, the following conditions apply to anticipative criminal investigations in order to guarantee the fairness of the criminal procedure:

1. A strict applicability of procedural and controlling mechanisms that aim to guard over the integrity of the state agency's investigative activities;
2. The involvement of a judicial body in the decision whether or not the prosecutor may introduce information as classified evidence. This decision shall concern: the necessity of keeping the information classified; the sufficiency of procedural safeguards that counterbalance the restriction on fair trial rights; and the relevance of the information as material evidence to the case.
3. The presence of counterbalancing procedures in the trial phase intended to give effect to the essence of defense rights;
4. The availability of procedural compensation at trial when the investigative agency has acted outside the confines of the law.

## 8.6 Conclusion

On the basis of the findings of this Chapter it is possible to answer the first part of the central research question, as formulated in Chap. 1: 'Can a preventive function of criminal investigation be part of a criminal justice system under the rule of law and, if so, under what conditions?' In Sect. 8.4 it was already concluded that prevention may indeed be a function of criminal investigation under the rule of law. Subsequently, Sect. 8.5 has formulated the conditions under which this preventive function shall be implemented in the regulation of the criminal justice system under the rule of law.

The legitimization for adopting a framework for anticipative criminal investigations in order to protect citizens against terrorist attacks can be found in the nature of the terrorist crimes and the effectiveness of an anticipative criminal investigative approach. The nature of the terrorist crimes requires the adoption of a hybrid framework pursuing both preventive and evidence-gathering objectives. Moreover, from the perspective of dealing most effectively with situations such as the hypothetical dilemma drafted at the beginning of this book, a hybrid framework shall be adopted by which both prevention and evidence-gathering can be realized. Lastly, this Chapter has addressed whether attributing a preventive function as such to the criminal justice system is legitimate from an institutional perspective. Also this question was answered in the affirmative: prevention and/or evidence-gathering are functions that may be pursued by different state institutions as long as the regulation applied to the investigative activities corresponds with the

175 Ashworth 2007, 216-217.

nature of the particular purpose(s) pursued. When the preventive purpose is thus pursued parallel to evidence-gathering for prosecution purposes, the investigative activities must meet the requirements following from the constitutive principles and parameters formulated in this Chapter.

Furthermore, this section has formulated, grouped in three pillars, the specific conditions which the regulation of anticipative criminal investigations shall meet. These conditions concern the legitimization of investigative action, the integrity of the investigating process and the fairness of the criminal proceedings. On the basis of these conditions, it is possible to draw a conclusion in the next Chapter with regard to the rule of law compatibility of the regulation of anticipative criminal investigations in the Netherlands and the United States.

The formulated conditions concern the architecture of anticipative criminal investigations in the light of the current circumstances in which states seek a solution to combine prevention with the prosecution and punishment of terrorists. Therefore, the assessment made in Sect. 8.4 has a more temporal character; the arguments addressed may give rise to a different interpretation when societal circumstances have changed (the building blocks may be positioned differently). The part of the architecture that concerns the foundation and the essential building blocks—the constitutive principles and parameters—have a permanent character: these are the fundamental rights and principles attached to the rule of law that shall always regulate the criminal investigative activities of state institutions in order to guarantee the fundamental, core, right of respect for human dignity.

# Chapter 9
# Conclusions

## 9.1 Introduction

Counterterrorism measures have been widely discussed during the past decade. Assessing newly adopted methods that have affected the criminal justice system has occurred from difficult angles. Some have considered a deviation from traditional protective guarantees to be justified, because the terrorist threat concerns an emergency situation.[1] Others have used a balancing approach addressing the question whether less liberty could help us to obtain more security.[2]

In this book the approach has been adopted that measures taken to control threats such as anticipative criminal investigations cannot be considered as a response to an emergency situation, because the measures are intended to function on a more permanent basis as a safety net around terrorist threats.[3] The terrorist threat is a very serious and complex form of dangerous behavior, likely to involve criminal behavior and also posing a threat to national security, rather than a 'mere' emergency situation. Because of this 'dual' character of the terrorist threat, it requires to be dealt with from the perspective of the protection of national security and from the perspective of the criminal justice system, dealing with serious crime through prosecution and punishment. Seeking a more permanent solution for dealing with terrorism, combining preventive and truth-finding purposes in the anticipative criminal investigative enterprise is, therefore, in principle a legitimate choice.[4] The conditions for adjustments to traditional frameworks regulating the government's criminal investigative powers have been formulated in the previous chapter. These conditions go beyond the often invoked need to "balance"

---

[1] See e.g. Ackerman 2006, Posner and Vermeule 2007 and Posner 2006.
[2] Concluding negatively, e.g. Cole and Lobel 2007. Understanding the achievement of more security by trading in on civil-liberties protection under certain conditions as the 'lesser evil', Ignatieff 2005.
[3] See Sect. 8.4.1.1.
[4] See Sects. 8.4.1.3, 8.4.1.4 and 8.4.3.

M.F.H. Hirsch Ballin, *Anticipative Criminal Investigation*,
DOI: 10.1007/978-90-6704-843-9_9,

conflicting interests, i.e. the interest of protecting civil liberties against the interest of promoting security: the "balancing" approach fails to acknowledge that the protection of certain interests is non-negotiable.[5]

This book reflects a rule of law approach, based on the core fundamental human right of respect for everyone's human dignity.[6] On this basis both the need and the value of using the criminal justice system for the prevention of terrorism has to be defended, as well as the limits on using the criminal justice system for this purpose, which follow from the fundamental rule of law principles underpinning the institutional organization and the regulation of government power in the context of the criminal justice system. As has been stated by Baker: "[t]he rule of law provides for the common defense of liberty and security."[7] Applied to the criminal justice system, this means that the synthesis between so-called shield and sword objectives should be achieved.

This rule of law approach has made it possible to determine the rule of law borders of the criminal investigation without rigidly upholding standards of traditional criminal investigative regulation, whilst acknowledging the need to act in the anticipative criminal investigation of terrorist activities for preventive purposes. This has resulted in the formulation of the conditions for the regulation of *anticipative* criminal investigations in order to comply with the rule of law.

The rule of law principles, identified in Chap. 8, always underpin the regulation of the criminal investigation. Therefore, it has been possible to formulate conditions surpassing the differences between legal systems that share these principles, even if these legal systems originate in different legal traditions. Nevertheless, a state's specific legal system continues to be the determining factor for the manner in which the state gives effect to a system of anticipative criminal investigation within (or transgressing) the context of this framework.

The previous chapter has tried to provide an answer to the first part of the research question. The question *whether* a preventive function of criminal investigative activities as such can be adopted in the criminal justice system under the rule of law has been answered in the affirmative. The justification for adopting a preventive purpose of criminal investigative activities can be found in the nature of the terrorist crimes and, considering this nature, the effectiveness of confronting this threat through combining a preventive function with the gathering of information that can be used for criminal prosecution. In addition, it has also been concluded that prevention can be adopted as the purpose of criminal investigative activities, where the regulation is based on a relation between the investigative purpose and the level of protective safeguards.[8] Hence, the prevention of terrorist

[5] See Sect. 8.1.1.

[6] See Sect. 1.2.3.

[7] Baker 2007a, 31.

[8] See Sect. 1.2.6 for the distinction between (an anticipative) criminal investigation and an intelligence/national security investigation on the basis of the purpose for which the information has been *gathered.*

crimes is a legitimate sword function of the criminal justice system under the rule of law. In addition, prevention is also, from an institutional perspective, a legitimate purpose of the criminal investigation, insofar as the relation between the purpose and the level of regulation is observed. Therefore, the combination of prevention realized by intercepting dangerous behavior that may point to the initial planning of concrete terrorist attacks before they have been committed and prevention in the long term through the prosecution and punishment of terrorists makes it possible to optimize the protection of national security and to achieve justice through applying the criminal justice system.[9] Whether the regulation adopted in the Netherlands and the United States to give effect to this preventive function in the criminal justice system also meets the required level of regulation under the rule of law forms the second part of the research question.

In order to answer this second part of the research question, the previous chapter has formulated the conditions for regulating anticipative criminal investigations on the basis of three building blocks. The constitutive principles, the parameters and the flexible area of the law (the foundation, the building blocks and the chosen position of the building blocks) have provided the reason for the adoption of specific conditions which any regulation of anticipative criminal investigations shall meet under the rule of law. These conditions have been grouped in *three pillars: legitimization, integrity and fairness*. The coherence between these three pillars enables the regulation of anticipative criminal investigations reflecting the required synthesis between the shield and sword functions under the rule of law.

This chapter will provide for normative conclusions with regard to the implications of realizing anticipative criminal investigations in the Netherlands and United States as identified in Chaps. 4 and 7. These conclusions are the product of applying the conditions of the three pillars to these implications and hence concern the (im)possibility of realizing coherence between, firstly, legitimization and integrity and, secondly, fairness and integrity. The pillar of 'integrity', covering the integrity of the institutions responsible for the investigative activities, concerns the connecting thread between the pillars of legitimization and fairness: in addition to procedural guarantees regarding legitimization and fairness, the integrity of the investigating institutions needs to be guaranteed in order to realize the legitimate investigation and fair procedure in practice.

The implications addressed in Chaps. 4 and 7 are only addressed here insofar as they need to be subjected to further scrutiny in the light of the findings of Chap. 8. On that basis the final conclusions can be drawn regarding the rule of law compatibility of the approach taken in the Netherlands and the United States to regulate the anticipative criminal investigation. The entirety of the implications of the measures and developments enabling an anticipative criminal investigation in the Dutch and US criminal justice systems has already been conclusively dealt with in Chaps. 4 and 7.

---

[9] Kris 2011, 5 and 9-10.

The three pillars of regulatory conditions formulated in Chap. 8 provide for a regulatory system that reflects the synthesis between shield and sword in anticipative criminal investigations. This regulatory system provides a coherent entity of, on the one side, the legitimization of such anticipative criminal investigative activities and the integrity of the investigating agencies and, on the other side, the fairness of the criminal proceedings following an anticipative criminal investigation and the integrity of the actors responsible for the preceding anticipative criminal investigation. Not only the rules for regulating anticipative criminal investigations shall be underpinned by the rule of law principles identified as the 'common ground of the regulation of criminal investigation' (Sect. 8.3). In addition, the manner in which the rules are applied in practice shall be compatible with the rule of law principles. For this reason the integrity of the investigating agency plays a crucial role: to guarantee compatibility with the rule of law where the rules grant discretion and to guarantee that the rules are not transgressed.

On the basis of the findings of Chap. 8 and the analysis of the regulation of anticipative criminal investigations in the Netherlands and the United States as provided in Parts I and II of this book, the relevant general perspectives will be identified (under 9.2). These general perspectives will be further elaborated in the subsequent sections (under 9.3), leading to recommendations for policy and legislation. A final conclusion as to the rule of law compatibility of anticipative criminal investigations in the Netherlands and the United States will be drawn in Sect. 9.4.

## 9.2 General Perspectives

### *9.2.1 Legitimization and Integrity*

The pillar of the 'legitimizing' conditions concerns the required procedural legitimization for initiating criminal investigative activities and, within that context, specifically the required legitimization for using special investigative techniques.[10] The integrity of the state institution responsible for the anticipative criminal investigation is realized under the second pillar through a combination of minimization mechanisms, controlling mechanisms and the availability of a remedy, intended to guarantee, through a structured approach, that the investigating agencies observe the procedural limits of legitimization.[11] Evaluating the regulation of anticipative criminal investigations in the Netherlands and the United States on the basis of these conditions concerning legitimization and integrity provides a reason for the following general perspectives, which will be further elaborated in Sect. 9.3.

---

[10] See Sect. 8.5.1.

[11] See Sect. 8.5.2.

In the regulation of (an anticipative) criminal investigation in the Netherlands the legitimizing grounds are insufficiently related to the specific *criminal* investigative purpose. This is important, because weaker legitimizing grounds are only sufficient for the specific investigative purpose for which these grounds have been adopted. The justification of adopting a lower threshold of application only appears when this lower threshold is exclusively used for the investigative purpose of evidence-gathering *and* preventing terrorism, whereas a stricter threshold is required for the criminal investigation of criminal behavior that does not justify preventive action. On the basis of an explicated relation between legitimizing grounds and investigative purpose, also the procedural mechanisms that are intended to guarantee the integrity of the investigative action can be used to limit the investigation to the legitimized scope.[12] In that way the risk that the anticipative criminal investigation will transgress rule of law limitations can be reduced.

In the United States the realization of an anticipative criminal investigation is characterized by two parallel developments. Firstly, in conventional criminal law a risk has been identified that through focusing on the Fourth Amendment ultimate touchstone of reasonableness the legitimizing grounds for *criminal* investigative activities are insufficiently observed (Sect. 7.2.2.2). Secondly, fitting within the development regarding Fourth Amendment interpretation in conventional criminal law, the relation between legitimization and the investigative purpose has been abandoned. Consequently, the FISA framework has obtained the status of a quasi-law enforcement framework, resulting in general, broad, investigative powers[13] that can be applied with wide discretion for the purpose of gathering evidence, for the purpose of protecting national security or, most likely, for both purposes. By using intrusive investigative techniques under FISA, a nexus between the persons under investigation and criminal activities is (logically) not required. This second development has been compensated through adopting a variety of procedural mechanisms that should guarantee an incorruptible institutional culture. At the same time, judicial overview, an important 'integrity guarantee' in US criminal investigations, is considerably reduced.[14] However, the *absence* of the required legitimization for *criminal* investigative activities cannot be compensated by increased procedural mechanisms to guarantee the integrity of the investigation. This would violate the constitutive principles of the presumption of innocence and the right to respect for one's private life.[15]

In comparison it can be observed that the relation between investigative purpose and legitimizing grounds as the dividing line between intelligence investigations and criminal investigations continues to be in force in the Netherlands but has been abandoned in the United States. Nevertheless, also in the Netherlands insufficient attention is attributed to the crucial relation between the required

---

[12] Compare Sect. 8.4.3.

[13] For an explanation of the nature of the specific powers see Sect. 7.3.

[14] See Sect. 7.2.3.

[15] See Sects. 8.3.1.1, 8.3.1.2 and 8.5.1.

legitimizing grounds and the specific investigative purpose within the context of the entire legal framework concerning the criminal investigative phase (under Article 132a CCP and also including the preliminary investigation).

On this basis a second comparative observation can be made. Because of the continued role of requiring a certain legitimization for *criminal* investigative activities, integrity guarantees applicable to the anticipative criminal investigation in the Netherlands have not been adjusted. In the United States, the broad investigative power and discretion has been compensated through a variety of enhanced integrity measures. This difference in approach may be explained by differences in the relation between the government and the citizens, as it has traditionally been understood in the Netherlands and in the United States. In the Netherlands, attributing the government powers in the field of criminal procedural law is strictly based upon the principle of legality: the legitimizing grounds for criminal investigative activities shall be provided in the law. In the United States, citizens harbor distrust with regard to a very powerful government interfering with its citizens' individual liberties. For this reason, the United States particularly focuses on mechanisms that shall protect against any governmental abuse of power. In addition, this distrust has been nourished by scandals in the 1960s and 70s involving abuses of the government's investigative power in order to discredit political opponents and activists, most notably, the Watergate scandal.

### *9.2.2 Fairness and Integrity*

The fairness conditions formulated apply to the information collected during the anticipative criminal investigation and introduced in criminal proceedings in order to guarantee a fair criminal procedure.[16] The integrity of the state institutions responsible for the gathering of information during the anticipative criminal investigation is in particular important when the criminal proceedings are dealing with the secretive products of the anticipative criminal investigation. The general perspectives provided below include recommendations in order to guarantee the fairness of the criminal process when involving information gathered in the anticipative criminal investigation. These recommendations will be further elaborated in Sects. 9.3.3 and 9.3.4.

On the basis of the analysis in Parts I and II, I have concluded that the Netherlands as well as the United States have been confronted with an 'infected criminal process' as a consequence of enabling anticipative criminal investigations.[17] These 'infections', however, have different underlying causes. In the Netherlands the infection follows from the 'preparatory investigative activities' of the anticipative criminal investigation conducted by the AIVD or CIE and from the

[16] See Sect. 8.5.3.

[17] See Sects. 4.3.4.3 and 7.4.3.

increased potential of AIVD influence during parallel investigations when the object of the investigation has attracted the shared interest of the AIVD, the PPS and the police. Consequently, criminal trials deal with a pre-trial phase containing secret elements and evidence originating from shielded sources and through shielded methods. In the United States, the infection follows directly from the manner in which evidence is gathered. Evidence in terrorism investigations is primarily (or maybe even exclusively) gathered by means of 'intelligence tools,' such as FISA surveillance, document production orders and national security letters.[18]

Dealing with this 'infected' criminal process, Dutch courts have strongly focused on the assumed integrity of intelligence agencies, warranted by the presence of procedural mechanisms that should guarantee the integrity of the intelligence service. As explained in Sect. 4.3.4.3, this 'basis of trust' is in many situations warranted. However, in order to guarantee control over the pre-trial phase courts should be careful not to exclude the exertion of control on the basis of an old-fashioned vision of the criminal investigative phase, leaving aside the reality of the anticipative criminal investigation. Integrity guarantees, such as internal supervisory mechanisms and parliamentary oversight, may warrant a more marginal examination of activities conducted for the purpose of intelligence gathering, but shall not bar any form of control over the legitimacy of pre-trial activities when these activities are *also* relevant for the anticipative criminal investigation.

The CIPA procedures that can be applied in criminal trials before US courts already provided for a solution regarding, although more limited, the exertion of control over the use of classified materials. However, especially in the criminal trials of terrorists, where basically all evidence has been obtained under the veil of secrecy which is applicable to national security investigations, the reality of the anticipative criminal investigation conflicts with criminal procedural fairness guarantees. In general, the impact of classified materials on the fairness of the proceedings is, as a consequence of the particular character of the anticipative criminal investigation in the US, considerably larger than in the Netherlands. Furthermore, courts confronted with evidence gathered under the FISA framework do not exert control with a view to realizing due process, but control the observance of the statutory requirements from the perspective of the FISA context: *in camera* and *ex parte* inspections of the affidavits in order to determine whether or not the order was clearly erroneous. In this way, control over the methods by which evidence has been gathered is excluded, which also touches upon the possibilities to challenge the evidentiary value of the materials gathered.

The difference in the underlying causes of the 'infected criminal process' and the manner in which 'shielded' investigative elements are dealt with, result in two

---

[18] Evidence directly gathered through the FISA framework or information gathered through typical intelligence tools, such as national security letters, may become part of criminal proceedings as a consequence of sharing obligations between, *inter alia*, the intelligence entities and federal prosecutors. See Sect. 7.4.3.

different recommendations in order to improve the realization of fair criminal proceedings. For the Netherlands, the complete bar on control over the investigative activities that have influenced the anticipative criminal investigation should be lifted in order to enable at least a marginal form of examination. A subtle adjustment regarding the approach taken by trial judges will be able to create the necessary 'spy holes' to control the integrity of the relevant activities of the intelligence agencies. These spy holes can be created through acknowledging the reality of the broad concept of 'anticipative criminal investigation'[19] when exerting control under Article 359a CCP through the procedure created by the Act on Shielded Witnesses.

The solution for establishing sufficient fairness guarantees during criminal trials following an anticipative criminal investigation in the United States shall not, in the first place, be sought in adjustments during the trial phase. The CIPA procedures themselves concern a procedural mechanism that is capable of enabling sufficient control over *some* shielded elements of the investigation. However, CIPA does not (yet) offer a solution in order to establish sufficient control over the most probable method of evidence gathering in the anticipative criminal investigation, namely under the FISA framework. Hence, the manner in which evidence is gathered in terrorist cases must be adjusted in order to reduce the veil of secrecy surrounding the anticipative criminal investigation. This can be realized by taking into account the observations made in the previous section. In the second place, when upholding the possibility to gather evidence through the FISA framework, courts confronted with the evidence gathered under FISA shall exert control on the basis of criminal procedural law principles, which is possible under the applicability of CIPA, and not exclusively through a 'national security law approach'.

## 9.3 Regulating Anticipative Criminal Investigations Under the Rule of Law: Conclusions and Recommendations

### *9.3.1 The Netherlands: Legitimization and Integrity*

#### 9.3.1.1 Relation Between Legitimizing Grounds and the Purpose of the Criminal Investigation

In the statutory regulation of SIT in the CCP, the purpose of the investigation is related to the required level of legitimization for initiating criminal investigative activities. This purpose of the investigation is related to the crimes under investigation; the making of prosecutorial decisions regarding the specific crimes under investigation; and, for terrorist crimes, additionally, the purpose of preventing

[19] For an explanation on this 'broad' concept of anticipative criminal investigation as opposed to the narrower interpretation on the basis of Article 132a CCP, see Sect. 4.3.3.

terrorist crimes.[20] In Sect. 8.4.1.3 the purpose of the investigation has been related to the nature of the terrorist crimes: because of the nature of the terrorist crime, prevention may be a legitimate purpose of the criminal investigation. In addition, the nature of a specific interference shall be related to additional protective safeguards. When the nature of the interference, considering the method used, is more intrusive, the statutory system provides for additional procedural safeguards.[21] The legitimization for initiating criminal investigations for a specific purpose (related to the crimes under investigation) with the help of SIT or search methods, however, remains the same.

This connection between the required legitimization and the specific purpose of the investigation is currently insufficiently recognized in the Netherlands.[22] The connection between the purpose of the investigation and the applicable procedural framework is not only important in order to distinguish intelligence investigation or administrative control from the criminal investigation, but also plays an important role within the context of a criminal investigation as such. The required legitimization within the entire concept of a criminal investigation (under Article 132a CCP and also including the preliminary investigation) is dependent on the specific purpose of the criminal investigation.

The lack of sufficient attention for this relation between the investigative purpose and the required legitimization has resulted in the stretching of the reasonable suspicion threshold, in order to be able to pursue multiple investigative purposes in the context of the classical investigation involving crimes with a differing nature. For example, the classical investigative domain is also used to pursue preventive investigative purposes upon the establishment of a reasonable suspicion of a terrorist crime.[23] This may be justified considering the specific circumstances of the case. However, as a consequence, the legitimization fades for investigative action where terrorist crimes or organized crime are not involved. Especially in order to enable the possibility to investigate for the purpose of prevention when a terrorist threat is involved, the legislature has created the possibility to act upon a weaker legitimization. Hence, a substantiated choice for a specific investigative domain, including the specific purpose of the investigation, strengthens the legitimization of specific investigative action for that purpose. This applies to the distinction between the investigative domains of classical investigation, organized crime investigation and terrorist crime investigation as well as to the distinction between a preliminary investigation and the (full) investigation in the context of one of these three domains.

Moreover, when the connection between the purpose of the investigation and the required level of legitimization is acknowledged and recognized in practice,

---

[20] See Sect. 4.2.1.2.

[21] Section 4.2.1.2.

[22] As concluded in Sect. 4.2.2.2.

[23] See Sect. 4.2.2.2. The classical investigative domain is also often used to pursue the proactive investigative purpose for targeting organized crime. See Sect. 2.3.2.3.2.2.

also the argument that the Act on the Criminal Investigation of Terrorist Crimes violates Article 8 ECHR and the principles of proportionality and subsidiarity, because of a lack of necessity, shall be rejected.[24] The Act on the criminal investigation of terrorist crimes does not violate the principle of necessity, considering that the *ultimum remedium* character of the criminal justice system is only upheld when, under the investigative domain for terrorist crimes, the purposes of prevention *and* evidence-gathering may be pursued.[25]

#### 9.3.1.2 Relating Legitimization to Integrity: Proportionality and the Legitimized Scope and Purpose

##### 9.3.1.2.1 The Legitimized Scope and Purpose

The main legislative change that has facilitated anticipative criminal investigations in the Netherlands exactly touches upon the legitimization of anticipative criminal investigative activities. The use of special investigative techniques and search methods is possible on the basis of 'indications of a terrorist crime', in order to enable the use of these investigative powers for the prevention of terrorism *and* truth-finding.

In order to be necessary and proportionate the investigative activities must have sufficient focus, which means that the legitimizing grounds must be sufficiently clear in order to reduce the investigative activities to identifiable (groups of) persons. In Sect. 2.3.2.3 it has been explained that the reasonable suspicion threshold in the classical investigative domain or organized crime investigative domain shall concern the crime and not a specific person. Furthermore, it must be possible to relate the persons investigated to that specific crime or to the serious crimes that are being planned or committed in an organized context. This is no different for the indications threshold. The difference with the reasonable suspicion threshold concerns the vaguer or softer information regarding a terrorist crime that may provide the legitimizing ground. The persons investigated on that basis shall still be related to that crime. Nevertheless, when applying the threshold in practice, it may be more difficult to relate specific persons or a group of persons to vaguer and softer information regarding a crime.

The decisive consideration for deciding whether the indications threshold is met concerns the 'interest of the investigation', or, in other words, whether

[24] The supposed lack of necessity has followed from the very limited use of the adopted legislation in practice and the sufficiency of the already existing investigative possibilities (using the classical investigative domain to prevent terrorism, because soft information has been accepted to establish a reasonable suspicion of crimes, including 'preparatory terrorist crimes'). When necessity is absent, the regulation of the investigative domain for terrorist crimes would also violate Article 8 ECHR and the principles of proportionality and subsidiarity. See Sect. 4.2.4.

[25] Section 8.3.2.3.

investigative action can, in the light of the information available, contribute to the prevention of terrorism.[26] Placing the prevention of terrorism at the forefront when deciding whether or not the information available provides sufficient legitimizing grounds for criminal investigative activities involves a risk that the threshold is stretched towards an impermissible scope.[27]

As explained, weaker legitimizing grounds, and thus an investigation with a broader scope, shall be restricted to the criminal investigation of crimes for which preventive action is justified, which are crimes that pose a threat to national security.[28] The procedural regulation of criminal investigative activities for the purpose of prevention provides for a threshold of 'indications of a *terrorist crime.*' Article 83 Penal Code lists the offenses that can be identified as terrorist crimes. One may discuss whether all these crimes also separately pose a threat to national security. Nevertheless, also the investigation of preparatory acts of larger terrorist crimes contributes to the prevention of these larger terrorist crimes and, hence, contributes to the protection of national security. In addition, offenses that are minor in themselves and which cannot be related to larger terrorist crimes also touch upon—because these offenses are committed with a terrorist intent—the essential aspects of the undisturbed functioning of the democratic state under the rule of law. The phenomenon of terrorism as such and, hence, any offenses committed with a terrorist intent, including those that do not directly threaten national security, concerns a threat to the essential aspects of the democratic state under the rule of law. The protection of national security involves the protection of these essential aspects of the democratic state under the rule of law. For that reason, the limitative enumeration of terrorist crimes in the Penal Code restricts the preventive use of SIT and search methods to investigating terrorist activities.

On paper, the threshold of indications to be used for the purpose of prevention and evidence gathering concerning terrorist crimes reflects the synthesis between shield and sword in the special circumstances of the anticipative criminal investigation. However, because preventing terrorism is the decisive consideration, there is a risk that the threshold is stretched towards an impermissible scope in practice. At this moment in time, there is insufficient clarity as to how the scope of the indications threshold shall be understood. Until now, this has resulted in reluctance concerning the use of the investigative domain for terrorist crimes.[29] When used, the information establishing the 'indications' seemed to be in conformity with the conditions of the rule of law. Also in comparison with the interpretation of the reasonable suspicion threshold, the scope of the terrorist crime investigation shall be limited to the investigation of persons who can be related to the, although weaker, information regarding a terrorist crime.[30]

---

[26] See Sect. 4.2.1.2.

[27] Compare Sects. 4.2.2.2 and 8.4.1.2.

[28] Section 8.5.1.

[29] See Sect. 4.2.2.2.

[30] See Sect. 4.2.1.2.

Nevertheless, to avoid the situation where the indications threshold will in the future be stretched into directions which are incompatible with the rule of law, judicial interpretation (which is currently still lacking), taking into account the legitimized scope and purpose, would be desirable.[31] In addition, it would be desirable for the PPS to formulate guidelines for the interpretation of the indications threshold. These guidelines should promulgate that the investigative domain for terrorist crimes can and shall be used, when needed, for the prevention of terrorism. Consequently, also the PPS and the police may start to feel more comfortable in using the investigative domain for terrorist crimes when the investigation deals with situations for which this investigative domain has been created.

In Sect. 4.2.1.2 the conclusion has been drawn that the indications threshold functions as a last resort, when a reasonable suspicion cannot be established. This shall *not* be the criterion for using the investigative domain for terrorist crimes. Rather, also in situations where it may be possible to establish a reasonable suspicion,[32] but the purpose of the investigation corresponds with the purpose of the investigative domain for terrorist crimes, a choice shall be made for the investigative domain for terrorist crimes. The situations described in Sect. 4.2.1.2 where the investigative domain could be used did not exclusively include situations where a reasonable suspicion cannot be established. Nevertheless, acting in these situations within the context of the investigative domain for terrorist crimes reflects the goal of the amendment of contributing to preventing terrorism. Therefore, the indications threshold shall not only be considered as a 'last resort,'[33] but primarily as a threshold that allows an investigation for the prevention of terrorism. When the investigative possibilities in relation to the permitted specific investigative purposes of the separate investigative domains are more clearly promulgated through guidelines, the use of the investigative domain for terrorist crimes for the purpose of preventing terrorism, combined with

[31] This would require an approach from the judiciary which is different from the current interpretation of the reasonable suspicion threshold (applicable in the classical investigation and the organized crime investigation) that is currently the leading approach in the case law, which has contributed to stretching the reasonable suspicion threshold so as to use it for purposes other than those for which the criminal investigative domain has been intended.

[32] Which is partly a consequence of the fact that the reasonable suspicion threshold has been stretched to pursue criminal investigative purposes that are actually attributed to specific investigative domains (the investigative domains for organized crime and for terrorist crimes).

[33] When, in the past, also the relation between the investigative purpose and the legitimized grounds had been accurately observed, the investigative domain for terrorist crimes would become a last resort: only for the investigation of terrorism is preventive action a necessity and, hence, also relying on the investigative domain for terrorist crime will become a necessity. However, because the reasonable suspicion threshold has been widely interpreted in the case law without restricting it specifically to the classical investigative domain or the investigative domain for organized crime, changing investigative policy as suggested would mean that the investigative domain for terrorist crime is not used as a 'last resort', which is currently the leading view in the field.

truth-finding, could be encouraged. This would avoid the further stretching of the reasonable suspicion threshold which is applicable to the classical investigative domain and more clearly demarcate the borders as well as the possibilities of specific investigative domains.

Furthermore, these guidelines by the PPS shall promulgate that the use of SIT or search methods within this investigative domain is limited to persons and/or organizations that can be identified as having a nexus with the terrorist crimes under investigation. The principle of proportionality shall be used to minimize the scope of the investigation to this specific legitimized scope and, thus, will avoid the stretching of the threshold to an impermissible scope. The use of 'proportionality' for this minimizing purpose will be addressed in the following sub-section.

#### 9.3.1.2.2 Proportionality as a Minimization Mechanism

Especially in the context of the regulation of anticipative criminal investigations, proportionality should be an important restrictive element. Proportionality[34] is in the context of the terrorist crime investigation strongly related to the legitimizing grounds: the information available shall be sufficiently concrete to foresee that the SIT sought to be used can contribute to preventing terrorism. In fact, the statutory requirement of being 'in the interest of the investigation' (reflecting a proportionality assessment) has a stronger regulatory influence limiting the scope of the investigation than the indications threshold.[35]

Also in the light of Article 8 ECHR other procedural conditions may compensate for a low threshold of application (legitimizing ground). The weaker legitimization of the indications threshold as introduced by the Act on the criminal investigation of terrorist crimes has not been accompanied with other procedural safeguards. Hence, the same procedural safeguards that apply to the other investigative domains shall be able to sufficiently minimize the scope of the criminal investigation of terrorist crimes. In Sect. 4.2.1.2.1.1 the conclusion has been drawn that especially the requirement of the 'interest of the investigation' and, hence, in fact the proportionality assessment, further tailors the scope provided by the legitimizing grounds in a specific case.

---

[34] For the (potential) regulatory role of the principle of proportionality in the criminal investigation, see Sects. 2.1.3.4.1 (as a principle of good governance), 2.3.1.1 (regulating police activities), 2.3.1.2 (regulating the activities of the PPS), 2.3.2.3.2.5 (as a statutory requirement in the regulation of SIT) and 2.3.2.1.1 (implied in the restrictive clause of Article 8 ECHR). Also the investigative activities of the AIVD are subjected to the principle of proportionality (and the principle of subsidiarity), as included in the WIV 2002 (Article 32). See Sect. 2.2.2.4.1. However, the investigative activities of the AIVD are, by definition, not included in the concept of anticipative criminal investigation.

[35] See Sect. 4.2.1.2.

However, partly under the influence of the growing social anxiety concerning insecurity and criminality, courts have granted investigative officers more discretion, using the principles of proportionality and subsidiarity, instead of protective, limiting, principles, primarily as principles that can also justify more investigative discretion when acting to prevent terrorism or to investigate serious crime in general. Hence, control over the observance of the principles of proportionality and subsidiarity is limited, which offers the investigative officers and the PPS more discretion. In addition, also investigative officers and the public prosecutor supervising the criminal investigation will be inclined to attach decisive weight to the interest of preventing terrorism in the proportionality assessment.[36]

Proportionality and subsidiarity are typically assessed on the basis of the information establishing indications in relation to the nature of the interference.[37] Consequently, it is likely that there will be a focus on the need for investigative action in order to exclude risks. As explained in the previous section, in the statutory system regulating SIT, the legitimizing grounds are specifically related to the purpose of the investigation, while the additional procedural safeguards shall be related to the nature of the interference. The government has used the latter in order to explain that additional procedural guarantees shall not be adopted in the regulation of the investigative domain for terrorist crimes. However, not only the nature of the technique as such shall be assessed. In addition, it is required to assess the possibility to limit the investigation to the legitimized scope and purpose, because also these factors contribute to the totality of the implications for the right of the persons concerned to have their private lives respected.

Because other minimizing procedural safeguards are absent and the legitimizing grounds are comparably weak, the (statutory) proportionality requirement obtains significant value. The proportionality requirement is adopted as a statutory requirement in the regulation of SIT and shall be observed by the public prosecutor and, for the most intrusive techniques, also the examining magistrate. Considering that proportionality is currently often explained as an argument to attach more value to the interest of preventing terrorism than to the interest of legal protection, the actual restrictive function of the principle should receive renewed attention. If the principle of proportionality is not used (exclusively) to justify more investigative discretion to benefit the prevention of terrorism, but also explicitly as a requirement to be met *before* using SIT under Title Vb, relating the information available to the use of a specific technique and the scope of the investigation, proportionality is able to function as a minimization mechanism. In this regard it is important to note that proportionality is not only a principle of the due administration of justice, but also a statutory requirement, warranting strict control by the public prosecutor, the examining magistrate and the trial judge on the observance of the principle. This, then, not only concerns the proportionality of the investigative action as such, considering the information available, but also the

[36] Sections. 4.2.1.2.1.1 and 4.2.3.1.

[37] Section 4.2.1.3.1.1.

proportionality of specific investigative action considering the information available and taking into account the scope of the investigation.

Also from the perspective of the requirements set by the ECrtHR in the light of Article 8(2) ECHR, involving the legitimized scope and purpose of the investigation in the proportionality assessment will contribute to compatibility with Article 8 ECHR.[38] As explained in Sect. 4.2.1.3.1.1, compatibility with Article 8 ECHR largely depends on the manner in which the procedural requirements are construed in practice. The previous section has signaled that considering the statutory system and considering the intention of the legislature in creating the investigative domain for terrorist crimes, the threshold of indications meets the rules formulated under the pillar of legitimization. Nevertheless, in order to reduce the risk that the scope of the investigation is in practice construed in a manner which exceeds these limits regarding the justified legitimization, the proportionality requirement has obtained significant meaning in the procedural regulation of Title Vb. If the statutory requirement of being 'in the interest of the investigation' is connected to the legitimized scope (only those persons or groups of persons that can be related to the present indications of a terrorist crime) and to the legitimized purpose (prevention and evidence gathering), the minimization achieved through the statutory proportionality requirement can guarantee that the anticipative criminal investigation is also conducted within the confines of the rule of law.

Furthermore, in Sect. 4.2.1.3.2 it was concluded that the regulation of Title Vb meets *in abstracto* the requirement of 'necessary in a democratic society'. However, because of the theoretical breadth of the legitimizing grounds and the related interpretation of the other procedural safeguards, there is a risk that the Act will be construed in a manner which lacks the focus required in order to render the investigative activities necessary to pursue the legitimate aim. Again, this is a reason, firstly, to explicitly relate the legitimization grounds to the specific purpose of the investigation and, secondly, to relate the proportionality assessment particularly to the legitimized scope and purpose in order to guarantee that it fulfills its important role as a minimization mechanism.

#### 9.3.1.2.3 Search Methods in Terrorist Crime Investigations

The situation is slightly different for the use of search methods in security zones. Because no order by the public prosecutor is required before investigative officers may apply investigative powers in security zones, the legitimizing ground (the presence of that person in a particular area labeled as a security zone by an administrative decree) does not relate the person searched to an actual crime that threatens national security. Rather, it relates all persons present in that area (in fact

[38] Compare ECHR 2 August 1984, App. no. 8691/79 (*Malone v. The United Kingdom*), para 68, see also Sect. 4.2.1.3.1.1.

a specific group of persons) to a place at a larger risk of terrorism attacks than other places.

Hence, it is difficult to uphold that the group of persons that qualify to be searched because of their presence in a security zone can be related to a terrorist crime. In the absence of a concrete current threat the nexus between these persons and a crime that threatens national security is insufficient. Also requiring an order by the public prosecutor in security zones before search methods may be applied against anyone present in that zone could restore this deficit. Urgent situations must be excluded from this requirement when the investigative officer present in the security zone cannot await the order of the public prosecutor in order to avert an urgent threat.[39] Additionally, in such an urgent situation a choice could be made for an *ex post* order from the public prosecutor.

Also proportionality is less strongly guaranteed for search methods, because the proportionality assessment does not require the involvement of the public prosecutor and is left to the discretion of the investigative officers. This applies especially to the use of search powers in security zones, where the public prosecutor is not involved at all. Because of the less strongly guaranteed proportionality requirement, the minimization achieved by the requirement of being 'in the interest of the investigation' is not capable of compensating the basically absent legitimizing grounds for search powers in security zones.[40] Amending the regulation for using search methods to include, similar to the use of search powers in security zones regulated in the Weapons and Ammunition Act, an order by the public prosecutor will provide for a stronger guarantee that the required legitimization is present within a particular time span.

#### 9.3.1.2.4 Preliminary Investigation of Terrorist Activities

The threshold which is applicable in the preliminary investigation[41] provides, in comparison to the indications threshold of Title Vb, for weaker legitimizing grounds, considering that the object of the indications threshold is not a specific terrorist crime, but a group of people in order to determine whether persons in that group can be related to indications of a specific terrorist crime. This also applies to preliminary investigative activities in preparation for the organized crime investigation, which was already in force prior to the adoption of the Act on the criminal investigation of terrorist crimes.

[39] As explained in Sect. 8.4.1.2: on an ad hoc basis situations of urgency may continue to justify an exception to the regular procedural framework.

[40] Compare the conclusion drawn in Sect. 4.2.1.3.1.3 that it is uncertain whether the regulation of the use of search methods under Title Vb can withstand an examination on the basis of the requirements of Article 8 ECHR.

[41] The preliminary investigation shall be considered as part of the entire concept of criminal investigation. See Sect. 2.3.2.2.4.

The legitimization for preliminary investigative activities is very weak. The nexus between the group investigated and the terrorist crime is indirect and the group investigated cannot be precisely determined. Only because persons are considered to be taking part in a specific group, while this group is, for example, known to be sensitive to radicalization and, thus, terrorist crimes, may they be included in preliminary investigative activities.[42] This involves a considerable risk that persons are arbitrarily and unnecessarily subjected to preliminary investigative activities.

At the same time it must be acknowledged that in the preliminary investigation only investigative methods may be applied that interfere, to a limited extent, with the privacy rights of the persons concerned. SIT or search methods cannot be applied upon the legitimizing standard for preliminary investigative activities only. In addition, the information collected has already been stored for other purposes and, hence, obtaining the information does not involve a new privacy intrusion. Nevertheless, obtaining information from sources where this information has not been stored for law enforcement purposes (from third parties) in order to analyze it for criminal investigative purposes does interfere with privacy rights. Considering that the privacy intrusion primarily follows from the fact that the information will be used for criminal law enforcement purposes, while collected and stored for other purposes, especially one of the newly introduced powers in the context of the preliminary investigation of terrorist crimes (Article 126hh CCP) gives reason for concern because of the weak legitimization and the privacy intrusion following from the ordering of personal data to be made available from third party automated information files. At the same time, the use of the technique of Article 126hh CCP is compensated by various procedural mechanisms, intended to guarantee the integrity of the collection of information, most notably, through minimization. The maybe otherwise insufficient legitimizing ground of the preliminary investigative power of Article 126hh CCP has been sufficiently counterbalanced by adopting strict minimization procedures through an automated filtering system, which is applicable in addition to the proportionality requirement. This automated minimization has particularly been adopted to guarantee that the technique is only applied for the legitimized purpose and scope.[43] In addition, it must be noted that the preliminary investigative technique of Article 126hh CCP has never been used in practice.

[42] For an explanation of the threshold of application in the preliminary investigation see Sects. 2.3.2.3.2.3 and 3.2.1.2.

[43] In Sect. 4.2.1.3.2 it was already concluded that the adopted minimization procedures in combination with the required authorization of the examining magistrate also make this relatively more intrusive preliminary investigative technique compatible with Article 8 ECHR, because the minimization procedures are able to limit the scope of the preliminary investigation to its legitimate aim, and thus makes it foreseeable to the persons concerned.

### 9.3.1.3 Control over the Legitimized Scope and Purpose

Making the relation between the required legitimization and the specific criminal investigative purpose explicit and also explaining the proportionality requirement of being 'in the interest of the investigation' in the light of the specific legitimized scope and purpose of the investigation also enable more transparent control over the anticipative criminal investigation.

The adoption of the investigative domain for terrorist crimes has not been accompanied with strengthened *ex ante* judicial control.[44] The central controlling role during the (anticipative) criminal investigation is attributed to the public prosecutor. The public prosecutor is confronted with the dilemma whether to risk subjecting possibly innocent persons to criminal investigative powers or to risk not averting a terrorist threat in time when receiving vague information involving such a threat. In addition, the controlling abilities of the public prosecutor with regard to the power to apply search methods in security zones have been reduced. Furthermore, the judiciary exerting control *ex post* has, as a consequence of the political and societal circumstances of the past decade, with a focus on security and the prevention of crime and threats, generally provided investigative officers with more discretion in their criminal investigative efforts. The principle of proportionality has been used to justify more discretion when the aforementioned interests are involved and the controlling scheme of Article 359a CCP is applied less strictly when the investigative officers have been dealing with serious crime or the prevention of terrorism.[45]

Hence, the anticipative criminal investigation has not left the controlling mechanisms for the criminal investigation unaffected. Especially the balance between the different actors with responsibility towards guaranteeing the fairness of the criminal process has been affected. As concluded in Sect. 4.2.4: investigative officers have been granted wide discretion to do what is necessary to prevent terrorism, whereas the controlling roles of the examining magistrate and the trial judge have been watered down, both as a consequence of the difficulty in exerting control on the basis of criteria affording wide discretion and as a consequence of the developments where security interests outweigh legal protective interests.[46]

At the same time it must be observed, as has followed from the empirical research into the Act on the Criminal investigation of terrorist crimes, that is seems that the public prosecutors have taken their central role as a controlling authority seriously. They seem to make a careful assessment of the interests involved, considering that the discretion offered to apply a variety of investigative powers is

---

[44] This does not apply to the newly adopted preliminary investigative technique of Article 126hh CCP, for which the authorization of the examining magistrate is required (unlike the other preliminary investigative techniques).

[45] See for an explanation of these findings Sect. 4.2.3.3.

[46] Section 4.2.4.

used restrictively when the information available is less concrete, by using less intrusive methods in order to exclude risks.[47]

Nevertheless, this reluctance among public prosecutors seems to follow primarily from uncertainty regarding the investigative possibilities as well as the limits on the investigative domain for terrorist crimes. Making the relation between the required legitimization and the specific criminal investigative purpose explicit and also explaining the proportionality requirement of being 'in the interest of the investigation' in the light of the specific legitimized scope and purpose of the investigation will also enable more transparent control over the anticipative criminal investigation. The public prosecutor and, for the more intrusive techniques,[48] the examining magistrate shall exert control over the use of the proportionality requirement in the recommended restrictive manner. The proportionality requirement then obtains an important protective role.

This cannot, however, be easily achieved. Exactly because proportionality as such provides a large margin of appreciation as to how to balance different interests in a particular case,[49] it cannot be said that proportionality is a very strong procedural guarantee. Hence, it would be desirable that the statutory requirement of being 'the interest of the investigation' will be further defined. Without depriving it of the required openness in order to deal with different situations, the connection between 'in the interest of the investigation' and the required legitimization needs to be made. This could be done in prosecutorial guidelines and in the case law. Such an approach would limit the anticipative criminal investigative phase to its legitimized scope and purpose and create the required transparency concerning its limitations to guarantee effective control. The protection of the right to respect for one's private life required in the criminal investigation, the presumption of innocence and the principles of proportionality and necessity are then sufficiently guaranteed also with regard to the manner in which the procedural guarantees are construed in practice.

#### 9.3.1.4 Some Comments on Notification

Including a requirement of notification in the regulation of anticipative criminal investigations is a prerequisite for guaranteeing the availability of a remedy. Because the persons involved in the anticipative criminal investigation will often not be prosecuted, the notification requirement is particularly important in order to provide an effective remedy and to realize the fundamental right to accountability,

---

[47] See Sect. 4.2.3.2.

[48] In particular for the more intrusive investigative techniques, prior judicial control is preferred, or in the light of the recent ECrtHR judgment in *Sanoma Uitgevers B.V. v. The Netherlands* (ECHR 12 September 2010, App. no. 38224/03) it may even be required. This prior judicial control through a warrant by the examining magistrate is in the Dutch regulation included for more intrusive techniques. Compare Sect. 8.5.2.2.

[49] Compare the rejection of a mere balancing approach in Chap. 8, Sect. 8.1.1.1.

through judicial review, once someone's individual liberty has been violated.[50] The applicability of the notification requirement has not been affected as a consequence of legislative measures enabling an anticipative criminal investigation. Article 126aa CCP requires records to be compiled and disclosure when the persons subjected to the criminal investigation are prosecuted. Article 126bb CCP provides for a mandatory requirement of notification to persons who are not subsequently prosecuted. An exception to notification is provided when the interest of the investigation (of the criminal investigation in question or of other criminal investigations) is adversely affected through notification.[51]

Currently, illegitimate actions that have occurred in the pre-trial phase are restrictively sanctioned in the context of trial proceedings. Proportionality is often used as an argument to avoid the procedural sanctioning of illegitimate conduct during the investigative phase. Also a violation of Article 8 ECHR is not necessarily remedied in the context of the trial proceedings, because sanctions only follow when an impairment of the right to a fair trial can be rectified through the procedural sanction. Nevertheless, this does not exclude the person in question from seeking remedies in the context of civil proceedings or before the National Ombudsman, which also concerns an effective remedy under Article 13 ECHR.[52] Hence, it can be concluded that, upon the observance of the notification requirement, persons subjected to investigative powers are provided with a remedy either in the context of trial proceedings or, if this is unsatisfactory or inapplicable, in civil proceedings or before the National Ombudsman.

In *Kruslin/Huvig v. France* the ECrtHR considered that only the possibility to challenge the legitimacy of investigative action after notification may be insufficient in order to realize also an *effective* remedy. According to the Court, in the absence of additional provisions facilitating a remedy, the effectiveness of the remedy may be doubted.[53] Hence, considering the decline of the effectiveness of the remedy provided at trial through procedural sanctions, it is recommendable that persons who are notified about the investigative action are also clearly notified about possibilities to challenge the legitimacy of the government's interference with their private lives in alternative proceedings, such as civil proceedings or a challenge before the National Ombudsman. This subject was also touched upon during the discussion of the Bill on the Act on the Criminal Investigation of Terrorist Crimes, but has never resulted in any actual measures.[54]

Especially the observance of the notification requirement as included in the statutory regulation is decisive for whether or not anyone subjected to anticipative criminal investigative activities has been provided with an effective remedy. From the evaluations of the Act on SIT it has appeared that, in practice, the notification

---

[50] See Sect. 8.3.2.1.

[51] See Sect. 2.3.1.6.

[52] See Sect. 4.2.3.2.

[53] See Sect. 2.3.1.6.

[54] See Borgers 2007, 53-55.

requirement is usually not observed. The exception of 'the interest of the investigation' can be easily relied upon in order to refrain from notification. This has resulted in a recommendation by the Board of Procurators-General to comply more effectively with the notification requirement. Considering the foregoing, this attention to better compliance with the notification requirement shall not lessen. Quite the contrary, especially in the context of an anticipative criminal investigation notification is of crucial importance in order to realize accountability, because the anticipative criminal investigative activities rarely result in criminal prosecution and the scope of the investigation is typically larger. In addition, not only an effective remedy but also control *ex post* is then realized concerning those investigative activities that have not resulted in a criminal prosecution.

## *9.3.2 The United States: Legitimization and Integrity*

### 9.3.2.1 Regarding the Anticipative Criminal Investigation in Conventional Criminal Law

#### 9.3.2.1.1 Attention to Legitimizing Grounds in the Reasonableness Assessment Under the Fourth Amendment

As a consequence of the focus on reasonableness in Fourth Amendment case law, especially in situations where the interest of preventing terrorism or protecting national security is involved, the protective value of the probable cause standard has lost some of its protective meaning.[55] The focus on reasonableness, through applying the 'totality of circumstances' test, and including the interest of preventing terrorism in the reasonableness assessments may result in reasoning where the probable cause requirement loses its meaning and the protective interest of this requirement is set aside. A risk has been identified where balancing the interests involved in the context of a reasonableness assessment, without including the probable cause requirement and warrant requirement, may justify *any* urgent need to investigate. This finding will be subjected to further scrutiny in order to determine whether the current focus on Fourth Amendment 'reasonableness' can offer sufficient legitimization for a criminal investigative action.

Probable cause can currently be better understood as a parameter whose presence is a clear indication with regard to the reasonableness of the search. Reasonableness being the ultimate touchstone of the Fourth Amendment, it will be crucial that the conditions regarding legitimization are included in the reasonableness assessment. When probable cause will be reaffirmed as a per se requirement under the Fourth Amendment, it will be clear that this will be in conformity with the conditions on legitimizing grounds for criminal investigative

[55] See Sects. 7.2.2.2.1 and 7.6.2.1.

activities that interfere with privacy rights. Nevertheless, in order to give the investigative agencies sufficient leeway to act also for preventive purposes during the criminal investigation, a lower threshold of application that still conforms to the conditions for the legitimizing grounds will be preferable. Reasonableness in itself, when applied through the totality-of-circumstances test is insufficiently capable of providing specific legitimizing grounds for criminal investigative activities. Hence, seeking to depart from probable cause by setting aside the probable cause requirement and focusing on reasonableness is not the right approach. As also concluded in Sect. 7.2.2.2.1 probable cause fulfills an important protective meaning, justifying *criminal* investigative activities where these activities interfere with the interests which the Fourth Amendment seeks to protect.[56] Because reasonableness, or in fact proportionality, implies a balancing of the interests involved, the specific legitimization of criminal investigative activities is not included. For this reason it was concluded that a form of suspicion concerns an essential restraint on the government's criminal search power as it concerns the core of Fourth Amendment protection.[57]

The foregoing warrants a conclusion that the current trend of focusing on reasonableness involves a risk that specific legitimization for the use of search methods in criminal investigations is set aside. At the same time, the probable cause standard may be too restrictive in order to reflect the current need to act proactively for a preventive purpose in order to serve the interest of preventing terrorism and protecting national security. For this reason, it may be recommendable to seek guidance within prior Supreme Court analysis where a lower form of suspicion was considered reasonable under the Fourth Amendment, such as the standard of reasonable suspicion legitimizing a *Terry* stop.[58]

Using a lower standard of suspicion to legitimize searches in cases involving the interest of preventing terrorism has, however, not been the explicit approach of the courts in dealing with investigations where the threat of terrorism was involved under the Fourth Amendment. Only the First Circuit Court in *United States v. Ramos* (2010), contrary to the district court that initially addressed the case, explicitly included in its assessment of the 'totality of circumstances' the legitimizing circumstances establishing a 'reasonable suspicion', which were the threat of terrorism, identified through objectifiable standards, in combination with another legitimizing circumstance. Although, similar to other courts in the post-9/11 era, the Court used a reasonableness assessment in order to justify the stopping of a vehicle for a brief investigation, it particularly focused on the legitimizing circumstances to reach its conclusion.

---

[56] Sections 7.2.2.2.1 and 7.2.2.2.2, where it has been concluded that the warrant requirement is not a per se requirement to render the search reasonable and that the developments in case law concerning the warrant requirement correspond with the general trend of focusing on reasonableness, where probable cause and a warrant are parameters instead of mandatory requirements, and Sect. 7.2.2.2.3 affirming the conclusion of an increasing focus on reasonableness as the ultimate touchstone of the Fourth Amendment.

[57] Section 7.2.2.2.1.

[58] See Sects. 5.3.2.1.1.1 and 6.2.2.

Although these specific legitimizing circumstances would normally have been insufficient to meet the standard of the *Terry* reasonable suspicion, they still provide sufficient legitimization thereby reducing the scope of the search to identifiable persons who can be related to information regarding a terrorist or other national security crime. Considering the specific circumstances of that case, involving a place at risk from terrorist crimes and the 'suspicious' behavior of the persons in the car, the limited intrusive stopping of the car was sufficiently legitimized. Such argumentation should be explicitly adopted in any Fourth Amendment reasonableness assessment.

This approach can be compared to the Supreme Court's reasoning in *Brigham City v. Stuart* and *Georgia v. Randolph*, where an interpretation of the probable cause standard different from the definition provided in *Brinegar*[59] has been accepted in order to give the police more leeway because of "compelling law enforcement needs".[60] The prevention of terrorism could be understood as such a 'compelling law enforcement need.'

Considering the mandatory presence of a standard reflecting the grounds upon which investigative powers can be used in the context of a criminal investigation, reasonableness may not be detached from the requirement of probable cause or, in the situation of a compelling law enforcement need, a lower version of suspicion (such as a reasonable suspicion as adopted in *Terry v. Ohio*). This will require courts to reflect on the importance of legitimizing grounds in their Fourth Amendment interpretation.

Currently, this attention to legitimizing grounds is insufficient, as a consequence of the one-sided focus on reasonableness, on which basis the parameters of probable cause and a warrant may eventually be set aside. Different gradations of a threshold are already included in the Mukasey Guidelines and the DIOG of the FBI, which provide a relation between the level of the applicable standard and the nature of the crimes investigated as well as the nature of the intrusion caused by the (criminal) investigation.[61] When courts seek to interpret the Fourth Amendment in cases where terrorism or other national security crimes are involved, it may be recommendable to focus also particularly on the, considering the circumstances, legitimizing grounds (meeting, as a minimum, the conditions formulated under the pillar legitimization in Sect. 8.5.1), for which purpose it may be possible to relate to the thresholds included in the investigating guidelines when interpreting 'lower versions' of probable cause under the reasonableness assessment. Reasonableness shall continue to play a role which minimizes interference with privacy rights. When this is done, while taking into account that a form of suspicion is required to render searches in the criminal investigation reasonable, the reasonableness standard will be able to minimize interference to its legitimized scope and purpose.

---

59 "[t]he facts and circumstances within their (the officers') knowledge and of which they had reasonably trustworthy information (are) sufficient in themselves to warrant a man of reasonable caution in the belief that an offense has been or is being committed" *Brinegar v. United States,* 338 U.S. 160, 69 S.Ct. 1392 (1949), 175-176. See Sect. 5.3.2.1.1.1.

60 See Sect. 6.2.2.

61 For an overview see Chap. 7, Table 7.2.

#### 9.3.2.1.2 Some Comments on the Special Needs Doctrine

Seeking to apply lower standards to searches involving the prevention of terrorism, courts have not only focused on the reasonableness of the search, but have also applied the special needs doctrine. The special needs doctrine has been used in the terrorism case of *Macwade v. Kelly* as an argument for deviating from the probable cause and the warrant requirement under the Fourth Amendment and a focus on reasonableness. Section 7.2.2.1 has in that regard drawn the conclusion that the special needs doctrine may only be used when the circumstances are defined by some particular conditions. Some proof regarding the presence of the special need of 'preventing a terrorist attack' or 'protecting national security' must be present in order to establish a 'social necessity' justifying a diminished expectation of privacy for the persons concerned. In addition, the special needs doctrine shall not be used for the primary purpose of evidence-gathering, but for the purpose of realizing the special need of preventing terrorism. Hence, 'plain view' evidence gathering is only allowed when the primary purpose of the search concerns the government's special need.

This conclusion corresponds with the approach defended in Sect. 8.4.1.2 concerning the argument of necessity or exigency justifying exceptions to shield elements within the traditional legal framework. Preventing terrorism or protecting national security shall not be used as categorical exceptions to protective elements, but may continue to function as *ad hoc* exceptions in situations of immediate danger to persons. Considering the preference for this approach it is not required to assess whether the use of investigative powers is sufficiently legitimized in accordance with the principles of Sect. 8.5.1, both because the search cannot be described as a criminal investigative search and because the doctrine may only be applied in circumscribed *ad hoc* situations of immediate danger to persons.

#### 9.3.2.1.3 Some Comments on Pen Registers and Trap and Trace Devices

The nature of pen registers and trap and trace devices has become more intrusive and, consequently, it is no longer self-evident that the use of these tools does not interfere with interests protected by the Fourth Amendment. In particular, the tools have become more privacy intrusive by making it possible to intercept Internet search terms and websites visited. Nevertheless, considering past Supreme Court judgments, it would be unlikely that courts will consider the regulation of the tools to be unconstitutional where, due to technological developments, the scope of the information that can be intercepted has increased.[62] Such an expansion of this scope cannot be considered to violate someone's reasonable expectation of privacy.

The more intrusive nature of the pen register and trap and trace devices raises questions with regard to the sufficiency of the legitimizing grounds to use these

---

[62] Section 7.2.1.3.

tools, in combination with procedural mechanisms guaranteeing the integrity of the application of these tools. For the use of pen registers and trap and trace devices 'specific and articulable facts' demonstrating the relevance of the information to the ongoing investigation is the threshold of application. Considering the limited interference with the right to respect for one's private life caused by the use of the pen registers and trap and trace devices, which—arguably with the exception of the interception of internet search terms and websites visited—do not violate someone's 'reasonable expectation of privacy' under Fourth Amendment jurisprudence, the conditions regarding the legitimization, as formulated in Sect. 8.5.1, do not need to be applied rigidly.

Nevertheless, because the distinction between content and non-content information is less clear under the current regulation of pen register and trap and trace devices, the potential for interferences with the right to respect for one's private life and thus the abuse of pen register and trap and trace investigative powers has increased. Therefore, procedural mechanisms guaranteeing the integrity of the use of pen registers and trap and trace devices are particularly important. For this purpose the FBI has adopted an automated system in order to filter the non-content information from content information without the intervention of a human being.[63] This thus concerns a minimization procedure in order to prevent information from being intercepted for which the regulation of pen registers and trap and trace devices lacks the required legitimization. Of course, such a system can still not completely rule out all forms of abuse or mistakes. Nevertheless, the entity of the regulation can be considered to contain sufficient guarantees that the use of pen registers and trap and trace devices is limited to its legitimized scope and purpose and, hence, does not violate someone's reasonable expectation to privacy.[64]

#### 9.3.2.1.4 Some Comments on Notification

Judicial review of violations of civil liberties has traditionally been strongly guaranteed through notification as well as a civil claim in the federal courts when investigative activities have occurred in violation of the Fourth Amendment such as constitutional rights.[65] This strong guarantee to achieve the accountability of

---

[63] Section 7.2.1.3.

[64] These findings are comparable with the findings with regard to the regulation and nature of the preliminary investigation in the Netherlands (see Sect. 9.3.1.2.4).

[65] The inclusion of a notification requirement in the warrant is an indication of "constitutional adequacy", *United States v. Freitas,* 800 F.2d 1324 (2nd Cir. 1990), 1456 (as firstly determined in *Berger v. New York* (1967)), see Sect. 7.2.1.2. In *Bivens v. Six Unknown Agents of the Federal Bureau of Narcotics,* 403 U.S. 388, 91 S.Ct. 1999 (1971) the Supreme Court established a federal cause of action to anyone subjected to search and/or seizure in violation of the Fourth Amendment. See Sect. 5.3.1.4.

criminal investigative activities through judicial review has been affected as a consequence of the expanded possibilities for delayed notice searches.[66] Considering the importance of subjecting the anticipative criminal investigative activities that interfere with the right to respect for one's private life, preferably *ex ante* but in any case a posteriori, to judicial scrutiny and to provide for an effective remedy, notification should continue to be strongly guaranteed.[67] Hence, as already recommended in Sect. 7.2.1.2 with regard to the constitutional adequacy of the regulation of the delayed notice warrant, the possibilities for a delayed notice shall be clearly circumscribed. This applies in particular to the current possibilities for a delay when the investigation would be seriously jeopardized or a trial would be unduly delayed because of notification and to the possibility to indefinitely extend the delay upon 'good cause shown'.[68]

#### 9.3.2.2 Regarding FISA as a Quasi-Law Enforcement Framework

The impact of the dismantling of the wall, enabling the anticipative criminal investigation to be conducted through the FISA investigative framework and enabling an unlimited sharing of information gathered in national security investigations, is significant.[69] It adds new intrusive methods[70] to the anticipative criminal investigation (under the Mukasey Guidelines a single investigation into terrorist activities may pursue multiple investigative purposes, whereas the tools of both the national security context and the conventional criminal law context are available) and, more importantly, it enables a criminal investigation (although only of terrorist or other national security crimes) for preventive purposes, without the protective requirements that would apply in conventional criminal law.

---

[66] See Sects. 6.2.1.3 and 7.2.1.2.

[67] See Sects. 8.3.2.1, 8.5.2.2 and 8.5.2.3.

[68] See Sect. 7.2.1.2.

[69] See for a detailed explanation as to why the anticipative criminal investigation may be conducted under the FISA framework and why the 'programmatic purpose' criterion will not be capable of excluding investigations with a primary purpose of gathering evidence for criminal prosecution: Sects. 7.4.1 and 7.4.2 For the implications see Sects. 7.4.2 and 7.4.4, which are reinforced as a consequence of the increase in investigative means in national security investigations regulated in the FISA (Sect. 7.3) and as a consequence of the possibility to share information gathered through FISA surveillance targeting non-US persons outside the US and national security letters with the law enforcement community (Sect. 7.5).

[70] Roving surveillance has been made possible (see Sect. 7.3.1.2), pen registers and trap and trace devices have obtained a more intrusive character (see Sect. 7.3.1.3) and the FISA document production order has become a very intrusive and broad investigative power that can be used (Sect. 7.3.2). See also Sect. 7.6.2 under 3.

#### 9.3.2.2.1 FISA Framework Inadequate for Legitimizing Criminal Investigative Activities

Because it has been concluded that under the current law the FISA is one of the investigative frameworks available in the anticipative criminal investigation, this means that the regulation provided should meet the conditions for the legitimizing grounds for anticipative criminal investigations. These legitimizing grounds may be weak in comparison to regular criminal investigations: on the basis of a low threshold investigative powers may be used for prevention and evidence-gathering in investigations involving a threat to national security.[71] Hence, at first sight the combination of the purpose of preventing terrorism and protecting national security with the gathering of information that can be used for a criminal prosecution through a looser framework than Title III may seem to be a legitimate choice.[72] However, as a minimum, the framework used for the purpose of gathering information to be used in criminal proceedings shall meet the conditions formulated in Sect. 8.5.1 in order to be legitimate under the rule of law.

When examining the threshold of 'probable cause' as applied under FISA with these conditions, it is clear that the FISA 'probable cause standard' does not meet the requirement of the availability of information establishing a nexus between the persons concerned and a terrorist crime or other national security crime. Rather, information that a target is a foreign power or an agent of a foreign power, which includes 'lone wolves,' suffices.[73] Hence, the crucial nexus between the target of the investigation and criminal activities that threaten national security is lacking.

As an additional requirement, the 'significant purpose' of the investigation shall be the gathering of foreign intelligence information. The definition of foreign intelligence information does not exclusively concern information regarding terrorist crimes or national security crimes, but may be broader: "[i]nformation that relates to, and if concerning a United States person is necessary to, the ability of the United States to protect against" certain national security threats that can be related to a foreign power or an agent of a foreign power.[74] Considering this definition, agents of a foreign power do not need to be related to terrorist crimes or national security crimes; they may be followed whenever this may result in obtaining information that can be defined as foreign intelligence information.

Furthermore, the Department of Justice and the FBI have adopted guidelines as a means of self-regulation. The two latest versions of the guidelines (issued by Attorneys General Ashcroft and Mukasey) were primarily used to optimize the investigative capabilities of the FBI. According to the current applicable Mukasey Guidelines the FISA investigative framework and Title III are available in the investigative domains of a 'full investigation' and an 'enterprise investigation'. The

---

71 See Sect. 8.5.1.

72 Compare Sect. 7.4.1.

73 See Sect. 7.3.1.1.

74 50 U.S.C. § 1801(e) (see for the precise definitions Sects. 5.2.2.3.1) and see Sect. 7.3.1.1.

entering of these investigative domains is subjected to a threshold. There are two alternatives: the one threshold could typically legitimize criminal investigative activities and the other could typically legitimize intelligence investigative activities. However, because a further distinction between criminal investigative purposes and national security investigative purposes is not made, the FBI may conduct a broad, single investigation into activities that may pose a threat to national security for multiple purposes legitimized by either threshold. Considering that the FISA framework is no longer limited to national security investigative purposes, the FBI may simply rely on the other threshold whenever the threshold that would provide the required legitimizing grounds for a criminal investigation cannot be met. This threshold of 'an articulable factual basis for the investigation that reasonably indicates that the investigation may obtain foreign intelligence' can barely impose a limitation. Considering the foregoing, the conclusion can be drawn that the FISA framework, in combination with the applicable Guidelines, does not provide for a threshold that meets the conditions in order to provide the grounds that can legitimize anticipative criminal activities.

In Sect. 8.4.2 it has been concluded that the relation between the state function (or the investigative purpose) and a specific set of limitations and guarantees regarding the protection of fundamental rights and accountability has a fundamental character. Considering that under the FISA framework a nexus between the persons investigated and criminal activities that threaten national security is not required and because neither the definition of foreign intelligence information nor the investigative guidelines provide for a further limitation to criminal activities, it shall be concluded that the FISA framework is not suitable for use in the anticipative criminal investigation. For that reason, also the reasoning of the FISA Court of Review is rejected as being incompatible with the rule of law. Whereas prior decisions from the Supreme Court in *Keith* and from the Fourth Circuit Court in *Truong* explicitly included in their Fourth Amendment analysis the relation between investigative purpose and the applicable regulatory standards, this fundamental relation (as concluded on the basis of the analysis provided in Sect. 8.4.2) was abandoned by the FISA Court of Review. Rather, the FISA Court of Review even suggested that such an explanation might have contributed to missing opportunities to anticipate the 9/11 attacks.[75] The case of *Mayfield* clearly demonstrates the risk that innocent persons are prosecuted and punished when evidence is gathered on the basis of the standards applicable under the FISA framework.[76]

Lastly, for the same reasons addressed in Sect. 9.3.2.1.2 also the FISA Court of Review's reasoning (*In re: Sealed* and *In re Directives Pursuant to Section 105B of the Foreign Intelligence Surveillance Act*) that its interpretation of the

[75] Section 7.4.2.

[76] See in detail Sect. 7.4.2.

'significant purpose language' can be justified on the basis of the special needs doctrine must be rejected: preventing terrorism or protecting national security may not be used as a categorical exception to Fourth Amendment requirements.[77]

#### 9.3.2.2.2 Re-Establishing the Required Legitimization for Anticipative Criminal Investigations

Two possible changes could contribute to bringing the current regulation of anticipative criminal investigations again within the borders of the rule of law.

In the first place, the interpretation of the FISA Court of Review could be rejected in order to re-establish the primary purpose language. This could be realized, for example, through explicitly interpreting the programmatic purpose[78] test as requiring a primary intelligence purpose and limiting the gathering of evidence to 'plain view gathering'. Consequently, the wall between the intelligence community and the law enforcement community would be rebuilt. However, it will not be required to raise the wall to the level it had prior to the 9/11 attacks; sharing can and should be allowed. In fact, also prior to changes during the post-9/11 era, such sharing was explicitly permitted: when information relevant for criminal proceedings was intercepted this could be shared with the law enforcement community; it was only prohibited that the FISA framework was used specifically for the purpose of evidence-gathering.[79] The operational wall—limiting such sharing prior to the events of 9/11 due to a cultural separation—shall not be rebuilt, whereas the investigative methods in terrorism investigations shall be used under the framework required considering the 'primary investigative purpose'. To do away with the operational wall and create "incentives for information sharing,"[80] bureaucratic changes, such as the establishment of the fusion centers of the Joint Terrorism Task Force,[81] could facilitate the sharing of information with the right agencies. In addition, it could be considered to promote the suggested approach under the Fourth Amendment reasonableness assessment (see Sect. 9.3.2.1.1), allowing for a weaker form of suspicion when terrorism is involved, in order to enable anticipative criminal investigations.

Alternatively, the solution could be sought in an adjustment to the Mukasey Guidelines and the DIOG of the FBI. Without necessarily rejecting the possibility

[77] It is also at odds with the federal court's analysis of the special needs doctrine. See Sects. 7.4.2 and 8.4.1.2.

[78] See on the programmatic purpose requirement and why this requirement is not able to protect against (ab)uses of FISA investigative powers for law enforcement powers Sect. 7.4.2.

[79] As acknowledged in *United States v. Rahman*, 861 F.Supp.247 (1994) and affirmed by the Second Circuit Court, 189 F.3d 88 (2nd Cir. 1999). See Sect. 5.2.2.3.2.

[80] "Provide incentives for information sharing" was one of the central recommendations of the 9/11 Commission. Report of the National Commission on Terrorist Attacks upon the United States 2004, 417.

[81] See Sect. 6.4.3.

to initiate single investigations, for multiple purposes, into terrorist activities, rules should be adopted connecting the specific investigative purpose with the available investigative tools under a specific statutory framework. This could be achieved rather easily by including a limitation on the basis of the current alternative thresholds in the full investigation or enterprise investigation.[82] The threshold that requires information relating an individual or group or organization to a crime or national security threat, capable of legitimizing criminal investigative activities, could justify the use of any lawful investigative techniques (including those under the FISA framework), because in that situation a sufficiently legitimizing standard applies in addition to the requirements of the FISA framework. However, this solution would continue to provide a weak legitimization, considering that the standards provided in the guidelines are not enforceable in the courts.

Therefore, when allowing the use of the FISA framework for anticipative criminal investigations, the condition that in addition the specific threshold which is suitable for legitimizing anticipative criminal investigative activities as provided in the guidelines must be observed, it needs to be assessed whether there are also sufficient guarantees in order to limit the use of the FISA investigative tools to their legitimized scope and purpose. In particular, judicial review shall be established concerning the legitimized scope and purpose in order to count as a sufficient integrity mechanism for the anticipative criminal investigation.[83] A new amendment to the FISA ‘purpose language’ reflecting two alternatives, with additional requirements for a criminal investigative primary purpose would be conceivable, but would make the system rather complex. Furthermore, control and the availability of a remedy shall be strongly established in the regulation, in order to guarantee the integrity of the FBI in conducting the anticipative criminal investigation with the help of FISA techniques. Because the legitimizing threshold for the investigation as such would then only be provided in guidelines, it is clear that there is a significant risk that the FISA investigative techniques used in the context of such an ‘ongoing’ investigation will be applied, in accordance with the statutory requirement, beyond the legitimized scope.

#### 9.3.2.3 Minimization and Alternative Controlling Mechanisms Instead of Judicial Control

Judicial control over the anticipative criminal investigation has generally been reduced. Exceptions to the warrant requirement have increasingly been accepted,

---

[82] See for the thresholds which are applicable to the different investigative levels under the Mukasey Guidelines and the DIOG of the FBI, Table 7.2 of Chap. 7. In addition, see Sects. 6.4.2.3 and 6.4.2.4.

[83] See Sect. 8.5.2.2.

especially when the 'expedient' circumstances of preventing terrorism are involved. Hence, *ex ante* judicial control is not always guaranteed.[84] This is not compensated through increased judicial control a posteriori. The meaning of the exclusionary rule as a controlling mechanism at trial in order to deter abuses of investigative power has been reduced.[85] Moreover, in general in the post-9/11 era the courts have exerted a more deferential review in order to grant the investigating agencies sufficient flexibility to act for the purpose of preventing terrorism.[86]

Notwithstanding these developments in conventional criminal law, judicial control over the anticipative criminal investigation has in particular been reduced as a consequence of using investigative techniques under the FISA framework. Although some form of judicial control is realized *ex ante* through the FISA Court judge, the review exerted is considerably more limited taking into account the standards which are applicable under FISA.[87] This applies to FISA surveillance orders, physical searches and document production orders. Where FISA surveillance targets non-US persons outside the US, the judicial control is even more marginal.[88] No prior judicial involvement is required for using the national security letter.[89]

Moreover, for some tools the possibilities for challenging the legitimacy of their use are limited, as a consequence of the applicability of a non-disclosure requirement.[90] Although since *Doe v. Mukasey* more meaningful judicial control has been established (mere certification by the government that disclosure may endanger national security may no longer be taken as conclusive), a solid and general level of accountability cannot be achieved. As a consequence of the non-disclosure requirement the persons actually affected are not notified that their records have been obtained, unless, firstly, the NSL or document production order recipient is willing to challenge the order, and, secondly, the judge finds sufficient reasons to bypass the government's national security claims.[91]

The lack of judicial control, characteristic of the investigative tools in national security investigations that are currently also being used in the anticipative criminal investigation, fits within the general development of reduced judicial control in Fourth Amendment interpretation. A lack of judicial control is typically compensated by the application of minimization procedures, control by the Inspector General and Congressional oversight. The controlling mechanisms of Congressional oversight and the reports of the Inspectors General have proven to be an effective means of control. Also

---

[84] See Sect. 7.2.2.2.2.

[85] See Sect. 7.2.2.2.4.

[86] See Sect. 7.6.2.1 under 2.

[87] See Sects. 7.3.1.1 and 7.3.2.1.

[88] Section 7.5.1.

[89] Section 7.5.2.

[90] FISA document production orders (see Sect. 7.3.2.2) and national security letters (see Sect. 7.5.2).

[91] Section 7.3.2.2.

civil litigation instigated by civil liberties advocates have brought to light the actual impact of 'national security investigative tools' as well as resulting in improvements. Civil litigation has resulted in revealing statistical information regarding document production orders, which has largely removed concerns regarding the use of the FISA document production orders in practice.[92] Reports of the Inspector General have brought to light abuses of investigative powers, such as the national security letter. This has resulted in adjustments to the regulation and the FBI's use of the NSL in practice.[93]

These controlling mechanisms and minimization procedures may function as effective integrity guarantees regarding the activities of the intelligence community. However, when 'intelligence powers' are actively and directly used in order to gather information for criminal investigative purposes, the investigative activities shall also be subjected to judicial scrutiny.[94] The manner in which the FISA judge exerts control is particularly geared towards the use of FISA investigative techniques for national security purposes. Hence, when seeking to continue to use the FISA framework in the anticipative criminal investigation, in the first place, measures shall be taken which limit the use of the FISA techniques to the required legitimizing grounds for criminal investigation (see the second alternative suggested in the previous section).

In addition, it shall be required that the FISA Court judge specifically oversees the legitimized scope and purpose of using FISA in the anticipative criminal investigation. Before issuing a FISA court order, the FISA judge shall include, in the assessment of the statutory requirements, the specific purpose of the investigation and whether this investigation has been initiated on the basis of the threshold provided in the guidelines legitimizing the investigation for that specific purpose. Furthermore, the thresholds provided in the guidelines in relation to the investigative purpose can be included in the reasonableness assessment under the Fourth Amendment in order to realize also *ex post* control over the observance of the required legitimizing grounds in investigative enterprises. Similarly, other intelligence tools available in an 'authorized investigation' can be legitimized through applying the correct threshold for initiating criminal investigations under the AG guidelines.

However, in order to realize the effective remedy of anticipative criminal investigative activities under FISA, notification must also be guaranteed when the FISA framework is used in the anticipative criminal investigation. Notification of FISA interceptions is currently generally not considered to be warranted, because it would affect the US' ability to protect national security.[95] Hence, especially realizing an effective remedy for those persons involved in FISA surveillance in the anticipative criminal investigation who are not prosecuted (which is usually the case) seems to be difficult to achieve.

---

92 Section 7.3.2.1.

93 See Sect. 6.5.2.

94 Compare the fourth 'integrity guarantee' formulated in Sect. 8.5.2.4.

95 Zabel and Benjamin Jr 2008, 80.

Notwithstanding these suggestions for an improvement with regard to integrity mechanisms, it shall be concluded that not only the required legitimizing grounds are lacking when using the FISA framework in the anticipative criminal investigation, but also the required minimization is difficult to realize. Hence, it can be concluded that the current regulation of control over the use of FISA investigative tools in the anticipative criminal investigation lacks the required judiciary control over the use of the investigative tools only for their legitimized scope and purpose in order to further the legitimacy of the procedure resulting in prosecution and punishment.

### 9.3.3 The Netherlands: Fairness and Integrity

In the Netherlands the anticipative criminal investigation is regulated in a manner which maintains the separation between the intelligence service and the law enforcement services on the basis of their separate tasks.[96] Although the concept of an anticipative criminal investigation is broader, including the preparatory investigative activities likely to be conducted by the AIVD or the CIE, it cannot be said that intelligence agencies have explicitly obtained an active and direct role in gathering information for criminal investigative purposes. For this reason, the anticipative criminal investigative phase corresponds in the procedural sense with the definition of Article 132a CCP. Nevertheless, the anticipative criminal investigation is significantly influenced by the preparatory investigative activities of the AIVD and CIE, which in particular has implications for control in order to guarantee the fairness of the criminal investigation.

On that basis an anticipative criminal investigation can, for the Netherlands, be defined as to cover the criminal investigation under the definition of Article 132a CCP, typically enabled through starting information from 'preparatory information-gathering activities' conducted by the AIVD or the CIE.[97] Without stretching the definition of the criminal investigation on the basis of the criminal investigative purpose provided in Article 132a CCP, these preparatory information-gathering activities provide the criminal investigation with its anticipatory character and have implications for the further criminal proceedings.

Hence, where in Sect. 9.3.1 the more limited concept of anticipative criminal investigation was the basis for assessing the required legitimization and the integrity mechanisms regarding this legitimization, the broader concept of the anticipative criminal investigation is the basis for assessing the fairness of the proceedings and the integrity mechanisms adopted for that purpose.

[96] See Sect. 4.3.3.

[97] Section 4.3.3 has defined and positioned the concept of an anticipative criminal investigation as it has taken shape in the Netherlands.

When the possibilities for control and a challenge are reduced in the trial phase because of the secrecy of certain aspects of the information-gathering process, guarantees with regard to the integrity of the investigating agencies are of the upmost importance. The information which is kept confidential in Dutch trial proceedings typically concerns the underlying information concerning starting information (an insight into preparatory information-gathering activities) and the subsequent AIVD reports shared with the police and the PPS and the background to the sharing of these reports concerning the course of events during parallel investigations.

The implications of the broader concept of anticipative criminal investigation become typically visible in the criminal trial of terrorist suspects. These implications are broader than one would suggest only on the basis of the Act on the criminal investigation of terrorist crimes, because preparatory information-gathering activities are typically conducted by the AIVD or CIE. These result in impediments for controlling the legitimacy of using investigative methods and, in the course of parallel investigations, on the use of investigative powers for the afforded purposes and the veracity of the information obtained in the context of the criminal investigation.[98] The central problem concerns the limited possibility, or maybe even the impossibility, of obtaining access to the underlying documents of the AIVD report and to the sources and methods by which the information has been gathered. Hence, to guarantee the fairness of the criminal proceedings, in particular the integrity of the activities of the AIVD, the PPS and the police, cooperation with the AIVD needs to be guaranteed. Therefore, this section will continue to address, firstly, the control over the AIVD and the CIE. Secondly, it will be addressed why the internal mechanisms of control applicable to the AIVD cannot replace the need for an examination by judges both *ex ante* and *ex post*.

#### 9.3.3.1 Control over the AIVD and CIE

Considering the broader concept of an anticipative criminal investigation, including the preparatory investigative activities conducted by the AIVD or CIE, also the integrity of these investigative activities shall be guaranteed. Because the primary purpose of both an intelligence investigation and a criminal investigation remains in place, the procedural and controlling mechanisms applicable within the broader concept of an anticipative criminal investigation shall correspond and thus differ in accordance with these distinguished purposes.[99] Accordingly, intelligence investigative activities are controlled through the independent oversight committee

---

[98] See Sect. 4.3.4.

[99] Compare the third condition for guaranteeing 'integrity', Sect. 8.5.2.4. The fourth condition shall thus not be applied to the Dutch regulation of anticipative criminal investigations.

and parliamentary control,[100] while the judiciary controls the criminal investigation.

As concluded in Sect. 4.3.4.3, there is no concrete reason to suspect the AIVD or CIE of illegitimate investigative activities. The following reasons were formulated for drawing this conclusion: controlling mechanisms are in place (the internal oversight committee and parliamentary control); the results of the examination of the oversight committee regarding the veracity of AIVD reports shared with the PPS on the basis of Article 38 WIV 2002; the fact that it is contrary to the AIVD's own interest to pursue law enforcement interests and, possibly most importantly, the procedure where the national public prosecutor for counterterrorism may 'look over the wall' in order to check the veracity of the AIVD report which the AIVD wants to share on the basis of the underlying documents.[101]

Procedural safeguards have also been adopted in order to exert control over investigative activities of the CIE and specifically over the use of CIE information as starting information for a criminal investigation. Internal controlling mechanisms apply and the public prosecutor for the CIE exerts random control.[102] In addition, it is common practice that CIE information in criminal proceedings is limited to functioning as starting information.[103]

Considering the presence of efficient controlling mechanisms to check the intelligence-gathering activities of the AIVD and CIE, marginal control, both *ex ante* and *ex post,* over the legitimacy of using this information as proactive steering information in criminal proceedings is justified. However, regardless of the presence of sufficient integrity guarantees that shall cover the activities conducted for 'intelligence' purposes, it must also be observed that the risk of abusing power has been increased in the course of 'parallel investigations' by the police/PPS and the AIVD, because prevention has become an investigative purpose of the criminal investigation and, consequently, the two intelligence and law enforcement communities have approached each other and cooperation has been intensified.[104] The impediments on control precisely concern these types of activities, covering the relation between the AIVD and the police/PPS, for which reason it has been concluded that the criminal process has been 'infected'.

#### 9.3.3.2 Integrity Guarantees Versus Judicial Control: The Fairness of Trial Proceedings

The fairness of the criminal process following an anticipative criminal investigation shall be guaranteed through a structured approach. Restrictions on the

[100] See in detail Sect. 2.2.2.4.1.

[101] See Sect. 4.3.4.3.

[102] See Sect. 4.3.4.1.

[103] See Sects. 2.3.2.1 and 4.3.4.3.

[104] See Sect. 4.3.1.

possibilities to challenge and exert control can be compensated by strong guarantees regarding the integrity of all the agencies responsible for information gathering in the broad concept of an anticipative criminal investigation and through counterbalancing procedures at the trial phase.[105]

The Act on Shielded Witnesses has been introduced in the Netherlands as a counterbalancing procedure to deal with intelligence in criminal proceedings. Under this counterbalancing procedure the examining magistrate may hear the AIVD officers on the background of an AIVD report and the AIVD investigation. The procedure is useful for examining the veracity of the AIVD reports used as starting information (although for this purpose the relevance is limited) and of AIVD reports introduced as evidence.[106] However, the procedure cannot be used to control the course of events in parallel investigations, for the simple reason that Article 359a CCP is interpreted as not covering control over intelligence investigative activities.

At this point the introduction of the anticipative criminal investigation clashes with the system of control over criminal proceedings. The trial judge adheres strictly to the separation between the PPS and police, on the one hand, and the AIVD, on the other, using the definition of Article 132a CCP as the strict borderline between an intelligence investigation and a criminal investigation. However, the reality of an anticipative criminal investigation is different, infecting the criminal process as a consequence of the fact that the preparatory investigative activities of the criminal investigation of terrorist crimes are typically conducted by the AIVD and the influence may continue to exist in the course of the anticipative criminal investigation.[107]

So far, the trial judge has only played a marginal role in the system of controlling the 'shielded' aspects of an anticipative criminal investigation. Only when the information is introduced as evidence is the trial judge willing to enter into an examination, because this is required under Article 6 ECHR. However, also the legitimacy of the evidence-gathering process and the reliability of the information collected in that process are relevant for the fairness of the trial proceedings as a whole, and for realizing accountability for investigative activities as required under the rule of law.[108] The realization of accountability *ex post* is even more pressing considering the reduced pre-trial control over the legitimacy of the preparatory investigative activities. Hence, it will be required that also the judiciary endorses the current reality of the anticipative criminal investigative phase in cases involving terrorism or other national security threats. On that basis it will be possible to open up the wall of secrecy which the defense currently faces when it seeks to challenge the legitimacy of anticipative criminal investigative activities,

---

105 See Sect. 8.5.3.

106 Section 4.3.4.3.

107 See the conclusion drawn at the end of Sect. 4.3.4.3.

108 See Sect. 8.5.3.

at least in a manner providing sufficient 'spyholes' to guarantee the fairness of the entire anticipative criminal investigative process.

These spyholes can be realized by a different interpretation of Article 359a CCP, which would provide the possibility to apply the procedure for hearing shielded witnesses in order to control the course of events during the AIVD investigation insofar as this has influenced the anticipative criminal investigation. This different interpretation can be achieved by not limiting the examination under Article 359a CCP strictly to the activities covered by the definition of Article 132a CCP, but also including those elements (the preparatory investigative activities) that have been included in Sect. 4.3.3 in the 'broad' definition of an anticipative criminal investigation.

The language of Article 359a CCP does not exclude such a broader interpretation of the scope of its applicability. However, attaching procedural sanctions to illegitimate actions that have not occurred under the direct responsibility of the public prosecutor is difficult to justify.[109] Nevertheless, the broadening of the examination, as proposed here, concerns preparatory investigative activities that touch upon the legitimacy of the criminal investigation, such as the impermissible influence of the AIVD on the criminal investigation or the circumvention of criminal investigative requirements by relying on the information shared by the AIVD. Moreover, the national public prosecutor for counterterrorism does have a 'bridging' function with regard to the information collected by the AIVD and the use of this information in criminal proceedings and bears, for that purpose, responsibility for the legitimacy of the use of AIVD information and the influence of AIVD investigative activities on the criminal proceedings. Hence, the character of Article 359a CCP does not oppose the realization of control over those aspects of the preparatory investigative activities which are relevant for the legitimacy and fairness of the criminal investigation.

Because of the applicable procedural and controlling mechanisms guaranteeing the integrity of the AIVD, the courts may continue to presume the legitimacy of the investigative activities of the AIVD. However, when confronted with challenges regarding the legitimacy of AIVD investigative activities that have influenced the anticipative criminal investigation, the fairness of the proceedings cannot be considered separately from these influences. Applying the counterbalancing procedure of hearing AIVD staff and/or the national public prosecutor for counterterrorism as shielded witnesses before the examining magistrate will provide the required structured approach for guaranteeing the fairness of criminal proceedings. When adopting this recommendation, the fairness of criminal proceedings can be guaranteed where the evidence has been gathered through an anticipative criminal investigation.[110]

---

109 Compare: Borgers 2009, 58. See also Sect. 4.3.3.

110 In particular the third and fourth condition, see Sect. 8.5.3.

### 9.3.3.3 Comment on the Use of Intelligence as Evidence

Except for controlling the *way* in which information introduced in criminal proceeding has been obtained, an anticipative criminal investigation may also result in an increase in intelligence in criminal proceedings. Classified information cannot be used as evidence in the Netherlands.[111] However, AIVD reports transferred to the law enforcement community may be used as evidence, while parts of the information and the underlying information remain classified. The defense, the public prosecutor and the trial judge all have access to the same materials: only the information that is contained in the AIVD report as such. Consequently, it cannot be examined whether the information that is kept shielded includes 'material evidence for or against the accused' covered by the disclosure obligation. To solve this issue, the counterbalancing procedure of hearing shielded witnesses before the examining magistrate has been adopted. The examining magistrate may hear AIVD staff with regard to this classified information, without obtaining any insight into the underlying information. When the AIVD officer invokes national security reasons in order to keep certain information shielded, this shall be considered as conclusive.[112]

The reasons for keeping information shielded cannot be examined by the examining magistrate. For this reason, it is difficult to control whether information is withheld that would fall under the disclosure obligation.[113] In fact, the most important controlling role is fulfilled by the national public prosecutor for counterterrorism, who shall examine the usefulness of AIVD information for criminal proceedings also in the light of the presence of exonerating information, which would touch upon the veracity of the AIVD report, before further transferring it to the law enforcement community. Of course, the examining magistrate can also question the national public prosecutor for counterterrorism on this aspect in order to give his judgment on the veracity of the AIVD report included in the file. Also the defense may ask or submit questions in that regard to the examining magistrate. Although, without obtaining an insight into the underlying information, a direct form of control is excluded, the procedure may be considered as a sufficient counterbalancing procedure to examine the veracity of any AIVD information included in the file.

In addition, it remains the decision of the trial judge whether or not limited disclosure with regard to the background of the information sought to be used as

[111] For this reason, the second condition formulated under the pillar of 'fairness' does not apply to the regulation of anticipative criminal investigations in the Netherlands. See Sect. 8.5.3.

[112] For the precise description of the procedure see Sect. 3.3.2.

[113] For this reason, Advocate General Machielse suggested establishing a disclosure judge, who can examine the reasons for the AIVD to keep information shielded. HR 15 maart 2011, *LJN* BP7544 (CPG 08/04418) (Conclusion of the AG, pending the decision of the Supreme Court), para 5.20. However, it cannot be expected that a judge is able to examine whether or not keeping information shielded is vital for the protection of national security and, hence, will necessarily generally follow any certifications of the AIVD in that regard.

evidence, and, hence, uncertainty about the reliability of the information, gives reason to exclude the AIVD report from the evidence. In the terrorism cases that have been dealt with by Dutch courts, it seems that trial judges are inclined to seek other sources of evidence in order to avoid using intelligence sources or, at least, to establish sufficient supporting evidence, which is also a fair trial requirement under Article 6 ECHR.[114]

## 9.3.4 The United States: Fairness and Integrity

### 9.3.4.1 Insufficient Control over FISA as a Quasi-Law Enforcement Framework

When the FISA framework is used to gather information for use in criminal proceedings, realizing fairness in the context of the criminal process requires the possibility at trial to control the legitimacy of using the FISA investigative techniques and the veracity of the information gathered through these techniques. For the latter purpose the CIPA procedures can be applied. For the first purpose, the trial judge does exercise control, but the manner in which the control is exerted is based upon the national security context. In fact courts dealing in the context of trial proceedings with the products of the anticipative criminal investigation—as has followed from the approach taken in *United States v. Abu-Jihaad* (2008) and *United States v. Warsame* (2008)—have not acknowledged that FISA has an important role in evidence gathering. Consequently, the control exerted was based upon the function of FISA in national security investigations, which is to gather foreign intelligence information without the direct purpose of using this information also as evidence in criminal proceedings. This means that the judge examines whether the statutory requirements for the order were met, which he or she will accept upon the certifications of the government in that regard unless they are 'clearly erroneous'. Moreover, the affidavits underlying the order are examined *ex parte* and *in camera.* As has been concluded in Sect. 9.3.2.3 also the integrity guarantees that apply to the FISA investigative tools and to national security letters are based upon the 'intelligence' nature of the tools. This is not compensated at trial through substantial judicial control a posteriori, again as a consequence of considering the investigative tools as intelligence tools for which alternative methods of control have been established.[115]

Hence, it can be concluded that enabling FISA to function as a quasi-law enforcement framework has not been accompanied by sufficient controlling mechanisms by subjecting the investigative activities to the required judicial

[114] See Sect. 4.3.4.3.

[115] Compare Sect. 7.4.3.

scrutiny[116] in order to make the framework (subject to the condition that the required legitimizing grounds are also included in the regulation) suitable for pursuing a criminal investigative purpose.

#### 9.3.4.2 CIPA as a Counterbalancing Procedure

CIPA procedures are based upon a presumption of disclosure and involve a judge in decisions on keeping the information classified, the need for disclosure and the question whether the use of summaries and substitutes will not put the defense in a more disadvantageous position than before.[117] The courts were already able to use CIPA procedures in a balanced way prior to the introduction of the anticipative criminal investigation in the post-9/11 era and, also, in the terrorist cases of the past decade CIPA has proven to function in practice as a fair counterbalancing procedure where national security interests in keeping information classified clash with disclosure obligations.[118]

CIPA corresponds with the conditions formulated for dealing with the products of an anticipative criminal investigation in order to guarantee the fairness of criminal proceedings. The judge decides on the applicability of CIPA, including the necessity of keeping information shielded, the sufficiency of procedural safeguards that counterbalance the restriction on fair trial rights and the relevance of the classified information as material evidence in the case.[119] Hence, CIPA may be considered as a counterbalancing procedure that intends to give effect to the essence of defense rights when classified materials are relevant to the criminal proceedings.[120]

#### 9.3.4.3 The Fairness of the Trial Proceedings

Considering the observations of the previous section, CIPA provides a counterbalancing procedure that makes it possible to guarantee, in principle, the fairness of the criminal proceedings when classified materials are involved in the trial proceedings. This does not mean that the CIPA procedures are in all circumstances a good alternative to regular criminal proceedings. Rather, it was observed that,

---

[116] Compare the fourth integrity condition, under b, Sect. 8.5.2.4, and the first and fourth fairness conditions, Sect. 8.5.3.

[117] See on CIPA procedures Sects. 5.3.1.2 and 5.3.1.3.

[118] See Sect. 7.4.3.

[119] The second 'fairness' condition, Sect. 8.5.3. Compare the second and third conditions to guarantee the fairness of the criminal procedure, Sect. 8.5.3.

[120] Compare the third 'fairness' condition, Sect. 8.5.3.

although intended to give effect to the essence of defense rights, the defense would not have a full possibility to challenge the veracity of the information.[121]

When using the FISA framework for the gathering of evidence within broad investigations for multiple purposes and introducing materials obtained in national security investigations (also without a criminal investigative purpose, e.g. obtained through national security investigations), the amount of classified information in criminal proceedings increases significantly. The CIPA procedures will apply as soon as the government certifies that declassification harms national security and judges are inclined to follow the government's certifications of national security interests, especially where these interests are more compelling, such as in terrorism cases. Consequently, CIPA becomes the rule instead of the exception and the enjoyment of the constitutional right to disclosure is significantly limited. Moreover, it will be particularly difficult for the judge applying CIPA to determine whether all the information that would fall under the disclosure obligation of the prosecutor is in fact taken into account, considering the wide variety of sources by which information that is material to the case may have been obtained, involving also various intelligence entities.[122]

Nevertheless, it has appeared that especially the possibility to control and challenge the legitimacy of the *manner* of evidence-gathering is impaired when information, relevant to the trial proceedings, has been gathered through the FISA framework.[123] In Sect. 9.3.4.1 it has been concluded that the manner in which control is exerted, both *ex ante* and *ex post*, is insufficient, because the procedural and controlling mechanisms which are applicable to the anticipative criminal investigation fail to provide sufficient guarantees as to the integrity of *criminal* investigative activities. In particular, the level of judicial review is insufficient and is typically organized from the perspective of the national security investigation instead of (also) the perspective of the criminal justice system.

Again, because the fairness of the criminal proceedings cannot be guaranteed as a consequence of the lack of control over the legitimacy of the anticipative criminal investigative activities, this is an indication that the FISA framework is not suitable for use in the anticipative criminal investigation. The only solution to guarantee the fairness of the criminal proceedings following an anticipative criminal investigation would be to restore the required legitimizing grounds when using investigative methods that interfere with privacy rights for the purpose of evidence-gathering, in one of the ways proposed in Sect. 9.3.2.2.2. Only on that basis can judicial control also be given a more meaningful role, in the sense that it will be examined whether the use of investigative methods for the purpose of evidence gathering is limited to its legitimized scope and purpose. With the broadening of the examination to that scope and thus the enabling of a judicial review not only from a FISA perspective, but also from a criminal procedural law

[121] Compare Sect. 7.4.3.

[122] See Sect. 7.4.3.

[123] See Sect. 7.4.3.

perspective, CIPA can play an important role in order to find the right balance between transparency with regard to the way in which evidence has been gathered and keeping certain aspects of the investigation shielded in order to protect national security.

## 9.4 Final Conclusions

On the basis of the conclusions drawn in Chaps. 4 and Chap. 7 several parallel developments can be identified in the Netherlands and in the United States with regard to enabling a system of anticipative criminal investigation. In the first place, the prevention of terrorism has become the top priority in both countries. The preventive paradigm, based on the presumption that security is achieved through prevention, underpins measures such as those enabling anticipative criminal investigations, and prevention has also obtained a central role within the regulation of anticipative criminal investigations in general. As a consequence, both in the Netherlands and in the United States intelligence-led policing has increased and the interest of preventing terrorism is understood as overriding criminal investigative interests. Furthermore, proportionality in the Netherlands and reasonableness in the United States, intended to restrict the large investigative discretion which is granted, are generally used in order to grant investigative officers the largest possible leeway in acting to prevent terrorism, instead of further restricting discretionary authority.

Secondly, both in the Netherlands and the United States attention to the imperative relation between the specific investigative purpose and the required legitimization and for the legitimization of criminal investigative activities in general has slackened. Because of the desire to realize both prevention and evidence gathering when conducting investigations into terrorist activities, the intelligence community and the law enforcement community have approached each other's fields of work. However, where in the Netherlands this development has stopped at the border of the required legitimizing grounds for criminal investigative activities, this border has been transgressed in the United States. Consequently, the US regulation of anticipative criminal investigations violates the fundamental restriction on governmental action for the purpose of gathering evidence to carry out the most far-reaching governmental power, namely prosecution and punishment.

A third parallel that can be identified concerns the manner in which courts deal with an 'infected criminal process,' caused by an increase in shielded elements in the trial proceedings as a consequence of the character of an anticipative criminal investigation. Both in the Netherlands and in the United States trial judges fail to acknowledge the specific character of the anticipative criminal investigation. Dutch courts have rigidly retained the definition of a criminal investigation according to Article 132a CCP and, on that basis, have excluded control over relevant intelligence investigative activities. In the United States the possibility to use the FISA framework for the purpose of gathering evidence has been approved by the federal courts. However, exercising control over the legitimacy of using FISA tools, as well as control over the veracity of the information obtained through these methods, occurs from a typical, traditional, national security perspective, where "*ex parte* and *in camera* inspections are the rule"[124] and limiting the control to a very marginal review as to whether, upon the information provided by the government, the statutory requirements have been met.

At the beginning of this book the central research question has been formulated:

*Can a preventive function of criminal investigation be part of a criminal justice system under the rule of law and, if so, under what conditions, and what does this mean for the current regulation of anticipative criminal investigations adopted in the Netherlands and the United States?*

It is now possible to formulate a final answer to this question. In the first place, a preventive function of the criminal investigation (the anticipative criminal investigation) can be part of a criminal justice system under the rule of law, considering the specific nature of terrorism. Because of this specific nature—terrorism has a diffuse and complex nature and constitutes both criminal activities as well as a threat to national security—it is a legitimate choice to adopt a hybrid framework to pursue both the purpose of prevention and the purpose of evidence-gathering. From this perspective, adopting a system of anticipative criminal investigation is also effective and, hence, necessary (and thus in line with the *ultimum remedium* character of the criminal justice system). However, giving the criminal investigation a preventive function is only compatible with the rule of law when the fundamental relation between the criminal investigative purpose and the regulatory framework is upheld. For this reason, the minimum conditions for regulating the anticipative criminal investigation have been formulated and are categorized in the pillars of legitimization, integrity and fairness, taking into account the non-derogable constitutive principles and parameters for criminal investigative activities. On the basis of these conditions, this chapter has evaluated the rule of law compatibility of the regulation of the anticipative criminal investigation in the Netherlands and the United States.

This evaluation makes it possible to provide also a final answer to the second part of the central research question, whether the anticipative criminal investigation as currently adopted in the Netherlands and the United States is compatible with the rule of law. This will be done for the Netherland and the United States separately.

*The Netherlands*

The Dutch regulation of anticipative criminal investigations complies with the fundamental relation between the purpose and the procedural regulation and, therefore, the approach chosen for regulating anticipative criminal investigations is as such compatible with the rule of law. However, a risk has been identified where

[124] *United States v. Abu-Jihaad,* 531 F.Supp.2d 299 (D.Conn 2008), 310.

the current regulation of anticipative criminal investigations in the Netherlands may be applied in a manner that is incompatible with the conditions formulated. In addition, the fairness of the criminal proceedings cannot in all circumstances be guaranteed.

In order to guarantee the rule of law compatibility of the regulation as currently in force, it should be considered to implement the recommendations as elaborated in Sects. 9.3.1 and 9.3.3. The caveats require adjustments to the established statutory framework in order to reduce the risks of transgressing rule of law borders during the execution of the anticipative criminal investigation. Currently the statutory regulation corresponds in general with the conditions formulated under the three pillars, and, hence, is on the regulatory level also compatible with the ECHR. However, concerning several aspects there is a clear risk that the borders of the anticipative criminal investigation will be transgressed when the statutory framework is applied in practice and, consequently, may also result in a violation of Article 8 ECHR and Article 6 ECHR. Both in the relation between legitimization and integrity and between fairness and integrity, improvements can be realized roughly by putting new life into the relation between the criminal investigative purpose and the legitimizing grounds, both in the executive phase and in the controlling phase, and embracing the reality of the broader concept of an anticipative criminal investigation in trial proceedings.

In order to implement this recommendation it will not be required to adjust the regulation. However, only through the issuing of guidelines by the Board of Procurators General can the investigative practice can be changed in order to realize that in practice the relation between legitimizing grounds and the investigative purpose is observed in order to realize adequate investigation and to limit preventive investigation to the criminal investigation of terrorist activities. In addition, also the examining magistrate and the trial judge shall control specifically the observance of the relation between legitimizing grounds and the criminal investigative purpose.

Lastly, it will be a task for the judiciary to embrace the reality of anticipative criminal investigations and, on that basis, to exert control over the 'preparatory investigative activities' to guarantee the fairness of the trial proceedings also where questions arise as to the legitimacy of the course of events during the anticipative criminal investigation. This is possible by extending the applicability of Article 359a CCP on the basis of the definition of the 'broader' concept of an anticipative criminal investigation as provided in Sect. 4.3.3. This includes the activities of the AIVD and CIE insofar as they touch upon the legitimacy of the criminal investigation and, for the preparatory activities conducted by the AIVD, where the national public prosecutor for counterterrorism has fulfilled his bridging function between the AIVD and the PPS. To deal with the classified nature of (some of the) activities of the AIVD and CIE and taking into account that a marginal examination is warranted because of the presence of adequate integrity mechanisms controlling the AIVD and CIE, the procedure of hearing shielded witnesses before the examining magistrate would concern an adequate counterbalancing procedure for dealing with examining the legitimacy of the anticipative criminal investigation under Article 359a CCP.

*The United States*

In the United States, the fundamental, imperative, relation between a procedural framework that includes the legitimizing grounds meeting the conditions formulated in Sect. 8.5.1 and the criminal investigative purpose has been abandoned. For that reason, the current regulation of anticipative criminal investigations in the United States affects the legitimacy of the criminal justice system under the rule of law, because the methods allowed for gathering information are not confined within the legitimizing grounds required for using the information gathered for the purpose of criminal prosecution. In order to restore the rule of law compatibility of the regulation adopted in the United States, the implementation of the recommendations as elaborated in Sects. 9.3.2 and 9.3.4 should be considered.

Seeking to adjust the regulation of anticipative criminal investigations to reflect the rule of law confines of criminal investigative action in the United States, the first and most essential demand would be to restore the relation between legitimization and the criminal investigative purpose. The regulation of investigative techniques under FISA lacks the required legitimization and integrity mechanisms in order to be suitable for use in the anticipative criminal investigation. Consequently, also the fairness of the criminal proceedings can no longer be guaranteed.

In order to comply with the fundamental relation between the investigative purpose and the procedural framework, there are two possibilities. Firstly, the procedural (not the operational) wall between criminal investigative activities and national security investigative activities could be rebuilt, which would disqualify the FISA framework from use in the anticipative criminal investigation. This would require an amendment to FISA in order to restore the primary purpose language. Alternatively, federal courts and, preferably, the Supreme Court should interpret the current FISA language in line with the Supreme Court's *Keith* decision and the Fourth Circuit's decision in *Truong* on the basis of the prior distinction in Fourth Amendment interpretation between criminal investigative purposes and national security investigation purposes. As a second possibility, the FISA framework could be adjusted in a manner that reflects the conditions required for regulating the anticipative criminal investigation. Such adjustments would touch upon the legitimizing grounds, the organization of integrity mechanisms (in particular the establishment of judicial control over the legitimized scope and purpose) and the possibility to guarantee the fairness of criminal proceedings by enabling control, during the trial, over the legitimacy of using the FISA investigative techniques (e.g. through CIPA).

Furthermore, in 'regular' criminal cases the courts should also take into account the importance of the presence of legitimizing grounds in Fourth Amendment analysis. The suggested changes to the use of the FISA framework in the anticipative criminal investigation would correspond and fit within Fourth Amendment analysis with an essential role for legitimizing grounds.

# Epilogue

Shortly after the killing of Osama Bin Laden, I heard a 9/11 victim state in reaction: '9/11 was the beginning of a book. Now we have reached the end of a Chapter, whilst it is still unknown how the story will end.' Ten years after 9/11 and a few months after the assassination of Osama Bin Laden, we may be able to close a decade that was dominated by a fear of terrorist attacks. This fear of terrorism has contributed to a changed political and societal climate, the initiation of a 'war against international (Islamic) terrorism' and a multitude of counterterrorism measures, which were partly successful, partly sharply criticized and for another part their effect is still unknown and may always be unknown. Ten years after 9/11 the threat of terrorism is not gone. Instead, we have recently been dramatically reminded that terrorism is not limited to Islamic terrorism, but can arise from any extreme ideology. The experience of devastating terrorist attacks committed by a right-wing extremist on July 22, 2011 in Norway may again change perceptions with regard to terrorism and counterterrorism policy. In any event, at this point we should be able to assess and judge the measures that were taken to counter terrorism in response to the threat of Islamic international terrorism with more hindsight and in a more balanced way.

In seeking the adoption of measures to confront threats previously unknown to the state that considers itself bound by the rule of law, it is generally insufficient to simply adjust a framework for the purpose of encompassing new investigative needs. This would affect the synthesis between shield and sword in the criminal justice system in an ill-considered manner. Ten years after the confrontation with the devastating attacks of September 11, 2001 and the implementation of many counterterrorism measures in the subsequent era, adopted under a widely felt haste—tomorrow the next attack may occur—it is possible to reassess our methods to confront threats such as terrorism at a greater distance. Sometimes it may be required to adjust the system traditionally adopted to deal with crime and threats of a different nature. However, this may only be done by first going back to the basic, fundamental, rule of law principles that should, at any time—with the exception of

M.F.H. Hirsch Ballin, *Anticipative Criminal Investigation*,
DOI: 10.1007/978-90-6704-843-9,

true and well circumscribed emergency situations—underpin a system of criminal procedural law.

This book has provided such a reconsideration of measures that aim to enable a form of investigation that could combine the prevention of terrorism with the desire to eventually prosecute and punish terrorists. As a result, the role of the criminal justice system in providing security under the rule of law has been repositioned, and the limits on the role of the criminal investigation in preventing terrorism prevention have been identified. It is not unlikely that in the future new forms of criminal behavior will arise, which place new demands on the character of the criminal investigation. For example, cybercrime may confront the government with new intangible threats, involving complex technological questions, requiring the government to explore new investigative challenges. Or, as another example, it may be required to reconsider the approach chosen to confront terrorism, in order to increase the capabilities of targeting lone wolves, such as Anders Behring Breivik. The normative framework adopted in Chap. 8 of this book has been particularly geared towards the anticipative criminal investigation of terrorist crimes. However, the constitutive principles and parameters identified and addressed will at any time continue to provide the architecture for the regulation of criminal investigations. And the line of reasoning provided can also be used for dealing with possible new investigative challenges, for which purpose it may be needed to set new preferences.

# Bibliography

Ackerman B (2006) Before the next attack. Preserving civil liberties in an age of terrorism. Yale University Press, New Haven

Addink GH (2010) Goed bestuur (inaugural lecture Utrecht). Kluwer, Deventer

Agamben G (2005) State of exception (translated by Kevin Attell). University of Chicago Press, Chicago

Aksu M (2007) Straatsburgse kaders voor terrorismebestrijding, EVRM, strafrecht en terrorisme (diss. Nijmegen). Wolf Legal Publishers, Nijmegen

Albrecht PA (2010) Kriminologie, Eine Grundlegung zum Strafrecht. Verlag CH Beck, München

Alink M (2004) AIVD-informatie als bewijs in het strafproces. In: Duyx PD (ed) Via Straatsburg. Liber amicorum Egbert Myjer. Wolf Legal Publishers, Nijmegen, pp 155–179

Allen RJ, Hoffmann JL, Livingston DA, Stuntz WJ (2005) Criminal procedure: investigation and right to counsel. Aspen Publishers, New York

Amar AR (1997) The constitution and criminal procedure, first principles. Yale University Press, New Haven

Amsterdam AG (1974) Perspectives on the fourth amendment. Minn L Rev 58:349–478

(Anonymous) Note (2008a) Mechanisms of secrecy. Harv L Rev 121:1556–1577

(Anonymous) Note (2008b) 'Shifting the FISA paradigm protecting civil liberties by eliminating ex ante judicial approval'. Harv L Rev 121:2200–2221

(Anonymous) Note (2009) Retreat: the supreme court and the new police. Harv L Rev 122: 1706–1727

Antkowiak BA (2007) Saving probable cause. Suffolk U L Rev 40:569–606

Arai Y (2006) Chapter 5. The system of restrictions. In: van Dijk P et al (eds) Theory and practice of the European convention on human rights. Intersentia, Antwerpen

Arcila F Jr (2010) The death of suspicion. Wm & Mary L Rev 51:1275–1341

Ashcroft J (2006) Never again. Securing America and restoring justice. Center Street, New York

Ashworth A (2007) Security, terrorism and the value of human rights. In: Goold BJ, Lazarus L (eds) Security and human rights. Hart Publishing, Portland, pp 201–226

Ashworth A (2009) Principles of criminal law. Oxford University Press, New York

Baaijens-van Geloven YGM, Simmelink JBHM (2002) Normering van de opsporing. In: Groenhuijsen MS, Knigge G (eds) Dwangmiddelen en rechtsmiddelen. Derde interim rapport onderzoeksproject strafvordering 2001. Kluwer, Deventer, pp 437–598

Baker JE (2007a) In the common defense, national security law for perilous times. Cambridge University Press, New York

M.F.H. Hirsch Ballin, *Anticipative Criminal Investigation*,
DOI: 10.1007/978-90-6704-843-9,

Baker JE (2007b) What's international law got to do with it? Transnational law and the intelligence mission. Mich J Int'l L 28:639–661

Bal P (2007) Uitsluiting van de uitsluitingsregel in de verenigde staten. De zaak Hudson v. Michigan. DD 2007 17:251–275

Barak-Erez D, Waxman MC (2009) Secret evidence and the due process of terrorist detentions. Colum J Transnat'l L 48:3–58

Barron JA, Dienes CT (2003) Constitutional law in a nutshell. West Group, St Paul

Bassiouni MC (2002) Legal control of international terrorism: a policy-oriented assessment. Harv Int'l L J 43:83–103

Bassiouni MC (2005) The regression of the rule of law under the guise of combating terrorism. Int Rev Penal Law 76:17–26

Bassiouni MC (2008) "Terrorism": Reflections on legitimacy and policy considerations. In: Karawan IA et al (eds) Values and violence, intangible aspects of terrorism. Springer, Dordrecht, pp 233–256

Beccaria C (1971) Over misdaden en straffen. Ingeleid, van aantekeningen voorzien en vertaald door Dr JM Michiels. Standaard Wetenschappelijke Uitgeverij, Antwerpen

Beccaria C (1986) On crimes, punishments (original edition 1764, translation by D Young). Indianapolis

Beck U (2005) Risk society. Towards a new modernity. Sage, London

Becker SW (2003) "Mirror, mirror on the wall": Assessing the aftermath of September 11th. Val U L Rev 37:563–626

Becker SW (2005) New developments: increased cooperation between law enforcement and intelligence agencies after September 11. Int Rev Penal Law 76:57–74

Becker SW (2007) Confronting the non-confrontational: reassessing the use of criminal evidence obtained extraterritorially in an age of global law enforcement and intelligence cooperation. Int Rev Penal Law 78:15–33

Becker SW (2008) Closing the door on justice. Secret evidence and the lack of transparency in court proceedings in the wake of the "war on terrorism". In: Becker SW, Derencinovic D (eds) International terrorism: the future unchained? faculty of law, University of Zagreb, Zagreb, pp 1–17

Beijer A (2006) Een andere kennismaking met de (wet) afgeschermde getuige. DD 2006 68:959–986

Beijer A, Bokhorst RJ, Boone M, Brants CH, Lindeman JMW (2004) De wet bijzondere opsporingsbevoegdheden – eindevaluatie. WODC, Ministerie van Justitie/Boom Juridische uitgevers, Meppel

Bekke AJGM, De Vries J (2007) U bent herkend. Aantreden en optreden van de nationaal coördinator terrorismebestrijding NCTb, Rapport Evaluatie NCTb, Apeldoorn/Leiden

Berkhout-van Poelgeest AM (2001) Enkele vragen over de legaliteit in het strafproces (artikel 1 Sv). In: Brants CH et al (eds) Legitieme strafvordering. Intersentia, Antwerpen, pp 23–36

Besselink LFM, Wessel RA (2009) De invloed van ontwikkelingen in de internationale rechtsorde op de doorwerking naar Nederlands constitutioneel recht. Een 'neo-monistische' benadering. Kluwer, Alphen aan den Rijn

Blaau LC (1990) The Rechtsstaat idea compared with the rule of law as a paradigm for protecting rights. S African L J 107:76–96

Bleichrodt E (2006) Chapter 11. Freedom from retrospective effect of penal legislation. In: van Dijk P et al (eds) Theory and practice of the European convention on human rights. Intersentia, Antwerpen, pp 651–662

Blom T (2007) Een ernstige inbreuk op de rechtsorde. DD 2007 51:626–638

Bloom R, Dunn WJ (2006) The constitutional infirmity of warrantless NSA surveillance the abuse of presidential power and the injury to the fourth amendment. Wm Mary Bill Rts J 15:147–202

Blum GL, Eclavea RP, Jacobs AJ, Surette EC (2010) III. Electronic surveillance. In: Wiretapping F Execution of warrant or order, 2 minimization. Am Jur 2d Searches and Seizures. 68:412–415 para

Boettke PJ, Oprea R (2004) The rule of law. In: Rowley C (ed) The encyclopedia of public choice, vol II. Kluwer Academic Publishers, Dordrecht, pp 507–510

Bokhorst RJ, De Kogel CH, Van der Meij CFM (2002) Evaluatie van de Wet BOB–fase 1. De eerste praktijkervaringen met de Wet Bijzondere opsporingsbevoegdheden. WODC, Ministerie van Jusitie, The Hague

Borgers MJ (2003) Rechtsstatelijkheid, doelmatigheid en transparantie van de strafrechtspleging. NJB 2003 11:553–556

Borgers MJ (2007) De vlucht naar voren (inaugural lecture amsterdam VU). Boom Juridische uitgevers, The Hague

Borgers MJ (2009) Het opsporingsbegrip anno 2009. In: Borgers MJ et al (eds) Politie in beeld. Liber amicorum Jan Naeyé. Wolf Legal Publishers, Nijmegen, pp 27–64

Borgers MJ (2011) De onderzoeksfase: toezicht, controle en opsporing. In: Kristen FGH et al (eds) Bijzonder strafrecht. Strafrechtelijke handhaving van sociaal-economisch en fiscaal recht in Nederland. Boom Lemma uitgevers, The Hague, pp 455–496

Borgers M, Van Sliedregt E (2009) The meaning of the precautionary principle for the assessment of criminal measures in the fight against terrorism. Erasmus L Rev 2(2):171–195

Brants CH, Rignalda A (2010/2011) Issues of convergence: inquisitorial prosecution in England and wales? Preadvies voor de Nederlandse vereniging voor rechtsvergelijking. Wolf Legal Publishers, Nijmegen

Brants CH, Van Lent L (2001) Externe openbaarheid. Van vanzelfsprekendheid tot probleem. In: Brants CH et al (eds) Legitieme strafvordering, Rechten van de mens als inspiratie in de 21ste eeuw. Intersentia Rechtswetenschappen, Antwerpen, pp 75–101

Brants CH, Field S, Jörg N (1995) Are inquisitorial and adversarial systems converging? In: Fennell P et al (eds) Criminal justice in Europe. A comparative study. Clarendon Press, Oxford, pp 41–56

Brants CH, Mevis PAM, Prakken E (2001) Legitieme strafvordering, rechten van de mens als inspiratie in de 21ste eeuw. Intersentia Rechtswetenschappen, Antwerpen

Brants CH, Mevis PAM, Prakken E, Reijntjes JM (2003) Op zoek naar grondslagen. In: Brants CH et al (eds) Op zoek naar grondslagen. Strafvordering 2001 ter discussie. Boom Juridische uitgevers, The Hague, pp 1–27

Brinkhoff S (2008) Anoniem melden startinformatie voor een strafrechtelijk onderzoek? NJB 2008 20:1224–1228

Brinkhoff S (2009) Controle op de criminele inlichtingeneenheden. DD 2009 10:112–139

Brouwer JG (2006) Van nachtbrakers tot terroristen. Over persoonsgericht verstoren (inaugural lecture Groningen). http://redes.eldoc.ub.rug.nl/FILES/root/2006/j.g.brouwer/Brouwer.pdf.. Accessed 28 April 2011

Buruma Y (2001) Buitengewone opsporingsmethoden. WEJ Tjeenk Willink, Deventer

Buruma Y (2004) Acht nieuwe wetten. De zin en onzin van gegevensbescherming. DD 2004 51:665–675

Buruma Y (2007) Formele bevoegdheden. In: Fijnaut CJCF et al (eds) Politie. Studies over haar werking en organisatie. Kluwer, Deventer, pp 525–558

Casey T (2008) Electronic surveillance and the right to be secure. U C Davis L Rev 41:977–1033

Cole D, Dempsey JX (2006) Terrorism and the constitution. Sacrificing civil liberties in the name of national security. The New Press, New York

Cole D, Lobel J (2007) Less safe less free. Why america is losing the war on terror. The New Press, New York

Coomans F, Kamminga M (2007) Rechten van de mens. In: Horbach N et al (eds) Handboek international recht. TMC Asser Press, The Hague, pp 469–507

Cooper Blum S (2009) What really is at stake with the FISA amendments act of 2008 and ideas for future surveillance reform. B U Pub Int L J 18:269–314

Coquillete DR et al (eds) (2007) Moore's federal practice—criminal. Matthew Bender & Company Inc., Newark

Corstens GJM (2005a) Dijkdoorbraken in de strafrechtspleging. NJB 2005 6:289

Corstens GJM (2005b) Het Nederlands strafprocesrecht. Kluwer, Arnhem

Corstens GJM (2008) Het Nederlands Strafprocesrecht. Kluwer, Deventer

Corstens GJM, Borgers MJ (2011) Het Nederlands Strafprocesrecht. Kluwer, Deventer

Coster van Voorhout JEB (2006) Intelligence as legal evidence. Comparative criminal research into the viability of the proposed Dutch scheme of shielded witnesses in England and Wales, and legislative compliance with Article 6 (3) (d) ECHR. Utrecht L Rev 2(2):119–143

Coveny AC (2007) When the immovable object meets the unstoppable force. Search and seizure in the age of terrorism. Am J Trial Advoc 31:329–387

Crocker ThP (2008) Overcoming necessity: torture and the state of constitutional culture. SMU L Rev 61:221–279

Damaška MR (1973) Evidentiary barriers to conviction and two models of criminal procedure. A comparative study. U Pa L Rev 121:506–589

Damaška MR (1986) The faces of justice and state authority, a comparative approach to the legal process. Yale University Press, New Haven

De Busser E (2009) Data protection in EU and US criminal cooperation. A substantive law approach to the EU internal and transatlantic cooperation in criminal matters between judicial and law enforcement authorities. Maklu, Antwerpen

De Hoog D (2008) Politiële terrorismebestrijding in Nederland: inrichting en uitdagingen van een bijzondere politietaak. In: Muller ER et al (eds) Terrorisme. Studies over terrorisme en terrorismebestrijding. Kluwer, Deventer, pp 579–612

De Moor-van Vugt A (1994) Maten en gewichten. Het evenredigheidsbeginsel in Europees perspectief (diss. Tilburg). WEJ Tjeenk Willink, Zwolle

De Poot CJ, Bokhorst RJ, Smeenk WH, Kouwenberg RF (2008) De opsporing verruimd? De wet opsporing terroristische misdrijven een jaar in werking. Cahier 2008–9 WODC, Ministerie van Justitie, The Hague

De Roos TA (2006) Kroniek van het straf(proces)recht. NJB 2006 31:1743–1752

De Roos TA (2010) Het gedoogakkoord en het repressieve veiligheidsbeleid, NJBlog 25 Oktober. http://njblog.nl/2010/10/25/het-gedoogakkoord-en-het-repressieve-veiligheidsbeleid. Accessed 2 May 2011

De Young K, Fletcher MA (2010) US was more focused on al-Qaeda's plans abroad than for homeland, report on airline bomb plot finds. Washington Post, January 8, 2010

Deelman P, Gunther Moor LGH (2010) Verschraalt de rol van de politie in het huidige integrale veiligheidsbeleid? Strafblad 2010 5:368–375 afl

Dinh VD (2002) Foreword: freedom and security after September 11. Harv J L Pub Pol'y 25:399–406

Donohue LK (2008) The costs of counterterrorism, power, politics and liberty. Cambridge University Press, New York

Dripps DA (2003) Terror and tolerance: criminal justice for the new age of anxiety. Ohio St J Crim L 1:9–43

Duncan RM Jr (2004) Surreptitious search warrants and the USA PATRIOT Act: "Thinking outside the box but within the constitution", or a violation of fourth amendment protections? NY City L Rev 7:1–38

Dworkin RM (1979) Taking rights seriously. Harvard University Press, Cambridge

Dworkin RM (2006) Is democracy possible here? Principles for a new political debate. Princeton University Press, Princeton

Dycus S, Banks WC, Raven-Hansen P (2007a) Counterterrorism law. Aspen Publishers, New York

Dycus S, Berney AL, Banks WC, Raven-Hansen P (2007b) National security law. Aspen Publishers, New York

Elliff JT (1984) Symposium: national security and civil liberties: the attorney general's guidelines for FBI investigations. Cornell L Rev 69:785–815

Elzinga DJ, Van Rest PHS, De Valk J (1995) Het Nederlandse Politierecht. WEJ Tjeenk Willink, Zwolle

Etzioni A (2004) How patriotic is the Patriot Act? Freedom versus security in the age of terrorism. Routledge, New York

Feld BC (2011) T.L.O. and reddings unanswered (Misanswered) fourth amendment questions: few rights and fewer remedies. Miss L J 80:847–954

Fenske D (2008) All enemies, foreign and domestic. Erasing the distinction between foreign and domestic intelligence gathering under the fourth amendment. Nw U L Rev 102:343–381

Feuth T (2002) Het verkennend onderzoek in strafzaken. Kluwer, Alphen aan de Rijn

Finn JE (1991) Constitutions in crisis. Political violence and the rule of law. Oxford University Press, Oxford

Fokkens JW, Kirkels-Vrijman N (2009) De artikelen 2 politiewet 1993 en 141 en 142 Strafvordering als basis voor opsporingsbevoegdheden. In: Borgers MJ et al (eds) Politie in beeld. Liber amicorum Jan Naeyé. Wolf Legal Publishers, Nijmegen, pp 105–124

Foqué R, Hart 't AC (1990) Instrumentaliteit en rechtsbescherming. Grondslagen van een strafrechtelijke waardendiscussie. Gouda Quint, Arnhem

Forgang JD (2009) "The right of the people": the NSA, the FISA amendments act of 2008, and foreign intelligence surveillance of americans overseas. Fordham L Rev 78:217–266

Franken AA (2004a) Voor de vorm (inaugural lecture Utrecht). Boom Juridische uitgevers, The Hague

Franken AA (2004b) Een effectief middel tegen vormverzuimen? In: Duyx PD, van Zeben PDJ (eds) Via straatsburg. Liber amicorum egbert myer. Wolf Legal Publishers, Nijmegen, pp 207–220

Franken AA (2006) De rol van de rechter-commissaris: tussen ideaal en praktijk. DD 2006 14:266–276

Franken AA (2008) Strafrechtswetenschappen en terrorismebestrijding. DD 2008 1:1–14

Franken AA (2009) Proportionaliteit en subsidiariteit in de opsporing. DD 2009 8:79–92

Garland D (2001) The culture of control. Crime and social order in contemporary society. Oxford University Press, New York

Glashausser A (2008) Treaties as domestic law in the United States. In: Miller RA, Bratspies RM (eds) Progress in international law. Martinus Nijhoff Publishers, Leiden, pp 219–242

Global Justice Information Sharing Initiative (2003) United States Department of Justice, The National Criminal Intelligence Sharing Plan, Solutions and approaches for a cohesive plan to improve our nation's ability to develop and share criminal intelligence. http://www.iir.com/GLOBAL/ncisp.htm. Accessed 24 Nov 2009

Global Justice Information Sharing Initiative (2006) United States Department of Justice, 'Fusion Center Guidelines, Developing and Sharing Information and Intelligence in a New Era, Guidelines for Establishing and Operating Fusion Centers at the Local, State, and Federal Levels, Executive Summary. http://www.iir.com/GLOBAL/ncisp.htm. Accessed 24 Nov 2009

Goldschmidt JE (2005) Mag het iets minder zijn? Hebben we een teveel aan mensenrechten? (Inaugural lecture utrecht). Universiteit Utrecht, Studie – en informatiecentrum mensenrechten (SIM), Utrecht

Griffiths J (1970) Ideology in criminal procedure or a third "Model" of the criminal process. Yale L J 79:359–417

Groenhuijsen MS (1991) Naar een geïntegreerde herziening van het wetboek van strafvordering. In: Doorenbos DR, en Verweij RJ (eds) Hercodificatie wetboek van strafvordering. Tijd voor een integrale herziening? Ars Aequi Libri 1991, Nijmegen, pp 35–60

Groenhuijsen MS, Knigge G (eds) (2001) Het onderzoek ter zitting. Onderzoeksproject strafvordering 2001. Eerste interimrapport. Gouda Quint, Deventer

Groenhuijsen MS, Kooijmans T (2010) Probleemoplossing door voortschrijdende wetgeving in het strafrecht? DD 2010 25:419–457

Groenhuijsen M, Simmelink J (2008) Criminal procedure in the Netherlands. In: Vogler R, Huber B (eds) Criminal procedure in Europe. Duncker & Humblot, Berlin, pp 373–481

Guiora NA (2008) Military Commissions and National Security Courts after Guantánamo. Nw U L Rev Colloquy 103:199–208

Habermas J (1996) Between facts and norms, contributions to a discourse theory of law and democracy (original edition 1992, translated by William Rehg). Massachusetts Institute of Technology, Cambridge

Handboek voor de opsporingspraktijk (2000–2007) Openbaar Ministerie. Sdu Uitgevers, The Hague

Harr JS, Hess KM (2002) Constitutional law and the criminal justice system. Wadsworth/ Thomson Learning, Belmont

Hart 't AC (1983) Strafrecht en beleid. Essays. WEJ Tjeenk Willink, Zwolle

Hart 't AC (1994) Openbaar ministerie en rechtshandhaving. Een verkenning. Gouda Quint, Arnhem

Hart HLA (2008) Punishment and responsibility. Essays in the philosophy of law. Oxford University Press, New York

Herman SN (2006) The USA PATRIOT Act and the Submajoritarian Fourth Amendment. Harv CR-CL L Rev 41:67–132

Hielkema J (2005) De rechter-commissaris in strafzaken: leidender of lijdelijker? In: Harteveld A et al (eds) Systeem in ontwikkeling. Liber amicorum G. Knigge. Wolf Legal Publishers, Nijmegen, pp 259–271

Hirsch Ballin MFH (2008) An inside view of dutch counterterrorism strategy. Countering terrorism through criminal law and the presumption of innocence. J Inst Just Int'l Stud 8:139–151

Hirsch Ballin MFH (2009) 'Een vreemde eend in de bijt van de opsporing'. DD 2009 22:281–302

Hirsch Ballin MFH (2012) Terrorism causing a shifting responsibility in criminal pre-trial investigation: from repression to prevention. In: van Coster Voorhout J et al (eds) Shifting responsibilities in criminal justice. Critical portrayals of the changing role and content of a fragmented globalizing law domain. Boom Juridische uitgevers, The Hague (forthcoming)

Hirsch Ballin MFH (2012) National security, international privacy and transnational data exchange. In: Scott Smith GP (ed) Obama, US Politics, and transatlantic relations: change or continuity? PIE-Peter Lang, Brussels (forthcoming)

Hitz FP (2002) Responses to the September 11 attacks. Unleashing the rogue elephant. September 11 and letting the CIA be the CIA. Harv J L Pub Pol'y 25:765–780

Hobbes Th (1998) Leviathan (reprinted, original edition 1651), edited with an introduction and notes by JCA Gaskin. Oxford University Press, New York

Hoffman B (2006) Inside terrorism. Columbia University Press, New York

Howell BA (2006) Foreign intelligence surveillance act: has the solution become a problem? In: Northhouse C (ed) Protecting what matters, technology, security and liberty since 9/11. Brookings Institution Press/Computer Ethics Institute, Washington

Huster S, Rudolph K (2008) Vom Rechtsstaat zum präventionsstaat (reprinted). Suhrkamp Verlag, Frankfurt am Main

Ignatieff M (2005) The lesser evil. Political ethics in an age of terror. Edinburgh University Press, Edinburgh

Israel JH (1993) Cornerstones of the judicial process. 2-SPG Kan J L Pub Pol'y 5–22

Israel JH, Kamisar Y, LaFave WR, King NJ (2006) Criminal procedure and the constitution. Leading supreme court cases and introductory text, 2006 edition. West a Thomson Business, St Paul

Israel JH, LaFave WR (2006) Criminal procedure, constitutional limitations, In a nutshell. Thomson/West, St Paul

Jackson AL, Brown M (2007) Ensuring efficiency, interagency cooperation, and protection of civil liberties. Shifting from a traditional model of policing to an intelligence-led policing (ILP) paradigm. Crim Justice Stud 20(2):111–129

Jones A (2009) The 2008 FBI guidelines: contradiction of original purpose. B U Pub Int L J 19:137–174

Keijzer N (1987) Enkele opmerkingen omtrent de praesumptio innocentiae in strafzaken. In: Enschedé CJ et al (eds) Naar eer en geweten. Liber amicorum journal remmelink. Gouda Quint, Arnhem, pp 235–253

Kelk C (1995) Criminal justice in the Netherlands. In: Fennell P et al (eds) Criminal justice in Europe: a comparative study. Clarendon Press, Oxford, pp 1–20

Kinports K (2009) Diminishing probable cause and minimalist searches. Ohio St J Crim L 6:649–660 Spring

Knigge G (2005) Verdachte en verdenking. In: Jordaans AHEC et al (eds) Praktisch strafrecht, Liber amicorum J.M. Reijntjes. Wolf Legal Publishers, Nijmegen, pp 351–365

Knigge G, Kwakman NJM (2001) Het opsporingsbegrip en de normering van de opsporingstaak. In: Groenhuijsen MS, Knigge G (eds) Het vooronderzoek in Strafzaken. Tweede interim-rapport onderzoeksproject strafvordering 2001. Gouda Quint, Deventer, pp 125–347

Krauß D (1971) Der Grundsatz der Unschuldsvermutung im Strafverfahren. In: Müller-Dietz H (ed) strafrechtsdogmatik und kriminalpolitik. Carl Heymanns Verlag KG, Köln/Berlin/Bonn/München, pp 153–178

Krips F (2009) Over de bruikbaarheid van AIVD-informatie in strafzaken. In: Scheltema A, Scheltema M, Dekerelaere K, Delvauw M, Tormans S, Krips F, Winants A, Kortmann J, Sieburgh C, Cauffman C, Weyts B (eds) Preadviezen 2009. Toezicht op de financiële markt en de energiemarkt. Staatsgeheimen en het strafproces. Rechtshandhaving door het privaatrecht (Vereniging voor de vergelijkende studie van het recht van België en Nederland). Boom Juridische uitgevers, The Hague, pp 129–194

Kris DS (2006) The rise and fall of the FISA wall'. Stan L & Pol'y Rev 17:487–529

Kris DS (2011) 'Law enforcement as counterterrorism tool'. J Nat'l Security L Pol'y 5:1–95

Kris DS, Wilson JD (2007) National security investigations and prosecutions. Thomson/West, Eagan

Krommendijk M, Terpstra J, Van Kempen PH (2009) De wet BOB: titels IVa en V in de praktijk, besluitvorming over bijzondere opsporingsbevoegdheden in de aanpak van georganiseerde criminaliteit. Boom Juridische uitgevers/WODC, Ministerie van Justitie, The Hague

Kuijer M (2005) Van lawless naar een rechtmatige bestrijding van terrorisme (inaugural lecture Amsterdam VU). Wolf Legal Publishers, Nijmegen

LaFave WR (2003) Principles of criminal law. West Group, St Paul

LaFave WR, Israel JH, King NJ (2004) Criminal procedure, fourth edition. West a Thomson business, St Paul

Lawson RA (1999) 'De internationale rechter en de Nederlandse rechtsorde', in Handelingen NJV 129[e] jaargang/1999-I, internationale rechtspraak in de Nederlandse rechtsorde, WEJ Tjeenk Willink, Deventer, 1–132

Lawson Mack R, Kelly MJ (2004) Equal justice in the balance. America's legal responses to the emerging terrorist threat. The University of Michigan Press, Ann Arbor

Lazarus L, Goold B (2007) Introduction, security and human rights: the search for a language of reconciliation. In: Goold BJ, Lazarus L (eds) Security and human rights. Hart Publishing, Portland, pp 1–24

Lindenberg K (2002) Van ort tot oro. Een verzameling van de werken die hebben geleid tot het oorspronkelijk regeringsontwerp van een nieuw Wetboek van strafvordering (1914). Rijksuniversiteit Groningen, Groningen

Lintz JM (2007) De plaats van de Wet terroristische misdrijven in het materiële strafrecht. Een onderzoek naar de wederzijdse beïnvloeding door de Wet terroristische misdrijven en het wetboek van strafrecht en enkele bijzondere wetten (diss. Rotterdam). Wolf Legal Publishers, Nijmegen

Lipton E, Schmitt E, Mazzetti M (2010) Review of jet bomb shows more missed clues, New York Times, January 18, 2010

Lobel J (2002) The war on terrorism and civil liberties. Univ Pitt L Rev 63:767–790

Locke J (1980) The second treatise of government (original edition 1690, edited by CB Macpherson), Hackett Publishing Company, Indianapolis

Loof JP (2000) Mag de overheid op zoek gaan naar de grenzen van haar bevoegdheid als daarbij de grondrechten in het geding zijn? NJCM-Bulletin 2000 25(2):666–667

Loof JP (2005) Mensenrechten en staatsveiligheid: verenigbare grootheden? Opschorting en beperking van mensenrechtenbescherming tijdens noodtoestanden en andere situaties die de staatsveiligheid bedreigen. Wolf Legal Publishers, Nijmegen

Luban D (2002) The war on terrorism and the end of human rights. Phil & Pub Poly Q 22:9–14

Luban D (2007) Legal ethics and human dignity. Cambridge University Press, New York

Luban D, O'Sullivan JR, Stewart DP (2010) International and transnational criminal law. Aspen Publishers, New York

Luchtman MJJP (2007a) Grensoverschrijdende sfeercumulatie. Over de handhavingssamenwerking tussen financiële toezichthouders, fiscale autoriteiten en justitiële autoriteiten in EU-verband (diss. Utrecht). Wolf Legal Publishers, Nijmegen

Luchtman MJJP (2007b) Sfeercumulatie in het verkeersrecht en het fiscale recht. DD 2007 53:657–681

Luchtman MJJP (2008) European cooperation between financial supervisory authorities, tax authorities and judicial authorities. Intersentia, Antwerpen

Luna E (2009) Criminal justice and the public imagination. Ohio St J Crim L 7:71–147

Manning PK (1977) Police work. The social organization of policing. Massachusetts Institute of Technology, Cambridge

Marcus P (1998) Symposium: the challenge of prosecuting organized crime in the United States. Procedural issues, XVI international congress of penal law, report submitted by the American National Section, AIDP: topic III: criminal procedure. Wayne L Rev 44:1379–1400

Mart SN (2008) The chains of the constitution and legal process in the library. A post-USA Patriot Reauthorization Act Assessment. Okla City U L Rev 33:435–503

Martin K (2002) Intelligence, terrorism and civil liberties. Human Rights, Winter 2002, 5–7

Mauriello TP (2007) Criminal investigation handbook. Mathew Bender & Company Inc, Newark

McConell JM (2008) Vision 2015. A globally networked and integrated intelligence enterprise, Report of the director of national intelligence, Washington. http://www.dni.gov/reports.htm. Accessed 4 Aug 2011

McCormack W (2007) Understanding the law of terrorism. LexisNexis, Newark

McCormack W (2008) Values implicated in the struggle with terrorism: war, Crime and Prevention. In: Karawan IA et al (eds) Values and violence, intangible aspects of terrorism. Springer, Dordrecht, pp 257–277

McCormack W (2010) Prosecuting terrorism. Models for confronting organized violence. SSRN: http://ssrn.com/abstract=1623847. Accessed 12 Aug 2011

McLaughlin K (2007) The fourth amendment and cell phone location tracking: where are we? Hastings Comm Ent L J 19:421–445

Mégret F (2010) Nature of obligations. In: Moeckli D et al (eds) International human rights law. Oxford University Press, Oxford, pp 124–149

Mevis PAM (2005a) Strafrecht, EVRM en grondwet. Enkele gedachten over het belang, de ontwikkeling en de versterking van een algemeen toetsingskader voor veranderingen binnen het strafrecht. In: Jordaans AHEC et al (eds) Praktisch strafrecht. Liber amicorum J.M. Reijntjes. Wolf Legal Publishers, Nijmegen, pp 453–469

Mevis PAM (2005b) De evaluatie van de wet BOB en van de wet herziening GVO. DD 2005 32:452–466

Mevis PAM (2009a) Nuttig recht op een eerlijk proces in de Grondwet. DD 2009 1:1–18

Mevis PAM (2009b) Wetsvoorstel versterking rol RC: toch maar doen. DD 2009 50:652–688

Moore K (2007) The role of federal criminal prosecutions in the war on terrorism. Lewis Clark L Rev 11:837–849

Muller ER (2007) Inlichtingendiensten in Nederland. In: Fijnaut CJCF et al (eds) Politie. Studies over haar werking en organisatie. Kluwer, Deventer, pp 169–190

Muller ER, Kummeling HRBM, Bron RP (2007a) Veiligheid en privacy. Een zoektocht naar een nieuwe balans. Boom Juridische Uitgevers/COT Instituut voor Veiligheids – en Crisismanagement/Universiteit Utrecht, Den Haag

Muller ER (2008) Trends in terrorisme en terrorismebestrijding. In: Muller ER et al (eds) Terrorisme. Studies over terrorisme en terrorismebestrijding. Kluwer, Deventer, pp 903–917

Muller ER, Dubelaar MJ, Cleiren CPM (2007b) Algemene beginselen van behoorlijke politiezorg. In: Fijnaut CJCF et al (eds) Politie. Studies over haar werking en organisatie. Kluwer, Deventer, pp 559–599

Muller ER, Rogier LJJ, Kummeling HRBM, Dammen R, Bron RP, Woltjer AJTh, Kalkhoven VC (2007b) Bestuur, recht en veiligheid. Bestuursrechtelijke bevoegdheden voor openbare orde handhaving en terrorismebestrijding, Onderzoeksrapport COT Instituut voorVeiligheids – en Crisismanagement, Erasmus Universiteit Rotterdam en Universiteit Utrecht. http://www.rijksoverheid.nl/documenten-enpublicaties/kamerstukken/2008/04/24/kabinetsstandpunt-rapport-bestuur-recht-en-veiligheid.html. Accessed 3 May 2011

Musch DJ (2003) Civil liberties and the foreign intelligence surveillance act, fourteenth volume, second series. terrorism: document of international and local control, oceana publications, Inc, Dobbs Ferry, NY. Myjer E (1997) De verdachte jager zonder stukken, EHRM 18 maart 1997, Fouchier t. Frankrijk, ann. E. Myer, NJCM-Bulletin 1997, 22(6):734–742

Myjer E (1997) De verdachte jager zonder stukken, EHRM 18 maart 1997, Fouchier t. Frankrijk, ann. E. Myer. NJCM Bull 1997, 22(6):734–742

Nakashima E (2010) White house proposal would ease FBI access to records of internet activity. Washington Post, 29 July 2010

Nakashima E (2010) Plaintiff who challenged FBI's national security letters reveals concerns. Washington Post, 10 Aug 2010

Nieland AE (2007) National Security Letters and the Amended Patriot Act. Cornell L Rev 92:1201–1236

Nokes SE (2011) Redefining the supremacy clause in the global age: reconciling medellin with original intent. Wm Mary Bill Rts J 19:829–855

Nowak JE, Rotunda RD (2004) Constitutional law. 7th edn. West, a thomson business, St Paul

Nowak JE, Rotunda RD (2005) Principles of constitutional law. West, a Thomson Business, St Paul

O'Harrow R Jr (2002) Six weeks in autumn. Washington Post Magazine, October 27, 2002

Ölçer FP (2008) Eerlijk proces en bijzondere opsporing. Wolf Legal Publishers, Nijmegen

Ölçer FP (2010) Preventief fouilleren zonder redelijk vermoeden van schuld, EHRM 12 januari 2010, Gillan en Quinton v. Het Verenigd Koninkrijk, appl. nr. 4158/05. Strafblad 2010 1:21–30 afl

Orth JV (2003) Due process of law, a brief history. University Press of Kansas, Lawrence

Packer H (1966) The courts, the police, and the rest of US. J Crim L Criminol Pol Sci 57(238): 238–243

Parry JT (2007) Terrorism and the new criminal process. Wm Mary Bill Rts J 15:765–835

Pati R (2009) Due process and international terrorism. An international legal analysis. Martinus Nijhoff Publishers, Leiden

Peçi I, Sikkema E (2008) De rechtsbeschermende functie van het opsporingsbegrip. In: Franken AA, de Langen M, Moerings M (eds) Constante waarden. Liber amicorum prof. mr. Constantijn Kelk. Boom Juridische Uitgevers, The Hague, pp 353–362

Perrine JB (2005) The USA PATRIOT Act: big brother or business as usual? Notre Dame J L Ethics Pub Pol'y 19:163–195

Peters AAG (1999) Het rechtskarakter van het strafrecht. In: Buruma Y (ed) 100 jaar strafrecht. Klassieke teksten van de twintigste eeuw. Amsterdam University Press, Amsterdam, pp 271–287

Pfeiffer C (2004) Feeling insecure? United States v. Bin laden and the merits of a foreign-intelligence exception for searches abroad. Rev Litig 23:209–237

Podgor ES (2004) Department of justice guidelines: balancing "Discretionary Justice". Cornell J L Pub Pol'y 13:167–202, Spring

Pompe WPJ (1959) Vooronderzoek of eindonderzoek beslissend? TvSTvS 1959:141–151

Pompe WPJ (2008) 'De persoon des daders in het strafrecht. Rede uitgesproken bij de aanvaarding van het hoogleraarsambt aan de Rijksuniversiteit te Utrecht op 8 oktober 1928'. In: Gedachten van Willem Pompe over de mens in het strafrecht. Willem Pompe Instituut/ Boom Juridische uitgevers, The Hague

Position paper Barack Obama (2008) Barack Obama: the war we need to win, Obama's plan to defeat terrorism worldwide. http://www.barackobama.com/pdf/CounterterrorismFactSheet.pdf. Accessed 25 Oct 2010

Posner R (2006) Not a suicide pact. The constitution in a time of national emergency. Oxford University Press, Oxford

Posner EA, Vermeule A (2007) Terror in the balance. Security, liberty and the courts. Oxford University Press, Oxford

Power RC (2010) "Intelligence" searches and purpose: a significant mismatch between constitutional criminal procedure and the law of intelligence-gathering. Pace L Rev 30: 620–687

Prakken E (2004) 'Naar een cyclopisch (straf)recht'. NJB 2004 45/46:2338–2344

Progress Report (2011) Implementing 9/11 commission recommendations. US Department of Homeland Security

Priest D, Arkin WM (2010) 'Top secret America, a Washington Post investigation', Washington Post, July 19, 2010

Ramraj VV (2007) Between idealism and pragmatism. Legal and political constraints on state power in times of crisis. In: Goold B, Lazarus L (eds) Security and human rights. Hart, Oxford, pp 185–202

Rawls J (1993) Political liberalism. Columbia University Press, New York

Reijntjes JM (2001) De toekomst van het voorbereidend onderzoek. DD 2001 31:264–284

Reijntjes JM (2006) Minkenhof's Nederlandse strafvordering. Kluwer, Deventer

Reis H (1970) Kant's political writings (edited with an introduction and notes by hans reiss, Translated by HN Nisbet). Cambridge University Press, Cambridge

Risen J, Lichtblau E (2005) Bush lets U.S. spy on callers without courts, New York Times, December 16, 2005. http://www.nytimes.com/2005/12/16/politics/16program.html. Accessed July 29, 2011

Rivers J (2006) Proportionality and variable intensity of review. Cambridge L Jo 65:174–207

Rodley NS (2010) Integrity of the person. In: Moeckli D et al (eds) International human rights law. Oxford University Press, Oxford, pp 209–232

Rosand E (2004) Security council resolution 1373 and the counter—Terrorism committee: the cornerstone of the United Nations contribution to the fight against terrorism. In: Fijnaut C et al (eds) Legal instruments in the fight against international terrorism. A transatlantic dialogue. Martinus Nijhoff Publishers, Leiden/Boston, pp 603–632

Rosenfeld M (2001) The rule of law and the legitimacy of constitutional democracy. S Cal L Rev 74:1307–1350

Roth MJ (2009) Berkemer revisited: uncovering the middle ground between Miranda and the New Terry. Fordham L Rev 77:2779–2833

Rozemond N (1998) Strafvorderlijke rechtsvinding (diss. Amsterdam VU). Gouda Quint, Deventer

Rozemond N (2000) Voorafgaande beschouwingen in de strafrechtspraak van de Hoge Raad. NJB 2000 13:706–712

Rozemond N (2003) De moraal van het strafrecht. DD 2003 33:595–613

Rozemond N (2006) Strafrechtelijke belangenafweging in de risicosamenleving. RMThemis 4:160–168

Sales NA (2007) Secrecy and national security investigations. Ala L Rev 58:811–884

Saul B (2006) Defining terrorism in international law. Oxford University Press, New York

Savage Ch (2011) Delayed miranda warning ordered for terror suspects. New York Times, March 24, 2011

Schalken T (2006) De jurist en de kunstenaar. Waar het verschil in denkstijlen toe kan leiden. NJB 2006 02:70–73

Schulhofer SJ (2005) Rethinking the patriot act. The Century Foundation Press, New York

Sen A (2010) The idea of justice. Penguin Books, New York

Senna JJ, Siegel LJ (1998) Essentials of criminal justice. Wadsworth Publishing Company, Belmont

Schmitt C (2005) Political theory, four chapters on the concept of sovereignty (original edition 1922, translated by George Schwab). University of Chicago Press, Chicago

Shumate BA (2006) From "Sneak and Peek" to "Sneak and Steal". Section 213 of the USA PATRIOT act. Regent U L Rev 19:203–234

Sidel M (2004) More secure less free? Antiterrorism policy & civil liberties after September 11. The University of Michigan Press, Ann Arbor

Sikkema E (2008) Aantekeningen op art. 27 (suppl. 169, oktober 2008). In: Melai/Groenhuijsen et al (eds) Het wetboek van strafvordering. Kluwer, Deventer (losbladig)

Simmelink JBHM (1987) De rechtsstaatgedachte achter art. 1 Sv. Gedachten over de betekenis van art. 1 Sv voor het handelen van de overheid in de opsporingsfase. Gouda Quint, Arnhem

Simmelink JBHM, Baaijens-van Geloven YGM (2001) Vervolging en rechtsbescherming. In: Groenhuijsen MS, Knigge G (eds) Het vooronderzoek in strafzaken. Tweede interimrapport onderzoeksproject Strafvordering 2001. Gouda Quint, Deventer, pp 387–496

Simmons R (2010) Searching for terrorists. Why public safety is not a special need. Duke L J 59:843–927

Slobogin C (2007) The liberal assault on the fourth amendment. Ohio St J Crim L 4:603–618

Smith JC (2003) The USA PATRIOT Act: violating reasonable expectations of privacy protected by the fourth amendment without advancing national security. N C L Rev 82:412–455

Snider B (2003) Congressional oversight of intelligence. Some reflections on the last 25 years. Center on Law Ethics and National Security, Durham

Special Report of the DoJ's Office of the Inspector General (2005) Federal Bureau of Investigation's Compliance with the Attorney General's Investigative Guidelines, US Department of Justice, Office of the Inspector General, September 2005

Soeteman A (2009) Rechtsbeginselen en positivisme!? R&R 2009 1(38):5–10

Sottiaux S (2008) Terrorism and the limitation of rights. The ECHR and the US constitution. Hart Publishing, Oxford

Stuckenberg CF (1997) Untersuchungen zur unschuldsvermutung (diss. Bonn University). Walter de Gruyter & Company, Berlin

Stuntz WJ (2002) Local policing after the terror. Yale L J 111:2137–2194

Subin HI, Mirsky IS, Weinstein IS (1993) The criminal process. Prosecution and defense functions. West Publishing Company, St Paul

Sunstein CR (2005) Laws of fear. Beyond the precautionary principle. Cambridge University Press, Cambridge

Swire PP (2004) The system of foreign intelligence surveillance law. Geo Wash L Rev 72:1306–1371

Sydejko RJ (2006) International influence on democracy. How terrorism exploited a deteriorating fourth amendment. J L Society 7:220–270

Tamanaha BZ (2004) On the rule of law: history, politics, theory. Cambridge University Press, Cambridge

Taslitz AE (2010) What is probable cause, and why should we care? The costs, benefits, and meaning of individualized suspicion. Law Contemp Probs 73:145–210

Trechsel S (2005) Human rights in criminal proceedings. Oxford University Press, Oxford

Tsakyrakis S (2008) Proportionality: an assault on human rights. Jean monnet working paper 09/08, available at: http://centers.law.nyu.edu/jeanmonnet/papers/08/080901.pdf. Accessed 12 Aug 2011

Van der Geest C (2008) Van daderschap naar intentie. Is er binnen het strafrecht, door de invoering van artikelen 140, 46 en 80 Sr en de invoering van de Wet Terroristische Misdrijven, sprake van een verschuiving richting intentiestrafrecht? Kennispunt Faculteit Recht, Economie, Bestuur en Organisatie, Universiteit Utrecht, Utrecht

Van der Meij PPJ (2010a) De driehoeksverhouding in het strafrechtelijk vooronderzoek. Een onverminderde zoektocht naar evenwicht in de rolverdeling tussen de rechter-commissaris, de officier van justitie en de verdediging. Kluwer, Deventer

Van der Meij PPJ (2010b) De rechter-commissaris als onmisbare schakel in het vooronderzoek? Trema 8:331–338

Van der Woude MAH (2010) Wetgeving in een Veiligheidscultuur. Totstandkoming van antiterrorismewetgeving in Nederland bezien vanuit maatschappelijke en (rechts)politieke context (diss. Leiden). Boom Juridische uitgevers, The Hague

Van der Woude M, Van Sliedregt E (2007) De risicosamenleving: overheid vs. Strafrechtswetenschap? Aanwijzingen voor het debat rondom veiligheid en risico's. Proces 2007 6:216–226

Van Gestel B, De Poot CJ, Bokhorst RJ, Kouwenberg RF (2009) Signalen van terrorisme en de opsporingspraktijk. De wet opsporing terroristische misdrijven twee jaar in werking. WODC, Ministerie van Justitie, The Hague

Van Gestel B, De Poot CJ, Kouwenberg RF (2010) De wet opsporing terroristische misdrijven drie jaar in werking. WODC, Ministerie van Justitie, The Hague

Van Ginkel B (2010) The practice of the United Nations in combating terrorism from 1946 to 2008. Questions of legality and legitimacy (diss. Utrecht). Intersentia, Leiden/Oxford/Portland

Van Kempen PHPHMC (2005) Terrorismebestrijding door marginalisering van strafvorderlijke waarborgen. NJB 2005 08:397–400

Van Kempen PHPHMC (2005b) Het conceptwetsvoorstel voorkoming, opsporing en vervolging van terroristische misdrijven. Terrorismebestrijding door marginalisering strafvorderlijke waarborgen. http://www.portill.nl/articles/vankempen/VanKempen_1.PDF. Accessed 13 May 2011

Van Kempen PHPHMC (2008) Repressie door mensenrechten. Over positieve verplichtingen tot aanwending van stafrecht ter bescherming van fundamentele rechten. Wolf Legal Publishers, Nijmegen

Van Kempen PHPHMC, Van de Voort J (2010) Nederlandse antiterrorismeregelgeving getoetst aan fundamentele rechten. Een analyse met meer bijzondere aandacht voor het EVRM. NCTb, WODC, Ministerie van Justitie/Radboud Universiteit, Nijmegen

Van Klink B, Lembcke O (2007) 'Can terrorism be fought within the boundaries of the rule of law? A review of recent literature in political philosophy'. R&R 2007 2:9–26

Van Sliedregt E (2006) Het verdenkingsbegrip. In: Cleiren CPM et al (eds) Jurisprudentie strafrecht select. Sdu Uitgevers, The Hague, pp 1–25

Van Sliedregt E (2009) Ten to one. A contemporary reflection on the presumption of innocence (inaugural lecture Amsterdam VU). Boom Legal Publishers, The Hague

Van Westerloo G (2006) Hoge Raad bezorgd over verharding strafklimaat. NRC Handelsblad, 6 May 2006

Van Wifferen L (2007) Terrorisme als gedraging in het strafprocesrecht. In: van Kempen PHPHMC et al (eds) De gedraging in beweging. Handelen en nalaten in het materiële strafrecht, strafprocesrecht en sanctierecht. Wolf Legal Publishers, Nijmegen, pp 195–209

Van Zuijlen RW (2008) Veiligheid als opdracht. Een onderzoek naar veiligheid als fundamenteel recht en als positieve verplichting van de staat in het licht van de politietaak tot strafrechtelijke rechtshandhaving (diss. Rotterdam). Wolf Legal Publishers, Nijmegen

Vellinga-Schootstra F, Vellinga WH (2008) 'Positive Obligations' en het Nederlandse straf (proces)recht (inaugural lecture Groningen). Kluwer, Deventer

Vermaas P (2011) AIVD en OM. Landelijke terreurofficieren willen informatie delen verbeteren. Opportuun 2:24–27, februari 2011

Verrest PAM (2011) Raison d'être. Een onderzoek naar de rol van de rechter-commissaris in ons strafproces. Boom Juridische uitgevers, The Hague

Verri P (1988) Osservazioni sulla tortura. Rizzoli Libre, Milano

Vervaele JAE (2005) 'Terrorism and information sharing between the intelligence and law enforcement communities in the US and the Netherlands: emergency criminal law?' Utrecht L Rev 1(1):1–27

Vervaele JAE (2008) The anti-terrorist law in the US: criminal law for the enemies. Inter-Am Europ Hum Rights J Revista Interame y Europea de Derechos Humanos 1(1):5–60

Vervaele JAE (2009) Special procedural measures and respect of human rights, general report. Int Rev Penal Law 1–2:75–123

Vervaele JAE (2012) Epilogue. In: van Coster Voorhout J et al (eds) Shifting responsibilities in criminal justice. Critical portrayals of the changing role and content of a fragmented globalizing law domain. Boom Juridische uitgevers, The Hague Forthcoming Fall

Vis T (2010a) De scheiding tussen de politieke inlichtingendienst AIVD en de politie. Strafblad 2010, afl 5:420–428

Vis T (2010b) Het vertrouwen tussen de AIVD en de politie: een brug te ver? In: Gaarthuis RST et al (eds) Vertrouwen in de strafrechtspleging. Kluwer, Deventer, pp 119–137

Vogler R (2008) Introduction. In: Vogler R, Huber B (eds) Criminal procedure in Europe. Duncker & Humblot, Berlin, pp 4–38

Walther S (2000) The position and structure of the prosecutor's office in the United States. Eur J of Crime, Crim L Crim Just 8/1(1):283–295

White JR (2004) Defending the homeland, domestic intelligence, law enforcement and security. Wadsworth Publishing Company, Belmont

Winter H (2006) Resurrecting the "Dead Hand" of the common law rule of 1789. Why Terry v. Ohio is in Jeopardy. 45:5 Crim Law Bull 2

Yeh BT, Doyle CH (2006) CRS report for congress. USA PATRIOT Act Improvement and Reauthorization Act of 2005. A legal analysis, congressional research service (updated December 21st 2006)

Zabel RB, Benjamin JJ Jr (2008) In pursuit of justice. Prosecuting terrorism cases in the federal courts. A white paper. Human Rights First 2008

Zabel RB, Benjamin JJ (2009) In pursuit of justice. Prosecuting terrorism cases in the federal courts. 2009 update and recent developments. Human Rights First 2009

# Reports

*Rapport Evaluatie Antiterrorismemaatregelen (2011) 'Antiterrorismemaatregelen in Nederland in het eerste decennium van de 21e eeuw. Over totstandkoming, toepassing, beoordeling en aanpassing van antiterrorismemaatregelen in Nederland 2001–2010'*, NCTb, Ministerie van Veiligheid en Justitie, The Hague (*Kamerstukken II* 2010/11, 29754, nr. 199).

*Rapport Staatscommissie Grondwet* (November 2010), available at: www.staatscommissiegrondwet.nl (accessed 27 January 27 2011) (*Kamerstukken II* 2010/11, 31570, nr. 17).

*Rapport van de Commissie Bestuurlijke Evaluatie Algemene Inlichtingen—en Veiligheidsdienst* (Commission Havermans). *De AIVD in verandering* (November 2004), available at: https://www.aivd.nl/actueel/aivd-publicaties/ (accessed 12 August 2011) (*Kamerstukken II* 2004/05, 29876, nr. 1).

*Rapport van de Commissie Evaluatie Antiterrorismebeleid* (Commission Suyver) *Naar een integrale evaluatie van antiterrorismemaatregelen* (May 2009), available at: http://www.nctb.nl/Images/Rapport_Suyver_tcm91-203904.pdf (accessed 12 August 2011).

*Rapport van de Commissie van Toezicht betreffende de Inlichtingen—en Veiligheidsdiensten inzake het onderzoek naar de door de AIVD uitgebrachte ambtsberichten in de periode van januari 2004 tot oktober 2005* (2006), CTIVD 9a, The Hague.

*Rapport van de Commissie van Toezicht betreffende de Inlichtingen—en Veiligheidsdiensten inzake het onderzoek naar de Contra Terrorisme Infobox* (2007), CTIVD 12, The Hague.

*Rapport van de Parlementaire Enquêtecommissie Opsporingsmethoden* (Commission Van Traa). *Inzake Opsporing* (1996), Sdu Uitgevers, The Hague (*Kamerstukken II* 1995/96, 24 072, nrs. 10–11).

*Report by the Commissioner for human rights Mr Thomas Hammarberg on his visit to the Netherlands* (2009), CommDH 2, available at https://wcd.coe.int/wcd/ViewDoc.jsp?id=1417061 (accessed May 22nd, 2011).

M.F.H. Hirsch Ballin, *Anticipative Criminal Investigation*,
DOI: 10.1007/978-90-6704-843-9,

***R****eport by the International Bar Association's Task Force on International Terrorism. International Terrorism, Legal Challenges and Responses* (2003), Transnational Publishers, Ardsley, NY.

***R****eport of the Eminent Jurists Panel on Terrorism, Counter—Terrorism and Human Rights. Assessing Damage, Urging Action* (2009), The International Commission of Jurists, Geneva.

***R****eport of the National Commission on Terrorist Attacks upon the United States* (The 9/11 Commission Report), (2004), available at: http://govinfo.library.unt.edu/911/report/911Report.pdf (accessed 29 July 2011).

***R****eport of the Office of the Inspector General* (2003) *The Federal Bureau of Investigation's Efforts to Improve the Sharing of Intelligence and Other Information*, US Department of Justice, Office of the Inspector General, Audit Division, Audit Report 04–10, December 2003 (Redacted and unclassified).

***R****eport of the Office of the Inspector General* (2006) *A Review of the Federal Bureau of Investigation's Handling of the Brandon Mayfield Case*, Department of Justice, Office of the Inspector General, Oversight and Review Division, March 2006.

***R****eport of the Office of the Inspector General* (2007) *A Review of the Federal Bureau of Investigation's Use of Section 215 Orders for Business Records*, US Department of Justice, Office of the Inspector General, March 2007.

***R****eport of the Office of the Inspector General* (2007) *A Review of the Federal Bureau of Investigation's Use of National Security Letters*, US Department of Justice, Office of the Inspector General, March 2007 (Unclassified).

***R****eport of the Office of the Inspector General* (2008) *A Review of the Federal Bureau of Investigation's Use of National Security Letters, Assessment of Corrective Actions and Examination of NSL usage in 2006*, US Department of Justice, Office of the Inspector General, March 2008 (Unclassified).

***R****eport of the Office of the Inspector General* (2010) *A Review of the Federal Bureau of Investigation's Use of Exigent Letters and Other Informal Requests for Telephone Records*, US Department of Justice, Office of the Inspector General, January 2010.

***R****eport of the Office of the Inspector General* (2011) *A Review of the FBI's Progress in Responding to the Recommendations of the Office of the Inspector General Report on the Fingerprint Misidentification in the Brandon Mayfield Case*, Department of Justice, Office of the Inspector General, June 2011.

***R****eport on the President's Surveillance Program* (2009) (prepared by the Offices of Inspectors General of the Department of Defense), Department of Justice, Central Intelligence Agency, National Security Agency, Office of the Director of National Intelligence, Report No. 2009-00013-AS, 10 July 2009 (Unclassified).

# List of Cases

## *European Court of Human Rights*

ECHR 6 September 1978, App. no. 5029/71 (*Klass and others v. Germany*).
ECHR 26 April 1979, App. no. 6538/74 (*Sunday Times v. United Kingdom*).
ECHR 25 March 1983, App. no. 5947/72; 6205/73; 7052/75; 7061/75; 7107/75; 7113/75; 7136/75 (*Silver and Others v. The United Kingdom*).
ECHR 25 March 1983, App. no. 8660/7 9 (*Minelli v. Switzerland*).
ECHR 2 August 1984, App. no. 8691/79 (*Malone v. The United Kingdom*).
ECHR 26 March 1987, App. no. 9248/81 (*Leander v. Sweden*).
ECHR 12 July 1988, App. no. 10862/84 (*Schenk v. Switzerland*).
ECHR 30 March 1989, App. no. 10461/83 (*Chapell v. The United Kingdom*).
ECHR 20 November 1989, App. no. 11454/85 (*Kostovski v. The Netherlands*).
ECHR 24 April 1990, App. no. 11105/84 (*Huvig v. France*).
ECHR 24 April 1990, App. no. 11801/85 (*Kruslin v. France*).
ECHR 30 August 1990, App. nos. 12244/86; 12245/86; 12383/86 (*Fox, Campbell and Hartley v. The United Kingdom*).
ECHR 28 August 1991, App. nos. 11170/84; 12876/87; 13468/87 (*Brandstetter v. Austria*).
ECHR 15 June 1992, App. no. 12433/86 (*Lüdi v. Switzerland*).
ECHR 16 December 1992, App. no. 13071/87 (*Edwards v. The United Kingdom*).
ECHR 16 December 1992, App. no. 13710/88 (*Niemietz v. Germany*).
ECHR 25 May 1993, App. no. 14307/88 (*Kokkinakis v. Greece*).
ECHR 23 June 1993, App. no. 12952/87 (*Ruiz-Mateos v. Spain*).
ECHR 24 November 1993, App. no. 13972/88 (*Imbrioscia v. Switzerland*).
ECHR 27 October 1994, App. no. 18535/91 (*Kroon and Others v. The Netherlands*).
ECHR 28 October 1994, App. no. 14310/88 (*Murray v. The United Kingdom*).
ECHR 22 November 1995, App. nos. 20166/92 and 20190/92 (*S.W. and C.R. v. United Kingdom*).
ECHR 8 February 1996, App. no. 18731/91 (*John Murray v. The United Kingdom*).

M.F.H. Hirsch Ballin, *Anticipative Criminal Investigation*,
DOI: 10.1007/978-90-6704-843-9,

ECHR 26 March 1996, Reports 1996-II (*Doorson v. The Netherlands*).
ECHR 15 November 1996, App. no. 22414/93 *NJ* 1997, 301, (*Chahal v. UK*).
ECHR 18 March 1997, Reports 1997-III (*Van Mechelen and others v. The Netherlands*).
ECHR 25 June 1997, App. no. 20605/92 (*Halford v. The United Kingdom*).
ECHR 25 March 1998, App. no. 23224/94 (*Kopp v. Switzerland*).
ECHR 30 July 1998, App. no. 27671/95 (*Valenzuela Contreras v. Spain*).
ECHR 24 August 1998, App. no. 23618/94 (Lambert v. France).
ECHR 9 June 1998, App. no. 25829/94 (*Teixeira de Castro v. Portugal*).
ECHR 23 September 1998, App. no. 24755/94 (*McLeod v. The United Kingdom*).
ECHR 28 October 1998, App. no. 23452/94 (*Osman v. The United Kingdom*).
ECHR 16 February 2000, App. no. 27798/95 (*Amann v. Switzerland*).
ECHR 16 February 2000, App. no. 28901/95 (*Rowe and Davis v. The United Kingdom*).
ECHR 4 May 2000, App. no. 28341/95 (*Rotaru v. Romania*).
ECHR 12 May 2000, App. no. 35394/97 (*Khan v. The United Kingdom*).
ECHR 10 October 2000, App. nos. 22947/93 and 22948/93 (*Akkoç v. Turkey*).
ECHR 3 April 2001, App. no. 27229/95 (*Keenan v. The United Kingdom*).
ECHR 5 July 2001, App. no. 41087/98 (*Phillips v. The United Kingdom*).
ECHR 25 September 2001, App. no. 44787/98 (*P.G. and J.H. v. The United Kingdom*).
ECHR 16 October 2001, App. no. 37555/97 (*O'Hara v. The United Kingdom*).
ECHR 24 April 2003, App. no. 24351/94 (*Aktaş v. Turkey*).
ECHR 28 October 2003 App. no. 44320/98 (*Baars v. The Netherlands*).
ECHR 22 July 2003, App. no. 39647/98 and 40461/98 (*Edwards and Lewis v. The United Kingdom*).
ECHR 24 June 2004, App. no. 59320/00 (*Von Hannover v. Germany*).
ECHR 28 October 2004, Requêtes n$^{os}$ 48173/99 et 48319/99 (*Y.B. et autres c. Turquie*).
ECHR 10 November 2005, App. no. 54789/00 (*Bocos-Cuesta v. The Netherlands*).
ECHR 17 November 2005, admissibility decision, App. no. 73047/01 (*Monika Haas v. Germany*).
ECHR 29 June 2006, admissibility decision, App. no. 45934/00 (*Weber and Saravia v. Germany*).
ECHR 6 February 2007, App. no. 14348/02 (*Garycki v. Poland*).
ECHR 25 October 2007, App. no. 38258/03 (*Van Vondel v. The Netherlands*).
ECHR 1 July 2008, App. no. 58243/00 *(Liberty and others v. The United Kingdom)*.
ECHR 12 January 2010, App. no. 4158/05 (*Gillan and Quinton v. The United Kingdom*).
ECHR 2 September 2010, App. no. 35623/05 (*Uzun v. Germany*).
ECHR 14 September 2010, App. no. 38224/03 (*Sanoma Uitgevers B.V. v. The Netherlands*).

## *Inter-American Court of Human Rights*

IACHR 29 July 1988, Series C No. 4 (*Velásquez Rodríguez v. Honduras*).

## *Supreme Court of the Netherlands*

HR 20 december 1926, *NJ* 1927, 85.
HR 2 december 1935, *NJ* 1936, 250, ann. WP.
HR 26 juni 1962, *NJ* 1962, 470, ann. WP.
HR 14 januari 1975, *NJ* 1975, 207.
HR 12 december 1978, *NJ* 1979, 142, ann. GEM.
HR 4 december 1979, *NJ* 1980, 356.
HR 18 november 1980, *NJ* 1981, 125.
HR 2 maart 1982, *NJ* 1982, 460.
HR 5 oktober 1982, *NJ* 1983, 297.
HR 20 maart 1984, *NJ* 1984, 549.
HR 30 oktober 1984, *NJ* 1985, 275.
HR 11 oktober 1986, *NJ* 1988.
HR 14 oktober 1986, *NJ* 1987, 564.
HR 14 oktober 1986, *NJ* 1988, 511, ann. ThWvV.
HR 26 april 1988, *NJ* 1989, 390, ann. ThWvV.
HR 14 september 1992, *NJ* 1993, 83.
HR 9 maart 1993, *NJ* 1993, 633.
HR 11 november 1994, *NJ* 1995, 400, ann. EAA/HJS.
HR 13 June 1995, *NJ* 1995, 684.
HR 19 december 1995, *NJ* 1996, 249, ann. Sch. *(Zwolsman).*
HR 19 maart 1996, *NJ* 1997, 85, ann. Knigge.
HR 7 mei 1996, *NJ* 1996, 687, ann. Sch.
HR 27 mei 1997, *NJ* 1997, 550.
HR 2 juni 1998, *NJ* 1998, 783.
HR 30 juni 1998 *NJ* 1998, 799, ann. Sch.
HR 18 mei 1999, *NJ* 2000, 104, ann. Sch.
HR 2 november 1999, *NJ* 2000, 162.
HR 30 november 1999 *NJ* 2000, 344 en 345 ann. Mevis.
HR 25 januari 2000, *NJ* 2000, 279.
HR 8 februari 2000, *NJ* 2000, 316.
HR 4 april 2000, *NJ* 2000, 735.
HR 20 juni 2000, *NJ* 2000, 502.
HR 7 november 2000, *LJN* AA8207.
HR 5 juni 2001, *NJ* 2001, 518.
HR 25 september 2001, *NJ* 2002, 97.
HR 12 februari 2002, *NJ* 2002, 301.
HR 14 januari 2003, *NJ* 2003, 288.
HR 18 maart 2003, *NJ* 2003, 527.
HR 8 april 2003, *NJ* 2003, 420.
HR 7 oktober 2003, *NJ* 2004, 118.
HR 24 februari 2004, *NJ* 2004, 226.
HR 30 maart 2004, *NJ* 2004, 376, ann. Y.B.

HR 20 april 2004, *NJ* 2004, 525.
HR 16 november 2004, *NJ* 2005, 171.
HR 29 maart 2005, *LJN* AS27527.
HR 6 september 2005, *NJ* 2006, 447.
HR 11 oktober 2005, *NJ* 2006, 625.
HR 7 februari 2006, *NJ* 2007, 396.
HR 13 juni 2006, *NJ* 2006, 346.
HR 5 september 2006, *NJ* 2007, 336, ann. Sch (*Eik*).
HR 17 oktober 2006, *NJ* 2007, 80, ann. Alkema.
HR 7 november 2006, *NJ* 2007, 108.
HR 21 november 2006, *NJ* 2006, 653.
HR 21 november 2006, *NJ* 2007, 233, ann. Mevis.
HR 23 oktober 2007, *LJN* BB3067.
HR 13 november 2007, *NJ* 2007, 614.
HR 22 januari 2008, *LJN* BC1375.
HR 12 februari 2008, *NJ* 2008, 248.
HR 11 maart 2008, *NJ* 2008, 328.
HR 11 maart 2008, *NJ* 2008, 329, ann. Borgers.
HR 10 juni 2008, *NJ* 2008, 348.
HR 20 januari 2009, *NJ* 2009, 225.
HR 12 mei 2009, *LJN* BH5249.
HR 7 juli 2009, *NJ* 2009, 528, ann. Buruma.
HR 8 september 2009, *NJ* 2009, 427.
HR 22 december 2009, *LJN* BJ8622.
HR 26 januari 2010, *NJ* 2010, 77.
HR 23 maart 2010, *NJ* 2010, 197.
HR 30 maart 2010, *NJ* 2010, 201.
HR 5 oktober 2010, *LJN* BL5629.
HR 15 maart 2011, *LJN* BP7544 (CPG 08/04418).
HR 22 maart 2011, *NJ* 2011, 144.

## *Courts of Appeal the Netherlands*

Hof Amsterdam 3 juni 1977, *NJ* 1978, 601.
Hof Amsterdam 9 juni 1994, *NJ* 1994, 709.
Hof Amsterdam 24 juni 2004, *NJ* 2004, 531.
Hof Arnhem 23 december 2002, *NJ* 2003, 134.
Hof 's-Gravenhage 31 mei 2002, *LJN* AE3708.
Hof 's-Gravenhage 15 november 2002, *NJ* 2003, 23.
Hof 's-Gravenhage 21 juni 2004, *NJ* 2004, 432 (*Eik*).
Hof 's-Gravenhage 22 februari 2005, *LJN* AU0235.
Hof 's-Gravenhage 1 maart 2007, *LJN* AZ9644.
Hof 's-Gravenhage 2 oktober 2008, *LJN* BF3987 (*Piranha*).

## District Courts the Netherlands

Rechtbank Amsterdam 1 december 2005, *LJN* AU7314.
Rechtbank Amsterdam 9 maart 2006, *LJN* AV4173.
Rechtbank Amsterdam 29 juni 2007, *LJN* BA9602 en *LJN* BA9586.
Rechtbank 's-Gravenhage 21 november 2000, *LJN* AA8414.
Rechtbank 's-Gravenhage 15 januari 2004, *NJ* 2004, 276.
Rechtbank Rotterdam 18 december 2002, *LJN* AF2141.
Rechtbank Rotterdam 5 juni 2003, *LJN* AF9546.
Rechtbank Rotterdam 1 december 2006, *LJN* AZ3589 (*Piranha*).

## Supreme Court United States

*Albright v. Oliver*, 510 U.S. 266, 114 S.Ct. 807 (1994).
*Berger v. New York*, 388 U.S. 41, 87 S.Ct. 1873 (1967).
*Berger v. United States*, 295 U.S. 78, 55 S.Ct. 629 (1935).
*Bivens v. Six Unknown Agents of Federal Bureau of Narcotics,* 403 U.S. 388, 91 S.Ct. 1999 (1971).
*Brady v. Maryland,* 373 U.S. 83, 83 S.Ct. 1194 (1963).
*Brigham City v. Stuart,* 547 U.S. 398, 126 S.Ct. 1943 (2006).
*Brinegar v. United States*, 338 U.S. 160, 69 S.Ct. 1302 (1949).
*Byod. v. United States,* 116 U.S. 616, 6 S.Ct. 524.
*California v. Ciraolo,* 467 U.S. 207, 106 S.Ct. 1809 (1968).
*California v. Greenwood*, 486 U.S. 35, 108 S.Ct. 1625 (1988).
*Camara v. Municipal Court*, 387 U.S. 523, 87 S.Ct. 1727 (1967).
*CIA v. Sims,* 471 U.S. 159, 105 S.Ct. 1881 (1985).
*City of Indianapolis v. Edmond*, 531 U.S. 32, 121 S.Ct. 447 (2000).
*Clinton v. Virginia,* 377 U.S. 158, 84 S.Ct. 1186 (1964).
*Coffin v. United States,* 156 U.S. 432, 15 S.Ct. 394 (1895).
*Coolidge v. New Hampshire,* 403 U.S. 443, 91 S.Ct. 2022 (1971).
*Dalia v. United States*, 441 U.S. 238, 247, 99 S.Ct. 1682, 1688 (1979).
*Delaware v. Arsdall*, 475 U.S. 673, 106 S.Ct. 1431 (1986).
*Dowling v. United States*, 493 U.S. 343, 110 S.Ct. 668 (1990).
*Duncan v. Louisiana*, 391 U.S. 145, 88 S.Ct. 1444 (1968).
*Florida v. Riley*, 488 U.S. 445, 109S.Ct. 693 (1989).
*Frank v. Mangum*, 237 U.S. 309, 35 S.Ct. 582 (1915).
*Georgia v. Randolph,* 547 U.S. 103, 126 S.Ct. 1515 (2006).
*Go-Bart Importing Co. v. United States,* 282 U.S. 344, 51 S.Ct. 153 (1931).
*Goldberg v. Kelly,* 397 U.S. 254, 90 S.Ct. 1011 (1970).
*Griffin v. Wisconsin*, 483 U.S. 868, 107 S.Ct. 3164 (1987).
*Griswold v. Connecticut,* 381 U.S. 479, 85 S.Ct. 1678 (1965).
*Hamdi v. Rumsfeld*, 542 U.S. 507, 124 S.Ct. 2633, 2648 (2004).
*Herring v. United States*, 555 U.S. 135,129 S.Ct. 695 (2009).

*Hoffa v. United States*, 385 U.S. 293, 87 S.Ct. 408 (1966).
*Hudson v. Michigan*, 547 U.S. 586, 126 S.Ct. 2159 (2006).
*Hudson v. Palmer,* 468 U.S. 517, 104 S.Ct. 3194 (1984).
*Illinois v. Gates*, 462 U.S. 213, 103 S.Ct. 2317 (1983).
*Illinois v. Krull*, 480 U.S. 340, 107 S.Ct. 1160 (1987).
*Illinois v. Lidster,* 540 U.S. 419, 124 S.Ct. 885 (2004).
*Joint Anti-Fascist Refugee Committee v. McGrath,* 341 U.S. 123, 71 S.Ct. 624 (1951).
*Katz v. Unites States,* 389 U.S. 347, 88 S.Ct. 507 (1967).
*Kyllo v. United States,* 533 U.S. 27, 121 S.Ct. 2038 (2001).
*Malloy v. Hogan*, 378 U.S. 1, 84 S.Ct. 1489 (1964).
*Mapp v. Ohio,* 367 U.S. 643, 81 S.Ct. 1684 (1961).
*Marbury v. Madison*, 5 U.S. 1 Cranch 137, 2 L.Ed. 60 (1803).
*Maryland v. Garrison,* 480 U.S. 79, 107 S.Ct. 1013 (1987).
*Matthews v. Eldridge,* 424 U.S. 319, 96 S.Ct. 893 (1976).
*McCulloch v. Maryland*, 17 U.S. (4 Wheat.) 316 (1819).
*Medellin v. Texas,* 552 U.S. 491, 128 S.Ct. 1346 (2008).
*Medina v. California*, 505 U.S. 437, 112 S.Ct. 2572 (1992).
*Michigan Department of State Police v. Sitz*, 496 U.S. 444, 110 S.Ct. 2481 (1990).
*Mugler v. State of Kansas,* 123 U.S. 623, 8 S.Ct. 273 (1887).
*Murray v. United States,* 487 U.S. 533, 108 S.Ct. 2529 (1988).
*Nardone v. United States,* 308 U.S. 338, 60 S.Ct. 266 (1939).
*National Treasury Employees Union v. Von Raab,* 489 U.S. 656, 109 S.Ct. 1348 (1989).
*New Jersey v. T.L.O.*, 469 U.S. 325, 105 S.Ct. 733 (1985).
*Nix v. Williams*, 467 U.S. 431, 104 S.Ct. 2501 (1984).
*Olmstead v. United States,* 277 U.S. 438, 48 S.Ct. 564 (1928).
*Pleasant Grove City, Utah v. Summum*, 555 U.S. 460, 129 S.Ct. 1125 (2009).
*Richards v. Wisconsin*, 520 U.S. 385, 117 S. Ct. 1416 (1997).
*Rochin v. California,* 342 U.S. 165, 72 S.Ct. 205 (1954)
*Sacramento v. Lewis,* 523 U.S. 833, 118 S.Ct. 1708 (1998).
*Safford Unified School District No. 1 v. Reddings,* 129 S.Ct. 2633 (2009).
*Samson v. California,* 547 U.S. 843, 126 S.Ct. 2193 (2006).
*Scott v. United States*, 436 U.S. 128, 98 S.Ct. 1717 (1978).
*Shadwick v. City of Tampa*, 407 U.S. 345, 92 S.Ct. 2119 (1972).
*Silverman v. United States,* 365 U.S. 505, 81 S.Ct. 679 (1961).
*Smith v. Maryland,* 442 U.S. 735, 99 S.Ct. 2577 (1979).
*Steele v. United States*, 267 U.S. 498, 45 S.Ct. 414 (1925).
*Tenet et al. v. Doe et Ux*, 544 U.S. 1, 125 S.Ct. 1230 (2005).
*Terminiello v. City of Chicago,* 337 U.S. 1, 69 S.Ct. 894 (1949).
*Terry v. Ohio,* 392 U.S. 1, 88 S.Ct. 1868 (1968).
*Totten, Administrator v. United States*, 92 U.S. 105, 1875 WL17758 (1876).
*United States v. Calandra*, 414 U.S. 338, 94 S.Ct. 613 (1974).
*United States v. Chavez*, 416 U.S. 562, 94 S.Ct. 1849 (1974).
*United States v. Giordano*, 416 U.S. 505, 94 S.Ct. 1820 (1974).

*United States v. Havens*, 466 U.S. 620, 100 S.Ct. 1912 (1980).
*United States v. Kahn,* 415 U.S. 143, 94 S.Ct. 997 (1974).
*United States v. Karo,* 468 U.S. 705, 104 S.Ct. 3296 (1984).
*United States v. Knights*, 534 U.S. 112, 122 S.Ct. 587 (2001).
*United States v. Knotts,* 460 U.S. 276, 103 S.Ct. 1081 (1983).
*United States v. Leon,* 468 U.S. 897, 104 S.Ct. 3405 (1984).
*United States v. Lopez*, 514 U.S. 549, 115 S.Ct.1624 (1995).
*United States v. Miller,* 425 U.S. 435, 96 S.Ct. 1619 (1976).
*United States v. Noble*, 422 U.S. 225, 95 S.Ct. 2160 (1975).
*United States v. Place*, 462 U.S. 696, 103 S.Ct. 2637 (1983).
*United States v. Ramirez,* 523 U.S. 65, 118 S.Ct. 992 (1998).
*United States v. R. Enterprises Inc.*, 498 U.S. 292, 111 S.Ct. 722 (1991).
*United States v. Sokolow,* 490 U.S. 1, 109 S.Ct. 1581 (1989).
*United States v. Verdugo-Urquidez,* 494 U.S. 259, 110 S.Ct. 1056 (1990).
*United States v. United States District Court for the Eastern District of Michigan (Keith)*, 407 U.S. 297, 92 S.Ct. 2125 (1972).
*United States v. White*, 401 U.S. 745, 91 S.Ct. 1122 (1971).
*Vernonia School District v. Acton,* 515 U.S. 646, 115 S.Ct. 2386 (1995).
*Virginia v. Moore*, 553 U.S. 164, 128 S.Ct. 1598 (2008).
*Whren v. United States,* 517 U.S. 806, 116 S.Ct. 1769 (1996).
*Wilson v. Arkansas,* 514 U.S. 927, 115 S.Ct. 1914 (1995).
*Wong Sun v. United States*, 371 U.S. 471, 83 S.Ct. 407 (1963).

## *Courts of Appeals United States*

*Bassiouni v. CIA,* 392 F.3d 244, (7th Cir. 2004).
*Bassiouni v. FBI,* 436 F.3d 712 (7th Cir. 2006).
*Catledge v. Mueller,* 323 Fed. Appx 464, 2009 WL 1025980 (7th Cir. 2009).
*Doe v. Gonzales,* 449 F.3d 415 (2nd Cir. 2006).
*Doe v. Mukasey,* 549 F.3d 861 (2nd Cir. 2008).
*In re Kevork,* 788 F2d 566 (9th Cir. 1986).
*In re Terrorist Bombings of U.S. Embassies in East Africa,* 552 F.3d 157 (2nd Cir. 2008).
*Macwade v. Kelly,* 460 F.3d 260 (2nd Cir. 2006).
*Mayfield v. United States,* 599 F.3d 964 (9th Cir. 2010).
*United States v. Abu Ali,* 528 F.3d 210 (4th Cir. 2008).
*United States v. Abu-Jihaad,* 630 F.3d 102 (2nd Cir. 2010).
*United States v. Biasucci*, 786 F.2d2d 504 (2nd Cir. 1986).
*United States v. Cox*, 342 F.2d 167 (5th Cir. 1965).
*United States v. Duggan,* 743 F.2d 59 (2nd Cir. 1984).
*United States v. Edwards,* 498 F.2d 496 (2nd Cir. 1974).
*United States v. Freitas,* 800 F.2d 1451 (9th Cir.1968).
*United States v. Johnson*, 952 F.2d 565 (1st Cir. 1991).

*United States v. Ning Wen,* 477 F.3d 896 (7th Cir. 2007).
*United States v. Pangburn*, 983 F.2d 449 (2nd Cir. 1993).
*United States v. Pelton*, 835 F.2d 1067 (4th Cir. 1987).
*United States v. Petti,* 973 F.2d 1441 (9th Cir. 1992).
*United States v. Rahman,* 189 F.3d 88 (2nd Cir. 1999).
*United States v. Ramos,* 629 F.3d 60 (1st Cir. 2010).
*United States v. Sarkissian*, 841 F.2d 959 (9th Cir. 1988).
*United States v. Simons,* 206 F.3d 392 (4th Cir. 2000).
*United States v. Skipwith,* 482 F.2d 1272 (5th Cir. 1973).
*United States v. Smith,* 780 F.2d 1102 (4th Cir. 1985).
*United States v. Stewart,* 590 F.3d 93 (2nd Cir. 2009).
*United States v. Truong Ding Hung*, 629 F.2d 908 (4th Cir. 1980).
*United States v. Villegas,* 899 F.2d 1324 (2nd Cir. 1990).
*United States v. Zacarias Moussaoui,* 382 F.3d 453 (4th Cir. 2004).
*Warshak v. United States,* 490 F.3d 455 (6th Cir. 2007).
*Warshak v. United States,* 631 F.3d 266 (6th Cir. 2010).

## *District Courts United States*

*ACLU v. United States Department of Justice* (*ACLU I*), 265 F.Supp.2d 20 (D.D.C. 2003)
*ACLU v. United States Department of Justice* (*ACLU II*), 321 F.Supp.2d 24 (D.D.C. 2004).
*Doe v. Ashcroft* (Doe I), 334 F.Supp.2d 471 (S.D.N.Y. 2004).
*Doe v. Gonzales* (Doe II), 386 F.Supp.2d 66 (D.Conn. 2005).
*Doe v. Gonzales* (Doe III), 500 F.Supp.2d 379 (S.D.N.Y. 2007).
*Doe v. Holder,* 665 F.Supp.2d 426 (S.D.N.Y. 2009).
*Doe v. Holder,* 703 F.Supp.2d 313 (S.D.N.Y. 2010).
*Doe v. Holder,* 04 Civ. 2614, 30 July 2010, p. 2 (Available at: http://www.wired.com/images_blogs/threatlevel/2010/08/Doe-vs-Holder_NSL.pdf, last visited at November 23, 2010).
*In re Application of the United States for an Order for Prospective Cell Site Information on a Certain Cellular Telephone,* 460 F.Supp.2d 448 (S.D.N.Y. 2006).
*In re Application of the United States of America for an Order Authorizing the Use of a Pen Register with Caller Identification Device Cell Site Location Authority on a Cellular Telephone,* 2009 WL 159187 (S.D.N.Y. 2009).
*In re Applications of the United States of America for Orders Pursuant to Title I8, United States Code, Section 2703(d),* 509 F.Supp.2d 76 (D.Mass. 2007).
*In re Kevork,* 634 F.Supp. 1002 (C.D.Cal. 1985).
*Martinez v. Ensor,* 958 F.Supp. 515 (D.Colo. 1997).
*Mayfield v. United States,* 504 F.Supp.2d 1023 (D.Or. 2007).
*People of State of New York v. Muka,* 440 F.Supp. 33 (N.D.N.Y. 1977).
*United States v. Abu-Jihaad,* 531 F.Supp.2d 299 (D.Conn. 2008).

*United States v. Bin Laden,* 126 F.Supp.2d 264 (S.D.N.Y. 2000).
*United States v. Duffey,* 2009 WL 2356156 (N.D.Tex. 2009).
*United States v. Falvey,* 540 F.Supp. 1306 (E.D.N.Y. 1982).
*United States v. Mubayyid,* 521 F.Supp.2d 125 (D.Mass. 2007).
*United States v. Rahman*, 861 F.Supp. 247 (S.D.N.Y. 1994).
*United States v. Ramos,* 591 F.Supp.2d 93 (D. Mass. 2008).
*United States v. Tomero*, 462 F.Supp.2d 565 (S.D.N.Y. 2006).
*United States v. Warsame,* 547 F.Supp.2d 982 (D. Minn. 2008).

## FISA Court and FISA Court of Review United States

*In re All Matters Submitted to the Foreign Intelligence Surveillance Court,* 218 F.Supp.2d 611 (Foreign Int. Surv. Ct. 2002).
*In re Directives Pursuant to Section 105B of the Foreign Intelligence Surveillance Act*, 551 F.3d 1004 (FISA Ct. Rev. 2008).
*In re Sealed Case,* 310 F.3d 717 (FISA Ct. Rev. 2002).

# Index




M.F.H. Hirsch Ballin, *Anticipative Criminal Investigation*,
DOI: 10.1007/978-90-6704-843-9,

**D**

Printed by Publishers' Graphics LLC USA
SO20120327-38
2012